HISTORY OF
THE SECOND WORLD WAR
UNITED KINGDOM MEDICAL SERIES
Editor-in-Chief:
SIR ARTHUR S. MACNALTY, K.C.B., M.A., M.D., F.R.C.P., F.R.C.S.

THE ARMY MEDICAL SERVICES

BY

F. A. E. CREW, F.R.S.

Campaigns

VOLUME IV

NORTH-WEST EUROPE

The Naval & Military Press Ltd

Published by

The Naval & Military Press Ltd
Unit 5 Riverside, Brambleside
Bellbrook Industrial Estate
Uckfield, East Sussex
TN22 1QQ England

Tel: +44 (0)1825 749494

www.naval-military-press.com
www.nmarchive.com

In reprinting in facsimile from the original, any imperfections are inevitably reproduced and the quality may fall short of modern type and cartographic standards.

EDITORIAL BOARD

Sir CYRIL FLOWER, C.B., F.S.A. (*Chairman*)

Sir WELDON DALRYMPLE-CHAMPNEYS, Bart., C.B., M.A., D.M., B.Ch., F.R.C.P. Sir FRANCIS R. FRASER, M.D., F.R.C.P.	*Ministry of Health*
Sir ANDREW DAVIDSON, M.D., F.R.C.P. Ed., F.R.C.S. Ed. A. K. BOWMAN, M.B., Ch.B., F.R.F.P.S.	*Department of Health for Scotland*
J. BOYD, C.B.E., M.D., F.R.C.P.I.	*Government of Northern Ireland*
Sir HAROLD HIMSWORTH, K.C.B., M.D., F.R.C.P., F.R.S. Dame JANET VAUGHAN, D.B.E., D.M., F.R.C.P.	*Medical Research Council*
Surgeon Vice Admiral Sir CYRIL MAY, K.B.E., C.B., M.C., Q.H.S., F.R.C.S.	*Admiralty*
Lt. General Sir ALEXANDER DRUMMOND, K.B.E., C.B., Q.H.S., F.R.C.S., D.L.O. Major General A. SACHS, C.B., C.B.E., M.Sc., Q.H.P., M.D., M.R.C.P.	*War Office*
Air Vice Marshal Sir PATRICK LEE POTTER, K.B.E., Q.H.S., M.D., D.T.M. & H.	*Air Ministry*
Brigadier H. B. LATHAM	*Cabinet Office*

Editor-in-Chief: Sir ARTHUR S. MACNALTY, K.C.B., M.A., M.D., F.R.C.P., F.R.C.S.

Secretary: W. FRANKLIN MELLOR

The following persons served on the Editorial Board for varying periods:

The Rt. Hon. R. A. Butler, P.C., M.A., F.R.G.S., M.P. (*Chairman*); Brigadier General Sir James E. Edmonds, C.B., C.M.G., D.Litt. (*Committee of Imperial Defence*); Surgeon Vice Admiral Sir Sheldon F. Dudley, K.C.B., O.B.E., M.D., F.R.C.P., F.R.C.S. Ed., F.R.S.; Surgeon Vice Admiral Sir Henry St. Clair Colson, K.C.B., C.B.E., F.R.C.P.; Surgeon Vice Admiral Sir Edward Greeson, K.B.E., C.B., M.D., Ch.B; Surgeon Vice Admiral Sir Alexander Ingleby-MacKenzie, K.B.E., C.B., B.M., B.Ch., Q.H.P. (*Admiralty*); Lt. General Sir William P. MacArthur, K.C.B., D.S.O., O.B.E., M.D., B.Ch., D.Sc., F.R.C.P.; Lt. General Sir Alexander Hood, G.B.E., K.C.B., M.D., F.R.C.P., LL.D.; Lt. General Sir Neil Cantlie, K.C.B.,

EDITORIAL BOARD

K.B.E., C.B., M.C., M.B., F.R.C.S.; Lt. General Sir Frederick Harris, K.B.E., C.B., M.C., M.B., LL.D., Q.H.S.; Major General H. M. J. Perry, C.B., O.B.E., F.R.C.P.; Major General L. T. Poole, C.B., D.S.O., M.C., M.B., Ch.B.; Brigadier Sir John Boyd, O.B.E., M.D., F.R.S.; Brigadier H. T. Findlay, M.B., Ch.B. (*War Office*); Air Marshal Sir Harold E. Whittingham, K.C.B., K.B.E., M.B., Ch.B., F.R.C.P., F.R.C.S., LL.D.; Air Marshal Sir Andrew Grant, K.B.E., C.B., M.B., Ch.B.; Air Marshal Sir Philip C. Livingston, K.B.E., C.B., A.F.C., F.R.C.S.; Air Marshal Sir James M. Kilpatrick, K.B.E., C.B., M.B., B.Ch., Q.H.P. (*Air Ministry*); Sir Edward Mellanby, G.B.E., K.C.B., M.D., F.R.C.P., F.R.S. (*Medical Research Council*); Professor J. M. Mackintosh, M.A., M.D., F.R.C.P. (*Department of Health for Scotland*); Lt. Colonel J. S. Yule, O.B.E., Philip Allen, Esq., G. Godfrey Phillips, Esq., M. T. Flett, Esq., A. M. R. Topham, Esq., D. F. Hubback, Esq., A. B. Acheson, Esq., C.M.G., C.B.E. (*Cabinet Office*).

EDITORIAL COMMITTEE

Sir ARTHUR S. MACNALTY, K.C.B., M.A., M.D., F.R.C.P., F.R.C.S.
(*Chairman*)

Surgeon Captain J. L. S. COULTER, D.S.C., F.R.C.S. (Barrister-at-Law)	*Admiralty*
Professor F. A. E. CREW, D.Sc., M.D., F.R.C.P. Ed., LL.D., F.R.S.	*War Office*
Squadron Leader S. C. REXFORD-WELCH, M.A., M.R.C.S., L.R.C.P.	*Air Ministry*
A. K. BOWMAN, M.B., Ch.B., F.R.F.P.S.	*Department of Health for Scotland*
J. BOYD, C.B.E., M.D., F.R.C.P.I.	*Government of Northern Ireland*
F. H. K. GREEN, C.B.E., M.D., F.R.C.P.	*Medical Research Council*
J. ALISON GLOVER, C.B.E., M.D., F.R.C.P.	*Ministry of Education*
A. SANDISON, O.B.E., M.D.	*Ministry of Pensions*
Sir ZACHARY COPE, B.A., M.D., M.S., F.R.C.S.	*Ministry of Health*

Secretary: W. FRANKLIN MELLOR

The following persons served on the Editorial Committee for varying periods:

Surgeon Commander J. J. Keevil, D.S.O., M.D.; Surgeon Lieutenant L. D. de Launay, M.B., B.S.; Surgeon Lieutenant Commander N. M. McArthur, M.D.; Surgeon Commander A. D. Sinclair, M.B., Ch.B. (*Admiralty*); Colonel S. Lyle Cummins, C.B., C.M.G., LL.D., M.D. (*War Office*); Wing Commander R. Oddie, M.B., B.Ch.; Wing Commander E. B. Davies, M.B., B.Ch.; Squadron Leader R. Mortimer, M.B., B.S. Squadron Leader H. N. H. Genese, M.R.C.S., L.R.C.P. (*Air Ministry*); Charles E. Newman, M.D., F.R.C.P.; N. G. Horner, M.D., F.R.C.P., F.R.C.S.; Lt. Colonel C. L. Dunn, C.I.E., I.M.S. (ret.) (*Ministry of Health*).

FOREWORD

BY THE EDITOR-IN-CHIEF

IN May 1944 Rear Admiral George Elvey Creasy, of the Royal Navy, Chief of Staff to Admiral Sir Bertram Ramsay, the Commander of the Allied Naval Expeditionary Force, in an address to Allied naval officers, referring to invasion of a foreign shore, said:

> 'Gentlemen, what Philip of Spain failed to do, what Napoleon tried and failed to do, and what Hitler never had the courage to try, we are about to do, and with God's grace we shall.'

Operation 'Overlord', the sea-borne invasion of France, was a magnificent conception. Three years of sustained, arduous and experimental preparation went to its making. The small-scale raids by the Commandos on the French coast had to be increased in scope and intensity as a prelude to greater operations. New engines of war and transport had to be devised, for example the 'Mulberry Harbours', the three Fighting Services were trained to fight as one team, supported by the industry of the nation, and the whole of Great Britain converted into an armed camp for launching, in the words of Admiral Ramsay, 'the greatest amphibious operation in history'. This was the necessary preliminary to the opening of the Western Front in Europe which, in conjunction with the great Russian advance, was to liberate Europe and to crush the fighting power of Germany.

At length D-day, the memorable June 6, dawned, preceded by an intense bombardment of the French coast from the air and the ships of the British Navy. The Germans concentrated their forces at the strongly defended Channel ports and were taken by surprise. A mighty armada of four thousand ships conveyed the Expeditionary Force of British, Canadians and Americans over mine-swept seas. The transports and barges were protected by a powerful umbrella of fighter aircraft. The Allied landings were made on the open beaches between Le Havre and Cherbourg. Invaders descended by parachute and by gliders behind the German defences. No invasion from the sea on a strongly defended coast was ever made before on so vast a scale. Tanks, reinforcements and supplies from Britain poured in on the footing secured in Normandy. On June 26 Cherbourg was taken and the Expeditionary Force now had captured a port. Caen was taken and the American Army surged forward, joined with the British and isolated the Channel ports. The French Forces of the Interior, the Maquis, rose all over France to attack the Germans. In August Paris was liberated and the Vichy Government collapsed.

In September five-sixths of France had been liberated and the greater part of Belgium. In the middle of the month the Allies invaded Holland and penetrated into Germany. By the early autumn of 1944 France had been freed, but the set-back at Arnhem halted the advance into Germany. On December 16 Field Marshal Rundstedt, at Hitler's command, began a German counter-offensive through the Ardennes which was overcome by a powerful attack, launched by General Eisenhower.

With dramatic swiftness the end of April 1945 saw the closing stages of the war in Europe. The main body of the Allied forces swept into Germany, while the Canadian First Army battled fiercely with the Germans in inundated Holland. The British Second Army advanced towards the Baltic. On April 17 the Russians renewed their offensive from the Oder and were in Berlin on April 29, the day before Hitler's death. On April 25 Russian and American forces had met at Torgau on the Elbe. The Germans in Italy surrendered unconditionally to Field Marshal Alexander on May 2. On April 28 Mussolini had been captured and shot by Italian partisans near Lake Como. All German forces in North-west Germany, Holland and Denmark surrendered unconditionally to Field Marshal Montgomery (21 Army Group) at Lüneburg on May 4. Germany's final submission was made at Rheims on May 7. The Allies set up a military administration in Germany according to the terms of the Yalta agreement.

The people of Great Britain had endured six years of Winston Churchill's promised 'blood, toil, tears and sweat'. Now the promised victory came.

To this great victory in North-west Europe the work of the British Army Medical Services made an important contribution. Its history is told in this fourth volume of the Campaigns. All the medical experience gained in previous campaigns, for example in North Africa, in Sicily, Italy and elsewhere, was brought to bear in the conduct of this campaign.

Professor F. A. E. Crew narrates in detail the prolonged medical planning that was required and the difficulties that were encountered. Sometimes the medical considerations prevailed; at other times they had to be abandoned in view of military necessities; or were met by some form of compromise. Accounts are furnished of the use of Landing Ship Tanks (L.S.T.), of air evacuation of the wounded which proved so valuable and indispensable, of the special arrangements on the landing beaches for medical care and of the elaborate hospital provision in France and in England. Then from the assault and lodgement in Normandy the medical features of the campaign are recorded at each step of the campaign culminating in Chapter 9 in the occupation of

Germany and the end of the war in Europe. The two concluding chapters deal with the health of the troops and 'Reflections on the Campaign'.

Professor Crew points out that there was a striking contrast between this and previous campaigns in respect of the degree of control over haemorrhage, shock and sepsis, the greatest of these being sepsis. To this satisfactory result early skilled treatment in the front line, treatment in specialist units, blood transfusion, a better appreciation of the causes and symptomatology of shock and the discovery of penicillin mainly contributed. The psychiatric organisation also played its part, particularly in the treatment of exhaustion. Nor must the benefits accruing from the air evacuation of casualties be forgotten. By air transport over a hundred thousand men were evacuated to base hospitals from front-line units. A great tribute was paid to the 'truly remarkable success of the medical organisation' by Field Marshal Montgomery in his Despatch of September 3, 1946 (*The London Gazette*), which is given here on p. 560. He observes that the exhilarating effect of success also played its part in reducing the rates of sickness, for the general morale of the troops was high.

The medical organisation and the application of medical knowledge not only preserved many lives that would inevitably have perished in previous wars but it also conserved medical man-power for the campaign. The medical account of the campaign in North-west Europe therefore embodies a fine record of medical achievements which in Professor Crew has found an enlightened historian and editor.

This volume of the Official Medical History of the War has been prepared under the direction of an Editorial Board appointed by Her Majesty's Government, but the Editor alone is responsible for the method of presentation of the facts and the opinions expressed.

CONTENTS

	Page
FOREWORD BY THE EDITOR-IN-CHIEF	ix
PREFACE	xli
Précis	1

CHAPTER 1: THE CAMPAIGN IN NORTH-WEST EUROPE, 1944–45 14

I

The Genesis and Development of Operation 'Overlord'   14

II

Operation 'Overlord'. Medical Planning   23

(A) Second Army	25
The Raising of the Medical Component	32
The Evacuation of Casualties	45
The Reception and Distribution of Casualties in the United Kingdom	61
Hospital Accommodation in the United Kingdom	70
Medical Supplies; Rations; Water	75
Precautions against Communicable Diseases	80
The Army Pathology Service. Second Army	85
The Army Transfusion Service. 21 Army Group	87
The Army Dental Service. Second Army	89
Assembly and Dispatch	91
The Reorganisation of Home Forces, 1944	97
Civil Affairs	101
(B) Canadian First Army. Medical Planning	101
Appendices I, II and III	104

CHAPTER 2: THE ASSAULT AND LODGEMENT . . . 114

I

The Operations. 'Neptune', 'Epsom', 'Jupiter' and 'Goodwood'   114

CONTENTS

II

The Assault and Lodgement. Medical Cover. 21 Army Group Formations

	Page
6th Airborne Division	127
50th (Northumbrian) Division	133
Canadian 3rd Division	138
Canadian II Corps	142
3rd Division	144
Guards Armoured Division	153
7th Armoured Division	154
11th Armoured Division	154
15th (Scottish) Division	155
43rd (Wessex) Division	162
49th (West Riding) Division	163
51st (Highland) Division	168
53rd (Welsh) Division	169
59th (Staffordshire) Division	172
79th Armoured Division	172

III

The Assault and Lodgement. Medical Arrangements. 21 Army Group Formations

	Page
I Corps	174
VIII Corps	176
XII Corps	180
XXX Corps	181
Second Army	184
The Army Dental Service (Second Army)	200
The Army Transfusion Service (21 Army Group)	203
The Army Psychiatric Service (Second Army)	206
Appendices IV and V	211

CHAPTER 3: THE BREAK-OUT AND THE ADVANCE INTO HOLLAND 214

I

The Operations

	Page
Operation 'Cobra'. U.S. First Army	214
Operation 'Bluecoat'. Second Army	215
The German Counter-attack at Mortain	216

CONTENTS

	Page
Operation 'Totalize'. Canadian First Army	219
The Advance to the Seine	221
Operation 'Anvil'. U.S. Seventh Army	222
The Pursuit to the Albert and the Meuse-Escaut Canals	222
Operation 'Market Garden'	226

II

The Break-out and the Advance into Holland. Medical Cover. 21 Army Group Formations

Guards Armoured Division	232
7th Armoured Division	234
11th Armoured Division	236
3rd Division	237
15th Division	238
43rd Division	242
49th Division	244
50th Division	250
51st Division	255
53rd Division	261
59th Division	267
1st Airborne Division	267
1st Airborne Division Military Hospital, Apeldoorn	278
The Lazarett at Stalag XIB	280
6th Airborne Division	283

III

The Break-out and the Advance into Holland. Medical Arrangements

I Corps	284
VIII Corps	284
XXX Corps	291
H.Q. Airborne Troops	299
Second Army	306
11 L. of C. Area	315
The Army Dental Service (Second Army)	319
The Army Transfusion Service (21 Army Group)	320
The Army Psychiatric Service (Second Army)	324
Canadian First Army	326
Appendices VI and VII	333

CONTENTS

CHAPTER 4: THE OPENING OF THE ESTUARY OF THE SCHELDT. CANADIAN FIRST ARMY . . . 335

I

The Operations   335

II

Medical Cover

Canadian 2nd Division. Operation 'Vitality I' . . .	341
Canadian 3rd Division. Operation 'Switchback' . .	342
Canadian 4th Armoured Division. Operation 'Suitcase' .	343
4th S.S. Brigade. Operation 'Infatuate II' . . .	343
52nd (Lowland) Division	345

III

Medical Arrangements

Canadian II Corps	347
Canadian First Army	347

CHAPTER 5: THE ADVANCE TO THE MAAS AND TO THE ROER AND THE GERMAN COUNTER-OFFENSIVE IN THE ARDENNES 351

I

The Advance to the Maas and to the Roer   351

II

The German Counter-Offensive in the Ardennes   353

III

The Clearing of the Roer Triangle (Operation 'Blackcock')   359

IV

Medical Cover

Guards Armoured Division	360
7th Armoured Division	360
6th Airborne Division	361

CONTENTS

	Page
15th Division	361
49th (West Riding) Division	366
51st (Highland) Division	369
53rd Division	377

V
Medical Arrangements

I Corps	380
XII Corps	380
XXX Corps	384
Second Army	390
L. of C.	400
The Army Psychiatric Service (Second Army)	403
Appendices VIII and IX	406

CHAPTER 6: THE ADVANCE TO AND THE CROSSING OF THE RHINE 413

I
The Operations

II
Medical Cover

Guards Armoured Division	419
7th Armoured Division	420
3rd Division	422
6th Airborne Division. Operation 'Varsity'	423
15th (Scottish) Division	426
43rd Division	436
51st (Highland) Division	440
52nd (Lowland) Division	445

III
Medical Arrangements

XII Corps	445
XXX Corps	450
Second Army	456
11 L. of C. Area	463
The Army Dental Service (Second Army)	464

CONTENTS

	Page
The Army Transfusion Service (21 Army Group)	465
Canadian First Army	466
Appendix X	474

CHAPTER 7: THE ADVANCE TO AND THE CROSSING OF THE ELBE 477

I

Operation 'Enterprise'

The Advance to the Elbe	477
The Crossing of the Elbe. Operation 'Enterprise'	481

II

Medical Cover

7th Armoured Division	484
11th Armoured Division	485
3rd Division	486
5th Division	487
6th Airborne Division	488
15th Division	489
43rd Division	493
52nd Division	494

III

Medical Arrangements

VIII Corps	495
XII Corps	496
XXX Corps. The Political Prisoners Camp, Sandbostel	498
Second Army	505

CHAPTER 8: THE LIBERATION OF HOLLAND. CANADIAN FIRST ARMY 516

CHAPTER 9: THE OCCUPATION OF GERMANY AND THE END OF THE WAR IN EUROPE 528

CONTENTS   xix

I
Page

Operation 'Eclipse'. (Second Army)

The Tasks of the Army Medical Services . . . 528
Second Army 530
I Corps District 536
VIII Corps 538
15th Division 540

II

The Specialist Services

The Army Dental Service (Second Army) . . . 541
The Army Transfusion Service (21 Army Group) . . 544
The Army Pathology Service (Second Army) . . . 553
The Army Psychiatric Service (Second Army) . . 554

CHAPTER 10: THE HEALTH OF THE TROOPS . . . 560

Appendix XI 595

CHAPTER 11: REFLECTIONS ON THE CAMPAIGN.
D.D.M.S. SECOND ARMY 636

Appendices XII to XVII 644

INDEX 659

APPENDICES

Chapter 1

		Page
I.	Operation 'Overlord'. The Allied Command	104
II.	Second Army. Order of Battle. January–June 1944	104
III.	21 Army Group. Medical Services (less Canadian Units)	106

Chapter 2

| IV. | The Development of the Administrative Command of Second Army in the Early Stages of Operation 'Overlord' | 211 |
| V. | 21 Army Group. Excerpts from 'A' Sitreps | 212 |

Chapter 3

| VI. | The Allied Command (Ground Forces). Autumn 1944 | 333 |
| VII. | 21 Army Group. Location Statement. General Hospitals. September 2 | 333 |

Chapter 5

| VIII. | Second Army. Skeleton Order of Battle and Medical Order of Battle. October–December 1944 | 406 |
| IX. | 21 Army Group. Location Statement. General Hospitals and Convalescent Depots. October–December 1944 | 409 |

Chapter 6

| X. | 21 Army Group. Location Statement. General Hospitals and Convalescent Depots. January–March 1945 | 474 |

Chapter 10

| XI. | Surgical Casualties. The Assessment of Battle Casualties in the Normandy Campaign. June–July 1944 | 595 |

Chapter 11

XII.	21 Army Group. Location Statement. General Hospitals. April–May 15, 1945	644
XIII.	21 Army Group. Medical Location Statement as at June 25, 1945	646
XIV.	21 Army Group. Medical Location Statement as at August 13, 1945	650
XV.	H.Q. Second Army. Successive Locations	654
XVI.	L. of C. Areas, and Sub-areas. November 1944–May 1945	655
XVII.	The Commando Medical Service	656

ILLUSTRATIONS

SKETCH MAPS AND DIAGRAMS

Fig.		Page

Chapter 1

1. Operation 'Neptune'. The Assault Landings 19

Chapter 2

2. The Assault Landings and Lodgement. D-day Gains . . 120
3. The Beachhead. June 13 122
4. The Beachhead. June 24 123
5. 50th Division. The Assault Landing and Lodgement. Medical Cover 132
6. 50th Division. Medical Cover. June 134
7. 50th Division. Medical Cover. July 136
8. The Inland Advance of the Canadians 140
9. 3rd Division. The Assault Landing and Lodgement . . 152
10. 15th Division. Medical Cover during the Period June 26–July 1, 1st Phase 157
11. 15th Division. Medical Cover during the Period June 26–July 1, 2nd Phase 158
12. 15th Division. Operation 'Greenline'. Medical Cover July 15–18 160
13. 49th Division. The Advance to Vendes–Rauray . . . 165
14. 51st Division. Medical Cover in the Bridgehead east of the Orne 168
15. 53rd Division. The Valley of the Odon. July . . . 169
16. I Corps. The Attack on Caen. Medical Arrangements . . 175
17. VIII Corps. Operations 'Epsom' and 'Jupiter'. Medical Arrangements 177
18. VIII Corps. Operation 'Goodwood Meeting'. Medical Arrangements 178
19. XXX Corps. The Medical Situation as at 2359 hours, June 18 . 183
20. The Distribution of the Medical Units under H.Q. 11 L. of C. Area, June 11 185
21. The Plan of the Bayeux Medical Area 191
22. Second Army. The Distribution of the Medical Units. June 30 . 192
23. The Evacuation System. Main Routes. July–August . . 195

Chapter 3

24. The Break-out. The German Counter-attack at Mortain. The Falaise Pocket. August 217
25. Canadian First Army. Operation 'Totalize' 218
26. The Advance from the Line of the Seine. August 26–September 4 224

xxi

ILLUSTRATIONS

Fig.		Page
27.	7th Armoured Division. Evacuation Plan during the Advance into Belgium	235
28.	49th Division. The Reduction of Le Havre. Medical Cover	246
29.	50th Division. The Advance to the Seine. Medical Cover	251
30.	50th Division. The Advance to the Somme. Medical Cover	252
31.	50th Division. The Crossing of the Albert Canal. Medical Cover	253
32.	50th Division. The Nijmegen Bridgehead. Medical Cover	254
33.	51st Division. Operation 'Totalize'. Medical Cover	257
34.	51st Division. The Advance to the Seine. Medical Cover	258
35.	51st Division. The Assault on Le Havre. Medical Cover	259
36.	1st Airborne Division Medical Area, Oosterbeek. September 18–26	271
37.	VIII Corps. Operation 'Bluecoat'. Medical Arrangements	285
38.	VIII Corps. 33 C.C.S. Lay-out of Tentage	287
39.	VIII Corps. 34 C.S.S. Lay-out of Tentage	288
40.	VIII Corps. Lay-out of a Corps Medical Area	289
41.	VIII Corps. Lay-out of Tentage for an Advanced Surgical Centre	290
42.	XXX Corps. The Crossing of the Albert and the Meuse–Escaut Canals. Medical Arrangements. Sept. 10	294
43.	XXX Corps. Operation 'Market Garden'. Medical Arrangements	296
44.	Operation 'Market Garden'. Medical Arrangements	303
45.	Second Army. The Medical Situation as at August 10	307
46.	Second Army. The Medical Situation as at August 23	308
47.	Second Army. The Medical Situation as at August 31	308
48.	Second Army. The Medical Situation as at September 6	310
49.	Second Army. The Medical Situation as at September 28	312
50.	The Distribution of the Medical Units in 11 L. of C. Area, August 31	315
51.	The Evacuation System. Late September	318
52.	The Caen–Falaise Road	327

Chapter 4

53.	Canadian First Army. The Clearance of the Scheldt Estuary. Medical Arrangements	338

Chapter 5

54.	The German Counter-Offensive in the Ardennes	354
55.	The Roer Triangle	358
56.	15th Division. The Attack on Tilburg. Medical Cover	362
57.	15th Division. The Crossing of the Deurne Canal. Medical Cover	363
58.	15th Division. The Attack on Blerick. Medical Cover	365
59.	51st Division. Eindhoven Airfield. Medical Cover. Oct. 2–23	369
60.	51st Division. Operation 'Colin'. Medical Cover, 1st Phase	371
61.	51st Division. Operation 'Colin'. Medical Cover, Later Phase	372
62.	51st Division. Operation 'Ascot'. Medical Cover, Early Phase	373
63.	51st Division. Operation 'Ascot'. Medical Cover, Later Phase	374
64.	51st Division. Nijmegen 'Island'. Medical Cover	375

ILLUSTRATIONS

Fig.		Page
65.	53rd Division. Operation 'Alan'. Medical Cover	377
66.	XII Corps. Medical Arrangements. October 22–25	381
67.	XII Corps. Medical Arrangements. October 26–November 2	381
68.	XII Corps. Operation 'Mallard'	382
69.	XXX Corps. Between the Waal and the Maas. October. Medical Arrangements	385
70.	XXX Corps. Operation 'Clipper'. Medical Arrangements	387
71.	XXX Corps. Medical Arrangements in connexion with the German Counter-Offensive in the Ardennes	389
72.	Second Army. The Medical Situation as at October 18	391
73.	Second Army. The Medical Situation as at November 9	392
74.	Second Army. The Medical Situation as at November 22	393
75.	Second Army. The Medical Situation as at December 7	395
76.	Second Army. The Medical Situation as at December 28	396

Chapter 6

77.	The Front Line. February 7	414
78.	Canadian First Army. The Battle of the Rhineland. February–March	415
79.	15th Division. Operation 'Torchlight'	431
80.	15th Division. Operation 'Torchlight'. Medical Cover	433
81.	43rd Division. Operation 'Veritable'	438
82.	51st Division. Operation 'Veritable'. Medical Cover, Early Phase	442
83.	51st Division. Operation 'Veritable'. Medical Cover, Later Phase	443
84.	XXX Corps. Operation 'Plunder'. Medical Arrangements	454
85.	Second Army. The Siting of the Forward Medical Units in support of XXX Corps. January 1, 1945	457
86.	Canadian First Army. Operation 'Veritable'. Medical Cover	468
87.	Canadian 2nd Division. Operations across the Rhine	473

Chapter 7

88.	The Advance to the Elbe (1)	478
89.	The Advance to the Elbe (2)	479
90.	Operation 'Enterprise'. The Crossing of the Elbe	482
91.	15th Division. Operation 'Enterprise'. Medical Cover	490

Chapter 8

92.	Canadian First Army. The Liberation of Holland	517

Chapter 10

93.	Casualties (Injured). Normandy. D-day to End of July 1944	610
94.	Casualties (Injured). Normandy. D-day to End of July 1944	612
95.	Casualties (Injured). Normandy. D-day to End of July 1944	616
96.	Casualties (Injured). Normandy. D-day to End of July 1944	617

ILLUSTRATIONS

PLATES

Chapter 2   *Between Pages*

I.	R.A.M.C. Personnel landing on the Normandy Shore from L.C.I. .	
II.	Disembarking from a L.C.T. on the Normandy Shore	
III.	An Ambulance Car leaves a L.C.T. for the Normandy Shore .	
IV.	A Bren Carrier used for the Evacuation of Casualties	
V.	Casualties of 6th Airborne Division being evacuated .	
VI.	Jeep-Ambulances moving forward	
VII.	Loading a Jeep-Ambulance	
VIII.	A Jeep-Ambulance crossing the Caen Canal Bridge .	
IX.	48 Field Dressing Station in the Abbey at Juaye-Mondaye .	154–155
X.	An Advanced Dressing Station in a Normandy Orchard	
XI.	Q.A.I.M.N.S. Nursing Officers in the Beachhead .	
XII.	Q.A.I.M.N.S. A Beachhead Dormitory . . .	
XIII.	Q.A.I.M.N.S. In a Beachhead Casualty Clearing Station .	
XIV.	A General Hospital in the Beachhead . . .	
XV.	A Water Pumping and Sterilising Unit . . .	
XVI.	A Beachhead Water Point	

Chapter 3

XVII.	Arnhem. A Casualty of 1st Airborne Division being taken to a Dressing Station .	
XVIII.	An Ambulance Railcar in La Gare du Midi, Brussels	250–251
XIX.	Belgian Civilians loading Casualties into a Dakota of R.A.F. Transport Command .	

Chapter 5

XX.	The Bridges over the Waal at Nijmegen . .	
XXI.	A Refrigerator Truck of a Field Transfusion Unit .	378–379
XXII.	The Advanced Blood Bank	

Chapter 6

XXIII.	The Crossing of the Rhine. 'Crocodiles' with Jeep-Ambulances aboard .	
XXIV.	A Casualty Evacuation Post on the East Bank of the Rhine .	442–443
XXV.	'Buffaloes' crossing the Rhine . . .	

ILLUSTRATIONS

Between pages

Chapter 7

XXVI.	A Half-track Ambulance Car crossing the Dortmund–Ems Canal	
XXVII.	Belsen Camp	
XXVIII.	Belsen Camp	506–507
XXIX.	11 Light Field Ambulance at Belsen Camp	
XXX.	Belsen Camp	
XXXI.	Belsen Camp. The Human Laundry	
XXXII.	Belsen Camp. Dusting with Anti-Louse Powder	

NOTE. *These plates are Crown copyright and were supplied by the Imperial War Museum to which acknowledgement is made.*

TABLES

Page

Chapter 1

1. The Bid for Labour in connexion with the Establishment of the General Hospitals on the Continent 40
2. Casualty Evacuation Schedule. British Sector . . . 58
3. The Disposal of Formations and Medical Units involved in the Reorganisation of Home Forces, 1944 100

Chapter 2

4. I and VIII Corps Casualties. July 18–19, 1944 . . . 127
5. 6th Airborne Division. R.A.M.C. Casualties up to June 20, 1944 130
6. 6th Airborne Division. Numbers admitted to the M.D.Ss. June 6–30, 1944 131
7. 50th Division. Casualties. June–July 1944 137
8. 3rd Division. The Build-up of the Medical Units in the Beachhead 150
9. 3rd Division. Casualties. June 6–30, 1944 153
10. Guards Armoured Division. Admissions to Medical Units. July 18–23, 1944 153
11. 15th Division. Admissions to Medical Units. June 26–July 1, 1944 159
12. 15th Division. Wounds by Anatomical Region. June 26–July 1, 1944 159
13. 15th Division. Casualties. July 15–18, 1944 161
14. 49th Division. Casualties. June 16–18, 1944 164
15. 49th Division. Casualties. June 25–29, 1944 166
16. 49th Division. Admissions to Medical Units. July 17–30, 1944 166
17. 53rd Division. Admissions to Medical Units. July 1944 . 171
18. I Corps Casualties. June 6–30, 1944 176
19. XXX Corps Casualties. June 6–30, 1944 182
20. Second Army. Admissions to and Evacuations from the Medical Units. June 6–July 1, 1944 184
21. Incidence of Psychiatric Casualties in 6th Airborne and 51st Divisions. June 17–July 1, 1944 207

Chapter 3

22. Guards Armoured Division. Casualties evacuated. July 31–September 19, 1944 234
23. 7th Armoured Division. Casualties. July–September 1944 . 235
24. 15th Division. The Distribution of Personnel among three Sections of a F.D.S. 240
25. 15th Division. Admissions to Medical Units. July–September 1944 241

		Page
26.	49th Division. Casualties. July–September 1944	247
27.	49th Division. Incidence of Gastro-intestinal Diseases. July–September 1944	249
28.	51st Division. Casualties. July–September 1944	260
29.	53rd Division. Casualties. Falaise. August 13–21, 1944	261
30.	53rd Division. Casualties. September 19–30, 1944	267
31.	Strengths of Medical Units of 1st Airborne Division taking part in Operation 'Market Garden'	268
32.	Types of Cases treated in the Lazarett in Stalag XIB	282
33.	Medical Supplies by Air to 1st Airborne Division at Arnhem	302
34.	1st Airborne Division. Scale of Re-supply by Air	304

Chapter 4

35.	52nd Division. Admissions to Field Ambulances. October–December 1944	346

Chapter 5

36.	49th Division. Casualties. October–December 1944	367
37.	51st Division. Casualties. October–December 1944	376

Chapter 6

38.	Guards Armoured Division. Casualties. Operation 'Veritable'	420
39.	7th Armoured Division. Casualties. January–March 1945	421
40.	6th Airborne Division. Casualties. March 24, 1945	425
41.	6th Airborne Division. Casualties. March 24–April 7, 1945	425
42.	15th Division. Casualties. January–March 1945	434
43.	43rd Division. Casualties. Operation 'Blackcock'	437
44.	43rd Division. Casualties. Operation 'Veritable'	439
45.	XXX Corps. Casualties. Operation 'Veritable'	453
46.	XXX Corps. Casualties. Operation 'Plunder'	456

Chapter 7

47.	7th Armoured Division. Casualties. April–June 1945	485
48.	3rd Division. Casualties. April 1945	487
49.	15th Division. Casualties. April–June 1945	492
50.	52nd Division. Admissions to Medical Units. April–June 1945	495

Chapter 8

51.	Canadian Casualties during the Campaign	526

Chapter 9

52.	The Army Dental Service. Summary of the Work performed June 1944–March 1945	543
53.	The Army Transfusion Service. Casualties Transfused and Total Fluids used during the Campaign	546

		Page
54.	XXX Corps. Psychiatric Casualties. February 8–March 10, 1945	555
55.	XXX Corps. Psychiatric Casualties. April 7–May 5, 1945	555
56.	21 Army Group. Psychiatric Casualties. June 6, 1944–May 9, 1945	557
57.	21 Army Group. Percentage of Exhaustion Cases returned to their Units without evacuation to the L. of C. February–March 1945	557
58.	Results of Review of Sentences passed on 373 Men serving Terms of Imprisonment for Desertion or Refusal to obey an Order. November 17–December 30, 1944	559

Chapter 10

		Page
59.	Comparison of Casualties in This and Other Campaigns	561
60.	I Corps. Casualties. July–September 1944. Principal Causes of Morbidity	564
61.	I Corps. Casualties. October–December 1944. Principal Causes of Morbidity	566
62.	I Corps. Casualties. March–June 1945. Principal Causes of Morbidity. April–June 1945	567
63.	VIII Corps. Principal Diseases affecting the Troops. July–September 1944	568
64.	XXX Corps. Casualties. January–March 1945	569
65.	VIII Corps. Casualties. Other Ranks. April 1945	570
66.	Second Army. Admissions to Medical Units classified by Cause and by Anatomical Region. Thirteen Weeks ending September 30, 1944	571
67.	Second Army. Infectious Diseases notified during the Thirteen Weeks ending September 30, 1944	572
68.	Second Army. The Average Weekly Incidence per 1,000 of the Principal Diseases affecting the Troops. October 1944–March 1945	573
69.	Second Army Troops. Incidence of Diseases. New Cases seen by R.M.Os. and in M.I. Rooms. June 1944–March 1945	573
70.	21 Army Group. Analysis of Admissions to British Medical Units. July–December 1944	576
71.	21 Army Group. Summary of Surgical Results (Forward Units) June 1944–February 1945 and March 1945	578
72.	21 Army Group. Analysis of Surgical Results. October–December 1944	579
73.	21 Army Group. Admissions to all British Medical Units. October 1944–January 1945	581
74.	21 Army Group (less Canadian First Army). Deaths in Medical Units. June 1944–April 1945	583
75.	21 Army Group. Hospital Bed State. December 1944–May 1945	583
76.	21 Army Group. Admissions to All Medical Units. Rates per 1,000 per Week. December 1944–May 1945	584

TABLES

		Page
77.	21 Army Group. Direct Admissions to the Medical Divisions of all British Hospitals (excl. 32 B.G.H.). January–March 1945 .	586
78.	21 Army Group. Numbers evacuated from the Theatre to the United Kingdom (excl. P.o.W.). December 1944–May 1945 .	588
79.	Medical Evacuations from North-west Europe expressed as Percentage of Admissions to Hospital (British Army only). 1914–18 and November 1944–April 1945 .	590
80.	21 Army Group. Summary of Work of Mobile Ophthalmic Units and of Ophthalmic Departments of General Hospitals. June–September 1944 .	590
81.	21 Army Group. Incidence of Skin Diseases among Patients admitted to British General Hospitals. July–September 1944 .	592
82.	21 Army Group. Venereal Disease. Rates per 1,000 per Week .	592
83.	13 Convalescent Depot. Summary of First, Second and Third Thousand Convalescents .	593
84.	Evacuation from Normandy; June–July 1944 .	603
84a.	Evacuation from Normandy; June–July 1944 .	604
85.	Ratio of Casualties caused by Enemy Action and Not by Enemy Action. Normandy; June–July 1944 .	604
86.	Disposal and Nature of Casualties not evacuated beyond the Forward Medical Units .	605
87.	Distribution of Casualties not evacuated, by Rank .	605
88.	Distribution of Casualties by Arm of Service .	606
89.	Limits of Overall Disposal and Nature of Casualties .	606
90.	Relationship between 'Days to Disposal' and Downgrading .	619
91.	Distribution of Category C and E Cases by 'Days to Disposal'	620
92.	Downgrading by Arm of Service .	621
93.	Downgrading by Rank .	621
94.	Deaths in Forward Medical Units .	622
95.	Days off Duty in Forward Medical Units .	622
96.	Percentage Disposed per 4-week Month—Cases evacuated to the United Kingdom .	623
97.	Percentage of Total Man-Day Wastage in Each Decile Group and at Each Stage of Treatment .	623
98.	Percentage of Cases in Each Group (including Officers) who attended Convalescent Depot .	624
99.	Mean Days for Each Group at Different Medical Levels .	624
100.	Percentage evacuated: (a) per Day after Wounding; (b) per Day after Wounding—Cumulative .	624
101.	Percentage discharged from Hospital: (a) per 4-weeks after Admission; (b) per 4-weeks—Cumulative .	625
102.	Percentage discharged from Convalescent Depot: (a) per Week after Admission; (b) per Week—Cumulative .	625
103.	Distribution of Injuries (E.A. and N.E.A.) by Site .	627
104.	Relative Severity of Injuries (E.A. and N.E.A.) at Different Sites .	627
105.	Overall Distribution of all Injuries by Site .	628

		Page
106.	Distribution of Hospitalised Injuries (E.A. and N.E.A.) by Number of Wounds	628
107.	Distribution of Hospitalised Injuries by Site and Arm of Service	628
108.	Distribution of Injuries by Type and Severity (single injuries only)	629
109.	Distribution of Hospitalised Single Injuries by Type and Site	629
110.	Overall Distribution of Wounds by Weapon and Severity Grades	631
111.	Distribution of Wounds by Weapon and Site of Injury	631
112.	Number of Wounds caused by Different Weapons (Evacuated Cases only)	632
113.	Percentage of Personnel wounded by Individual Weapons downgraded to Categories C and E	632
114.	Distribution of Trivial Wounds by Weapon and Arm of Service	633
115.	Distribution of Evacuated Wounds by Weapon and Arm of Service	633
116.	Distribution of Lethal Wounds by Weapon and Arm of Service	634
117.	Distribution of Wounds by Weapon and Rank	634

ABBREVIATIONS

A.	The Adjutant-General's Branch
A/	Acting
A.A.	Anti-aircraft
A.A.G.	Assistant Adjutant-General
A.B.	Airborne
A. and D.	Admission and Discharge (Book)
A.C.C.	Ambulance Car Company, R.A.S.C.
A.C.I.	Army Council Instruction
A.D. Corps	The Army Dental Corps (now The Royal)
A.D.D.S.	Assistant Director, Dental Service
A.D.H.	Assistant Director of Hygiene (now Health)
Adm.	Administrative
A.D.M.S.	Assistant Director, Medical Services
A.D.S.	Advanced Dressing Station
Adv.	Advanced
Adv. Depot Med. Stores	Advanced Depot of Medical Stores
Adv. Surg. Centre	Advanced Surgical Centre
A.F.	Army Form
A.F.D.A.G.	Airborne Forward Delivery Airfield Group
A.F.V.	Armoured Fighting Vehicle
A.G.R.A.	Army Group. Royal Artillery
A.G.R.E.	Army Group. Royal Engineers
A/L	Airlanding or Anti-louse
Amb.	Ambulance
A.M.D.	The Army Medical Directorate of the War Office
A.M.P.C.	The Auxiliary Military Pioneer Corps
A.M.S.	The Army Medical Services
A.N.E.F.	Allied Naval Expeditionary Force
A.P.C.	Army Pioneer Corps
Armd.	Armoured
A.S.C.	Advanced Surgical Centre
A.S.H.	The Army School of Hygiene
A/T, A.T.	Anti-tank
A.V.R.E.	Armoured Vehicle, Royal Engineers
B.A.O.R.	The British Army of the Rhine
B.C.	Battle Casualties
B.D.	Battle Dress
Base Depot Med. Stores	Base Depot of Medical Stores
Bde.	Brigade
B.D.O.	Blood Distribution Officer

ABBREVIATIONS

B.D.S.	Beach Dressing Station
B.E.F.	The British Expeditionary Force, France 1939–1940
B.G.H.	British General Hospital
B.L.A.	The British Army of Liberation
Black Watch	The Black Watch (Royal Highland Regiment)
Bn.	Battalion
B.O.R.	British Other Rank
Border	The Border Regiment
Br.	British
B.R.C.S.	The British Red Cross Society
B.S.A.	Beach Sub-area or Base Sub-area
B.T.	Benign Tertian (Malaria)
B.T.U.	Base Transfusion Unit
Bty.	Battery
B.W.	Bomb wound
C.A.	Civil Affairs
C.A.E.C.	Casualty Air Evacuation Centre
C.A.E.U.	Casualty Air Evacuation Unit (R.A.F.)
Cameronians	The Cameronians (Scottish Rifles)
C.A.O.F.	Canadian Army Occupation Force
Capt.	Captain
C.B.D.	Corps Base Depot
C.C.P.	Casualty Collecting Post
C.C.S.	Casualty Clearing Station
C.D.L.	'Canal Light Defence.' An infantry tank fitted with a powerful projector that emitted a beam that illuminated a wide field and dazzled the eye.
Cdn.	Canadian
Cdn. G.H.	Canadian General Hospital
Cdo.	Commando
C.D.P.	Casualty Disembarkation Post or Point, where casualties were off-loaded from craft that had crossed a water obstacle
C.E.E.S.	Captured Enemy Equipment Section
C.E.P.	Casualty Embarkation Post, where casualties were loaded into craft to cross a water obstacle; or Casualty Evacuating Point
C. in C.	Commander- or Commanding-in-Chief
C.M.F.	The Central Mediterranean Force
C.M.O.	Chief Medical Officer
C.O.	Commanding Officer
Col.	Colonel
Con. Depot	Convalescent Depot
C.O.S.S.A.C.	The Chief of Staff to the Supreme Allied Commander
Coy.	Company

ABBREVIATIONS

C.P.	Car Post
Cpl.	Corporal
C.R.E.	Commanding Royal Engineers
C.R.S.	Camp Reception Station
C.S.	Clearing Station (U.S.)
C.S.F.	Cerebro-spinal Fever
C.S.M.	Cerebro-spinal Meningitis
C.V.	Command Vehicle
D.A.D.H.	Deputy Assistant Director of Hygiene
D.A.D.M.S.	Deputy Assistant Director, Medical Services
D.A.D.M.S. (E)	Deputy Assistant Director, Medical Services (Evacuation)
D.A.G.	Deputy Adjutant-General
D.C.L.I.	The Duke of Cornwall's Light Infantry
D.D.	Duplex Drive
D.D.D.S.	Deputy Director of Dental Service
D.D.H.	Deputy Director of Hygiene
D.D.M.S.	Deputy Director, Medical Services
D.D.O.S.	Deputy Director, Ordnance
D.D.P.	Deputy Director of Pathology
D.D.T.	Dichloro-diphenyl-trichlorethane
Det. or Detach.	Detachment
D.G.	Dragoon Guards
D.G.A.M.S.	Director General Army Medical Services
D.I.D.	Detail Issue Depot
Div.	Division
D.L.I.	The Durham Light Infantry
D.M.S.	Director of Medical Services
D.O.	Dental Officer
Dorset	The Dorsetshire Regiment
D.P.	Displaced Person
D.R.	Despatch Rider
D.R.L.S.	Despatch Rider Letter Service
D.S.	Dressing Station
D.U.K.W.	An amphibious 2½ ton vehicle
D.W.R.	The Duke of Wellington's Regiment
D.Z.	Dropping Zone
E.A.	Enemy Action (caused by)
E.M.S.	The Emergency Medical Services of the Ministry of Health and of the Department of Health for Scotland
E.N.T.	Ear, Nose and Throat
E.T.O.U.S.A.	European Theatre of Operations, United States Army
Evac.	Evacuation
E. Yorks	The East Yorkshire Regiment (Duke of York's Own)

ABBREVIATIONS

Fd. Amb.	Field Ambulance
F.D.C. or Fd. Dent. Centre	Field Dental Centre
Fd. Dent. Lab.	Field Dental Laboratory
Fd. Hosp.	Field Hospital (U.S.A.M.C.)
Fd. Hyg. Sec.	Field Hygiene Section
Fd. San. Sec.	Field Sanitary Section
F.D.S.	Field Dressing Station
F.F.I.	Les Forces Françaises de l'Intérieur
F.S.	Field Service
F.S.U.	Field Surgical Unit
F.T.U.	Field Transfusion Unit
Fwd. Del.	Forward Delivery (truck)
G.1098	Mobilisation Equipment Scale
G. (S.D.)	Operations Branch of the General Staff (Staff Duties)
G.D.O.	General Duty Officer or Orderly
Gds.	Guards
Gen. Hosp.	General Hospital
G.H.Q.	General Headquarters
Glasgow Highlanders	The Glasgow Highlanders (T.A.)
G.O.C.	General Officer Commanding
Gp.	Group
Green Howards	The Green Howards (Alexandra, Princess of Wales' Own Yorkshire Regiment)
G.R.O.	General Routine Order
G.S.	General Service
G.S.W.	Gunshot wound
H.	Hussars
Hallams	The Hallamshire Battalion, York and Lancaster Regiment (T.A.)
Hamps.	The Hampshire Regiment
H.E.	Higher Establishment
H.L.I.	Highland Light Infantry (City of Glasgow Regiment)
H.P.	Hospital Pattern
H.Q.	Headquarters
Hy. Sec.	Heavy Section
I.1248	Scale of Medical Mobilisation Equipment, Apparatus and Drugs
I.A.T.	Inflammation of the Areolar Tissue
i/c	in command or in charge of
Indep.	Independent
Inf.	Infantry
I.O.F.B.	Intra-ocular foreign body

ABBREVIATIONS

'Kangaroo'	Troop-carrying Tank
Kensingtons	The Kensington Regiment (T.A.)
K.O.S.B.	The King's Own Scottish Borderers
K.O.Y.L.I.	The King's Own Yorkshire Light Infantry
K.S.L.I.	The King's Shropshire Light Infantry
K.W.M.	Killed: Wounded: Missing
L.C.I.	Landing Craft Infantry
L.C.P.	Landing Craft Personnel
L.C.T.	Landing Craft Tank
L. of C.	Lines of Communication
L/Cpl.	Lance-Corporal
L.E.	Lower Establishment
Leicesters	The Leicestershire Regiment
Lincolns	The Lincolnshire Regiment
L.O.	Liaison Officer
L.S.T.	Landing Ship Tank
Lt.	Light
Lt. Col.	Lieutenant-Colonel
L.V.T.	Landing Vessel Tank (The 'Buffalo')
L.Z.	Landing Zone
M.A.C.	Motor Ambulance Convoy
M.A.L.O.	Medical Air Liaison Officer
M.B.U.	Mobile Bath Unit
M/C or M.C.	Motor Cycle
M.D.S.	Main Dressing Station
M.D.U.	Mobile Dental Unit
M.E.	The Middle East
Med.	Medical
M.E.F.	Middle East Force
M.F.S.U.	Maxillo-facial Surgical Unit
M.G.S.O.	Marquee General Service, Oval
Mil. Gov.	Military Government
M.I. Room	Medical Inspection Room
M.N.S.U.	Mobile Neuro-surgical Unit
M.O.	Medical Officer
Mob. Bact. Lab.	Mobile Bacteriological Laboratory
Mob. Hyg. Lab.	Mobile Hygiene Laboratory
M.O.U.	Mobile Ophthalmic Unit
m.p.h.	miles per hour
M.R.C.	The Medical Research Council
M.T.	Mechanical Transport or Malignant Tertian (Malaria)
N.C.O.	Non-commissioned Officer
N.E.A.	Not Enemy Action (not caused by)
N.M.O.	Non-Medical Officer

ABBREVIATIONS

N.O.	Nursing Orderly
N.S.R.	The North Shore Regiment (Canadian)
N.Y.D.	Not Yet Diagnosed
N.Z.	New Zealand
O.B.D.	Ordnance Base Depot
O.C.	Officer Commanding
Offrs.	Officers
Op.	Operational
O.R.A.	Operating Room Assistant
Ord.	Ordnance
O.Rs.	Other Ranks
P.A.C.	Prophylactic Ablution Centre
Para.	Parachute
Pln.	Platoon
P.L.U.T.O.	Pipeline under the Ocean
Pol.	Polish
P.O.L.	Petrol, Oil, Lubricants, supply systems
P.o.W.	Prisoner-of-War
Pte.	Private
P.U.O.	Pyrexia of Unknown Origin
P.W.X.	ex-Prisoners-of-War other than Germans
Q.	The Quartermaster-General's Branch dealing with food, quarters, clothing, equipment, stores and movement
Q.(A.E.) Stats.	The Quartermaster-General's Branch dealing with the statistical side of the Area Engineer's stores (Arms and Equipment)
Q.A.I.M.N.S.	Queen Alexandra's Imperial Military Nursing Service (now Q.A.R.A.N.C.)
Q.M.	Quartermaster
Q.M.S.	Quartermaster-Sergeant
Q.O.R.	The Queen's Own Rifles of Canada
R.A.	The Royal Regiment of Artillery
R.A.F.	The Royal Air Force
R.A.M.C.	The Royal Army Medical Corps
R.A.M. College	The Royal Army Medical College
R.A.O.C.	The Royal Army Ordnance Corps
R.A.P.	Regimental Aid Post
R.A.S.C.	The Royal Army Service Corps
R.C.A.M.C.	The Royal Canadian Army Medical Corps
R.C.A.F.	The Royal Canadian Air Force
R.C.T.	Regimental Combat Team (U.S.)
R.E.	The Corps of Royal Engineers
Recce.	Reconnaissance
Regt.	Regiment

ABBREVIATIONS

R.E.M.E.	The Royal Electrical and Mechanical Engineers
Res.	Reserve
Rft.	Reinforcement
R.H.	Railhead
R.H.O.	Regional Hospital Officer (E.M.S.)
'Rhino' ferry; 'Rhinoceros'	A steel raft about 150 ft. long, built up of rectangular steel caissons bolted together and powered by two 60 h.p. petrol engines at the stern. Vehicles were lifted by ship's derricks on to the ferry which then transported them to the beach or shore
R.H.U.	Reinforcement Holding Unit
R.M.	The Royal Marines
R.M.A.	Rear Maintenance Area
R.M.O.	Regimental Medical Officer
R.N.	The Royal Navy
Royal Berks.	The Royal Berkshire Regiment (Princess Charlotte of Wales's)
Royals	The First Royal Dragoons
R.S.	The Royal Scots (The Royal Regiment)
R.S.F.	The Royal Scots Fusiliers
R.T.	Radio Telegraphy
R.Tks.	The Royal Tank Regiment
R.T.U.	Returned to Unit
R.W.R.	The Royal Winnipeg Regiment (Canadian Army)
S.A.	Sub-area or Small arm
S. and T.	Supply and Transport
S.B.	Stretcher Bearer
Seaforth	The Seaforth Highlanders
Sec.	Section
S.G.	Selection Grade
S/Sgt.	Staff-Sergeant
Sgt.	Sergeant
S.H.A.E.F.	Supreme Headquarters Allied Expeditionary Force
Shropshires or K.S.L.I.	King's Shropshire Light Infantry
S.I.	Self-inflicted
Sitrep.	Situation Report
S. Lancs. or S. Lan. R.	The South Lancashire Regiment (The Prince of Wales's Volunteers)
S.M.O.	Senior Medical Officer
Somersets or Som. L.I.	The Somerset Light Infantry (Prince Albert's)
S.P.	Self-propelled
Sp.	Support (Group)
Sqn.	Squadron
S.R.	Special Reserve

ABBREVIATIONS

S.S.	Special Service or in the German Army Schutzstaffel. Originally the Führer's personal bodyguard, later a State Military Police Force of 3 divisions. By 1941 it had expanded to 30 divisions with priorities in respect of man-power and equipment.
S. Staffords.	The South Staffordshire Regiment
Str.	Stretcher
Surg. Team	Surgical Team
S.W.	Shell Wound
T.A.	The Territorial Army
T.A.B.	Typhoid, Para-typhoid A and B
T.A.F.	The Tactical Air Force
T.A.T.	Temporary Ambulance Train
T.B.	Tuberculosis
T.C.P.	Traffic Control Post
T.C.V.	Troop-carrying Vehicle
Tk.	Tank
T.O.	Transfusion Officer
Tps.	Troops
Tyne. Scot.	The Tyneside Scottish (T.A.)
u/c	under the command of
U.K.	The United Kingdom
U.N.R.R.A.	United Nations Relief and Rehabilitation Association
U.S.A. or U.S.	The United States of America
U.S.S.R.	The Union of Soviet Socialist Republics
V.D.	Venereal Diseases
V.D.T.C.	Venereal Diseases Treatment Centre
W.E.	War Establishment
Wilts.	The Wiltshire Regiment (The Duke of Edinburgh's)
W.T.	Wireless Telegraphy

BIBLIOGRAPHY

PUBLISHED SOURCES

Despatches

EISENHOWER, General DWIGHT D. *Report of the Supreme Commander to the Combined Chiefs of Staff on the Operations in Europe of the Allied Expeditionary Force, 6 June, 1944—8 May, 1945*. 1946. H.M.S.O.

MONTGOMERY, Field Marshal the Viscount. *Operations in North-west Europe from 6th June, 1944 to 5th May, 1945*. 1946. H.M.S.O.

RAMSAY, Admiral Sir BERTRAM. *The Assault Phase of the Normandy Landings*. 1947. H.M.S.O.

Books

BRADLEY, General OMAR. *A Soldier's Story*. 1951. Eyre & Spottiswoode.

BRIGHT, PAMELA. *Life in Our Hands*. 1955. Macgibbon & Kee.

BUTCHER, Captain H. C. *My Three Years with Eisenhower*. 1946. New York. Simon & Schuster.

By Air to Battle. The Official Account of the British First and Sixth Airborne Divisions. 1945. H.M.S.O.

CHURCHILL, WINSTON S. *The Second World War*. Vol. 5: *Closing the Ring*. 1952. Vol. 6: *Triumph and Tragedy*. 1954. Cassell.

CLAY, Major E. W. *The Path of the 50th*. The Story of the 50th (Northumbrian) Division in the Second World War 1939–45. 1950. Gale & Polden.

DARBY, H. and CUNLIFFE, M. *A Short Story of 21 Army Group*. Gale & Polden.

EDWARDS, Commander K. *Operation 'Neptune'*. 1946. Collins.

EISENHOWER, General D. D. *Crusade in Europe*. 1948. Heinemann.

FALLS, CYRIL. *The Second World War*. 1948. Methuen.

FOLEY, C. *Commando Extraordinary*. 1954. Longmans.

FULLER, Major General J. F. G. *The Second World War*. 1948. Eyre and Spottiswoode.

GUINGAND, Major General Sir FRANCIS de. *Operation 'Victory'*. 1947. Hodder and Stoughton.

HARRIS, Marshal of the Air Force Sir ARTHUR. *Bomber Offensive*. 1947. Collins.

History of 7th Armoured Division, June 1943–July 1945. 1945.

LIDDELL HART, Captain B. H. *The Other Side of the Hill*. 1951. Cassell.

LINDSAY, Lt. Colonel M. *So Few got Through*. Hutchinson.

LOCKHART, Sir ROBERT BRUCE. *The Marines were There*. 1950. Putnam.

MARTIN, Lt. General H. G. *The History of the Fifteenth Scottish Division 1939–45*. 1948. Blackwood.

MONTGOMERY, Field Marshal the Viscount. *Normandy to the Baltic*. 1946. Hutchinson.

MORGAN, Lt. General Sir FREDERICK. *Overture to 'Overlord'*. 1950. Hodder & Stoughton.

BIBLIOGRAPHY

NORTH, JOHN. *North-West Europe, 1944–45*. The Achievement of 21 Army Group. 1953. H.M.S.O.
PATTON, General GEORGE S. *War as I Knew it*. 1947. Boston. Houghton Mifflin.
PHILLIPS, R. *The Belsen Trial*. 1948. Hodge.
RANDEL, Major P. B. *A Short History of 30 Corps in the European Campaign 1944–45*. 1945. Limited Edition.
SALMOND, J. B. *The History of the 51st Highland Division, 1939–1945*. 1953. Blackwood.
SAUNDERS, HILARY ST. GEORGE. *The Red Beret*. The Story of the Parachute Regiment at War 1940–45. 1950. Michael Joseph.
—— *The Green Beret*. The Story of the Commandos. 1949. Michael Joseph.
SCARFE, NORMAN. *Assault Division*. A History of the 3rd Division. 1947. Collins.
SCHULMAN, MILTON. *Defeat in the West*. 1947. Cassell.
STACEY, Colonel C. P. *The Canadian Army, 1939–45*. 1948. Ottawa. King's Printer.
Taurus Pursuant. A History of the 11th Armoured Division, 1945.
URQUHART, Major General R. E. *Arnhem*. 1958. Cassell.
WATTS, Lt. Colonel J. C. *Surgeon at War*. 1955. Allen & Unwin.
WILMOT, CHESTER. *The Struggle for Europe*. 1952. Collins.
WILSON, Field Marshal the Lord. *Eight Years Overseas*. 1950. Hutchinson.
WINGFIELD, R. M. *The Only Way Out*. 1955. Hutchinson.

UNPUBLISHED SOURCES

War Diaries, Quarterly Reports and other official documents.
Letters from officers of the Army Medical Services.
Provisional Narrative prepared by the Official Canadian Medical Historian.

In the interval between the writing and the publication of this volume there appeared:

BRYANT, Sir ARTHUR. *The Turn of the Tide*. 1957. Collins.
—— *Triumph in the West*. 1959. Collins.
HOWARTH, D. *Dawn of D-Day*. 1959. Collins.
MERRIAM, ROBERT E. *The Battle of the Ardennes*. 1958. Souvenir Press.
MONTGOMERY, Field Marshal the Viscount. *The Memoirs of*. 1958. Collins.
RYAN, CORNELIUS. *The Longest Day, June 6, 1944*. 1959. Gollancz.
THOMPSON, R. W. *The Eighty-Five Days*. 1957. Hutchinson.
—— *The Battle for the Rhineland*. 1958. Hutchinson.
TURNER, J. F. *Invasion '44*. 1958. Harraps.
WOOLLCOMBE, R. *Lion Rampant*. 1955. Chatto & Windus.

PREFACE

UPON the Army, in war, is focused the alert and anxious attention of the entire civilian population, and those who are responsible for its training and employment are at all times exposed to the hazards of violent criticism. This is particularly so when defeat and disaster occur, for then the tendency is to impute their causes to gross incompetence or to criminal neglect. There is no component of an army more open to such criticism and none more sensitive to it than its medical services. The general public may know little of military matters in general but claims, because of its own experience during illness, to be well informed concerning doctors, dentists and nurses, their work and their responsibilities. The sick and especially the wounded soldier attracts the compassionate interest of everybody and any rumour or suspicion of professional indexterity or carelessness on the part of the administration or of any member of the Army Medical Services quickly arouses clamorous protestation. The gratitude that is showered upon those who tend the sick and the hurt when all goes well is equalled only by the blame that is heaped upon them when things go wrong.

During the war years a constant stream of complaints flowed into the Army Medical Directorate of the War Office, from relatives of soldiers or from their Members of Parliament. Since all medical officers, all dentists, all nurses were not equally experienced and equally competent and since patients display so wide a range of variability in respect of their reactions to one and the same disease-evoking agency and to the same system of therapy, the outcome of medical intervention was not invariably successful. The occasional mistake in diagnosis and in treatment did occur. But in the overwhelming majority of instances it was found, after careful and thorough enquiry, that these complaints were without foundation, usually being born of misunderstanding on the part of the patient and worry on the part of his relatives. Some, however, were, beyond all doubt, displays of fierce prejudice, chagrin or even downright malice. The experience of the Army Medical Services differed in no way and in no degree from that of the National Health Service since the war.

Certain wars have been notable for 'medical scandals', the administration of the medical services being charged with glaring inefficiency. Such a charge was made in 1915 after the battle of Ctesiphon in Mesopotamia. At no time during the Second World War was there any rumour or suspicion of any such break-down of medical arrangements. The Army Medical Services were never embarrassed from any inherent cause. The despatches testify that in every campaign and in every theatre, whenever the tactical situation permitted them to discharge their responsibilities, they did so with marked success, the efficiency of their administration and the competence, fidelity, endurance and courage of their members attracting the warm commendation of those they served.

The practice of military medicine can never be easy. It is invariably associated with difficulties that derive from the climatic, geographic or demographic features of the theatre and from the variable conditions and circumstances that warring creates. These difficulties were fewer and smaller in the campaign in North-west Europe, 1944–45 than in any of those that preceded it. Problems in plenty were encountered but none of them over-taxed the resourcefulness or the resources of the Army Medical Services. Evacuation from the Normandy beaches and across the floods of Holland and the great rivers of Germany evoked a reasonable anxiety during the period of preparation but, in the event, proved to be a simple and straightforward affair for the reason that intelligent use was made of the abundant resources that had been made available. The swift advance following the break-out from the Normandy bridgehead made it difficult for those concerned to provide adequate hospital cover for the formations in the van. But the skilful use of the more mobile field medical units and the full exploitation of all evacuation facilities solved such problems as presented themselves.

In respect of training and experience the medical services of Second Army were better equipped than had been any of those of any other expeditionary force thus far considered. Into their preparation all that had been learnt in previous campaigns, and that was applicable, had been incorporated. The senior administrative medical officers were men whose competence had been thoroughly tested in war. Of the personnel of the field medical units a large proportion had long records of active service and had attained a high degree of efficiency in their various rôles. The material resources available to them were the very best that could be provided. Into their hands abundant tools of power and precision were placed.

Second Army had been passed through the sieve of selection and to a large extent had been ridded of its inadequates. Its morale was high and remained high. The campaign opened with a dramatic success and throughout its course victory followed swiftly upon victory. The campaign was fought in a country which was not remote from and was in every way similar to Great Britain. The campaign was brief.

In such circumstances the tasks of the Army Medical Services are greatly lightened. In the presence of swift victory sickness wanes and the healing of wounds is quickened.

It is therefore hazardous to attempt to compare the 'efficiency' of the Army Medical Services in this and in the preceding campaigns of the Second World War or in this war and in the First World War. Professional competence is, of course, directly reflected in the outcome of medical intervention. But these results are profoundly affected by the conditions and the circumstances in which such intervention occurs. For example, if the length of time between the receipt of the wound and admission to a medical unit adequately equipped to deal with it surgically was twice as great, on the average, in the Italian campaign as it was in the campaign in North-west Europe, it would not be expected that the results of surgical intervention of the same standard would be the same in both theatres. Nor would it be expected, if the campaign in Italy lasted three years and that in North-west Europe less than one, that the over-all sick rate in both theatres during the period June 1944–May 1945 would be the same. In 1944–45 the power to prevent, to control and to cure disease and hurt possessed by members of the Army Medical Services was infinitely greater than it had been in 1914–18. Moreover the conditions and circumstances of the two wars were so utterly different that the soldier patients were likewise different in respect of their capacity to respond to medical and surgical intervention. In 1944–45 the medical units did not encounter those wraiths with grey, expressionless faces drained of vitality, dead tired, debilitated, beyond caring, with wounds fouled with the mire of the trenches who, in 1914–18, stumbled or were carried into the dressing stations in their hundreds.

It will be agreed that if the quality of the medical arrangements and the adequacy of the medical cover in any given situation is to be examined, it is necessary to make this examination against the operational background. In the source material of the medical historian—the quarterly reports of the senior administrative medical officers—there is a section that briefly describes the operational plan and the tactical situation. It is to be noted that such accounts are in accord with the information that was possessed by the senior administrative medical officer at that time. It is to be noted further that the actions taken and the policy adopted by the senior administrative medical officer were fashioned by the information that was then available.

It has to be acknowledged that it is but seldom that a D.M.S., a D.D.M.S. or an A.D.M.S. is fully informed of the tactical plan or is aware of the actual progress of an operational enterprise. These 'operational' sections in the quarterly reports are therefore very unsafe sources of information. Moreover, the interest in operational matters, as judged by what is included in the quarterly report, varies greatly. It is quite certain that the content of the operational sections of this volume will be found to be imperfect and often incorrect when the volume of the Official History that deals with this campaign makes its appearance. However, it is what was thought to be the situation and what was understood to be the plan that determined the policy and action of the Army Medical Services and not what actually was the situation and what precisely was the plan.

To provide the appropriate operational setting for this medical narrative is indeed difficult. The medical chronicler's knowledge of operational matters is necessarily limited and imperfect and considerable powers of discriminative selection are demanded. The prime purpose of this volume is to present an adequate account of the activities of the medical services of 21 Army Group. Condensed and curtailed descriptions of the operational activities of Second Army and of Canadian First Army are therefore given. But since these are not to be understood without some knowledge of the operational activities of U.S. 12 and 6 Army Groups, brief reference to these is made. The reader will not need to be reminded that the course and outcome of the campaign in North-west Europe were profoundly influenced by the happenings on the eastern front and in the Italian theatre and in the Far East. But considerations of these matters can claim no place in this volume with its very restricted purpose.

The reader may find reason to note that in the sections that deal with 'medical cover' and 'medical arrangements' there are omissions. A particular division or corps that demands mention is not included. The reason for this, invariably, is that the quarterly report of the A.D.M.S. or D.D.M.S. for this particular period was not received by the Army Medical Directorate and is not to be traced. The deficiencies in respect of these quarterly reports make this campaign somewhat remarkable; they are so numerous. To find an adequate reason for this is indeed difficult. During the course of a war of this magnitude and importance to most people it must seem somewhat absurd to give much thought or time to checking the safe arrival and safe keeping of documents of this kind. Yet, if a volume such as this is to be written, such source material is of the greatest importance; indeed without it the chronicler's task is made well-nigh impossible.

During the preparation of this volume much use was made of John North's *North-West Europe 1944-45*, of Chester Wilmot's *Struggle for Europe* and of the other books listed in the bibliography. In so far as the Canadian material is concerned full use was made of the provisional narrative of the Canadian Official Medical Historian, Dr. W. R. Feasby.

From Colonel Graeme Warrack (A.D.M.S. 1st Airborne Division) and Colonel Hamilton Kerr (A.D.M.S. 15th (Scottish) Division) much valuable help was received. The former guided me skilfully through the far from simple story of the divisional medical services' activities during the Arnhem adventure, the latter was able to, and good enough to provide me with a precise and detailed account of the work of the divisional medical services throughout the campaign.

PREFACE

This campaign was remarkable for the extent to which the system of evacuation of casualties by air was developed. In this respect it stands between the earlier campaigns of the Second World War and the final campaign in Burma. In the former air evacuation was a subsidiary method of evacuation. It was known to possess many advantages but since the supply of aircraft for evacuation purposes was for the most part uncertain, its development remained somewhat tardy. In the Burma campaign, the narrative of which falls to be written after this, more often than not evacuation by air was the only possible method. As the development of air evacuation is traced during this war from the campaign in Libya to the campaign in Burma it becomes revealed that nothing affected medical policy and action more than did the use of the aeroplane in a systematic way for this purpose.

To the preparation of this volume Mr. J. Basset Scott and Lieut. General Sir Treffry O. Thompson made considerable contributions, the former to its earliest, the latter to its penultimate forms. Very great help was received from the members of the staffs of the Historical Section of the Cabinet Office and of the Editor-in-Chief. For the assistance, the advice and the criticism that were given so generously, the writer is indeed grateful. It is but fair, however, to make it clear that he alone is responsible for the decision as to whether or not that which was offered was accepted or disregarded, for the selection of the material and for such opinions as are expressed.

F. A. E. C.

Edinburgh.
1955.

PRÉCIS

IT was accepted that Germany could not be purged of the evils which the Nazi régime represented without a military invasion of the country and the complete defeat of her armed forces in battle. As early as 1940 plans for the return of a British expeditionary force to the Continent of Europe were being considered, but it was recognised that before Germany's dominion over the countries she had overrun could hopefully be challenged certain conditions would have to be satisfied—a considerable proportion of her military might would have to be inextricably involved in an area far removed from the western sea-board; the industrial and military strength of Britain and of the Commonwealth countries would have to be strongly reinforced by that of other great Powers; the Atlantic supply routes of Great Britain would have to be made safe and the command of the sky over Western Europe would have to be gained. It was not until 1944 that the cross-Channel invasion of the Continent became a feasible enterprise, that sufficient numbers of trained men, sufficient quantities of warlike material in sufficient variety and sufficient means of transportation became available.

The chosen point of re-entry into the Continent was in the Bay of the Seine because it was protected against the prevailing westerly winds by the Cotentin Peninsula and because by bombing the bridges over the Seine and the Loire the north-west quarter of France could, strategically, be isolated. Two large ports lay on its flanks and these, like the bay itself, were within fighter range of England, and one of them, Cherbourg, situated at the tip of the Cotentin Peninsula, once the peninsula was overrun, could be completely invested. The stretch of coast on which the assault landings were to be made was some seventy miles in extent between Quinéville on the east coast of the Cotentin Peninsula and the estuary of the River Orne in which the inland port of Caen lies.

The invasion force was to consist ultimately of three army groups, U.S. 6 and 12 and British 21, together with Allied First Airborne Army. 21 Army Group consisted of Canadian First and British Second Armies; U.S. 6 Army Group of U.S. Seventh and French First Armies; and U.S. 12 Army Group of U.S. First, Third and Ninth Armies. The formations involved in the initial phase of Operation 'Overlord' were to be the U.S. First Army and British XXX and I Corps, the latter with Canadian 3rd Division under command. In addition, two U.S. and one British airborne divisions were to be dropped on the flanks of the beachhead that was to be seized. General Eisenhower was the Supreme Commander. General Montgomery, commanding 21 Army Group, was to be in operational charge of the land forces during the initial phase of the operation.

In brief, the tactical plan involved the establishment of two beach-heads, U.S. on the right, British on the left respectively; the expansion of these to form one continuous front; and the further extension of this foothold north-west, west and south but not appreciably east or south-east. British I Corps was to hold Caen against all attacks while British XXX Corps and U.S. V Corps of U.S. First Army thrust southwards to secure the high ground along the line St. Lô–Caumont–Villers-Bocage and while U.S. VII Corps struck west to seal off the Cotentin Peninsula and then north to capture Cherbourg.

As the build-up in the expanding beachhead proceeded it was General Montgomery's intention, by powerful thrusts by the British and Canadians, to create the impression that the attempt to break-out from the beachhead would be made from the vicinity of Caen so that the German High Command would react by concentrating the bulk of its available forces opposite the British–Canadian sector and so make the real break-out by U.S. First Army in the St. Lô area all the easier. The Americans were to advance on Brittany with the object of capturing the ports southwards to Nantes, and finally to drive east on the line of the Loire and north across the Seine with the purpose of destroying as many as possible of the German forces in this area of the west. While the Germans south of the Seine were thus being cut off, U.S. Seventh Army was to land in the south of France and advance up the valley of the Rhône to join up with the American formations moving eastwards from the Normandy beachhead.

Prior to D-day much effort was expended in persuading the German High Command that the assault landings of the invasion that obviously was imminent would take place in the Pas-de-Calais and that any landings on the Normandy shore were mere diversions. The chosen area and its hinterland were isolated by the systematic crippling of the French and Belgian railways, by the demolition of bridges in north-western France and by consistent attacks upon the airfields within 130 miles radius of the beaches. The coastal batteries and radar installations along the coast were repeatedly bombed, and on D-day – 1 ten large batteries on the Normandy coast were heavily bombed as well as the whole of the northern coast of France. The French Resistance Movement was alerted.

Operation 'Overlord' was launched on June 6, 1944. The time-table of the assault was as follows: (i) 0200 hours, the dropping of the three airborne divisions; (ii) 0315 hours, aerial bombardment of all enemy strong-points in the beachhead area; (iii) 0550 hours, naval bombardment of beach obstacles and coastal defences; (iv) 0630 hours, under

PRÉCIS

cover of a standing barrage from the warships and under a cover provided by the air forces, the first wave of the assaulting armour and infantry to land. The objective for the first day of the invasion was the line Ste. Mère-Église–Carentan–Bayeux–Caen. Though in places stubborn opposition was encountered and although Caen and its airfield were not captured, within twenty-four hours of the initial landing a fairly secure foothold in France had been gained. By June 11 the separate beachheads, by enlargement, had become merged to form one continuous front. The synthetic ports—'Mulberries'—were towed across the Channel and manœuvred into position, one off the U.S. beaches, the other off Arromanches in the British sector. Then came the storm of June 19–23 to impede the build-up, to wreck the American 'Mulberry' and to damage several hundreds of the vessels at a most critical moment in the operation.

While the British and Canadians were heavily engaged in a series of battles in the areas of Caen and Villers-Bocage, U.S. VIII Corps succeeded in thrusting across the base of the Cotentin Peninsula and then turning north to invest Cherbourg. The port fell on June 26, but so great was the damage done that it could not be brought into use for another month. The Americans then regrouped and on July 3 began to press southwards. The plan was for the British and Canadians to drive across the Orne from Caen towards the south and south-east, exploiting in the direction of the Seine basin and for the Americans to launch a major attack across the St. Lô–Périers line and thereafter, if a break-through occurred, to swing west towards Coutances and then towards Avranches. The British–Canadian attack was initially successful but a break in the weather brought it to an end. The American advance was therefore postponed until July 25 when U.S. First Army reached and crossed the St. Lô–Périers road. Then on the 26th armoured and motorised columns were unleashed and by the evening of the 29th were swarming down all the main roads between Coutances and the River Vire. U.S. Third Army now became operational and General Patton whipped U.S. VIII Corps through a gap in the German line near the coast. Coutances was entered on July 30 and then the columns fanned out, some heading for Brest in the west, others for Nantes in the south and still others for Le Mans in the east. On August 1, U.S. 12 Army Group became operational with General Bradley in command. Meanwhile, U.S. First Army had captured Mortain.

On July 29, U.S. Third Army's leading elements were across the Sienne south of Coutances and two days later were in Avranches. At the same time General Montgomery thrust south of Caumont and Evrecy, and Esquay and Villers-Bocage were occupied. U.S. Third Army was in Rennes on August 2 and in Nantes on the 6th, on which day U.S. 6th Armoured Division stood before Brest.

In this fashion the first phase of the invasion was brought to a successful end.

On August 7 the Germans attempted to cut the communications of U.S. Third Army by a counter-attack from the Vire–Mortain area towards Avranches. But U.S. VII Corps stood firm and the weather was such that rocket-firing Typhoons were able to attack the German armour with devastating effect. The Germans in the salient they had formed were threatened with envelopment as Canadian First Army, now operational, thrust southwards towards Falaise and as U.S. Third Army thrust northwards from the direction of Le Mans and Alençon towards Argentan. On August 12 the Americans were in Alençon, and by the evening of the following day had reached the vicinity of Argentan. The Canadians entered Falaise on the 16th and, together with the Polish Armoured Division, pressed on towards Trun and Chambois so as to close the only exit from the Falaise pocket in which were gathered, in desperate plight, the remnants of fifteen German divisions. On August 19 the Americans and the Poles met in Chambois and the pocket was closed. As the Germans strove to break-out towards the east they were consistently attacked from the air while the escape routes were drenched with artillery fire. Many thousands did manage to escape, withdrawing hurriedly in disorder towards the Seine, but in the pocket there remained 10,000 dead and some 50,000 who were taken prisoner on the 22nd. German losses in respect of tanks, guns and transport were exceedingly heavy. Though the disaster at Falaise did not destroy completely the German forces west of the Seine it did ensure that the Germans, if relentlessly pursued, could not stand until the Rhine itself was reached.

By August 17 U.S. Third Army was in Chartres and Dreux, and two days later the Seine was reached and crossed at Mantes-Gassicourt. It was crossed again at Melun on the 23rd. Orleans had been entered on the 17th and Fontainebleau on the 20th. Sweeping east of Paris the Americans continued to advance. These swift moves rendered the position of the German forces in Paris untenable and they withdrew. On August 25 French and American troops marched into the liberated capital. Following the elimination of the Falaise pocket U.S. First Army, Canadian First Army and British Second Army all moved up to the line of the Seine to occupy its entire length north of Paris.

On August 26 General Montgomery issued orders for the advance beyond the Seine, and on September 1 he handed over the command of the Allied land forces in France to General Eisenhower, was promoted to the rank of Field Marshal and retained the command of 21 Army Group. The tasks assigned to the different armies were as follows: Canadian First Army was to advance towards the Ruhr along the coast; British Second Army was to complete the isolation of the Ruhr by advancing through central Belgium; U.S. First Army was to advance on the line Duchy of Luxembourg–Liège and U.S. Third Army on Nancy–Verdun sending a column towards Belfort to link up with U.S. Seventh Army which had landed on August 15 on the southern coast of France between Agay and Cavalaire (Operation 'Anvil'). The assault landings had been completely successful, Toulon and Marseilles were occupied on August 28 as the German formations in this area withdrew. The advance up the valley of the Rhône was uneventful and swift, and on September 11 U.S. Seventh and Third Armies met in Sombernon, near Dijon.

21 Army Group moved forward from the Seine without encountering any serious opposition. Amiens was entered on August 31; Brussels was liberated on September 3, and on the following day Antwerp, its docks intact, was occupied. This port could not be used, however, for there were strong German forces on both sides of the estuary of the Scheldt commanding the approaches to this great inland port.

At this particular time the Germans were incapable of presenting any continuous front against the Allies' advance, their losses in the beachhead, in the counter-attack at Mortain, in the Falaise pocket and during the retreat to and the crossing of the Seine had been crippling. But because of the lack of large ports supply difficulties had been progressively increasing as the Allied Armies grew in size and as the distance from the beachhead increased. Formations had to be grounded and their transport used for the supply of others. General Montgomery then suggested that all available supplies should be allotted to 21 Army Group to enable it to drive northwards and cross the Rhine between Arnhem and Düsseldorf, occupy the Ruhr, the industrial heart of the Reich, and press on to Berlin. General Bradley proposed that all available supplies should be allotted to U.S. 12 Army Group, which would advance eastwards through the Frankfurt corridor and cut Germany into two and take Berlin from the south. General Eisenhower accepted neither of these proposals but decided to advance on a wide front, lining up his armies against the Rhine and establishing bridgeheads across the river whereever possible. At the same time he required that the port of Antwerp should be opened with the minimum of delay.

Within three weeks of the fall of Paris the Germans had succeeded in reorganising their forces and were holding a coherent line. By their skilful and stubborn resistance they had brought the mobile form of warfare, in which they were greatly handicapped, to an end. By their defence of the Channel ports, by the demolition of those which they were forced to surrender and by the continued possession of the approaches to Antwerp they were denying to the Allies the supplies which were necessary for the maintenance of the momentum of their swift advance. The only chance of recreating the conditions of mobile warfare and of dealing a decisive blow which might bring the war to an end in 1944 was to succeed in Operation 'Market Garden' which was now being mounted.

In the first week of September British Second Army was faced by determined resistance along the line of the Albert Canal. After severe fighting this was overcome and a foothold gained on the northern side of the Escaut Canal, fifteen miles south of Eindhoven. In western Holland at this time there were some 350,000 German troops and their lines of communication ran eastwards between the Zuider Zee and the Escaut Canal. General Montgomery proposed to cut these and to isolate the Germans in western Holland by using Second Army to attack through Eindhoven and Arnhem towards the Zuider Zee. This operation, if successful, could lead to the outflanking of the Siegfried Line and to the establishment of a powerful force on the edge of the North German Plain. This advance through Arnhem towards the Zuider Zee involved the swift capture of the great bridges over the Maas at Grave, the Waal at Nijmegen and the Lower Rhine at Arnhem. To secure these bridges intact it was proposed to lay a carpet of airborne troops along the road between Eindhoven through Veghel, Uden, Grave, Nijmegen, to the north side of Arnhem so that these could create a corridor along which XXX Corps could drive furiously and thrust westwards towards the Zuider Zee and eastwards to outflank the Siegfried Line, which ended in the vicinity of Aachen. Success would mean that the Germans in western Holland would be isolated and moreover that the V.2 bases near The Hague would be cut off from their sources of supply. The first of these great rockets had fallen on London on September 8. Since there were not enough transport planes to carry all three airborne divisions in one lift a very great deal depended upon the weather remaining good during the period of the build-up.

On September 17 the first flights of the airborne divisions went in. British 1st A.B. Division landed west of Arnhem and one brigade proceeded to organise the defence of the dropping zones while another advanced on the bridge in Arnhem. About 500 officers and men reached the north end of the bridge to find the south end securely held by a party of S.S. troops. Those on and around the dropping zones were quickly and heavily engaged by German troops that had been hastily gathered and rushed forward. U.S. 82nd A.B. Division, dropped in the Nijmegen–Eindhoven stretch of the corridor, met little opposition and quickly captured the bridge at Grave and another over the Maas–Waal Canal. Advancing towards the Nijmegen bridge they found it strongly defended. South of the Maas and still in the Nijmegen–Eindhoven stretch U.S. 101st A.B. Division took all four of the bridges in the vicinity of Veghel but failed to prevent the Germans blowing the one over the Wilhelmina Canal at Son. Nevertheless the canal was crossed and the leading elements of the division moved on Eindhoven there to meet the armour of XXX Corps that was to drive up the corridor from the Escaut Canal.

Under a rolling barrage from the guns and supported by a constant stream of rocket-firing Typhoons the tanks of Guards Armoured Division rolled forward to reach the first objective, Valkenswaard, five miles south of Eindhoven. By the afternoon of the 18th the Guards and U.S. 101st A.B. Division had joined up in Eindhoven. Meanwhile, XII Corps on the left of XXX Corps and VIII Corps on the right moved forward on either side of the corridor but slowly because for them there were no roads. The blown bridge at Son was being repaired.

On the 18th the British paratroops at the north end of the Arnhem bridge were under continuous attack and were forced back when the houses in which they sheltered were set alight. The rest of the division was heavily engaged, and those who had moved towards Arnhem were forced back to Oosterbeek, where a defensive perimeter, enclosing the north end of the Heveadorp ferry, was being formed. The Germans in this area, as also on the flanks of the airborne corridor, were reacting more speedily and more vigorously than had been thought possible. Moreover, the weather had deteriorated. The flights due on the 18th arrived but were late; on D-day +2 the greater part of the third flight was unable to leave the bases in England; on the following day flying was impossible; on D-day+4 the aircraft took off from the bases but less than half of them found the dropping zones; on the following day flying was again impossible and by D-day+6 the situation around Arnhem was beyond redemption by airborne troops.

The Nijmegen bridge was captured intact as a result of a magnificent feat of arms by U.S. 504th Para. Regiment of U.S. 82nd A.B. Division. In broad daylight and in the face of stern opposition, about 200 officers and men managed to scramble across the fast-running river and to establish a slender foothold on the far bank. During the afternoon this bridgehead was gradually expanded and ultimately its occupants were able to break out of it and reach the northern end of the bridge. By this time the Guards Armoured Division had crossed the repaired bridge at Son and was in the vicinity of the stoutly defended southern end of the bridge. Five tanks rushed it; two got through the defences and across the bridge to join up with the Americans; the bridge was won and the way to Arnhem was opened.

But in Arnhem the paratroops had been forced back from the bridge and German tanks were now crossing it and moving south to block the path of XXX Corps. The defended locality around the Hartenstein Hotel was under constant and very heavy pressure, food and water stocks were nearing exhaustion and ammunition was running low. The several attempts on the part of XXX Corps to reach Arnhem during the next three days were thwarted; the Nijmegen–Arnhem road itself —the corridor—was cut temporarily on several occasions. On September 25 the remnants of British 1st A.B. Division were withdrawn across the Neder Rijn. VIII Corps on the right of XXX Corps reached the Maas. The break in the weather, the speed with which the Germans collected and organised their forces in the area, the break-down of intercommunications, the reluctance on the part of British commanders to endure heavy casualties, these were factors that have been regarded as major reasons for the failure of Operation 'Market Garden'. Another was the adoption of the broad-front policy and the consequent inability to provide Second Army with resources sufficient to ensure success. The corridor itself was widened and held against repeated attacks.

Antwerp lies some fifty miles from the open sea. At the mouth of the estuary of the Scheldt the Germans had strongly fortified the island of Walcheren on the north and the Breskens pocket on the south. The coastal guns in these areas had to be silenced before any ship could reach Antwerp. The land approach to Walcheren from the mainland is by the long narrow isthmus and peninsula of South Beveland and across a slender causeway. Walcheren is shaped like a saucer. The R.A.F. blew in the encircling dykes and by the middle of October three-quarters of the island were deep under water and the German garrison confined to three small strips of coast and to the towns. Canadian First Army was assigned the task of subduing the German garrisons of Walcheren and the Breskens pocket. Four weeks were required to overcome the very stubborn resistance of the German division in the Breskens pocket. During this time to the north of the Scheldt the Canadians had secured the Beveland Peninsula and had reached the causeway that links Beveland with Walcheren. Then as the Canadians attacked along the causeway the main assault went in from the sea. Commandos landed in Flushing and also sailed through the gaps in the dykes in 'Buffaloes'. 52nd Division followed and the German garrison surrendered. The first convoy entered the port of Antwerp on November 28.

Meanwhile the U.S. armies had been pressing on. By September 12, First Army had crossed the German frontier in the Aachen and Trier areas and on September 15 U.S. Third Army had entered Nancy. U.S. Seventh and French First Armies were moving steadily towards the Belfort gap. After very heavy fighting Aachen, reduced to ruins, was entered on October 13 and cleared a week later.

Then in November a general offensive was opened, having for its purpose the occupation of the left bank of the Rhine from its mouth to Düsseldorf, or if possible to Bonn or even Mainz. It was opened by 21 Army Group in the north on November 15, but because of the exceptionally bad weather it was not until December 4 that the last pocket on the west bank of the Maas was cleared. At the same time U.S. First and Ninth Armies, covered by intensive air and artillery bombardments, attacked west of Düren and advancing slowly reached the River Roer on December 3. South of the Ardennes U.S. Third Army's offensive, which had opened on November 8, made more rapid progress. Metz was entered on the 22nd though seven of its forts continued to hold out until December 13 and bridgeheads were established over the Moselle near Saarlautern. On U.S. 6 Army Group front French First Army cleared Belfort by November 22, whereupon the Germans in front of U.S. Seventh Army fell back and Sarrebourg on the Moselle was occupied on November 21. A week later the French entered Strasbourg. By December 15 U.S. Seventh Army had bitten deep into the Siegfried Line north-east of Wissembourg but the French were unable to drive the Germans out of Colmar.

While these events were taking place information to the effect that the Germans were about to launch an ambitious counter-offensive continued to accumulate. This information proved to be correct for on December 16 a violent counter-offensive was launched. At this time, of the thirty-one divisions of U.S. 12 Army Group, all deployed for attack, there were sixteen on a forty-mile sector between Geilenkirchen and Monschau, north of the Ardennes, and ten on a sixty-mile sector facing the Saar south of the Ardennes. Between these two sectors, along a stretch of 100 miles in the Ardennes, there were but five divisions, some of them battle-worn, others inexperienced. The terrain was regarded as being totally unsuitable for the passage of large mechanised forces and was therefore lightly held. Before dawn on the 16th of December the leading elements of three armies, Fifth Panzer, Sixth S.S. Panzer and Seventh, moved through the forests of the Eifel towards this thinly held sector of the line, between Monschau in the north and Echternach in the south. The objectives, it was learnt later, were the capture of Liège and the occupation or destruction of Antwerp. The initial attack between St. Vith and Wiltz carried all before it and the German armour swept onwards towards the River Meuse. At once General Eisenhower ordered the cessation of all Allied attacks along the whole front and moved every available reserve towards the haunches of the rapidly deepening salient. U.S. 101st A.B. Division, hurriedly moving up, reached Bastogne. Next General Eisenhower ordered General Patton to attack northwards towards Bastogne and placed U.S. First Army and part of U.S. Ninth Army, north of the salient, under command of General Montgomery. Bastogne held firm, as did the haunches of the salient, so that the Germans were unable to widen the base, to safeguard their communications and to gain room for manœuvre. Between December 18 and 23 the battleground was blanketed by a dense fog, but on the 24th the weather cleared and the

Allied air fleet of some 5,000 aircraft swept in to destroy the German supply system and to isolate the battlefield. This intervention was decisive, for having advanced to within a few miles of the Meuse the Germans were compelled to begin to withdraw. By January 1, 1945, they were in full retreat and by the 31st of this month the salient had been completely eliminated.

By this audacious and perilous adventure the Germans temporarily disrupted the Allied advance and gained time, but at a catastrophic cost to themselves for it consumed their only mobile reserves. From the first the odds against this counter-offensive succeeding were exceedingly heavy, but the situation in Germany was so desperate that any chance that seemed to proffer even a remote hope of success had to be seized. When it was over General Eisenhower proceeded to plan on the assumption that one more full-blooded attack on a broad front would end the war. His plan was as follows: 21 Army Group was to seize the west bank of the Rhine from Nijmegen to Düsseldorf, after clearing the Lower Rhineland with converging attacks—from the Reichswald by Canadian First Army and from the River Roer by U.S. Ninth Army, which was to remain under General Montgomery's command for the Rhine crossing.

During these operations, apart from capturing the Roer dams and covering U.S. Ninth Army's southern flank, U.S. 12 Army Group formations on the Ardennes front were to maintain an aggressive offensive. Next, while 21 Army Group was preparing for a set-piece assault across the Lower Rhine, U.S. 12 Army Group was to secure the west bank of the Rhine from Düsseldorf to Coblenz. U.S. First Army was to drive its left wing through to Cologne and then strike south-east into the flank and rear of the Germans in the Eifel. Thereupon U.S. Third Army was to take up the offensive, attacking eastwards from Prüm to Coblenz. Finally, while 21 Army Group was assaulting the Lower Rhine, U.S. Third and Seventh Armies were to clear the Moselle–Saar–Rhine triangle and secure crossing places on the Mainz–Coblenz sector for the forces which were to carry out the southern envelopment of the Ruhr.

The first stage was opened by Canadian First Army on February 8. The weather was appalling and the advance slow. Cleve was taken on the 11th and on the 14th the Rhine opposite Emmerich was reached. Meanwhile U.S. Ninth Army, which should have opened its offensive between the 10th and 15th, was delayed by the breaching of the Roer dams by the Germans and it was not until the 23rd that the resulting floods had subsided sufficiently to permit the Americans to thrust northwards towards the Canadians. In the Jülich sector the Roer was crossed and Düren cleared on February 25. By March 1 München-Gladbach, Grevenbroich, Neuss and Venlo had been entered and two days later contact was made with the Canadians in Geldern. In this fashion the whole of the west bank of the Rhine between Düsseldorf and the sea, except for a small bridgehead at Wesel, was occupied. The bridgehead was eliminated on March 10.

Then U.S. First Army's drive towards Cologne opened. By February 10 the River Erft was reached and on the following day its western bank was cleared. Bridgeheads were then established and on March 5 the leading elements of U.S. VII Corps entered Cologne, and two days later the whole of the city west of the Rhine was occupied. Further to the south U.S. 9th Armd. Division on March 7 was able to seize the bridge across the Rhine at Remagen before the German guards could blow it. At once a lodgement on the far bank was made and by the 25th this had grown into a bridgehead twenty-five miles long by ten miles deep. From it the Ruhr was threatened from the south.

Meanwhile, U.S. Third Army had overcome all resistance in the Saar–Moselle–Rhine triangle by February 23. On March 2 Trier was entered and on the 9th the Rhine was reached at Andernach where contact was made with the U.S. First Army. The next day the western bank of the Rhine from Andernach to Coblenz was cleared; by the 19th this clearance was extended from Coblenz to Bingen. Then with surprising suddenness and without special preparations Third Army crossed the Rhine at Oppenheim, south of Mainz on the night of March 22nd. All resistance in Mainz itself ceased and on the following day Speyer was reached.

The third stage of the operation was opened in the middle of March when U.S. 6 Army Group, having eliminated the Colmar pocket, began its advance to the Rhine. By the 25th all organised resistance west of the river had ended.

The Allied armies were now confronted with the greatest water obstacle in Western Europe and to cross it required the largest and most difficult amphibious operation since the crossing of the Channel. It had to be assumed that the line of the Rhine would be defended with the utmost resolution. The crossing north of the Ruhr was to be undertaken by 21 Army Group and U.S. Ninth Army between Rheinberg and Rees, U.S. Ninth Army on the right, south of Wesel, Second Army on the left, to the north of Wesel. To facilitate Second Army's advance U.S. 17th A.B. and British 6th A.B. Divisions of Allied First Airborne Army were to drop amid the German positions north of Wesel. On its left Second Army was to be protected by Canadian First Army.

Prior to the assault crossing of the river the Ruhr was isolated by air attack, and rail centres, bridges and vital points were very thoroughly bombed. Then on March 23 the attack opened with a heavy air attack upon Wesel and a crushing artillery bombardment of the German positions along a front of twenty-five miles by over 3,000 guns. A commando brigade crossed the river almost undetected and infiltrated into Wesel, and on either side of this town two American and two British divisions got across without much difficulty. By dawn on the 24th three firm bridgeheads had been established and the infantry were moving forward supported by D.D. tanks that had swum the river. During the morning of the 24th the airborne divisions descended in the midst of the German defences, thus deepening the bridgehead and disrupting the defences. By the evening of the 28th the bridgehead was thirty-five miles wide with an average depth of twenty miles, and, as the pressure within it increased, the German cordon snapped and the way into the Westphalian Plain was open for the twenty divisions and 1,500 tanks that had been assembled east of the Rhine within a week of the initial crossing. General Montgomery now issued orders for Canadian First Army to turn northward to cut off the German forces in western Holland and to clear the Frisian coast while Second Army and U.S. Ninth Army were to drive for the line of the River Elbe and so gain possession of the plains of northern Germany. During this advance Ninth Army was to seal the northern and eastern exits from the Ruhr and establish contact with U.S. First Army, which was advancing from the south.

In the third week in March while 21 Army Group was preparing to cross the Rhine and U.S. Third Army was racing through the Palatinate, General Eisenhower instructed General Bradley of U.S. 12 Army Group to broaden the Remagen bridgehead and to move U.S. First Army across the Rhine. By March 24 the left bank from Bonn almost to Coblenz was in American hands and the Rhine had been bridged in a dozen places. On the morning of the 25th U.S. First Army struck east along the valley of the River Sieg and south-east towards the Lahn in order to link up with U.S. Third Army, which was along the Rhine from Mainz to Coblenz and which had established three bridgeheads over the river. On the 28th the two armies joined up near Giessen and drove up the Frankfurt–Kassel corridor in a great sweep which would take them east of the Ruhr. U.S. VII Corps, during this sweep, wheeled abruptly north into the rear of the German forces clinging to the Rhine between Cologne and Duisburg. At Paderborn, the panzer training area, the staff of the school and students fought valiantly but were finally overwhelmed on April 1 and the envelopment of the Ruhr was completed when U.S. First and Ninth Armies joined up at Lippstadt. Some 325,000 German troops were trapped. This garrison of the Ruhr gradually disintegrated and finally surrendered.

The western front was now wide open, for the occupation of the Ruhr had created a 200-mile breach which the German High Command had no chance of closing. There were no field armies, no prepared defences and no physical barriers between the front line and Berlin.

Supply difficulties had been overcome and it was possible for the Allies to move forward in irresistible strength. General Eisenhower did not move on Berlin, however; he decided that instead of this U.S. First and Third Armies should advance from Kassel towards Leipzig and that Ninth Army should become dissociated from 21 Army Group on April 4.

Kassel was cleared by U.S. Third Army on April 4, Weimar was reached on the 11th; Jena and Chemnitz on the 13th and the frontier of Czechoslovakia crossed on the 18th. Meanwhile U.S. Ninth Army had advanced through Brunswick to reach the Elbe on April 12. After severe fighting Magdeburg was taken on the 18th. On April 11 U.S. First Army, south of the Harz mountains, advanced rapidly, reaching Dessau on the 14th and clearing the whole of the Harz area by April 21. Meanwhile Second Army had advanced on Bremen and Hamburg and Canadian First Army had begun to clear north-east Holland. Second Army crossed the Weser on April 5, Lüneburg was reached on the 18th and Hamburg masked. The Elbe was crossed on the 29th and the advance was continued until Lübeck was entered. U.S. 6 Army Group had meanwhile moved on Bayreuth where it linked up with U.S. 12 Army Group, and on the 16th Nürnberg was entered. At the same time the French First Army captured Karlsruhe and Pforzheim. These remarkable advances, some of them as much as 100 miles a day, were made possible because the armoured columns were supplied by air; 1,500 troop carrier aircraft, supplemented by heavy bombers converted for the purpose, flew more than 20,000 sorties during April and carried nearly 60,000 tons of freight including 10,000,000 gallons of petrol to the forward elements of the advancing armies.

While the Allied armies were halted on the line of the Elbe, the Mulde and the Czechoslovakian border, save in the north where they had advanced to the Baltic near Lübeck, the Russians swiftly advanced from the Oder westwards and from the Niesse northwards.

On April 25 Berlin was completely encircled and the Russian and American patrols had met in Torgau on the River Elbe. On April 29 the German forces in Italy, nearly a million strong, had surrendered unconditionally. On April 30 the German Führer shot himself in his bunker beneath the Chancellery in Berlin. On May 2 the remnants of the Berlin garrison surrendered. On May 5 all the German forces in northern Germany, Holland, Schleswig-Holstein and Denmark surrendered. At 0800 hours on this day, May 5, the cease-fire was sounded all along the front of 21 Army Group. Two days later the Instrument of Surrender was signed at Supreme Headquarters in Rheims and on May 9 this act was ratified in Berlin. The war in Europe thus ended at midnight of May 8/9, 1945.

CHAPTER 1

THE CAMPAIGN IN NORTH-WEST EUROPE, 1944-45

(i)

The Genesis and Development of Operation 'Overlord'

WITHIN a month following the violent expulsion of the B.E.F. from France in June 1940 a Combined Operations Command was created and charged with the duty of preparing the way for a return to the Continent of Europe by means of a direct assault launched from the English shore and, in the meantime, of carrying out a series of harassing raids upon the occupied coastline. On October 5, 1940, the Joint Planning Staff began to study the possibility of more ambitious offensive operations in Europe, including the establishment of a bridgehead on the Cherbourg Peninsula. Such planning became more realistic when, in June 1941, the Germans invaded Russia. Almost immediately the first of a long series of requests from the U.S.S.R. to Britain to open a second front in France was received. But at this time, and indeed for long thereafter, it was far beyond Britain's power to comply. However, in September 1941 the Joint Planning Staff was instructed to complete, as a matter of urgency, the examination of the plan for operations on the Continent in the final phase of the war with particular reference to all types of special craft and equipment both for the actual operations and for the training of the necessary forces. By December an outline plan had been produced for the invasion of France in the summer of 1943.

The entry of the United States of America into the war, consequent upon the Japanese attack upon Pearl Harbour on December 7, profoundly affected every aspect of such planning. The entire military and economic resources of the two nations were pooled under the direction of a common command, the Combined (U.S. and Br.) Chiefs of Staff, operating under the general direction of the President of the United States and the Prime Minister of Great Britain. All planning and all preparations for the eventual cross-Channel assault thereafter proceeded on an Anglo-American basis.

In January 1942, a body known as the Combined Commanders was formed to prepare an outline plan for operations on the Continent in the final phase of the war. It consisted of Cs. in C. Home Forces, Portsmouth, Fighter Command, the Chief of Combined Operations and the Commanding General E.T.O.U.S.A.

On April 8, 1942, General Marshall, Chief of Staff U.S. Army, recommended that preparations should begin forthwith for a large-scale cross-Channel invasion to be launched in the spring of 1943 (Operation 'Round-up') and suggested that in the autumn of 1942 the Allies should be prepared to establish a small bridgehead to serve as a foothold for the major offensive in the spring of 1943 (Operation 'Sledgehammer').

In June 1942 M. Molotov, the Russian Foreign Secretary, visited President Roosevelt in Washington, where a communiqué was drafted stating that the Allies had reached full understanding with regard to the urgent task of creating a second front in Europe in 1942. On his way back to Russia M. Molotov was privately informed by Mr. Churchill, who agreed to the issue of the communiqué, that the British Government could not guarantee to open a second front in 1942. The British point of view was made clear in an *aide memoire* which stated that 'we are making preparations for a landing on the Continent in August or September 1942. . . . Clearly, however, it would not further either the Russian cause or that of the Allies as a whole if, for the sake of action at any price, we embarked on some operation which ended in disaster. . . . It is impossible to say in advance whether the situation will be such as to make this operation feasible when the time comes. We can therefore give no promise in the matter.'

In June 1942, during the discussions in Washington between the President, the Prime Minister and the Combined Chiefs of Staff, the British delegation presented the view that if any major Anglo-American amphibious operation was to be launched in 1942 it should and could only be against French North Africa (Operation 'Torch'). The Americans, on the other hand, maintained the view that nothing must be allowed to interfere with Operation 'Bolero' (the build-up of U.S. forces in Britain for the cross-Channel invasion).

General Eisenhower, assuming command of the United States Army in the European theatre (E.T.O.U.S.A.), informed himself of the views of the British planning staffs, who were convinced that there could be no successful invasion of France in 1942, and learnt that in the opinion of the Prime Minister the most urgent problem was that of saving the Middle East. Following the receipt of General Eisenhower's report on the matter, General Marshall and Admiral King (Chief of Staff U.S. Navy) came to London to press for the mounting of Operation 'Sledgehammer.' The discussions, which began in London on July 18, were both exhaustive and prolonged. The British finally rejected the 'Sledgehammer' plan on July 22. On the 25th President Roosevelt intervened to say that the invasion of North Africa should proceed but that it must take place not later than October 30.

In August the Prime Minister flew to Moscow to confer with M. Stalin concerning these matters and returned confirmed in his view that Operation 'Torch' was the correct immediate action. The bitter outcome of the Dieppe reconnaissance in force, August 1942, by the Canadians provided overwhelming support for the view that no fortified Channel port could be taken by direct assault with the resources available at that time.

At the Casablanca Conference in January 1943, the Combined Chiefs of Staff concluded that a cross-Channel assault, to be successful, could not be launched before the spring of 1944. It was at this conference that the British delegation proposed that when Operation 'Torch' was successfully ended Sicily should be invaded to provide a stepping-stone to the mainland of Italy. After much discussion it was finally agreed that Operation 'Husky' (the invasion of Sicily) should be mounted, it being understood that this would in no way interfere with the maturation of Operation 'Overlord.'

At the 'Trident' Conference in Washington at the end of May 1943 the target date of 'Overlord' was fixed for May 1, 1944. The British delegation proposed that General Eisenhower should be given sufficient resources to enable him to invade Italy when Operation 'Husky' ended, and it was agreed that he should mount such operations in exploitation of the invasion of Sicily as might be calculated to eliminate Italy from the war. On July 20 the U.S. members of the Combined Chiefs of Staff Committee gave their assent to the invasion of the Italian mainland but insisted that a considerable proportion of the amphibious equipment and of the U.S. air force should, at the end of Operation 'Husky', begin to move away from the Mediterranean theatre. General Eisenhower was also informed that four U.S. and three British divisions would be withdrawn for Operation 'Overlord' and were to be ready to move on November 1. He was allowed to retain 18 L.S.T. for use in connexion with Operation 'Avalanche' (the landing at Salerno).

Meanwhile, on March 12, 1943, it was decided to appoint a chief of staff to the Supreme Allied Commander (yet to be nominated), C.O.S.S.A.C., who would be charged by the Combined Chiefs of Staff, together with his Anglo-American staff, to take over from the Combined Commanders and to give cohesion and impetus to the preparations for 'Overlord.'

The C.O.S.S.A.C. plan was presented to the 'Quadrant' Conference at Quebec in August 1943. It proposed the invasion of Normandy with three seaborne divisions and two airborne brigades in the assault and two further divisions, preloaded in landing craft, in the immediate follow-up. After securing a foothold between Caen and Carentan the

Anglo-American forces were to concentrate on the capture of Cherbourg. The bridgehead was to be supplied, until Cherbourg was usable, through two artificial harbours which would be prefabricated in the United Kingdom and towed across the Channel. Eighteen divisions were to be landed during the first fourteen days, at the end of which time the bridgehead would, it was postulated, include Cherbourg and western Normandy as far as the line Mont St. Michel–Alençon–Trouville. Into this area the main strength of the U.S. Army would be shipped direct from the United States until the Allies had assembled up to one hundred divisions for the invasion of Germany. The plan gained the approval of the Combined Chiefs of Staff.

General Marshall then proposed that as a diversion in connexion with 'Overlord' the amphibious resources available in the Mediterranean should be used for an invasion of Southern France to establish a lodgement in the Toulon–Marseilles area and to exploit northwards (Operation 'Anvil' or 'Dragoon').

At the Teheran Conference in November it was explained to M. Stalin that shortage of shipping, and especially of landing craft, had prevented the launching of 'Overlord' in 1943 and he was assured that it would take place on May 1, 1944. He was told that the desirability of a further offensive in the Mediterranean theatre as a prelude to 'Overlord' was being seriously considered. He placed but little importance on the campaign in Italy and argued that the only direct way of striking at the heart of Germany was through France. He favoured Operation 'Anvil' and promised that when 'Overlord' was launched the Russians would step up their offensive in the East.

In December 1943 General Eisenhower was nominated as Supreme Commander of the Anglo-American forces which were to invade the Continent. The directive given to him stated that the object of Operation 'Overlord' was 'to mount and carry out an operation, with forces and equipment established in the United Kingdom and with target date May 1, 1944, to secure a lodgement on the Continent from which further offensive operations could be developed. The lodgement area must contain sufficient port facilities to maintain a force of some twenty-six to thirty divisions and enable that force to be augmented by follow-up shipment from the U.S.A. or elsewhere of additional divisions and supporting units at the rate of three to five divisions per month.'

Supreme Headquarters, Allied Expeditionary Force (S.H.A.E.F.), came into being and General Montgomery, commanding 21 Army Group (Second Army and Canadian First Army), was given operational control over the Anglo-American land forces in the assault phase of the operation, it being understood that when a U.S. army group took the field under General Omar Bradley, who was to lead the U.S. assault force as Commanding General U.S. First Army, General Eisenhower would himself assume direct command of the land operations.

General Eisenhower formed the opinion that the assault would need to be given greater weight and a broader front and he instructed General Montgomery to revise the C.O.S.S.A.C. plan in conjunction with the Chief of Staff S.H.A.E.F. and the Commanders-in-Chief of the Naval and Air Forces.

The modified plan took the following form. Two or, if possible, three airborne divisions would be flown in, followed within a few hours by a seaborne assault by five divisions with two more, preloaded in landing craft, for the immediate follow-up. This meant that the frontage of the assault would need to be extended from twenty-five miles to fifty and that the weight of the assault landings from the sea would have to be increased by 40 per cent. and from the air by 200 per cent. Far more landing craft were thus made necessary, as was also a much stronger naval escort. Since these could not possibly be made available by May 1 it was recommended that D-day be postponed until early June, that landing craft be borrowed from the Mediterranean, even though this would mean that Operation 'Anvil' must be postponed, and that the U.S. Navy be requested to provide a task force for escort duties.

The Combined Chiefs of Staff agreed to the postponement of 'Overlord' and ultimately also to that of 'Anvil.' On April 15 it was agreed that the U.S. task force should be made available.

The final pattern of the plan for Operation 'Neptune,' the assault phase of 'Overlord,' was as follows:

1. During the night preceding the seaborne invasion 6th Airborne Division would be dropped in the Orne Valley and U.S. 82nd and 101st Airborne Divisions at the base of the Cotentin Peninsula to secure the flanks of the bridgehead and weaken the beach defences at keypoints by attacks from the rear.
2. (a) U.S. First Army would land north and east of the Vire Estuary.
   U.S. VII Corps on the right on Utah Beach;
   U.S. V Corps on the left on Omaha Beach;
   Four U.S. tank battalions would accompany the assault divisions.
   (b) Second Army would land between Bayeux and Caen.
   XXX Corps on the right on Gold Beach; using 50th Division and 8th Armd. Bde., followed by 7th Armd. and 49th Divisions;
   I Corps on the left, Canadian 3rd Division and Canadian 2nd Armd. Bde. followed by Commandos of 4th S.S. Bde. on Juno Beach. 3rd Division and 27th Armd. Bde. followed by 1st S.S. Bde., 51st Division and 4th Armd. Bde. on Sword Beach.
   These would be preceded by special assault teams of 79th Division.

The immediate task of these forces was to be that of forming two bridgeheads on D-day, one between the Rivers Vire and Orne, including

Isigny, Bayeux and Caen, the other on the coast of the Cotentin north of the Vire extending to the line of the Carentan Canal and beyond the River Merderet. It was not expected that these two bridgeheads would become linked up before D-day+1 at the earliest.

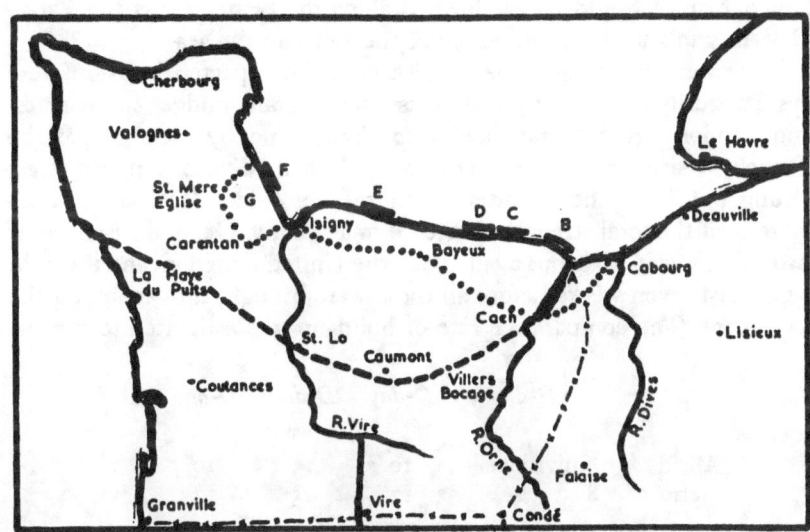

FIG. 1. Operation 'Neptune'. The Assault Landings.

A. Dropping Zone. 6th Airborne Division
B. Sword Beach. 3rd Division. I Corps
C. Juno Beach. Canadian 3rd Division. I Corps
D. Gold Beach. 50th Division. XXX Corps
E. Omaha Beach. U.S. V Corps
F. Utah Beach. U.S. VII Corps
G. Dropping Zone. U.S. 82nd and 101st Airborne Divisions

```
........  = D-day objective
--------  = D-day+9 objective
—x—x—     = D-day+17 objective
```

General Montgomery intended that this foothold should then be expanded north-west, west and south but not appreciably east or south-east. The rôle of I Corps was to hold Caen and the open ground immediately south of the city as a pivot and a bastion while XXX Corps and U.S. V Corps attacked southwards to secure, by D-day+9, the high ground along the line St. Lô–Caumont–Villers-Bocage so as to gain depth sufficient to protect the artificial harbours from direct fire. Meanwhile U.S. VII Corps would strike westwards, seal off the base of the Cotentin Peninsula and move northwards to capture Cherbourg, by D-day+8 if possible. When Cherbourg was taken U.S. First Army would concentrate for a southwards drive with the object of enlarging the bridgehead into a substantial lodgement area.

The further aim was that by D-day + 50 the Allies would be holding an area which included the Brittany ports and extended south to the Loire and east to the line Deauville–Tours and that by D-day + 90 the Allied Armies would be established along the Seine, across the Paris–Orleans gap and down the valley of the Loire to the sea.

The German preparations to withstand the expected invasion were systematically followed by reconnaissance aircraft, midget submarines, commandos, agents parachuted into France and by members of the French Resistance. There were sixty German divisions in the west strung out from the Mediterranean to the Zuider Zee, about one-quarter of the total strength of the German Army. General Eisenhower had thirty-seven divisions available in the United Kingdom and it would be at least seven weeks before all these were brought into action on the Continent. The comparative rate of build-up was estimated to be

	D-day	D-day +1	D-day +3	D-day +7	D-day +10
Allied	8 divisions	10	13	16	18
German	8 ,,	12	15	22	27

so that the critical phase of the operation would be during the first week or ten days. It became evident that the Germans meant to oppose and defeat the invasion on the beaches.

Among the measures taken to redress this imbalance were the following:

1. General Eisenhower required that the rail communications leading to the invasion area should be paralysed by aerial bombardment. In March 1944 the Strategic Air Forces were placed under the operational control of S.H.A.E.F. and Air Chief Marshal Tedder chose as his primary targets railway workshops and locomotive sheds. Railway experts chose eighty key targets in Northern France and of these thirty-nine were to be dealt with by Bomber Command. The offensive opened on March 6/7 and by the middle of May very great damage and disruption had been caused. Then on May 21 the attacks were switched to bridges, viaducts, locomotives and railway tracks. By June 5 eighteen of the twenty-four bridges over the Seine, Oise and Meuse had been destroyed, three were closed for repairs and the remaining three so incessantly attacked that they could not be used for large-scale movement during the day-time. At the same time the Luftwaffe had been subdued and the launching sites of the V-weapons and

every airfield within 130 miles of the Channel had been consistently bombed.

2. Operation 'Fortitude' was launched to persuade the Germans that the assault was aimed at the Pas-de-Calais and that the Normandy landing was but a feint. Air reconnaissance and bombing were concentrated on this area. Large concentrations of troops were made discreetly visible in the areas in England opposite to the Pas-de-Calais. Dummy landing craft were accumulated in the Thames Estuary and dummy gliders on the airfields in Kent and East Anglia. From wireless traffic it was to be learnt that Canadian First and U.S. Third Armies were to land in the Pas-de-Calais.

3. To overcome the defences of the 'Atlantic Wall', which included underwater obstacles and mines, a wide variety of new weapons was to be used and novel tactics adopted. 79th Armoured Division had been transformed into an experimental formation charged with the task of devising and developing special armour and equipment for the cross-Channel enterprise. Its commander was uniquely fitted for the job assigned to him. A seemingly endless series of novelties were either invented or else further developed—the 'Bobbin' tank that laid a carpet of matting as it moved over treacherous ground, the 'Crab' tank with flails that beat the ground and set off buried mines, the D.D. (duplex drive) amphibious tank, the C.D.L. tank that carried a searchlight which, flickering, could temporarily blind the defence, the 'Buffalo', a tracked amphibious tank, the armoured bulldozer, the 'A.V.R.E.' (Armoured Vehicle Royal Engineers), with a variety of machines that could be attached to it for the undertaking of special tasks, bridge-carrying tanks, flame-throwing tanks and many more. General Montgomery decided to place these 'Bobbin', 'Crab' and D.D. tanks in the first wave of the assault, other specialised armour in the second and the infantry in the third.

4. The Prime Minister's ideas of concrete caissons and floating piers were explored by Combined Operations Command and the outcome was the production of two prefabricated harbours, Mulberry A and Mulberry B, each the size of Dover harbour and consisting of an outer floating breakwater, an inner fixed breakwater of concrete caissons, and four floating piers. While they were being assembled shelter was to be provided by breakwaters formed of sunken obsolete ships. C.O.S.S.A.C. also provided P.L.U.T.O. (pipelines under the ocean).

5. As D-day approached the security ring around Britain was tightened. In February 1944 all civilian travel between the United

Kingdom and Eire was stopped. In April a coastal belt ten miles deep, from the Wash to Land's End and on either side of the Firth of Forth, was closed to all visitors. Foreign diplomats and their couriers were not permitted to enter or to leave the country and the diplomatic bag was subjected to censorship. During the last week of May the closely guarded and wired camps wherein the first flights of the invading armies waited were sealed and the troops were briefed by means of aerial photographs, sketches, maps and large-scale models. Confidence mounted as the troops came to realise that nothing had been left to chance and that every detail had been considered.

All that now remained was the fixing of the actual day and hour. On May 17 General Eisenhower tentatively selected June 5 as D-day and turned to his meteorological experts for their predictions of the weather. What was wanted was a calm D-day followed by three calm days, surface winds not exceeding 8–12 m.p.h. on shore nor 13–18 m.p.h. off shore, visibility at least three miles, and half moonlight for the airborne landings. During May there had been eighteen days which met all these requirements but June 1 dawned dull and grey. On June 2 when the meteorologists reported to General Eisenhower and his three Commanders-in-Chief at his H.Q. near Portsmouth they were obliged to be somewhat pessimistic concerning the immediate future. On the 3rd their reports were even more pessimistic. When at 0415 hours on Sunday, June 4, they reported again, they forecast rising winds and thick low cloud and General Eisenhower decided that the assault must be postponed by one day. At 1100 hours the Admiralty issued a gale warning to all shipping in the Irish Sea and as the day dragged on the storm gathered in fury and a high wind piled white-crested breakers on the fogbound beaches of Normandy. Out in the Channel and in the crowded harbours from Harwich to Falmouth the troops in the tossing ships watched the weather worsen as they endured the strain of waiting. At 2100 hours the meteorologists reported again. They were now able to predict that the storm front was quickly passing and that following in its wake there would come a brief period of fair conditions which would probably last until Tuesday, June 6. Thereafter the weather would become variable with considerable fair periods until Friday.

The issue facing General Eisenhower and his Commanders was now clear-cut, to accept the risks and unleash the invading forces on Tuesday, and this decision, if made, had to be made there and then, or else to postpone the operation for a fortnight for the next suitable tide. The hazards of postponement, being examined, were manifestly greater than those which would attend the earlier launching. However, it was decided to wait for a further meteorological report at 0415 hours on the

THE CAMPAIGN IN N.W. EUROPE 23

morrow. When the conference reassembled the weather was clearing and the meteorologists were able to report that the outlook was propitious in that the fair weather was likely to last into the late forenoon or afternoon of Tuesday the 6th. General Eisenhower then gave the word that was to loose the troops that were straining at the leash and within two hours the invasion convoys were slipping out to sea. By mid-afternoon five hundred warships and three thousand landing craft were moving toward the opening of the swept Channel which began south of the Isle of Wight at a point designated Area Z immediately north of the Normandy beaches. Above the convoys swarms of fighters formed a protective screen and on their flanks aircraft of Coastal Command and warships ceaselessly patrolled to strengthen the protection afforded by the minefields which they had already laid. Flotillas of minesweepers swept ten channels from Area Z to the Bay of the Seine. The leading flotilla arrived in sight of the Normandy coast at 1957 hours, three hours before dark, and before nightfall two flotillas were in full view of the shore but were not fired upon.

Meanwhile the Royal Navy and the R.A.F. took appropriate steps to jam the German radar installations between Cherbourg and Le Havre and to persuade those between Le Havre and Calais that an invasion fleet was heading toward this sector of the coast.

(ii)

Operation 'Overlord'. Medical Planning

The Medical Branch, H.Q. 21 Army Group, had its beginnings on July 9, 1943, at Kneller Hall, Twickenham, when D.D.M.S. and A.D.M.S. joined. A.D.M.S. (Personnel) joined on September 1, D.M.S. on September 14. During December, D.D.D.S., Principal Matron, D.D.H., Matron, Consulting Physician and the Adviser in Psychiatry joined. On July 26, 1944, Main H.Q. 21 Army Group moved to Southampton to embark for the Continent and Rear H.Q. to Wentworth. Main H.Q. opened in La Corderie near Bayeux on July 29. In September 1944 H.Q. 21 Army Group moved forward to Brussels where it remained until the end of the campaign.

It came to consist of D.M.S., D.D.M.S., 4 A.Ds.M.S., 3 D.A.Ds.M.S., D.D.H., A.D.H., D.D.P., A.D.P., D.D.D.S., A.D.D.S., Chief Principal Matron and A/Matron, consultants in medicine and surgery (brigadiers) and advisers in anaesthesia, blood-transfusion, dermatology, neurology, ophthalmology, orthopaedics, penicillin and chemotherapy, psychiatry, radiology and venereology (lieut. colonels). These consultants and advisers were available to the Canadians as well as to Second Army. The Canadians had their own consulting surgeon, physician and psychiatrist with Canadian First Army. In so far as purely medical matters were concerned, the medical branch of H.Q. 21 Army Group dealt directly with the Army Medical Directorate of the War Office.

Second Army Headquarters, Main and Rear, at Slade Camp and Cowley Barracks, Oxford, had completed its plans for training and equipping the Army by the end of January 1944 and in the last week of that month began to consider details of the assault landings. For this purpose all branches of the H.Q. were divided into: (*a*) personnel whose presence was essential for this project; and (*b*) those who could be engaged more profitably in matters relating to the preparation of the Army for Operation 'Overlord'. The former group moved to London in order to facilitate liaison with S.H.A.E.F., H.Q. 21 Army Group, U.S. First Army and the like and was designated Advanced Headquarters. The latter group—Static H.Q.—remained in Oxford.

Planning being completed by the third week of April, Static H.Q. moved to London to become merged with Advanced H.Q. On April 24 H.Q. Second Army moved to its concentration area, Rear H.Q. to Fort Purbrook, Main H.Q. to Fort Southwick, both overlooking Portsmouth Harbour and Spithead. For the sake of convenience these were designated also as Army H.Q. marshalling and embarkation areas. At the same time the formations and units of Second Army moved to their appointed concentration areas, movement to the marshalling areas being carried out only shortly before the time of embarkation. Troops of the assault formations moved into sealed camps in mid-May. A full-dress rehearsal of the assault landings was staged on the beaches of Hayling Island on May 4, (Exercise 'Fabius'). On June 1 General Montgomery, C. in C. 21 Army Group, delivered a briefing lecture to all officers of lieut. colonel's rank and upwards and on June 3 all ranks of Second Army were addressed by General Dempsey, commanding Second Army.

Within 21 Army Group the Canadian and British Army Medical Services were integrated in the sense that they were both directed by the Medical Branch, H.Q. 21 Army Group. But as far as possible the Canadian medical services, personnel and units, were employed with Canadian First Army and Canadian casualties were, as far as possible, evacuated along a Canadian chain of medical installations. Behind the Canadian medical services of Canadian First Army was the Directorate of Medical Services, Canadian Military Headquarters in the United Kingdom. This, in its development, came to consist of:

        D.M.S. (Major General)
        D.D.M.S. (Col.)
        V.D. Control Officers (1 Lieut. Col., 1 Maj.)

A.M.D.1 (Personnel)
  A.D.M.S. (Col.)
  D.A.M.D.S. (Maj.)

A.M.D.2 (Hospitalisation)
  A.D.M.S. (Col.)
  D.A.D.M.S. (Maj.)
  Medical Officers (2 Majs.)

A.M.D.3 (Equipment)
  Lt. Col. non-medical
  Majors, non-medical 2
  Captains 2, one a radiological engineer

A.M.D.4 (Nursing Service)
  Matron-in-Chief (Lieut. Col.)
  Principal Matron (Maj.)
  Matron (Capt.)

A.M.D.5 (Hygiene and Sanitation)
  D.D.H. (Col.)
  D.A.D.H. (Maj.)
  D.A.D.H. (Nutrition) (Maj.)
  Medical Officer (Chemical Warfare) (Maj.)
  Medical Officer (Medical Intelligence) (Maj.)
  Medical Officer (Medical History) (Maj.)

Medical Inspection Room Staff
  S.M.O. (Maj.)
  Medical Officers (4 Majs. or Capts.)

Consulting Staff

Consultants in medicine (brigadier), surgery (brigadier), neurology (colonel), radiology (lieut. colonel).

Advisers in ophthalmology (lieut. colonel), oto-rhino-laryngology (lieut. colonel), anaesthesia (lieut. colonel) and neuro-psychiatry (lieut. colonel). Four specialists in psychiatry (majors). An adviser in pathology was provided from within the W.E. of a static Canadian general hospital. A total of 43 officers and 62 O.Rs.

This directorate exercised a close supervision over the whole of the Canadian Army Medical Services until such time as the personnel and units passed to a field force.

(A) SECOND ARMY

Apart from matters of military strategy and tactics bound up in the operational plan for the conduct of the campaign, this enterprise entailed two primary considerations essentially distinct one from the other. The first was the raising, training and welding together into one cohesive whole of units from various arms of the Service to constitute the expeditionary force complete in all respects. This was a process which, subject only to the restrictions of man-power, was dictated by the principles of military organisation evolved by time and experience. It was therefore capable of accomplishment largely through the normal machinery. The second consideration, however, that of assembling and concentrating the force when ready for action, of embarking it, of transporting it overseas, of landing it in the face of enemy opposition and of maintaining it thereafter on a hostile shore, constituted a combined operation of the first magnitude and necessitated the most detailed planning and complete co-operation not only between the three Fighting Services but also with the civil defence authorities and with the organisations controlling shipping, ports and harbours, railways, roads, etc. So extensive and complicated were the issues involved that a special Administrative Planning Staff was constituted and charged with the duty of preparing and co-ordinating the administrative arrangements essential to ensure the successful accomplishment of the plan of operations devised by those in command of the naval, military and air forces taking part in the enterprise. This Administrative Planning Staff or, as it were, this central planning authority, then proceeded to develop a sectional organisation by which the various administrative questions were delegated to groups or committees of staff officers, specialist experts and representatives of the several Service branches and civil departments intimately concerned with one or other of the many features of the general scheme. Each section was placed under the control of a permanent convener and, in respect of the subject allocated to it, was made responsible, working through the normal staff channels, for the formulation of an administrative plan and for taking preparatory measures for putting that plan into effect. Each section was required to maintain touch with other sections dealing with associated matters and to ensure interchange of essential information one with the other; sections were instructed to refer all questions needing a decision or definition of general policy to the Administrative Planning Staff who were to be notified periodically of progress made and of executive action taken.

Planning in respect of the medical services was entrusted to a section which included representatives from the staffs of the Naval Commander, the Admiralty, the Army Commander, the War Office, the Air Commander, the Air Ministry, the Chief of Combined Operations, the Headquarters of E.T.O.U.S.A., the U.S. Navy, the Headquarters of Services of Supply, U.S.A., the Ministry of Health and the Department of Health for Scotland. D.G.A.M.S. was appointed convener of this section.

For the guidance of the various planning sections the Administrative Planning Staff issued to each convener a memorandum which broadly outlined the scope of the proposed operations, surveyed the conditions likely to be encountered and enunciated certain basic principles to serve as a foundation upon which to build the complex administrative structure which the project involved. This document contained much that was of primary significance to the medical services. First in importance was a tentative estimate of sick and battle casualties for whom provision must be made. The following rates were given as a working basis:

(a) during concentration in the United Kingdom—2 per cent. of the total forces per month;
(b) during the assault phase—25 per cent. of the forces engaged;
(c) during subsequent operations—10 per cent. per month.

It was also determined that the reception and distribution of patients arriving in England from the Continent would remain under War Office control and that existing arrangements for the pooling of all hospital accommodation in the United Kingdom would continue. Consequently it was intended that casualties should be admitted to military or E.M.S. hospitals indiscriminately.

Other hypotheses of a more problematical nature were put forward for the guidance of those responsible for medical planning. Difficulty was expected in the provision of adequate surgical facilities for the seriously wounded at the time of, and shortly after, the initial assault. Attempts would be made to extend the area occupied by the assault force in such a way as to include buildings suitable for the accommodation and treatment of casualties; nevertheless, it would be unsafe to assume, and to rely upon, success in this direction. In the absence of these facilities the provision of sufficient medical attention on the spot and for all classes of case would clearly be impossible. Large-scale evacuation, on the other hand, would involve heavy demands upon transport craft. A definition of policy to govern the retention or evacuation of casualties from the beaches was therefore essential. It was proposed that casualties should be assessed as follows:

(a) seriously wounded unfit for embarkation and evacuation;
(b) lying cases requiring evacuation by hospital ship or hospital carrier;
(c) walking wounded capable of evacuation by landing craft; and
(d) sitting cases fit to travel in whatever shipping might be available.

This classification would form a basis upon which to arrange provision of hospital ships, home ambulance trains and motor-boats for ferrying between shore and ship. The matter of supplying air ambulance transport presented difficulties. Its provision in the early stages would conflict with operational requirements and it would therefore not be available at the time when it was most urgently needed. Consequently, this form of evacuation must be largely discounted until later in the campaign when more stabilised conditions would permit of an organisation for the evacuation of casualties by air. Hospital ships and carriers would be restricted to disembarkation at designated ports provided with all necessary medical facilities, but during the assault phase all landing craft were liable to suffer casualties among the personnel in transit and to pick up others before leaving the beaches. These craft on return to their loading ports in the United Kingdom were therefore likely to arrive carrying casualties; thus each port and hard (a firm beach or foreshore) used as a loading point would need to be furnished with a medical organisation. Mention was made also of the fact that certain modifications in the usual arrangements for the transport of casualties from front line to place of embarkation were certain to be required for some time after the landing of the force. It was unlikely that ambulance trains could operate satisfactorily within a period of two or three months. While the fitting of 'Brechot' apparatus to ordinary rolling stock might be possible, yet reliance would have to be placed mainly on motor ambulance transport for the carriage of casualties. These methods would necessitate either the establishment of medical units to hold casualties in forward areas, an undesirable expedient, or the organisation of a fleet of motor ambulance convoys operating between front and base and the setting up of medical staging posts at intervals along the route.

As regards the medical component of the force, it was prescribed that its constitution and organisation should conform to the new system devised by the 'Hartgill' Committee* for the medical services in the field, and that provision for medical units and personnel should be made on that basis; detailed information as to the number and type of units required would be supplied to A.M.D. as soon as the battle order of the force had been settled. Adequate facilities would be given for the training of field medical units and they were to be released from functioning in any way as static units.

It was thus apparent that in estimating the medical needs and providing the medical services of a force engaged in an enterprise of this kind, preparations were required in respect of two entirely different situations widely divergent in their demands and necessitating totally different measures to meet them. To supply the needs of the army in the field the usual methods employed in any overseas theatre of war were to a great extent applicable. It was for A.M.D. to organise the raising, training, mobilisation and equipping of the number of field medical units authorised for a force of the dimensions it was proposed to employ; to arrange for the establishment, on the Continent or at home, of sufficient hospitals, either in tents or huts or by taking over civil hospitals or other buildings; to supply accommodation on the scale requisite for the number of sick and wounded expected; to ensure the provision of surgical facilities in such degree, time and place as would afford a maximum of succour to battle casualties. The vigilance of the medical services was necessary to translate into practical application the accepted principles that the force should be fully protected by inoculation and vaccination; that all personnel were correctly graded as regards medical

---

* *See* Army Medical Services, Vol. 1, Administration, p. 465.

category; that sufficient attention was paid to such obvious but none the less all-important matters as supplying them with well-fitting boots; that a satisfactory standard of field sanitation was enforced and adequate control exercised over sources used for obtaining drinking water; that prompt steps were taken to restore public water supplies and sewerage systems damaged or destroyed by the enemy; and that the spread of infectious disease to the armies from the civil population was reduced to the absolute minimum.

In all these things there were precedents and the experience of military operations elsewhere to act as guides in designing the pattern of medical provision. Very different was the situation presented by the opening phases of this undertaking. No adventure of the kind on the scale proposed had ever before been attempted. The task of supplying adequate medical facilities for a large force engaged in landing upon open and defended beaches, in assaulting coast fortifications and in seizing a bridgehead in the face of fierce resistance was beset with many perplexing problems, the more so because any medical arrangements must perforce be limited by, and made subordinate to, tactical considerations even more insistent and compelling in their application. The formulation of a plan for the medical services during the early stages of the undertaking was therefore influenced by the dictates of necessity rather than by freedom of choice.

At its first meeting in July 1942, the Medical Planning Section constituted as described above, discussed a paper prepared by D.G.A.M.S. in the light of the circumstances revealed by the Administrative Planning Staff's memorandum and sought to clarify matters by establishing a number of premises acceptable as a guide to further investigation and preparatory action. In the first place the projected operations were divisible into three distinct phases presenting different conditions and requiring different treatment. These phases were those of assault, of seizing a bridgehead and of subsequent consolidation.

In the assault phase it was estimated that the peak of casualties suffered would be reached during the first and second days after the landing. The total of casualties to be dealt with during this time was placed at 22,500, composed as follows:

(a) lying cases requiring urgent surgical attention—2,000 (8 per cent.);
(b) lying cases not requiring urgent surgical attention—8,125 (36 per cent.);
(c) sitting cases—12,375 (56 per cent.).

The question then arose as to alternative methods of disposal. Were casualties to be retained and accommodated on the beaches or were they to be immediately evacuated to the United Kingdom? The first would call for a very large medical organisation in addition to the normal field medical component of the formations taking part; the second implied the provision and employment of transport craft specially reserved for the purpose. Until an answer to these questions was forthcoming little could be accomplished in the way of preparatory arrangements. The Medical Planning Section, however, was in no doubt as to which would prove the more desirable and satisfactory course to adopt. It was considered that, in any case, provision would have to be made for the accommodation and retention of the 2,000 for whom life-saving surgery would be necessary and who would not be in a fit state for evacuation until several days later. The remaining 20,500 would be available for evacuation at once and should be evacuated as soon as it was possible to make the appropriate arrangements. It was expected that similar conditions requiring the same methods would obtain throughout the assault stage. Large hospital ships were unsuitable for use under the conditions visualised and would not be employed during this, the first, phase. Smaller hospital carriers, although primarily intended for transport between port and port, would be used to the number of twelve and, given full loads, could carry some 6,000 of the 8,125 lying cases, leaving 2,125 to be transported by other craft equipped and staffed for the carriage of casualties. It was decided that while the Army Medical Services would undertake the care of casualties transported in hospital carriers, responsibility for medical attention to those carried in other craft would devolve upon the Royal Naval Medical Services. All loading ports and harbours, not only those designated as medical ports, in the United Kingdom would be supplied with a medical embarkation staff and facilities for giving medical and surgical treatment, including resuscitation, to wounded arriving in personnel ships and other craft. M.A.Cs. and, in certain places, ambulance trains would be available and ready for the distribution of casualties to selected hospitals.

During the phase of seizing a bridgehead it would be necessary to land additional field ambulances, motor ambulance convoys and casualty clearing stations to undertake the collection and urgent surgical treatment of casualties. It would still be necessary to effect the evacuation of all cases, other than those unfit to travel, direct to the United Kingdom and to do so from open beaches, a procedure liable to interference by weather or by enemy action. Large-scale crisis expansion of accommodation in the bridgehead would therefore be necessary to cope with, perhaps, large numbers of cases whose evacuation was delayed by either of these agencies.

The main task during the phase of consolidation would consist of a gradual building up of hospital beds on the Continent to a scale of 6 per cent. of the strength of the force. Evacuation from battle zone to casualty clearing station would be by motor ambulance and possibly by water transport in the form of barges, but evacuation from casualty clearing station to general hospital would be undertaken, to a gradually increasing extent, by ambulance train instead of by motor transport. Evacuation by sea from the Continent to the United Kingdom would be more restricted as general hospital accommodation became available for the retention of less serious cases in which the process of recovery was likely to be rapid. Opportunity was taken to stress the necessity for evacuation of selected casualties by air and to urge that for this purpose there should be provided as early as possible in the operation a more comprehensive organisation than the somewhat haphazard use of returning transport planes.

To the closer examination of these and kindred questions the Medical Planning Section then turned its attention and during the succeeding six months accomplished the investigatory and preparatory work, much of it of an arduous and detailed nature, which served to lay the foundation of the final medical plan.

In the meantime, however, and before the close of that year, 1942, the military situation had been profoundly changed by developments in the Mediterranean where extensive commitments had been undertaken, including the landing of an expeditionary force in French North Africa. With the expansion of the Mediterranean theatre of war and the prospect of operations in Italy any question of an immediate attack upon Western Europe by an Anglo-American force receded into the background and the possibility of military action in that direction during the year 1943, as previously intended, became remote. As has been related, it was decided that Operation 'Overlord', hitherto provisionally fixed for the summer of 1943, should be postponed until the spring of 1944. This postponement and the consequent absence of a clear-cut operational plan put an end, for the time being, to any precise or detailed planning and, as far as the medical aspect of affairs was concerned, little further progress of importance can be recorded as having taken place during the first half of the year 1943.

In May of the same year the organisation for the control of preparatory planning underwent radical changes by which the central Administrative Planning Staff constituted in 1942 was abolished and its functions transferred to the various authorities concerned with the conduct of the prospective undertaking. The Chief of Staff to the Supreme Allied Commander (C.O.S.S.A.C.), pending the appointment of the Supreme Commander himself, had assumed responsibility for the planning and execution of operations based upon the United Kingdom, detailed military planning being delegated to the commanders of the army groups concerned in conjunction with the appropriate naval and air force commanders. The War Office, in collaboration with the staff of E.T.O.U.S.A., accepted responsibility for the military arrangements required in the United Kingdom for launching the forces engaged in the operation. The C. in C. Home Forces was made responsible for the defence of Great Britain, for supplying the troops required to staff assembly areas and for providing such administrative services as would be necessary to assist in the dispatch of the expeditionary force. These functions were exercised by delegation to general officers commanding-in-chief of commands and thence to commanders of districts and sub-districts. In order to ensure the production of a single harmonious plan arrangements were made to secure complete co-ordination between all military and civil authorities involved. At the centre of affairs this was achieved by the Home Defence Executive and the Home Defence Committee, bodies which included representatives of the Service departments, the civil ministries and the C. in C. Home Forces. Locally, steps were taken to set up planning committees and co-ordination committees which comprised in their membership representatives of general officers commanding in commands, regional commissioners, local military and civil defence officers and officers of the various county and municipal authorities concerned.

The abolition of the central Administrative Planning Staff implied the consequent abolition of the Medical Planning Section which it had brought into being; in point of fact, however, this body continued its existence as a medical planning committee under the chairmanship of D.G.A.M.S. and was entrusted with the duty of initiating or co-ordinating all medical arrangements made in connexion with the plan of operations. With the experience and achievements of a year's preliminary work to assist it the committee proceeded to develop its plans in greater detail and in conformity with a situation which had changed in many respects since the day when it first entered upon its labours.

THE RAISING OF THE MEDICAL COMPONENT

When, at the beginning of the year 1943, the first steps were taken towards raising the medical component of the new expeditionary force, the Army Medical Services were in process of reorganisation on the lines recommended by the Hartgill Committee and subsequently approved by the Army Council. The adoption of these recommendations involved changes in the establishment of existing medical units in respect of personnel, equipment and transport; alterations in the standard scale of allotment of medical units to a field force in relation to the composition of the force; and, above all, the formation of units of an entirely new kind, such as the field dressing station (F.D.S.), the field surgical unit (F.S.U.) and the field transfusion unit (F.T.U.). In formulating this scheme of reorganisation it had been accepted as a basic principle that whatever changes were made there could be no aggregate increase in

THE CAMPAIGN IN N.W. EUROPE 33

personnel over and above the total already authorised under the previous organisation. This stipulation was the more insistent in regard to medical officers. Any additions occasioned either in the establishments of existing units or by the raising of units of a new type were therefore to be counterbalanced by reductions elsewhere. The standard allotment sanctioned in respect of the F.D.S., a unit comprising personnel to the number of 90 all ranks, was on the scale of two to a division, one to a corps and an additional increment, as army troops, equivalent to one for each division in the force. Smaller units such as the F.S.U. and the F.T.U. were added, but on a lower scale. On the other hand, the provision of C.C.Ss. was reduced. At the same time numerous alterations were made in the composition of previously existing units. Consequently a somewhat intricate readjustment of medical assets was involved, and thus it was that although the new organisation had been introduced in August 1942 it had not been brought into general application when the Medical Planning Committee began its task of providing medical units for the expeditionary force, the medical services of which were to be constituted throughout in accordance with the latest developments.

The provision of medical units was undertaken in conformity with a prescribed programme for the preparation of the force at large. This programme was divided into several phases during which the several formations constituting the force were successively brought up to strength in units and personnel, equipped, trained and finally mobilised. In so far as their medical units were concerned but few of the divisions nominated for inclusion in the order of battle had yet been placed on the basis of the new organisation for the medical services in the field. In most cases, therefore, it was necessary to reconstitute them in this respect by providing each with two F.D.Ss. anew and by mobilising or remobilising their existing field ambulances and field hygiene sections on the revised scale of personnel, transport and equipment. Medical units for corps, army, G.H.Q. and lines of communication, such as F.S.Us., F.T.Us., C.C.Ss., general hospitals, etc., were provided either by nominating and mobilising units already in being or by raising, forming and mobilising new units of the kind and in the numbers required.

New units were formed by one of three methods. By the first a unit which was surplus to immediate requirements, or which had become redundant for any reason, was selected for disbandment, whereupon its personnel were used to form one or more of the type in demand. Deficiencies in establishments were then made good by posting additional personnel of the ranks and trades necessary for completion. Conversely, any excess was dissipated by transfer to other units. This method was particularly applicable in the case of the F.D.S., for a field ambulance or light field ambulance surplus to requirements sufficed on disbandment to form two F.D.Ss. By the second method an existing unit of the same, or even of a different, kind was required to throw off a cadre to provide a nucleus for the new unit, which was then gradually built up by adding to this cadre the personnel necessary to complete the establishment. The third method consisted of selecting a unit to act as parent unit and posting to it the personnel required to form the new unit, which was administered by its parent until such time as it became self-supporting. A unit having been raised and formed by any one of these methods was subsequently brought to a state of mobilisation by filling any outstanding deficiencies in its personnel and by supplying its equipment and transport as prescribed by field service scales.

In February 1943 orders were received to effect the provision of medical services to complete the component denoted by the first phase of the programme for the preparation of the expeditionary force. This component, which was to be mobilised by April 1 of that year, comprised one corps, consisting of one infantry division and two divisions (mixed) with corps troops and a quota of army, G.H.Q. and lines of communication troops. Medical units thus required, including those on lines of communication such as general hospitals, depots of medical stores and laboratories as well as those for the operational zone such as field ambulances, F.D.Ss. and C.C.Ss., amounted to a total of 48. Steps were then taken by A.M.D., acting through the usual staff channels, to allocate to the force specific units of the types and in the numbers necessary. This was done (*a*) by nominating units already mobilised, about a quarter of the number; (*b*) by effecting the remobilisation of those already mobilised but requiring reorganisation on revised establishments, as mentioned above; (*c*) by initiating the mobilisation of other units available and under the control either of the War Office or of Home Forces; (*d*) by arranging for the raising and formation of new units necessary to complete the medical quota, approximately one-third of the total.

At the end of March 1943 authority was given to proceed with the second phase of the programme involving the provision of a second corps and a corresponding addition to the medical services. In the following month a third corps was assigned to the potential expeditionary force, which was thereby increased to a total of three corps, including in all two armoured divisions, three divisions (mixed), three infantry divisions, one independent infantry brigade, two tank brigades, one parachute brigade, with corps, army, G.H.Q. and lines of communication troops and the usual ancillary services. The whole included some 190 medical units of one kind and another, of which only about a third, and these mostly divisional units, were immediately available. Shortly afterwards instructions were issued calling for acceleration in the process of preparation and mobilisation, particularly in the case of units belonging to G.H.Q. and lines of communication. This edict produced something of a problem in its application to the medical component. The position then, in June 1943, was that all divisional and basic corps units were due to complete mobilisation not later than August 1, while a number of units for allocation to army headquarters, G.H.Q. and lines of communication had already been mobilised under the first phase of the programme of preparation. These, it was considered, would suffice to meet the immediate requirements of any military operation of a limited nature, the only kind of operation likely to be undertaken in the immediate future. Indiscriminate acceleration in the process of mobilising medical units, many of which would in all probability not be required for some time to come, was attended by serious disadvantages in that mobilisation of a unit involved completion of its establishment and thus the tying of personnel. If, as it was proposed, all units were to be mobilised immediately, then large numbers of medical officers and medical personnel would be consigned to a state of relative inactivity, and for an indefinite period, while their services were in urgent demand elsewhere. At that time the Army Medical Services were in the midst of an acute crisis in the matter of medical man-power and the numbers of M.Os. and of specialists in particular required both for the field force and for the static forces at home, were not forthcoming. The state of affairs was such that adequate medical attention to the Army in the United Kingdom could be supplied and maintained only by using the staffs of field force units pending their dispatch overseas to assist the static medical services at the disposal of home commands. These being the facts, A.M.D. recommended, as a solution to the difficulty, that the mobilisation of the smaller specialist units such as transfusion units, special surgical teams, etc., should be postponed until shortly before the date fixed for the opening of military operations and that some of the larger units, e.g. general hospitals, should be formed in the first instance with a minimum cadre and completed at a later date as dictated by the supply of personnel and the programme of unit training. This suggestion was approved and mobilisation time-tables were amended accordingly. Ultimately, and consequent upon postponement in the date of completion for the expeditionary force as a whole, a revised phased programme for the raising and mobilisation of medical units was prepared and brought into operation, although afterwards somewhat altered in so far as general hospitals were concerned by subsequent changes in the prescribed scale of hospital provision.

In August 1943 the Army at Home, including the expeditionary force, now designated 21 Army Group, underwent reorganisation and reconstitution. Certain formations previously included in the force were withdrawn and others substituted in their place; each of the three divisions (mixed) in the force was converted into an infantry division by removing its tank brigade and replacing it by a third infantry brigade and the three tank brigades, so released, were retained with the expeditionary force as independent tank brigades. This reorganisation entailed the provision of more medical units, for whereas the allotment of field ambulances to a mixed division was two, that to an infantry division was three. Furthermore, the retention of the tank brigades in an independent capacity involved the allocation of a light field ambulance to each. The required units were made available as the result of disbandment, or reduction in establishment, of formations belonging to Home Forces which were undergoing reorganisation at the same time.

Shortly afterwards further changes were made in the composition of the expeditionary force, this time owing to a deterioration in the general man-power situation. It now appeared that the intake to the Army during the last few months of 1943 was likely to reach only a third of the presumed total. Thus the numbers forthcoming would be insufficient to supply the reinforcements necessary to replace wastage from battle casualties on the scale to be anticipated in a force of the size hitherto conceived. There was therefore no alternative but that the battle order of 21 Army Group should be reduced to a strength for which provision could be made in accordance with an amended man-power budget. It was decided to achieve the necessary decrease by reducing provision in respect of personnel or services which could be regarded as not wholly indispensable or which were capable of reduction below the normal standard scales. The latter expedient was made applicable to the medical services, where a reduction of 1,150 personnel was imposed. At the instigation of the staff of 21 Army Group it was proposed that the saving should accrue from a reduction in the number of hospitals to be included in the force. The standard scale for provision of hospital beds had been fixed at 10 per cent. of the strength of the force, including 6 per cent. overseas and 4 per cent. in the United Kingdom. It was now suggested that the proportions might be reversed by limiting beds overseas to 4 per cent. and increasing those in the United Kingdom to 6 per cent., the extra 2 per cent. at home being provided by hospitals of the E.M.S. This, it was held, would permit the elimination of two general hospitals of 600 beds, three general hospitals of 1,200 beds, one convalescent depot for 1,000 men and two convalescent depots each for 2,000 men.

A.M.D. contested the wisdom of this step and declared that in the end it would prove neither a practical proposition nor a measure of economy. In the first place reduction of hospital beds overseas would aggravate the burden of the E.M.S., which were already finding difficulty in meeting the additional military commitments devolving upon them as the result of a falling off in the recruitment of medical officers for the Army. Secondly, reduction in hospital accommodation overseas could but increase the number of cases evacuated from the Continent to the

United Kingdom. This of itself must involve increased wastage in the man-power of the force and the loss would be the greater by reason of the fact that military patients treated in hospitals of the E.M.S., and the majority would be so treated, were invariably longer in returning to duty than those admitted to military hospitals. The elimination of convalescent depots providing accommodation for 3,000 men was even more objectionable, on the grounds that their absence would entail the occupation of hospital beds by patients no longer in need of hospital treatment and would still further reduce the hospital accommodation available for casualties. Furthermore, lack of means for rehabilitation would necessitate the evacuation to the United Kingdom of a large number of slight cases of sickness or wounds, cases which, given the proper facilities, might well be retained with the force and rendered fit to return to duty in a minimum period of time. It was eventually agreed that the full complement of convalescent depots should be retained but that the hospitals should be reduced to the extent of 4,800 beds, thereby decreasing the total provision to 26,700 beds, that is to say to 5 per cent. of the strength of the force. It is of interest to note that within a few weeks of this decision being made the administrative staff of 21 Army Group expressed their concern at this departure from the previous intention to provide hospital beds overseas on the scale of 6 per cent. of the force and, basing their opposition upon arguments identical with those set out above, naïvely enquired if this reversal of policy had been initiated by the War Office!

Towards the end of the year 1943 it was resolved that the strength of the expeditionary force should be further augmented and that the required increment should be derived from the Mediterranean theatre of operations. This increment consisted of one corps comprising one armoured division, two infantry divisions, two armoured brigades and corps troops.

All these required reorganisation and remobilisation on arrival in the United Kingdom and, not having been converted to the new medical organisation, the allocation of the standard number of F.D.Ss. Besides the divisional and corps medical units belonging to these formations other units were brought home from Italy, North Africa and the Middle East to supply the additional quota necessary to complete the medical services on the lines of communication and at the base. These included general hospitals, depots of medical stores, mobile laboratories, etc. It was intended that reorganisation and remobilisation should be completed during the months of January and February 1944 but the delayed return of some units made a considerably later date of completion unavoidable.

The acquisition of this increment to the expeditionary force, and the substantial increase in strength occasioned thereby, reopened the question of the provision to be made in respect of hospital beds on the

Continent. A.M.D. had already called attention to the fact that since the decision in the previous September to limit hospital beds to the scale of 5 per cent. the force had expanded by approximately 40,000 all ranks while the number of hospitals had remained unchanged. A deficiency of some 2,000 beds on the revised scale of 5 per cent. had thus been produced. In response to this it was contended that the increase in the force was in respect of administrative rather than fighting troops and so did not call for the full scale of provision, but in any case the number of hospitals already authorised represented the maximum permitted by the man-power situation.

The position was now worse than ever because the hospitals included in the increment drawn from the Mediterranean were insufficient to supply beds on the scale of 5 per cent. even for that increment alone. The deficiency had therefore become greater than before. With the total strength of the expeditionary force estimated at 691,968, including the component from the Mediterranean, 34,594 beds were required to afford hospital accommodation at a ratio of 5 per cent. strength. Yet the total number of beds for which provision had actually been made, also including those of units from the Mediterranean, amounted to no more than 31,500. Thus even according to the revised scale there was a deficiency of more than 3,000 beds. Once again the matter was raised by A.M.D., the previous warnings in regard to inadequate hospital resources being reiterated and the necessity of adhering to the prescribed standard being urged. While not gaining all that was desired, the efforts made on this occasion were not without result for sanction was given to bring home three more general hospitals from the Middle East and so add 1,400 beds to the total, which now became 32,900, a ratio of 4·7 per cent. strength of the force. At this point finality was reached, and it was with hospitals provided on this scale that the expeditionary force was eventually dispatched. In point of fact the hospital resources of 21 Army Group, regarded as a whole, just reached the ratio of 5 per cent. of the force, for although the scale for the British component did not exceed 4·7 per cent. that for the Canadian component was as high as 6·7 per cent.; in all there were 40,100 beds available for a force of 799,894 and the prescribed standard was thus met.

There can be little doubt that in first urging the necessity of supplying hospital beds on a basis of 6 per cent. and in subsequently resisting reductions in this scale, the Army Medical Services were handicapped by their inability to adduce conclusive factual evidence with which to support their contentions. In the absence of basic facts to serve as a foundation for their recommendations, they were forced to rely upon a somewhat arbitrary statement of probabilities and the reiteration of out-dated, even if time-honoured, precedents, neither of which sufficed to carry conviction in higher councils.

THE CAMPAIGN IN N.W. EUROPE

Before the end of the year 1943 it was decreed that all units destined for service with the expeditionary force should on mobilisation pass under the direct control of 21 Army Group, mainly in order that the operational training and preparation of units and formations might be directed and co-ordinated by the command under which they were to serve. As many units of the engineer, supply and medical services were engaged, wholly or partly, in performing static functions, certain reservations were prescribed in order that the preparation of these units for war and their existing static obligations were as far as possible made compatible. These provisions applied with special force to general hospitals and also to other medical units such as F.S.Us. where the medical staff consisted chiefly of specialists. General hospitals of the field force were indispensable in providing beds and staff for the maintenance of the normal routine medical services in the United Kingdom; specialists everywhere were already fully occupied. As a means of meeting the requirements of operational training, on the one hand, and of supplying the needs of the hospital service on the other, a scheme was devised to free a certain number of general hospitals from static hospital functions and to permit of their undertaking training with field force equipment while other general hospitals were required, as a priority duty, to serve in the capacity of static military hospitals. By the allocation of field force general hospitals successively, first in one and then in the other capacity, it was intended that all would eventually receive their field training at the cost of a minimum of interference in the maintenance of normal military hospital services.

Early in 1944 all general hospitals allocated to the expeditionary force were reorganised on the new system evolved towards the end of the previous year by which their establishments were made to include within their total number of beds one or more sections of 100 beds for the treatment of cases belonging to one or other special group—e.g. ophthalmic, orthopaedic, psychiatric, etc. In the case of the hospital of 600 beds there was one such section; in the hospital of 1,200 beds there were two. As regards personnel establishments were made flexible in order to provide the staff required according to the category chosen for the special section or sections; thus of the total number of specialists authorised four were selective and variable as circumstances demanded. Further, as a measure of economy in man-power, machinery had been devised for the expansion of existing hospitals, when authorised, by extensions of 100 beds each carrying a fixed establishment of officers, nursing sisters and other ranks. Thirty-three of these extensions, nine for hospitals of 600 beds and twenty-four for those of 1,200 beds, had been authorised and were in process of formation. It remained, therefore, to designate the special sections and to allocate the 100-bed extensions among the hospitals being mobilised. An exception to the general scheme of organisation was made in the case of one general hospital of 600 beds reserved for the treatment of neuropathic cases only.

The last step required in the preparation of general hospitals was that of arranging for their release from the performance of static functions when required for service overseas. A phased programme of departure was prepared in conformity with the estimated requirements of the force and the facilities likely to be available for the establishment of hospitals at successive intervals after the initial landing on the far shore. In this programme the hospitals were placed in order of priority according to their several functions. It was therefore necessary to devise a schedule of moves and transfers so arranged that those hospitals placed early in the programme of departure but still undertaking static hospital duties were relieved and released by other hospitals not due for dispatch until later. In this way it was possible to ensure that all military hospitals hitherto staffed by personnel of field force hospitals would continue to function, by the same means, until a date some ten weeks after the opening of military operations on the Continent. Thence onwards there would be no replacement by units of the field force and, as the remaining hospitals were withdrawn, so the static military hospitals served by them must cease to function unless staff could be obtained from other sources.

The bid for labour in connexion with the establishment of the general hospitals on the Continent was as follows:

TABLE 1

Period	Mobile Labour		Static Labour		Totals		Cumulative Totals	
	Initial	Permanent	Initial	Permanent	Initial	Permanent	Initial	Permanent
D-day–D-day+18	480	120	300	80	780	200	—	—
D-day+19–D-day+30	160	40	450	120	610	160	1,390	360
D-day+31–D-day+60	—	—	750	200	750	200	2,140	560
D-day+61–D-day+90	—	—	525	140	525	140	2,665	700
D-day+91–D-day+120	—	—	825	220	825	220	3,490	920
D-day+121–D-day+180	—	—	—	—	—	—	3,490	920
D-day+181–D-day+240	—	—	—	—	—	—	3,490	920

Military operations taking the form of an assault from the sea and a landing on a hostile coast necessitated the early establishment of an organisation to control the movement of personnel, vehicles and stores across the beaches from landing craft to assembly areas, transit areas and supply dumps and also to provide a maintenance area for the holding and issuing of stores and commodities required by the troops engaged in developing the attack and securing a bridgehead. Equally there was need to establish a system for the treatment and disposal of casualties evacuated to the beaches from the fighting zone. The organisation charged with these responsibilities and intended to exercise these functions until such time as it would be possible to establish the normal system of lines of communication and base was furnished by a specially devised composite formation termed the 'beach group', built around an infantry battalion to supply the necessary labour and including various elements concerned with engineer, signal, supply, medical and ordnance services. Two or more beach groups constituted a 'beach sub-area' the commander of which was responsible for the control of all services within the beach groups. In the final plans for the assault provision was made for six of these beach groups. In order to spare operational formations from these additional obligations the units used to constitute the beach groups were, for the most part, those ultimately destined for the rearward organisation of the force, e.g. lines of communication sub-areas and base sub-areas, into which they would be absorbed in due course.

In order to meet the requirements of the beach group it was essential that its medical component should consist of units sufficiently simple in composition and light in equipment that they could be easily landed and rapidly established within a short time of the opening of the assault. On the other hand, it was no less necessary that they should be capable of affording such a measure of first-aid treatment, including life-saving surgery, as would permit the immediate evacuation of the majority of casualties with a reasonable degree of safety under conditions in which the possibilities for further treatment during the voyage to the United Kingdom would be slight. An additional requirement was that these units should possess facilities for the retention of those casualties, now estimated at 5 per cent. of the total, unfit for immediate evacuation. Two C.C.Ss. belonging to the assault corps were due to land on the second tide of the first day of the operation but it appeared probable that they would not be in a position to receive patients until the following day at the earliest. In the meantime, therefore, beach groups had to be supplied with units having the staff and capacity for emergency surgery and the means of retaining cases after operation or in need of resuscitation.

It was therefore decided that the units best fitted to fulfil these conditions were the F.D.S. and the F.S.U., which in combination provided the advanced surgical centre (A.S.C.) as devised by the Hartgill Committee. In view of the heavy casualties expected, it was considered that a beach group would require two of these centres; consequently two F.D.Ss. and two F.S.Us. were allocated to each of the six beach groups. In point of fact, as eventually arranged, only the heavy section of the F.D.S. was employed with the F.S.U. to form the advanced surgical centre; the light section, consisting of one medical officer and fifteen other ranks, was allotted the special function of establishing a subsidiary dressing station to deal with local casualties on the beach.

In accordance with the dictum that units of beach groups should not be found at the expense of fighting formations, the F.D.Ss. selected were those included in the force as army troops and providing the additional increment of F.D.Ss. intended to supplement divisional and corps F.D.Ss. as required. F.S.Us. were, in any case, G.H.Q. troops and the field hygiene sections chosen to supply detachments were those allotted to lines of communication. There was some debate as to whether this policy was the correct one in its application to F.D.Ss. It was argued that the allocation to beach groups of all the F.D.Ss. available as army troops for the reinforcement of any operational zone requiring them might unduly retard the evacuation of casualties or even lead to a breakdown in the chain of medical organisation. The suggested alternative was that dressing stations for beach groups should be provided by the divisions engaged in the initial assault since these, not being required to effect any deep penetration from the coast, would not need their own divisional F.D.Ss. in addition to those of the beach groups. Other F.D.Ss. for the beach groups might well be supplied by formations not due to land until the later stages of the operation. This scheme gained some support but was eventually discarded in favour of the original arrangements. There was also a proposal to reduce the number of F.D.Ss. allocated to a beach group from two to one, but here again the previous decision was reaffirmed.

Medical units nominated for duty with beach groups were required to undergo special training; firstly, a course of instruction in beach organisation attended by one or two officers of each unit; secondly, unit training at a centre specially devised for training in amphibious warfare and combined operations generally; and, thirdly, further training with the beach group constituted as a complete organisation. Some difficulty was experienced in fulfilling this programme in respect both of F.D.Ss. and of F.S.Us. As regards the former, F.D.Ss. nominated to serve with beach groups, being those allotted to the force as army troops, were less far advanced in the stage of preparation than were their opposite numbers belonging to divisions and corps, units higher in order of priority for formation and mobilisation. Thus it happened that when required to undergo their special training they were not infrequently in possession of only a part of their field service equipment and vehicles. Obstacles in the way of unit training for F.S.Us. were attributable mainly to the prevalent shortage of all specialists, including surgeons. It was not always possible to make definite allocation of personnel to these units or to assemble them complete with their equipment for any lengthy course of training, the more so because, as already mentioned, the mobilisation of these and similarly constituted units had been deferred until a relatively late date.

Eventually, indeed, it was found necessary to rescind arrangements for the postponement of mobilisation in respect of specialist units as it proved impossible to adhere to the programme of deferment and at the same time to ensure adequate technical training of their personnel. As a result of previous experience in other campaigns elsewhere it was generally agreed that, apart from the training of the unit as a unit, the personnel of a surgical team of any kind required at least one month's training as a team in order to acquire and practise the special technique essential for the satisfactory treatment of battle casualties. Attempts had been made in this direction but without achieving any substantial measure of success. In fact the extent to which it had been possible to arrange for the training of surgeons for the expeditionary force in general had, up to the end of the year 1943, been disappointing. Several factors were responsible; there was a shortage of surgeons everywhere; the employment of field force hospitals in the capacity of static hospitals had restricted the release of their surgeons for special training; operational unit training, e.g. that of beach group units referred to above, had occupied much time; and there were then in the United Kingdom but few surgeons having personal experience in dealing with battle casualties and therefore in a position to give instruction to others. Moreover, at that date it had not yet been found possible to post the total number of surgeons authorised for units of the force.

Having regard to the fact that training by means of lectures and the circulation of reports and memoranda had been tried without obtaining satisfactory results, it was decided to proceed at once with the raising of these surgical teams, including those of a specialised category, and to assemble in each command a F.S.U. attached to a F.D.S. or general hospital in order to demonstrate the lay-out of a surgical centre and to provide something comparable to battle training for surgical teams. At the same time arrangements were made for the raising of the special maxillo-facial surgical teams, the mobile neuro-surgical team and the surgical team for chest surgery. These units were formed by the general hospital to which they would eventually be attached. After formation they received technical training at centres already established within the E.M.S. for similar special work.

With the object of strengthening the expeditionary force in respect of surgeons having experience of battle casualties, a proposal was put forward for bringing home a proportion of the surgical specialists in the Mediterranean and replacing them by others from the United Kingdom. It was suggested that if the two theatres of war shared the more experienced staff who could impart their knowledge to their less experienced colleagues the general standard of surgical performance would be raised, with advantage to the Army as a whole. Just then, however, the forces in the Mediterranean were heavily engaged and it was considered undesirable that they should be denuded of their experienced surgeons on account of projected operations elsewhere. Moreover, an interchange of this kind would undoubtedly cause some disorganisation, even if only of a temporary nature. In the circumstances it was decided that while there was much to be said for the underlying principle, yet practical difficulties precluded any extensive application of the scheme. The result was that, although it was found possible in some cases to arrange transfers, the number effected was small.

The importance of providing hygiene services as early as possible on the beaches and for a rapid advance inland was fully recognised in 21 Army Group and in Second Army. Hygiene units, therefore, appeared early in the phasing tables. The order of priority given to field hygiene units varied from formation to formation but the principle of giving these units early shipping space was generally accepted.

In the first plan each of the six beach groups included a detachment of two N.C.Os. provided from the field hygiene sections of the assault formations. This plan was reconsidered as it depleted units which would be required to accompany their formations in the advance and the detachments were eventually found by 45 Fd. Hyg. Sec. (G.H.Q. Troops) and the four field sanitary sections mobilised for the L. of C. Two N.C.O. sanitary assistants were therefore detached for duty with each beach group battalion and were attached to one of the field dressing stations.

One of these N.C.Os. was charged, at the request of the General Staff, with gas detection duties and general hygiene supervision of the area administered by the beach group. The second was to be employed on the supervision of water supplies in the beach group area. The beach group detachments were permanently attached to their groups for training under D.A.Ds.M.S. beach group sub-areas and each detachment was supplied with one motor cycle from the parent field hygiene section or field sanitary section; 100 per cent. reserves were also trained.

It was accepted that the passage of very large numbers of troops through the beach transit areas would require careful attention to sanitation by the beach groups themselves and by all units passing through to the beach assembly areas which were outside the areas administered by the beach group battalions. A clear directive was therefore issued which contained instruction on the following matters:

(a) the early selection and marking of 'foul' areas with conspicuous direction signs.
(b) the provision of shallow trench latrines in these foul areas at the earliest possible opportunity, followed by deep trench latrines covered by the flat squatting type of superstructure evolved in the Middle East.
(c) the prevention of fly-breeding and the disposal of rubbish and garbage.

THE EVACUATION OF CASUALTIES

BY SEA

The most cursory examination of the plan of campaign and of the conditions under which it was likely to be fought was sufficient to show that, from the medical aspect, the outstanding question presented was the task of evacuating the presumably heavy casualties likely to be suffered by the expeditionary force in the assault stage of the invasion. Consequently, from the day when the Medical Planning Section came into being and throughout its subsequent existence and that of its successor, the Medical Planning Committee, this matter was one of deep concern to those responsible for preparing an organisation adequate to perform the functions required of it. This subject was rendered the more difficult by reason of the fact that it included many primary considerations outside the control of the medical services, some of them indeed, for example the weather, being beyond the power of any human agency.

The situation, as visualised by the Medical Planning Section at its first meeting in July 1942, involved arrangements vastly different and more complicated than the normal routine by which fully equipped hospital ships, providing every facility for medical and surgical treatment, were engaged in supplying what was in effect a travelling hospital service between an overseas theatre of war and the home base. Under the conditions to be expected no such system would, at first, be possible and special methods would need to be devised. As no port would be available and as the evacuation of casualties would be undertaken by embarkation from open beaches, it was necessary at the outset to discover what vessels would be available and which of them were suitable, or could be adapted, for use in these unusual circumstances. On investigating the matter a variety of obstacles was encountered. In the first place it appeared that the use of hospital carriers, that is to say ships specially modified and equipped for the carriage of casualties over a short sea passage, might be found impracticable during the initial forty-eight hours on account of the exposed position they would occupy and their liability to attack from sea, land or air, the more so because at least two journeys of their water ambulances, small landing craft adapted to carry six stretcher cases and upwards of ten sitting or walking cases, between shore and ship would be required to provide them with a full load. In any case the usual method of loading, i.e. by hoisting the water ambulance on specially constructed davits to the level of the deck of the carrier, was likely to prove difficult, especially in unfavourable weather. Subject to contingencies so restrictive in their effects, the scope of hospital carriers could but be confined within limits that precluded the possibility of extensive evacuation of casualties by this means.

The use of other craft as substitutes for hospital carriers was then examined. The assault force, its weapons and mechanised transport were to be ferried across the Channel in a variety of shipping, including deep-draught transports such as merchant ships and specially built landing craft, designed to go close in shore and land their human or material cargoes direct on to the beaches. Consideration was given as to the suitability and availability of these craft for the carriage of casualties on the return voyage to the United Kingdom. It appeared that personnel ships or transports were unsuitable for employment as carriers. In the first place they were not fitted with the special davits necessary for the use of water ambulances and there were objections to holding them off shore during the slow process of embarking wounded because any delay in their departure from the scene of operations would render them more liable to be sunk by enemy action. Infantry landing craft (L.C.I.), owing to their form of construction, were out of the question for any but walking wounded; certain types of transport landing craft were subjected to trial and found suitable for stretcher cases but their number was limited and it was stated that they would be available for this work only at certain periods of the assault and then only provided they were occasioned no appreciable delay, a phrase likely to prove as restrictive in its application as it was vague in definition. Moreover, it was recognised that in the stress and urgency of battle it would be difficult to obtain the degree of co-ordination among craft commanders, beach masters and embarkation medical officers necessary to ensure a smooth and efficient system of evacuation by this method. It was decided to recommend that a number of landing craft be allocated solely for casualty evacuation and that certain modifications in construction be made to render them suitable for the purpose. This suggestion was regarded as impracticable and so failed to gain general support. It was contended that all available landing craft would be required for their primary function of transporting troops and equipment; none could be spared for exclusive use by the medical services. Further, any question of alteration in the construction of these craft would inevitably entail delay in their production and was therefore to be deprecated.

In the face of these difficulties the consideration of alternative methods became imperative. It was therefore decided to examine the possibility of restricting evacuation during the first two days to walking wounded only and of providing on shore a medical organisation sufficient for the treatment and accommodation of all other classes of casualty during this period. It was estimated that if this procedure were adopted not more than 10 per cent. of the casualties would be evacuated; the number remaining on shore to be dealt with by other means might therefore be expected to reach a total of 20,000. A special sub-committee was appointed to work out details of the minimum medical organisation that would be needed on the beaches to provide essential requirements in that event. This sub-committee regarded it as axiomatic that this organisation must be additional to the field medical units forming part of the force undertaking the assault, since it was essential that divisional field ambulances should at all times be ready to advance with their formations and could not be permitted to run the risk of becoming immobilised by the retention of casualties, a duty outside their function and one for which they were neither intended nor equipped. The sub-committee was of the opinion that the medical provision necessary during the first two days of the battle would suffice to meet all demands up to and including D-day + 10; requirements were assessed at six F.D.Ss., four F.T.Us., eight F.S.Us., four C.C.Ss., six general hospitals of 1,200 beds each and two general hospitals of 600 beds each. These units included R.A.M.C. personnel to the number of 4,248, which, with an allowance for the replacement of casualties and pioneers for labour purposes, represented a total amounting to 8·9 per cent. of the assault force. Additional equipment, e.g. stretchers, blankets and water, to be provided was estimated at no less than 647 tons, apart from tentage and hospital rations. Last but not least, a medical or hospital area, of considerable size and remote from military installations likely to invite attack, would need to be set aside for the exclusive use of this organisation. The report of the sub-committee was sufficient to demonstrate the utter impossibility of giving practical effect to any scheme of this kind; it also served to emphasise the inevitable necessity of contriving the evacuation of casualties from the very beginning of the action. Thus, after several months of discussion, something of a deadlock had been reached in regard to medical arrangements for the assault stage of the proposed military operations. On the one hand, in the opinion of the central Administrative Planning Staff, suitable craft were not available or could not be spared in numbers sufficient to give effect to the policy of maximum evacuation; on the other hand, the retention of casualties on shore and the establishment of a large medical organisation would make even greater inroads on transport resources and would involve almost insuperable obstacles in other directions.

From this quandary the Medical Planning Section was delivered through the agency of a memorandum on the subject of hospital and ambulance transport at sea submitted in September 1942 by the Naval C. in C. of the expeditionary force. Here it was clearly and succinctly stated that it was the intention to use hospital carriers to the utmost both by night and by day but that their employment was in great measure dependent upon enemy action and the weather. Embarkation of casualties in these circumstances must always be a matter of uncertainty, and what might be called planned evacuation would not, in the full sense of the term, be possible. Similar restrictions applied to the use of transports for carriage of casualties. Even under favourable conditions their use for this purpose involved delay in turn-round and therefore an appreciable increase in the risk of loss by enemy attack. Both these factors implied waste of shipping and therefore loss of carrying power for the build-up of the expeditionary force. The C. in C. declared that planned evacuation was possible only by means of landing craft working from the beaches direct to disembarkation points on the English coast and that a sufficiency of such craft must be allocated to the medical services for this purpose. The naval staff suggested that three flotillas of transport landing craft, i.e. thirty-six vessels in all, should be reserved solely for the carriage of casualties, even at the expense of operational requirements.

Confronted with this dictum of the Naval C. in C., with the insistent pressure exercised by D.G.A.M.S. and with the findings of the special sub-committee already mentioned, the Administrative Planning Staff had no option but to accept the original recommendation of the Medical Planning Section and to give provisional approval to the principle of maximum evacuation of casualties from the outset of the assault stage of the operation. It was also agreed that a number of transport landing craft should be allocated for the purpose of transporting casualties from shore to shore and that certain structural modifications to provide increased medical facilities should be considered and recommendations submitted in due course. This decision was regarded as remaining operative throughout the course of further preparatory work undertaken during the following months, in fact until July 1943 when, in the light of new developments, the subject was re-opened by the new planning organisation that had come into being in the circumstances already described.

Evacuation of casualties was at that time, as at every other time, the subject above all others causing concern to those responsible for organising the medical services of the expeditionary force. It had become an established fact that, until the time should arrive when it would be possible to operate a regular service of hospital ships plying between continental and home ports, casualty evacuation must depend largely upon improvisation and upon the utilisation of resources available under circumstances of compulsion rather than of discretion, resources which, however well employed, could by no means supply facilities of the standard regarded as essential for the accommodation, treatment and comfort of wounded men while in transit from shore to shore. This unsatisfactory state of affairs was rendered the more significant by reason of the fact that any shortcomings were bound to be most in evidence at the beginning of the assault when the majority of wounded to be evacuated could have received little more than first-aid treatment on the beaches.

Not only was the use of hospital ships out of the question, but not more than eight hospital carriers could be made available, so great was the demand upon shipping for various purposes. As these hospital carriers in the early days of the campaign would be functioning much in the manner of A.D.Ss., steps had been taken to supply them with facilities additional to those which, in the normal course of events, sufficed for the needs of a hospital carrier. Arrangements had been made to carry out structural alterations providing treatment rooms, resuscitation wards, operating rooms and extra store rooms. Nevertheless it had been confirmed that, as previously stated and for the reasons already elaborated, hospital carriers could not be used until at least forty-eight hours after the opening of the assault and that, even when brought into service, their use would suffice for the evacuation of a relatively small number of casualties only; reliance would therefore have to be placed upon other types of craft for the transport of the very large remainder.

In the course of the preceding few months a new type of vessel had been devised for service in the transit of the expeditionary force. This vessel, known as a tank landing ship (L.S.T.), was of very much larger size than the transport landing craft previously considered in relation to the carriage of casualties. Designed primarily for the conveyance of tanks and heavy vehicles, it was also a troop-carrying craft of some 1,500 tons displacement, almost 330 feet in length and 50 feet in beam. Although an ocean-going vessel, it was of shallow draught intended to discharge heavy vehicles direct on to the beaches by means of a specially constructed ramp. The vessel might be described as comprising a tank garage, 240 feet in length and 30 feet in width, with a parking deck above, connected by a lift for raising vehicles, and ballast compartments and store rooms below. It included crew's living quarters with galley, etc., and accommodation for troops. Unfortunately, owing to its form of construction, the vessel tended to roll heavily in a sea-way.

It appeared that the 'behemothian' L.S.T. was far better suited to the transport of casualties than any of the other smaller landing craft previously considered, for, with the large tank deck fitted with stretcher racks, it would be capable of accommodating some 300 casualties, while its larger size and more extensive accommodation would present greater scope for adaptation and for the provision of medical facilities in the form of dressing and resuscitation rooms for the treatment of those carried. Moreover, the ramp used for the loading and unloading of vehicles could be used for the loading of casualties by the employment of the new 2½-ton dual-drive, amphibious motor truck, known as a D.U.K.W., which, adapted for the purpose by being fitted to carry stretchers, would provide the necessary water ambulance to ferry both lying and sitting cases between shore and ship.

The use of L.S.T. for the transport of casualties and the provision of D.U.K.Ws. for loading them were discussed at a meeting of the principal staff officers of C.O.S.S.A.C. in July 1943. It was appreciated that these ships would suffer neither loss of space nor reduction in carrying capacity by the structural modifications necessary to fit them for the carriage of casualties, but there was some doubt as to whether their use for this purpose, by prolonging the time of turn-round both at the beaches and at their loading points, would not interfere with their operational function and thus retard the programme of building up the expeditionary force. D.G.A.M.S. agreed that the question was one primarily of military expediency, but urged that it was necessary to accept either a delay in the building up of the force or a delay in the evacuation of casualties with a consequent lowering in the morale of the troops caused by the sight of large numbers of wounded on the beaches awaiting evacuation. In the end it was agreed that the adaptation of L.S.T. for the transport of casualties between the far shore and home ports and the provision of D.U.K.Ws. as water ambulances for loading purposes provided the best solution to this difficult question. Subject to the extra delay in the turn-round of these ships being operationally acceptable, it was proposed to determine by trial and experiment the structural modifications which should be carried out in those then under construction. It was also decided that such ships as were to be allotted for the transport of casualties should be placed at the disposal of the medical services only. These recommendations, however, were made subject to reservation in that further examination of all the factors involved was necessary to ascertain their feasibility.

Steps were then taken to investigate the question of the number of L.S.T. required. This involved calculations based not only on the total casualties expected from day to day during the assault, a number subject to repeated alteration as estimates were revised from time to time, but also upon the daily number of cases actually requiring evacuation. A certain percentage of each day's casualties would be unfit to travel and must therefore be retained ashore; on the other hand, as time passed, casualties at first retained for urgent surgical treatment would have recovered and become ready for evacuation. Furthermore, consideration had to be given not only to the carrying capacity of L.S.T. but also to the number that would be available on each tide daily for casualty evacuation, for, despite the recommendation mentioned above, it was apparently thought unlikely that any of these vessels could be reserved solely for medical purposes; on the contrary, it was assumed that the primary function of all of them would be the transport of vehicles and troops, in which case their arrival at the beaches would be dictated by the time-table for the building up of the force. As a result of the added delay in turn-round occasioned by the loading and unloading of casualties, some twelve hours would be added to the round voyage, thus increasing it from two and a half to three days. Moreover, no L.S.T. would be available at the beaches between the second tide of the first day after the landing and the first tide of the third day of the assault because they would all be returning from their first voyage. However, it was found possible to estimate requirements in L.S.T. according to the day of the assault and in terms of a complete voyage of three days. The numbers were as follows: D-day 22, D-day+1 6, D-day+2 9, D-day+3 5—that is to say, a total of 42 would suffice to provide the carrying capacity required during the first few days of the operation and therefore for the remainder of the time that would elapse before a port could be made available for hospital ships. To this total of 42 it was necessary to add an allowance to cover losses by sinking or damage, estimated respectively at 10 per cent. and 20 per cent. on D-day and 5 per cent. and 20 per cent. thereafter. The total thus became 59 and it was thought advisable to allow a further margin and to request that 70 L.S.T. be fitted for the carriage of casualties. This decision was approved and arrangements made in the U.S.A., where these ships were being constructed, for the necessary structural alterations to be made.

A few months afterwards, in November 1943, it was discovered that some 60 L.S.T. had been equipped as required but that all of them had been assigned to the forces of the U.S. D.G.A.M.S. thereupon communicated with C.O.S.S.A.C., expressing his anxiety at finding first that no arrangements had been made to supply the British forces with converted L.S.T. and, second, that apparently it was not the intention to allocate any of these ships solely for medical purposes and, as he understood the position, that the number of D.U.K.Ws. to be provided was no more than would be required for their operational function of unloading supply ships. The reply of the Chief of Staff was to the effect that at no time had there been any decision to allocate L.S.T. solely for medical use. D.U.K.Ws., in any case, were never likely to reach the numbers ordered; there would be a shortage of these, as in most other vital resources, but it would be for the operational commanders to say how the best use could be made of those available and much must be left to the common sense of the man on the spot. At the same time, the staff of the Commander of the Allied Naval Expeditionary Force stated that as many as possible of the 189 L.S.T. allocated to the operation would be adapted for the purpose of evacuating casualties and manned by medical personnel. This statement clearly implied the intention that all L.S.T. would carry their normal loads of transport and personnel on the outward voyage and on the return voyage would carry wounded to home ports. The advantage of this arrangement was that all these vessels could be used for operational purposes and for the conveyance of casualties without restriction on account of their potentialities in either direction. D.G.A.M.S. objected that the use of all these craft with a two-fold object in the manner proposed must result in adding to the number of the ports and hards in the United Kingdom at which casualties would arrive, thus increasing the number of medical personnel required for their reception. The naval staff, however, assured him that this was not so, for only Southampton and Gosport would be used as ports of reception in the systematic evacuation of British casualties. Tilbury would be used if necessary but would be avoided if possible owing to the length of the sea passage involved.

Subsequently, in January 1944, at a meeting of principal staff officers at Supreme Headquarters, Allied Expeditionary Force, which had now replaced the former organisation known as C.O.S.S.A.C., several important decisions were made in regard to casualty evacuation:

(a) It would not be possible to allot L.S.T. specifically for casualty evacuation but the naval and military staff of the expeditionary force would issue instructions for the control of these ships so as to ensure adequate provision in due priority;

(b) The number of these ships required would be based on a carrying capacity of not more than 200 lying cases and 100 sitting cases;

(c) As many L.S.T. as possible would be adapted for the carriage of casualties, a minimum of 70 being required for the British forces;

(d) Not less than 45 of these vessels would be permanently manned by medical personnel, 40 by the Navy and the remaining 5 by the Army, who would also man a further 25 to be held in reserve as well as 27 unadapted vessels to be used for walking wounded;

(e) Provided the number available was sufficient, 100 D.U.K.Ws. would be allotted by the Commander-in-Chief for the sole purpose of casualty evacuation;

(f) The ruling of the Commander-in-Chief, Naval Expeditionary Force, that L.S.T. should be beached and 'dried out' only in emergency was accepted;

(g) No landing craft other than L.S.T. would be employed in the organised evacuation of casualties;

(h) Arrangements would be made by the War Office at all ports and hards for the reception of odd casualties arriving by other than the organised system of evacuation;

(i) Casualties among personnel of the Navy and Merchant Navy would be evacuated by the Army through the normal system of evacuation.

To D.G.A.M.S. certain of these decisions implied the negation of the principles he had advocated as essential to the success of the medical plan for the operation; indeed in his considered opinion they were such as to invite catastrophe. He therefore prepared for the attention of the Adjutant-General a detailed statement of the position and of the events that had led to it. He recalled the fact that in the course of the previous eighteen months and throughout the many discussions on the subject during that time he had demanded and consistently pressed for transport to be allocated solely for the purpose of evacuating casualties and placed wholly at the disposal of the medical services until such time as the normal hospital ship or hospital carrier service could be established. The necessity for these facilities at a time when evacuation would be most difficult—i.e. from the beaches during the early stages of the assault—had been recognised, but only after much persuasion and argument. Recognition, however, had not been followed by effective action. As long before as September 1942, the naval staff had agreed to the reservation of landing craft for casualty evacuation and in July 1943 the subject had been reopened and, as he understood it, the previous conclusion reaffirmed. Now, in January 1944, this decision had been reversed. Thus, despite his constantly reiterated opinion that craft should be allotted for the transport of casualties no less than for the transport of tanks and personnel, he now found himself forced to accept a state of affairs in which operational necessity and scarcity of craft available precluded the reservation of vessels specially for the purpose of casualty evacuation and imposed upon the medical services the obligation of undertaking this task by means of vessels engaged primarily in performing other functions. The reason given, that of operational necessity, made any continuance of medical representation useless. Previous experience of improvisation of this kind had shown only too clearly the liability of such measures to break down. Responsibility for any failure in medical arrangements due to this decision must be with the operational staff and could not be imputed to the medical services. Bearing in mind the public reaction to any suffering imposed upon casualties by inadequate medical facilities, and realising that any such shortcomings would occur under the eye of the people of this country, he desired the facts to be brought to the notice of the Secretary of State.

When forwarding the D.G's. protest to the Secretary of State, the Adjutant-General agreed that to provide a satisfactory means of evacuating casualties from the beaches during the assault it was desirable that some form of landing craft, suitably designed or adapted, should be allocated solely for that purpose. He explained that everything possible had been done to arrange for this provision but, nevertheless, the fact was that such vessels did not exist and improvisation was therefore necessary. Much as he disliked improvised methods in this connexion he could see no alternative.

Following a visit of inspection to a L.S.T. in company with representatives of other naval and military departments, D.G.A.M.S. amplified his previous statements. He felt that as a means of casualty evacuation these ships were unsatisfactory and any system based on their use for that purpose was likely to fail. Nor was he convinced as to the facility of loading them by D.U.K.Ws. plying between shore and ship. It appeared that even in a moderate sea this process was likely to prove impossible, in which case the ships must be beached and loaded direct from the shore. Once beached a ship could not leave the shore immediately on completion of loading but must await refloating by the next tide, thus causing delay in evacuation during which time casualties would be exceedingly vulnerable to enemy attack. There were also objections to the vessels from the aspect of the treatment of patients carried. Facilities existed for only the simplest surgical procedure and many cases requiring life-saving surgery would not receive it. Seriously wounded men were likely to suffer severely from the rolling to which they would be subjected and their extrication in any emergency—for example enemy attack upon the ship—would be most difficult. He once more stated his opinion that tank landing ships were unsuitable for casualty evacuation and that the prospects for wounded men embarked in them for a voyage of fourteen to sixteen hours, after receiving only first-aid treatment, were grim and such as to arouse the indignation of the public. He thought it probable that the whole system would break down unless favoured by fair weather and calm seas and he foresaw the medical arrangements for this operation being made the subject of an enquiry at some future date. He denied that the medical services had approved of the use of L.S.T.; they had asked that special craft be provided for the evacuation of casualties and had to presume that the vessels supplied would, when adapted, prove suitable for the purpose.

In order to provide better conditions for the seriously wounded and to afford greater opportunity for the treatment of those requiring operative surgery as distinct from first-aid treatment, some 12 per cent. of all casualties, endeavours were made to find two more hospital carriers and thus increase the total number from eight to ten, to be shared equally between the British and American forces. This was a matter of some difficulty for it had already been established that the decision at the end of 1943 to increase the number of personnel ships allotted for the transit of the force had withdrawn the last reserves of shipping available as potential hospital carriers. Eventually two vessels, suitable although smaller than desirable, were obtained and it was decided that, as soon as operationally possible, a service of hospital carriers between the far shore and home ports should be maintained on a basis of daily sailings, irrespective of whether or not they carried a full load on each voyage.

The estimate of their average load was placed at 200 sitting and 100 lying cases. Carriers would sail to ports on the south coast as previously determined and the complete voyage, including turn-round time, was expected to occupy not more than forty-eight hours. The intention was that, as far as possible, wounded treated on the beaches should be subjected to a process of selection. By this means the more serious cases and those likely to need surgical attention during the voyage would be evacuated by hospital carrier and the less serious, or less urgent, cases by L.S.T.

The result of all this discussion, proposal and counter-proposal was that the Secretary of State referred the question to the War Cabinet for decision and, in doing so, submitted a memorandum giving an account of the relevant events and circumstances and summarising the points at issue from the operational and medical aspects. Expressing his own opinion in the matter, the Secretary of State said that the existing arrangements for the evacuation of casualties admittedly represented an improvisation which had been imposed by the hard facts of the situation. In particular, the extensive use of L.S.T. in a dual function and, consequently, with fewer amenities for the carriage of casualties than similar vessels used solely for the purpose, might give rise to criticism. It was, however, to be borne in mind that the evacuation of casualties during the assault phase had always presented the thorniest problem to those planning a combined operation. The success or failure of the plan in this respect depended largely upon such uncertain factors as the weather, the number of casualties, the proportion of seriously wounded and the scale of the enemy's air attack.

With this statement of the position D.G.A.M.S. was unable to concur. In recording his views he maintained that it was too optimistic in outlook and did not stress the likelihood of a complete breakdown in the medical services and consequently a demand by the public for an enquiry into medical arrangements. In similar circumstances in the past, heads of medical services had been blamed for failing to stress the grave risk of disaster attaching to inadequate medical provision; it was for him to ensure that there should be no such omission on this occasion and he therefore regarded it as his duty to exercise his right of approach to the Secretary of State in the matter. In point of fact, however, D.G.A.M.S. was not given the opportunity of personally representing his views to the Secretary of State and eventually, in March 1944, the Cabinet assented to the view that, much as it was to be deplored, there was no option but to accept restricted facilities for the evacuation of casualties as dictated by operational necessity.

Further trials and exercises were then carried out in connexion with the handling of casualties on beaches and in L.S.T. and with the loading of these ships by means of D.U.K.Ws. The Chief Medical Officer to the Supreme Allied Commander eventually expressed the opinion that, having in mind the restrictions imposed upon the medical services by the character of the operation, the evacuation of casualties in L.S.T. afforded an acceptable means for the carriage and treatment of wounded other than those of the more serious type requiring operative surgery.

While discussions were in progress on the subject of the use of L.S.T. for the conveyance of casualties, attention was directed to the medical staff and equipment with which these vessels should be supplied in order to fit them for the function they were to undertake. Representatives of the Royal Naval Medical Services and of the Army Medical Services investigated the question and recommended that each ship be staffed by four medical officers, including a surgical team and two G.D.Os., twenty sick-berth attendants or nursing orderlies, ten general duty men and two operating-room assistants. Scales of equipment were drawn up on the recommendations of the consulting surgeons of the Navy and the Army and courses of instruction were arranged at the R.A.M. College for medical officers detailed for duty in these ships.

The recommendation made in regard to the provision of surgical teams was subsequently revised as the result of further investigation of the resources available. It was found that the allocation of a surgical team to each L.S.T. staffed by the Army Medical Services would necessitate the posting of thirty surgeons from the hospitals of the expeditionary force due for later dispatch overseas. This would involve the risk of loss through battle casualties of a high proportion of the surgeons of the force. On the other hand, it seemed that the scope, and therefore the life-saving value, of a surgical specialist under the primitive conditions pertaining to a L.S.T. were so limited as to render his services superfluous. The work to be undertaken in these vessels was comparable to that of a field ambulance rather than that of an A.S.C.; moreover, almost all the wounded embarked would have received treatment at the hands of the surgical teams of the beach groups and should therefore be fit to travel to the United Kingdom without further surgical attention of the kind performed in an operating theatre. It therefore appeared to be of advantage to all concerned that, rather than surgical teams, general duty officers having some knowledge of surgery should be allocated for employment in this connexion. This view was accepted, and the medical staff for L.S.T. manned by the Army Medical Services was fixed at three G.D.Os. for each vessel adapted for the carriage of casualties and one G.D.O. for vessels not so adapted and to be used for walking wounded only.

Final arrangements for casualty evacuation were then completed and summarised in special instructions issued to those concerned. Hospital ships would not be employed until suitable ports were available for their use. In the initial stages of the operation casualties would be evacuated over the beaches from specified casualty evacuation points. Ten hospital carriers, five for the British forces and five for those of the U.S., were to be available from the afternoon of the day following the landing. These ships would lie well off shore and would load from water ambulances alongside or hoisted to their davits as convenient. Hospital carriers would be used as far as possible for the accommodation of the more seriously wounded or of cases likely to require surgical attention during the voyage. The average load to be carried by hospital carriers was estimated at 100 lying cases and 200 sitting cases. The bulk of casualties, however, would be evacuated by L.S.T. available from the beginning of the operation. By that date some 70 of these vessels, adapted for the carriage of casualties, would be available on the British sector of the beaches; all of them were to be medically manned, 40 by the Navy and 30 by the Army. The load of these ships was approximately 200 lying cases and 100 sitting cases. In addition there were to be available a number of unconverted L.S.T., also medically manned and capable of carrying 100 sitting cases. Normally L.S.T. would lie off shore and would be loaded by D.U.K.Ws., 100 of which would be reserved for this purpose, in the manner already described. If, owing to bad weather, loading by D.U.K.Ws. were to become impracticable, tank landing ships would be beached and 'dried out' in order that casualties might be carried aboard direct from the beaches. L.S.T. were to be beached only at the discretion, and upon the authority, of the naval commander. Other types of landing craft, personnel ships and transports would take no part in the evacuation of casualties except in an emergency, when any craft available might be used for the purpose. These vessels, however, were to be provided with medical personnel and medical equipment, inasmuch as they were liable to suffer casualties among their crews and the troops they carried and, in addition, were likely to pick up odd casualties from various sources.

The process of evacuation was to be controlled by medical staff officers of the grade of D.A.D.M.S. attached as embarkation medical officers, one to each of the three beach sub-areas. It was the duty of the embarkation medical officers to keep the naval officers in charge of the beaches informed as to the number of casualties, sitting and lying, awaiting evacuation. It was then for the staff of the Naval Commander, Expeditionary Force, to arrange for the retention of the requisite number of vessels in order that they might be loaded under the direction of the embarkation medical officers. One company of pioneers was due to be provided in each beach sub-area to act as stretcher-bearers. Other personnel for this duty would be found from the infantry battalion belonging to each beach group. To assist in arranging for evacuation from the beaches a schedule or time-table of embarkation was prepared

TABLE 2
CASUALTY EVACUATION SCHEDULE
British Sector

Day	Total casualties occurring	Approximately			Tide	Cases available for evacuating on tides each day		Number of converted tank landing ships required ÷ 25 per cent. Note (b)	Casualties carried by tank landing ships shown in column 9		Number of converted tank landing ships available	Number of hospital carriers available	Casualties carried by hospital carriers		Number of unconverted tank landing ships required
		50 per cent. Sitting	45 per cent. Lying	5 per cent. Lying, movable after 5 days		Sitting Note (a)	Lying Note (a)		Sitting	Lying			Sitting	Lying	
1	2	3	4	5	6	7	8	9	10	11	12	13	14	15	16
D-day	4,700	2,400	2,000	Note (f)	D-day D-day + ½	400 1,200	— 1,000	3(h) 8 }11	300 800	600 1,600	5 11 }16	—	—	—	16
D-day + 1	1,500	800	600	Note (f)	D-day + 1 D-day + 1½	1,000 300	1,000 200	8 3(h) }11	800 300	1,600 600	11 3 }14	—	—	—	(d) 4(d)
D-day + 2	2,200	1,100	1,000	Note (f)	D-day + 2 D-day + 2½	300 700	300 500	3 4 }7	300 400	600 800	5 6 }11	2	400	200	(d)
D-day + 3	1,000	500	450	Note (f)	—	700	700	5	500	1,000	8	2	400	200	(d)
D-day + 4	1,100	550	500	Note (f)	—	500	500	3	300	600	8	2	400	200	(d)
D-day + 5	1,200	600	500	300	—	600	800	5	500	1,000	8	2	400	200	—
D-day + 6	1,400	700	600	100	—	700	600	3	300	600	8	2	400	200	—
D-day + 7	1,500	700	700	100	—	700	750	4	400	800	8	2	400	200	—
D-day + 8	1,300	700	500	50	—	700	680	4	400	800	8	2	400	200	—
D-day + 9	1,400	700	600	50	—	600	450	3	300	600	8	2	400	200	—
D-day + 10	1,600	800	700	100	—	800	700	4	400	800	8	2	400	200	—
D-day + 11	1,600	800	800	100	—	800	825	4	400	800	8	2	400	200	—
D-day + 12	1,800	900	800	100	—	850	900	5	500	1,000	8	2	400	200	—
D-day + 13	1,900	900	900	100	—	750	700	5	500	1,000	8	2	400	200	—
D-day + 14	2,000	1,000	900	100	—	900	1,000	6	600	1,200	8	2	400	200	—

NOTES:

(a) Casualties stated in columns (3), (4) and (5) are those that occur daily. A percentage of these will not be immediately available for evacuation—the following assumptions have therefore been made for planning: D-day to D-day+8, 50 per cent. lying cases and 33 per cent. sitting cases will not be available on beaches for evacuation until day following; D-day+9 to D-day+12, 75 per cent. lying cases and 50 per cent. sitting cases will not be available and D-day+13 onwards 100 per cent. lying cases and 66 per cent. sitting cases will not be available, until following day.

(b) As casualties awaiting evacuation on various beaches are unlikely to correspond exactly to the number of converted L.S.T. arriving off each beach, it will be necessary to allow a margin of L.S.T. to cover higher proportions on some beaches than others. For planning purposes an overall allowance of 25 per cent. has been made. This applies only until approximately D-day+8 after which day all casualties will be collected at casualty collecting points and L.S.T. brought to these as required.

(c) The number of L.S.T. shown as available is the suggested distribution of the converted L.S.T. in order to meet the requirements shown under columns (7) and (8) after making allowance for casualties for converted L.S.T. on the outward trips.

(d) Only 5 converted L.S.T. are brought in on the first tide in order that no more of these valuable ships with their medical detachments should be hazarded than is absolutely necessary. It will be necessary therefore to embark some sitting cases in unconverted L.S.T.

(e) Planning date. It has been assumed that of the 70 converted L.S.T. available to the British Sector only 45 will be available on D-day and of the 8 hospital carriers available 4 will be allotted to the British Sector.

Capacities

L.S.T. converted . . . . 200 lying 100 sitting
L.S.T. unconverted . . . . 100 sitting
Carrier . . . . 100 lying 200 sitting

Round Trip Times

L.S.T. when used for lying casualties . . . 3 days
Carrier . . . . . . 2 days

(f) The lying cases (movable after 5 days) on D-day to D-day+4 are shown on D-day+5 *et seq.* All these cases are available for evacuation on that day *et seq.*

(g) No L.S.T. arrive on certain tides. To provide the lift required for casualty evacuation on these tides, L.S.T. as needed will remain on the far shore from previous tides.

(h) One per beach sub-area.

for general guidance but subject to alteration as required by the exigencies of the situation. This schedule set out in tabular form for each day during the first two weeks of the operation the estimated number of casualties of each category, the estimated number available for evacuation on each tide, the number of hospital carriers and L.S.T. necessary to provide the required transport and the number of these vessels available for the purpose. This schedule is shown in Table 2.

BY AIR

The evacuation of casualties by air,* having so clearly proved its usefulness in the Middle East, was manifestly a question of primary importance in medical plans for any subsequent military operation. From the earliest days of preparation for a campaign in Western Europe the Army Medical Directorate had urged the establishment at the first possible moment of an organisation designed to undertake the systematic evacuation of casualties by air from battle zone to base and from the Continent to the United Kingdom. At first the outlook was not propitious, for it had been laid down that sufficient aircraft were not available to permit of any being allocated solely for this purpose and, in any case, owing to operational considerations no such evacuation would be possible during the first ten days of the battle. Nevertheless a strong recommendation was made for the ultimate provision of twelve large and twelve small air ambulances within an organisation concerned exclusively with the conveyance by air of casualties, medical personnel and medical stores. For future planning air ambulance provision was estimated on the scale of one heavy and one light air ambulance for every 50,000 troops composing the force. As an interim measure it was proposed that fifteen transport aircraft would be required daily, after the first ten days, for the evacuation of suitable casualties from the Continent to the United Kingdom and that all transport aircraft should be adapted to render them capable of loading and carrying stretcher cases.

As time went on it became possible to obtain more tangible results and to develop something in the way of a definite system of air evacuation. As regards the expeditionary force itself, light transport aircraft were to be allotted for the evacuation of a limited number of casualties from forward landing-strips near F.D.Ss. to advanced airfields in the neighbourhood of C.C.Ss. or general hospitals. Casualty evacuation units to hold cases awaiting transit at forward landing grounds and advanced airfields were to be provided by the R.A.F.

No air evacuation from the Continent could be guaranteed until D-day + 9, when light transport aircraft on their return journey to the United Kingdom could be used for the conveyance of casualties, but

---

* See R.A.F. Medical Services, Vol. 1, Chapter 10.

it was estimated that the number of cases so evacuated would not be much greater than 100, and would certainly not exceed 200, daily. At the end of the sixth week more and larger transport aircraft would become available and from that date onwards a daily total of 600 cases could be expected. Eventually the system might be extended to greater proportions, but that was a matter for consideration as the campaign progressed.

THE RECEPTION AND DISTRIBUTION OF CASUALTIES IN THE UNITED KINGDOM*

BY SEA

Arrangements for the reception and distribution of casualties returning to the United Kingdom from the Continent were determined on the one hand by the scheme of evacuation and, on the other, by the resources of the country in hospital accommodation and by the geographical disposition of that accommodation. Here again demands were expected to be heaviest at the beginning of the campaign when casualties were likely to be most numerous and when they would all require to be evacuated, and once again it could be said that medical considerations were influenced largely by operational factors.

It was not possible to produce a precise or detailed scheme for the reception of casualties in this country until such time as the operational plan had been developed and a stage reached when specific functions were assigned to selected ports. More rapid progress was made after settlement of the main issues in regard to evacuation of casualties. It having been decided that systematic evacuation would be by hospital carrier and L.S.T. only, Southampton was designated as the port of disembarkation for all hospital carriers, Southampton and Gosport for L.S.T. operating with the British forces and Portland and Brixham for those of the United States. Portsmouth and Tilbury were to be held as ports in reserve but Tilbury was to be avoided if possible owing to the length of the sea passage involved. Dover, while not included among the ports prescribed for purposes of systematic evacuation, was to be organised for the reception of casualties arriving from various sources by emergency means or resulting from enemy attack upon vessels passing through the Strait.

The estimate of casualties from the British sector was subject to revision from time to time as a result of various changes which took place in the general plan of operations during the two years that preparatory work was in progress. The trend was towards decrease and the numbers originally put forward underwent progressive reduction. Estimates as finally revised indicated that it would be necessary to prepare for the

---

* *See* Emergency Medical Services, Vol. 1, Chapter 6.

reception of 6,900 casualties, i.e. 3,900 sitting cases and 3,000 lying cases, from the British and Canadian forces during the first three days of the assault, the largest number in any one of those three days being 2,600 or, in terms of vessels, two hospital carriers and eleven L.S.T. After the first three days the numbers to be dealt with were expected to be very much lower. Of the total casualties arriving by the method of systematic evacuation 60 per cent. would be disembarked at Southampton and the remaining 40 per cent. at Gosport. The organisation for their reception was thus to devolve for the most part upon one circumscribed area and, so far as medical provision for the British and Canadian forces was concerned, upon D.D.M.S., Southern Command, who was charged with responsibility for local administration in that respect. Executive authority was put in the hands of an officer appointed for the purpose in the capacity of A.D.M.S. (Evacuation); he was to be assisted by an embarkation staff officer and a representative of the Ministry of Health. Embarkation headquarters were to be established at Southampton, Gosport and Portsmouth and a staff of medical officers and other ranks R.A.M.C. would be placed under his orders for duty in connexion with the actual disembarkation of casualties arriving at these ports.

Medical arrangements at these reception ports included, in addition to the administrative machinery, the provision of a medical organisation to undertake two functions: first, to afford treatment to casualties in urgent need at the time of disembarkation and, second, to carry out the selection of cases in accordance with the scheme of casualty disposal. The first was rendered necessary by the probability that after a voyage of some ten to sixteen hours spent in craft not attaining a high standard of medical and general amenity under the best conditions and markedly unsteady in a sea-way, the condition of many patients would have deteriorated to a state requiring immediate life-saving treatment, including resuscitation and blood transfusion. As regards the second of these functions, the system regulating the distribution of casualties to hospitals of various categories was in no small measure dependent for its successful operation upon the careful selection and skilful sorting of cases at the time of disembarkation. Two field ambulances were therefore allocated to the reception ports of Southampton and Gosport for the purpose of establishing dressing stations staffed and equipped to undertake preliminary sorting of cases, first-aid treatment, resuscitation and urgent surgery. In each the medical staff was reinforced by the temporary attachment of surgeons with special experience in the selection of battle casualties. Similar organisations, but on a smaller scale, were required at Tilbury in Eastern Command and at Dover in South-Eastern Command. As already stated, Tilbury as a reception port was to be avoided if possible and a special function was assigned to Dover.

At each of these places provision was made to deal with a maximum of 300 casualties daily.

So much for the ports designated as reception ports in connexion with systematic casualty evacuation; there remained numerous other ports and hards along the east, south-east and south coasts to which transports, personnel ships and landing craft returning in accordance with their operational functions might bring casualties, either from among their own personnel or from personnel picked up during the voyage. While the numbers of cases to be expected from casual evacuation of this kind were not great, yet measures for their disposal were none the less necessary. To this end it was proposed to take advantage of medical provision to be made in connexion with the ultimate assembly and dispatch of the expeditionary force, arrangements which included the establishment of dressing stations or first-aid posts in all embarkation areas and at all embarkation points, and the allocation of field ambulances to supply the required medical staff and transport. These field ambulances were therefore given a dual function; in addition to their responsibilities in respect of the outgoing troops they undertook the duties of disembarkation, treatment when necessary, and disposal of the odd cases expected to arrive from time to time at the various loading ports and hards along the coast. Mobile teams of medical officers and nursing orderlies with medical equipment and motor ambulance cars would be made available to go to any point where and when casualties were to be disembarked.

Subsequent distribution of British casualties after arrival in the United Kingdom postulated the formation of three geographical and functional groups of hospitals. In the first group were those situated in the neighbourhood of ports. These 'port' hospitals, as they were called, were reserved for the reception of casualties who, on disembarkation, appeared to be in urgent need of hospital treatment or unfit for further travel. The second group consisted of certain hospitals, other than port hospitals, in the area south of a line drawn from the Thames Estuary to Bath. It was to this group, termed 'transit' hospitals, that all casualties except the urgent cases already mentioned were to be sent direct from ports of disembarkation in the first instance for primary treatment and selective disposal. It was expected that about half the number of casualties received at transit hospitals would be in need of operative surgery; complete diagnostic and surgical facilities, with the appropriate staff, were therefore required in all of these hospitals, which would in fact serve in the capacity of military C.C.Ss. That being their function, they would retain only those cases whom it was not desired to move or subject to further travel. The remainder would be evacuated as soon as possible to the third group of hospitals, i.e. 'home base' hospitals, situated north of the line of demarcation already described, cases of a special kind requiring specific treatment of one sort or another being dispatched to selected hospitals. At home base hospitals casualties would be accommodated in the usual way and retained until fit for disposal or transfer to other establishments.

Conveyance of casualties between port of disembarkation and hospital was to be effected partly by road and partly by rail. It was arranged that hospitals of the port group should be established within a short distance of all ports and hards at which casualties were likely to arrive, whether by systematic evacuation or by adventitious means. Urgent cases for admission to port hospitals, therefore, would invariably be sent by means of motor ambulance cars placed at the immediate disposal of the medical staff in charge of disembarkation and subject to general control by the D.D.M.S. of the command. The same arrangements were made for the conveyance of casualties from ports to transit hospitals where the number involved was small and insufficient to warrant the use of an ambulance train, as for example in the case of the small parties expected to arrive at ports and hards by casual evacuation. In the ordinary way, however, carriage of casualties from reception ports to transit hospitals would be undertaken by ambulance train, centrally controlled by the War Office but moved under the authority of the appropriate command in accordance with the requirements of the medical staff in charge of disembarkation. Conveyance of casualties from transit hospitals to home base hospitals and their transfer from one base hospital to another was to take place entirely by ambulance train, as arranged between the Emergency Medical Services of the Ministry of Health and the War Office.

Both the Ministry of Health and the military authorities being concerned with the distribution of British casualties and therefore with their movements, a clearly defined allocation of responsibility was essential. It was prescribed that the A.M.S. would undertake all movement of casualties by road between ports of disembarkation and port hospitals or transit hospitals and also movement by rail between ports of disembarkation and transit hospitals as far as ambulance train detraining points; they would, of course, continue to carry out all transfers between military hospitals or other military medical establishments. Movement of casualties between E.M.S. transit hospitals and home base hospitals and between one base hospital and another was to be the responsibility of the Ministry of Health, which was also to undertake the duty of intermediate road movement between ambulance train detraining points and transit hospitals.

For the carriage of casualties by rail there were three types of ambulance train in existence: first, the 'casualty evacuation train', of which there were twenty-one belonging to the Ministry of Health and intended for the evacuation of civilian air-raid casualties; second, 'military home ambulance trains', twelve in number, employed in the normal service of conveying invalids from overseas between ports of disembarkation and hospital; and, third, 'military overseas ambulance trains', of which ten had been completed, designed and built for service overseas with the expeditionary force but available for use in the United Kingdom until required on the Continent. The total carrying capacity of all these trains amounted to more than 11,500 cases and was regarded as more than adequate for the combined needs of the British, Canadian and American forces.

These trains were distributed as follows: eight of the casualty evacuation trains of the Ministry of Health were assigned to maintain a shuttle service between reception ports and transit hospitals; the other thirteen casualty evacuation trains and seven of the home ambulance trains were detailed for the longer distance service between transit hospitals and home base hospitals; the remaining five home ambulance trains and all ten of the overseas ambulance trains were handed over to the military authorities of the United States, who were to maintain with their own personnel a distinct system of casualty distribution between the reception ports allocated to them and their own hospitals in the United Kingdom. Of the twenty-one casualty evacuation trains eighteen were staffed by personnel of the E.M.S.; staff for the remaining three were to be found by transferring to them R.A.M.C. personnel from overseas ambulance trains handed over to the United States forces. Immediately before the day fixed for the beginning of military operations each ambulance train was to be manned and moved to its operational stabling point, from which it would be called forward to entraining stations as and where required and to which it would return after completing its journey and detraining its patients, unless needed at once to undertake another journey. Each of these stabling points would provide a headquarters for the train and its personnel and a means of replenishing equipment and supplies, including rations, both for personnel and for patients. In addition, depots were established at certain stations on the scheduled train routes for the issue of clean linen and perishable foodstuffs for patients. Reserves of stretchers and blankets were accumulated at selected places. In order to avoid undue handling of wounded and to save time in their disembarkation and distribution it was decided that, as far as possible, each patient should remain upon the same stretcher throughout the process of conveying him from ship to hospital, including entraining and detraining. The adoption of this procedure involved changes in the casualty evacuation trains allocated to the shuttle service between ports and transit hospitals. These trains, designed for the carriage of civilian casualties, were equipped with steel stretchers of the civil type which could not be used with military ambulance cars. Stretchers of the Army pattern had therefore to be substituted. It was also a matter of considerable importance that adequate measures should be taken to prevent any deficiencies of stretchers and blankets in vessels and vehicles used for the conveyance of casualties. Deficiencies were most likely to arise through failure to replace these articles at the time of disembarking or detraining patients. A system of interchange was therefore instituted to ensure that whenever patients were removed from a vessel or vehicle stretchers and blankets, corresponding in numbers to those removed with the patients, were immediately handed over in replacement by the personnel receiving the patients. This interchange was continued throughout the course of transfer from ship to ambulance car, from ambulance car to ambulance train, from ambulance train to ambulance car again and, finally, from ambulance car to hospital bed.

The movement of ambulance trains involved a somewhat complicated chain of administrative arrangements. Control of all these trains, civil as well as military, allocated to the British forces for the conveyance of British and Canadian casualties was vested centrally in the War Office, by which executive authority was delegated to the usual organisation for the regulation of troop movements in commands and districts. As regards trains allocated to the maintenance of the service between reception ports and transit hospitals, proceedings were initiated by the A.D.M.S. (Evacuation), who notified his requirements to the Movement Control Officer at Southampton. This officer, in collaboration with the Docks and Marine Manager of that port, then settled details as to the selection of the train, the time and place of loading, the estimated load, the expected time of departure, the destination of the train and the disposal of the train after detrainment of patients. The actual movement of the train was then effected by action on the part of the railway executive. Having completed his arrangements, the Movement Control Officer at Southampton notified the War Office and warned the movement control organisation in the district to which the train was to be sent; thence the information was transmitted to the appropriate E.M.S. regional or sector hospital officer, who was thus enabled to arrange with his detraining officer for the reception of the train and the provision of motor ambulance transport to convey the patients to the transit hospital indicated. After detrainment all responsibility for attention to casualties, their transport, distribution to hospital and reception at the hospital passed into the hands of the hospital officer.

Ambulance trains required for the transfer of casualties from transit hospitals to base hospitals were regulated by a procedure somewhat different in that their movement was initiated by E.M.S. regional hospital officers. Each hospital officer was kept informed, from daily statements rendered by hospital superintendents, of the number of patients in his area available for transfer from transit hospitals to base hospitals. When the numbers were sufficient to warrant it, the hospital officer called for a train by application direct to the War Office, stating the number of patients to be conveyed and the entraining station at which the train was required. The War Office then selected the train to be used, nominated the detraining station by reference to a schedule of priorities determined by the Ministry of Health, arranged with the Railway Executive Committee for the movement of the train and notified the military movement control organisation of the district from which the train was to depart and of the district at which the train was to arrive. On receipt of this notification the military movement control organisation in the dispatching district notified the regional hospital officer who had asked for the train and who now arranged for the entrainment of the patients at the appointed place and time. Meanwhile the movement control organisation in the receiving district notified the hospital officer there and the latter then made provision for detraining the casualties and distributing them among the receiving base hospitals. It will be obvious, therefore, that in the movement of casualties between transit hospitals and base hospitals the Army Medical Services were concerned only with the internal administration of the train and its personnel and with responsibility for medical attention to the patients during their journey between entraining station and detraining station.

The movement of casualties by road presented some difficulty from the aspect of adequate provision of transport. In the first place, a large number of ambulance cars was necessary for the carriage of urgent cases from designated reception ports to port hospitals and for the conveyance of small parties of casualties from these ports to transit hospitals. Again, the number supplied must be such as would permit of motor ambulance cars being available at the numerous ports and hards along the coast where at any time casualties might be landed by emergency methods of evacuation. Finally, a large fleet of ambulance cars formed an essential part of the special medical services to be provided in connexion with the assembly and dispatch of the expeditionary force.

Motor ambulance transport belonging to the Civil Defence Services was already fully committed to supplying the ambulance service that would be required for the conveyance of military casualties between ambulance train railheads and hospitals of the E.M.S. Little or no assistance could be expected from that quarter and therefore all ambulance cars in demand for the additional military duties mentioned must be found from military sources.

At the beginning of the year 1943 the total number of motor ambulance cars, of all types, held by military establishments, including field medical units, command pools, anti-aircraft medical services, etc., throughout the United Kingdom was approximately 3,300, of which number some 1,200 belonged to units of the expeditionary force and would therefore be sent overseas with that force. It was estimated that in the commands concerned with the special medical arrangements made for the dispatch of the expeditionary force and the reception of its casualties the number of motor ambulance cars likely to be forthcoming, including those of the field ambulances allocated to these commands for special duty, was considerably below the minimum number required, the deficiency being well over 300 in all. It was at first intended to make good this deficiency by the temporary allocation of ambulance cars belonging to units of the expeditionary force low in the order of dispatch overseas, but later it was discovered that none of these would be available owing to the necessity of calling in all vehicles for water-proofing at a date well in advance of the day fixed for the dispatch of the force. Eventually, after further examination of the question, it was found possible to obtain the temporary release of three units of the expeditionary force, i.e. two ambulance car companies and one ambulance unit of the B.R.C.S., for periods of nineteen days, twenty-four days and forty-four days respectively from the date of the assault. At the end of the periods specified these units would join the expeditionary force.

These additions, however, did not suffice to cover the estimated total requirements, which tended to rise as preparatory arrangements developed. Assistance was forthcoming from the B.R.C.S., which undertook to raise another ambulance unit of 100 cars with drivers. Even so, a deficiency of more than 100 motor ambulance cars remained to be met. Eventually the additional number required was made available by issuing, from transport reserves, ambulance cars in excess of their normal complement to the field ambulances allocated to Eastern, South-Eastern and Southern Commands for special duty in connexion with the projected military operations. Drivers for the extra ambulance cars were found within the field ambulances concerned by using personnel normally employed in driving other types of vehicles belonging to these units—e.g. lorries, trucks, etc. Where necessary the number of drivers was supplemented by drawing upon other units elsewhere.

Final arrangements for the reinforcement of ambulance resources in commands were as follows: Eastern Command one ambulance car company of 120 cars from the expeditionary force and 57 extra cars issued to field ambulances; South-Eastern Command one B.R.C.S. ambulance car company of 25 cars belonging to the expeditionary force and 36 extra cars issued to field ambulances; and Southern Command, whose commitments far exceeded those of the other two commands, one ambulance car company of 120 cars belonging to the expeditionary force, the specially raised B.R.C.S. ambulance car company of 100 cars and 36 extra cars issued to field ambulances.

BY AIR

A distinct system of reception and disposal was required for casualties arriving in the United Kingdom by air.* An Air Evacuation Headquarters was established at H.Q. Salisbury Plain District (The Close, Stratton St. Margaret). Attached to it were representatives of the three Services, of the Canadian Army and of the E.M.S. Its function was to control the arrival of casualties coming by air from the Continent and their subsequent distribution. Transport aircraft allocated for the conveyance of casualties were all to return to airfields situated within a short distance of Swindon. Three airfields—Blakehill Farm, Down Ampney and Broadwell—would come into service and would receive all casualties evacuated by air, except just before and during periods of airborne operations when, for security reasons, the airfield at Watchfield would be used. Each of these airfields required medical and transport arrangements comparable with those established at ports of reception for seaborne casualties. The R.A.F. accepted responsibility for the reception of airborne casualties and proposed to establish at each airfield a casualty air evacuation centre of 200 beds with facilities for urgent surgery and resuscitation; responsibility for their distribution and conveyance to hospital rested with the Army Medical Services. For purposes of disposal cases were to be divided into two classes, those requiring immediate hospital treatment and those fit for onward transmission by ambulance train. Urgent cases would be conveyed by motor ambulance car to the E.M.S. hospital at Stratton St. Margaret, near Swindon, except that such as were received at the Broadwell airfield would be dispatched to hospitals at Oxford, the distance involved being appreciably less.

All who were fit to travel would be taken by ambulance car to an ambulance train railhead established at Shrivenham, near Swindon, where extra sidings had been built, and thence by ambulance train to selected detraining stations for distribution among home base hospitals under the same system as that applicable to seaborne casualties. Special arrangements were made by which patients suffering from wounds of the head would go to the Hospital for Head Injuries at St. Hugh's College, Oxford, and cases of maxillo-facial injury or burns to Gloucester City Hospital.

The reception and distribution of casualties evacuated by air thus implied an extensive motor ambulance service. This was to be undertaken by the special ambulance unit of 100 cars raised by the B.R.C.S. and allocated to Southern Command under arrangements for supplementing motor transport resources in commands.

---

* For a comprehensive account of this, see R.A.F. Medical Services, Vol. 1, Administration, Chapters 5 and 10.

HOSPITAL ACCOMMODATION IN THE UNITED KINGDOM*

The ultimate disposal of casualties from the Continent again raised the hoary question of hospital accommodation available for military patients in Great Britain. The special features of the projected campaign precluded the usual military procedure by which general hospitals, as part of the medical component of an expeditionary force, were established at an early date in the theatre of operations. Indeed, in the circumstances, it appeared certain that some weeks must elapse before conditions would be sufficiently stable to permit development of the medical services to that extent. During this time the force would be denied its own hospitals upon which it would normally rely for the accommodation of a large proportion of its battle casualties and sick. It followed that, in the opening phases of the attack and until the force was sufficiently consolidated to permit of the retention of casualties overseas, all sick and wounded, irrespective of type or degree of severity, must be evacuated to the United Kingdom. General hospitals belonging to the expeditionary force could not be relied upon to render much assistance in respect of the accommodation and treatment of battle casualties at this stage for, although still located at home, they would for the most part be standing by with their equipment packed awaiting the call for dispatch abroad. Thus at first, and for some time after the launching of the assault, the provision of beds for casualties from the forces engaged must devolve upon static military hospitals and hospitals of the E.M.S. in Great Britain. It was a matter for decision as to whether the accommodation thus available was sufficient, without further provision, to meet the demands arising from a campaign in Western Europe in addition to those presented by commitments in other directions.

In order to supply the answer to this question it was sought to determine the number of hospital beds that would be required for military purposes and then to ascertain the total number of beds available, or likely to become available, in hospitals of various categories throughout the United Kingdom. As regards requirements, the General Staff's estimate of the battle casualties that would be incurred during the first six months of the campaign and the medical estimate of the probable average duration of their hospital treatment were subjected to statistical examination, from which it was possible to obtain an indication of the maximum number of beds for which provision must be made on account of battle casualties alone. To this number it was necessary to add beds required in respect of the sick of the expeditionary force, calculated at the rate of 3 per cent. of strength, and those necessary to provide for the sick of the forces remaining in the United Kingdom, also calculated at

---

* See Emergency Medical Services, Vol. 1, Chapter 6.

the rate of 3 per cent. The sum thus obtained yielded the total hospital accommodation required for military purposes. In the circumstances that existed in July 1942, when the investigation was made, the estimate of accommodation required was 83,750 beds.

In collaboration with the Ministry of Health a survey was made of beds available in military hospitals, in hospitals of the E.M.S. in England and Wales, and in civil hospitals under the control of the Department of Health for Scotland. It was found that the number of Class A beds, that is to say beds equipped and ready for use, in contradistinction to reserve beds, available in military and civil hospitals amounted to a total of 87,200, excluding those in hospitals situated in some of the larger towns and other areas regarded as specially vulnerable to enemy attack. There was thus a safety margin between maximum requirements and accommodation available, a margin likely to be increased by a forthcoming revision in the schedule of vulnerable areas and the consequent release from restriction in the use of certain hospitals.

In December 1943 the question of hospital accommodation for military casualties was re-examined when the position in regard to accommodation required and accommodation available was again investigated in the light of alterations recently made in the constitution of the expeditionary force and of certain changes that had taken place in the hospital situation. It was now estimated that, at maximum rates of 10 per cent. for the field force and 3 per cent. for the forces in the United Kingdom, the Army would need 86,600 beds, while the R.N. and R.A.F. would need 5,000 more. Thus the sum total of hospital requirements for the British forces on the Continent and in the United Kingdom was increased to 91,600 beds. Statistical investigation of the probable incidence of casualties, however, had shown that on the 29th and 59th days after the landing of the force there would be a peak-load upon hospital accommodation calling for further provision, which would raise the number of beds necessary at the period of maximum demand to 95,000 in all.

Towards the provision of these 95,000 beds there were but 16,800 in static military hospitals. The general hospitals of the expeditionary force would eventually establish 32,900 more on the Continent but these, for the reason already given, would not be available at the outset and certainly not before the date at which maximum accommodation might be necessary. Consequently, in order to meet all possible exigencies, it would be necessary to rely upon the resources of the E.M.S. for the provision of hospital beds up to a maximum of 78,200 in the first instance and subsequently in numbers gradually decreasing to 45,300 after the complete establishment overseas of the general hospital component of the expeditionary force.

The E.M.S. had at their disposal in the hospitals under their control a total of 191,000 beds, including 84,000 already equipped and staffed, 25,000 more equipped and staffed for a short period (about seven days) to deal with emergency demands, 47,000 that could be made available at short notice by discharge of patients sufficiently recovered to return home and 35,000 in reserve equipped but not staffed. In addition to calls made upon them in respect of military casualties, these hospitals were required to provide accommodation for civilian air-raid casualties, to supply the ordinary hospital needs of the civil population and to be prepared to cope with any special demands that might arise in connexion with the prevalence of epidemic diseases such as influenza. However, it was agreed that the resources available would suffice for all liabilities and that full provision could be made to supply the needs of the Armed Forces.

Having regard to the small number of beds provided by military hospitals in relation to the total required, it was obvious that the majority of patients would be treated in civil hospitals by civil medical and surgical staffs and subject to the control of the civil medical organisation. The E.M.S. being so largely involved in the accommodation and treatment of returning casualties, administrative arrangements governing the hospital service to be provided in connexion with the forthcoming military operations were matters in which the Ministry of Health was as much concerned as was the War Office. The general scheme subsequently evolved and the numerous points of detail finally elaborated were the result of joint planning by these two authorities and were made possible only by frequent consultation and co-ordinated action. In this way a system was devised for the allocation of hospitals into three groups, port, transit and home base, already described in relation to the reception and distribution of casualties. Similarly, it was agreed that, as a means of simplifying procedure, the sick of the forces at home should be concentrated in military hospitals whenever possible while casualties from overseas would, for the most part, enter hospitals of the E.M.S.

In order to have ready a maximum of hospital accommodation conveniently accessible to ports of disembarkation and available for the first flow of casualties, it was necessary that action should be taken in good time to empty, as far as was practicable, all hospitals of the port and transit groups and some of the less distant home base hospitals. Consequently, well in advance of the date fixed for the landing on the Continent, patients fit to return home were discharged and those requiring prolonged treatment—i.e. more than twenty-eight days—transferred to other hospitals situated in the northern and western parts of the country. It was essential from the point of view of security that the process should be gradual and so relatively inconspicuous. The Ministry of Health was satisfied that this movement of patients could be undertaken and completed satisfactorily within thirty days of their receiving notice to do so. They did not require, and indeed did not desire, precise information as to the date of the operation. It was also agreed, again in the interests of security, that civil medical practitioners and nurses who were being held in reserve to reinforce the staffs of certain hospitals when the invasion took place should remain at their usual places of residence until after the attack on the Continent had actually begun, when they would be conveyed to their destinations by road transport.

It is to be noted that the foregoing account of the arrangements made in respect of hospital accommodation for casualties returning from overseas refers to the British forces only, the Canadian and American military authorities having undertaken to provide in the United Kingdom sufficient hospitals of their own to receive casualties among their forces.

Long before the completion of medical plans for the campaign it became apparent in the course of consultation between the War Office and the Ministry of Health that the E.M.S., entrusted as they were with a large share of responsibility for the treatment and the distribution of battle casualties, would be unable to fulfil their obligations in their entirety unless afforded some measure of assistance by the Army Medical Services. While no difficulty was likely to be encountered in providing the hospital beds required, it appeared that considerable help would be needed in supplementing the surgical staffs of E.M.S. hospitals belonging to the port and transit groups. These hospitals during the early stages were due to function in the place of the military C.C.Ss. which usually accompany a fighting force. They would therefore be called upon to undertake a volume of operative surgical work which would undoubtedly prove greater than could be performed by the normal staff unaided. Although arrangements were being made by the Ministry of Health for the transfer to the smaller hospitals of staff from E.M.S. hospitals elsewhere, nevertheless it seemed improbable that sufficient surgeons could be made available without having recourse to those of the R.A.M.C. Another direction in which assistance would be needed was that of supplying the personnel required by R.H.Os. to undertake the handling of casualties at entraining and detraining stations in the process of transfer between ambulance trains and E.M.S. hospitals.

It was therefore to be expected that fairly heavy demands would be made upon the Army Medical Services for surgeons, anaesthetists, nursing sisters and operating-room assistants and for stretcher-bearers, clerks and cooks. Accordingly, attempts were made early in 1944 to determine the number of personnel of various categories that would be needed to supplement the civil organisation. The E.M.S. therefore submitted a tentative estimate of their requirements. No precise statement could be made until such time as it would be possible to obtain a decision in several matters still unsettled in the general plan of operations, such as the use of certain ports for the reception of casualties.

In fact the provisional figures quoted underwent continual revision until the last moment. They were, however, sufficient to permit of preparatory action. As then estimated it appeared that the medical services would be required to provide twenty-three surgical teams, including a theatre sister in each, and fourteen transfusion officers; other ranks to the number of 1,483, including 1,347 stretcher-bearers, 69 clerks and 67 cooks, would also be needed. Of the stretcher-bearers 767 were required for hospitals and 580 for ambulance train railheads. It was agreed that where the E.M.S. were unable to provide accommodation for R.A.M.C. personnel billets would be found by the commands concerned, but that feeding arrangements would be made by the E.M.S., military rations being supplied.

No difficulty was to be expected in making available medical officers and sisters in the numbers demanded. Their services would be required for not longer than a week or two from the beginning of the campaign, during which time casualty clearing stations and general hospitals of the expeditionary force would still be located in the United Kingdom. It would therefore be possible to call upon these units for the temporary loan of their surgical specialists, anaesthetists, etc., to E.M.S. hospitals in need of reinforcement. On the other hand the finding of 1,483 additional other ranks for attachment to the E.M.S. organisation presented something of a problem, the more so as the liabilities of home commands in regard to the special medical services for the assembly and embarkation of the expeditionary force had already given rise to a demand for some 500 other ranks, R.A.M.C., over and above normal establishments. The situation had, however, been foreseen and there was at the time in the United Kingdom an accumulated surplus of some 3,000 other ranks available to meet reinforcement demands and to supply overseas drafts. Authority was therefore given to D.Ds.M.S. of all commands in the United Kingdom to retain as reserved and unavailable for posting elsewhere the number of other ranks required for their own additional needs and for assistance to the E.M.S.

In the course of the next few months the requirements in R.A.M.C. personnel, as thus assessed, underwent alteration in several respects. The decision that Tilbury should not be used as a port of reception for systematic casualty evacuation removed the necessity for seven surgical teams and the number of teams to be lent to E.M.S. hospitals was thus reduced to sixteen. On the other hand the demand for stretcher-bearers was increased and the number of other ranks, R.A.M.C., reserved for duty with the E.M.S. finally reached the total of 1,589. In addition to these a small number of despatch riders was required for attachment to various E.M.S. regional headquarters. These were produced without difficulty by drawing upon the personnel of one of the field ambulances.

Special arrangements were made in regard to hospitals in the neighbourhood of the casualty reception airfields near Swindon. The E.M.S. intimated that the staff of the hospital at Stratton St. Margaret was insufficient to cope with a large influx of serious cases. As the function of this hospital was to provide surgical aid for cases found to be in urgent need of treatment when landed at the airfields, a C.C.S. was to be located nearby, sufficiently accessible to enable the staff of the unit to reinforce the hospital and thus provide the required assistance.

MEDICAL SUPPLIES. RATIONS. WATER

MEDICAL SUPPLIES

Not the least noteworthy nor, indeed, the least vital feature in preparations for the medical component of the expeditionary force was that of supplying medical stores and equipment. In addition to providing a great variety of units with their appropriate scales of field service equipment it was necessary to evolve a system of maintenance and replenishment adapted to the peculiar circumstances of the operation.

The supply of mobilisation stores and equipment was remarkable chiefly for the quantity involved and the celerity with which it was accomplished. No fewer than 385 medical and dental units of some thirty different types were included in the force, yet their field service requirements were, in the main, built up at the Army Medical Store at Ludgershall within six months, despite the fact that some of the units included in the medical component were added to the order of battle only towards the end of that period. During the same time approximately 500 combatant units were provided with regimental medical equipment for the use of their R.M.Os. By the end of March 1944 this formidable undertaking had been completed save for a large number of demands for new items or for items in excess of authorised scale received up to almost the last moment. Many of these demands were made as the result of recent experience in other theatres of war and were doubtless a means of increasing the efficacy of the treatment which the wounded ultimately received during the campaign; even so, their belated appearance was a cause of some embarrassment and additional strain upon the already fully extended resources of the Army Medical Store. Nevertheless, by the time of their arrival in their assembly areas units were in possession of their mobilisation stores and equipment complete to scale in all respects but for minor last-minute demands; indeed most of these were supplied before the actual date of embarkation except in the case of some items involving fresh provision.

A notable development in connexion with the mobilisation equipment of general hospitals was the adoption of a new method of issue, packing and dispatch. Previously the equipment of general hospitals had been issued from ordnance and medical stores direct to the port of shipment whence it was dispatched, as a complete entity, to the scene of operations overseas, no account being taken of relative urgency as among the various constituent parts or of the gradual nature of the process which the establishment of a hospital entailed. It was now arranged that, in the first instance, field service equipment, both ordnance and medical, should be issued from store to the unit concerned. Here the equipment was broken down into blocks, each to provide for 50 beds. These blocks were then reassembled in such a way that the whole of the stores and equipment was contained in four sections to correspond with four stages in the establishment of the hospital, articles in demand from the outset being included in the first section, those least urgently required being placed in the last section. Each section and each block in the sections were clearly numbered and the whole returned to store for consignment to the port of loading. Equipment could thus be called forward for dispatch as required. Besides being convenient from the point of view of the unit, this system reduced priority demands for shipping in respect of general hospitals and therefore permitted more advantageous use of the space allotted. For example, the total equipment of a general hospital of 600 beds included 3,886 packages weighing 580 tons, whereas the first section amounted to no more than 1,536 packages or 215 tons. This, having regard to the vast calls upon shipping involved in the transit of a large expeditionary force, represented an economy of some significance. As it happened the application of the system was restricted to general hospitals of 600 beds; time did not permit of the very much greater task of reorganising the equipment of general hospitals of 1,200 beds on the same basis.

To maintain the supply of medical stores and equipment to the force after its landing special measures were required. During the assault stage of the operation, and probably for some time afterwards, it would be impossible to establish overseas the depots of medical stores that normally accompanied an expeditionary force. This being so, there would be no means of following the usual procedure by which units were supplied with the articles they required by advanced, or base, depots of medical stores and by which these depots were replenished in response to considered demands. In the meantime, therefore, the only way of maintaining supplies was to assemble blocks of stores, consisting of articles of pre-determined category and quantity, for shipment and delivery in accordance with a pre-arranged time-table based on estimated requirements.

Two kinds of maintenance block of prescribed weight and contents were therefore prepared. The first was the 'beach block' intended for the daily replenishment of forward medical units, e.g. field ambulances, F.D.Ss., F.S.Us. and C.C.Ss. In deciding the form which the beach block should take it was necessary to consider not only the kind and quantity of the drugs, dressings, instruments, etc., to be included but also such matters as size and weight convenient for man-handling, protection of contents against weather or immersion, allowance for losses in transit, and packing in such a manner as to permit of dispersal in order to reduce risk of loss by enemy action. As the result of trial and experiment the first beach block was assembled in July 1943. After further trial and modification the final pattern was approved in December 1943 and assembly at the Army Medical Store then followed. As finally designed, the whole block weighed 2½ tons and consisted of two identical half-blocks each of 47 packages and weighing 1¼ tons. The original plan provided for the dispatch of 100 blocks at the rate of two each day during the first fifty days of the operation. In the event, however, all 100 blocks were delivered within the first three weeks.

The second type of maintenance block was the '15-tons maintenance block'. This block, being intended for the maintenance of the medical services in general, comprised a much wider selection of stores and more elaborate equipment. In design it was much the same as the maintenance block previously devised for the landing in North Africa. Experience had suggested minor alterations and, as ultimately assembled and approved in March 1944, the block actually weighed only 14 tons. The programme of supply provided for the delivery of eighteen of these blocks within the first eight weeks of the campaign.

During the preparatory period stores and equipment were assembled and built up at the Army Medical Store on the principles described. Final detailed analyses of requirements for the force were received by the War Office during April and the beginning of May 1944. Before the end of April particulars of stowage space required in respect of medical stores to provide for the day of the landing were submitted to the authorities responsible for the allocation of shipping and all tonnage applications to cover the first four weeks of the operation were forwarded by the middle of May. The first consignment of maintenance stores was required to reach the loading ports on May 12 and subsequent calling forward of stores was arranged direct with the Army Medical Store.

Provision was also made for the supply of medical stores by air. This was the only method applicable to troops engaged in certain special operations and was also one well suited to supplement the ordinary process in such circumstances as rapid movement by advanced units. In addition to the normal medical equipment for two airborne divisions, stores and equipment representing four days' maintenance supplies for 1st Airborne Division were assembled and placed at the disposal of the D.D.M.S., Airborne Troops. A duplicate consignment was retained at the Army Medical Store in case of need. A bulk consignment of medical stores, including five days' maintenance supplies packed for dropping by parachute, was prepared for the use of paratroop units. Stores were assembled to provide, in case of need, for the dropping by parachute of maintenance supplies for one brigade group for three days and for one division for five days. In this connexion it is of interest to note that for the delivery of medical supplies from the air it was intended to rely to some extent upon the beach maintenance block already described, experiment having shown that this block, as ordinarily packed, was also suitable for dropping by parachute.

The air route was chosen as the best method of supplying fresh transfusion fluids for the use of medical units of the force and to this end arrangements were made for the delivery of approximately one ton daily. The same means were used for the dispatch of special stores or equipment urgently needed and for supplementing the supply of any articles required in quantities greater than those provided by the maintenance blocks. The contents of these blocks, being pre-determined as regards both category and quantity, could not be varied to suit special requirements. After assembly nothing could be added and nothing could be removed; the blocks had therefore to be accepted as a whole if accepted at all. Thus additional quantities of any one article could not be made available through the routine method of supply without, at the same time, increasing the receipt of other articles the reserves of which were already ample. Hence the value of maintenance by air as a means of supplying those articles for which special demands arose at any time.

Generally speaking, the process of planning and providing the medical stores and equipment of the force was completed smoothly and with but few complications of any kind, although the staff at the Army Medical Store laboured under increasing difficulty by reason of the fact that, in the course of time, much of the space normally available for assembling and packing goods became occupied by stores already packed and retained pending the date of dispatch.

RATIONS

As regards arrangements for the rationing of the expeditionary force, there could be no doubt that the usual method of provisioning an army engaged in operations overseas by the issue of the field service ration in bulk and including fresh foods, would be impracticable until the invading forces were well established and in a position to set up the normal lines of communication and organisation for supply. It was therefore thought best to plan on the assumption that after the assault and throughout the first six weeks of the campaign all rations would take the form of the composite (14-men) ration pack. This pack, the successor of the old 'compo' (12-men) pack, was now produced in two varieties, with and without biscuit, the latter intended for use when fresh bread was available. There were seven types of the first and three types of the second. Each was made up entirely of tinned commodities so arranged as to provide a sufficient well-balanced diet, and the several types differed in their contents in order to allow of some measure of change and variety daily during the week. The use of this composite pack in the ordinary course of events required cooking facilities under unit arrangements. For isolated detachments improvised cooking was necessary; in exceptional circumstances 'tommy' cookers would be supplied.

During the assault stage of the operation troops would depend entirely upon the twenty-four hours' ration pack, which was a revised and improved form of mess-tin ration designed to yield the greatest food value possible within the limits of permissible space and weight. The principal items in the pack were: (a) a meat block composed of precooked dried meat which, if necessary, could be eaten cold but which was intended for reconstitution into a mince or stew by the addition of water and subsequent heating; (b) two oatmeal blocks consisting of rolled oats, sugar and fat for the preparation of sweet porridge, and (c) several tea, sugar and milk blocks, each producing two pints of tea. Other items included were biscuits, vitaminised chocolate, meat extract, sugar, salt and boiled sweets. All these articles of food were packed in a waxed cardboard waterproof container measuring about $6 \times 5 \times 2\frac{1}{2}$ ins. and weighing 2 lb. 3 oz. The total energy value of the ration was 4,000 Calories. With this pack there would be issued a tommy cooker, fuel tablets, a water sterilising outfit and 20 cigarettes, as a supply for forty-eight hours.

For the feeding of troops on the voyage between ports of embarkation and landing beaches all personnel ships and landing craft were to carry a forty-eight hours' supply of a sea passage ration consisting of the composite (14-men) ration pack, type F, including biscuits, preserved meat, tea, sugar, milk, jam, cheese and chocolate. In addition to this ration each man would be given one tin of self-heating soup in each twenty-four hours and assault troops were to receive also one tin of self-heating cocoa in the same period. Further, all ships would be provisioned with a reserve ration of preserved meat, biscuits, tea, etc., for use in the event of a prolonged or delayed voyage. Water was to be provided on the scale of one gallon per head per day with an equal quantity as ship's reserve in case of need. Apart from all the rations mentioned above, every man would carry the usual emergency ration of chocolate concentrate to be consumed only if all other sources of supply failed and then only at the order of an officer.

The organisation for the supply of rations included arrangements whereby each man, immediately before or at the time of embarkation, was issued with (a) one emergency ration, and (b) two twenty-four hours' ration packs with cigarettes, tommy cooker and fuel, water sterilising outfit, and, in the case of personnel landing during the first three days of the assault, one tin of preserved meat. Every man was thus rendered capable of subsisting upon what he himself carried and independent of other sources of supply for a period of at least forty-eight hours after landing on the far shore. The bagged ration consisting of biscuits, boiled sweets and chewing gum, intended as a preventative against seasickness, was issued at the same time.

WATER

Until bulk water supplies could be made available as soon as possible after the landing, all water for consumption by the assault force was to be carried with them in $4\frac{1}{2}$-gallon containers. Provision was made for a daily allowance of one gallon per man with an additional gallon per day for casualties. Individual water-sterilising outfits were issued to each man in order to render him independent of bulk supplies or unit water vehicles in an emergency. Personnel were specially trained in the purification of water in small containers.

A water tank truck (230 gallons) was added to the establishment of all general hospitals and a recommendation made that, if piped water could not be delivered by the R.E. within forty-eight hours, storage in canvas tanks and small containers, to hold 10 gallons per bed, should be made available. It was found that without storage one water tank truck was insufficient to satisfy the needs of a 200-bed hospital.

It was the intention ultimately to employ large plants for bulk chlorination of water supplies, some of them capable of an output as high as 50,000 gallons per hour. Hygiene officers and sanitary assistants were, for the most part, unfamiliar with apparatus of this kind, but as it was highly desirable that they should have some insight into the working and performance of plant so closely concerned with a subject upon which they would be called upon to advise, arrangements were made for them to attend demonstrations given by water engineers employed by the manufacturers of the apparatus.

PRECAUTIONS AGAINST COMMUNICABLE DISEASES

Among the many factors necessary to ensure the success of this military enterprise was the inception of measures to obviate loss of efficiency to the expeditionary force through wastage caused by communicable disease. This question was the more compelling because the probable sequence of events attending the landing and advance of the force was such as to invite large-scale outbreaks of epidemic disease as the result of unavoidable destruction of public utility undertakings and of inevitable breakdown of administrative services, including the organisation responsible for protecting the health of the civilian population in the liberated territories.

Some knowledge as to the diseases, infectious and otherwise, prevailing on the Continent was available through intelligence reports received from time to time through secret agents and civilians escaping from countries in the hands of the enemy. Collection of information of this kind from various sources had been in progress for some years and a detailed appreciation of the state of the public health in occupied territories, as far as it was possible to estimate, was prepared for the use of the Administrative Planning Staff. From the facts thus presented it appeared that the danger to the Allied Armies through infectious disease communicated to them from the civilian population was likely to be greatest in respect of typhus, the enteric fevers, dysentery and venereal disease.

It was ascertained that an outbreak of typhus had occurred in the Cherbourg area during the early part of 1944 and although on this occasion no epidemic had developed there was reason to believe that undernourishment and louse-infestation were widespread and that further outbreaks were likely to follow, especially under the conditions that would be brought about by military operations. Additional precautionary measures in this respect were therefore adopted in the preparation of the expeditionary force. It was decided that all officers and men should receive anti-typhus inoculation. Arrangements were made for the issue of 750,000 shirts, (two per man), impregnated with a louse-repellent substance (D.D.T.) to personnel of divisional, corps, airborne and special service units at the time of their passage through the marshalling areas in the United Kingdom immediately before embarkation. Anti-louse powder was provided in a quantity sufficient for the protection of all troops and medical units and regimental medical establishments were each supplied with hand dust-sprayers for the application of the powder and all medical officers were taught how they should be used. Special instruction in methods of eradicating lice was given by hygiene officers to units generally and, in greater detail, to personnel of mobile laundry and bath units. Two field sanitary sections and two mobile laundry and bath units were furnished with a special scale of equipment, including protective clothing, additional disinfestors, etc., devised for intensive anti-typhus measures. Adequate reserves of special clothing, repellent powder and apparatus were provided and made readily available for the use of the force as required.

Dobbin's Hand Dust Sprayers were issued to units in 21 Army Group on the following scale:

Fd.Hyg.Secs. . . 25	Gen.Hosps. . . 6
Fd.San.Secs. . . 25	C.C.Ss. . . 6
M.B.Us. . . . 25	Fd.Ambs. . . 6
	F.D.Ss. . . 6
R.M.Os. . . 1	

Mechanical Compressor Spray Units were to be supplied to field hygiene and field sanitary units on a scale of two per section.

Localised outbreaks of typhoid and paratyphoid fevers were known to be of frequent occurrence in France and other Continental countries and risk of these diseases appearing in epidemic form was certain to increase as the result of damage to water supplies and sewerage systems following bombing and artillery fire. Steps were therefore taken to obtain for every individual soldier the full measure of protection afforded by preventive inoculation and to ensure that the best possible environmental conditions were achieved and constantly maintained, not only by the provision of an efficient hygiene service but also by inculcating a high standard of sanitary discipline in the training of all personnel of the force.

The prevention of dysentery was dependent almost entirely upon the observance of elementary sanitary principles by all concerned, but with special attention to constant and vigorous efforts aimed at the destruction of flies and their breeding places. It was foreseen that the presence of a large force operating in the restricted area of a bridgehead would be conducive to fly-infestation, which must inevitably be aggravated by the presence of unburied dead and animal carcases on the battle field. Arrangements were therefore made for supplying the force with a generous scale of meat-safes, fly-swatters, fly-traps, etc., and for the issue of a special spray consisting of 5 per cent. D.D.T. in kerosene with hand-sprayers to field hygiene and field sanitary sections. Every R.M.O. was supplied with 500 0·5 gramme tablets of sulphaguanidine.

As a probable cause of wastage venereal disease presented a more difficult problem than typhus, enteric or dysentery, if only because it was less amenable to concerted measures aimed at its control. Administrative and disciplinary action was a matter for the force itself after its deployment overseas. From the aspect of preparatory planning the primary considerations were education, the provision of facilities for individual preventive measures and arrangements for general welfare. As regards the first, an intensive campaign was undertaken with the object of ensuring that every man was made aware of the dangers to which he would be exposed and of the means whereby infection could be avoided or prevented. This was done by strict enforcement of the order requiring compulsory attendance at lectures given by R.M.Os., by the issue to all ranks of a special pamphlet on the subject and by the exhibition of printed posters in unit lines. Arrangements were made to exhibit a training film produced by the United States forces on the subject of venereal disease. It was the intention that all troops of 21 Army Group should see the film when passing through the marshalling areas before embarkation. Unfortunately some units were not given this opportunity owing to the decision that command cinema sections which comprised female personnel should not handle the film, the showing of which was therefore limited to the number of exhibitions that could be undertaken by the cinema service of 21 Army Group. There was also undue delay in the issue of the pamphlet and posters mentioned above. In so far as preventive measures were concerned, provision was made for a total of twenty prophylactic ablution centres (P.A.Cs.) to be included in the war establishments of the force. The personnel of each included N.C.Os. and special treatment orderlies, R.A.M.C. The allocation and distribution of these centres was a question for decision by the staff of the force itself. Measures for promoting the general welfare of the troops lay in the direction of providing adequate facilities for recreation, including games, entertainments, institutes and canteens, matters which were not directly within the scope of the Medical Planning Committee.

The British, Canadian and United States staffs agreed that the arguments in favour of closing brothels, where possible, and of placing them out of bounds at all times outweighed all others. This was therefore accepted as the policy of 21 Army Group. It was also agreed that no medical examination of prostitutes should be undertaken' by the military medical services. A *pro forma*, based on that used in France in 1939–40, was designed in conjunction with Civil Affairs for the identification of infected civilian contacts. Plentiful supplies of prophylactic packets and condoms were assured. In addition to the large stock of condoms held by the P.A.Cs., the depots of medical stores held 100,000 in advanced depots and 3,000 gross in base depots. It was not the policy to issue condoms in the United Kingdom. Some units, however, drew them for a proportion of their strength for issue in Normandy, as occasion demanded, on arrival.

Mention must be made of another disease, malaria, as a cause of some concern during the later stages in the preparatory planning for the campaign in North-west Europe. Reference has been made to the decision, in the autumn of 1943, to increase the strength of 21 Army Group by the addition of a fourth corps including several divisions to be withdrawn from the Mediterranean. The formations selected for this transfer had been operating in Sicily throughout the malaria season and consequently had continued routine suppressive treatment for one month after leaving the infected area. There was, however, reason to expect that despite this precaution troops from so highly malarious a region would, even after their return to the United Kingdom, be liable to suffer from malaria in the form of spring relapses early in the coming year. It was therefore prescribed that units on their way home should receive a week's intensive course of treatment before arrival in Great Britain. This order, however, was not issued in time for its application to the first arrivals and those who returned later and received the intensive course of treatment had not been exposed to so great a risk of infection; thus the value of the treatment was not easy to assess.

In any case, spring relapses made their appearance in large numbers during the month of March 1944. It now became a question as to the best course to adopt, and here there was some divergence between the medical and operational aspects. Medical opinion appreciated the fact that spring manifestations of this kind were a well recognised characteristic of the disease and that they would come to an end in late spring or early summer. Moreover, the interests of the patient himself were best served by allowing the attack to develop and then effecting a complete cure by administering the standard course of treatment in a military hospital. On the other hand, in consequence of these widespread relapses certain units became seriously depleted. The consequent interference with military training coupled with the near approach of the date fixed for the opening of the campaign caused some alarm among those in command. The matter thus became one of morale and, therefore, of operational importance. The upshot was that a special investigation of the state of affairs in all infected units was carried out by consultants in malariology, medicine, pathology and hygiene. In some units a still more exhaustive examination was conducted by teams of clinicians and pathologists nominated for the purpose. As a result certain units were selected for a further period of suppressive treatment; others were subjected to the intensive course of shorter duration. Special arrangements were made for men giving a history of having suffered from malaria previously. Notwithstanding these precautions the occurrence of spring relapses continued into the late spring and early summer, when the incidence declined as already foreseen. In point of fact, although cases were still coming to light, malaria did not at any time prove an embarrassment during the assault stage of the operations on the Continent.

In addition to bringing T.A.B. inoculation and vaccination up to date in all units, it was decided that all ranks of 21 Army Group should receive anti-typhus inoculation and that a booster dose of tetanus toxoid should be given to those who had not received a third re-inoculation dose. This dose was to be given not less than six weeks after the second. It was also decided that normal re-inoculation on the Continent should be by one dose of 1 c.c. annually. In the presence of typhus, however, the dose for this inoculation would be repeated quarterly.

Prior to the concentration period units and formations of 21 Army Group were scattered over the United Kingdom including Northern Ireland. Their medical administration was in the hands of home commands and many small units, especially those of G.H.Q. and L. of C. troops, carried no medical officer on their W.E. It was therefore necessary to issue the orders for inoculation and vaccination and also those calling for progress reports through staff channels, through the medium of G.R.Os., copies of which were received by home commands and by officers commanding units.

Progress reports of the inoculation and vaccination states of units consolidated by formations were prepared by Q.(A.E.) Stats. Branch and sent to the D.A.G. and D.M.S. monthly. From these reports, which showed the percentage protected, partially protected and unprotected, the D.M.S. was able to indicate to the D.A.G. instances in which progress was considered to be unsatisfactory. Unsatisfactory progress was chiefly noted among corps and army troops, G.H.Q. and L. of C. units and some Allied contingents isolated from their formations and without medical officers. 21 Army Group took the field, however, over 90 per cent. protected against all diseases for which inoculation was required and progress reports were discontinued after May.

Owing to the unsatisfactory nature of the records of vaccination in Army Book 64, disclosed by a survey carried out by D.D.M.S. VIII Corps (in which it was found that out of 1,068 men examined the result of vaccination confirmed by examination of scars on the men had been recorded in 12 per cent. of the books only), an immediate review of the vaccination records was ordered and re-vaccination, in the absence of evidence of a successful operation, insisted upon.

Civilian and welfare workers were also recommended to receive inoculation and vaccination.

THE ARMY PATHOLOGY SERVICE. SECOND ARMY

The many-sided duties of the Pathology Service called for detailed and careful planning. A very close liaison was maintained with the Director of Pathology at the War Office, with the Officer Commanding, the Army Blood Supply Depot, and with colleagues in the Royal Naval Medical Services, the Royal Air Force Medical Services and the Medical Services of the United States Army.

ORGANISATION OF LABORATORIES AND RESEARCH

The laboratories coming under control of 21 Army Group on D-day were:

Laboratories, British General Hospitals	30
Laboratories, Canadian General Hospitals	8
Mobile Bacteriological Laboratories, British	4
Mobile Bacteriological Laboratories, Canadian	1

The experience gained in previous campaigns was of value. Only one important modification was introduced—the issue to general hospital laboratories of panniers of ready-made media. They retained the apparatus for making media if required.

Serological Diagnosis of Syphilis. It was decided to make the Kahn reaction the standard test for the diagnosis of syphilis and for the control of treatment.

Mobile Bacteriological Laboratories. Provided on the scale of one per corps. Their function was to carry out laboratory work for the 200-bed general hospitals and the C.C.Ss. in the corps and to conduct special investigations. Experience had shown that the amount of 'forward' laboratory work was necessarily limited and it was therefore decided to employ two of the five mobile bacteriological laboratories for special investigations—one was specially equipped for the investigation of anaerobic infections of wounds and the other for the control of penicillin therapy.

Pathologists. Senior pathologists were posted to the mobile bacteriological laboratories. It might be thought that a robust junior officer would have been more suitable for such a post but, in fact, there was not much 'roughing' to be done in such a laboratory and the additional weight carried by the opinion of an older and more experienced officer was very important in the independent position he occupied. A card index of all laboratory assistants was compiled to facilitate the distribution of talent among the different laboratories. A preliminary conference of pathologists in 21 Army Group was held at the Royal Army Medical College. Matters of policy and technique were discussed and pathologists became acquainted with each other.

It was clear that, in the European campaign, the more important work in research would be surgical rather than medical. At the invitation of the Director of Pathology, D.D.P., 21 Army Group, attended meetings of the War Wounds Committee of the Medical Research Council and co-operated in a scheme for the investigation of anaerobic infection of war wounds; it was arranged that most of the actual laboratory work would be carried out by M.R.C. workers in the United Kingdom. In addition, as penicillin had become increasingly available, it was decided to set up machinery for the scientific investigation of its use in more specialised ways. For this purpose the post of Adviser in Penicillin and Chemotherapy was created under the joint direction of the Consulting Surgeon and D.D.P. In addition, 3 Mobile Bacteriological Laboratory was allocated for the control of penicillin therapy. It was also decided to continue the prophylaxis of wound infection by sulphonamide drugs under the general supervision of the officer commanding 1 B.T.U. who had pioneered their use during the Middle East campaign —one example of which was the introduction of micro-crystalline sulphadiazine into the peritoneal cavity in cases of abdominal wounds.

All ranks were actively immunised against smallpox, typhoid and paratyphoid fevers, tetanus and typhus fever. The possibility of carrying out active immunisation against gas gangrene was explored by the War

Wounds Committee but no potent toxoid was forthcoming until it was too late to make use of it. The gas gangrene antitoxin in use was polyvalent against *Cl. welchii, Cl. septicum* and *Cl. oedematiens*, the unitage per prophylactic dose being *Cl. welchii*, 9,000 units, *Cl. septicum*, 4,500 units and *Cl. oedematiens*, 9,000 units.

THE ARMY TRANSFUSION SERVICE. 21 ARMY GROUP

The structure of the Transfusion Service for the campaign in Northwest Europe was modelled on the organisation which had been evolved over a long period in the Middle East. It consisted of:

(a) a base transfusion unit with
(b) two forward distribution sections;
(c) 17 field transfusion units.

In addition there were also included:

(d) transfusion departments in base hospitals.

In general, the functions of the B.T.U. were to act as the parent unit, to receive, store and distribute all transfusion material supplied to 21 Army Group by the Army Blood Supply Depot, Bristol; to produce crystalloid solutions and transfusion apparatus; to undertake supply of whole blood from local resources in case of necessity; to train and maintain a pool of transfusion personnel for medical units; and, finally, the O.C. being adviser in blood transfusion to D.M.S., to act in a general advisory capacity on all matters relating to transfusion and allied technical problems.

WAR ESTABLISHMENT

The war establishment used for this campaign allowed of a much larger unit than heretofore and also permitted of its expansion in accordance with the size and composition of the force. Moreover, for the first time the B.T.U., which had always previously been attached to a parent unit, usually a general hospital, was made a complete self-contained unit by the addition of A.C.C. personnel, while an increased scale of transport rendered the unit operationally self-mobile and independent.

The unit consisted of:

(i) H.Q. with two officers and 42 O.Rs.;
(ii) a blood-collecting section with one officer and 13 O.Rs.;
(iii) two forward distribution sections, each with one (non-medical) officer and 14 O.Rs.;
(iv) increments: small increases in personnel and transport were allowed for additional corps and armies.

Personnel included, in addition to N.Os. and T.Os., R.A.M.C., engine fitters, R.E., to maintain refrigerators, drivers and vehicle mechanics, R.A.S.C., and cooks A.C.C. The transport included a total of 18 vehicles equipped with refrigerators, as well as M/Cs., cars and load-carrying vehicles.

The main duties of (i) the H.Q. officers were to administer the unit and to deal with the transfusion requirements of general hospitals in its area, i.e. base and rearward L. of C. areas. As the force was being supplied with whole blood from outside the theatre, the officer of (ii) the blood-collecting section was to be employed as blood distribution officer and supply the vitally important liaison between the F.T.Us., the forward distributing sections, and base. He was to be in constant touch with D.Ds.M.S. corps and armies so that he could ascertain the tactical situation and the requirements for impending operations, and by frequent visits to F.T.Us., field medical units and forward distributing sections he would be able to advise on distribution problems and, as far as possible, on technical difficulties and developments.

His work was of extreme importance to the smooth working of the service and though it was largely non-medical in character it was essential that he should be a medical officer, with considerable experience in dealing with battle casualties, who could talk to surgeons and other M.Os. on equal terms and who was able to deal with the medical administrative staff of divisions, corps and armies.

In the case of (iii) the forward distribution sections, which became known as advanced blood banks, medical qualifications were not essential for the officers in charge. Their work was carried out for the first time by non-medical officers, R.A.M.C., an extremely successful innovation. These advanced blood banks, one to each of Canadian and Second Armies, were to be sited at or near the rear H.Q. of the Army under the control of the D.D.M.S. They carried four refrigerator vehicles each of which enabled them to store substantial amounts of blood and also allowed them to send out as light sections forward trucks to be attached to C.C.Ss. at the level of rear H.Q. of corps and thus bring a constant supply of blood to the doorsteps of the most forward medical units capable of using it with advantage.

The final link in the chain was supplied by the F.T.Us., which were allocated to the force on the scale of three per corps, plus one additional unit per army. Their establishment was one officer, one refrigerator vehicle with driver and two transfusion orderlies. They were mainly to be sited with corps C.C.Ss. which acted as parent units, a few being sent further forward along with F.S.Us. to act as advanced surgical centres attached to F.D.Ss.

Though not officially recognised as specialists, the officers had come to have the status of such and to be employed exclusively on transfusion work, though this was frequently widened to include supervision of the pre-operative department of the C.C.Ss. whether or not the cases required transfusion. A considerable amount of post-operative treatment, such as saline transfusions and gastric suctions, was also being done by F.T.U. officers.

Each general hospital had a transfusion department with one officer and two transfusion orderlies. These units carried out almost as many transfusions as the forward medical units and a very large part of the work of the base transfusion unit was concerned with supplying them. It was intended that they should, as soon as possible, maintain their own blood banks with a panel of local donors.

THE ARMY DENTAL SERVICE. SECOND ARMY

The training of A.D. Corps officers and O.Rs. attached to general hospitals, C.C.Ss., field ambulances and F.D.Ss. was carried out as part of the training of the units themselves. The dental personnel took part in the various exercises and performed a wide variety of duties—
—e.g. S.B. officer, liaison officer, recce. officer, gas officer. Dental clerk orderlies were usually employed as 'A. & D.' clerks or with the equipment loading parties. The mobile dental units trained as field units, the course lasting one month and including instruction in administration, message writing, map reading, camouflage, weapon training, night driving, loading and unloading, setting up and striking the unit. A majority of the dental officers of Second Army attended the special maxillo-facial course and a course in anaesthetics at the E.M.S. hospital, East Grinstead. A.D.D.S. Second Army re-tested all dental clerk orderlies and dental mechanics. Dental mechanics were sent to refresher courses conducted by the command dental laboratories. The supply of dental and ordnance equipment was satisfactory save that sufficient penthouses for the 15-cwt. 4 × 4 trucks, intended for use by dental officers attached to F.D.Ss., could not be obtained owing to the considerable demand throughout Second Army for tentage.

The task of making Second Army dentally fit was undertaken in the main by the dental services in the home commands. On December 22, 1943, it was estimated that of the formations derived from Home Forces 19·49 per cent. required dental treatment, while among the formations returning from C.M.F. to join Second Army 40·53 per cent. were in need of treatment and 4·66 per cent. required denture work. By the end of April 1944 only 4·34 per cent. required treatment and 1·74 per cent. denture work. This work was continued right up to the time of the assault landings lest any cessation might indicate the approach of D-day. Arrangements were made whereby the Army Post Office would despatch the completed denture work to Normandy.

A.D.D.S. Second Army was appointed in October 1943 in order to reduce dental sick wastage in Second Army to a minimum. The following policy was adopted:

1. To raise the standard of dental health to the highest possible degree during mobilisation.
2. To maintain this standard by every possible means during the campaign with a minimum disturbance of the soldier's normal duties.

The attainment of the first of these aims was made somewhat difficult by the movements of units until arrangements were made whereby the A.D.D.S. of the district was informed of such impending moves. This objective was reached by mid-May.

The dental sick rate was about 0·3 per cent. per day. With a war establishment of one dental officer per 3,700 men this meant a daily dental sick parade per dental officer of 11 men. But a number of complicating factors had to be considered. Owing to operational activities and movements of formations there would be many days when, on the Continent, the dental officers would not be able to function professionally. There would be losses of dentures during the crossing of the Channel and the assault landings and also during subsequent actions. Acute ulcerative gingivitis and stomatitis could be expected to assume a certain prevalence. The dental condition of reinforcements could affect the amount of dental work to be done in Second Army after the assault landings and lodgement.

To mitigate or counter the action of these and other unpredictable factors the following steps were taken:

1. Of the twelve M.D.Us. at the disposal of Second Army one was allotted to Army troops and the remainder to corps for employment on the scale of one per division.
2. Instructions were issued to ensure that, during the campaign,
    (a) patients should not travel rearwards of a unit capable of undertaking the treatment required;
    (b) patients reporting sick would have all other necessary treatment required completed at a single visit if possible;
    (c) divisional dental work would be carried out at the M.D.U. in the shortest possible time;
    (d) M.D.Us. would be well route-signed and would remain open for the maximum period between moves;
    (e) whenever possible dental officers would be aggregated at a suitable situation in the divisional administrative area and form a divisional dental centre;
    (f) the incidence of acute ulcerative gingivitis would be closely observed and rigorous measures taken to control its spread and to eradicate it. Cases requiring hospitalisation would be held at the most forward level possible;
    (g) in no circumstances would purely dental casualties (other than maxillo-facial) leave the Army area.

THE CAMPAIGN IN N.W. EUROPE

3. Arrangements were made to issue from advanced depots of medical stores equipment for use in reinforcement holding units by dental officers and O.Rs. held there.

A.D.D.S. Second Army remained at Oxford when H.Q. Second Army divided into Advanced and Static H.Q. and joined the H.Q. in London on April 1, moving to Fort Purbrook on April 24. For reasons of security the dental personnel of field units temporarily posted elsewhere were recalled by telephone, ostensibly for the purpose of further training. The M.D.Us. were concentrated at Luton and were there briefed by A.D.D.S. When the first flight of Second Army went into the sealed camps the dental officers, lacking their dental equipment which had been pre-loaded, had to depend upon the contents of their dental haversacks.

The withdrawal by units in the latter part of April of A.F. I.5033 (Dental Treatment Card) of Second Army personnel for despatch to G.H.Q. 2nd Echelon 21 Army Group gave rise to minor administrative difficulties. A.Ds.D.S. districts, no longer able to distinguish Second Army units, were unable to give dental states with the desired accuracy. The value of the fortnightly dental states despatched by static districts to Second Army therefore became much diminished and these returns were discontinued at the end of the first week in May.

A review of this period of preparation, in so far as the Army Dental Service is concerned, suggests that the senior administrative dental officer to a mobilising field formation should be appointed at the earliest possible stage and that he should have dental laboratory experience behind him, should have served with a field unit and, if possible, should have attended a course of instruction in staff duties. It suggests too that during the period of mobilisation all field unit dental personnel should be placed at the disposal of the A.Ds.D.S. of districts and be employed solely with the treatment of field troops, save that they should take part in unit and formation exercises.

The phasing of the dental units was made without reference to A.D.D.S. Second Army. A.D.D.S. and his clerks landed on D-day+8, six of the M.D.Us. on D-day+11 and the remainder on D-day+12.

ASSEMBLY AND DISPATCH

The assembly of the expeditionary force before its transit from the English coast to the Continental shore in a vast collection of shipping under the command of the Naval Commander, Allied Expeditionary Force, constituted a movement of very great magnitude requiring a special administrative plan for its execution.

The dispatch of the force was to take place in three phases: first, the departure of the large initial increment of assault troops; second, the following up by another large increment and, third, the smaller and continuous flow of units and formations to complete the building up of the force. The whole evolution was scheduled to occupy approximately ten weeks.

The process of assembly was also one of three stages. In the first place the force was to move to concentration areas within a distance of 75 to 100 miles from the points of embarkation. The expeditionary force itself, through its staff, undertook the arrangement and conduct of this movement and continued in the usual way to be responsible for administrative and supply services to its formations and units while they remained in the concentration areas, units providing for their own domestic needs by the normal routine procedure. When called forward for embarkation formations and units moved under War Office control to marshalling areas where they were broken up into parties and ship-loads dictated by their operational functions. Only troops and vehicles essential for the assault and initial stage of the operation were allotted shipping space in the first convoys, the remainder being held back for dispatch at a later date. This procedure broke up unit administration and made it impossible for units to provide for themselves. A complete administrative service, including accommodation, cooking, messing and general welfare, was therefore required in the camps used for the reception and occupation of troops passing through the marshalling areas. The final stage was the move forward from marshalling areas to embarkation areas situated in the immediate vicinity of ports and hards at which troops embarked in the vessels to which they had been allocated. Here also special arrangements for administrative and supply services were necessary.

The assembly and dispatch of the force thus necessitated the provision of medical facilities peculiar to the needs of the situation in the localities concerned. The normal routine was followed in the concentration areas, and so R.M.Os. and field medical units of the force continued to perform their usual functions in regard to the units and formations to which they belonged, relying on hospitals and reception stations in the neighbourhood for the accommodation of their sick as in the manner applicable to any other part of the country. In the marshalling areas and embarkation areas, however, it was necessary that the medical care of troops in transit should be taken over by the local static medical services of the three commands and the one district in which the marshalling areas and embarkation areas were situated, that is to say in Eastern, South-Eastern and Southern Commands and in London District. D.Ds.M.S. at the headquarters of these commands were charged with the responsibility of making the medical arrangements required and, through their A.Ds.M.S. of districts, with putting those arrangements into effect.

The plans and preparations made in the three commands were based on the same general lines and differed little in their application. It was proposed to set up in each marshalling area an administrative headquarters to which a medical officer was to be attached as S.M.O. in charge of local medical arrangements. All C.R.Ss., including those of the A.A. medical service, situated within the marshalling areas were to be expanded to full capacity and reinforced with medical officers and other ranks. In camps where there was no C.R.S. a medical inspection room would be established and staffed with a medical officer and nursing orderlies. Similar arrangements would be made in embarkation areas. At ports and hards used for the embarkation of the force a somewhat different organisation was required. Not only was it necessary to deal with the ordinary occurrence of sickness and injury but, as these vital points were likely to invite intensive air attack on the part of the enemy, provision must be made against the possibility of heavy casualties among the force during embarkation. Here also it was necessary to provide accommodation and staff to deal with odd casualties brought into port by vessels which had been subject to enemy attack during the passage of the force across the Channel or which had picked up survivors from other vessels sunk or damaged. Medical officers and other ranks, R.A.M.C., including transfusion orderlies, were therefore allocated to ports and hards for the purpose of establishing dressing stations or R.A.Ps. varying in size according to local conditions and equipped to undertake these three distinct functions. Each administrative headquarters in the marshalling areas was to be supplied with a mobile reserve of medical officers and nursing orderlies for duty as and where required in an emergency and ambulance cars were to be stationed at all C.R.Ss., dressing stations, medical inspection rooms and first-aid posts throughout the marshalling and embarkation areas. To supervise and control sanitary conditions in the various camps sanitary assistants were allocated to the administrative headquarters of marshalling areas.

The medical organisation necessary to undertake the duties occasioned by the dispatch of the expeditionary force was to some extent combined with the special scheme already described as required in connexion with the reception, in southern England, of casualties sustained by the force in the assault phase. The normal establishments of the static medical units stationed within the commands charged with these additional responsibilities were insufficient in respect both of officers and other ranks to provide the personnel needed. In order to obtain the necessary reinforcements it was decided to have recourse to the field medical units of formations remaining in the United Kingdom and not assigned to the expeditionary force and to reserve them for the purpose of contributing towards the supply of medical officers, other ranks and ambulance cars. In all, eleven field ambulances and three field hygiene sections were allocated for special duty in the commands affected. Two field hospitals, recently returned from overseas and due for disbandment, were also held in reserve to provide further assistance.

Among the numerous questions arising in connexion with medical arrangements for personnel of the expeditionary force immediately before their departure one matter of considerable importance, and one requiring special measures, was the admission to hospital of troops who fell sick or suffered injury after they had been instructed as to the part they and their units were to play in the assault landings. It was obvious that if such personnel were sent to any convenient hospital in the ordinary way leakage of information would occur and it would be impossible to secure the degree of secrecy in regard to pending events vital to the success of the enterprise.

It was proposed that troops forming part of the assault force would be briefed while in the marshalling areas and elaborate precautions were to be taken to prevent their coming into contact with personnel not belonging to the force, other than personnel included in the administrative staff of the camps in which they were accommodated, personnel who for security purposes were regarded as belonging to the force. In conformity with general arrangements for security requirements in respect of all troops while in the marshalling and embarkation areas, special instructions were issued in regard to admission to hospital of sick and injured among personnel in camp or in transit for embarkation. It was decided that after troops had been briefed cases of sickness among them would, whenever possible, be retained with their units or accommodated in C.R.Ss. situated within the boundaries of their camps. Cases referred for specialist opinion would be confined to those of extreme urgency and in no circumstances would personnel be referred to a medical board. Cases would be admitted to hospital only if retention in camp was likely to have a permanent ill effect upon their health or to involve danger to others. Specific military hospitals and reception stations were designated for the admission of briefed personnel and wards were specially reserved for their accommodation. Staff attending them were made subject to special security measures. There remained the possibility that, as a result of air raids or road accidents during transit from marshalling areas to embarkation areas, briefed personnel might be admitted direct to hospitals of the E.M.S. As the E.M.S. authorities felt themselves unable to do more than instruct their staff in the vital importance of maintaining security, it was arranged that on admission of briefed personnel to an E.M.S. hospital the hospital officer would then notify the military registrar of the hospital group concerned. This officer would then notify the local commander who was responsible for taking the necessary security precautions. Briefed personnel were not to be allowed out of hospital or reception station during their stay, their correspondence was to be censored and they were not to receive visitors unless they were seriously or dangerously ill, and then only under military supervision. After discharge from hospital they would be returned to their own units or to a reinforcement camp under escort.

A consideration of the very greatest consequence in regard to the transit of the assault force across the Channel was that everything be done to ensure that the troops engaged should arrive at the other side in the best of physical condition to undertake their strenuous and exacting task. Hence the necessity for measures to combat seasickness, the ravages of which in rough weather might prove so severe and universal as to jeopardise the successful outcome of the venture. This question, therefore, was one occupying the close attention of the medical planning organisation. Hyoscine in doses of $\frac{1}{100}$ grain had been used with success during training in combined operations. More recent experience in the Middle East, however, had suggested that better results were obtained by employing a combination of hyoscine and benzedrine, 1·2 mgm. and 10 mgm. respectively. At the same time other observers urged the merits of a Canadian preparation known as the 'Canadian Pink Pill', containing hyoscine, hyoscyamine and nicotinic acid, and of the 'American Motion-Sickness Preventative', consisting of sodium amytal, scopolamine and atropine.

In order to determine the relative efficacy of these various remedies it was arranged by the Directorate of Medical Research to subject them all to practical tests during assault exercises using a large number of troops carried in craft of the types to be used for the invasion. A test of this kind took place at the end of January 1944 but was inconclusive owing to the calm weather which prevailed at the time. Steps were taken to repeat the trial but it was not until the following March that it was found possible to obtain the release of sufficient craft, which were in constant use for training purposes. Again the weather was consistently fine throughout the ten days of the exercise, with the exception of one day when there was a moderate swell. Nevertheless, there was forthcoming sufficient evidence to show that medication did in fact reduce the incidence of seasickness, although there was no clear indication that any one of the remedies tried was superior to the others. The ultimate decision, therefore, was to make no change and to continue with the drug already in use, i.e. hyoscine in doses of $\frac{1}{100}$ grain.

The intention was that the drug should be issued under regimental arrangements and that not more than two doses should be given to each officer and man of the assault force, the first dose to be taken one hour before reaching rough water and the second six hours later, if considered necessary by the craft commander. The reasons for this arrangement were: first, many small craft were unaccompanied by medical officers and could not therefore depend on administration of the drug under medical advice, hence the issue must be in the hands of regimental officers and N.C.Os., but at the same time the risk of over-medication must be avoided by restricting the issue to two doses only; second, seasickness usually appeared within the first two hours of exposure to rough weather; third, the greater part of the first assault formation would reach the far shore within twelve hours of leaving their ports of embarkation.

Other precautions to be observed in the prevention of seasickness were: the placing of officers, N.C.Os. and other key men amidships and aft; the avoidance of overcrowding in assault craft; the keeping of as many men as possible in the fresh air when aboard; the provision of ground-sheets as cover against the wet and of vomit bags to be thrown overboard after use; the taking of the last meal two hours before embarkation and the issue of boiled sweets, biscuits and chewing gum for consumption during the voyage, the first two to allay nausea and the last to counteract dryness of the mouth occasioned by the taking of hyoscine.

A directive setting forth the accepted instructions for the prevention of seasickness, including the issue of hyoscine and the procedure to be adopted, was issued through staff channels as an administrative instruction. The intention was that this should reach all formations and units through staff channels, but unfortunately this plan was wrecked by Second Army H.Q. which passed it over to D.D.M.S. to be dealt with through medical channels. As soon as this was discovered urgent representations were made to Second Army, pointing out that the subject should not be confined to medical channels. But the matter had gone too far and although adequate instructions were issued by D.D.M.S. Second Army no staff directive was issued. The result was that certain small units were omitted when the hyoscine was issued. In reports made after the operation D.D.M.S. Second Army recommended that in future operations of the same kind seasickness remedies should be issued along with the voyage ration by the R.A.S.C. One factor was entirely overlooked. The first dose of hyoscine was issued to many of the units with orders that it was to be taken at a time to be determined by the officer commanding troops on the ship or craft. This dose had already been taken when the orders postponing the operation were received.

Three lessons may perhaps be learnt from this experience. A clear staff directive must reach every unit commander. Issues of drugs, biscuits, sweets and vomit bags must be made at one and the same time. Every craft should carry a reserve of drugs, say 50 per cent. for a short sea voyage to allow for unforeseen delays.

Assault formations reported favourably on the efficiency of the measures adopted. D.D.M.S. Second Army reported that seasickness never assumed the magnitude of a problem and that it seemed certain that the

THE CAMPAIGN IN N.W. EUROPE

steps taken were successful in preventing incapacity. One formation reported that the troops in the first wave of the assault suffered far more than those who followed though all had received hyoscine. It was thought that the difference might be due to the differences in respect of nervous tension.

THE REORGANISATION OF HOME FORCES, 1944

Early in 1944 it became evident that, in order to provide reinforcements for overseas, it would be necessary to draw heavily upon the formations and units constituting the Army at Home. Shortage of man-power being such as to suggest little possibility of replacement, it followed that units of the divisions which, already placed on a lowered establishment, constituted the field army component of the forces in the United Kingdom would eventually be reduced to a strength that rendered them inoperative. At the same time some organisation, in addition to the normal drafting and holding machinery, would be required in the United Kingdom for the retraining of casualties from the expeditionary force returned to duty after rehabilitation. To provide for these two contingencies some reorganisation of the divisions of Home Forces was clearly necessary.

It was therefore decided that the one armoured division remaining in Great Britain should be disbanded and that the five infantry divisions maintained on a lower scale of establishments should be reconstituted. Two of them were to be converted into field force divisions on full order of battle but with units on a cadre basis until such a time as brought up to normal establishment by absorption of casualties returned to duty. The remaining three of these divisions were to be reduced to reserve scale and used to replace existing reserve and holding divisions, three of which would then be disbanded. Thus a total of four divisions, including the armoured division, would be disbanded, and instead of five lower establishment divisions there would be two divisions constituted on field force scale, while the number of reserve and holding divisions, although changed in identity, would remain unchanged in number.

No less than nine divisions and their constituent units were therefore involved in this scheme of reorganisation, and the selection of the divisions and units to be retained or disbanded became a matter of some importance as affecting the traditional or sentimental interests of those concerned, including the T.A. Associations. The fate of these divisions, as formations and apart from their contained units, was determined by four factors: first, the existence in the field force of any other divisions with similar T.A. connexions, in order to ensure as far as possible that each territorial area in the United Kingdom should be represented by at least one field force division; second, their relative seniority as T.A. formations; third, the degree of disturbance likely to be occasioned in each case by reorganisation and, finally, the standard attained in training and fighting efficiency. As regards the individual units, priority for retention was to be given to regular units and, thereafter, to units of the S.R. and to original or duplicate units of the T.A. in preference to units formed during the War. A proper balance was to be maintained between units, having in view the capacity of their respective geographical areas to provide reinforcements. Other administrative considerations such as affiliation between units and training centres, the proportionate allocation of units administered by the various record offices, etc., were also to be taken into account.

This reorganisation manifestly entailed a somewhat complicated readjustment of the units of all arms constituting the formations involved, first by reason of the fact that the proposed changes, raising or lowering the scale of establishment of divisions, also implied changes in the number and kind of units included in those establishments and, second, in order to avoid the disbandment of units which, in accordance with the precepts mentioned above, it was desirable to preserve.

Medical units of the lower establishment divisions consisted only of two field ambulances and one field hygiene section, whereas those of a field force division included three field ambulances, two F.D.Ss. and one field hygiene section. Consequently, the raising of two lower establishment divisions to full field force scale created the need for supplying each of them with one additional field ambulance and two F.D.Ss. Two field ambulances and four F.D.Ss. had therefore to be found from elsewhere. On the other hand, while the lower establishment divisions included two field ambulances and one field hygiene section the reserve and holding divisions each contained only one field hygiene section. The reduction of three lower establishment divisions to reserve status and the disbandment of three reserve or holding divisions therefore made available six field ambulances and three field hygiene sections. Further, the disbandment of the armoured division released one field ambulance, one light field ambulance and one field hygiene section. Thus the total of medical units rendered surplus by reduction or disbandment amounted to seven field ambulances, one light field ambulance and four field hygiene sections. It was from this surplus that units were taken to supply the deficiencies of the divisions raised to field force status. Priority for retention was given to those units considered to have the strongest claim in terms of the factors already mentioned. The light field ambulance was accordingly reorganised and converted to field ambulance establishment and then transferred to one of the field force divisions. One of the surplus field ambulances was similarly transferred to the other field force division, thus completing the quota of field ambulances. Four others of these surplus field ambulances were converted into F.D.Ss., retaining their original numerical designations for sentimental reasons, and transferred two to each of the field force divisions, which were now rendered complete in respect of medical units. The remaining two field ambulances and all four of the surplus field hygiene sections were then available for reallocation to some other commitment or for disbandment.

As already stated, the function of units belonging to the two divisions raised to field force category was primarily that of training or retraining returned casualties and other personnel as reinforcements for the expeditionary force. In due course the absorption of personnel from one source or another would bring these units up to the full war establishment applicable to normal field force units, but as the result of a continuous process of intakes on the one hand and outgoing reinforcement drafts on the other their personnel would be constantly changing. In order to obtain continuity of training it was necessary to evolve a system which ensured retention of training instructors. To this end each unit was required to maintain a minimum training cadre as a permanent staff consisting of officers and men unavailable for drafting on account of low medical category, age or other cause rendering them ineligible for service overseas. The capacity of each unit to accept returned wounded, etc., would thus be the difference between normal unit war establishment and the strength of the minimum training cadre. If the number of personnel for retraining rendered it necessary, units were to be filled in excess of war establishments, subject to accommodation being available.

The medical units affected in this way were the field ambulances, F.D.Ss. and field hygiene sections of the divisions concerned. Steps were taken to work out the minimum number of officers and other ranks necessary to provide a permanent staff for instructional and administrative duties. The smaller and more technical the unit the larger was the minimum training cadre in proportion to total establishment. The cadres as finally approved were as follows: field ambulance, 7 officers and 91 other ranks as against a total establishment of 15 officers and 245 other ranks; F.D.S., 5 officers and 55 other ranks as against 7 officers and 90 other ranks; field hygiene section, 1 officer and 19 other ranks as against 1 officer and 27 other ranks. Training cadres were formed in each unit from a nucleus of suitable low-category men selected for the purpose by the commanding officer; the cadre was then completed by other suitable low-category men posted from units due for disbandment.

The scheme of reorganisation here described was formulated and approved some time before the opening of military operations in France in June 1944. Its immediate application to the medical units concerned was, however, precluded by the operational functions assigned to these units. Field ambulances and field hygiene sections of the lower establishment divisions were called upon to contribute largely towards providing the special medical services entailed by the dispatch of the expeditionary force and the reception of casualties from the Continent in the assault stage of the campaign. The performance of these duties being manifestly incompatible with a process of reorganisation and conversion, the latter was postponed until the establishment of a normal cross-Channel service for casualty evacuation permitted the release of these units from their special functions and their return to normal conditions. The disposal of formations and medical units in this reorganisation is shown in detail in Table 3.

Table 3

Formation	Disposal	Medical Units	Disposal
9th Armd. Div.	Disbanded	7 Fd. Amb.	For disbandment
		201 Lt. Fd. Amb.	Converted to field ambulance and transferred to 61st Div.
		81 Fd. Hyg. Sec.	For disbandment
38th Div. L.E.	Replaced 80th Res. Div.	207 Fd. Amb.	Converted to 207 F.D.S. for 55th Div.
		209 Fd. Amb.	For disbandment
		80 Fd. Hyg. Sec.	Retained in 38th Res. Div.
45th Div. L.E.	Replaced 77th Holding Div.	190 Fd. Amb.	Converted to 190 F.D.S. for 61st Div.
		191 Fd. Amb.	Converted to 191 F.D.S. for 61st Div.
		55 Fd. Hyg. Sec.	Retained in 45th Holding Div.
47th Div. L.E.	Replaced 76th Res. Div.	180 Fd. Amb.	To 55th Div.
		199 Fd. Amb.	Converted to 199 F.D.S. for 55th Div.
		68 Fd. Hyg. Sec.	Retained in 47th Res. Div.
55th Div. L.E.	Reorganised as an infantry division on full order of battle	177 Fd. Amb.	Retained in 55th Div.
		178 Fd. Amb.	Retained in 55th Div.
		28 Fd. Hyg. Sec.	Retained in 55th Div.
61st Div. L.E.	Reorganised as an infantry division on full order of battle	171 Fd. Amb.	Retained in 61st Div.
		172 Fd. Amb.	Retained in 61st Div.
		7 Fd. Hyg. Sec.	Retained in 61st Div.
48th Res. Div.	Remained as such	73 Fd. Hyg. Sec.	Retained in 48th Res. Div.
76th Res. Div.	Disbanded	74 Fd. Hyg. Sec.	For disbandment
80th Res. Div.	Disbanded	72 Fd. Hyg. Sec.	For disbandment
77th Holding Div.	Disbanded	79 Fd. Hyg. Sec.	For disbandment
52nd Div. H.E.	Not affected		
55th Div.		177 Fd. Amb. and 178 Fd. Amb.	Retained
		180 Fd. Amb.	From 47th Div.
		199 F.D.S.	From 199 Fd. Amb. 47th Div.
		207 F.D.S.	From 207 Fd. Amb. 38th Div.
61st Div.		171 and 172 Fd. Ambs.	Retained
		201 Fd. Amb.	From 9th Armd. Div.
		190 F.D.S. and 191 F.D.S.	From 190 and 191 Fd. Ambs. of 45th Div.
38th Reserve Div.		80 Fd. Hyg. Sec.	Retained

47th Reserve Div.	68 Fd. Hyg. Sec.	Retained
48th Reserve Div.	73 Fd. Hyg. Sec.	Retained
45th Holding Div.	55 Fd. Hyg. Sec.	Retained

CIVIL AFFAIRS

The Civil Affairs Staff was much handicapped during the planning stages of Operation 'Overlord' by the fact that on the establishment there were no medical officers. The shortage of medical personnel was such that no medical officer on the active list could be spared for employment with Civil Affairs. Both S.H.A.E.F. and 21 Army Group emphasised the need for the attachment of Civil Affairs medical officers to the staffs of armies, corps, L. of C. and base areas and certain appointments were made, a senior medical staff officer (C.A.) with 21 Army Group, hygiene officers (C.A.) with Canadian First Army and Canadian II Corps and an officer was seconded from the United States forces to act as Health Officer (C.A.) with Second Army. The Supreme Commander asked that medical officers of health should be released from civil employment to serve with C.A. staffs. It was also decided that the Civil Affairs policy of 21 Army Group should be determined by D.M.S. Second Army on behalf of the C. in C. An instruction to this effect was issued. The chief points in this instruction dealt with the supply of medical and epidemiological information concerning the civil population by C.A. staffs to A.Ds.M.S. and with the approval by these of plans proposed by Civil Affairs for dealing with outbreaks of disease. Because of the shortage of medical personnel in Civil Affairs it had to be expected that much additional work would have to be undertaken by the hygiene personnel of 21 Army Group. A short course of instruction was therefore staged by D.D.H. 21 Army Group at the Civil Affairs staff centre at Wimbledon. Some 70 hygiene officers and N.C.Os. attended this three-day course.

(B) CANADIAN FIRST ARMY. MEDICAL PLANNING

Canadian First Army, together with British Second Army, constituted 21 Army Group. In general the Group medical planning covered the Canadian and British components equally. But because the Canadian Expeditionary Force was based in North America and not in the United Kingdom and because it was the accepted policy that Canadian casualties should, as far as possible, be tended by the Canadian Army Medical Services in order that the Canadian Expeditionary Force might more easily retain its own structure and manage its own affairs, in certain ways the British and Canadian plans diverged.

Canadian 3rd Division and supporting regiments of Cdn. 2nd Armd.

Bde., u/c I Corps, were to take part in the initial landings. When the beachhead was secure Canadian 2nd Infantry Division and Canadian 4th Armoured Division were to land and H.Q. Canadian II Corps and H.Q. Canadian First Army would follow and assume command of all Canadian troops on the Continent.

Casualties were classified as (*a*) drowned, (*b*) sick and non-battle, and (*c*) battle. It was expected that of the landing craft lost or damaged during the assault phase 60 per cent. would become so on the outward journey when loaded with troops, that 70 per cent. of the troops on those lost would become casualties and that 20 per cent. of those that were damaged would be casualties. It was estimated that 0·17 per cent. of the troops in the beachhead would become sick or injured.

Battle casualties were estimated on the following scale:

Formations	Light Day per cent.	Severe Day per cent.	Maximum Day per cent.
Brigade	2·50	15·00	25·00
Division	1·00	8·00	15·00
Corps	0·50	3·00	5·00
Army	0·35	1·00	2·50
L. of C. and Service units not included in other estimates	0·25	0·60	

These estimates were further sub-divided:

<pre>
D-day and D-day+1
    Killed, P.o.W., Missing   30 per cent.
    Wounded   70   ,,
D-day+2 and afterwards
    Killed, P.o.W., Missing   25 per cent.
    Wounded   75   ,,
</pre>

Assuming that 70,000 British and Canadian personnel were ashore on D-day, the total casualties to be expected on D-day were estimated to be 6,250, of whom 4,495 would require medical attention.

With Canadian 3rd Division were 14, 22 and 23 (Cdn.) Fd. Ambs. These alone were to take part in the assault landings. In so far as specialist units were concerned the Canadians were to make use of British facilities. Each of the field ambulances was to supply a section to each of the three battalions of the brigade to which the field ambulance was attached. The brigades were to attack with two battalions up and one in support. The sections serving the two battalions were to land twenty minutes after the battalions got ashore. The third section was to acompany the supporting battalions.

The Canadian Army Medical Services aimed to provide hospital beds in numbers equal to 10 per cent. of the Canadian troops on the Continent, i.e. 22,100. By March 1944 there were 10,104 Canadian beds in England. By expansion a further 2,277 could readily be provided. It was proposed to bring the total number up to the target figure by using hospital units already mobilised or authorised for mobilisation in Canada. Early in May 1944 it was agreed that the Canadian hospitals proceeding to the Continent would be scaled in accordance with the British standard.

On May 3, 2 Cdn.G.H. at Bramshott, 3 Cdn.G.H. at Aldershot and 17 Cdn.G.H. at Crowthorne were placed on the list of transit hospitals by the E.M.S. Then 9 Cdn.G.H. at Horsham, 13 Cdn.G.H. at Cuckfield and 12 Cdn.G.H. at Horley were designated as coastal hospitals which would receive 'unorganised' casualties—casualties arriving in non-medical vessels—in the area east of Portsmouth. Their patients were transferred to 11 Cdn.G.H. at Taplow, 20 Cdn.G.H. at Leavesden, to the Roman Way Canadian Convalescent Hospital at Colchester and to 4 Cdn. Con. Depot at Hunmanby. So it was that by D-day 2, 4, 9, 12, 13 and 17 Cdn.G.Hs. and the Basingstoke Neurological and Plastic Surgery Hospitals were practically empty.

The Canadian hospitals which were to function as base hospitals— 18 Cdn.G.H. at Cherry Tree, 20 at Leavesden and 11 at Taplow—were issued with extra tentage and to them were attached additional stretcher-bearers, ambulance drivers and ambulance cars. Canadian casualties arriving at this time from Italy were sent to 19 Cdn.G.H. at Marston Green and all minor injury cases among Canadian personnel in the United Kingdom were dealt with by 1 Cdn. Special Hospital at Alton. 18 Cdn.G.H. at Cherry Tree became a 'security' hospital from the end of May, and just before D-day 13 Cdn.G.H. at Cuckfield was likewise designated. To these were sent all Canadians needing hospitalisation from the camps in which the troops had been briefed for the assault phase.

So many of the Canadian hospitals had been designated as coastal, transit and security hospitals that it was decided not to attempt to separate Canadian casualties from the general evacuation streams except in numbers sufficient to fill the 600 beds in 11 and 20 Cdn.G.Hs.

In May 1944, 7, 8, 10 and 16 Cdn.G.Hs. were placed on a field establishment basis and thereafter underwent special training under canvas before moving into the marshalling area. On May 11, the Canadian personnel selected to assist in the manning of the L.S.T. went to Hythe for special training in the loading of casualties into D.U.K.Ws and in the transfer of casualties from D.U.K.W. to L.S.T.

(The composition of the forces employed by Allied Command for Operation 'Overlord' is given in Appendix I. Second Army's Order of

104　　THE ARMY MEDICAL SERVICES

Battle, January–June 1944 is shown in Appendix II. In Appendix III the Medical Order of Battle of 21 Army Group, less the Canadian medical units, is given.)

APPENDIX I

OPERATION 'OVERLORD'. THE ALLIED COMMAND

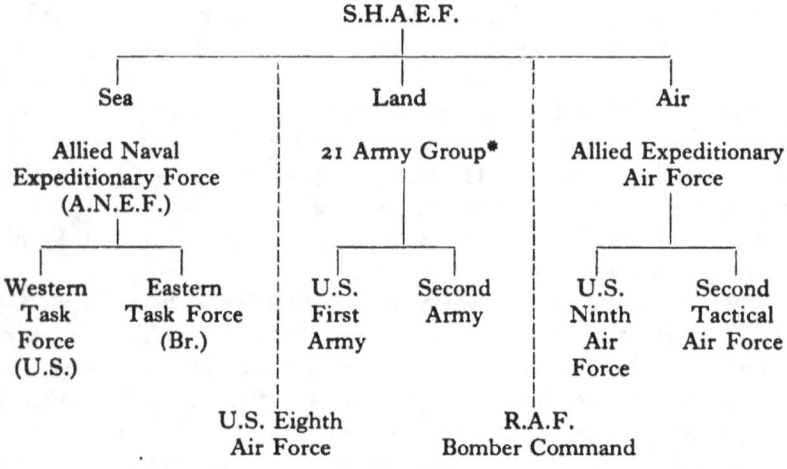

APPENDIX II

SECOND ARMY. ORDER OF BATTLE (ABBREVIATED)

January–February 1944

VIII Corps
    Corps H.Q. Stamford Bridge   Yorks
        Guards Armoured Division   North Riding area
        11th Armoured Division   East Riding area
        15th (Scottish) Division   West Riding area

---

* 21 Army Group was composed of Canadian First and British Second Armies. General Montgomery, commanding 21 Army Group was placed in charge of the land forces during the initial stages of the operation. In the actual assault landing (Operation 'Neptune') formations belonging to U.S. First and British Second Armies were employed. Canadian 3rd Division was under command I Corps of British Second Army at this time.

XII Corps
   Corps H.Q. Tunbridge Wells
      43rd (Wessex) Division   Sussex area
      53rd (Welsh) Division   South Kent area
      59th (Staffordshire) Division North Kent area
XXX Corps (*en route* from C.M.F.)
   Corps H.Q. Newmarket
      7th Armoured Division   North Norfolk area
      50th (Northumbrian) Division   Cambridgeshire, Suffolk and
                                       Essex area
      51st (Highland) Division   Hertfordshire and Bucking-
                                       hamshire area

March 1944

VIII Corps   As above
XII Corps   As above
XXX Corps   As above, save 49th (West Riding) Division in place of 51st
             Division (in East Norfolk area)

I Corps
   Corps H.Q. Chobham   Surrey
      3rd Division   Inverness and Nairn area
      51st (Highland) Division   Hertfordshire and Bucking-
                                       hamshire area
      Canadian 3rd Division   Southampton area

As at June 5, 1944

H.Q. Second Army
   6th Airborne Division, less 5th Para. Bde. Gp.
   H.Q. 1st S.S. Bde.
      3rd, 4th, 6th and 45th Cdos.
   H.Q. 4th S.S. Bde.
      41st, 46th, 47th and 48th Cdos.
   Royal Marine Armd. Sp. Gp.
   100th A.A. Bde.
   106th A.A. Bde.
   3rd, 4th, 5th, 8th and 9th A.Gs. R.A.
   30th Armd. Bde.
   1st Assault Bde. R.E.
   H.Q. Second Army Tps.
   5 L. of C. Sub-area
   H.Q. I Corps
      3rd Infantry Division with u/c 27th Armd. Bde.
      Canadian 3rd Division with u/c Cdn. 2nd Armd. Bde.
      51st Infantry Division
      4th Armd. Bde.
      80th A.A. Bde.
      I Corps Tps.

H.Q. VIII Corps
  Guards Armoured Division
  11th Armoured Division
  15th Infantry Division
  VIII Corps Tps.
H.Q. XII Corps
  43rd Infantry Division
  53rd Infantry Division
  59th Infantry Division
  34th Tk. Bde.
  XII Corps Tps.
H.Q. XXX Corps
  7th Armoured Division
  50th Infantry Division with u/c 8th Armd. Bde. and 56th Inf. Bde.
  49th Infantry Division with u/c 22nd Armd. Bde.
  76th A.A. Bde.
  XXX Corps Tps.
H.Q. 11 L. of C. Area
  101, 102 and 104 Beach Sub-areas
  4 L. of C. Sub-area
  10 Garrison

APPENDIX III

21 ARMY GROUP (LESS CANADIAN UNITS). MEDICAL SERVICES

Medical Staff for Headquarters of Formations

  21 Army Group—1st Echelon
    ,, ,,   ,, —2nd Echelon

Second Army

Airborne Troops
I Corps
VIII Corps
XII Corps
XXX Corps

Guards Armoured Division
7th   ,,   ,,
11th   ,,   ,,
79th   ,,   ,,

3rd Infantry Division
15th   ,,   ,,
43rd   ,,   ,,
49th   ,,   ,,
50th   ,,   ,,
51st   ,,   ,,
53rd   ,,   ,,
59th   ,,   ,,

1st Airborne Division
6th   ,,   ,,

Lines of Communication
11 L. of C. Area
12   ,,   ,,

4 L. of C. Sub-Area
5   ,,   ,,

7 Base Sub-Area
8   ,,   ,,

101 Beach Sub-Area
102   ,,   ,,
104   ,,   ,,

Field Medical Units

2 Lt. Fd. Amb.	7th Armoured Division
11 ,, ,, ,,	27th Armoured Brigade
14 ,, ,, ,,	4th ,, ,,
16 ,, ,, ,,	30th ,, ,,
18 ,, ,, ,,	11th ,, Division
19 ,, ,, ,,	Guards ,, ,,
21 ,, ,, ,,	31st Tank Brigade
22 ,, ,, ,,	33rd Armoured Brigade
23 ,, ,, ,,	34th Tank Brigade
168 ,, ,, ,,	8th Armoured Brigade
8 Fd. Amb.	3rd Division
9 ,, ,,	3rd ,,
128 ,, ,,	Guards Armoured Division
129 ,, ,,	43rd Division
130 ,, ,,	43rd ,,
131 ,, ,,	7th Armoured Division
146 ,, ,,	49th Division
147 ,, ,,	53rd ,,
149 ,, ,,	50th ,,

153 Fd. Amb.	15th Division
160 ,, ,,	49th ,,
162 ,, ,,	L. of C.
163 ,, ,,	56th Bde.
174 ,, ,,	51st Division
175 ,, ,,	51st ,,
176 ,, ,,	51st ,,
179 ,, ,,	11th Armoured Division
186 ,, ,,	50th Division
187 ,, ,,	49th ,,
193 ,, ,,	15th ,,
194 ,, ,,	15th ,,
200 ,, ,,	50th ,,
202 ,, ,,	53rd ,,
203 ,, ,,	59th ,,
210 ,, ,,	59th ,,
211 ,, ,,	59th ,,
212 ,, ,,	53rd ,,
213 ,, ,,	43rd ,,
223 ,, ,,	3rd ,,
16 Para. Fd. Amb.	1st Airborne Division
133 ,, ,, ,,	1st ,, ,,
224 ,, ,, ,,	6th ,, ,,
225 ,, ,, ,,	6th ,, ,,
181 A/L Fd. Amb.	1st ,, ,,
195 ,, ,, ,,	6th ,, ,,
1 F.D.S.	Second Army (7th Beach Group)
2 ,,	,, ,, ,, ,, ,,
3 ,,	XXX Corps
4 ,,	XII ,,
5 ,,	51st Division
6 ,,	51st ,,
7 ,,	11th Armoured Division
8 ,,	Guards Armoured ,,
9 ,,	Second Army (6th Beach Group)
10 ,,	3rd Division
11 ,,	3rd ,,
12 ,,	Second Army (6th Beach Group)
13 ,,	53rd Division
14 ,,	43rd ,,
15 ,,	43rd ,,
16 ,,	49th ,,
17 ,,	49th ,,
20 ,,	Second Army (5th Beach Group)
21 ,,	,, ,, ,, ,, ,,

22 F.D.S.		15th Division
23 ,,		15th ,,
24 ,,		VIII Corps
25 ,,		Second Army (10th Beach Group)
26 ,,		53rd Division
27 ,,		59th ,,
28 ,,		59th ,,
29 ,,		7th Armoured Division
30 ,,		I Corps
31 ,,		Second Army (10th Beach Group)
32 ,,		,, ,, 9th ,, ,,
33 ,,		,, ,, 8th ,, ,,
34 ,,		,, ,, ,, ,, ,,
35 ,,		,, ,, 9th ,, ,,
47 ,,		50th Division
48 ,,		50th ,,
49 ,,		11 L. of C.
50 ,,		Second Army Tps.
6 Fd. Hyg. Sec.		I Corps
10 ,, ,, ,,		XII ,,
22 ,, ,, ,,		50th Division
26 ,, ,, ,,		3rd ,,
27 ,, ,, ,,		VIII Corps
29 ,, ,, ,,		51st Division
30 ,, ,, ,,		59th ,,
31 ,, ,, ,,		XXX Corps
35 ,, ,, ,,		49th Division
38 ,, ,, ,,		43rd ,,
40 ,, ,, ,,		15th ,,
45 ,, ,, ,,		L of C.
53 ,, ,, ,,		53rd Division
60 ,, ,, ,,		Guards Armoured Division
61 ,, ,, ,,		Second Army
70 ,, ,, ,,		7th Armoured Division
75 ,, ,, ,,		Second Army
76 ,, ,, ,,		11th Armoured Division
1 Fd. San. Sec.		Second Army
2 ,, ,, ,,		L. of C.
3 ,, ,, ,,		L. of C.
4 ,, ,, ,,		Second Army
6 F.S.U.		Second Army
12 ,,		XII Corps
13 ,,		Second Army
14 ,,		,, ,,

15 F.S.U.		XII Corps
27	,,	XII ,,
33	,,	Second Army
34	,,	I Corps
37	,,	I ,,
38	,,	Second Army
39	,,	I Corps
40	,,	Second Army
41	,,	I Corps
42	,,	XII Corps
43	,,	Second Army
44	,,	,, ,,
45	,,	,, ,,
46	,,	,, ,,
47	,,	,, ,,
48	,,	,, ,,
49	,,	,, ,,
50	,,	,, ,,
51	,,	,, ,,
52	,,	VIII Corps
53	,,	VIII ,,
54	,,	Second Army
55	,,	,, ,,
56	,,	,, ,,
6 F.T.U.		Second Army
7	,,	,, ,,
13	,,	XII Corps
14	,,	I Corps
21	,,	VIII Corps
22	,,	VIII ,,
24	,,	Second Army
29	,,	,, ,,
30	,,	,, ,,
31	,,	XII Corps
35	,,	Second Army
36	,,	,, ,,
37	,,	XII Corps
3 C.C.S.		XXX Corps
10	,,	XXX ,,
16	,,	I ,,
23	,,	XII ,,
24	,,	XII ,,
32	,,	I ,,
33	,,	VIII ,,
34	,,	VIII ,,
35	,,	Second Army

Base and L. of C. Medical Units

General Hospitals		Normal No. of Beds	Extensions 100 Beds	Total Beds	Special Function
6 B.G.H.	L. of C.	1,200	2	1,400	General
8 ,,	,,	600	—	600	,,
9 ,,	,,	600	3	900	Orthopaedic
20 ,,	,,	600	—	600	General
23 ,,	,,	1,200	5	1,700	,,
24 ,,	,,	1,200	—	1,200	V.D.
25 ,,	,,	600	—	600	,,
29 ,,	,,	1,200	2	1,400	Orthopaedic
30 ,,	,,	600	2	800	,,
32 ,,	,,	600	—	600	Neuropathic
39 ,,	,,	600	—	600	Psychiatric
73 ,,	,,	1,200	2	1,400	V.D.
74 ,,	,,	600	3	900	General
75 ,,	,,	600	—	600	,,
77 ,,	,,	600	—	600	Orthopaedic
79 ,,	,,	600	—	600	,,
81 ,,	Second Army	200	—	200	Ophthalmic
84 ,,	,,	200	—	200	,,
86 ,,	,,	200	—	200	,,
88 ,,	,,	200	—	200	,,
101 ,,	L. of C.	1,200	—	1,200	Orthopaedic
102 ,,	,,	1,200	—	1,200	General
105 ,,	,,	1,200	4	1,600	,,
106 ,,	,,	1,200	—	1,200	Orthopaedic
107 ,,	,,	1,200	4	1,600	General
108 ,,	,,	1,200	3	1,500	,,
109 ,,	,,	1,200	—	1,200	Orthopaedic
110 ,,	,,	1,200	2	1,400	General
111 ,,	,,	1,200	—	1,200	,,
112 ,,	,,	1,200	—	1,200	,,
113 ,,	,,	1,200	—	1,200	Orthopaedic
114 ,,	,,	1,200	—	1,200	General
115 ,,	,,	1,200	—	1,200	,,
121 ,,	,,	600	1	700	V.D.

General Medical and Surgical Beds	17,900
Orthopaedic	9,100
Venereal Disease	3,900
Ophthalmic	800
Neuropathic	600
Psychiatric	600
	32,900

6 M.N.S.U.   L. of C.
3 Surg. Team Chest Surgery   ,,
5 M.F.S.U.   ,,
6 ,,   ,,

1 B.T.U.   L. of C.
6 ,,   ,,

5 Con. Depot   L. of C.
12 ,, ,,   ,,

13 Con. Depot			L. of C.	
14 ,,	,,		,,	
15 ,,	,,		,,	
16 ,,	,,		,,	

6 Adv. Depot Med. Stores				Second Army	
8 ,,	,,	,,	,,	,,	,,
9 ,,	,,	,,	,,	,,	,,
11 ,,	,,	,,	,,	,,	,,

5 Base Depot Med. Stores				Second Army
11 ,,	,,	,,	,,	L. of C.
12 ,,	,,	,,	,,	,,
13 ,,	,,	,,	,,	,,

3 Mob. Bact. Lab.			L. of C.
4 ,,	,,	,,	Second Army
7 ,,	,,	,,	L. of C.
8 ,,	,,	,,	,,

4 Mob. Hyg. Lab.   L. of C.

20 Port Detachment			Second Army	
21 ,,	,,		,,	,,
22 ,,	,,		,,	,,
23 ,,	,,		,,	,,
24 ,,	,,		,,	,,
25 ,,	,,		,,	,,
26 ,,	,,		,,	,,
27 ,,	,,		,,	,,
28 ,,	,,		L. of C.	
29 ,,	,,		,,	
30 ,,	,,		,,	

40 Amb. Train		L. of C.
41 ,,	,,	,,
42 ,,	,,	,,
43 ,,	,,	,,
44 ,,	,,	,,
45 ,,	,,	,,
46 ,,	,,	,,
47 ,,	,,	,,
48 ,,	,,	,,
49 ,,	,,	,,
50 ,,	,,	,,
51 ,,	,,	,,
52 ,,	,,	,,
53 ,,	,,	,,

60 Prophylactic Ablution Centre			Second Army
61	,,	,, ,,	L. of C.
62	,,	, ,,	,,
63	,,	,, ,,	,,
64	,,	,, ,,	XXX Corps
65	,,	,, ,,	VIII ,,
66	,,	,, ,,	XII ,,
67	,,	,, ,,	I ,,
68	,,	,, ,,	Second Army
69	,,	,, ,,	L. of C.
70	,,	,, ,,	,,
71	,,	,, ,,	,,
72	,	,, ,,	,,
73	,,	,, ,,	,,
74	,,	,, ,,	,,
75	,,	,, ,,	,,
76	,,	,, ,,	,,
77	,,	,, ,,	,,
78	,,	,, ,,	,,
79	,,	,, ,,	,,

134 Mobile Dental Unit			Second Army	
204	,,	,, ,,	,,	,,
205	,,	,, ,,	,,	,,
206	,,	,, ,,	,,	,,
207	,,	,, ,,	,,	,,
208	,,	,, ,,	,,	,,
209	,,	,, ,,	,,	,,
210	,,	,, ,,	,,	,,
211	,,	,, ,,	,,	,,
212	,,	,, ,,	,,	,,
214	,,	,, ,,	,,	,
215	,,	,, ,,	,,	,,

CHAPTER 2

THE ASSAULT AND LODGEMENT

(i)

Operation 'Neptune'

FOR the assault landings and seizure of the beachhead, 21 Army Group had under command the following formations belonging to U.S. First, Canadian First and British Second Armies:

To be dropped on the extreme right
U.S. 82nd Airborne Division
U.S. 101st Airborne Division

To be dropped on the extreme left
6th Airborne Division

	1st Flight	*Preloaded Follow-up*	*Preloaded Build-up*
U.S. VII Corps Landing on Utah Beach	U.S. 4th Division	359th R.C.T. U.S. 90th Division	U.S. 90th Division less 359th R.C.T. U.S. 9th Division
U.S. V Corps Landing on Omaha Beach	U.S. 1st Division	U.S. 29th Division	U.S. 2nd Division
XXX Corps Landing on Gold Beach	50th Division 8th Armd. Bde.	7th Armd. Division	49th Division
I Corps Landing on Juno Beach	Canadian 3rd Division Canadian 2nd Armd. Bde.	4th S.S. Bde.	51st Division
I Corps Landing on Sword Beach	3rd Division 27th Armd. Bde.	1st S.S. Bde.	

The task of the U.S. airborne divisions was made difficult by the nature of the terrain. The Germans had flooded large areas close to Utah beach so that immediately behind the line of the coastal defences

THE ASSAULT AND LODGEMENT

there was a mile-wide lagoon crossed by five narrow causeways. Ten miles to the west and south-west of Utah beach the inundations in the valleys of the Merderet and Douve were even more extensive.

U.S. 101st Airborne Division was to drop two parachute regiments just west of this coastal lagoon to silence a heavy battery and seize the western exits of the causeways. Another parachute regiment was to drop north of Carentan, destroy the main rail and road bridges over the Douve and hold the line of the Douve and of the Carentan Canal and so afford protection to U.S. VII Corps as this came ashore.

U.S. 82nd Airborne Division was to drop astride the Merderet south and west of Ste. Mère-Eglise, extend the protective flank by destroying two more bridges over the Douve and secure the crossings over the Merderet (see Fig. 1).

Night fighters covered the approach of the Pathfinders as these flew in just before midnight on June 5/6. The troop carriers following these were greatly impeded by heavy cloud and were greeted by severe A.A. fire. 101st Airborne Division became widely scattered over an area 25 × 15 miles. U.S. 82nd Division was more fortunate and about three-quarters of the division landed within three miles or so of the selected dropping zone and by 0400 hours on the 6th had taken Ste. Mère-Église, thus blocking the Carentan–Cherbourg road. The parachutists became so heavily involved in fighting that they were unable to seize the bridges over the Merderet or to destroy those over the Douve. 101st Division had dropped into an area with but few defenders and, being reinforced by glider-borne troops before daylight, the parachutists were able to secure the western exits of the causeways and to occupy the battery position which the Germans had abandoned.

At 0200 hours on June 6, the 1,000 ships carrying 30,000 troops of U.S. VII Corps and 3,500 vehicles began to assemble in an area twelve miles north-east of Utah beach. At 0530 hours U.S. naval units and bombers began to pound the strong-points along the shore. Then two squadrons of D.D. tanks were launched two miles from the shore, 28 of the 32 reaching it and about a dozen of them touching down with the first wave of the infantry at 0630 hours. The resistance encountered was slight and by 0900 hours the 'Atlantic Wall' in this sector had been breached on a two-mile front between the sea and the coastal lagoon. In the wake of the infantry engineers landed to clear lanes through the beach obstacles. The infantry then set out across the causeways with amphibious armour in close support and by 1300 hours the airborne and seaborne forces had met. The beachhead, 4,000 yards wide and 10,000 yards deep at the point of greatest penetration, was secure.

The assault landing of U.S. V Corps on Omaha beach, on the other hand, was bitterly contested and for a time seemed likely to end in disaster. Of the thirty-two amphibious tanks that were launched all but five quickly foundered and of these five one was knocked out immediately it reached the shore. The landing craft carrying the infantry were flung out of formation by the rough sea. The naval and aerial bombardment in this sector had been largely ineffective and the coastal defences were strongly garrisoned. So it was that there was great congestion on the beach and not a little confusion and that casualties were heavy. It was only towards the end of the day that the line of the coastal road was forced. At dark the grip on the slender beachhead was far from secure. Its full sweep was under fire from artillery and mortars and in it there was an acute shortage of armour and of guns. The area held was about six miles wide and less than two miles deep at the point of greatest penetration. Two critical days were to pass before U.S. V Corps joined up with XXX Corps on its left in the Port-en-Bessin area and three before the beachhead had been so enlarged and so reinforced that it could be regarded as secure.

In so far as the terrain was concerned Second Army was perhaps more favoured than U.S. First Army, but it had to expect a more dangerous and a more violent immediate reaction on the part of the Germans for their panzer divisions were known to be stationed east and south of Caen. It was therefore imperative that the landings should be smooth, the advance inland rapid and the build-up swift. The task of this British and Canadian force was that of capturing an area which included Bayeux and Caen, the line of the main road between these cities and the bridgehead east of the Orne by the evening of D-day. From this base it was intended that armoured columns should thrust aggressively southwards, on D-day if possible, to seize the high ground about Villers-Bocage and Evrecy, twenty miles inland.

6th Airborne Division was to capture, between midnight and dawn on June 6, the bridges on the only through road over the Orne, north of Caen, to capture a coastal battery at Merville near the mouth of this river, to demolish five bridges in the flooded valley of the Dives, some six miles east of the Orne, and to gain control of the high wooded ground between the Orne and the Dives. These objectives were to be gained by 3rd and 5th Para. Bdes. and a small glider-borne force and these were to be reinforced around midday by commandos of 1st S.S. Bde., which would land on Sword beach. In the evening the rest of 6th Airborne Division would be flown in, after the landing zones had been cleared of obstacles.

The bridges over the Orne were captured according to plan by the occupants of gliders that were crash-landed near to them at 0200 hours on D-day. But the high wind carried the Pathfinders well to the east of the selected dropping zones and because of the shortness of the time they were obliged to set up their signals where they were. Thus it was that 5th Para. Bde. was dropped wide of its mark and much scattered.

THE ASSAULT AND LODGEMENT

However, it managed to clear the main landing zone east of the Orne before the gliders carrying the heavy equipment of the division came in at 0330 hours. It then drove the Germans out of Ranville. 3rd Para. Bde. was likewise widely scattered. Nevertheless, the five larger bridges in the flooded area were duly blown, four quite easily, the fifth, the one at Troarn, by an officer and seven men who, landing far away, piled into a jeep and stormed it. 9th Para. Bn., which was to capture the Merville battery, was dropped miles from its target and greatly scattered. Two hours later only 150 men, one machine-gun and far too little explosive for the job could be mustered. However, at 0430 hours this party rushed the battery and overwhelmed its occupants. In this fashion the last of 6th Airborne Division's D-day objectives was gained (see Fig. 2).

Forty minutes before sunrise warships of the Royal Navy began to bombard the coastal defences in Second Army's sector, concentrating on the coastal batteries which had already been heavily attacked by Bomber Command.

On XXX Corps' sector the sole response was from a battery at Longues, north of Bayeux. This was quickly silenced and thereafter the assembly of the assault force proceeded without interruption save from a wind-whipped sea. So rough was it that it was decided to land the D.D. tanks direct on to Gold beach immediately following the infantry.

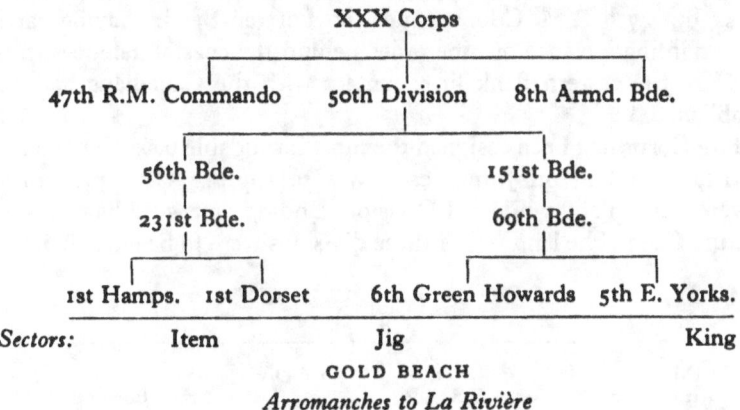

GOLD BEACH
Arromanches to La Rivière

The D-day objectives of 50th Division were the town of Bayeux and the high ground in the vicinity of St. Léger. Shortly before 0730 hours the leading companies of 1st Hamps. of 231st Bde. of 50th Division waded ashore to find the specialised armour already engaging the defences. One strong-point, unscathed by the bombardment, at Le Hamel gave much trouble and checked the advance. Asnelles was not taken until midday. 1st Dorset, the other assault battalion of 231st Bde., strongly supported by armour, moved steadily inland until checked to the south of Arromanches. This resistance was overcome in the afternoon and the advance continued.

At the eastern end of 50th Division's front when the armour had silenced a pillbox near La Rivière 5th East Yorks. fought their way through the village while 6th Green Howards reached the Meuvaines Ridge, a mile inland, by 0930 hours and 7th Green Howards with supporting armour were moving up to continue the advance. When the follow-up brigades, 56th and 151st, landed about 1100 hours the assault gained fresh power, and by 1230 hours the beachhead was two and a half miles deep and three miles wide, although the garrison in Le Hamel continued to resist until 1630 hours. Then the Hampshires turned westward to roll up the coastal defences, naval units putting down a barrage ahead of them. By 2100 hours they were in Arromanches. Meanwhile the main weight of XXX Corps had been directed south and south-west. During the afternoon 56th Bde. advanced six miles and sent patrols into the outskirts of Bayeux while advanced elements of 151st Bde. reached the Bayeux–Caen road three miles to the south-east of Bayeux. On the left 69th Bde. ended the day six miles south of the assault beach.

At nightfall the Gold beachhead measured roughly six miles by six. The leading battalions were some two to three miles short of their D-day objectives. Between Gold and Omaha beaches there was a gap of seven miles, but 47th R.M. Cdo. was nearing Port-en-Bessin, having carried out a fighting advance of nine miles behind the coastal defences in this gap. On the eastern flank firm contact with the Canadians had been established.

To I Corps had been assigned the most formidable task. Canadian 3rd Division, landing on Juno beach was to capture Carpiquet airfield eleven miles inland while 3rd Division, landing on Sword beach, was to capture Caen. The landings of these divisions were to be later than those

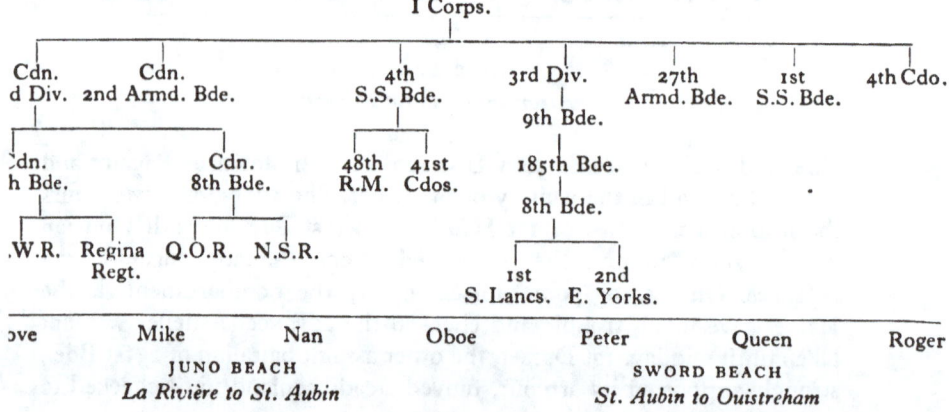

elsewhere because of the tide and the presence of rocks and so the Germans would have been alerted. The two beaches were separated by outcrops of rock.

Canadian 3rd Division landed on Juno beach astride the mouth of the River Seulles. Delayed by the rough sea the leading assault craft came in nearly half an hour late and were borne by the tide through the belt of heavily mined obstacles. Many of the craft were sunk or damaged but casualties were few. The infantry arrived ahead of the armour to find the defences almost unscathed by the bombardment. Cdn. 7th Bde., assisted by D.D. tanks, stormed the main strong-points on the water front at the mouth of the Seulles and by mid-morning were two miles inland. Further east Cdn. 8th Bde., landing without D.D. tanks in support, captured Bernières and thrust beyond Bény-sur-Mer. By dusk the foremost Canadian troops were seven miles inland and at nightfall two battalions were within three miles of Caen itself.

Behind a screen of gunfire 8th Bde. of 3rd Division landed on Sword beach and with D.D. tanks of 13th/18th Hussars and specialised armour in the lead got ashore at 0730 hours. The defences were quickly overwhelmed and Hermanville was captured at 0930 hours, 4th Cdo. entering the western outskirts of Ouistreham. Thereafter the advance slowed down and it was not until eight hours later that Ranville was reached.

2nd K.S.L.I. of 185th Bde. set out for Caen along the Hermanville–Caen road. By 1600 hours they were through Biéville, only four miles from Caen, but then were checked by German armour. This being driven off, the Shropshires then advanced another mile before they came under heavy fire and were halted.

Between Canadian 3rd and 3rd Divisions lay a belt of territory running right down to the coast at Luc still in German hands. The danger that the Germans might thrust down this corridor in strength was removed when at 2100 hours 250 tugs and 250 gliders escorted by a host of fighters brought 6th Air-Landing Bde., the reconnaissance regiment, light tanks and guns of 6th Airborne Division to land in the fields beside the Orne.

Thus at the end of D-day the Allies had broken into Festung Europa on a front of thirty miles. The Utah beachhead was isolated, the hold on Omaha precarious, between U.S. V Corps and XXX Corps was a gap of seven miles and another of three miles between the Canadians and 3rd Division. None of the D-day objectives had been reached and the unloading was some ten to twelve hours behind schedule. The weather was threatening.

The losses of men had been far less than expected, probably in the region of 2,500 killed and missing and 8,500 wounded. The most severe losses had been those endured by U.S. V Corps at Omaha.

On June 7 U.S. 82nd Airborne Division, which during the night had

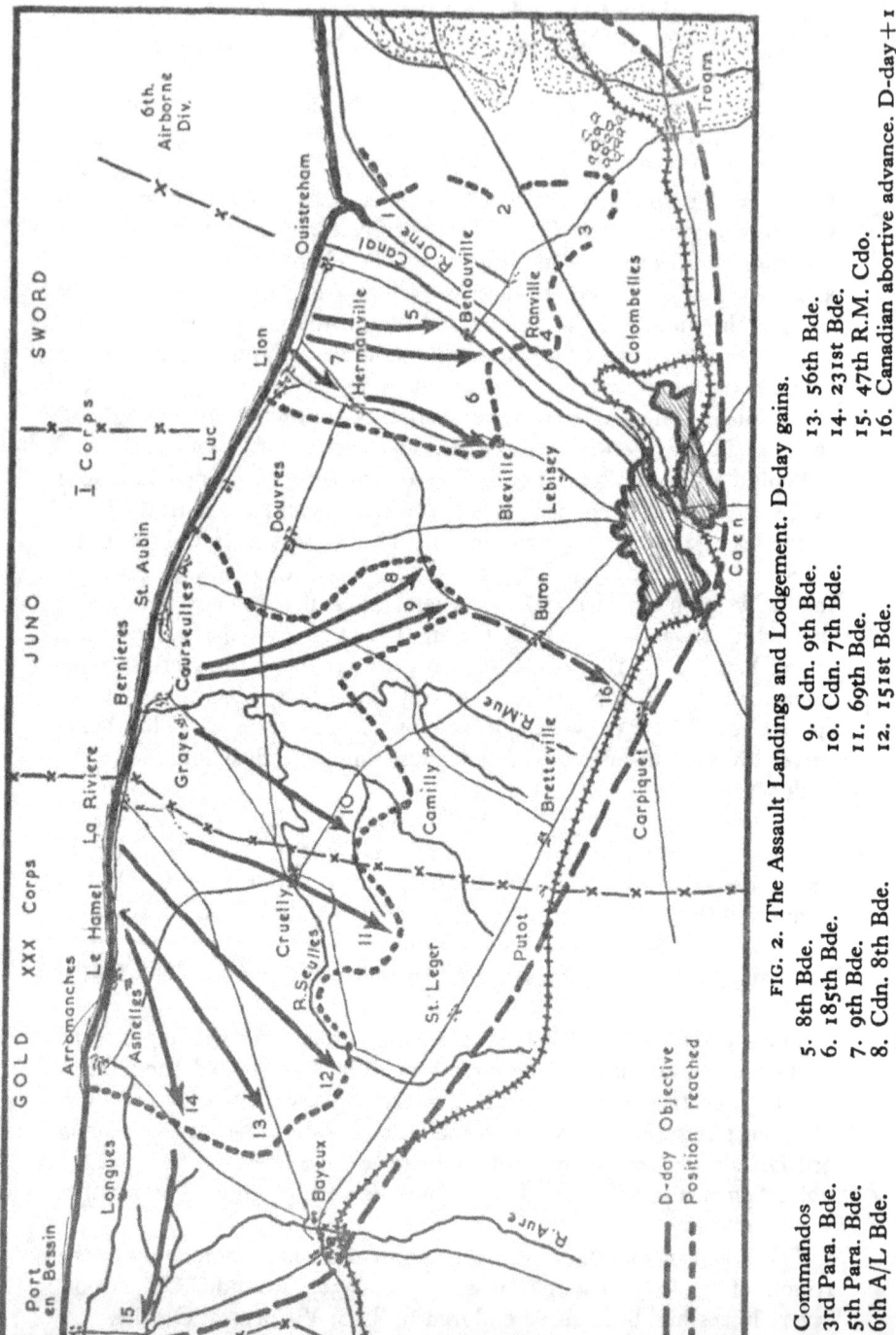

FIG. 2. The Assault Landings and Lodgement. D-day gains.

1. Commandos
2. 3rd Para. Bde.
3. 5th Para. Bde.
4. 6th A/L Bde.
5. 8th Bde.
6. 185th Bde.
7. 9th Bde.
8. Cdn. 8th Bde.
9. Cdn. 9th Bde.
10. Cdn. 7th Bde.
11. 69th Bde.
12. 151st Bde.
13. 56th Bde.
14. 231st Bde.
15. 47th R.M. Cdo.
16. Canadian abortive advance. D-day + 1

been heavily attacked across the Merderet and which in the morning was reinforced by glider-borne troops, held on to its positions along the Merderet. U.S. 4th Division advanced two miles to the north-west and so by dark the beachhead was eight miles deep and nine miles wide. By the morning of June 9 U.S. 82nd and 101st Airborne Divisions had further expanded the bridgehead west and south across the flood lines but still there was no link between U.S. VII and U.S. V Corps.

Efforts to widen the Omaha beachhead were strenuously opposed and U.S. 29th Division was able to make but minor advances. But the opposition weakened as U.S. 1st Division gained ground to the south to secure a bridgehead across the Aure.

50th Division of XXX Corps moved on Bayeux and the Canadians reached the Bayeux–Caen road which as far east as Bretteville l'Orgueilleuse was now in Second Army's possession. The Canadians then advanced from Villons-les-Buissons towards Authie, two miles from Caen. There they met head-on a large-scale counter-attack by German armour and were pressed back to their start line.

Thus by nightfall on D-day+1 Second Army had a solid beachhead twenty-two miles wide and five to ten deep and occupied positions which could be confidently defended and from which further advances could hopefully be made.

While preparations for the capture of Carentan and Caen were proceeding the Utah beachhead was further expanded and secured. By the 9th its maximum depth had become ten miles. On the same day U.S. 29th Division of U.S. V Corps captured Isigny and on the 10th the two American corps linked up east of this town and on the left of U.S. V Corps U.S. 1st Division made contact with 50th Division of XXX Corps to the west of Bayeux. On the 8th commandos had captured Port-en-Bessin and established firm contact with U.S. V Corps.

On June 8 the Canadians, dug in astride the Caen–Bayeux road at Pûtot-en-Bessin and Bretteville, were heavily attacked by German armour and driven out of Pûtot. But a counter-attack by 1st Canadian Scottish retook the village and restored the line. A British armoured column thrust to the outskirts of Tilly-sur-Seulles but being unaccompanied by infantry could not consolidate its gains.

On June 11, U.S. 101st Airborne Division forced the outer defences of Carentan, from which the Germans then withdrew. This American advance was then exploited by XXX Corps on the 12th. 7th Armoured Division was ordered to break off its direct attack upon Tilly and carry out a right hook to Villers-Bocage and thrust on toward Evrecy. 22nd Armd. Bde. advanced six miles before being checked at Livry, northeast of Caumont. Next morning the advance to Villers-Bocage was continued unopposed. Villers-Bocage was held until nightfall when the British troops withdrew to a knoll a mile to the west.

50th Division attacked at Tilly but was repulsed and 7th Armoured Division was then withdrawn to Bricquessard, two miles east of Caumont. 51st Division, attempting to expand the bridgehead east of the Orne, failed to do so. It then became clear that Caen could be taken only by a set piece assault. The arrival of VIII Corps with 11th Armoured, 15th and 43rd Divisions was awaited.

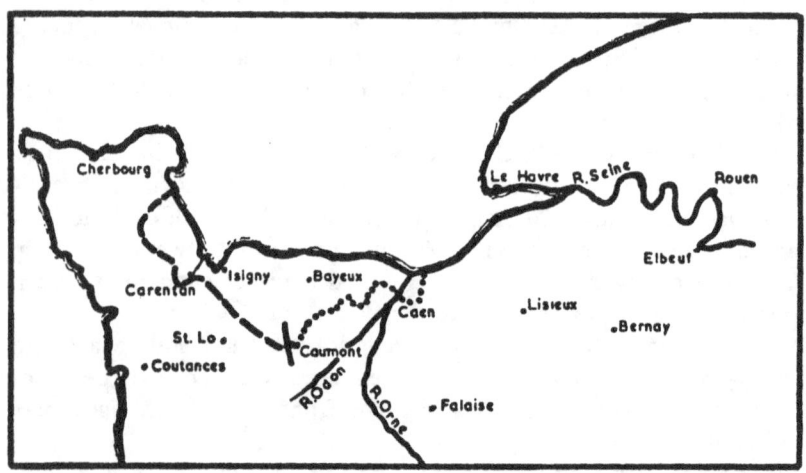

FIG. 3. The Beachhead. June 13.

The countryside south and south-west of the Caen–Bayeux road is an area of undulating wooded hills and steep-sided valleys with innumerable streams. The hill slopes are covered with farms with their small fields encircled with broad banks three to four feet in height with a ditch on either side and topped with stout thorn hedges. There are also many orchards surrounded by stout stone walls. Through the maze run few straight roads and these run south-west. XXX Corps was attempting to advance south-east along sunken lanes. The bocage (= copse, woody, bosky) was a most effective barrier to armour and to manœuvre. The Germans thoroughly exploited the natural defensive strength of the terrain in order to gain time, but nevertheless, owing to the aggressiveness of their opponents, they had to continue to use their armour to hold the line from Caen to Caumont which had been captured by U.S. 1st Division on June 14.

It was General Montgomery's aim to attract the greatest enemy strength opposite Second Army in order that U.S. First Army might expand and extend more quickly. In this he had succeeded. He now planned, using VIII Corps, to cut through the German defences between Caen and Tilly, cross the Odon and the Orne and establish his armour astride the Caen–Falaise road on the high ground between

THE ASSAULT AND LODGEMENT 123

Bourguébus and Bretteville-sur-Laize. Caen would then be outflanked and almost enveloped and this threat would, General Montgomery hoped, keep the German panzer divisions away from the St. Lô–Coutances area where the Americans were to make the main Allied effort, in preparation for which U.S. VII Corps was to attack south from the flooded Douve valley in order to gain sufficient room for the mounting of the break-out offensive.

The preparations for the attack by VIII Corps were profoundly affected by a storm of gale force which broke on June 19 and lasted three days. By the 21st the 'Mulberry' harbour in the U.S. sector was wrecked beyond repair and that at Arromanches severely damaged. When the storm abated there were some 800 craft stranded on the beaches. The storm had done five times more damage to Allied shipping than the Germans had caused since D-day. It also slowed down or postponed all operations on the part of the Allied armies.

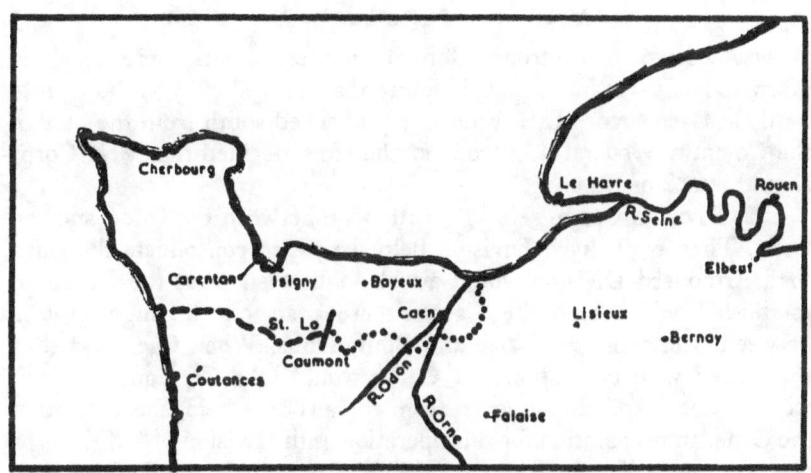

FIG. 4. The Beachhead. June 24.

U.S. VII Corps, with its strength doubled since D-day, was now heading towards Cherbourg, fighting its way through bocage country of the most difficult kind. On June 15 the Americans crossed the upper Douve at St. Sauveur, the last natural defence line in front of Cherbourg. By the 17th they were in sight of the sea on the west coast of the peninsula. On the 18th they were in Barneville and the base of the peninsula was sealed. While U.S. VIII Corps guarded the southern front General Collins, commanding U.S. VII Corps, with U.S. 4th, 79th and 9th Divisions overran the defences on either side of Montebourg, reached Valognes and broke the main German positions on June 19th. On the 20th the three divisions reached the outer defences of Cherbourg. The garrison commander ignored a formal summons to surrender on the 21st. On the 22nd the Americans attacked and gained some ground. The 23rd was a day of bitter hand-to-hand fighting while the defences progressively crumbled. On the 24th, U.S. 4th Division reached the coast three miles east of Cherbourg and by the evening of the 26th all organised opposition in the city itself had collapsed. The garrison commander was captured and the garrison of the arsenal surrendered. The harbour forts held out for two more days and the resistance of the German right wing in the north-west corner of the peninsula continued until July 1.

Because of mines, obstructions and demolitions no supply ships could enter the port until July 16 and it was another three weeks before ships could tie up alongside the quays and two months before the port could handle in a day as much cargo as was unloaded every 24 hours over Utah beach.

OPERATIONS 'EPSOM' AND 'JUPITER'

It was known that strong German reinforcements were reaching Normandy. It was important therefore that these should be drawn into battle at Caen before U.S. First Army attacked south from the base of the Cotentin. General Montgomery therefore decided that VIII Corps should attack on June 26.

15th Division was to seize a broad ridge between the Odon and the Orne. Then while 43rd Division helped 15th to consolidate the gains 11th Armoured Division would attack south-east, cross the Orne and establish itself astride the Caen–Falaise road on the high ground between Bretteville-sur-Laize and Bourguébus. When Caen was thus threatened with envelopment I Corps would take Carpiquet airfield, west of Caen, and thrust south from the airborne bridgehead, east of the Orne. In preparation for this operation 49th Division of XXX Corps was to capture Rauray Ridge on the 25th to protect the flank of 15th Division and thereafter XXX Corps was to exploit southwards through Noyers to Aunay-sur-Odon. The start was inauspicious, for the weather grounded the air forces based on Britain and a thick ground mist so impeded 49th Division that it was still a mile short of Rauray Ridge on the evening of the 25th. However, two hours after dawn on the 26th, 15th (Scottish) Division with 31st Armd. Bde. in support moved into battle. The opposition encountered was stubborn and the advance greatly impeded by mines and the torrential rain. Ultimately the Caen–Villers-Bocage railway at Colleville was reached, some four miles south of the morning's start line and a mile from the Odon.

On the 27th a German counter-attack was repulsed, 49th Division captured Rauray and a bridge across the Odon was captured intact and 11th Armoured Division got across. On the 28th strong German reinforcements began to arrive and it was decided that VIII Corps should not attempt to cross the Orne until the positions north of the Odon had been consolidated. The corridor created by VIII Corps was only about a mile and a half wide.

On the 29th the R.A.F. went into action early, so to disrupt the German concentrations that it was 1430 hours before the expected attack on the Odon bridgehead began. When it was unleashed it was bloodily repulsed.

The Americans now had four corps and fourteen divisions ranged along a fifty-mile front but the terrain in this sector was such that General Bradley could not reap advantage from this great numerical superiority. On July 3 he struck with U.S. VIII Corps in the vicinity of La Haye-du-Puits. After seven days of fighting the Germans had been driven back only five miles and still held the hills south of La Haye. Meanwhile U.S. VII Corps had encountered even greater difficulty in breaking through the slender bottleneck on the Carentan–Périers road and after nine days the attack down this road was abandoned. Further east U.S. XIX Corps had crossed the Vire seven miles north of St. Lô on July 7 but inundations prevented the extension of the bridgehead (*see* Fig. 1).

Meanwhile Second Army had been maintaining pressure from the Odon salient and had continued its attempts to secure Caen. On July 4 the village of Carpiquet was taken by the Canadians but the airfield remained in German hands. It was then reluctantly decided that Caen must be bombed. On the evening of July 7, 2,560 tons of bombs were dropped on the northern outskirts of the ancient city by Bomber Command and at dawn next morning I Corps with 3rd Division on the left, 59th Division in the centre and Canadian 3rd Division on the right, attacked. By dark 3rd Division had reached the northern fringe of the city and the following morning, while patrols made their way to the city centre, bulldozers struggled to clear the streets and the Canadians reached the river from the west to find every bridge down and the far bank strongly held. The city was in British hands but the road to the Falaise plain was still blocked.

OPERATION 'GOODWOOD MEETING'

By July 10 the situation was causing anxiety. Cherbourg harbour was not yet open; only one 'Mulberry' was functioning; the Carpiquet airfield had not yet been captured; reinforcements were reaching the Germans in a steady stream; the path of Second Army was blocked by the Germans in the eastern half of Caen and the American offensive had lost its momentum. General Montgomery decided to strike from the 'airborne bridgehead' east of the Orne in order to halt the transfer of the German armour to U.S. First Army's sector.

It was decided that this operation ('Goodwood') would begin on July 18, that it would be preceded by a feint from the Odon salient on the night of July 15/16 and be followed by Operation 'Cobra'—the breakout of U.S. First Army—on the 20th. General Montgomery asked for the strongest possible support for both these operations from the strategical and tactical air forces. It was planned that the three armoured divisions, 7th, 11th and Guards, under VIII Corps should debouch in rapid succession from the Orne bridgehead and charge through the corridor to Cagny and then fan out, 7th driving straight on to Garcelles-Secqueville, 11th swinging south-west towards Bourguébus and the Guards turning south-east for Vimont. Canadian II Corps would secure the area from Colombelles to Vaucelles and I Corps on the left would clear the string of villages from Touffréville to Emiéville and then capture Troarn. The air forces were to neutralise the German strongholds on the flanks of the attack and to obliterate Cagny while the area beyond the Caen–Cagny–Vimont railway would be carpeted with fragmentation bombs, to avoid cratering.

It was on July 17, while making a final survey of his defensive dispositions that General Rommel sustained severe concussion. His car was chased by a British aircraft, the driver struck down and the car wrecked.

Shortly after dawn on July 18 the air forces opened the battle with the heaviest and most sustained bombardment so far attempted in support of ground forces. At 0745 hours, 11th Armoured Division moved forward behind a rolling artillery barrage while bombers swept in to strike at strong-points further ahead. It was not until Cagny was reached that opposition was encountered. In the wrecked village German infantry and anti-tank guns had remained unscathed and to their aid heavy German armour moved up from the south. 11th Armoured Division was checked, as was also the Guards Armoured Division when it turned south-east towards Vimont. Before 7th Armoured Division could reinforce the offensive the German armour attacked and though the Panthers were harried by rocket-firing Typhoons they were successful in halting the British armour.

After a battle which continued far into the night the Canadians cleared Colombelles and gained a foothold in Vaucelles. The Germans withdrew from the Caen suburbs to the western end of the Bourguébus ridge. 3rd Division by-passed Touffréville, which had escaped the bombing, mopped up several wrecked villages and reached the outskirts of Troarn. During the next two days in a number of local actions the Canadians and the British drove the Germans from all the villages on the northern slope of Bourguébus ridge except La Hogue. But before the crest of the ridge could be attacked the weather broke to turn the soil of the Caen plain into a quagmire. General Montgomery therefore withdrew the armoured divisions into reserve.

THE ASSAULT AND LODGEMENT

All the objectives of Operation 'Goodwood' had not been gained, but it was in a sense successful in that the way through Caen had been cleared, the airborne bridgehead had been substantially expanded and German reinforcements were diverted to the Caen area away from that of St. Lô. The losses in killed, wounded and missing during the operation are given in Table 4.

TABLE 4

	Guards Armd. Division	7th Armd. Division	11th Armd. Division	Totals
VIII Corps				
July 18	137	48	336	521
July 19	33	67	399	499
I Corps				
July 18				651
July 19				541
				2,212

(ii)

The Assault and Lodgement. Medical Cover (21 Army Group Formations)

6TH AIRBORNE DIVISION

This division was formed in April 1943. To complete its medical establishment 224 and 225 Parachute Field Ambulances were raised. A nucleus for each of these medical units was readily obtained but it soon became evident that, owing to the generally low medical categories of R.A.M.C. personnel, it would be impossible to recruit sufficient volunteers of the high standard of physical fitness required from within the Corps. War Office approval was therefore sought to call for volunteers from the many groups of conscientious objectors who had been drafted to bomb disposal squads throughout the country. Some 450 volunteers were obtained from this source. They were interviewed by senior R.A.M.C. officers who selected from them some 130 as being suitable in all respects for training as parachutists and these were posted to the Airborne Forces Training Depot where they were enrolled. It is worthy of note that their records indicated that they were conscientious objectors, that it was clearly understood that they were not to be called upon to bear arms against their wish and that they would not be eligible for promotion to non-commissioned rank unless they renounced their objections. It is noteworthy, too, that although many of them subsequently elected to carry arms in action, there was no instance of a conscientious objector renouncing his objections in order to gain N.C.O. rank, although many of them were in every way suitable for such promotion.

Once the personnel of the field ambulances had qualified as parachutists they entered upon a long period of intensive individual and unit training. This was largely based upon the lessons learnt from the experiences of 16 Para. Fd. Amb. of 1st Airborne Division in North Africa and Sicily. From the frequent brigade and divisional exercises it was learnt that it was advantageous to divide the personnel of the field ambulance into a number of teams, every man being so trained that he could undertake any one of the many tasks that a team must perform with equal efficiency and so to distribute the equipment that partial loss did not completely dislocate the work of the unit. It was found that the load that could be placed on a man who had to jump and then carry it over long distances during an approach march was limited to 20–25 lb. in the pack plus 8–10 lb. hung on the person. This meant that surgical instruments and gear had to be rationed severely. It was decided therefore to run the surgical theatre on a 'cafeteria' system in which all the available instruments were kept sterilised on a central table, the surgeons drawing from this pool whatever they required for each case.

It was accepted that during the assault landing phase of Operation 'Overlord' there would be a flood of casualties that would strain the resources of the medical units to the limit and result in a great accumulation of patients awaiting operation. It was necessary, therefore, to adopt a system of selection which would pick out those cases which would suffer most from delay. Priority was to be given to open fractures, particularly of the femur, abdominal cases who would be reasonable risks following resuscitation, extensive flesh wounds in which gas gangrene was likely to develop and open chest wounds. It was decided that head injuries should wait for better facilities, following first-aid measures. It was accepted that the cases requiring surgical intervention would be major ones, each demanding about an hour on the table so that each surgeon could deal with 12 to 16 cases in the 24 hours. It was decided to make the officer in charge of resuscitation responsible for determining the order of the cases in the operating list and so to train the nursing orderlies that they could assume responsibility for post-operative care. It was agreed that within the division a common plan of progressive treatment for each category of casualty should be adopted. It was assumed that all casualties would have to be held for a period up to 72 hours until the ground force joined up with the airborne. So, in order that the field ambulances might hold as well as collect and treat their patients, six surgeons were included within the divisional medical establishment. Each of the three field ambulances had, in addition to the usual complement of medical officers, nursing orderlies, stretcher-bearers, cooks, clerks and drivers, two surgeons and a dental officer well versed in anaesthesia. One section of the field ambulance was made responsible for the reception, recording and sorting of the admissions, these being classified as (1) those requiring minor treatment only and (2) those requiring surgery and/or resuscitation. The first category was directed to the second section of the unit in the minor treatment centre where they were either retained for subsequent evacuation or else discharged to their units. The second category of casualties was referred to the third section of the unit in the resuscitation wing. Each of the two surgical teams of each field ambulance consisted of a surgeon, an anaesthetist, 2 O.R.As., 3 N.Os. and 1 G.D.O. In action one orderly 'scrubbed up', one was responsible for the sterile instruments, one for the pressure stoves for the sterilisers, the dirty instruments and jaconet towels, one for preparing the next patient or for plastering after operation and the remaining two for the post-operative care of the patients in the 'ward' and for the supervision of any extra orderlies that had been provided.

When the division moved into the sealed camps every officer and other rank was thoroughly briefed for the impending operation. Everyone was told exactly what he was to do, shown aerial photographs and maps of the area around the dropping zone, given all available information concerning the German positions and defensive plans and also concerning the local F.F.I. and shown photographs of the château in Ranville in which the first M.D.S. was to be established, and of alternative routes to it from the dropping zone.

Each battalion had with it a section of the field ambulance that was assigned to the brigade to which the battalion belonged. D.A.D.H. 6th Airborne Division accompanied 8 Fd. Amb. of 3rd Division ashore to act as liaison officer, for this division was to be responsible for the evacuation of 6th Airborne Division's casualties once contact between these two divisions had been made.

The *coup de main* party which crash-landed near the bridges had with it one medical officer, 2 medical orderlies and 6 stretcher-bearers. Before it was withdrawn at 1700 hours on D-day 18 British and 6 German casualties were collected and treated by this medical detachment.

225 Para. Fd. Amb. was the first of the medical units to drop. The drop at 0100 hours on June 6 was accurate and there were no casualties. The personnel quickly gathered at the appointed unit rendezvous and moved at once to the preselected château where by 0330 hours the M.D.S. was established. When the roar of the rockets from the assault craft four miles away was first heard, one of the surgical teams was

already operating. The second surgical team reached the château shortly afterwards and thereafter the two teams worked without ceasing until the evening of D-day + 1. The A.D.S. established by the medical detachment attached to 7th Para. Bn. on the west side of the bridge over the canal was captured by the Germans but the personnel managed to escape.

224 Para. Fd. Amb., dropping, became widely scattered and was obliged to function in the form of a number of detachments deficient in respect of equipment. Its M.D.S. was eventually established at Le Mesnil at 0850 hours on D-day and casualties from 8th and 9th Para. Bns. and from Cdn. 1st Para. Battalion were admitted. As two surgeons and about two-thirds of the O.Rs. were late in joining the M.D.S. its staff was hard pressed. There were many casualties among R.A.M.C. personnel attached to the battalions. It was not until the early hours of D-day + 1 that A.D.M.S. 6th Airborne Division was able to make contact with this unit.

195 A/L Fd. Amb. emplaned during the afternoon of June 6 in 6 gliders. The equipment was distributed among all the machines. With the unit went 3 jeeps and trailers. Every man carried two bottles of plasma in his pouches (a total of 200 bottles). The unit landed at 2100 hours on D-day on landing zones on either side of the River Orne and the Caen Canal and proceeded to the château in Ranville. Early on June 7 the unit moved to Le Mariquet and opened its M.D.S. which continued to function until the end of June 8.

During the rest of the month of June there was no further movement of these field ambulances. The link-up of ground and airborne forces occurred on D-day + 2. Thereafter evacuation of 6th Airborne Division's casualties from the M.D.Ss. to the beaches began. There was much fighting and many casualties during the rest of the month but no medical problems of unexpected complexity presented themselves. The co-operation which 6th Airborne Division received from I Corps, 3rd Division and S.S. Bde. medical services enabled those of the Airborne Division to discharge their functions satisfactorily.

D.D.M.S. Airborne Troops disembarked on Mike beach on June 18 and joined H.Q. 6th Airborne Division.

TABLE 5

Casualties, R.A.M.C., up to 1200 hours June 20

Numbers brought in by air	Offrs.	O.Rs.
195 A/L Fd. Amb.	12	112
224 Para. Fd. Amb.	12	120
225 Para. Fd. Amb.	12	135
Divisional H.Q.	2	5

THE ASSAULT AND LODGEMENT

Table 5 continued

	Killed	Wounded	Missing	Totals
H.Q. 6th Airborne Division	—	1	2	3
195 A/L Fd. Amb.	3	8	—	11
With battalions of 6th A/L Bde.	1	1	—	2
224 Para. Fd. Amb.	—	—	47	47
With battalions of 3rd Para. Bde.	—	—	25	25
225 Para. Fd. Amb.	4	6	11	21
With battalions of 5th Para. Bde.	1	9	5	15
Cdn. Para. Bn.	—	—	4	4
	9	25	94	128

TABLE 6

Admissions to the M.D.Ss. of 6th Airborne Division. June 6–30

Date	195 A/L Fd. Amb.			224 Para. Fd. Amb.			225 Para. Fd. Amb.			Totals
	B.C.	Sick	P.o.W.	B.C.	Sick	P.o.W.	B.C.	Sick	P.o.W.	
June 6	—	—	—	—	—	—	181	—	14	195
7	154	—	10	84	—	7	174	—	5	434
8	105	5	13	62	1	10	53	—	2	251
9	156	—	1	32	—	7	30	—	—	226
10	224	—	41	29	1	13	24	1	4	337
11	47	4	—	126	—	2	24	3	11	217
12	40	1	4	121	1	—	18	2	4	191
13	124	—	2	95	1	3	191	2	20	438
14	34	1	2	34	3	—	16	2	—	92
15	23	2	—	13	—	1	19	5	1	64
16	76	—	3	47	1	1	40	22	—	190
17	36	12	—	33	4	—	12	13	—	110
18	73	—	—	32	5	2	1	9	—	122
19	98	—	1	21	2	1	—	—	—	123
20	83	16	—	—	—	—	—	—	—	99
21	60	16	—	—	—	—	—	—	—	76
22	37	11	—	—	—	—	1	4	—	53
23	36	10	—	—	—	—	2	9	—	57
24	22	5	—	—	—	—	2	4	—	33
25	62	7	—	—	—	—	—	5	—	74
26	23	10	—	—	—	—	1	5	—	39
27	20	4	—	—	—	—	4	8	—	36
28	25	8	—	—	—	—	3	12	—	48
29	27	8	—	—	—	—	6	16	—	57
30	40	8	—	—	—	—	4	6	—	58
	1,625	128	77	729	19	47	806	128	61	3,620
Totals		1,830			795			995		

On July 1 the divisional H.Q. moved from Ranville to the quarries at Ecarde. It now became possible for the field ambulances to set up a skin and V.D. centre with a P.A.C. (224 Para. Fd. Amb.) and a disinfestation

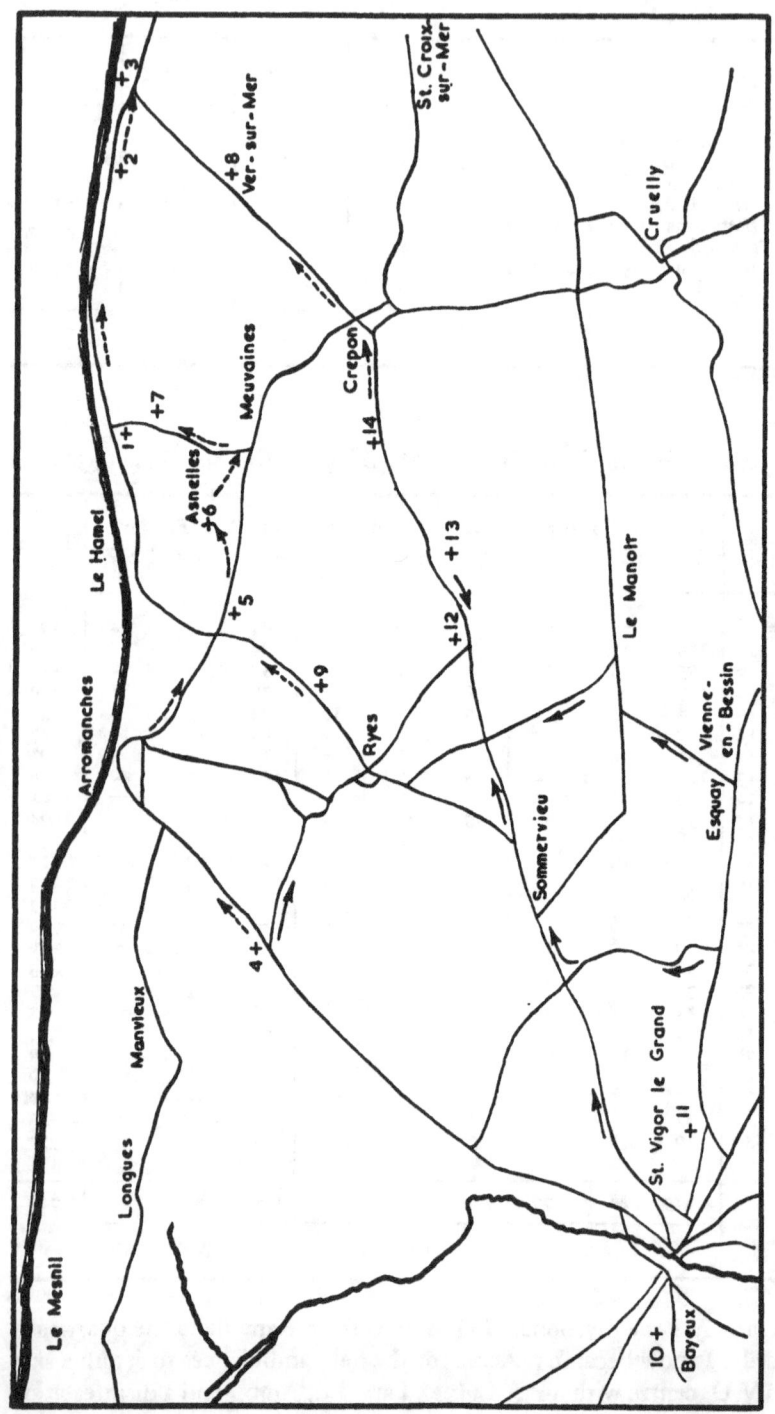

Fig. 5. 50th Division. The Assault Landing and Lodgement. Medical Cover.*

THE ASSAULT AND LODGEMENT

centre (225 Para. Fd. Amb.) and to pay careful attention to the hygiene of the divisional units.

50TH (NORTHUMBRIAN) DIVISION

For the assault phase, to this division with its 69th, 151st and 231st Bdes. were added 56th Independent Bde., 8th Armd. Bde. and 104 Beach Sub-Area. Its medical component consisted of:

A.D.M.S. and Staff

50th Division	56th Bde.	8th Armd. Bde.	
149, 186 and 200 Fd. Ambs.	203 Fd. Amb.	168 Lt. Fd. Amb.	3 C.C.S. attached from Corps
47 and 48 F.D.Ss.			
22 Fd. Hyg. Sec.			

104 Beach Sub-Area
Beach Group B.D.Ss.
 „   „   F.D.Ss.

The 50th Division that landed was the product of much experience in the Western Desert and Sicily. Its medical services had developed clear-cut ideas concerning the medical equipment necessary for battle conditions and while preparing for Operation 'Overlord' had obtained

---

* *Key to Fig. 5*

1. B.D.S. June 6
2. B.D.S. June 6
3. C.E.P.
4. C.C.P. 200 Fd. Amb. June 8–10
5. A.D.S. 200 Fd. Amb. June 7–9
6. Beach F.D.S. June 6–8
7. C.C.P. 200 Fd. Amb. June 6
8. A.D.S. 186 Fd. Amb. June 6 till 2100 hrs.
   Beach F.D.S. after 2100 hrs.
9. C.C.P. 203 Fd. Amb. June 6
   A.D.S. 203 Fd. Amb. June 8–12
10. C.C.P. 203 Fd. Amb. June 7–12
    A.D.S. 203 Fd. Amb. June 12–14
    A.D.S. 200 Fd. Amb. June 9–23
    C.C.P. 200 Fd. Amb. June 10–12
    A.D.S. 186 Fd. Amb. June 14–19
11. 10 C.C.S. June 12–19
12. 3 C.C.S. June 8–12
13. A.D.S. 149 Fd. Amb. June 7–9
14. A.D.S. 186 Fd. Amb. June 6 after 2100 hrs.

- - - -→ Route of evacuation to Beach F.D.S.—B.D.S.—C.E.P. June 6–8

⎯⎯→ Evacuation route to 3 C.C.S. June 8–12

much that was not standard. Sufficient canvas was collected for the making of 40 × 40 ft. penthouses, which added to the No. 14 Lorry Shelter produced an excellent replica of the New Zealand Penthouse. It was proposed to issue five of these to each field ambulance and two to each F.D.S. but XXX Corps decided to undertake this work for all its divisions with the result that 50th Division got only three per ambulance and one per F.D.S. (In this connexion it is to be noted that canvas was in very short supply and that it would have been quite impossible at the time to make these penthouses a general issue.) 40-gallon tanks with taps

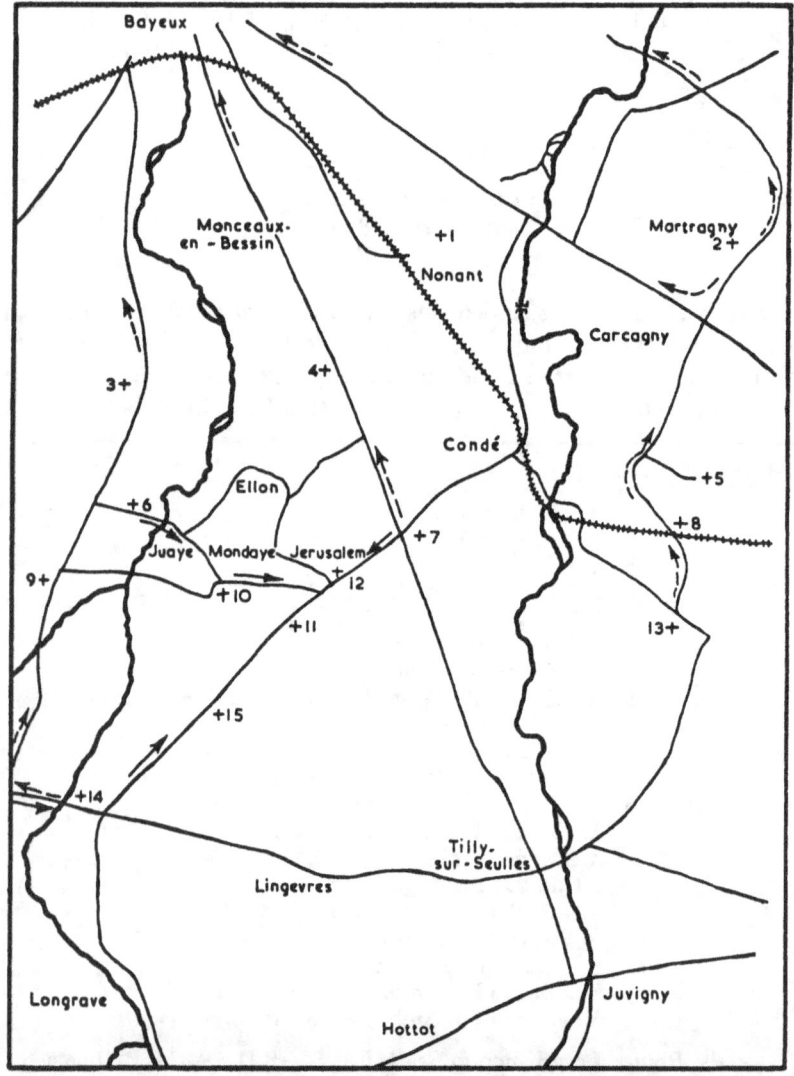

FIG. 6. 50th Division. Medical Cover. June.*

THE ASSAULT AND LODGEMENT

for the penthouse lorry were obtained from C.R.E. on the scale of two per unit. Large tea urns with taps were obtained from the B.R.C.S. on the scale of one per unit for use in connexion with these penthouses.

The Bergen jacket was adopted for the assault. An extra medical pannier was issued to each field ambulance and extra items of medical supplies obtained. These included plaster-of-paris, sterile vaseline gauze, morphia syrettes and whole blood.

The assault went very much according to plan. The field ambulances opened C.C.Ps. as soon as transport began to come ashore (*see* Plates I–III). Prior to this the assault sections of the field ambulance attached to the battalions followed on the battalion axis, nesting casualties which were later evacuated by jeep to the B.D.Ss. and later on to the F.D.Ss. By the time 3 C.C.S. was established the medical units were functioning normally, the assault sections were recalled and each field ambulance established a forward C.C.P. with 3 M.Os., 1 N.M.O. and some 60 O.Rs. R.A.M.C. and behind this an A.D.S. consisting of the remainder of the field ambulance.

The A.D.Ss. of 186 and 200 Fd. Ambs. served 151st Bde. and 56th Bde. until D-day+3 when 149 and 203 Fd. Ambs. also opened their A.D.Ss. and the whole four then served these brigades for a few days for the reason that each of them had a very wide and separate frontage (*see* Plate X). Later one A.D.S. proved to be sufficient to serve both

* *Key to* Fig. 6

1. C.C.P. 149 Fd. Amb. June 7–11
   A.D.S. 149 Fd. Amb. June 9–14
2. C.C.P. 186 Fd. Amb. June 7–10
   A.D.S. 186 Fd. Amb. June 9–14
3. C.C.P. 200 Fd. Amb. June 12–19
4. C.C.P. 203 Fd. Amb. June 12–15
   A.D.S. 203 Fd. Amb. June 14–15 (left command)
   A.D.S. 168 Lt. Fd. Amb. June 13
5. C.C.P. 186 Fd. Amb. June 12–14
6. A.D.S. 200 Fd. Amb. June 23–30
7. C.C.P. 149 Fd. Amb. June 12–14
   A.D.S. 149 Fd. Amb. June 15–30
8. C.C.P. 186 Fd. Amb. June 15–30
9. A.D.S. 186 Fd. Amb. June 23–30
10. 48 F.D.S. June 14–30
11. C.C.P. 186 Fd. Amb. June 15 (on wheels)
12. 3 C.C.S. June 19–30
13. C.C.P. (Lt.) 186 Fd. Amb. June 19–30
14. C.C.P. 186 Fd. Amb. June 16–30
    A.D.S. 186 Fd. Amb. June 19–21
15. C.C.P. 200 Fd. Amb. June 19–30
    A.D.S. (Lt.) 200 Fd. Amb. June 19–23

- - - - → Evacuation route to 3 C.C.S. June 8–12 or to 10 C.C.S. June 12–19
———→ Evacuation route to 3 C.C.S. June 19–30

brigades. When 3 C.C.S. moved to Jerusalem the A.D.Ss., with the exception of that of 149 Fd. Amb., were closed, for the C.C.S. was only three miles from the front line and the C.C.Ps. could evacuate direct to it. When 47 F.D.S. arrived its resuscitation team, with lorry and penthouse and full equipment, was brought forward and allocated to that C.C.P. most heavily employed. 48 F.D.S., arriving on June 14, was established in the Abbey at Juaye-Mondaye to take all minor sick and to hold and treat malaria relapses (*see* Plate IX).

Evacuation from R.A.P. to C.C.P. was by 5-cwt. ambulance cars and 2-stretcher ambulance cars, and from C.C.P. to A.D.S. or C.C.S. by 2-stretcher and 4-stretcher ambulance cars. M.A.C. cars were not required or called for by the division during the assault phase.

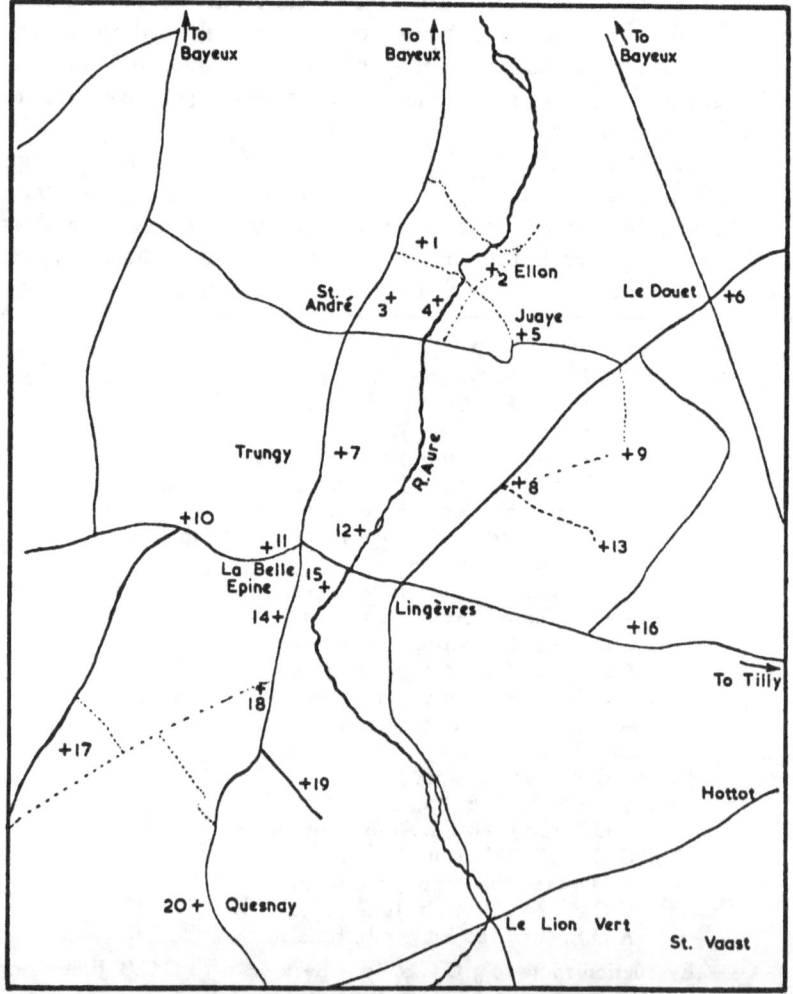

FIG. 7. 50th Division. Medical Cover. July.*

THE ASSAULT AND LODGEMENT

During July, 50th Division was continuously involved in the fighting south-west of Tilly-sur-Seulles, all the brigades being in the line. A constant stream of casualties flowed into the divisional medical units. Evacuation was direct from brigade C.C.P. to 3 C.C.S., the greatest distance between these being six to seven miles.

TABLE 7
50th Division. Casualties. June–July
Admissions to Divisional Medical Units (149, 186, 200, 203 Fd. Ambs. and 48 F.D.S.)

June 6	29	June 6–30	Offrs.	O.Rs.
7	169	149 Fd. Amb.	52	710
		186 ,, ,,	52	550
		200 ,, ,,	54	715
		203 ,, ,,	6	108
		48 F.D.S.	—	2
			164	2,085

---

* *Key to Fig. 7*
  1. A.D.S. 200 Fd. Amb. July 1–28
     C.C.P. 200 Fd. Amb. July 22–28
  2. A.D.S. 200 Fd. Amb. July 29–31
  3. 48 F.D.S. July 25–31
  4. C.C.P. 186 Fd. Amb. July 27–31
  5. 48 F.D.S. July 1–25
     47 F.D.S. July 25–31
  6. C.C.P. 149 Fd. Amb. July 1–7
     A.D.S. 149 Fd. Amb. July 1–27
  7. A.D.S. 203 Fd. Amb. July 4–20 (left command)
     47 F.D.S. July 21
  8. C.C.P. 200 Fd. Amb. July 1–9
  9. C.C.P. 149 Fd. Amb. July 8–10
  10. A.D.S. 203 Fd. Amb. July 1–7
  11. C.C.P. 168 Lt. Fd. Amb. July 17–20
      A.D.S. 149 Fd. Amb. July 28–29
  12. C.C.P. 186 Fd. Amb. July 1–19
      A.D.S. 168 Lt. Fd. Amb. July 21–31
  13. C.C.P. 149 Fd. Amb. July 11–21
  14. C.C.P. 203 Fd. Amb. July 9
  15. A.D.S. 149 Fd. Amb. July 29–31
  16. C.C.P. 149 Fd. Amb. July 22–31
  17. C.C.P. 203 Fd. Amb. July 1–8
      C.C.P. 203 Fd. Amb. July 10–20 (left command)
  18. 47 F.D.S. July 22–25
      C.C.P. 163 Fd. Amb. July 25–28 (relieved 203 with 56th Bde.)
  19. C.C.P. 186 Fd. Amb. July 20–26
      C.C.P. 200 Fd. Amb. July 27–31
  20. C.C.P. 163 Fd. Amb. July 30–31

Table 7 continued

Casualties admitted direct to B.D.S.

	Offrs.	O.Rs.
	23	146

Killed and Missing. June 6–30

	Offrs.	O.Rs.
Killed . . .	60	473
Missing . . .	33	939
	93	1,412

Battle Casualties admitted to Divisional Medical Units. July

	Offrs.	O.Rs.
	43	873
56th Bde.	17	265
Killed . . .	19	167
Missing . . .	2	40
	21	207

Week ending	Malaria and Pyrexia N.Y.D.	Exhaustion
June 10	85	6
17	112	77
24	130	85
July 1	172	120

CANADIAN 3RD DIVISION*

The assault sections of 14, 22 and 23 (Cdn.) Fd. Ambs. were attached to Cdn. 7th, 8th and 9th Bdes. respectively and landed with them. For the first few days or so they remained in the beach area collecting, treating and nesting casualties and then as the battalions moved inland they followed close behind. Then 22 (Cdn.) Fd. Amb. landed at about 1800 hours and established its A.D.S. at Bény-sur-Mer. On the morning of June 7 its assault sections rejoined the unit. C.C.Ps. were set up at Cairon and at Neuf Mer. Admissions were few, averaging about twelve per day. The field ambulance remained at Bény until July 4.

14 (Cdn.) Fd. Amb., landing, set up an A.D.S. (on wheels) at Banville and on the 7th at Pierrepont. Evacuation from the three assault sections

---

* For a fuller account of the affairs of this division the *Official History of the Canadian Medical Services 1939–1945* should be consulted.

THE ASSAULT AND LODGEMENT 139

with the battalions was by jeeps sent forward from the A.D.S. On June 8 a C.C.P. was set up at Secqueville-en-Bessin and this cleared 115 casualties to the A.D.S. during the next three days. When the fighting died down an exhaustion centre was organised by the divisional neuro-psychiatrist in association with the A.D.S. at Pierrepont. During the period D-day to D-day + 24 the field ambulance dealt with 977 casualties.

23 (Cdn.) Fd. Amb. landed on D-day + 1 and established itself in a quarry near Reviers where its assault sections rejoined it on June 9, when evacuation was through the C.C.S. at Reviers. On June 14 a section of the unit was sent to Fontaine-Henri to deal with casualties in the divisional administrative area and the ambulance itself moved to a site near Amblie. On June 26 the headquarters of the unit moved to Bény-sur-Mer.

For the assault 102 Beach Sub-area was under the command of the Canadian division. Following the assault sections of the field ambulances ashore it established a beach maintenance area. The B.S.A. was composed of a headquarters and two beach groups, one to each brigade. The medical component of each beach group consisted of two F.D.Ss., two F.S.Us., one F.T.U., one surgical team, a detachment of a field sanitary section, a Pioneer company and a C.E.P. (half of a F.D.S.). Each light section of the F.D.Ss. set up a B.D.S. Of the main sections one combined with the surgical team, the two F.S.Us. and the F.T.U. to form an advanced surgical centre, the other functioned normally as a F.D.S. The B.D.Ss. were established early in the assault phase and when the beaches were secure two advanced surgical centres were established about a mile inland, one at Bernières-sur-Mer and the other at Graye-sur-Mer. During the next four days they performed some 200 major operations and treated about 1,800 casualties. They continued to function until June 19.

There was no evacuation by sea on D-day but on June 7 a few scattered groups of casualties were taken off in the assault craft to the L.S.T., and D.U.K.Ws. were used to move casualties from the beach to the F.D.Ss. a mile or so inland. On June 8 a L.S.T. was made available for evacuation purposes and over 300 casualties were taken off. Thereafter, until the hospitals were established in the bridgehead area, a constant stream of L.S.T. kept the area clear of casualties and save for the period of the great storm—June 15–19—no interruptions were experienced in the flow of casualties from Normandy to the United Kingdom. The policy of using medically adapted L.S.T. and the allocation of D.U.K.Ws. for medical purposes worked most satisfactorily.

The medical officers and other ranks assigned to the L.S.T. joined their craft on May 30. These vessels made the outward trip heavily laden with personnel and material but were fitted to carry 300 casualties

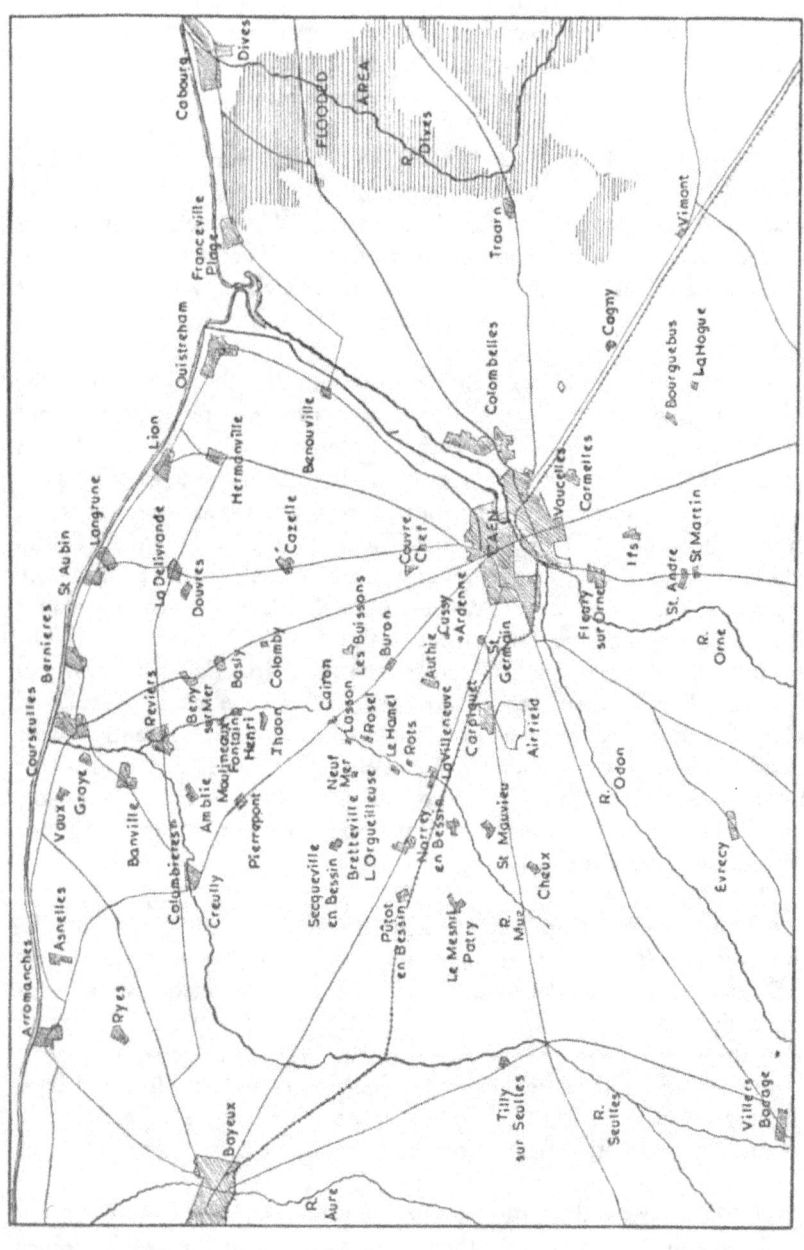

Fig. 8. The Inland Advance of the Canadians.

on the return journey. They each made about five trips. On the lower deck was an improvised operating theatre. By June 17 the need for medical crews from Army sources had passed and the personnel rejoined their parent units.

On July 4 the Canadians attacked with the Carpiquet airfield as their objective. Carpiquet village was taken but only part of the airfield could be held. On July 8 the attack on Caen opened. Cdn. 8th Bde. took Buron and Authie and Cdn. 7th Bde. drove on to Cussy and Ardenne. On July 9–10 Caen was occupied as far as the Orne.

17 (Cdn.) Lt. Fd. Amb. arrived on June 13 and proceeded to a location on the River Seulles near Colombiers-sur-Seulles. On the 22nd its headquarters moved to Bény-sur-Mer and two sections were detached to serve the regiments of Cdn. 2nd Armd. Bde. A third section was sent to Moulineaux to serve the brigade troops in this area.

For the attack on Carpiquet 22 (Cdn.) Fd. Amb. established a C.C.P. at St. Mauvieu, three miles west of Carpiquet, in addition to the one at Cairon. 14 (Cdn.) Fd. Amb. sent six heavy ambulance cars and two jeeps to a point just north of Bretteville-l'Orgueilleuse where 17 (Cdn.) Lt. Fd. Amb. set up a C.C.P.

Casualties were heavy and were evacuated through Neuf Mer and St. Mauvieu. 343 casualties were evacuated to 33 C.C.S. near Secqueville-en-Bessin.

In preparation for the attack on Caen on July 8, 23 (Cdn.) Fd. Amb. established a C.C.P. of two sections at Les Buissons to clear Cdn. 9th Bde. 22 (Cdn.) Fd. Amb. maintained its C.C.P. at St. Mauvieu to clear 8th Bde. and 14 (Cdn.) Fd. Amb. set up a C.C.P. at Cairon and maintained the one at Neuf Mer to clear 7th Bde. 17 (Cdn.) Lt. Fd. Amb. established a C.C.P. near Rots to evacuate casualties from Cdn. 2nd Armd. Bde. As the battle progressed these units moved forward with the armoured regiments, evacuating to Pierrepont or Bény-sur-Mer.

Twenty additional ambulance cars were assigned to Canadian 3rd Division for this operation. Twelve of them were attached to the advanced surgical centre at Pierrepont and eight at Bény-sur-Mer. Evacuation from Bény and Pierrepont and from 33 C.C.S. at Secqueville-en-Bessin was to the medical centre at La Délivrande. For the first twenty-four hours evacuation from the C.C.Ps. was along the Buron–Cairon road to Pierrepont. When the A.D.S. there was more than fully occupied 23 (Cdn.) Fd. Amb's. A.D.S. at Bény received for four hours, evacuation being by way of Cairon–Thaon–Basly for the reason that the more direct route was under shellfire. This was also the reason why 23 (Cdn.) Fd. Amb's. C.C.P. at Les Buissons had not been able to go forward to Buron to clear the casualties of Cdn. 9th Bde. During this action the Canadian medical units dealt with 744 casualties, of whom 684 were Canadians. By the evening of the 9th the whole of Caen north of the Orne was in Allied hands but as mopping up operations proceeded further casualties flowed into the divisional medical units, 356 including 308 Canadians and 36 P.o.W. on July 9 and 112 including 110 Canadians on the 10th.

On July 9, 22 (Cdn.) Fd. Amb's. A.D.S. at Bény-sur-Mer moved up to the vicinity of La Villeneuve and that of 14 (Cdn.) Fd. Amb. from Pierrepont to Cairon. Casualties from Cdn. 8th Bde. were thereafter evacuated to Secqueville, all others to La Délivrande.

CANADIAN II CORPS

On July 10, Canadian 2nd Division with 10, 11 and 18 (Cdn.) Fd. Ambs., 4 and 21 (Cdn.) F.D.Ss. and 13 (Cdn.) Fd. Hyg. Sec. arrived and on the following day Canadian II Corps, with Canadian 2nd and 3rd Divisions and Cdn. 2nd Armd. Bde. under command, took over the Caen sector. During Operation 'Goodwood' the task of the Canadians was that of advancing across the Orne and seizing the heights west of the Caen–Falaise road. But by July 22 the Germans had been driven back only about four miles south and east of Caen.

For this operation a medical centre was formed in the Secqueville-en-Bessin area. Here 2 and 3 (Cdn.) C.C.Ss. and 9 (Cdn.) Fd. Amb. (the corps field ambulance), together with F.S.Us. and F.T.Us., were concentrated. 6 (Cdn.) C.C.S. was at Cazelle u/c Canadian II Corps with 10 (Cdn.) F.D.S. alongside. 6 (Cdn.) F.D.S. was located at Thaon and to it was attached 1 (Cdn.) V.D.T.U. and 1 (Cdn.) Exhaustion Unit. 5 and 7 (Cdn.) F.D.Ss. and 7 (Cdn.) Fd. Hyg. Sec., belonging to Canadian 3rd Division but held in reserve during the assault phase, had by this time arrived in Normandy.

The field ambulances supported their respective brigades:

Canadian 2nd Division			*Canadian 3rd Division*		
11	with Cdn.	4th Bde.	14	with Cdn.	7th Bde.
18	,,	5th ,,	22	,,	8th ,,
10	,,	6th ,,	23	,,	9th ,,

Evacuation was from the A.D.S. of 18 (Cdn.) Fd. Amb. at Caen to the Canadian medical area at Secqueville for Canadian 2nd Division and from the A.D.S. of 23 (Cdn.) Fd. Amb. at Couvre Chef for Canadian 3rd Division. Because of the shelling D.U.K.Ws. could not be used and Canadian 3rd Division casualties had to be moved across the bridge at Bénouville and on to the medical centre at La Délivrande. By July 19 two bridges had been constructed across the Orne and so the evacuation route was greatly shortened. On Canadian 3rd Division front casualties were thereafter directed to 5 (Cdn.) F.D.S. at Couvre Chef and thence to Secqueville.

18 (Cdn.) Fd. Amb. evacuated 75 casualties on the night of July 18/19 from Canadian 2nd Division south of Caen, on July 19, 160 and on July 20, 341. In Canadian 3rd Division sector 23 (Cdn.) Fd. Amb. was used as the forward collecting post in conjunction with 5 (Cdn.) F.D.S. as the A.D.S. to receive casualties evacuated by both 14 and 22 (Cdn.) Fd. Ambs.' C.C.Ps. in the city. In the six days July 16–22 the A.D.S. of 23 (Cdn.) Fd. Amb. treated 338 casualties, almost all of them from Canadian 3rd Division area.

Then, while holding on to their positions, the Canadians prepared for Operation 'Spring', designed to seize the high ground on either side of the Falaise road south of Caen, on July 25. For this operation the Guards and 7th Armoured Division came u/c Canadian II Corps.

14 and 22 (Cdn.) Fd. Ambs. established A.D.Ss. at Fleury-sur-Orne and Caen and C.C.Ps. in Ifs. The A.D.Ss. were bombed on three consecutive nights and had fourteen casualties among unit personnel. On Canadian 3rd Division front the fighting along the Verrières Ridge was fierce and the Canadians were checked. 10 (Cdn.) Fd. Amb. and 21 (Cdn.) F.D.S. opened in caves at Fleury-sur-Orne. 11 (Cdn.) Fd. Amb. in Caen was held in reserve. 18 (Cdn.) Fd. Amb. on wheels in Caen was prepared to receive overflow cases. 2 (Cdn.) M.A.C. had its headquarters in Caen. During the fighting on July 25 the A.D.S. of 10 (Cdn.) Fd. Amb. cleared over 400 casualties in the twenty-four hours and 11 (Cdn.) Fd. Amb. some 250. On the 26th these two units admitted 285 casualties. Evacuation from the A.D.S. was by M.A.C. to the medical centre at St. Germain. Exhaustion cases were dealt with by 7 (Cdn.) F.D.S. at Beauregard Château (Canadian 3rd Division) and by the corps exhaustion centre at Thaon (Canadian 2nd Division).

By July 26, 7, 8 and 10 Cdn.G.Hs. (a total of 2,400 beds) were in Normandy and had been established in the Medical Area, Bayeux. On the 31st, 6 Cdn.G.H. (Canadian Army) opened at Douvres-la-Délivrande. Nevertheless, the policy of evacuating all casualties not likely to be fit for duty within seven days was continued. 16, 20 and 21 Cdn.G.Hs. were in the United Kingdom awaiting transport to the Continent.

In the United Kingdom 9 Cdn.G.H. at Horsham, 12 Cdn.G.H. at Horley and 13 Cdn.G.H. at Cuckfield had been classified as 'coastal hospitals'. 9 Cdn.G.H. received its first casualties on June 8, 12 Cdn.G.H. on the 9th and 13 Cdn.G.H. not until the 21st, and these all P.o.W.

2 Cdn.G.H. at Bramshott, 4 Cdn.G.H. at Aldershot and 17 Cdn.G.H. at Crowthorne had been designated as 'transit hospitals'. 22 Cdn.G.H. took over from 2 Cdn.G.H. on July 1. 2 Cdn.G.H. received 238 casualties on the 8th by ambulance train. On the same day 4 Cdn.G.H. received 278. On June 9, 17 Cdn.G.H. received its first group of 213.

The number of casualties received by these Canadian hospitals during the assault phase was far less than expected and among these there were but few Canadians. Thus, for example, of 2,191 casualties received by 17 Cdn.G.H. up to June 16 not more than 20 per cent. were Canadians. The hospital was therefore instructed to retain all Canadian casualties. On July 31 this hospital ceased to function as a transit hospital.

Because these coastal and transit hospitals were at no time overtaxed the 'home base hospitals' received far fewer casualties than had been expected and so their main function continued to be the hospitalisation of Canadian troops remaining in the United Kingdom.

3RD DIVISION

The divisional medical planning, as revealed in 3rd Division Medical Operations Instruction No. 1, was most detailed and comprehensive and will serve to illustrate the prevailing policy as interpreted at divisional level.

1. *Information*
   (a) 3rd Infantry Division is part of a force landing on the Continent of Europe.
   (b) Order of Battle (medical), *see* Appendix to this Instruction.

2. *Intention*
   (a) To collect and render first aid to all casualties.
   (b) To evacuate to the United Kingdom all transportable casualties.
   (c) To retain and treat any casualties unfit to be moved.

3. *Method*
   Allotment of Divisional Medical Units.
   (a) One Fd. Amb. to each Bde. Group.
   (b) One sec. of above at assault scales will land with each bn. and maintain contact.
   (c) Remainder of Fd. Amb. at assault scales will land at approximately the same time as Bde. H.Q.

4. *Beach Medical Units*
   (a) Each Beach Group is allotted two F.D.Ss., two F.S.Us. and one F.T.U.
   (b) Following will land first tide:
       Medical units of 5 Beach Group.
       Lt. Secs. of F.D.Ss. 6 Beach Group.
       1 Casualty Evacuating Point.
       303 Pioneer Coy. for medical use.
       Marching personnel of 16 C.C.S.
   (c) Following will land second tide:
       Medical units of 6 Beach Group (less Lt. Secs. of F.D.Ss.).
       20 Port Detach. R.A.M.C.

THE ASSAULT AND LODGEMENT

16 C.C.S. (less marching personnel)
55 F.S.U. (attached 16 C.C.S.) } allotted by I Corps
29 F.T.U. („ „ „)

5. *Opening of Medical Installations*
   (a) One B.D.S. will be established on each beach by H-hour+90.
   (b) Medical units of 5 Beach Group will be sited together and will be ready to receive casualties by H-hour+240.
   (c) C.E.P. will be established by H-hour + 360.
   (d) Medical units of 6 Beach Group will be open by 2300 hours D-day.
   (e) 16 C.C.S. (with 55 F.S.U. and 29 F.T.U. attached) will be ready to receive casualties by 1000 hours D-day+1.
   (f) For locations of these units see First Key Plan: concerned addressees may verify at this office.
   (Map references and place names not given for security reasons.)
   (g) Fd. Ambs. will open C.C.Ps. and A.D.Ss. as circumstances dictate.
   (h) 11 Lt. Fd. Amb. will land D-day+2 to D-day+6 and will join Armd. Bde. on arrival.
   (i) Divisional F.D.Ss. will land D-day+4 to D-day+5 when they will proceed to Div. Adm. Area.

6. *Build-up of Medical Units*
   See Appendix to this Instruction (Table 8).
   Divisional medical units will resume their normal rôle as soon as circumstances permit.

7. *Collection of Casualties*
   (a) R.N. is responsible for casualties afloat.
   (b) Army is responsible for all casualties ashore, including naval.
   (c) Casualties in ships will remain in ships.
   (d) Casualties in first flight of assault craft return to parent ship (or ship nominated by R.N.).
   (e) Casualties in subsequent flights will be landed and taken to B.D.S.
   (f) Casualties on beaches and up to main (third) lateral will be collected by S.Bs. of Beach Bn. reinforced by S.Bs. of Pioneer Coy. and taken to the nearest medical installation by hand carriage or amb. jeep.
   (g) Inland casualties will be collected by S.Bs. of Infantry and R.A.M.C.; they will be given first aid and rested on the axis of advance until arrival of transport of Fd. Ambs. which will convey them to F.D.Ss. of Beach Group (*via* A.D.S. when opened).
   (h) Each Fd. Amb. Comd. is responsible for collection of all casualties on his own Bde. front.
   (i) Pending arrival of 11 Lt. Fd. Amb., 9 Fd. Amb. will be prepared to detach two self-contained secs. to support a thrust by Armd. Bde.

8. *Airborne and S.S. Troops*
   (a) Airborne Divisions are landing their own medical units and are establishing a M.D.S. where they will collect and treat casualties from

Airborne Troops and S.S. Troops under command; 3rd Division is responsible for evacuation from this M.D.S.; 8 Fd. Amb. will carry out this evacuation in accordance with instructions already communicated. One liaison medical officer from Airborne Division is landing with 8 Fd. Amb.
- (b) S.S. Troops operating on the beaches will nest their casualties and notify sites of nests to nearest B.D.S. which will arrange collection.

9. *Evacuation to United Kingdom*
- (a) Evacuation to the U.K. will be by specially fitted L.S.T. staffed by R.N. or Army medical personnel and allotted by R.N.; when ready to receive casualties they will fly the 'Mike' international flag.
- (b) One platoon (33) D.U.K.Ws. is allotted for medical use to transport casualties from C.E.P. to L.S.T. Twenty-two D.U.K.Ws. will land on first tide, remainder on D-day + 2.
- (c) D.A.D.M.S.(E) will co-ordinate arrangements on shore. He will notify travel officer in charge ashore (or his representative—naval medical liaison officer) of the numbers of casualties for evacuation. Naval officer in charge will arrange allotment of L.S.T.
- (d) Casualty Evacuation Officer (O.C., C.E.P.) will arrange for loading and despatch of D.U.K.Ws. to L.S.T. He will co-ordinate movement of D.U.K.Ws. with Principal Beach Master and R.A.S.C. officer i/c Medical D.U.K.W. platoon. To prevent delay to L.S.T. a 'cushion' of casualties will be maintained at C.E.P.
- (e) D.A.D.M.S.(E) will notify naval officer in charge when L.S.T. are loaded.
- (f) Hospital carriers will arrive off beaches on second tide D-day + 1. They will be loaded by their own water ambulances (L.C.P.) which will evacuate from C.E.P. direct to hospital carriers.
- (g) Hospital ships will be available when a port is open.
- (h) Air evacuation will probably be available by D-day + 14.

NOTE.—The success of the arrangement for evacuation by sea depends on close personal liaison being maintained on shore between R.N. and Army officers concerned.

10. *Treatment*
- (a) Cases unfit for evacuation to the U.K. will be retained for treatment in: Beach F.D.Ss., F.S.Us. and F.T.Us. open D-day

    C.C.S.   D-day + 1
    General Hospital   D-day + 4
- (b) Surgical. In early stages surgery will be limited to life-saving operations and rendering casualties fit to travel.
- (c) Ophthalmological Section will be attached to a 200-bed general hospital, landing D-day + 4.
- (d) Resuscitation. Plasma will be available in the assault and whole blood by end of D-day. Replenishments of plasma will be in medical maintenance blocks; replenishment of whole blood will be in insulated boxes

THE ASSAULT AND LODGEMENT

each containing 10 bottles and weighing 50 lb., which will be brought ashore from a depot ship and delivered to C.E.P. from D-day+1 onwards; 29 F.T.U. will collect from C.E.P. and arrange distribution. All used transfusion and infusion apparatus will be salvaged. One Advanced Blood Bank will be landed D-day+4 and will be attached to 16 C.C.S.

(e) Venereal Disease. In early stages V.D. will be treated in unit lines—i.e. until a V.D.T.C. is established.

(f) Exhaustion cases will in early stages be transferred as other cases. Copies of a directive by I Corps psychiatrist have been distributed to medical units and R.M.Os.

11. *P.o.W.*
    (a) Wounded P.o.W. will receive normal treatment.
    (b) If a static enemy medical unit is captured enemy wounded therein will not be evacuated until the situation clarifies.

12. *Civilians*
    (a) Military medical administrative authorities are responsible for action necessary to prevent civilian epidemic diseases interfering with Army efficiency.
    (b) Civilians will receive treatment under Civil Affairs Organisations, military medical units assisting where necessary, provided the treatment of military personnel is not thereby prejudiced. During the early stages 8 R.A.M.C. officers and 16 O.Rs. R.A.M.C. from 600-bed hospitals are being loaned to Chief Civil Affairs Officer. These personnel will revert to their units when these arrive on D-day+13. They are not under orders 3rd Division.

13. *Stretchers and Blankets*
    (a) In addition to G.1098 scale, 1,200 stretchers will be landed on D-day in divisional vehicles; a further 750 will be landed in D.U.K.Ws. on first tide as divisional reserve. Each stretcher carries 3 blankets.
    (b) Additional stretchers, blankets and pyjamas will be available in O.B.D. from D-day+1 onwards.

14. *Medical Stores*
    (a) All medical units will carry ashore on the man and in unit transport sufficient medical supplies to last four days.
    (b) Medical maintenance blocks are being landed daily from D-day+1 and will be available at 16 C.C.S.
    (c) It is anticipated that a complete Adv. Depot Med. Stores will be open on D-day+14 at site of 16 C.C.S., with which an advance party lands on D-day+1.

15. *Shell Dressings*
    Two per vehicle will be carried.

16. *Supplies for Casualties*
   (a) Casualties occurring in first forty-eight hours carry their own rations.
   (b) Each Fd. Amb. and F.D.S. will take ashore sufficient tea, sugar and milk to make 100 pints of tea, also a reserve of 100 'compo' rations.
   (c) Rations, water, extra tea, sugar and milk for casualties will be drawn from D.I.D. on D-day+1 onwards.

17. *Medical Pioneer Company*
   The medical Pioneer Company will be used for digging in medical units, stretcher-bearing and loading of D.U.K.Ws. D.A.D.M.S.(E) will allot sections as required.

18. *Sign-posting*
   All medical units and the roads leading thereto will be adequately sign-posted by night and day.

19. *Ambulance Transport*
   Pending arrival of M.A.C. cars on D-day+5, all ambulance transport is liable to be pooled should the necessity arise. Medical units will detach transport as under:

   (a) 8 Fd. Amb.

Amb. car, 2 str. and driver	1	to report to 20/21 F.D.S. by H-hour+4. Subsequently they will be attached to Div. H.Q. for all purposes.
Amb. jeep and driver	1	
D.R. and M/C	1	

   (b) 223 Fd. Amb.

Amb. jeeps and drivers	2	to report to 20/21 F.D.S. by H-hour+5. Subsequently attached to Div. H.Q.
D.R. and M/C	1	

   (c) 9 Fd. Amb.

Jeeps and drivers	2	to report to 20/21 F.D.S. by H-hour+7. Subsequently attached to Div. H.Q.
D.R. and M/C	1	

   NOTE: (i) Transport under (b) and (c) above (less D.Rs.) will remain at disposal of 20/21 F.D.S. until beaches are clear of wounded.
   (ii) As soon as possible 9 and 223 Fd. Ambs. will replace two jeeps by one heavy ambulance car.

20. *Documentation*
   (a) The procedure for the documentation of casualties described in the pamphlet 'Unit Guide to Documentation in a Theatre of War (Overseas) 1944', as modified by Appendix 'B' to 21 Army Group General Routine Order No. 31, dated 21 April 1944, and 'R.A.M.C. Training Pamphlet No. 2 1943', as amended by Amendment No. 1 notified in A.C.I. 12 April 1944, will be followed.
   (b) A.F. W.3118 (Field Medical Card and envelope) will be used for clinical entries at all medical units forward of general hospitals. On discharge

to duty or death of the patient the A.F. W.3118 will be sent to D.M.S. 21 Army Group; otherwise it must accompany the patient to the United Kingdom.
- (c) A.F. W.3211—Sulphanilamide Label. This label will be completed for all surgical or other cases in which sulphonamide drugs have been used; it serves as a record of the total dosage given during evacuation.
- (d) A.F. W.3034 (Reprint) and A.F. W.3034B (Admissions and Discharges in Expeditionary Forces) will be rendered in accordance with instructions printed on these forms.
- (e) It is particularly important that a complete record is maintained of all casualties embarked. C.E.P. is responsible for this and will use either A.F. W.3210 (Revised) or A.F. W.3083 (Revised).
- (f) Every case embarked will have attached A.F. W.3118 in envelope, also A.F. W.3211 if applicable.
- (g) Air Evacuation. Os.C. corps medical units transferring patients by air will ensure that all patients are accompanied by their relevant documents (A.F. W.3118 and A.F. W.3118A), Sulphanilamide Label (A.F. W.3211) where necessary and that special Air Evacuation Label R.A.F. Form 2074 is completed as per instructions on the reverse of the form and is firmly tied to all patients.

21. *Estimate of Casualties*

It is not possible to give an accurate forecast of casualties for evacuation. For working purposes there may be assumed to be on the whole divisional front (including airborne and S.S. Troops) 2,000 per day for first 2 days, 1,000 per day for third and fourth days and 400 per day thereafter.

22. *Hygiene and Sanitation*

Copies of a directive by D.D.M.S. I Corps have been distributed to all medical units and R.M.Os.

23. *Intercommunication*
- (a) A.D.M.S. will land at approximately H-hour+$3\frac{1}{2}$ and will be based initially on 20/21 F.D.S., thereafter at Main Divisional H.Q. when established.
- (b) D.Rs. report to A.D.M.S. as in para. 19.

Appendix—3rd Division Medical Services

A.D.M.S.

3rd Division	27th Armd. Bde.	Attached from Corps
8, 9 and 223 Fd. Ambs.	11 Lt. Fd. Amb.	16 C.C.S.
10 and 11 F.D.Ss.		55 F.S.U.
26 Fd. Hyg. Sec.		29 F.T.U.

101st Beach Sub-area (Corps)
20 Port Detach. R.A.M.C.
I C.E.P. ($=\frac{1}{2}$ of a F.D.S.)

5th Beach Group
  20 and 21 F.D.Ss.
  39 and 40 F.S.Us.
  109 Surg. Team
  21 F.T.U.
  1 Fd. San. Sec.

6th Beach Group
  9 and 12 F.D.Ss.
  37 and 38 F.S.Us.
  22 F.T.U.
  2 Fd. San. Sec.

TABLE 8

The Build-up of the Medical Units of 3rd Division

	D-day 1st tide		D-day 2nd tide		D+1 3rd tide		D+1 4th tide		D+2		D+4		D+5		D+6		D+10		D+11		Subsequent to D+17	
	P	V	P	V	P	V	P	V	P	V	P	V	P	V	P	V	P	V	P	V	P	V
8 Fd. Amb.	194	26	—	—	6	3	—	—	—	—	33	6	2	1	—	—	2	1	2	1	12	10a
9 " "	194	26	—	—	6	3	—	—	—	—	33	6	2	1	—	—	2	1	2	1	12	10a
223 " "	194	26	—	—	6	3	—	—	29	4	4	2	2	1	—	—	2	1	2	1	12	10a
11 Lt. Fd. Amb.	—	—	—	—	—	—	—	—	18	3	—	—	89	10	66	17	—	—	—	—	20	10
10 F.D.S.	—	—	—	—	—	—	—	—	—	—	89	10	—	—	—	—	—	—	2	1	6	3
11 "	—	—	—	—	—	—	—	—	—	—	—	—	—	—	89	10	—	—	2	1	6	3
26 Fd. Hyg. Sec.	b	—	—	—	—	—	—	—	20	2	—	—	—	—	—	—	—	—	1	1	1	1
1 C.E.P.	45	4	—	—	—	—	—	—	—	—	—	—	3	2	—	—	—	—	1	1	—	—
20 Port Detach.	—	—	3	—	—	—	—	—	—	—	—	—	—	—	—	—	—	—	—	—	—	—
20 F.D.S. incl. 109 Surg. Team	92	8	—	—	—	—	2	1	—	—	—	—	1	1	—	—	—	—	—	—	6	5
21 F.D.S.	88	8	—	—	—	—	2	1	—	—	—	—	1	1	—	—	—	—	—	—	6	5
39 F.S.U.	9	1	—	—	—	—	—	—	—	—	—	—	1	1	—	—	—	—	—	—	1	1
40 "	9	1	—	—	—	—	—	—	—	—	—	—	1	1	—	—	—	—	—	—	1	1
21 F.T.U.	5	1	—	—	—	—	—	—	—	—	—	—	—	—	—	—	—	—	—	—	—	—
1 Fd. San. Sec. detach.	2	—	—	—	—	—	—	—	—	—	—	—	—	—	—	—	—	—	—	—	—	—
9 F.D.S.	16	1	72	7	2	1	—	—	—	—	—	—	2	1	—	—	—	—	—	—	5	5
12 "	16	1	72	7	2	1	—	—	—	—	—	—	1	1	—	—	—	—	—	—	6	5
37 F.S.U.	—	—	9	1	—	—	—	—	—	—	—	—	1	1	—	—	—	—	—	—	1	1
38 "	—	—	9	1	—	—	—	—	—	—	—	—	1	1	—	—	—	—	—	—	1	1
22 F.T.U.	—	—	5	1	—	—	—	—	—	—	—	—	—	—	—	—	—	—	—	—	—	—
2 Fd. San. Sec. detach.	—	—	2	—	—	—	—	—	—	—	—	—	—	—	—	—	—	—	—	—	—	—
303 Medical Pioneer Coy.	290	3	—	—	—	—	—	—	—	—	—	—	—	—	—	—	—	—	—	—	—	—
Totals:	1,154	106	172	17	22	11	4	2	67	9	159	24	107	23	155	27	6	3	12	7	96	71

(a) Includes 4 heavy ambulance cars replacing 10 jeeps used in the assault.
(b) O.C. and 5 O.Rs. landing with field ambulances first tide D-day.

P = personnel; V = vehicles

3rd Division had been training for over a year for this operation and its medical units had taken part in a series of exercises which closely simulated the actual assault landing. The division with its 8th, 9th and 185th Inf. Bdes. was reinforced for the initial phase of the operation by 27th Armd. Bde. Its medical units were 8, 9 and 223 Fd. Ambs., 10 and 11 F.D.Ss. and 26 Fd. Hyg. Sec. For the assault 101st Beach Sub-area was placed under command of the division; this included four F.D.Ss.,

THE ASSAULT AND LODGEMENT

four F.S.Us. and two F.T.Us. In addition 16 C.C.S. with a F.S.U. and a F.T.U. was allotted by corps to the division, pending the arrival of D.D.M.S. corps. The strength of the division prior to the assault was well over 30,000; when the non-divisional units reverted to corps the figure dropped to approximately 20,000.

3rd Division formed the left flank of Second Army; it landed at assault scale on the beaches just west of Ouistreham with the object of seizing Caen and securing the left flank by holding the line of the Orne between Caen and the sea. To assist in the operation 6th Airborne Division landed in the early morning of June 6 and seized the bridges over the Caen Canal and the Orne at Bénouville and established itself on the rising ground to the east, being reinforced by 1st S.S. Bde. 3rd Division landed according to plan, one brigade up in the order 8th, 185th and 9th. H-hour was 0725 on June 6. The beach defences were overcome and the river line secured, but inland the advance was checked, the furthest penetration being to the wood at Lébisey. The division settled itself on a line running roughly from Blainville through Biéville to Cazelle. Save for a minor advance towards La Lande and Cambes the position remained unaltered until July 8.

On July 8, 3rd Division, in conjunction with Canadian 3rd Division and reinforced by a brigade of 59th Division on the right, resumed the attack and Caen up to the line of the Orne, was captured. Then, on July 16 and 17, 3rd Division moved to the east of the Orne and concentrated in the area Hérouvillette preparatory to an attack south of Sannerville and Troarn. The attack opened in the early morning of July 18. Much ground was gained but Troarn was not taken.

For the assault landings there was but little deviation from the plan outlined above. The main divergences were:

(i) instead of two B.D.Ss. joining up to work together on each beach they were set up separately so that there was a B.D.S. for roughly every 400 yards of the beach;
(ii) the transport of the two F.D.Ss. of 6th Beach Group did not arrive and so these F.D.Ss. could not open until D-day+1. Their personnel were attached to those of 5th Beach Group;
(iii) the site allotted to 16 C.C.S. was not clear of the enemy until D-day+2. The unit was therefore held in the Hermanville area and opened there on June 8;
(iv) the sites allotted to the F.D.Ss. of 6th Beach Group were untenable and so they were opened on D-day+1 adjacent to the F.D.Ss. of 5th Beach Group.

On D-day+1 it was found possible to evacuate the casualties of 6th Airborne Division by ambulance cars from the M.D.S. direct to 1

C.E.P. Evacuation was greatly simplified by the use of the stretcher-carrying jeep, by the presence of the Pioneer Company and by the availability of D.U.K.Ws. Evacuation by sea commenced on the evening of D-day, 272 casualties being embarked by nightfall. Many more could have been sent away if the D.U.K.Ws. could have found the L.S.T. during the hours of darkness (*see* Plates IV–VII). On D-day+1 844 casualties were embarked and 543 on D-day+2.

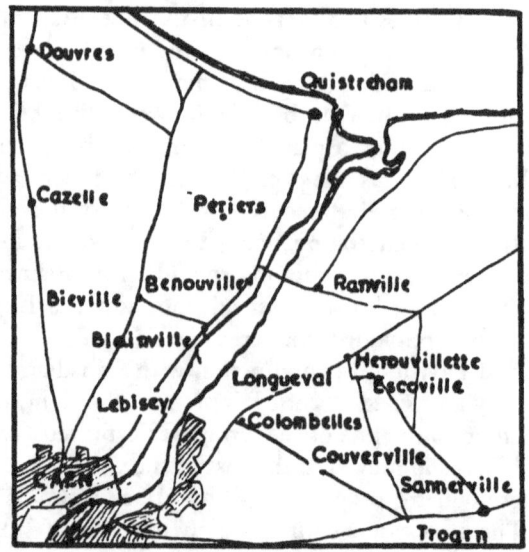

FIG. 9. 3rd Division. The Assault Landing and Lodgement.

On the morning of D-day+3 A.D.M.S. 3rd Division handed over responsibility for the beaches and evacuation therefrom to D.D.M.S. I Corps. In the medical installations there were at this time approximately 350 casualties who were unfit to travel.

For the attack on Caen on July 8, 223 Fd. Amb. opened an A.D.S. at Périers. On the 8th 422 casualties passed through this A.D.S. It was then closed, casualties being switched to the A.D.S. of 9 Fd. Amb. at Biéville to which 146 battle casualties were admitted during the 9th.

For the attack south of Sannerville and Troarn on July 18, 8 Fd. Amb. established an A.D.S. north of Ranville which dealt with 195 wounded and 45 exhaustion cases on the first day. 223 Fd. Amb. opened north of Escoville on the 19th and admitted 245 wounded and 102 cases of exhaustion. The total wounded during this operation was 839, including three R.M.Os.

On July 31, 3rd Division was withdrawn to the west of the Orne preparatory to joining VIII Corps.

TABLE 9

3rd Division. Casualties June 6–30

Battle Casualties

Wounded . . . 2,280
Exhaustion . . . 273

Medical Personnel

	Killed	Wounded	Missing (believed killed)	Died of Wounds	Totals
Officers	2	9	1	1	13
O.Rs.	3	32	18	–	53
	5	41	19	1	66

GUARDS ARMOURED DIVISION

The Guards Armoured Division consisted of 5th Gds. Armd. Bde. and 32nd Gds. Bde. Its medical units were 19 Lt. and 128 Fd. Ambs., 8 F.D.S. and 60 Fd. Hyg. Sec.

For Operation 'Goodwood' it was planned that 8 F.D.S. should open to receive casualties occurring on the west bank of the Orne and that 19 Lt. and 128 Fd. Ambs. should move as far forward as possible to serve 5th Gds. Armd. and 32nd Gds. Bdes. respectively. A section of 128 Fd. Amb. would be attached to each of the infantry battalions of the brigade; three sections of 19 Lt. Fd. Amb., forming a company, would move with the armoured brigade. Casualties would be evacuated to the nearest A.D.S. of I Corps until one of the divisional field ambulances opened. Each field ambulance would have six cars, twelve being left with the M.A.C. which would move with H.Q. 19 Lt. Fd. Amb.

8 F.D.S. opened in a field to the north of St. Aubin d'Arquenay on July 18, 19 Lt. Fd. Amb. at Ranville at 2000 hours and 128 Fd. Amb. in a cornfield south of Cuverville at 2200 hours. On July 19, 19 Lt. Fd. Amb. moved forward to a site between Cuverville and the A.D.S. of 128 Fd. Amb., which then closed. On the 20th the two field ambulances

TABLE 10

Casualties treated in Divisional Medical Units. July 18–23

	Offrs.	O.Rs.
Guards Armoured Division	15	210
Others	17	138
	32	348

opened a conjoint A.D.S. on the road near Cuverville (*see* Fig. 9) for the heavy rain had made cross-country travel impossible. Later 19 Lt. Fd. Amb. moved to the church in Cuverville itself. Next day 19 Lt. Fd. Amb. handed over to 128 Fd. Amb. and moved to Colombelles where it opened an A.D.S. 128 Fd. Amb. moved to Longueval, near Colombelles, on the 23rd. The division remained in reserve u/c Canadian II Corps until the 29th and on the 30th moved to the vicinity of Bayeux.

7TH ARMOURED DIVISION

This division consisted of 22nd Armd. Bde., 131st Inf. Bde. and 56th Inf. Bde. with divisional troops and services. Its medical units were 131 Fd. Amb., 2 Lt. Fd. Amb. (56th Bde.), 29 F.D.S., 134 (later 500) M.D.U. and 70 Fd. Hyg. Sec. Landing in Normandy it went into action on June 9. 2 Lt. Fd. Amb. was under command 22nd Armd. Bde. for operational purposes only, one company 131 Fd. Amb. was under command 131st Bde. for operational purposes only, H.Q. and one company 131 Fd. Amb. and 29 F.D.S. were under command A.D.M.S. division. 134 M.D.U. was attached to the F.D.S.

R.M.Os. of the armoured regiments and infantry battalions had one ambulance car attached for the evacuation of casualties to the sections of the light field ambulance or to the company of the field ambulance, these always being situated in the vicinity of main brigade H.Q. As a general rule the H.Q. and the 'link' section of the light field ambulance were situated near rear brigade H.Q. on the divisional axis. The H.Q. and one company of the field ambulance together with the F.D.S. formed a divisional medical area near rear divisional H.Q., eight to ten miles behind the forward elements. A car post was established in the divisional medical area by D.D.M.S. corps for the rearward evacuation of casualties to the C.C.S.

Casualties were evacuated to the divisional medical area, being received there by the field ambulance. The seriously wounded were transferred to the F.D.S., in which they were treated and sent on to the C.C.S. But since such were few in number and since the C.C.S. was well forward this system was changed. The F.D.S. received the minor sick and was prepared to move forward at short notice and the field ambulance received, resuscitated and evacuated the battle casualties to the C.C.S. direct. When the division advanced the F.D.S. received all casualties while the H.Q. of the field ambulance was cleared, closed and moved up to the new divisional medical area.

11TH ARMOURED DIVISION

11th Armoured Division consisted of 29th Armd. Bde. and 159th Inf. Bde. Its medical units were 18 Lt. Fd. Amb. and 179 Fd. Amb., 7 F.D.S. and 76 Fd. Hyg. Sec. It landed in Normandy on June 14.

PLATE I. R.A.M.C. Personnel landing on the Normandy shore from L.C.I.

[Imperial War Museum

PLATE II. Disembarking from a L.C.T. on the Normandy shore.

[*Imperial War Museum*]

PLATE III. An Ambulance Car leaves a L.C.T. for the Normandy shore.

[*Imperial War Museum*

PLATE IV. A Bren Carrier used for the evacuation of casualties. A German Tiger Tank in the background.

[*Imperial War Museum*]

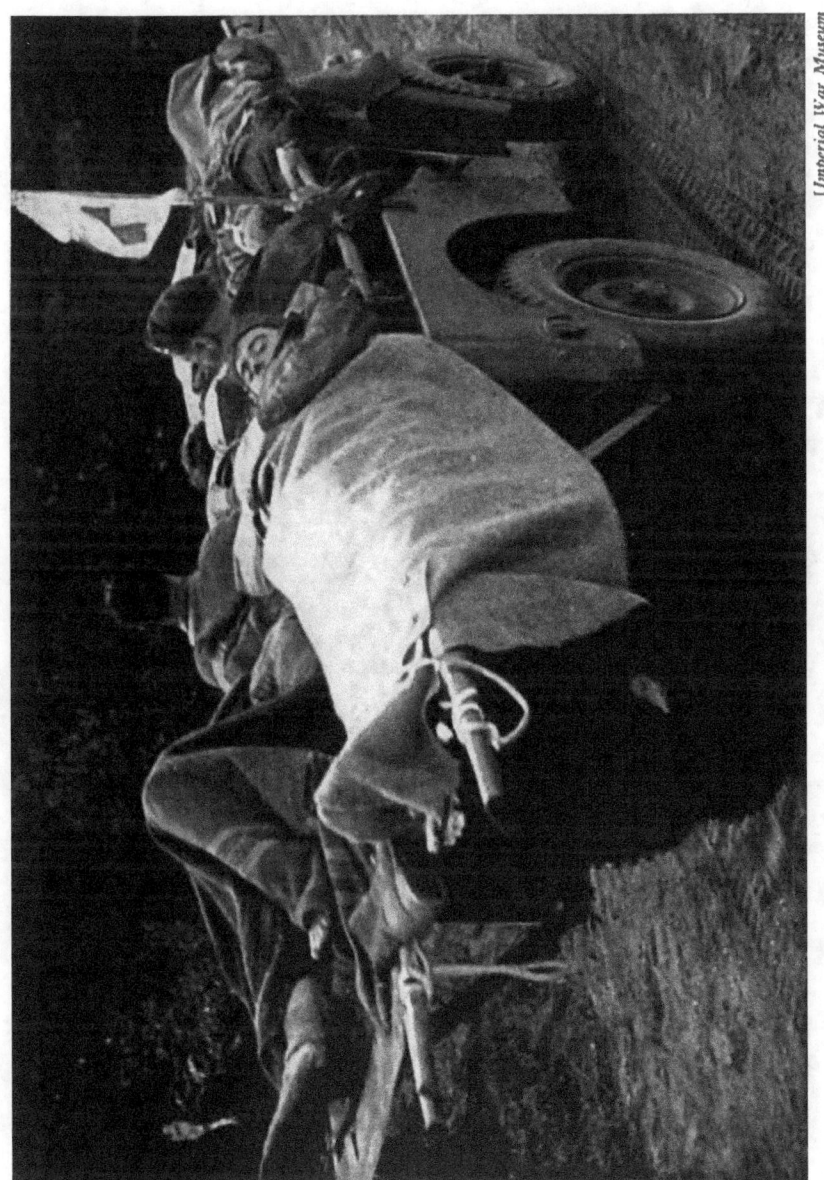

PLATE V. Casualties of 6th Airborne Division being evacuated.

[*Imperial War Museum*

PLATE VI. Jeep Ambulances moving forward to evacuate casualties.

[*Imperial War Museum*]

PLATE VII. Loading a Jeep Ambulance.

PLATE VIII. A Jeep Ambulance crossing the Caen Canal Bridge, June 9. Crashed gliders in the background.

[*Imperial War Museum*

[*Imperial War Museum*

PLATE IX. 48 Field Dressing Station. Double-tier bunks in the abbey at Juaye-Mondaye.

PLATE X. An Advanced Dressing Station of a Field Ambulance in a Normandy Orchard.

[*Imperial War Museum*]

PLATE XI. Q.A.I.M.N.S. Nursing Officers in the Beachhead.

[Imperial War Museum

PLATE XII. Q.A.I.M.N.S. A Beachhead Dormitory.

[Imperial War Museum

PLATE XIII. Q.A.I.M.N.S. In a Beachhead Casualty Clearing Station.

[Imperial War Museum

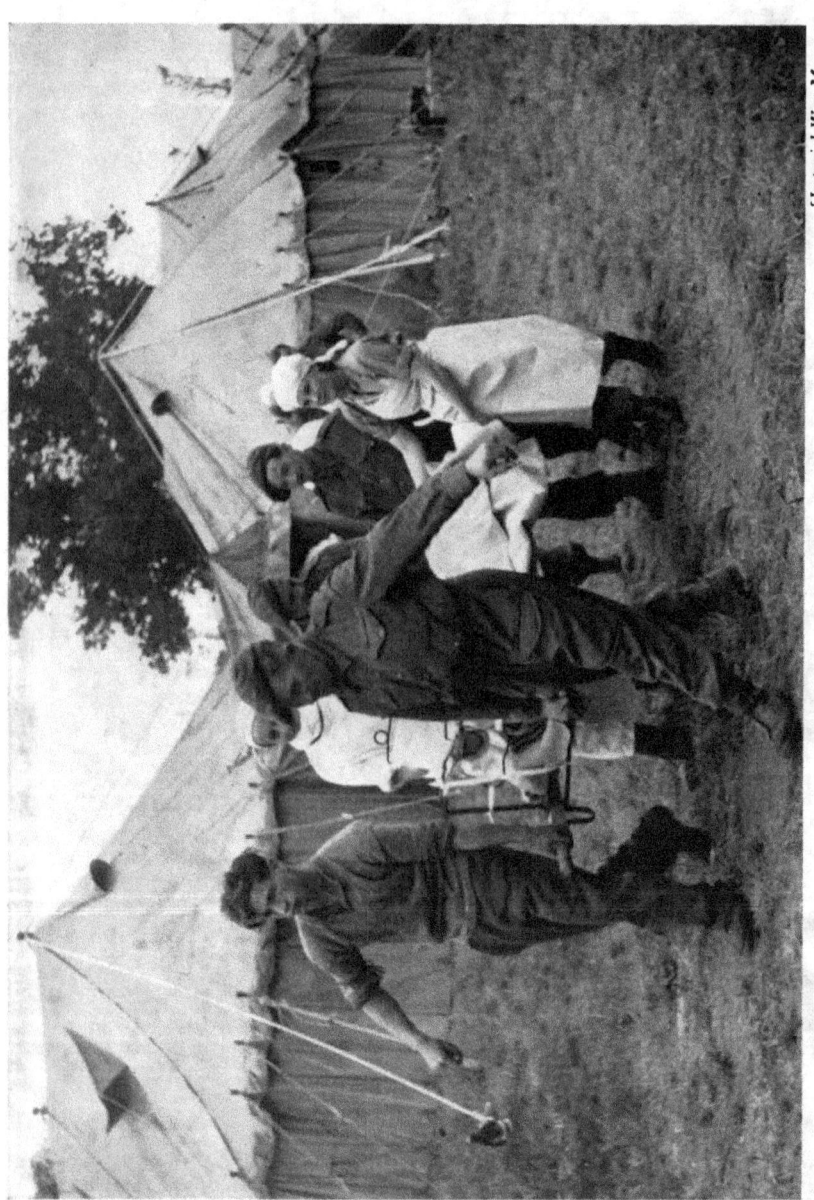

PLATE XIV. From the Operating Theatre to the ward of a Beachhead General Hospital.

[Imperial War Museum

[*Imperial War Museum*

PLATE XV. A Water Pumping and Sterilising Unit.

PLATE XVI. A Beachhead Water Point.

THE ASSAULT AND LODGEMENT

To begin with the divisional casualties were evacuated to the medical units of 15th (Scottish) Division, those of 11th Armoured Division remaining on wheels. On the afternoon of June 29 the armoured brigade and two battalions of the infantry brigade crossed the Odon at Mondrainville to enter a very narrow and congested bridgehead, the flanks of which were held by 15th and 43rd Divisions.

18 Lt. Fd. Amb. established a two-section C.C.P. just across the river and 179 a C.C.P. a mile to the west thereof. 179 Fd. Amb. itself was located half a mile from Cheux (*see* Fig. 10) near to 194 Fd. Amb. of 15th Division. When the latter became overtaxed 179 Fd. Amb. opened to become fully occupied almost at once. Evacuation by M.A.C. was exceedingly difficult owing to the great congestion of traffic on the roads and also because the A.D.S. came to be the centre of numerous gun positions. The work of the A.D.S. was much impeded, documentation suffering in consequence. By 1000 hours on June 30 the situation had become eased. Between 1500 hours on June 29 and 1500 hours on June 30, 179 Fd. Amb. dealt with 545 casualties, less than one-fifth of these belonging to 11th Armoured Division.

Then until July 6 the division held the line of the Odon. During this period 179 Fd. Amb. was sited just east of Cheux. On July 16 the division moved to the east of the Orne along with the Guards and 7th Armoured Divisions to take part in Operation 'Goodwood'.

The difficulty of getting casualties back over the Orne was overcome by setting up an evacuation post by 18 Lt. Fd. Amb. at a footbridge and by hand-carriage across this. Thence casualties were evacuated to the corps medical centre at La Délivrande. During the course of Operation 'Goodwood' 455 casualties passed through this evacuation post.

15TH (SCOTTISH) DIVISION

This division consisted of 44th (Lowland), 46th (Highland) and 227th (Highland) Infantry Brigades with supporting arms and services including 153, 193, and 194 Fd. Ambs., 22 and 23 F.D.Ss. and 40 Fd. Hyg. Sec. A.D.M.S's. office was particularly well equipped, a C.V. and a 3-ton lorry being allotted for accommodation in addition to a 15-cwt. truck for the R.A.P. equipment. A wireless vehicle with Signals personnel was allotted to each field ambulance and a rover set was fitted to the A.D.M.S's. car.

The move to France of H.Q. Med. was uneventful and it opened near St. Gabriel on June 16. By the 23rd, 193 and 194 Fd. Ambs. and 22 F.D.S. were ashore but 153 was not expected before June 28.

The division went into action on June 26. It was to attack on a narrow front and to secure crossings over the Odon, and 11th Armoured Division was then to pass through and exploit. The operation was to be carried out in four phases.

1. 46th Bde., plus a battalion of tanks, was to advance along route 'Oban.'

    44th Bde., plus a battalion of tanks, was to advance along route 'Hawick'.

    These were to secure Le Haut du Bosq–Cheux–La Gaule–St. Mauvieu.

2. 227th Bde., preceded by recce. and armoured elements, was to pass through and advance on the roads to the river line, there to secure bridges and bridgeheads over the Odon.

3. 46th and 44th Bdes. were to be relieved by brigades of 43rd Division.

4. 46th Bde. was to close up behind 227th Bde. in the bridgehead and be prepared to follow 11th Armoured Division. 44th Bde. was to move up on the left flank and exploit towards Verson.

A C.C.P. formed by a whole company of a field ambulance would be opened on each route as far forward as possible before the battle. 193 Fd. Amb. would establish an A.D.S. at Pûtot-en-Bessin and 194 Fd. Amb. an A.D.S. at Bretteville-l'Orgueilleuse. To 193 would be attached the main portion of 22 F.D.S. and its light section would be attached to 194. 31 F.T.U., having been allotted to 15th Division by corps, would also be attached to 193 Fd. Amb. The reserve company of 194 Fd. Amb. would be moved to the area immediately north of Cheux and there establish a C.C.P. as soon as the first objectives had been taken. A company of 193 Fd. Amb. would move in support of 227th Bde. The A.D.S. of 194 at Bretteville would close as quickly as possible following the capture of the first objectives and open in the location of the C.C.P. immediately north of Cheux. On relief by the field ambulances of 43rd Division, 193 Fd. Amb. would close at Pûtot and move with 46th Bde.

The first objectives were quickly taken. Casualties were numerous and both field ambulances were fully employed. Both C.C.Ps. came under severe mortar and shell fire and casualties to medical personnel were sustained. 227th Bde. was held up on its start-line at Cheux and it was not possible to move the company of 194 Fd. Amb. along route 'Hawick' to Cheux. So 'A' Coy. 194 Fd. Amb. went forward along route 'Oban' to reach Cheux and there establish a C.C.P. The company then moved forward in support of 227th Bde.

On June 27, 227th Bde., advancing, was checked south of Le Haut du Bosq and so 46th Bde., on relief by 43rd Division, moved to support 227th Bde. and to attack Grainville sur Orne and Le Valtru.

193 Fd. Amb's. A.D.S. at Pûtot was relieved by a field ambulance of 43rd Division and by 1900 hours on the 27th was established north of

Cheux. 22 F.D.S. and 31 F.T.U. were attached to this A.D.S. 'A' Coy. 193 Fd. Amb. established a C.C.P. at Colleville on the 28th. When 44th Bde. attacked to clear the area west of route 'Oban', 'B' Coy.

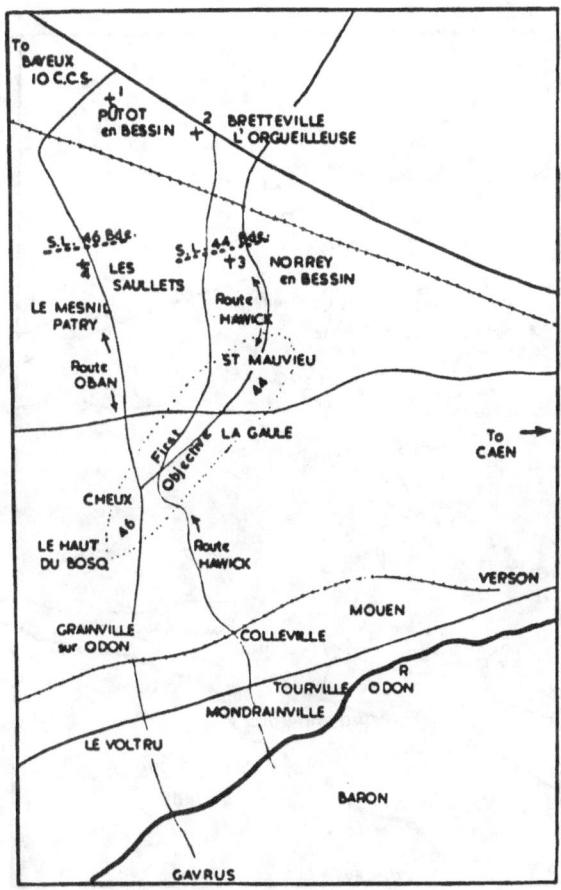

FIG. 10. 15th Division. Medical Cover. June 26–July 1. First Phase.

1. A.D.S. 193 Fd. Amb.
   22 F.D.S.
   31 F.T.U.
2. A.D.S. 194 Fd. Amb.
   Lt. Sec. 22 F.D.S.
3. C.C.P. 194 Fd. Amb.
4. C.C.P. 193 Fd. Amb.

194 Fd. Amb. moved in support. During the night of June 28/29, H.Q. Coy. 194 Fd. Amb. relieved the A.D.S. of 193 Fd. Amb. north of Cheux.

On the 29th the Germans counter-attacked strongly and the C.C.P. at Colleville was withdrawn but returned to its site on the following morning when the situation had become stabilised. 153 Fd. Amb., arriving, relieved 194 Fd. Amb. at Cheux on the 30th and 193 Fd. Amb., which had moved to Le Mesnil-Patry in reserve, was opened there to deal with local casualties.

This operation presented peculiar medical problems. The salient in

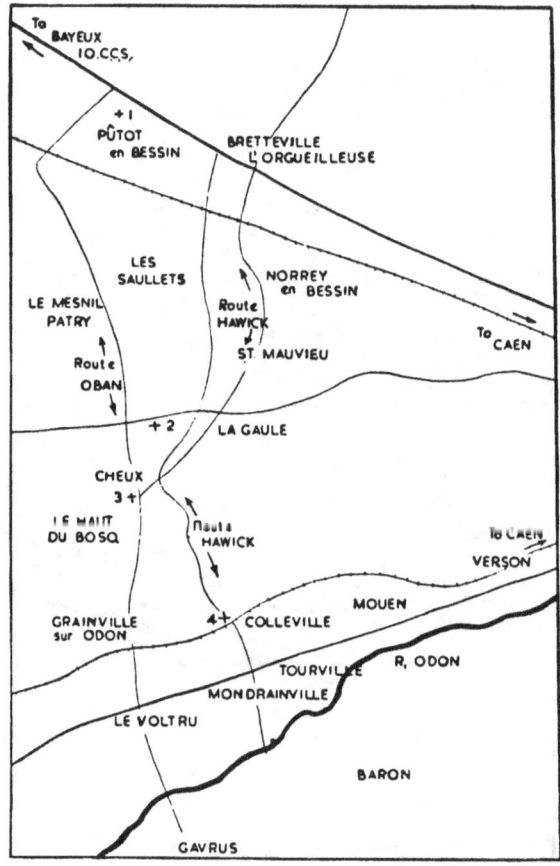

Fig. 11. 15th Division. Medical Cover. June 26–July 1. Second Phase.

1. A.D.S. of 43rd Division
2. A.D.S. 193 Fd. Amb.
   22 F.D.S.
   31 F.T.U.
3. C.C.P. 'A' Coy. 194 Fd. Amb.
4. C.C.P. 'A' Coy. 193 Fd. Amb.

which the division was operating was a long and narrow one and was under heavy fire from both flanks. The operation opened in pouring rain and the roads and tracks were soon deep in mud. Traffic congestion added greatly to the difficulties of evacuation. The average interval between time of wounding and arrival at a C.C.S. on the first day of battle was $2\frac{1}{2}$–$4\frac{1}{2}$ hours.

TABLE 11

Casualties admitted to the Field Medical Units of 15th Division.

June 26–July 1

	193 Fd. Amb.	194 Fd. Amb.	153 Fd. Amb.	22 F.D.S.	Totals
June 26.	126	216	—	134	476
27.	105	128	—	206	439
28.	229	—	—	77	306
29.	55	195	—	152	402
30.	38	177	—	25	240
July 1.	46	1	182	12	241
	599	717	182	606	2,104

1,642 of 15th Division

Casualties among Medical Personnel.

June 26–July 1

	Killed	Wounded
Medical Officers	—	4
O.Rs.	6	14

TABLE 12

15th Division. Wounds by Anatomical Region. June 26–July 1

Wounds by Anatomical Region and by Missile

	G.S.W.	Splinter unclassified	Splinter Shell	Splinter Mortar	Burns	Fractures	Totals	Percentage of Total
Head	34	38	2	10	1	7	92	6·18
Face	26	47	6	9	11	3	102	6·99
Neck	14	11	—	5	—	—	30	2·01
Shoulder	41	27	3	12	—	2	85	5·71
Arm and Hand	150	92	6	45	6	27	326	21·90
Chest and Thorax	41	26	—	10	—	4	81	5·44
Abdomen	21	19	2	4	—	—	46	3·09
Back	21	36	5	11	—	—	73	4·91
Buttock	32	33	1	5	—	1	72	4·83
Thigh	57	40	4	9	—	17	127	8·51
Leg	92	100	10	29	2	26	259	17·40
Foot	60	25	3	13	—	3	104	6·93
Multiple	27	47	1	10	5	1	91	6·11
Totals	616	541	43	172	25	91	1,488	100·00
Percentage	41·39	36·29	2·89	11·55	1·68	6·11		

44th and 46th Bdes. with 'A' Coy. 194 and 'B' Coy. 193 Fd. Ambs. served u/c 43rd Division at the beginning of July, casualties being evacuated to 130 Fd. Amb. of 43rd Division.

Then, on July 15, 15th Division passing through 43rd Division

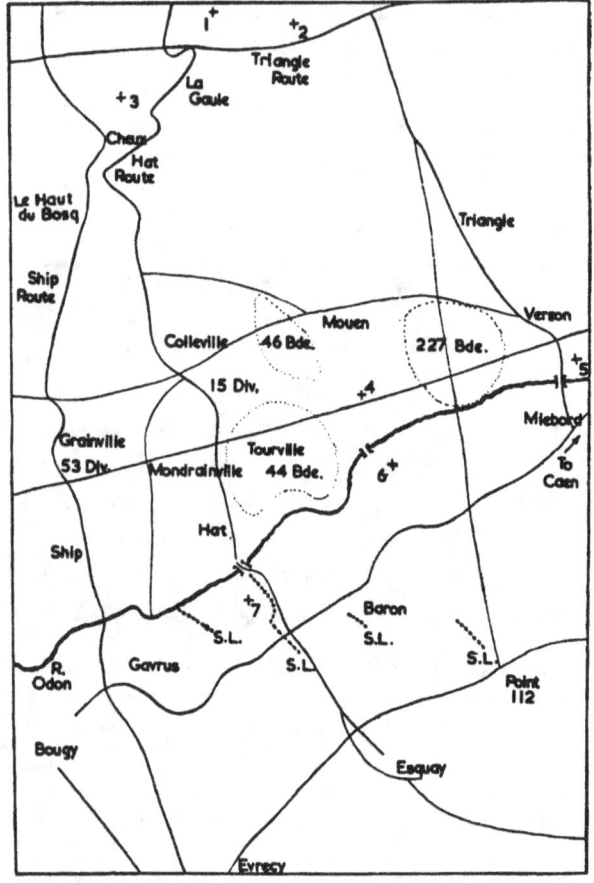

Fig. 12. 15th Division. Operation 'Greenline'. July 15-18. Medical Cover.

1. M.A.C. Control
2. Forward Medical Area. 1st Position.
   A.D.Ss. 153 and 194 Fd. Ambs., 22 F.D.S.
3. Forward Medical Area. 2nd Position.
   A.D.Ss. 193 and 21 Lt. Fd. Ambs.
4. C.C.P. Lt. Sec. 23 Lt. Fd. Amb.
5. C.C.P. 'A' Coy. 153 Fd. Amb. 1st Position
6.   ,,   ,,   ,,   ,,   ,,   ,,   2nd Position
7. C.C.P. 'A' Coy. 194 Fd. Amb.

S.L. = Start Lines. Ship, Hat and Triangle = Evacuation Routes

THE ASSAULT AND LODGEMENT

attacked towards Esquay, Gavrus, Bougy and, finally, Evrecy. Heavy casualties were expected and it was certain that evacuation would be difficult. It was decided therefore to form a forward medical area on a lateral road joining the main divisional axis and so make provision for evacuation by routes 'Triangle', 'Hat' or 'Ship'.

Companies of the field ambulances were allotted to the brigades and these moved over the river before the attack and established C.C.Ps. A section of 23 Lt. Fd. Amb. of 34th Tk. Bde. (u/c 15th Division) formed a C.C.P. at the Traffic Regulating H.Q. to deal with casualties on the bridge approaches. The officer commanding this C.C.P. was in wireless communication with A.D.M.S. Seventeen carriers were allotted to the divisional medical services for evacuation from R.A.P. to C.C.S.

When the forward lateral route became impassable the C.C.P. of 153 Fd. Amb. moved to the second position shown in the sketch map.

The forward medical area consisted of 22 F.D.S. and the A.D.Ss. of 153 and 194 Fd. Ambs. During the battle a rear medical area was also formed; it consisted of 23 F.D.S., 193 Fd. Amb. and 23 Lt. Fd. Amb. on wheels and in reserve.

On July 16 the divisional maintenance route was changed from 'Triangle' to 'Hat' route and arrangements were made with A.D.M.S. 43rd Division whereby 43rd Division took over 15th Division's medical area and used the 'Triangle' route for evacuation while 15th Division used 'Hat' route exclusively for evacuation purposes, 193 Fd. Amb. and 23 Lt. Fd. Amb. opening to form a new forward medical area sited as shown in Fig. 12. 151 cases of exhaustion (17·5 per cent. of the total casualties) were evacuated to the divisional F.D.S.

TABLE 13

15th Division. Casualties. July 15–18

	Killed	Wounded	Missing
Officers	9	33	1
O.Rs.	92	687	40
	101	720	41

Since June 24, when 15th Division first went into action, the loss of vehicles had been severe and had led to much loss of efficiency and no little anxiety.

On July 18 the division was withdrawn, being relieved by 53rd Division, and moved to the right flank of Second Army taking over from a U.S. division and coming u/c XXX Corps.

43RD (WESSEX) DIVISION

This division, consisting of 129th, 130th and 214th Inf. Bdes. with supporting arms and services including 129, 130 and 213 Fd. Ambs., 38 Fd. Hyg. Sec., 14 and 15 F.D.Ss. and 22 F.T.U., landed on Juno beach on June 24 to pass u/c VIII Corps. 213 Fd. Amb. established itself near Loucelles with a C.C.P. in Les Saullets. 129 and 130 Fd. Ambs. opened in Bretteville-l'Orgueilleuse on the 27th. 14 and 15 F.D.Ss. were in the divisional gun and administrative areas, 14 taking the divisional sick and the exhaustion cases. On the 28th, 32nd Guards Bde. came under command and 128 Fd. Amb. took over from 129 and 130 Fd. Ambs., opening an A.D.S. 129 Fd. Amb. then moved to Pûtot-en-Bessin and 130 joined its brigade.

When, on the 29th, 129th Bde. passed through 214th Bde. over the Odon, one company of 129 Fd. Amb. was in support, a section accompanying each battalion to form a C.C.P. at Mouen. Early on the 30th, 129 Fd. Amb. moved to a position south-east of Cheux to reinforce 130 Fd. Amb. and 14 F.D.S. was brought up nearby in reserve.

On July 1 the locations of the divisional units were as follows:

129 Fd. Amb. at Pûtot-en-Bessin, 130 and 213 Fd. Ambs. and 14 F.D.S. at Les Saullets, 15 F.D.S. in the administrative area and 128 Fd. Amb. in Bretteville-l'Orgueilleuse. Late that day 129 moved to the crossroads north of Cheux. On the 5th, 130 Fd. Amb. and 14 F.D.S. moved to the Château de Mouen and opened an A.D.S. and F.D.S. while 129 closed. On the 6th, 213 Fd. Amb. moved to Cheux and 129 moved back to Les Saullets.

For Operation 'Jupiter' the company of 129 Fd. Amb. with 214th Bde. moved to a quarry on the Odon and opened on the evening of July 9 and after dark two sections of 130 Fd. Amb. opened sectional C.C.Ps. at the bridges over the river. 22 F.T.U. opened at the Château de Mouen with 130 Fd. Amb., 14 F.D.S. and a company of 194 Fd. Amb. Early on the 10th the brigade company of 130 Fd. Amb. moved across the Odon and opened a C.C.P. at Fontaine. Because its work was greatly impeded by gun and mortar fire it was later withdrawn and the brigaded company of 213 Fd. Amb. established a C.C.P. at Mirbord, half a mile to the west.

During the morning of the 11th the C.C.Ps. at the bridges were withdrawn, being no longer necessary. At 1630 hours the A.D.S. and F.D.S. in the Château de Mouen closed, having dealt with over 1,500 casualties during the previous thirty-six hours. 130 Fd. Amb. went into rest at Les Saullets and 14 F.D.S. took over the divisional sick in the administrative area. 213 Fd. Amb. in Cheux opened an A.D.S. and was joined by 15 F.D.S.

On the 14th the C.C.P. of 213 Fd. Amb. at Mirbord closed and was withdrawn to rest. 130 Fd. Amb. reopened its C.C.P. in the Odon valley at the site of the bridge. On the 15th, 14 Lt. Fd. Amb. came under command and remained closed beside the medical area of 15th Division on 'Triangle' route (see 15th Division). When in the afternoon this route was assigned to 43rd Division 14 Lt. Fd. Amb. opened to take all divisional casualties.

On the 17th, 129 Fd. Amb. opened alongside 14 Lt. Fd. Amb. and 213 Fd. Amb. and 14 F.D.S. closed and moved back into rest. The C.C.P. of 213 took over from the C.C.P. of 129 in the quarry by the Odon. On the 19th, 14 Lt. Fd. Amb. passed from command and closed and 14 F.D.S. joined 129 Fd. Amb., 15 F.D.S. assuming responsibility for the sick in the divisional administrative area.

On the 25th the division moved into rest at Carcagny and, on the 29th, u/c XXX Corps moved into the line again, 130 Fd. Amb. opening at La Prévotière, the C.C.Ps. being brigaded.

49TH (WEST RIDING) DIVISION

This division was trained as an assault division under the command of I Corps but before the invasion was transferred to XXX Corps and became a 'follow-up' division. It consisted of 146th, 147th and 70th Bdes. and to it was attached 8th Armd. Bde. Its medical units were 146, 160 and 187 Fd. Ambs., 16 and 17 F.D.Ss., 35 Fd. Hyg. Sec and 205 (502) M.D.U. With 8th Armd. Bde. was 168 Lt. Fd. Amb. When the division embarked 17 F.D.S. was left in the United Kingdom with the residues of other medical units. 16 F.D.S. was loaned to XXX Corps and landed on D-day + 1, rejoining the division on D-day + 10.

The division with its medical units landed in Normandy between D-day + 4 and D-day + 8. During the period June 16–30 the division took part in a series of actions in *bocage* country, advancing to the general line St. Pierre (east of Tilly)–Tessel–Rauray.

146 Fd. Amb. opened an A.D.S. in St. Léger on June 14, being joined there on the following day by 187 Fd. Amb. Single sections of the field ambulance were placed in support of battalions and formed C.C.Ps. For the attack on St. Pierre by 10th D.L.I. on June 17 the C.C.P. serving this battalion was reinforced with an additional section. The C.C.P. with 6th D.W.R. attacking Parc de Boislonde was similarly reinforced but not in time to enable the C.C.P. adequately to deal with the large number of casualties that had occurred. Thereafter the C.C.P. was always formed with two or three sections and sited in the rear of a brigade sector, dealing with the casualties of all the battalions of the brigade. This was tantamount to a reversal to the older system of A.D.S. and M.D.S.

TABLE 14

49th Division. Casualties. June 16–18

	1st/4th K.O.Y.L.I. 146th Bde.	6th D.W.R. 147th Bde.	7th D.W.R. 147th Bde.	10th D.L.I. 70th Bde.
June 16				
Killed	2			
Wounded	32			
Missing	1			
June 17				
Killed		22	1	17
Wounded		65		29
Missing		30	1	13
June 18				
Killed		3	5	3
Wounded		63	79	26
Missing		56	18	4

The division then participated in the operation commencing on June 25 with the object of advancing to the general line Vendes–Rauray, thus securing a firm base for a further advance to secure the Noyers area. The operation was divided into three phases:

A. The capture of La Caude Rue–Fontenay.
B. The advance to the north edge of Tessel.
C. The advance to the line Vendes–Rauray.

The advance did not proceed as swiftly as had been hoped and at the end of five days the line ran from Tessel to the south of Rauray.

For phase A 146 Fd. Amb. and 16 F.D.S. opened an A.D.S. at St. Léger. A C.C.P. of two sections and with two more sections in reserve was established at Le Haut d'Audrieu. A C.C.P. of one section was established at Cristot and another of two sections north of St. Pierre. 187 Fd. Amb. was in St. Léger closed but ready to open at one hour's notice. 160 Fd. Amb. was in reserve on wheels. An ambulance car pool of all the 4 stretcher cars was established in the vicinity of Ducy Ste. Marguerite.

During the afternoon of the 25th the A.D.S. at St. Léger was under stress so 187 Fd. Amb. opened. The C.C.P. at Le Haut d'Audrieu was reinforced by personnel from the two sections in reserve.

As soon as Fontenay was secured a C.C.P. was opened there. On June 27, 146 Fd. Amb. closed at St. Léger and prepared to move forward. 187 Fd. Amb. and the C.C.P. at Cristot likewise closed. When the offensive died down the field ambulances moved to the vicinity of Ducy Ste. Marguerite. During these events 16 F.D.S. had remained in St.

THE ASSAULT AND LODGEMENT

Léger holding the divisional sick. It supplied a transfusion section to each open A.D.S. Medical officers from the divisional R.E., from the A/T Regt. and from 2nd Kensingtons were attached to the A.D.Ss. during the operation.

Evacuation difficulties were greatly eased by the provision by the battalions of jeeps and carriers for the conveyance of casualties to the R.A.Ps. One or two 2-stretcher 4×4 ambulances were posted to each R.A.P. These plied between R.A.P. and C.C.P. The 4-stretcher ambulances were used between C.C.P. and A.D.S. During one very wet night the ambulances were halted by the mud and casualties were brought back to the A.D.S. on carriers and half-tracked vehicles borrowed from the R.M.Os. of 8th Armd. Bde. On June 25 four of the ambulances were wrecked by mortar and mine. As a result of this experience A.D.M.S. 49th Division formed the firm opinion that the transport allotted to field ambulances and R.M.Os. for the carriage of casualties was unsuitable and inadequate and suggested that jeeps and carriers were necessary and that regimental S.Bs. should be trained as drivers of these vehicles.

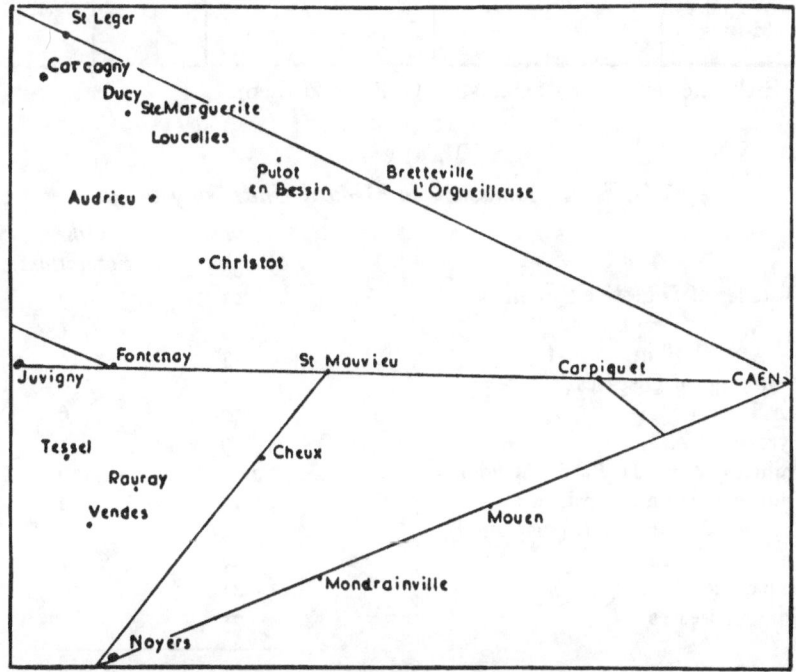

FIG. 13. 49th Division. The Advance to Vendes–Rauray.

Table 15
49th Division. Casualties. June 25–29

	4th Lincolns 146th Bde.	1st/4th K.O.Y.L.I. 146th Bde.	Hallams 146th Bde.	11th R.S.F. 147th Bde.	1st Tyneside Scots 70th Bde.	10th D.L.I. 70th Bde.
June 25						
Killed	11	13	15	10	—	—
Wounded	62	54	67	150	—	9
Missing	10	—	36	133	—	—
June 26						
Killed	—	1	1	—	5	1
Wounded	3	8	26	3	41	1
Missing	—	2	—	—	2	2
June 27						
Killed	3	6	—	—	—	—
Wounded	8	16	13	32	—	—
Missing	—	1	—	—	—	—
June 28						
Killed	1	8	2	—	3	9
Wounded	6	5	17	—	84	60
Missing	—	—	—	—	—	—
June 29						
Killed	—	4	—	—	—	—
Wounded	4	9	9	8	11	32
Missing	—	—	6	—	—	3

Sick rate (excluding exhaustion) 0·8/1,000/diem.

Table 16
49th Division. Admissions to Medical Units. July 17–30

	49th Division	Other Formations
Diseases of Digestive System	15	7
„ Respiratory „	9	1
„ Skin	13	1
Neurological Diseases	1	—
I.A.T.	50	6
Pyrexia N.Y.D.	9	3
Injuries, Wounds, Battle Accidents	1,607	136
Injuries, Wounds Accidental	49	4
Injuries, Wounds S.I. (suspected)	4	—
Injuries, Burns	20	1
Exhaustion	281	32
Other Diseases	75	7
Totals	2,133	198

THE ASSAULT AND LODGEMENT

Total evacuated out of Divisional Area		2,033	164
Total R.T.U. from Divisional Medical Units		70	10
Total Deaths in Divisional Medical Units		21	3
	Totals	2,124	177

Total Casualties admitted to A.D.S.   2,331
- Battle   1,743   74·7 per cent.
- " Accidents   53   2·2 "
- Sick   222   9·5 "
- Exhaustion   313   13·4 "

Killed during same period   284
Ratio wounded to killed   6·8 : 1

Causal Agent (1,550 cases):
- G.S.W.   341   22·0 per cent.
- S.W. (including mines)   258   16·6 "
- B.W. (mortar)   712   46·0 "
- Burns   14   0·9 "
- Other Weapons and (?)   225   14·6 "

Wounds by Anatomical Region (a series of 1,529 cases):
- Head and Face   154   10·1 per cent.
- Neck   26   1·7 "
- Chest   89   5·8 "
- Abdomen   32   2·1 "
- Upper Limb   414   27·0 "
- Lower Limb   490   32·0 "
- Buttocks   68   4·4 "
- Back   71   4·7 "
- Multiple   185   12·1 "

In a series of 442 Admissions to one medical unit there were:
- Intra-cranial   3   0·7 per cent.
- Intra-thoracic   15   3·4 "
- Intra-abdominal   8   1·76 "
- Compound Fracture
  - Humerus   7   1·6 "
  - Radius and Ulna   4   0·9 "
  - Femur   11   2·4 "
  - Tibia and Fibula   17   3·8 "
  - Foot   18   4·0 "
  - Buttocks   15   3·4 "

Severity of Wounds (a series of 1,538 cases):

Slight	822	53·4 per cent.
Severe	556	36·2 ,,
Dangerous	160	10·4 ,,

Of 982 evacuated, 62·7 per cent. were lying cases.

51ST (HIGHLAND) DIVISION

51st Division consisted of 152nd, 153rd and 154th Inf. Bdes. Its medical units were 174, 175 and 176 Fd. Ambs., 5 and 6 F.D.Ss. and 29 Fd. Hyg. Sec.

After landing the division held positions in the bridgehead east of the Orne. Casualties from the units in the line were evacuated through the medical units of 6th Airborne Division until June 15 when 174 Fd. Amb. relieved 225 Para. Fd. Amb. and opened a divisional A.D.S. in Ranville and 176 Fd. Amb. opened an A.D.S. in St. Aubin d'Arquenay for

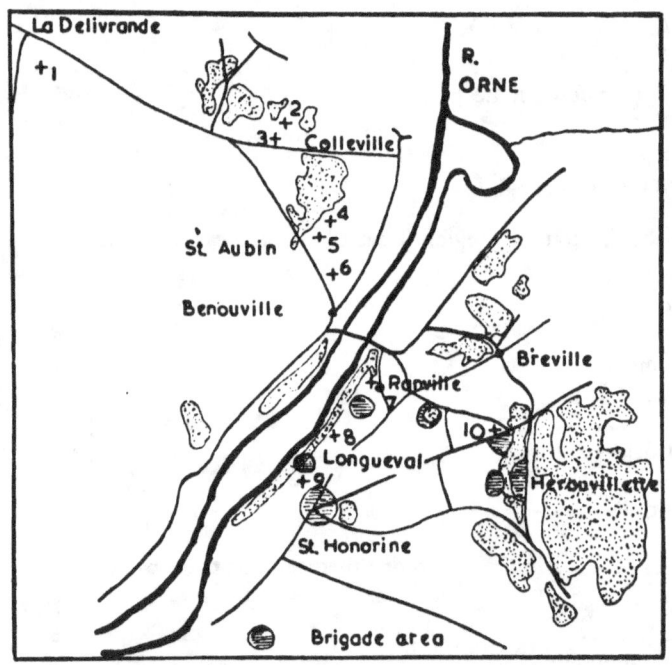

FIG. 14. 51st Division. Medical Cover in the Bridgehead east of the Orne.

1. Medical Area. 86 and 88 B.G.Hs. 16 C.C.S.
2. 5 F.D.S.
3. A.D.M.S.
   174 Fd. Amb.
4. 6. F.D.S.
5. 176 Fd. Amb.
6. C.C.P. 176 Fd. Amb.
7. 175 Fd. Amb.
8. C.C.P. 175 Fd. Amb.
9. C.C.P. 175 Fd. Amb.
10. C.P. 176 Fd. Amb.

THE ASSAULT AND LODGEMENT

the reception of the sick and lightly wounded. Evacuation was by M.A.C. to La Délivrande.

During July the essential rôle of the division was the holding of part of the perimeter east of the Orne on the right of 6th Airborne Division. On the night of July 10/11, 153rd Bde. attacked the Colombelles factory area but was unsuccessful. On July 18, 152nd Bde., u/c 3rd Division, attacked east of the Orne towards Troarn, Cagny and Bourguébus.

175 Fd. Amb. had its A.D.S. in Ranville for battle casualties. 176 Fd. Amb. had its A.D.S. for sick and minor battle casualties in St. Aubin but, suffering casualties from bombing, was obliged to move to Colleville-sur-Orne on the 24th. 174 Fd. Amb. and 5 F.D.S. were in Colleville in reserve. With each brigade was a company of a field ambulance which formed C.Ps. and C.C.Ps. as required. Evacuation was to La Délivrande and Hermanville.

53RD (WELSH) DIVISION

This division, consisting of 71st, 158th and 160th Bdes. with supporting arms and services including 147, 202 and 212 Fd. Ambs., 13 and 26 F.D.Ss., 27 and 31 M.D.Us., 53 Fd. Hyg. Sec. and 'C' Pln. 302 M.A.C., landed at Arromanches on June 27–28 and moved to an area south-east of Bayeux.

It straightway entered the line in the Cheux–Colleville–Mondrainville

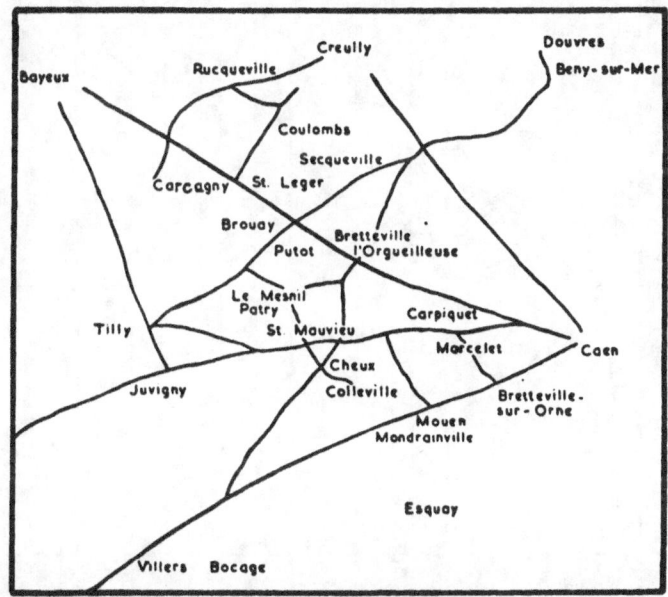

FIG. 15. 53rd Division. The Valley of the Odon. Movements of the Medical Units. July.

170 THE ARMY MEDICAL SERVICES

53rd (Welsh) Division. Location of Medical Units. July 1944

Date	A.D.M.S. Main Div. H.Q.	H.Q. Med. 53 Fd. Hyg. Sec.	147 Fd. Amb.	202 Fd. Amb.	212 Fd. Amb.	13 F.D.S.	26 F.D.S.	M.A.C.	
July 1	Brouay	Coulombs	Bény-sur-Mer	Bretteville-l'Orgueilleuse	Brouay then Le Mesnil Patry A.D.S. open Coy. C.C.P. Colleville	Subles then N. of Cheux Resuscitation	Juno Beach then Rucqueville minor sick	—	u c VIII Corps
2	,,	Brouay	Secqueville-en-Bessin C.C.P. in Rucqueville (closed)	N. of Cheux A.D.S. open	,,	,,	,,		,,
3	,,	,,	Rucqueville (closed)	,,	,,	,,	,,		
8	,,	,,	,,	Coy. C.C.P. Cheux	,,	,,	,,	St. Léger	
10	,,	,,	Coy. C.C.P. Colleville	,,	,,	,,	,,	,,	u c XII Corps Coy. 149 Fd. Amb. 50th Div. u/c
11	,,	,,	,,	,,	Coy. C.C.P. Château de Mouen	,,	,,	,,	
13	,,	,,	N. of Cheux A.D.S. open	Brouay	,,	,,	Brouay minor sick	,,	
14	,,	,,	,,	,,	,,	,,	,,	,,	
18	St. Mauvieu	St. Mauvieu	,,	Cheux	,,	,,	,,	St. Mauvieu	
19	,,	,,	Cheux A.D.S. open	,,	,,	,,	,,	,,	23 Lt. Fd. Amb. u c Cheux
22	,,	,,	,,	Marcelet A.D.S. open	,,	,,	,,	,,	
23	,,	,,	,,	,,	St. Mauvieu	St. Mauvieu	St. Mauvieu	,,	
24 28	,,	,,	,,	,,	,,	,,	,,	,,	23 Lt. Fd. Amb. closed. 'B' Sec. to 34th Tk. Bde. Admin. Area, Bessin
29	,,	,,	,,	,,	,,	,,	,,	,,	23 Lt. Fd. Amb. A.D.S. open

sector u/c VIII Corps. On July 11 the division passed to XII Corps which, with 15th, 43rd and 53rd Divisions, continued the efforts VIII Corps had been making to extend the bridgehead in the Odon valley. Then, when VIII and XXX Corps made their thrust to the south to capture Villers-Bocage, Aunay-sur-Odon and Mont Pinçon, 53rd Division with 59th Division u/c XII Corps kept up pressure to prevent the withdrawal of enemy forces on its front.

The medical cover provided during these events is depicted in the location statements of the divisional medical units for the month of July.

Evacuation in front of the R.A.P. was by hand-carriage, jeep and carrier, and rearwards of the R.A.P. by two-stretcher ambulance. Up to July 6 exhaustion cases were sent to the corps evacuation centre at Creully but thereafter the divisions were instructed to retain these in their own medical units.

Table 17

53rd Division. Admissions to Medical Units. July

	B.C.	Sick	P.o.W.		B.C.	Sick	P.o.W.
July 1	34	10	1	July 16	132	54	18
2	35	24		17	84	23	5
3	7	28	1	18	147	165	6
4	23	35	1	19	42	35	
5	17	24		20	66	58	
6	16	27		21	29	43	2
7	37	44		22	15	71	
8	60	57		23	35	40	1
9	32	58		24	28	109	1
10	31	43		25	17	32	1
11	119	58	5	26	36	55	
12	56	58	5	27	3	38	
13	54	46		28	28	58	
14	32	33		29	26	36	
15	26	37		30	5	25	
				31	16	40	

Two O.Rs. of 212 Fd. Amb. and one O.R. of 13 F.D.S. were among the wounded on July 3. On the 4th one O.R. of 212 Fd. Amb. was killed and one wounded and on the 5th two O.Rs. of the same unit were wounded and one missing. On the 14th two O.Rs. of 147 Fd. Amb. and one O.R. of 212 Fd. Amb. were among the wounded. Around July 22 a mild type of gastro-enteritis accounted for much of the sickness.

59TH (STAFFORDSHIRE) DIVISION

The departure from the United Kingdom of this division, consisting of 176th, 177th and 19th Inf. Bdes. with supporting arms and services including 203, 210 and 211 Fd. Ambs., 30 Fd. Hyg. Sec. and 27 and 28 F.D.Ss., was delayed for a week by the weather. It reached the area of Esquay-sur-Seulles on June 27, 28 and 29. Under command I Corps it took part, along with 3rd and Canadian 3rd Divisions, in the attack on Caen, opening on July 8. Later it took part in an operation subsidiary to Operation 'Goodwood'. In the interval it was in the line engaged in offensive patrolling.

The method of employment of the divisional medical units was as follows:

(a) Jeep and carrier were used almost exclusively for the evacuation of casualties from company aid posts to the R.A.P.
(b) The old lay-out of the A.D.S. and M.D.S. was adopted, the brigade C.C.P. being the equivalent of the A.D.S. and the A.D.S. that of the former M.D.S.

When the division was in the line O.C. field ambulance detailed an 'operational company' to support the brigade. This operational company was employed as follows:

During battle periods O.C. Coy. assigned one N.C.O. and 60 O.Rs. R.A.M.C. to each battalion of the brigade. These worked under the R.M.O. at the R.A.P. One was allotted to each jeep or carrier, plying between company aid post and R.A.P.

O.C. Coy. with the remainder of the company set up a C.C.P. on the brigade axis.

During quiet periods O.C. Coy. established a C.C.P.

A.D.M.S. decided at all times which of the field ambulances would open A.D.Ss. The A.D.S. was located near a divisional downroute away from crossroads and other obvious artillery targets and, if possible, beyond mortar range.

When the division was not in the line one medical orderly with one light ambulance car and driver was attached to each battalion R.A.P. The rest of the field ambulance was concentrated in its brigade area and opened a C.C.P. for the admission of casualties. In battle periods one of the F.D.Ss. was used for the reception of exhaustion cases.

At no time during this period were the divisional medical services overtaxed.

79TH ARMOURED DIVISION

This was an unusual formation in respect of its size (over 22,000), arms and employment. It was composed of:

THE ASSAULT AND LODGEMENT 173

1. Divisional H.Q. and three brigade H.Qs.
2. A three-regiment brigade of Flails.
3. A three-regiment brigade of assault troops, R.E. (two regiments of A.V.R.Es.; one regiment of landing vehicles, tracked (Buffaloes).
4. Two regiments of flame-throwing tanks (Crocodiles).
5. One regiment of duplex-drive tanks (D.D. tanks).
6. Two regiments of armoured personnel carriers (Kangaroos).
7. One regiment of landing vehicles, tracked (Buffaloes) plus twenty-two units representing R.A.S.C., R.E.M.E., Ord. and medical. Of these R.E.M.E. formed a large proportion, there being nine units with a total establishment of 1,800. There was also an assault training regiment, R.E. The medical units were 16 and 21 Lt. Fd. Ambs. There were thirteen R.M.Os. and the usual medical staff at divisional H.Q.

The division was not employed in battle as a complete entity, nor were the brigades. A regiment occasionally was, but usually it was broken down to squadrons or even troops which fought in support of different formations on different sectors. The division was composed of specialised units which acted in support of the normal formations and at the conclusion of an operation these units and sub-units returned to 79th Division.

Such an exceptional formation had peculiar requirements in respect of medical services. A.D.M.S. therefore placed before D.M.S. 21 Army Group a scheme for the reorganisation of the light field ambulances and obtained his approval. The objects of the scheme were:

(1) To increase the evacuating potential in the most forward areas for casualties incurred by any squadron of the division, irrespective of the number of squadrons that were operating at any one time, in support of 'user' formations.
(2) To provide for the evacuation and treatment of casualties in the forward area in the event of the troops consisting entirely or almost entirely of those of 79th Division.
(3) To provide the means during non-operational periods for the treatment of in-patients of the division who were not serious cases but who otherwise would have to be admitted to a C.C.S. or general hospital and who thus might be lost to the division for a considerable time.
(4) To provide the medical personnel and equipment for first-aid treatment for every squadron of every regiment of the division in non-operational periods.

It was proposed that four brigade medical sections should be formed, two to be provided by each of the light field ambulances, and that each brigade medical section should be divisible into nine sub-sections, each consisting of four stretcher-bearers. With three of the brigade medical sections so sub-divided, the other being held in reserve, it would be possible to provide for every squadron, excluding those with the A.P.C.

regiments, a sub-section R.A.M.C. To two out of every three sub-sections a 2-stretcher ambulance car could be allotted.

The scheme proved to be very satisfactory in action. The H.Q. of the light field ambulance established an A.D.S. and those of the brigade medical sections sick bays. A total of 70 beds was available in these installations. Some 73 per cent. of those admitted to them were returned to their units, the rest being transferred to C.C.S. or general hospital.

(iii)
The Assault and Lodgement. Medical Arrangements 21 Army Group Formations

I CORPS

In addition to the medical services of 3rd, Canadian 3rd, 51st and 6th Airborne Divisions and units under the command of these divisions, I Corps for the assault landings had the following medical order of battle:

Corps Troops (D.D.M.S.)	101 Beach Sub-area		102 Beach Sub-area	
	20 Port Detach. R.A.M.C.		21 Port Detach. R.A.M.C.	
16 C.C.S.				
29 F.T.U.	C.E.P. 1		C.E.P. 2	
55 F.S.U.				
32 C.C.S.	5 Beach Gp.	6 Beach Gp.	7 Beach Gp.	8 Beach Gp.
36 F.T.U.	20 F.D.S.	9 F.D.S.	1 F.D.S.	33 F.D.S.
56 F.S.U.	21 F.D.S.	12 F.D.S.	2 F.D.S.	34 F.D.S.
23, 24, 29 and	39 F.S.U.	37 F.S.U.	33 F.S.U.	45 F.S.U.
73 Surgical	109 Surg.	38 F.S.U.	34 F.S.U.	112 Surg.
Teams	Team	22 F.T.U.	13 F.T.U.	Team
6 Fd. Hyg. Sec.	40 F.S.U.	2 Fd. San.	4 Fd. San.	46 F.S.U.
	21 F.T.U.	Sec. Detach.	Sec.Detach.	14 F.T.U.
	1 Fd. San.			3 Fd. San.
	Sec.Detach.			Sec.Detach.

Planning for this operation had been thorough and the medical units were well rehearsed in their respective parts. In the event things went very much according to plan, save that on landing many of the medical units could not occupy their pre-selected sites. These were either in enemy hands or proved to be totally unsuitable. The pre-selection of Hermanville as a site for a C.C.S. was unfortunate for it turned out that this site was wanted for an ammunition dump. The move of 16

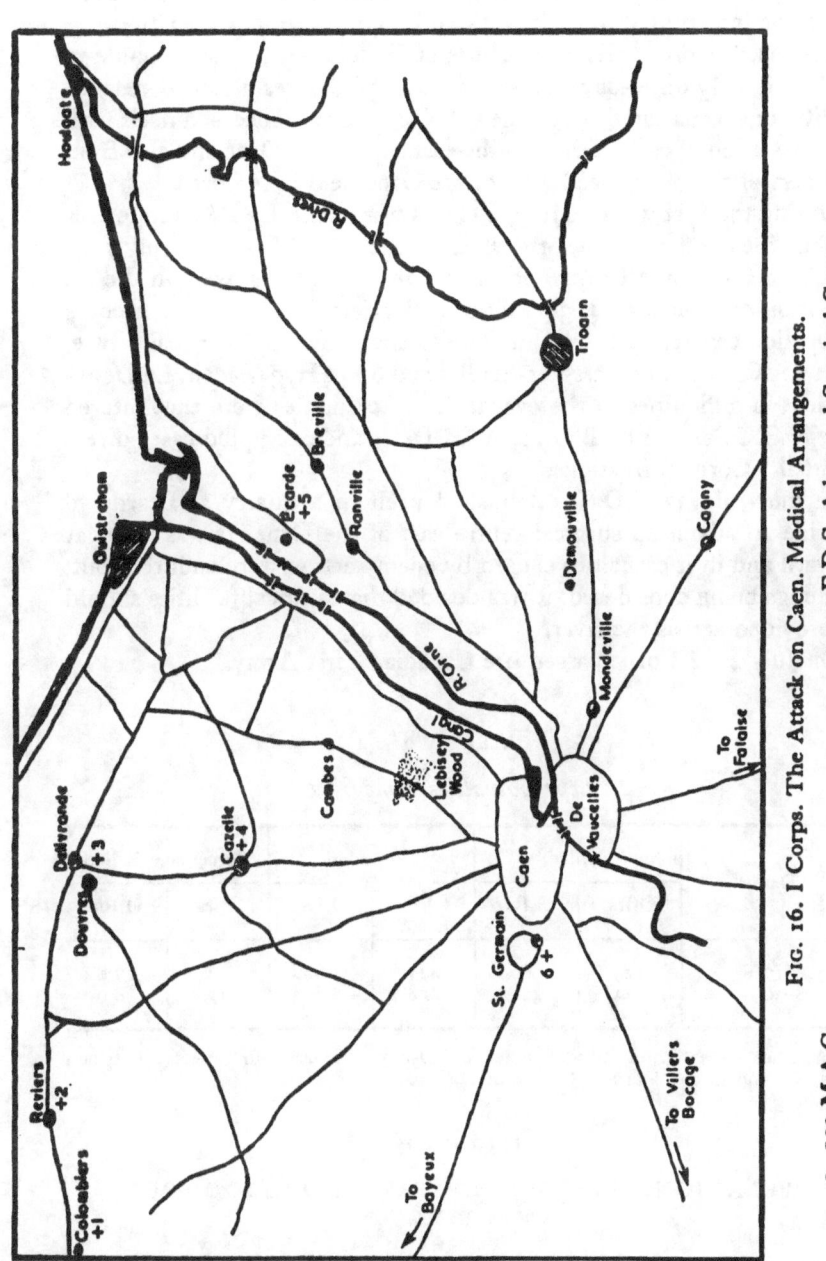

Fig. 16. I Corps. The Attack on Caen. Medical Arrangements.

1. 132 M.A.C.
2. 30 F.D.S. (Corps Exhaustion Centre)
3. 16 and 32 C.C.Ss. 6 Fd. Hyg. Sec.
4. 33 F.D.S. Advanced Surgical Centre
5. " " " (Mid-July)
6. 100 beds in Civil Hospital for 3rd Division

C.C.S. to La Délivrande on June 16 caused considerable trouble for it was fully functioning and had many immobiles in its care. The B.D.Ss. had to be interrupted in their work and required to look after these.

D.D.M.S. Corps arrived off-shore at H-hour+9 but was unable to land until early on D-day+2. When 11 L. of C. Area assumed responsibility for evacuation through the C.E.Ps. I Corps concerned itself with the evacuation of casualties from the east side of the Orne and also from that part of the bridgehead west of the Orne held by I Corps.

During the first week of July, I Corps was in the La Délivrande area holding the left flank of the bridgehead in the area of Caen. On July 7 the attack on Caen by I Corps opened. 16 and 32 C.C.Ss. were in the La Délivrande medical area, 30 F.D.S. in Reviers functioning as a corps exhaustion centre, 33 F.D.S. in Cazelle as an advanced surgical centre, 132 M.A.C. in Colombiers-sur-Seulles and 6 Fd. Hyg. Sec. in La Délivrande. No difficulties in the evacuation of casualties were encountered for the C.C.Ss. and 86 B.G.H. in La Délivrande accepted cases direct from all I Corps formations.

In mid-July 33 F.D.S. established itself in a quarry at Ecarde to provide an advanced surgical centre east of the Orne. It was very far forward and in it casualties caused by enemy action were endured, but, all things being considered, it was decided that surgical facilities should be provided across the river.

On July 22, I Corps passed u/c Canadian First Army.

TABLE 18

I Corps Casualties. June 6–30

Date	Killed		Wounded		Percentage Killed	
	Offrs.	O.Rs.	Offrs.	O.Rs.	Offrs.	O.Rs.
June 6–17 .	129	996	411	4,606	24	17·8
June 18–30 .	44	220	298	2,238	12	8·9

Casualties were lighter than expected on D-day, heavier than expected between D-day+1 and D-day+11 and lighter thereafter.

VIII CORPS

OPERATIONS 'EPSOM', 'JUPITER' AND 'GOODWOOD MEETING'

Operation 'Epsom'—the initial attack from the line of the Bayeux–Caen road—succeeded in gaining a small bridgehead over the Odon. This was followed by a period during which subsidiary operations were

THE ASSAULT AND LODGEMENT

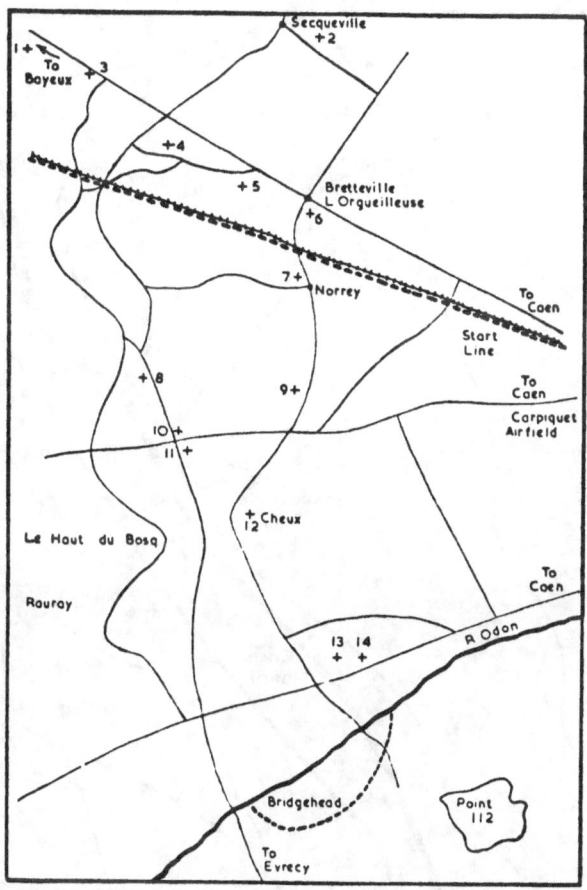

FIG. 17. VIII Corps. Operations 'Epsom' and 'Jupiter'. Medical Arrangements.

1. Medical Area
   3 C.C.S.
   79 B.G.H.
2. Medical Area
   Two C.C.Ss.
   One F.D.S.
   One light field ambulance
3. M.A.C. Control Post
4. A.D.S. and F.D.S.
5. A.D.S.
6. 32 C.C.S.
7. A.D.S.
8. M.A.C. Control Post
9. M.A.C. Control Post
10. F.D.S.
11. A.D.S.
12. A.D.S.
13. A.D.S.
14. F.D.S.

Operation 'Epsom'. Evacuation to Bayeux and when the line was lengthened to 32 C.C.S. 3, 4 and 5 were established prior to H-hour. Then as the operation progressed 7, 8, 9, 10, 11 and 12 were established and 5 remained open.

Operation 'Jupiter'. In addition to the above 13 and 14 were established prior to H-hour.

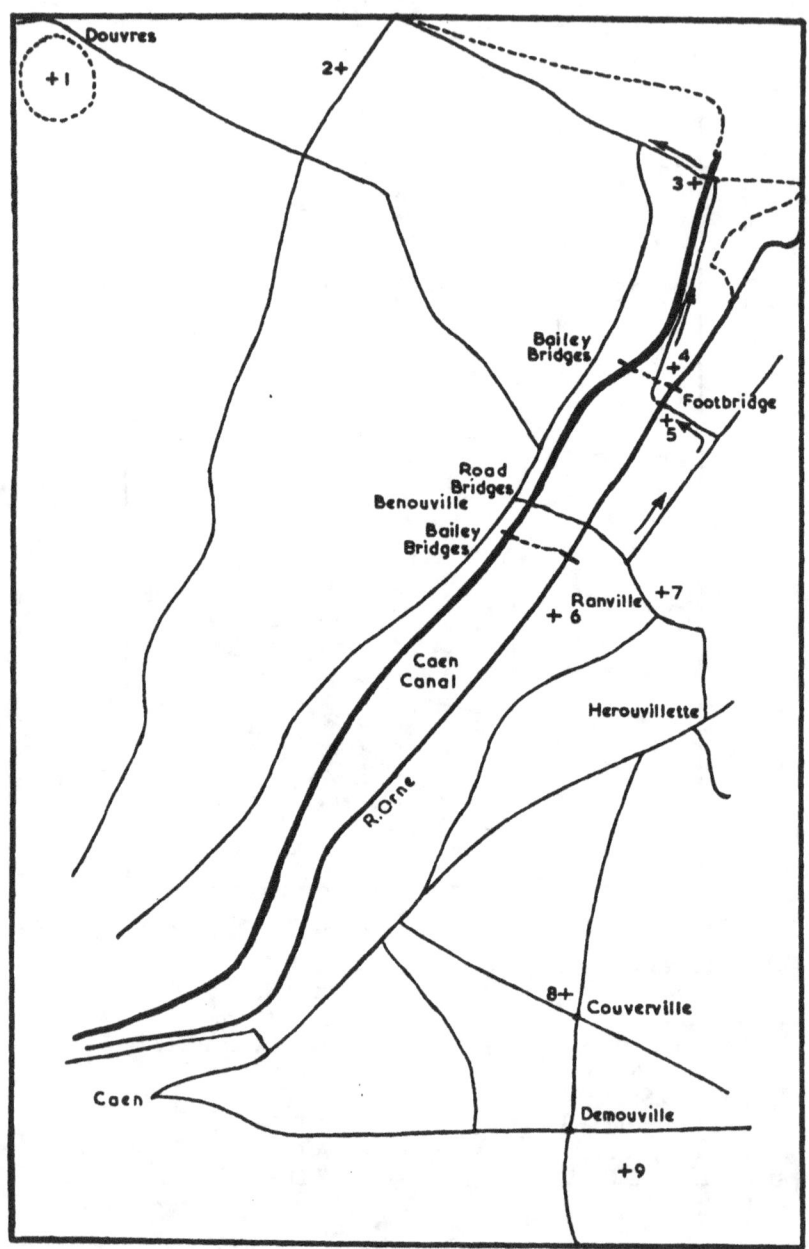

Fig. 18. VIII Corps. Operation 'Goodwood Meeting'. Medical Arrangements.*

undertaken to strengthen the flanks—e.g. the capture of the Rauray ridge and the capture of Carpiquet by the Canadians. Operation 'Jupiter' had for its purpose the enlargement of the bridgehead over the Orne and the capture of Pt. 112 and the high ground overlooking Evrecy.

Three infantry and one armoured divisions, one infantry brigade (32nd Gds.), one armoured brigade and one tank brigade were involved. Because the front was so narrow the medical tactical plan was a corps and not a divisional one. The main concern was the prevention of the unnecessary opening of medical units.

As the bad weather had caused a delay in the landing of VIII Corps' C.C.Ss. use was first made of 3 C.C.S. of XXX Corps and 79 B.G.H. at Bayeux and later of 32 C.C.S. loaned by I Corps. 33 C.C.S. (VIII Corps), landing, opened on July 1, 34 C.C.S. (VIII Corps) on July 5.

In the early stages the axis of evacuation was a central one with one M.A.C. control point. As the front widened and additional roads were constructed two lateral axes each with a control post were used.

For Operation 'Goodwood', the massive thrust of three armoured divisions, which involved the concentrating secretly of one of them in the very narrow and congested bridgehead east of the Orne, set the medical services a difficult problem. All evacuation had necessarily to be back against the heavy stream of fighting troops and across two waterways. It was imperative that nothing should impede the forward movement. It was therefore decided that no ambulance traffic should pass back over any of the bridges unless permission was given by 'Q Movements'. It was assumed that such permission would not be given until 1800 hours, H-hour being 0800 hours. A footbridge over the Orne was therefore strengthened so that casualties could safely be hand-carried over it. The light ambulance of an independent brigade was posted to this footbridge. Casualties were transferred to M.A.C. cars waiting on the island between the Orne and the canal and then driven along a track to the bridge at Ouistreham and on to the La Délivrande hospital area past a F.D.S. which admitted the sick and lightly wounded.

To insure against the possibility that a major obstacle to evacuation

---

* Key to Fig. 18

1. Douvres Medical Area. 33 C.C.S.
2. F.D.S. for walking wounded and sick
3. Second M.A.C. Reserve
4. M.A.C.
5. Light field ambulance.
6. F.D.S. and F.S.U. in reserve
7. A.D.S. and F.D.S. Section
8. A.D.S.
9. A.D.S.

The Bailey bridges and road bridges were reserved for combatant troops. Evacuation was over the footbridge to M.A.C. car in a strip of ground between the river and the canal.

might occur and also to make possible the early forward movement of a medical unit should the advance be rapid and deep, one F.D.S. with F.S.U. and F.T.U. attached was placed across the river the day before the operation started. If necessary these could form an advanced surgical centre.

33 and 34 C.C.Ss. were not required for the La Délivrande medical area was within easy distance of the line. However, 33 was opened in the outskirts of Douvres as a precautionary measure.

33 C.C.S. was loaned to Canadian II Corps and VIII Corps undertook to supervise the arrangements for the admission to and the use of the two Canadian F.S.Us. and the two Canadian and one British C.C.Ss. The F.D.Ss., working alternately, served as a filter to the C.C.Ss. and when one C.C.S. had admitted 95–130 total cases, casualties were diverted to another.

XII CORPS

D.D.M.S. landed with corps H.Q. on June 25. The corps medical units landed as follows:

    4 F.D.S. and 23 Lt. Fd. Amb. on June 25;
    23 C.C.S. and 302 M.A.C., less residue, on June 26;
    10 Fd. Hyg. Sec. on June 30;
    24 C.C.S. on July 1.

On landing all the divisions then under command and the majority of corps troops passed to the command of other formations. Only the armoured brigade of Guards Division and 34th Tk. Bde. remained u/c XII Corps. One platoon of 302 M.A.C. was lent to A.D.M.S. L. of C.; 4 officers and 200 O.Rs. of 23 C.C.S. to D.D.M.S. XXX Corps for instructional purposes; 4 officers and 20 O.Rs. of 24 C.C.S. to D.D.M.S. VIII Corps and 4 officers and 20 O.Rs. of 4 F.D.S. to D.D.M.S. XXX Corps.

On June 30, 4 F.D.S. opened for the reception of minor casualties from corps troops and 23 Lt. Fd. Amb. opened to serve 34th Tk. Bde. A dental centre was established in connexion with each of these medical units.

When about to proceed to the marshalling area in the United Kingdom XII Corps had provided 74 N.Os. from 23 and 24 C.C.Ss. and from 302 M.A.C. for duty in pairs in the L.S.T. under 21 Army Group arrangements. It was understood at that time that they would return to XII Corps by June 13. But by July 13 only 8 of them had rejoined their units and so the C.C.Ss. were so shorthanded as to be incapable of functioning. However, XII Corps remained unemployed until July 11.

On July 12, 15th, 43rd and 53rd Divisions were placed u/c XII Corps as were the following Army medical units:

THE ASSAULT AND LODGEMENT

9 F.D.S.
12, 13, 15, 27 and 42 F.S.Us.
13, 30 and 37 F.T.Us.
211 and 215 M.D.Us.
68 P.A.C.

24 C.C.S. opened in St. Léger and 9 F.D.S. opened to act as a sieve to the C.C.S., draining off the walking wounded. 4 F.D.S. took the minor sick and exhaustion cases.

The usual scheme for the utilisation of medical units in XII Corps at this time was as follows:

The divisional F.D.Ss. were used for the holding of cases likely to be fit to fight again in a few days or to reinforce A.D.Ss. The corps F.D.Ss. were used as small C.C.Ss. with two F.S.Us., one F.T.U. and two nursing officers attached, sometimes under the command of divisions. The C.C.Ss., when no considerable advance was made, were grouped in pairs together with a F.D.S. A C.C.S. admitted 100 cases and then the flow was directed to the other. When the advance was considerable the corps C.C.Ss. leap-frogged each other.

XXX CORPS

In addition to the medical services of 7th Armoured, 49th and 50th Divisions and of the units that were attached to these divisions XXX Corps' medical order of battle for the assault landings was as follows:

Corps Troops (D.D.M.S.)	Army Tps. u/c XXX Corps	104 Beach Sub-area	
		9 Beach Gp.	10 Beach Gp.
3 and 10 C.C.Ss.	25, 31, 32, 35 F.D.Ss.	47, 48 F.S.Us.	41, 42 F.S.Us.
3 F.D.S.			
31 Fd. Hyg. Sec.		24 F.T.U.	30 F.T.U.
111 M.A.C.		22 Port Detach. R.A.M.C.	23 Port Detach. R.A.M.C.

3 F.D.S. had been mobilised only just prior to D-day. XXX Corps therefore borrowed 16 F.D.S. from 49th Division for use as the corps F.D.S. during the assault landings.

XXX Corps, like I Corps, was compounded out of divisions with long service in a theatre of war and of others which had no experience of battle. 7th Armoured Division had come from C.M.F. as had also 3 C.C.S., 6 F.S.U., 7 F.T.U., 131 Fd. Amb., 2 Lt. Fd. Amb. and 70 Fd. Hyg. Sec. They all had to be remobilised on the new war establishment and completely re-equipped. Since the policy was to spread those with battle experience throughout the corps there was much crossposting. This inevitably caused much disgruntlement for it could mean that an officer of senior rank but without any service overseas was placed in command of a unit or of a company thereof which consisted of officers and men long trained in actual battle.

On February 5, 1944, following the example set by Second Army, XXX Corps H.Q. divided itself into two parts, an advanced and a static H.Q. The former, including D.D.M.S. and D.A.D.M.S., moved to London to concern itself with planning, the latter, including the A.D.H., remained in Cambridge. The work of remobilising and equipping the units was so arduous that it was found necessary to attach a second officer to A.D.H. as staff captain. Adv. H.Q. shut down and rejoined Static H.Q. on March 26. The medical units underwent intensive training and a number of R.A.M.C. personnel were instructed in wireless procedure.

As in I Corps, so also in XXX Corps, everything went more or less according to plan on D-day. There was some delay in the landing of the vehicles and, to begin with, in the evacuation of the casualties. On D-day + 2, twenty-four hours late, 3 C.C.S. and 16 F.D.S. came ashore and opened in their pre-selected sites near Ryes. On D-day + 5 the Corps was well established well south of Bayeux. 10 C.C.S. was moved to the vicinity of Bayeux to open on June 12. Thereafter evacuation was smooth, 3 C.C.S. and 16 F.D.S. being able to transfer their more serious cases to 81 B.G.H. which had moved in and was taking over. 16 F.D.S. reverted to 49th Division on June 14 and on the 17th 3 C.C.S. with 3 F.D.S. moved to Jerusalem. On June 18 casualties from VIII Corps on the left of XXX Corps inundated 10 C.C.S. and XXX Corps' casualties were therefore diverted to 3 C.C.S. As soon as the fighting quietened down nursing officers from 81 B.G.H. joined 3 C.C.S. 35 F.D.S. (Army) was attached to 10 C.C.S. and with it went the corps psychiatrist to open a corps exhaustion centre. But this centre soon became overtaxed, commanding officers taking advantage of it to get rid, along medical channels, of grossly unsatisfactory men. This abuse had to be checked.

TABLE 19

XXX Corps Casualties. June 6–30

Strength:
  Assault phase . . . . . . 90,000 approximately
  Thereafter . . . . 65,000 approximately

Killed	Wounded	Sick
1,176	5,730 plus 386 P.o.W.	2,833

THE ASSAULT AND LODGEMENT

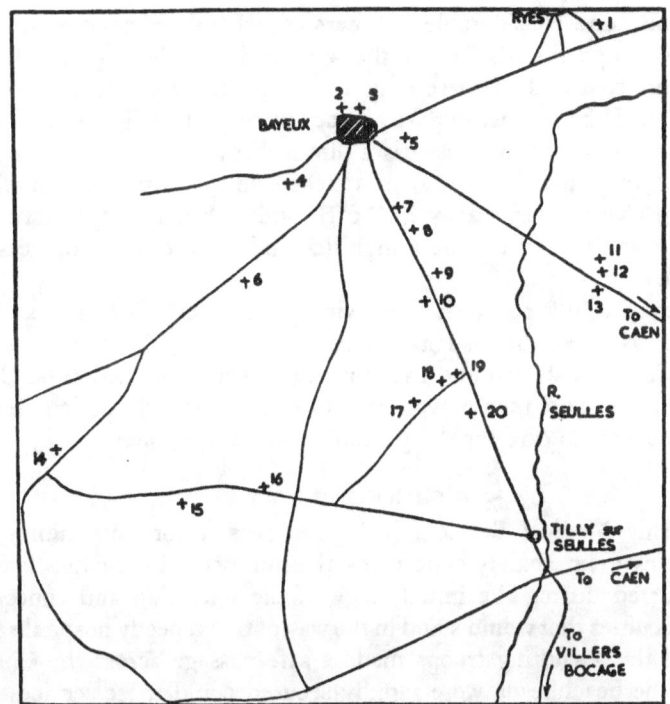

FIG. 19. XXX Corps. The Medical Situation as at 2359 hours, June 18.

1. 81 B.G.H.
2. 186 Fd. Amb. 50 Div.
3. 200 Fd. Amb. 50 Div.
4. 79 B.G.H.
5. 10 C.C.S. XXX Corps.
   35 F.D.S.
   111 M.A.C.
   31 Fd. Hyg. Sec. XXX Corps
6. 131 Fd. Amb. 7 Armd. Div.
7. 168 Lt. Fd. Amb. 8 Armd. Bde.
8. D.D.M.S. XXX Corps
9. A.D.M.S. 50 Div.
10. 203 Fd. Amb. 59 Div.
11. 16 F.D.S. 49 Div.
    187 Fd. Amb. 49 Div.
12. A.D.M.S. 49 Div.
13. 146 Fd. Amb. 49 Div.
14. A.D.M.S. 7 Armd. Div.
15. 2 Lt. Fd. Amb. 7 Armd. Div.
16. 29 F.D.S. 7 Armd. Div.
17. 48 F.D.S. 50 Div.
18. 3 C.C.S. XXX Corps.
19. 3 F.D.S. XXX Corps.
20. 149 Fd. Amb. 50 Div.

160 Fd. Amb. of 49th Division was located further to the south-east along the Bayeux–Caen road.

At the beginning of July when XXX Corps had consolidated its position south of Tilly from Touteval–Juvigny–Grainville, 10 C.C.S., 35 F.D.S., the corps psychiatrist and the corps venereologist were at St. Vigor-le-Grand, east of Bayeux, the C.C.S. receiving battle casualties and 35 F.D.S. the minor sick, psychiatric and V.D. cases. 3 C.C.S. and 3 F.D.S. were open at Jerusalem, receiving battle casualties. To the F.D.S. 43 and 47 F.S.Us. and 7 F.T.U. were attached.

At this time considerable numbers of exhaustion cases were being admitted to 35 F.D.S. During the week ending July 1, 524 such cases were admitted and of these only 10 per cent. were returned to their units. 9 F.D.S. was temporarily attached to 35 to help. As the weeks passed the numbers of these cases diminished.

When, on July 6, 56th Bde. attacked and captured Grainville its casualties were received by 3 C.C.S. and 3 F.D.S. At this time 10 C.C.S. was catering for the minor sick and for the numerous cases of malaria.

When, on July 16, 56th Bde. with 33rd Armd. Bde. attacked and captured Noyers, 465 casualties were admitted to 3 C.C.S. On the 17th the C.C.S. was shelled and two nursing officers wounded. The C.C.S. and 3 F.D.S. were then moved back to Nonant from Jerusalem, leaving adequate staff to care for the 50 non-transportable cases.

SECOND ARMY

The Army Medical Services had good reason for entertaining and expressing great anxiety concerning the numbers of casualties likely to be incurred during the initial stage of the operation and concerning the difficulties that would stand in the way of their speedy hospitalisation. Only if the assaulting troops made a safe passage across the Channel and if the beachheads were rapidly secured could these services hope to function with efficiency. This anxiety was stilled when it became known that success had been achieved. Difficulties still remained but they were of a kind that had been weighed and that could be removed or lessened by administrative elasticity. It had not been expected that everything would proceed according to plan. In general, however, nothing presented itself, save the storm of June 19, that seriously interfered with the arrangements that had been so carefully prepared.

Having regard to the nature of the operation casualties were few.

TABLE 20

Second Army. Admissions to and Evacuations from the Medical Units June 6–July 1, 1944

		Average rate per 1,000 per week
June 6–10 inclusive	5,259 (not classified)	
June 11–July 1	20,492	
Injuries and wounds:		
Battle Casualties	14,224	17·39
Accidental	1,213	1·42
Self-inflicted	52	0·06
Burns	331	0·39
Exhaustion	1,853	2·11

Diseases of Digestive System	565	0·21
,, ,, Respiratory ,,	397	0·16
,, ,, Skin	591	0·27
Neurological Diseases	88	0·10
I.A.T.	585	0·63
P.U.O.	593	0·65
	20,492	

Exhaustion Cases:

June 11–17	6·74 per cent. of total admissions
13–24	10·13 ,, ,, ,, ,,
25–July 1	10·88 ,, ,, ,, ,,

Of the battle casualties 50 per cent. were caused by shell and mortar bomb fragments.

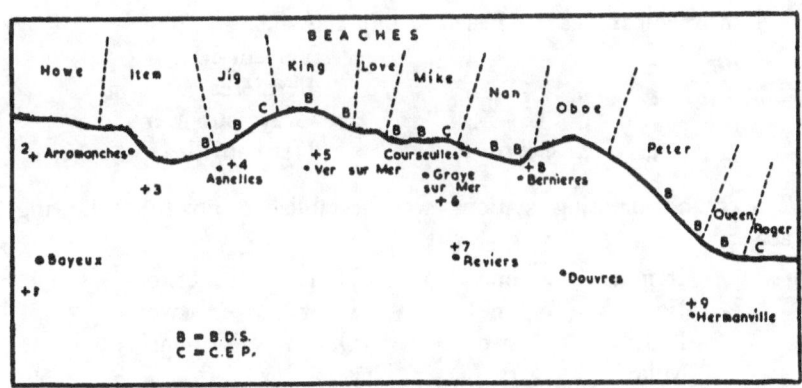

Fig. 20. Distribution of the Medical Units under H.Q. 11 L. of C. Area as at June 11.

1. 79 B.G.H.
2. 74 Fd. Hyg. Sec.
3. 49 F.D.S. and 54 F.S.U.
4. Joint Medical Area. 10 Beach Group. Asnelles.
   25 and 31 F.D.Ss.; 41 and 42 F.S.Us.; 30 F.T.U.
5. Joint Medical Area. 9 Beach Group. Ver-sur-Mer.
   32 and 35 F.D.Ss.; 47 and 48 F.S.Us.; 24 F.T.U.
6. Joint Medical Area. 8 Beach Group. Graye-sur-Mer.
   1 and 2 F.D.Ss.; 33 and 34 F.S.Us.; 13 F.T.U.
7. H.Q. 11 L. of C.
8. Joint Medical Area. 7 Beach Group. Bernières-sur-Mer.
   33 and 34 F.D.Ss.; 45 and 46 F.S.Us.; 14 F.T.U.; 112 Surgical Team.
9. Joint Medical Area. 5 and 6 Beach Groups. Hermanville.
   5 Beach Group. 20 and 21 F.D.Ss.; 39 and 40 F.S.Us.; 21 F.T.U.
   6 Beach Group. 9 and 12 F.D.Ss.; 37 and 38 F.S.Us.; 22 F.T.U.

Table 20 continued

Numbers evacuated to the United Kingdom
By sea . . 16,598
By air . . 3,073
_____
19,671

The following figures are given in the *Official History of the Canadian Medical Services*, Vol. I:

Second Army Casualties up to D-day+23 . . 21,016 (approx.)
                      including . . 2,968 Canadians.

19,748 of these were evacuated to the U.K. up to June 30. 46,300 including sick had been evacuated to the U.K. by sea and air by July 28.

The beach groups banded themselves together into medical areas.

Joint medical area	10 Beach Group at	Asnelles
,, ,, ,,	9 ,, ,,	Ver-sur-Mer
,, ,, ,,	7 ,, ,,	Bernières
,, ,, ,,	8 ,, ,,	Graye-sur-Mer
,, ,, ,,	5 & 6 ,, ,,	Hermanville

The beach dressing stations were established on the following beaches:

Item .	. one	Nan .	. two
Jig .	. one	Peter .	. two
King .	. two	Queen .	. one
Mike .	. two		

Casualty evacuation points were located as under:

C.E.P. 3 on Jig Beach . . one
C.E.P. 2 ,, Mike Beach . one
C.E.P. 1 ,, Roger Beach . one

Thus all the beach medical units were committed and there was none in reserve. However, the medically fitted L.S.T. beached from D-day + 1 and many more casualties were evacuated than would have been the case had the L.S.T. lain off shore and been loaded by D.U.K.Ws. and so the lack of a reserve was not felt.

On D-day and D-day + 1 B.D.Ss. evacuated direct to the C.E.P., but from D-day + 2 they sent their cases to the joint medical areas. When shelling of Roger beach rendered the loading of L.S.T. *via* the C.E.P. impossible the casualties from 101 Beach Sub-area were diverted to

C.E.P. 2 on Mike beach. Time came when only one C.E.P. was needed. C.E.P. 3 on Jig beach was closed and 2 F.D.S. established a C.E.P. at Courseulles. But when 1,000–2,000 casualties had to be held overnight at this C.E.P., as the tide was unsuitable for L.S.T. to beach and the weather too rough for carriers to load at sea, it became necessary to reinforce the unit. A château at Vaux was taken over and staffed with a composite medical unit, 2 and 34 F.D.Ss., 45 and 46 F.S.Us. and 13 F.T.U. Sixteen nursing officers were attached to it as was also a company of A.M.P.C. 7 ambulance cars, 8 3-ton lorries, and up to 30 D.U.K.Ws. were available for evacuation from the C.E.P. to the point of evacuation.

This C.E.P., with a staff of 38 officers, 16 nursing officers and some 600 O.Rs., developed an organisation that enabled it to function efficiently in difficult circumstances. It had accommodation for about 300 patients in buildings and 400 under canvas. Admitted to it and evacuated from it were 200 to 2,200 a day so that very frequently the numbers that had to be cared for far exceeded the available accommodation. Commonly patients had to remain in the ambulances that had brought them to the C.E.P. until these could proceed to the embarkation point. Owing to the vagaries of the weather there could be no steady stream of evacuation and so the C.E.P. had to be prepared to hold patients for indefinite periods of time. However, it was found that a demand for rations for 350 patients a day was quite adequate.

Duties within the C.E.P. were distributed as follows:

O.C. C.E.P.	The senior of the two O.Cs. F.D.Ss.
2nd i/c	The junior „ „ „ „ „
Evacuation officers (2)	The 2 i/c F.D.Ss. (Selection of cases for evacuation by (i) L.S.T. (24–36 hours' journey) or (ii) hospital carrier (10–12 hours))
Control officers (2)	The non-medical officers of the F.D.Ss. (Supervision of the embarkation of casualties)
Os. i/c ship-loading (4)	The subalterns of the Pioneer Coy. (Supervision of the actual loading of the ships. The L.S.T. could take 144 lying cases, in racks, 100 walking, on the troop decks plus a number of stretchers lashed to the tank decks. The largest number carried by one such L.S.T. was 450.)
Evacuation transport officer	The O.C. D.U.K.W. platoon (24 ambulance cars, 8 3-ton lorries and 33 D.U.K.Ws.)

Within the C.E.P. there were:

 Reception . . . 3 M.Os.
 Surgical wing . . . The F.S.Us. and F.T.U.
 (40 beds)
  A 1 ward (cases for immediate evacuation by hospital carrier)
  A 2 ward (cases needing further treatment before evacuation)
 (For record purposes this wing was designated 2 F.D.S.)

Documentation demanded most careful attention. A nominal roll of each ship-load was made by a clerk stationed at the gangway of each ship as it was loaded. Of this nominal roll one copy was sent to G.H.Q. 2nd Echelon, one to D.A.D.M.S.(E) Beach Sub-area and one was filed. Loading was restricted to the hours of daylight.

On D-day a strong wind made the handling of small craft in the surf very difficult and the 'Rhino' ferries (steel raft-like craft) were immobilised, many being stranded. There was some delay in the landing of vehicles and in the evacuation of the wounded but some 200 casualties were embarked. At nightfall the situation was satisfactory, the medical units still having ample holding space.

On D-day + 1 evacuation was at a standstill for the D.U.K.Ws. could not live in the heavy sea that was running. Towards the evening the medical units were overfull. The Navy, however, agreed to beach the L.S.T. for loading and the threat of a crisis passed. D.D.M.S. XXX Corps landed early on this day, as did also A.D.M.S. 11 L. of C. Area.

On D-day + 2 the sea went down and the D.U.K.Ws. were able to resume their amphibious rôle. Because of the difficulties that attended the off-loading of L.S.T. by 'Rhino' ferry, the majority of the L.S.T. were beached and dried out and the D.U.K.Ws. were required to swim their casualty loads out to the ships. D.D.M.S. Second Army landed with Tactical H.Q. early on this day.

The energies of the Army Medical Services were at this time necessarily focused upon the organisation of the system of evacuation over the beaches. The most difficult part of the procedure was the transportation of the casualties from the beach F.D.S. to the C.E.P. The beachheads were exceedingly congested and in them all movement was difficult. It became necessary to invoke the aid of the Provost Branch, representatives of which thereafter led the convoys of D.U.K.Ws. and cleared the roads for them.

The policy of using medically adapted L.S.T. and setting aside D.U.K.Ws. for medical purposes worked very satisfactorily; there were, however, misunderstandings and difficulties concerning the arrival of the hospital carriers. Eventually it became routine for an officer of the C.E.P. to meet the carriers in a D.U.K.W. and guide them to the proper anchorage. The policy of sending representatives of the follow-up medical units with the units landing before them proved to be very satisfactory for by it the time required for the follow-up units to become established was greatly shortened.

The personnel of the C.C.Ss. did not always land at the times scheduled; the vehicles arrived at odd times, sometimes twenty-four hours before, sometimes twenty-four hours after, the scheduled time. The pre-selected sites for these units were not in all cases available and alternative sites had to be chosen by A.Ds.M.S. in conjunction with divisional A/Q.

In the early days of the invasion the F.S.U. abundantly proved its worth, the wounded receiving therein a much higher grade of surgical care than had been contemplated during the planning phase.

D.A.D.M.S., D.A.D.H., 11 L. of C. Area and a number of 'pool' medical officers landed on D-day + 3, as did A.D.M.S's. clerical staff later in the day. The remainder of the pool M.Os. remained aboard a 'Rhinoceros' ('Rhino' ferry) to land dry-shod next morning. H.Q. L. of C. Area was established at Reviers on D-day + 4, to remain there until September 3.

H.Q. Second Army took over from I and XXX Corps in Normandy on June 11, Main H.Q. being at Cruelly and Rear H.Q. first at Banville and later, on July 6, at Vaux-sur-Seulles. The control of rear areas was exercised through H.Q. Second Army Troops, 5 L. of C. Sub-area and 11 L. of C. Area. The last of these was placed in control of the local administration of 101, 102 and 104 Beach Sub-areas and through 4 L. of C. Sub-area of 10 Garrison and of the local administration of Mulberry B and Port-en-Bessin. H.Q. Second Army Troops took over command of the depots and installations in the beach maintenance areas now being expanded into two Army road-heads to serve Second and Canadian First Armies respectively. The rear maintenance area, formed from 2 Army Road-head in the Bayeux area, was placed under the local administration of 5 L. of C. Sub-area. On July 11, 101 Beach Sub-area was made responsible for the ports of Caen and Ouistreham. On July 25, 7 Base Sub-area relieved 101 Beach Sub-area of its responsibilities, the beach sub-area in its turn relieving 10 Garrison at Port-en-Bessin. 10 Garrison was then placed u/c Second Army for forward duties.

The arrival of Canadian First Army H.Q. necessitated the separate administration of the rear areas and on July 13 this responsibility was assumed by H.Q. L. of C. On July 22 H.Q. Second Army relinquished operational control of 2 Army Road-head and on the 23rd the rear Army boundary was defined and Second Army was relieved administratively as well as operationally of all rearward commitments.

On June 11 the distribution of the medical units was as follows:

Beaches

Right	. . .	49 F.D.S. at Arromanches where construction of the Mulberry harbour had begun.
		25 and 31 F.D.Ss. with field surgical and transfusion units at Asnelles-sur-Mer.
		32 and 35 F.D.Ss. with field surgical and transfusion units at Ver-sur-Mer.
Centre	. . .	1 and 2 F.D.Ss. at Graye-sur-Mer.
		33 and 34 F.D.Ss. at Bernières-sur-Mer.
Left	. . .	9, 12, 20 and 21 F.D.Ss. at Hermanville.

Inland

XXX Corps	. . .	3 C.C.S. open at Ryes.
		10 C.C.S. preparing to open at St. Vigor-le-Grand (just east of Bayeux).
I Corps	. . .	16 C.C.S. open at Hermanville.
		32 C.C.S. open at Reviers.
Army	. . .	81 B.G.H., which had landed on June 10, was closed alongside 3 C.C.S. at Ryes.
		84 B.G.H. was closed at La Délivrande.
		35 C.C.S., landing on June 9, opened alongside 32 C.C.S. at Reviers on June 11.

From these three medical areas at Ryes, Reviers and La Délivrande developed the Army lay-out which remained in operation until the break-out from the bridgehead occurred. A fourth medical area, just west of Bayeux, was earmarked for 79 B.G.H. This was afterwards to become the main area for L. of C. hospitals in Normandy. 79 B.G.H. landed on June 14 and first began to receive casualties on June 20.

Evacuation by air began on June 13, which was a week earlier than had been anticipated in planning. Air evacuation was more uncertain than sea evacuation because the airfields on which suitable aircraft arrived changed constantly and there was always uncertainty as to the number of aircraft available. The problem was also complicated by the fact that no facilities existed on the airstrip for holding casualties. Consequently no preparations could be made for evacuation until the aircraft had landed and in a congested beachhead it was not always possible to deliver casualties at the airstrip on time. The necessity for dual documentation was another factor which caused a heavy strain on the medical unit. On June 18, however, the whole air evacuation scheme was centralised under 11 L. of C. Area. A Medical Air Liaison Officer (M.A.L.O.) was attached to 83 Group R.A.F. and 81 B.G.H.; later 77 B.G.H. at Reviers was made the principal collecting centre for those to be evacuated by air. A single airstrip was selected for evacuation purposes. R.A.F. casualty air evacuation units began to arrive at this time and assisted in holding casualties on the airfield until aircraft were

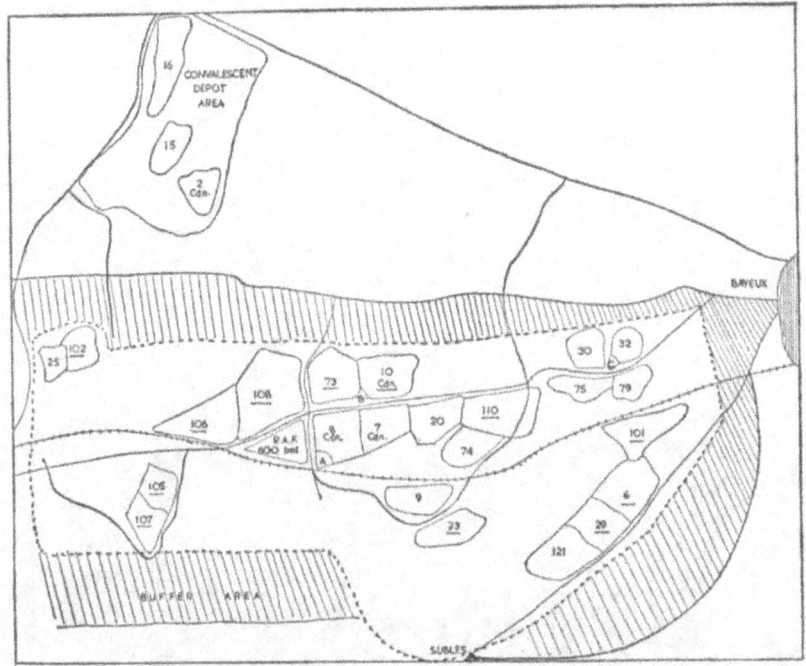

FIG. 21. The Plan of the Bayeux Medical Area.

The figures underlined represent 1,200-bed hospitals, the rest 600-bed. 7, 8 and 10 Canadian General Hospitals had a total capacity of 2,400 beds.

        A = 2 Cdn. Base Depot of Medical Stores
        B = 12 and 13 Base Depots of Medical Stores
        C = 5 Base Depot of Medical Stores

available. The holding capacity of these units was not large enough to deal with the numbers to be evacuated and on several occasions a F.D.S. or C.C.S. was sited to help in this task. During June 3,176 casualties (2,113 lying) were evacuated by air (*see* Appendix V).

By June 18 it was possible to lay down a definite scheme for disposal of casualties to become operative on June 20. Two evacuation sectors, east and west, roughly corresponding to the corps areas, were defined. The policy of evacuating all cases not likely to be fit in forty-eight hours was continued. Evacuation in the western sector was to be to 79 B.G.H. in Bayeux and 81 and 84 B.G.Hs. at Ryes. Evacuation in the eastern sector was to be to 86 and 88 B.G.Hs. at La Délivrande and 32 and 35 C.C.Ss. at Reviers.

Corps were to be responsible for evacuating to these centres with their M.A.Cs. 257 A.C.C. was responsible for evacuation to the C.E.P. and airfields.

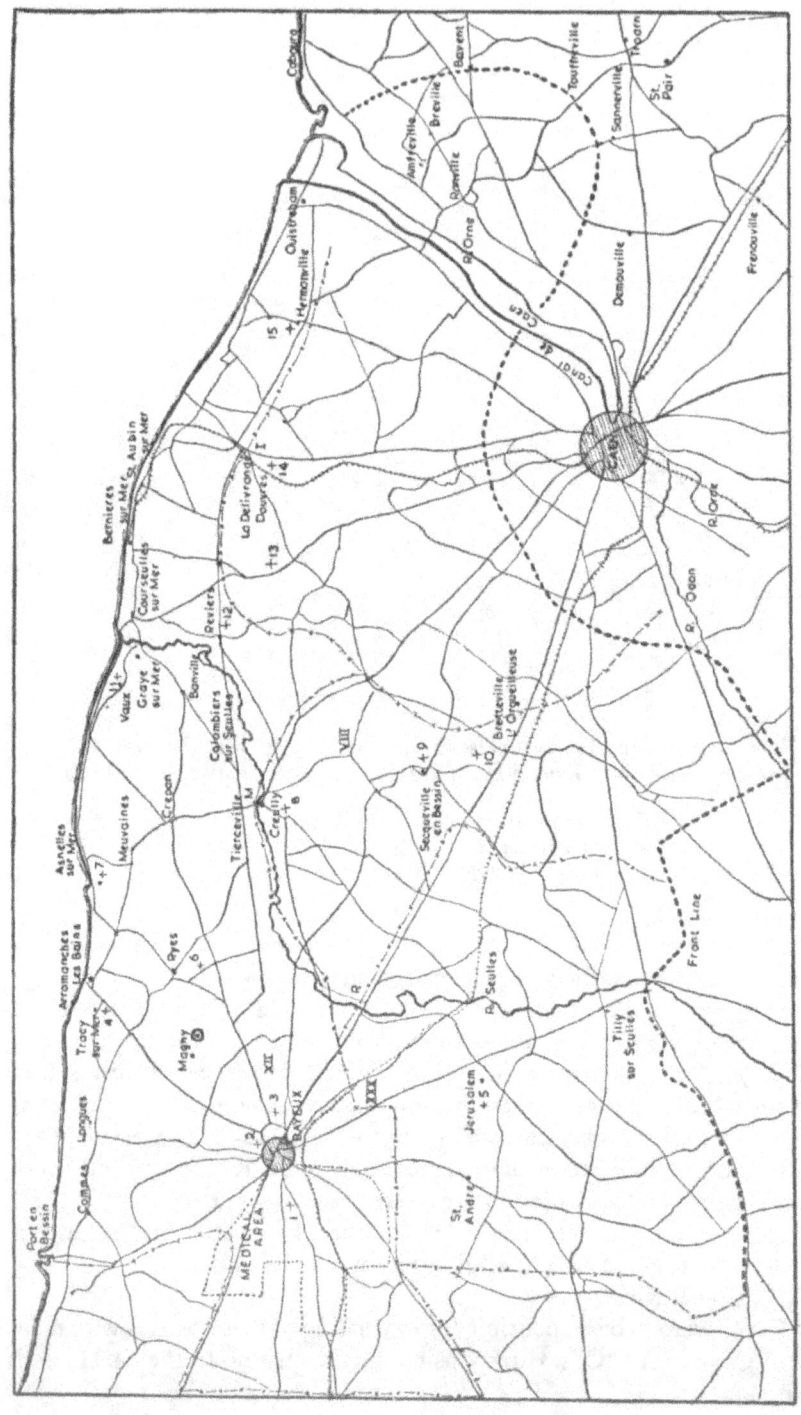

Fig. 22. Second Army. Distribution of Medical Units as at June 30 (D-day+24).

THE ASSAULT AND LODGEMENT

31 F.D.S. at Ryes, 50 F.D.S. at Reviers and 20 F.D.S. at La Délivrande were to screen the minor sick and walking cases in order to relieve pressure on hospitals.

3 C.C.S. (XXX Corps) left the Ryes area on June 18 and its place was taken by 84 B.G.H., which landed on June 17. 88 B.G.H., which landed on the same day, moved into the La Délivrande area. 16 C.C.S. (I Corps) had been transferred to this area on June 16 from Hermanville.

20, 75 and 77 B.G.Hs. landed on the night of 22nd/23rd and were located as follows: 20 in La Lazarette at Bayeux, 75 in reserve in the Ryes area and 77 in Reviers, where it began to take over from 32 C.C.S. (I Corps). (Plates XI–XIV illustrate conditions in the Beachhead Medical Area.)

32 C.C.S. on relief went to Bretteville-l'Orgueilleuse in support of VIII Corps, which went into action on June 20 without its own C.C.Ss. However, by June 25, 33 C.C.S. (VIII Corps) had arrived and opened at Secqueville, to which area 32 C.C.S. was withdrawn.

By June 23 it was possible to elaborate the scheme further. 20 B.G.H. joined the Bayeux group, which now received from the western sector, and Ryes was allotted for overflow cases and minor sick. 77 B.G.H. was to open in Reviers to take over that area and to receive primarily from VIII Corps. The La Délivrande group continued to receive from I Corps. The Army A.C.C. now took over the evacuation from the corps C.C.Ss., except that XXX Corps continued to evacuate direct to Bayeux. 218 A.C.C. under A.D.M.S. 11 L. of C. Area evacuated from Army medical areas to the C.E.P. and the airfields.

During this period a number of the F.D.Ss. had been withdrawn from the beaches and 2 and 34 F.D.Ss. were made responsible for evacuation over the beaches. Of the F.D.Ss. withdrawn one had been given to each corps then ashore (XII Corps arrived at the end of the month) to assist them with psychiatric and exhaustion cases which were

---

* *Key to Fig. 22*

1. 30, 32, 75 and 79 B.G.Hs.
2. 20 B.G.H.
3. 10 C.C.S.
4. 49 F.D.S
5. 3 C.C.S..
6. 81 and 84 B.G.Hs.
   31 F.D.S.
7. 25 F.D.S.
8. 1 F.D.S.
9. 33 and 34 C.C.Ss.
10. 24 F.D.S.
11. C.E.P. 2 and 34 F.D.Ss.
    Rest Centre 32 F.D.S.
12. 77 B.G.H.
    35 C.C.S. (closed)
    50 F.D.S.
13. 257 A.C.C.
14. 86 and 88 B.G.Hs.
    16 and 32 C.C.Ss.
15. 12 and 21 F.D.Ss.

M = Main Army H.Q.   R = Rear Army H.Q.
I, VIII, XII and XXX = Corps H.Q.

beginning to show an increase. It was planned to open an Army psychiatric centre at Vaux, near the C.E.P., at the beginning of July where cases could be held up to seven days. The C.E.P. was moved from the now congested area of Graye-sur-Mer to Vaux.

During the rest of the time before the break-out from the bridgehead the medical base at Ranchy, near Bayeux, was gradually built up. It was a somewhat slow process because of the delays in the arrival of equipment. Save for 20 B.G.H. in the Lazarette all the hospitals were tented. The supply of water was a major problem and even after the R.E. had installed a pipe-line water carts were fully occupied in delivering water within the hospital area. By July 26 there were nineteen general hospitals and twelve C.C.Ss. in the bridgehead. As a result of the slow build-up the policy of retaining patients in the theatre could not be implemented and so it was that all patients unlikely to be fit to return to duty in a week were evacuated to the United Kingdom.

On July 13, H.Q. 11 L. of C. Area assumed control of the rear areas and so took over the Bayeux medical area, 77 B.G.H. at Reviers and responsibility for evacuation to the United Kingdom by sea and air.

As the Bayeux medical area expanded it became possible to close that at Ryes. On July 21, Canadian First Army assumed responsibility for the La Délivrande area, 86 and 88 B.G.Hs. passing under its command. At the end of July 86 B.G.H. was relieved by 6 Cdn.G.H. and moved to Ryes on reversion to Second Army. There it remained closed. 81 B.G.H. in Ryes also closed and prepared to move forward. 84 B.G.H. remained open to serve the local sick.

During the operations at the end of July Army F.D.Ss. were moved forward by bounds to take over the immobiles for the corps C.C.Ss. and to act as staging posts on the long road journeys back to Bayeux. One F.D.S. was associated with each of the 200-bed hospitals to deal with the lightly wounded and 50 F.D.S. was allotted to Army troops for the sick and V.D. cases.

Evacuation by air and sea proceeded smoothly during July. The daily bid of one medically equipped L.S.T. on each tide and one hospital carrier had to be stepped up to three L.S.T. and one carrier in the later part of July. If six L.S.T. were not forthcoming then a second carrier had to be called forward.

In July the medical branch of H.Q. 11 L. of C. Area was assigned the task of meeting all L. of C. medical units as they came ashore and routeing them to their appointed destinations. It was found that it was impossible to do these things for only rarely was H.Q. informed of their impending arrival and only infrequently were the sites allotted to them available when they landed. The need was felt for a medical staging camp in the Bayeux area.

It was found that the attachment to the medical branch of H.Q. 11 L.

THE ASSAULT AND LODGEMENT

of C. area of a R.A.S.C. liaison officer to control the movement of ambulance cars was exceedingly helpful.

All was not satisfactory, however, for in the C.A.E.C. only stretchers were available and these were not suitable for the seriously wounded or sick who had to be held overnight. So it was that 200 beds in 77 B.G.H. at Reviers were set aside for such casualties as awaited evacuation by air. During July, 7,567 casualties, 5,252 by air, were evacuated, a total since D-day of 10,743 (see Appendix V).

The system of evacuation during the latter part of June, July and August is shown in diagrammatic form in Fig. 23.

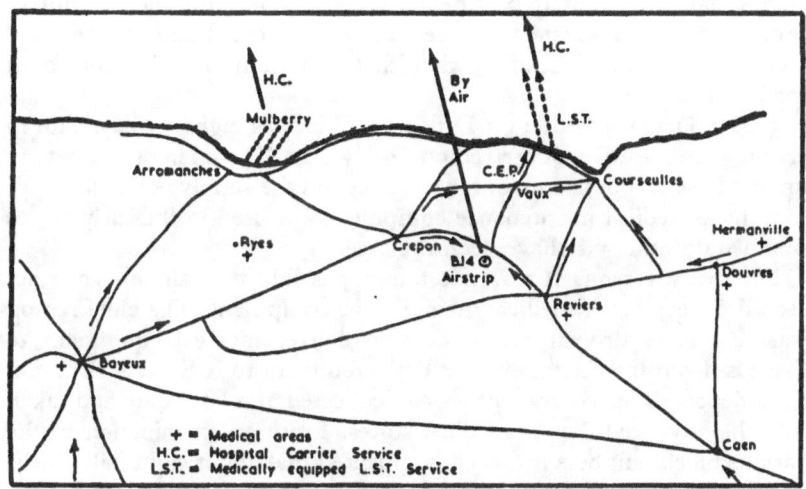

FIG. 23. The Evacuation System. Main Routes. July–August.

The supply of medical equipment by the block system arrived daily by sea in accordance with the agreed programme. Equipment was transferred from the beaches to the O.B.Ds. of the Beach Sub-areas. A Port Detachment R.A.M.C. (1 N.C.O. and 2 men) was employed at each O.B.D. in recognising and sorting medical stores until collected for transfer to advanced depots medical stores. This system of supply worked well and, with a few minor exceptions, all reasonable demands for medical equipment were met in the early stages of the campaign.

Two advanced depots (6 and 9) were phased in on a 'piecemeal' basis between D-day+3 and D-day+10 in five- to ten-ton loads. This was considered necessary in view of possible sickness. In addition, six tons of medical equipment were pre-loaded on R.A.S.C. transport to augment the medical maintenance blocks (beach), should this be necessary. The two remaining advanced depots (8 and 11) arrived on D-day+13 as total consignments. The Canadian advanced depot arrived shortly afterwards on the Canadian sector.

6 Adv. Depot Med. Stores	La Délivrande	open
8 ,, ,, ,, ,,	Ryes	closed, in reserve
9 ,, ,, ,, ,,	Ryes	open
11 ,, ,, ,, ,,	Reviers	open

The stores were thus located so as to enable the supply to be carried out on a geographical basis. Owing to the short distances involved at this time the supply of medical equipment worked smoothly.

Seven 15-ton medical maintenance blocks were phased in after the cessation of receipt of the medical maintenance blocks (beach). These were situated to maintain base depots medical stores until normal indent procedure was established. These stores were sorted and checked and handed over to H.Q. L. of C. when that formation took over control of the beaches.

5 Base Depot was due on D-day + 13 but was eighteen days late in arriving. 12 Base Depot arrived on D-day + 22. The lateness in opening up of 5 Base Depot had no untoward effect on the supply position except that more medical maintenance equipment was used in the early stages than would otherwise have been the case.

For many reasons it was not found possible to maintain an exact record of receipts of medical maintenance equipment. The chief reason was that lorry drivers with orders to deliver medical equipment to C.B.Ds. from the beaches in fact delivered them to R.E., R.A.S.C. and C.A. depots. This equipment was all collected at a later date and taken into the advanced depots medical stores. From an examination of the various block numbers recorded it appeared that about eight half blocks failed to arrive. Approximately three tons arrived which had been immersed in sea water and had to be destroyed. Minor losses of medical equipment of advanced depots medical stores occurred. Fortunately the type of items lost was easily replaced from the medical maintenance blocks and no undue inconvenience resulted.

Rations were supplied as composite packs and were adequate. Arrangements were made for medical units to draw for their patients the type of pack which contained the particular articles required, e.g. rice puddings, tinned fruits, etc. A good supply of medical comforts was brought in by the units and the R.A.S.C. supplied certain items from a very early date following D-day.

Water supply was from water-points established by the R.E., water being taken from small rivers in the bridgehead. All Army water-points were visited by personnel of 61 Fd. Hyg. Sec. The lack of water-carts and water-tanks caused difficulties in R.H.Us. where for the most part water had to be drawn in jerricans.

To deal with the number of casualties as estimated by 'G', approximately 20,000 stretchers and 60,000 blankets were shipped from the United Kingdom to the beaches on an agreed programme. Supplies arrived well, but for the following reasons it became necessary to freeze stocks and to issue only on the authority of H.Q.

(i) daily loss due to evacuation by sea.
(ii) daily loss due to evacuation by air.
(iii) issues to medical units, particularly to the 600-bed hospitals, in excess of G.1098 scales.

As the situation improved and as the formation of a battle reserve became possible, authority for the issue of these items was delegated to medical administrative officers. When the responsibility for the evacuation of casualties by sea and air was taken over by 11 L. of C., demands for stretchers, blankets, pyjamas and the like, decreased.

In the Normandy landings sanitary discipline was well maintained by the fighting troops who first occupied the beaches but not by those following. Slit trenches dug by the assault troops were used as latrines by later arrivals and growing accumulations of food tins began to appear. Many weeks' work was required to clear up areas around the beaches.

It was planned that on leaving beach transit areas, where M.E. squatting latrines would be provided, units were to become responsible for their own sanitation and would have to improvise. A study was made of the materials likely to be available for the improvisation of the necessary sanitary appliances.

The Army School of Hygiene had suggested the utilisation of 'compo' ration cases as covers for shallow trench latrines and to provide footboards between the trenches. A list of other non-returnable containers was obtained from the S. & T. staff and embodied in a hygiene technical instruction on improvisation.

The 'compo' boxes proved to be most useful. It was possible to make them into crude latrine seats for use until permanent fixtures could be provided. In some instances these boxes were combined with the M.E. superstructure to make a temporary deep trench latrine and seat. Empty 105 m.m. shell boxes were later used for a similar purpose.

It was considered to be desirable to provide a reserve of M.E. superstructures for use in forward areas. Experience of the Desert campaign had proved that although these appliances could be carried flat in a 15-cwt. truck they were too heavy (66 lb. complete) to be carried by field units during operations. This was confirmed when the question was taken up with lower formations. M.E. latrine covers could not be carried in unit transport. It was decided to hold a reserve of 2,000 in R.E. stores, to be drawn upon as required. This reserve also provided useful field latrines for P.o.W. camps under construction.

Geological reports of the Normandy coast suggested that in many places loose sandy soil might be encountered in which the water table was high. On this account it was considered that incineration by oil and water A.S.H. faeces destructors was likely to be the most satisfactory method of disposal and the Works Directorate was advised accordingly. It was also recommended that these destructors should be constructed in pairs for any number of men over 500. This was in order to effect economy in building materials, conserve heat and provide a spare destructor should one be out of order or should the camp be temporarily overcrowded.

Drawings for standard covers for Otway pits were also prepared. It was decided to limit the size of such pits to that capable of dealing with latrine contents for 250 men. In practice the ground in most parts of the bridgehead was found to be light and absorbent and well suited for disposal by burial. In the Bayeux area deep boreholes and Otway pits were successfully employed. The former were sunk by 3-ft. well-boring apparatus to an average depth of 12–15 ft. and dealt with large quantities of urine and faeces but filled up rapidly with the greasy water from sullage wastes.

The disposal of sullage water produced in very large quantities by laundries was a problem that claimed early attention. In order to avoid pollution of the many small rivers in the bridgehead, from which water was taken for all purposes (*see* Plates XV and XVI), instructions were issued that no untreated effluent would be discharged into a watercourse by laundries. Base laundries were to precipitate effluents by the ferrous sulphate and lime process and mobile laundries, if unable to carry this out, were to use improvised methods of treatment.

The disposal of the large collection of food tins following the use of the 14-man 'compo' packs was most conveniently carried out by controlled tipping, a method which was also successfully used in cleaning up back areas in the vicinity of Caen. Units eventually cleared their own camps with their own transport but in some instances it was necessary at first to employ pioneer labour and transport on a 'milk round' to clear to a selected site for disposal.

The disposal of the carcasses of cattle and horses and the burial of the dead in battle areas gave rise to problems in the solution of which hygiene officers were much concerned. Artillery fire and bombing caused many casualties among the horses and cattle in the well-stocked Normandy pastures and carcasses gave rise to great offence and caused fly-breeding. The battlefields contained many dead and the work of burial parties was frequently hampered by the presence of mines and booby-traps attached to corpses.

Many carcasses were successfully burned with petrol but the most generally adopted method of disposal was by oiling and burial. The carcass was sprayed with a mixture of creosol and diesel oil or sump oil in the proportion of one pint of creosol to two of diesel or sump oil and burned, or buried with a covering of oil-soaked earth. Bulldozers were used for the burial of carcasses wherever possible; indeed without their assistance the disposal of large numbers of carcasses, many of which were in an advanced state of decomposition, could not have been effected. Shortly after the landing one beach group employed hand-grenades to make craters for the burial of carcasses.

The organisation for the burial of the dead had been worked out in advance. Burial parties were established and did excellent work. Their equipment included a 50-yard rope for attachment to corpses to test for booby-traps. Supervision was necessary to ensure that corpses were buried at a sufficient depth as there was a tendency, which was understandable, for burial parties to hurry over their unpleasant task and get clear of battle grounds with as little delay as possible. Sanitary assistants did excellent work in supervising and giving advice to these parties and the presence of R.A.M.C. personnel in this work did much to help and encourage. Many of the corpses had to be sprayed with the oil mixture referred to previously and afterwards wrapped in an oily blanket before burial. Some chaplains took exception to this practice but the necessity for it was obvious to the majority. A special oil had been provided for spraying dead in armoured fighting vehicles. This oil, which had been successfully used in the Desert, was composed of creosote oil with the addition of a lighter oil. The oil issued to armoured and R.E.M.E. units in 21 Army Group was a heavy creosote oil undiluted. To begin with this oil was only issued to R.E.M.E. recovery units but later it was issued to all armoured regiments, including those of the R.E. operating flails, etc. A directive on the subject of the spraying of dead and remains in A.F.Vs. was issued and included details of the scale of issue of equipment for this purpose.

During operations in Normandy the problem of dealing with dead in tanks and A.F.Vs. was not encountered on the scale experienced by Eighth Army in the Desert campaign. A.F.Vs. were recovered more rapidly and, heat and flies were not present in the same degree as in the Desert. Instances in which remains in such vehicles had reached an unpleasant and difficult state of putrefaction were comparatively infrequent. Calls on field hygiene section personnel were made chiefly by R.E.M.E. recovery units, but armoured units also sought their assistance in carrying out this unpleasant task. No call of this nature was refused by the field hygiene sections.

For the application of oil the disinfector sprayer Mark II was provided and two of these were already carried by field hygiene sections. This sprayer was portable and easy to use but required two operators. In practice a sprayer of a wider delivery type was found to be preferable, such as the 'Mysto' (Four-Oaks type) knapsack sprayer which could be operated by one man. Stirrup pumps were also employed but were rather wasteful and better results were obtained with the pressure cylinders of fire extinguishers.

Supplies of D.D.T. residual spray (5 per cent.) arrived by air towards the close of the fly season and was used with excellent results in the damaged areas in Caen where flies abounded.

On the beaches divisional field hygiene sections improvised shower-baths before the arrival of mobile laundry and bath units. One of these was set up at Graye-sur-Mer. The German bathhouse at Bayeux was later put into full operation and bathed some hundreds daily. During the hot summer days many men availed themselves of the pools afforded by the rivers and streams for swimming and bathing. It was thought wiser to allow this to continue, with due regard to the safeguarding of intakes for drinking water supplies, as it was unlikely that an order forbidding such bathing could be enforced. One or two cases of infectious jaundice were reported but no particular pool or stream was incriminated.

Mobile laundry and bathing arrangements were available early and included issues of clean underclothing and shirts to bathers. Bulk issues of clean garments in exchange for dirty were also made to units. Formations reported that the prejudice which soldiers have against this method, on the grounds that they may receive back the wrong size of underclothes, was diminishing, and in one formation had been met by allowing the men to choose their own size of garments from a heap of clean clothes.

D.D.O.S. also arranged that showers should be added to the equipment of base hospital laundries—36 showers to each.

To tide over the period before the arrival of Ordnance laundries arrangements had been made for clean bundles of hospital laundry to be supplied by a general hospital in the United Kingdom to hospitals on the beaches. Shower-baths could not, however, be provided by the base laundries. These were chiefly employed in laundering returned clothing and blankets.

The C.C.S. laundry trailer apparatus was reported to be heavy and cumbersome during operations. It was suggested by the Ordnance staff that the two C.C.S. laundries should be combined to provide a corps laundry in the corps maintenance area.

THE ARMY DENTAL SERVICE (SECOND ARMY)

The dental personnel of the field ambulances of 6th Airborne Division dropped with the field ambulance personnel during the night of June 5/6, emergency dental treatment becoming available at once with the equipment carried in the dental haversacks. Full field dental equipment was later obtained by the issue to them of panniers from the advanced depots of medical stores.

The dental personnel of the field ambulances of 50th, Canadian 3rd and 3rd Divisions, of 5, 7 and 8 Beach Group F.D.Ss. (1, 2, 20, 21, 33 and 34), of 35 F.D.S. (9 Beach Group) and of 31 F.D.S. (10 Beach Group) all landed on D-day. The arrival of the dental officers of 10 C.C.S. (XXX Corps) and of 16 and 17 F.D.Ss. of 49th Division brought the total number of A.D. Corps officers ashore in Normandy on the evening of D-day to 20, or 1 D.O. to every 3,000 men. Until the full equipment arrived, in most cases a few days later, only emergency dental treatment could be offered. Many of the dental officers acted as anaesthetists.

During the remainder of June and during July there was much movement of field ambulances and F.D.Ss. and the dental officers with these were able to open for dental treatment only on fourteen days a month. The dental officers of divisional M.D.Us. worked about 2–3 miles behind the line and were able to open for about twenty-four days a month. Some of these M.D.Us. moved in such close association with the divisions to which they were attached that it was decided that the Red Cross emblem must be removed from their vehicles. Until the arrival of the M.D.Us. on D-day + 16 and D-day + 18 the pressure of dental work on the general hospitals and C.C.Ss. was heavy, particularly for repairs to dentures. With their arrival it became possible to define the responsibilities of dental officers at various levels:

1. *Divisional Units*

Field Ambulance
- (a) operative dental surgery for the brigade;
- (b) chairside prosthesis for the brigade;
- (c) maxillo-facial first aid for the brigade.

F.D.S.
- (a) operative dental surgery for divisional administrative area troops;
- (b) chairside prosthesis for neighbouring divisional administrative troops;
- (c) resuscitation and adjustment (if necessary) to maxillo-facial cases of the division;
- (d) acute ulcerative gingivitis/stomatitis cases of division.

M.D.U.
- (a) operative dental surgery for divisional H.Q. troops;
- (b) chairside prosthesis for divisional H.Q. troops;
- (c) laboratory prosthesis for division.

2. *Corps Units*

C.C.S.
- (a) operative dental surgery for corps and army troops in the neighbourhood;

(b) chairside prosthesis for corps and army troops in the neighbourhood;
(c) adjustments (if necessary) to maxillo-facial cases;
(d) minor oral surgery of total corps.

F.D.S.
(a) operative dental surgery for corps and army troops in the neighbourhood;
(b) chairside prosthesis for corps and army troops in the neighbourhood; (laboratory prosthesis by C.C.S.)
(c) acute ulcerative gingivitis/stomatitis cases of corps and army troops in the neighbourhood.

3. *Army Units*

200-bed Hospital }
C.C.S. }
(a) operative dental surgery for all troops in neighbourhood;
(b) chairside and laboratory prosthesis for all troops in the neighbourhood;
(c) laboratory prosthesis for associated F.D.Ss.
(d) minor oral surgery for all troops in the neighbourhood.

F.D.S.
(a) operative dental surgery for all troops in neighbourhood;
(b) chairside prosthesis for all troops in neighbourhood;
(c) acute ulcerative gingivitis/stomatitis cases of all troops in the neighbourhood.

M.D.U.
Comprehensive dental surgery and prosthesis.

This allocation of duties was not meant to be interpreted rigidly; all who came to a unit were treated; but it was a guide and as such was helpful. By mid-July it was agreed that the M.D.U. could, and did, function with advantage independently of a parent unit. In 50th Division the dental officers were all brought together and a divisional dental centre formed in Juaye-Mondaye, about two miles behind the line and under control of the officer commanding 204 M.D.U. This experiment showed that under the stable conditions that then obtained this arrangement had much to commend it.

The dental work at this time consisted in the main of single extractions or conservations. The demand for denture work, mainly for the repair of fractured dentures, was high. During this period 1,472 dentures were received from the United Kingdom, being delivered in special mailbags. The three dental mechanics held at 34 R.H.U. were withdrawn in the last week of June and attached to 204, 207 and 208 M.D.Us. At the end of July one more dental mechanic was attached

THE ASSAULT AND LODGEMENT

to each Army M.D.U. These men were withdrawn from 1,200-bed hospitals by D.D.M.S. 21 Army Group, A.D.M.S. L. of C. having stated that he could make them available. So the number of dental mechanics in forward areas was raised to 23, and four more were serving with the two M.D.Us. in the rear Army area.

At first the incidence of maxillo-facial injuries was lower than had been expected, but during the battles for Caen the rate rose and by the first week in July, 6 M.F.S.U. was dealing with an average of 10 cases a day. 5 and 6 M.F.S.Us. had arrived by July 5 but without their equipment. This deficiency was made good by loans from the parent hospitals to which they were attached.

A.D.D.S. had no transport of his own, but within five days of his arrival he acquired a motor cycle of the airborne pattern and thereafter he regularly visited the dental units and officers in the bridgehead. He was permitted to sign orders on behalf of 'G' (S.D.) and 'A' branches at Army H.Q. authorising the movement of dental units and the posting of dental personnel. During the first week of July orders were issued which placed the M.D.Us. under both operational and administrative command of the divisions. The effect of this action was soon manifest; the division displayed increased interest in the M.D.U. and the personnel of the dental unit enjoyed the satisfaction of belonging to and being a component part of a particular formation, this enjoyment being reflected in the enthusiasm with which their services were rendered.

THE ARMY TRANSFUSION SERVICE (21 ARMY GROUP)

The first transfusion personnel to land were the F.T.Us. with the beach groups, which went ashore on D-day soon after the assault troops. They were followed by five more on D-day+1 with corps C.C.Ss. and F.D.Ss. Three further units were landed by D-day+7 to complete the total for the initial phase. The two forward distribution sections, now called 'X' and 'Y' Advanced Blood Banks, went in on D-day+5, each with three refrigerator vehicles, and the remainder of the B.T.U. arrived in two sections on D-day+20 and D-day+42 respectively.

It had been foreseen during the planning for the operation that the supply and distribution of blood to the F.T.Us. in the beachhead would be extremely difficult during the first few days until the distribution sections of the B.T.U. landed and were able to undertake this function. The following arrangements were made for the supply of transfusion fluids during this phase.

Firstly, a considerable amount of plasma was landed with each medical unit, field ambulance, F.D.S., C.C.S. and 200-bed hospital.

Secondly, a large amount of plasma and saline was included in the composite blocks of general medical stores called 'beach bricks', which were landed daily in each beach group from D-day onward.

Thirdly, all F.T.Us. except two carried 80 bottles of blood in their refrigerators. Similarly, both advanced blood banks landed with three full refrigerators. This latter arrangement was achieved with great difficulty in the days immediately preceding D-day because all the units were already 'sealed' in their concentration areas long before the days of embarking. The sudden bleeding of hundreds of o/4 donors and the delivery of the blood into these widely separated 'sealed' areas might easily have endangered security. However, it was successfully accomplished, with the result that supplies of whole blood, though limited and tending towards over-age (14 days), were available from the beginning.

Finally, from D-day + 1 onwards 400 pints of blood in insulated containers were sent by the Army Blood Supply Depot from Portsmouth by Naval despatch boats to the H.Q. ship of the force, whence it was delivered ashore to the Naval Medical Liaison Officer who was sited at or near the C.E.P. He in turn delivered it to the nearest F.T.U. from which other units were able to draw supplies.

In practice this system functioned adequately, mainly because of the liberal supplies and the proximity of the F.T.Us. to each other within the narrow confines of the beachhead; though in I Corps' sector, which had the heavier casualties and was receiving twice as much blood as XXX Corps, the D-day + 1 delivery did not arrive and transfusion officers had to bleed a few local donors to tide them over till the next day's delivery arrived.

On D-day + 5 the blood distribution officer landed and later the same day the two advanced blood banks went ashore. From then on the supply situation gradually evolved and stabilised and was working smoothly by the time the main body of the B.T.U. arrived on D-day + 20.

The two banks continued to collect their own supplies, which were landed separately on the two halves of the beachhead until D-day + 10 when all the blood was landed at a central point and was collected by a refrigerator truck detached from one of the banks to act as receiver for both. Until the institution of supply by air from the United Kingdom on D-day + 17 this method of sea delivery worked well. For a few days just before the change to air supply the blood was landed at the 'Mulberry' at Arromanches.

From then on air transport was used exclusively for the supply of whole blood from England until the end of the campaign, with the exception of a short period during the winter when the weather interfered with flying and sea transport had to be substituted. Other transfusion stores, however, plasma, solutions and equipment, continued to be landed by sea throughout the campaign.

The advantages of short lines of communication within the small but expanding beachhead were largely discounted by the enormous congestion and confusion on the few roads and tracks available. It required the most determined efforts on the part of those trying to distribute supplies equally between one unit and the next to make their way for even a short distance through seething masses of vehicles of all types—trucks, tanks, bulldozers, motor cycles, jeeps, ambulances and the rest. Nor was communication with England sufficiently easy to allow of changes in the amount of blood per day according to the rise or fall of demand, but by the end of June, about D-day + 25, it was decided to keep the demands at the figure of 400 pints per day, this having been the average consumption on the previous month's working.

By this time the remainder of the B.T.U. had arrived and set up in the middle of the circle of general hospitals which were beginning to arrive and to assume the duties previously performed by the C.C.Ss. and 200-bed hospitals. These latter had now moved forward as the boundaries of the beachhead, or bridgehead as it was now becoming, gradually expanded, taking with them sections of the two advanced blood banks.

The B.T.U. was located under canvas in a field and orchard adjoining a small civilian medical building in the outskirts of Bayeux. For a short time it actually occupied this building but was ultimately ejected therefrom by the Civil Affairs Branch in order to house wounded civilians. It retained only one small outhouse to accommodate its solution preparing department.

Gradually there began to take shape the structure outlined at the beginning; the B.T.U. received all stores as they arrived and distributed them to the advanced banks, now out with their armies. Second and Canadian First Armies, and the forward trucks up with corps supplied the transfusion units in corps medical areas as well as divisional medical units.

The work of the B.T.U. was increased by the gradual expansion of the base hospital area. 600 and 1,200-bed hospitals were arriving and opening in increasing numbers. At one time there were twenty of them, all functioning in the Bayeux medical area.

Casualties were very heavy about this time from the Caen battles and many cases were reaching general hospitals without preliminary treatment. Consequently the amount of resuscitation being done in base hospitals was almost as great as that being done in forward medical units. It was about this time that incoming supplies of whole blood were barely sufficient to meet the needs and for a period of ten days local bleeding was undertaken. 1,500 bottles were taken in all, though quite a large proportion of this was given to the American Army blood banks in the adjoining sector to the south which were also having supply difficulties.

The other main function of the B.T.U., the production of transfusion equipment and solutions, began as soon as the local water and electricity supplies allowed.

THE ARMY PSYCHIATRIC SERVICE (SECOND ARMY)

In the light of previous experience in the organisation of psychiatric services in forward areas in other theatres of war, a psychiatric organisation was built up in 21 Army Group before the opening of the Second Front. This included an adviser in psychiatry who was appointed in February 1944, one psychiatrist to the H.Q. of each corps of this army group, one psychiatrist attached to each of six general hospitals available also for duty with the Army or in the L. of C., and 32 B.G.H. with 600 beds for psychiatric cases. During the four months in the United Kingdom prior to the landing in Normandy the corps psychiatrists were engaged in the training of regimental medical officers in the care of acute psychiatric casualties; advice on the handling of disciplinary and morale problems was given and the weeding out of unsuitable men from combatant units carried out. By D-day this preparatory work had come to an end.

Films were found useful in the training of medical officers. The first film, 'Field Psychiatry for the Medical Officer', was made prior to the campaign and emphasised the importance of early diagnosis and first aid in dealing with psychiatric battle casualties.

The forward organisation came into being during the first six weeks of the campaign. Psychiatrists landed with the troops in the early days and the first corps exhaustion centre opened on D-day + 8. Two F.D.Ss. under Army control opened as exhaustion centres on D-day + 11 and by the end of June each operating corps had its exhaustion centre and these were backed up by three Army exhaustion centres and a large rehabilitation centre (Second Army Rest Centre). The latter was built on the nucleus of a F.D.S. Its purpose was to retain psychiatric casualties for adequate convalescence and for subsequent down-grading in medical category if necessary. On July 20 it was taken over by 13 Con. Depot which carried on the same task. During July this rehabilitation centre admitted approximately 100 psychiatric convalescents per day for several weeks and thus effected a considerable saving in man-power.

During the first ten days of the campaign the percentage of psychiatric battle casualties gradually rose to approximately 13 per cent. of all casualties and it remained at approximately that level until the end of the month. Seasoned divisions produced as many cases as 'green' divisions. A good contrast was 6th Airborne Division and 51st (Highland) Division, fighting alongside each other and under similar strain. The first was almost wholly 'green', the second full of old campaigners. The incidence of psychiatric casualties and of battle wounds in these two divisions was:

TABLE 21

Psychiatric Casualties. June 17–July 1

Week ending	Battle Wounds	Psychiatric Casualties	Psychiatric Casualties as a percentage of Battle Wounds
6th Airborne Division			
June 17	1,871	54	3
„ 24	229	29	13
July 1	164	10	6
51st (Highland) Division			
June 17	205	30	15
„ 24	394	35	9
July 1	177	76	43

The relatively small number of psychiatric casualties among the Airborne troops was again commented upon by the psychiatrist to Second Army after the fighting in September. The rigorous selection of personnel for these formations was considered to be the most probable explanation.

The psychiatrist to Second Army in his report for June 1944 writes:

> 'The importance of good leadership in preventing psychiatric casualties has been brought out clearly again and again in the last few weeks. A common story is a sudden influx of cases following the death or wounding of the commanding officer. One anti-tank unit was known before coming overseas to be in an unhealthy state from a psychiatric point of view. The explanation was provided a few days ago when the commanding officer was evacuated showing a severe state of anxiety. A whole platoon of a certain battalion was evacuated to the corps exhaustion centre owing to the irresponsible behaviour of its subaltern commander and the presence in its midst of a severe chronic neurotic (with the exception of whom all made good recoveries and returned to duty).
>
> 'A unit medical officer by energetic tackling of the prophylactic side and by careful examination and assessment of men sent to him can certainly help to keep down the number of cases of exhaustion. But the implications of a rise in number are, of course, wider than the medical aspects. The number of cases coming from a given unit is an index to that unit's quality of men and of its wellbeing and morale. In fact, it is as good a guide to the unit's state of mental health as is the temperature chart in a case of fever. As a corollary to this, any measures which are taken to reduce the incidence of neurotic breakdown by direct restriction can accomplish no more than an antipyretic given to a febrile patient. Before any effective measures can be taken the cause or causes of the rise must be found'.

Lack of accommodation, lack of skilled personnel for treatment, etc., made it impossible in June to hold cases in medical units for longer than forty-eight hours. In spite of the dangers of such a procedure, many psychiatric casualties had therefore to be evacuated to the United Kingdom who would, given a few days' treatment in the beachhead, have been fit to return to their units for full duty. In June only some 10 per cent. of cases were returned to duty; the remainder had, of necessity, to be evacuated to England. Corps exhaustion centres were swamped. The psychiatrist with XXX Corps reported on the situation in June:

> 'When cases from 43rd Division began to arrive at the corps exhaustion centre it was soon apparent that a fair proportion should never have been allowed to reach corps level. Large numbers arrived with the briefest of documentation, making it extremely difficult to assess the true picture. Accordingly, a medical officer with psychiatric experience was detailed by D.D.M.S. XXX Corps to work at a more forward F.D.S., which was acting as a sorting house for C.C.Ss., and arrangements made whereby cases could be returned to their divisions direct. From the report he submitted it was clear that our observations were justified, for he sent back to their units some 70 per cent. of cases, referring the remainder to the corps exhaustion centre'.

The need for divisional as well as corps exhaustion centres was therefore clear, and their establishment and opening in July was a major step forward. Such centres were first set up by XXX Corps and other corps followed suit. By the middle of July exhaustion centres were functioning at divisional, corps and Army levels. The advantages of having divisional centres were considerable. Divisions were continually switching about within corps so that the division was the only stable entity; men treated at a divisional centre were still within the 'family' and intimate contact was possible between the centre and the R.M.Os. of the division; treatment at a forward medical unit within sound of battle was easier than at more rearward centres; the number of casualties was such that corps centres working alone were swamped. The medical unit principally used in the forward treatment of psychiatric casualties was the F.D.S. At divisional level these were run by specially selected medical officers under the guidance of the corps psychiatrist, and though at first resistant to the new rôle they eventually showed great keenness in this work. At corps level the exhaustion centre established in a F.D.S. was run by the corps psychiatrist. The Army exhaustion centre, also established in a F.D.S., was located in the area of the roadhead and thus suitably placed in relation to R.H.Us. and Army hospitals.

In July the incidence of psychiatric casualties steadily rose until during the week ending July 22 it was 21·7 per cent. of total casualties, or 28·5 per cent. of battle surgical casualties. The actual incidence was 2,370 from Second Army during the week ending July 22. This, however, was the 'peak' of the campaign; the following week the incidence was 12·5 per cent. of all casualties, or 22·5 per cent. of battle surgical casualties.

Throughout the campaign the incidence of self-inflicted wounds bore no relation to the incidence of psychiatric casualties as a whole but remained comparatively steady at ·06 per 1,000 per week, whereas the neurotic breakdown rate fluctuated widely.

During July it was possible to retain psychiatric casualties for seven days' treatment. Results were immediate, approximately 50 per cent. were returned to full combatant duties in their original units and 10 to 20 per cent. were returned to L. of C. or base duties. Many of the latter passed through the Army Rest Centre or 13 Con. Depot and were discharged in lowered medical categories. Their re-allocation to suitable L. of C. or base duties presented at first a considerable problem, but this was partially solved by the dispatch from the United Kingdom of a selection team of personnel selection officers and two psychiatrists. With G.H.Q., 2nd Echelon, still in the United Kingdom, the reposting of down-graded men remained a cumbersome procedure until the end of July, when an advanced reinforcement section was established in Normandy with the authority to post men to new duties.

The great frequency with which unit reinforcements broke down was stressed by the psychiatrist, Second Army, during July. He writes in his report for July:

> 'Apart from the general quality of reinforcements, three points stand out. The first is that a unit that has suffered a very large number of casualties consists almost entirely of reinforcements and can hardly be considered a coherent body of men. . . . When such a unit goes into action a very high breakdown rate must be expected, since the emotional ties among the men, and between the men and their officers (which is the most single potent factor in preventing breakdown) barely exist. . . . The second is that reinforcements should be integrated into their units in sizeable bodies. . . . The third point is that untrained reinforcements frequently become psychiatric casualties. Stories of clerks, cooks, storemen and the like being sent forward as riflemen reinforcements are all too frequent. Such men, apart from breaking down themselves, can be a real menace to their units'.

H.Q. 21 Army Group intended that 32 B.G.H. should be used in two sections; an advanced section of 200 beds to proceed overseas on D-day + 18 and a rear section of 400 beds to proceed on D-day + 48. This split of the hospital was required to be carried out without any increase in staff, equipment and transport, and though excellent in theory was more difficult in practice. The advanced section arrived in Normandy on D-day + 19 and opened near Bayeux with 200 beds on July 6. The intention was to use this section as far forward as possible to provide treatment of up to three weeks' duration and to return the maximum number to their original units. The number of psychiatric casualties at this time was, however, so large that the advanced section could itself only operate as an exhaustion centre retaining cases for a limited period of three to four days. No effective treatment could therefore be given and only some 18 per cent. of patients were returned to duty. The remainder were evacuated to England.

The Development of the Administrative Command of Second Army in the early stages of Operation 'Overlord' is shown in Appendix IV. Plates I–XVI illustrate some of the activities of the various medical units during the landings, assault and lodgement operations and the organisation providing for the collection, transport, treatment and evacuation of the casualties from the beachhead areas.

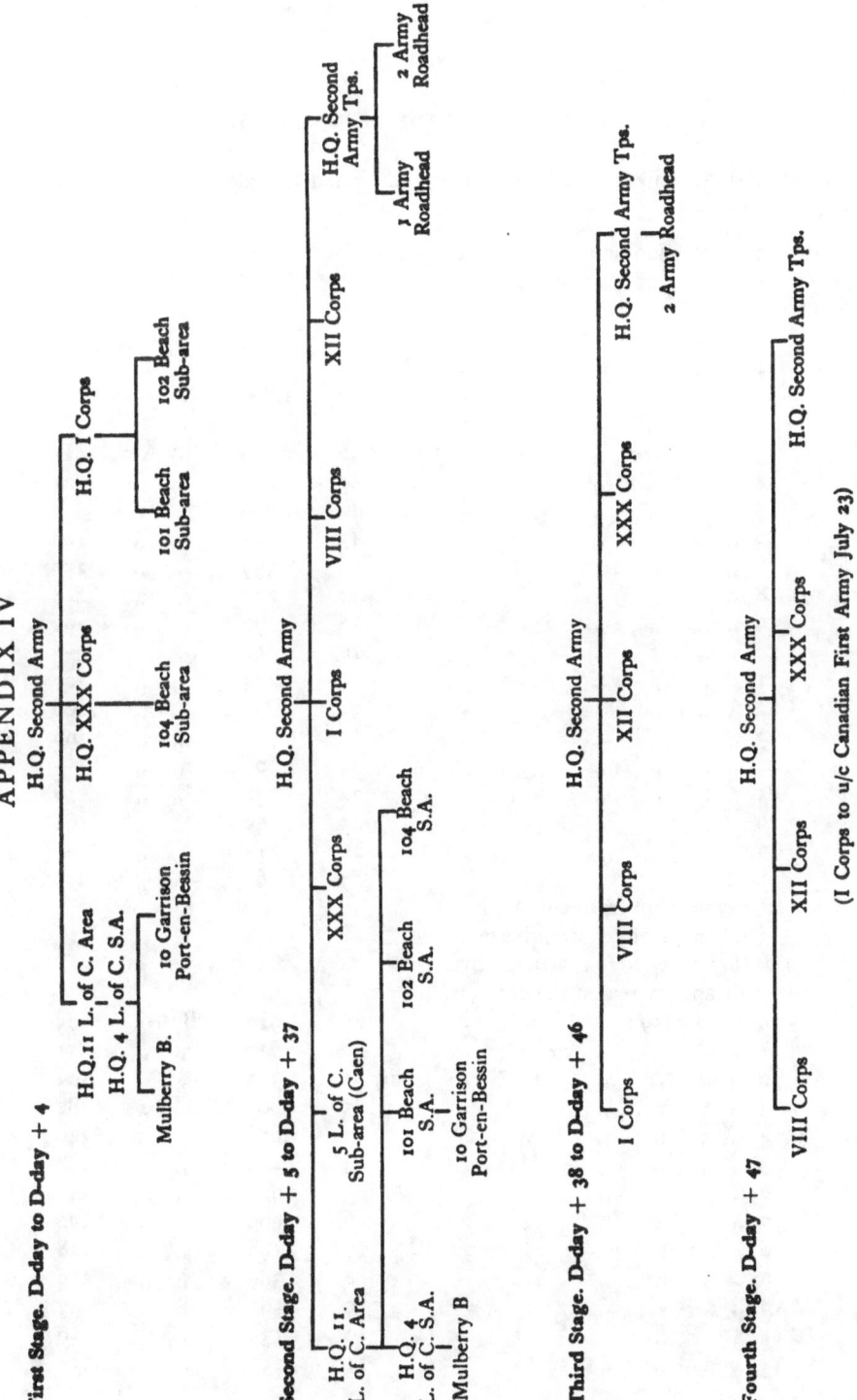

APPENDIX V

21 ARMY GROUP. EXCERPTS FROM 'A' SITREPS

Casualties evacuated to and received in the United Kingdom:
Sitrep* of:

Date					
June 7 up to 0900 hours	. .	June 7	70		
8 ,, ,, 0900 ,,	. .	7	238		
		8	79		
9 ,, ,, 2359 ,,	. .	8	1,471		
10 ,, ,, ,, ,,	. .	9	1,817		
11 ,, ,, ,, ,,	. .	10	1,897		
12 ,, ,, ,, ,,	. .	11	575		
13 ,, ,, ,, ,,	. .	12	2,189	By Air	11
14 ,, ,, ,, ,,	. .	13	807	,, ,,	23
15 ,, ,, ,, ,,	. .	14	1,259	,, ,,	2
16 ,, ,, ,, ,,	. .	15	1,011	,, ,,	106
17 ,, ,, ,, ,,	. .	16	359	,, ,,	230
18 ,, ,, ,, ,,	. .	17	240	,, ,,	248
19 ,, ,, ,, ,,	. .	18	290	,, ,,	402
20 ,, ,, ,, ,,	. .	19	59	,, ,,	—
21 ,, ,, ,, ,,	. .	20	453	,, ,,	407
22 ,, ,, ,, ,,	. .	21	—	,, ,,	206
23 ,, ,, ,, ,,	. .	22	722	,, ,,	196
24 ,, ,, ,, ,,	. .	23	607	,, ,,	—
25 ,, ,, ,, ,,	. .	24	732	,, ,,	16
26 ,, ,, ,, ,,	. .	25	536	,, ,,	191
27 ,, ,, ,, ,,	. .	26	414	,, ,,	—
28 ,, ,, ,, ,,	. .	27	1,267	,, ,,	238
29 missing but from cumulative totals given it would seem that 2,347 were evacuated by air and by sea on the 28th					
30 up to 2359 hours	. .	29	917	By Air	675
July 1 ,, ,, ,, ,,	. .	30	710	,, ,,	51
2 ,, ,, ,, ,,	. .	July 1	1,342	,, ,,	103
3 ,, ,, ,, ,,	. .	2	693	,, ,,	82
4 ,, ,, ,, ,,	. .	3	1,076	,, ,,	340
5 ,, ,, ,, ,,	. .	4	400	,, ,,	158
6 ,, ,, ,, ,,	. .	5	939	,, ,,	145
7 ,, ,, ,, ,,	. .	6	609	,, ,,	272
8 ,, ,, ,, ,,	. .	7	198	,, ,,	148
9 ,, ,, ,, ,,	. .	8	399	,, ,,	250
10 ,, ,, ,, ,,	. .	9	503	,, ,,	83
11 ,, ,, ,, ,,	. .	10	1,135	,, ,,	336
12 ,, ,, ,, ,,	. .	11	253	,, ,,	252

THE ASSAULT AND LODGEMENT

July 13 up to 2359 hours				12	1,305	By Air	234
14 ,, ,, ,, ,,				13	579	,, ,,	191
15 ,, ,, ,, ,,				14	669	,, ,,	219
16 ,, ,, ,, ,,				15	475	,, ,,	296
17 ,, ,, ,, ,,				16	146	,, ,,	266
18 ,, ,, ,, ,,				17	172	,, ,,	208
19 ,, ,, ,, ,,				18	791	,, ,,	376

July 31. Cumulative Total   50,601

Battle Casualties, Accidental Injuries and Sick

	Offrs.	O.Rs.
Strength . . 560,170	27,851	532,319

Killed . . 7,803
Wounded . 38,846
Missing . . 8,572

               55,221

Beds equipped	6,790
British . . 44,788 occupied	3,822
Canadian . . 10,433 vacant	2,968

It is to be understood that the figures given in these Sitreps* are tentative; they are the best available at the time and serve a useful purpose. They are corrected as fuller and more precise information is gathered. They are given here in order to illustrate the kind of information that, day by day, during the assault landings and lodgement flowed into G.H.Q. 21 Army Group, S.H.A.E.F. and the War Office.

---

* Situation Reports.

CHAPTER 3

THE BREAK-OUT AND THE ADVANCE INTO HOLLAND

(i)
The Operations

OPERATION 'COBRA' (U.S. FIRST ARMY)

THIS break-out attempt was to have been made on the day following the opening of Operation 'Goodwood' but bad weather caused its postponement. General Bradley was to attack on a 6,000 yards front, five miles west of St. Lô.

At 0940 hours on July 25 fighter-bombers struck at the German outpost line along the St. Lô–Périers road. Then for an hour Fortresses and Liberators saturated an area four miles wide and a mile and a half deep covering the whole frontage of the sector to be attacked and the whole depth of the German positions. Then at 1100 hours U.S. 9th, 4th and 30th Divisions of U.S. VII Corps moved forward, preceded by an aerial barrage. When the Marigny–St. Gilles road was reached the two divisions on the flanks swung outwards and U.S. 1st Infantry and 2nd and 3rd Armoured Divisions passed through. By dark they had advanced about two miles. Early on the 26th medium bombers laid carpets of bombs along the main roads leading to the south as the armoured and motorised infantry divisions moved relentlessly forward. Columns of tanks, infantry in armoured half tracks, motorised artillery and engineers followed the armoured bulldozer tanks as these tore their ways through the high hedgerows. To overcome the *bocage* the Americans had invented a contraption consisting of eight steel teeth welded on to the front of a Sherman tank. Overhead Thunderbolts functioned as aerial artillery controlled from the ground.

On July 27, while U.S. 2nd Armoured Division thrust towards the Bréhal–Tessy road, U.S. 1st Division and 3rd Armoured Division advanced on Coutances. By the evening of the 28th there were columns swarming down all the main roads between Coutances and the River Vire. U.S. VII Corps was checked for a time in front of Coutances but the armoured divisions of U.S. VIII Corps broke through and captured the town. During the next two days, while U.S. VII Corps widened the area of the break-through by attacking towards Mortain, U.S.

BREAK-OUT AND ADVANCE INTO HOLLAND

VIII Corps thrust between the German flank and the coast, U.S. 4th Armoured Division advancing twenty-five miles in thirty-six hours to reach Avranches at dusk on July 30. By the following night a bridgehead across the Selune at Pontaubault had been firmly secured.

OPERATION 'BLUECOAT' (SECOND ARMY)

In support of Operation 'Cobra' General Montgomery on July 28 instructed General Dempsey to transfer his armour from the Orne to Caumont and to attack on the 30th, employing VIII and XXX Corps, with the object of seizing Hills 361 and 309 (the western half of the Mont Pinçon ridge), exploiting towards Vire.

VIII Corps
15th (Scottish) Division, 6th Guards Tk. Bde., 11th and Guards Armoured Divisions.
XXX Corps
43rd and 50th Divisions, 8th Armd. Bde. and 7th Armoured Division.

The task set was indeed a difficult one. The Germans east of the Vire were full of fight. U.S. V Corps had been attacking strongly between Caumont and St. Lô since the 26th but had moved forward only about three miles. South of Caumont the *bocage* country conferred much advantage on the defenders and in it the Germans were firmly entrenched on the slopes and ridges of the Mont Pinçon feature. Bad flying weather nullified the preliminary bombardment of the German positions from the air.

When 43rd Division went in on the left it was soon checked by a dense minefield and the supporting tanks were halted by a steep-sided stream. On the other flank 11th Armoured Division was likewise checked but in the centre 15th Division with 6th Guards Tk. Bde. made good progress, gaining the slopes and then the crest of Hill 309.

During the night of July 30/31 an infantry battalion moved by a woodland track to the outskirts of St. Martin-des-Besaces and soon after dawn a few armoured cars slipped past the village through the Forêt L'Evêque to reach the River Souleuvre, five miles south of St. Martin. Finding an intact bridge west of Le Bény-Bocage they called the tanks forward and an armoured regiment of 11th Armoured Division, with infantry riding on the tanks, reached the bridge just in time to repel a German counter-attack. On the following morning 11th Armoured Division entered Le Bény-Bocage, patrols probing southwards towards Vire encountering but slight opposition. Vire was entered by these patrols during the night of August 1/2.

Since Vire lay on the American side of the inter-army boundary VIII Corps did not press its attack in this direction but instead swung south-east towards Flèrs while XXX Corps continued its attack upon Mont Pinçon.

On August 2, 11th Armoured Division made good progress towards the Vire–Vassy road but the Guards Armoured Division was checked at Estry, south-east of Le Bény-Bocage. Meanwhile 43rd Division had captured Hill 361, but neither 7th Armoured nor 50th Division had made any appreciable gains towards Aunay-sur-Odon and Villers-Bocage.

Operation 'Bluecoat' was therefore brought to an end. VIII Corps had not gained as much ground as had been hoped but it had done that which had been required of it; it had prevented the reinforcement of the German forces facing U.S. First Army.

On August 4/5, the Germans withdrew from the area north of Mont Pinçon, abandoning the ruins of Villers-Bocage, Aunay and Evrécy to hold the line Bourguébus ridge–Thury Harcourt–Mont Pinçon–Vire. On August 5, 43rd Division began its attack on the steep-sided Mont Pinçon. By midday on the 6th, 129th Bde. was on the line of the Druance at the foot of the western slopes with tanks of 13th/18th Hussars in support. As the barrage began to creep up the slopes 5th Wilts. and 4th Somersets waded across the stream but were quickly pinned to the ground by heavy machine-gun and mortar fire. The Hussars rushed the bridge on the La Varinière road and drove to the crest, there to be joined by the infantry. The German defensive line in this sector was thus broken.

THE GERMAN COUNTER-ATTACK AT MORTAIN
(U.S. 12 ARMY GROUP)

On August 1, U.S. 12 Army Group, consisting of U.S. First and Third Armies, was constituted. General Montgomery as Commander Ground Forces continued to direct the operations of both 21 Army Group (British Second and Canadian First Armies) and U.S. 12 Army Group. General Bradley assumed command of U.S. 12 Army Group.

While U.S. First Army was seizing the area Vire–Mortain, U.S. Third Army was instructed to secure the line St. Hilaire–Fougères–Rennes and then turn westwards into Brittany. General Patton, commanding U.S. Third Army, at once ordered U.S. VIII Corps to drive deep into Brittany, sending one armoured and one infantry division down the centre of the peninsula to Brest and a similar force through Rennes to Quiberon Bay. The presence and activities of Les Forces Françaises de l'Intérieur (F.F.I.) greatly facilitated these operations. By August 4, Rennes had been captured and the Americans were in Vannes, sealing off the peninsula. On the 7th they reached the vicinity of Brest.

Meanwhile U.S. First Army had continued its attacks east and south-east. U.S. VII Corps captured Mortain on August 2. On August 3, General Patton was instructed to drive eastwards, leaving minimum forces in Brittany. This eastward drive began on August 4 and in the

BREAK-OUT AND ADVANCE INTO HOLLAND 217

next three days U.S. XV Corps advanced seventy-five miles almost to Le Mans, cutting deep into the rear of the German forces in Normandy.

The Germans then launched a vicious counter-attack on the night of August 6/7 and pierced the American line between Mortain and Sourdeval to advance some seven miles toward Avranches, but they were checked by U.S. 3rd Armoured Division. South of this thrust the Germans retook Mortain but failed to dislodge U.S. 30th Division from the

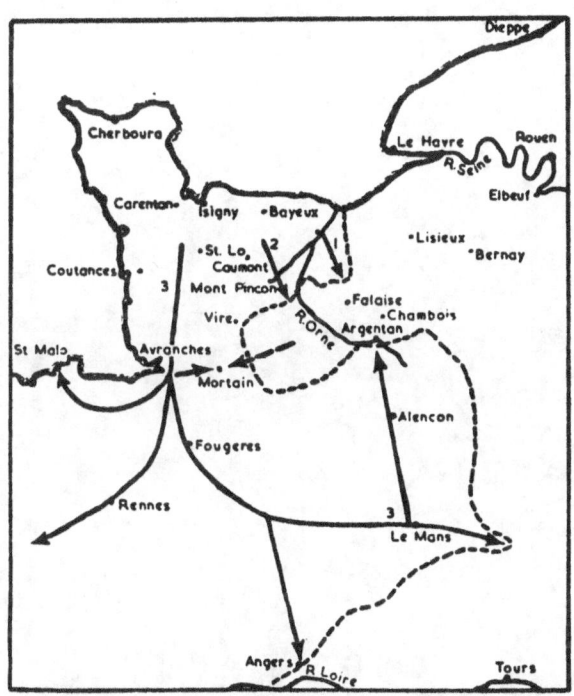

Fig. 24. The Break-out and the German Counter-attack at Mortain. The Falaise Pocket. August.

1. Canadian First Army
2. Second Army
3. U.S. Forces

←---- The German Counter-offensive August 6.

heights west and north-west of the town. Toward midday the fog that had so greatly advantaged the Germans lifted and the Allied Air Forces intervened to bring the German advance to an abrupt halt and to cause great havoc among the German armour and transport. Then the Americans passed to the offensive. On August 7, U.S. 2nd Armoured Division made a forced march through St. Hilaire to Barenton and halfway to Ger to strike at the rear of the Germans around Mortain.

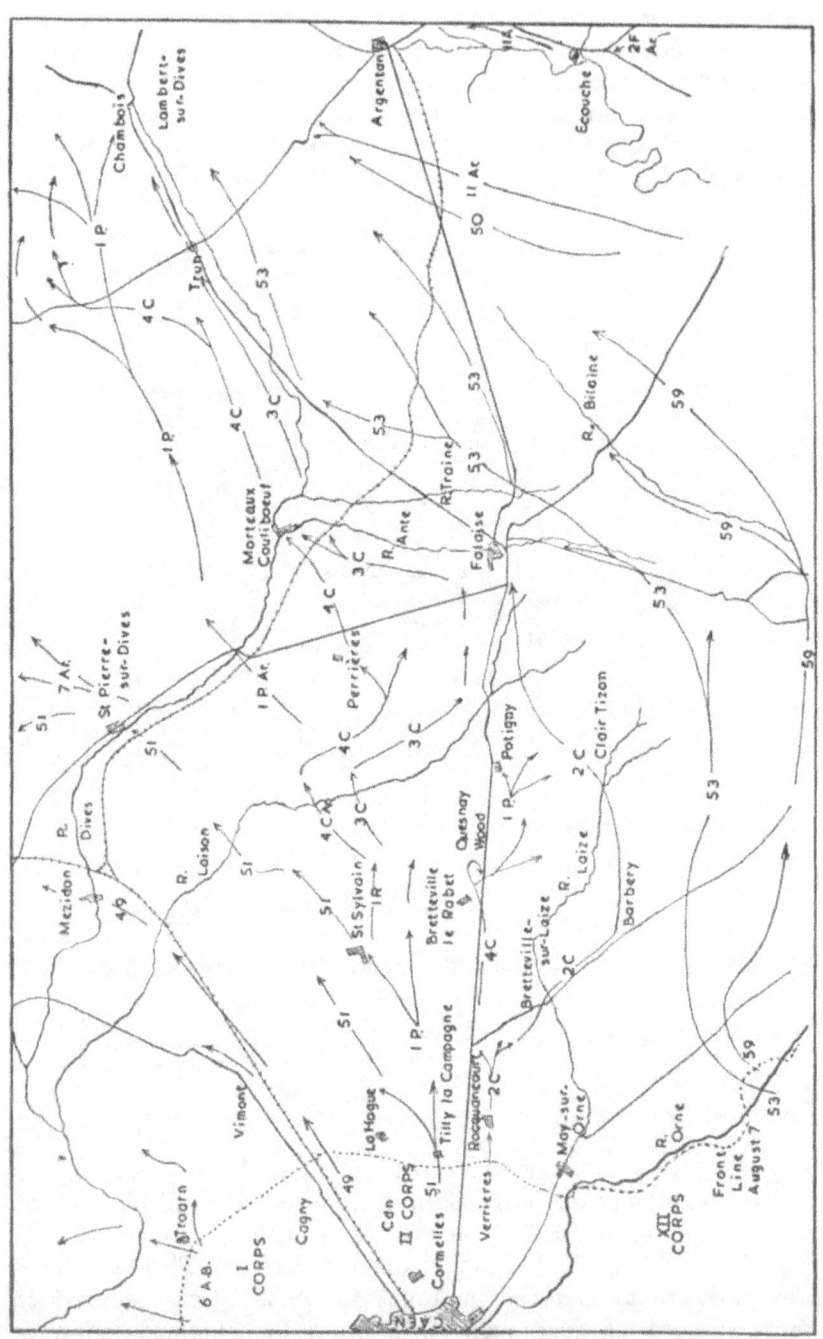

Fig. 25. Canadian First Army. Operation 'Totalize'.*

BREAK-OUT AND ADVANCE INTO HOLLAND

On August 8, U.S. Third Army, by a deep outflanking movement, reached Angers to the south and Le Mans to the east.

OPERATION 'TOTALIZE' (CANADIAN FIRST ARMY)

As an outcome of the eastward drive of U.S. XV Corps of U.S. Third Army a large German salient had developed with its base on the line Falaise–Argentan and its apex about Mortain. Within it were large German forces west of the Orne. It was now decided to encircle and destroy them. To the Canadians was assigned the task of breaking through to Falaise. Canadian First Army at this time consisted of Canadian II and I Corps.

I Corps was placed u/c Canadian First Army with effect from July 23. With it went 6th Airborne, 49th and 51st Divisions. The association of I Corps with Second Army was not renewed until April 1945. 7th Armoured Division was transferred to I Corps on August 16 from XXX Corps, was restored to Second Army on the 27th and thereafter with rare intervals remained with Second Army. The other divisions with I Corps were only occasionally placed u/c Second Army for short periods. The changes of corps command of divisions were numerous, sudden and often of short duration. They did not entail any serious administrative disturbance. During August 59th Division was disbanded in order to maintain the flow of trained reinforcements to the remaining infantry divisions.

On the evening of August 7, Canadian 2nd and 51st Divisions assembled south of Caen in six closely packed columns of tanks, flails, armoured infantry carriers and self-propelled A/T artillery. To the west of the Caen–Falaise road were Cdn. 4th Inf. and Cdn. 2nd Armd. Bdes.; to the east of the road were 154th Highland Bde. and 33rd Armd. Bde. In the line were Canadian and Highland infantry whose task it would be to mop up any strong-points by-passed by the advancing columns.

At 2300 hours the bombing from the air of targets marked by flare shells opened and half an hour later the columns moved forward on either side of the road. By dawn they were firmly established three miles inside the German positions. Then at midday U.S. 8th Airforce began

---

* *Key to Fig. 25.*

6 A.B.	6th Airborne Division
7 Ar.	7th Armoured Division
11 Ar.	11th Armoured Division
2 Fr. Ar.	French 2nd Armoured Division
1 P or 1 P.Ar.	Polish 1st Armoured Division
49, 50, 51, 53, 59	Infantry Divisions
2 C, 3 C	Canadian 2nd and 3rd Infantry Divisions
4 C	Canadian 4th Armoured Division

bombing the Bretteville–Cintheaux–St. Sylvain area in preparation for an advance by Canadian 4th and Polish 1st Armoured Divisions. But when this advance began it was quickly checked by A/T gunfire. However, during August 9 the Germans pulled back to the line of the Laison and by the following morning Canadian II Corps had moved forward some nine miles and its leading elements were within seven miles of Falaise.

On August 12 the Americans captured Alençon and were threatening Argentan. Between Canadian II Corps and U.S. XV Corps the gap measured some twenty miles.

On August 14 the Canadians launched another major attack towards Falaise. Canadian 2nd Division moved to outflank the German positions in Quesnay Wood and on Potigny Ridge while Cdn. 2nd Armd. Bde., Canadian 3rd Infantry and Canadian 4th Armoured Divisions, moving in solid phalanxes, forced the line of the Laison under cover of a smoke screen. By dusk the leading elements of Canadian 3rd Division were within three miles of Falaise. Heavy fighting continued until August 16 when Canadian 2nd Division broke into Falaise from the west.

Meanwhile U.S. XV Corps had been fiercely engaged in the Argentan area. It did not attempt to continue its northward advance lest it should collide with the Canadians. Two of its divisions were sent to Dreux to reinforce the eastward drive. But on August 17 General Montgomery decided that this risk should be taken. U.S. V Corps took over the U.S. divisions still in the Argentan area and prepared to drive north to Trun and Chambois.

In the north Canadian 4th and Polish 1st Armoured Divisions ultimately broke out across the Dives in the Morteaux–Coulibœuf area and made a wide sweep to the south-east and by the evening of August 17 were within two miles of Trun. In the south the Americans captured Bourg-St.-Léonard. The gap was now only six miles and within an area twenty miles wide and ten miles deep there were some 100,000 German troops subjected to remorseless pressure and pounded by bomb and shell. Their only paths of escape were now the narrow roads through Chambois and St. Lambert and these were under fire from both sides and from the air.

On the 18th a fierce battle raged north of Chambois. The Canadians captured Trun and at nightfall were within two miles of Chambois itself. From the south U.S. 90th and French 2nd Armoured Divisions were nearing Chambois.

On the 19th the Germans within the pocket were concerned only with escape. The roads leading to the east were choked with tanks, guns and transport. In the evening the Poles, the Americans and the French were in Chambois and the encirclement of the German forces within the pocket was complete.

On the 20th the encircling line was pierced between Trun and

BREAK-OUT AND ADVANCE INTO HOLLAND

Chambois by a desperate German thrust which kept the road through St. Lambert open for a while. It was firmly closed again in the evening. On the 21st a final attempt to relieve the forces in the pocket was made but it was unavailing and the Germans, leaving 10,000 dead and 50,000 prisoners-of-war, some 500 tanks and guns behind, withdrew beyond the Seine on either side of Paris.

THE ADVANCE TO THE SEINE

The advance to the Seine was begun by U.S. Third Army on August 15 while the battle of the Falaise pocket was still raging. On the 16th, U.S. XII Corps was in Orleans, U.S. XX Corps in Chartres and U.S. XV Corps in Dreux. By dark on the 18th, U.S. 79th Division was in Mantes-Gassicourt, west of Paris and only three miles from the Seine. On the 19th a patrol found an intact footbridge across the river and without interference a firm bridgehead was established on the 20th. On the 23rd, U.S. 7th Armoured Division secured a second bridgehead at Melun, south-east of Paris.

In front of Second Army the Germans, fighting a skilful rearguard action, withdrew in an orderly fashion towards the Seine, followed up by XXX, XII, Canadian II and I Corps in this order from right to left. But the American advance to the Seine endangered the German forces facing Second Army for the reason that for them the only bridge across the river was the damaged railbridge at Rouen. To cut this way of escape General Bradley despatched U.S. XIX Corps northwards from the area of Verneuil on August 20. In the next four days U.S. 2nd Armoured Division advanced sixty miles into the flank of the retreating Germans but at Elbeuf encountered strong opposition from armoured forces covering the escape route through Rouen. For two days the advance was checked and so it was that the retreat was not transformed into a rout. Suffering very heavy losses of men and, especially, of material the Germans, by means of ferries, pontoon bridges, rafts and small boats, got across the river. Second Army, following upon their heels, took over its sector of the Seine front in the face of almost negligible resistance as U.S. XIX Corps turned south across the front of the advancing British and Canadian formations.

43rd Division crossed the Seine against slight opposition near Vernon on August 25. By the 26th Canadian 3rd Division and Canadian 4th Armoured Division were crossing the Seine near Elbeuf, 15th Division of XXX Corps was across in the vicinity of Vernon and, on the 27th, I Corps reached the Seine on a broad front with 7th Armoured Division on its right. On August 31, 49th and 51st Divisions began to cross.

Meanwhile Paris had been liberated. On August 19, 3,000 armed gendarmes had turned the Île de la Cité into a fortress and the F.F.I. gained control over the centre of the city. The German commandant asked for an armistice to permit him to withdraw his troops to the eastern sector of the city and offered to recognise the F.F.I. as belligerents, to leave them in possession of the centre of the city and to allow French food convoys to enter. This was agreed. But on the night of the 20th a proclamation was broadcast which seemed to suggest that the Germans were not to observe the conditions of the armistice and fighting flared up again.

On August 22, French 2nd Armoured and U.S. 4th Divisions of U.S. V Corps began to move on the capital and at dawn on the 25th the French from the west and the Americans from the south entered the city. By dusk all organised opposition had been overcome.

The crossing of the Seine in the original 'Overlord' planning had been scheduled for D-day+90. Despite the fact that the capture of Caen was rather more than a month behind schedule, the first crossing of the Seine had beaten it by a fortnight.

OPERATION 'ANVIL' (OR 'DRAGOON')

On August 15, U.S. Seventh Army landed on the Côte d'Azur. All German troops in Southern France, save the garrisons of Toulon and Marseilles, were promptly withdrawn. By the end of August these two ports had been captured and American and French columns were advancing up the valley of the Rhône. On September 5, French 2nd Infantry Division made contact with French 2nd Armoured Division near Dijon and the forces of 'Anvil' and 'Overlord' joined to yield a continuous front from the Swiss border to the Channel. U.S. Seventh Army and French First Army became the components of U.S. 6 Army Group operating on the extreme right flank of the Allied Armies.

THE PURSUIT TO THE ALBERT AND MEUSE–ESCAUT CANALS

General Montgomery was firmly of the opinion that following the crossing of the Seine the Allies should, by means of a swift and powerful thrust on a narrow front, cut clean through the considerably disorganised German armies and strike at the Ruhr area which was the source of more than half of Germany's hard coal and steel. He foresaw that it would be exceedingly difficult if not impossible to maintain a general advance on a broad front to the Rhine and planned that the Canadian and Second Armies should be directed on the Pas-de-Calais and Antwerp and U.S. First and Third Armies on Brussels and Aachen with their right flank on the Ardennes.

But his views did not prevail. General Eisenhower, whose operational headquarters were to open officially on the Continent on September 1, decided, for a variety of reasons, that it was necessary for the advance to be a general one and on a broad front to secure the whole length of the Rhine, the left wing thrusting north-eastward to open the Channel ports and Antwerp, clear the V-weapon sites and directly threaten the Ruhr while the right wing moved eastwards to threaten the Saar basin and to link up with U.S. 6 Army Group in the Vosges. General Eisenhower assumed direct control over the ground forces and so the command of General Montgomery, soon to become a Field-Marshal, became restricted to 21 Army Group now consisting of fourteen divisions and seven armoured brigades.

The immediate tasks of 21 Army Group were the destruction of the enemy in north-east France, the capture of the Belgian airfields and the opening of the port of Antwerp. Second Army was to advance from the Seine with all possible speed and advance to the area Arras–Amiens–St. Pol, irrrespective of the progress of the armies on its flanks. From that area it was to be prepared to drive forward through the industrial area of Northern France and into Belgium. Canadian First Army was to operate along the central coastal belt initially as far as Bruges. Dieppe was to be seized and a corps swung into the Le Havre Peninsula to secure the port.

The advance had to be nourished by supplies brought by road from Bayeux, two hundred and fifty miles away. There was an acute shortage of transport. The second line transport of VIII Corps and half its first line transport had to be used for the maintenance of XII and XXX Corps. Not more than two corps, therefore, could be supplied as the L. of C. lengthened. For the advance XII Corps had under command 7th Armoured, 15th and 53rd Divisions and an armoured brigade, XXX Corps, the Guards and 11th Armoured, and 50th Divisions and an armoured brigade.

XXX Corps advanced from its bridgehead across the Seine on August 29 with 11th Armoured Division in the lead. By midday on the 30th, 11th Armoured Division was within forty miles of Amiens and was meeting only light opposition. The division drove on through the night to enter the city next morning and to cross the Somme over a bridge that, owing to the intervention of the local Resistance Movement, was intact. 50th Division also reached Amiens on this day and the Guards Armoured Division came up on the right to the Albert–Amiens road. By September 2, armoured cars had reached the Franco-Belgian border south-east of Lille. Further east two U.S. armoured divisions crossed into Belgium as far as the Lille–Mons road along which the German troops from the Pas-de-Calais were attempting to escape. XXX, U.S. XIX and U.S. VII Corps were ranged along the frontier within a day's march of Brussels.

XII Corps moved out of the Seine bridgehead on August 30. Followed by 53rd Division, which dealt with such enemy resistance as had been by-passed by the armour, 7th Armoured Division moved swiftly to within fifteen miles of the Somme.

During the next three days the pace of the advance quickened. The Guards Armoured Division, with the Belgian Bde. under command, crossed the Franco-Belgian border during the afternoon of September 3 and headed straight for Brussels. 11th Armoured Division by-passed Lille and leaguered that night a few miles east of Alost. 50th Division reached Alost on the morning of the 4th and on this day 11th Armoured Division swept into Antwerp in time to prevent serious damage being done to the docks. XXX Corps was now well established in the area Antwerp–Malines–Brussels–Louvain.

XII Corps, leaving 53rd Division and the armoured brigade to deal with such opposition as was encountered, by-passed Lille and moved on Ghent, which was entered on the evening of September 5.

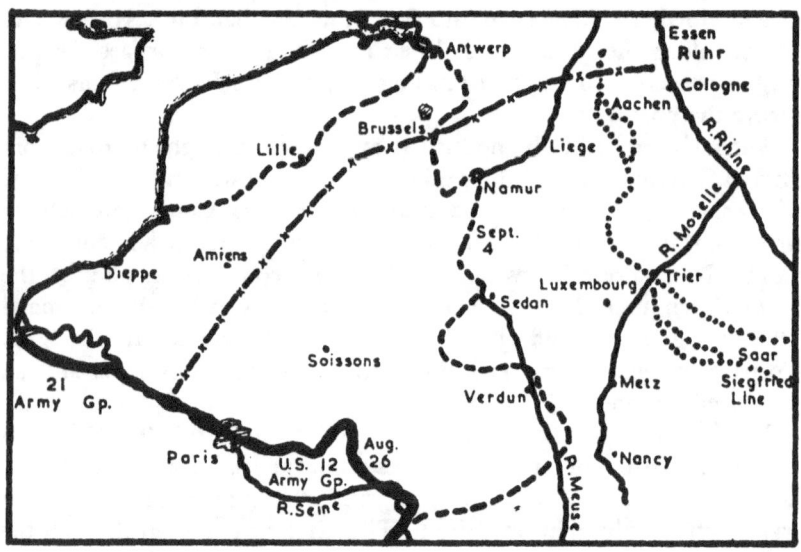

FIG. 26. The Advance from the Line of the Seine.
August 26–September 4.

So at the beginning of September, Second Army's front stretched along a general line between Hasselt and Antwerp. Ahead of it lay a number of water obstacles including the Albert and the Meuse–Escaut Canals and beyond these the Maas and the Rhine. On September 6 and 7, 11th Armoured Division tried to break out northwards from Antwerp and failed. 50th Division, given a similar task at Gheel on September 7, gained a bridgehead over the Albert Canal, but could not expand it. Further east, Guards Armoured Division secured a bridgehead at Beeringen on September 6, but not until the 10th, after much hard

BREAK-OUT AND ADVANCE INTO HOLLAND

fighting against German counter-attacks, was it able to seize the bridge over the Meuse–Escaut Canal at Neerpelt. All 21 Army Group's resources were now being concentrated towards the north-east. By September 9, XII Corps had relieved XXX Corps of Alost and Antwerp and on the 12th it took over the Gheel bridgehead with 15th Division which secured a small bridgehead over the Meuse–Escaut Canal but was unable to expand it. Further to the west Canadian II Corps took over Ghent from XII Corps on September 11.

The task of clearing the Channel ports was assigned to Canadian 3rd, 49th and 51st Divisions. I Corps began its advance from the Seine bridgehead on September 1, 49th Division swinging left into the Le Havre Peninsula, 51st Division heading for St. Valéry, which was entered on September 2. Then 51st Division turned down the coast to come in on the right of 49th Division and to take over the northern sector of the perimeter around the strongly defended port of Le Havre. The defences having been thoroughly softened up by the Royal Navy and the R.A.F., 49th Division on the afternoon of September 10 broke through the perimeter and by midnight 51st Division had done likewise. The garrison surrendered during the morning of the 12th. Canadian 3rd Division closed in on Boulogne and Calais on September 5. The majority of the civilian population of Boulogne was evacuated, the R.N. and the R.A.F. bombarded the defences, and on September 17 two brigades of Canadian 3rd Division supported by a large concentration of guns began their attack upon the great concrete forts. The town was cleared by September 20 and on the 22nd the last of the forts surrendered.

Three days later the attack on Calais opened. A heavy air bombardment preceded the evacuation of the civilian population and by it the resistance of the German garrison was much diminished. The Citadel fell on September 27, the Cap Gris Nez position twelve miles to the west of Calais was overrun on the 29th and by October 1 Calais itself was in Canadian hands. The flying bomb sites had been captured.

Canadian 2nd Division, advancing by way of Dieppe by-passed Dunkirk which was soon to be invested by the Czech Armoured Brigade, and occupied Ostend and Canadian 4th Armoured Division with the Polish Armoured Division on its right was directed on the Bruges–Ghent Canal. A crossing over the canal was secured on September 9. Light forces on the coast approached Zeebrugge and the Poles moved in to the Ghent area, there to take over from XII Corps. The task now facing Canadian First Army was that of clearing the banks of the Scheldt Estuary in order that the port of Antwerp, some fifty miles from the sea, could be brought into use.

The phase of swift movement which had conferred such great advantage upon the Allies had now ended. The Germans were holding a coherent line. Field Marshal Montgomery now planned to recreate the conditions of mobile warfare and to make use of the Allied Airborne Army for a bold and unorthodox stroke which, he hoped, would force the Germans out of their defensive positions and bring about a rapid break-through and penetration deep enough to carry Second Army across the Rhine in one bound. He proposed to lay a carpet of airborne troops, some 35,000 in all, to seize the canal and river bridges ahead of Second Army and thus clear the way for the swift advance of its armoured divisions over the Maas and the Rhine, outflanking the Siegfried Line which ended north of Aachen and establishing a powerful armoured force on the edge of the North German Plain (Operation 'Market Garden').

OPERATION 'MARKET GARDEN'

East of Nijmegen where the Rhine swings west and crosses into Holland the river divides into the Neder Rijn, which flows through Arnhem, and the Waal, which flows through Nijmegen. To the south is the Maas with a bridge at Grave and over the Maas–Waal Canal was a bridge at Heumen. The bridge at Arnhem, protected by strong-posts at either end and with A.A. guns posted to the south with a field of fire straight down the bridge, was the last barrier in front of the lightly fortified German frontier twenty miles to the east. Ten miles south of Arnhem was the bridge at Nijmegen, eight hundred yards long. At both Arnhem and Nijmegen both road and rail bridges were known to be intact.

Second Army for this operation had under command four corps, one of which was I Airborne Corps of Allied First Airborne Army. 1st Airborne Division reinforced by the Polish Para. Bde. was to be dropped beyond the Neder Rijn west of Arnhem to capture the bridge at Arnhem. U.S. 82nd Airborne Division was to be dropped between the Maas and the Waal, south of Nijmegen, to capture the bridges at Nijmegen, Grave and Heumen. U.S. 101st Airborne Division (under XXX Corps' command) was to be dropped between Veghel and Son, north of Eindhoven, to open the main road connecting 1st and U.S. 82nd Airborne Divisions with Second Army. 52nd (Lowland) Division (Airportable) was to be flown in as soon as air strips had been prepared north of Arnhem.

The airborne troops were to be landed in depth so as to form a corridor fifty miles long. Along the Meuse–Escaut canal line were:

VIII Corps
 11th Armoured and 3rd Divisions
XXX Corps
 Guards Armoured, 43rd and 50th Divisions; 8th Armd. Bde. and the Royal Netherlands Brigade Group.
XII Corps
 7th Armoured, 15th and 53rd Divisions; 4th Armd. Bde.

But VIII Corps on the right was not ready for immediate action. XII Corps was facing a belt of difficult country. In any case there were sufficient supplies forward to maintain a deep penetration by one corps only and so the relief and reinforcement of the airborne forces depended on XXX Corps, especially on the Guards Armoured Division. Second Army began this operation with very small reserves. For the armour there was but one clear route and this passed over a number of water obstacles, at any one of which its advance might be checked. Lest some of the bridges should be blown much bridging material, many D.U.K.Ws. and assault boats were brought forward. Along the narrow 'airborne corridor' some 20,000 vehicles would have to move. It was hoped that Second Army would be able to reach the Zuider Zee in the area of Nunspeet, isolating the German forces in western Holland and would establish bridgeheads to the east of the Ijssel, preparatory to an advance on the Ruhr.

There were not sufficient aircraft to transport all the airborne troops in one lift. It was decided therefore that on the first day U.S. 82nd and 101st Divisions should each land their three parachute regiments (each equal in strength to a British brigade) and that 1st Airborne Division should send in one parachute brigade and the bulk of its airlanding brigade. On D-day+1 and D-day+2 the American glider-borne artillery and infantry and a British and a Polish parachute brigade would be sent in. At least three days of fair weather were therefore required.

It was decided that the only feasible dropping and landing areas for 1st Airborne Division were north of the river six to eight miles west of the Arnhem road bridge. General Urquhart commanding the division decided that because his force was to arrive in three instalments he must deploy his airlanding brigade outside Arnhem to protect the dropping zone at least until the second lift arrived on D-day+1. For the attack on the bridge he had therefore only his lightly armed parachute battalions and his reconnaissance squadron which could not be reinforced for another twenty-four hours. Much therefore would depend on the speed and strength of the German reaction and on the weather.

On the morning of Sunday, September 17, the Allied air fleet flew from England into Holland in two great sky trains, over 1,000 troop-carriers and nearly 500 gliders carrying a total of 20,000 men. The airfleet itself was escorted by 1,240 fighters. The way had been prepared by more than 1,000 bombers which struck at German A.A. batteries along the route and around the dropping zone. By 1330 hours that afternoon the sky over Arnhem, Nijmegen and Veghel was filled with the throb of engines. West of Arnhem the paratroops and gliders of 1st Airborne Division landed accurately and with little interference. None of the division's 358 gliders had been shot down but 38 failed to arrive because of broken tow ropes and in these were some of the armoured jeeps of the Recce. Sqn. which was to have rushed the road bridges. 1st A/L Bde. organised the defence of the dropping zones while 1st Para. Bde. set out for Arnhem with 2nd Para. Bn. in the lead. As 'C' Coy. reached the railway bridge it was blown. The other two companies pressed on but at Den Brink, less than two miles from the road bridge, they encountered stern opposition. Leaving 'B' Coy. to deal with this the battalion H.Q. and 'A' Coy. and some engineers pressed on to secure the northern approaches to the bridge shortly after 2000 hours.

By this time the southern end of the bridge was strongly held and when a platoon of the Para. battalion attempted to cross the bridge it was quickly thwarted. Soon 'B' Coy. and part of Bde. H.Q. arrived, but the 500 men with only one troop of A/T guns could do naught else but hold on to the northern end of the bridge and wait for reinforcements.

Meanwhile the rest of the brigade had become heavily engaged within two miles of the dropping zone and German reinforcements, including tanks, took up blocking positions between Oosterbeek and Arnhem. The five hundred troops at the bridge were thus isolated and 1st and 3rd Para. Bns., each fighting its own battle, were separated. The airlanding brigade was widely dispersed in defence of the dropping zone.

The Americans in the Nijmegen–Eindhoven part of the corridor enjoyed more success for the opposition they encountered was far less. A battalion of U.S. 82nd Airborne Division, dropping astride the Maas bridge at Grave, gained it within an hour of landing. Before dark one of the bridges over the Maas–Waal canal at Heumen had been captured and the road to Nijmegen secured. But the Waal bridge in Nijmegen itself was stoutly held and the Americans were checked about four hundred yards from it.

U.S. 101st Airborne Division captured all four of the bridges in Veghel intact and that at Son over the Wilhelmina Canal was blown as they reached it. However, one parachute regiment got across the canal during the night and by dawn was nearing Eindhoven.

At 1425 hours on September 17 the guns of XXX Corps began to put down a rolling barrage one mile wide and five miles deep along the Eindhoven road. Typhoons in a continuous stream reinforced this barrage. Then the tanks of the Irish Guards moved forward to smash through a barricade five hundred yards north of the Dutch border and to engage the German defences in the cypress plantation that bordered the road. After fighting strenuously and losing a number of tanks the resistance was overcome and the Irish Guards reached Valkenswaard, five miles from Eindhoven. 50th Division, following, mopped up the pockets by-passed by the armour. By the afternoon of the 18th the Guards and U.S. 101st Airborne Division had joined up in Eindhoven and when the engineers had repaired the bridge at Son the road to

Nijmegen was clear for the armour to continue its drive down the corridor.

Of the 1,203 gliders that took off from England on the 18th only 13 were shot down. But they were much delayed by fog. The Germans, counter-attacking, overran the landing zones of U.S. 82nd Airborne Division just before the gliders were due to arrive. The Americans counter-attacked at once and drove the Germans back just in time. The gliders landed under fire. Being so heavily engaged the Americans were unable to capture the Nijmegen bridge that day.

The troop carriers and gliders for Arnhem were five hours late. By this time 1st and 3rd Para. Bns. had fought their way into Arnhem but had been cut to pieces in a series of bitter actions around the St. Elizabeth Hospital so that their combined strength was now less than 250. They were unable to break through to the 700 men at the north end of the bridge who were forced back when the houses they were holding were set alight.

By the evening of the 18th the situation north of the Neder Rijn was extremely confused. Communications within the division and between the division and the outside world had broken down. 4th Para. Bde. was directed to drive the Germans from the high ground north of Oosterbeek and thus strengthen the divisional perimeter. This attack failed and two battalions lost half their strength. Two battalions were sent into Arnhem. Though they reached the St. Elizabeth Hospital and the survivors of 1st Para. Bde. they could get no nearer the bridge. On the 19th they repeatedly attacked but German tanks and S.P. guns now covered every approach to the bridge and ultimately they were forced back to Oosterbeek. On September 19 because of thick fog in England most of the Polish Para. Bde. and the glider infantry regiment of U.S. 82nd Airborne Division were not able to leave their airfields. Of 655 troop carriers and 431 gliders that did take off from other airfields only 60 per cent. reached their destinations and 112 gliders and 40 transport planes were lost.

Altogether, 8,905 officers and men of 1st Airborne Division and 1,100 glider pilots landed in the Arnhem area.

Practically none of the supplies dropped by air reached 1st Airborne Division; they fell almost entirely into the hands of the Germans. The R.A.F., in attempting to deliver these supplies, initially to an area which 1st Airborne Division never reached, endured heavy loss.

The force at the north end of the bridge was now completely cut off and its situation was fast becoming desperate. It held about a dozen houses and a school which were under continuous shell and mortar fire. The cellars were full of wounded and the nearby houses were ablaze. German tanks were systematically demolishing its defences. On the morning of Wednesday, the 20th, this force regained contact with divisional H.Q. through the Arnhem telephone exchange which was still being operated by Dutch patriots. Its commander then learnt that there was no hope of rescue unless he could hold on until the ground forces arrived from Nijmegen.

On the 19th the Grenadier Guards Group had driven rapidly from Son to the woods south of Nijmegen where they found U.S. 82nd Airborne Division hard pressed by attacks from the Reichswald. Together with an American parachute battalion the Guards pressed on toward both the road and the rail bridges but could not reach them.

During the night of September 19/20 preparations were made for U.S. 504th Para. Regt. to cross the Waal a mile down stream to seize the northern end of the bridges as the Grenadier Guards and a parachute battalion attacked their southern defences. The mopping up of the town of Nijmegen occupied all Wednesday morning. At 1500 hours the 504th launched their boats. Only half of these reached the north bank and some 200 men scrambled ashore to establish a slender foothold which was gradually reinforced and expanded. By 1830 hours the Americans, by a magnificent feat of arms, had routed their opponents and secured the northern end of the railway bridge. Then the Guards pressed home their attack and before 1900 hours five tanks, with their guns firing, raced for the road bridge. Two made it, crossed and joined up with the Americans. The road to Arnhem was open.

In Arnhem the force at the bridge was now only about 140 strong. The school had collapsed in flames. Three hours before the first tank crossed the bridge at Nijmegen, heading north, the first German tank broke through and crossed the bridge at Arnhem, heading south.

North of the Maas there were the Guards Armoured and U.S. 82nd Airborne Divisions which were fully engaged in repelling the frequent German counter-attacks from the Reichswald flank. In the Nijmegen bridgehead there were one parachute regiment and two groups of Guards but the latter could not resume the offensive until they had been relieved by 43rd Division which was only just crossing the Maas. It was not until the afternoon of the 21st that the Irish Guards were able to attack from the Nijmegen bridgehead and then they were halted almost at once by an anti-tank screen south of Bessem. A direct attack by infantry and an outflanking movement by the Welsh Guards was no more successful. The Polish Para. Bde. was dropped that day between Elst and Driel in the face of heavy opposition but by the time the Poles reached the south bank of the Neder Rijn the ferry at Heveadorp had been sunk and the northern end of the ferry site was in German hands.

The remnants of 1st Airborne Division, some 3,500 altogether, were now within an area one thousand yards wide and two thousand yards deep around the Hotel Hartenstein in Oosterbeek which was under constant heavy and continuous fire from three sides.

On Friday, September 22, 43rd Division attacked along the main road through Elst to Arnhem and along the side road through Oosterhout to the Heveadorp ferry. The division made very slow progress during the day's fighting and accomplished little. At 1800 hours, however, 5th D.C.L.I. on tanks of 4th/7th D.G., carriers and D.U.K.Ws., loaded with supplies and ammunition, drove through Oosterhout and joined the Poles in Driel. It was then discovered that the banks of the Neder Rijn were so soft and steep that the D.U.K.Ws. could not be launched. Only some fifty men of the Polish Bde. got across in reconnaissance boats.

Then the Germans cut the corridor between Veghel and Uden and 32nd Gds. Bde. had to be sent back to re-open it.

By the evening of the 23rd, 1st Airborne Division was desperately in need of ammunition and during the night supplies were ferried across. 250 Poles got across but of these only 150 reached the Hartenstein perimeter.

On Sunday, September 24, the R.A.F. was able for the first time in eight days to provide strong air support for 1st Airborne Division. Then at night about 250 men of 4th Dorset crossed in the few assault boats that were available, but owing to the blackness of the night and to the swiftness of the current the landings on the far side were widely spread and before the Dorsets could find the perimeter the Germans closed in around them.

On this day the corridor was cut again, to remain closed for forty-eight hours. It was decided that 1st Airborne Division, now only 2,500 strong, should be withdrawn across the Neder Rijn.

On the night of the 25th, under a barrage of the guns of XXX Corps, they slipped away in small parties to the boats, manned by British and Canadian engineers, which were waiting for them at the river's edge. Their wounded who could not be moved kept up the usual pattern of radio traffic and defensive fire. By daybreak on the 26th, 2,163 men of 1st Airborne Division and the Glider Pilot Regiment, 160 Poles and 75 Dorsets had reached the safety of the southern bank. 300 wounded within the perimeter and 200 men of 4th Dorset were taken prisoner to swell the number of those captured in and around Arnhem to more than 6,000, of whom nearly half were wounded before they fell into German hands. Several hundred more remained at large, sheltered by the Dutch. The majority of these eventually found their way back across the river.

By the end of the month, after VIII Corps on the right of XII Corps on the left had filled out its flanks, the corridor was broadened. By early November 21 Army Group was established on the Maas from Grave to the sea and Canadian II Corps then took over the Nijmegen bridgehead. On December 2 the Germans cut the dykes on the southern side of the Neder Rijn west of Arnhem and flooded most of it. On December 4 the

Germans fiercely attacked what was left of it and were sternly repulsed by 49th Division. Thereafter the Arnhem gateway into the Ruhr remained closed. Seven months were to pass before Arnhem was again entered by Allied troops.

(ii)

The Break-out and the Advance into Holland. Medical Cover (21 Army Group Formations)

GUARDS ARMOURED DIVISION

For the exploitation of the break-through by VIII Corps three battle groups were formed. To these were attached:

(1) a section of 128 Fd. Amb.
(2) three sections of 19 Lt. Fd. Amb.
(3) 128 Fd. Amb., less one section.

H.Q. 19 Lt. Fd. Amb. was to move forward and open an A.D.S. as soon as possible; H.Q. 128 Fd. Amb. was to open as late as possible. 8 F.D.S. and 60 Fd. Hyg. Sec. were to remain in the divisional administrative area and deal with the minor sick and exhaustion cases. Evacuation was to be down the divisional axis to VIII Corps' medical area at Perigny.

On July 31, Group 1 advanced to the area of Le Tourneur, Group 2 to St. Martin-des-Besaces and Group 3 to the area of Sallen north-west of Caumont. 19 Lt. Fd. Amb. opened north of Caumont and VIII Corps' F.D.S. formed an advanced surgical centre at St. Jean-des-Essartiers.

On August 1, 8 F.D.S. moved to a site north of Sallen, 19 Lt. Fd. Amb. to St. Jean-des-Essartiers and 128 Fd. Amb. to Sept Vents.

On August 3 all three groups were in the vicinity of Estry. On the 5th Group 1 became isolated and suffered about 40 casualties, which were evacuated in an escorted convoy to 18 Lt. Fd. Amb. of 11th Armoured Division at Bény-Bocage.

On August 6 the advance continued with 15th Division followed by 11th Armoured Division on the left and 3rd Division followed by the Guards Armoured Division on the right. The advance was checked at the Vassy–Vire road on August 11. C.C.Ps. were opened and 19 Lt. Fd. Amb. at Le Bocq evacuated casualties to 128 Fd. Amb.

Between August 28 and September 6 the division advanced to the Albert Canal u/c XXX Corps. It passed through the bridgehead held by 43rd Division over the Seine at Vernon. On the 31st the division crossed the Somme at Condé. On September 1 Arras and Douai were reached.

BREAK-OUT AND ADVANCE INTO HOLLAND 233

Opposition was slight and casualties few. Evacuation was direct to 3 C.C.S. at Allonville. 128 Fd. Amb. with 32nd Gds. Bde. harboured in Ficheux.

On the 3rd, 231st Bde. of 50th Division with 200 Fd. Amb. came under command. The few casualties incurred were evacuated to 10 C.C.S. at Fresnoy. 32nd Gds. Bde. entered Brussels. The German hospital annexe to Hôpital St. Pierre was captured intact. On September 4 the division made a triumphal entry into Brussels and harboured for the night in the Parc Royal.

On September 6, the division advanced to the Albert Canal and 231st Bde. moved to Antwerp. 32nd Gds. Bde. secured a bridgehead at Beeringen. 19 Lt. Fd. Amb. opened south-west of Tessenderloo and 128 Fd. Amb. near the bridge that was being constructed in the bridgehead. Evacuation was to 86 B.G.H. in Brussels. On the 7th, 8 F.D.S. moved up to a site east of Schaffen. On the 8th the division crossed the canal and, on the 9th, 128 Fd. Amb. opened in the village of Heusden. On the 10th the division moved up to the Escaut Canal. Three sections of 19 Lt. Fd. Amb. opened at Vlasmer and H.Q. established an A.D.S. at Spiekelspode. On the 12th Hechtel was captured.

On September 18 the division moved to Eindhoven leading 43rd and 50th Divisions in Operation 'Market Garden'. On the 19th the advance continued, casualties being left with the medical centre of U.S. 101st Airborne Division at Veghel. Nijmegen was reached and 19 Lt. Fd. Amb. opened north of Malden. On the 20th, twenty M.A.C. cars were lent to D.D.M.S. Airborne Corps to move U.S. 82 Evac. Hosp. to Brakkenstein. On the 21st a section of 19 Lt. Fd. Amb. opened in the Jonker Bosch hospital, there to be joined in the evening by 35 F.D.S. and Lt. Sec. 10 C.C.S.

The divisional medical units at this time had the following composition and average strength:

	Officers	O.Rs.
19 Lt. Fd. Amb.		
H.Q. and four secs.	10	175
128 Fd. Amb.		
H.Q. and two Bearer Corps each of three secs.	13	220
8 F.D.S. divisible into heavy and light secs.	7	90
60 Fd. Hyg. Sec.	1	26

Their normal employment was as follows:

19 Lt. Fd. Amb.
Three secs. formed a C.C.P. in the area of H.Q. 5th Guards Armd. Bde. The sections were separated only when units of the brigade were operating in independent rôles. H.Q. and one sec. remained

under divisional control but during a rapid advance they too were placed u/c 5th Guards Armd. Bde.

128 Fd. Amb. (less one sec. without a M.O.)
was placed u/c 32nd Gds. Bde. One sec. with ambulance cars moved with each battalion. The section without a M.O. was placed u/c M.O. R.A.S.C. and sited in Adm. H.Q. area.

8 F.D.S. and 60 Fd. Hyg. Sec.
remained in Adm. H.Q. Area and moved with it. The F.D.S. took over the patients of the field ambulances at the start of any advance in order that the two field ambulances should be fully mobile.

During the advance each brigade was organised into two battle groups each consisting of one armoured regiment and one infantry battalion. It was found that the light field ambulance and the field ambulance were both equally capable of dealing with the casualties of these mixed groups when the sections of the light field ambulance were strengthened by the addition of personnel from the H.Q. of the unit. At no time were the field medical units taxed.

TABLE 22

Guards Armoured Division. Casualties Evacuated

July 31–August 6	345
August 11–August 12	314
August 31	14
September 1	28
September 2	6
September 3	25
September 4	6
September 7–12	596
September 18	55
September 19	16

7TH ARMOURED DIVISION

In mid-July the division passed under command VIII Corps and moved to Cazelle in preparation for the battle for Caen. Toward the end of July the division passed to the command of XXX Corps, moving to the east of Caumont and then by way of Villers-Bocage to Aunay-sur-Odon.

During these actions 2 Lt. Fd. Amb. and 29 F.D.S. were engaged, the latter functioning in the rôle of a field ambulance headquarters. 131 Fd. Amb. was held in reserve.

On August 16 the division returned to I Corps and fought at Livarot, Lisieux and St. Georges during the advance to the Seine. 2 Lt. and 131 Fd. Ambs. with 29 F.D.S. worked together in the divisional medical

BREAK-OUT AND ADVANCE INTO HOLLAND 235

area. Two of them were alongside each other, one open and the other closed, while the third moved forward to open in the next divisional medical area. After the vicinity of Ghent had been reached to 29 F.D.S. was assigned the care of the 'B' Echelon of 22nd Armd. Bde., 131st Bde. and divisional troops and the holding of key personnel who were sick. The unit was prepared to receive battle casualties if necessary. The two field ambulances were with their brigades, one company of 131 and two sections of 2 Lt. being forward. Evacuation was to the corps advanced surgical centre.

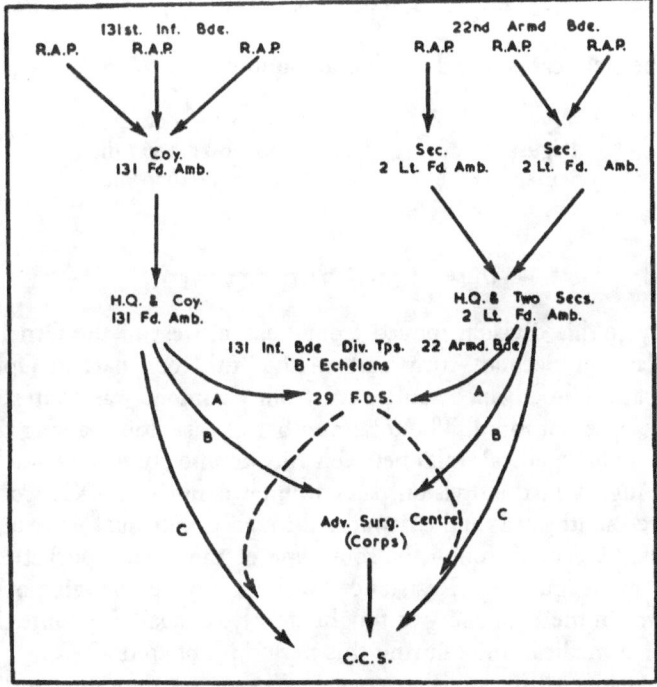

FIG. 27. 7th Armoured Division. Evacuation Plan during the Advance into Belgium.

    A. Key men and minor sick
    B. Groups 1* and 2* cases
    C. Group 3*.

TABLE 23

7th Armoured Division. Casualties. July–September

Head	18·0 per cent.
Chest	8·2 ,,
Abdomen	3·3 ,,

* *See* definition on page 448.

Upper Limb . . . . . 38·0 per cent.
Lower Limb . . . . . 35·5 ,,
Multiple . . . . . 3·0 ,,
Burns . . . . . . 4·0 ,,

Evacuated from Divisional Area (average strength 15,000)

	Battle Casualties		Sick and Accidental Injuries	
July	361	0·86/1000/diem	576	1·37/1000/diem
August	657	1·2/1000/diem	591	1·1/1000/diem
September	261	0·62/1000/diem	267	0·63/1000/diem

Of the sick, cases of exhaustion amounted to:

July	130	0·32/1000/diem
August	70	0·15/1000/diem
September	9	0·02/1000/diem

11TH ARMOURED DIVISION

On July 29 this division moved from Lasson, west of the Orne, to the right flank of Second Army and on the 30th took part in Operation 'Bluecoat'. The advance southward from Caumont was contested and progress was not rapid. The total number of casualties passing through the divisional medical units between July 30 and August 12 was 820.

On August 13 the division passed under command XXX Corps and advanced southwards and eastwards through Condé-sur-Noireau, Flers, Ecouché, Argentan, round the south end of the Falaise pocket to reach Laigle on August 23. Resistance was not severe though pockets of Germans in the Ecouché area fought stoutly. Casualties admitted to the divisional medical units during this period numbered 287.

On August 28 the division reached Vernon on the Seine and on the 29th began a rapid advance, to reach Amiens on the 30/31st and Antwerp on September 4. On September 3 an advanced surgical centre was established at Renaix. Between August 29 and September 8 the number of casualties admitted to the divisional medical units numbered 261.

On September 9 the division moved to the Albert Canal to protect the right flank of XXX Corps. By the 12th the division was in the area of Peer. Between September 9 and 12 the casualties admitted numbered 75.

On September 17, 11th Armoured Division reverted to the command of VIII Corps with 3rd Division and on the 20th advanced northwards into Holland, moving as a right flank protection to XXX Corps, and on the 26th reached Gemert, twelve miles west of the Maas. 204 casualties were admitted to the medical units of the division between September 20 and 26.

Casualties. July–September

Battle Casualties	2,561
Battle Injuries and Sick	1,528

3RD DIVISION

This division passed from I to VIII Corps on August 2 and moved to an area south of Bayeux. 185th Bde. with 223 Fd. Amb. was u/c 11th Armoured Division when, on August 6, it occupied a position on the high ground Le Bas Perrier–Sourdeval and there repulsed a heavy attack; 248 men of the brigade were wounded in this action. On August 6 the division moved into the line east of Vire and during the next ten days made a series of advances to reach the vicinity of Flers. On September 3 it crossed the Seine near Les Andelys and on the 16th moved into Belgium to an area south of the Escaut Canal near Peer. On the 19th, 9th Bde. made an assault crossing of the canal at Lille St. Hubert. On September 23 the division moved into Holland in support of 11th Armoured Division which was protecting the eastern flank of the Airborne corridor to Nijmegen. By the end of the month the division was in the area Helmond–Gemert–Asten with U.S. 7th Armoured Division on its right.

During August the ratio of exhaustion cases to wounded was 2 : 7, an improvement on the 2 : 5 of July. During the period June 6–August 31, exhaustion cases constituted 14·5 per cent. of the cases admitted to divisional medical units. Until August 6 these cases were evacuated to corps medical installations and of them not more than 50 per cent. returned to duty after treatment. Thereafter these cases were retained in 11 F.D.S. and the proportion of those returning to their units after seven days of treatment was much greater.

As the fighting became more open the divisional medical units were no longer distributed among the brigades but were used on the divisional axis, leap-frogging over each other. One F.D.S. was reserved for Priority 1 cases but as there were relatively few of these it was decided to attach the unit to whichever A.D.S. was functioning.

When the division moved into Belgium 44 non-transportable patients in the divisional medical units were concentrated in 11 F.D.S. which was left behind.

For the crossing of the Meuse–Escaut Canal 9 Fd. Amb. opened an A.D.S. at Petit Broghel and a C.C.P. on the near bank of the canal. A detachment of one M.O. and 13 O.Rs. R.A.M.C. was attached to each assaulting battalion. One M.O. and 22 O.Rs. R.A.M.C. were assigned the task of establishing a C.C.P. on the far side of the canal as soon as this became possible and casualties were to be ferried across pending the construction of a bridge.

For the advance into Holland the field ambulances were brigaded.

3rd Division. Casualties (wounded)

August	848
September	277

15TH DIVISION

On July 18, 15th Division was relieved by 53rd Division in the Evrecy area and moved to the right flank of Second Army, taking over in the Caumont sector from U.S. 5th Division and passing u/c XXX Corps. On the 28th the division reverted to the command of VIII Corps for Operation 'Bluecoat'.

For the opening phase of this battle a forward and a rear medical area was the lay-out of choice as the division was operating on a single axis and heavy casualties were expected. The forward medical area contained the A.D.Ss. of 194 and 153 Fd. Ambs. with 23 F.D.S. responsible for resuscitation. In the rear area were 193 Fd. Amb. and 11 Lt. Fd. Amb. (6th Gds. Tk. Bde.) on wheels and ready to move forward. 22 F.D.S. was open for the divisional sick and exhaustion cases. Each brigade had a field ambulance company under command.

Rapid progress was made and it became necessary to move 193 Fd. Amb. forward to open an A.D.S. 11 Lt. Fd. Amb. also moved forward but remained closed and on wheels. 22 F.D.S. was moved up alongside the A.D.S. of 193 Fd. Amb.

On July 30, some 300 casualties passed through the divisional medical units. On July 31, 194 Fd. Amb. leap-frogged over 196 and opened an A.D.S. in Hervieux. This was reinforced later by 23 F.D.S. and 11 Lt. Fd. Amb.

43rd Division on the left, however, had not been able to keep pace with the advance of 15th Division and so it was that the open left flank lengthened as the division continued to advance. To meet the difficulties inherent in such a tactical situation, two A.D.Ss. were disposed in echelon, both being supported by detachments from 23 F.D.S. for resuscitation work. 22 F.D.S. in the rear dealt only with the minor sick and exhaustion cases. During the rest of the operation one of the field ambulances leap-frogged over another, the rearmost closing and preparing to move forward. In the final stages of the battle the divisional axis became dichotomised to yield two evacuation routes with an A.D.S. on each. The C.C.Ps. became exposed to heavy fire from the flank, that of 193 Fd. Amb. receiving a direct hit, three men being killed and three others wounded. That of 153 Fd. Amb. also received a direct hit and suffered casualties.

BREAK-OUT AND ADVANCE INTO HOLLAND 239

On August 14, the division was withdrawn on relief and moved to the vicinity of Amayé-sur-Orne and thence to the area of Fresney-le-Vieux to pass u/c XII Corps.

On August 23 the division advanced to the Seine on three routes. A field ambulance was allotted to each of the brigades and a section of the M.A.C. was attached to each field ambulance. The F.D.Ss., leapfrogging, were used to form collecting points at pre-selected nodal points related to the main axis and, where possible, at points where the three roads converged. Casualties accumulated at these nodal points were evacuated by M.A.C. to the nearest C.C.S. or general hospital. G.O.C. 15th Division agreed that Medical H.Q. should be included in Main Divisional H.Q. for this advance.

By August 25, the distance to the C.C.Ss. had become somewhat overlong and so two F.S.Us. and one F.T.U. were attached to one of the F.D.Ss. to constitute an advanced surgical centre should this become necessary. In the event, it did not.

During the crossing of the Seine at Portejoie, St. Pierre-du-Vauvray and Muids, near Louviers, casualties were few and very easily dealt with by the field ambulances which had sections across the river at an early stage of the crossing. The field ambulances were under divisional control. Two A.D.Ss. were formed by 193 and 153 Fd. Ambs. on the near side of the river and these received the casualties until 194 Fd. Amb. had crossed the river and opened on the far side.

For the advance into Belgium *via* St. Pol–Lens–Lille–Roubaix the field ambulances were placed u/c the brigades and the F.D.Ss. leapfrogged along the line of the divisional axis to receive and stage casualties *en route* for the nearest corps medical unit. During this advance 23 F.D.S. with two F.S.Us. and one F.T.U. formed an advanced surgical centre which received casualties from 7th Armoured Division, which was ahead of 15th Division. Contact with the enemy was made north of Autryve when 193 and 194 Fd. Ambs. both opened to receive a small number of casualties and 22 F.D.S. took these over so that the field ambulances might close and move on.

On September 10, the division moved to an area between Antwerp and Brussels and on the 12th took over the bridgehead at Gheel from 50th Division. On the 13th, 194 Fd. Amb. opened an A.D.S. in the bridgehead in a mental hospital in Gheel. On the following day 44th Bde. forced its way across the canal and established a bridgehead against stiffening resistance. Casualties began to increase in number and a corps F.D.S. with F.S.Us. and F.T.U. joined the A.D.S. of 194 Fd. Amb. in Gheel on September 14. Later this advanced surgical centre was joined by 22 F.D.S. which took over the minor sick and exhaustion cases.

The bridgehead over the canal was small and in it the fighting was severe. The R.A.Ps. were in deep cellars and casualties—80 to 90 a day—had to be evacuated by ferry. On the 17th, 153 Fd. Amb. relieved 194. On September 24, the division came out of the line to take over an area north of Eindhoven, still functioning as the flank guard to the main axis of Second Army's thrust. It took over a small bridgehead at Best on the Wilhelmina Canal west of Eindhoven. In this bridgehead the fighting was violent. It was decided not to move a complete field ambulance into it but to allot a company of a field ambulance to each of the three brigades therein to form a C.C.P. 193 Fd. Amb. opened an A.D.S. in a school on the route from the bridge leading into the bridgehead. Casualties were passed from the A.D.S. to 23 F.D.S. which was functioning as an advanced surgical centre at Meerveldhoven, whence evacuation by air from Zeelst to Brussels was now possible.

In this division at this time it was the practice to use one of the F.D.Ss. for the reception and treatment of the minor sick and for exhaustion cases and the other for resuscitation duties. This second F.D.S. was always associated with the A.D.S. that was receiving battle casualties. The F.D.S. was divided into three sections, each self-contained, and not into a light and a heavy section.

TABLE 24

15th Division. Distribution of Personnel of a F.D.S.

	S/Sgt.	Sgt.	Cpl.	L/Cpl.	Pte.
Section 1	–	1	2	–	8
2	–	1	2	–	8
3	–	1	2	–	8 (including dental corporal)
Evacuation	–	1	1	–	6 (including two amb. orderlies)
Q.M.	–	1	–	1	5 (including dispenser Sgt., carpenter and cobbler)
Cookhouse	–	1	1	–	6 (including three G.D.Os.)
Office	–	1	–	1	3
Staff employed	1	–	–	2	4 (including 1 L/Cpl. water duties, 1 L/Cpl. and 1 Pte. sanitation and 3 batmen)

Medical officers were attached to sections as required.
The equipment was distributed according to a plan born of experience.

TABLE 25

15th Division. Casualties admitted to Medical Units.

July 1–September 30

	Battle Casualties	Non-Battle Casualties
193 Fd. Amb.	1,441	881
194 ,, ,,	1,213	603
153 ,, ,,	930	835
22 F.D.S.	62	689
23 ,,	66	787
	3,712	3,795

Total 7,507

Exhaustion Cases admitted to Divisional F.D.Ss. July 1–September 30	692
Transferred out of Divisional Area	357
R.T.U.	335

Of the admissions only 68 were re-admissions.

R.A.M.C. Casualties

	Killed	Wounded	Missing
Officers	—	5	1
O.Rs.	13	51	3
	13	56	4

Sick

	July				
	1–7	8–14	15–21	22–29	Av.
Ratio per 1,000 reporting sick daily	7·4	5	7·8	8·9	7·2
,, ,, ,, Scabies.	0·56	0·21	0·06	0·5	0·33
,, ,, ,, Pediculosis	0·69	0·07	0·06	0·19	0·25
,, ,, ,, V.D.	0·06	—	0·12	0·06	0·06
Total cases Infectious Diseases	5	3	—	3	2·7
,, ,, Other Skin Diseases	54	80	75	113	80·5
,, ,, Exhaustion.	22	18	1	21	15·5
,, ,, admitted to Medical Units	109	268	406	123	—

Table 25 (Sick) continued

	August				
	30/5	6–12	13–19	20–26	Av.
Ratio per 1,000 reporting sick daily	6·3	9·7	12·9	10·7	9·9
,, ,, ,, Scabies	0·24	0·14	0·19	—	0·14
,, ,, ,, Pediculosis	—	0·55	0·19	0·12	0·21
,, ,, ,, V.D.	0·06	—	—	0·06	0·03
Total cases Infectious Diseases	4	2	2	1	2·2
,, ,, Other Skin Diseases	71	71	117	96	88·75
,, ,, Exhaustion	66	160	26	4	64
,, ,, admitted to Medical Units	314	680	152	186	—

	September				
	27/1	2–9	10–16	17–23	24–30	Av.
Ratio per 1,000 reporting sick daily	12·5	6·9	6·8	9·1	10·7	9·2
,, ,, ,, Scabies	0·16	0·14	0·21	0·07	0·21	0·15
,, ,, ,, Pediculosis	—	—	0·07	0·21	0·21	0·05
,, ,, ,, V.D.	—	0·06	0·14	0·07	0·14	0·08
Total cases Infectious Diseases	—	1	5	2	1	2·2
,, ,, Other Skin Diseases	82	72	60	82	57	70·6
,, ,, Exhaustion	10	3	98	75	77	52·6
,, ,, admitted to Medical Units	108	119	337	282	401	—

43RD DIVISION

On August 1 the division advanced on the general axis Caumont–Cahagnes–Jurques–Le Mesnil Auzouf. 213 Fd. Amb. opened its A.D.S. south of Caumont, where 14 F.D.S. joined it. The C.C.Ps. moved forward with the brigades. The advance continuing, 129 Fd. Amb. leap-frogged over 213 and opened at St. Pierre-du-Fresne, north of Jurques. On the 5th, in preparation for the attack on Mont Pinçon, 15 F.D.S., clearing its patients to the C.C.S., prepared to move forward and 130 Fd. Amb., remaining on wheels, joined 129 at St. Pierre-du-Fresne. In preparation for the assault across the Noireau 129 Fd. Amb. moved to La Londe, west of Aunay, opening here on the morning of the 15th. On the 17th, 130 Fd. Amb. opened two miles north of the Noireau. The field ambulances crossed the river with their brigades and the rapid movement towards the Seine began. 129 and 130 Fd. Ambs. moved to the vicinity of Ecouché on the 22nd, 213 Fd. Amb. to the east of Argentan. On the 24th the division was split into three groups for the advance to the Seine; 129 Fd. Amb. moved with the first of these to Breteuil, 213 with the second to Gacé, 130 Fd. Amb., 15 F.D.S. and 38 Fd. Hyg. Sec. with the third to Exmes.

Medical cover for the crossing of the Seine was as follows:

An ambulance car and six S.Bs. of 129 Fd. Amb. were allotted to each

BREAK-OUT AND ADVANCE INTO HOLLAND 243

of the four R.M.Os. to cross with the battalions. The rest of the field ambulance company with the brigade formed a C.C.P. first on the near bank and then on the far bank. Two D.U.K.Ws. were allotted to Group 1 for medical purposes. Two sections of the second company of the field ambulance with the brigade established detachments at the two ends of each bridge. A car post of at least four cars was established as near the bridge site as possible. The remainder of the field ambulance with 49 F.S.U. established an A.D.S. on a site selected by the brigade. Six M.A.C. cars were attached to 129 Fd. Amb. to ply behind the A.D.S.

An ambulance car and six S.Bs. of 213 Fd. Amb. were allotted to each R.M.O. A detachment of 168 Lt. Fd. Amb. was with the armoured regiment of 3rd Armd. Bde. A C.C.P. was established on the near bank and the rest of the field ambulance crossed and established an A.D.S. on the further side. Six M.A.C. cars were attached to the field ambulance.

By the 27th the C.C.Ps. of all the field ambulances were open at the eastern end of the bridges and a further C.C.P. of 130 Fd. Amb. was open on the west bank in Vernon for staging. Evacuation across the river was by bridge and ferry.

While 43rd Division remained astride the Seine from August 27 onwards, 8th Armd. Bde. and 11th Armoured and 50th Divisions passed through the bridgehead at Vernon and drove northwards. Then, on September 1, 43rd Division began to move forward. 129 and 130 Fd. Ambs. opened near Giverny and Tilly (N.E. of Vernon) respectively and, on the 3rd, 14 F.D.S. moved to Heubécourt.

When, on September 8, 7th Hamps. went forward to garrison Brussels one ambulance car of 130 Fd. Amb. accompanied them. On the 11th, 130th Bde. moved to Brussels accompanied by one company of 130 Fd. Amb. On the 14th the rest of the division set out for Belgium, 129 and 213 Fd. Ambs. with their brigades, 130 Fd. Amb. and 15 F.D.S. with the administrative group. On the 15th the division reached the Albert Canal at Beeringen. 14 F.D.S. was sent to Bourg-Léopold to join the medical area there and to come u/c XXX Corps.

For Operation 'Market Garden' the division was divided into thirteen groups with extra troops under command. The distribution of medical personnel among these groups was as follows:

1. 3 amb. cars
2. 130 Fd. Amb., less dets.
4. 1 amb. car
5. 1 amb. car and det. 130 Fd. Amb.
6. 213 Fd. Amb., less dets.
7. Royal Netherlands Bde. medical services; 3 amb. cars
8. 15 F.D.S. and 168 Lt. Fd. Amb.
9. 2 amb. cars

10. 129 Fd. Amb., less dets.
13. Det. 129 Fd. Amb.

On September 17, 130 Fd. Amb. with 130th Bde. moved to the area of Hechtel and on the 20th the group moved northwards, to cross the Dutch frontier and to pass through Eindhoven, St. Oedenrode, Uden and Grave to the vicinity of Nijmegen. 213 Fd. Amb. opened near Grave on the 21st. On the 22nd, 214th Bde. broke out of the Waal bridgehead and 129 Fd. Amb. crossed the river and opened an A.D.S. The C.C.P. of 213 Fd. Amb. was now established in Nijmegen and 15 F.D.S. opened to function as an A.D.S. in the Children's Hospital in Nijmegen.

On the 23rd, 130th Bde. crossed the Waal and 130 Fd. Amb., moving with the brigade, opened an A.D.S. near Valburg. 163 Fd. Amb. (XXX Corps) moved up alongside the A.D.S. to receive casualties from 1st Airborne Division as this withdrew from Arnhem.

On the 24th the C.C.P. of 213 Fd. Amb. moved to the area of Valburg and that of 130 Fd. Amb. to Driel. To receive casualties from 1st Airborne Division, withdrawing across the Neder Rijn, a collecting post was established south of Driel and two car posts were placed on the south bank of the river at the points where 1st Airborne Division would cross.

On the 26th, 129 Fd. Amb. recrossed the Waal and moved to a point south of Valburg, remaining closed, and arrangements were made to evacuate some 300 43rd Divisional troops still on the north bank of the Neder Rijn. But none of these could be found.

On September 28, the C.C.P. of 213 Fd. Amb. moved to Andelst and heavy shelling necessitated the withdrawal of 15 F.D.S. from Nijmegen.

49TH DIVISION

On July 24 the division moved to the area across the Orne, east of Caen, under command of I Corps. Two brigades took over the line from 51st Division on the 25th. The division remained in this sector until August 7–8 when the Germans withdrew.

One A.D.S., that of 187 Fd. Amb., was opened in Ranville and two C.C.Ps. were established in the rear of the brigades. 146 and 160 Fd. Ambs. and 16 and 17 F.D.Ss. remained west of the river in the vicinity of Cazelle. 160 Fd. Amb. continued to function as the divisional exhaustion centre and 146 supplied reliefs for R.M.Os. who were brought out of the line for forty-eight hours' rest periods. 16 F.D.S. held the divisional sick and 17 F.D.S. was lent to I Corps for a short period to act as the corps exhaustion centre.

On August 8 the division began to press on the heels of the Germans as they withdrew beyond the Seine, fighting sharp actions on the line

BREAK-OUT AND ADVANCE INTO HOLLAND 245

of each of the five rivers—Dives, Vie, Touques, Calonne and Risle. The advance was made on a two-brigade front. The divisional centre line passed through Démouville, Vimont, Mézidon, Crèvecœur-en-Auge, Bonnebosq, Ouilly-le-Vicomte, Le Pin, Cormeilles, La Poterie Mathieu, Pont-Audemer on the Risle, Bourneville, Routot and Caudebec-en-Caux on the Seine. During this advance the officers commanding the field ambulances lived at brigade H.Q. and had under their command four sections which they used for the establishment of C.C.Ps. To these sections extra ambulance cars were allotted.

At a river crossing a section was attached to the R.A.P. of the leading battalion in order that it might get across as early as possible. Two more sections were attached to the R.A.P. of the second battalion to cross. The headquarters of the field ambulances was leap-frogged forward so as always to have an A.D.S. no more than 10 kms. behind the leading elements of the division. The F.D.Ss. were similarly moved forward to deal with the sick. The F.D.S. was pushed as far forward as possible and then allowed to fall as much as thirty miles behind before it was moved again. Then it would leave its patients with the other F.D.S. as it passed this on its way forward. Some 600 sick were dealt with in this fashion during the advance and were not lost to their units. When the Seine was reached a C.C.P. was established at each of the ferry sites and an A.D.S. was opened in Le Plessis. An officer of 187 Fd. Amb. crossed the Seine in a rowing boat, made contact with the F.F.I. in Caudebec and with their aid and using one small boat got a C.C.P. across the river. Three ambulance cars and one 15-cwt. lorry with the personnel of two sections were sent to Rouen to filter across the bridge there. This they did and a C.C.P. was established. A company of 146 Fd. Amb. got across at Rouen and established an A.D.S. at Lillebonne, whence evacuation was to Rouen.

49th Division, along with 51st Division, next took part in the reduction of Le Havre. 34th Tk. Bde. with 23 Lt. Fd. Amb. and other units came under command of the division. Prior to the assault 23 Lt. Fd. Amb. opened an A.D.S. in Hermeville. 146 Fd. Amb. established its A.D.S. in St. Romain. 17 F.D.S. functioned as a walking wounded annexe to 146 Fd. Amb. 187 Fd. Amb. opened a brigade C.C.P. in Montivilliers and another in Rolleville.

The assault of 56th Bde., u/c 49th Division, went well. Casualties were admitted direct to the C.C.P. in Montivilliers and it was possible to close the C.C.P. in Rolleville.

To provide medical cover for 147th Bde. was difficult owing to the congestion in the gaps that had been made in the minefields. Sections of 160 Fd. Amb. were therefore issued with assault packs similar to those used in the initial landings.

Three sections, one half-track and four ambulances were assigned to

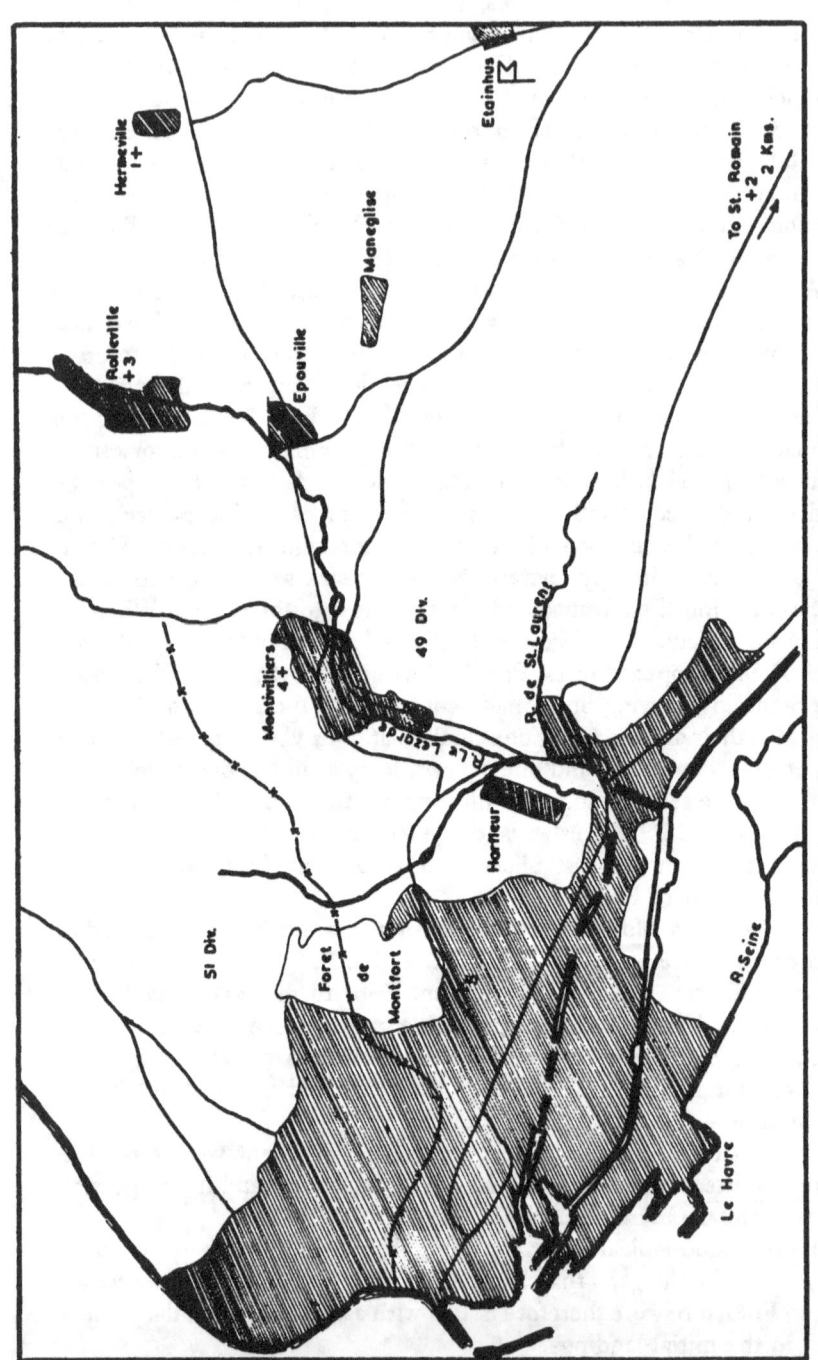

Fig. 28. 49th Division. The Reduction of Le Havre. Medical Cover.
1. 23 Lt. Fd. Amb. 2. 17 F.D.S., A.D.S. 146 Fd. Amb. 3. C.C.P. 187 Fd. Amb. 4. C.C.P. 187 Fd. Amb., A.D.S. 160 Fd. Amb. 5. 187 Fd. Amb.

BREAK-OUT AND ADVANCE INTO HOLLAND 247

1st Leicesters, two sections and three ambulances to 11th R.S.F. and one section and two ambulances to 7th D.W.R., the sections to form C.C.Ps. and the ambulances car posts as near to the C.C.Ps. as possible. It became necessary to resort to hand carriage and to make use of jeeps, carriers and P.o.W. for the ambulances could make no headway because of the congestion. Fortunately casualties were relatively few.

For 146th Bde's. crossing of the Lézarde boats were obtained for the company of 146 Fd. Amb. which was to accompany the brigade and bearer squads of 1 N.C.O. and 12 O.Rs. R.A.M.C. were attached to each battalion. However, the success of the attack by 147th Bde. greatly simplified this operation and the battalions and their R.A.M.C. attachments crossed the river over an intact bridge. C.C.Ps. were then established in support of the battalions in the normal manner.

160 Fd. Amb. opened an A.D.S. in Montivilliers at 1900 hours on D-day + 1, taking over the site of the C.C.P. of 187 Fd. Amb. 23 Lt. Fd. Amb. in Hermeville now closed.

After Le Havre had capitulated 187 Fd. Amb. moved in to render assistance to the civil authorities and to deal with German casualties. However, no assistance was required.

Casualties during this operation were: Killed, 32; Wounded, 260; Missing, 38. In addition 271 P.o.W. and 9 civilians were evacuated through the divisional medical units.

The division was then withdrawn into rest in the area of Dieppe. On September 20 it began to move to the area of Lierre. For this move the field ambulances were placed under the command of the brigades. On September 24 the division established a bridgehead over the Albert Canal north of Lierre and advanced to establish another over the Turnhout Canal north of Oostmalle. 146 Fd. Amb. opened an A.D.S. in Oostmalle and C.C.Ps. were established across the canal as early as possible.

TABLE 26

Admissions to 49th Divisional Medical Units (including 23 Lt. Fd. Amb.). July 1–September 30

	49th Division	Other Formations	P.o.W.	Civilians
Battle Casualties	2,551	348	530	98
Sick	2,781	457	3	26
Exhaustion	475	44	—	—
	5,807	849	533	124

Ratio of Exhaustion to Battle Casualties 1 : 5·3

Causal Agents. A series of 3,425 Battle Casualties

G.S.W.	876	25 per cent.
B.W. (mortar)	725	21 ,,
S.W.	1,093	31 ,,

Wound by Anatomical Region (a series of 3,315)

Head and Face	394	11·9 per cent.
Neck	53	1·6 ,,
Chest	234	7·0 ,,
Abdomen	159	4·8 ,,
Upper Limb	797	24·0 ,,
Lower Limb	1,030	31·1 ,,
Buttocks	61	1·8 ,,
Back	119	3·6 ,,
Multiple	468	14·1 ,,

Severity of Wound

Slight	1,514	47·4 per cent.
Severe	1,453	45·5 ,,
Dangerous	225	6·8 ,,

60 per cent. (approx.) of the casualties were evacuated as stretcher cases.
Deaths in divisional medical units numbered 74, including a large number dead when brought in. Ratio of wounded to killed was 4·9 : 1.

Admissions to 49th Divisional Medical Units (excluding 23 Lt. Fd. Amb.). July 1–September 30

	49th Division	Other Formations
Diseases of Digestive System	783	146
,, Respiratory ,,	147	14
,, Skin	194	31
Neurological Diseases	13	1
I.A.T.	341	27
Pyrexia N.Y.D.	123	21
Injuries, wounds. Battle casualties	2,426	348
,, ,, Accidental	515	127
,, ,, S.I. (suspected)	17	1
,, Burns	77	23
Exhaustion	475	42
Other diseases	515	68
Totals	5,626	849

Total evacuated out of divisional area	4,316	676
Total deaths in medical units	42	12
Total returned to units from divisional medical units	1,331	109
	5,689	797

Diseases. Equivalent Annual Ratio per 1,000

	Average Strength July	Average Strength August	Average Strength September
	16,425	16,989	17,045
Digestive	65·8	419·3	88·9
Respiratory	33·7	32·3	34·9
Skin	43·3	66·2	30·7
I.A.T.	90·4	85·4	75·4
Exhaustion	350·7	62·3	36·2
Other Diseases	147·7	156·2	82·2

TABLE 27

49th Division. Incidence of Gastro-Intestinal Diseases. July 1– September 30

Week ending	Admitted to Medical Units	First Attendances at R.A.P.
July 8	14	47
15	30	77
22	24	113
29	22	110
August 5	27	158
12	80	357
19	258	754
26	150	862
September 2	61	350
9	31	118
16	13	97
23	4	74
30	31	72
Totals	745	3,189

There was an epidemic of diarrhoea and dysentery (Flexner) during August when the division moved into the Caen sector which was in a filthy condition consequent upon the bitter fighting. Exhaustion was far more common during the severe fighting in the *bocage* country than during the open fighting that followed the break-out. In August septic mosquito bites were responsible for many admissions; every derelict building in the Caen area was a breeding ground.

50TH DIVISION

During July the division was continually engaged in the fighting south-west of Tilly-sur-Seulles. Casualties rose to a maximum on July 30 and 31 during the attack on Hottot when 283 battle casualties, mostly from 231st Bde., were evacuated in the course of thirty-six hours direct from the brigade C.C.Ps. to 3 C.C.S.

During the period August 1–3 the division pressed on to Villers-Bocage at a cost of 5 officers and 126 O.Rs. wounded. These were evacuated through the A.D.S. of 149 Fd. Amb. and later through that of 200 Fd. Amb. to 10 C.C.S.

Then, following the battle for the Mont Pinçon feature, the division moved forward to take the ground between Le Plessis and the approaches to Condé-sur-Noireau. During the period August 9–13, 35 officers and 598 O.R. battle casualties were evacuated through the A.D.S. of 186 Fd. Amb. to 3 C.C.S.

During the advance into the Falaise pocket and onwards to the Seine, August 18–23, the division moved behind 11th Armoured Division and mopped up isolated pockets of resistance and collected German stragglers. By the 23rd the division had reached Laigle. For this advance the divisional field ambulances were under command of their respective brigades and had attached to them three M.A.C. cars each. The F.D.Ss. brought the sick they were holding forward with them.

From August 23 to 29 the division paused at Laigle while 43rd Division passed through to secure a bridgehead over the Seine at Vernon. During this time 149 Fd. Amb. established a divisional A.D.S. and took over the light sick from 47 F.D.S. Evacuation was to the nearest corps medical units, some 70 kms. away and along exceedingly congested roads. The division began to cross the Seine on the 29th and 30th behind 11th Armoured Division.

Then came the swift advance to the Somme and then on to the Albert Canal, August 30–September 8. The field ambulances moved with the brigade groups and 47 F.D.S. passed to XXX Corps for staging duties. 48 F.D.S. moved with Rear Divisional H.Q. The few casualties were evacuated in M.A.C. cars to Beauvais. On September 2, 231st Bde. and 200 Fd. Amb. passed to the command of the Guards Armoured Division. The field ambulance reached Brussels on the 4th and thence proceeded

PLATE XVII. Arnhem. A casualty of 1st Airborne Division being taken to a Dressing Station. September 1944.

[*Imperial War Museum*]

PLATE XVIII. An Ambulance Railcar standing in La Gare du Midi, Brussels.

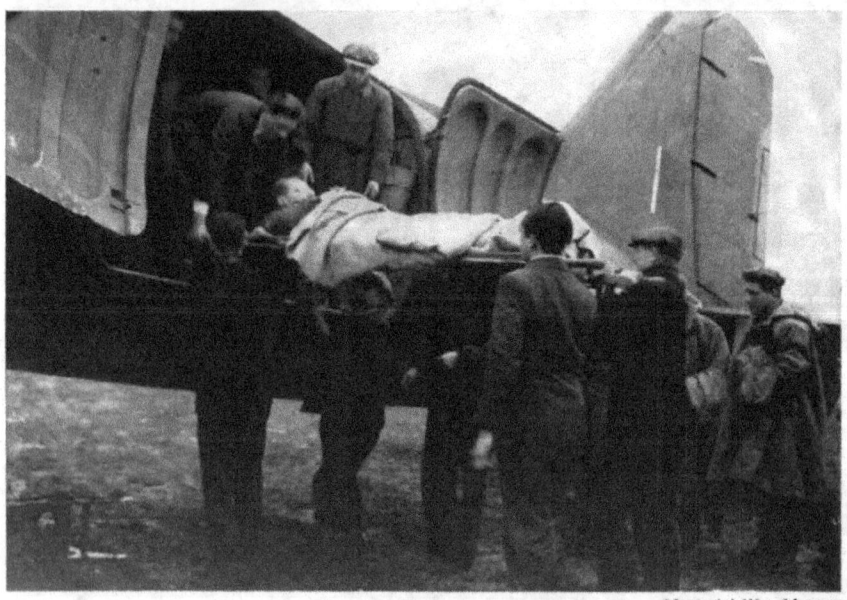

PLATE XIX. Belgian civilians loading casualties into a Dakota of R.A.F. Transport Command.

BREAK-OUT AND ADVANCE INTO HOLLAND 251

to Antwerp. On September 3 and 4, 151st Bde. was involved in fighting south-west of Lille while 69th Bde. cleared the route Tournai–Renaix–Alost–Brussels. Evacuation west of Tournai was to

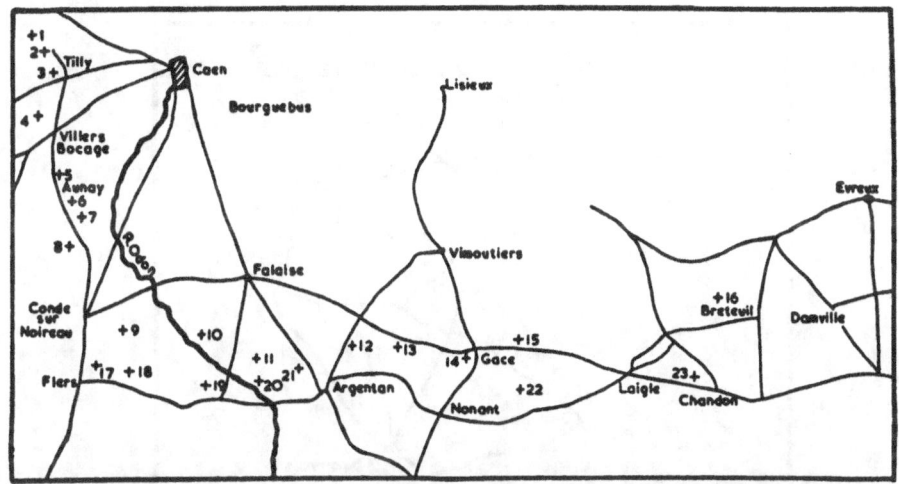

FIG. 29. 50th Division. The Advance to the Seine. Medical Cover.

1. A.D.S. 200 Fd. Amb. Aug. 1–8
   48 F.D.S. Aug. 1–7
   A.D.S. 186 Fd. Amb. Aug. 1–6
2. 47 F.D.S. Aug. 1–9
3. A.D.S. 149 Fd. Amb. Aug. 1–6
4. A.D.S. 149 Fd. Amb. Aug. 6–10
   A.D.S. 186 Fd. Amb. Aug. 6–8
   47 F.D.S. Aug. 9–17
   48 F.D.S. Aug. 7–9 and 12–15
5. A.D.S. 186 Fd. Amb. Aug. 8–9
   A.D.S. 200 Fd. Amb. Aug. 8–12
   A.D.S. 149 Fd. Amb. Aug. 10–17
   47 F.D.S. Aug. 17–22
   48 F.D.S. Aug. 15–24
6. A.D.S. 186 Fd. Amb. Aug. 9–18
   A.D.S. 200 Fd. Amb. Aug. 12–19
   A.D.S. 149 Fd. Amb. Aug. 17–18
7. 48 F.D.S. Aug. 9–12
8. 47 and 48 F.D.Ss. Aug. 24–28

9. A.D.S. 149 Fd. Amb. Aug. 18
   A.D.S. 200 Fd. Amb. Aug. 19–21
10. A.D.S. 149 Fd. Amb. Aug. 19–20
11. A.D.S. 186 Fd. Amb. Aug. 21–22
12. A.D.S. 149 Fd. Amb. Aug. 21
13. A.D.S. 149 Fd. Amb. Aug. 22
14. A.D.S. 200 Fd. Amb. Aug. 22–23
15. A.D.S. 186 Fd. Amb. Aug. 22–23
16. A.D.S. 186 Fd. Amb. Aug. 26–27
17. A.D.S. 186 Fd. Amb. Aug. 18–19
18. A.D.S. 186 Fd. Amb. Aug. 19–20
19. A.D.S. 186 Fd. Amb. Aug. 20–21
20. A.D.S. 149 Fd. Amb. Aug. 20
21. A.D.S. 149 Fd. Amb. Aug. 21
    A.D.S. 200 Fd. Amb. Aug. 21–22
22. A.D.S. 200 Fd. Amb. Aug. 23–24
23. A.D.S. 149 Fd. Amb. Aug. 23–27
    A.D.S. 200 Fd. Amb. Aug. 24–27
    47 F.D.S. Aug. 24–28

10 C.C.S. at Fresnoy on the Arras–Lens road. When 151st Bde. reached Brussels on September 6 evacuation was direct to 86 B.G.H.

On the night of September 7/8, 69th Bde. established a bridgehead over the Albert Canal south of Gheel and 151st Bde. reverted to the command of 50th Division and moved into this bridgehead on the 8th. 186 Fd. Amb. was opened in the rear of the C.C.Ps. of these two brigades and evacuated to 86 B.G.H. 48 F.D.S. moved up alongside 186 Fd. Amb. on September 9 to hold the sick.

The division was relieved by 15th Division on September 12/13 and

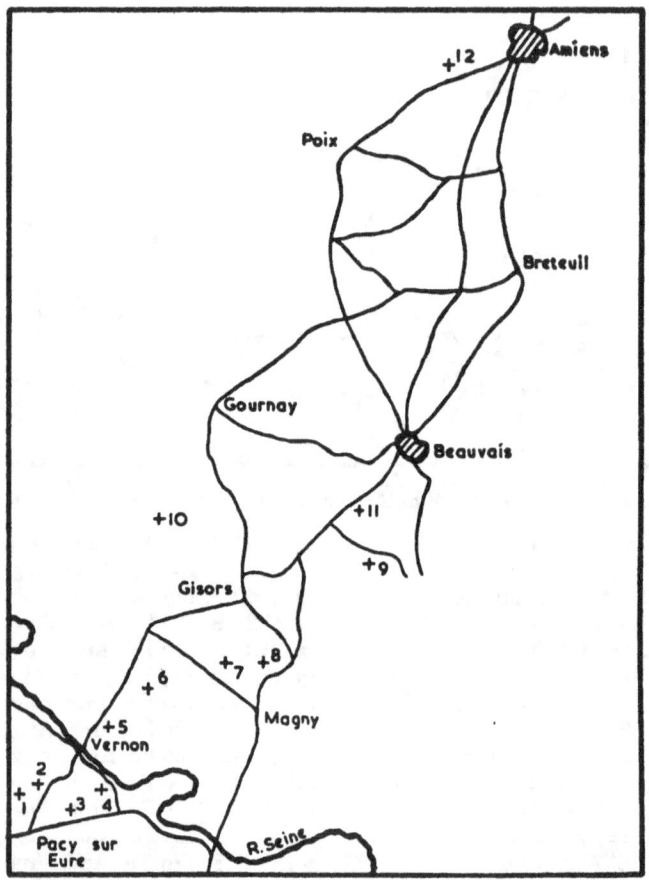

Fig. 30. 50th Division. The Advance to the Somme. Medical Cover.

1. 47 and 48 F.D.Ss. Aug. 28–30
2. A.D.S. 200 Fd. Amb. Aug. 27–30
3. A.D.S. 149 Fd. Amb. Aug. 27–30
4. A.D.S. 186 Fd. Amb. Aug. 27–30
5. A.D.S. 149 Fd. Amb. Aug. 30
6. 47 and 48 F.D.Ss. Aug. 30–31
7. A.D.S. 200 Fd. Amb. Aug. 30–31
8. A.D.S. 186 Fd. Amb. Aug. 30–31
9. A.D.S. 200 Fd. Amb. Aug. 31
10. A.D.S. 149 Fd. Amb. Aug. 30–31
11. A.D.S. 186 Fd. Amb. Aug. 31
12. A.D.S. 149 Fd. Amb. Aug. 31

was then deployed to guard the bridge over the Albert Canal at Beeringen and to support the Guards Armoured Division in the bridgehead over the Meuse–Escaut Canal north of Hechtel. Evacuation was now to 10 C.C.S. at Diest and later to 86 B.G.H.

BREAK-OUT AND ADVANCE INTO HOLLAND

During the earlier phases of Operation 'Market Garden', 50th Division passed to VIII Corps and was employed in widening the corridor and protecting its flanks. 200, 186 and 149 Fd. Ambs. in turn provided the divisional A.D.S., each closing as its brigade moved forward. Evacuation was by M.A.C. to 14 F.D.S. at Bourg-Léopold which was staging on the route to Diest.

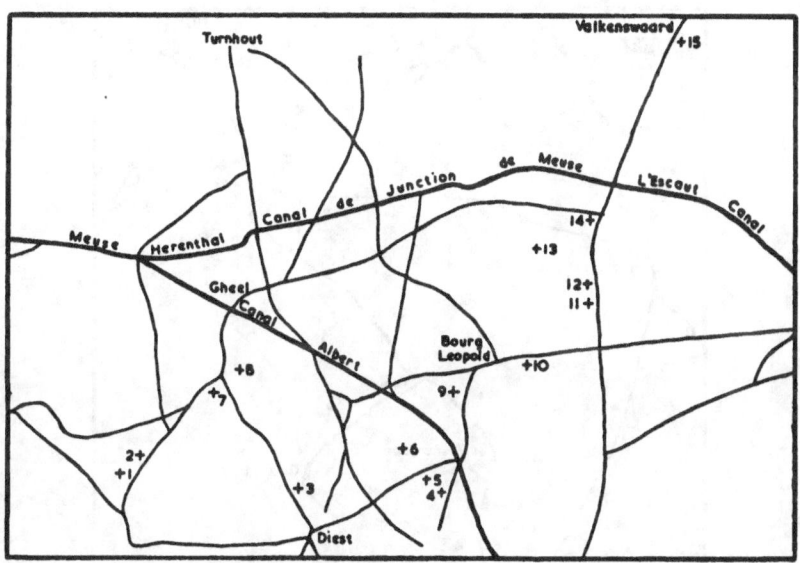

FIG. 31. 50th Division. The Crossing of the Albert Canal. Medical Cover.

1. A.D.S. 149 Fd. Amb. Sept. 8–9
2. A.D.S. 149 Fd. Amb. Sept. 9–11
3. A.D.S. 186 Fd. Amb. Sept. 12–13
4. A.D.S. 149 Fd. Amb. Sept. 14–15
5. A.D.S. 186 Fd. Amb. Sept. 13–15
6. A.D.S. 149 Fd. Amb. Sept. 13–16
7. A.D.S. 186 Fd. Amb. Sept. 7–12
   48 F.D.S. Sept. 9–14
8. A.D.S. 149 Fd. Amb. Sept. 12–13
9. A.D.S. 186 Fd. Amb. Sept. 15–18
10. 48 F.D.S. Sept. 15–19
11. A.D.S. 200 Fd. Amb. Sept. 15–20
12. A.D.S. 186 Fd. Amb. Sept. 18–23
13. A.D.S. 149 Fd. Amb. Sept. 16–21
14. A.D.S. 149 Fd. Amb. Sept. 21–23
15. A.D.S. 200 Fd. Amb. Sept. 20–23

During the period September 20–27 the division moved up to the area St. Oedenrode–Veghel. On the 21st, 69th Bde. u/c XXX Corps moved up to Nijmegen and crossed into the bridgehead north of the Waal. 151st Bde. assisted in the restoration of the corridor after it had been cut on the 24th. Evacuation north of Eindhoven was first to 48 F.D.S. in the St. Joseph's Hospital, Eindhoven, to which a F.S.U. and a F.T.U. were attached, and later to 35 C.C.S. which opened in Eindhoven on the 25th.

On the 26th the division passed to VIII Corps and evacuation was to

254   THE ARMY MEDICAL SERVICES

34 C.C.S. at Geldrop. On the 27th the division began to move to the area between the Zuid Willems Vaart and the Maas.

The high incidence of exhaustion during the hard fighting round Tilly was the cause of considerable concern to this experienced division. It was noted that it occurred usually among the reinforcement elements and that it was associated with heavy casualties among officers and

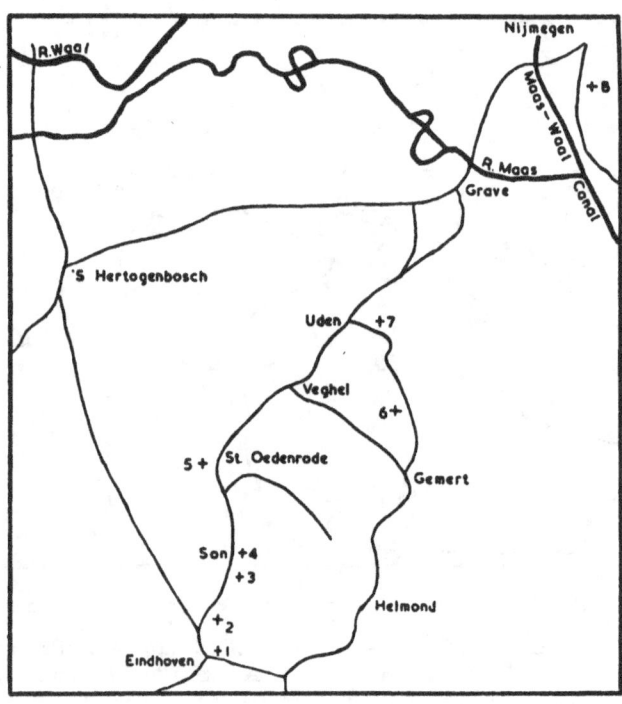

FIG. 32. 50th Division. Nijmegen Bridgehead. Medical Cover.

1. 48 F.D.S. Sept. 19–30
2. A.D.S. 149 Fd. Amb. Sept. 23–26
3. A.D.S. 200 Fd. Amb. Sept. 23–26
4. A.D.S. 186 Fd. Amb. Sept. 23
5. A.D.S. 186 Fd. Amb. Sept. 23
6. A.D.S. 149 Fd. Amb. Sept. 27–30
7. A.D.S. 200 Fd. Amb. Sept. 26–30
8. A.D.S. 186 Fd. Amb. Sept. 24–30

senior N.C.Os., with prolonged periods of heavy mortar fire, with no periods out of the line and with lack of success. To prevent man-power wastage from this cause 200 Fd. Amb. was assigned the task of holding and treating such cases in the divisional area. By doing this it was found that about 46 per cent. of the cases could safely be returned to their units. The corps psychiatrist spent some time with the division and advised the medical officers concerning the treatment of these cases. At this time malaria relapses were common; those cases in which complications occurred were boarded and placed in category C for a period of three months.

The corps medical units were so distributed that quite commonly the A.D.S. was not required, the casualties being evacuated from the C.C.Ps. direct to the C.C.S. The C.C.P. was maintained at full field ambulance company strength and to it was added a transfusion team of one M.O., 2 N.C.Os. and 8 O.Rs. R.A.M.C. with a 3-ton truck, a 40 × 40 New Zealand pattern penthouse and full equipment.

At no time were more than three C.C.Ps. or two A.D.Ss. required to deal with all the divisional battle casualties. One A.D.S. or F.D.S. was used to hold the sick, another was sometimes employed as a minor convalescent depot of 200 capacity.

In November 50th Division returned to the United Kingdom there to become a training division.

51ST DIVISION

On July 31, 51st Division was relieved by 49th Division in the Cagny area and moved to the area of Biéville to take part in Operation 'Totalize' u/c II Canadian Corps. The rôle assigned to the division was that of advancing on the left flank of II Canadian Corps and of capturing Tilly-la-Campagne, Secqueville-la-Campagne, Garcelles-Secqueville and Cramesnil, all to the south of Bourguébus. 154th Bde. was to be conveyed from the assembly area in two columns of armoured vehicles through the German front line into the rear defensive positions, the columns passing on either side of Tilly-la-Campagne which was to be reduced by 152nd Bde. Tanks of 33rd Armd. Bde. were to move with each of the columns and the route from the start-line was to be marked by searchlights and tracer. A concentrated attack from the air lasting three-quarters of an hour was to precede the attack, which was to be launched on August 17, H-hour being 2300 hours.

From the start the operation was successful. On August 9, 51st Division reverted to I Corps. St. Sylvain fell on the 10th and a general advance to the east started on the 12th. St. Pierre-sur-Dives, St. Julien-le-Faucon and Lisieux were entered on August 22 and the Risle crossed on the 27th. On the following day the Seine was reached south of Duclair and a small bridgehead across the river secured. On September 1 the division crossed the Seine by way of the Canadian bridgehead at Elbeuf and on the 3rd reached St. Valéry-en-Caux without encountering any opposition north of the Seine.

In June 1940 the 51st Division that was part of the B.E.F. had been destroyed at St. Valéry-en-Caux. Now, in September 1944, the 51st Division that was part of B.L.A. passed through St. Valéry-en-Caux. There it paused for a while. A memorial service was held in Cailleville and on this Sunday afternoon the massed pipes and drums played the Retreat.

Then on September 4 the division moved on towards Le Havre to take part, with 49th Division, in the attack on the port. When the garrison capitulated the divisional first-line transport helped to lift 49th Division to Antwerp and the divisional artillery moved to the Boulogne area. On September 24, 154th Bde. Gp. moved to Dunkirk to relieve 4th Special Service Bde. 154th Bde. was relieved by the Czech brigade on October 8 and 9 and thereupon set out to rejoin the division in the vicinity of St. Oedenrode.

For Operation 'Totalize' the medical cover was as under:

> 174 Fd. Amb. opened an A.D.S. in Cormelles for the lightly wounded.
> 176 Fd. Amb. opened an A.D.S. in Cormelles for the seriously wounded.
> 5 F.D.S. opened in Cormelles for the divisional sick.
> 175 Fd. Amb. and 6 F.D.S. closed in reserve in Cambes, south of Cazelle.
> 22 Lt. Fd. Amb. (33rd Armd. Bde.) opened in the Canadian medical area for the overflow of minor cases.
> One C.C.P. (one company of a field ambulance) was placed under command of each brigade.

One M.O. and 12 O.Rs. R.A.M.C. accompanied each column, riding in the rear four T.C.Vs. These vehicles, returning from the debussing areas behind the German front line, under the command of the M.O. along the line of the advance searched all disabled vehicles for casualties; 16 were discovered and brought back to the A.D.Ss. whence they were evacuated by the Canadian M.A.C. to the Canadian medical area at St. Germain, west of Caen.

When the division reverted to the command of I Corps on August 9 evacuation was to the hospital area at Cazelle by 132 M.A.C. until an advanced surgical centre was opened at Pédouzes.

During the rapid advance to St. Valéry-en-Caux and Le Havre the field ambulances leap-frogged in the usual manner.

Since casualties were few it was generally found sufficient to have a single A.D.S. open for the battle casualties and a F.D.S. in the same location for the minor sick. The closed units were moved up as close as possible to the open A.D.S. ready for the next forward bound.

Except in the area between St. Sylvain and the River Ifs where the divisional axis was a cross-country track, evacuation was along good roads. In this particular area evacuation by night was impracticable but the opening of an advanced surgical centre at Pédouzes on August 18 and later of 16 C.C.S. at Ingonville so shortened the line of evacuation that no difficulty was thereafter experienced.

For the attack on Le Havre on August 10/11 the following medical cover was provided:

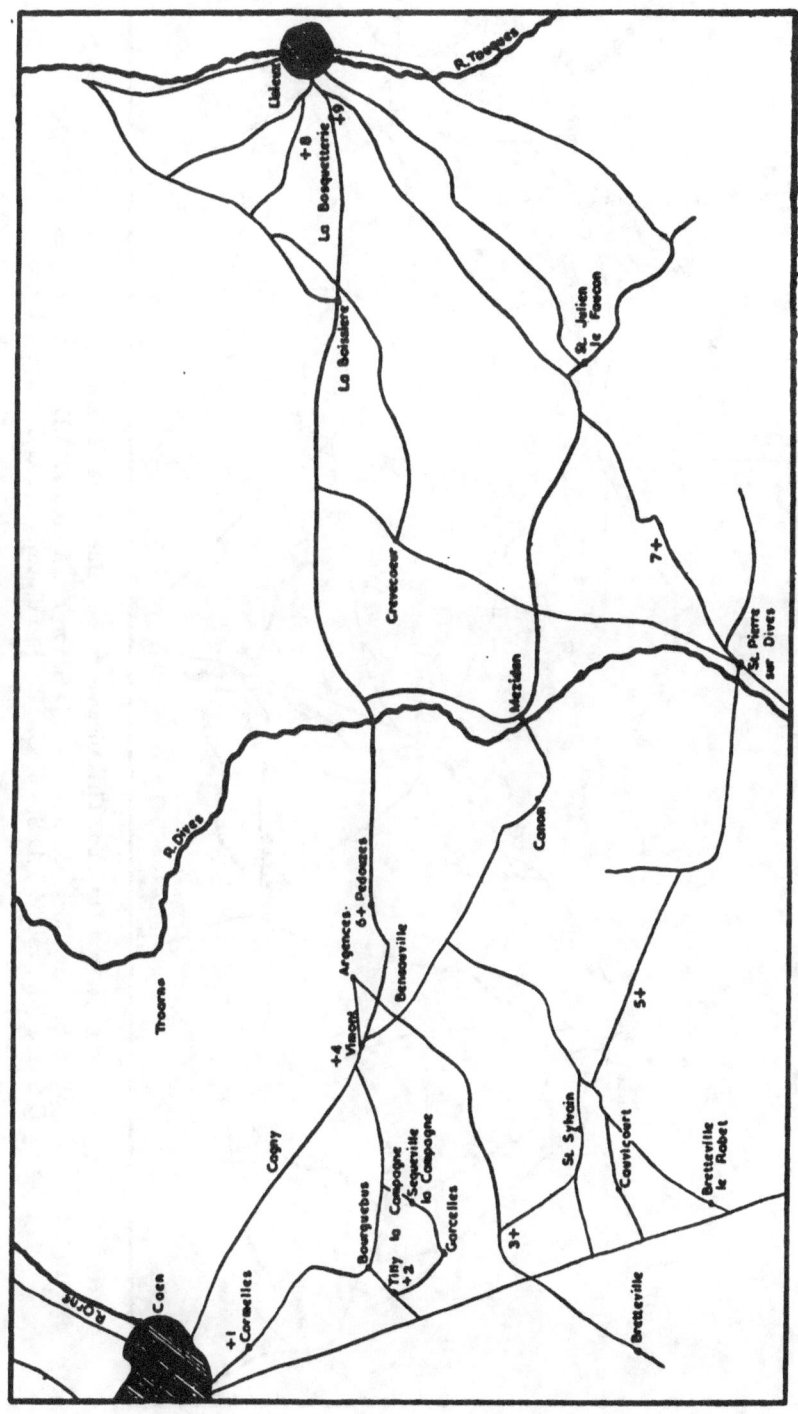

Fig. 33. 51st Division. Operation 'Totalize'. Medical Cover.

1. 174 and 176 Fd. Ambs. 2. C.C.P. 3. 175 Fd. Amb. 4. 16 C.C.S. 5. A.D.S. 175 Fd. Amb.
6. Adv. Surg. Centre 7. A.D.S. 174 Fd. Amb. 8. 32 C.C.S. 9. A.D.S. 175 Fd. Amb.

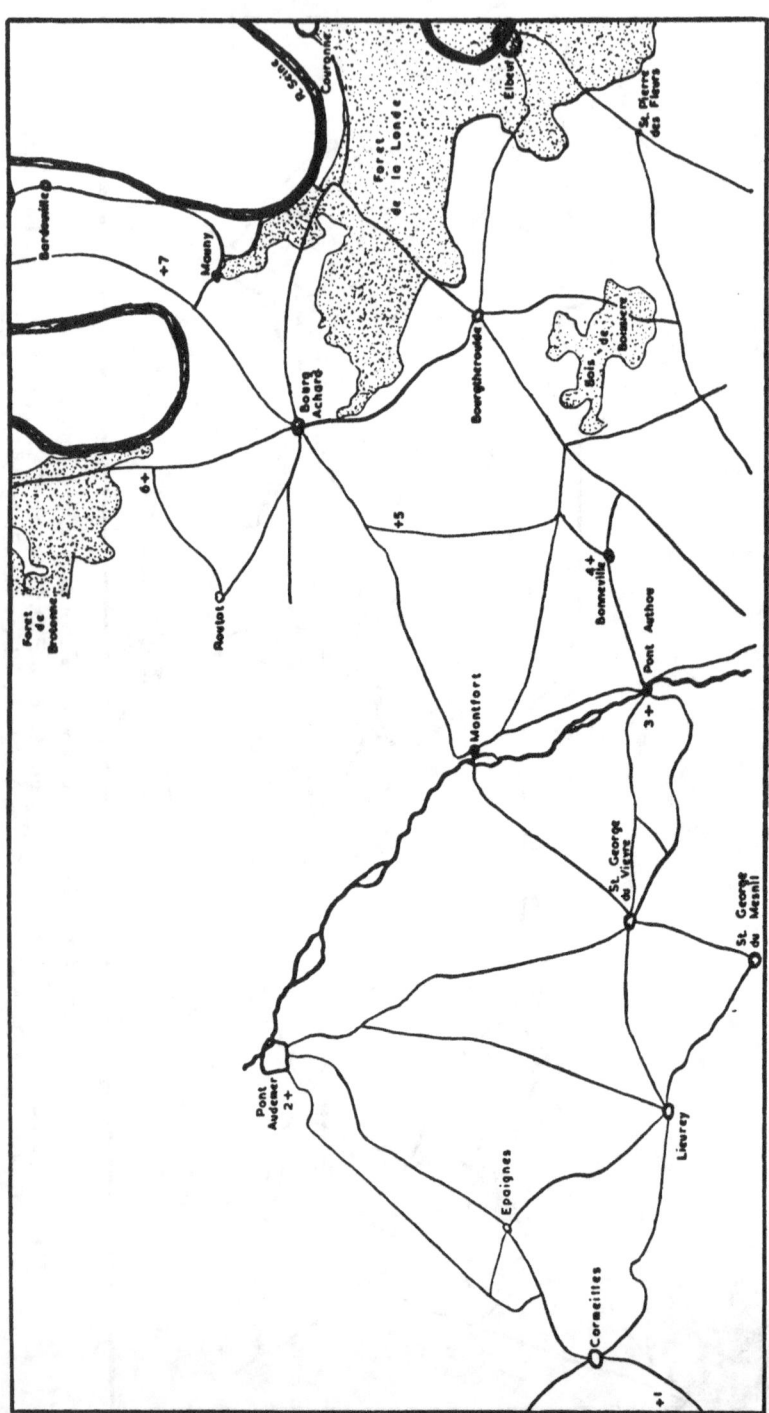

Fig. 34. 51st Division. The Advance to the Seine. Medical Cover.

1. 16 C.C.S.   2. 30 F.D.S. (Adv. Surg. Centre)   3. A.D.S. 176 Fd. Amb.   4. A.D.S. 176 Fd. Amb, 5 F.D.S.
5. A.D.S. 174 Fd. Amb, 6 F.D.S.   6. C.C.P. 174 Fd. Amb.   7. C.C.P. 176 Fd. Amb.

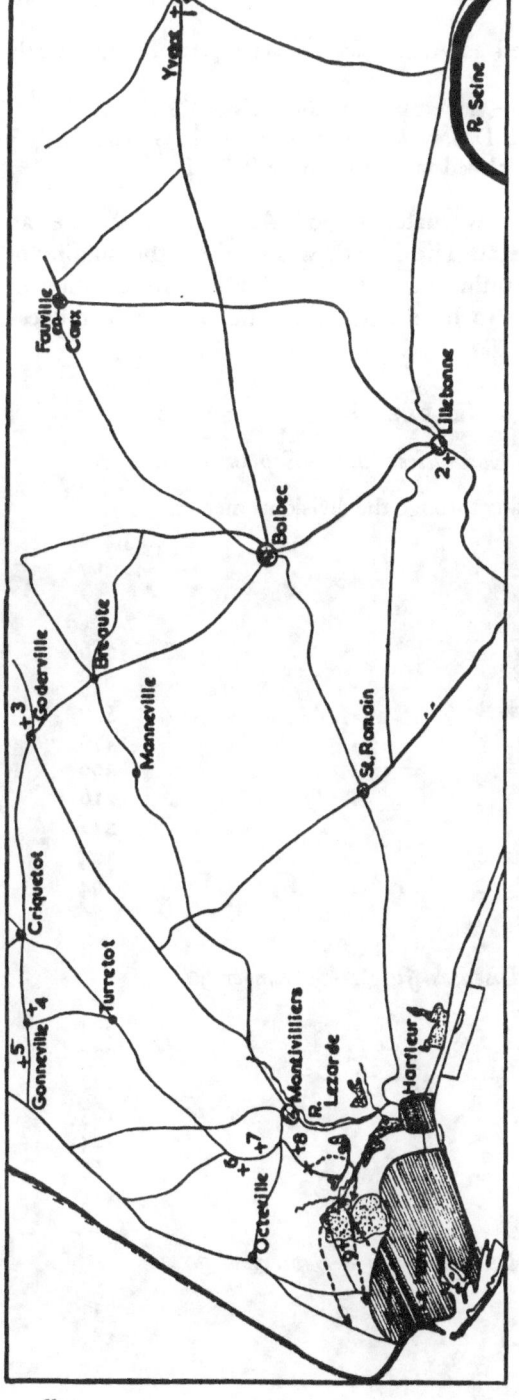

FIG. 35. 51st Division. The Assault on Le Havre. Medical Cover.

1. 32 C.C.S.
2. Adv. Surg. Centre 20 F.D.S.
3. 175 Fd. Amb. } In reserve
6 F.D.S.
4. A.D.S. 174 Fd. Amb.
5 F.D.S.
5. A.D.S. 176 Fd. Amb.
6. C.C.P. 174 Fd. Amb.
7. C.C.P. 175 Fd. Amb. (1st position)
8. C.P.
9. C.C.P. 175 Fd. Amb. (2nd position)

× = Gap in Minefield.

174 Fd. Amb. opened an A.D.S. in Gonneville-la-Mallet for the seriously wounded.

176 Fd. Amb. opened an A.D.S. in the same place for the lightly wounded.

5 F.D.S. opened in the same place for the divisional sick.

175 Fd. Amb. and 6 F.D.S. were closed in reserve in Goderville.

22 Lt. Fd. Amb. was closed in reserve in Le Tilleul.

Urgent surgical cases were evacuated to 20 F.D.S. at Lillebonne, all others to 32 C.C.S. at Yvetot. The F.D.S. was used for the holding of the minor sick but for training purposes and for the preservation of morale, efforts were made to have battle casualties admitted to these units occasionally.

TABLE 28

51st Division. Casualties. July 1–September 30

Battle Casualties passing through the divisional medical units	3,479
Died from Wounds	67
Types of Wound:	
Upper extremity	726
Lower extremity	678
Back and Buttock	570
Head, Neck and Face	470
Multiple	309
Fractures	216
Chest	212
Blast and Concussion	124
Abdomen	94
Burns	80

Principal Diseases. July 1–September 30

Exhaustion	504
Digestive System	225
Pyrexia N.Y.D.	224
I.A.T.	163
Skin	124
Respiratory	67
Neurological	15

Infectious Diseases. July 1–September 30

Malaria relapse	633
Malaria, fresh	183
Scabies	37

Infective Jaundice	19
Pediculosis pubis	14
Gonorrhoea	8
Urethritis N.Y.D.	8
Influenza	6
V.D. N.Y.D.	4
Pediculosis corporis	4
Syphilis	1
Balanitis	1
Penile wart	1

53RD DIVISION

Following the break-through, 53rd Division, along with 7th Armoured and 15th Divisions u/c XII Corps, advanced to the Seine and into Belgium. It was 53rd Division's task to deal with opposition in the Béthune–St. Pol area while 7th Armoured Division by-passed Lille and headed for Ghent. Then when XII Corps took over from XXX Corps in the Alost and Antwerp area 53rd Division went to Antwerp.

At the beginning of August the division was holding the Maltot–Bougy sector of the line with 158th Bde. (202 Fd. Amb.) on the left, 160th Bde. (212 Fd. Amb.) in the centre and 71st Bde. (147 Fd. Amb.) on the right. On August 2 the division extended its line by taking over part of that held by 59th Division as far as Bordell. Preparations were being made for a swift advance and the field ambulances in support of the brigades were to pass u/c brigade, reverting to A.D.M.S. when an A.D.S. was opened.

When, on August 4, the Germans in the divisional sector began to withdraw to the line of the Orne, the division at once moved forward. On August 9, 158th Bde. u/c 59th Division secured a bridgehead over the Orne and linked up with the Canadians on the left. On August 13 the division, with the Canadians on the left and 59th Division on the

TABLE 29

53rd Division. Casualties. Falaise. August 13–21

	B.C.	Sick	Exhaustion
August 13	106	64	21
14	153	76	26
15	45	42	1
16	61	48	4
17	32	54	6
18	35	48	–
19	7	24	1
20	30	24	1
21	2	24	1

right, moved on Falaise and was assigned the task of blocking the roads leading to Falaise from the south-west and south.

The weather was now very bad with heavy rain. The medical and most other units were under canvas. An epidemic of gastro-enteritis yielded a high sick rate—there were 150 cases in the division in the week ending August 5, 287 in that ending August 12 and 446 in that ending August 19. Most of these cases were treated in unit lines but about 20 per cent. of them had to be admitted to the divisional medical units, mainly to the F.D.S. taking minor sick. Dead horses and cattle littered the countryside and there was a plague of flies. Sulphaguanidine was in short supply and had to be reserved for the more severe cases. Quite a number of German military hospitals were uncovered and considerable numbers of German battle casualties were admitted to the divisional medical units. For the Germans military hospitals tentage, stretchers and blankets were obtained from XII Corps, for they were all grossly overcrowded.

On August 24, the division began to prepare for the advance to and beyond the Seine. Owing to shortage of transport the brigades were to move forward by bounds. On the 26th the advance began—Brieux, Orville (August 24), La Haye St. Sylvestre (August 27), La Chapelle (29th), Le Thuit (30th), Mesnil-Verclives (30th)—crossing the Seine at Les Andelys and advancing north-eastwards to the Somme. Little opposition was encountered and casualties were almost exclusively cases of gastro-enteritis, the worst of them being evacuated to 26 F.D.S.

On September 3, the division resumed its advance and reached Hornoy, the medical units moving with their brigade groups, Bonneville (September 4), Caucourt (4th), Grenay (5th), Fleurbaix (6th), into Belgium to Gheluvelt (8th) and Antwerp (9th).

In the German Military Hospital in Antwerp were 190 German wounded, 2 M.Os., 7 nursing sisters and 90 orderlies. These became the responsibility of A.D.M.S. 7 B.S.A.

On September 16, the division moved to the Veerle area and 158th Bde. prepared to make an assault crossing of the Escaut Canal into Holland from Lommel. On the following day the division moved to Baelen and the attack by 158th Bde. opened. The task of the division was to protect the left flank of XXX Corps between the Escaut and Wilhelmina Canals along with 15th Division on the left operating west of the Turnhout Canal.

158th Bde's. casualties in this action admitted to the divisional medical units were 65 wounded, 24 sick and 4 exhaustion.

160th Bde. (with 212 Fd. Amb.) was to clear the right bank of the Turnhout Canal, 71st Bde. to seize Duizel, Eersel, Meerveldhoven, Veldhoven and Riethoven, 158th Bde. to protect the Escaut Junction Canal crossings. These operations were successful.

BREAK-OUT AND ADVANCE INTO HOLLAND

53rd Division. Location Statement of the Divisional Medical Units. August and September 1944

Date	A.D.M.S. with Main Div. H.Q.	Med. H.Q. 53 Fd. Hyg. Sec.	147 Fd. Amb.	202 Fd. Amb.	212 Fd. Amb.	13 F.D.S.	26 F.D.S.	'C' Pln. 302 M.A.C.	Remarks
Aug. 1	St. Mauvieu	St. Mauvieu	St. Mauvieu closed	Marcelet A.D.S. open	Cheux A.D.S. open	St. Mauvieu	Marcelet	St. Mauvieu	u/c XII Corps 23 Lt. Fd. Amb. A.D.S. open in Cheux alongside 212 Fd. Amb.
4	,,	,,	Château de Mouen	,,	,,	,,	,,	,,	,,
5	Mondrainville	Grainville-sur-Odon	,,	,,	,,	Tourville	,,	,,	,,
7	,,	,,	Baron	,,	Château de Mouen A.D.S. open Coy. C.C.P. Gavrus	,,	,,	,,	
8	,,	,,	,,	,,	,,	Mondrainville minor sick	,,	Mouen	
9	Le Mesnil	Le Mesnil	Vacognes closed (S.W. of Evrecy)	Gournay A.D.S. open	,,	,,	,,	,,	158th Bde. with 202 Fd. Amb. u/c 59th Div.
10	,,	,,	,,	Brieux closed	,,	,,	,,	,,	,,
11	,,	,,	,,	Les Moutiers-en-Cinglais A.D.S. open	,,	,,	,,	,,	,,
12	St. Laurent-de-Condel	St. Laurent-de-Condel	Les Moutiers C.C.P. Freaney-le-Vieux	,,	Le Mont	Vacognes	Les Moutiers	Les Moutiers	,,

53rd Division. Location Statement of the Divisional Medical Units, August and September 1944—continued

Date	A.D.M.S. with Main Div. H.Q.	Med. H.Q. 53 Fd. Hyg. Sec.	147 Fd. Amb.	202 Fd. Amb.	212 Fd. Amb.	13 F.D.S.	26 F.D.S.	'C' Pln. 302 M.A.C.	Remarks
13	St. Laurent-de-Condel	St. Laurent-de-Condel	Bois Halbout A.D.S. open	Les Moutiers-en-Cinglais A.D.S. open	Le Mont	Vacognes	Les Moutiers	Les Moutiers	
14	,,	,,	,,	,,	nr. Meslay	,,	,,	,,	
15	Bois Halbout	Bois Halbout	,,	,,	Aubigny	Forêt Grimbosq	,,	,,	
16	St. Germain-Langot	St. Germain-Langot	,,	Leffard A.D.S. open	,,	,,	Leffard	Grimbosq	
17	,,	,,	'B' Coy. C.C.P. Noron-l'Abbaye	,,	,,	,,	,,	Bois Halbout	
18	,,	,,	,,	,,	St. Clair A.D.S. open	Meslay	,,	,,	
19	Villers-Canivet	Villers-Canivet	,,	,,	,,	,,	,,	,,	
20	,,	,,	,,	Nécy	,,	,,	S.W. of Falaise	,,	
21	Brieux	Brieux	,,	,,	,,	St. Martin-de-Mieux	,,	,,	
22	,,	,,	Brieux	,,	,,	Nécy	,,	,,	
23	,,	,,	Nécy	,,	,,	,,	nr. Vignats	Nécy (S.E. of Falaise)	
24	,,	,,	,,	,,	,,	,,	,,	Vignats	
25	,,	,,	,,	Bailleul	Les Moulins (S.E. of Thury Harcourt)	,,	,,	,,	
26	Orville	Orville	Orville	,,	Grand Val (closed)	Fresnay	,,	,,	

Aug. 27	La Haye St. Sylvestre	La Haye St. Sylvestre	"	Mardilly (closed)	Les Bottereaux	Chambord	"	"		
28	"	"	"	Glos-la-Ferrière then Fontaine A.D.S. open	"	"	Marnefer	Marnefer		
29	La Chapelle-du-Bois	La Chapelle-du-Bois	Les Faux	"	Les Planches	La Chapelle-du-Bois	"	"		
30	Le Thuit then Mesnil-Verclives	Le Thuit then Mesnil-Verclives	"	"	Mesnil-Lieubray	Saussay-la-Campagne	Sacquenville	Sacquenville		
31	"	"	Montroty nr. Gournay	Ecouis then Bosquentin	"	"	Touffreville minor sick	Touffreville		
Sept. 1	"	"	"	"	"	"	"	"		
2	"	"	Méricourt-en-Vimeux	Domart	Selincourt	"	"	"		
3	Hornoy	Hornoy	Epecamps	Pernes A.D.S. open	Nune	Bonneville	Avesnes-le-Comte	Avesnes-le-Comte		
4	Bonneville then Caucourt	Bonneville then Caucourt	Mingoval	"	"	Le Sevich	"	"		
5	Grenay	Grenay	Pt. Sains	"	Béthune	Bully Grenay	"	"		
6	Fleurbaix	Fleurbaix	Fleurbaix	Fleurbaix	Neuve Eglise	Fleurbaix	Nœux-les-Mines minor sick	Nœux-les-Mines		
7	"	"	Coy. in Armentières	Werwicq	Reusel nr. Ypres	Gheluvelt	"	"		
8	Gheluvelt	Gheluvelt	nr. Menin	Antwerp	"	Borsbeek	"	"		

53rd Division. Location Statement of the Divisional Medical Units. August and September 1944—continued

Date	A.D.M.S. with Main Div. H.Q.	Med. H.Q. 53 Fd. Hyg. Sec.	147 Fd. Amb.	202 Fd. Amb.	212 Fd. Amb.	13 F.D.S.	26 F.D.S.	'C' Pln. 302 M.A.C.	Remarks
9	Antwerp	Antwerp	Lierre nr. Antwerp A.D.S. open	A.D.S. open	Ranst nr. Antwerp	Borsbeek	Nœux-les Mines minor sick	Nœux-les-Mines	
10	,,	,,	,,	,,	Borsbeek	,,	,,	,,	
14	,,	,,	Antwerp A.D.S. open	Lierre	,,	,,	,,	,,	
15	,,	,,	,,	Zammel	,,	,,	,,	,,	
16	Veerle	Veerle	A.D.S. closed	Kattenbosch A.D.S. open	Oxelear nr. Diest	Veerle	Baelen	Baelen	
17	,,	,,	Wezel	,,	Kerkhoven	Baelen	,,	,,	
18	,,	,,	,,	,,	Luyksgestel A.D.S. open	,,	,,	,,	
19	,,	,,	Riethoven A.D.S. open	,,	,,	,,	,,	,,	
20	Hof	Hof	,,	Luyksgestel	,,	Bergeyk	Bergeyk	Bergeyk	
21	,,	,,	Oerle A.D.S. open	Eersel A.D.S. open	,,	,,	,,	,,	46th Bde. and 193 Fd. Amb. u/c
23	,,	,,	,,	,,	,,	,,	,,	,,	46th Bde. left command
24	,,	,,	,,	,,	Postel A.D.S. open	Eersel	,,	,,	
25	Eersel	Eersel	,,	,,	,,	,,	,,	,,	
27	,,	,,	,,	St. Oedenrode	,,	open as A.D.S.	,,	,,	158th Bde. and 202 Fd. Amb. to command 15th Div.

TABLE 30

53rd Division. Casualties. September 19–30

	B.C.	Sick	Exhaustion
September 19	72	13	4
20	39	30	6
21	44	26	7
22	79	29	3
23	41	35	10
24	53	26	8
25	53	46	11
26	24	26	3
27	32	37	16
28	12	40	12
29	23	37	5
30	23	10	0

The medical cover provided for these operations is depicted in the location statement of the divisional medical units for the months of August and September as shown on pages 263–266.

59TH DIVISION

This division took part in the thrust toward Falaise beginning on August 10. During this period nothing of unusual interest occurred in so far as the divisional medical services were concerned.

On August 19 orders for the immediate disbandment of the division were received and all the divisional medical units proceeded to the west of the Orne.

1ST AIRBORNE DIVISION

The following divisional medical units took part in Operation 'Market Garden':

(A) *Airborne* (see Table 31)

(B) *Seaborne*

Each medical unit had a seaborne tail which consisted of the bulk of the unit transport, including 7 ambulances per unit, all available drivers and five days re-supply of medical and ordnance equipment. D.A.D.H. was i/c medical detachments of the seaborne tail; with him was one other medical officer and the Q.M. of 181 A/L Fd. Amb. One month's supply of M.I. Room stores was carried in each battalion's seaborne tail.

TABLE 31

	Emplaning Strength		No. of Aircraft	No. of Gliders	Jeeps	Trailers	M/C 350 c.c.	M/C 125 c.c.
	Offrs.	O.Rs.						
16 Para. Fd. Amb.	10	125	6	6	6	6	4	5
133 ,, ,, ,,	10	119	6	6	8	6	2	3
181 A/L Fd. Amb. Reserve Sec.	10	104	—	9 }	8	4	—	5
	1	23	—	3 }				
Medical personnel with Para. Bns. (6).	6	108	—	—	—	—	—	—
Para. Bde. H.Q.	1	3	—	—	—	—	—	—
A/L Bns. (3)	3	39	—	3	3	3	—	—
Recce. Sqn.	1	4	—	—	—	—	—	—
Indep. Para. Coy.	—	4	—	—	—	—	—	—
Lt. Regt. R.A.	1	4	—	1	1	1	—	—
H.Q. R.A.	1	2	—	1	1	1	—	—
A.D.M.S. staff	2	7	—	1	1	1	—	—
	46	542	12	30	28	22	6	13

THE MEDICAL TACTICAL PLAN

(a) Field ambulances would be under command of brigades during the initial stages of the operation and would be responsible for the clearing of their own dropping zones to the dressing station in the L.Z./D.Z. area.

(b) 181 A/L Fd. Amb. would be responsible for a temporary dressing station in the L.Z./D.Z. area and for the care and treatment of all these early casualties.

(c) When the situation had stabilised and Arnhem had been occupied the field ambulances would open in the following Dutch hospitals:

    16 Para. Fd. Amb.   St. Elizabeth Hospital
    133 Para. Fd. Amb.   the hospital in the brigade area
    181 A/L Fd. Amb.   Municipal Hospital

(d) Units were then to revert to A.D.M.S. control and efforts would be made to open dressing stations in rotation and start evacuation by road and air as quickly as possible.

(e) The reserve section of 181 A/L Fd. Amb. would remain under A.D.M.S. control from the beginning and be prepared to open a casualty air evacuation centre when the local airfield had been captured and was operating.

On Sunday, September 17, between 1000 and 1100 hours 1st Para. Bde. with 16 Para. Fd. Amb. and 1st A/L Bde. with 181 A/L Fd. Amb. emplaned on airfields in Lincolnshire and Oxfordshire respectively.

BREAK-OUT AND ADVANCE INTO HOLLAND 269

Between 1315 and 1400 hours these brigades dropped over the appointed D.Zs. after an uneventful flight and with but few casualties.

A dressing station was opened in four small houses near the railway by 181 A/L Fd. Amb. in the area of Wolfheze and its location notified to A.D.M.S. By the evening about 60 casualties had been admitted and one of the surgical teams was functioning. A.D.M.S. received no report from 16 Para. Fd. Amb. during this day but it was known that the unit had dropped safely and had moved off with its brigade. Later it was learnt that the unit had moved into St. Elizabeth Hospital in Arnhem, there to find casualties already waiting on the doorstep. The surgical teams started operating under excellent conditions at 2200 hours.

At 0700 hours on September 18, divisional H.Q., which thus far had been dug in on the edge of the L.Z., moved towards Arnhem and the R.M.O. attached H.Q. R.A. established a divisional H.Q. R.A.P. in a house adjacent to divisional H.Q. on the Arnhem–Wageningen road. The R.A.P. of 1st Border was in Johanna Hoeve in the middle of the L.Z. and D.Z. for the second lift. The landing of this lift was opposed and large numbers of casualties were brought by jeep to this R.A.P. which was under mortar and small arms fire. (Plate XVII illustrates the collection of a casualty after air landings.)

At 1700 hours the divisional commander ordered the A/L and 4th Bdes. and the divisional troops to move nearer the town and so the dressing station at Wolfheze had to move with all its patients to the Hotel Schoonoord in Oosterbeek. It was intended that when the division moved into Arnhem the dressing station would move into the Municipal Hospital there but as things turned out this was not to be and the Hotel Schoonoord became the main medical installation in the Oosterbeek area, which was soon to become a battleground. The unit also took over a nursing home, the Hotel Tafelberg, two hundred yards away, and to this the surgical teams were sent.

At 2030 hours elements of 133 Para. Fd. Amb. arrived at Wolfheze. This unit had become somewhat dispersed owing to opposition during landing. As the brigade was staying in the area for the night the party of 133 Para. Fd. Amb. took over the dressing station.

Thus at the end of the second day the distribution of the medical units was as follows:

> 16 Para. Fd. Amb.
>> In St. Elizabeth Hospital, Arnhem (the unit had already been captured but was still functioning).
>
> 133 Para. Fd. Amb.
>> In the dressing station at Wolfheze (not yet complete).
>
> 181 A/L Fd. Amb.
>> In Hotels Schoonoord and Tafelberg in Oosterbeek. Reserve section at the dressing station in Wolfheze.
>
> A.D.M.S. at divisional H.Q. in the Hotel Hartenstein, Oosterbeek.

Early on September 19, the bulk of the personnel of 133 Para. Fd. Amb. had reached Wolfheze and the reserve section of 181 A/L Fd. Amb. with all transportable casualties moved from Wolfheze to Oosterbeek and was placed u/c 181 A/L Fd. Amb.

A.D.M.S. was informed by G.O.C. 1st Airborne Division, who had been into Arnhem, that 16 Para. Fd. Amb. was settled in St. Elizabeth Hospital and suggested that contact might be made by telephone. Telephonic communication was established on a civil line—a Dutch doctor's telephone was used—and A.D.M.S. learnt that the whole unit had arrived safely but that it had been captured, the officer commanding together with other officers and a number of O.Rs. having been removed by the Germans. The two surgical teams had been allowed to continue their work on parole, there being some 100 casualties in urgent need of surgical intervention.

In Oosterbeek 181 A/L Fd. Amb. had been obliged to take over further buildings for the stream of casualties had grown in volume. The glider-borne element of 16 Para. Fd. Amb., having been unable to link up with its parent unit, reported to 181 A/L Fd. Amb. and was straightway employed.

4th Para. Bde. had attempted to get into Arnhem by making a detour north of the railway but had been unsuccessful. The brigade then thrust along the main road. A party of 133 Para. Fd. Amb. with this brigade and including the two surgical teams established itself in houses near the M.D.S. of 181 A/L Fd. Amb. in Oosterbeek and from then on became part of this medical area.

At the end of the third day, therefore, the distribution of the divisional medical units was as follows:

16 Para. Fd. Amb.
Surgical teams only functioning in St. Elizabeth Hospital in Arnhem, the rest of the unit being P.o.W.
133 Para. Fd. Amb.
About half of the unit running an annexe to the M.D.S. in Oosterbeek. The other half missing.
181 A/L Fd. Amb.
Running the D.S. in Oosterbeek.
A.D.M.S. at divisional H.Q. in the Hotel Hartenstein.

On September 20, the Germans attacked Oosterbeek. The M.D.S. in the Hotel Schoonoord was captured with all its staff. The Germans allowed the staff to continue its work for there were some 300 casualties, including Germans, needing attention. A.D.M.S., removing his rank badges, reduced himself to the ranks and was able to watch the proceedings. A German soldier was posted as guard over the D.S. Shortly afterwards a S.P. gun and an A/T gun, one on either side of the D.S.

BREAK-OUT AND ADVANCE INTO HOLLAND 271

which was plainly marked with the Red Cross, fought a duel and the D.S. was hit four times, a chaplain and the orderly room sergeant of 181 A/L Fd. Amb. being wounded. Several of the patients were rewounded by mortar fragments. Soon, however, the firing became desultory and it was then learnt that the Hotel Tafelberg and the reserve

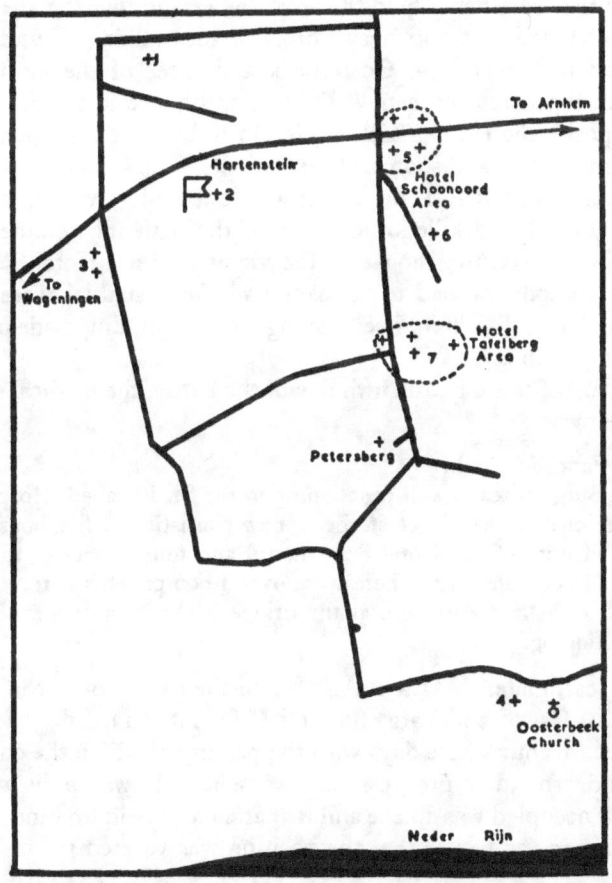

FIG. 36. 1st Airborne Division Medical Area, Oosterbeek. September 18–26.

1. R.A.P. K.O.S.B.
2. R.A.P. Divisional H.Q.
3. R.A.P. 1st Border
4. R.A.P. Gunners
5. M.D.S. 181 A/L Fd. Amb.
6. School destroyed September 21
7. D.S., A.D.M.S.

section of 181 A/L Fd. Amb. in the school had not been captured. By 2300 hours all was quiet in the D.S. area and A.D.M.S. left, the German guard's attention being distracted for the moment, and returned to divisional H.Q. in the Hotel Hartenstein. It is to be noted that though the D.S. was captured the Germans at no time and in no way interfered with its functioning.

During the night of September 20/21, 4th Para. Bde. had advanced eastward so that the D.S. in the Hotel Schoonoord was relieved and evacuation to it became possible again, though distinctly hazardous. A.D.M.S., visiting the R.A.P. of the Light Regt. R.A., found that nearly 100 casualties were being held there for the reason that the area around it was under constant and heavy fire. All the walking wounded were despatched to the D.S. in Oosterbeek and three of the most serious cases were evacuated by jeep. A.D.M.S. and his staff now moved to a house opposite the Hotel Tafelberg in Oosterbeek. It was opened as an annexe to the D.S. and soon had 90 patients. The school in which the reserve section of 181 A/L Fd. Amb. was functioning was hit, an officer and five O.Rs. being killed and many of the patients wounded again. The section moved to a house in the vicinity of the Hotel Tafelberg. More accommodation had to be taken over for casualties were mounting. In the Hotel Tafelberg itself damage to the building made operative surgery impossible.

At the end of this day, the fifth day of the battle, the medical situation was as follows:

> 16 Para. Fd. Amb.
> Surgical teams still functioning in the St. Elizabeth Hospital.
> The medical area in Oosterbeek, now consisting of five houses in the vicinity of the Hotel Schoonoord and four houses in that of the Hotel Tafelberg. There were over 1,000 patients here.
> R.A.P. of 2nd Para. Bn. at the bridge in Arnhem presumably functioning.

(It was learnt later that the R.A.P. established at the bridge in Arnhem by the R.M.Os. of 2nd Para. Bn. and H.Q. 1st Para. Bde. had in fact functioned for four whole days with the passing of which the conditions within and around it progressively worsened. It was only when the building it occupied was ablaze and its patients were in imminent danger of perishing in the flames that the position was vacated.)

> R.A.P. 2nd S. Staffords in the vicinity of St. Elizabeth Hospital.
> R.A.Ps. in the divisional area, the gun area near the church and in the 1st Border area functioning comparatively smoothly. The R.A.P. of the K.O.S.B. had been captured and the R.M.O. replaced.

On September 21 the Germans captured the M.D.S. in the Hotel Schoonoord once again. During the day the situation progressively deteriorated, evacuation to the medical area was very spasmodic and the medical units were under continuous mortar fire. Several of the buildings were hit and some of the casualties were killed or re-wounded, for the medical area was a battlefield and for the patients there could be no

BREAK-OUT AND ADVANCE INTO HOLLAND

protection. Those who were there and lived speak highly of the fortitude that was displayed by these patients and of the coolness and solicitude of those who tended them.

On September 22 evacuation from the R.A.Ps. to the D.S. ceased for medically no more could be done in the latter than in the former; the danger of re-wounding was just as great in one as in the other and evacuation had become exceedingly hazardous. Medical supplies were still adequate for a certain amount of re-supply by air had got through. Food was getting somewhat short and the troops were obliged to begin to live on the land; sheep were slaughtered and the contents of the local shops brought into use. Water shortage was becoming acute for almost all of the 10-cwt. trailers had been hit and the water supply to the area had been cut off by the Germans. For a time the Germans allowed medical personnel to collect water from outside the perimeter but soon, in desperation, it became necessary to make use of the water in the central heating systems of the houses. R.A.M.C. personnel and the ambulance jeeps carried Red Cross flags which indeed seemed to protect them from direct small arms fire.

The perimeter near the medical area was held by the Independent Para. Coy., that is to say these troops were in neighbouring houses. Glider pilots were also dug in around the area. The mortar fire had become so fierce that it became necessary to move the A.D.M.S's. D.S. into the cellar of a cottage across the way. Rest, warmth and fluids for the patients could now be provided only with the greatest difficulty. Supplies of morphia and bandages were running out. Many of the wounded were lying on the floor with one blanket between two. All that could be done was to hang on and hope.

On September 23, one of the houses of the D.S. was repeatedly hit, set on fire and had to be evacuated. A.D.M.S. discussed the medical situation with the G.O.C. and it was agreed that he should try to arrange with the German senior medical officer for the evacuation of the wounded to a safer area in German held territory, evacuation across the river being impossible. A.D.M.S. was instructed to ask that fire on the medical area and R.A.Ps. might be lifted for a period during that afternoon to allow the battlefield to be cleared of wounded so that both sides could get on with the fight. Accompanied by a Dutch liaison officer and a local doctor, A.D.M.S. approached a German medical officer who was now in charge of the D.S. in the Hotel Schoonoord and who turned out to be the S.M.O. of the German forces. He was taken by this officer into Arnhem, there to interview the German G.O.C. who agreed to help in the matter of the collection of the wounded of both sides.

A.D.M.S. then visited St. Elizabeth Hospital and found that the patients were well cared for. When he returned to Oosterbeek he found that the Germans were now in possession of the Tafelberg group of buildings. During the afternoon all the walking wounded, some 200, were moved out of these buildings and taken to the German rear.

Ambulances and lorries bearing the Red Cross came across from the German lines and evacuated the German wounded and then the British. Jeeps were passing back from R.A.Ps. direct to St. Elizabeth Hospital. The S.M.O. of St. Elizabeth Hospital visited Oosterbeek and returned with some of the patients. But at 1600 hours the Germans moved up in force to the Hotel Schoonoord, seemingly with the intention of attacking under cover of the casualty evacuation. The officer commanding 181 A/L Fd. Amb. intervened and managed to persuade the Germans to restore peace in the area. The ambulances and lorries retired for the night but their drivers promised to return on the morrow. By this time the whole medical area was invested by the Germans, but the combatants of both sides were kept out of the buildings.

On September 25, A.D.M.S. was told of the decision to withdraw to the south of the Rhine. It was decided that it would be impossible to take the wounded and that it would be necessary to leave them behind together with the whole of the medical personnel. The divisional area was to be swept for casualties on the morning following the withdrawal, which was to be carried out during the night of the 25th/26th. A.D.M.S. visited H.Q. R.A. and gave the positions of the various R.A.Ps. and other medical installations and asked that the information be transmitted to the gunners on the other side of the river.

In Oosterbeek the situation in the medical area deteriorated to such an extent that it became necessary to transfer as many casualties as possible from the Hotel Tafelberg and elsewhere to the Hotel Schoonoord dressing station. By 1800 hours this was filled with casualties brought thereto by stretcher-bearer parties of 181 A/L Fd. Amb. by hand-carriage, by cart and by jeep, under fire the whole time. That night, when the division withdrew across the Neder Rijn, there were some 200 wounded in the Hotel Schoonoord, about 100 in the R.A.P. of the Lt. Regt. R.A., about 70 in the R.A.P. of 1st Border and about 30 in the dressing station at Petersberg.

A strange and oppressive silence attended the lightening of the sky on the morning of the 26th, a silence soon to be shattered by occasional bursts of S.A. fire as the Germans searched for stragglers. A.D.M.S., taking a jeep from a German soldier, drove down the routes taken by the division on the previous night and found German medical services personnel tending the wounded. Returning to the dressing station in Oosterbeek, he found that the officer commanding 181 A/L Fd. Amb. was controlling the evacuation of British casualties. The Germans had provided about 36 ambulances and lorries bearing the Red Cross emblem. A plaster clinic was opened in order to immobilise fractures. It was learnt that the casualties were being taken to Apeldoorn. The

BREAK-OUT AND ADVANCE INTO HOLLAND

German officer who was supervising this evacuation, accompanied by A.D.M.S., examined the whole of the Airborne Divisional area and was shown the many R.A.Ps. and C.C.Ps. Many of those who became casualties during the withdrawal had been taken to Petersberg and to the gunner R.A.P. About twenty casualties were found on the right bank of the river. The attitude of the Germans was completely correct during these events. By 1800 hours all the wounded and all the British medical personnel, except for a small party on the river bank, had been evacuated. A.D.M.S., D.A.D.M.S., H.Q. 181 A/L Fd. Amb. and the Dutch nurses, who insisted on accompanying their patients, left in the last of the lorries and as the party passed through Oosterbeek and Arnhem on the way to Apeldoorn and captivity they were able to measure the fierceness of the fighting that had taken place by the numbers of the dead that lay everywhere, by the destruction of the buildings and by the mass of debris that had replaced the neatness of the Dutch countryside.

No records of the work of the several medical units could possibly be maintained during the battle; but on the memories of those who were there the unforgettable events engraved deep impressions and so it is that from the reports compiled long afterwards by certain of the officers who were involved it is possible to provide further illustrations of the exceptional difficulties which beset the divisional medical services and of the manner in which the members of the R.A.M.C., A.D. Corps and R.A.S.C. maintained the proud record of their Corps.

16 PARA. FD. AMB.

September 17. H.Q. and 2 Sec. dropped seven miles west of Arnhem, complete save for one surgical pack which was lost when a kitbag rope broke in mid-air, and moved with the brigade into Arnhem. St. Elizabeth Hospital was reached about 2330 hours and arrangements for accommodation made with the Dutch medical staff.

September 18. At 1100 hours the hospital was captured by the Germans, who agreed to leave two surgeons, two anaesthetists, a sergeant N.O. and about 16 O.Rs., on parole for the period of the battle, to continue the work of the unit. The other members of the unit were taken away. Many casualties were being brought in by Dutch Red Cross personnel and by the Germans themselves.

September 19. The German troops were pressed back and the hospital freed; but only for a little while. The Germans returned and the unit was cut off from the rest of the divisional medical services. During these actions troops passed through the hospital, firing along the corridors.

September 20 and 21. The area around the hospital became quieter. Casualties continued to be brought in and both surgical teams were fully occupied. The staff was reinforced by the arrival of two medical officers and several O.Rs. R.A.M.C. belonging to other units. The

Dutch nurses on the staff of the hospital volunteered to stay on and the help they gave was of the highest order. Catering was undertaken entirely by the civilian staff, which included a number of German nuns. Lighting and water supplies ceased.

September 22. The walking wounded were evacuated by the Germans to the German rear.

September 23. The transportable cases were removed by the Germans to Apeldoorn. The Germans sent to the hospital a quantity of medical supplies, some of these being British in origin. In the evening the officer commanding 163 Fd. Amb. (XXX Corps), who had crossed the Neder Rijn, reached the hospital and asked for help in the establishment of a hospital for British casualties in Apeldoorn. Two officers and about 20 O.Rs. R.A.M.C. with equipment went with him to Apeldoorn.

September 24. Several hundred casualties were transferred to St. Elizabeth Hospital from Oosterbeek. On the 25th and 26th the numbers of admissions progressively decreased.

September 27. The Germans evacuated all the transportables to Apeldoorn, leaving only about 30 patients with one of the surgical teams. These were removed to Apeldoorn about ten days later.

It will be noted that the Germans, having captured the hospital and removed most of the staff, then evacuated large numbers of casualties, British and German, into it. The field ambulance personnel could not possibly have treated these casualties in comparatively satisfactory conditions had it not been for the help they received from the Dutch medical and nursing staff of the hospital. The medical personnel were on parole but quite a number of their patients, with the aid of the Dutch Underground Movement, escaped.

133 PARA. FD. AMB.

Dropping, this unit became somewhat dispersed. One medical officer and two O.Rs. dropped a few hundred yards north of the D.Z. were fired upon (one of the O.Rs. being killed), captured by a party of Dutch S.S. troops and taken to the German R.A.P. in Ede and thence to Apeldoorn. Of the unit's transport only three vehicles were available. When 4th Para. Bde. moved off the D.Z. a staff sergeant and 4 O.Rs. R.A.M.C. were left behind to look after the casualties. These were taken prisoner almost immediately. The unit moved into Oosterbeek and evacuated its casualties to the M.D.S. of 181 A/L Fd. Amb.

Next morning H.Q. 133 Para. Fd. Amb., consisting of four officers and thirty O.Rs., moved with 4th Para. Bde. and established a C.C.P. under the railway bridge on the road to Arnhem. Then, when the brigade was withdrawn into the divisional defence perimeter, the medical unit moved into Oosterbeek where its affairs became merged with those of the divisional medical area.

181 A/L FD. AMB.

September 17. The M.D.S. party arrived safely and complete at 1319 hours and at once moved into Wolfheze, there to open in a house. By 1500 hours casualties were being admitted and seven other houses had to be taken over to accommodate them.

September 18. There were about 120 patients and a large mental hospital across the railway was taken over and the casualties transferred thereto. The officer commanding, with A.D.M.S., went into Oosterbeek to choose a site for the M.D.S. and selected the Hotel Schoonoord. This hotel was taken over and 210 casualties moved into it. The affairs of 181 A/L Fd. Amb. thereafter became merged with those of the divisional medical area which have already been described. But the report of the officer commanding gives details which portray the very exceptional difficulties which surrounded the work of the unit. The unit, on September 20, was occupying three of the houses at the cross-roads in the Hotel Schoonoord area and combatant troops were in a fourth. A German officer under a flag of truce arrived and demanded that this fourth house should be vacated. If this were done the Germans undertook not to fire on the houses occupied by the medical unit. The troops were withdrawn, but on the 22nd Polish troops, who had crossed the river, occupied this house and the Germans promptly mortared the whole area. When, on the 23rd, the Germans again captured the M.D.S. they were fired on by Poles from the windows of houses across the street. The officer commanding 181 A/L Fd. Amb. interviewed the Poles and the Germans, obtaining from the former a promise not to fire into the houses occupied by this unit and from the Germans an undertaking that they would not show themselves at the windows of these houses.

During the battle one officer and four O.Rs. of 181 A/L Fd. Amb. were killed and two officers and 15 O.Rs. wounded. Of the 12 Dutch women and 8 Dutch men who worked with the unit throughout the battle, one male nurse was killed and another wounded. 'They were quite magnificent. They fed and washed the patients, acted as bearers, always willing to do anything required of them. Without their help we would not have been able to cope as we did'. They accompanied the unit into captivity but at Apeldoorn the Germans turned them away.

SEABORNE ECHELON

The seaborne echelon proceeded by way of Gisors, Crèvecœur, Franvillers, Halle, Louvain, Helchteren, Valkenswaard, Eindhoven to Grave, which was reached on September 22. The S.M.O. reported to D.D.M.S. Airborne Corps in Nijmegen and was instructed to join 163 Fd. Amb. with all the medical personnel of the echelon and to move with this unit to Valburg. On September 23 the Polish element of the echelon, with its vehicles, joined the Polish brigade south of Driel.

In connexion with the attempt to get medical supplies across the river to 1st Airborne Division, S.M.O. Seaborne Echelon established a report centre east of Driel at 1500 hours on September 24.

On September 28 the medical stores in charge of the echelon were handed over to 3 C.C.S. and the echelon, together with the remnants of those who had reached Arnhem by air, set out for Brussels *en route* for the United Kingdom.

THE 1ST AIRBORNE DIVISION MILITARY HOSPITAL, APELDOORN SEPTEMBER 25–OCTOBER 26, 1944

After the withdrawal of 1st Airborne Division across the Neder Rijn there remained in the Arnhem area over 2,000 British wounded, together with 25 officers and about 400 O.Rs. R.A.M.C. and battalion stretcher-bearers. The German medical services were more than fully occupied in looking after their own casualties and the two Dutch hospitals in Apeldoorn, the Algemeene and the Katholijke Ziekenhuizen, were rapidly filling with wounded Dutch civilians, Germans and British. There was no other choice open to the German senior medical administrative officer (=A.D.M.S. Area) than to encourage the British medical personnel to run their own hospital. Three barrack blocks of the Kazerne Willem III in Apeldoorn were assigned to them for conversion. These barracks were modern in construction, exceptionally well appointed and well suited for the purpose. The three blocks were enclosed in concertina barbed wire and on three of the sides by a 10-ft. high steel fence.

The following staff was elected:

1. H.Q. Commanding Officer	A.D.M.S. 1st A.B. Division
Second in Command / Liaison Officer	O.C. 163 Fd. Amb.
2. Administrative Wing	O.C. 181 A/L Fd. Amb.
3. Medical Wing	O.C. 133 Para. Fd. Amb.
4. Registrar	D.A.D.M.S. 1st A.B. Division

The barrack rooms were used as wards and accommodation for 900 patients was provided. The following policy was agreed to by the German and British senior medical administrative officers and by the head of the Dutch Red Cross Society in the Gelderland Province:

1. All British wounded would be treated in this hospital, but those then in the German military hospitals in the area—St. Joseph's Kriegs Lazarett and the Het Loo (the summer Palace of Queen Wilhelmina)—would remain there until fit to move when they would either be transferred to the Airborne Military Hospital or else be evacuated into Germany, according to their condition.
2. Since there were no nurses and no comforts and since the diet would necessarily be somewhat rough and ready, the more serious cases in

BREAK-OUT AND ADVANCE INTO HOLLAND

the Airborne Military Hospital would be transferred to the Katholijke or the Algemeene Ziekenhuizen.
3. Radiology would be carried out in these Dutch hospitals.
4. The Germans would provide bedpans and urinals, blankets, sheets, soap, towels, tooth brushes, etc.
5. The Germans would do everything possible to replenish expendible medical stores. It was recognised that this would be difficult because of the number of the German casualties and of the paucity of transport. A.D.M.S. 1st Airborne Division suggested that an attempt should be made to have supplies brought in or dropped from Second Army but the German command did not approve.
6. The Germans would do everything possible to augment the P.o.W. standard ration.
7. The Dutch would provide comforts and deal with the matter of Red Cross parcels and notification cards. They also undertook to make available six complete surgical teams, including a neuro-surgical team, and to provide whole blood for transfusion purposes.

On September 25, when the medical staff consisted solely of two officers and 8 O.Rs. R.A.M.C., some 700 wounded were admitted. On September 26 about 650 more arrived. Thereafter the numbers of the admissions rapidly fell and the evacuation of the convalescents to Germany during the next two weeks reduced the number of patients to about 120.

On September 26, 500 walking wounded were sent to Germany in cattle trucks. On October 2, 200 of the more lightly wounded were sent away on a Red Cross train, which was in fact composed of cattle trucks with straw on the floor. Strong protests were made by the senior British officers. On October 6, 500 of the patients were removed on a proper ambulance train staffed with German medical and nursing personnel. On these trains a number of the medical staff of the Airborne Hospital travelled. On October 18, 150 of the staff of the hospital were despatched to Germany and, on October 26, the remaining 80 patients and the 5 officers and 20 O.Rs. R.A.M.C. were transferred to other hospitals in Apeldoorn. The Airborne Military Hospital closed down.

Most excellent medical work was done in this hospital and hundreds of the wounded have reason to be grateful for the care they received therein. The way in which the Dutch people and the Dutch medical profession rallied to the aid of the hospital commanded the respect and admiration of staff and patients. The staff had every reason to acknowledge that the German medical services personnel were more than punctiliously correct in their behaviour for within the limits of their ability they were truly helpful. It is to be noted, however, that had it not so happened that a compact divisional medical group with equipment and supplies was able to take charge of the British casualties the local German medical services would certainly have been overtaxed and overwhelmed, and this under the observation of the critical and distinctly unfriendly Dutch.

The composition of the hospital staff and patients, being divisional, ensured that the atmosphere of the place was tinged with an optimistic impudence. To them escape became not only a duty but an adventure in accord with the tradition of the division. It became necessary for the Germans to transfer all the British wounded from the Het Loo hospital because so many of them, with the ardent help of the Dutch Underground, escaped. Four officers (3 R.A.M.C. and 1 A.D. Corps) travelled on the first Red Cross train. They found themselves locked in a compartment and unable to tend the patients. So they decided that three of them should attempt to get away. One of them was shot and killed while doing so but the other two escaped. When, by October 15, the numbers of the staff had become greatly out of proportion to the numbers of the patients, A.D.M.S. 1st Airborne Division called his officers together and encouraged those who wished to escape to do so. When several of them were missing the Germans instituted a daily counting parade. Then two of the surgeons left and to cover their departure operations were staged by O.Rs. disguised in full surgical garb. Then the second in command and one of the padres could not be found and the Germans decided to move everybody, with the exception of five officers and 20 O.Rs., and they were warned to be ready within half an hour. This time was stretched into three hours and during this period the A.D.M.S. himself disappeared. (He reached the British lines four months later.) Thereafter the whole hospital was compressed into one of the blocks and the guards were doubled until the hospital closed.

THE LAZARETT AT STALAG XI B

One of the surgical specialists of 133 Para. Fd. Amb. found himself the senior British medical officer in this P.o.W. camp following capture at Arnhem. In October approximately 1,700 British wounded were added to the 50 British P.o.W. already in the camp and the 200 who were in working camps in the neighbourhood. Thereafter, until February 1945 inclusive, about 250 British and American wounded reached the camp each month to be admitted to the lazarett, in addition to about 1,000 walking wounded each month who were accommodated in the camp itself. In February 1945, 900 sick, considered unfit to march, arrived from Görlitz. In March the flow of wounded P.o.W. ceased but sick men, who had marched from Poland and East Germany, arrived in such numbers that it became impossible to keep any accurate record. Certainly over 4,500 of these came to the camp, almost every one of them suffering from malnutrition and 2,000 of them from diarrhoea, mainly dysenteric.

On October 9, 1944, there were seven medical officers, but by the end of the month three of these had been sent away. It was not until February 1945 that other R.A.M.C. officer P.o.W. came to this camp, two in February and one more in March. Plentiful O.Rs. R.A.M.C. reached the camp but the Germans would not permit more than 35 to live and work in the lazarett. A daily working party of 20 orderlies from the camp was provided but the arrangement was so unsatisfactory that it was soon discontinued. The difficulty was got over by admitting fit orderlies to hospital with a diagnosis of malaria and the like and in this way 50 were added to the staff.

Until February the lazarett consisted of three barrack huts holding about 130 men. They were full at all times and patients had to be discharged long before they should have been in order to make room for more serious cases. Each hut was divided into wards 30 × 17 ft. and holding 22 patients in double-tier bunks. But the number of beds had to be reduced as it was found to be impossible to nurse many of the patients in beds of this type. Each patient had one blanket only during the first three months, then two. Each ward had a stove but the fuel ration was sufficient for only one day a week. There were no cleaning materials and no brooms. Lighting was uncertain and the current was shut off centrally at night. Each barrack hut had one hurricane lamp but no oil. Torches were not allowed. There was an ablution room in each hut but no facilities for hot showers or bathing. Water was strictly rationed and none of the P.o.W. ever knew when it was to be cut off. The British medical officers were accommodated in one of the huts and locked in every night.

Each barrack hut had one small treatment room. In these all dressings were done, as was all minor surgery and all out-patient work. There was no heating and no running water and in only one of these rooms was there an electric steriliser. The operating theatre, in one of the huts, was slightly less primitive, being electrically heated and having running water. The French medical officer P.o.W. used this room extensively for 'cold' surgery so that the British medical officers had to make still further use of the treatment rooms for serious surgery.

Medical supplies were utterly inadequate at all times for the reason that the British component in the camp was unable to compete in the black market run by the German dispenser. At times only 100 paper bandages per hut per week could be obtained. Periodically wounds could not be dressed for lack of dressings. Dysentery had to be treated with charcoal and tannic acid, and of these there was but little. Had it not been for the Red Cross supplies that reached the camp, medical officers would have been almost powerless to help those in their charge.

The beds were of wood with straw palliasses. There were two bed-pans, three urinals and two washing bowls per hut. There was one razor per 20 men, one hairbrush per 10, one spoon to each four and no toothbrushes. Though many of the patients were completely naked no clothes were supplied until a man was fit for discharge. There was one Thomas' splint. From the Red Cross six pairs of pyjamas and two air pillows arrived.

Only post-operative abdominal and fractured jaw cases were allowed a hospital diet—this differing from the ordinary in that the potatoes were mashed and the bread was white. One pudding per day was supplied but no sugar. A patient arriving after 0800 hours received no rations for that day. If this was a Saturday he got none until Monday. Had not Red Cross food supplies been received it is certain that mortality would have reached a very high figure. The Germans failed to provide any means for the cooking and preparing of Red Cross food.

Under these conditions and in spite of German demands for the treatment of herniae, haemorrhoids and the like, the British medical officers refused to undertake 'cold' surgery. The following table illustrates the type of cases treated during six months:

Table 32

Surgical

Fracture	
Humerus	60
Radius or/and Ulna	50
Femur	15
Fibula and Tibia	30
Skull (vault)	7
Jaw	10
Severe wound	
Wrist and Hand	30
Ankle and Foot	20
Severe Frostbite of Feet	100
Suppurative Arthritis of major joints	30
Empyemas	12
Major amputations	80
Loss of one or both eyes	30
Aneurysm of major vessels	8
Hemiplegias and paraplegias	9
Peripheral nerve injuries	150

Medical

Pneumonias (excl. terminal)	50
Diphtheria	50
Dysentery (treated in lazarett)	250
Erysipelas (severe)	15

BREAK-OUT AND ADVANCE INTO HOLLAND

Most of the surgical cases arrived during the third week after wounding. There were also a few cases of bladder and bowel injury, carcinoma of the stomach, intestinal volvulus, appendicitis, severe burns, cerebral abscess, pulmonary tuberculosis, scarlatina, nephritis, meningitis and psychiatric disorders. Over 90 per cent. of the admissions were lousy and this made the wearing of plaster fracture cases well-nigh intolerable. Adequate treatment of fractures of the femur was impossible. Bed sores were almost unavoidable.

30 patients died from medical causes, 15 from surgical. Of the 30 medical cases 29 deaths were largely, if not mainly due to malnutrition; so also were 3 of the 15 surgical.

In these circumstances the medical officers could do but little for their cold, hungry, lousy patients save attempt to keep them alive until the end of the war and share with them the universal misery. In retrospect it is possible to make allowances, for the Germans themselves were very hard pressed during the last phase of the war, but it remains impossible to conclude that more could not have been done to lessen the sufferings of the wounded and the sick in this nightmarish lazarett.

6TH AIRBORNE DIVISION

This division was not involved in any of the major battles of July. When, following the break-out 21 Army Group advanced to the Seine and beyond, it, with the Belgian and Royal Netherlands Brigades under command, moved along the coast towards Le Havre. It was not involved in any considerable engagement. During the first week of September the division moved back to Arromanches and to the United Kingdom.

Before the break-out 224 Para. Fd. Amb. opened a rest camp for the division west of the Orne. On August 9 the division regrouped preparatory to the advance and 195 A/L Fd. Amb. moved from Le Mariquet to Ecarde. On the 17th this unit moved again to Le Plein. For the crossing of the River Dives at Troarn this unit opened its M.D.S. in Amfreville. 225 Para. Fd. Amb. at Le Mariquet set up a car post in Le Mesnil and 224 Para. Fd. Amb. opened its A.D.S. in the vicinity of St. Richier, the rest of the unit moving up to St. Samson. On the following day the whole of 225 was in St. Richier and a M.D.S. was established there. 224 Para. Fd. Amb. opened an A.D.S. in Dozulé on the Troarn–Pont l'Evêque road.

On August 23 195 A/L Fd. Amb. opened a M.D.S. in Villers-sur-Mer where 225 Para. Fd. Amb. took over a deserted German military hospital and it was joined by 20 F.D.S. and 48 F.S.U. The journey back to the medical area at La Délivrande had grown so long that it became necessary for 225 Para. Fd. Amb. to hold its patients until evacuation into 32 C.C.S. became possible on the 24th. 195 A/L Fd. Amb's. next forward move was to St. Gatien-des-Bois while 224 remained back in

Dozulé on wheels. On the 25th 224 Para. Fd. Amb. opened in St. André d'Herbetot to serve 3rd and 5th Para. Bdes. On the 26th 225 Para. Fd. Amb. moved into the Casino in Trouville. This was the last move of the divisional medical units before that back to Arromanches.

(iii)

The Break-out and the Advance into Holland Medical Arrangements

I CORPS

I Corps was not involved in the Falaise operations, but 33 F.D.S. in the vicinity of St. Germain passed temporarily u/c Canadian II Corps and 32 C.C.S. admitted casualties from the formations that were engaged.

During the latter part of August, I Corps moved along the axis Lisieux–Pont-l'Evêque–Pont-Audemer to cross the Seine and turn westwards towards Le Havre. On August 27, 30 F.D.S. formed an advanced surgical centre at Pont-Audemer, evacuating to 16 C.C.S. at Cormeilles. On September 1, 32 C.C.S. moved from St. Aubin-sur-Algot to Yvetot where it opened in the buildings of the School of Agriculture for the period of the attack upon Le Havre and its capture on September 12. 20 F.D.S. formed an advanced surgical centre in Lillebonne on September 4. After the fall of Le Havre 30 F.D.S. took over the underground German hospital in the town. When Le Havre had been finally cleared I Corps moved to the area of Lierre in Belgium, 16 C.C.S. opening in the town.

6 Fd. Hyg. Sec. (I Corps) was called upon to undertake a most distressful task in Le Havre. On August 4, during an Allied air raid, the entrance to an underground air-raid shelter had been blocked and the inmates incarcerated. On September 13 the R.E. cleared the entrance and forced compressed air into the shelter. Then personnel of the field hygiene section went in to spray the place and its contents with 20 per cent. Creosol. Thereafter the French civilians were helped to remove their dead.

30 F.D.S. (I Corps) established itself in the German underground hospital to care for the large number of German wounded. When these had been evacuated the unit rejoined I Corps in northern Belgium.

VIII CORPS

Operations 'Bluecoat' and 'Grouse' constituted the breaks-through at Caumont and the further movement south that was the beginning of the

BREAK-OUT AND ADVANCE INTO HOLLAND

drive into Holland. For Operation 'Bluecoat', VIII Corps for the first time on the Continent was as constituted in the United Kingdom; the units and services which had trained together now fought together.

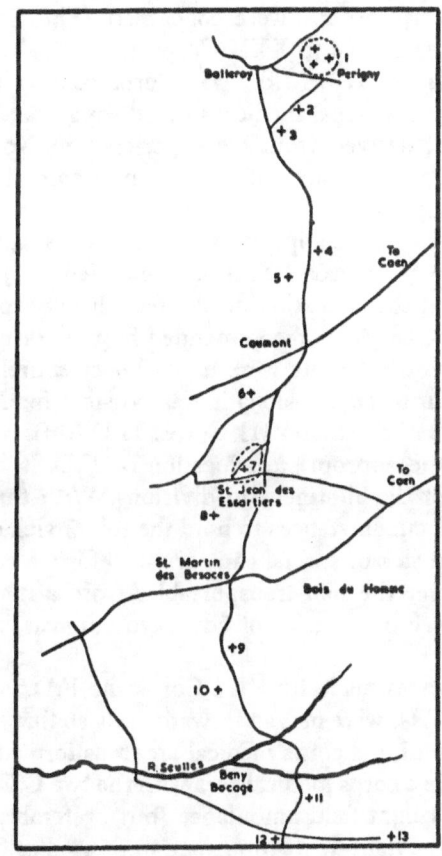

FIG. 37. VIII Corps. Operation 'Bluecoat'. Medical Arrangements.

1. Medical Area
   One C.C.S. and two F.D.Ss. open
2. M.A.C.
3. A.D.S.
4. M.A.C.
5. A.D.S. and F.D.S.
6. A.D.S.
7. Second Medical Area
   One C.C.S., one F.D.S. and one light field ambulance
8. A.D.S.
9. M.A.C.
10. A.D.S.
11. M.A.C.
12. A.D.S.
13. A.D.S.

1–7 inclusive were established at the beginning of the operation. The F.D.S. at 7 opened first, the C.C.S. could not do so with safety for two and a half days. The single line of communications and its length created difficulties.

A medical area was established prior to the operation and then, as the advance proceeded, an advanced surgical centre was set up by the two F.D.Ss. and three attached surgical teams.

During the drive to the Somme, VIII Corps became pinched out in so far as its corps troops were concerned. The Guards and 11th Armoured Division passed to XXX Corps.

The observations of D.D.M.S. VIII Corps concerning the employment of corps and divisional medical units during operations and other pertinent matters, derived from his experience in Normandy are, in general, representative of those of all the senior administrative medical officers in 21 Army Group.

VIII Corps started the campaign with two C.C.Ss. and one F.D.S. as the basic allotment. A second F.D.S. was added on June 29. It was quickly found that the allocation of one base F.D.S. to corps and one per division in the corps, as recommended by the Hartgill Committee, did not happen as these units were used almost entirely in Army and L. of C. areas. On three occasions it was possible for Army to release a third F.D.S. for the use of VIII Corps. D.D.M.S. reached the firm conclusion that the appropriate allocation of F.D.Ss. to a corps was three, exclusive of the allotment to divisions. With three it would be possible under all circumstances to hold the minor sick during a winter campaign, to hold sick of special categories, to form a corps exhaustion centre, to take over the non-transportables from a moving C.C.S. or other unit and to form a series of advanced surgical centres during a rapid advance.

In all the advances made by VIII Corps the F.D.Ss. with attached F.S.Us. and a F.T.U. were moved forward early so that forward surgery could be available until a corps medical area was formed. It was always the aim to build up a corps medical area with the two C.C.Ss. and at least one F.D.S. and a light field ambulance (but preferably two F.D.Ss.). The F.D.S. and the light field ambulance were used as filters to take all walking wounded, sick and exhaustion cases. In this way the work of the C.C.S. was greatly lightened. On July 11, for example, the C.C.Ss. dealt with 459 admissions, the associated F.D.S. with 108 exhaustion cases and the light field ambulance with 666 sick and walking wounded. The holding of such exhaustion cases not sufficiently severe to warrant evacuation proved to be a whole-time job, in most periods, for one F.D.S. functioning as the corps exhaustion centre.

When the two corps C.C.Ss. were together in the corps medical area they were used in two ways; in quieter periods on a basis of twenty-four hours on and twenty-four hours off, in rush periods by the number of cases awaiting surgical intervention. The supervision of the latter arrangement and the general control of admissions and evacuation were undertaken by the officer commanding the F.D.S. that was acting as a

BREAK-OUT AND ADVANCE INTO HOLLAND

filter. In the rush periods the C.C.Ss. had perforce to pass the less serious cases through as rapidly as possible and as the number of the immovables mounted it was not always easy to provide adequate post-operative care. It was felt that a case could be made for an increase in the number of nursing officers in a C.C.S. When the fighting was relatively static better post-operative attention became possible and the effect of this was reflected in the increased percentages of recovery.

When only one C.C.S. could be assigned to an advanced surgical centre one F.D.S. with an attached F.S.U. was associated with it to deal with any overflow of surgical cases during rush periods. Cases transferred to the F.D.S. were confined, as far as possible, to fractures and movables. When the C.C.S. moved the F.D.S. took over its immovables.

Both 33 and 34 C.C.Ss. finally decided that the ideal lay-out of the tentage of a C.C.S. was in three main blocks.

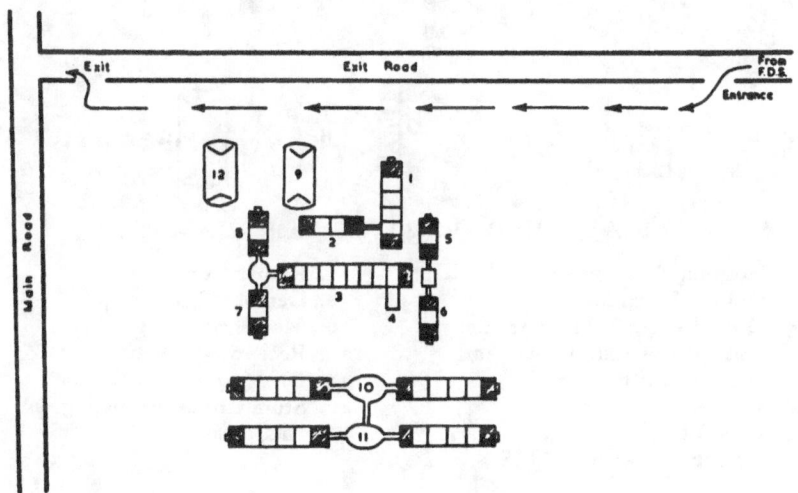

Fig. 38. VIII Corps. 33 C.C.S. Tentage Lay-out.

1. Reception
2. Dressing
3. Resuscitation and Pre-operative Ward
4. X-ray (No. 10 shelter)
5. C.C.S. Theatre
6. C.C.S. Theatre
7. 33 F.S.U.
8. 38 F.S.U.
9. Evacuation (Store tent)
10. Two Retention Wards joined by M.G.S.O.
11. Two Retention Wards joined by M.G.S.O.
12. Blankets and Stretchers (Store tent)

The main essential in field ambulance, F.D.S. or C.C.S. was to have adequate space in 'reception'. Without it chaos soon reigned. It was soon found to be greatly advantageous to have the 'Evacuation' Ward close to Reception since such an arrangement saved much unnecessary carrying of the less serious cases, which passed from the filter F.D.S. at the entrance to the medical area direct to Evacuation. The evacuation ward was used as an overflow for Reception in rush periods and so increased the holding capacity that evacuation by night could be avoided.

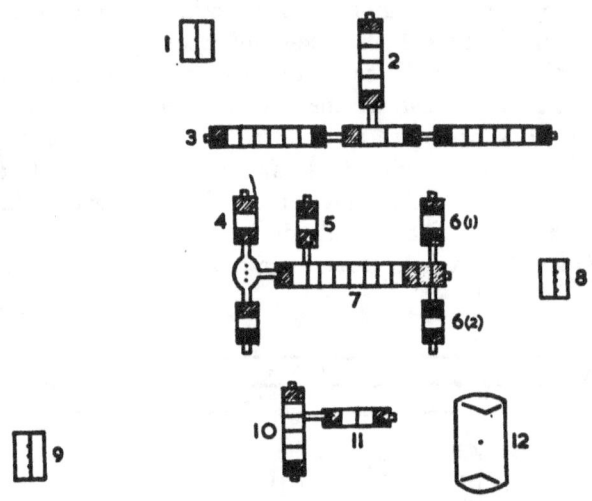

Fig. 39. VIII Corps. 34 C.C.S. Tentage Lay-out.

1. Hospital Cookhouse
2. Officers Retention
3. O.Rs. Retention (Two-section marquee as central pivot and duty rooms for wards)
4. 38 F.S.U.
5. 54 F.S.U.
6. Operating theatres (C.C.S.)
7. Resuscitation
8. Dental Officer
9. Mortuary
10. Reception
11. Dressing
12. Store tent as evacuating marquee.

Resuscitation required a large ward which usually consisted of a marquee of two ends and nine sections. The operating theatres, four in number and one holding two tables, led directly off Resuscitation so that the surgeons could easily watch the waiting cases and determine the order of operation. The post-operative wards containing serious cases must not be too large lest adequate supervision should become difficult.

Whenever possible it was the practice so to arrange the lay-out that the ward tentage of an advanced surgical centre was very close to the post-operative block so that no moving of surgical cases was necessary when the C.C.S. moved and left the immovables in charge of the F.D.S. Some difficulty arose on occasion when a C.C.S., moving, had to leave behind marquees with immovables. It was thought that the holding of a

BREAK-OUT AND ADVANCE INTO HOLLAND

small reserve of tentage by Army, on which a C.C.S. could draw, would solve this problem.

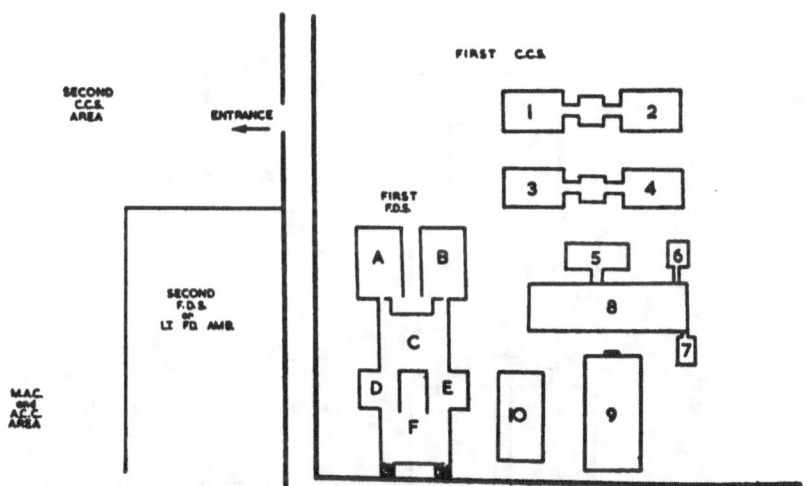

FIG. 40. VIII Corps. Lay-out of a Corps Medical Area.

C.C.S.
1, 2, 3, 4. Wards
5, 6, 7. Theatres
8. Resuscitation and Pre-operative
9. Reception
10. Evacuation

F.D.S.
A. Ward (major and minor)
B. Ward (minor)
C. Post-operative (major)
D and E. Theatres
F. Resuscitation

Save when the F.S.Us. were attached to F.D.Ss. to form advanced surgical centres or where one was left behind in charge of immovables, it was the practice to attach them to the C.C.Ss., three to each. With the filtration of minor cases at the entrance to the medical area this arrangement enabled the surgeons to give their full attention to the serious cases and, in all save the peak periods, to work in eight-hour shifts. With five surgeons available four teams were able at all times and without overstrain to cope with all demands. The attachment of three F.S.Us. to a C.C.S. greatly increased the holding capacity and beddage of the unit and endowed it with considerable flexibility and mobility. When immovables were left behind one F.S.U. and two nursing officers always remained with them.

The F.T.Us. were normally employed at C.C.S. level. It was found to be essential to have two T.Os. at each C.C.S. to enable proper reliefs to be carried out. Exceptionally they worked at divisional F.D.S. level when large numbers of casualties were expected, and were in fact incurred, and when evacuation by road was expected to be far from easy.

Nevertheless it was the opinion of D.D.M.S. that the F.D.S. itself could have undertaken the work done by the F.T.U. and that the latter unit would have been better employed at C.C.S. level.

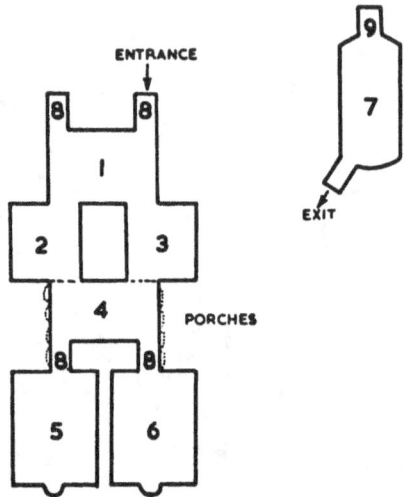

Fig. 41. VIII Corps. Lay-out of Tentage for an Advanced Surgical Centre.

1. Resuscitation
   (Marquee H.P. Extdg. 2 Secs.)
2 and 3. Theatres
   (Tents Universal)
4. Post-operative ward, major
   (Marquee H.P. Extdg. 2 Secs.)
5 and 6. Post-operative wards, minor
   (Marquee H.P. Extdg. 2 Secs.)
7. Reception
   (Store tent G.S.)
8. Entrances
   (160 lb. tents)
9. Annexe
   (Shelter No. 10)

D.D.M.S. recorded the opinion that the A.M.P.C. personnel attached to the C.C.Ss. rendered most excellent service and that indeed they were indispensable.

In battles of narrow frontages and with comparatively heavy casualties it was found to be a good plan to use either a whole or part of a divisional F.D.S. in conjunction with the A.D.S. of a divisional field ambulance working in a divisional medical area. In this area, in which the tentage was more widely dispersed than in the corps medical area, the F.D.S. could in rush periods take all the walking wounded and the moribund who required to be carefully transfused. This enabled the field ambulance to give more time and attention to the more serious cases and to fractures. In quiescent periods the field ambulance could also deal with the walking wounded.

On wide frontages when more than one divisional field ambulance was employed, sections and not the whole F.D.S. were frequently employed, enabling all the field ambulances to be provided with extra transfusion facilities. The Guards Armoured Division so increased the potentiality of the light section of the F.D.S. that it was capable of an independent existence. 15th Division divided the F.D.S. into three more or less equal sections so that a section could be attached to each of the divisional field ambulances when all of them were actively engaged. One of the field ambulances devised a scheme for its division into three teams for use when this was the only field ambulance in action. When this occurred it was possible to attach one of the sections of the F.D.S. to each of the parts of the field ambulance.

Since commonly both armoured brigade groups and tank brigades were under command VIII Corps it was possible to make a comparison of the uses made of the light field ambulances serving with these formations. The armoured brigade group consisted of some 5,000 troops and was often employed in an independent rôle. The light field ambulance proved to be an essential component of such a group. When an armoured brigade group was employed in close co-operation with or u/c an infantry division the light field ambulance should always remain under the operational control of D.D.M.S. corps. Tank brigades, on the other hand, very seldom undertook any independent mission but worked in the closest co-operation with infantry divisions. The need for a medical unit of its own was never apparent provided that the brigade was under a higher formation for administrative purposes.

D.D.M.S. Corps was with main corps H.Q., his office with rear corps H.Q. and A.Ds.M.S. of the component divisions with main divisional H.Qs. All problems of evacuation have their origins in the forward areas and by this arrangement the senior administrative medical officers informed themselves at the earliest possible moment of plans and projects and were able to make their own plans in good time. For example, in Operation 'Bluecoat' this early knowledge made it possible to move medical units by night in advance of the movement of VIII Corps.

XXX CORPS

In preparation for the coming offensive 10 C.C.S., 35 F.D.S., 163 Fd. Amb., 111 M.A.C. and 31 Fd. Hyg. Sec. were moved from St. Vigor-le-Grand to Balleroy. The minor sick, psychiatric and V.D. cases were diverted to 3 F.D.S. at Nonant, to which the corps psychiatrist and venereologist moved. Later, the operational plan being changed, 10 C.C.S., 35 F.D.S. and 163 Fd. Amb. moved, on July 28, to the vicinity of Trungy, the C.C.S. and the ambulance opening and the F.D.S. remaining on wheels.

During the action on July 30–August 4 when 7th Armoured, 50th and

43rd Divisions captured Orbois, Cahagnes, Canteloup and the high ground west of Ondefontaine, 336 casualties were admitted to 10 C.C.S. on July 30 and 332 on August 3. 3 F.D.S., 6 F.S.U., 44 F.S.U., 35 F.T.U. and Lt. Sec. 3 C.C.S. with additional canvas moved from Nonant to join 10 C.C.S. at Trungy.

Following the capture of Mont Pinçon on August 6, 3 C.C.S., 35 F.D.S. and a company of 163 Fd. Amb. were moved from Nonant to a site to the south of Villers-Bocage. 6 and 44 F.S.Us. and 35 F.T.U. moved from 10 to 3 C.C.S. 49 F.D.S. with 40 F.S.U. (Army) then relieved 10 C.C.S., which then closed and prepared to move.

As Second Army advanced toward Argentan, 10 C.C.S., 3 F.D.S. and 163 Fd. Amb. were moved from Trungy to La Blanchère on August 18. 21 F.D.S. (Army) relieved 3 C.C.S. and 35 F.D.S. and these units closed and prepared to move. On August 20, 3 C.C.S., 35 F.D.S. and a company of 163 Fd. Amb. moved from Aunay to Montgaroult and, on the 22nd, 163 Fd. Amb. moved again to a site west of Gacé in the vicinity of Croisilles.

When the advance to the Seine began 10 C.C.S. and 3 F.D.S. moved from La Blanchère to join 163 Fd. Amb. 3 F.D.S. was again relieved by 49 F.D.S. (Army) and made mobile. 49 F.S.U. and 7 F.T.U. were temporarily attached to 129 Fd. Amb. of 43rd Division for the advance to the Seine and for the assault crossing of this river.

On August 25, 10 C.C.S., 3 F.D.S. and 163 Fd. Amb. moved from Gacé behind 43rd Division to Caillouet. When 43rd Division had secured its bridgehead at Vernon 129 Fd. Amb. with 49 F.S.U. opened six miles west of Vernon and 10 C.C.S. with its associated units in the vicinity of Evreux. Casualties were few during the advance and river crossing.

By August 29, the leading elements of Second Army were twenty miles beyond the Seine. 3 C.C.S. with 35 F.D.S. and 163 Fd. Amb. moved forward in two stages from Montgaroult across the Seine to Beauvais, which they reached on August 31. 11th Armoured Division was now in Amiens. Lt. Sec. 3 C.C.S. and 163 Fd. Amb. were therefore moved to Allonville (north-west of Amiens) where they were joined by the heavy section on the following day. 35 F.D.S. remained at Beauvais for staging duties and took over the local hospital which had been hurriedly evacuated by the Germans.

On September 1, 10 C.C.S. and 3 F.D.S. moved forward eighty-seven miles from Caillouet to join 3 C.C.S. at Allonville, remaining closed. The forward troops were now in Arras, Douai and Lens. In the local hospitals were many groups of German casualties with German medical personnel looking after them. To each of these a small British medical detachment was assigned. These remained behind until relieved by Army or 10 District. Wounded P.o.W. were sent to these hospitals.

BREAK-OUT AND ADVANCE INTO HOLLAND

47 F.D.S. (50th Division) was opened at Cahaignes (halfway between Vernon and Gisors) on the L. of C. for staging duties and passed to Army on August 2. 16 F.D.S. (Army) relieved 35 F.D.S. at Beauvais on September 2.

When on September 3, 11th Armoured, Guards Armoured and 50th Divisions made their rapid advance to Alost, Assche, Tournai and Brussels, 10 C.C.S. and 163 Fd. Amb. moved from Allonville to Fresnoy, forty miles away, where they opened. A second lift moved 3 C.C.S. from Allonville to Fresnoy. 3 F.D.S. was left at Allonville to take care of the immobiles. On September 4, 3 C.C.S., 35 F.D.S. and 163 Fd. Amb. moved from Fresnoy to Assche, seventy-eight miles away. 'B' Coy. 163 Fd. Amb. was dropped at Renaix and to it 50 F.S.U. (50th Division) was attached for staging duties. 'A' Coy. 163 Fd. Amb. remained with 3 C.C.S. but H.Q. moved on to Willebroeck to serve 11th Armoured Division which was heading for Antwerp. 31 F.D.S. (Army) relieved 3 F.D.S. at Allonville and then moved to Fresnoy on September 4.

10 C.C.S. moved from Fresnoy to Assche on September 6, remaining on wheels. 3 C.C.S. and 35 F.D.S. took over the Hôpital St. Pierre in Brussels, 500 German wounded therein being transferred with the German medical personnel to the Military Hospital, Avenue de la Couronne. Later 86 B.G.H. took over from 3 C.C.S. On September 6, 47 F.D.S. relieved 3 F.D.S. at Fresnoy. Lt. Sec. 35 F.D.S. was posted to the Airport at Brussels pending the arrival of a R.A.F. medical unit.

XXX Corps' next task was that of securing crossings over the Albert and Meuse–Escaut Canals. Bridgeheads were secured at Beeringen and south-west of Gheel, and Bourg-Léopold and the Hechtel crossroads were reached.

On September 9, 10 C.C.S. and 163 Fd. Amb. were moved from Assche to Diest, remaining on wheels. But as 50th Division was encountering much resistance 10 C.C.S. and associated units opened a forward medical area just north of Diest. 3 C.C.S. and 35 F.D.S. were brought forward from Assche to Diest, Lt. Sec. 35 F.D.S. with 43 F.S.U. remaining in Assche to take care of the immobiles. The mobile element of the advanced depot of medical stores joined 10 C.C.S. on September 10 and thereafter moved with it.

In preparation for Operation 'Market Garden', 3 and 10 C.C.Ss., 3 and 35 F.D.Ss., 163 Fd. Amb., 111 M.A.C. and one platoon 257 A.C.C. were all concentrated on wheels in the vicinity of Laak. 14 F.D.S. with 31 Fd. Hyg. Sec. were installed in the hospital at Bourg-Léopold to receive the early casualties and evacuate them forward to 48 F.D.S. in the hospital at Eindhoven should rearward evacuation become impossible.

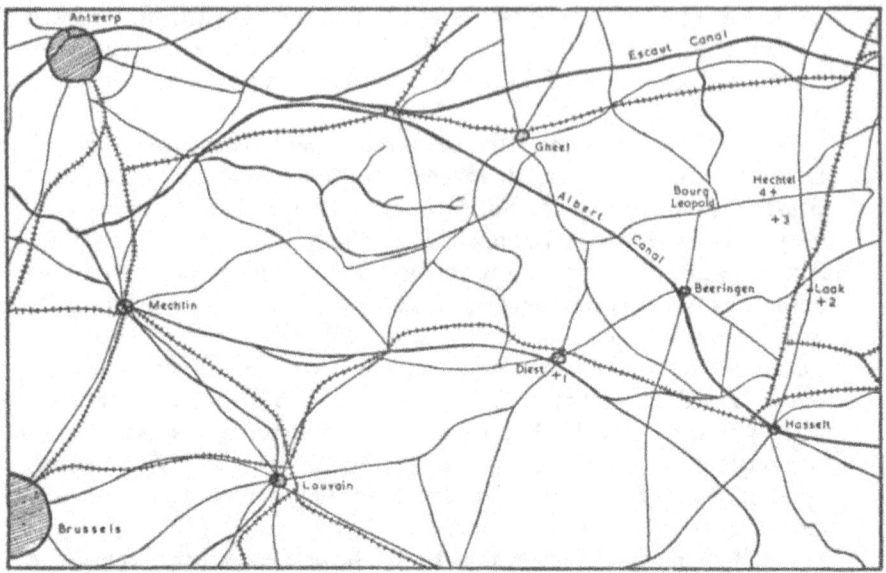

Fig. 42. XXX Corps. The Crossing of the Albert and the Meuse–Escaut Canals. Medical Arrangements. September 10.

1. 3 C.C.S. and 35 F.D.S. (closed)
   10 C.C.S., 3 F.D.S.
   163 Fd. Amb.
2. Concentration area
   3 C.C.S. 35 F.D.S.
   10 C.C.S. 3 F.D.S.
   H.Q. 111 M.A.C.
   257 A.C.C.
   10 U.S. ambulance cars
3. Concentration area
   'B' Coy. 163 Fd. Amb.
   4 T.C.Ps.
   6 U.S. ambulance cars
4. U.S. 24 Evac. Hosp.

(Mechlin = Malines)

For this operation the following U.S. medical units were allotted to XXX Corps, together with a U.S. medical liaison officer:

24 Evac. Hosp.
384 Amb. Coy.
a Collecting Coy.
a Clearing Coy.

These were sited west of Hechtel crossroads. Ten ambulance cars were attached to 10 C.C.S. with instructions to retain contact with the medical services of U.S. 82nd Airborne Division in the area of Nijmegen. Detachments from the medical units of 50th Division were allotted to the Traffic Control Points in the Hechtel area and one company of 163 Fd. Amb. was sited at St. Oedenrode on the L. of C. To this company six ambulance cars of U.S. 384 Ambulance Company were attached and instructed to move with the company and make contact with the medical services of U.S. 101st Airborne Division in the Son area. Other T.C.Ps. with similar medical detachments were to open at the Escaut Canal, Eindhoven, Veghel and Grave. It was expected that the medical units of U.S. 101st and 82nd Airborne Divisions would open at Son and Nijmegen respectively.

On September 17, XXX Corps moved forward and reached Valkenswaard. On the 18th Son was reached and contact made with U.S. 101st Airborne Division. On the 19th, sixteen ambulance cars were sent forward to Son and 450 casualties evacuated to U.S. 24 Evac. Hosp. at Hechtel. XXX Corps joined up with U.S. 82nd Airborne Division. Casualties were light. Evacuation in front of Son was impossible at first but rearwards from Son it proceeded smoothly.

Lt. Sec. 3 C.C.S. and 35 F.D.S. moved into Eindhoven on September 20, remaining on wheels. Some 300 U.S. casualties had been accumulated in a civil hospital in Nijmegen; these were evacuated by U.S. 384 Amb. Coy.

On September 20, 48 F.D.S. with 49 F.S.U. and 7 F.T.U. opened in the St. Joseph Hospital in Bourg-Léopold, and, on the 21st, 3 C.C.S. and 35 F.D.S. opened in the Jonker Bosch Hospital, Nijmegen. 10 C.C.S. with 3 F.D.S., 163 Fd. Amb., Hy. Sec. 3 C.C.S., 111 M.A.C. and 257 A.C.C. moved, though with great difficulty, towards Nijmegen.

On the 22nd when the corridor was cut north of Veghel and St. Oedenrode D.D.M.S. was out of touch with the forward medical units for a day. 10 C.C.S. less its light section which, with the heavy section of 3 C.C.S., had been sent on ahead, 3 F.D.S., 111 M.A.C. and 257 A.C.C. were held up south of St. Oedenrode.

Casualties on the L. of C. were light and were dealt with by 'B' Coy. 163 Fd. Amb. at St. Oedenrode and thence evacuated to 48 F.D.S. at Eindhoven. U.S. casualties were evacuated to Son and thence to U.S. 24 Evac. Hosp. at Hechtel.

On the 23rd, the corridor having been opened again, Hy. Sec. 10 C.C.S. and 3 F.D.S. pushed on to the Jonker Bosch Hospital, Nijmegen, where Lt. Sec. 10 C.C.S. and 35 F.D.S. were open. 3 C.C.S. was open in the Pensionaat Marienbosch, Nijmegen, and 3 F.D.S. opened in Hees, Nijmegen, with the corps psychiatrist and venereologist to deal with the minor sick, exhaustion and V.D. cases. Had the corridor not been re-opened and these C.C.Ss. enabled to move forward, a critical medical situation would certainly have arisen.

The corridor was cut again on September 24. Rear corps H.Q. was held up south of St. Oedenrode and could not reach Grave until the 26th. No corps medical units were open north of Nijmegen. 163 Fd. Amb. was placed u/c D.D.M.S. Airborne Troops for the assault crossing of the Maas by 43rd Division east of Arnhem. The unit moved to a site south of Valburg.

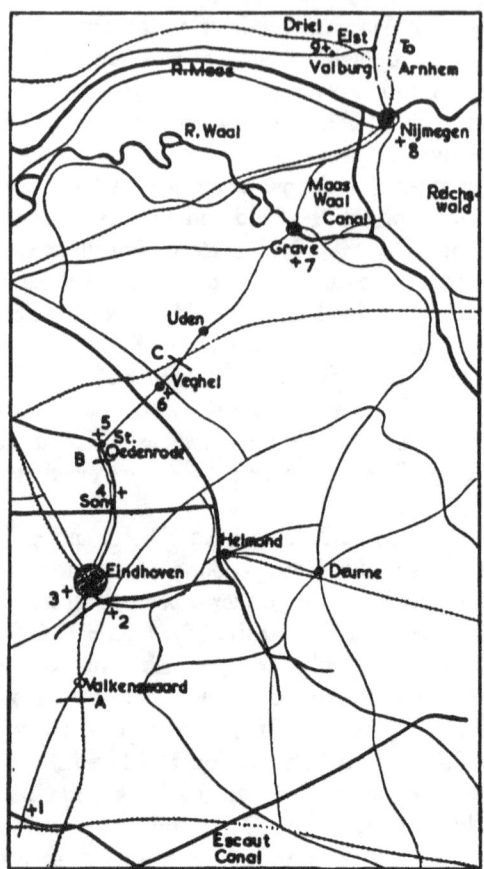

Fig. 43. XXX Corps. Operation 'Market Garden'. Medical Arrangements.

—— A. The Advance checked September 11
—— B. The Forward Movement of 10 C.C.S., 3 F.D.S., 111 M.A.C. and 257 A.C.C. checked September 22
—— C. Road cut September 22–24

1. T.C.P. Medical Detachment
2. T.C.P. Medical Detachment
3. 3 C.C.S.
   35 F.D.S. (staged September 20)
   48 F.D.S.
   49 F.S.U.
   7 F.T.U.
4. Med. Coy. U.S. 101st A/B Division
5. 'B' Coy. 163 Fd. Amb.
6. T.C.P. Medical Detachment
7. T.C.P. Medical Detachment
   35 F.D.S. (Grave airfield)
8. 10 C.C.S.
   35 F.D.S.
   257 A.C.C. (Jonker Bosch Hospital)
   3 F.D.S.
   111 M.A.C. (Hees)
   3 C.C.S. (Pensionaat Marienbosch)
9. 163 Fd. Amb.
   Med. Coy. U.S. 82nd A/B Division

In an orthopaedic hospital in Nijmegen there were some 400 German battle casualties with German medical personnel left behind to look after them. To this hospital all wounded P.o.W. were admitted and 186 Fd. Amb. and then 35 F.D.S. were placed in charge of it. 3 C.C.S. was now fully established in Marienbosch, 10 C.C.S. with 35 F.D.S. in the Jonker Bosch, 'B' Coy. 163 Fd. Amb. at St. Oedenrode, 3 F.D.S. at Hees, U.S. 307 Medical Company at Brakkenstein, the medical company of U.S. 101st Airborne Division at Son and 163 Fd. Amb. at Valburg.

A transit area was organised near Driel and to this all personnel of 1st Airborne Division crossing the river were directed. Thence transport conveyed them to 163 Fd. Amb. which was made responsible for their reception, examination and conveyance to two barracks in Nijmegen or, alternatively, to the C.C.Ss. All the medical stores and comforts held by the seaborne tail of 1st Airborne Division were made available to 163 Fd. Amb. 130 Fd. Amb. of 43rd Division, with an A.D.S. in Driel and a C.C.P. on the south bank of the river, was made responsible for the collection, treatment and disposal of all casualties from the south bank of the Neder Rijn.

D.D.M.S. Airborne Corps established a medical H.Q. in Driel and generally supervised the arrangements.

As a result of enemy action during the withdrawal some 220 casualties were admitted to the A.D.S. of 130 Fd. Amb. On the 26th 163 Fd. Amb. returned to Nijmegen and reverted to command XXX Corps.

35 F.D.S. was moved from the Jonker Bosch Hospital to the airfield at Grave and on the 27th 300 British and 200 American casualties were moved to the airfield for evacuation by air. But this did not take place and the casualties were evacuated by road to 35 C.C.S., now at Eindhoven. 35 F.D.S., being withdrawn from the airfield, joined 3 C.C.S. at Marienbosch on September 28. On the 28th 350 casualties were similarly evacuated and 270 on the 29th.

The general policy which determined the tactical handling of the corps medical units during the advance from the Meuse–Escaut Canal line into Holland was as follows:

163 Fd. Amb., one C.C.S. and one F.D.S. were moved forward as the tactical situation permitted to open a forward medical area. The other C.C.S. and the other F.D.S. remained open until this forward medical area was established. Then they closed and moved forward, remaining on wheels until the situation allowed them in turn to leap-frog over the open C.C.S. and F.D.S. and, with 163 Fd. Amb., open a new forward medical area. 163 Fd. Amb. always moved with the C.C.S. in the lead. 111 M.A.C. normally evacuated from divisional medical units to the rear open corps C.C.S. Rearward of this evacuation was an Army responsibility by A.C.C. Coy. A pool of M.A.C. cars was maintained with each division, moving with the division but remaining under

corps command. One platoon of 257 A.C.C. was usually attached to the open C.C.S. and evacuated therefrom to the general hospitals. When a C.C.S. closed and moved forward its immobiles were placed in the care of a corps F.D.S. until an Army medical unit took over. Similarly, pockets of German casualties left behind in hospital were placed in charge of a corps medical unit until relieved by an Army medical unit.

The Leap-frogging of the C.C.Ss.

July	19	10 C.C.S.	Bayeux to Balleroy
	22	3 C.C.S.	Jerusalem to Nonant
Aug.	4	10 C.C.S.	to Trungy
	6	3 C.C.S.	to Aunay
	18	10 C.C.S.	to La Blanchère
	20	3 C.C.S.	to Montgaroult
	24	10 C.C.S.	to Gacé
	27	10 C.C.S.	to Caillouet
Sept.	1	3 and 10 C.C.Ss.	to Allonville
	2	10 C.C.S.	to Fresnoy
	3	3 C.C.S.	to Fresnoy
	4	3 C.C.S.	to Assche
	6	10 C.C.S.	to Assche
	9	10 C.C.S.	to Diest
	11	3 C.C.S.	to Diest
	16	3 and 10 C.C.Ss.	to Laak
	20	3 C.C.S.	to Nijmegen
	21	10 C.C.S.	to Nijmegen

Total distance about 480 miles

3 C.C.S. group   9 bounds
10 C.C.S. group 11 bounds

On September 24, it was decided by D.Ds.M.S. XXX and Airborne Corps that attempts should be made to replenish the medical units of 1st Airborne Division. The officer commanding 163 Fd. Amb. then obtained permission from H.Q. 130th Bde:

(1) to make an attempt to take supplies over in daylight under cover of the Red Cross flag;
(2) to send two medical officers and 12 O.Rs. R.A.M.C. in 6 D.U.K.Ws., each carrying half a ton of medical supplies obtained from the seaborne tail of 1st A.B. Division, this party to cross the river during the night of September 24/25;
(3) to send across one officer and 30 O.Rs., each carrying an assault pack of medical supplies in assault boats at night.

At 1430 hours on September 24, accompanied by a medical officer of Airborne Corps H.Q. and four O.Rs. R.A.M.C. of 163 Fd. Amb., he went to the river bank near Driel, displaying the Red Cross flag. The

BREAK-OUT AND ADVANCE INTO HOLLAND

party was carrying about 6 cwt. of emergency medical supplies. An assault boat was found and the party paddled across. Leaving the rest on the bank, the officer commanding 163 Fd. Amb. then went forward alone into the German lines where he asked to be taken to a senior officer. He was blindfolded and a German soldier, taking the Red Cross flag, went to the river bank to bring in the rest of the party. In Ede at the German headquarters he requested permission to pass, with his party and stores, through the German lines. His status was discussed and it was decided that he was not an envoy bearing a flag of truce but that he should be regarded as a special type of P.o.W. He was sent to the German chief regional medical officer who had been instructed to give all possible assistance in the evacuation of British casualties. The rest of the party were not permitted to proceed but were allowed to recross the Neder Rijn in safety.

At 1900 hours on September 24, the medical officer of Airborne Corps H.Q. and the quartermaster of 181 A/L Fd. Amb. loaded an assault boat with medical stores and went across the river with 4th Dorset. They landed safely but became separated when the Dorsets were overwhelmed on the 25th. The Q.M. got away and swam to the south bank.

On September 25, the officer commanding 163 Fd. Amb. learnt that the evacuation of British casualties had already begun in accordance with arrangements made with A.D.M.S. 1st Airborne Division and was taken to Arnhem, there to see a German S.S. general of the medical services and to request permission to go back across the river and arrange for the sending of medical supplies and a surgical team from 133 Para. Fd. Amb. The general undertook to consider these requests. But on the 26th the officer commanding 163 Fd. Amb. joined the staff of the 1st Airborne Military Hospital in Apeldoorn as second-in-command. He was now regarded as a P.o.W. without any kind of qualification.

On October 16, with the permission and encouragement of A.D.M.S. 1st Airborne Division, he and a chaplain left this hospital by way of a window and, following tracks through moor and forest, reached Otterloo on the 17th. There they were hidden and fed by a Dutchman, who then set them on their way towards Wolfheze and the river bank. In their attempts to avoid German patrols they became separated. The officer commanding 163 Fd. Amb. swam across the river, met an American patrol and was taken to U.S. 101st Division H.Q. and then on to H.Q. XXX Corps.

H.Q. AIRBORNE TROOPS
MEDICAL TACTICAL PLAN. OPERATION 'MARKET GARDEN'

D.D.M.S. H.Q. Airborne Troops.

Adv. H.Q. was with H.Q. Second Army; Main H.Q. still in U.K.

Medical Operation Instruction No. 1 (extracts from)

1. Information
(a) The main axis of the advance of Second Army is Eindhoven–Grave–Nijmegen–Arnhem.
   The Airborne Corps will capture and hold crossings over the canals and river on this axis of advance.
(b) Order of Battle for the Force:

   1. H.Q. Airborne Corps
   2. 1st Airborne Division (1st A/L and 1st and 4th Para. Bdes.)
   3. 2nd A/L Lt. A.A. Bty. R.A.
   4. 1st Polish Independent Para. Bde. Gp.
   5. 52nd (Lt.) Division (Airportable)
   6. U.S. 82nd Airborne Division
   7. U.S. 101st Airborne Division
   8. U.S. 878th Airborne Aviation Engineer Bn.
   9. Airborne Forward Delivery Airfield Group (A.F.D.A.G.)

2. Intention
To collect and treat and hold casualties until evacuation by air or by road can be established.
To provide facilities for essential surgery.

3. Order of Battle (medical units)

1st Airborne Division	16 and 133 Para. Fd. Ambs.
	181 A/L. Fd. Amb.
52nd Division	155, 156 and 157 Fd. Ambs.
	32 Fd. Hyg. Sec.
	18 and 19 F.D.Ss.
Polish 1st Para. Bde.	1 (Pol.) Para. Fd. Amb.
U.S. 82nd A.B. Division	U.S. 307 Airborne Medical Coy.
U.S. 101st A.B. Division	U.S. 326 A.B. Med. Coy.
	Two platoons U.S. Fd. Hosp.

4. Method
(a) Divisional medical units will be established in divisional areas and will be prepared to collect and treat casualties.
(b) Casualties will be retained by divisional medical units until evacuation by air has been established (D-day+3 to D-day+4) or until contact has been made with the medical services of the Supporting Force.
(c) Formations will be instructed by H.Q. Airborne Tps. to detail a sub-unit to establish C.A.E.Cs. when facilities for evacuation by air are available.
(d) On instructions from H.Q. Airborne Tps., formations will be notified by Os. i/c C.A.E.Cs. of the number of walking and lying cases which can be emplaned and time at which these should arrive at the notified C.A.E.C.

BREAK-OUT AND ADVANCE INTO HOLLAND

(e) No corps medical units are available for the British formations. One platoon of a U.S. Fd. Hosp. will be attached to each of the U.S. airborne divisions and will be placed to begin with u/c Surgeons 82nd and 101st Divisions respectively and will be established in the divisional areas.

(f) Jeeps modified to take stretchers are being allocated from corps pool to assist in the evacuation of casualties. These jeeps will be u/c D.D.M.S. Airborne Tps. and will be used to assist in the evacuation of casualties from divisional areas to C.A.E.Cs.

5. Command

The responsibility for the collection, treatment and evacuation of casualties within divisional areas is as shown:

A.D.M.S. 1st A.B. Division	1st A.B. Division Area
	Polish Para. Bde. Area
Surgeon U.S. 82nd A.B. Division	U.S. 82nd A.B. Div. Area
Surgeon U.S. 101st A.B. Div.	U.S. 101st A.B. Div. Area
A.F.D.A.G.	A medical officer R.A.M.C. will be instructed by H.Q. Airborne Tps. to which medical unit he will evacuate casualties.

The responsibility for the medical care of casualties in the undermentioned units will be notified when the location of these units is known:

2nd A/L Lt. A.A. Bty.
U.S. 878th A.B. Aviation Engineer Bn.
H.Q. Airborne Tps. will be responsible for liaison with the medical services of the Supporting Force and will issue instructions as to the evacuation of casualties when orders are received from D.D.M.S. XXX Corps in the initial stage and, later, from D.D.M.S. Second Army. In the case of 52nd Division, which is under direct command of XXX Corps, A.D.M.S. 52nd Division will receive his instructions from D.D.M.S. XXX Corps.

6. Special Treatment

Surgical. Surgery limited to life-saving operations will be carried out by the surgical teams attached to divisions.

Exhaustion cases will at first be evacuated as other cases. An exhaustion centre u/c corps psychiatrist will be established as soon as possible and formations notified of the action then to be taken.

7. Medical Supplies

The u/m supplies are being flown in with aircraft of A.F.D.A.G. (*see* Table 33):

TABLE 33

1st Airborne Division Medical Supplies by Air

Medical stores
   ½ beach blocks   1

Ordnance stores	1st A.B. Div.	Pol. 1 Para. Bde.	52nd Div.	Totals
Stretchers (airborne or mountain)	300	100	300	700
Blankets	900	300	900	2,100
Sheets	300	100	300	700
Pyjamas	100	75	100	275

D.D.M.S. Reserve
  Ordnance Supply
    Stretchers (airborne or mountain)   250
    Blankets   500

A medical dump will be established in the forward maintenance control; the location will be notified to all concerned. Supplies will be obtained on demand by A.Ds.M.S. of divisions or S.M.Os. of brigades.

Resupply by Air.

The responsibility for the supply of the medical units of the U.S. airborne divisions is that of the medical services of U.S. XVIII Corps.

The scale of supply by air, the transport to be employed and the estimates of casualties to be evacuated are detailed in Table 34.

Points of interest in the planning for this operation are to be found in the 'Hygiene' recommendations. Chlorination of water was to be by means of the individual water sterilising outfit. For the initial stages 'Cat Sanitation' would be the only feasible method of excreta disposal, each man covering his excrement with earth.

Main H.Q. Airborne Troops embarked for Normandy. D.D.M.S.

Key to Fig. 44
1. Dressing Station. 181 A/L Fd. Amb. Wolfheze
2. M.D.S. 181 A/L Fd. Amb. Oosterbeek
3. Dressing Station. 133 Para. Fd. Amb. Oosterbeek
4. M.D.S. 16 Para. Fd. Amb. Arnhem
5. C.P. 130 Fd. Amb. (43 Div.)
6. C.P. 130 Fd. Amb. and Polish Fd. Amb. Dressing Station
7. M.D.S. 163 Fd. Amb. (XXX Corps)
   M.D.S. 130 Fd. Amb.
   Platoon U.S. 50 Fd. Hosp.
8. 3 F.D.S.

(continued on next page)

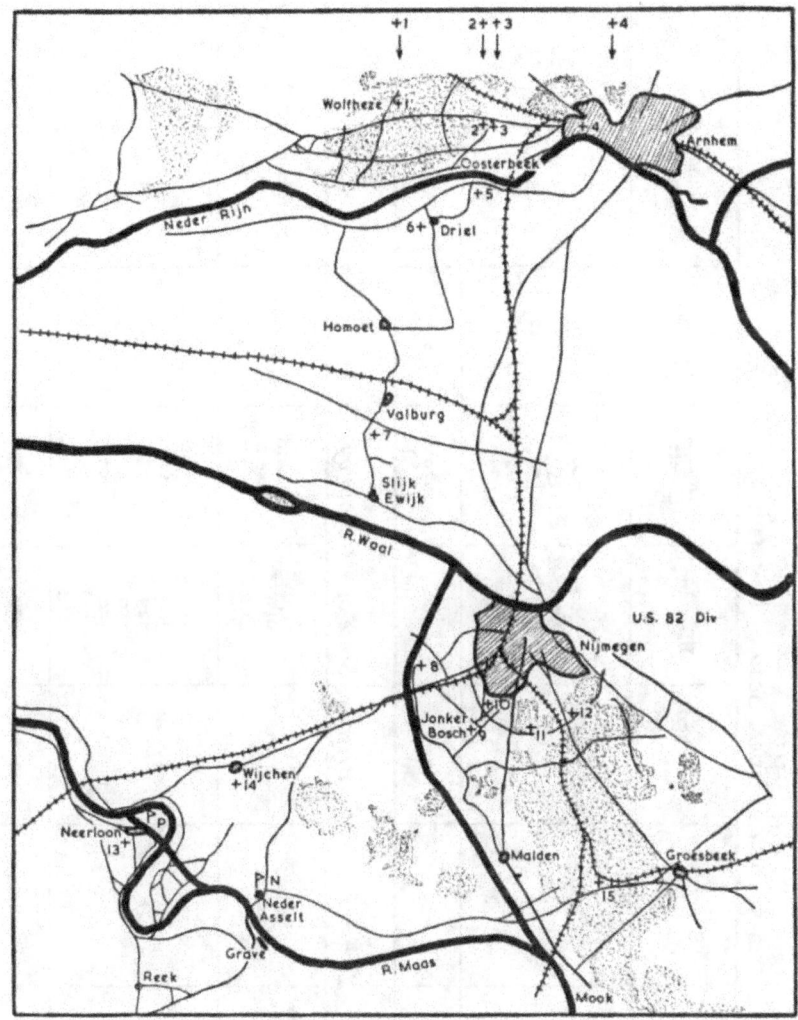

Fig. 44. Operation 'Market Garden'. Medical Arrangements.

Key to Fig. 44—continued

9. 10 C.C.S.
10. C.S. U.S. 101st A.B. Division
11. C.S. U.S. 82nd A.B. Division
12. 3 C.C.S.
13. Polish Fd. Amb.
14. 157 Fd. Amb. (52 Div.)
15. C.S. U.S. 82nd A.B. Division

P = Polish Bde.
N = Royal Netherlands Bde.

TABLE 34

1st Airborne Division. Scale of Re-supply by Air

	Medical Stores Panniers or Containers	Shelters airborne	Stretchers	Blankets	Ground Sheets	Pyjamas	Sleeping Bags	Thomas' Splints
Night of								
D-day/D+1	15 or 30	3	300	900	300	150	150	18
D+1/D+2	15 or 30	3	150	600	150	144	75	12
D+2/D+3	15 or 30	3	150	300	150	120	75	12
D+3/D+4	15 or 30	3	75	150	75	135	42	12
D+4/D+5	15 or 30	3	75	150	75	72	33	9
	75 or 150	15	750	2,100	750	621	375	63

Polish Parachute Brigade. Scale of Resupply by Air

	Medical Stores Panniers or Containers	Shelters airborne	Stretchers	Blankets	Ground Sheets	Pyjamas	Sleeping Bags	Thomas' Splints
Night of								
D-day/D+1	6 or 12	1	100	300	100	75	50	6
D+1/D+2	6 or 12	1	75	225	75	50	25	6
D+2/D+3	6 or 12	1	50	150	50	25	25	3
D+3/D+4	6 or 12	1	50	150	50	25	25	3
D+4/D+5	6 or 12	1	25	75	25	25	25	3
	30 or 60	5	300	900	300	200	150	21

Transport

	Airborne Jeeps	Road Convoy	Ambulances
A.F.D.A.G.	3	—	—
1st Airborne Division	13	—	18
52nd Division	46	—	32
Polish 1st Para. Bde.	5	—	7
U.S. 101st Airborne Division	54	—	—

Estimates of Casualties to be Evacuated

	H.Q. Airborne Corps	2nd A/L L.A.A. Bty.	A.F.D.A.G.	1st A.B. Division	1st Polish Para. Bde.	52nd Division	U.S. 82nd A.B. Div.	U.S. 101st A.B. Div.	U.S. 878th A.B. Aviation Engineer Bn.	Totals
D-day	24	18	61	616	154	—	740	740	37	2,390
D+1	6	5	15	149	38	—	150	150	10	523
D+2	6	5	14	141	37	—	174	174	9	560
D+3	21	15	56	564	132	293	628	628	31	2,368
D+4	5	3	13	127	32	149	152	152	7	640
D+5	5	3	12	124	31	225	148	148	7	703
D+6	5	3	12	121	30	219	145	145	7	687

Note: Based on 10 per cent. D-day and D-day+1 casualties, killed or missing
2½ ,, ,, the rest
25 per cent. casualties, killed or missing
2 per 1,000 sick.

went by air to Brussels and Diest and on to Neerpelt and Nijmegen. He made arrangements for obtaining medical supplies from XXX Corps for U.S. 82nd A.B. Division and for the taking over of Berchmanium College in Nijmegen for the use of this division. The rest of the activities of D.D.M.S. Airborne Troops were so intertwined with those of D.D.M.S. XXX Corps that to record them would be largely to duplicate the account that is offered concerning the affairs of XXX Corps and Second Army.

H.Q. Airborne Troops returned to the United Kingdom on October 9.

Polish 1st Para. Bde., less the gliders which landed with 1st Airborne Division on September 19, was dropped in the Driel area on the 21st with the intention of crossing the river to reinforce 1st Airborne Division. Out of a total of 110 aircraft 4 returned without dropping, 13 were missing and 3 landed at Brussels. The strength of the medical services of the brigade was, as a result, reduced by 3 officers and 33 O.Rs. and it was found impossible to collect and move to the dressing station all the medical stores and equipment on the D.Z. On the 22nd, a dressing station was established in the school at Driel. It was repeatedly hit by mortar and artillery fire. On the 26th the brigade moved to the south-west of Nijmegen and the dressing station to Neerloon.

From the D.S. at Driel casualties were evacuated to 3 C.C.S. In all 159 casualties were admitted to the D.S. and of these 62 were operated on by the surgical team.

In the original plan, after the capture of Deelen airfield, north of Arnhem, the Airborne Forward Delivery Airfield Group, U.S. 878th Airborne Aviation Engineer Bn. and 52nd Division were to be flown in.

157th Bde. of 52nd Division moved up with the supporting force and had under command the seaborne tail of the division. The units of this brigade were constantly being moved about and placed under a variety of commands. The policy adopted was to attach a section of 157 Fd. Amb. to any unit which was moved out of the brigade area. The A.D.S. of 157 Fd. Amb. evacuated its casualties to 10 C.C.S. at Jonker Bosch.

The S.M.O. of the Royal Netherlands Bde. established his H.Q. at Nederasselt and evacuated casualties from his medical detachments to the A.D.S. of 157 Fd. Amb.

SECOND ARMY

When the break-out occurred 81 B.G.H. was moved to Aubigny, near Falaise, on August 24. This unit remained open for a few days only for the rapidity of the advance soon left it too far in the rear. 49 F.D.S. took over its immobiles and acted as a staging post. On August 25, 86 B.G.H. was moved to Rugles where for a few days it functioned as a hospital before assuming a staging rôle. By August 29, 84 B.G.H. was open in Caillouet there to receive the casualties from the Seine crossing

BREAK-OUT AND ADVANCE INTO HOLLAND   307

and to act as a centre for air evacuation from the airfield at Evreux. During August, 12,106 casualties (8,955 lying cases) were evacuated by air, a total of 22,849 since D-day.

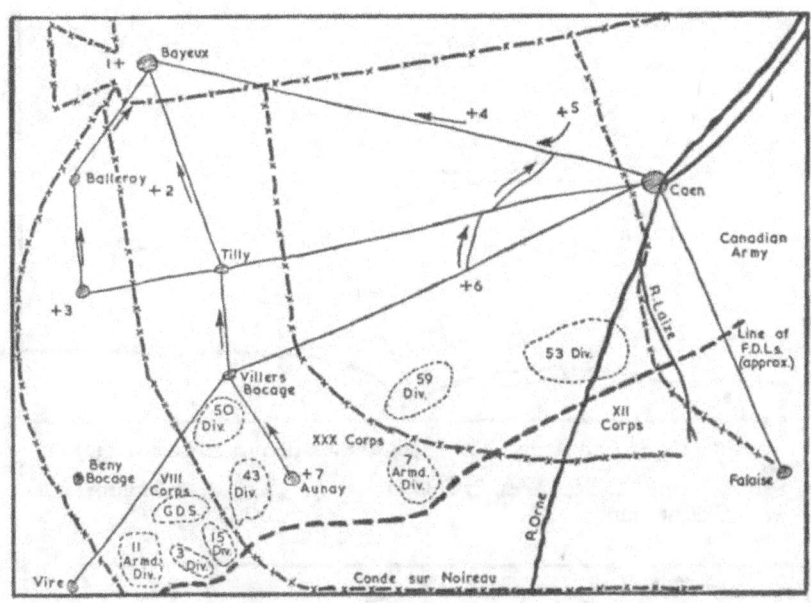

FIG. 45. Second Army. Medical Situation as at August 10.

1. Army Medical Area
    81 and 86 B.G.Hs. closed
    84 B.G.H. Open for local sick
2. 10 C.C.S.
3. 33 and 34 C.C.Ss.
4. 24 C.C.S.
5. 35 C.C.S.
6. 23 C.C.S.
7. 3 C.C.S.

By the end of August the tactical situation was such that the medical planners of 21 Army Group were able to publish an administrative order outlining the proposed development of medical operations for the immediate future. The proposed plan was divided into five phases.

1. The base hospital area at Bayeux; a hospitalisation period of 14 days on the Continent and evacuation from Normandy ports and airstrips to the United Kingdom.

2. Advanced hospital area of 600-bed hospitals north of the Seine; evacuation by air direct to the United Kingdom or, if this proved to be impracticable, to the base hospital area and thence to the United Kingdom as in phase 1.

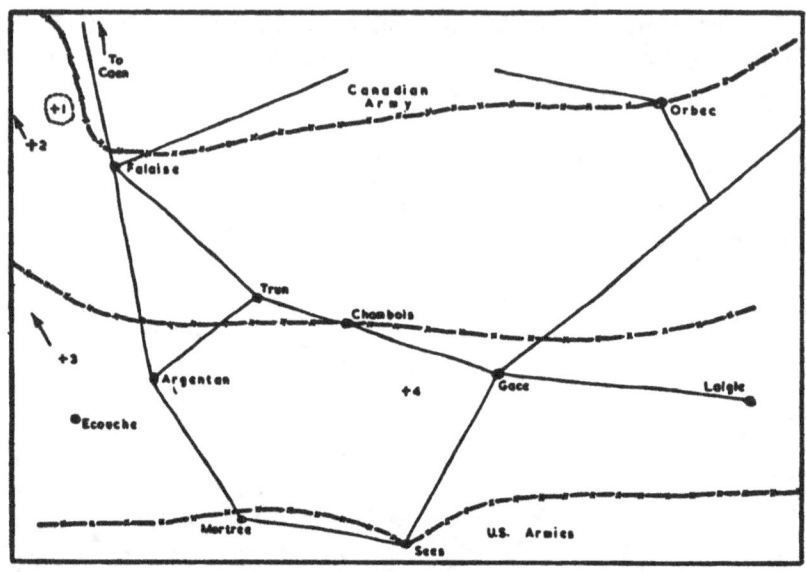

Fig. 46. Second Army. The Medical Situation as at August 23.

1. Second Army Medical Area. 81 B.G.H.
2. 23 C.C.S. at Ouilly
3. 3 C.C.S. at Montgaroult
4. 10 C.C.S.

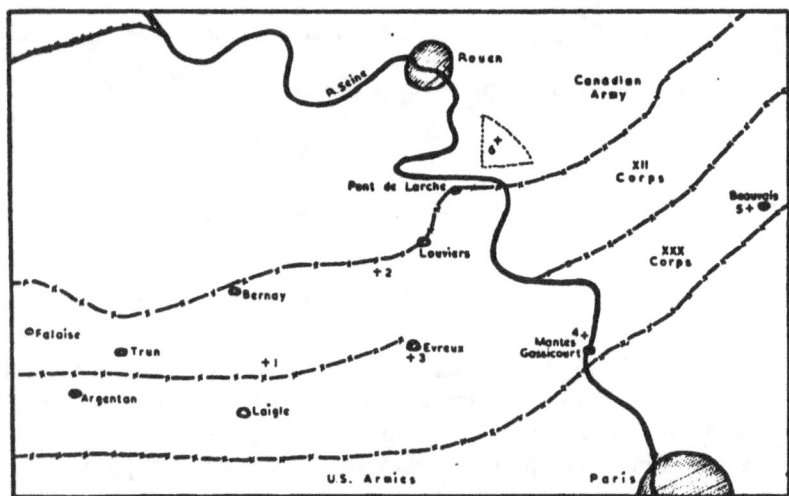

Fig. 47. Second Army. The Medical Situation as at August 31.

1. 86 B.G.H. Open for local sick
2. 23 and 24 C.C.Ss. closed, moving to Amiens
3. 35 C.C.S. closed, moving to Poix
4. 84 B.G.H. Open for wounded and air evacuation
5. 3 and 10 C.C.Ss.
6. Proposed site for 600-bed hospitals

BREAK-OUT AND ADVANCE INTO HOLLAND 309

3. The opening of the port of Dieppe for casualty evacuation; the evacuation of all casualties in the advanced hospital area through Dieppe or by air, after the minimum period of hospitalisation. During this phase (which actually developed during September) the hospitals in the Bayeux medical area were to be brought forward to Dieppe. Other hospitals were to be brought from the United Kingdom to this Dieppe medical area on the highest priority but their number was to be kept to the minimum necessary to meet operational requirements.

4. A new medical area to be established and the period of hospitalisation on the Continent to be progressively lengthened. The number of the hospitals in the Bayeux and the Dieppe medical areas to be reduced to the minimum required for the local casualties. These developments assumed the continuation of active operations during the winter months.

5. The setting up of hospitals on an area basis throughout the occupied territories following the collapse of German resistance (*see* Appendix VII).

On September 4, 81 B.G.H. was moved to Amiens and on the 6th an advance party of 86 B.G.H. reached Brussels and took over the Hôpital St. Pierre in which there were many German wounded. The remainder of the unit arrived on the 7th and 8th and the hospital then opened. 84 B.G.H. reached Brussels and opened in the Hôpital Brugmann on September 14.

Meanwhile, on September 12, 25 B.G.H. (200 beds) had taken over from 81 B.G.H. in Amiens and 8 B.G.H. (600 beds) from 86 B.G.H. in Brussels on September 11 and 35 C.C.S., which had been relieving pressure on the corps C.C.Ss. and assisting in air evacuation from Evreux, had moved to Antwerp where it opened on September 12.

In preparation for Operation 'Market Garden' 81 and 86 B.G.Hs. were established in Diest by September 17 and 84 B.G.H. had been relieved by 39 B.G.H. (600 beds) in the Hôpital Brugmann and had moved to the Hôpital St. Gilles in Brussels and was ready either to open or to move forward. 35 C.C.S. in Antwerp was about to be relieved by 9 B.G.H. 31 F.D.S. was established in the Diest area to assist 81 and 86 B.G.Hs.

On September 23, 35 C.C.S. moved into Eindhoven to stage casualties and to act as a holding unit for air evacuation.

During the early stages of the advance 257 A.C.C. cleared rearwards of corps to Bayeux. As the distance extended it became necessary to obtain assistance from 227 M.A.C. (VIII Corps). By the time the Seine was reached, though a certain number of casualties were evacuated by road staging at Rugles and Falaise, the principal evacuation method was by Sparrow aircraft from Evreux, the cases being held by 84 B.G.H. at Caillouet. When 81 B.G.H. opened in Amiens the air evacuation centre was moved forward to Amiens. Evacuation was by Sparrow aircraft to

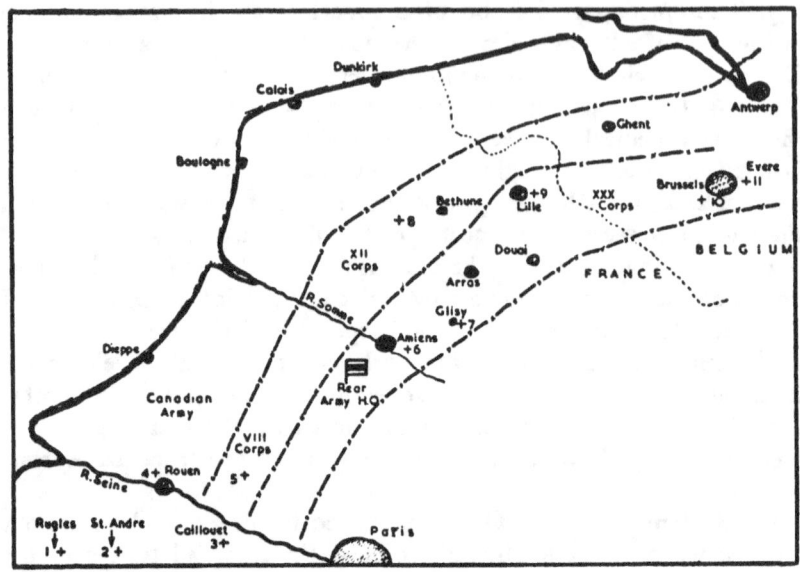

Fig. 48. Second Army. Medical Situation as at September 6.

1. 86 B.G.H.
2. Air Evacuation Centre for Bayeux
3. 84 B.G.H.
4. 9 B.G.H.
5. VIII Corps Medical Area
6. 81 B.G.H.
7. Air Evacuation Centre for Bayeux and the U.K.
8. 23 C.C.S.
9. 10 C.C.S.
10. 3 C.C.S.
11. Air Evacuation Centre for the U.K. (September 7)

Bayeux or by Dakota to the United Kingdom. Exceptionally, casualties were evacuated by road to Rouen.

From Brussels there was but one method of evacuation at first, by air, mostly by Dakota to England, some ferried by Sparrow to Amiens; a steady lift of 500–700 cases daily was organised. (Plate XIX illustrates casualties being loaded into a Transport Command Dakota at Brussels.)

As during the period of evacuation from the beaches so also now during the rapid advance into Belgium medical units found it extremely difficult to conserve their stocks of stretchers and blankets. Plentiful supplies reached the beaches but owing to the daily depletion due to the evacuation of large numbers of casualties and also because it was necessary to issue these commodities to general hospitals in excess of their

BREAK-OUT AND ADVANCE INTO HOLLAND

G.1098 scales, it became necessary to 'freeze' the stocks and to issue these items only on the authority of H.Q. It was noted that when the responsibility for evacuation passed to H.Q. L. of C. the demands for stretchers, blankets and pyjamas appreciably decreased.

When air evacuation at Brussels airport began a stock of 2,000 stretchers, 6,000 blankets and 1,500 pairs of pyjamas was established, sufficient for one week's requirements. The stock quickly became depleted and emergency demands for replenishments from local sources were unavailing. The situation was saved by the arrival of 1,000 stretchers and 3,000 blankets from the United Kingdom within thirty-six hours of the despatch of a request for them from 21 Army Group. It became evident that the loss of these stretchers, etc., consequent upon large-scale evacuation by air could not be made good by replacements sent by sea and road and that it was essential that large reserves should be maintained in Army area.

When the hospital opened in Diest the forward shuttle service was by Sparrow to Brussels where, on the airfield, 83 Gp. R.A.F. and 2 F.D.S. were in charge. At the end of September the Sparrows plied between Eindhoven and Brussels.

During this period 257 A.C.C. was supplemented by two platoons from 403 A.C.C., one from 218 A.C.C. and one from 753 A.C.C. 257 worked on the main axis from Nijmegen to Diest, 218 cleared XII Corps, one platoon of 403 cleared VIII Corps to Brussels, the other was in Brussels itself and 753 worked from Antwerp to Brussels.

On September 23, A.D.M.S. 4 L. of C. Sub-area took over the Brussels area and by the 25th, when the flow of casualties from XXX Corps and the Airborne division was diminished, it became possible to revert to the normal distribution of the A.C.Cs., 257 A.C.C. clearing corps to Diest and the L. of C. S.A. assuming responsibility for keeping Diest clear. On September 20 an ambulance train formed out of recaptured British and Belgian stock found in Brussels was made available. Staff and equipment were provided by the Belgian Red Cross and the Belgian Railways and the train made its first run from Brussels to Amiens on this day. Further runs were made on the 23rd and 26th and then the train passed to H.Q. L. of C. (Plate XVIII illustrates an ambulance railcar in the Gare du Midi, Brussels.)

P.o.W. hospitals were organised at Amiens (31 F.D.S.), Brussels (49 F.D.S.) and in Antwerp. A 600-bed P.o.W. hospital was established at Bourg-Léopold by 14 F.D.S.

Prior to the rapid advance to the Seine and beyond 13 Con. Depot functioned as the Army exhaustion centre. The incidence of exhaustion dropped markedly when the advance began.

The Army Medical Services were being required to tackle and solve a set of problems very different indeed from those with which they had dealt during the earliest phase of Operation 'Overlord'. In the confined bridgehead the distance from the front line to the hospital area was nowhere great and much of the surgery was done in the C.C.S. The F.D.Ss. were not, as a rule, called upon to form A.S.Cs. but worked in conjunction with the C.C.Ss. undertaking triage and assisting in evacuation. During this phase too transport facilities by land, sea and air were

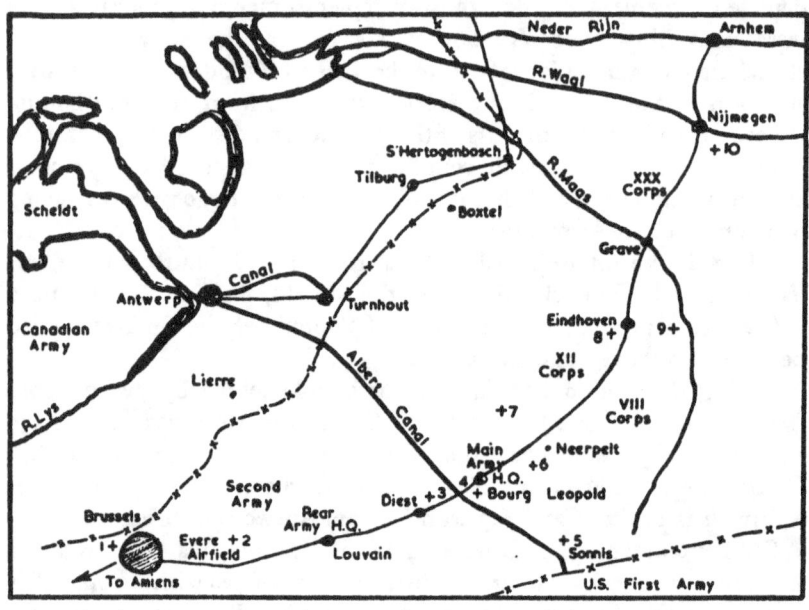

Fig. 49. Second Army. The Medical Situation as at September 28.

1. 84 B.G.H.
   11 Adv. Depot Med. Stores
2. 2 F.D.S.
3. 81 and 86 B.G.Hs.
   31 F.D.S.
   9 Adv. Depot Med. Stores
4. 14 and 47 F.D.Ss.
5. 34 C.C.S.
6. U.S. 24 Evac. Hosp.
7. 24 C.C.S.
8. 23 and 35 C.C.Ss. 49 F.D.S.
9. 33 C.C.S.
10. 3 and 10 C.C.Ss.

Evacuation by air or by road to Brussels and thence by rail to the hospitals in France or by air to the United Kingdom.

excellent for the greater part of this period and evacuation did not constitute too serious a problem. Suddenly this period of almost static warfare gave place to one of rapid pursuit. The advance to the Seine did not bring in its train any serious difficulty for the line of evacuation did not become excessively long and casualties were not so numerous as to strain the resources of the medical services. But after the Seine had been crossed the speed of the advance became greatly increased and as the

BREAK-OUT AND ADVANCE INTO HOLLAND

armies raced through Belgium these resources were severely strained, especially during the first half of September.

As has been stated, the medical plan for this phase of the operation involved the evacuation of casualties from Dieppe to the United Kingdom, rail evacuation to the medical area at Bayeux, air evacuation either to the United Kingdom or else to Bayeux and the establishment of an advanced hospital area north of the Seine pending the establishment of a new medical base in the Antwerp–Rotterdam area. But the port of Dieppe could not be used for the evacuation of casualties until September 16. Evacuation by rail became increasingly difficult as the railhead was left further and further behind. An evacuation airstrip north of the Seine was constructed but owing to bad flying conditions could not be used until September 11. So that for a time casualty evacuation depended almost entirely upon the motor ambulance. The ambulance car companies were obliged to haul their own fuel. So it was that in the forward medical units there came to be serious overcrowding, made worse by the influx of wounded P.o.W. The establishment of an advanced hospital area was much delayed by the shortage of transport vehicles, for these had to be used for the forward movement of fuel, food and ammunition over the greatly lengthened lines of communication stretching back to Bayeux. The same factors prevented the early movement forward of C.C.Ss.

The general circumstances were such that of necessity the bulk of the forward surgery was performed in A.S.Cs. formed, for the most part, by F.D.Ss. But even these failed to keep pace with the advancing formations and as many as eighteen to twenty-four hours could elapse between the receipt of a wound and the admission to an A.S.C. When in Normandy the C.C.S. and the F.D.S. worked in conjunction, the latter unit did triage. But now, with the F.D.S. functioning as an A.S.C., the need was felt for triage to be carried out in front of the F.D.S.

During September the problems that had to be solved by the Army Medical Services increased in magnitude and complexity. The combatant formations and the services that maintained their power were given priority in respect of transport and of roads. The left flank of 21 Army Group stretched from Dieppe to the Dutch border, some 200 miles, so that the problem of providing and maintaining an efficient evacuation system became and remained acute. Any medical unit that depended upon borrowed transport for its forward movement quickly found itself far behind the battle line. Air evacuation rendered assistance of the utmost value at a time when other methods of evacuation were being strained to breaking point.

Those who understand the nature of the needs of the severely wounded man will grant that the conditions and circumstances that obtained during this swift advance were such as to test to the full the competence of the senior administrative medical officers of 21 Army Group and to demand the highest degree of devotion to duty from the personnel of every kind of medical unit and of M.A.C. and A.C.C. Too rapid an advance, like too rapid a retreat, can greatly diminish the quality of the aid which the Army Medical Services can give to those who most need their help.

With the advance after the break-through the advanced depots of medical stores made the following moves:

- 8 Adv. Depot Med. Stores moved from Ryes to St. Léger on July 26, to Estrues on August 18, to Aubigny on August 25 and to Diest on September 8.
- 9 Adv. Depot Med. Stores moved from Ryes to Perigny on July 30, to Montgaroult on August 21, to Rugles on August 27, to Allonville on September 8 and to Diest on September 14.
- 11 Adv. Depot Med. Stores moved from Reviers to Ardenne on July 27, to Aunay-sur-Odon on August 10, to Caillouet on September 1, to Brussels on September 8 and to Eindhoven on September 30.
- 6 Adv. Depot Med. Stores (I Corps) passed to Canadian First Army on July 21.
- 2 (Cdn.) Adv. Depot Med. Stores with Canadian II Corps passed to Canadian First Army on July 31.

These moves were planned so as to supply each corps from one specified source but owing to the constant switching of divisions from corps to corps this arrangement was defeated. Occasion arose when two corps were drawing upon one and the same depot which soon became depleted. It was then necessary to switch them to another depot, when the situation permitted, in order to maintain a balance.

Since these advanced depots could not move forward in step with the formations they were intended to serve, it was decided to create a mobile element out of each of them. This consisted of two 3-ton lorries with drivers, one N.C.O., R.A.M.C. and one Pioneer. Approval was obtained for the lorries but the drivers had to be found from local sources. To each mobile element a modified medical maintenance block (beach) was issued from its parent depot and the element was attached to the forward C.C.S. of the corps.

During this advance from the beachhead into Holland these advanced depots were based for maintenance upon the base depots of medical stores at Bayeux and Dieppe. Supplies were sent forward by rail, road and by air to meet the fortnightly demands that were submitted. Changes in surgical technique and the activities of the specialist units— e.g. M.N.S.U., M.F.S.U.—required many modifications in the quantities and varieties of medical supplies carried by the advanced depots.

11 L. OF C. AREA

By August the evacuation system had become stabilised and was functioning smoothly. D.A.D.M.S.(E) 21 Army Group was attached to H.Q. 11 L. of C. Area on August 19 in order that he might familiarise himself with its details. On the 25th he and his staff assumed full responsibility for the evacuation of casualties from Normandy to the United Kingdom. It was at this time that evacuation from the pier at Arromanches began. This part of the evacuation scheme was controlled by 4 L. of C. S.A., 5 L. of C. S.A. and D.A.D.M.S.(E) 21 Army Group conjointly. This was a period of rapid changes, medical units leaving the area and others coming in. 5 L. of C. S.A. took over the Bayeux area from 11 L. of C. Area on July 4, coming u/c of 11 L. of C. Area but passing to command 12 L. of C. Area on August 31. 104 B.S.A. was disbanded and 102 B.S.A. became 6 L. of C. S.A., to pass on July 25 from the command of Second Army to that of 11 L. of C. S.A.

On August 31, 11 L. of C. Area handed over to 12 L. of C. Area and on September 3 left Reviers for Amiens. At the time of the take-over the lay-out of the medical units under command was as shown in Fig. 50.

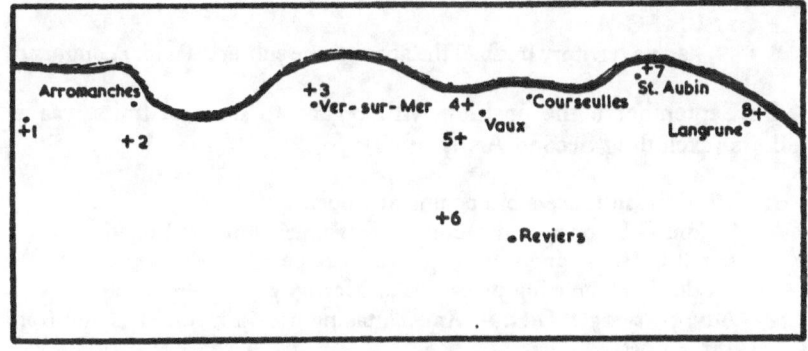

FIG. 50. Distribution of the Medical Units in 11 L. of C. Area as at August 31.

1. 75 Fd. Hyg. Sec.
2. C.R.S. Coy. 162 Fd. Amb.
3. 4 Fd. San. Sec.
4. C.E.P. 34 F.D.S.
   45 F.S.U.
5. 12 Con. Depot
6. 77 B.G.H.
   H.Q. 11 L. of C. Area
7. C.R.S. Hy. Sec. 12 F.D.S.
8. 3 Fd. San. Sec.

By September 5 it was learnt that 6 L. of C. S.A. was to control the Dieppe area and was to come u/c 11 L. of C. Area and that 5th Royal Berks. was to garrison Rouen under command of H.Q. 11 L. of C. Area, which was to control the town of Amiens. At this time the territory between the Seine and the Belgian frontier was under the administration of Second Army and Canadian First Army and it was not until September 18 that a firm boundary line between Army and L. of C. was defined. 4 L. of C. S.A. reached Lille on September 9 and moved on to Brussels on the 17th. 6 L. of C. S.A. moved from Amiens to Dieppe on September 9, taking over from the Canadians. Though 4 L. of C. S.A. in Brussels and 8 B.S.A. at Ostend lay within Army area both were u/c 11 L. of C. Area. 15 L. of C. S.A. arrived at Amiens on September 20, moved to Samer the same day and later took over the Boulogne area. 16 L. of C. S.A. also reached Amiens on the 20th, moved to Saleux and assumed responsibility for the administration of Amiens and its surroundings. On September 28 the inter-sub-area boundaries were fixed. Roughly they were as follows:

6 L. of C. S.A.
Dieppe up to the line of the Somme, less Rouen which passed to 12 L. of C. Area.
15 L. of C. S.A.
from the Somme to the Belgian frontier, including Boulogne.
16 L. of C. S.A.
a narrow strip of territory south of 6 and 15 from the Seine to the Belgian frontier.
11 L. of C. Area
had no territory but had the above three sub-areas under command.

On September 6 the position with regard to medical units was as follows (excluding Second Army units):

9 B.G.H. in process of opening at Rouen.
8 Cdn. G.H. open under canvas eight miles north of Rouen.
121 B.G.H. moving into Arques-la-Bataille.
7 Cdn. G.H. erecting its canvas at Martigny.
Adv. party 25 B.G.H. in Amiens taking over a mental hospital from 81 B.G.H.
31 F.D.S. running a P.o.W. hospital at Amiens.
Sites for two more 1,200-bed B.G.Hs. were being prepared in Dieppe.

On September 10, planning was based on the assumption that the territory of 11 L. of C. would be extended up to the Belgian frontier. 13 Base Depot Medical Stores was sited at Arques-la-Bataille. 21 F.D.S. took over the P.o.W. hospital from 31 F.D.S. Arrangements were made for the collection of all German P.o.W. sick and wounded scattered throughout the countryside into the P.o.W. hospital in Amiens. Three platoons of 753 A.C.C. (R.A.S.C.) arrived and were distributed among Rouen, Dieppe and Amiens areas. Pool M.Os. were distributed among M.I. rooms in areas in which there were the greatest concentrations of troops.

BREAK-OUT AND ADVANCE INTO HOLLAND

On September 19, 6 B.G.H. took over from 9 B.G.H. in Rouen. 12 F.D.S. joined 25 B.G.H. in Amiens and acted as an overflow for minor sick. 32 F.D.S. moved to Ostend on September 26, there to establish a C.R.S. A psychiatrist joined H.Q. 11 L. of C. Area to organise the treatment and disposal of psychiatric cases occurring locally or being evacuated from the forward areas. On September 30, 34 F.D.S. moved up to Lille to establish a C.R.S. in the Hospital for Incurables.

Evacuation from the rearward units during this period was as follows:

1. By air from Glisy, by Dakotas to the United Kingdom; by Sparrows to the Bayeux area. This service ceased on September 14.
2. By Army ambulance car to 8 Cdn. G.H. and 9 B.G.H. at Rouen. On September 12 three platoons of 753 A.C.C. replaced the Army cars.
3. By ambulance train from R.H. at Mézidon and later at Forêt-de-la-Londe, draining these two general hospitals and running between R.H. and Bayeux.

When the carrier service Dieppe–United Kingdom began to run on September 20 the above system came to an end. 121 B.G.H. and 7 Cdn.G.H. were both established in Dieppe by this date.

When preparations in connexion with the Canadian drive on the Channel ports and Operation 'Market Garden' were being made the estimate of casualties was such as to overwhelm completely the accommodation and the evacuation facilities available to 11 L. of C. Area. The hospitals beyond the Seine were cleared by ambulance train on September 23, 24 and 25. The Dieppe hospitals were allotted to the Canadians, those in Amiens and Rouen to Second Army. All trains from the forward area were stopped at Corbie and later, when the line was through Corbie to Amiens on September 21, at Amiens. Two T.A.Ts. were stabled at Amiens and casualties arriving at Amiens were transferred to these and sent on to Dieppe or to Rouen or off-loaded to 25 B.G.H. in Amiens itself. On the 28th the two T.A.Ts. moved to Brussels and thereafter evacuation by rail was as follows:

1. Two T.A.Ts. working in front of Brussels.
2. Two British and one Belgian ambulance train between Brussels and Amiens, one reaching Amiens each day.
3. One British ambulance train stationed at Amiens and running between Amiens and Rouen or Amiens and Dieppe as necessary.

Since the inflow of casualties into the area always exceeded the outflow to the United Kingdom this was a trying period. There were no convalescent depots in the area and undoubtedly many cases were evacuated to the United Kingdom that should have been retained. The fact is, however, that there was no accommodation for them in the area. U.S. casualties were evacuated by road to the U.S. hospitals in Paris.

In spite of the many difficulties that beset him at this time, A.D.M.S. 11 L. of C. Area formed the opinion that in the majority of cases A.Ds.M.S. sub-areas were redundant for, save for purely local matters, most of the medical administration of hospitals and matters concerning the distribution and evacuation of casualties, bedstates, rations, equipment and personnel are best handled by A.D.M.S. area so as to avoid delay.

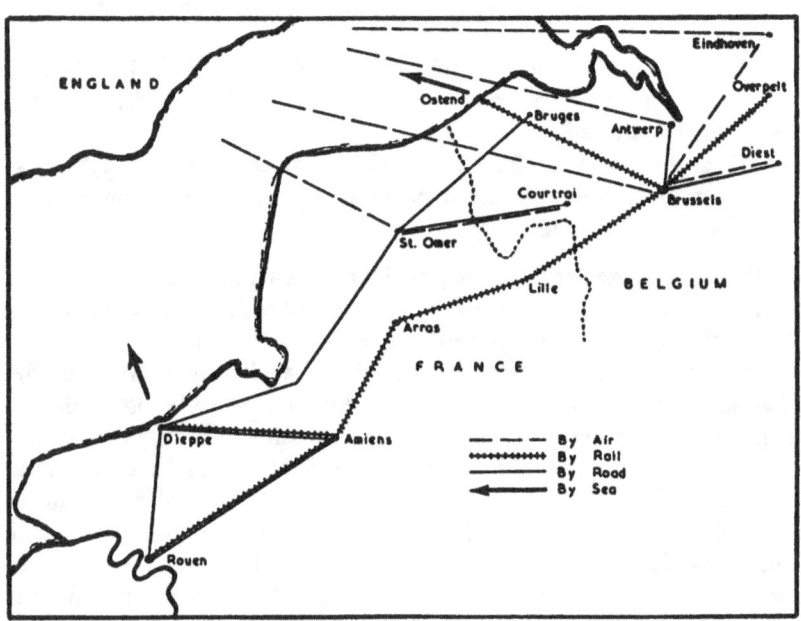

FIG. 51. The Evacuation System. Late September.

Following the battle of Falaise and during the subsequent advance the numbers of P.o.W. swamped the facilities created for their reception. P.o.W. camp staffs urgently needed at the head of the L. of C. were immobilised at the base by the arrival of large numbers of P.o.W. Staffs for the forward camps had to be improvised; in one instance a heavy A.A. regiment had to be employed for this purpose.

Dusting with A.L. 63 Mark III was carried out in corps and Army cages by means of the Dobbins hand sprayer. When large numbers had to be dealt with this arrangement broke down and the P.o.W. were passed on to the base undusted, though body-louse infestation was exceedingly common among them. In the base camps dusting teams were formed out of German medical personnel and although the prisoners

BREAK-OUT AND ADVANCE INTO HOLLAND

generally were eager to be treated much supervision was required to ensure that the dusting was thoroughly done. It quickly became clear that trained British teams were required at each cage and camp and that compressor spray units were necessary. Personnel of the M.B.Us. were trained by Ordnance. All P.o.W. who were retained in the theatre were dusted every ten days and were examined to ensure that their vaccination and inoculation state was satisfactory. In the Middle East it had been learnt that reliance could not be placed on the German T.A.B. vaccine and it was decided therefore to inoculate all P.o.W. with British vaccine. The evidence set forth in the 'paybook' concerning vaccination and inoculation against smallpox and typhus was accepted as trustworthy.

THE ARMY DENTAL SERVICE (SECOND ARMY)

During the battle of Falaise and thereafter until the pause on the Meuse–Escaut Canal line, contact with dental officers of formations by A.D.D.S. became increasingly difficult. These officers made their professional services available at every opportunity offered by the brief halts between periods of movement. In certain instances, e.g. 210 M.D.U. with 11th Armoured Division, the dental officers with 131 Fd. Amb. and 2 Lt. Fd. Amb. both with 7th Armoured Division, obtained through divisional administrative channels a 3-ton lorry converted by R.E.M.E. into a mobile dental surgery. Dental officers during the advance undertook a variety of duties other than the professional, not the least important being that of recce. officers for night leaguers. 210 M.D.U. with 11th Armoured Division entered Antwerp and 209 M.D.U. with Guards Armoured Division entered Brussels shortly after their capture. 204 and 207 M.D.Us. with 50th Division and 134 M.D.U. with 7th Armoured Division accompanied the pursuit formations, being sited in the divisional administrative area. On September 7, 212 M.D.U. with H.Q. Second Army Troops and 214 M.D.U. with Second Army Rear H.Q. were sited about eight miles west of Brussels.

Of the 19,172 attendances for dental treatment during August and September, 10,480 were in divisional areas, 2,828 in corps areas and 5,864 in Army rear areas, proportions in keeping with the relative number of troops in these areas.

During the latter part of July all dental officers of Second Army were instructed to:

1. Draw medical and dental stores sufficient to make them independent of further supplies for one month.
2. Maintain the closest possible contact with their parent units in the absence of movement orders.
3. Arrange for the liberal signposting of the unit, particularly on routes leading away from the formation axis of advance.

Because of the frequency and rapidity of movement the M.D.Us. had so to organise their affairs that repairs to dentures could be completed in one day and new and remodelled dentures in forty-eight hours.

So it was that though C.C.Ss. and general hospitals were unable to keep pace with the advancing formations owing to the difficulty of obtaining transport, their dental departments therefore not being available to the forward troops, treatment continued to be readily available in the forward areas and no shortage of equipment arose.

The monthly rate of attendance for dental treatment fell from 76 to 34 per 1,000 during the period of this advance. This fall was partly due to the unavoidable unavailability of dental treatment owing to the movement of formations and partly to the disregard of trivial discomforts on the part of the troops during a period of exaltation.

The pressure of denture work on rearward Second Army dental personnel, mainly those attached to the 200-bed hospitals and certain C.C.Ss., was eased by the transfer of L. of C. units under their care to the expanding dental service of L. of C.

Of 1,604 men who during July, August and September required the provision of new dentures, the treatment of 1,407 was completed by the end of September, 589 of these being carried out by ten M.D.Us.

The incidence of acute ulcerative gingivitis/stomatitis showed a steady and marked decline during this period. As casualties were light few maxillo-facial cases presented themselves.

D.D.M.S. Second Army instituted an unofficial medical tactical headquarters consisting of D.D.M.S., A.D.D.S. and four O.Rs. with suitable tentage and transport to permit attachment to Main H.Q. On the move forward of Rear H.Q. to Bazoches-en-Houlme this unofficial tactical H.Q. moved to La Trinité des Laitiers in association with Army Main H.Q. This arrangement continued until after Operation 'Market Garden'. Army Rear H.Q. was rejoined on September 29. From this mobile H.Q. it was possible to maintain contact with the advancing units and by travelling an average distance of 720 miles a week the entire front and much of the area immediately in the rear of it could be covered. A.D.D.S. had by this time added a jeep to his motor cycle. In the bridgehead A.D.D.S. had acted as officer i/c medical wireless net. He had temporarily to relinquish this duty during the advance. The central set at Rear H.Q. had a range of up to twenty-five miles. The sub-sets were with the medical branches of corps H.Q. and with the H.Q. of the A.C.C.

THE ARMY TRANSFUSION SERVICE (21 ARMY GROUP)

The work of the B.T.U. continued on an increasing scale as the Armies, having burst out of the bridgehead, advanced with amazing rapidity across northern France and into the Low Countries.

BREAK-OUT AND ADVANCE INTO HOLLAND

In the first few days of September it was obvious that the unit could not possibly continue to supply units which were now three hundred miles away, even though internal air transport and air evacuation of casualties to base had begun. So, on September 6, a detachment consisting of the O.C., the Blood Distribution Officer and 13 O.Rs. moved to a general hospital in Amiens. They took with them sufficient stores and refrigerators to act as an advanced depot, supplying 'X' Advanced Blood Bank with Canadian First Army moving along the coast to the west of Amiens and 'Y' Bank to the north and east with Second Army towards Brussels. Local hospitals in the intervening areas were supplied by B.T.U. vehicles which were gradually ferrying stores from Bayeux to Amiens and Brussels, detours being made where necessary.

As the advance continued it became obvious that a further forward movement of the whole unit was essential and it was decided to establish the unit in Brussels. Accordingly, the Amiens detachment moved on September 16 to Brussels with stores and refrigerator and set about finding and preparing accommodation for the arrival of the complete unit. Meanwhile, a further detachment left Bayeux for Amiens to deal with local commitments and act as a staging post for unit vehicles, stores and personnel in transit to Brussels. For a period of about three weeks therefore the B.T.U. was functioning in three sections along an axis three hundred miles in length. The larger general hospitals were now moving from Normandy and were spread out along the lines of communication from Brussels backward. Those remaining in Bayeux were no longer receiving the acute type of casualty and would, with the departure of the remainder of the B.T.U., be able to provide their own modest requirements of whole blood by local bleeding. Arrangements were made by the local A.D.M.S. for the allocation to each hospital of certain static local Army units which were used by the transfusion officers and pathologists to provide voluntary donors. Refrigeration was provided by the two paraffin-burning refrigerators carried by each hospital. Sufficient material for making transfusion giving-sets and a reasonable amount of consumable stores, plasma, saline, penicillin, etc., were given to each hospital. In addition, a dump of transfusion stores was left with the local base depot of medical stores, from which hospitals acquired their other medical equipment, and this was available to them on indent.

Having thus provided for this group of hospitals, the rear party of the B.T.U. left for Brussels, where it was soon joined by the detachment from Amiens which had made similar provision for the needs of its groups of hospitals. The move was completed within four weeks of the first detachment having moved to Amiens and had been carried out without interruption of the supply of materials to units. The round trip by road from Bayeux to Brussels and back took four days and, as the amount of stores to be moved totalled nearly 220 tons, a very considerable strain was placed on the transport section, which was given no extra vehicles for this herculean task. A certain amount of stores and personnel were moved by air, but this mode of transport was somewhat erratic and could not be relied on to any great extent.

Very suitable and commodious premises had been found in a disused chocolate factory in Brussels but it was some time before solution production, which had been interrupted by the move, reached its former level. This was mainly due to unexpected difficulties in securing a constant supply of water and electricity. The unit continued to operate from this location until the end, when the sudden cessation of hostilities found the service again stretched out over enormous distances and again contemplating a forward movement in order to shorten them.

Two small units whose work was related to that of the B.T.U. were attached to and moved with the main body of the unit. 3 Mob. Bact. Lab. was engaged on investigations on penicillin, the storage and distribution of which was undertaken by the Transfusion Service. The work included assays of samples and testing of apparatus used for continuous penicillin therapy, it having been found that certain types of equipment, particularly synthetic rubber, were highly deleterious to penicillin. It also prepared sulphanilamide-penicillin powder for wound treatment, investigated slow release vehicles and tried out a variety of therapeutic techniques and dosages.

There was attached to the B.T.U. the Adviser in Penicillin and Chemotherapy, 21 Army Group, who advised on the distribution and technical problems.

7 Mob. Bact. Lab. conducted an investigation on gas gangrene, also a subject bound up with transfusion, sulphanilamide and penicillin.

When the force broke out after the bitter fighting at Caen and the chase down the Falaise road began, new difficulties arose connected with the greater distances involved and the highly mobile nature of the fighting. The two Advanced Banks had to follow the two armies, Canadian and British, under order of the D.Ds.M.S. and the officers in charge had the greatest difficulty in maintaining contact with medical units which were opening, closing and leap-frogging each other at intervals of a few hours. Fortunately casualties were very light and lack of information about the positions of units had been foreseen by the blood-bank officers and provided for by stocking up the refrigerators of those involved in the forward rush. Distances became too great for Advanced Banks to communicate with the B.T.U. by D.R. and it became necessary to send out trucks with supplies from the base at regular intervals every day or every other day, the returning vehicles bringing back information about locations and requirements.

Until the crossing of the Seine the two armies had played the same type of rôle, but subsequently their functions began to differ. Canadian First Army, the concern of 'X' Bank, was involved in a slow steady advance occupying the wide area of the Pas-de-Calais, whereas Second Army, the concern of 'Y' Bank, was thrusting ahead along a narrow axis for great distances through Amiens to Brussels and beyond.

Canadian First Army moved mainly along the bulge of the coast, by-passing the enemy garrisons at Le Havre, Boulogne, Calais and Dunkirk. 'X' Bank placed itself centrally in the bulge with two forward trucks out, one with I Corps in the Le Havre peninsula and another with Canadian II Corps towards Calais. By this time the B.T.U. had sent forward its detachment to Amiens where it was well placed to supply both 'X' Bank to the west and 'Y' Bank to the east and north. As the advance north along the coast towards Ostend continued, 'X' Bank moved up to St. Omer and left the supplying of the relatively quiet south-west corner of the Pas-de-Calais, now being gradually occupied by general hospitals, to the care of the Amiens detachment and to vehicles plying between there and Bayeux. Air transport did not play a large part in communications between Normandy and the Canadian sector, which was off the main axis of the advance, and 'X' Bank relied on road transport throughout. Communications within this area were not difficult. Although distances were long, 'X' Bank being a hundred and twenty miles behind its two forward trucks along the arms of a wide letter 'Y' and a hundred and twenty miles away from Amiens along the stem of the 'Y', progress was slow and steady and moves of medical units, and therefore of transfusion units, were deliberate and easy to keep up with by routine visits of vehicles delivering stores.

The movements of 'Y' Bank with Second Army after the battle for the Seine were far more erratic. The two forward trucks crossed very early with their corps C.C.Ss. and for some days were lost to the main 'Y' Blood Bank, still sitting on the south side of the river. The F.T.Us. and forward trucks were carried by the precipitate rush of the Army through Beauvais, Amiens and Brussels. No one was unduly perturbed by the loss of contact; the casualties were light and the Bank had wisely supplied all F.T.Us. and forward trucks with liberal amounts of blood on the eve of the Seine crossing.

A large medical centre composed of C.C.Ss. and 200-bed hospitals was now set up at Diest, forty miles east-north-east of Brussels, during the short lull before the battle for the canals which barred the way into Holland. 'Y' Bank had followed up through Amiens, where it stayed a few days till replaced by the first detachment of the B.T.U. from Bayeux, next to Brussels, where it stayed a week, and then on to Diest, leaving behind a refrigerator vehicle to collect blood arriving by air in Brussels.

The large airport on the outskirts of Brussels was now in full working order. The armies had outstripped their supply organisation and masses of material, chiefly petrol and ammunition, were being flown directly from England, hundreds of aircraft arriving daily. These same planes were also used to evacuate casualties direct to the United Kingdom instead of sending them back the long distances to Amiens and Bayeux. Supplies of whole blood, from England too, began to arrive at Brussels instead of in Normandy, which was obviously passing into the background.

'Y' Bank was not allowed to pause for very long. The bitter fighting for the canals and the rapid build-up with air transport heralded the epic combined operation by Second Army and the airborne troops which established the Nijmegen corridor and all but succeeded in extending it to Arnhem. The corridor was secure as far as Eindhoven from the beginning, but beyond this the situation was extremely delicate and on several occasions the road between Eindhoven and Nijmegen, where 'Y' Bank had two F.T.Us. and a forward truck with XXX Corps' C.C.Ss., was cut. However, the stocks of the three refrigerators were sufficient to last until the officer of the Bank succeeded in bringing through supplies. The Bank was now set up in Eindhoven, half-way between Brussels and Nijmegen, where it remained for the next five months.

'X' Bank, in the meantime, continued to supply the Canadians as they fought their hard battles to clear the coasts of France, Belgium and Holland up to the line of the south bank of the Maas, culminating in the brilliant amphibious operation on Walcheren which completed the freeing of the port of Antwerp. Its moves brought it gradually nearer to the B.T.U.; from St. Omer it moved to Lierre, between Brussels and Antwerp, and then to Tilburg, two hours by road to the north-north-east of Brussels.

THE ARMY PSYCHIATRIC SERVICE (SECOND ARMY)

The rear section of 32 B.G.H. joined the advanced section in Normandy on July 26, but through delay in the arrival of equipment it was not possible for it to function until August 8, when the hospital had its full complement of 600 beds. This was still not sufficient and only a few vacancies could be allotted to the hospital in 13 Con. Depot. During the week ending August 12, the admissions totalled 436; the following week this figure rose to 696. As the type of case admitted was usually a severe unrecovered one from forward exhaustion centres, the short stay permissible in 32 B.G.H. made any good results impossible. Though the greater bedstate made it possible to improve on the results attained by the advanced section and approximately 68 per cent. of cases were returned to duty, this figure could have been raised to at least 90 per cent. had it been possible to provide up to three weeks' treatment. Of those returned to duty, 7 per cent. returned to front-line units in medical category A.

After the advance of Second Army from the bridgehead it became more profitable, owing to the distance involved, to evacuate cases from Army level to the United Kingdom and, in consequence, the number of admissions to 32 B.G.H. gradually diminished during September. The hospital closed down in Normandy on September 25 and moved to Wavre Notre Dame. Its usefulness in Normandy had been impaired by three factors; it arrived after the main problem had developed; in view of the size of the force, 600 psychiatric beds were inadequate; and by the end of August the hospital was too far to the rear to serve its purpose as a psychiatric base.

During August there was a drop in actual incidence of psychiatric casualties to 52 for the week ending the 26th. The percentage incidence among all casualties fell to 3·02 per cent. The incidence shown as a percentage of surgical battle casualties was, however, 24 per cent. The downward trend during August was due mainly to the gradually increasing pace of the advance against a diminishing opposition. Return to duty rate remained at approximately 68 per cent. It was estimated that over 80 per cent. of men previously returned to combatant units remained with their units for at least six weeks.

During September the incidence remained low, at approximately 3·5 per cent. of all casualties or 10 per cent. of surgical battle casualties. The rapid advance of over four hundred miles from the medical base at Bayeux made inevitable a return to the situation of June. Beds in Belgium were too few to retain casualties for long and, in the circumstances, the aim of forward retention of psychiatric casualties for treatment had to go by the board. Fortunately these casualties were few and most were chronic cases who would anyhow have required evacuation to base.

In September 1944, psychiatrists in the L. of C. were allotted to certain L. of C. areas, as the L. of C. lengthened, to open out-patient centres, treat those cases with a favourable prognosis and examine psychiatric cases among men undergoing detention.

During the rapid advance, the organisation for the treatment of psychiatric casualties became disrupted, but towards the end of September divisional psychiatric centres were re-established and the corps centres became busier. The material now being evacuated from these centres was quite different from that dealt with at the beginning of the campaign. It consisted in the main of men with long histories of psychiatric disorder who required, not treatment in the centre, but evacuation to the base and re-allocation. This was just as well for at this time beds of all kinds were comparatively few in Belgium and Holland.

During this period the number of men leaving their units for treatment, though within the range predicted, was at times distressingly large and led to certain complications. The man who goes sick on account of exhaustion undoubtedly suffers from a sense of guilt which is damaging to the personality. To repair this damage is difficult. Among those treated in the psychiatric centre and returned to full duty were many whose performance was reduced.

The second complication stemmed from the fact that whereas some men went sick and were evacuated, others suffering from much the same condition ran away, were charged and awarded penal servitude. The psychological escape of the former and the physical escape of the latter were expressions of the same mechanism yet while one was sympathetically treated in hospital the other was severely punished. At the end of July the number of deserters was large and many of them, contrasting themselves with those whose reactions to the same conditions had taken another pattern, considered that injustice had been done when they were awarded stiff punishment.

CANADIAN FIRST ARMY[*]

Canadian First Army, with I Corps under command, assumed responsibility for the section of the front running from the coast inland for twelve miles on July 23. On the 31st, when Canadian II Corps passed under command, its front was enlarged to include the area running from the Orne, four miles south of Caen, to the sea coast east of the mouth of this river. On August 1 Canadian 2nd Division unsuccessfully attacked Tilly-la-Campagne as did also Canadian 4th Armoured Division on the following day. On August 1 casualties were very numerous and were evacuated through a C.C.P. in Ifs to the A.D.S. of 11 (Cdn.) Fd. Amb. in Caen and thence to the medical centre at St. Germain la Blanche Herbe where there were two C.C.Ss. and two F.D.Ss. On the 2nd, 15 (Cdn.) Fd. Amb. was greatly impeded in its work by mortar fire. On August 4 the Canadians prepared to attack from Caen in the direction of Falaise (Operation 'Totalize'). The field ambulances were attached to the brigades and sections of these units to the battalions. 11 (Cdn.) Fd. Amb. served Cdn. 2nd Armd. Bde., 10 (Cdn.) Fd. Amb., was with Cdn. 5th Inf. Bde. and 18 (Cdn.) Fd. Amb. with Cdn. 6th Inf. Bde. 10 established its C.C.P. in Ifs and 18 had its A.D.S. in Fleury-sur-Orne which was the ambulance R.H. for Cdn. 2 M.A.C. 21 (Cdn.) F.D.S. established a resuscitation centre in Fleury and 4 (Cdn.) F.D.S. a divisional exhaustion centre. Evacuation was to be to St. Germain la Blanche Herbe, and thence to the medical area at Bayeux.

During the first day of the operation, August 7, the A.D.S. of 18 (Cdn.) Fd. Amb. in Fleury admitted 503 casualties and 10 (Cdn.) Fd.

---

[*] For a fuller account the Canadian Official Medical History should be consulted.

BREAK-OUT AND ADVANCE INTO HOLLAND 327

Amb., which was on wheels waiting to move forward, was obliged to open and admit some 400 casualties. At St. Germain la Blanche Herbe were 2 and 3 (Cdn.) C.C.Ss. with attached surgical and transfusion units. They admitted casualties alternately and dealt with some 520 on the 8th. In Cazelle was 6 (Cdn.) C.C.S.; it was ordered to open immediately in the afternoon of the 8th and during the remainder of this day admitted 221 casualties. Total admissions to 2, 3 and 6 (Cdn.) C.C.Ss. during August 8 and 9 amounted to 1,347. Most of the casualties on the

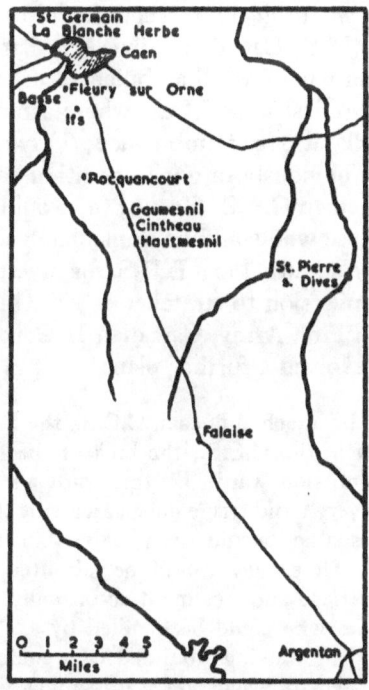

FIG. 52. The Caen–Falaise Road.

9th were in Cdn. 4th Armd. Bde. and during this day 12 (Cdn.) Lt. Fd. Amb. evacuated 215. On August 10, 14 (Cdn.) Fd. Amb. opened its A.D.S. in Rocquancourt where it was reinforced by sections of 23 (Cdn.) Fd. Amb. 22 (Cdn.) Fd. Amb. had a C.C.P. at Cintheaux and through this 153 casualties passed during the day.

On August 15 the advance towards Falaise was resumed. 11 (Cdn.) Fd. Amb. of Canadian 2nd Division opened an A.D.S. while 10 and 18 (Cdn.) Fd. Ambs. remained on wheels. Canadian 3rd Division's A.D.S. was provided by 14 (Cdn.) Fd. Amb. and 7 (Cdn.) F.D.S. in Rocquancourt. 15 (Cdn.) Fd. Amb. opened an A.D.S. in Gaumesnil to serve Canadian 4th Armoured Division while 12 (Cdn.) Lt. Fd. Amb.

remained on wheels. On the afternoon of August 14 the R.A.F. and R.C.A.F. bombed behind the Canadian line to cause some 200 casualties. These added greatly to the difficulties of the Canadian C.C.Ss. and F.D.Ss. 2 and 3 (Cdn.) C.C.Ss. admitted a total of 537 casualties during this day, 9 and 10 (Cdn.) F.D.Ss., in the same area, admitted 569 and it became necessary to open 6 (Cdn.) C.C.S. as well as 33 C.C.S. in Cazelle to which a further 694 casualties were directed.

Experience had shown that very considerable strain was put upon the surgical capacities of a C.C.S. by the accumulation within the unit of such as required urgent surgical intervention and of walking wounded. On August 14, D.D.M.S. Canadian First Army and O.C. 10 (Cdn.) F.D.S. evolved a plan whereby 'all ambulance cars that come into the medical area would go first to a F.D.S. where a rapid triage could be done: (a) walkers—all get out of ambulance; (b) lying cases apparently lightly wounded and obviously in good condition admitted to F.D.S.; (c) all others—to go on to C.C.S. Group; (a) would then very quickly be divided into (i) those who could be immediately sent on to hospital; (ii) those who must be admitted to a F.D.S. for investigation, for change of dressing or for conversion to stretcher cases'. On the following day D.Ds.M.S. Canadian First Army, Canadian II Corps and I Corps met in St. Germain and evolved a further plan:

> 'One F.D.S. to be attached to each C.C.S., the F.D.S. to be set up as an integral part of the C.C.S., the bulk of the F.D.S. canvas being used as the admission ward. To this ward all casualties would be admitted and a very rapid triage done as a result of which about 20 per cent. of the casualties would need to be transferred to the C.C.S. admission tent. Here they would be admitted to the C.C.S. and receive further triage and treatment accordingly. Of the 80 per cent. of total casualties who could be handled by a F.D.S. approximately one-third would be walking wounded who could be dealt with very quickly and passed to evacuation wards almost immediately. Of the remaining two-thirds most would require only change of dressing, rest, fluids, food, etc., and these, too, could be dealt with very quickly and transferred to evacuation. A very few would, on closer examination, perhaps have to be transferred to a C.C.S. for resuscitation or treatment. Such a scheme really involves pooling F.D.S. and C.C.S. completely, both personnel, tentage and equipment. . . . It is felt that such a scheme would result in using the F.D.Ss. to their maximum efficiency and at the same time enable the C.C.Ss. to give the most serious casualties the best possible treatment.'

This plan was put into effect on August 16 by 2 (Cdn.) C.C.S. and 9 (Cdn.) F.D.S. to the satisfaction of all concerned.

When the Falaise gap was closed Canadian 4th Armoured Division and Polish 1st Armoured Division stood athwart the path of the German

BREAK-OUT AND ADVANCE INTO HOLLAND

retreat and sustained many casualties. The medical units had difficulty in evacuating the casualties because of the congestion and the confusion that abounded. 15 (Cdn.) Fd. Amb. on August 19, for example, found itself in possession of two German troop carriers and two ambulances with a German medical officer, 10 German medical orderlies and 40 German wounded aboard.

The advance to the Seine and beyond brought to the Canadian medical planners the same acute problems that had to be tackled by those of Second Army. The Canadian Army was to operate at an ever-increasing distance from its base and along a single thrust line. So, on August 17, 6 (Cdn.) C.C.S. with 9 and 10 (Cdn.) F.S.Us. and 7 (Cdn.) F.T.U. were moved from Cazelle to Hautmesnil, half-way between Caen and Falaise. On the following day 10 (Cdn.) F.D.S. joined and an A.S.C. was established. Evacuation from this was to the Bayeux medical area, except for such as could not endure the forty-mile journey. These were to be admitted to 2 (Cdn.) C.C.S. at St. Germain until 88 B.G.H. opened in Ardenne near St. Germain la Blanche Herbe on August 23 to stage casualties on their way back to the base. In Canadian 2nd Division the field ambulances were placed with their respective brigades and the foremost of them established C.C.Ps. and dressing stations along the axis of advance. One of the C.C.Ps. acted at roadhead for the M.A.C. and remained open until the whole of the division had passed by. Later this arrangement was changed and 4 (Cdn.) F.D.S. took over the rôle of divisional A.D.S. Canadian 3rd Division also placed the field ambulances with their respective brigades and 23 (Cdn.) Fd. Amb. always kept one section in a known position while the others moved forward with the brigade. Canadian 4th Armoured Division had its field ambulance sections forward with the advancing column and the H.Q. in the centre. The F.D.S. was in the rear acting as a dressing station and despatch point for the M.A.C. In two days this division moved forward 100 miles. In a three-day period 109 casualties were evacuated from the division.

On August 18 Canadian II Corps medical area at Hautmesnil included 5 and 10 (Cdn.) F.D.Ss. and 6 (Cdn.) C.C.S. On the 20th 6 (Cdn.) F.D.S. established an A.S.C. at St. Pierre-sur-Dives, thirteen miles north of Falaise. From this centre some 500 casualties were evacuated to Hautmesnil. On August 24, 11 (Cdn.) F.D.S. established an A.S.C. in Le Hamel, ten miles south-east of Lisieux. On the 27th 2 (Cdn.) C.C.S. opened in Brionne and 5, 6 and 11 (Cdn.) F.D.Ss. thereupon closed and prepared for the crossing of the Seine.

For the pursuit Canadian First Army had Canadian II Corps and I Corps under command but since each of these had its own axis of advance and since the two axes were widely separated it was impossible to pool the medical resources of the corps. Each had to move its medical units in relation to the speed of its own advance while Army had to attempt to keep up evacuation to the base hospital area. The medical situation during the advance was satisfactory on the whole but this was only because casualties were relatively few and their evacuation to the base therefore possible. The roads were very congested. The medical units had to leave small detachments behind to look after pockets of casualties. The medical units had to admit casualties while on the move. It was by no means easy to keep in touch with forward medical units and thus control the flow of casualties to particular C.C.Ss. or F.D.Ss. D.Rs. had great difficulty in making their way along the crowded roads. The weather was not helpful for the last week of August in Normandy was rain-filled.

These difficulties were in part overcome by the adoption of a 'trickle' system of movement. Thus, 6 (Cdn.) F.D.S. moved several times without closing. On August 18 it moved from Basse to Cintheaux while admitting patients. For the first part of the move these were admitted to the rear portion of the unit in Basse and later to the forward portion of the unit, as this grew increasingly larger as the rear portion grew progressively smaller, in Cintheaux. All patients still with the rear party of the unit when this moved forward were taken along. The medical units of Canadian 2nd Division were provided with wireless detachments by the division and the 'Slidex' Code was used for intercommunication. By August 28 the Canadians were on the line of the Seine and the line of evacuation had become stretched to more than ninety miles. 6 Cdn. G.H. opened in St. Hymer on this day. On September 1 air evacuation from Brionne to Bayeux began and the aircraft on their return journeys brought forward quantities of medical supplies.

The medical area of St. Germain la Blanche Herbe was closed on August 18. 3 (Cdn.) C.C.S. moved forward to Livarot, nine miles east of St. Pierre-sur-Dives, handing over its residual patients to 2 (Cdn.) C.C.S. which reverted to Army command. 88 B.G.H. was *en route* for Brionne, half-way between Falaise and Rouen.

During the month of August Canadian casualties numbered 9,369 of whom 2,258 lost their lives.

2 and 12 Cdn.G.Hs. (1,200 bed) arrived in Normandy during August to bring the total number of Canadian hospital beds to 5,000. 2 (Cdn.) Con. Depot. had also arrived and had opened in the Bayeux medical area.

Canadian 2nd Division was in Dieppe during the first week of September and thence moved on to Dunkirk. On September 18 it set out for Antwerp. By the 22nd it had secured a bridgehead across the Albert Canal immediately east of Antwerp and then crossed the Antwerp–Turnhout Canal. During these moves evacuation from the divisional medical units was to Antwerp where there was a British medical centre

BREAK-OUT AND ADVANCE INTO HOLLAND

or to Canadian medical units in Steenvoorde. 9 (Cdn.) F.D.S., with F.S.Us. and F.T.Us. attached, was functioning as an A.S.C. in Antwerp after September 29.

Canadian 3rd Division advanced against Boulogne, the attack upon which began on September 17. The field ambulances established C.C.Ps. and an A.D.S. to serve their respective brigades and, with 7 (Cdn.) F.D.S., to serve also the artillery and engineer units with the division. On the 5th when a German naval hospital in Hardinghem was over-run, 14 (Cdn.) Fd. Amb. went forward to take it over. This unit remained there until October 2. It was joined in the naval hospital by 5 (Cdn.) F.D.S. and being reinforced with F.S.Us. and F.T.Us. an A.S.C. was established. Evacuation from this A.S.C. was to 6 Cdn. G.H. in Wailly-Beaucamp.

During the attack upon Boulogne 22 (Cdn.) Fd. Amb. evacuated directly into 6 Cdn.G.H. and admitted casualties from the C.C.P. of 23 (Cdn.) Fd. Amb. By September 22 the town was in Canadian hands. Its capture had cost the Canadians 634 casualties. On the 25th the Canadians were beseiging Calais. For this operation the field ambulances again were with their respective brigades. The C.C.Ps. of 14 and 22 (Cdn.) Fd. Ambs. cleared their casualties to the A.S.C. in Hardinghem, as did also 17 (Cdn.) Lt. Fd. Amb. while 23 (Cdn.) Fd. Amb. evacuated its patients from its own A.D.S. direct to 6 Cdn. G.H. in Wailly-Beaucamp. By October 1 all resistance had been overcome. During this operation the medical units of Canadian 3rd Division evacuated 687 casualties, 236 of them being P.o.W.

Canadian 4th Armoured Division moved forward on Bruges. The field ambulances were with their respective brigades with one or two sections detached to serve main and rear divisional headquarters. 12 (Cdn.) F.D.S. moved at the rear of the division. At Soex a German military hospital was over-run and an officer of 12 (Cdn.) Lt. Fd. Amb. was left in charge. In Dixmude 12 (Cdn.) F.D.S. took over another hospital on September 8. On September 13 Bruges was entered and on the following day an unsuccessful attempt was made to force a crossing of the Léopold Canal. For the rest of the month Canadian 4th Armoured Division continued to patrol the line of this canal. Evacuation from the field ambulances with the brigades was to the A.S.C. at Hardinghem and to 3 (Cdn.) C.C.S. at Lokeren until September 25 on which date an A.S.C. was established at Eecloo.

Canadian II Corps during September had at its disposal four C.C.Ss., five F.D.Ss., eight F.S.Us., five F.T.Us., a field hygiene section, a V.D.T.U., an exhaustion unit, an advanced depot of medical stores and a special employment company to which post-exhaustion cases could be sent for recovery. But the advance was so fast that not all of these units remained available for use. 3 (Cdn.) C.C.S. crossed the Seine on

September 1 and moved to Wailly-Beaucamp, opening there on September 10. 2 (Cdn.) C.C.S. closed in Brionne on September 5 and went forward to Steenvoorde to open there on the 15th. Two days later 3 (Cdn.) C.C.S. closed at Wailly-Beaucamp and moved forward to Lokeren. Thus it was not until September 10 that a Canadian C.C.S. was open north of the Seine. 6 (Cdn.) C.C.S. was closed between September 1–13 during its move to St. Omer.

5, 6, 9 and 11 (Cdn.) F.D.Ss. with attached F.S.Us. and F.T.Us. took the place of the C.C.S., functioning as a series of A.S.Cs. 6 was open in Les Authieux beyond the Seine on September 1 and moved forward to Wailly-Beaucamp on the 5th and again on the 11th to Dixmude. 5 crossed the Seine on September 3 and opened in Le Translay whence after four days it moved forward to Hardinghem. 11, crossing the Seine, likewise moved to Le Translay where it remained until the 26th. 9 (Cdn.) F.D.S. crossed the Seine on September 7 and proceeded to Steenvoorde where it opened on the 9th. Eight days later the unit moved forward again to Lokeren. But even these rapid leaps of the medical units failed to keep pace with certain of the Canadian formations and it was necessary occasionally to leave casualties in civilian hospitals.

To shorten the line of evacuation and so relieve the ambulance car companies, general hospitals were brought forward whenever possible. As has already been stated 88 B.G.H. moved from Ardenne to Brionne on September 1. 8 Cdn. G.H. was then moved from Bayeux to St. André-sur-Cailly, north-east of Rouen, to open there on September 4. 6 Cdn. G.H. was in St. Hymer at this time. Next, 6 and 7 Cdn. G.Hs. were opened in Wailly-Beaucamp and Martigny on September 11. Railhead was pushed forward first to Mézidon and then on September 9 to Lisieux. Air evacuation was inclined to be uncertain at this time because of bad weather. During the last week of September the speed of the advance slackened and so the medical situation was eased. Air evacuation to the Bayeux medical area continued until September 23, after which evacuation by air was to the United Kingdom. 6 and 16 Cdn. G.Hs. admitted all casualties from the Canadian First Army front and from these medical units evacuation was either by air to the United Kingdom or else by road to Dieppe.

BREAK-OUT AND ADVANCE INTO HOLLAND

APPENDIX VI

THE ALLIED COMMAND (GROUND FORCES) AUTUMN 1944

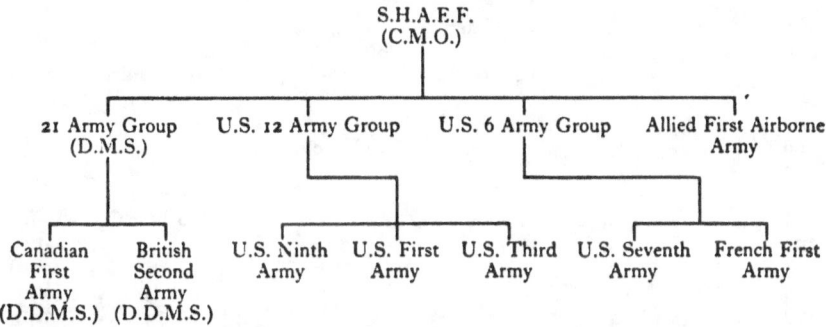

APPENDIX VII

21 ARMY GROUP. LOCATION STATEMENT. GENERAL HOSPITALS. SEPTEMBER 2

With Second Army
  81, 84, 86, 88 B.G.Hs. and 6 Cdn. G.H. (all 200 beds)
In Bayeux Hospital Area
  8, 9, 20, 25, 32, 39, 74, 75, 77, 79, 121 B.G.Hs.
  7, 8 and 16 Cdn. G.Hs. (all 600 beds)
  6, 23, 24, 29, 73, 101, 102, 105, 106, 107, 108, 110 B.G.Hs.
  2, 10 and 12 Cdn. G.Hs. (all 1,200 beds)
Still in the U.K.
  109, 111, 112, 113, 114, 115 B.G.Hs.
  20 and 21 Cdn. G.Hs. (all 1,200 beds)

Tentative proposals concerning their movements (1) in the immediate and (2) in the more remote future were:

		(1)	(2)	
8 B.G.H.	Bayeux	—	Forward Zone	
9 ,,	,,	Rouen	,,	
20 ,,	,,	—	—	To War Office when situation permitted
25 ,,	,,	Amiens	Forward Zone	
30 ,,	,,	—	,,	
32 ,,	,,	—	,,	
39 ,,	,,	—	,,	
74 ,,	,,	—	,,	
75 ,,	,,	—	—	

			(1)	(2)	
77 B.G.H.		Reviers	—	Forward Zone	
79	,,	Bayeux	—	—	
121	,,	,,	Dieppe	Forward Zone	
7 Cdn. G.H.		,,	,,	,,	
8	,,	,,	Rouen	,,	
16	,,	,,	St. Omer	,,	
6 B.G.H.		,,	—	Rouen	
23	,,	,,	Cherbourg	—	If required, otherwise to War Office
24	,,	,,	—	—	
29	,,	,,	—	Le Havre	
73	,,	,,	—	—	To War Office, 5th in order
101	,,	,,	—	—	To War Office (7th)
102	,,	,,	—	—	,, ,, ,, (4th)
105	,,	,,	—	—	,, ,, ,, (2nd)
106	,,	,,	—	—	,, ,, ,, (6th)
107	,,	,,	—	—	,, ,, ,, (3rd)
108	,,	,,	—	—	,, ,, ,, (1st)
109	,,	U.K.	—	Antwerp	Direct
110	,,	Bayeux	—	—	To War Office
111	,,	U.K.	—	Antwerp	Direct
112	,,	,,	—	—	To War Office
113	,,	,,	—	Arques-la-Bataille	
114	,,	,,	—	—	To War Office
115	,,	,,	—	Antwerp	Direct
2 Cdn. G.H.		Bayeux	—	Forward Zone	
10	,,	,,	—	,,	
12	,,	,,	—	Boulogne	
20	,,	U.K.	—	Antwerp	Direct
21	,,	,,	—	Dieppe	Direct

CHAPTER 4

THE OPENING OF THE ESTUARY OF THE SCHELDT

(i)
The Operations

IT will have been noted that after Antwerp was entered by 11th Armoured Division on September 4, no bridgehead to the north was secured immediately and then all resources were applied north-eastward; thus no serious and sustained attempt was made to advance to and secure the base of the South Beveland Isthmus leading to the Island of Walcheren and so deprive the German forces on the mainland north of the Léopold Canal and on the Island of Walcheren of their easiest road and rail connexion with the east. So it was that the German forces retreating from the Pas-de-Calais were able to make full use of it, passing by way of Breskens and Flushing. They left behind them two divisions to hold positions north and south of the Scheldt Estuary and two more in the area between Antwerp and Bergen-op-Zoom to guard the approaches to the Beveland Isthmus from the east.

S.H.A.E.F., far away at Granville in Normandy, was thinking of and planning for the capture of (i) Antwerp and the Ruhr and (ii) the Saar and Frankfurt, for it seemed that German resistance was fast collapsing. It soon became manifest, however, that this was not so and the war of swift movement came to an end. The outcome of Operation 'Market Garden' was disappointing but Field Marshal Montgomery was still of the opinion that, given the means, it was possible to drive through the Reichswald into the Rhineland and occupy the Ruhr. At a conference with his senior commanders at Versailles on September 22, General Eisenhower decided that the envelopment of the Ruhr from the north by 21 Army Group, supported by U.S. First Army, should be the main Allied effort in the immediate future. He decided that 21 Army Group should also take steps to open the port of Antwerp. By the end of the first week in October, Field Marshal Montgomery found it necessary to advise General Eisenhower that the Rhineland offensive would have to be postponed until the German forces had been driven east of the Maas on his right flank. General Eisenhower did not agree to this sector having priority over Antwerp and on October 16 the Field Marshal issued orders closing down all offensive operations save those concerned with the opening of the Scheldt Estuary by Canadian First Army. Second Army was instructed to regroup so as to bring its weight to bear in the west. In order to shorten the Canadian line, Second Army took over its right sector.

At this time VIII Corps, holding the eastern side of the Nijmegen salient, was conducting an offensive towards the Maas from Grave in the direction of Venraij and Venlo. This offensive had been checked by water obstacles in the area of Venraij. 3rd Division entered Venraij on October 18 and thereafter the offensive was abandoned. In its place Second Army was to launch an offensive to clear the Germans out of the area south of the Maas from 's Hertogenbosch westwards.

The need for a major port not too remote from the line now held by the Canadian, British and United States armies in the north had become increasingly urgent. Their supplies had to come by road from the Normandy shore, five hundred miles away. Their strength was progressively increasing. Antwerp was but eighty miles away and its facilities were sufficient to maintain a force of two millions and more. But it lay some fifty miles from the open sea and the sea-lane to it was completely dominated by the German positions on either side of the Scheldt Estuary. Merxem, a suburb of Antwerp, was held by the Germans and the docks of Antwerp were within range of their guns. The German positions in the Breskens pocket and on the Island of Walcheren were parts of the strongly fortified Atlantic Wall. The only land approach to Walcheren was along the narrow isthmus of South Beveland and across a causeway which carried the road and a single railway track. Walcheren was almost entirely land reclaimed from the sea (polder), lying below the sea level. On the mainland the Léopold Canal provided a perimeter for the Breskens pocket in which flooded areas gave protection to its garrison, which consisted of first-class troops abundantly supported by artillery. The terrain gave every advantage to the Germans and the task assigned to Canadian First Army could not have been more difficult.

It was to involve a frontal and a flank attack on the Breskens pocket, two amphibious assaults by commandos on Walcheren, an amphibious operation by 52nd Division, trained in mountain warfare, transformed into an air-portable formation and now to fight as much in water as on land, an operation by Canadian and British troops to secure the right flank in the area Bergen-op-Zoom–Roosendaal and a series of frontal assaults along the South Beveland Isthmus and across the causeway to Walcheren. The complementary drive to the Maas was to involve 15th, 51st and 53rd Divisions and 7th Armoured Division of Second Army and 49th Division, Canadian 4th Armoured Division, the Polish Armoured Division and U.S. 104th Division under Canadian First Army.

THE OPENING OF THE SCHELDT ESTUARY

The first of these interrelated and complex enterprises was Operation 'Switchback' undertaken by Canadian 3rd Division, supported by an infantry battalion, a field regiment and the reconnaissance regiment of 52nd Division, which was launched on October 6. Under cover of flame throwers, two battalions in assault boats got across the Léopold Canal, to be followed by a third battalion on the following day. Seven days were to pass before the bridgehead was large enough to permit the canal to be bridged. On October 9, a brigade embarked in 'Buffaloes' which had travelled from Ghent and crossed the Scheldt from Terneuzen to land at the north-east tip of the Breskens pocket. The third brigade of the division then crossed and the division fought its way from dyke to dyke to link up on October 19 with troops of 52nd Division in the bridgehead across the Léopold Canal.

On this day Breskens was entered after prolonged air and artillery bombardment.

The German forces in the Breskens pocket were now cooped up in the heavily waterlogged area around the sea end of the Léopold Canal between Zeebrugge and Knocke-sur-Mer. On November 3, their resistance was finally overcome and the whole of Belgium had been liberated. Moreover, the Allies were in possession of the south shore of the Scheldt.

Operation 'Vitality I' had for its aim an advance along the Beveland Isthmus. On October 1, after crossing the Antwerp–Turnhout Canal some fifteen miles north-east of Antwerp, through the bridgehead established by I Corps on September 25, Canadian 2nd Division moved westwards along the further side of the canal to Merxem and then began to thrust northward towards Woensdrecht. During the following week the resistance encountered was not particularly stubborn, but when the base of the isthmus was neared it stiffened and the advance was checked. It was not until a fortnight later that the neck of the isthmus was finally sealed.

On October 23, Canadian 4th Armoured Division came up on the right of the Canadian infantry and made it possible for Canadian 2nd Division, with its right flank secure, to swing into the isthmus itself. Operation 'Vitality I' opened on October 24 and, often waist-deep in water, the Canadians fought their way to reach within six miles of the Beveland Canal on the 26th. This was crossed during the following night and two bridgeheads secured.

Meanwhile Operation 'Vitality II' had opened. On October 26, two brigades of 52nd Division embarked at Terneuzen and Ossenisse in 'Buffaloes' and crossed the Scheldt to land in the area of Baarland at the south-east corner of South Beveland. A bridgehead was quickly secured and reinforced. On October 29, a brigade of Canadian 2nd Division, thrusting south from the main road that traverses South

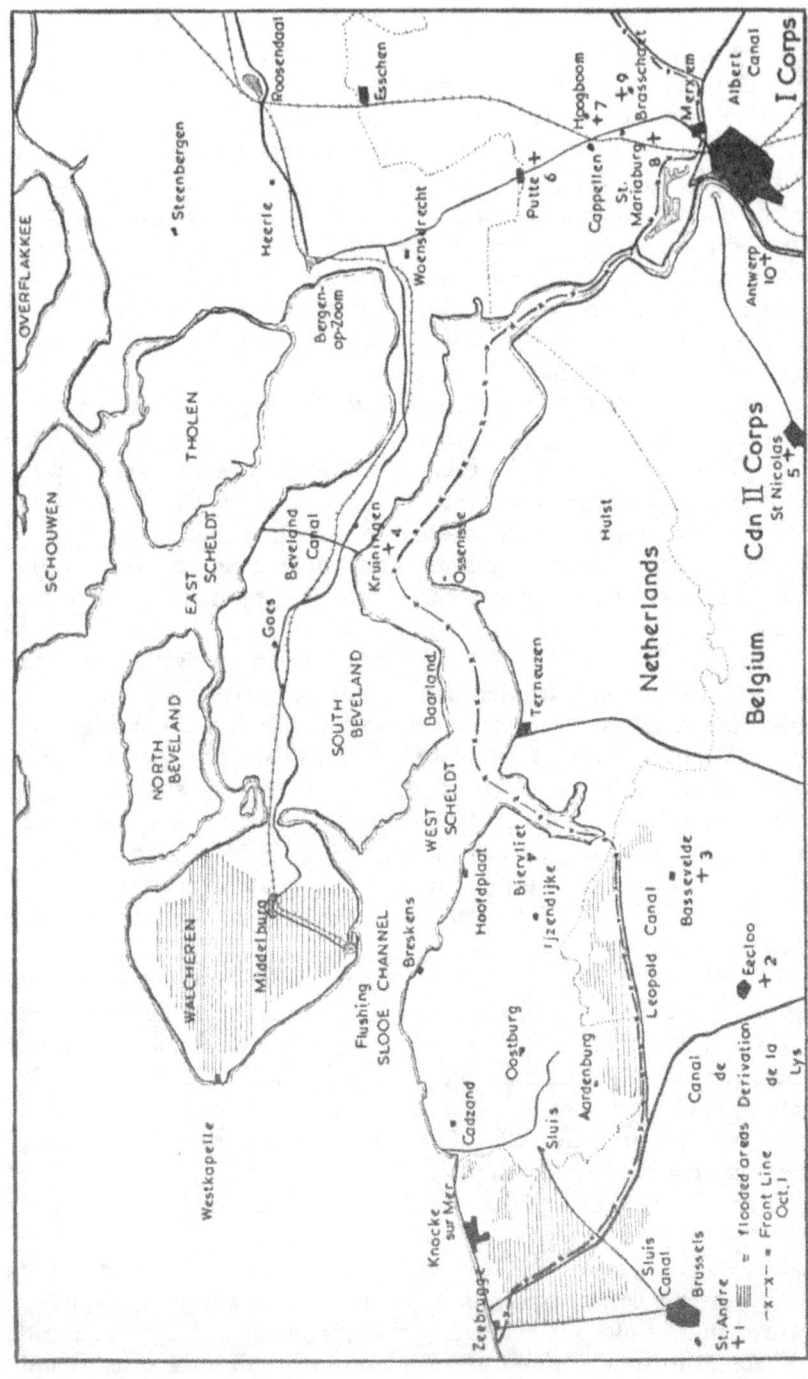

FIG. 53. Canadian First Army. The Clearance of the Scheldt Estuary. Medical Arrangements. (*See* key on page opposite.)

THE OPENING OF THE SCHELDT ESTUARY

Beveland, linked up with the right-hand brigade of 52nd Division and South Beveland was quickly cleared. A reconnaissance squadron promptly crossed to North Beveland.

The moment had now arrived for the launching of Operation 'Infatuate', the assault on Walcheren. In order to remove the advantage given to the German garrison by the water obstacles on the island and to permit the use of amphibious craft inside the rim, R.A.F. Bomber Command had breached the sea dykes at four points. Three-quarters of the island were now under deep water and the German garrison confined to three small strips of coast and to the towns of Flushing and Middelburg.

The advance of Canadian 2nd Division along the causeway was an operation to which no special code name was given but it was indeed a most dangerous adventure. On October 31 the Royal Regiment of Canada cleared a small pocket of Germans at its eastern end and the Canadian Black Watch then thrust along it to reach within seventy-five yards of its western end. Then during the night the Calgary Highlanders burst through to secure a small bridgehead on Walcheren. Next morning they were pressed back by a furious German counter-attack but the Régiment de Maisonneuve attacked and re-established the bridgehead. On the morning of November 2, Canadian 2nd Division was relieved by 52nd Division and was withdrawn to rest.

The Glasgow Highlanders held on to the bridgehead, withstanding several fierce counter-attacks. Then, on November 3, rocket-firing Typhoons intervened and 6th Cameronians crossed the Slooe Channel to take the Germans completely by surprise and to join up with the Highlanders on the evening of the 4th.

On November 1, Operation 'Infatuate I', the assault on Flushing, and

---

Key to Fig. 53

1. 12 Cdn. G.H. (from September 30)
2. Adv. Surg. Centre
    6 (Cdn.) F.D.S. September 25–October 25
    5 (Cdn.) F.D.S. October 25–November 8
3. 7 (Cdn.) F.D.S. October 11–November 8
4. 21 (Cdn.) F.D.S. October 31–November 2
5. 3 (Cdn.) C.C.S. October 7–20
6. 4 (Cdn.) F.D.S. October 10–November 10
7. Adv. Surg. Centre
    5 (Cdn.) F.D.S. October 17–28
8. 21 (Cdn.) F.D.S. October 6–30
9. 12 (Cdn.) F.D.S. October 19–November 3
    6 (Cdn.) C.C.S. October 18–November 8
10. 9 (Cdn.) F.D.S. September 28–October 24
    6 Cdn. G.H. September 30
    8 Cdn. G.H. October 2

Operation 'Infatuate II', the assault on Westkapelle, opened, being launched from Breskens and Ostend respectively. The third brigade of 52nd Division with 4th Cdo. set out for Flushing. Ships of the Royal Navy, Typhoons of the R.A.F. and the guns on the Breskens shore covered the assault landings and 4th Commando and 4th K.O.S.B. were quickly ashore. The seafront and the centre of Flushing were soon cleared. On November 3, 7th/9th R.S. attacked the German Command H.Q. in the Hotel Britannia which had been transformed into a veritable fortress. After most bitter hand-to-hand fighting the Germans surrendered.

A company of 7th/9th R.S. then embarked in 'Buffaloes' and, crossing the flooded and mined central area of the island, proceeded to Middelburg, to enter it and to accept the surrender of its garrison on November 6. The Royal Scots were joined there by 5th and 6th H.L.I. who had crossed the Slooe Channel.

'Infatuate II' was a combined operation of considerable magnitude. H.M.S. *Warspite* and two monitors, *Erebus* and *Roberts*, engaged the coastal guns but the spotting planes were fog-bound in England and so the bombardment was not very effectual. Twenty-five landing craft mounting rockets and light artillery drove inshore and joined battle. Very heavy losses in landing craft and in men were endured. But while they engaged the attention of the defences 41st, 47th and 48th R.M. Cdos. and 10th Inter-Allied Commando of 4th S.S. Bde. landed on either shoulder of the Westkapelle Gap. Indeed some of them actually sailed through the gap in their 'Buffaloes' and took the village of Westkapelle from the east. Before nightfall the commandos on the western side of the island had captured the two main coastal batteries but on the eastern side it took till November 3 to overpower the batteries and reach the gap just west of Flushing.

The Royal Navy began to sweep the Scheldt Estuary on November 4. The clearing of the heavily strewn mines from the seventy-mile channel took more than three weeks and it was November 28 before the first convoy could dock at Antwerp.

Following these events and until February 8, 1945, the Canadian Army took part in no major operation. Having cleaned up the left bank of the Maas Canadian 4th Armoured Division was used in a patrolling rôle on this line and Canadian 2nd and 3rd Infantry Divisions moved into the Nijmegen salient where they remained until the opening of the spring offensive.

(ii)
Medical Cover

CANADIAN 2ND DIVISION. OPERATION 'VITALITY I'*

The field ambulances (10, 11 and 18) were attached to their respective brigades and each furnished an A.D.S. and a C.C.P. 21 (Cdn.) F.D.S. carried out triage on casualties received from 10 and 18 (Cdn.) Fd. Ambs., evacuating the minor sick and injured and exhaustion cases to 9 (Cdn.) F.D.S. which was functioning as an A.S.C. in Antwerp and all others to 6 Cdn. G.H. also in Antwerp. 11 (Cdn.) Fd. Amb. evacuated its casualties directly into 6 Cdn. G.H. Evacuation from the C.C.P. to the F.D.S. was by field ambulance transport and from F.D.S. rearwards by 2 (Cdn.) M.A.C. As the division moved up towards the entrance of the peninsula the C.C.Ps. moved with their respective brigades. When the attack upon the strongly defended village of Woensdrecht opened during the second week of October, 4 (Cdn.) F.D.S. was moved up to Putte, halfway between Antwerp and Woensdrecht to function as a resuscitation centre and roadhead for the M.A.C. 21 (Cdn.) F.D.S. took over the rôle of divisional recovery centre. On October 13 heavy casualties were endured as the Canadians crossed the open flooded fields in the entrance to the Beveland Peninsula. The wounded were evacuated from the forward C.C.P. of 18 (Cdn.) Fd. Amb. to 4 (Cdn.) F.D.S. at Putte where a new system of triage was being tested. Cases requiring urgent surgery were passed to the A.S.C. of 9 (Cdn.) F.D.S. in Antwerp; minor sick, injured and exhaustion cases were sent to 21 (Cdn.) F.D.S. at Ste. Mariaburg and all others to 6 Cdn. G.H. in Antwerp. When a foothold in the entrance to the peninsula had been secured the division prepared to advance against South Beveland itself. Casualties from the area of Putte and north of it were to be evacuated to 4 (Cdn.) F.D.S. in Putte, those from south of this area to 6 (Cdn.) C.C.S. in Brasschaet. Both 4 and 21 (Cdn.) F.D.Ss. were to function as recovery centres, retaining those suffering from minor sickness, injury or exhaustion and evacuating all others to 6 (Cdn.) C.C.S. by cars of 2 (Cdn.) M.A.C.

On October 24 the advance began and five days later Canadian 2nd Division linked up with 52nd (Lowland) Division which had landed on the coast behind the Beveland Canal. By the 31st the whole of South Beveland, with the exception of a small area at the east end of the causeway linking South Beveland and Walcheren, had been captured. By November 2 this small pocket had been eliminated and a

---

* For a fuller account the Canadian Official Medical History should be consulted.

bridgehead had been secured on Walcheren itself. Canadian 2nd Division then handed over to 52nd Division and withdrew to Antwerp to rest.

During these actions 10 (Cdn.) Fd. Amb. opened an A.D.S. in Krabbendijke on October 28 and 11 (Cdn.) Fd. Amb. an A.D.S. in Goes on the 31st. 21 (Cdn.) F.D.S. was moved to Kruiningen on October 31 to serve as the roadhead for 2 (Cdn.) M.A.C.

CANADIAN 3RD DIVISION. OPERATION 'SWITCHBACK'

While Canadian 2nd Division was involved in Operation 'Vitality I', Canadian 3rd Division was attacking the German positions behind the Léopold Canal. On October 7, Cdn. 7th Bde. secured a bridgehead while Cdn. 9th Bde. in an amphibious attack upon the enemy's rear provided support. Cdn. 8th Bde. followed 9th Bde. across the Braakman Inlet while Cdn. 4th Armoured Division attacked the land gap west of this inlet. By November 3 the Germans had been cleared from this last pocket of occupied Belgium.

For this operation each infantry brigade had one field ambulance company attached to it. 14 (Cdn.) Fd. Amb. established a C.P. south of the Léopold Canal for Cdn. 7th Bde. casualties and 23 (Cdn.) Fd. Amb. opened one just west of Terneuzen to cover Cdn. 9th Bde's. amphibious assault. Evacuation from these C.Ps. was to the A.D.Ss. established by these two field ambulances. 12 (Cdn.) Lt. Fd. Amb. received from 14 (Cdn.) Fd. Amb. and carried out triage. Evacuation therefrom was to the A.S.C. at Eecloo (Priorities I and II) and to 12 Cdn. G.H. at St. André near Bruges, (the rest). 23 (Cdn.) Fd. Amb. evacuated its casualties from its own A.D.S. to 2 (Cdn.) C.C.S. in Ghent.

Between R.A.P. and C.C.P. and between C.C.P. and A.D.S. the hand-carriage of casualties was the rule during this operation. Only from the ambulance C.Ps. and the A.D.Ss. was use made of jeeps and the M.A.C. For evacuation across the Braakman no amphibious vehicles were allotted for medical purposes exclusively and it took from two to eight hours to get casualties back, especially at night. As the Germans were pressed westwards it became possible on October 15 to evacuate casualties by road around the southern tip of the Braakman. Then 14 (Cdn.) Fd. Amb. moved to Biervliet on the 19th and to Groede on the 30th, while on the 21st 23 (Cdn.) Fd. Amb. was able to open south of Ijzendijke. By the 31st evacuation had become possible along the Oostburg–Aardenburg–Maldegem road. Priority I and II cases were then sent to 5 (Cdn.) F.D.S. at Eecloo and the rest to 22 (Cdn.) Fd. Amb. in Maldegem and thence either to 2 (Cdn.) C.C.S. in Ghent or else to 12 Cdn. G.H. in St. André. Minor sick were treated in 22 (Cdn.) Fd. Amb. and exhaustion cases in 7 (Cdn.) F.D.S. at Bassevelde.

THE OPENING OF THE SCHELDT ESTUARY 343

CANADIAN 4TH ARMOURED DIVISION.
OPERATION 'SUITCASE'

Canadian 4th Armoured Division came under command of I Corps on October 17. It was to advance towards Esschen on two parallel axes, a battle-group on each. Casualties incurred by Cdn. 4th Armd. Bde. on the left or 'Green' route were to be cleared by 12 (Cdn.) Lt. Fd. Amb.; those incurred by Cdn. 10th Inf. Bde. Gp. on the right or 'Blue' route were to be collected and evacuated by 15 (Cdn.) Fd. Amb. 12 (Cdn.) Lt. Fd. Amb. established an A.D.S. in a Belgian Red Cross building in Cappellen on the 19th, leaving one section with rear H.Q. of Cdn. 4th Armd. Bde. and sending two sections forward to form a C.C.P. to move with the brigade. This A.D.S. dealt with 49 battle casualties, 9 sick, 3 exhaustion cases and 8 accident cases on October 20–22. Evacuation was to 12 (Cdn.) F.D.S. which was functioning in association with 6 (Cdn.) C.C.S. in Brasschaet as a triage unit and a holding centre for minor sick, lightly wounded and exhaustion cases. Serious cases were passed on to the C.C.S. 15 (Cdn.) Fd. Amb. moved up to a point three-quarters of a mile north-east of Brasschaet on October 19 but did not open. Casualties on the 'Blue' route were being evacuated directly from the C.C.Ps. to 12 (Cdn.) F.D.S. in Brasschaet. As the C.C.Ps. moved forward the A.D.S. was established in Achterbroek on October 21. By the 22nd Esschen was firmly in Canadian hands.

The division then turned west towards Bergen-op-Zoom, Cdn. 4th Armd. Bde. pressing on to Wouwsche Plantage. 12 (Cdn.) Lt. Fd. Amb. opened its A.D.S. in Huijbergen, receiving its first patients on October 26. 15 (Cdn.) Fd. Amb. with Cdn. 10th Inf. Bde. remained in Achterbroek until the 29th and then moved forward to establish its A.D.S. two miles south of Bergen. The next objective was Steenbergen. Cdn. 4th Armd. Bde. thrust northwards and pressed the Germans back to within three miles of the town. Then Cdn. 10th Inf. Bde. passed through and captured it. Once again the field ambulances moved with their respective brigades, evacuating casualties through the A.D.S. of 15 (Cdn.) Fd. Amb. near Bergen-op-Zoom to 12 (Cdn.) Lt. Fd. Amb. now in Heerle, to 12 (Cdn.) F.D.S. in Bergen and 30 F.D.S. in Roosendaal where it had formed an A.S.C. From these units the less urgent of the casualties were evacuated to 6 (Cdn.) C.C.S. at Brasschaet while the minor sick were retained in the divisional recovery centre that was being run by 12 (Cdn.) F.D.S.

4TH SPECIAL SERVICE BRIGADE. OPERATION
'INFATUATE II'

For the amphibious operation against Walcheren the R.C.A.M.C. provided the medical cover. On October 8, 17 (Cdn.) Lt. Fd. Amb., of

Canadian 4th Armoured Division, joined 4th Special Service Brigade for special training. On the 21st this medical unit was joined by 8 and 9 (Cdn.) F.S.Us. and 5 (Cdn.) F.T.U. 10 (Cdn.) F.D.S. was also attached to the brigade for the operation.

17 (Cdn.) Lt. Fd. Amb. had one section attached to 41st Commando which landed on the left of the Westkapelle Gap and another with 48th Cdo. which landed on the right of the gap. Casualties were numerous. Those on the left of the gap were nested in a shell-hole on the edge of the dyke until Westkapelle had been cleared when they were moved into a house in the village. On the right of the gap a C.C.P. was established on the inside of the sea wall and there the casualties were held until 10 (Cdn.) F.D.S. came ashore at 1400 hours and established a B.D.S. Most of the casualties were taken off during the night by L.C.T. and conveyed to 6 (Cdn.) F.D.S. in Ostend. On November 2 a C.C.P. was established in the village of Zoutelande. Bad weather prevented the evacuation of casualties during the period November 2–6 and so the F.S.Us., which had taken over a German hospital dug-out, were kept very busy. On November 6 a house in Domberg was taken over for use as an A.S.C.

On this day the walking wounded were evacuated by sea to Ostend. On November 13 the Canadian medical units left the island and returned to the base at St. Michel, near Bruges.

During the course of this operation 6 (Cdn.) F.D.S. in Ostend received 512 casualties from Walcheren, mainly naval personnel on November 1 and 2 and a further 220 when evacuation was resumed. In Ostend the casualties were met on the dock, given interim treatment and then sent on to 108 B.G.H. in Ostend. Casualties to the number of 57 were received on November 9 and 10 and were taken by road to Antwerp.

The Canadian medical units did most excellent work in conditions which taxed their resources to the utmost. For the first two days of the operation the sites of these units were under fire. Storms obliged these units to hold their patients for nearly a week. The amount of canvas which the units had brought with them was barely sufficient to provide shelter for these patients. Nevertheless the quality of the attention given to them was in all respects exceptionally high.

One point of interest during this period was the provision of transfusion services for the landing on Walcheren. 5 (Cdn.) F.T.U. took part in the operation with its refrigerator mounted in an amphibious tank, which carried also all its other stores and personnel. It left with adequate supplies of blood and arrangements were made for replenishing them. Fortunately casualties were light and its work was not unduly heavy; neither personnel nor refrigerator suffered any damage in this experimental venture.

THE OPENING OF THE SCHELDT ESTUARY

52ND (LOWLAND) DIVISION

This division, consisting of 155th, 156th and 157th Inf. Bdes. with supporting arms and services including 155, 156 and 157 Fd. Amb., 18 and 19 F.D.Ss., 32 Fd. Hyg. Sec. and 533, 534 and 501 M.D.Us., had been trained for mountain warfare and so possessed special equipment appropriate for this rôle. In addition to its three brigades it had two regiments of mountain gunners and two animal transport companies. It was then converted into an air-portable division and briefed as such for several operations, including 'Market Garden'. It was not until October 23 that the division embarked for the Continent without its animal transport companies and without the normal infantry divisional transport but with the jeeps and trailers of an air-portable formation. One of its brigades, less two battalions and with a field ambulance attached, had preceded the division and was u/c XII Corps in the Nijmegen sector.

Because of its designation as an air-portable division there were certain peculiarities about the organisation of its medical services. 18 F.D.S. carried on its staff one surgical specialist, one graded surgeon, one graded anaesthetist, one medical officer for anaesthetist duties, one transfusion officer, one transport officer (from a field ambulance) and four O.R.As. The transport officer, on landing, would attempt to form an improvised M.A.C. out of any available vehicles.

155 and 156 Fd. Ambs. each had 17 jeeps, 15 trailers and 2 water trailers. 18 F.D.S. had 17 jeeps, 15 trailers and 2 water carriers; 19 F.D.S. had 14 jeeps, 12 trailers and 2 water carriers; 157 Fd. Amb., which had reached the Continent along with 157th Bde., had 32 heavy ambulance cars.

The division at once moved to the forward area to take part in the opening of the Scheldt Estuary.

The casualties of 156th Bde. in its attack on South Beveland were dealt with by 156 Fd. Amb. This unit crossed the Scheldt with the assault force, carrying only skeleton equipment on man-pack and taking only one jeep. The casualties were evacuated in 'Buffaloes' to Molenhoek (south-east of Eecloo) where the field ambulance had a car post and thence to 6 (Cdn.) F.D.S. Owing to a break in the dyke the C.P. had to be moved to Terneuzen.

With 155th Bde. in its attack on Flushing went 155 Fd. Amb. on an assault scale. Casualties were evacuated to Breskens where the field ambulance had a car post and thence to 18 F.D.S. at Biervliet which was functioning as an advanced surgical centre. The F.D.S. admitted 227 battle casualties (including civilian and P.o.W.) and performed 38 major operations, and gave blood transfusions to 51 cases. The evacuation of casualties from Flushing was greatly facilitated by the use of amphibious craft which loaded direct on to the assault craft offshore.

When 157th and 156th Bdes. launched the attack across the causeway leading from South Beveland to Walcheren casualties were evacuated *via* 156 Fd. Amb's. car post to its A.D.S. at Goes, thence to 6 (Cdn.) F.D.S. and, finally, to Antwerp. At the time of its surrender the German garrison included 306 wounded who had to be evacuated.

TABLE 35

52nd Division. Admissions to Field Ambulances. October–December 1944

	Sick	Exhaustion	Battle Casualties	Totals
British and Allied Tps.	1,015	88	624	1,727
P.o.W.	121	8	575	704
Civilian	11	—	118	129
	1,147	96	1,317	2,560

Of the 1,317 battle casualties the distribution of wounds by anatomical region was:

Head	149
Chest	103
Abdomen	31
Limbs	875
Multiple and Burns	159
	1,317

Of a series of 38 major operations carried out in the advanced surgical centre of 18 F.D.S. the distribution was:

Abdominal	15
Compound Fractures	5
Amputation	3
Others	15
	38

(iii)
Medical Arrangements

CANADIAN II CORPS*

During these events the medical units under command Canadian II Corps made few moves. 6 (Cdn.) F.D.S., with 4 (Cdn.) F.T.U. and 10 and 11 (Cdn.) F.S.Us. attached, formed an A.S.C. in Eecloo, remaining there until October 25 and receiving casualties from Canadian 3rd Division during Operation 'Switchback'. It was impossible to site an A.S.C. beyond the Léopold Canal for the reasons that no suitable building was available and the ground was too boggy to permit the use of canvas. When 6 (Cdn.) F.D.S. was moved to Ostend in connexion with Operation 'Infatuate', its place was taken by 5 (Cdn.) F.D.S. The F.S.Us. and the F.T.U. remained with this unit which between October 1 and November 3 dealt with 841 casualties. Evacuation was to 2 (Cdn.) C.C.S. in Ghent or to 12 Cdn. G.H. at St. André.

To serve Canadian 2nd Division for Operation 'Vitality', 9 (Cdn.) F.D.S. with 5 (Cdn.) F.T.U. and 8 and 9 (Cdn.) F.S.Us. attached, formed an A.S.C. in Antwerp. Evacuation was to 6 and 8 Cdn. G.Hs. and to 9 and 30 B.G.Hs., all in Antwerp. On October 16, 5 (Cdn.) F.D.S. moved from Lokeren to Hoogboom there to form an A.S.C. Evacuation was to 6 (Cdn.) C.C.S. in Brasschaet. The F.D.S. was moved back to Eecloo on October 25 for the reason that in Hoogboom it was not fully occupied. It relieved 6 (Cdn.) F.D.S. in Eecloo, freeing this unit to participate in Operation 'Infatuate II'. Between October 23 and November 3, 5 (Cdn.) F.D.S. in Eecloo dealt with 331 casualties from Canadian 3rd Division. 6 (Cdn.) F.D.S. opened in Ostend to serve 4th S.S. Bde. in its assault upon Westkapelle and also sent a light section with 52nd Division to Flushing. Casualties from 52nd Division during this operation were few and were evacuated to 12 Cdn. G.H. at St. André, Bruges, and to 2 (Cdn.) C.C.S. in Ghent.

CANADIAN FIRST ARMY

On October 6 the distribution of the Canadian general hospitals was as follows:

Antwerp Area	6 (200) and 8 (600) Cdn. G.Hs. (also 9 and 30 B.G.Hs.)
St. André, Bruges	12 Cdn. G.H. (1,200)
St. Omer	16 Cdn. G.H. (600)
Bayeux medical area	2 and 10 Cdn. G.Hs. (both 1,200)
Martigny	7 Cdn. G.H. (600)
Mesnières-en-Bray nr. Dieppe	21 Cdn. G.H. (1,200)

* For a fuller account the Canadian Official Medical History should be consulted.

Air evacuation from Antwerp began on October 8 and sea evacuation from Ostend on October 21. Ambulance railhead was opened in Antwerp on the 20th and thereafter ambulance trains ran from Antwerp through Ghent and Bruges to Ostend. Thus far in the campaign although there were times when the forward hospitals were almost filled to capacity only about 30 per cent. of the total beds available in the Canadian general hospitals had been used. During the rapid advance through northern France and Belgium it had been found to be more practicable to evacuate casualties from the forward zone directly to the United Kingdom than to the base hospitals. It had also been impossible to move the larger base hospitals forward and had this difficulty been overcome it would have been exceedingly difficult to find appropriate accommodation for them. At one time the lack of accommodation was so serious that six British general hospitals which had become redundant in the Bayeux medical area were shipped to the United Kingdom there to remain until suitable accommodation for them had been discovered in the new advanced base area. Tented accommodation for the sick and wounded during the winter months in north-west Europe would be most unsatisfactory. It was held to be undesirable to dislocate civilian life in the liberated areas by requisitioning such buildings as schools and hospitals. All that could reasonably be done was to take over such buildings as had been used by the Germans as military hospitals and to augment this accommodation by making use, with the approval of the civil authorities, of convent, hospital, school and such like buildings. Until such arrangements had been made it was inevitable that considerable numbers of such as were suffering from minor ailments and slight wounds and injuries and who might have remained in the Army area were evacuated beyond the divisional recovery centres and even out of the theatre. During October the forward movement of the Canadian general hospitals from Bayeux began and by the beginning of November hospital facilities were such that it was possible to increase the holding period in the theatre to thirty days. At the end of November there were eight general hospitals north of the Seine.

Ghent	2 Cdn. G.H.	St. André, Bruges	12 Cdn. G.H.
Antwerp	6 and 8 Cdn. G.Hs.	St. Omer	16 Cdn. G.H.
Turnhout	7 and 10 Cdn. G.Hs.	Mesnières-en-Bray	21 Cdn. G.H.

12 and 21 were functioning as holding hospitals for casualties being evacuated by air, 16 for those going by sea. Casualties among the troops containing the German garrison in Dunkirk were also admitted to 16 Cdn. G.H.

The almost continuous fighting and the onset of cold, wet weather during October yielded a noticeable increase in the incidence of minor sickness and of exhaustion in Canadian First Army. In Canadian

2nd Division 4 and 21 (Cdn.) F.D.Ss. provided the divisional recovery centre. In Canadian 3rd Division it was the practice to return exhaustion cases and the minor sick to 7 (Cdn.) F.D.S. although up to thirty minor sick a day were held at 22 (Cdn.) Fd. Amb. in Maldegem. In Canadian 4th Armoured Division 12 (Cdn.) F.D.S. provided the divisional recovery centre in Brasschaet.

During this period, while the weather remained consistently wet with temperatures of 40°–50° F., the collection of casualties had to be carried out without any undue delay and resuscitation had to be commenced well forward. During the second week of October there was some discussion concerning the value of the practice of employing divisional F.D.Ss. as A.S.Cs. But since in the Canadian First Army sector the seriously wounded needed to be moved only a few miles before they received extended medical and surgical attention it was decided that the A.S.Cs. should remain under the control of corps.

The cost of clearing the Channel ports and the Scheldt was heavy; 703 officers and 12,170 O.Rs. were killed, wounded or missing and of these 355 officers and 6,012 O.Rs. were Canadians.

Between the first week of November 1944 and the second week of February 1945 when Operation 'Veritable'—the crossing of the Rhine—began, Canadian First Army did not take part in any large-scale fighting. During the long winter months while Canadian 4th Armoured Division patrolled the south bank of the Maas the divisional field ambulances were attached to their respective brigades and when out of the line opened dressing stations capable of holding thirty patients suffering from minor illnesses or injuries.

On January 26, 1945, the division mounted Operation 'Elephant' to dislodge a nest of German para-troopers from a small bridgehead on the south side of the Maas at Kapelsche Veer. For this operation 15 (Cdn.) Fd. Amb. reinforced its C.C.P. in Loon-op-Zand and transformed it into an A.D.S. The 406 casualties from this operation were evacuated to 2 (Cdn.) C.C.S. in Tilburg.

Canadian 2nd and 3rd Divisions moved into the Nijmegen salient and remained there until the opening of the spring offensive. The field ambulances of Canadian 2nd Division established C.C.Ps. in their respective brigade areas and 21 (Cdn.) F.D.S. opened a divisional recovery centre to hold the minor sick and injured. In Canadian 3rd Division the medical arrangements were somewhat different. For the first part of their stay in Nijmegen, 23 (Cdn.) Fd. Amb. and 5 (Cdn.) F.D.S., with F.S.Us. and F.T.Us. attached, formed an A.S.C. and a divisional recovery centre in a Jesuit college on the outskirts of the city. During December and January, 22 (Cdn.) Fd. Amb., along with 7 (Cdn.) F.D.S. and 6 (Cdn.) F.S.U., took over the divisional recovery centre. 14 (Cdn.) Fd. Amb., serving Cdn. 7th Inf. Bde., moved to Mook on

December 26 and returned to Nijmegen on January 31. After its return from Walcheren, 17 (Cdn.) Lt. Fd. Amb. spent a fortnight in Bruges, refitting and replacing lost equipment and then went into action again providing C.C.Ps. to serve Cdn. 2nd Armd. Bde. near Grave. During December and January the unit functioned as a brigade recovery centre.

In November the corps and Army medical units were, for the first time, able to function in a semi-static rôle and to adopt an evacuation policy designed to conserve the strength of the force. Minor sick, likely to recover within a fortnight could now be held. 12 Cdn. G.H. at St. André which had only 50 beds on October 5 had its full 1,200 on November 4. During this period it had dealt with 3,934 admissions and the number of operations performed totalled 1,860. After the first week of November the admission rate dropped rapidly, only 3,407 casualties being admitted during November and December. On November 24, 7 Cdn. G.H. moved up from Martigny to Turnhout and, in December, 6 and 8 Cdn. G.Hs. moved out of Antwerp, to escape the persistent rocket attacks, to St. Michielsgestel. 16 Cdn. G.H. remained in St. Omer until January 8, 1945, when it moved to Oost Dunkerke.

During the first six months of this campaign Canadian battle casualties totalled 29,393, of whom 7,828 lost their lives. During the same period the hospitals admitted 29,944 sick.

CHAPTER 5

THE ADVANCE TO THE MAAS AND TO THE ROER AND THE GERMAN COUNTER-OFFENSIVE IN THE ARDENNES

(i)

The Advance to the Maas and to the Roer

ON October 16 Field Marshal Montgomery decided to utilise all his resources in clearing the Scheldt and in bringing his left flank on to the Maas. This was accomplished by early November. He then turned his attention to his right and by early December had driven the Germans east of the Maas on this flank. These operations had left a small pocket in the triangle between the Roer and the Maas and this had to be liquidated before the line of the Rhine opposite the Ruhr could be attacked. In early December the waterlogged state of the ground in this triangle made an attack upon it difficult. Then came the German counter-offensive in the Ardennes which for the time being occupied all the energies of the Allies. However, by the end of January the triangle had been cleared (*see* page 359).

Another problem that had to be tackled was that created by the possession by the Germans of the Schmidt dams on the upper waters of the Roer. The release of these waters would cause a short but wide flood, or a controlled rise in the river. In the latter case for about a fortnight no floating bridges could be maintained on the Roer, across which the right wing was due to attack. The left wing would not suffer this disadvantage as the floods would be much less severe as far downstream as Grave. These dams were on U.S. First Army front and the battle for them was to last for almost three months. They were not secured until the second week in February and before withdrawing the Germans blew the charges which ensured the controlled rise in the river. During U.S. First Army's fight towards these dams through the Hürtgen Forest, east of Aachen, the village of Hürtgen changed hands no less than fourteen times and the village of Vossenach no less than twenty-eight times.

While Canadian First Army was freeing the banks of the Scheldt, XII Corps of Second Army and I Corps of Canadian First Army were engaged in clearing the area south of the Maas from 's Hertogenbosch westwards. While these operations were developing the Germans launched a sharp counter-attack on VIII Corps' front and penetrated several miles south of Venraij along the road to Helmond. 15th Division was rushed across from the western sector of the salient where, on October 22, XII Corps had launched Second Army's westward drive. By the end of the month the position on VIII Corps' front had become stabilised again. Second Army's objective was the general line Geertruidenberg–Oosterhout–Poppel; I Corps' from there to the west. I Corps began its first task on October 20 when Canadian 4th Armoured Division and 49th Division advanced to seal off the South Beveland Isthmus by securing Bergen-op-Zoom and Roosendaal. These divisions then continued to advance to the Maas with U.S. 104th Division and Polish Armoured Division on their right.

Meanwhile, on October 22, XII Corps struck west of the general line Oss–Veghel–St. Oedenrode towards 's Hertogenbosch and Tilburg. 7th Armoured and 53rd Divisions moved on 's Hertogenbosch followed by 51st Division and, on the left, 15th Division advanced on Tilburg. 's Hertogenbosch was finally cleared by 53rd Division on October 27 on which day 15th Division was in Tilburg. On the 30th, 49th Division entered Roosendaal. Then 7th Armoured Division thrust towards Oosterhout to make contact with the Polish Armoured Division advancing from Breda, which it had captured on the 29th. By November 5, XII Corps had completed its task when 51st Division crossed the last canal in front of the river line and was then switched to VIII Corps' front.

I Corps finished its task four days later when the last pockets of resistance in the vicinity of the Moerdijk bridges at the confluence of the Maas and Waal were overcome. The Germans destroyed these bridges before they could be captured. On November 9 Canadian II Corps from the Scheldt area took over the Nijmegen area from XXX Corps. On November 14, the advance of Second Army to the line of the Maas was resumed. VIII Corps pushed on towards the river through mud and minefield, and XII Corps with 7th Armoured, 51st and 53rd Divisions attacked east towards Roermond and north-east towards Venlo. By November 16, XII Corps had completed the clearance of the west bank of the Maas opposite Roermond and by the end of the month the last German bridgehead west of the river in VIII and XII Corps' sectors was at Blerick facing Venlo on the far bank.

On December 3, 15th Division, supported by Flails and A.V.R.Es. of 79th Division, eliminated this bridgehead at a cost of only 50 casualties.

On November 18 on XXX Corps' front between the Maas and the Würm an attack was launched in the Geilenkirchen sector in conjunction with U.S. Ninth Army's operations on the flank of the main American thrust towards Cologne. With 43rd Division on the right and Guards Armoured Division on the left and with U.S. 84th Division under command, XXX Corps took Geilenkirchen on November 20, but heavy rain then made the ground impassable to both tracked and wheeled vehicles and so the operation came to an end.

By the end of November U.S. Ninth Army had reached the Roer between Jülich and Linnich and by the middle of December U.S. First Army was on the river line opposite Düren. So after a month's bitter fighting the Americans in this sector had advanced only some seven or eight miles and there was no sign of any weakening in the German defence. Further south U.S. Third Army had captured Metz by the middle of November and had reached the line of the Moselle, but heavy rain had so swollen the river that all the pontoon bridges were swept away. In the extreme south U.S. 6 Army Group had advanced into Alsace Lorraine; U.S. Seventh Army had captured Strasbourg and had advanced towards Karlsruhe and French First Army had reached the Rhine between the Swiss frontier and Mulhouse. The offensive along the entire Allied front had become bogged down.

It was decided that U.S. Ninth Army should accept responsibility for the elimination of the German salient in the Heinsberg area in the Roer triangle and should take over XXX Corps' sector of the line and that XXX Corps, with Guards Armoured, 15th, 43rd and 53rd Divisions, should concentrate under Canadian First Army for their thrust through the Reichswald towards Krefeld.

But these plans came to nought for on December 16 the Germans launched the Ardennes counter-offensive which was, for the time being, to wrest the initiative from the Allies.

(ii)

The German Counter-Offensive in the Ardennes

Displaying truly remarkable powers of recovery, the Germans had succeeded in halting the swift advance of the Allied Armies. The Allies were preparing for a resumption of this advance from the Roer and the Reichswald as soon as U.S. V Corps had captured the Roer dams and, to the south, U.S. Third Army was about to make a further attempt to capture the Saar. 21 Army Group was regrouping. U.S. 12 Army Group was everywhere committed along a front of some two hundred miles but in different sectors of its line varied greatly in respect of strength. Between Geilenkirchen and Monschau on a forty-mile sector there were sixteen U.S. divisions; south of the Ardennes on a sixty-mile sector facing the Saar there were ten; but between these two sectors on a ninety-mile front in the Ardennes there were but five. This was a quiet sector to which formations in need of rest were sent. In mid-December there were in the sector under U.S. VIII Corps of U.S. First Army, U.S. 106th Infantry Division, which had only recently arrived there, U.S. 4th and 28th Infantry Divisions, which had suffered severely in the

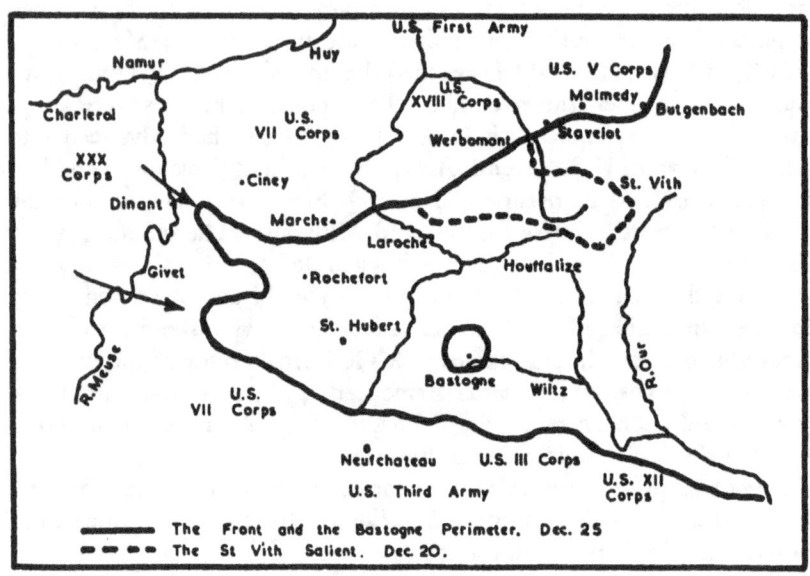

FIG. 54. The German Counter-Offensive in the Ardennes.

fighting in Hürtgen Forest, and U.S. 9th Armoured Division, which was comparatively inexperienced. There was not a single division in army group reserve. At Rheims was U.S. XVIII Airborne Corps with U.S. 82nd and 101st A.B. Divisions resting and refitting after the fighting between Nijmegen and Arnhem.

At 0530 hours on December 16 in darkness and fog the German guns laid down an exceptionally heavy barrage on U.S. VIII Corps' front between Monschau and Echternach and the battle of the Ardennes began.

It was learnt later that this desperate counter-offensive in great strength had for its aim a decisive victory in the west, an attempt to snatch victory from defeat. Three German armies had been gathered

ADVANCE TO MAAS AND ROER: ARDENNES

and equipped for this adventure. Sixth Panzer Army, which had lain concealed in the Eifel, the mountainous woodland on the German side of the Luxembourg border, was to advance on a narrow front of about fifteen miles on the axis Malmédy–Liége and strike north-west, crossing the Meuse between Liége and Huy, and drive for Antwerp. On its left Fifth Panzer Army on a front of about thirty miles was to advance on the axis Marche–Namur, cross the Meuse between Namur and Dinant and drive for Brussels. On the southern flank of the attack the German Seventh Army was to occupy and hold a line stretching from the Moselle across Luxembourg to Dinant. On the third or fourth day of the attack the German Fifteenth Army was to make a converging attack from the Roer sector towards Maastricht to assist Sixth Panzer Army's drive on Antwerp and, for the final phase, another attack was to be mounted from Utrecht across the Maas and directed on Antwerp.

But, at the time, these intentions were not known to S.H.A.E.F. and so during the earlier phases of the battle there was much uncertainty concerning both the magnitude of this German counter-offensive and its objectives.

U.S. 28th Division, strung out on a front of nearly thirty miles along the River Our, was quickly overwhelmed and the German armoured columns, crossing the river, drove west. In the Schnee Eifel two of the regiments of U.S. 106th Division were encircled and the way to the important road junction of St. Vith opened. South of Bütgenbach a cavalry group at the junction of U.S. V and VIII Corps was over-run. By the evening of December 17, Sixth Panzer Army was twenty miles inside Belgium, one powerful battle group having reached Stavelot.

But though the line was pierced certain critical sections were holding firm. U.S. 2nd and 99th Divisions were standing fast in the Monschau–Elsenborn sector despite the dropping of a German parachute battalion in their rear. A regiment of U.S. 1st Division, moving south by night, reached Bütgenbach and held it against attack. At St. Vith, U.S. 7th Armoured Division (U.S. Ninth Army), which had been rushed from the north of Aachen, succeeded in throwing a horseshoe-shaped defensive line around the town and had forced the advancing German columns to divide into two streams flowing north and south of the town. U.S. 30th Division, coming down from the Roer sector, struck against the flank of the northern stream and recaptured Stavelot. U.S. 82nd A.B. Division, moving swiftly from Rheims to the area of Werbomont, checked the German column moving west from Stavelot.

By the morning of December 18, the German 116th Panzer Division was approaching Houffalize, 2nd Panzer and Panzer Lehr Divisions, Bastogne. In Bastogne at this time there were only the corps troops of U.S. VIII Corps and remnants of U.S. 28th Division. But U.S. 10th

Armoured Division's Combat Command 'B' (U.S. Third Army) from Luxembourg and U.S. 101st A.B. Division from Rheims were racing for the town. The C.C. 'B' was the first to arrive and at once blocked the roads leading into Bastogne from the east and north-east. The airborne division arrived during the night.

On the 19th the Germans captured Wiltz and Houffalize and, leaving their infantry to complete the encirclement of Bastogne, their armour drove west.

General Bradley ordered U.S. Third Army to cancel its offensive against the Saar, planned to open on the 21st, and to move instead to the aid of U.S. First Army. General Eisenhower met his American commanders at Verdun and outlined his plans 'to plug the holes in the north and launch a co-ordinated counter-attack from the south'. But on his return to Versailles on the evening of the 19th he learnt that the situation had worsened. The northern and southern shoulders of the break-through were still holding firm but the position at St. Vith was obscure; German columns, having driven far beyond the town on either flank, were within fifteen miles of Liége and approaching Laroche, Marche and St. Hubert. Between Bastogne and Werbomont there was a gap of about twenty miles and through this German columns were driving towards the Namur–Dinant–Givet section of the Meuse, which was virtually undefended. It seemed likely that the Germans would reach the Meuse within the next twenty-four hours. Though U.S. divisions were moving from the Roer and the Saar sectors they could not reach the line for several days. An armoured division, then disembarking at Le Havre, and two airborne divisions in the United Kingdom could not be brought into action in time to affect the existing crisis. So General Eisenhower gave orders that U.S. engineer and supply units were to guard the Meuse bridges. Field Marshal Montgomery, on his own initiative, was already moving XXX Corps, which had been preparing for the Reichswald offensive, into the potential danger zone between the Meuse and Brussels. The four divisions of XXX Corps constituted the only reserve immediately available for placing athwart the path along which the advancing Germans were driving.

The German penetration had so split the American front that there was now no direct contact between the tactical H.Q. of U.S. 12 Army Group in the city of Luxembourg and H.Q. U.S. First Army now at Chaudfontaine, near Liége. General Eisenhower therefore, on December 20, placed Field Marshal Montgomery in command of all the Allied forces north of the break-through.

For this reason, and also because XXX Corps was to be involved, it is necessary to include an account of the 'Battle of the Bulge' in this volume. It was essentially an American affair, the outcome of which was primarily determined by the quality of the American soldiery.

ADVANCE TO MAAS AND ROER: ARDENNES

On December 20, a concentrated attack by several German divisions drove U.S. 7th Armoured Division and the remnants of two of the infantry divisions of U.S. VIII Corps that had been overrun at the outset of the offensive out of St. Vith.

On the 21st the Germans launched a series of fierce attacks against U.S. First Army's front. The first of these was on the Malmédy–Bütgenbach–Monschau sector and was maintained for forty-eight hours. The Germans gained no ground. The second crushed in the sides of the St. Vith salient and U.S. 7th Armoured Division was compelled to withdraw across the Salm to the line that was being built up by U.S. VII Corps. The third attack was against U.S. 82nd A.B. Division, which was likewise forced back from the Salm. The fourth attack took the German armour to within five miles of Dinant by the evening of the 23rd.

On December 19, General Eisenhower had ordered U.S. Seventh Army to sidestep to the north in order to release U.S. Third Army for its northward march against the southern flank of the 'bulge'. In beleaguered Bastogne, its north and south exits cut, U.S. 101st A.B. Division was entrenched, supported by two armoured combat commands of U.S. 10th Armoured Division. On December 23 the weather was good enough for supplies to be dropped from the air. That evening the Germans launched an attack which stove in the south-eastern corner of the perimeter and a number of tanks broke through into the town itself. These were destroyed, the supporting infantry flung back and the line restored. On Christmas morning the Germans attacked again, this time from the north and north-west, and again the perimeter was breached and again restored. On Boxing Day the Germans resumed their attack, but before it could develop a small relief column of U.S. Third Army drove through the encircling German line to penetrate the town. The bitterest phase of the battle followed its arrival and the Germans continued their assaults until January 5, by which time the Allies on the north flank of the bulge were counter-attacking and Bastogne was safe.

On December 19, as has been recalled, Field Marshal Montgomery cancelled the move of XXX Corps to Canadian First Army and ordered it to concentrate, with Guards Armoured, 43rd, 51st and 53rd Divisions under command, in the area Louvain–St. Trond.

It was echeloned behind the front and suitably placed to prevent the Germans crossing the river and to cover the routes leading from the south-east to Brussels and Antwerp and to cover Liége itself. It was to provide a stop-line for U.S. VII Corps of U.S. First Army.

It was west of Celles on Christmas Eve that 3rd R. Tks. of 29th Armd. Bde. made contact with a German battle group. The brigade had left Ypres on December 20 and on the following day took over the responsibility of guarding the bridges at Namur, Dinant and Givet. 23rd Hussars was sent to Givet on Christmas Day, moved across the Meuse and for four days lay in wait for an enemy who did not arrive.

On Christmas morning, when 3rd R.Tks. began to push forward from a small bridgehead at Dinant, they found their progress barred by a combat team, the spearhead of U.S. 2nd Armoured Division, which was striking from the north against Rochefort and Celles. For two days the battle raged west of Rochefort but by the evening of the 27th U.S. 2nd Armoured Division had finally brought to a complete standstill the German advance to the west. 6th Airborne Division joined XXX Corps on the Meuse on this day.

On January 3, U.S. VII and XVIII Corps of U.S. First Army counter-attacked from the north and XXX Corps conformed and attacked on the west flank until it was pinched out. This counter-attack was directed on Houffalize, the centre of the salient. On January 9, U.S. Third Army launched an attack on Houffalize from the south. On January 16 these two armies met and thereafter turned eastwards. At the beginning of February they were back in the positions held on December 16, up against the Siegfried Line.

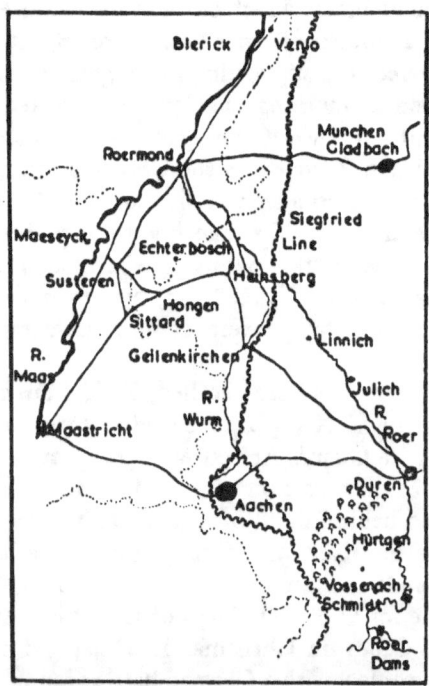

FIG. 55. The Roer Triangle.

(iii)

The Clearing of the Roer Triangle (Operation 'Blackcock')

As a preliminary to the operations designed to bring the Allied armies up to the line of the Rhine, Second Army undertook the task of clearing the area bounded by the Maas, the Roer and the Würm and of reaching the line of the Roer along a twelve-mile front (Operation 'Blackcock'). The attack was to be launched by 7th Armoured Division with 8th Armd. Bde. and a brigade of 52nd Division under command, up the Roermond road through Susteren. 43rd Division, acting in conjunction with the left-hand division of U.S. Ninth Army, operating on the east bank of the River Würm, would then move in support and clear the area. In support of the armoured and infantry divisions was an abundant variety of the A.F.Vs. of 79th Armoured Division and also the Canadian 1st Rocket Unit.

The terrain was of an exceptionally difficult nature. There were numerous water obstacles, of which the Saeffeler Beck, a twenty-foot wide stream with a steep far bank, was the worst. The whole of the area was mine-strewn and studded with hamlets that had been converted into strongpoints. In it there were three defensive belts running east and west and the middle one of these was part of the Siegfried Line.

On January 16, 4th/5th R.S.F. crossed the minefield, passed through the belt of wire and got across the Saeffeler Beck under cover of the bombardment provided by the Canadian rocket unit. 6th Cameronians followed and thrust along the road to Heinsberg. This town was taken by 7th/9th R.S. and 4th K.O.S.B., with the support of 8th Armd. Bde. and 'Crocodiles' of 79th Armoured Division, on January 24. 52nd Division was the first British formation to establish its headquarters on German soil, at Höngen. Meanwhile, 7th Armoured Division and 43rd Division, on the flanks of 52nd Division, had been moving forward and by January 26 the task of XII Corps had been completed, the Germans blowing the last bridge across the Roer as they retreated.

On February 4 U.S. First Army captured the first of the seven Roer dams and Canadian First Army's preparations for the postponed Reichswald attack were almost complete.

(iv)
Medical Cover

GUARDS ARMOURED DIVISION

This division was not involved in any major action following Operation 'Market Garden' until Operation 'Veritable' in February 1945. During early October it was in the Nijmegen area with a counter-attack rôle. 5th Gds. Armd. Bde. Gp. with 19 Lt. Fd. Amb. was north of the Waal u/c 43rd Division. 32nd Gds. Bde. u/c U.S. 82nd A.B. Division and with 128 Fd. Amb. was concentrated in a counter-attack rôle between the Maas–Waal Canal and the Maas. 128 Fd. Amb. was open in Hasselt. 8 F.D.S., south of Wijchen, was open for the reception of minor sick. Evacuation was by M.A.C. to 3 or 10 C.C.S. in Nijmegen.

On November 10, the division moved to Sittard to take over part of the line between Geilenkirchen and the Maas from a U.S. formation. 128 Fd. Amb. opened a forward A.D.S. in Sittard, sections of the unit being with the battalion groups. Sections of 19 Lt. Fd. Amb. were with 5th Gds. Bde. on the left flank. 8 F.D.S. and 60 Fd. Hyg. Sec. were at Lanklaar. Evacuation was to 3 F.D.S. at Nuth or 10 C.C.S. at Eysden.

On December 20, the division moved to the Louvain–Diest area to form part of a mobile reserve force. During the move all except divisional H.Q. and 32nd Gds. Bde. Gp. were diverted to the area St. Trond–Tirlemont and on the following day 32nd Gds. Bde. Gp. was in Tirlemont and 5th Gds. Armd. Bde. Gp. at St. Trond. 128 Fd. Amb. opened in Gossoncourt, 19 Lt. Fd. Amb. in Halle-Boyenhoven and 8 F.D.S. in Wommerson. The division was now under command of XXX Corps. Evacuation was to 101 B.G.H. Heverlee or 39 and 81 B.G.Hs. at Hasselt.

7TH ARMOURED DIVISION

In early October this division was in the Veghel area holding the line defending the main road running north to Nijmegen. The division remained in this area until the beginning of the attack which cleared the Germans out of Western Holland, south of the Maas. For this 7th Armoured Division was directed on Loon-op-Zand, north of Tilburg. Thereafter the division held the river and canal line from Geertruidenberg to 's Hertogenbosch. When in November, Canadian First Army took over this sector 7th Armoured Division moved to the Bree–Kinroy area to protect the right flank of XII Corps. On December 7, the division moved to Sittard where it remained until the end of the year.

131 Fd. Amb. was in Veghel and 2 Lt. Fd. Amb. in Uden until the 's Hertogenbosch operation when 2 Lt. Fd. Amb. moved to Udenhout.

ADVANCE TO MAAS AND ROER: ARDENNES

When the division moved to the Bree area both the field ambulances and 29 F.D.S. were in the town itself for suitable accommodation for them elsewhere in the area could not be found. The field ambulances had sub-units forward with the brigades. When the division moved to the Sittard area the same difficulty was encountered but eventually 131 Fd. Amb. moved to a site near Geleen and 29 F.D.S. to Lanklaar.

The first operation in the New Year in which the division took part was the clearing of the Meuse–Roer–Würm triangle when it attacked the village of Dieteren. For a period of forty-eight hours evacuation was rendered difficult because no vehicles could be used. A detachment of 131 Fd. Amb. was sent forward, practically into the front line, there to hold casualties under shell, mortar and small-arms fire. The farmhouse in which this detachment was functioning was ultimately burnt out. The remainder of the field ambulance company followed the detachment twelve hours later and set up an A.D.S. in Dieteren. 'Kangaroos' were then used for evacuation until the main Roermond–Sittard road was opened.

This operation being completed, 7th Armoured Division, under command U.S. Ninth Army, held the line Roermond–Vlodrop until the middle of February when it was withdrawn to the Weert–Heeze area to rest and refit.

6TH AIRBORNE DIVISION

This division which had returned to the United Kingdom after the break-out from the Normandy beachhead and the crossing of the Seine, was recalled to the Continent in December when the German counter-offensive was at its height. Leaving Tilbury for Ostend, the division moved across Belgium to Mettet, west of the Meuse, there to link up with 29th Armoured Brigade, holding a long stretch of the river line. When the Germans withdrew the division moved forward first to Celles and thence to relieve 15th Division on the Maas in the vicinity of Venlo on the Dutch-German frontier. There the division functioned as an infantry division until February 25 when once more it returned to the United Kingdom.

Concerning its medical units during this period there is nothing of great interest to record for the division was not involved in any major action.

15TH DIVISION

By October 4 this division was concentrated in the area Gemert–Helmond–Bakel, 22 F.D.S. being open in Helmond for the reception of the divisional sick. On October 17 the division passed u/c XII Corps and prepared for an operation having for its object the capture of Tilburg.

The division moved to the Best–St. Oedenrode area and 227th Bde. relieved 51st Division which was to take part in the operation on the right of 15th Division. As 51st Division had A.D.Ss. already open in this area only 153 Fd. Amb. opened a C.C.P. in the initial stage of the battle.

The Germans withdrew from their positions in the Best area and so the operation developed into a rapid advance along the axis Best–Oirschot. 194 Fd. Amb. was moved to Best and there opened an A.D.S. on October 25. Field ambulance companies moved in support of the brigades. 22 F.D.S. had been divided into three resuscitation units, one moving with each field ambulance.

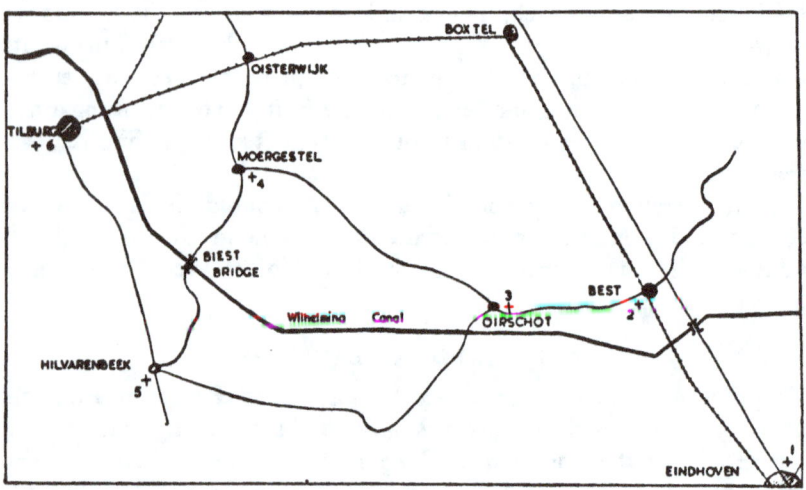

FIG. 56. 15th Division. The Attack on Tilburg. Medical Cover.

1. 1st A.D.S. 153 Fd. Amb.
2. 2nd A.D.S. 194 Fd. Amb.
3. 3rd A.D.S. 193 Fd. Amb., 23 F.D.S. after 2nd Phase
4. 4th A.D.S. 153 Fd. Amb., later relieved by 193 Fd. Amb.
5. 5th A.D.S. 194 Fd. Amb.
6. 6th A.D.S. 153 Fd. Amb.

By the afternoon of the 25th, 193 Fd. Amb. had opened an A.D.S. in Oirschot. As the leading brigade had now cleared Moergestel and was approaching Oisterwijk, 153 Fd. Amb. moved up to Moergestel and opened an A.D.S. there on the 26th. 44th Bde. was approaching the Wilhelmina Canal at Biest and 194 Fd. Amb. opened its A.D.S. at Hilvarenbeek on the 27th.

As it was intended that 227th Bde. should be in the lead after Tilburg had been taken, 193 Fd. Amb. relieved 153 Fd. Amb. in Moergestel and the latter, on wheels, moved to the rear of this brigade and, on the 28th, entered Tilburg. 23 F.D.S. was moved to Oirschot. The wounded in this operation numbered 114.

ADVANCE TO MAAS AND ROER: ARDENNES

In this operation it was always possible to have one A.D.S. close to the C.C.Ps. and to have another ready to leap-frog or to move to a lateral axis. Six successive A.D.S. locations were occupied without any interruption of the flow of casualties, two A.D.Ss. being open in echelon at one and the same time while the third was moving. In the control of such movements the wireless intercommunication proved to be most valuable.

The division then moved to the area south-east of Helmond where

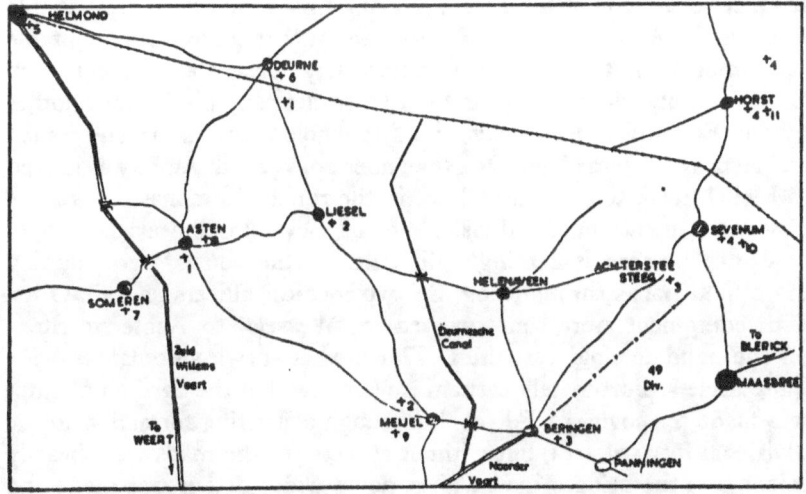

FIG. 57. 15th Division. The Crossing of the Deurne Canal. Medical Cover.

1. C.C.Ps. 1st Phase
2. C.C.Ps. 2nd Phase
3. C.C.Ps. 3rd Phase
4. C.C.Ps. 4th Phase
5. 22 and 23 F.D.Ss.
6. A.D.S. 194 Fd. Amb. 1st Phase
7. A.D.S. 153 Fd. Amb. 1st and 2nd Phases
8. A.D.S. 193 Fd. Amb. 2nd Phase
9. A.D.S. 194 Fd. Amb. 3rd Phase
10. A.D.S. 153 Fd. Amb. 4th Phase
11. A.D.S. 153 Fd. Amb. Final Position

U.S. 7th Armoured Division was hard pressed. On October 30, 15th Division took over from U.S. 7th Armoured Division. 194 Fd. Amb. opened an A.D.S. at Deurne and 153 Fd. Amb. at Someren, 193 being kept in reserve. 22 F.D.S. opened in Helmond for minor sick and 23 F.D.S. remained at Oirschot to deal with the sick admitted during the Tilburg operation. Field ambulance companies were with the brigades. The German attacks were held and divisional casualties on this day totalled 167.

Then the division attacked, and during the following days the Germans were driven out of Liesel, into which village a company of 194

Fd. Amb. moved on November 2. On the 4th, 193 Fd. Amb. opened an A.D.S. in Asten. 23 F.D.S. opened in Helmond and took over the treatment of minor sick from 22 F.D.S.

The division, attacking the German positions at Meijel encountered such stern resistance that the attack was abandoned. By November 15, however, the attack was resumed and the area west of the Deurne Canal, including Meijel, cleared.

By November 17 a bridgehead over the Deurne Canal east of Meijel and south-east of Liesel had been established and the division began its advance to the line of the Maas. During this period it was impossible to move the A.D.Ss. forward for the reason that there was no suitable accommodation, the area being completely devastated. A company C.C.P. was opened in Meijel on the 18th to clear 227th Bde. and another by 193 Fd. Amb. in Helenaveen. The whole area was heavily mined and so progress was slow. On November 20, 194 Fd. Amb. was moved to Meijel, there to open an A.D.S. in the ruins of a monastery. As the forward elements of the division neared Sevenum the evacuation of casualties became increasingly difficult for the routes were nothing more than tracks through bog. So two medical officers and six O.Rs. with equipment were sent forward in 'Weasels' to Achterste Steeg on the 22nd to hold casualties. The 2-wheel-drive ambulances were quite useless. Fortunately casualties were few. On the 23rd an attempt was made to move 153 Fd. Amb. through a flanking formation to the divisional forward area, but without success for the roads were heavily mined and the bridges down. Next day a wider detour was made and 153 Fd. Amb. managed to reach Sevenum and opened an A.D.S. there. The pace of the advance now quickened and, on the 25th, 153 Fd. Amb. was moved to Horst, there to join a C.C.P. that had been established by 193 Fd. Amb. The line of the Maas was reached by the division on November 28 and 15th Division then proceeded to take over from 49th Division on its right.

The divisional front on the Maas extended from Grubbenvorst to the German perimeter round Blerick and thence southward along the river to the junction with the Derivation Canal. Two brigades were in the line and 227th Bde. in reserve. The A.D.S. of 193 Fd. Amb. was opened in Sevenum, that of 194 in Maasbree and that of 153 in Meijel.

On December 3, 44th Bde. attacked the strongly fortified defences of Blerick. Pathways through the extensive minefield were beaten by Flail tanks, the anti-tank ditch was bridged by bridging tanks and the infantry went forward in 'Kangaroos' (armoured troop-carrying tanks).

R.M.Os. followed their battalions in 'Kangaroos', setting up their R.A.Ps. in cellars and the like. Casualties were evacuated in returning 'Kangaroos' to the C.C.Ps. where they were transferred to ambulance cars. To deal with casualties occurring during the advance from the

ADVANCE TO MAAS AND ROER: ARDENNES

start-line the following arrangements were made. There were six lanes through the minefield and across the anti-tank ditch. 'Gap Control' had posts, in tanks, at the entrances and exits of these lanes and all of these were in contact with brigade H.Q. on the Gap Control wireless net. The forward C.C.P. was linked up with this net and was informed of the whereabouts of any wounded. A 'Kangaroo' was then sent forward from the C.C.P. to collect these. The C.C.P. was also on the medical net and so could get into touch with the A.D.S. The casualties evacuated during this action up to 1500 hours on December 3 totalled 57.

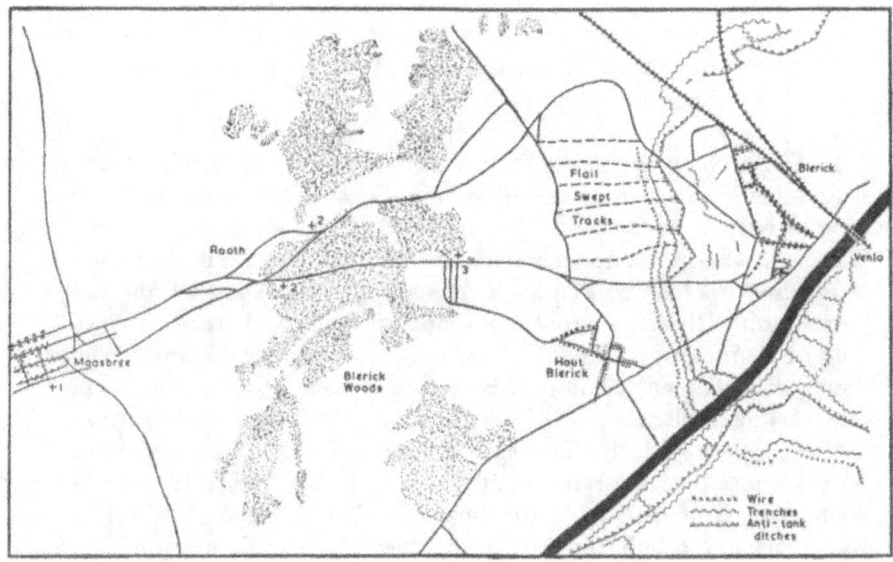

FIG. 58. 15th Division. The Attack on Blerick. Medical Cover.

1. A.D.S. 194 Fd. Amb.
2. C.C.Ps.
3. Gap Control R.A.P. (with wireless on Medical Net)

This was the first time 'Kangaroo' tanks had been used for casualty evacuation in this division. Before the stretchers could be loaded into these vehicles it was found necessary to saw off the handles, and this meant that the stretchers had to be changed at the C.C.P.

Following the capture of Blerick this sector of the line became comparatively quiet. But as the roads leading to Blerick were under direct observation, half-track armoured personnel carriers had to be used for evacuation purposes.

The division, under command of VIII Corps, continued to hold the line of the Maas until January 25 when it passed to XXX Corps in

Canadian First Army for Operation 'Veritable', the breaching of the Siegfried Line.

49TH (WEST RIDING) DIVISION

The operational activities of the division were as follows:

1. October 1–November 9. u/c I Corps in Canadian First Army operating in the Turnhout–Roosendaal–Maas area.
2. November 9–November 30. u/c XII Corps in Second Army operating in the Venlo sector about Nederweert, Maasbree and Sevenum towards Blerick and the River Maas.
3. December 1–31. u/c Canadian II Corps in Canadian First Army operating in the Nijmegen salient and holding a bridgehead on an 'island' north of the Waal.

1. The division was located south and south-west of Turnhout with a strong bridgehead over the Turnhout Canal. This bridgehead was progressively extended until by October 18 it reached the line Poppel–Baarle-Nassau–Dépôt de Mendicité–St. Léonard. A sector in the middle of this line was held by Polish 1st Armoured Division and a composite force of 49th Division—'Bobforce'—held the extreme left.

187 Fd. Amb. opened two A.D.Ss., one of them at Ryckevorsel consisting of a company reinforced by a section from 160 Fd. Amb. The other field ambulances opened C.C.Ps., but otherwise were in reserve.

On October 18, the division began to regroup for Operation 'Rebound' —an advance over the canal at St. Léonard led by 56th Bde. 187 Fd. Amb. opened an A.D.S. at Westmalle leaving the second A.D.S. at Ryckevorsel. 146 and 160 Fd. Ambs. were with their brigades, less sections left in support of Cdn. 2nd Armd. Bde. (u/c 49th Division) and 'Bobforce'. The fighting was confused until Roosendaal fell and the evacuation of casualties difficult over very bad tracks. Many C.C.Ps. were established and some of them functioned as car posts too. Casualties were passed from C.C.P. to C.C.P. Several A.D.Ss. were opened, but only one at a time.

From November 1–7 the division was involved in Operation 'Humid' —the clearing of the area north of Roosendaal to the Maas. 187 Fd. Amb. opened an A.D.S. in the civil hospital in Roosendaal and this dealt with all the divisional casualties during this operation. I Corps lent three jeeps from the M.A.C. to assist in the very difficult evacuation in marshy country.

2. Between November 8–16 the division moved to XII Corps area and concentrated round Hamont, Budel and Lille St. Hubert. 16 and 17 F.D.Ss. dealt with the local sick; the other units remained closed.

ADVANCE TO MAAS AND ROER: ARDENNES

On November 19, 49th Division moved up between 51st Division on the right and 15th Division on the left for the advance towards Blerick and the Maas, and 146 Fd. Amb. opened an A.D.S. at De Heibloem to support 146th Inf. Bde. On November 21, 14 Lt. Fd. Amb. (4th Armd. Bde.) opened an A.D.S. at Everlo (north-east of Panningen). 56th Bde. moved up on the left of 146th Bde. on November 22 and, on the 23rd, 147th Bde. passed through 56th Bde. On the 26th, 146 Fd. Amb. moved from De Heibloem to Everlo to take over from 14 Lt. Fd. Amb. as 4th Armd. Bde. was leaving XII Corps. The other field ambulances remained closed in Weert as there was no accommodation for them further forward. As the advance continued 146 Fd. Amb. moved forward to open an A.D.S. at Maasbree on November 27 and 187 Fd. Amb. was brought forward to establish an A.D.S. at Sevenum. XII Corps attached a F.S.U. and a F.T.U. to 187 Fd. Amb. in preparation for the final attack on Blerick but in this attack 49th Division was not involved.

3. On November 29/30, the division moved into the Nijmegen salient to pass u/c Canadian II Corps and took over from 50th Division. 160 Fd. Amb. opened an A.D.S. at Oosterhout and the field ambulances sent C.C.Ps. forward with their brigades. On December 8, 16 F.D.S. opened for light sick in the orthopaedic hospital in Nijmegen where 187 Fd. Amb. (closed) was also accommodated. 17 F.D.S. was in Bergharen with 146 Fd. Amb. nearby in farm buildings. During this period operational activity was confined to patrolling.

TABLE 36

49th Division. Admissions to Medical Units. October–December 1944

	49th Div.	Other	P.o.W.	Civilian	Totals
Battle Casualties	1,237	268	160	180	1,845
Sick	2,109	419	—	72	2,600
Exhaustion	176	23	—	—	199
	3,522	710	160	252	4,644

Wounds by Causal Missile (a series of 1,545):

	Actual Numbers	Percentages
S.W.	939	61
G.S.W.	342	22
Others	264	17

Wounds by Anatomical Region (a series of 1,525):

	Actual Numbers	Percentages
Multiple	193	12·6
Head and Face	218	14·3
Neck	33	2·2
Chest	126	8·3
Abdomen	49	3·2
Upper Limb	315	20·6
Lower Limb	504	33·1
Buttocks	36	2·4
Back	51	3·3

Severity of Wound (a series of 1,528):

	Actual Numbers	Percentages
Slight	725	47·4
Severe	588	38·5
Dangerous	215	14·1

Deaths: 41, of which 23 were dead on admission.
Exhaustion: Ratio of Exhaustion Cases to Battle Casualties 11 : 7.

Diseases: Equivalent Annual Rates per 1,000:

	Oct.	Nov.	Dec.
Average Strength	17,075	17,538	17,947
Digestive	43·2	44·1	42·9
Respiratory	78·6	88·2	91·8
Skin	43·2	38·5	24·4
I.A.T.	78·6	70·2	45·3
Exhaustion	72·4	31·4	20·9
Others	126·5	123·2	100·5

Venereal Disease: Average Weekly Numbers and Weekly Rate per 1,000 Strength:

	Cases	Rates
Oct. 7	4	0·23
14	6	0·11
21	7	0·11
28	5	0·23
Nov. 4	2	0·11
11	6	0·34
18	6	0·34
25	17	0·97
Dec. 2	7	0·40
9	6	0·34
16	14	0·77
23	8	0·44
30	5	0·27

ADVANCE TO MAAS AND ROER: ARDENNES

51ST (HIGHLAND) DIVISION

In the early days of October the division, less 154th Bde., moved into Holland and took over a sector of the line from St. Oedenrode to Best from 15th Division and took part, u/c XII Corps, in a series of operations

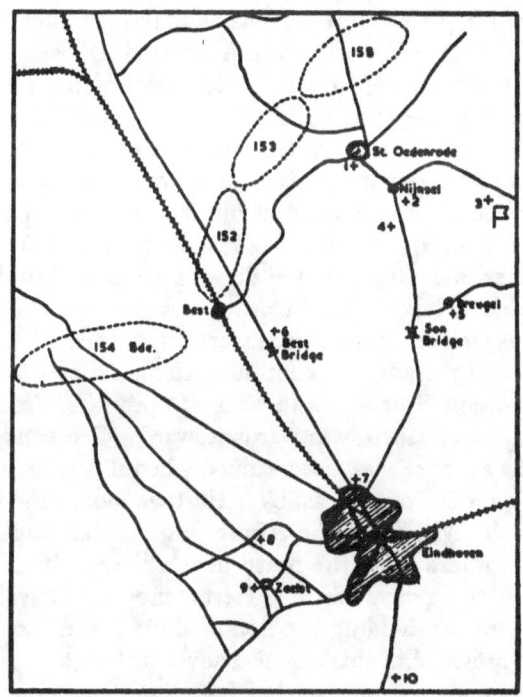

FIG. 59. 51st Division. Eindhoven Airfield. Medical Cover. October 2–23.

1. C.C.P. 174 Fd. Amb.
2. A.D.S. 175 Fd. Amb. (closed)
3. A.D.M.S.
4. A.D.S. 202 Fd. Amb.
5. 5 F.D.S.
6. C.C.P. 175 Fd. Amb.
7. A.D.S. 174 Fd. Amb.
   6 F.D.S.
   A.D.S. 176 Fd. Amb. (closed)
8. C.C.P. 176 Fd. Amb.
9. 23 C.C.S.
10. 79 B.G.H.

to the north of Eindhoven, to the north-east of Weert towards Venlo and, finally, in the Nijmegen area. Then on Christmas Day it moved back into Belgium to the east bank of the Meuse a few kilometres from Liége.

When it took over from 15th Division, 158th Inf. Bde. of 53rd Division with 202 Fd. Amb. was in the line and came u/c 51st Division. On October 9, 154th Bde., having been relieved at Dunkirk, rejoined the division and was assigned the task of safeguarding the Eindhoven airfield until 158th Bde. returned to its own division, when 154th Bde. took over the eastern sector of the divisional front. The medical cover provided at this time is depicted in Fig. 59.

The division took part in Operation 'Colin' to establish bridgeheads over the Dommel and Halsche Water and to clear the area in order to open up a route for 7th Armoured Division to pass through and advance on Tilburg. 53rd Division with 7th Armoured Division opened the attack on October 22, advancing on 's Hertogenbosch on the axis Oss–'s Hertogenbosch while 15th Division, which had taken over the line St. Oedenrode–Best from 51st Division, attacked towards Tilburg. 51st Division's attack opened at 2300 hours on October 23 and all the objectives were reached without difficulty and with comparatively few casualties. The medical cover provided is shown in Fig. 60.

On October 24 and thereafter the division continued to advance and captured Schijndel, Boxtel and St. Michielsgestel and the intervening countryside was cleared. Bridgeheads were established over the Halsche Water at Hals and the advance continued along the axis Vught–Udenhout–Loon-op-Zand–Sprang–south bank of the Maas. From Loon-op-Zand one brigade pushed westwards towards Geertruidenberg. By October 30, the advance was discontinued when it was found that, save in the 'island' bounded on the east by 's Hertogenbosch and in the north and south by the Maas and the Afwaterings Canal respectively, the Germans had withdrawn to the north of the river. The division then concentrated in the general area 's Hertogenbosch–Helvoirt with the Derbyshire Yeomanry holding the line of the Afwaterings Canal. The medical cover provided at this time is shown in Fig. 61.

On November 4, planning started for Operation 'Guy Fawkes' to clear the whole of Afwaterings 'island,' which entailed an assault crossing of the Afwaterings Canal from the south by 153rd and 152nd Bdes. and an entry into the 'island' from the east to capture Engelen and Fort Crèvecœur by 154th Bde. The assault opened at 1600 hours on November 4 and from the onset was a great success, the Germans being taken completely by surprise. The attack was covered by the guns of the tanks of 33rd Armd. Bde. which were moved up behind the high banks of the canal. At H-hour the tanks mounted the banks and deluged the German positions with high explosive while the infantry crossed the canal in assault craft. Divisional casualties in the action passing through the A.D.Ss. were 1 officer and 56 O.Rs.

This was the first occasion when casualties in the division had to be evacuated across a water obstacle before this was bridged. The medical arrangements worked smoothly and well. Car posts were sited near the bridging points on the south side of the canal and C.C.Ps. moved across with the assault troops and established themselves on the far bank.

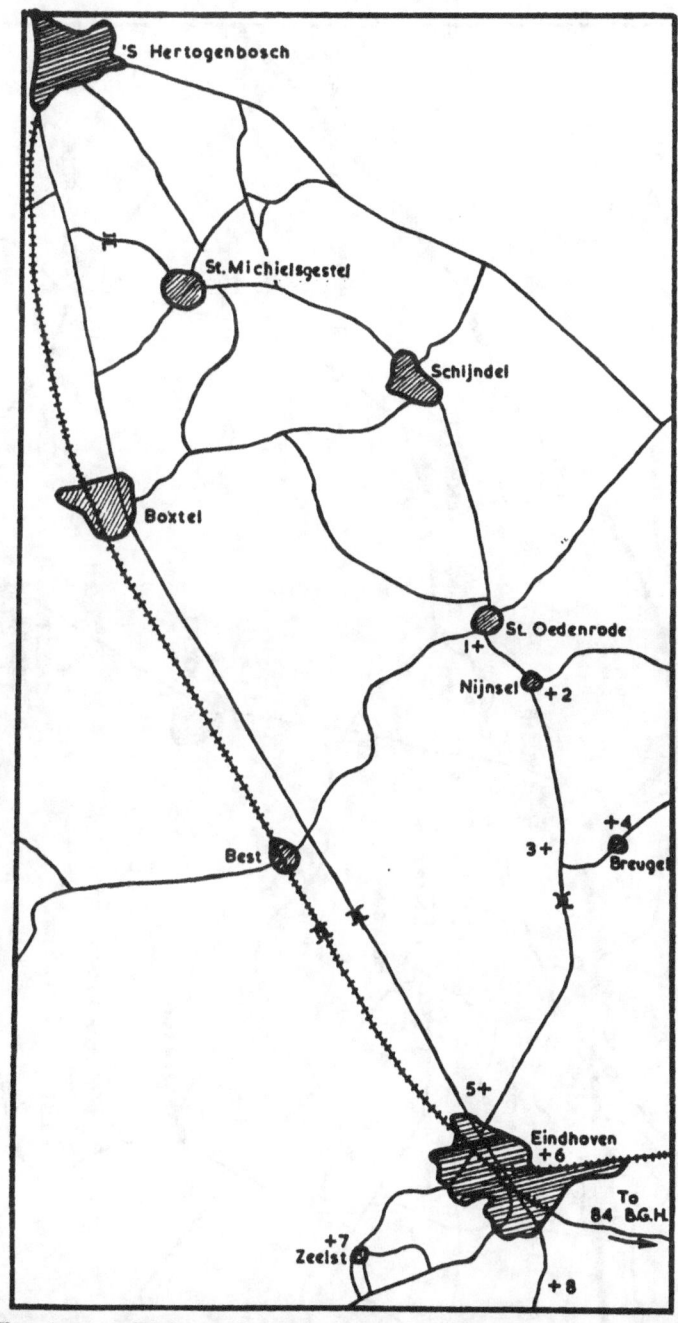

Fig. 60. 51st Division. Operation 'Colin'. Medical Cover. 1st Phase.

1. A.D.S. 175 Fd. Amb.
2. 176 Fd. Amb. (closed)
3. M.A.C. Control Post
4. 5 F.D.S.
5. A.D.S. 174 Fd. Amb., 6 F.D.S.
6. A.D.S. 22 Lt. Fd. Amb.
7. 23 C.C.S.
8. 79 B.G.H.

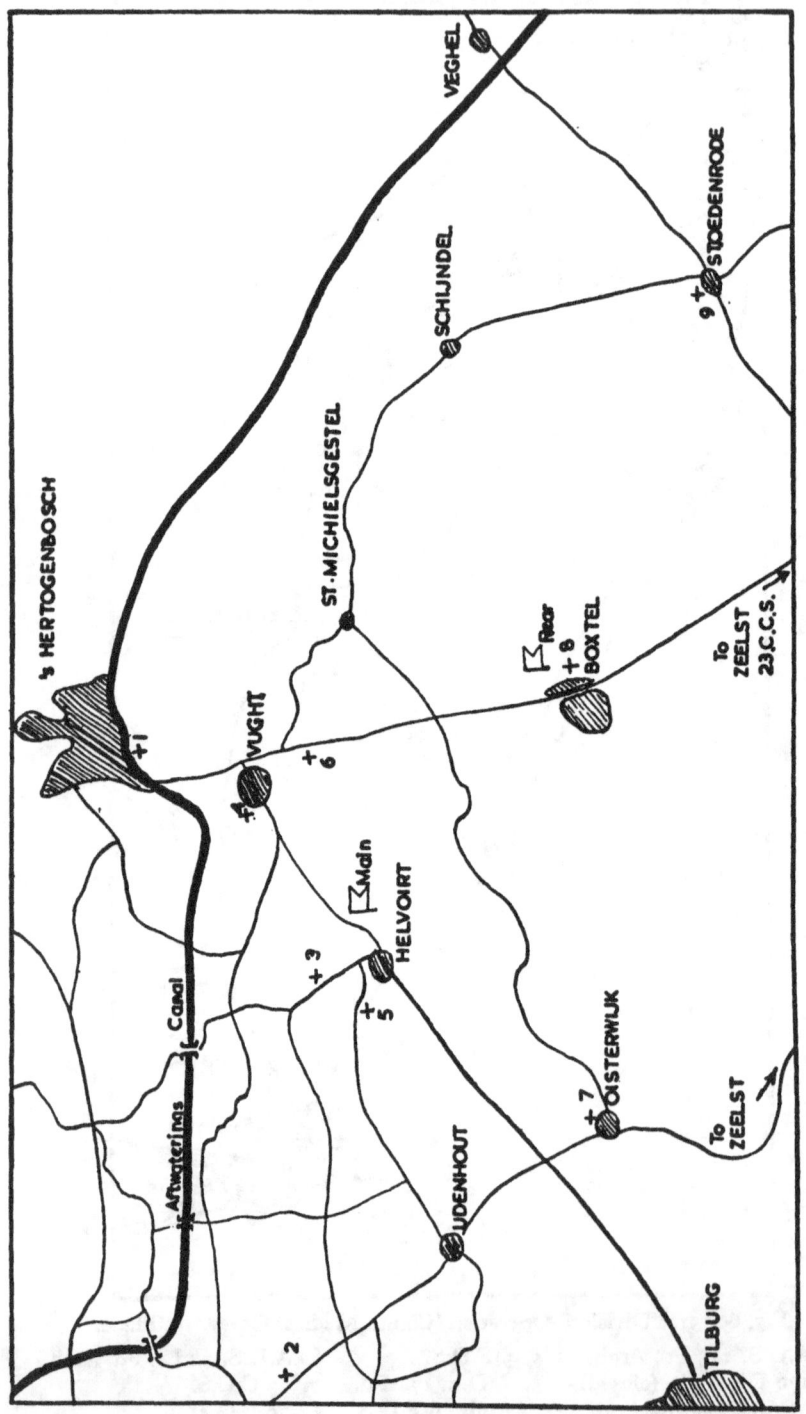

FIG. 61. 51st Division. Operation 'Colin'. Medical Cover. Later Phase.

1. C.C.P. 176 Fd. Amb. 2. C.C.P. 175 Fd. Amb. 3. C.C.P. 174 Fd. Amb. 4. 5 F.D.S. 5. 175 Fd. Amb. 6. A.D.S. 176 Fd. Amb. 7. A.D.S. 174 Fd. Amb. 8. Adv. Surg. Centre 9. 6 F.D.S.

ADVANCE TO MAAS AND ROER: ARDENNES

Casualties were sent across the canal in returning assault craft until bridges became available.

On November 7, the division handed the 'island' over to 7th Armoured Division and moved to the south-east of Eindhoven to take up positions on the Noorder Canal and the Wessem Canal. There was a great lack of accommodation for the medical units and initially the divisional battle casualties and sick were evacuated from the C.C.Ps. to the A.D.S. of 153 Fd. Amb. of 15th Division.

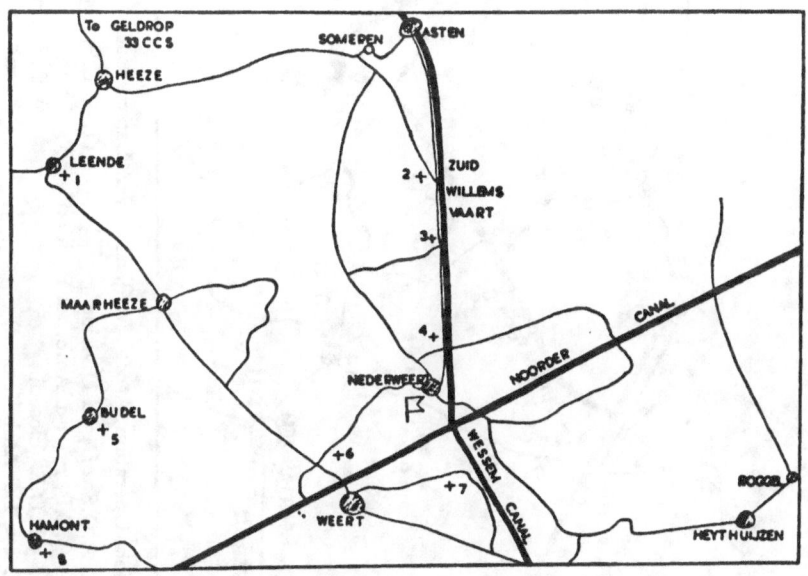

FIG. 62. 51st Division. Operation 'Ascot'. Medical Cover. Early Phase.

1. 6. F.D.S.
2. A.D.S. 175 Fd. Amb.
3. C.C.P. 176 Fd. Amb.
4. C.C.P. 175 Fd. Amb.
5. 4 F.D.S. (XII Corps)
6. A.D.S. 174 Fd. Amb.
7. C.C.P. 174 Fd. Amb.
8. 24 C.C.S.

On November 14 the division took part in Operation 'Ascot'—an assault crossing of the Noorder Canal east of Nederweert by 152nd Bde. and of the Wessem Canal by 153rd Bde. followed by the clearing of the 'island' at the junction of these canals by a battalion of 154th Bde. Evacuation was somewhat complicated for these canals ran at right angles to one another and their point of junction was in German hands and dominated the approaches from the north and from Weert to the south-west. It was necessary therefore in the early stages of the operation to evacuate casualties from 152nd Bde. northwards to 33 C.C.S. (VIII Corps) at Geldrop and those from 153rd and 154th Bdes. to 24 C.C.S.

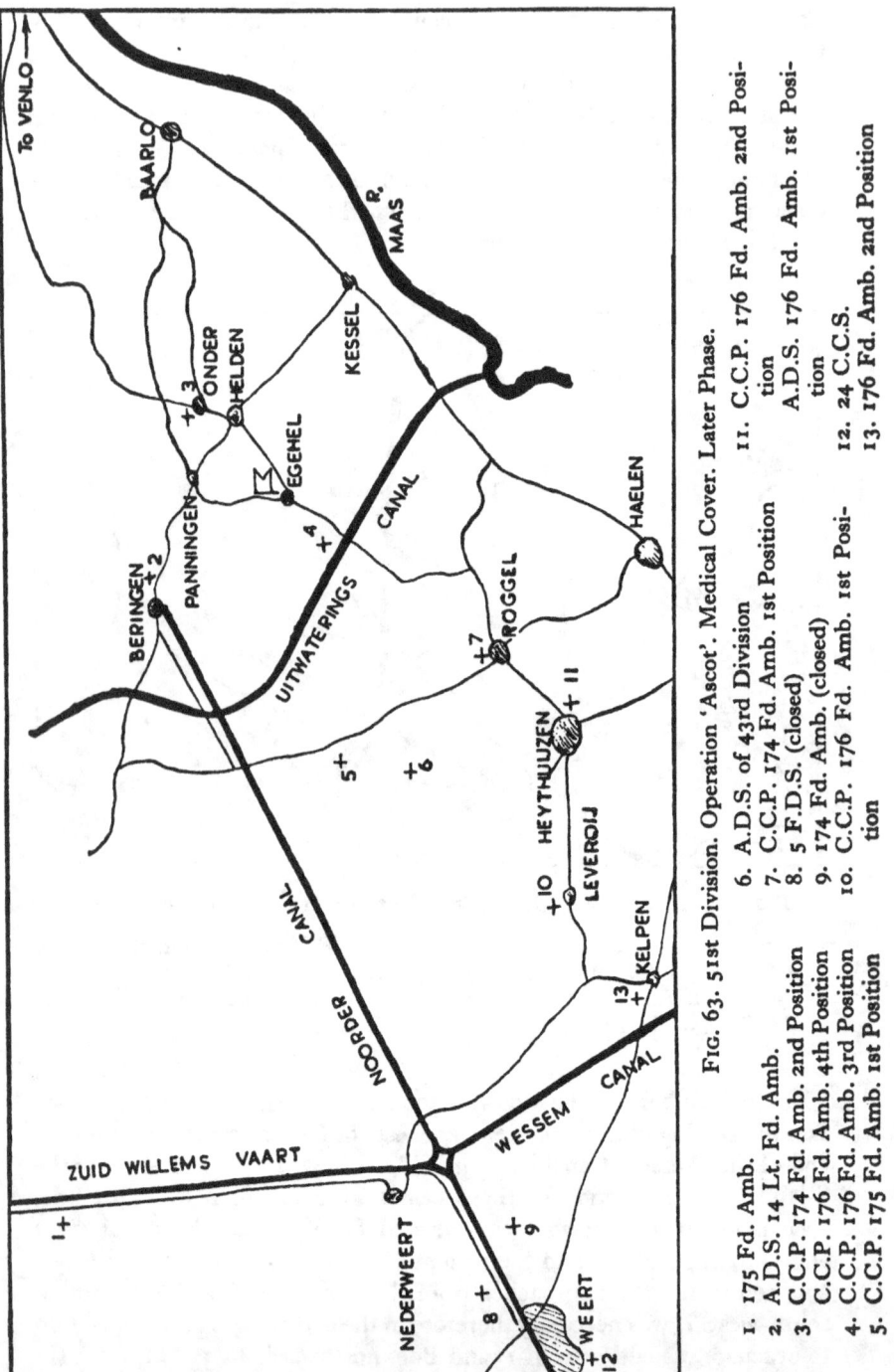

FIG. 63. 51st Division. Operation 'Ascot'. Medical Cover. Later Phase.

1. 175 Fd. Amb.
2. A.D.S. 14 Lt. Fd. Amb.
3. C.C.P. 174 Fd. Amb. 2nd Position
4. C.C.P. 176 Fd. Amb. 4th Position
5. C.C.P. 175 Fd. Amb. 1st Position
6. A.D.S. of 43rd Division
7. C.C.P. 174 Fd. Amb. 1st Position
8. 5 F.D.S. (closed)
9. 174 Fd. Amb. (closed)
10. C.C.P. 176 Fd. Amb. 1st Position
11. C.C.P. 176 Fd. Amb. 2nd Position
12. 24 C.C.S.
13. 176 Fd. Amb. 2nd Position

ADVANCE TO MAAS AND ROER: ARDENNES

(XII Corps) at Hamont. By dawn on November 15, however, it had become possible to evacuate all casualties to 24 C.C.S. for secure and deep bridgeheads had by then been established. The operation proceeded satisfactorily. Leveroij, Heythuyzen and Roggel were quickly occupied and the area west of the Meijel–Roggel road cleared. 152nd and then 153rd Bde. crossed the Uitwaterings Canal and moved to the line Beringen–Panningen–Helden and 154th Bde., passing through, continued to advance towards Onder, Baarlo and the River Maas. The medical cover provided during the later stages of the operation is shown in Fig. 63.

49th Division now took over this sector from 51st Division, which began to move to the Nijmegen sector on November 24 there to take over

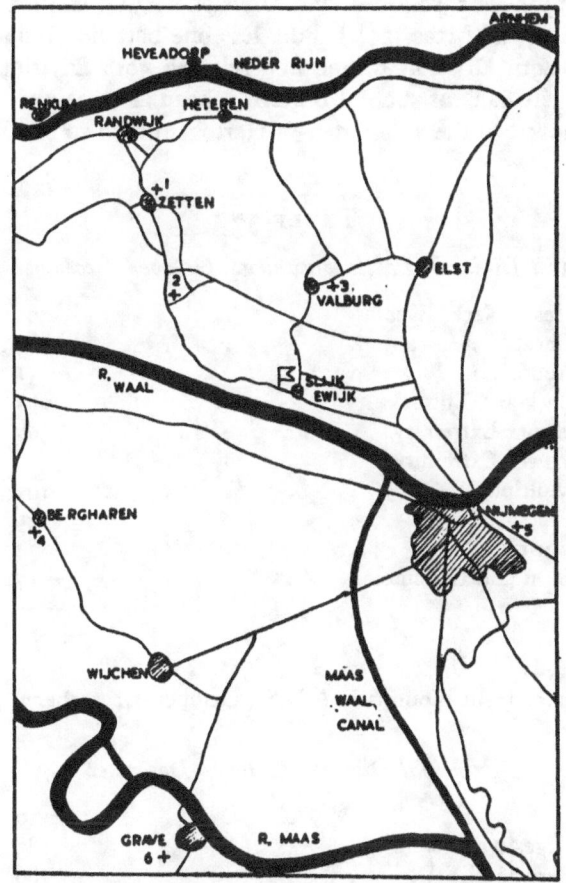

FIG. 64. 51st Division. Nijmegen 'Island'. Medical Cover.

1. C.C.P. 174 Fd. Amb.
2. C.C.P. 176 Fd. Amb.
3. C.C.P. 175 Fd. Amb.
4. A.D.S. 174 Fd. Amb.
5. A.D.S. 175 Fd. Amb.
6. 3 (Cdn.) C.C.S.

from U.S. 101st Airborne Division and to come u/c Canadian II Corps. By the 27th Main Divisional H.Q., three brigades and one field regiment were on Nijmegen 'island' and the rest of the division south of the Waal. Because of the lack of suitable accommodation no A.D.S. was opened on the 'island.' C.C.Ps. remained under command of the brigades. 175 Fd. Amb. opened an A.D.S. in Nijmegen for battle casualties and 174 Fd. Amb. an A.D.S. in Bergharen for the divisional sick. Evacuation was to 3 (Cdn.) C.C.S. in Grave. The medical cover provided is depicted in Fig. 64. (Plate XX shows casualties being evacuated across the River Waal by ferry.)

On the night of December 2/3 the Germans breached the dykes on the south side of the Neder Rijn east of Arnhem and the 'island' was inundated. 152nd, 153rd Bdes. and Divisional H.Q. in turn withdrew to the south of the Maas, 154th Bde. less one battalion remaining and passing u/c 49th Division, which had relieved 50th Division and was holding the left flank of such of the bridgehead as remained. The division then moved to the area Uden–'s Hertogenbosch to rest.

TABLE 37

51st Division. Battle Casualties. October–December

Head, Neck, Face	265
Chest	85
Abdomen	51
Back and Buttocks	264
Upper Extremity	307
Lower Extremity	332
Multiple	193
Fractures	99
Burns	34
Blast and Concussion	57
	1,687

Deaths from Wounds in A.D.Ss. October–December = 9

Principal Diseases. October–December

Exhaustion	110
Digestive System	183
Pyrexia N.Y.D.	86
I.A.T.	134
Skin	90
Respiratory	153
Neurological	10

ADVANCE TO MAAS AND ROER: ARDENNES

Infectious Diseases. October–December

Gonorrhoea	37
Syphilis	1
Urethritis N.Y.D.	84
Balanitis	8
Penile Wart	25
V.D. N.Y.D.	7
Pediculosis corporis	11
Pediculosis pubis	11
Influenza	8
Infective Jaundice	10
Scabies	66
Malaria (fresh)	6
Malaria (relapse)	153

53RD DIVISION

At the beginning of October this division, u/c XII Corps and less 158th Bde. Gp. and 202 Fd. Amb. which were with 51st Division in the

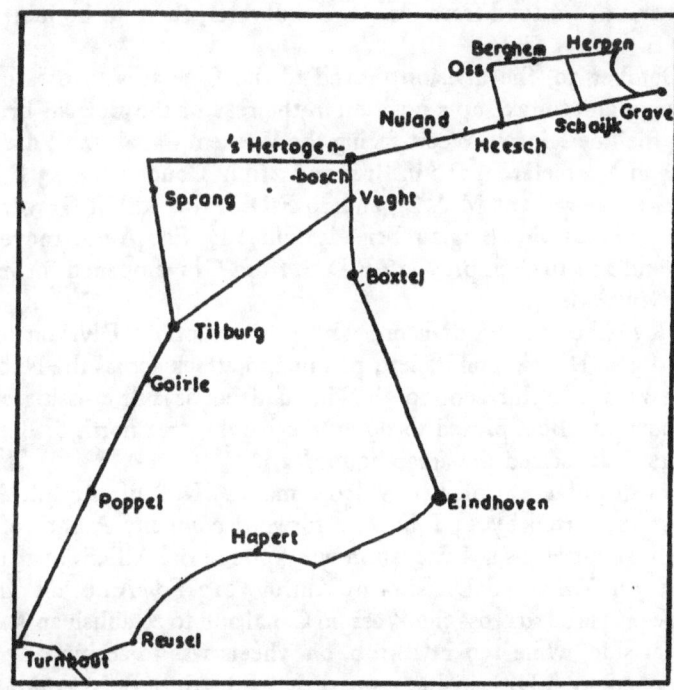

FIG. 65. 53rd Division. Operation 'Alan'. Medical Cover.

Schijndel area, the A.D.S. of the field ambulance being in St. Oedenrode, was holding a line covering the L. of C. south of Eindhoven. 147 Fd. Amb. had its A.D.S. in Oerle, 212 Fd. Amb. in Postel. There were C.C.Ps. in Hapert, Reusel and Voorheide. 13 F.D.S. was in Bergeyk and 26 F.D.S. in Steensel, the former functioning as an A.D.S. covering the centre of the divisional front, the latter admitting minor sick.

On October 7 the division passed to XXX Corps and moved into the Nijmegen 'island'. 147 Fd. Amb. moved to Nijmegen, 212 Fd. Amb. and 13 F.D.S. to Huis Oosterhout (north-west of Nijmegen), 26 F.D.S. to Grave and 'C' Pln. 302 M.A.C. to Nijmegen. On the 9th the division returned to XII Corps and on the 17th, being relieved by 50th Division, moved to Schaijk. 202 Fd. Amb. moved to Schaijk, 212 to Oss and 13 F.D.S. to Berghem. On the 19th the division moved again to an area south of the Maas and 147 Fd. Amb. moved to Herpen.

On October 22, the division became involved in Operation 'Alan'—XII Corps' attack on 's Hertogenbosch and Tilburg. The medical tactical plan for this provided for an A.D.S. of 212 Fd. Amb. in Oss, an A.D.S. of 147 Fd. Amb. and 13 F.D.S. in Heesch and 202 Fd. Amb. in reserve ready to open in Nuland. The attack on 's Hertogenbosch was successful and when this town was entered 202 Fd. Amb. opened in Nuland and 212 moved from Oss to Coudevater, there to be joined by 13 F.D.S.

On October 30, the division moved to the Bree area to pass under VIII Corps and to take up a position in the rear of the Belgian brigade holding the line Kinroy–Weert facing the Wessem Canal. 147 Fd. Amb. was now in Neeroeteren, 202 in Bree and 212 in Coudevater. 13 F.D.S. was in Bree, as was the M.A.C., and 26 F.D.S. was still in Grave. The division relieved the Belgian brigade and 147 Fd. Amb. moved to Kinroy and 202 to Stamproy. 26 F.D.S. from Grave opened for minor sick in Gruitrode.

On November 12 the division, with 7th Armoured Division on its right and 51st Division on its left, planned to attack across the Noorder Canal towards Heythuyzen. 160th Bde. made an assault crossing of the canal and 158th Bde. passed through to seize the area north of Baexem while 71st Bde. seized the area about Horn.

The medical tactical plan provided a main A.D.S. of 202 Fd. Amb. in Weert supported by 13 F.D.S., a forward company A.D.S. of 212 Fd. Amb. about Hunsel. Evacuation was to be to the A.D.S. of 131 Fd. Amb. of 7th Armoured Division in Kinroy. 212 Fd. Amb. on wheels was to be prepared to cross the Wessem Canal and to establish an A.D.S. on the far side, while 147 Fd. Amb. on wheels was to accompany 71st Bde. to open an A.D.S. in Baexem. 14 Lt. Fd. Amb. (4th Armd. Bde. u/c 53rd Division) was to be in Keent for minor sick and evacuation

PLATE XX. The bridges over the Waal at Nijmegen, November 1944. An Ambulance Car that has crossed the river by ferry.

[Imperial War Museum]

PLATE XXI. A Refrigerator Truck of a Field Transfusion Unit. December 1944.

PLATE XXII. The Advanced Blood Bank. December 1944.

ADVANCE TO MAAS AND ROER: ARDENNES

was to 24 C.C.S. at Hamont and 4 F.D.S. (corps exhaustion centre) at Budel.

Operation 'Mallard' opened on the 14th and good progress was made, the canal being bridged on the following day. Then came mopping up operations between the Wessem Canal and the river at Roermond. 212 Fd. Amb. moved to Oler and 147 Fd. Amb. to Baexem. The medical cover proved to be entirely satisfactory. A company of a field ambulance was with each brigade and the rest of the field ambulance in support of that brigade. When the brigade was on the move the field ambulance company with it broke up into sections and a section moved in support of each battalion. Open A.D.Ss. were always under the control of A.D.M.S. division.

December opened with 53rd Division holding the line of the Maas opposite Roermond from Wessem to Kessel. The medical units were disposed as follows:

    147 Fd. Amb. and M.A.C. in Baexem
    202 Fd. Amb. and 13 F.D.S. in Weert
    212 Fd. Amb. in Helden
    26 F.D.S. in Bocholt.

Evacuation was to 23 C.C.S. and 9 F.D.S. in Weert, to 24 C.C.S. in Hamont and 4 F.D.S. (V.D.T.C. and corps exhaustion centre) in Budel. 84 B.G.H. was in Steensel and 79 B.G.H. in Eindhoven.

On December 17, the division moved to an area east of Antwerp to pass u/c Canadian First Army. 53 Fd. Hyg. Sec. went to Pulle, 202 Fd. Amb. to Hoogstraten, 147 Fd. Amb. to Boom, 13 F.D.S. to Boekel. 212 Fd. Amb. went to Kessel with 160th Bde.

Then came the German Ardennes counter-offensive and 53rd Division was quickly moved to the Louvain–Brussels area to pass u/c XXX Corps. 160th Bde. went to the Louvain area and 212 Fd. Amb. opened an A.D.S. in Heverlee, 158th Bde. to an area south-east of Brussels and 202 Fd. Amb. opened an A.D.S. in Overyssche. 147 Fd. Amb. with 71st Bde. opened an A.D.S. in La Hulpe. 22 Lt. Fd. Amb. of 33rd Armd. Bde. at Erps-Querbs came under command 53rd Division, as did 18 Lt. Fd. Amb. of 29th Armd. Bde. at Biesme. On December 30, 212 Fd. Amb. with 160th Bde. moved forward to the Château Liblion and 202 Fd. Amb. with 158th Bde. to Celles.

53rd Division with 33rd Armd. Bde. was holding the sector Houyet–Aye with 158th Bde. on the right and 160th Bde. on the left and 71st Bde. and 33rd Armd. Bde. in reserve. U.S. 84th Division was on the left and 6th Airborne Division on the right.

(v)
Medical Arrangements

I CORPS

During the winter months I Corps was south of the Maas on the Netherlands–Belgium frontier. At the beginning of October, 16 C.C.S. was in Lierre and 32 C.C.S. in Turnhout. Then the corps was engaged in clearing the area up to Tilburg and Breda along the Brasschaet and Turnhout roads leading to the north. When this area had been cleared the corps became practically static. 16 C.C.S. was moved to Breda and 32 C.C.S. to Goirle. 30 F.D.S. with attached F.S.Us. and F.T.Us. formed an advanced surgical centre in Roosendaal in the civil hospital there and 20 F.D.S. in a sanatorium south of Poppel looked after convalescents.

The composition of the corps underwent constant change as formations joined and left it. At the end of the year only Canadian 4th and Polish 1st Armoured Divisions remained.

XII CORPS

At the beginning of October, XII Corps with U.S. 101st Airborne Division, 50th and 53rd Divisions and 4th Armd. Bde. under command moved to the Nijmegen area to undertake the protection of the Nijmegen bridgehead north of the River Waal.

Of the corps medical units 23 C.C.S. was open at Zeelst, 24 C.C.S. and 4 F.D.S. were open at Grave, 9 F.D.S. was functioning as an advanced surgical centre in Uden and 13 F.S.U. was attached to 212 Fd. Amb. across the bridge at Nijmegen so that should the bridge be destroyed surgical facilities would still be available. The remaining corps medical units were 12, 15, 27 and 42 F.S.Us., 13, 30 and 37 F.T.Us. and 10 Fd. Hyg. Sec.

On October 18, D.D.M.S. moved with corps H.Q. to Zeeland and XII Corps, with 7th Armoured, 15th, 51st and 53rd Divisions and 30th Armd. Bde., left Nijmegen to take part in Operation 'Alan' which commenced on October 22 and had for its objectives 's Hertogenbosch, Tilburg and the clearing of the south bank of the Maas. 's Hertogenbosch was captured on October 25.

The distribution of the corps medical units October 22–25 is depicted in Fig. 66.

When 's Hertogenbosch was taken 9 F.D.S. moved to Boxtel to form an advanced surgical centre. The corps V.D.T.C. and exhaustion centre joined 22 Lt. Fd. Amb. in Eindhoven.

On October 28, D.D.M.S. moved to St. Michielsgestel.

ADVANCE TO MAAS AND ROER: ARDENNES

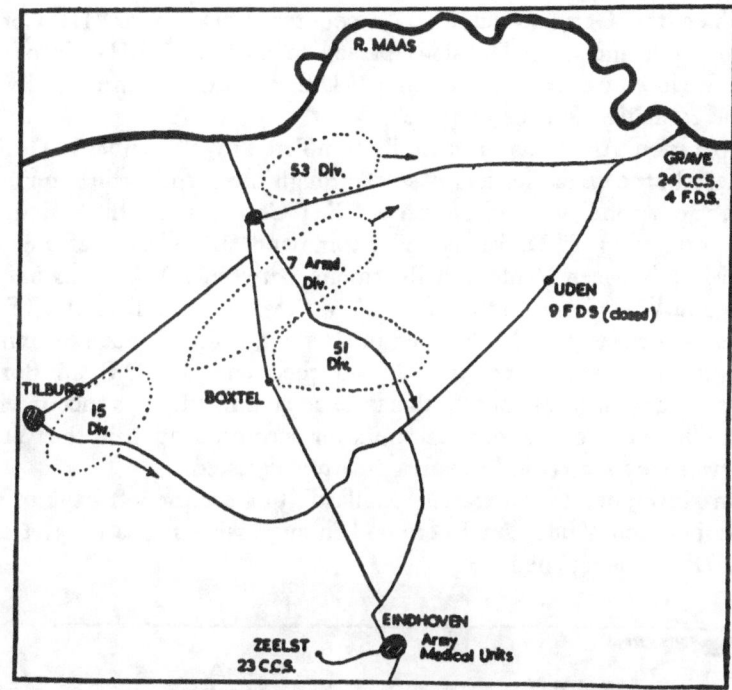

Fig. 66. XII Corps. Medical Arrangements. October 22–25.

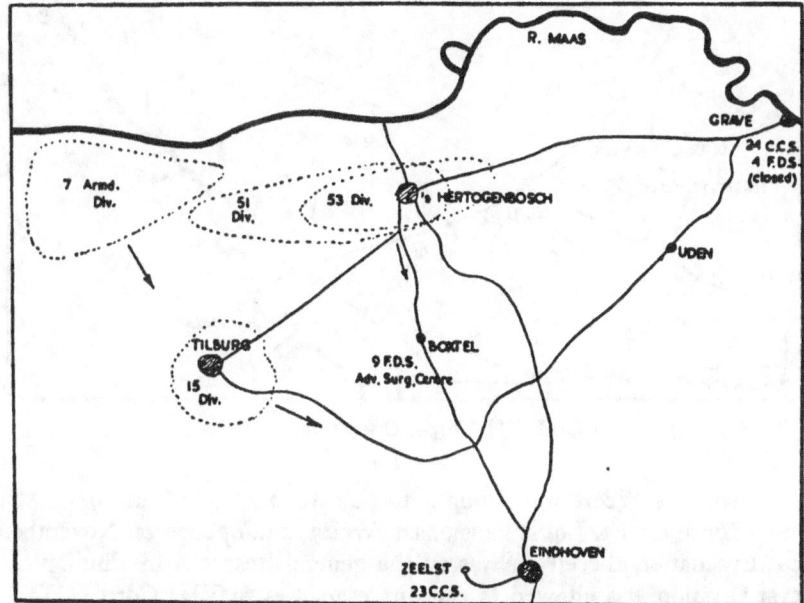

Fig. 67. XII Corps. Medical Arrangements. October 26–November 2.

When the Germans launched a counter-attack upon VIII Corps' sector 15th and 53rd Divisions passed to command VIII Corps. 24 C.C.S. closed on October 31 and 4 F.D.S. remained open to deal with battle casualties and the light sick.

Operation 'Alan' was successfully completed by November 2. During it 1,480 battle casualties had passed through the corps medical units.

In the second week in November XII Corps, with 7th Armoured, 49th, 51st and 53rd Divisions under command, moved to an area facing the Maas between Venlo and Roermond between XXX Corps on the right and VIII Corps on the left. D.D.M.S. was in Kaulille. 23 C.C.S. at Zeelst was closed, 24 C.C.S. open in Hamont, 4 F.D.S. open for minor sick in Budel with the V.D.T.C. attached and 9 F.D.S. in Boxtel admitted urgent cases only. At this time much difficulty was encountered in finding sites for the medical units for accommodation in the Weert area was very scarce and the area greatly congested.

On November 14, Operation 'Mallard', to clear the left bank of the Maas between Venlo and Roermond in successive stages by 51st and 53rd Divisions, opened.

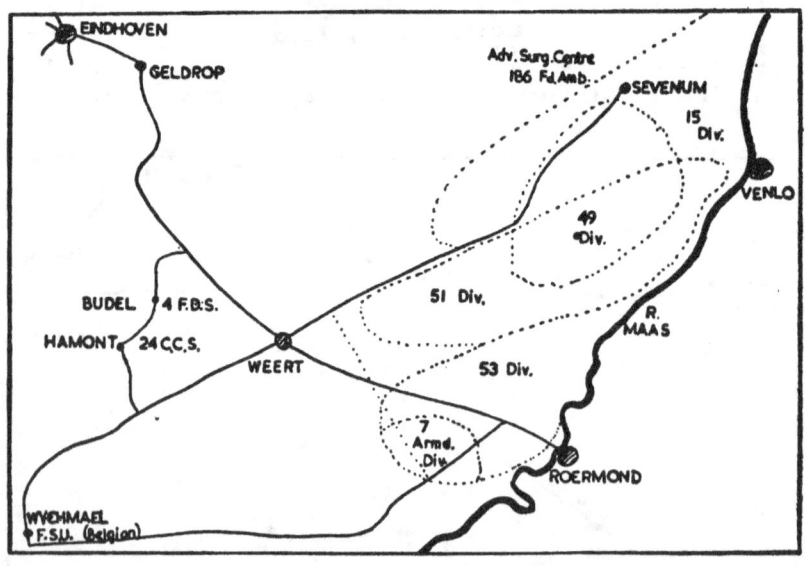

Fig. 68. XII Corps. Operation 'Mallard'.

As soon as Weert was thought to be safe, 23 C.C.S. and 9 F.D.S. moved into the St. Louis Pensionaat, Weert, and opened on November 20. Evacuation therefrom was to the general hospitals in Eindhoven. 51st Division was allowed to send its casualties to VIII Corps' C.C.S. at Geldrop.

ADVANCE TO MAAS AND ROER: ARDENNES

22 Lt. Fd. Amb. passed to Canadian First Army and so the corps exhaustion centre was attached to 4 F.D.S. in Budel. On the 26th, 15 F.S.U. and 30 F.T.U. joined 187 Fd. Amb. in Sevenum to serve as an advanced surgical centre in connexion with the attack on the western defences of Venlo and to reduce the length of the evacuation route.

At the end of the month 49th Division left XII Corps and was replaced by 15th Division.

During Operation 'Mallard', November 14–December 4, casualties passing through the corps medical units totalled 1,186.

On December 13, H.Q. XII Corps took over the locations of H.Q. XXX Corps at Beek and Mechelen to undertake Operation 'Shears' with XXX Corps formations and units. This operation was cancelled owing to bad weather and later, when the German break-through in the Ardennes occurred, there was a regrouping of the corps of Second Army and XXX Corps was ordered to move to the south of Namur. So it was that for a time the medical units under XII Corps were 3 and 10 C.C.Ss. at Bies and Eysden respectively, 3 F.D.S. at Nuth and 35 F.D.S. at Eysden. On December 20, Guards Armoured Division, 43rd Division and 35 F.D.S. left XII Corps. On the 24th, 3 C.C.S. left and was replaced by 24 C.C.S. and on the 28th, 3 F.D.S., 43 and 49 F.S.Us. and 7 F.T.U. rejoined XII Corps.

At the end of the year therefore XII Corps had under command 7th Armoured Division, 51st and 52nd Divisions, 8th Armd. Bde. and 6th Gds. Tk. Bde. The corps medical units were:

   10 C.C.S., with 14 and 50 F.S.Us. and 24 F.T.U. at Eysden
   24 C.C.S., with 12 and 15 F.S.Us. and 13 F.T.U. at Bies
   9 F.D.S. with the corps V.D.T.C. and exhaustion centre at Eysden
   10 Fd. Hyg. Sec. in Stein.

In the first week of January 1945, 43rd Division came under command of XII Corps and from January 15–26 the corps was engaged in Operation 'Blackcock'. For this operation the following medical arrangements were made:

(i) 131 Fd. Amb. with 41 F.S.U. formed an A.S.C. to receive Groups I and II cases (Priorities I and II) from 7th Armoured Division. On January 16, 9 F.D.S. replaced 131 Fd. Amb.

(ii) Lt. Sec. 9 F.D.S., the corps V.D.T.C. and the corps exhaustion centre remained in the College in Mechelen.

(iii) 10 C.C.S. remained in Eysden to admit all types of cases from 7th Armoured Division.

(iv) 24 C.C.S. at Bies received all types of cases from 43rd and 52nd Divisions.

(v) 14 F.D.S., under the control of D.D.M.S. Corps, at Nuth, received all Group III cases and sick from 43rd and 52nd Divisions.

On January 21, 10 C.C.S. left XII Corps to rejoin XXX Corps, 23 C.C.S. coming to XII Corps in its place.

After Operation 'Blackcock' there was a complete regrouping, all the divisions leaving the operational control of XII Corps.

XXX CORPS

XXX Corps with the Guards Armoured, 43rd and 50th Divisions and 8th Armd. Bde. was, at the beginning of October, in the Nijmegen sector and on the defensive. On November 10 it handed over all local commitments to Canadian II Corps and moved to take over a sector from the American forces in the Geilenkirchen–Maeseyck area where it participated in the operations that led to the capture of Geilenkirchen. On December 13, XXX Corps H.Q. handed over its troops to XII Corps and began to plan for its next operation. This was interrupted on December 23 when the corps became operational again to take part in the reaction to the German thrust through the Ardennes Gap and moved to a position north of the Meuse between Liége and Namur, later operating offensively south of the river against the German salient between U.S. VII and VIII Corps.

The Germans from their prepared defences along the Neder Rijn and in the Reichswald area launched frequent attacks on XXX Corps' front in attempts to regain the Nijmegen bridge or, failing this, to destroy it. XXX Corps was disposed with 43rd Division and 8th Armd. Bde. on the right flank in the Reichswald sector alongside U.S. 82nd Airborne Division and 50th Division holding defensive positions in the 'island' north of Nijmegen facing the south bank of the Neder Rijn. Guards Armoured Division was in support of both these infantry divisions.

The corps medical units were disposed as under:

1. 10 C.C.S. group with 163 Fd. Amb. — Jonker Bosch Hospital, Nijmegen
2. 3 C.C.S. group with 35 F.D.S., less lt. sec. — Marienbosch, Nijmegen
3. Lt. Sec. 35 F.D.S. — St. Maartins Orthopaedic Klinick, Nijmegen, supervising the organisation of some 800 German wounded and the German medical staff
4. 3 F.D.S. with the corps V.D.T.C. and corps psychiatrist — Hees
5. U.S. 307 Med. Coy. of U.S. 82nd Airborne Division — Brakkenstein Hospital
   U.S. 326 Med. Coy. of U.S. 101st Airborne Division — Son
6. 111 M.A.C. — Hees
7. 31 Fd. Hyg. Sec. — Bourg-Léopold supervising the organisation of the hospital there.

ADVANCE TO MAAS AND ROER: ARDENNES

The following Army medical units were in support of XXX Corps:

1. One pln. 257 A.C.C.	Jonker Bosch
2. 8 Adv. Depot Med. Stores	Nijmegen
3. 1 Fwd. Del. Truck 'Y' Blood-bank	With 10 C.C.S.
4. Mobile element of an advanced depot of medical stores	Jonker Bosch

On October 4 fighting flared up in the 'island' north of Nijmegen and casualties, American and British, averaged some 400 a day. U.S.

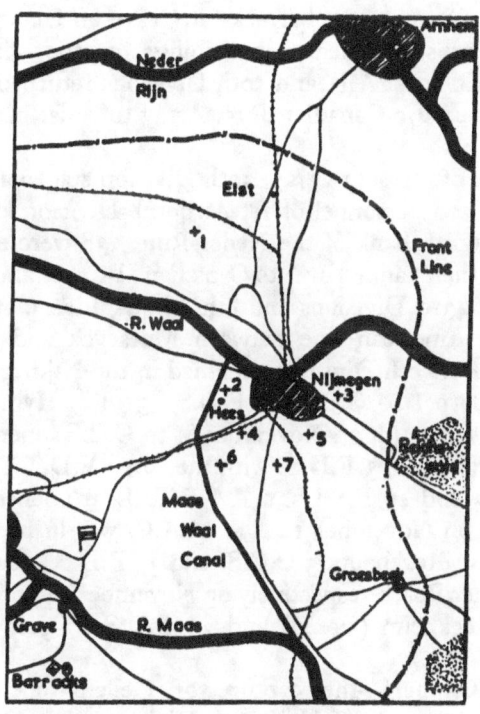

FIG. 69. XXX Corps. Between the Waal and the Maas, October. Medical Arrangements.

1. U.S. 326 Med. Coy.
2. 3 F.D.S., V.D.T.C., Corps Psychiatrist, 111 M.A.C.
3. 35 F.D.S., 8 Adv. Depot Med. Stores
4. U.S. 326 Med. Coy.
5. 3 C.C.S., 35 F.D.S. (October 1)
6. 10 C.C.S., 35 F.D.S., 163 Fd. Amb.
7. U.S. 307 Med. Coy.
8. 24 C.C.S.

101st A.B. Division moved into the 'island' and 50th Division took up defensive positions. British casualties were evacuated to 3 and 10 C.C.Ss. on alternate days, U.S. casualties to U.S. 307 and 326 Med. Coys. On October 5, U.S. 24 Evac. Hosp. moved from Hechtel to Uden and received casualties from the two medical companies. On October 6, 163 Fd. Amb. reverted to Second Army and moved on the 8th to Diest alongside 81 B.G.H. 35 F.D.S. left 3 C.C.S. and moved to the site vacated by 163 Fd. Amb. adjoining 10 C.C.S. to deal with minor sick.

On October 9, XXX Corps handed over all commitments on the 'island' to XII Corps, U.S. 101st A.B. and 50th Divisions passing to XII Corps and XXX Corps remaining responsible for the defences between the Maas and the Waal facing the Reichswald. 24 C.C.S. was moved by XII Corps to the barracks at Grave on October 11. On the 16th, XXX Corps resumed responsibility for the defences on the 'island' and U.S. 101st A.B. and 50th Divisions returned to command. XII Corps passed u/c Canadian First Army to assist in the capture of Antwerp.

On the night of October 22/23, 50th Division staged an operation to evacuate some 200 personnel of 1st Airborne Division known to be in hiding on the north bank of the Neder Rijn; 138 were evacuated.

XXX Corps then handed over to Canadian II Corps and, with Guards Armoured and 43rd Divisions and 8th Armd. Bde., moved south to a section of the American line between Maeseyck and Geilenkirchen across the Meuse. 50th Division remained in the Nijmegen 'island' u/c Canadian II Corps. 10 C.C.S., 3 F.D.S., 31 Fd. Hyg. Sec. and 111 M.A.C. all moved south on November 8. 10 C.C.S. opened in a school in Eysden on the 10th, 3 F.D.S. with the corps V.D.T.C. was in Nuth where, with 43 and 49 F.S.Us. and 7 F.T.U., it opened an advanced surgical centre on November 14, 111 M.A.C. was in Mechelen and 31 Fd. Hyg. Sec. in Reckheim. 3 C.C.S. and 35 F.D.S. closed at Marienbosch and Jonker Bosch respectively on November 11 and moved south, 3 C.C.S. to Reckheim (closed) and 35 F.D.S. to join 10 C.C.S. in Eysden.

Operation 'Clipper'—the capture of Geilenkirchen—opened on November 18. A R.C.T. of U.S. 84th Division advanced eastward on the south side of Geilenkirchen and a brigade of 43rd Division advanced eastward on the north side; a second R.C.T. then attacked the town directly. The operation was successful and losses were few, 112 American and 22 British casualties occurring on the first day; on the second, casualties totalled 152.

A U.S. clearing company with a light section of 35 F.D.S. served the R.C.T. Casualties were evacuated to 3 F.D.S. in Nuth. 10 C.C.S. at Eysden received all casualties from XXX Corps. 3 F.D.S. received urgent and V.D. cases only.

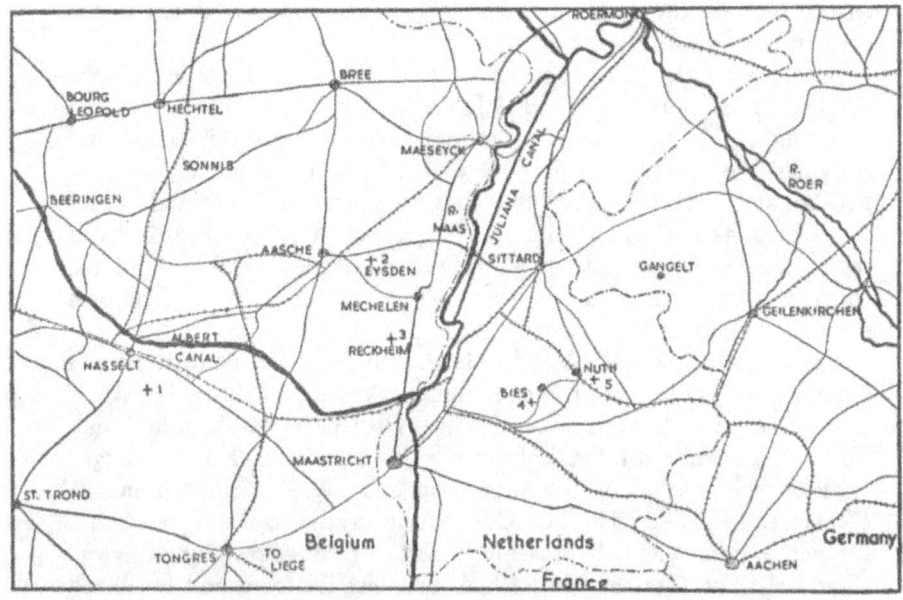

Fig. 70. XXX Corps. Operation 'Clipper'. Medical Arrangements.

1. 39 and 81 B.G.Hs.
   8 Adv. Depot Med. Stores
2. 10 C.C.S.
   35 F.D.S.
3. 3 C.C.S. (withdrawn to Sittard)
   31 Fd. Hyg. Sec.
4. 3 C.C.S. (from Sittard)
5. 3 F.D.S. (Adv. Surg. Centre)

On November 21, Lt. Sec. 3 C.C.S. moved to the civil hospital in Sittard and opened as an advanced surgical centre.

Following Operation 'Clipper' the weather conditions rapidly deteriorated. The Meuse was in spate and the two bridges in XXX Corps sector were out of action. The bridge at Maastricht in the U.S. sector had to be used and traffic congestion caused much delay in the evacuation of casualties.

On December 19, XXX Corps became operational again after a period of planning for Operation 'Veritable', which was postponed as an immediate result of the German break-through on U.S. First Army front. On the following day the corps, with Guards Armoured, 43rd and 51st Divisions, 29th and 33rd Armd. Bdes. and 34th Tk. Bde. under command, moved to Hasselt from Boxtel. 53rd Division formed a firm infantry base for the corps on the line of the Dyle and was made responsible for the defence of Brussels. On the right Guards Armoured Division and on the left 43rd Division concentrated north of the Meuse, watching the river crossings and prepared to counter-attack. 51st Division was concentrated to the north of 53rd Division. 29th

Armd. Bde. operated to the south of Charleroi and moved east to the river in the area of Dinant.

No corps medical units opened since 81 and 39 B.G.Hs. in Hasselt, 101 B.G.H. in Louvain and 8 B.G.H. in Brussels were so near. 3 C.C.S., reverting to XXX Corps, was moved from Bies to Wijchmaal and remained closed. 10 C.C.S. (XII Corps) was in Eysden. 3 and 35 F.D.Ss. and 111 M.A.C. reverted to XXX Corps but remained in XII Corps area. 34 C.C.S. at Helmond was placed u/c XXX Corps but was replaced later by 24 C.C.S. 35 F.D.S. with the V.D.T.C. and the corps psychiatrist moved on December 23 to Tirlemont to deal with the minor sick and V.D. cases.

On December 24, 29th Armd. Bde. encountered German patrols and armour a few miles east of Dinant and checked them. 18 Lt. Fd. Amb. in support of this brigade was in Biesme. On December 25, 29th Armd. Bde. was committed offensively across the Meuse. 13 F.D.S. of 53rd Division was opened in Gerpinnes and to it were attached 6 and 44 F.S.Us. and 35 F.T.U. from 3 C.C.S. to form an advanced surgical centre.

On the 26th, 3 C.C.S. was moved into the university buildings in Charleroi. The German thrust had now lost its force and improved weather conditions enabled the Allied air forces to intervene. Guards Armoured and 43rd Divisions remained in their positions north of the river. 6th Airborne Division came u/c XXX Corps and along with 53rd Division and 29th Armd. Bde. operated offensively east from the Meuse between Givet and Dinant towards St. Hubert. On the 27th, 43rd Division left XXX Corps and on the following day the corps, with the exception of Guards Armoured Division, was committed south of the river between U.S. VII Corps on the left and U.S. VIII Corps on the right and so forward medical units became necessary. 3 F.D.S. with 43 and 49 F.S.Us. and 7 F.T.U. were moved from Nuth in XII Corps area to Ciney to form an advanced surgical centre. 33 C.C.S. from VIII Corps was placed u/c XXX Corps and was moved to St. Servais near Namur since 3 C.C.S. in Charleroi was too far to the flank and off the line of evacuation. 35 F.D.S. was moved to Namur. 31 Fd. Hyg. Sec. was now in Rhisnes and 111 M.A.C. in Maillen.

On January 6, 53rd Division suffered a slight and temporary reverse on the left flank, but the position was quickly restored.

Casualties were being evacuated by 111 M.A.C. from the divisional medical units, Group I to 3 F.D.S. and the rest to 33 C.C.S. 3 C.C.S. was moved from Charleroi to Ciney and then absorbed 3 F.D.S.

On January 8, 51st Division relieved 53rd Division, one brigade of the latter division remaining behind in support of 51st Division. As the German forces withdrew from the salient and the Allied forces pressed on their heels 3 F.D.S. was moved from Ciney to Marche where it opened an advanced surgical centre for Group I cases on the 9th.

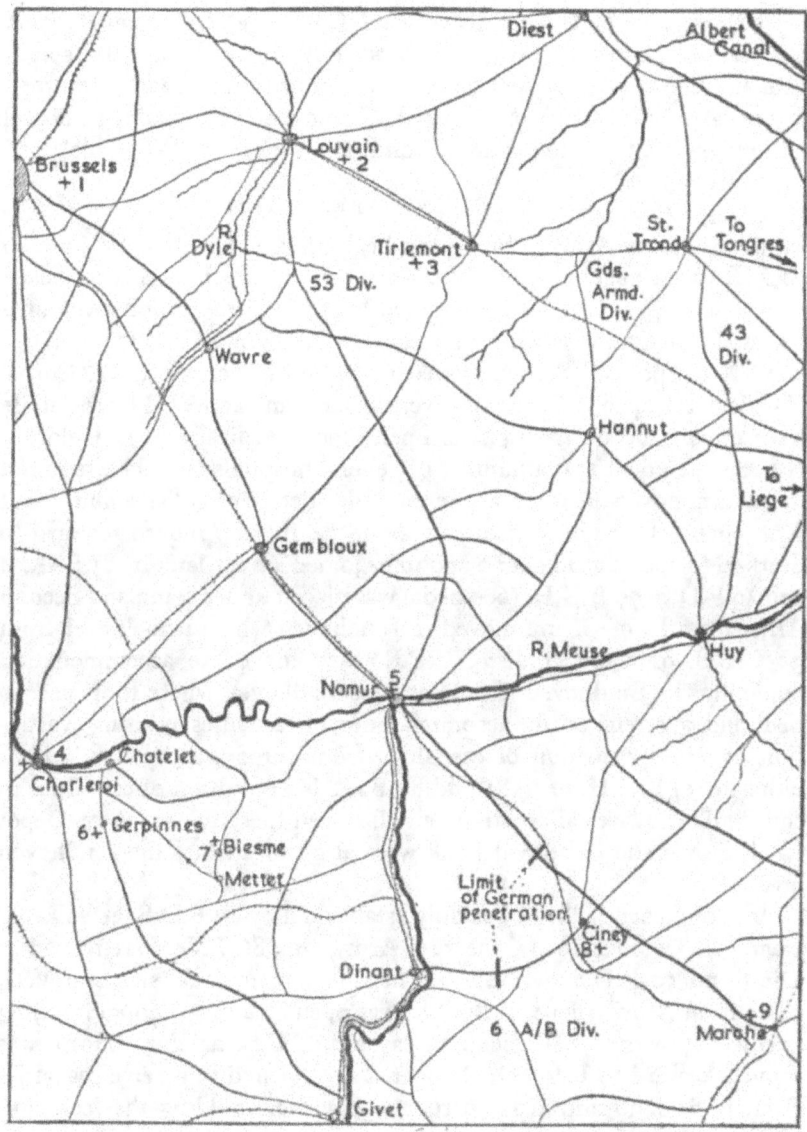

Fig. 71. XXX Corps. Medical Arrangements in connexion with the German Counter-Offensive in the Ardennes.

1. 8 B.G.H.
2. 101 B.G.H.
3. 35 F.D.S. (December 23)
4. 3 C.C.S. (December 26)
5. 33 C.C.S. (December 28)
   35 F.D.S. (December 29)
6. 13 F.D.S. (Adv. Surg. Centre)
7. 18 Lt. Fd. Amb.
8. 3 F.D.S. (December 28)
9. 3 F.D.S. (Adv. Surg. Centre)

By the 12th, XXX Corps' front had become considerably reduced by the convergence of U.S. VII and VIII Corps and arrangements were therefore made to pull it out of the line. 29th Armd. Bde. with its light field ambulance was the first formation to be withdrawn and it returned to 11th Armoured Division. Corps H.Q. moved from Namur to Boxtel on January 18, there to resume planning for Operation 'Veritable'.

SECOND ARMY

In the forward Army area at the beginning of October, 81 and 86 B.G.Hs. were open with 31 F.D.S. at Diest and 84 B.G.H. was closed in Brussels. 35 C.C.S. had only recently arrived in the Eindhoven area and was functioning as an air cushion for Eindhoven airfield.

XXX Corps' C.C.Ss. were open in the Nijmegen area, XII Corps' C.C.Ss. were open in Zeelst to cover the left flank and VIII Corps' units were moving up on the right to open a new medical area in Geldrop. It became evident that a number of general hospitals would be required in the Eindhoven area. It was therefore decided to establish a number of Army general hospitals in this area and 84 B.G.H. moved forward to Sterksel to open on October 5 and to be joined a week later by 81 B.G.H. and 49 F.D.S. 79 B.G.H. (600 beds) was placed under command Second Army from L. of C. and moved to Eindhoven where it took over from 35 C.C.S. on October 9. 35 C.C.S. then moved to accommodation adjoining the Eindhoven airfield at Meerveldhoven where it opened 50 beds and 50 stretchers for accommodation of casualties awaiting evacuation by air. Evacuation of casualties from corps was by 257 A.C.C. either to 79 B.G.H. or to 81 and 84 B.G.Hs., reception of casualties in the Eindhoven area alternating daily between these two. 11 Adv. Depot Med. Stores and 'Y' Blood Bank were also moved into the Eindhoven area.

An ambulance railhead was duly established by 47 F.D.S. at Valkenswaard on October 10. In the rear Army area 86 B.G.H. remained at Diest and 50 F.D.S. was opened in Louvain for local sick and V.D. cases from Army troops. 14 F.D.S. was open at Bourg-Léopold dealing exclusively with P.o.W. sick and casualties. U.S. 24 Evac. Hosp. was moved forward to Uden on October 8 and opened to receive casualties from U.S. 82nd and 101st Airborne Divisions holding the 'corridor' to Nijmegen.

At the end of October it was possible to increase the hospital beds available in Eindhoven by bringing up 86 B.G.H. from Diest to St. Augustine's College, Eindhoven. About the same time 31 F.D.S., which had moved to Wijchmaal to cover medical requirements of Army roadhead, was allotted two F.S.Us. and one F.T.U., thus forming an advanced surgical centre covering the Belgian brigade holding the right flank of Second Army. 2 F.D.S. opened in Diest to provide accommo-

ADVANCE TO MAAS AND ROER: ARDENNES

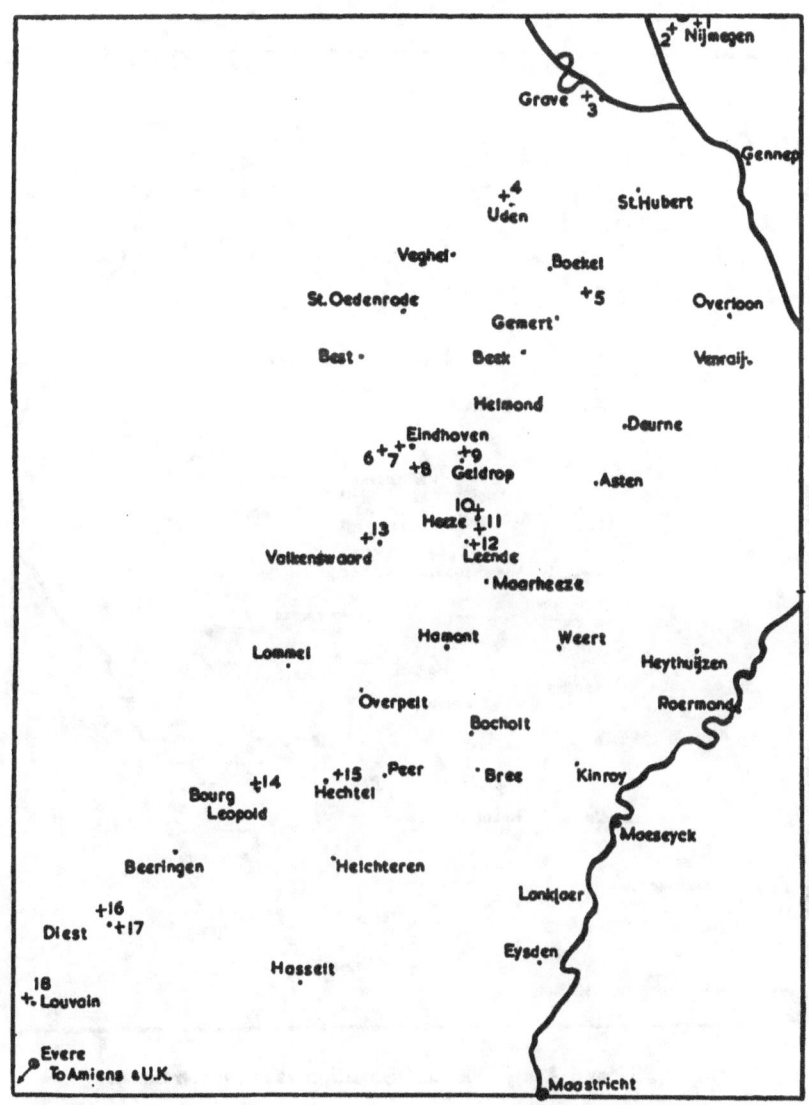

FIG. 72. Second Army. Medical Situation as at October 18.

1. 3 C.C.S.
2. 10 C.C.S.
3. 24 C.C.S.
4. U.S. 24 Evac. Hosp.
5. 34 C.C.S.
6. 35 C.C.S.
7. 23 C.C.S.
8. 79 B.G.H.
9. 33 C.C.S.
10. 49 F.D.S.
11. 84 B.G.H.
12. 81 B.G.H.
13. 47 F.D.S.
14. 14 F.D.S.
15. 31 F.D.S.
16. 2 F.D.S.
17. 86 B.G.H.
18. 50 F.D.S.

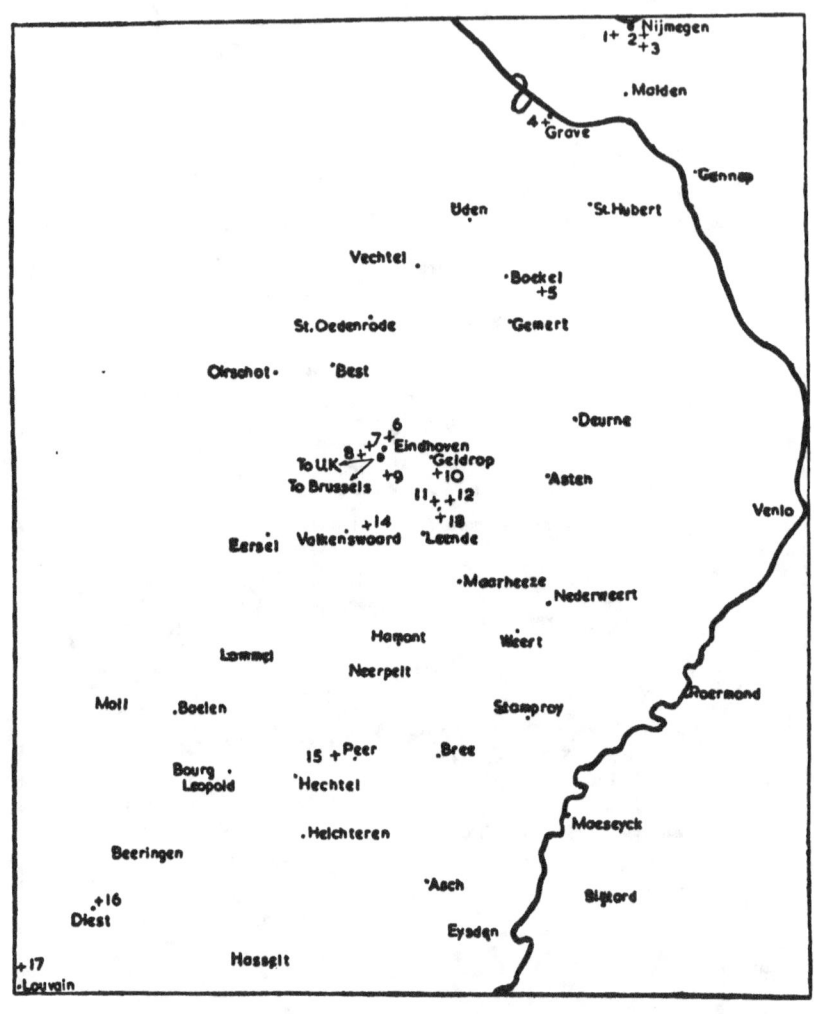

Fig. 73. Second Army. Medical Situation as at November 9.

1. 10 C.C.S.
2. 3 C.C.S.
3. U.S. 24 Evac. Hosp.
4. 24 C.C.S.
5. 34 C.C.S.
6. 86 B.G.H.
7. 35 C.C.S.
8. 23 C.C.S.
9. 79 B.G.H.
10. 33 C.C.S.
11. 81 B.G.H.
12. 84 B.G.H.
13. 49 F.D.S.
14. 47 F.D.S.
15. 31 F.D.S.
16. 2 F.D.S.
17. 50 F.D.S.

ADVANCE TO MAAS AND ROER: ARDENNES

dation for minor sick and casualties and facilities for emergency surgery in the rear Army area.

Apart from the move of 50 F.D.S. from Louvain to the Army troops area at Moll, there was no major change in dispositions of Army medical

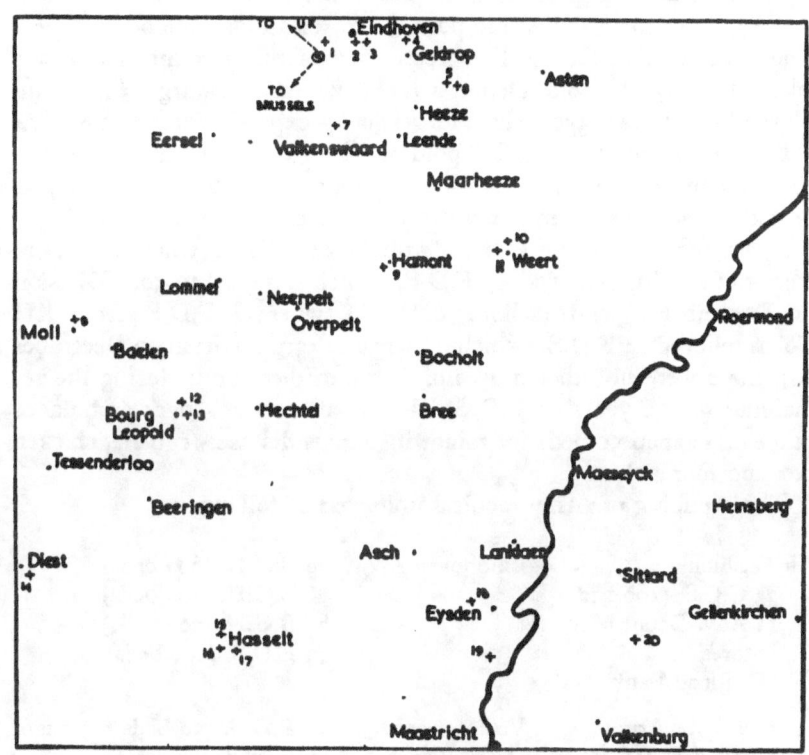

FIG. 74. Second Army. Medical Situation as at November 22.

1. 35 C.C.S.
2. 79 B.G.H.
3. 86 B.G.H.
4. 33 C.C.S.
5. 84 B.G.H.
6. 49 F.D.S.
7. 47 F.D.S.
8. 50 F.D.S.
9. 34 C.C.S.
10. 9 F.D.S.
11. 23 C.C.S.
12. 13 Con. Depot
13. 14 F.D.S.
14. 2 F.D.S.
15. 39 B.G.H.
16. 31 F.D.S.
17. 81 B.G.H.
18. 10 C.C.S.
19. 3 C.C.S.
20. 3 F.D.S.

units until mid-November when the regrouping of Second Army (after the move south of XII and XXX Corps) necessitated the opening of a subsidiary hospital area in Hasselt. This was effected by moving 81 B.G.H. from Sterksel to Hasselt and opening 31 F.D.S. in adjoining buildings as a screen for minor sick and casualties. 39 B.G.H. (600 beds) was placed under command Second Army from L. of C. and moved up to Hasselt to the New Barracks and 8 Adv. Depot Med. Stores opened in a cinema adjoining 81 B.G.H.

In the Bourg-Léopold area, as the numbers of sick and wounded P.o.W. diminished, it became possible to release accommodation previously used by 14 F.D.S. The greater part of this accommodation was taken over by 13 Con. Depot, which opened at Bourg-Léopold on November 13 with 550 beds and gradually expanded to 750 beds. 14 F.D.S. remained at Bourg-Léopold and became the Army psychiatric centre. This unit worked in close conjunction with 13 Con. Depot, providing facilities for minor treatment of convalescents.

Apart from reliefs of F.D.Ss. at ambulance railhead (where 21 F.D.S. from the L. of C. relieved 47 F.D.S., which returned to 50th Division on December 2) and at Bourg-Léopold (where 4 F.D.S. from XII Corps relieved 14 F.D.S., which returned to 43rd Division on December 19), there were no other moves of Army medical units during the remainder of the year. 21 F.D.S., shortly after taking over ambulance railhead, opened 50 beds for minor infectious diseases (rubella, chicken pox and mumps).

The grouping of Army medical units was as follows:

Air Cushion	Eindhoven Area	79 B.G.H. (600 beds)
35 C.C.S. (100 beds)		86 B.G.H. (200 beds)
11 Adv. Depot Med. Stores		84 B.G.H. (200 beds)
'Y' Blood Bank		49 F.D.S. (100 beds)
50 F.D.S.-Army Tps. V.D.T.C. at Moll	Valkenswaard (Ambulance Railhead)	21 F.D.S. (50 beds for minor infectious diseases)
		9 Adv. Depot Med. Stores
		H.Q. 257 A.C.C.
13 Con. Depot (750 beds)	Bourg-Léopold	
14 F.D.S. (100 psychiatric beds)		
	Hasselt (Ambulance Rail Halt)	39 B.G.H. (600 beds)
		81 B.G.H. (200 beds)
		31 F.D.S. (120 beds)
		8 Adv. Depot Med. Stores

The first six months of the campaign had shown that, sited alone, the capacity of the 200-bed hospital units was too small, even with daily evacuation, to deal with the casualties evacuated from one corps during battle periods. It was invariably necessary (1) to augment its surgical

ADVANCE TO MAAS AND ROER: ARDENNES

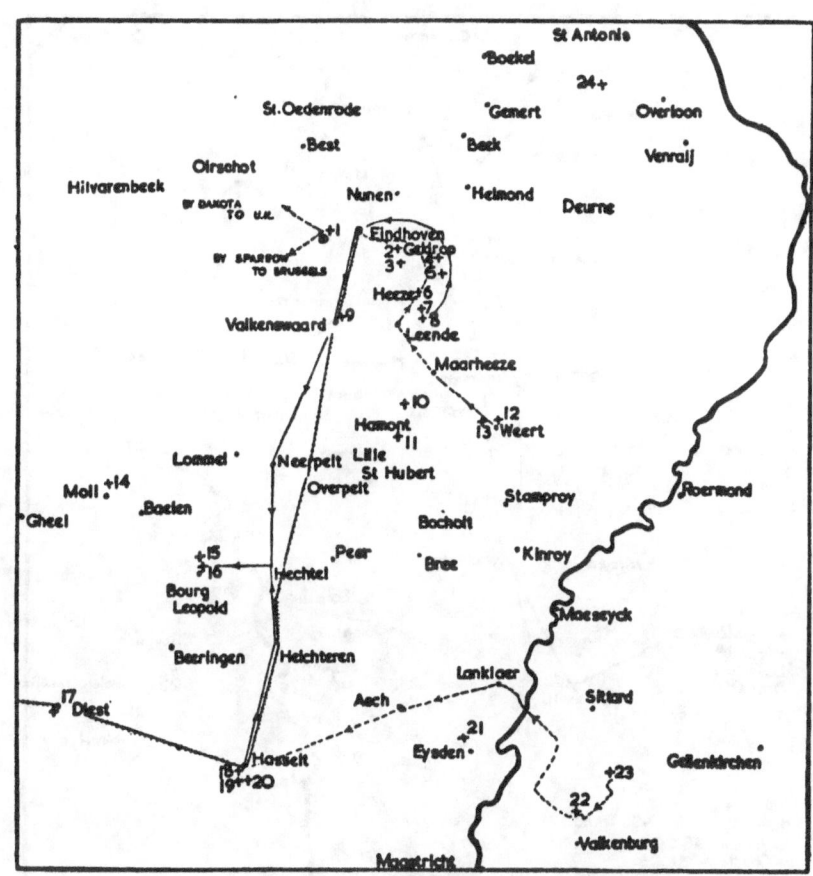

FIG. 75. Second Army. Medical Situation as at December 7.

1. 35 C.C.S.
2. 86 B.G.H.
3. 79 B.G.H.
4. 33 C.C.S.
5. 24 F.D.S.
6. 1 F.D.S.
7. 49 F.D.S.
8. 84 B.G.H.
9. 21 F.D.S.
10. 4 F.D.S.
11. 24 C.C.S.
12. 9 F.D.S.
13. 23 C.C.S.
14. 50 F.D.S.
15. 13 Con. Depot
16. 14 F.D.S.
17. 2 F.D.S.
18. 39 B.G.H.
19. 31 F.D.S.
20. 81 B.G.H.
21. 10 C.C.S.
22. 3 C.C.S.
23. 3 F.D.S.
24. 34 C.C.S.

——————— Evacuation by road of convalescents, psychiatric and exhaustion cases to 14 F.D.S.
+++++++ Evacuation by rail
- - - - - Evacuation from corps

By air. Those with hospital expectancy of over 6 weeks to the U.K., under 6 weeks to Brussels

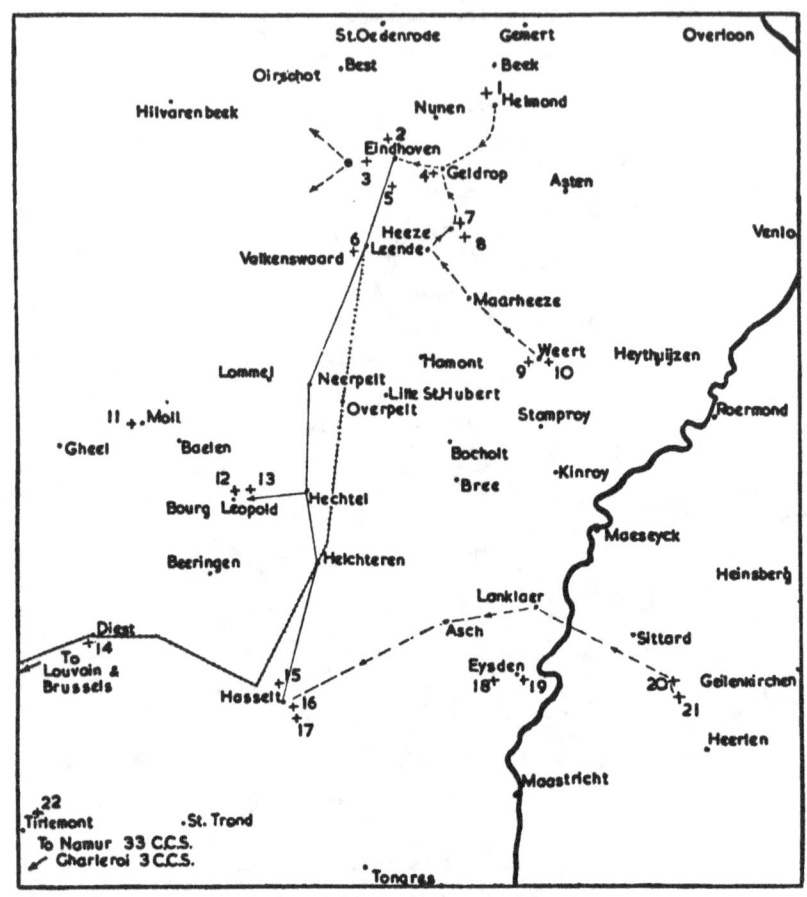

Fig. 76. Second Army. Medical Situation as at December 28.

1. 34 C.C.S.
2. 86 B.G.H.
3. 35 C.C.S.
   (Evacuation by air, Long-term cases (over 6 weeks hospital expectancy) to U.K.; short-term and neurosurgical cases to Brussels)
4. 24 F.D.S.
5. 79 B.G.H.
6. 21 F.D.S.
7. 84 B.G.H.
8. 49 F.D.S.
9. 33 C.C.S.
10. 1 F.D.S.
11. 50 F.D.S.
12. 13 Con. Depot
13. 4 F.D.S.
14. 2 F.D.S.
15. 39 B.G.H.
16. 31 F.D.S.
17. 81 B.G.H.
18. 9 F.D.S.
19. 10 C.C.S.
20. 24 C.C.S.
21. 3 F.D.S.
22. 35 F.D.S.

——— = Evacuation by road for convalescents and psychiatric patients to 4 F.D.S. at Bourg-Léopold
++++++ = Evacuation by rail
- - - - - = Evacuation from corps by road

ADVANCE TO MAAS AND ROER: ARDENNES

facilities by attaching a F.S.U. and (2) to increase its holding capacity by opening alongside it a F.D.S. with 100 beds for sick and minor casualties evacuated from forward areas.

The importance of placing one 600-bed general hospital, and later a second one, under command Army was forcibly demonstrated. One 600-bed general hospital was required in Army area to provide the necessary capacity for receiving cases from larger scale operations involving two corps. A second 600-bed general hospital in the area served a most useful purpose by increasing hospital holding capacity within the Army area and thus saving wastage of man-power through evacuation of shorter term cases out of the Army area to L. of C. hospitals.

Two F.D.Ss. were fully employed at all times in special rôles for Army troops, one as the Army Troops V.D.T.C. (also admitting minor sick from Army troops in area) and a second as the Army psychiatric centre, for which 50 to 100 beds were continually required.

One F.D.S. was also required for each 200-bed general hospital whenever these units were located some distance from other general hospitals. Normally two F.D.Ss. were utilised in this way to provide additional accommodation for 200-bed general hospitals working alone. Other valuable rôles carried out by Army F.D.Ss. were:

1. provision of accommodation for minor infectious diseases during winter months;
2. with F.S.Us. and F.T.Us. attached, providing an advanced surgical centre for independent brigades operating directly under Army in an independent flank rôle;
3. forming a special P.o.W. hospital when the numbers of sick and wounded P.o.W. required the provision of more than 50 special beds;
4. with an attached F.S.U. and F.T.U., forming an Army air cushion.

The Army C.C.S. was mainly employed as an air cushion. Its functions could have been carried out equally well by a F.D.S. with F.S.U. and F.T.U. attached and with a number of nursing officers to ensure good nursing attention for post-operative cases.

A general policy for holding cases for treatment within the Army area was introduced at the beginning of November. Initially the object was to hold cases of 7–10 days' hospital expectancy in general hospitals in Second Army area. With the opening of 13 Con. Depot the holding policy was extended to a total period of 21 days' combined hospital and convalescent depot treatment.

1. Minor cases (3–5 days) treated in Army F.D.Ss.
2. Cases of 7–10 days' hospital expectancy with subsequent convalescent depot treatment were retained and treated in 200-bed hospitals.

3. Cases of 10–14 days' hospital expectancy were retained and treated in 600-bed general hospitals in Army area before transfer to 13 Con. Depot for 10–14 days' convalescent treatment.
4. Cases of more than 14 days' hospital expectancy were evacuated to L. of C. hospitals; those requiring six weeks' hospital treatment were evacuated to the United Kingdom by air if their condition permitted.

During battle periods the holding policy was reduced to seven days for hospitals admitting battle casualties but the original policy outlined above was restored when operations were completed.

257 A.C.C. evacuated by road all casualties from corps C.C.Ss. When any one corps had two C.C.Ss. open in separate areas but both admitting casualties at the same time, the policy was to restrict the responsibility of the ambulance car company to evacuating casualties from the railhead C.C.S. There were, however, frequent occasions when 257 A.C.C. did, for operational reasons, evacuate from forward and railhead C.C.Ss. in a corps.

In addition to the three platoons employed in evacuating from corps C.C.S., a fourth platoon was employed in clearing general hospitals to ambulance railhead and in mobile road evacuation of 'overflow' casualties.

A temporary ambulance train ran daily from Overpelt station from October 1–10. Thereafter it was possible to establish ambulance railhead at Valkenswaard and a proper ambulance train ran daily from ambulance railhead to Brussels. Later, as L. of C. hospital areas developed, ambulance trains ran to Lille, Amiens, Renaix, Louvain and Ostend, in addition to Brussels.

Special arrangements were made for detraining certain types of cases *en route* so that they could readily be transferred to the appropriate special hospital; for example, maxillo-facial and neurosurgical cases were detrained in Brussels area for 8 B.G.H. and psychiatric cases were similarly detrained and transferred to 32 B.G.H. at Wavre Notre Dame.

By mid-November, with the reduction in the number of battle casualties and the increasing holding capacity within Army hospitals, a daily ambulance train was no longer necessary and arrangements were made for trains to be reduced first to four or five trains per week and later to one train on alternate days. Finally, towards the end of December, one train every three days proved sufficient.

35 C.C.S., acting as Army air cushion at Eindhoven, handled 6,000 casualties between October 20 and December 31; of these cases 150 required surgical treatment.

As a general rule air evacuation was possible five or six days every week; the longest period during which weather made air evacuation

ADVANCE TO MAAS AND ROER: ARDENNES

impossible was three consecutive days. A daily provision of two Dakotas for evacuating casualties to the United Kingdom covered requirements for priority casualties to the United Kingdom; the remaining casualties for air evacuation were evacuated either to Brussels, by Sparrow aircraft, or to the United Kingdom in returning Dakotas. The R.A.F. casualty evacuation staff gave every assistance.

The steady flow of P.o.W. sick and casualties from operations in the Nijmegen area and along the Maas necessitated the establishment of a P.o.W. hospital. 14 F.D.S. moved to Bourg-Léopold, taking over accommodation that had previously been used as a German military hospital. At the end of the first week in October German P.o.W. casualties were diverted to this F.D.S., where cases were retained and treated. Help was given by the Dutch Red Cross and full use was made of captured enemy protected personnel, including nursing sisters. By the end of October there were 637 sick and wounded P.o.W. in this centre. The German protected personnel staffing the P.o.W. hospital numbered 150. The majority of cases were discharged to the Army P.o.W. cage when fit and separate arrangements were made for the evacuation of the remaining cases and for the transfer of protected personnel. The centre closed on November 9.

With the approach of winter advanced depots of medical stores were sited to meet the changed conditions and were accommodated in buildings wherever possible. At the end of September three advanced depots medical stores were under command. These were sited as follows:

8 in Nijmegen (later in Hasselt)
9 in Diest (later in Valkenswaard)
11 in Eindhoven.

The base depots were originally at Bayeux and Dieppe but were later brought forward and the distances between these units and advanced depots were greatly reduced, thus easing supply difficulties.

A mobile element of an advanced depot medical stores was allotted to and was at the disposal of each D.D.M.S. corps. The mobile element comprised two 3-ton lorries with drivers and was stocked with items likely to be required by forward medical units. One lorry was located with a corps medical unit selected by D.D.M.S. corps. The second lorry ferried unit demands and replenishments to the forward lorry or proceeded, completely stocked, and replaced it. In the latter case the replaced vehicle could be maintained and overhauled and completely restocked at the parent advanced depot. On the move of an advanced depot the lorries could be stocked before the move and opened for issue immediately on arrival at the new location. When not required by D.D.M.S. corps the advanced element was located at the parent advanced depot. The mobile element amply proved its worth and on the only occasion on which one was given up by a corps its return was requested for the next operation on which the corps was engaged. The provision of one N.C.O. R.A.M.C., one Pioneer (for general duties) and two drivers for a mobile element was more than justified by the saving in time, personnel and vehicles of medical units whose resources were fully committed.

To provide for the supply of small quantities of medical equipment to R.M.Os. and isolated detachments in Second Army troops area a detailed issue medical store was located at 50 F.D.S. at Moll with a detailed issue dispensary at 31 F.D.S. at Hasselt. Supply to the detailed issue medical store was made from a nominated advanced depot medical stores, thus preventing depletion of stocks in general hospitals, C.C.Ss. and F.D.Ss.

The policy of treating as many minor sick as possible in forward areas where they could more readily be returned to their units for duty, necessitated advanced depots medical stores holding greater quantities of some consumable items and the provision of medicine, or their ingredients, ointments, etc., not included in A.F. I.1248 scales for advanced depots medical stores but normally supplied for the treatment of minor sick. Existing I.1248 scales for some items were quite inadequate for actual requirements in this theatre and, consequently, most demands from medical units for such items were in excess of the normal scales. It was possible to meet all reasonable demands for most of these requirements.

Captured German medical equipment was handed in to the nearest advanced depot medical stores whence it was taken to No. 1 Captured Enemy Equipment Section (Medical) for classification and reissue.

L. OF C.

The rapid advance of the armies had left the majority of the hospitals in the rear maintenance area. It was therefore of primary importance to move at once as many as possible into northern France and Belgium, since at the beginning of this period there were only 6,100 beds to serve the bulk of 21 Army Group located north of the Seine compared with the 11,400 beds which remained in Normandy.

Despite the urgency of the situation only one general transport company could be allotted to the task, and this was fully employed up to the end of December in moving the required medical units forward. Apart from the question of transport, the speed at which the hospital area in the advanced base was built up also depended on finding and adapting adequate covered accommodation, for since winter was approaching it was not feasible to site hospitals under canvas. At one time the lack of accommodation was so serious that six general hospitals which had become redundant in the R.M.A. were shipped back to the United

Kingdom to wait until suitable buildings were available in the advanced base. The problem was gradually surmounted by taking over all existing civilian and German military hospitals and by converting many large schools and convents to medical uses. By January 7, 29,600 beds were equipped and functioning within the theatre while 1,400 beds were closed but ready to open when required.

At this time the lack of adequate convalescent depot facilities adversely influenced the intention to lengthen the holding period. Nevertheless by October 27, cases which were likely to return to duty or to be convalescent within 28 days were, whenever possible, held in the theatre and, by December 7, the holding period had been extended in most cases to 30 days.

The opening of convalescent depots was delayed by lack of suitable accommodation, the need to wait until completion of the necessary engineering work and the difficulty in obtaining essential accommodation stores such as beds or double bunks. A 500-bed depot was eventually opened at St. Pol on October 30 and another, with a capacity of 300 beds, at De Haan in November. By the first week in January, 3,700 beds were available in convalescent depots.

The main hospital areas in the L. of C. were in the vicinity of Brussels, Antwerp, Ghent, Bruges, Ostend, Lille, Tournai, Amiens and St. Omer. Early in the period there were hospitals at Rouen and Dieppe. When U.S. forces took over these areas and when Dieppe closed as a port, these medical units moved into Belgium. The medical area of the R.M.A., which figured so importantly in the earliest phases of the campaign, now existed only in the shape of a 'winterised' 1,600-bed general hospital in Bayeux.

Evacuation by hospital carrier from the R.M.A. continued from Arromanches until mid-December, although by this time the commitment had dwindled to only one carrier weekly. When this service ceased, casualties unfit for evacuation by air were accepted by the U.S. authorities and taken to the United Kingdom from Cherbourg. Air evacuation continued from Carpiquet, but by the end of the year it was more usual for casualties to be shuttled forward to an airfield near St. Omer. Hospital carriers continued to evacuate casualties north of the Seine from Dieppe until mid-November, but the main port for sea evacuation was Ostend, which despatched its first hospital carrier on October 21. Movement to Ostend from other hospital areas was through ambulance railheads. The Brussels area, which received shuttle cases from Second Army and also, until early November, most of the ambulance trains, was the main centre for air evacuation. Air evacuation from Antwerp started at the beginning of October, but as Antwerp became untenable as a medical centre owing to attacks by V.1 weapons the air evacuation unit was moved to Bruges and continued to function from there.

In December H.Q. 11 L. of C. Area moved to Malines, there to take over the accommodation previously occupied by H.Q. L. of C., and H.Q. 12 L. of C. Area replaced H.Q. 11 L. of C. Area in Amiens. A search for suitable hospital sites began again and the usual difficulties were encountered. Lack of interchange of information between the R.A.F. and Army Medical Services added to these difficulties, leading as it did to a competition for sites.

The V.1 rocket attacks on Antwerp caused great damage and many casualties, civilian and military. It became necessary to reduce the staff of 9 B.G.H. so that it came to function as a C.C.S., evacuating to 109 B.G.H. at Duffel. 20 Cdn. G.H. in Antwerp was kept closed with only a caretaker staff. 109 B.G.H. itself was in the target area and so it was kept as clear as possible.

When the German counter-offensive in the Ardennes opened H.Q. 11 L. of C. Area, H.Qs. 4 L. of C. Sub-area and 7 Base Sub-area stood to and the mobile medical units were put into a state of readiness to move at a moment's notice. But after three days the emergency passed in so far as these H.Qs. were concerned. The office of D.D.M.S. remained with Rear Army H.Q. except for a small detachment comprising the Army psychiatrist and his clerk who were located with 'A' Branch at Main Army H.Q., thus facilitating the work of the psychiatrist in connexion with review of sentences in conjunction with A.A.G's. Branch.

The supply of officer reinforcements was quite satisfactory; a large number of officers sent forward as reinforcements were most anxious to serve in forward areas either as R.M.Os. or M.Os. in field ambulances. 31 R.A.M.C. officer reinforcements were received to replace officer casualties within Second Army (killed 3; wounded 6; missing 1; sick 21).

The supply of other rank reinforcements was also satisfactory. The delay occasioned in obtaining replacements for certain R.A.M.C. tradesmen who became casualties (especially clerks, hospital cooks and masseurs) was unavoidable.

Documentation within the Army was based on a weekly return from all R.M.Os. showing under the headings of various diseases the attendance at M.I. Rooms and admission to medical units. Formations submitted a weekly return showing admissions to medical units according to disease and a weekly infectious disease return. It was considered that these returns would form a good basis from which to obtain the figures of sick wastage in the Army. Unfortunately it did not take into consideration the return to the fighting units of minor sick. A new return was instituted which was completed by all medical units showing the admissions due to battle casualties, injuries (non-enemy action) and sickness (including exhaustion). This return also showed the numbers discharged by each medical unit back to duty or to the reinforcement holding unit. A further sub-division into British Army, Canadians and Allies completed the return.

ADVANCE TO MAAS AND ROER: ARDENNES

The Army medical R/T net was retained and proved to be of value on several occasions when line communication was broken. This net was also used during operations for passing urgent messages from the medical branch at one corps to that at a neighbouring corps.

The policy of maintaining close liaison with the Surgeon's Office of the flanking U.S. Ninth Army by attachment of a R.A.M.C. liaison officer proved immensely useful.

The scheme for the treatment of venereal disease in unit lines was changed. Previously, fresh cases of gonorrhoea were treated in the lines and only resistant or relapsing cases, as well as penile sores, were referred to the V.D.T.C. at corps. Under the new arrangement a field ambulance unit was nominated by A.D.M.S. division to receive and treat fresh cases of gonorrhoea with penicillin and the V.D.T.C. still remained at corps level where all cases of penile sore and resistant cases of urethritis were admitted.

The use of penicillin in the treatment of syphilis was now extended to all V.D.T.Cs., thus achieving a vast saving in man-hours since an in-patient in a F.D.S. was discharged back to duty after only nine days and required only to attend a V.D.T.C. at intervals of 2, 4, 6, 9, 12, 18 and 24 months afterwards for surveillance. The weekly visit to medical units for arsenical injections thus became a thing of the past.

The optical section, with an ophthalmologist from 81 B.G.H., was detached to Grave to provide forward ophthalmic facilities for XII and XXX Corps during October and was later moved up to Nijmegen where it remained until XXX Corps was withdrawn. The supply and repair of spectacles was satisfactory. There was undoubtedly a high wastage rate of spectacles in Army area and efforts to check this were unsuccessful. The use of old respirator face-pieces to protect face and eyes from fragments during mine-lifting operations proved very effective and undoubtedly reduced casualties from this cause.

A dermatologist was attached to 79 B.G.H. at Eindhoven and was responsible for general supervision of treatment of skin cases within Army. Minor skin conditions were treated in divisional, corps or Army F.D.Ss.; the more serious cases requiring specialist attention were referred to 79 B.G.H. for admission.

In addition to these arrangements, minor infectious cases (rubella, chicken pox and mumps) were admitted to 21 F.D.S., located at ambulance railhead. The specialist in dermatology from 79 B.G.H. paid regular visits to F.D.Ss. where skin cases were retained for treatment.

THE ARMY PSYCHIATRIC SERVICE (SECOND ARMY)

After closing down in Normandy, 32 B.G.H. moved to Belgium and opened at Wavre Notre Dame near Malines, on October 24. Here the bedstate was increased to 1,200 and, in addition, one division of 14 Con.

Depot, equipped and staffed for 600 patients, was attached to the hospital. Thereafter, the return to duty rate rose to 92 per cent. though it later fell, in February 1945, to 82 per cent. following a reduction in the bedstate to 800 and the removal of the convalescent depot beds. Those evacuated to the United Kingdom were mainly chronic constitutional neurotics and mental defectives.

Experience in the handling of psychiatric casualties in 32 B.G.H. showed that the whole organisation of a military psychiatric hospital in the field should have a preponderantly military orientation. To prevent the onset of the military degeneration which is inseparable from a spell in hospital, it was necessary to provide an organisation in which men ceased, as far as possible, to be regarded as hospital patients but were placed under a much more military influence, with the twofold object of assisting their recovery in the military sense and of preventing any undue exploitation of neurotic symptoms. Each patient had to fit into this organisation as soon as he was in a fit state of health to do so. There was, however, unfortunately no provision made in the establishment of a psychiatric general hospital for the necessary staff required for this military rehabilitation. In Normandy, convalescent officer and senior N.C.O. patients ran the organisation, but this was not satisfactory for various reasons. The attachment to the hospital in Belgium of one division of a convalescent depot solved the problem. The original intention had been for this division to function as such and for convalescent patients to be transferred to it from the adjacent hospital. This arrangement had disadvantages and the staff of the convalescent division eventually took over the entire training programme of the patients in the hospital so that military rehabilitation was initiated at the earliest possible stage. Something akin to the usual convalescent depot training programme was incorporated into the hospital and patients entered this as soon as fit to do so. Each ward represented a platoon under a senior N.C.O. patient of the ward and platoons were grouped in companies under a C.S.M. of the convalescent depot staff. Ward morale was good and a well-ordered ward routine gave the individual patient on his first entry into his ward a measure of confidence and security and helped in the restoration of self respect. Convalescence and rehabilitation took place simultaneously with treatment, and the time the patient spent away from his unit was considerably less than if he had been discharged to a convalescent depot after completion of psychiatric treatment. He was under the control of one psychiatrically trained medical officer from first to last.

In the early months of the campaign, L. of C. psychiatrists in the United Kingdom were engaged in the psychiatric 'screening' of reinforcements to 21 Army Group. Many unstable men were found in the stream of reinforcements. This vital prophylactic work, designed to prevent potential psychiatric casualties from being sent to fighting units, acted as a filter for general reinforcements and for ex-hospital casualties, both surgical and medical, returning to 21 Army Group from military and E.M.S. hospitals. The valuable work of 'screening' the reinforcement stream in the United Kingdom had to cease as the need became urgent for psychiatrists for clinical work in the L. of C. and in the hospital base developing around Bayeux. By the middle of September the psychiatric selection work in 21 Army Group was concentrated at 37 R.H.U. in Normandy, to which an increased staff, including a standing medical board and personnel selection teams, were added. This unit was, however, swamped with ex-hospital cases, predominantly psychiatric, who required placement, but for whom neither adequate accommodation nor adequate staff was made available. Provision for dealing with this problem was never adequate until the arrival of 10 Holding and Selection Centre in February 1945.

A considerable 'bottleneck' developed and men awaiting re-allocation accumulated. This delay, together with the general conditions prevailing in the R.H.U., had a serious effect on the morale of the low-grade reinforcements. The personnel of 10 Holding and Selection Unit included two psychiatrists and placed the process of re-allocation on a sound basis.

During October, November and December the incidence of psychiatric casualties was 4·8 per cent. of all casualties, or 14·3 per cent. of surgical battle casualties. All reports from corps psychiatrists of Second Army commented on the frequency with which reinforcements figured among the cases seen. Many were described as young, immature lads who had not been long enough with their units to develop a group spirit; others were men of low morale and low combatant temperament who should have been combed out before leaving the United Kingdom, and a fair number were men who had previously been for long periods in 'employed' jobs and who had had little preparation for a change to an active combatant rôle. The question of the disposal of the 'war weary' soldier cropped up repeatedly in a variety of ways. He was frequently an officer or N.C.O. of good personality with a good previous record, whose service in different theatres of war was considerable and who had now reached the end of his resources to deal with further battle stress. He was almost certainly a reliable man, since the less efficient and less robust had been weeded out in earlier campaigns. Many suffered from a mild chronic anxiety state and were often embittered and paranoid in their outlook. Owing to this attitude some became disciplinary cases; others broke down during battle and were evacuated; the majority remained with their units, showing an inadequate performance and power and an ineffective drive in battle.

(Second Army's Order of Battle and Medical Order of Battle from

October to December 1944 will be found in Appendix VIII and the Location Statement of 21 Army Group's General Hospitals for the same period in Appendix IX.)

APPENDIX VIII

A. SECOND ARMY. SKELETON ORDER OF BATTLE
B. SECOND ARMY. MEDICAL ORDER OF BATTLE

OCTOBER–DECEMBER 1944

A 1. Order of Battle on October 1, 1944, and December 31, 1944

October 1, 1944:
VIII Corps
    11th Armd. Division
    3rd Division
    50th (N.) Division
    4th Armd. Bde.
    6th Gds. Tk. Bde.
    Belgian Bde.

XII Corps
    7th Armd. Division
    15th (S.) Division
    53rd (W.) Division

XXX Corps
    Gds. Armd. Division
    43rd Inf. Division
    8th Armd. Bde.
    Royal Netherlands Bde.

December 31, 1944:
VIII Corps
    11th Armd. Division
    3rd Division
    15th (S.) Division

XII Corps
    7th Armd. Division
    43rd Inf. Division
    51st (H.) Division
    52nd (L.) Division
    8th Armd. Bde.
    6th Gds. Tk. Bde.

XXX Corps
    Gds. Armd. Division
    6th Airborne Division
    53rd (W.) Division
    29th Armd. Bde.
    33rd Armd. Bde.
    34th Tk. Bde.

A 2. Formations under command Second Army during period October 1–December 31, 1944

Formation	Period
Gds. Armd. Division	Oct. 1–Dec. 31
7th Armd. Division	Oct. 1–Dec. 31
11th Armd. Division	Oct. 1–Dec. 31
6th Airborne Division	Dec. 27–Dec. 31
3rd Division	Oct. 1–Dec. 31
15th (S.) Division	Oct. 1–Dec. 31
43rd Inf. Division	Oct. 1–Dec. 31
50th (N.) Division	Oct. 1–Nov. 9
49th Inf. Division	Nov. 9–Nov. 30

ADVANCE TO MAAS AND ROER: ARDENNES

51st (H.) Division	Oct. 2–Oct. 9
	Oct. 18–Nov. 25
	Dec. 20–Dec. 31
52nd (L.) Division	Dec. 6–Dec. 31
53rd (W.) Division	Oct. 1–Dec. 18
	Dec. 20–Dec. 31
4th Armd. Bde.	Oct. 1–Dec. 31
6th Gds. Tk. Bde.	Oct. 1–Dec. 17
	Dec. 25–Dec. 31
8th Armd. Bde.	Oct. 1–Dec. 31
33rd Armd. Bde.	Oct. 18–Nov. 29
	Dec. 20–Dec. 25
29th Armd. Bde.	Dec. 22–Dec. 31
34th Tk. Bde.	Oct. 9–Dec. 31
U.S. 7th Armd. Division	Oct. 25–Nov. 9
U.S. 82nd Airborne Division	Oct. 10–Nov. 5
U.S. 101st Airborne Division	Oct. 19–Nov. 9
Belgian Bde.	Oct. 1–Nov. 25
Royal Netherlands Bde.	Oct. 1–Nov. 8

B. Medical Order of Battle

General Hospitals	39	Nov. 15–Dec. 31
	79	
	81	
	84	
	86	
C.C.S.	35	
F.D.Ss.	1	allotted to VIII Corps
	2	
	4	Dec. 18–Dec. 31
	9	allotted to XII Corps
	14	Oct. 11–Dec. 18
	21	Dec. 2–Dec. 31
	31	
	35	allotted to XXX Corps
	47	Oct. 1–Dec. 2
	49	
	50	
Con. Depot	13	Nov. 12–Dec. 31
F.S.Us.	6	
	12	
	13	Oct. 1–Dec. 12
	14	
	15	
	27	

F.S.Us.	33		
	38		
	40		
	41		
	42		
	43		
	44		
	45		
	46		
	47		
	49		
	50		
	51		
	52		
	53		
	54		
	56		Dec. 12–Dec. 31
Special Surgical Teams .	6	M.N.S.U.	Oct. 1–Oct. 15
	5	M.F.S.U.	Oct. 1–Oct. 15
F.T.Us.	6		
	7		
	13		
	21		
	22		
	24		
	30		
	31		
	35		
	37		
Blood Distribution Units	'Y'	Blood Bank	
Field Hygiene Sections .	30	allotted to 10 Garrison	
	61		
Adv. Depots Med. Stores	8		
	9		
	11		
Laboratories	4	Mob. Bact. Lab.	
	4	Mob. Hyg. Lab.	Dec. 16–Dec. 31
A.C.C.	257		
Port Dets. R.A.M.C.	25		
	28		Dec. 9–Dec. 31
P.A.Cs.	62		
	64		
	65		
	66		
	68		

APPENDIX IX

21 ARMY GROUP. LOCATION STATEMENT GENERAL HOSPITALS AND CONVALESCENT DEPOTS.

OCTOBER–DECEMBER 1944

General Hospitals

At the beginning of October the distribution of the general hospitals of 21 Army Group was as follows:

Second Army		81, 84, 86 and 88 B.G.Hs. — all 200 beds
		6 Cdn.G.H.
L. of C.		
11 L. of C. Area (Northern France)	Martigny	21 Cdn.G.H. (1,200)
	Dieppe	
	Amiens	25 B.G.H. (600)
12 L. of C. Area (south of the Seine and Rouen)	Rouen	6 B.G.H. (1,200)
4 L. of C. Sub-Area	Brussels	8 and 39 B.G.Hs. (600)
5 L. of C. S.A.	Bayeux	20, 32, 74, 75 and 79 B.G.Hs. (600)
		23, 24, 29, 73, 101, 102, 105, 106, 107, 108 and 110 B.G.Hs. (1,200)
		2 and 10 Cdn. G.Hs. (1,200)
	Reviers	77 B.G.H. (600)
6 L. of C. S.A.	Arques-la-Bataille	113 B.G.H. (1,200)
	Dieppe	121 B.G.H. and 7 Cdn. G.H. (600)
15 L. of C. S.A.	St. Omer	16 Cdn.G.H. (600)
7 Base Sub-Area (Antwerp)	Antwerp	9 B.G.H. and 8 Cdn. G.H. (600)
	Duffel	30 B.G.H. (600)
8 B.S.A. (Ostend)	Bruges	12 Cdn. G.H. (1,200)

Base Depots Medical Stores:

Bayeux	5
Antwerp	11
Bayeux	12
Dieppe	13
Bayeux	2 Cdn. (closed)

The following moves took place:

During October:

20, 23, 24 and 29 B.G.Hs. closed and returned to the United Kingdom, there to pass under the control of the War Office.

73, 102 and 107 B.G.Hs. closed, the personnel returning to the United Kingdom and the equipment being stored in Normandy against the return of the personnel to the Continent.

32 B.G.H.	moved from	Bayeux	to Wavre Notre Dame	(7 B.S.A.)
77 ,,	,,	,,	Reviers	,, St. André, Lille	(11 L. of C. A.)
79 ,,	,,	,,	Bayeux	,, Eindhoven	(Second Army)
121 ,,	,,	,,	Dieppe	,, Amiens	(16 L. of C. S.A.)
7 Cdn. G.H.	,,	,,	Dieppe	,, Turnhout	(Cdn. First Army)
101 B.G.H.	,,	,,	Bayeux	,, Louvain	(4 L. of C. S.A.)
105 ,,	,,	,,	Bayeux	,, Ostend	(8 B.S.A.)
108 ,,	,,	,,	Bayeux	,, Brussels	(4 L. of C. S.A.)
109 ,,	,,	,,	United Kingdom	,, Duffel	(7 B.S.A.)
111 ,,	,,	,,	United Kingdom	,, Brussels	(4 L. of C. S.A.)
115 ,,	,,	,,	United Kingdom	,, De Haan	(8 B.S.A.)
2 Cdn. G.H.	,,	,,	Bayeux	,, Ghent	(8 B.S.A.)

During November:

81 B.G.H.	Second Army	Sterksel, then Hasselt
84 ,,	,, ,,	Heeze, nr. Sterksel
86 ,,	,, ,,	Eindhoven
88 ,,	Cdn. First Army	Bouchout, then Tilburg
6 Cdn. G.H. ,,	,, ,,	Antwerp

30 B.G.H.	moved from	Duffel	to Lille	(15 L. of C. S.A.)
39 ,,	,,	,,	Brussels	,, Hasselt	(Second Army)
74 ,,	,,	,,	Bayeux	,, Bruges	(8 B.S.A.)
110 ,,	,,	,,	Bayeux	,, Bruges	(8 B.S.A.)
10 Cdn. G.H.	,,	,,	Bayeux	,, Turnhout	(Cdn. First Army)

During December:

6 Cdn. G.H.	moved from	Antwerp	to St. Michielsgestel	(Cdn. First Army)
75 B.G.H.	,,	,,	Bayeux	,, Brussels	(4 L. of C. S.A.)
77 ,,	,,	,,	Lille	,, Ghent	(16 L. of C. S.A.)
8 Cdn. G.H.	,,	,,	Antwerp	,, St. Michielsgestel	(Cdn. First Army)
6 B.G.H.	,,	,,	Rouen	,, Oostakker nr. Ghent	(16 L. of C. S.A.)

113 B.G.H. moved from Arques-la-
                     Bataille   to Renaix   (13 Garrison)
20 Cdn. G.H.   ,,   ,,   United
                     Kingdom ,, Antwerp   (7 B.S.A.)

Convalescent Depots

At the end of October the distribution of the convalescent depots was as follows:

5 Con. Depot   still in the United Kingdom ⎫
12 ,,   ,,   Bayeux, closed, to move to Ostend ⎪
14 ,,   ,,   Bayeux   ⎬ 2,000 beds
15 ,,   ,,   Bayeux, closed   ⎪
2 Cdn. Con. Depot Bayeux, closed   ⎭
13 Con. Depot   Bayeux, closed, to move to St. Pol ⎫ 1,000 beds
3 Cdn. Con. Depot Bayeux   ⎭

By mid-November:

12 Con. Depot had moved from   Bayeux to De
                                        Haan   (16 L. of C. S.A.)
15 ,,   ,,   ,,   ,,   ,,   Bayeux ,, St. Pol (5 L. of C. S.A.)
2 Cdn. Con. Depot had moved from Bayeux ,, Knocke (16 L. of C. S.A.)
13 Con. Depot had moved from   Bayeux ,, Bourg-
                                        Léopold (Second Army)

In December:

5 Con. Depot arrived from the United Kingdom in Knocke
                                               (5 L. of C. S.A.)
14 ,,   ,,   moved from Bayeux to Tournai   (13 Garrison)
3 Cdn. Con. Depot moved from Bayeux to Knocke (5 L. of C. S.A.)

The Location Statement as at the end of the year was therefore as follows:

General Hospitals

	Present Location	Expansions	Formation	Remarks
200 beds				
81 B.G.H.	Hasselt		Second Army	
84 ,,	Sterksel		,, ,,	
86 ,,	Eindhoven		,, ,,	
88 ,,	Tilburg		Cdn. First Army	
6 Cdn. G.H.	St. Michiels-gestel		,, ,, ,,	
600 beds				
8 B.G.H.	Brussels		4 L. of C. S.A.	
9 ,,	Antwerp	3 × 100	7 B.S.A.	
25 ,,	Amiens	3 × 100	6 L. of C. S.A.	
30 ,,	Lille	2 × 100	15 L. of C. S.A.	
32 ,,	Wavre Notre Dame		7 B.S.A.	
39 ,,	Hasselt		Second Army	
74 ,,	Bruges		8 B.S.A.	

	Present Location	Expansions	Formation	Remarks
75 B.G.H.	Brussels		4 L. of C. S.A.	Opening
77 ,,	Ghent		16 L. of C. S.A.	
79 ,,	Eindhoven		Second Army	
121 ,,	Amiens	1 × 100	6 L. of C. S.A.	
7 Cdn. G.H.	Turnhout		Cdn. First Army	
8 ,,	St. Michiels-gestel (closed)		,, ,, ,,	
16 ,,	St. Omer		15 L. of C. S.A.	To move to Oost Dunkerke when relieved by 21 Cdn.G.H.

1,200 beds

	Present Location	Expansions	Formation	Remarks
6 B.G.H.	Oostakker, nr. Ghent		16 L. of C. S.A.	
23 ,,	Lille (St. André)		15 L. of C. S.A.	Opening
29 ,,	United Kingdom			Called forward for Eecloo
96 ,,	United Kingdom			Called forward for St. Amands in January
101 ,,	Heverlee nr. Louvain	7 × 100	4 L. of C. S.A.	
105 ,,	Ostend	4 × 100	8 B.S.A.	
106 ,,	Bayeux	5 × 100	5 L. of C. S.A.	
108 ,,	Brussels	3 × 100	4 L. of C. S.A.	
109 ,,	Duffel		7 B.S.A.	
110 ,,	Bruges	1 × 100	8 B.S.A.	
111 ,,	Brussels		4 L. of C. S.A.	
113 ,,	Renaix		13 Garrison	
115 ,,	De Haan	2 × 100	8 B.S.A.	
2 Cdn. G.H.	Ghent		16 L. of C. S.A.	
10 ,,	Turnhout		Cdn. First Army	
12 ,,	Bruges		8 B.S.A.	
20 ,,	Antwerp		7 B.S.A.	
21 ,,	Château Mesniéres, nr. Dieppe		6 L. of C. S.A.	To relieve 16 Cdn.G.H.

Convalescent Depots

	Present Location	Formation	Remarks
2,000 beds			
5 Con. Depot	Knocke	8 B.S.A.	
12 ,, ,,	De Haan	8 B.S.A.	
14 ,, ,,	Tournai	13 Garrison	One division with 32 B.G.H.
15 ,, ,,	St. Pol	15 L. of C. S.A.	
2 Cdn. Con. Depot	Knocke	8 B.S.A.	
1,000 beds			
13 Con. Depot	Bourg-Léopold	Second Army	
3 Cdn. Con. Depot	Knocke (closed)	8 B.S.A.	

CHAPTER 6

THE ADVANCE TO AND THE CROSSING OF THE RHINE

(i)

The Operations

GENERAL EISENHOWER's plans for the advance to the Rhine took the following form: 21 Army Group, with U.S. Ninth Army under command, would seize the west bank of the Rhine from Nijmegen to Düsseldorf, after clearing the Lower Rhineland with converging attacks by Canadian First Army from the Reichswald and U.S. Ninth Army from the Jülich–Linnich area, the two attacks converging on the Rhine opposite Wesel. While 21 Army Group was preparing for these operations U.S. First Army would press forward to Cologne and capture the Roer dams. Then while 21 Army Group was clearing the Rhineland, U.S. 12 Army Group would assume an aggressive defence on its whole front except on the extreme left where it would advance to protect U.S. Ninth Army's right flank. When the early and complete achievement of objectives in the Rhineland was assured, U.S. 12 Army Group would invest Cologne and close to the Rhine north of the Moselle. When the success of this operation was assured, U.S. Third and Seventh Armies would clear the Moselle–Saar–Rhine triangle and secure crossings over the Rhine in the Mainz–Mannheim sector.

Canadian First Army was now set the task of attacking south-eastwards from Nijmegen through the Reichswald to the general line Geldern–Xanten and then to bridge the Rhine at Emmerich, while U.S. Ninth Army attacked north-eastwards from the Jülich–Linnich sector of the Roer towards the Rhine, between Düsseldorf and Mörs. U.S. First Army in the Cologne sector was to protect the right flank of the operation up the Erft (*see* Figs. 77 and 78).

At the start of this battle Canadian First Army had under command seven divisions for the actual battle, one in reserve and two more holding the front from Nijmegen to the west. Later, three more divisions were allotted to it for the battle, one joined it from reserve and one went from the battle to reserve. Of the eleven divisions that took part in the battle eight were British.

XXX Corps was placed in charge of the whole front during the initial stage—the attack on the Reichswald—and to it were allotted seven divisions, three armoured brigades and eleven regiments of 79th Armoured Division, over 200,000 men in all, supported by over 1,000 guns.

The initial attack was to be undertaken by Canadian 2nd and 15th, 53rd and 51st Divisions in this order from north to south, while Canadian 3rd Division attacked on the extreme northern flank. The task of piercing the Siegfried Line at the northern tip of the Reichswald was assigned to 15th Division. The fortifications of the Siegfried Line did not extend as far north as the Reichswald but the Germans had developed

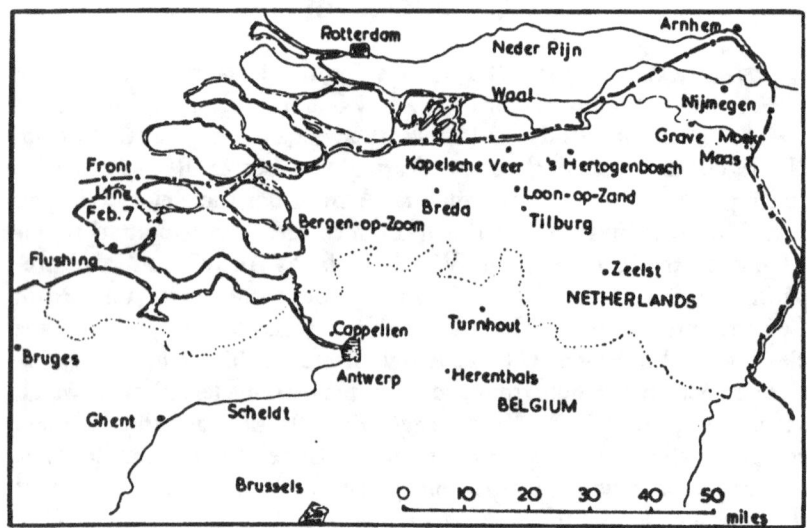

FIG. 77. The Front Line. February 7.

the forest's natural defensive qualities to the full and had breached the banks of the Rhine and flooded part of the area. Beyond the Reichswald they had fortified the towns of Goch and Cleve. At the time of the operation the ground, previously frozen firm, had become soft and the rain had turned the forest tracks into quagmires.

The battle opened at 0500 hours on February 8. The preliminary barrage lasted five and a half hours. Then five infantry divisions, supported by three armoured brigades and the specialised armour, attacked on a seven-mile front. 51st Division advanced to capture the high ground at the south-west corner of the Reichswald and 53rd Division to seize the high ground at the north-west corner. 15th Division thrust towards Kranenburg. On the left of 15th Division, Canadian 2nd Division advanced on Wyler and on the extreme left of

ADVANCE TO AND CROSSING OF THE RHINE

the attack Canadian 3rd Division in 'Buffaloes' and 'Weasels' set out to clear the flooded area between the Nijmegen–Cleve road and the Waal. All the minor roads between Groesbeek and the Reichswald broke up so that the advance was delayed; the rising flood waters started to flow

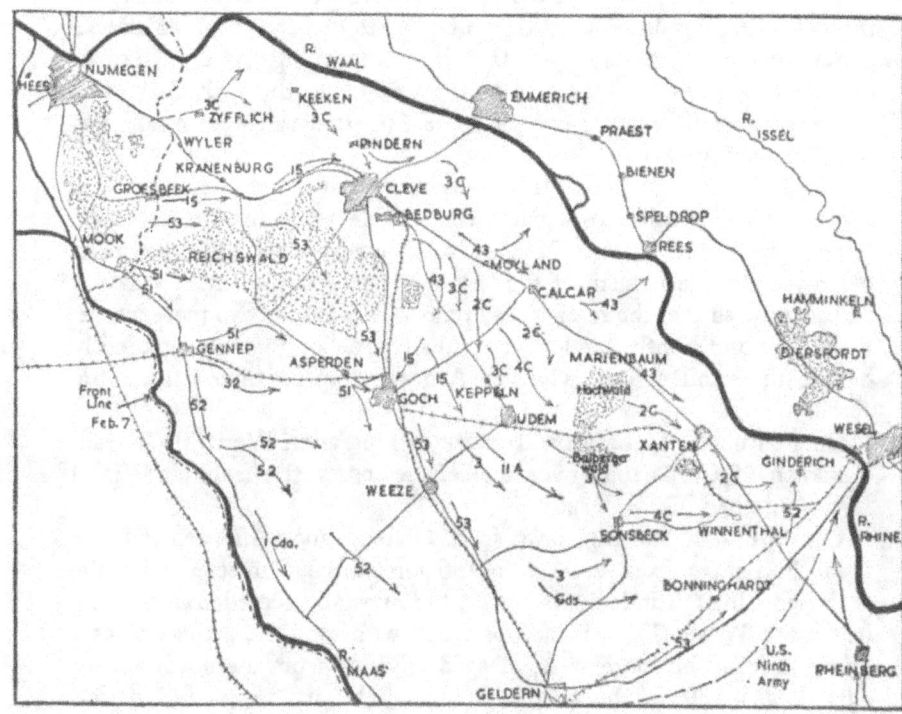

FIG. 78. Canadian First Army. The Battle of the Rhineland. February–March.

3, 15, 43, 51, 52 and 53 = 3rd, 15th, 43rd, 51st, 52nd and 53rd Divisions
2C, 3C = Canadian 2nd and 3rd Infantry Divisions
4C = Canadian 4th Armoured Division
32 = 32nd Guards Brigade
Gds. = Guards Armoured Division
11A = 11th Armoured Division
1 Cdo. = 1st Commando Brigade

over the Nijmegen–Cleve road on February 11th and next day the road was impassable.

On the 9th, 15th Division reached the high ground overlooking Cleve. 43rd Division was moved up to exploit the success of 15th Division and arrived before the latter had secured its final objectives. In the darkness and the rain some confusion ensued but 43rd Division managed to get a brigade into Cleve just before German reinforcements arrived to augment the garrison. A brigade of Canadian 3rd Division turned the Siegfried Line in the north. 51st Division fought its way through the Reichswald and cut the main road from Mook to the south. During the night of February 10/11 the division got across the Niers and entered Gennep in the early hours of the 11th. 53rd Division was now emerging from the Reichswald and fighting off a series of fierce counter-attacks at its south-east corner. 43rd Division was rolling up the German positions along the eastern face of the forest. On the 11th Cleve was finally secured but it was not until the 13th that the Reichswald was completely cleared.

The Germans had been able to reinforce this sector of their line because U.S. Ninth Army had been unable to launch its offensive (Operation 'Grenade') on February 10 as was planned. The Germans destroyed the mechanism of the last of the Roer dams on February 9 and so ensured that the river would remain in flood for two more weeks. U.S. First and Ninth Armies were thus compelled to wait impatiently behind the swollen Roer while 21 Army Group continued the battle alone.

On February 15, the second phase of Operation 'Veritable' began. Canadian II Corps took over the left sector of the front and 52nd Division joined XXX Corps.

52nd Division, moving down from Gennep, took Afferden but was then checked in front of a wide anti-tank ditch connected with the Siegfried Line. Ultimately, however, the division succeeded in fighting its way to Wesel. The garrison of Goch withstood the attacks of 51st Division from the south-west, of 53rd Division from the north and of 43rd Division from the north-east. On February 18, 15th Division moved down from the north to lead the final assault on Goch's formidable defences and on the 19th its garrison surrendered. Nevertheless, it took two more days for 15th and 51st Divisions, with the help of the specialised armour of 79th Armoured Division, to clear the town.

While XXX Corps was capturing Goch, Canadian II Corps, with a brigade of 15th Division under command, south-east of Cleve was thrusting towards Calcar. The Germans had thrown a strong screen of anti-tank defences and guns along the Goch–Calcar road and beyond Calcar on the Xanten road and were holding the Hochwald and the Balberger Wald in force. This third defensive belt ran from the west bank of the Rhine, near Rees, through the Hochwald and Balberger Wald, through Geldern and along the east bank of the Roer to Düren. U.S. Ninth Army was to clean up the southern part of this defensive system and Canadian II Corps was to drive across the plateau between Calcar and Üdem (Operation 'Blockbuster'). The operation was launched on February 26 with 11th and Canadian 4th Armoured Divisions and 43rd and Canadian 2nd and 3rd Divisions under command

ADVANCE TO AND CROSSING OF THE RHINE 417

but not until March 4 had the Hochwald and the Balberger Wald been cleared. During this time XXX Corps advanced to Geldern where, on March 3, contact was made with the Americans; XXX Corps then turned east towards Wesel, tightening the net around the shrinking German bridgehead.

By March 8 the divisions attacking this bridgehead had become reduced through lack of space to U.S. 35th Division, 52nd Division, Guards Armoured Division, Canadian 4th Armoured Division and 43rd Division. Xanten fell to the last two of these on March 8 and by the 11th the bridgehead had been eliminated (*see* Fig. 78).

On February 23, U.S. Ninth and First Armies began crossing the Roer and quickly established a firm bridgehead. On the last day of the month the armour broke out and two days later the Americans reached the Rhine south of Düsseldorf. Opposite Düsseldorf, on the night of March 2/3, an American column slipped through the disintegrating German lines and penetrated ten miles to reach within sight of the Rhine at Oberkassel, but as the Americans approached the town the Germans blew the bridge. The same thing happened at Uerdingen. On March 5, U.S. First Army reached Cologne to find the bridge down and turned south-east to strike into the flank and rear of the Germans in the Eifel while U.S. Third Army fell upon them with a frontal attack. The American armour covered fifty-six miles in three days to reach the Rhine near its confluence with the Moselle. All the bridges over the Rhine between Coblenz and Duisburg were down. On March 7, twenty-five miles downstream, U.S. 9th Armoured Division was leading the advance of U.S. First Army along the northern edge of the Eifel. In its path lay the town of Remagen, the outskirts of which were reached in the early afternoon. The Americans saw before them the Ludendorf railway bridge across the Rhine still intact. A motorised platoon raced through the town, choked with stragglers, and dashed for the western end of the bridge. Engineers cut the demolition cables and the infantry rushed across and overpowered the German guards. A shallow bridgehead was hurriedly established. The last barrier in the west had been breached.

There now remained the third phase of the operational schedule, the clearing of the west bank of the Rhine by a converging attack by U.S. Third and Seventh Armies to eliminate the German forces in the Moselle–Saar–Rhine triangle. U.S. Third Army was to strike southeast across the Moselle and through the wooded heights of Hunsrück while U.S. Seventh Army was to attack across the Saar between Saarbrücken and Hagenau, break the Siegfried Line and close on the Rhine. French First Army was to protect the right flank.

By March 12, U.S. Third Army had closed up to the Moselle between

Coblenz and Trier. On the 14th the river was crossed. Coblenz was occupied and on March 22 all resistance had ceased in Mainz and the Americans crossed the Rhine at Oppenheim, and by the 25th, U.S. Third and Seventh Armies had closed to the Rhine from Coblenz to Karlsruhe.

21 Army Group's preparations for the assault crossing of the Rhine (Operation 'Plunder') were elaborate. The water obstacle facing the armies was the greatest in Europe and when the plans were being prepared it had to be assumed that it would be strongly defended. A comprehensive programme of interdiction bombing, designed to isolate the battlefield and prevent the movement of German reinforcements into the Westphalian Plain, was therefore undertaken by the Allied air forces. By March 23, vast quantities of ammunition, stores and bridging equipment had been brought up to dumps on the west bank of the Rhine.

That night the attack began, preceded by an exceedingly heavy bombardment and by a heavy air attack on Wesel, into which 1st Cdo. Bde. (XII Corps) made its way to overcome its dazed defenders. The assault was launched on a twenty-five mile front between Emmerich and Rheinberg. 51st (XXX Corps) and 15th (XII Corps) Divisions of Second Army and U.S. 30th and 79th Divisions of U.S. Ninth Army were the assault formations. The crossing was effected without much difficulty for most of the German reserves had been drawn to the south as a consequence of the American crossings at Remagen and Oppenheim. By dawn on the 24th three firm bridgeheads had been established and the infantry divisions, supported by D.D. tanks, were moving forward (*see* Fig. 78).

U.S. XVIII Corps, with 6th and U.S. 17th Airborne Divisions under command, dropped to deepen the bridgehead (Operation 'Varsity') and by dusk the Allied forces were six miles east of the Rhine. By the evening of the 26th, twelve bridges were spanning the river and by that of the 28th the bridgehead had become thirty-five miles wide with an average depth of twenty miles.

The way into the Westphalian Plain was open but the forward movement of the armour was greatly impeded by the rubble of the towns which had been bombed with such severity. On the left of 21 Army Group the German garrison in North-east Holland was still holding fast, prepared to deny the Allies the north German ports and air bases; on its right the Germans were standing firm in the Ruhr; but in the centre the way was open to the Elbe. Field Marshal Montgomery therefore ordered Canadian First Army to turn north to cut off the German garrison in North-west Holland and to clear the Frisian coast, and Second Army and U.S. Ninth Army to drive hard for the Elbe while the latter

ADVANCE TO AND CROSSING OF THE RHINE 419

also sealed the northern exits from the Ruhr and established contact with U.S. First Army, which was advancing rapidly from the south to close the trap.

By March 24, U.S. First Army was holding the east bank of the Rhine from Bonn almost to Coblenz and had bridged the river in a dozen places. On the 25th it struck east along the valley of the Sieg and southeast towards the Lahn in order to link up with U.S. Third Army which was in the process of establishing further bridgeheads between Mainz and Coblenz. On March 28 the two armies joined forces near Giessen and drove together up the Frankfurt–Kassel corridor in a great sweep which took them east of the Ruhr. U.S. VII Corps wheeled northward into the rear of the Germans holding the line of the Sieg south of the Ruhr.

On April 1, Paderborn was taken and the envelopment of the Ruhr completed by the junction of U.S. First and Ninth Armies at Lippstadt. More than a quarter of a million German troops were trapped. While the mopping up of the Ruhr area proceeded the U.S. armies pressed on without pause for the Elbe. In front of them there were no prepared defences and no field armies.

(ii)

Medical Cover

GUARDS ARMOURED DIVISION

For Operation 'Veritable' this division, under XXX Corps, was required to move from its concentration area around Tilburg and 's Hertogenbosch to Nijmegen through Cleve and on to its objective, the high ground north-east of Sonsbeck, moving through 15th Division round Cleve and following 43rd Division until it reached this town, when it would come up on the left of 43rd Division.

32nd Gds. Bde. with 128 Fd. Amb. was to lead. Two sections of the field ambulance would be with each battalion group. Divisional H.Q. and the light section of 8 F.D.S. with the M.A.C. control post and a pool of ambulance cars would follow. Then would come 5th Gds. Armd. Bde. Gp. with 19 Lt. Fd. Amb. at the rear of the group. Last of all would be 2nd Scots Guards with a section of 128 Fd. Amb.

On February 13, 32nd Gds. Bde. Gp. was put u/c 51st Division and, on the 14th, successfully attacked Hommersum, west of Goch, 128 Fd. Amb. opening a C.C.P. in Ottersum. Evacuation therefrom was to 176 Fd. Amb. at Mook. The light section of 8 F.D.S. opened at Mill for minor sick. On the 15th, the C.C.P. of 128 Fd. Amb. moved to Gennep station whence evacuation was direct to XXX Corps medical centre at Nijmegen. On the 17th, 32nd Gds. Bde. Gp. captured Hassum, west of Goch.

On the 23rd the division, less 32nd Gds. Bde. Gp., moved to an area north of Goch and took over part of the line from 15th Division. Divisional H.Q. moved to the east corner of the Reichswald. Lt. Sec. 8 F.D.S. moved into Goch.

The division was now to advance on the axis Goch–Weeze–Kevelaer–Winnekendonk–Kapellen–Issum (the last on the Geldern–Wesel road south of Xanten). On March 3 the objective was changed from Issum to Bonninghardt, further to the east (*see* Fig. 79). The medical plan was as follows. 19 Lt. Fd. Amb. would evacuate casualties from 5th Gds. Armd. Gp. to 128 Fd. Amb. with 32nd Gds. Bde. Gp. and evacuation therefrom would be to Lt. Sec. 8 F.D.S. in Goch by M.A.C. Abdominal cases were to be sent to the Canadian hospital in Bedburg and all others to 23 C.C.S. in Mook. Minor sick were to be retained by Lt. Sec. 8 F.D.S. or sent on to the heavy section of this unit in Nijmegen.

The operation proceeded very much according to plan and casualties were not numerous. 19 Lt. Fd. Amb. opened a C.C.P. at Winnekendonk which cleared its cases to 212 Fd. Amb. of 53rd Division in Kevelaer. On March 5, 19 Lt. Fd. Amb. established its C.C.P. in Wetten and, on the 6th, 128 Fd. Amb. opened an A.D.S. in Kapellen to cover the attack of 1st Welsh Gds. and 2nd Scots Guards on Bonninghardt. Evacuation was to 10 C.C.S.

The division moved to the area Mook–Gennep on March 12.

TABLE 38

Guards Armoured Division. Casualties. Operation 'Veritable'

		Offrs.	O.Rs.
Evacuated by Divisional Medical Units:	Sick	38	1,176
	Wounded	47	415
,, ,, Medical Units of Flanking Formations:	Sick	2	114
	Wounded	4	77
Casualties of Other Formations evacuated by Guards Division Medical Units:	Sick	5	147
	Wounded	4	103

7TH ARMOURED DIVISION

At the beginning of the year 7th Armoured Division was holding the line of the Maas from just south of Maeseyck to Gangelt. It then took part in the clearing of the area between the three rivers, Maas, Roer and

ADVANCE TO AND CROSSING OF THE RHINE

Würm. During this operation 8th Armd. Bde., 157th Bde. of 52nd Division and 1st Cdo. Bde. were under command at various times. The initial attack was on Dieteren, the central one of three fortified villages. The approach was along a bad track and over two dykes, which were initially to be bridged by assault footbridges, and for a period of up to forty-eight hours no wheeled vehicle could be used. It was decided to send a detachment of 131 Fd. Amb. forward on foot with the R.A.P. of the attacking battalion. This section established itself in a stoutly built farmhouse and held casualties for thirty-six hours under shell, mortar and small-arms fire until at last the house was set alight and was burnt to the ground. The remainder of the company of the field ambulance followed the section and set up an A.D.S. in Dieteren. No casualty suffered unduly and none was re-wounded.

Later in the operation, when the Roermond–Sittard road had been opened, evacuation became straightforward and simple.

The division then passed to command U.S. Ninth Army and remained in the line, holding the sector running from immediately south of Roermond to Vlodrop until the middle of February. Then for the first time since it landed in Normandy the division was pulled out of the line to rest and refit in the Weeze–Weert area. During this time the divisional medical units were all under cover in Geleen and Buchten.

On March 25, 7th Armoured Division crossed the Rhine to play its part in the final battle of the campaign and to thrust towards Hamburg.

TABLE 39

7th Armoured Division. Casualties. January–March

Battle Casualties:

January	. . .	$366 = 0\cdot6/1{,}000/\text{diem}$
February	. . .	$33 = 0\cdot06/1{,}000/\text{diem}$
March	. . .	$124 = 0\cdot23/1{,}000/\text{diem}$

Sick and Accidental Injuries:

January	. . .	$296 = 0\cdot53/1{,}000/\text{diem}$
February	. . .	$272 = 0\cdot53/1{,}000/\text{diem}$
March	. . .	$286 = 0\cdot53/1{,}000/\text{diem}$

Exhaustion:

January	. . .	$18 = 0\cdot03/1{,}000/\text{diem}$
February	. . .	$2 = 0\cdot003/1{,}000/\text{diem}$
March	. . .	$5 = 0\cdot009/1{,}000/\text{diem}$

Venereal Diseases reported from R.A.Ps. and M.I. Rooms:

January	. . .	$76 = 0\cdot12/1{,}000/\text{diem}$
February	. . .	$124 = 0\cdot25/1{,}000/\text{diem}$
March	. . .	$158 = 0\cdot28/1{,}000/\text{diem}$

3RD DIVISION

The division was holding the line of the Maas from Boxmeer to Lottum until February 8 when it was relieved by 52nd Division and moved to the Louvain area to prepare for Operation 'Veritable'. Then, on the 25th, it moved to the area of Goch under command XXX Corps and took over from 15th Division.

Its first task was that of cutting the Weeze–Üdem road. This was completed on February 27. 9 Fd. Amb., covering this operation, dealt with:

	Battle Casualties	Sick	Exhaustion
3rd Division	154	41	32
Other Formations	49	14	6
P.o.W.	67	—	—

On February 28, 8 Fd. Amb. opened an A.D.S. in Goch in two brick kilns and to it a transfusion team from 11 F.D.S. was attached. On this day there was much fighting before a rapid advance towards Kervenheim was made. During this day 8 Fd. Amb. dealt with:

	Battle Casualties	Sick	Exhaustion
3rd Division	144	8	33
Other Formations	16	5	2
P.o.W.	18	—	—

On March 2, Kervenheim and Weeze were cleared and Winnekendonk captured and 223 Fd. Amb. established an A.D.S. in Kervenheim (*see* Fig. 79). On the 4th, Kapellen was entered and a hospital therein taken over as an A.D.S. by 8 Fd. Amb., which was joined by 3 F.D.S. On the 5th Wesel was cleared and thereafter the division was withdrawn, taking over from 43rd Division an area between the Rhine and the Cleve–Xanten road (*see* Fig. 78).

Divisional Casualties. March 1–12

Wounded	319
Battle Accidents	43
Sick	312
Exhaustion	43

On March 19, D.D.M.S. XXX Corps required 3rd Division's medical units to receive all casualties occurring during the initial phases of Operation 'Plunder' from 51st and 43rd Divisions and from one

ADVANCE TO AND CROSSING OF THE RHINE

Canadian brigade. This arrangement was to continue until M.A.C. cars were able to run from across the Rhine to the C.C.Ss.

3rd Division was the holding division in this operation. 8 Fd. Amb. established an A.D.S. in a most suitable building in Botzelaer which was reinforced with a resuscitation team from 9 Fd. Amb. 223 Fd. Amb. opened a tented A.D.S. further north. 21 M.A.C. cars and one T.C.V. were attached to 8 Fd. Amb., 6 cars to 223. British casualties were evacuated to 10 C.C.S. and Canadian to 3 (Cdn.) C.C.S.

Casualties admitted to the field ambulances of 3rd Division from March 23-28 totalled:

Wounded	1,298
Battle Accidents	64
Sick	304
Exhaustion	154

On March 27, 9th Inf. Bde. crossed the Rhine to occupy Rees and Groin. 9 Fd. Amb. established an A.D.S. in Rees and a C.C.P. in Groin. On the 29th the remainder of the division crossed and 9th Inf. Bde. was set the task of establishing a bridgehead over the Holtwicker Bach. This was done and the division then waited to follow the Guards Armoured Division through Holland.

At the end of March, in accordance with Second Army policy, one of the F.D.Ss. with the division was withdrawn. This loss meant that the sick of non-divisional, corps and Army units could no longer be held in the divisional medical units but would have to be evacuated. In the recent operations the divisional field ambulances were often required to use tentage for the A.D.S. It happened that each of them had a few 40 ft. × 40 ft. N.Z. shelters in fair condition and so were enabled to function with efficiency.

6TH AIRBORNE DIVISION (OPERATION 'VARSITY')

This division returned from the Continent to the United Kingdom in February 1945 to re-equip and prepare for the crossing of the Rhine. This was to involve a daylight landing among prepared defences and, it was assumed, in the face of considerable opposition. The glider-borne element of the division was to land in the same zone as the paratroops after an interval of twenty minutes during which time no gunfire could be directed on the zone for the reason that it would be occupied by the paratroops. It was taken for granted that the glider-borne troops would meet stiff and fully aroused opposition. However, it was planned that the ground forces would quickly link up with the airborne and would advance swiftly thereafter. In this advance 6th Airborne Division would assume an infantry rôle.

The medical units had to expect to be called upon to deal with large numbers of casualties. These would have to be nested until such time as the link-up between ground and airborne forces took place. Since the period of isolation was expected to be very brief it was possible for the medical units to take with them relatively small quantities of drugs and dressings and relatively large numbers of blankets and stretchers, having regard to the numbers of casualties to be dealt with. It was planned that when the division moved forward immobile casualties would be left with a rear party of one of the field ambulances, this rear party rejoining the division along the divisional axis of advance about ten days later.

The field ambulances were attached to their respective brigades and were instructed to clear the brigade D.Z. and L.Z., to establish a M.D.S. in the brigade area, to hold casualties until evacuation became possible and to undertake Priority I surgery and resuscitation. 195 A/L Fd. Amb. was to detail a M.O. to be in charge of the divisional D.Z. and to reinforce the R.A.P. that was to be established by the R.M.O. attached to H.Q. R.A. in the divisional area.

Jettison drops were to be on the Para. brigade's D.Zs. and so it was arranged that all jettison drop medical equipment would be collected by the parachute field ambulances and that 11 extra panniers would be provided for 195 A/L Fd. Amb. in Hamilcars. One day's re-supply (15 panniers) was also to be carried in Hamilcars. Eight tons of medical stores including a medical maintenance brick were preloaded in D.U.K.Ws. and were to be ferried across the Rhine at H-hour + 14.

D.A.D.M.S. 6th Airborne Division spent some time with 15th Division making the final arrangements for the evacuation of the airborne casualties. The medical officer attached to H.Q. R.A.S.C. acted as M.O. i/m/c Land Element. A.D.M.S. 6th Airborne Division did not drop with the division but remained with Second Army to supervise arrangements for the evacuation of the division's casualties.

The briefing of the medical units was as thorough as it had been for the original landing in France. The division emplaned on the airfields of East Anglia at 0745 hours and landed at 1020 hours. All three field ambulances established their M.D.Ss. on the preselected sites, that of 195 A/L Fd. Amb. having to be cleared of its German occupants before the medical unit could take it over. 195 A/L Fd. Amb. opened in Hamminkeln, 224 on the western edge of the forest and 225 Para. Fd. Amb. in a large farm about a mile east of the divisional L.Z. Casualties during the fly-in and drop were severe and the surgical teams were fully occupied. The M.O. H.Q. R.A. was seriously injured in a crash-landing of a glider. D.A.D.M.S. 6th Airborne Division established a R.A.P. in the vicinity of rear divisional H.Q. This quickly became untenable and so the casualties were moved to the M.D.S. of 225 Para. Fd. Amb. D.A.D.M.S. then went to main divisional H.Q. where a medical officer

ADVANCE TO AND CROSSING OF THE RHINE

and a party of O.Rs. from 195 Fd. Amb. had established a R.A.P. after clearing the southern half of the L.Z.

TABLE 40

6th Airborne Division. Casualties. March 24

	Killed		Wounded	
	Officers	O.Rs.	Officers	O.Rs.
3rd Para. Bde.	10	40	2	105
5th Para. Bde.	1	60	10	132
6th A/L Bde.	20	140	22	342
Divisional Tps.	9	59	14	109
	40	299	48	688

Contact between the ground and airborne forces occurred later on the 24th and evacuation from the M.D.S. of 224 Para. Fd. Amb. to the medical units of 15th Division began that night. The ambulances and heavy equipment of the medical units reached the M.D.Ss. during the morning of the 25th and the M.D.Ss. were promptly cleared. Leaving 10 seriously ill patients in the care of one of its surgical teams, 225 Para. Fd. Amb. moved forward with its brigade on the 26th. By the evening of this day all 6th Airborne's wounded had been cleared to the C.C.P. at Bislich.

TABLE 41

Casualties Admitted to the Field Ambulances of 6th Airborne Division. March 24–27

195 A/L Fd. Amb.	520
224 Para. Fd. Amb.	251
225 Para. Fd. Amb.	384
	1,155

Casualties among R.A.M.C. Personnel. March 24–27

	Killed		Wounded		Missing	
	Offrs.	O.Rs.	Offrs.	O.Rs.	Offrs.	O.Rs.
195 A/L Fd. Amb.	—	4	—	11	1	9
224 Para. Fd. Amb.	1	3	2	8	—	11
225 Para. Fd. Amb.	1	4	—	11	—	17
	2	11	2	30	1	37

6th Airborne Division Casualties. March 25–April 7

	Killed		Wounded		Missing	
	Offrs.	O.Rs.	Offrs.	O.Rs.	Offrs.	O.Rs.
3rd Para. Bde.	5	29	6	97	1	62
5th Para. Bde.	1	17	5	79	6	74
6th A/L Bde.	4	33	11	143	3	61
Divisional Tps.	—	6	13	51	13	147
	10	85	35	370	23	344

15TH (SCOTTISH) DIVISION

On January 27 planning began for Operation 'Veritable', the breaching of the Siegfried Line. The operation was to be on a five-divisional front. 51st Division on the right was to advance through the Reichswald to block the southern entrance to the forest and to be prepared to assist in the attack on Goch. In the right centre 53rd Division was to seize Feature 8053 and to clear the edge of the Reichswald as far as Stoppel Burg. In the left centre 15th Division was to break through north of Reichswald, breach the Siegfried Line and secure the high ground west of Cleve. On the left Canadian 2nd Division was to capture Wyler, Den Heuvel and Hochstrasse while Canadian 3rd Division was to clear the area north of the Wyler–Cleve road as far as Spoy Canal. On the success of 15th Division depended the passing through of 43rd Division directed on Goch and later of Guards Armoured Division.

15th Division's task was planned in five phases:

1. Two brigades to secure the high ground between Auf den Heuvel and Kranenburg and then Kranenburg and the surrounding area;
2. One brigade to cross the anti-tank ditch and obstacle belt and secure Wolfsberg, Hingstberg and Nütterden;
3. To secure the high ground south-west and north-west of Cleve;
4. The clearance of Cleve;
5. Reconnaissance in force by small armoured columns towards Üdem and Calcar (*see* Fig. 78).

ADVANCE TO AND CROSSING OF THE RHINE

The main route for evacuation was 'Ayr' or 'Pearl Red' and in order to relieve the inevitable congestion on this it was intended to open as soon as possible a route to the north—'Pearl Black'—which could not be used during the early stages of the operation since the area of Wyler was held by the Germans.

The field ambulances at this time had only one jeep apiece and so the R.M.Os.' scout cars or half-tracks were modified for the carriage of stretchers. A generous supply of self-heating soups and the like was obtained and a quantity of twenty-four-hour ration packs for the field ambulance personnel. Each field ambulance was issued with 80 square yards of glass substitute for use in making damaged buildings habitable. During February 4–6 the division concentrated in the Nijmegen area, full precautions to secure secrecy being taken.

On the evening of D-day – 1, C.C.Ps. were established in the Groesbeek area. 194 Fd. Amb. opened an A.D.S. at Berg-en-Dal to provide for the possibility of the opening of Route 'Pearl Black' before an A.D.S. could be opened in Kranenburg. 23 F.D.S. opened in Nijmegen to deal with the sick and exhaustion cases. 22 F.D.S. remained in Tilburg to look after the divisional administrative area. The M.D.Us. were attached to the F.D.Ss.

On February 8, five and a half hours before H-hour (1030 hours), the artillery barrage opened and at 0700 hours 193 Fd. Amb. established an A.D.S. in the monastery in Nebo. Despite the very heavy going the infantry had got beyond Kranenburg and Frasselt by 1800 hours. The field ambulance companies moving in support of the brigades had very great difficulty in getting forward and in evacuating casualties since even the stretcher-carrying jeeps had to be towed by carriers. In many stretches hand-carriage was necessary. In the late afternoon 193 Fd. Amb's. C.C.P. at Groesbeek was reinforced and was functioning as a light A.D.S. in echelon with the A.D.S. at Nebo. Although the C.C.S. at Marienboom was only four miles away from this light A.D.S. the time taken to reach it was excessively long owing to traffic and blocks. Many cases were severely shocked on arrival at the C.C.S. despite drip transfusions administered *en route* between C.C.P. and C.C.S. A resuscitation team of 22 F.D.S. was attached to the light A.D.S.

Before the start of the second phase, as 'Ayr' Route forward of the German frontier had become impassable, 44th Bde's. axis was changed and the armoured breaching force moved forward on 'Pearl Black'. This change of axis left the C.C.P. of 'A' Coy. 194 Fd. Amb. isolated and its vehicles could not in fact be extricated from the mud for two days, and in order to have a C.C.P. open for the battle one section of 'B' Coy. was moved to Kranenburg before the passage of the armoured columns, a car post being established there to cover the interim period. A car post was also established in the vicinity of the intended Gap

Control organised to trans-ship cases from 'Kangaroos' to ambulance cars.

At 0400 hours on February 9 the second phase began and by 0700 hours two battalions were across the anti-tank ditch and by 0900 hours the outskirts of Nütterden were reached. By 1530 hours the leading troops were established on the high ground overlooking Cleve from the west and the north-west. 153 Fd. Amb. opened an A.D.S. in Kranenburg by 1230 hours and the C.C.P. of 194 Fd. Amb. moved from Kranenburg to Bomshof.

During the afternoon of this day the roads were packed with the transport of the two brigades of 43rd Division moving forward and so 15th Division's reconnaissance regiment, to which a section of 11 Lt. Fd. Amb. was attached, had much difficulty in advancing.

On February 10, battalions of 43rd Division were engaged in confused street fighting in Cleve and traffic blocks in Nütterden and on the roads prevented 227th or 44th Bde. being passed through into the town until the morning of February 11, when battalions of 15th Division were mopping up in Cleve.

On February 12, while the relief of 44th Bde. by Canadian 7th Bde. was in progress, a mobile column of 7th Seaforth supported by tanks reached Frasselt but withdrew. The village was again occupied by the Seaforth on the 13th.

Flooding of the Nijmegen–Kranenburg road now stopped all evacuation by M.A.C. and a D.U.K.W. evacuation point was established during the night of February 12/13 by a section of 153 Fd. Amb. Through this D.A.D.M.S. 15th Division organised the evacuation of 350 cases from the A.D.Ss. of 15th, 43rd and 53rd Divisions during the night. On the 13th, 193 Fd. Amb. opened an A.D.S. near Donsbrüggen, the site chosen in Cleve having been heavily shelled. Here a more permanent D.U.K.W. evacuation point was established; the original one when no longer needed by 202 Fd. Amb. was closed. Altogether some 500 casualties had passed through it. 193 Fd. Amb. at the second D.U.K.W. evacuation point cleared over 4,000 casualties and D.D.M.S. XXX Corps caused a non-medical officer to be posted to this D.U.K.W. evacuation point to assist in the organisation thereof.

In the meantime, 51st Division was advancing on Gennep, 53rd Division was advancing south-west from the north-east edge of the Reichswald, Canadian 3rd Division had reached the line of the Spoy Canal and 43rd Division was advancing south-east from the Materborn area and was in the outskirts of Hau. By midnight on February 13 the Reichswald had been cleared and 51st Division had crossed the Niers.

On February 14, 15th Divisional Main H.Q. moved into Cleve and 46th Bde. began to clear the woods and ridge west of Moyland, passing u/c Canadian II Corps from February 15–18. Evacuation from the

ADVANCE TO AND CROSSING OF THE RHINE 429

C.C.P. to the A.D.S. of 193 Fd. Amb. in Cleve was smooth. 153 Fd. Amb. in Kranenburg was closed but dealt with local casualties.

By the 17th, 52nd Division, which had joined XXX Corps on the 15th, was in Afferden, 51st Division in Asperden, 53rd Division had passed through the Staatsforst Cleve and 43rd Division was in Asperberg.

On February 18 at 1330 hours 44th Bde. attacked Goch and had cleared it by 1740 hours on the 19th. It was impossible to open an A.D.S. for this operation as no suitable site could be found. 15th Division casualties were therefore evacuated to an A.D.S. of 43rd Division in the sanatorium at Bedburg. H.Q. 194 Fd. Amb., which had been marooned in Berg-en-Dal by flooding, now managed to move to Kranenburg.

On February 20, 227th Bde. advanced to reach Bucholt by 1145 hours and Schloss Calbeck by 1400 hours. Again no site for an A.D.S. could be obtained. Next came the clearing of the woods east of the Niers and south of Schloss Calbeck. Four of the R.A.Ps. were in the cellars of the Schloss and 193 Fd. Amb. ran a divisional C.C.P. nearby. The clearing of Goch was completed by 51st Division on the 22nd.

While 53rd Division continued the advance towards Weeze and 51st Division cleared the area around Siebengewald, 15th Division was relieved by 3rd Division and moved to the Tilburg, Turnhout and Boxtel area to rest.

15th Division casualties during Operation 'Veritable' totalled 67 officers and 1,423 O.Rs. killed, wounded and missing. The wounded numbered 51 officers and 1,033 O.Rs. There were 46 cases of exhaustion during the first four days of the battle, a ratio of 1 to 7·9 battle casualties. The incidence of exhaustion then fell, to rise again during the fighting in the forests near Moyland and Schloss Calbeck. The total number of exhaustion cases between February 8-24 was 155 (1 exhaustion: 7 battle casualties).

The conditions in which the troops had fought had been wretched; the weather was bad, much of the ground waterlogged and the countryside devastated and insanitary. Yet the health of the division remained good, the daily admission rate on account of sickness never much exceeding 2/1,000/diem. 40 Fd. Hyg. Sec. reached Nütterden on February 16 and thereafter was much involved in supervising the sanitation of refugee collecting posts, in conjunction with personnel of Military Government, and the use of flood water by unit water carts. As pigs were being slaughtered and eaten, warnings concerning the danger of worm infestation were published.

During the operation the value of the 'Weasel' was again recognised. These vehicles were needed by the medical services not only for evacuation but also for reconnaissance. The C.C.P. had to be established before the assault battalions moved forward. Under the conditions that obtained nothing short of a special route for evacuation could be satisfactory. Close liaison with the Gap Control officer was essential since he regulated all traffic through the minefield gaps and could direct 'Kangaroos' carrying casualties to the car post or C.C.P. The stationing of a medical officer at the car post where the 'Kangaroos' off-loaded the casualties proved to be a wise insurance for then the C.P. could function as a Gap R.A.P. and deal with casualties occurring in and around the gaps. An A.D.M.S. of a typical infantry division, finding himself possessed of a strange and wide variety of 'funnies'—the modified armoured fighting vehicles created by 79th Division—doubtless regarded them, on first acquaintance, as a distinct liability, but having come to appreciate their unique value in actions such as the attack on Blerick and Operation 'Veritable', he came to number them among his greatest assets.

15th Division then passed to XII Corps for Operation 'Torchlight'— the crossing of the Rhine—and moved to the area of Frasselt. The corps plan freed the assaulting division from medical responsibilities on the near bank other than the provision of a F.D.S. for its minor sick. Casualties from the assault were to be cleared from the near bank *via* casualty disembarkation posts set up by 11 Lt. Fd. Amb. in relation to the return routes of 'Buffaloes', one for each assaulting battalion, one per assault brigade near the storm-boat ferry and one on the return circuit of the D.U.K.Ws. at Birten. 11 Lt. Fd. Amb. had stretcher squads of Pioneers along the near bank. Evacuation from these posts of 11 Lt. Fd. Amb. was to be to the A.D.Ss. of 52nd Division.

15th Division's task was that of making contact with the airborne divisions and the division was responsible for getting across the river, liaison officers and the A.Ds.M.S. of the airborne divisions, its own ambulance cars to clear the airborne M.D.Ss. as well as detachments of U.S. 183 Medical Battalion.

15th Division was to force the passage of the Rhine between Bislich and Vynen, starting at 0200 hours on March 24, five hours after 1st Cdo. Bde. on the division's right had got across near Wesel and four hours after 51st Division of XXX Corps on the division's left had crossed near Rees, and to advance to relieve 6th Airborne Division in the Hamminkeln area. 6th A.B. Division was to drop at 1000 hours and U.S. 17th A.B. Division at 1100 hours on March 24. 44th Bde. on the right was to capture and hold the Bislich area, Löh and Schüttwick, 227th Bde. on the left was to capture and hold Haffen and Mehr and 46th Bde. was to capture and hold the area Clasenho–Mehrhoog and the high ground and woods south-east of Haldern. Then a mobile striking force was to cross and seize the area about Wissman. After the assault wave had crossed the river in 'Buffaloes' a ferry service conveying jeeps and carriers was to start and the reserve battalions were to cross in storm-

ADVANCE TO AND CROSSING OF THE RHINE

boats. Raft ferries and a D.U.K.W. ferry were then to be instituted and bridges built.

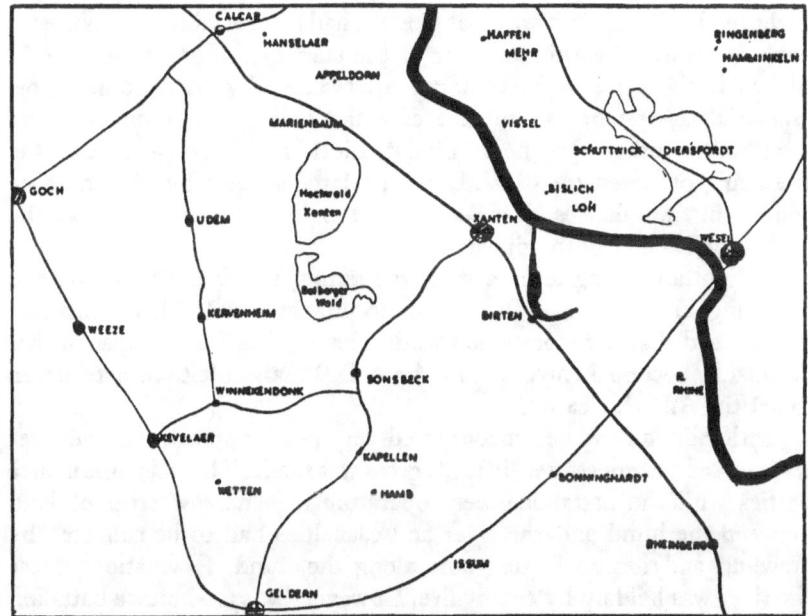

FIG. 79. 15th Division. Operation 'Torchlight'.

The medical plan was as follows:

1. The R.M.O. in a jeep would cross with his battalion;
2. One medical officer and 13 O.Rs. of a field ambulance without transport would cross with each assaulting battalion;
3. A R.A.P. and a C.C.P. for each assaulting battalion would be set up at once on the far bank;
4. A brigade evacuation medical officer would cross in the first wave, or as soon as possible by the ferry service, to co-ordinate evacuation;
5. Two stretcher jeeps per battalion and four stretcher jeeps per field ambulance would cross by the ferry service;
6. Four 'Weasels' per field ambulance and five 'Weasels' per battalion would be available for evacuation;
7. Four light ambulance cars and two jeep ambulances per brigade would be given high priority on the raft ferry service.

During the night of March 21/22 the brigades concentrated in the Hochwald Xanten (*see* Fig. 79). Field ambulance companies were with the brigades and the rest in Hamb. 23 F.D.S. opened in Wetten. The field ambulance vehicles and D.U.K.Ws. were preloaded.

44th Bde's. attack went well and Bislich was cleared by 0900 hours on March 24. By 1400 hours the brigade had linked up with U.S. 17th Airborne Division south of Diersfordt and by 1600 hours with 6th Airborne Division. So it was that C.E.Ps. had been established on the far bank of the river within an hour of the start of the operation, one in Bislich itself being opened shortly afterwards. By 0900 hours jeeps, 'Weasels', 4-stretcher ambulance cars and other field ambulance cars were across and at 1530 hours nine medical D.U.K.Ws. arrived at the site being prepared for the A.D.S. in a large school. By 1600 hours a convoy of ambulances, jeeps and a 3-ton lorry set out to clear the M.D.Ss. of the airborne divisions.

At nightfall, owing to damage to the ramps, the D.U.K.Ws. stopped operating and casualties began to accumulate. A.D.M.S. remained uninformed that a minor crisis was developing, but it so happened that D.D.M.S. Second Army, visiting the A.D.S., was able to initiate action to get the A.D.S. cleared.

227th Bde. on the left encountered very fierce opposition. The river was crossed but thereafter little progress was made. The field ambulance parties with the battalions were operating in a narrow strip of land between the bund and the river and casualties had to be collected by crawling and nested in dug-outs along the bund. Evacuation across the river was held up by enemy fire. However, by 1700 hours a battalion of 227th Bde. was advancing on Haffen and the company of 193 Fd. Amb. with the reserve brigade (46th) was able to open an A.D.S. (*see* Fig. 80). Not until late evening could the ambulance cars get across and evacuation by 'Buffaloes' begin. (Plates XXIII to XXV show medical units crossing the Rhine.)

On March 25 good progress was made by 44th, 46th and 157th Bdes.; the river was bridged and the ferries were working. A site for the next A.D.S. was found at Vissel. That afternoon the A.D.S. of 194 Fd. Amb. was reinforced by a team from 193 Fd. Amb. and by personnel of 9 F.D.S., sent by D.D.M.S XII Corps. Later in the day 'C' Pln. of 302 M.A.C. joined the A.D.S.

On the 26th, 44th Bde. reached the Issel and 157th Bde. entered Ringenberg. The whole of 193 Fd. Amb. was now across the Rhine, its A.D.S. open in Vissel in echelon with that of 194 in Bislich. All the airborne M.D.Ss. had been cleared and a section of 193 Fd. Amb. took over the post-operative immobiles from 224 Para. Fd. Amb. 'A' Coy. 193 Fd. Amb. was in support of 46th Bde. for its advance on Haffen. 4th Armd. Bde., between 44th and 46th Bdes., was being served by C.C.Ps. of 11 Lt. Fd. Amb.

The 27th was a day of heavy fighting, but by nightfall the Germans were retreating and the armour was in pursuit.

On the 28th the remainder of 194 and 153 Fd. Ambs. crossed the

ADVANCE TO AND CROSSING OF THE RHINE

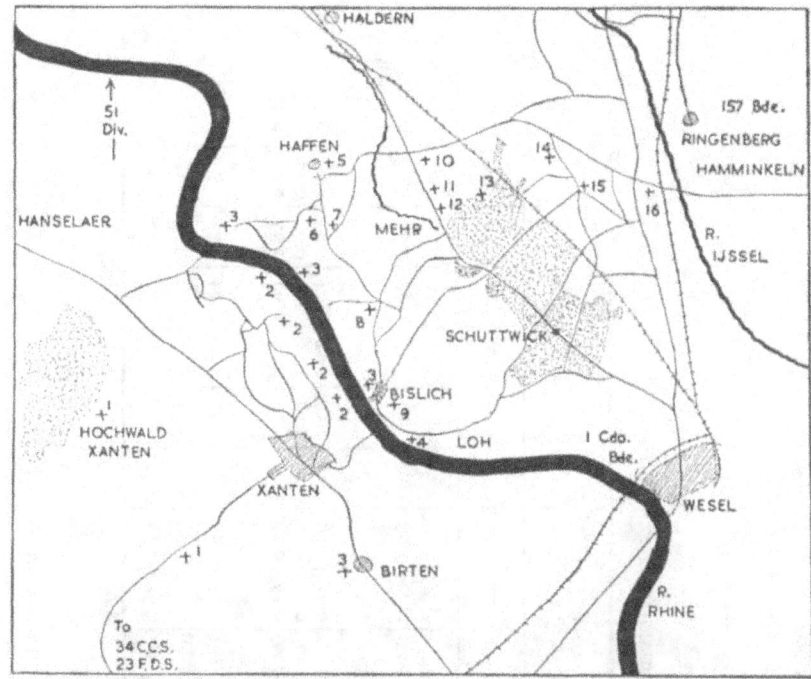

Fig. 80. 15th Division. Operation 'Torchlight'. Medical Cover.

1. A.D.Ss. of 52nd Division
2. C.D.Ps. of 11 Lt. Fd. Amb.
3. C.E.Ps. for the river crossing
4. D.U.K.W. Ferry C.C.P.
5. C.C.P. 153 Fd. Amb.
6. C.C.P. 193 Fd. Amb.
7. C.C.P. 153 Fd. Amb.
8. A.D.S. 193 Fd. Amb.
9. A.D.S. 194 Fd. Amb.
   23 F.D.S. (March 28)
10. C.C.P. 193 Fd. Amb.
11. A.D.S. 153 Fd. Amb.
12. A.D.S. 224 Para. Fd. Amb.
13. C.C.P. 194 Fd. Amb.
14. A.D.S. 225 Para. Fd. Amb.
15. C.C.P. 194 Fd. Amb.
16. A.D.S. 195 A.L. Fd. Amb.
    C.C.P. 157 Fd. Amb. (later)

Rhine. They had been held up by 53rd Division passing through. 23 F.D.S. reached Bislich. On the 29th, 15th Division passed into corps reserve.

During Operation 'Torchlight' about 1,000 battle casualties and sick of 6th Airborne Division passed through the field medical units of 15th Division. In addition 137 battle casualties and sick of other formations and 289 P.o.W. were evacuated through 15th Divisional channels. The casualties of 15th Division totalled 48 officers and 824 O.Rs., of whom 35 officers and 630 O.Rs. were wounded. There were 35 cases of exhaustion and of these only 15 were admitted to 23 F.D.S. Of these 15, 8 were relapses. The daily admission rate on account of sickness was only 1·56 per 1,000.

TABLE 42

15th Division Casualties. January–March 1945

	January week ending					February week ending					March week ending					Total Average
	6	13	20	27	Av.	3	10	17	24	Av.	3	10	17	24	31	Av.	
Daily average reporting sick	202	220	210	168	200	255	125	143	132	163	93	84	235	183	136	168	0·9 per cent. daily
Average weekly incidence of																	
Scabies	0·88	0·71	0·53	0·41	0·63	0·93	0·23	1·0	0·23	0·59	1·17	0·59	1·82	0·94	0·93	1·09	0·77
Pediculosis	0·23	0·12	0·12	0·47	0·23	0·76	0·11	0·17	0·17	0·30	0·41	0·18	0·11	—	0·06	0·15	0·22
V.D.	0·29	0·12	0·24	0·12	0·19	0·23	0·35	0·29	0·17	0·26	0·23	0·12	1·72	0·62	0·32	0·61	0·35
Total cases: Other Skin Diseases	111	107	91	61	92	76	79	61	55	67	88	95	118	93	72	93	85
Total cases: Exhaustion	—	—	1	2	0·7	18	26	40	89	43	5	1	2	—	35	8·3	16

Medical Boards:

	January	February	March
Number examined	27	24	42
" down-graded	26	21	34
" up-graded	1	—	1
" retained in category	—	3	7

Wounds by Anatomical Region and by Causal Missile:

	G.S.W.	S.W. artillery	S.W. mortar	B.W.(M) mine	Burns	Fractures	Totals	Percentages of wounds by anatomical area
Head	14	81	—	—	—	6	101	5·92
Face	8	43	3	4	6	—	64	3·68
Neck	16	10	2	—	—	—	28	1·61
Shoulder	30	71	2	—	—	14	117	6·21
Arm and Hand	79	161	6	6	4	24	280	13·51
Chest and Thorax	29	35	4	—	—	—	68	5·84
Abdomen	21	51	18	—	—	—	90	4·18
Back	19	41	14	—	—	—	74	4·18
Buttocks	21	29	5	—	—	—	55	4·31
Thigh	48	139	15	—	—	—	202	15·38
Leg	50	146	21	31	—	20	268	7·35
Foot	38	46	5	39	—	5	133	16·23
Multiple	61	121	40	37	8	11	278	11·6
Totals	434	974	135	117	18	80		
Percentage of wounds by missile	25·2	55·12	7·51	6·6	1·1	4·47		

Total Admissions. January–March 1945:

	Battle Casualties	Non-Battle Casualties
193 Fd. Amb.	678	529
194 " "	648	195
153 " "	408	522
22 F.D.S.	—	293
23 "	7	357
	1,741	1,896

3,637

Table 42—*continued*

Dental Treatment. January–March 1945

Numbers inspected	2,110
Attendance for treatment	4,188
Teeth extracted under local anaesthesia	15
Teeth extracted under general anaesthesia	28
Teeth conserved without root treatment	1,126
Teeth conserved with root treatment	16
Teeth conserved with silver nitrate	3
Scalings completed	390
Cases of Acute Ulcerative Gingivitis	
New	75
Relapses	30
Cases completed	53
Personnel supplied with new dentures	70
Dentures supplied	122
Dentures remade	119
Dentures repaired	225
Personnel for whom treatment was completed	942

44th Bde's. assault crossing moved more swiftly than had been expected and in retrospect it seemed that the quickly established A.D.S. would have been greatly advantaged had a F.S.U. been attached to it. As things turned out the field ambulance parties of 194 Fd. Amb. which accompanied the assaulting battalions found themselves functioning forward of the normal field ambulance sphere. On the left flank, on the other hand, had these parties not got across with the assault wave it is doubtful if they would have been able to cross until very much later and then might have had considerable difficulty in getting into touch with the R.A.Ps. During Operation 'Torchlight' it became manifest that many of the battalions had far too few men trained as regimental stretcher-bearers and it became necessary to remind the S.M.Os. of brigade groups of their responsibilities in this matter.

43RD DIVISION

43rd Division u/c XII Corps relieved 52nd Division in the Brunssum–Geilenkirchen area on January 12. 129 Fd. Amb. moved to Treebeek, 213 Fd. Amb. to Brunssum, 15 F.D.S. to Hoensbroek, 130 Fd. Amb. to Gangelt and 14 F.D.S. to Nuth. 6th Gds. Tk. Bde. with 11 Lt. Fd. Amb. came u/c 43rd Division for Operation 'Blackcock'. For this twelve 'Weasels' were allotted to the medical services of the division. They were held in a pool by 130 Fd. Amb. to be re-allotted to battalions as required.

ADVANCE TO AND CROSSING OF THE RHINE

In support of 130th Bde's. advance on January 26, the C.C.P. of 130 Fd. Amb. moved forward to Erpen and the C.C.P. of 213 Fd. Amb. to Retersbeek. On the 28th, 130th Bde. and 130 Fd. Amb. passed to command 52nd Division. The A.D.S. of this field ambulance remained in Gangelt.

On January 31, Operation 'Blackcock' being concluded, the division moved to the area of Turnhout–Lierre.

TABLE 43
43rd Division. Casualties. Operation 'Blackcock'

	Admitted	Evacuated	R.T.U.
Battle Casualties	166	144	15
Sick	830	346	434
Exhaustion	31	20	10
	1,027	510 +7 died	459

On February 5, the division moved to its concentration area near Eindhoven to take part in Operation 'Veritable'.

During February 8, the division moved forward to Nijmegen. During the evening of the 9th, 129th Bde. moved forward along the main Cleve road with 129 Fd. Amb. in support. The C.C.P. of this medical unit opened in Cleve. On the 10th, because difficulties in connexion with evacuation were increasing owing to the deterioration of the roads, 129 Fd. Amb. opened an A.D.S. about 4 km. west of Cleve. Arrangements were made to evacuate casualties from this A.D.S. *via* an A.D.S. of 15th Division in Kranenburg, where they could be staged if necessary. The journey of 5 km. between the two A.D.Ss. took anything up to four hours. By midnight of February 10/11 all the other divisional medical units had reached Nijmegen. By this time 129th Bde. was firmly established on the Materborn feature and one battalion of 214th Bde. was in Hau and the C.C.P. of 213 Fd. Amb. was open in Nütterden.

By the 11th, 51st Division on the extreme right had crossed the Niers and was threatening Gennep. 53rd Division was clearing the northern fringe of the Reichswald and 15th Division was mopping up west of Cleve and Duffelward. Part of Cleve was holding out and, during the morning of the 11th, 44th Bde. of 15th Division took over the task of clearing the rest of the town from 129th Bde.

On the 12th, 214th Bde. took Bedburg. By about 2000 hours on this day the road had become impassable to all but amphibious vehicles and 120 D.U.K.Ws. which were transporting stores forward were used to bring casualties back. Forward and rearward casualty relay posts were established near Nütterden and in Nijmegen evacuation was by M.A.C. to 3 C.C.S.

The field ambulances of each of 15th, 43rd and 53rd Divisions were now freely admitting casualties of all of the divisions and consequently it became necessary to ensure that none of them became overtaxed. The A.D.S. of 129 Fd. Amb. was exposed to this danger for communication with it had become exceedingly difficult. So, on February 13, 213 Fd. Amb. was ordered up from Nijmegen and moved with 130th Bde. to the Materborn area.

During February 13, 129th Bde. pressed down the Cleve–Üdem road

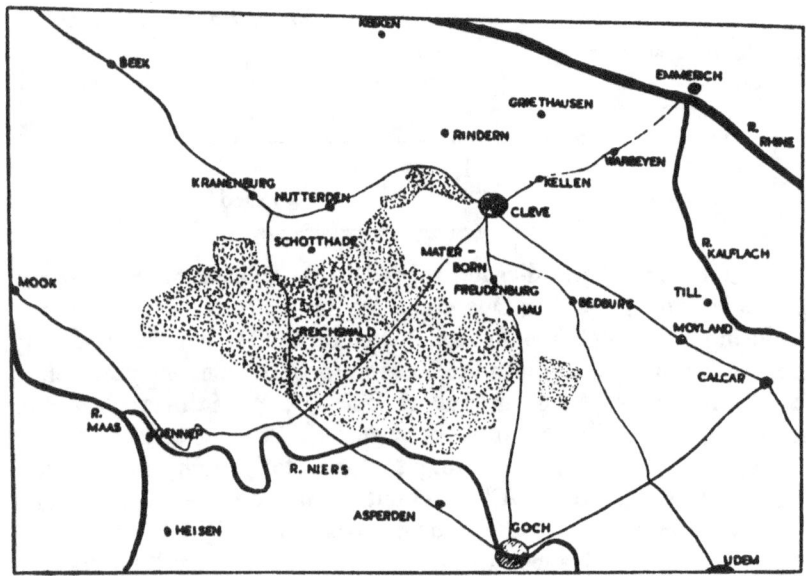

FIG. 81. 43rd Division. Operation 'Veritable'.

and the C.C.P. of 129 Fd. Amb. opened in Freudenburg. The A.D.S. of this unit was moved up to the outskirts of Cleve on the morning of the 14th. It evacuated its casualties to the A.D.S. of 193 Fd. Amb. of 15th Division. The C.C.P. of 130 Fd. Amb. opened near Bedburg. During the 15th, 129th Bde. continued to make progress down the Cleve–Üdem road and on the 16th the division advanced southward in successive brigade leaps to reach within 1 km. of Goch. 213 Fd. Amb's. C.C.P. opened in Bedburg alongside that of 130 Fd. Amb. On the 16th the advance continued. 129 Fd. Amb's. A.D.S. was closed and rested and 213 Fd. Amb. moved forward in its place to open in Bedburg at 1300 hours. 168 Lt. Fd. Amb. (8th Armd. Bde.) opened in Nijmegen to take exhaustion cases. 129 Fd. Amb's. C.C.P. joined those of 130 and 213

ADVANCE TO AND CROSSING OF THE RHINE

Fd. Ambs. in Bedburg and all three closed, the A.D.S. alone admitting casualties.

By the 18th, 43rd Division's tasks were completed. 130th Bde. was pulled out of the line to the Materborn area. It was arranged that casualties from 15th Division, attacking Goch, should pass through the A.D.S. of 213 Fd. Amb. in Bedburg.

On the 20th, 130th Bde. u/c Canadian 3rd Division took over certain of the islands in the flood water in the areas of Keeken, Griethausen and Warbeyen from Canadian 8th Bde. Each of these islands had a medical post and from this evacuation was by D.U.K.W. to C.D.Ps. complete with M.Os. and ambulance cars in Cleve and Beek. Fig. 81 shows the area in which the division was operating during this period.

129th Bde. was concentrated west of Cleve and only 214th Bde. u/c 15th Division was in the line.

By midday on the 20th evacuation by the A.C.C. in the normal fashion had become possible again.

On February 21 the division passed from XXX Corps to Canadian II Corps.

TABLE 44

43rd Division. Casualties. Operation 'Veritable'

	Offrs.	O.Rs.
Battle Casualties	30	651
Sick	7	268
Exhaustion	3	129
Total casualties of all formations evacuated by the medical services of 43rd Division:		
Battle Casualties	79	1,151
Sick	11	349
Exhaustion	3	259

Following Operation 'Veritable', 43rd Division rested in the Cleve–Calcar area. 129, 130 and 213 Fd. Ambs. and 38 Fd. Hyg. Sec. were with the division but 14 F.D.S. was still in Turnhout and 15 F.D.S. in Nijmegen. On March 2, 130 Fd. Amb. moved to Cleve and 14 F.D.S. from Turnhout to Nijmegen. On the 8th, 129 Fd. Amb. opened in Calcar to cover 129th Bde's. attack on Xanten and thereafter returned to Cleve.

On the 12th the division passed to command XXX Corps and moved to the area Goch–Well. On the 23rd the division participated in Operation 'Plunder' in a follow-up rôle. 130th Bde. Gp. with the C.C.P. of 130 Fd. Amb. crossed the Rhine on the 25th and on the following day

129 and 130 Fd. Ambs. moved across. The complete division was in the bridgehead by April 1.

51ST (HIGHLAND) DIVISION

This division moved from Maastricht on Christmas Day and by January 1 was concentrated south of Liége, which at this time was being subjected to continuous attacks by V.1 rockets, some 50–60 falling in the area each day. On January 1, 153rd Bde. Gp. moved to the Namur area to pass under command XXX Corps and was shortly followed by divisional H.Q. and 154th Bde. Gp., which moved into the Namur–Ciney–Marche area. 152nd Bde. Gp. and the divisional troops followed in their turn. On January 8, 154th Bde. took over the high ground dominating the Marche–Hotton road from 53rd Division and through this brigade 153rd Bde. passed to attack north-eastward towards Hotton in the early hours of the 10th. Against weak opposition, but in bitter weather, 153rd Bde. pressed forward and captured Hotton. Then 152nd Bde. passed through and advanced to take Rendeux and Cheoux and pressed on toward Halleux and Champlon. Next 154th Bde. took up the attack and, advancing on the axis Rendeux–Laroche, soon entered Laroche and continued south to capture Ortho. 153rd and 154th Bdes. thereafter continued to advance against lessening opposition and, on January 15, these brigades linked up on the line of the Ourthe with U.S. forces advancing from the south. At the conclusion of these operations, 51st Division, still in XXX Corps, moved on January 18 to the general area Itegem–Herenthals–Turnhout.

During these operations, despite the severe frost and the deep snow, no great difficulty was experienced in casualty evacuation.

In Operation 'Veritable', 51st Division's main task was to attack on the right of 53rd Division, as the right division of XXX Corps, and to capture the high ground on the western edge of the Reichswald, clear the southern part of this forest and gain control of the area Hekkens–Asper Bridge.

Planning for this operation was begun early in November. As originally planned, the operation was to consist of a seven-division attack with the object of capturing and clearing the area between the Maas and the Rhine as far south as Geldern. 154th Bde., the leading brigade, was to concentrate in the Mill–Beers area west of the Maas, move to an assembly area east of the river and there remain concealed until the move to the start-line just before H-hour. When 154th Bde. left its concentration area its place was to be taken by 153rd and 152nd Bdes. in succession, prior to their moving across the Maas. The line at this time was held by Canadian 2nd Division. Because of the nature of the ground, of the universal devastation and of the concentration of large numbers of troops in very limited space, it was certain that the medical units would

ADVANCE TO AND CROSSING OF THE RHINE

be unlikely to find suitable accommodation throughout the whole operation. Nevertheless, it was considered imperative that at least one complete field ambulance should be functioning east of the Maas not less than 12–18 hours before H-hour. Severe winter weather conditions prevailed and a thick mantle of snow covered the ground, the temperature fell below freezing point both by day and by night and commonly a bitter north-east wind blew. Few metalled roads were available. The main axis ran from Mook along the road through the woods to Groesbeek and thence turned sharply south-west to pass in twists and turns through Breedeweg to the western border of the Reichswald. In the forest the axis ran south-eastwards along a track, eventually to cut the Kranenburg–Hekkens road a mile or so north-west of Hekkens. The main Nijmegen–Mook–Hekkens road could not be used until the Reichswald had been cleared, Gennep, Ottersum and Hekkens captured and the area of the Niers cleared. The country roads in and around the villages of Horst, Bruk, Breedeweg and Grafwegen could be expected to degenerate into tracks under the weight of the traffic. C.C.Ps. had to be sited as far forward as possible therefore.

On January 29, the snow and frost gave place to rain and mud and the problems of evacuation became even more complex. The division went into the operation with an overall shortage of six medical officers. So the officer commanding 29 Fd. Hyg. Sec. and two R.M.Os. were attached to the A.D.Ss.

Operation 'Veritable' opened in wretched weather, the infantry crossing the start-line at 1100 hours on February 8. Progress against bitter opposition was slow but steady. Before dark the high ground had been captured and the outskirts of the Reichswald entered. For the next three weeks operations continued without intermission; the southern part of the Reichswald was gradually cleared first by 154th Bde. and then by 152nd Bde. On the 11th, Gennep fell to 154th Bde. which, on the night of the 13th, crossed the Niers to enter Kessel from the east, and by the 17th the western outskirts of Goch were entered. Thus 51st Division continued, with 52nd Division and a brigade of the Guards Armoured Division on its right, until February 28 when it was relieved by 53rd Division. Fig. 82 shows the medical lay-out at the beginning of Operation 'Veritable' and Fig. 83 the distribution of the medical units on February 28.

As the operation developed there inevitably arose fresh day-to-day problems in the evacuation of casualties, due to modifications of the original tactical plan, to obstacles encountered, to new objectives given to the division, to the progress of flanking formations and to the reactions of the enemy. Nevertheless, evacuation proceeded satisfactorily during the attack by 154th Bde. on February 13, when casualties had to be brought across the Niers and during the attack by 1st Gordons on

Thomashof on February 21, when the casualties had to be evacuated by half-tracks under cover of a smoke screen.

The paucity of accommodation was overcome by holding the divisional sick in 5 and 6 F.D.Ss. west of the Maas, by opening only one divisional A.D.S. east of the Maas between February 8–13, by providing the C.C.Ps. with extra tentage, by the use of German medical installations in the Reichswald and by the improvised repair of partly demolished buildings.

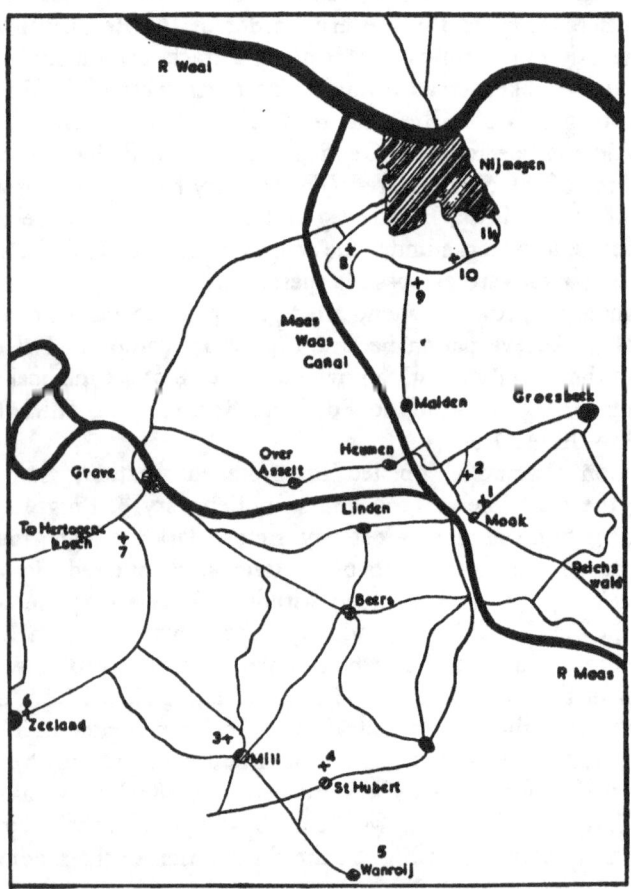

FIG. 82. 51st Division. Operation 'Veritable'. Medical Cover. Early Phase.

1. C.C.P. 176 Fd. Amb.
2. A.D.S. 176 Fd. Amb.
3. A.D.S. 174 Fd. Amb. (closed)
4. A.D.S. 175 Fd. Amb. (closed)
5. 5 F.D.S.
6. 35 F.D.S.
7. 10 C.C.S.
8. 6 (Cdn.) C.C.S.
9. Amb. Control Post
10. Adv. Surg. Centre
11. 3 C.C.S.

PLATE XXIII. The crossing of the Rhine. March 1945. 'Crocodiles' with Jeep-Ambulances aboard going over the flood-bank.

PLATE XXIV. A Casualty Evacuation Post on the east bank of the Rhine. March 1945.

PLATE XXV. 'Buffaloes' crossing the Rhine. March 1945.

[Imperial War Museum

ADVANCE TO AND CROSSING OF THE RHINE

The adverse weather conditions were combated by providing extra blankets, stoves, self-heating soups and cocoa, wind-proof clothing to car drivers and covers for the stretcher-bearing jeeps.

Evacuation difficulties were diminished by the provision of a reserve of stretcher-bearer squads at C.C.Ps. and of sledges. The medical unit jeeps were pooled, the R.M.Os'. 'Weasels' were used between R.A.P. and C.C.P., 'Buffaloes' for evacuation between R.A.P. and jeep car post and armoured half-tracks of 107th R.A.C. were held ready to collect and evacuate casualties to the C.C.P.

During Operation 'Veritable', February 8–28, a total of 96 officers and 1,300 O.R. battle casualties passed through the medical units of

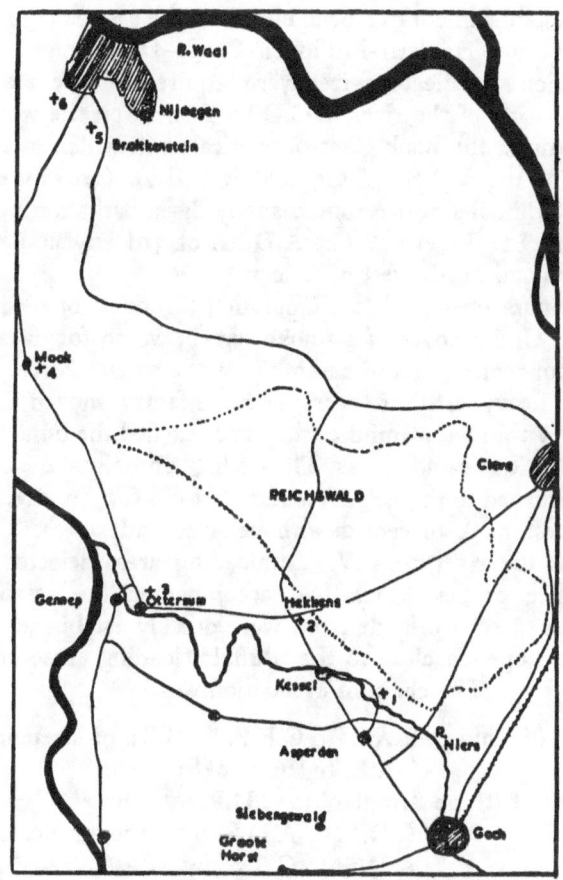

FIG. 83. 51st Division. Operation 'Veritable'. Medical Cover. Later Phase.

1. A.D.S. 176 Fd. Amb.
2. A.D.S. 175 Fd. Amb.
3. A.D.S. 174 Fd. Amb.
4. 23 C.C.S.
5. 3 C.C.S.
6. 3 (Cdn.) C.C.S.

51st Division. Of these, 72 officers and 1,004 O.Rs. belonged to 51st Division.

Then, on March 6–8, the division moved to the Weert area to prepare for Operation 'Plunder'. Full-scale exercises by day and by night were carried out across the Maas and evacuation by 'Buffalo', D.U.K.W. and storm-boats rehearsed. Then, on March 20, the division moved to the assembly area around Calcar–Marienbaum–Üdem.

51st Division was to be the assault division of XXX Corps and was to cross the Rhine in the vicinity of Rees on a two-brigade front with 153rd Bde. on the right, 154th Bde. on the left. These brigades were to be followed respectively by 152nd Bde. and Canadian 9th Bde. (Canadian 3rd Division) and the general tasks were (1) the clearing of Rees and (2) the establishment of a bridgehead on the east bank of the Rhine on the general line Haldern–Millingen–Praest–Dörnick.

51st Division's medical services were required to evacuate casualties from the east side of the river to C.D.Ps. formed on the west bank by 14 Lt. Fd. Amb., the Bank Control medical unit, which in turn transferred them to the A.D.Ss. of the holding division (3rd) for evacuation to the C.C.Ss. in Bedburg. Four casualty disembarkation points were formed by 14 Lt. Fd. Amb. The A.D.Ss. of 3rd Division were open in Appeldorn and north-west of Calcar.

At 2100 hours on March 23, Operation 'Plunder' opened on XXX Corps front. Under cover of a smoke screen, which for days had concealed the concentration and assembly of the assault force, and of an exceedingly heavy artillery barrage the infantry moved forward in 'Buffaloes'. Within a few minutes they had reached the bund, were over it and into the Rhine and across. The leading 'Buffaloes' deposited their loads and returned to the L.V.T. loading areas a few hundred yards beyond the west bank to reload with vehicles and stores. These were taken across the river to L.V.T. unloading areas selected by small reconnaissance parties which had accompanied the assault troops. Two C.E.Ps. to each brigade front were quickly established while the C.D.Ps. were opened close to the 'Buffalo' loading areas on the near bank of the river. The chain of evacuation was:

East bank of Rhine   R.A.P. to C.E.P. by S.Bs. or stretcher jeep.
                                    C.E.P. to 'Buffalo' by S.Bs.
West Bank of Rhine   'Buffalo' to C.D.P. by S.Bs.
                                    C.D.P. to A.D.S. by ambulance car.
                                    A.D.S. to C.C.S. by M.A.C.

By 1900 hours on the 24th, jeep scale C.C.Ps. of 174 and 176 Fd. Ambs. were across the river together with three ambulance cars. Five jeeps over and above the numbers allotted to C.C.Ps. got across and were distributed between the two C.C.Ps. On the 25th, 175 Fd. Amb.

ADVANCE TO AND CROSSING OF THE RHINE

crossed. On the 26th, XXX Corps' D.U.K.W. C.E.P. was established close to the L.V.T. unloading area west of Rees and direct evacuation by D.U.K.W. to the A.D.S. at Appeldorn began. Evacuation from the more distant C.C.Ps., 1 and 4, continued to be by 'Buffalo'.

On March 27, 174 Fd. Amb. was open in Rees and with the first bridge now available evacuation was direct to the C.C.Ss. at Bedburg. Six M.A.C. cars joined this unit on the 28th. On the 29th the remainder of 174 and 176 Fd. Ambs. crossed.

The bridgehead was quickly enlarged. Rees was cleared, Canadian 3rd Division was thrusting towards Emmerich, 43rd Division was advancing eastwards and, on March 29 and 30, 154th Bde. captured Isselburg and established a bridgehead over the Issel through which Guards Armoured Division passed. 51st Division passed into XXX Corps reserve on March 30.

Between March 23–31, 51st Division sustained a total of 48 officer and 654 O.R. battle casualties. Of these 12 officers and 109 O.Rs. passed through 51st Division A.D.Ss., the remainder passed through the A.D.Ss. of 3rd Division.

52ND (LOWLAND) DIVISION

This division, now functioning as an ordinary infantry formation, relinquished the peculiarities in respect of equipment and transport that had distinguished it when it was air-portable. Like other divisions of Second Army it had lost its second F.D.S. and its medical units were now 155, 156 and 157 Fd. Ambs., 18 F.D.S. and 32 Fd. Hyg. Sec. 533, 534 and 501 M.D.Us. were attached to it.

The division took part in the capture of Heinsberg, the clearing of the Wesel pocket and the crossing of the Rhine, but during these operations the work of the divisional medical units called for no special mention. They came to appreciate the usefulness of the 'Weasel' M.29 when the ground was impassable to all other wheeled or tracked vehicles. During Operation 'Veritable' the medical units of the division were used for the evacuation of the casualties from the assaulting divisions and established two A.D.Ss. and numerous C.C.Ps. in the assembly area. During this operation they dealt with 818 casualties.

(iii)

Medical Arrangements

XII CORPS

After Operation 'Blackcock' there was a complete regrouping; all the divisions leaving the operational control of XII Corps. H.Q. corps and corps troops moved to the area of Aerschot to plan for Operation 'Plunder'. 24 C.C.S. with 56 F.S.U. opened in Betekom for emergency cases. 9 F.D.S. with 42 F.S.U. and the corps psychiatrist opened in Haecht for minor sick. 4 F.D.S. rejoined XII Corps and along with the V.D.T.C. opened in Diest. 23 C.C.S. and 302 M.A.C., less 'B' Pln., moved to XXX Corps for operations in the Goch–Xanten area.

For Operation 'Plunder' the order of battle was as follows:

Assault Division	15th Division
	1st Cdo. Bde. (with 21 Lt. Fd. Amb.)
Holding Division	52nd Division
Follow-up Divisions	7th Armoured Division
	53rd Division

THE HOLDING DIVISION

A.D.M.S. Holding Division (52nd Division) was made responsible for medical arrangements on the west bank for formations in his divisional area. He was to establish C.C.Ps., particularly in the gun areas, and two A.D.Ss., one for each assault brigade front. Groups I and II casualties were to be evacuated to 24 C.C.S. and Group III and exhaustion cases to 9 F.D.S., all by 302 M.A.C. Of the ambulance cars six were to be attached to each of the A.D.Ss.

O.C. 11 Lt. Fd. Amb. was appointed S.M.O. bank control and corps medical evacuation Officer. He was made responsible for medical arrangements for the actual assault and for the evacuation of casualties in the assault division on the west bank. He was also made responsible for assisting 6th Airborne Division in the loading of casualties into D.U.K.Ws. on the east bank. He was to establish C.D.Ps. at (1) the L.V.T. collecting areas, (2) the storm-boat ferry and (3) the D.U.K.W. ferry. He was to establish car posts as necessary where ambulance cars could not drive up to the C.D.P. Evacuation of casualties to such C.Ps. would be by stretcher jeep or 'Weasel'. To him for use as S.Bs. would be attached two sections of A.M.P.C. S.B. patrols would be established in the vicinity of the Class 9 Raft Ferry and of the storm-boat ferry to evacuate cases to the Storm-boat C.D.P. He would obtain stretchers and blankets from the corps dump and establish a dump near the D.U.K.W. C.D.P., replenishing the assault division as required and when notified by the brigade evacuation medical officers.

S.M.O. 31st Armd. Bde. and R.M.Os. in the vehicle waiting areas would be responsible for the collection of casualties occurring in these areas.

THE ASSAULT DIVISION

A.D.M.S. Assault Division (15th Division) was made responsible for medical arrangements for the assault. He had no responsibilities on the

ADVANCE TO AND CROSSING OF THE RHINE

west bank other than the opening of a F.D.S. in the divisional marshalling area for the minor sick. His brigade evacuation medical officers were to cross in the first wave and R.A.Ps. were to be opened on the east bank as soon as possible, always being ready to move forward with their battalions. He was to establish C.E.Ps. on the east bank in the vicinity of (1) the L.V.T. unloading area, (2) the storm-boat ferry east bank terminal and (3) the D.U.K.W. ferry unloading area. Casualties were to be evacuated from R.A.Ps. to C.C.Ps., thence to returning L.V.T., storm-boats and Class 9 rafts across the river to C.C.Ps. of S.M.O. Bank Control. He was to be responsible for loading the assault division stretcher and blanket dump previously established at one of the S.M.O. Bank Control L.V.T. C.D.Ps. by him on to a L.V.T. returning from the first wave. He would provide one S.B. officer and two S.Bs. from his divisional F.D.S. to accompany the dump to the C.E.P. indicated by the brigade evacuation medical officer. He was to arrange through the brigade evacuation medical officer to select a site at the D.U.K.W. ferry for a C.E.P. to be established in preparation for the opening of the D.U.K.W. ferry evacuation service, which was not to commence before H-hour + 14. Nine D.U.K.Ws. were to be assigned to him, including one for 6th Airborne Division.

The C.E.P. at the D.U.K.W. ferry was to be built up to a C.C.P. and then into an A.D.S. and when the D.U.K.W. ferry was fully working the L.V.T. and the storm-boat C.E.Ps. would shut down.

To help him in connexion with the evacuation of casualties of the airborne divisions a detachment from 11 Lt. Fd. Amb. and a detachment of 4 officers and 40 O.Rs. from U.S. 17th Airborne Division were provided. A.D.M.S. 15th Division was to be responsible for the evacuation of airborne casualties after the link-up until the airborne divisions were self-supporting, their 'land tails' having joined them. Liaison officers from each of the airborne divisions were to be attached to him and he would attach a liaison officer to each of these divisions.

AIRBORNE DIVISIONS (6th and U.S. 17th)

A.D.M.S. 6th Airborne Division and Surgeon, U.S. 17th Airborne Division, would be prepared to hold casualties up to forty-eight hours but after the link-up casualties would be evacuated to the assault division's C.E.Ps. until the airborne divisions became self-supporting. A medical D.U.K.W., pre-loaded with equipment, would be allotted to 6th Airborne Division by the assault division. A detachment of 11 Lt. Fd. Amb. would be attached to 6th Airborne Division for loading of casualties at the D.U.K.W. C.E.P. U.S. 17th Airborne Division would provide a medical detachment to assist 15th Division at the D.U.K.W. C.E.P. and a platoon to assist S.M.O. Bank Control at the D.U.K.W. C.D.P.

1ST COMMANDO BRIGADE

21 Lt. Fd. Amb. was placed under 1st Cdo. Bde. Its A.D.S. would be established in Menzelen and a detachment of 1 officer and 13 O.Rs. would establish a C.C.P. and C.D.P. on the west bank. On the east bank a detachment of 1 Sgt. and 6 O.Rs. would establish a C.E.P. One officer and 14 O.Rs. would proceed to the brigade's objective and set up a C.C.P. One officer and 14 O.Rs. were to collect casualties *en route* from the perimeter of the bridgehead to the objective assisted by 60 O.Rs. acting as S.Bs. One 'Weasel' for equipment and two for casualties would be provided on the east bank. Evacuation across the river would be by L.V.T. and evacuation from C.D.P. to A.D.S. by six jeeps of the commando brigade.

CORPS MEDICAL INSTALLATIONS

24 C.C.S. with 15, 42 and 56 F.S.Us., 13 and 21 F.T.Us., 'Y' Blood Truck and the mobile element of 9 Adv. Depot Med. Stores would receive Groups I and II casualties from:

1. Holding Division's A.D.Ss. prior to the bridging of the river. Thereafter normal evacuation from the assault division's A.D.Ss.
2. Holding Division's F.D.Ss.

23 C.C.S. with 12, 27, 38 and 41 F.S.Us. and 30 and 37 F.T.Us. would be the rear C.C.S. 9 F.D.S. would function as the corps exhaustion centre and would receive Group III cases from the A.D.Ss. of the holding division.* When normal evacuation commenced these cases

---

* Triage, the classification of the wounded according to their immediate needs in respect of surgical intervention, was carried out at the A.D.S. There they were sorted into the following three categories preparatory to further evacuation:

Group 1: Those requiring resuscitation before any question of operation or further evacuation could be considered. Usually these were transferred to a F.D.S. functioning as a resuscitation centre.

Group 2: Those requiring immediate operation if life and limb are to be saved and who therefore must be held, after the operation, until fit to move. These were sent from the A.D.S. to the advanced surgical centre, commonly a F.D.S. with one or two F.S.Us. and a F.T.U. attached.

Group 3: These were they whose further treatment could safely be delayed until they reached the next unit in the evacuation chain. This group included the non-urgent, lying, sitting and walking wounded, and the sick. It was therefore by far the largest group. Its destination was the C.C.S.

There was, in fact, another group, the apparently moribund. These were segregated in the A.D.S. and not evacuated.

The F.D.S. had a staff of 6 officers R.A.M.C. (two non-medical), 1 officer A.D. Corps and approximately 90 O.Rs. It had twenty light beds for the more serious cases and was designed to hold and nurse patients either before or after operation until they were fit for further evacuation.

The F.S.U. consisted of one surgical team:

Surgeon (specialist)—1	G.D.Os.—7	Laundry orderly
Anaesthetist (Graded)—1	Steriliser	Water orderly
O.R.A. (Cpl.)—1	Preparation of patients	Generator orderly
	Plaster orderly	Runner

It, like the F.D.S., carried 20 light beds.

The C.C.S., with its two surgical teams was capable of holding 120 patients, sick or wounded, 50 beds, 70 stretchers.

One surgeon, it was estimated, could deal with 15 cases in twenty-four hours.

ADVANCE TO AND CROSSING OF THE RHINE

would be received from the assault division's A.D.Ss. 4 F.D.S. with the corps V.D.T.C. would be open for V.D. cases and for casualties and minor sick from west of the Rhine. A platoon of a U.S. Fd. Hosp. would be attached to 24 C.C.S. and U.S. cars would be routed therefrom. 23 and 24 C.C.Ss. would be cleared by 'B' Pln. 257 A.C.C. to Venraij (Second Army hospital area). 10 Fd. Hyg. Sec. would provide personnel for corps P.o.W. cage, Corps Tps. R.E., Bank Control and the Holding Division area. Civilian casualties would be evacuated through the usual military channels to A.D.S. level whence they would be evacuated in military ambulance cars to the civil hospital, Kevelaer.

The evacuation plan is shown below:

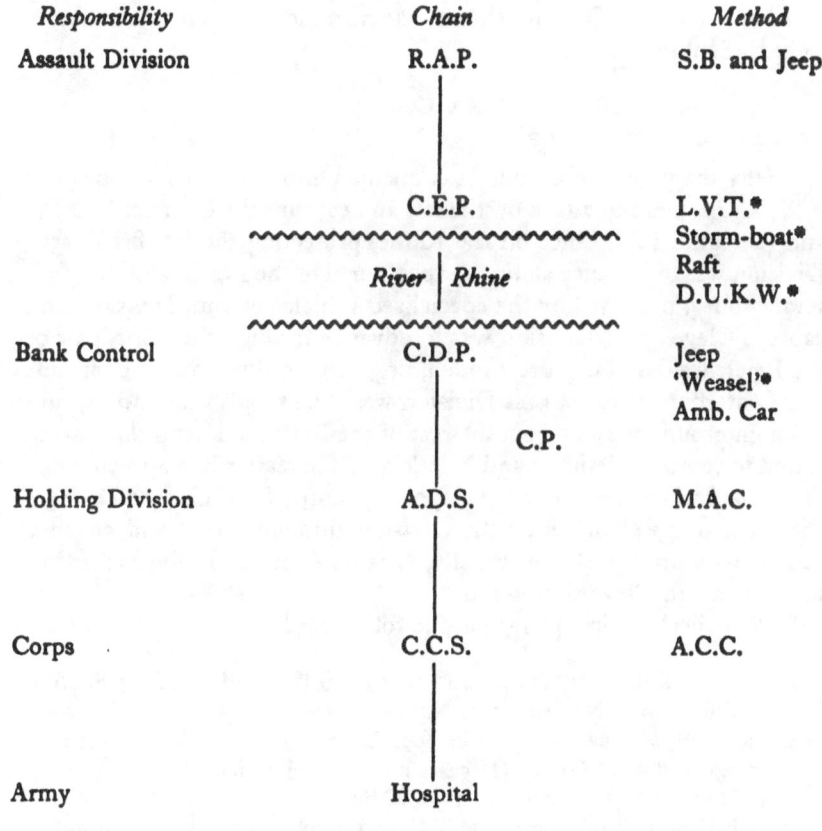

Responsibility	Chain	Method
Assault Division	R.A.P.	S.B. and Jeep
	C.E.P.	L.V.T.* Storm-boat*
	*River	Rhine*	Raft D.U.K.W.*
Bank Control	C.D.P.	Jeep 'Weasel'* Amb. Car
	C.P.	
Holding Division	A.D.S.	M.A.C.
Corps	C.C.S.	A.C.C.
Army	Hospital	

---

* Storm-boat: A light wooden craft with an outboard motor. Could take 4 stretchers.
L.V.T. ('Buffalo'): Landing Vessel, Tank. Type IV with door that could be lowered so that vehicles such as jeeps and 'Weasels' could drive aboard. Type II had no door and carried personnel only.
'Weasel': A small tracked vehicle which could take 2 stretchers.
D.U.K.W.: A 2¼ ton amphibious vehicle. Could take 9 stretchers.

Operation 'Plunder' was very successful and evacuation was smooth and according to plan. 23 and 24 C.C.Ss. opened and closed alternately.

On March 26, 4 F.D.S. moved up to Kevelaer, taking over from 9 F.D.S. 33 C.C.S. of VIII Corps admitted the overflow of cases from 23 and 24 C.C.Ss. during the time in which the very numerous airborne casualties were evacuated.

A total of 1,095 casualties, plus 291 German wounded, passed through the C.D.Ps. of 11 Lt. Fd. Amb. during the period March 24–26.

On March 28, 9 F.D.S., with 38 and 41 F.S.Us. and 30 F.T.U., crossed the Rhine and formed an advanced surgical centre in Hamminkeln.

On March 29, 34 C.C.S. was ordered to move to Borken, 23 C.C.S. to Ahaus and 4 F.D.S. to Hamminkeln. 9 Adv. Depot Med. Stores went to Schloss Wissen.

XXX CORPS

OPERATION 'VERITABLE'

Briefly the plan was as follows. Canadian 2nd and 3rd Divisions u/c XXX Corps were to attack on the left and capture the German F.D.Ls. and thereafter to advance on the Rhine, protecting the left flank. 15th Division was to advance along the road north of the Reichswald through Kranenburg, preceded by the specialised vehicles of 79th Division, and capture Cleve. 53rd Division was to advance through the north part of the Reichswald and capture Bradenburg, Stoppel Burg and the formidable Materborn feature. 51st Division was then to advance and capture the high ground west and south-west of the Reichswald and then swing round to capture Riethorst and Middelaar. Thereafter it was to clear the Goch road which was to be developed as a corps L. of C. 43rd Division was then to pass through 15th Division through Cleve and advance south-east on to the Rhine. Finally, Guards Armoured Division was to thrust through Cleve southwards.

The medical tactical plan took the following form:

1. 3 C.C.S. with 6, 14, 43, 44, 49 and 50 F.S.Us., and 7 and 35 F.T.Us. to be open in Marienbosch, Nijmegen.
2. 10 C.C.S. with 24 F.T.U. to be open in the barracks at Grave to receive the overflow of Group III cases and to receive sick.
3. 3 F.D.S. to be with and assist 3 C.C.S.
4. 35 F.D.S. with the corps V.D.T.C. and psychiatrist to be at Zeeland.
5. 111 M.A.C. at Boxtel; 302 M.A.C. at Gemonde.

It was agreed that as XXX Corps was under command of Canadian First Army for this operation the medical resources of Canadian II Corps and XXX Corps should be pooled under arrangements made by D.D.M.S. Canadian First Army.

ADVANCE TO AND CROSSING OF THE RHINE

The Canadian medical units were distributed as follows:

1. 3 (Cdn.) C.C.S. with a Cdn. F.S.U. and a Cdn. F.T.U. at Hees, near Nijmegen.
2. 6 (Cdn.) C.C.S. with two Cdn. F.S.Us. and a Cdn. F.T.U. at Jonker Bosch Hospital, Nijmegen.
3. 5 (Cdn.) F.D.S. with two Cdn. F.S.Us. and a Cdn. F.T.U. at Brakkenstein Hospital, Nijmegen.

Army units in support were:

1. 6 Cdn. G.H.	. . . . . .	St. Michielsgestel
2. 7 Cdn. G.H.	. . . . . .	Turnhout
3. 8 Cdn. G.H.	. . . . . .	St. Michielsgestel
4. 10 Cdn. G.H.	. . . . . .	Turnhout
5. Fwd. Del. Truck 'X' Blood Bank	. . .	With 6 (Cdn.) C.C.S.
6. Fwd. Del. Truck 'Y' Blood Bank	. .	With 3 C.C.S.
7. 11 Adv. Depot Med. Stores	. . .	Eindhoven

Ambulance cars were allotted as follows:

111 M.A.C.	one pln. to	15th Division
	three secs. to	51st Division
	three secs. to	53rd Division
302 M.A.C.	one pln. to	Guards Armoured Division
	one pln. to	43rd Division

Ambulance control posts were established at the crossroads on the axis of evacuation.

Battle casualties would be evenly distributed among the Canadian and British medical units, British V.D. and exhaustion cases to 35 F.D.S., sick to 10 C.C.S.

At 0500 hours on February 8, about 1,000 guns opened on the Siegfried Line and at 1030 hours the infantry attacked. By last light the leading divisions had taken all their objectives, including Kranenburg, Frasselt, Zyfflich and Wyler, and 178 casualties had been admitted to the corps medical units. On the 9th there was heavy fighting around Cleve, about half of the Reichswald was cleared and Gennep neared. On this day 341 casualties were admitted to the corps medical units. The main road through Kranenburg began to deteriorate rapidly as a consequence of the volume of heavy traffic flowing along it and of the Germans having flooded the area north of the Reichswald, which included the main Kranenburg–Cleve road. It therefore became necessary to make use of D.U.K.Ws. for evacuation purposes.

On the 11th, Cleve was captured at a cost of some 300 casualties. On the 12th the floods had risen so that evacuation by ambulance car became impossible. By the morning of the 13th some 250 casualties had been evacuated to 3 C.C.S. by D.U.K.Ws. On this day the clearing of the Reichswald was completed. Enemy resistance then stiffened and casualties increased in number, rising to 328 on February 15 with the capture of Kessel.

On February 16, 52nd Division joined XXX Corps and passed through 51st Division while 43rd and 15th Divisions attacked southward to Goch; 358 casualties were admitted to the corps medical units on this day. 3 C.C.S. was filled to capacity and all casualties were diverted to 3 and 6 (Cdn.) C.C.Ss.

On the 19th, 52nd Division on the right was checked by an anti-tank ditch but 51st Division captured Goch. On the 20th the floods subsided and evacuation by ambulance car became possible once more. On February 22, 23 C.C.S. moved into the convent at Mook. The main corps L. of C. now being along the Mook road, all evacuation was on this route. Evacuation from Guards Armoured, 3rd and 53rd Divisions was now to 23 C.C.S., from 43rd, 51st and 52nd to 3 C.C.S., Group I cases of 51st and 52nd Division being sent to an advanced surgical centre in Bedburg. This was a small township consisting of 35 large blocks of buildings used as hospitals and refugee centres. In it there were some 500 psychotics and considerable numbers of T.B. and diphtheria cases. In addition there were some 7,000 refugees.

On February 24, the American offensive in the Roer valley opened to the south of XXX Corps front. At this time 52nd Division was on the right, 15th Division was being relieved by 3rd Division, 53rd Division was in reserve, 51st Division was holding a line south of Goch while Guards, 11th and Canadian 4th Armoured Divisions were preparing to make a three-pronged thrust towards Wesel.

On February 28, the Canadians captured Calcar and Üdem Ridge. Weeze fell to 53rd Division and the Canadians became involved in heavy fighting on the left in the Hochwald. Casualty figures mounted again, numbering 445 on March 1. 23 C.C.S. was closed, evacuation being switched to 3 C.C.S.

By March 3, German resistance had weakened and it appeared that the Germans were thinning out and withdrawing across the Rhine while holding firmly on to their positions in the Hochwald and forming a perimeter defence around Wesel. Guards Armoured Division attacked and broke through these defences on March 4.

On March 5, 10 C.C.S. was moved to Schloss Wissen. Casualties forward of Weeze were evacuated thereto, those in rear of Weeze to 23 C.C.S. at Mook. 3 F.D.S. with 43 and 49 F.S.Us. and 7 F.T.U. moved to open an advanced surgical centre in the convent at Kapellen.

By the 10th, Operation 'Veritable', the penetration of the northern tip of the Siegfried Line, had been completed.

TABLE 45

XXX Corps. Casualties. Operation 'Veritable'

Feb.	8	178	Feb.	24	246
	9	341		25	240
	10	200		26	155
	11	293		27	289
	12	198		28	194
	13	235	March	1	311
	14	256		2	213
	15	328		3	196
	16	358		4	84
	17	464		5	202
	18	234		6	202
	19	307		7	58
	20	196		8	57
	21	247		9	157
	22	189		10	157
	23	257			

Total admissions Feb. 8–March 10 5,832
Total admissions on account of Exhaustion of which 280 were evacuated from corps area 735
Of 5,200 casualties reaching surgical departments Feb. 8–23, 105 died (2 per cent. mortality). Of these 5,200, 1,327 required operation and of these 55 died (4 per cent. mortality).

OPERATION 'PLUNDER'

Preparatory to this operation—the crossing of the Rhine—3 C.C.S. was moved from Marienbosch to Bedburg on March 11, handing its immobiles over to a Canadian F.D.S. which took over its site. 35 F.D.S. also moved to Bedburg on the 12th to deal with V.D. and psychiatric cases. 302 M.A.C. left XXX Corps on March 12 and, on the 17th, 23 C.C.S. moved from XXX to XII Corps and took over the site of 10 C.C.S., which moved to Bedburg. 3 F.D.S. moved to Qualburg and 43 and 49 F.S.Us. and 7 F.T.U. joined 35 F.D.S. in Bedburg.

Operation 'Plunder' involved the crossing of the Rhine by Second Army with Canadian II, VIII, XII and XXX Corps under command. XXX Corps' task was that of capturing Rees and Haldern, establishing a bridgehead and advancing into Germany. 51st Division was to lead the assault, followed by 43rd Division and Canadian 3rd Division in succession. Finally, Guards Armoured Division was to pass through the bridgehead and thrust towards Groenlo or Bocholt. 3rd Division was to hold the line of the Rhine within the corps boundaries.

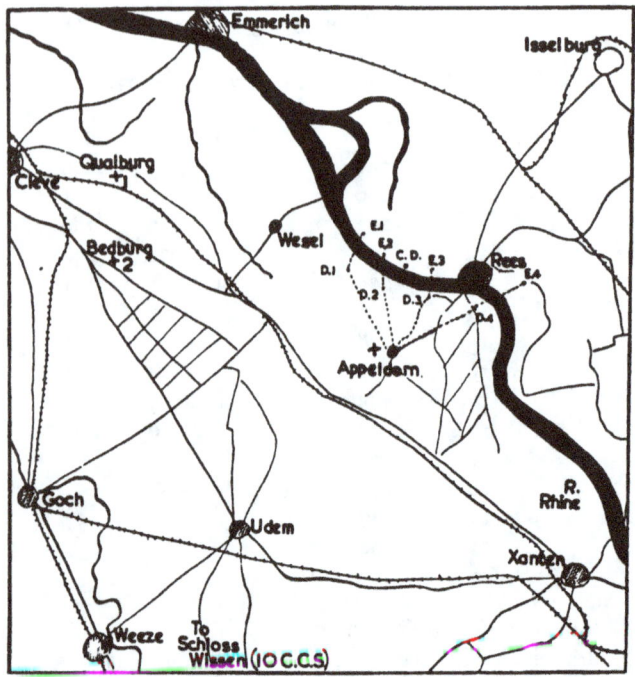

Fig. 84. XXX Corps. Operation 'Plunder'. Medical Arrangements.

E 1, 2, 3, 4. C.E.Ps.
D 1, 2, 3, 4. C.D.Ps.
C.D. Corps D.U.K.W. C.E.P.

1. 3 F.D.S.
2. 3 and 10 C.C.Ss.
   35 F.D.S.

The medical tactical plan was as follows:

51st Division would make the initial medical arrangements on the east bank of the river. The bank group—the Royals with 14 Lt. Fd. Amb.—would function as a beach group and the officer commanding the light field ambulance would make the initial medical arrangements on the west bank, evacuation being to the medical units of the holding division (3rd). 51st Division was to establish four C.E.Ps. by H-hour + 2 hours and divisions were to be responsible for the evacuation of their casualties to these C.E.Ps. A corps D.U.K.W. C.E.P. was to be established near the centrally placed D.U.K.W. control post by the light section of 35 F.D.S. with additional tentage and equipment. This C.E.P. was to cross the river in the first flight in D.U.K.Ws., eight D.U.K.Ws. being allotted with a call on all returning D.U.K.Ws. through the control post. Adequate supplies of blankets and stretchers were to be accumulated in the D.U.K.W. trans-shipment area for the replenishment of the medical units on the far side of the river. Casualties initially were to be

ADVANCE TO AND CROSSING OF THE RHINE

evacuated by 'Buffalo' from the C.E.Ps. to the four C.D.Ps. to be established by 14 Lt. Fd. Amb. on the west bank. From the C.D.Ps. evacuation would be to 8 Fd. Amb. of 3rd Division at Botzelaer.

8 and 223 Fd. Ambs. were responsible for the reception of casualties from the C.D.Ps. and from the D.U.K.Ws. and for evacuation by M.A.C. to Bedburg where 10 C.C.S. would admit battle casualties. 3 C.C.S. received the sick and any overflow of surgical cases from 10 C.C.S. V.D. and exhaustion cases would be sent to 3 F.D.S. at Qualburg. 35 F.D.S. with 43 and 49 F.S.Us. and 7 F.T.U. was closed ready to move across the Rhine to open an advanced surgical centre. When the river had been bridged and ambulance transport was running freely evacuation would be direct from the divisional medical units to 8 and 223 Fd. Ambs. and onwards to Bedburg.

Operation 'Plunder' commenced on March 22 with heavy air attacks on the German positions and communications. Then on the 23rd at 1700 hours the guns opened. The weather was fine. The assaulting infantry began to cross the Rhine at 2100 hours. By 2359 hours 22 casualties had been admitted to 8 Fd. Amb. and by 0300 hours on the 24th 10 C.C.S. had admitted 150 and was temporarily closed, 3 C.C.S. taking over. By 0900 hours on the 24th 3 C.C.S. had admitted 100. At 1000 hours 10 C.C.S. opened again and 3 closed. Casualties on the 24th totalled about 500.

The morning of the 25th found 51st Division in possession of most of its initial objectives but Rees was not completely clear. Evacuation was still by 'Buffalo'. The corps D.U.K.W. C.E.P. was established by the evening of this day. By the 26th two bridges were in use. Rees was finally cleared. On this day 143 casualties were admitted to corps medical units. On the 27th evacuation by D.U.K.W. across the bridges was proceeding and by nightfall ambulance cars were evacuating direct to the C.C.Ss. through 8 Fd. Amb. On the 28th 35 F.D.S. opened an advanced surgical centre just north of Rees.

By March 30, XXX Corps was across the Rhine, Guards Armoured, 43rd and 51st Divisions in hot pursuit of a defeated and disorganised enemy. 3rd Division moved into Rees to form a firm corps base.

The evacuation system adopted for this operation was as interesting as it was satisfactory. Evacuation at first was by 'Buffalo' from the assault divisional C.E.Ps. to the bank group C.D.Ps., thence by ambulance car to the field ambulances of the holding division and thence to the medical area in Bedburg. Some 630 casualties were thus evacuated. When the corps D.U.K.W. C.E.P. opened casualties were evacuated by D.U.K.W., swimming and later running over the bridges, to the field ambulances of the holding division and thence to the medical area. The 'Buffaloes' continued to run until the D.U.K.Ws. were fully operating and the D.U.K.Ws. continued in use until evacuation by ambulance car over the bridges was well established. A total of 404 casualties were evacuated by D.U.K.Ws. swimming and a further 118 by D.U.K.Ws. running over the bridges.

TABLE 46

XXX Corps. Casualties. Operation 'Plunder'

March 23	20	March 28	272
24	495	29	145
25	372	30	141
26	268	31	56
27	166		

Total admissions March 23–31 . 1,935

SECOND ARMY

The new year opened with Second Army composed of three corps, VIII, XII and XXX, together with Army troops. XXX Corps passed u/c Canadian First Army for Operation 'Veritable' but returned to Second Army during the second week of March for Operation 'Plunder'. At the end of March U.S. XVIII Airborne Corps came under command Second Army.

At the beginning of January VIII Corps was holding the northern portion of Second Army's sector along the line of the Maas from Nijmegen to Maeseyk. To the south XII Corps was deployed east of the Maas in the area north and east of Sittard. XXX Corps had been moved to the area Marche–Rochefort with 6th Airborne and 53rd Divisions and 29th Armd. Bde. Gp. under command to take part in the checking of the German thrust from the Ardennes towards Brussels and Antwerp. Meanwhile XII Corps was preparing for Operation 'Blackcock', which was successfully completed on January 26.

XXX Corps passed to Canadian First Army for Operation 'Veritable' with Guards Armoured, 15th, 51st and 53rd Divisions under command. XII Corps withdrew to the rear area for training and planning and VIII Corps held the line of the Maas. During the later phases of Operation 'Veritable', 11th Armoured, 3rd and 52nd Divisions left Second Army to pass u/c XXX Corps and so Second Army became non-operational for a time. With the final withdrawal of the Germans from the Wesel bridgehead across the Rhine on March 11 the task of Canadian First Army was completed and XXX Corps with its eight divisions returned to Second Army.

On March 23 Operation 'Plunder' opened. XXX Corps quickly captured Esserden and Wardmannshof. U.S. XVIII Airborne Corps entered the battle (Operation 'Varsity'). In XII Corps' sector 15th Division quickly linked up with 6th Airborne Division. VIII Corps with

ADVANCE TO AND CROSSING OF THE RHINE

11th Armoured Division crossed the Rhine and moved into the lin south of XII Corps, taking under command 15th and 6th Airborn Divisions.

Second Army now began to advance on a wide front with four corps in the line. In the north XXX Corps moved on a north-easterly axis directed on Bremen and by March 31 had reached Groenlo and Eibergen. On its right XII Corps met stubborn opposition in the Rheine area. To the south VIII Corps advanced rapidly to cross the Ems at Greven.

The distribution of the Army Medical units in support of XXX Corps during the period of the German counter-offensive in the Ardennes is shown in Fig. 85.

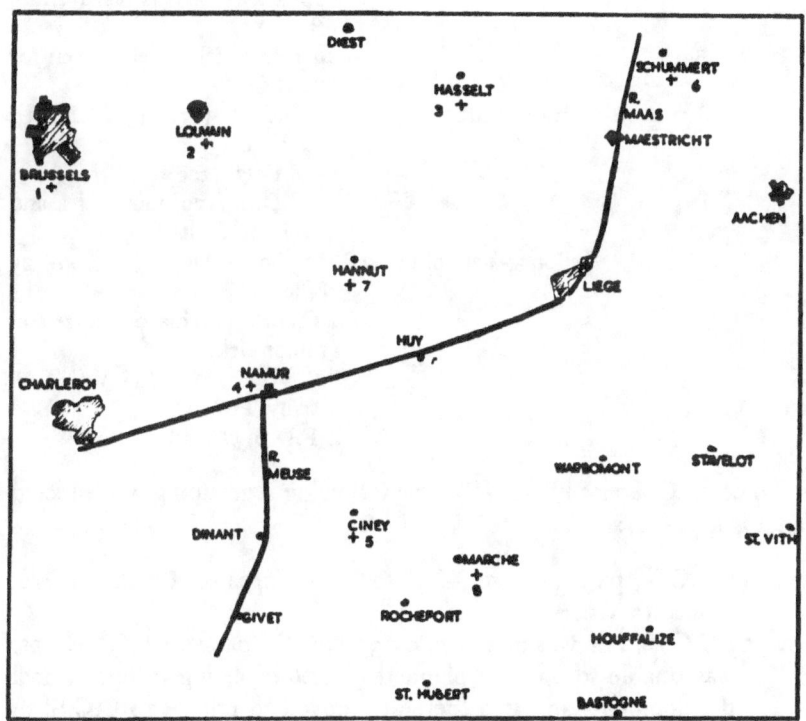

FIG. 85. Second Army. The Siting of the Forward Medical Units in support of XXX Corps. January 1, 1945.

1. 8 and 108 B.G.Hs.
2. 101 B.G.H.
3. 39 and 81 B.G.Hs.
   31 F.D.S.
   8 Adv. Depot Med. Stores
4. 33 C.C.S.
   35 F.D.S.
5. 3 C.C.S.
6. 24 C.C.S.
7. 11 Lt. Fd. Amb.
8. 3 F.D.S.

The distribution of Army medical units in connexion with Operation 'Blackcock' (*see* page 359) is shown below:

VIII Corps	.	34 C.C.S. open in Technical College, Helmond
		23 C.C.S. open in Weert
XII Corps	.	10 C.C.S. open in Eysden
		24 C.C.S. open in Bies
XXX Corps	.	33 C.C.S. open in Asile Ave Maria, St. Servais, near Namur (asile = a mental hospital)
		3 C.C.S. open in Ciney
Army	.	Eindhoven area — 79 B.G.H. (600)
		84 B.G.H. (200)
		86 B.G.H. (200)
		35 C.C.S. (150) (air cushion)
		21 F.D.S. (Valkenswaard) Amb. R.H.
		49 F.D.S. (Sterksel) screen for 84 B.G.H.
		Hasselt area — 39 B.G.H. (600) (5 M.F.S.U. attached)
		81 B.G.H. (200)
		31 F.D.S. (120) minor sick and Amb. R. Halt
		Bourg-Léopold area — 13 Con. Depot (1,000+25 officers)
		2 F.D.S. (psychiatric centre and minor sick)
		50 F.D.S. (Moll) V.D.T.C. Army Tps.
		4 F.D.S. (Diest)

To cover Operation 'Veritable' the following regrouping was effected (*see* Figs. 74–76):

1. 33 C.C.S., passing from XXX to VIII Corps on January 19/20, moved to Weert.
2. 23 C.C.S., relieved in Weert by 33 C.C.S., passed to XII Corps, was unable to open as planned in Sittard owing to operational developments and was therefore moved to relieve 10 C.C.S. in Eysden.
3. 10 C.C.S., thus relieved, moved into XXX Corps Troops concentration area on January 23.
4. 4 F.D.S. in Diest passed u/c XII Corps.
5. As U.S. forces took over Second Army's sector east of the Maas, 23 and 24 C.C.Ss. were withdrawn, 23 C.C.S. moving to Tremeloo under command XXX Corps and 24 C.C.S. to Betekom under command XII Corps.

ADVANCE TO AND CROSSING OF THE RHINE

In preparation for Operation 'Plunder' the following moves took place:

VIII Corps	33 C.C.S. moved from Weert to Geldern.
	34 C.C.S. remained in Helmond.
XII Corps	24 C.C.S. moved from Betekom to Kapellen on March 14.
	23 C.C.S. from Tremeloo relieved 10 C.C.S. at Schloss Wissen.
XXX Corps	3 C.C.S. from Ciney moved to Bedburg and was joined there by 10 C.C.S. on March 17
Army	The Hasselt group of hospitals was gradually closed down, 39 B.G.H. alone being left there under command L. of C. to accept overflow cases. At the same time a hospital area was built up at Venraij.
	The Eindhoven group was reduced.
	Units of the Bourg-Léopold group were phased forward.

Forward Hospitals:
Venraij area:

Oostrum	81 B.G.H. (200) opened March 9
Venraij	9 B.G.H. (600) opened March 22
	84 B.G.H. (200) ,, ,, 21
	21 F.D.S. screen for 81 and 84 B.G.Hs., opened March 21 and later formed Amb. R.H.
Helmond	31 F.D.S. temporary Amb. R.H. and local minor sick, opened March 15.

Rearward Hospitals:

Eindhoven	79 B.G.H. (600)
	86 ,, (100+100 for special surgery, 6 M.N.S.U. and 5 M.F.S.U.)
	35 C.C.S., air cushion
Sterksel	49 F.D.S. Army Psychiatric Centre, opened March 18
	13 Con. Depot forward wing (500) opened March 19
Geldrop	50 F.D.S. (V.D.T.C. Army Tps. and infectious cases) opened March 21
Bourg-Léopold	2 F.D.S. (local Troops sick and V.D.)
Army Tps. Rear Area	13 Con. Depot rear wing (500)

During the initial phase of Operation 'Plunder' the following moves took place:

Each assaulting corps was allotted one light field ambulance to cover casualty disembarkation and evacuation from the river bank. C.C.Ss. were placed under Army control for movement and siting.

VIII Corps

33 C.C.S. remained in Geldern to cover the right flank, including 1st Cdo. Bde. and U.S. XVIII Airborne Corps. A U.S. field hospital was established nearby so that U.S. casualties could be evacuated along U.S. channels.

34 C.C.S. crossed the Rhine on March 29 to open in Gemen.

XII Corps

11 Lt. Fd. Amb. was allotted to XII Corps to provide C.D.Ps. and C.C.Ps. to cover the assault crossings in the Xanten area.

23 C.C.S. remained at Schloss Wissen. It was later relieved by 86 B.G.H. and prepared to move across the Rhine.

24 C.C.S. remained at Kapellen. One platoon of a U.S. field hospital was established nearby to filter off U.S. casualties from U.S. XVIII Corps' sector.

11 Lt. Fd. Amb. carried out special training with D.U.K.Ws. and L.V.T. for the assault crossing of the Rhine. This unit trained with the Bank Control Group and thereby, besides acquiring technical training, was able to fit itself into the control organisation and ensure smooth working of casualty evacuation in the actual operation. One section of Pioneers was attached to and trained with this field ambulance. The unit was organised to set up two C.D.Ps. for storm boats and a further two for L.V.T. C.D.Ps. evacuated to an A.D.S. formed by H.Q. of the ambulance. Later C.D.Ps. for storm boats were replaced by D.U.K.W. C.D.Ps.

XXX Corps

14 Lt. Fd. Amb. was allotted to XXX Corps to provide C.D.Ps. and C.C.Ps. in the Rees sector.

3 and 10 C.C.Ss. remained in Bedburg.

Army

35 C.C.S. moved from the Eindhoven airfield to Hees but still functioned as an air cushion with 120 beds.

86 B.G.H. closed at Eindhoven and moved to Schloss Wissen where it replaced 23 C.C.S. of XII Corps on April 1.

One of the two F.D.Ss. with each infantry division was withdrawn immediately before the Rhine crossing. These F.D.Ss. were placed under Army control and sub-allotted as follows:

11 F.D.S. (from	3rd Div.)	allotted to	XXX Corps			
14 ,,	,,	43rd ,,	,,	,,	XII	,,
22 ,,	,,	15th ,,	,,	,,	VIII	,,
19 ,,	,,	52nd ,,	} retained under Army control for Army roadhead area and to meet Operation 'Eclipse' commitments later			
6 ,,	,,	51st ,,				
26 ,,	,,	53rd ,,				

At the beginning of the year ambulance R.H. was at Valkenswaard (21 F.D.S.) with an ambulance train halt at Hasselt for general hospitals in the Hasselt area. Ambulance trains were required to run on alternate days, but this was later reduced to two ambulance trains per week, with

ADVANCE TO AND CROSSING OF THE RHINE

the proviso that ambulance trains could be called upon to run twenty-four hours ahead of the scheduled timings, if necessary, on twenty-four hours' notice being given to Q (Mov.).

Ambulance R.H. moved to Helmond on March 18 and was later moved to Horst-Sevenum, adjoining the Venraij hospital area, on March 24. During the first few days of Operation 'Plunder' ambulance trains were scheduled to leave ambulance R.H. twice daily. In practice it proved possible to reduce the number of ambulance trains to one per day after the fourth day.

During January and February air evacuation continued from Eindhoven. 35 C.C.S. had established an air evacuation cushion with accommodation for 80 lying cases and 70 walking cases. Cases of less than six weeks expectancy of hospital treatment were evacuated to hospitals in the Brussels area; longer term cases were evacuated direct to the United Kingdom.

During the early part of January there were two periods, one of four days and one of five days, during which no air evacuation was possible owing to bad weather. Apart from these two periods it was possible to evacuate cases by air on at least five days each week.

During the later stages of Operation 'Veritable' 'B' Flight 1 C.A.E.U., R.A.F., was moved to Eindhoven where it relieved 35 C.C.S. as casualty air cushion and the C.C.S. underwent training for an air transportable rôle with equipment and load tables based on an overall lift of 25 Dakotas (53½ tons).

It was then possible during the last week of March to move 35 C.C.S. forward to Hees to establish air evacuation. The totals of cases evacuated by air from Second Army area during the initial phases of the Rhine crossing are given below:

	To Brussels	To United Kingdom	Totals
March 25	196	17	213
,, 26	185+21	—	206
,, 27	305+12	117	434
,, 28	234+139	—	373
,, 29	366	80	446
,, 30	231+295	114	640
,, 31	357	83	440
			2,752

During the winter months 257 A.C.C. was responsible for evacuation from corps C.C.Ss. and for the road evacuation within Army area (including transfers to the convalescent depot). One platoon of ambulance cars was allotted to each operational corps and one platoon retained under Army control for evacuation within Army area, including ambulance cars required to cover air evacuation and ambulance trains.

During Operation 'Plunder' two platoons of 218 A.C.C. were placed under command Second Army. The following allotment of ambulance cars was made:

257 A.C.C.
>One platoon to VIII Corps
>One platoon to XII Corps
>One platoon to XXX Corps
>One platoon for road evacuation to airfield and within Second Army area (including evacuation of special cases from forward hospitals at Venraij to rearward hospitals at Eindhoven).

218 A.C.C.
>Two platoons for evacuation from Venraij to Amb. R.H. (One of these platoons later took over road evacuation of special and minor cases from Venraij to Eindhoven.)

With winter conditions prevailing, the three advanced depots medical stores were accommodated in buildings. During this period their locations were as follows:

>8 at Hasselt, moving to Venraij on March 16
>9 at Valkenswaard, moving to Venraij on March 30
>11 remained in Eindhoven.

Advanced depots at this time obtained supplies from base depots in Brussels and Louvain.

Mobile elements continued to be invaluable and the additional load-carrying vehicles they provided enabled advanced depots to function efficiently when roads were in a very bad condition due to ice and snow.

The detailed issue medical stores continued to function and relieved general hospitals and advanced depots medical stores, but most of the work involved supplying the needs of R.M.Os. in Second Army Troops area.

The supply of medical equipment generally was satisfactory. Some difficulty was, however, experienced in meeting many of the expendible requirements of R.M.Os., F.D.Ss. and V.D.T.Cs. This was due to the fact that the A.F. I.1248 scale of equipment for advanced depots medical stores did not include many of the medicines necessary for the treatment of minor sick, who can easily be retained and treated in unit sick bays and divisional medical units. Many of these items were, in fact, available to those R.M.Os. and medical units in rear areas who were able to obtain their requirements from the dispensaries of general hospitals.

Treatment of large numbers of minor sick in the unit sick bays and in divisional medical units effected a considerable saving in man-power.

ADVANCE TO AND CROSSING OF THE RHINE 463

If cases were carefully selected, ambulance cars and hospital beds were saved for longer term cases and, moreover, minor sick so treated could be discharged direct to their units instead of to reinforcement holding units with consequent delay in their return to duty. For the success of this policy it is essential for the A.F. I.1248 scales for consumable items of medical equipment held by advanced depots medical stores to be sufficiently elastic to permit of additional essential items being obtained without a special authority being necessary for each and every demand by medical units and R.M.Os.

This period witnessed a wide variety of operational activity, active and offensive patrolling, defensive actions, clearing of pockets of stubborn resistance and set battles of great magnitude culminating in the crossing of the Rhine, the largest assault of a great river obstacle undertaken during the campaign. These activities took place in a wide range of climatic conditions, from the snow of the Ardennes, the rain of Operations 'Blackcock' and 'Veritable' to the perfect weather of Operation 'Plunder'.

Throughout this period the Army Medical Services were never overextended. The more static rôles of the C.C.Ss. and the general hospitals permitted them to pay more attention to post-operative cases. Evacuation was difficult in Operation 'Veritable' when the flooded roads made the standard methods impracticable so that D.U.K.Ws. had to be used extensively, and in Operation 'Plunder' in which the bank control group, including a strong medical element had to be devised.

11 L. OF C. AREA

The V.1 rocket attacks on Antwerp progressively increased in intensity to reach a climax in February when a gradual decline set in to end in an abrupt cessation on March 30. The damage to property was enormous but casualties were not as heavy as might have been expected. In mid-January it was decided to change the personnel of 9 B.G.H. for periods of a month. On January 25 the annexe of the hospital was hit, but apart from broken windows no great damage was done and there were no severe casualties. Then on the 31st the officers mess was hit and badly wrecked and two officers were injured.

In late February 9 B.G.H. passed to command Second Army and so closed and prepared to move. 163 Fd. Amb. thereupon took over the Belgian Military Hospital from 20 Cdn. G.H. and opened a 120-bed hospital (60 underground) plus 80 C.R.S. beds. To the field ambulance two F.S.Us., a F.T.U., a radiologist, a physician, 4 nursing officers and a number of O.Rs. R.A.M.C. were attached. The combined units were known as the British Military Hospital (163 Fd. Amb.) Antwerp and served the Antwerp area until April when 106 B.G.H. moved from Wavre Notre Dame to Antwerp and took over from 163 Fd. Amb.

THE ARMY DENTAL SERVICE (SECOND ARMY)

The reduced movement and limited aims of the winter operations resulted in a lessening of the operational activities of the dental units and the adoption by them of a more static rôle in buildings centrally situated in the area of concentration of the formations to which they were attached.

The routine dental inspection of units was found to be impracticable, save at 13 Con. Depot and 101 Rft. Gp. In order to divert the daily dental sick from the hospitals, the dental officers of the hospitals concerned and of the medical units in their vicinity were concentrated in a central dental centre in Eindhoven in November. A similar concentration was formed at 101 Reinforcement Group, Bourg-Léopold, based on 207 F.D.C. (Op.) Type B. The dental personnel held there as reinforcements were employed in the centre and for their use one field dental outfit for two mechanics was obtained from 11 Base Depot Medical Stores in Antwerp.

125 F.D.C. (Op.) Type A came u/c Second Army early in December and was sited at Bourg-Léopold to serve 113 Transit Camp. 147 F.D.C. (Op.) Type B was withdrawn in February from 34 R.H.U. (renumbered 33 R.H.U.) and sited at Diest to cover the units in this area, one dental mechanic and field dental outfit for two mechanics being provided for the unit. 517 M.D.U. was thus freed for duty with 4th Armd. Bde.

The more stable conditions led to an increase in the attendances at dental units. In November these had averaged 70/1,000/diem; in January the figures were 87/1,000/diem. The figure fell again with the flare-up of operational activity in the Ardennes and in the Roer triangle.

By March about half of the troops who had landed in Normandy were no longer with Second Army; they had become casualties. The dental condition of their replacements was generally satisfactory. Among them there was a rising proportion of men of the higher age groups and so the demand for denture work rose from 8 per 1,000 in October to 10·9 in March.

The incidence of acute ulcerative gingivitis/stomatitis rose from 0·47/1,000/mensem to 1·78 in December and 2·52 in March.

5 M.F.S.U. came u/c Second Army on February 19 and was attached to 86 B.G.H. in Eindhoven.

Twenty-three M.D.Us., having been mobilised, were equipped with medical and other equipment and vehicles.

It was necessary to divert to Base Depot Med. Stores the heavy demands made on Adv. Depots Med. Stores by dental units of 83 Group T.A.F. As an additional safeguard against unexpected depletion of stocks at Adv. Depots Med. Stores a system was instituted whereby the officers commanding the three stores under the control of Second Army submitted weekly stock statements to A.D.D.S. Three corporal dental

ADVANCE TO AND CROSSING OF THE RHINE

clerk orderlies held at 32 R.H.U. were attached for duty to 8, 9 and 11 Adv. Depots Med. Stores during December.

The number of M.D.Us. was raised in November to a total of 36 by the remobilisation of F.D.Ss. In January this number was reduced by one when 514 M.D.U. passed to command 21 Army Group. It was now possible to provide an adequate means of meeting the denture demands of Second Army.

    Three M.D.Us. were attached to each infantry division
    Two   „   „   „   „   „   armoured „
    One   „   was   „   „   „   corps
    Eight „   were employed in Army rear area.

In March this distribution was changed to:

    Three M.D.Us. per infantry division
    Three   „   „   armoured „
    Two   „   „   corps
    Two   „   in Army area

and the attachment of M.D.Us. to independent brigades, A.G.R.A. and A.Gs.R.E. by corps became possible.

Throughout the winter A.D.D.S. was with Rear H.Q. Second Army in Sonnis but on March 19 he moved to Main H.Q. at Walbeck in connexion with the preparations for the crossing of the Rhine. During the last fortnight of December and the first week of January he was much occupied with the remobilisation of the F.D.S. dental personnel as M.D.Us.

THE ARMY TRANSFUSION SERVICE (21 ARMY GROUP)

The work of the B.T.U. was now becoming of a routine nature. Throughout the winter no important moves took place, except for a brief moment when XXX Corps hurriedly rushed down from northeast of Brussels to the south-east, in the line of the German advance from the Ardennes. 'Y' Bank had to send a forward truck with this force, but it was within easy distance of the B.T.U. which supplied it with stores.

Base hospitals, Canadian and British, had gradually been increasing in numbers in Belgium and Holland and regular delivery schedules by base vehicles were begun to cover the areas Antwerp–Louvain and Ghent–Bruges–Ostend, one tour of each being done every three days. It was still necessary to do a round of hospitals in the rearward areas, Amiens–Dieppe–Rouen, for a short time but this was gradually discontinued as the hospitals became independent or moved up to Belgium.

Incoming supplies of blood continued to arrive steadily by air, though during the very bad weather they had to be sent by sea to the port of Ostend, a quite satisfactory arrangement.

The disposition of the service remained the same throughout most of the winter; base unit at Brussels, 'X' Bank at Tilburg (two hours away) with one section out at Breda, 'Y' Bank at Eindhoven (three and a half hours away) with sections out at Nijmegen and Eysden. There were no great movements of armies or overrunning of territory during this time; it was a period of continuous bitter fighting in very adverse climatic conditions with a steady stream of casualties, and all the sections were fully occupied with distribution and transfusion.

The first moves began when Second Army, facing eastwards along a line just this side of the Rhine from Nijmegen down towards the American sector at Maastricht, began to straighten its line and clear all the territory up to the river. 'Y' Bank moved one of its forward trucks into this sector for the short sharp engagement; casualties were fairly heavy and consumption of blood rose considerably.

At the same time, the Canadians, considerably reinforced by British units, were also pushing out towards the Rhine at the north end of this sector. The fighting through the Reichswald Forest across seas of water-logged country, to turn the north end of the Siegfried Line, was largely amphibious and was as severe as any during the campaign.

To deal with the heavy casualties expected, an enormous advanced surgical centre with one of the C.C.Ss. was set up in Nijmegen. Eight F.S.Us. and three F.T.Us. were concentrated in this centre and a large dump of transfusion stores was built up by 'X' Bank from Tilburg preparatory to its move into Nijmegen when 'Y' Bank moved out to follow Second Army. This arrangement greatly eased the B.T.U's. supplying work when the battle began and casualties increased. 'Y' Bank moved out to Venraij towards the south-east on March 18. The enormous congestion on the roads at this time increased the transport difficulties, but fortunately air evacuation of casualties from this sector was functioning on a large scale and a very close liaison was worked up between 'Y' Bank and the casualty air evacuation unit which carried up in empty planes large amounts of transfusion stores and also provided the all-important communication between Bank and base. (Plates XXI and XXII illustrate a transfusion unit in action in the field.)

CANADIAN FIRST ARMY*

The estimated casualties in Operation 'Veritable' were 1,000 a day with a peak of 2,300 to 5,000 on the third day. The medical planners had ample time to make their preparations. Casualties would be evacuated from R.A.P. to C.C.P. by jeep ambulance, and by 'Weasel'

---

* For a fuller account, the Canadian Official Medical History should be consulted.

ADVANCE TO AND CROSSING OF THE RHINE 467

and 'Buffalo' if water obstacles had to be crossed. Evacuation from C.C.P. to A.D.S. would be by the same types of vehicle. From the A.D.S. the casualties would be taken by M.A.C. to one or other of three control posts which would be under the control of A.D.M.S. Army Troops, manned by F.D.S. personnel and situated on the roads leading from the battle to Nijmegen. At the control post the M.A.C. cars would be directed to corps C.C.Ss. or F.D.Ss. in the Nijmegen area at every one of which surgical facilities would be available. From the corps C.C.S. or F.D.S. casualties would be conveyed along the Nijmegen–'s Hertogenbosch road to another control post at which the ambulance car would be directed to one or other of the eight general hospitals in the Army area. Certain of these hospitals were equipped to treat special types of wound, e.g. 8 Cdn. G.H. in St. Michielsgestel had a maxillo-facial surgery team attached to it, 6 Cdn. G.H. a neurosurgical team, 10 Cdn. G.H. in Turnhout a chest surgery team. Civilian casualties would be sent to St. Canisius Hospital, Nijmegen, military personnel with communicable diseases to 3 (Cdn.) C.C.S. at Hees and minor sick would be held in the divisional F.D.Ss.

It was arranged that in the forthcoming attack 18 (Cdn.) Fd. Amb. would clear casualties in Cdn. 5th Inf. Bde. Gp. to its C.C.P. in Berg-en-Dal and that the casualties in Cdn. 4th and 6th Inf. Bde. Gps. would be evacuated through the C.C.P. of 10 (Cdn.) Fd. Amb. in Malden. From these C.C.Ps. casualties would be taken by M.A.C. to 5 (Cdn.) F.D.S. at Brakkenstein, to 3 C.C.S. in Marienbosch, to 6 (Cdn.) C.C.S. in Jonker Bosch or to 3 (Cdn.) C.C.S. in Hees. Jeep ambulances would be assigned to the brigades and additional ambulance cars would be provided for the conveyance of casualties from C.C.Ps. and A.D.Ss.

C.C.Ps. were opened by 10 (Cdn.) Fd. Amb. at Bisselt and Malden and by 18 (Cdn.) Fd. Amb. in Berg-en-Dal. A.D.Ss. were established by 10 and 11 (Cdn.) Fd. Ambs. in Nijmegen and by 18 (Cdn.) Fd. Amb. at Slijk-Ewijk, some five miles north-west of Nijmegen on the Waal.

On the morning of February 8 Canadian 2nd Division launched an attack to clear a triangular area dominating the main road from Nijmegen to Cleve. Its C.C.Ps. evacuated 145 casualties during the first three days of Operation 'Veritable' and of these only 75 were Canadians. During the afternoon of the 8th, Canadian 3rd Division began its advance into the flooded area between the Nijmegen–Cleve road and the Waal. Its 7th Brigade reached Zyfflich while its 8th Brigade passed through Zandpol and Leuth by the evening of this day. At times the water was three feet deep and so both the advance and the evacuation of casualties were greatly impeded. 22 (Cdn.) Fd. Amb. established a C.C.P. on the bank of the Waal, four miles north-east of Nijmegen but because of the floods it was forced to move the C.C.P. back into Nijmegen itself and thereafter casualties were ferried from the forward R.A.Ps. by 'Buffaloes',

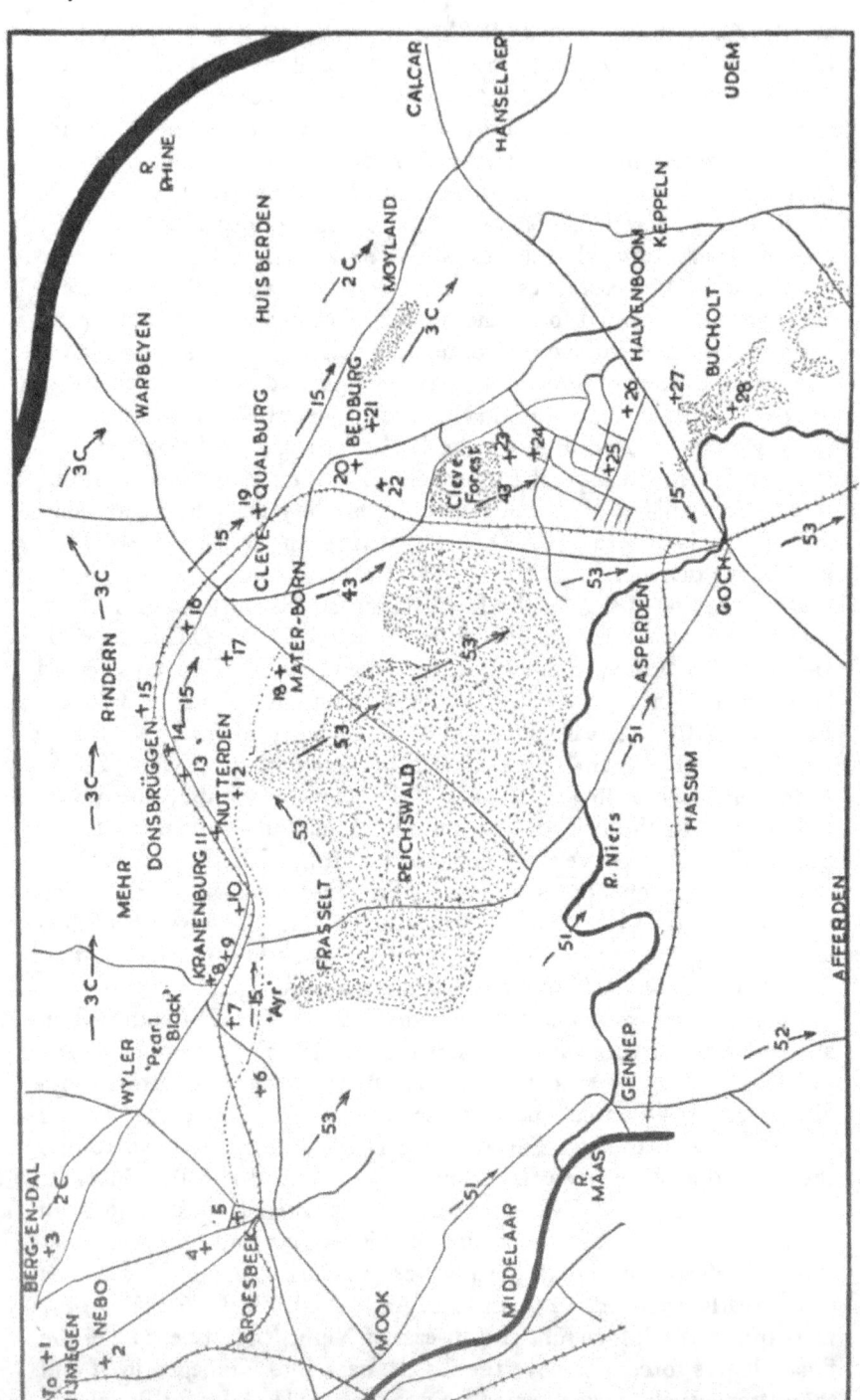

Fig. 86. Canadian First Army. Operation 'Veritable'. Medical Cover.
See opposite page for key

ADVANCE TO AND CROSSING OF THE RHINE 469

'Weasels' and D.U.K.Ws. From the C.C.P. they were evacuated to the A.D.S. of 14 (Cdn.) Fd. Amb. in Nijmegen and thence to the ambulance control post where they were directed to one or other of the C.C.Ss. or F.D.Ss. in this area.

As the operation progressed Cdn. 8th Bde. replaced Cdn. 7th Bde., held the cleared bank of the river and proceeded to take Kekerdom, Millingen and Keeken. Casualties were cleared by 23 (Cdn.) Fd. Amb's. C.C.P. in Beek, on the Nijmegen–Cleve road, and thence were evacuated to the A.D.S. of 22 (Cdn.) Fd. Amb. just south of this road. As the advance continued casualties were evacuated to the A.D.S. of 193 Fd. Amb. of 15th Division in Cleve. This A.D.S. was a trans-shipment post and from it the casualties were evacuated in D.U.K.Ws. which had to cross about two miles of deeply flooded country between Kranenburg and Wyler on their way back to Nijmegen. These D.U.K.Ws. conveyed their casualties to 3 C.C.S. just outside Nijmegen where an ambulance post had been established. From this post heavy ambulance cars could operate and the casualties were taken thence to the corps F.D.S. or C.C.S. Evacuation by ambulance car from Cleve was never possible during the operation. On February 25 15th Division's D.U.K.W. loading-point in Cleve was taken over by 11 (Cdn.) Fd. Amb. By this time Canadian 3rd Division was in Keppeln and was preparing to continue with the next phase of the attack, Operation 'Blockbuster'.

On February 15 Canadian 2nd Division passed under command Canadian II Corps and having regrouped began to move from the vicinity of Nijmegen to that of Cleve. 11 (Cdn.) Fd. Amb. sent its H.Q. and one company forward with Cdn. 4th Inf. Bde. Gp. The H.Q. opened an A.D.S. in Cleve and the company established a C.C.P., evacuating

---

Key to Fig. 86.

15, 43, 51, 52, 53 = 15th, 43rd, 51st, 52nd, 53rd Divisions
2 C, 3 C = Canadian 2nd and 3rd Infantry Divisions

1. 3 C.C.S.
2. A.D.S. 193 Fd. Amb.
3. A.D.S. 194 Fd. Amb.
4. C.C.P. 153 Fd. Amb.
5. C.C.P. 193 Fd. Amb.
6. C.C.P. 194 Fd. Amb.
7. C.C.P. 153 Fd. Amb. (closed)
8. H.Q. and A.D.S. 153 Fd. Amb.
9. C.C.P. 194 Fd. Amb.
10. D.U.K.W. Evacuation Post
11. C.C.P. 153 Fd. Amb.
12. C.C.P. 194 Fd. Amb.
13. H.Q. 193 Fd. Amb. (closed)
14. C.C.P. 153 Fd. Amb.
15. C.C.P. 193 Fd. Amb.
16. A.D.S. 193 Fd. Amb. D.U.K.W. Evac. Pt.
17. C.C.P. 194 Fd. Amb.
18. C.C.P. 193 Fd. Amb.
19. C.C.P. 193 Fd. Amb.
20. A.D.S. 43rd Div.
21. C.C.P. 194 Fd. Amb.
22. H.Q. 153 Fd. Amb. (closed)
23. C.C.P. 194 Fd. Amb.
24. A.D.S. 153 Fd. Amb.
25. C.C.P. 153 Fd. Amb.
26. C.C.P. 193 Fd. Amb.
27. C.P.
28. C.P.

casualties to the D.U.K.W. loading-point in Cleve. On the 17th, Cdn. 7th Inf. Bde. Gp. with a company of 10 (Cdn.) Fd. Amb., and on the following day, Cdn. 5th Inf. Bde. Gp. with a company of 18 (Cdn.) Fd. Amb., moved into the Cleve area. C.C.Ps. were opened whence evacuation was to the A.D.S. of 11 (Cdn.) Fd. Amb. in Cleve. On the 19th Canadian 2nd Division, with 43rd Division on its left and Canadian 3rd Division on its right, began to drive south-east towards Xanten. 11 (Cdn.) Fd. Amb. opened a C.C.P. in Bedburg. By the evening of the 19th, 18 (Cdn.) Fd. Amb. moved to a site alongside this C.C.P. and established an A.D.S., the C.C.P. being reinforced to become a divisional recovery centre. All casualties, other than those for the divisional recovery centre, were sent to the D.U.K.W. loading-point in Cleve.

Cdn. 4th Inf. Bde. made good progress along the Goch–Calcar road during the afternoon of February 19 but the supporting armour became bogged and the Germans in front of the brigade strongly reinforced. For a while the situation was desperate but was restored on the 20th. 18 (Cdn.) Fd. Amb., which was providing an A.D.S. to serve the whole division, admitted 131 casualties during the 20th. On the following day Moyland Wood was cleared and the road to Calcar opened.

Canadian casualties passing through the medical units of Canadian 2nd and 3rd Divisions between February 8–25 totalled 1,532, of whom 1,100 were from Canadian 2nd Division.

By the 25th Canadian II Corps was ready to launch Operation 'Blockbuster' which involved an assault against the heavily defended Hochwald across the plateau between Calcar and Üdem. In preparation for this an A.S.C. was established in Bedburg by 5 (Cdn.) F.D.S. and on February 25, 3 (Cdn.) C.C.S. moved into a block of buildings adjoining the F.D.S. It was arranged that the F.D.S. should take care of the abdominal and chest cases while other Priority I and II cases would be admitted to the C.C.S. Less serious cases, minor injuries and such as were unlikely to recover in the divisional recovery centres were to be taken to 6 (Cdn.) C.C.S. in Nijmegen. 11 (Cdn.) Fd. Amb. opened the divisional recovery centre for Canadian 2nd Division in Cleve, 7 (Cdn.) F.D.S. for Canadian 3rd Division in Bedburg and 12 (Cdn.) F.D.S. in Bedburg for Canadian 4th Armoured Division.

On February 26 all three Canadian divisions attacked. Their field ambulances established A.D.Ss. and C.C.Ps. well forward and as the operation progressed the A.D.Ss. leap-frogged forward and the C.C.Ps. cleared their casualties to the nearest open A.D.S. whence they were taken back to Bedburg. During the 26th, 18 (Cdn.) Fd. Amb. in Bedburg treated 107 wounded P.o.W. in addition to 260 Canadian and British casualties. On March 1 the fighting in the Hochwald and Balberger Wald was very bitter and it was not until the evening of the 4th that these forests were clear of Germans. As the battle progressed the forward medical units advanced in association with their respective brigades. 18 (Cdn.) Fd. Amb. opened an A.D.S. in Üdem on March 1 to serve Canadian 2nd Division. On March 4, 12 (Cdn.) F.D.S. established an A.S.C. in a building next to that occupied by the A.D.S. to receive very urgent cases, the rest being evacuated to the medical centre at Bedburg. Then 10 (Cdn.) Fd. Amb. moved up to the western edge of the Hochwald on March 4 and two days later on to Marienbaum. The D.U.K.W. loading-point in Cleve, now being operated by 11 (Cdn.) Fd. Amb., was called upon to deal with as many as 500 casualties in a single day.

14 (Cdn.) Fd. Amb. in Üdem cleared the casualties of Canadian 3rd Division through its A.D.S. while the C.C.Ps., which moved forward as the division advanced, were provided by 22 and 23 (Cdn.) Fd. Ambs. To serve Canadian 4th Armoured Division 12 (Cdn.) Lt. Fd. Amb. provided an A.D.S. which as the operation proceeded was leap-frogged by 15 (Cdn.) Fd. Amb. as the division advanced. 12 (Cdn.) F.D.S. functioned both as an A.S.C. and as a divisional recovery centre at Üdem from March 2.

In respect of casualties Operation 'Blockbuster' was slightly more costly than Operation 'Veritable' had been. During 'Veritable' Canadian First Army casualties totalled 5,422, these being about equally divided between Canadian II Corps and XXX Corps. During Operation 'Blockbuster' the total was 5,805 with a slightly higher proportion of Canadians among them. 'Schu' mines accounted for a large number of fatalities and injuries during the opening stages of the battle.

The widespread destruction of buildings by air and artillery bombardment during this long drawn-out battle often made it difficult for the medical units to find accommodation in the forward zone. Usually a building was secured for the accommodation of casualties and the medical personnel had to be content with canvas. The flooding between Kranenburg and Nijmegen made the use of amphibious vehicles for evacuation purposes necessary but no really serious impediment to the clearance of the A.D.Ss. and to the conveyance of the casualties to the general hospitals was encountered. From February 10 to March 10, 20,640 casualties of all types were evacuated from the battle area, 5,689 by road, 4,275 by air and 10,676 by ambulance train.

The leading elements of Canadian I Corps from Italy began to arrive in southern Belgium during February. By mid-March Canadian 5th Armoured Division was complete and by the end of the month Canadian 1st Division units had arrived. Corps and divisional troops were concentrated in Courtrai, Ypres and Grammont. Their casualties were accepted by any of the numerous general hospitals situated in or near these concentration areas. On March 9, 4 (Cdn.) C.C.S. and elements of 1 (Cdn.) M.A.C. arrived. The C.C.S. was opened at Petegem and evacuation therefrom was to 2 Cdn. G.H. in Ghent. On March 13 Canadian I Corps moved to Wijchen in the Nijmegen area and two days later, with 49th Division under command, assumed responsibility for the sector held at that time by this division. Canadian I Corps now had Canadian II Corps on its right and I Corps on its left.

In front of Canadian I Corps were formidable water obstacles and until April 2 activity was restricted to patrolling along the Maas. During this relatively quiet period Canadian 5th Armoured Division was reorganised. On its arrival in the Low Countries the division had consisted of one armoured and two infantry brigades. Now it lost one of its infantry brigades. It arrived with three light field ambulances and one field hygiene section. These units were reorganised to provide the division with one field ambulance, one light field ambulance, one field dressing station and one field hygiene section. 8 (Cdn.) Lt. Fd. Amb. became 8 (Cdn.) F.D.S. and its surplus personnel were transferred to 24 (Cdn.) Lt. Fd. Amb. to bring this unit up to strength. Vehicles and equipment were similarly redistributed. By March 15 this medical reorganisation was complete. 24 (Cdn.) Lt. Fd. Amb. had become 24 (Cdn.) Fd. Amb.; 8 (Cdn.) Lt. Fd. Amb. was now 8 (Cdn.) F.D.S. and had reverted to the command of Canadian I Corps; 13 (Cdn.) F.D.S. from Canadian I Corps passed to the command of Canadian 5th Armoured Division; 11 (Cdn.) Fd. Hyg. Sec. lost its typhus increment which had been authorised in C.M.F.

On March 27 Canadian 5th Armoured Division began to move from its concentration area around Ypres towards Nijmegen coming under command of Canadian I Corps on April 1. Canadian 1st Division, not yet complete, began to move from its concentration area around Grammont to another concentration area in the Reichswald on April 4.

For the crossing of the Rhine, Operation 'Plunder', Canadian First Army was assigned the task of holding the front while the rest of 21 Army Group regrouped. The Canadian front ran from Emmerich to the sea. Canadian II Corps passed to Second Army for the initial phase of the operation. Cdn. 9th Inf. Bde. was placed under command of 51st Division. In the Nijmegen medical area the bed capacity of the hospitals was augmented by the addition of 1 Cdn. G.H. (600) newly arrived from Italy. To this hospital were attached 1 (Cdn.) M.N.S.U. and 6 M.F.S.U. The chest surgery team that was attached to 10 Cdn. G.H. in Turnhout was brought forward to join 8 Cdn. G.H. in St. Michielsgestel.

It was agreed that casualties occurring among Canadian units serving with Second Army should be evacuated along a Canadian chain of medical installations. An arrangement was made whereby they would be evacuated from divisional medical units across the Rhine in the vicinity of Rees to 3 (Cdn.) C.C.S. at Bedburg and thence to the Nijmegen group

ADVANCE TO AND CROSSING OF THE RHINE 473

of hospitals from which they would be transferred by air, road or rail to the base hospitals on the Continent or in the United Kingdom.

Cdn. 9th Inf. Bde., u/c 51st Division, crossed the Rhine near Rees on March 24 some seven hours after the leading elements of the Highland Division had done so. It attacked the village of Speldrop three miles beyond the river but encountered such stiff opposition that it was not until the 25th that it was cleared. The assault C.C.P. of 23 (Cdn.) Fd. Amb. crossed the Rhine in the early hours of March 24 along with Cdn. 9th Inf. Bde. and established a C.C.P. in the bridgehead, evacuating casualties to one of four C.E.Ps. formed by 51st Division on the east bank of the river. Thence casualties were taken by assault craft to the disembarkation points on the west bank and on to the A.D.Ss. of 8 or 223 Fd. Ambs. and from these to 3 (Cdn.) C.C.S. at Bedburg. During the night of March 27/28 the A.D.S. of 23 (Cdn.) Fd. Amb. crossed 'Waterloo' bridge and joined up with its C.C.P. which was then divided into two parts, one remaining where it was and the other moving about three miles further south. On March 28 the A.D.S. moved to a new site near Praest.

On March 28 Canadian 3rd Division had returned to Canadian II Corps and this A.D.S. at Praest was excellently placed to receive casualties from Cdn. 7th and 8th Bdes. which were attacking Emmerich. At the end of March all the field ambulances of Canadian 3rd Division were east of the Rhine. C.C.Ps. were established in Emmerich and the A.D.S. of 23 (Cdn.) Fd. Amb. remained in Praest and continued to evacuate the divisional casualties. 7 (Cdn.) F.D.S. remained in Cleve to serve divisional troops west of the Rhine. During Operation 'Plunder' Canadian 3rd Division's medical units evacuated 205 battle casualties and 55 others.

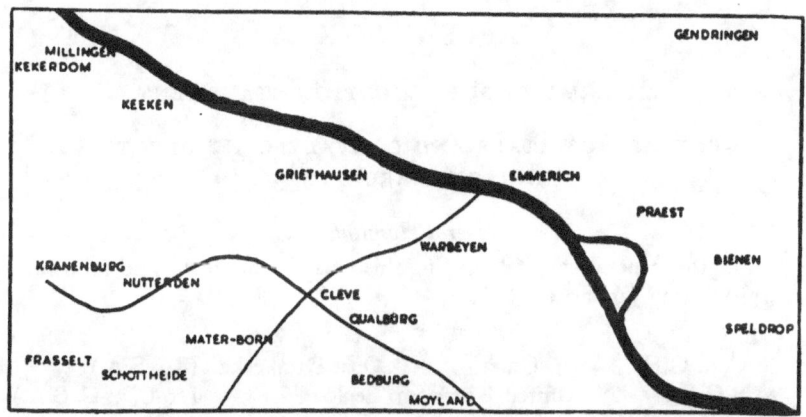

FIG. 87. Canadian 2nd Division. Operations across the Rhine.

Following Operation 'Blockbuster', Canadian 2nd Division had been concentrated in the Reichswald area. On March 28 it re-entered the battle when its 6th Bde. crossed the Rhine to relieve Cdn. 9th Bde. of Canadian 3rd Division in the area between Bienen and Praest. 10 (Cdn.) Fd. Amb. accompanied the brigade and established its A.D.S. in Bienen. During the next two days 18 and 11 (Cdn.) Fd. Ambs. crossed with their respective brigades. By the end of the month the division was operating on a one-brigade front north from Gendringen. All the brigades were evacuating their casualties through the A.D.S. of 18 (Cdn.) Fd. Amb. in Gendringen. 4 (Cdn.) F.D.S. was open in Cleve to serve divisional troops in the rear areas and to hold minor sick and injured.

Canadian 4th Armoured Division, following Operation 'Blockbuster', went into Army reserve in the Tilburg area. From March 23 to 30 the division gave effective fire support to the Rhine crossing with its whole tank strength functioning as artillery. 12 (Cdn.) Lt. Fd. Amb. evacuated casualties from the armoured brigade group, the engineers and the artillery while 15 (Cdn.) Fd. Amb. served the rest of the division. On March 31 the division began to cross the river and to concentrate in the Speldrop area preparatory to a thrust north-east.

During these operations the regiments of Cdn. 2nd Armd. Bde. were used almost exclusively to support the infantry of Canadian 2nd and 3rd Divisions. So, 17 (Cdn.) Lt. Fd. Amb. found itself split up into sections scattered over wide areas. Some of them set up C.C.Ps. from which casualties were evacuated to the A.D.S. of the division to which the regiment was attached. Other elements of the field ambulance were loaned to a brigade of the Royal Marines for the latter part of March.

At midnight on April 1 Canadian II Corps returned to the command of Canadian First Army.

APPENDIX X

21 ARMY GROUP. LOCATION STATEMENT

GENERAL HOSPITALS AND CONVALESCENT DEPOTS.
JANUARY–MARCH 1945

General Hospitals

Moves of the general hospitals during this period were few. The following occurred during January:

	From	To	
16 Cdn. G.H.	St. Omer	Oost Dunkerke	(8 B.S.A.)
29 B.G.H.	United Kingdom	Eecloo	(16 L. of C. S.A.)
96 ,,	United Kingdom	Kain, nr. Tournai	(13 Garrison)

ADVANCE TO AND CROSSING OF THE RHINE

	From	To	
21 Cdn. G.H.	Dieppe	St. Omer, detach. at Hardinghem	(15 L. of C. S.A.)

During February:

32 B.G.H.	Wavre Notre Dame	Thildonck	(4 L. of C. S.A.)
106 ,,	Bayeux	Wavre Notre Dame, detach. left at Bayeux	(7 B.S.A.)

In March:

1 Cdn. G.H.
3 ,, } arrived in the theatre
16 ,,

81 B.G.H.	Hasselt	St. Paschale, Oostrum	(Second Army)
84 ,,	Sterksel	Venraij	
9 ,,	Antwerp	Venraij	(Second Army)
20 Cdn. G.H.	St. Omer	Turnhout	(7 B.S.A.)
13 Con. Depot	Bourg-Léopold	Sterksel	

At the end of March the distribution was as follows:

81 B.G.H.	St. Paschale, Oostrum	Second Army
84 ,,	Venraij	,, ,,
86 ,,	Eindhoven	,, ,,
88 ,,	Nijmegen	Canadian First Army
3 Cdn. G.H.	Tilburg	,, ,, ,,
6 ,,	St. Michielsgestel	,, ,, ,,
8 B.G.H.	Brussels	4 L. of C. S.A.
9 ,,	Venraij	Second Army
25 ,,	Amiens	12 L. of C.A.
30 ,,	Lille	15 L. of C. S.A.
32 ,,	Thildonck	4 L. of C. S.A.
39 ,,	Hasselt	L. of C.
74 ,,	Bruges	4 L. of C. S.A.
75 ,,	Brussels	4 L. of C. S.A.
77 ,,	Ghent	16 L. of C. S.A.
79 ,,	Eindhoven	Second Army
121 ,,	Amiens	12 L. of C. A.
1 Cdn. G.H.	Nijmegen, Nebo	Canadian First Army
7 ,,	Turnhout	7 B.S.A.
8 ,,	St. Michielsgestel	7 B.S.A.
16 ,,	Oost Dunkerke	8 B.S.A.
6 B.G.H.	Oostakker	16 L. of C. S.A.
23 ,,	Lille (St. André)	15 L. of C. S.A.
29 ,,	Eecloo	16 L. of C. S.A.

96 B.G.H.		Kain	13 Garrison
101	,,	Heverlee, nr. Louvain	4 L. of C. S.A.
105	,,	Ostend	8 B.S.A.
106	,,	Wavre Notre Dame (detach. Bayeux)	7 B.S.A.
108	,,	Brussels	4 L. of C. S.A.
109	,,	Duffel	7 B.S.A.
110	,,	Bruges	8 B.S.A.
111	,,	Brussels	4 L. of C. S.A.
113	,,	Renaix	13 Garrison
115	,,	De Haan	8 B.S.A.
2 Cdn. G.H.		Ghent	16 L. of C. S.A.
10	,,	Turnhout	7 B.S.A.
12	,,	Bruges	8 B.S.A.
20	,,	Turnhout	7 B.S.A.
21	,,	St. Omer (detach. Hardinghem)	15 L. of C. S.A.

Convalescent Depots

5 Con. Depot	Knocke	8 B.S.A.
12 ,, ,,	De Haan	8 B.S.A.
14 ,, ,,	Tournai	13 Garrison
15 ,, ,,	St. Pol	15 L. of C. S.A.
2 Cdn. Con. Depot	Knocke	8 B.S.A.
13 Con. Depot	Sterksel (detach. Bourg-Léopold)	Second Army
3 Cdn. Con. Depot	Vught	Canadian First Army

CHAPTER 7

THE ADVANCE TO AND THE CROSSING OF THE ELBE

(i)

Operation 'Enterprise'

1. THE ADVANCE TO THE ELBE

SECOND Army was to advance to the line of the Elbe on a three-corps front, VIII Corps—11th Armoured and 6th Airborne Divisions, 6th Guards Armd. and 1st Commando Bdes.—on the right and directed on Osnabrück, Celle and Uelzen; XII Corps—7th Armoured, 15th, 52nd and 53rd Divisions—in the centre, directed on Rheine and its airfields, Nienburg and Lüneberg; and XXX Corps—Guards Armoured, 3rd, 43rd and 51st Divisions—on the left, directed on Enschede, Lingen, Bremen and Hamburg.

Canadian First Army was to open a supply route through Arnhem and to clear the Dutch and German coast as far as the Elbe and thereafter to liberate Western Holland.

VIII Corps advanced from the Rhine on two axes, with 6th Airborne Division on the right and 11th Armoured Division on the left. By April 5 it had captured Osnabrück and had reached the Weser; on April 7 the corps advanced to the Leine. Celle, on the Aller, was entered by 15th Division, which had taken over on the right from 6th Airborne Division, on the 12th. Four days of hard fighting then secured Uelzen and on the same day, April 18, 11th Armoured Division held firm across the roads north of Uelzen while 15th Division cleared the town. The armoured division then turned north to occupy Lüneburg and to reach the Elbe on the 19th. By the 24th the west bank of the river had been cleared throughout VIII Corps' sector.

On XII Corps' front the task of securing the main axis of advance devolved upon 7th Armoured Division, with 53rd Division protecting its left flank. By April 1 the Ems had been reached at Rheine and the Dortmund–Ems Canal beyond the river. 52nd Division was ordered to bridge the river and the canal at Rheine and 7th Armoured Division swung to the right in search of a possible crossing and found that 11th Armoured Division had secured an intact bridge. Crossing the canal and being unable to overcome the stubborn resistance which was encountered south of Ibbenbüren, 7th Armoured Division by-passed it to the right as 11th Armoured Division had also done. The Weser was reached at Hoya on April 7. Turning north-east toward Bremen 7th Armoured Division again ran into stiff opposition. Meanwhile, Ibbenbüren was secured after three days of bitter fighting, 52nd Division advanced slowly beyond Rheine, 53rd Division came forward to force a crossing over the Weser and the Aller and 3rd Division of XXX Corps was brought up to relieve 7th Armoured Division which then broke out of the Aller bridgehead on April 15, captured Soltau and made a wide

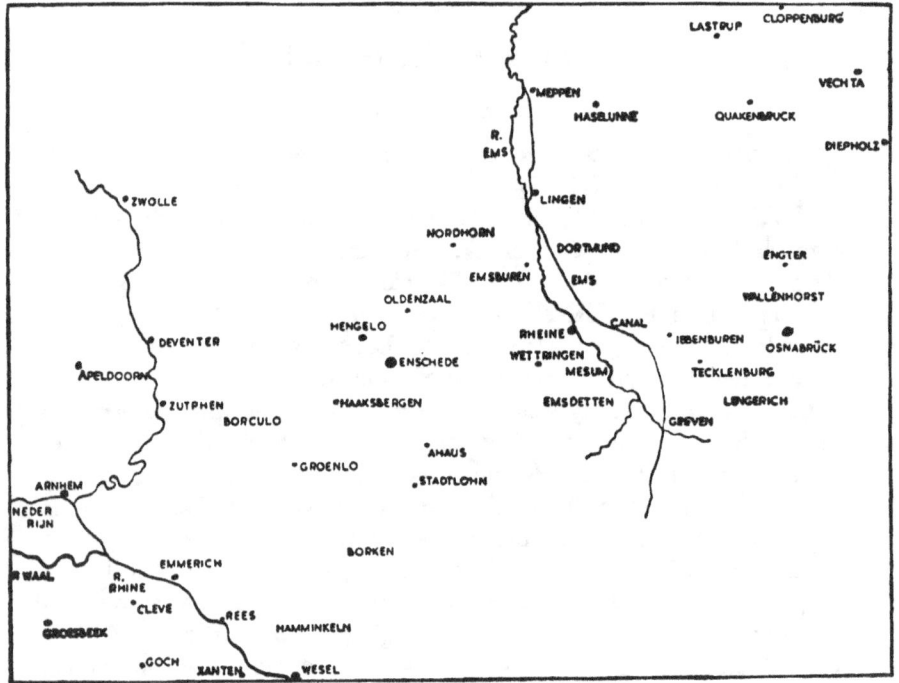

Fig. 88. The Advance to the Elbe (1).

sweep to cut the Bremen–Hamburg autobahn some fifteen miles from Hamburg. Harburg was entered on April 23 and XII Corps closed to the Elbe alongside VIII Corps. Guards Armoured Division joined XII Corps from XXX Corps on April 16 and operated on the left flank toward Bremervörde.

On XXX Corps' sector fierce opposition was encountered along the line of the Dortmund–Ems Canal and it was not until April 6 that Lingen was finally cleared. Then for the attack on Bremen 3rd and 52nd Divisions came under command from XII Corps and the city was captured from the south-east with two divisions north of the Weser and one south of the river. By April 26 the last pockets of resistance had

ADVANCE TO AND CROSSING OF THE ELBE

been eliminated. Guards Armoured Division now reverted from XII Corps and reached Stade on May 1, while 51st and 43rd Divisions advanced north-west into the Cuxhaven Peninsula between the Elbe and the Weser. In this fashion all three corps closed on the Elbe between Neu Darchau and Stade.

During this advance no great set piece battle was fought; the German armies were rapidly disintegrating and the opposition Second Army formations encountered was from hastily assembled and improvised battle groups which fought fiercely and skilfully, demolishing everything

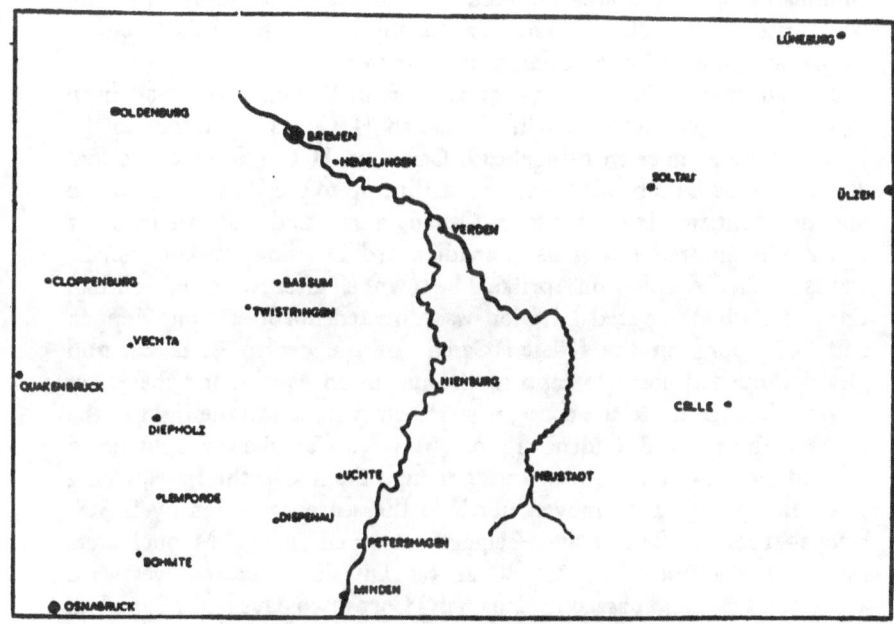

FIG. 89. The Advance to the Elbe (2).

that might facilitate the advance of their opponents. No less than five hundred bridges had to be constructed by Second Army engineers during this advance of two hundred miles in under four weeks. This advance was an excellent example of the dexterous use of armour and infantry in combination. 11th Armoured Division of VIII Corps, 7th Armoured Division of XII Corps and Guards Armoured Division of XXX Corps were the armour, 3rd, 15th, 43rd, 51st and 53rd Divisions, the infantry. On the right where the opposition was weakest, the airborne troops moved faster than did the armoured divisions on their left. On the left where opposition was strongest, armour and infantry moved more or less at the same pace. Across the whole front and especially on the left the German demolition policy determined the nature of the advance, reducing it to a series of dashes from obstacle to obstacle with the intervals filled with bridge-building. Each defended major obstacle on an armoured division's axis necessitated the securing of a bridgehead by the infantry, either by a brigade or by a division; when pockets of resistance were by-passed, infantry were required for mopping-up; when a long leap forward occurred infantry were needed for the protection of the flanks of the armoured divisions.

To ease the administrative burden of Second Army, I Corps left Canadian First Army on April 14 and assumed responsibility for the administration of the area between the Maas and the Rhine, wherein was located 10 Roadhead. When 12 Roadhead was opened in Rheine I Corps' area was extended so as to include this.

The advance of XXX Corps on the left of Second Army had been carried out in conjunction with Canadian II Corps, operating to the north of the Emmerich bridgehead. Canadian II Corps' task was that of clearing the Dutch and German coastline up to the Weser and thus to outflank Arnhem. It consisted of Canadian 1st, 2nd and 3rd Infantry and 4th Armoured Divisions. Canadian 3rd Division, striking northwards reached Zutphen on April 6. The town fell after two days' fighting. Canadian 4th Armoured Division was directed north-east on Meppen and Oldenburg on the Küsten Canal. In the centre Canadian 2nd Division pushed north to capture Groningen on April 6 and thereafter cleared the area up to the coast; it was then switched to the right of the corps and captured Oldenburg on May 3. Canadian 3rd Division entered Deventer on the 10th and then held the line of the Ijssel, facing west, and on the 12th moved north to the sea coast aided by S.A.S. troops—French, British and Belgian—dropped in the Meppel area, east of the Zuider Zee. Canadian 1st Division attacked westward across the Ijssel and passed to Canadian I Corps two days later. Canadian 5th Armoured Division from Canadian I Corps and Polish 1st Armoured Division then joined Canadian 3rd Division to clear north-west Holland, a task that was completed by April 20 save for a small pocket west of the Ems which was eliminated on May 2.

After the fall of Bremen, Canadian II Corps began to clear the Ems-Wilhelmshaven Peninsula. These operations were still in progress when the final surrender came.

Meanwhile (*see* Chapter 8), Canadian I Corps from the Nijmegen area had opened the route through Arnhem. By April 5 the whole area between Nijmegen and the Neder Rijn was in Canadian hands and Arnhem was seized by a right hook. While Canadian 5th Armoured Division and Canadian 1st Armd. Bde. gave support from south of the river 49th Division crossed the Neder Rijn near its confluence with the Ijssel on April 12 and then thrust west to take Arnhem in the rear on the 14th. Canadian 5th Armoured Division then crossed the Neder Rijn and drove

ADVANCE TO AND CROSSING OF THE ELBE

north to seize the high ground south of the Zuider Zee. Canadian 1st Division captured Apeldoorn on April 17. On the 18th the Canadians were in Amersfoort and all the German forces north of the Maas were isolated. On the 28th a virtual truce came into force on Canadian I Corps' front and Canadian First Army and the Allied Air Force, by agreement with the Reichskommissar for the Netherlands, turned to the task of feeding the people of Western Holland. On April 29, 500 tons of food were dropped by Allied bombers and from May 2, Canadian I Corps assumed responsibility for the provision of 1,000 tons a day.

Then, after a week's pause on the Elbe, came the advance to the Baltic. For this 21 Army Group had the aid of U.S. XVIII Airborne Corps consisting of U.S. 7th Armoured, U.S. 82nd Airborne and U.S. 8th Divisions. The task of this corps was to protect the right flank of Second Army's bridgehead across the Elbe and to secure a line from Darchau on the Elbe to Wismar on the Baltic.

VIII Corps was to cross the Elbe, establish a bridgehead fifteen miles wide and eight miles deep and break out to the north and seize Lübeck. Then XII Corps, passing through, was to swing west to mask Hamburg.

15th Division, reinforced by 1st Cdo. Bde., was to be the leading formation of VIII Corps and the assault was to be launched in the early hours of April 29. U.S. XVIII Corps was to make its crossing twenty-four hours later with U.S. 82nd Division at Bleckede.

II. THE CROSSING OF THE ELBE. OPERATION 'ENTERPRISE'

The Operation opened with a great artillery bombardment and then, just before 0200 hours on April 29, 'Buffaloes' loaded with infantry emerged from the main street of Artlenburg and made their way down to the river. The bridgehead was quickly established in the face of but light opposition and was rapidly expanded. U.S. 82nd Division attacked astride Bleckede the next night and crossed the river with equal ease. 6th Airborne Division crossed by a newly constructed bridge at Artlenburg. U.S. 7th Armoured Division by another at Darchau.

On May 1, 5th Division, from Italy, on the right and 11th Armoured Division on the left, led the advance from the bridgehead. 15th Division, following the north bank of the river, reached Geesthacht, only about sixteen miles from Hamburg.

On May 2, 2nd Battalion of the Argyll and Sutherland Highlanders received emissaries who wished to parley. They were sent to VIII Corps H.Q. XII Corps' formations passed through VIII Corps' bridgehead and headed for Hamburg. The city surrendered to 7th Armoured Division. 11th Armoured Division of VIII Corps with 5th Division on its right reached Lübeck and entered the town without opposition.

To the east U.S. XVIII Corps captured Ludwigslust, 6th Airborne

Division, transferred from VIII Corps the day before, advanced forty miles on May 2 with Canadian 1st Para. Bn. leading, occupied Wismar on the Baltic coast and made contact with the Russians.

On March 26 the advance of U.S. First Army out of the Remagen bridgehead began. U.S. V Corps thrust to the south-east and overran Limburg. U.S. Third Army in the Oppenheim area tightened its grip on the small bridgehead. On March 28, these two armies by converging

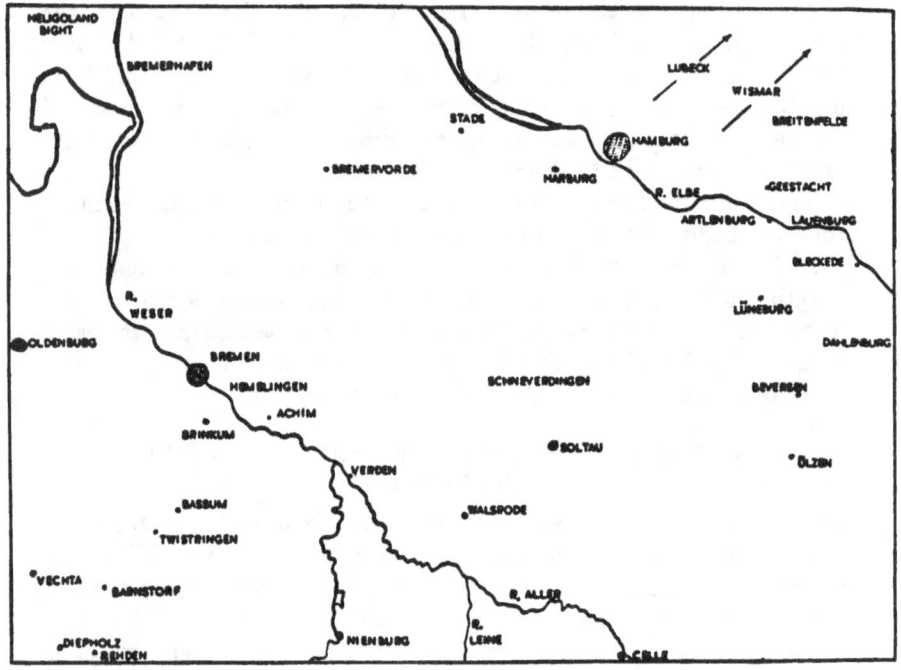

Fig. 90. Operation 'Enterprise', the Crossing of the Elbe.

thrusts from the west and the south joined forces near Giessen on the Lahn about thirty miles north of Frankfurt. This city was entered and cleared on the 29th and armoured spearheads then thrust towards Kassel, well behind the area of the Ruhr.

Still further south U.S. Seventh Army of U.S. 6 Army Group forced a crossing of the Rhine near Worms on March 26–27 and promptly linking up with U.S. Third Army pushed on to capture Mannheim. Further south still French First Army got across at Philippsburg, near Karlsruhe, on April 1 and began at once to strike in the direction of Stuttgart and to clear the east bank of the Rhine right down to the Swiss border.

ADVANCE TO AND CROSSING OF THE ELBE

In the north the Ruhr was threatened from the north by U.S. Ninth Army which had crossed the Rhine along with Second Army on March 23-24. It was threatened from the south by U.S. First Army. The Germans in this area had withdrawn behind the Sieg. By April 1, U.S. Ninth and U.S. First Armies met at Lippstadt, near Paderborn, and the Ruhr was encircled and its large garrison trapped. The German forces in the Ruhr pocket made two strenuous attempts to break out but failed. On April 14, an American attack cut the pocket in two and two days later the eastern half collapsed. On the 18th the remaining garrison surrendered. Some 325,000 were taken prisoner.

Meanwhile, U.S. Third Army had struck south in the direction of the Czechoslovakian border to reach Chemnitz on April 13-14. U.S. First Army on the left of U.S. Third Army advanced rapidly to reach Dessau on the 14th and to cut off some 15,000 German troops in the Harz Mountains. These held out until April 21.

On the left of U.S. First Army, U.S. Ninth Army had advanced in conformity and by April 5 had established a bridgehead over the Weser and had crossed the Leine on the 8th. It then drove for the Elbe, which it reached just south of Magdeburg on April 11. On the following day U.S. 2nd Armoured Division got across and established a small bridgehead which, being severely counter-attacked, was abandoned. But another bridgehead established by U.S. 83rd Division was firmly held. On April 25, patrols of U.S. 69th Division of U.S. V Corps met patrols of Russian Guards Division at Torgau, about seventy-five miles south of Berlin.

In the south the Germans continued to resist stubbornly. When U.S. Seventh Army reached the Neckar it had to fight hard to get across. The garrison of Heilbronn held out for a whole week. U.S. XV Corps reached Nuremburg on April 16 but here again several days of fighting were required before the defence was overcome.

French First Army captured Stuttgart and at the same time, far to the west, French forces liberated Bordeaux.

U.S. Third Army began to advance down the Danube on April 22. Bridgeheads on either side of Regensburg were quickly established and on May 5 the German garrison of Linz surrendered. U.S. V Corps was now attached to Third Army and it was sent eastwards into Czechoslovakia. The corps captured Pilsen on May 6. U.S. Seventh Army on April 22 began to move down the Danube and then turned southward to strike at Munich, which was captured on May 3. On the following day Berchtesgaden and Salzburg were occupied. On May 3, Innsbruck was captured and the Brenner Pass reached. Here U.S. 88th Division of U.S. Fifth Army, advancing from Italy, was encountered.

The first capitulation came in Italy. Negotiations for a local surrender resulted in the cessation of hostilities in that theatre on May 2.

At 0800 hours on May 3, emissaries of Grand Admiral Doenitz, Hitler's successor as President of the Reich and Supreme Commander of the Wehrmacht, were brought into the lines of 7th Armoured Division. The delegation was received at Second Army H.Q. and sent on to Tactical H.Q. 21 Army Group, which was situated on a singularly inhospitable, wild and windswept strip of country known as Lüneburg Heath. Here Field Marshal Montgomery received them. They were informed that the only matter that could be discussed was the unconditional surrender of all forces—land, sea and air—still resisting in Holland, the Frisian Islands, Heligoland, Schleswig-Holstein, Denmark and those parts of Germany west of the Elbe still in German possession. Certain of the delegates then returned whence they came. On the following afternoon, 11th Hussars of 7th Armoured Division met these delegates on the Flensburg road, north-west of Hamburg, and arranged for their escort to Lüneburg Heath. At 1830 hours on May 4 the Instrument of Surrender was signed. It became effective from 0800 hours on May 5.

The German forces facing U.S. Seventh Army surrendered on May 5, the capitulation becoming effective on May 6. On May 5, representatives of Admiral Doenitz reached General Eisenhower's H.Q. in Rheims and signed the Instrument of Surrender in the early hours of May 7. It became effective at midnight on May 8/9. On May 9 the formal Ratification of the Surrender was signed in Berlin. In this fashion the war in Europe ended.

(ii)
Medical Cover

7TH ARMOURED DIVISION

This division, crossing the Rhine on March 25 after a month's rest, thrust forward round the left flank of the German forces facing Second Army. The advance consisted of long runs punctuated by short periods of bitter fighting. The advance was through Stadtlohn, Ahaus, Wettringen, Rheine, Ibbenbüren (where heavy fighting took place), Lemforde, Diepholz, Barnstorf (whence for several days the division threatened Bremen), across the Aller (against heavy opposition), Walsrode, Soltau, to the area south of Harburg and Hamburg.

During this rapid advance the field ambulances were placed under command of the brigades. At one stage the F.D.S. was no less than eighty miles behind the more forward of the two field ambulances. Bad roads, bad weather and congested axes (VIII and XII Corps shared the same main axis for a distance of thirty miles) made evacuation difficult and arduous. Difficulty was also caused by the number of the

ADVANCE TO AND CROSSING OF THE ELBE

German medical installations that were overrun during the advance. XII Corps provided extra medical officers and the division a battery of the A/Tk. Regt. to act as guards. Every village near Hamburg had one or more reserve lazarette and every farm house contained a small dump of medical stores. These arrangements had been made imperative by the Allied bombing of the city. Fortunately the responsibility of controlling and guarding enemy medical installations and of ensuring that the patients were adequately tended was not one that was required to be undertaken while severe fighting was in progress. Medical man-power was also required in connexion with the small camps of displaced persons and Allied P.o.W.; but of these there were not many in the divisional area.

TABLE 47

7th Armoured Division. Casualties. April–June 1945

Battle Casualties:
    April . . . 334 = 0·654/1,000/diem
    May 1–8 . . 10 = 0·074/1,000/diem

Sick and Accidental Injuries:
    April . . . 335 = 0·656/1,000/diem
    May . . . 214 = 0·406/1,000/diem
    June . . . 395 = 0·774/1,000/diem

Exhaustion:
    April . . . 18 = 0·35/1,000/diem
    May 1–8 . . 1 = 0·007/1,000/diem

Venereal Disease reported from R.A.Ps. and M.I.Rooms:
    April . . . 48 = 0·094/1,000/diem
    May . . . 66 = 0·125/1,000/diem
    June . . . 92 = 0·18/1,000/diem

Following the end of hostilities the division moved first to the north of the Kiel Canal and then to Itzehoe in Kreis Steinburg to become involved in the rounding up of the German troops in Schleswig-Holstein.

11TH ARMOURED DIVISION

Having crossed the Rhine the division advanced to cross the Ems and to harbour near Elte on April 1. The next day 159th Bde. met severe opposition from the senior N.C.Os.' school, Hanover, and sustained about 100 casualties, but 29th Armd. Bde. reached Tecklenburg without much difficulty. While the armoured brigade pressed on to the north of

Osnabrück 159th Bde. was still involved in heavy fighting in the Teutoburger Wald until relieved by 7th Armoured Division. Then 11th Armoured Division advanced to reach the Weser.

Detachments of the field ambulances followed the brigades on two centre lines. Evacuation was made difficult by the shortage of ambulance cars for ten M.A.C. ambulances were required for the evacuation of Allied P.o.W. and only two cars were with 179 Fd. Amb. 21 Lt. Fd. Amb. was placed u/c A.D.M.S. 11th Armoured Division and one section of it was allotted to 1st Cdo. Bde. When 81 B.G.H. opened in Wettringen 22 F.D.S. ceased to function as an advanced surgical centre and assumed the rôle of a V.D.T.C. and exhaustion centre. 1 F.D.S. opened as an advanced surgical centre in Uchte.

On April 8 the division followed 159th Bde. over the Weser by way of 6th Airborne Division's bridge at Petershagen and advanced to the Aller. Part of the division passed through Belsen to reach the Elbe and capture Lüneburg on April 18. On the 19th, 22 F.D.S. and 33 C.C.S. opened in Lüneburg.

On May 1 the division crossed the Elbe and on the following day captured Lübeck.

During this advance of about 420 miles 1,136 battle casualties were admitted to the divisional field medical units.

Following the cessation of hostilities the division was committed in the province of Schleswig-Holstein on Operation 'Eclipse'.

3RD DIVISION

On April 1 the division, following Guards Armoured Division, began to advance through Holland into Germany, passing through Groenlo, Eibergen, Haaksbergen, Enschede, Oldenzaal and Nordhorn. On April 3 a battle group of Guards Armoured Division seized intact a bridge over the Ems and 3rd Division exploited this success by forcing a crossing of the Dortmund–Ems Canal at Altenlingen.

Thus far casualties had been few and the field ambulances with the brigades encountered no difficulties. Then followed the battle for Lingen which began on April 4. For this 223 Fd. Amb. established a C.C.P. on the west bank of the river, casualties being evacuated to 9 Fd. Amb., staged at 8 Fd. Amb. at Nordhorn and thence to 81 B.G.H. at Rheine on the Ems south of Lingen. (Plate XXVI shows an ambulance car crossing the canal while evacuating casualties.) In Lingen a P.o.W. camp hospital was uncovered. It was commanded by an officer of 16 Para. Fd. Amb. and the conditions in it were satisfactory, food and medical supplies being ample.

On April 5, all three brigades of the division were committed and 223 Fd. Amb. established its A.D.S. in Lingen. At last Guards Armoured Division was able to overcome the resistance facing it and to

ADVANCE TO AND CROSSING OF THE ELBE

break out to the east, and, by the 7th, Lingen and the roads leading to the north, south and east had been cleared.

A P.o.W. camp, containing Russians, was uncovered in Wietmarschen. D.A.D.M.S. 3rd Division visited the camp and found that 1,200 out of the 1,800 prisoners-of-war were gravely ill, very many of them with advanced pulmonary tuberculosis. The division provided rations and XXX Corps blankets and medical supplies, while 26 Fd. Hyg. Sec. cleaned up the camp and deloused its inmates.

On April 8 the division passed under command XII Corps. 185th Bde. moved to the Lembruch-Lemforde-Reiningen-Hunteburg-Schagen-Wallenhorst area north of Osnabrück and 223 Fd. Amb. opened its A.D.S. in Engter. 9th Bde. moved to the Diepholz-Barnstorf-Twistringen area and 9 Fd. Amb. established its A.D.S. at Rehden. 8th Bde. followed to concentrate in the Scholen area.

Then, on April 13, the division reverted to XXX Corps and was set the task of capturing Brinkum. This was completed by the 16th. On the following day Mittelschucting was captured after bitter house-to-house fighting and on the 19th the Delmenhorst-Bremen road was cut.

The division then advanced on Bremen and that portion of the city south of the Weser was quickly captured. For this operation 8 Fd. Amb. had its A.D.S. in Erichshof, 223 its A.D.S. in Sudweyhe. 9 and 223 Fd. Ambs. established C.C.Ps. at their respective brigade 'Buffalo' embarkation points. Evacuation was to 10 C.C.S. and 3 F.D.S. in Bassum.

TABLE 48

3rd Division. Casualties. April 1945

Wounded	526
Battle Injuries	135
Sick	440
Exhaustion	13
P.o.W. Wounded passing through the divisional medical units	311

5TH DIVISION

This division, consisting of 13th, 15th and 17th Inf. Bdes. with supporting arms and services including 141, 158 and 164 Fd. Ambs. and 24 Fd. Hyg. Sec., moved from Palestine to Italy in November-December 1944 and thence to the United Kingdom and then to the Continent. It remained in billets in the Ghent area until April 14, 1945. To it was allotted 53 F.D.S. On April 18, the division moved to an area south of Uelzen to come under command VIII Corps.

It then advanced in a north-easterly direction towards the Elbe on a two-brigade front. 13th Bde. (164 Fd. Amb.) on the left had Bleckede as its left boundary and 17th Bde. (141 Fd. Amb.) Neu Darchau as its right objective. 15th Bde. (158 Fd. Amb.) was in reserve. Each brigade had a C.C.P. under command. On the 20th, 164 opened an A.D.S. in a farm at Ripdorf. Evacuation therefrom was to 24 F.D.S. in the vicinity of Uelzen where VIII Corps had its advanced surgical centre.

13th Bde. reached the Elbe with little opposition and, on April 21, 141 Fd. Amb. opened an A.D.S. in a factory two miles west of Dahlenburg, whence evacuation was to 33 C.C.S. in Lüneburg, fourteen miles away. 17th Bde., on the other hand, encountered fairly stiff opposition. Its casualties were sent to the A.D.S. of 164 Fd. Amb. at Ripdorf. By the evening of the 17th the forest of Gehrde had been cleared and 17th Bde. casualties could be evacuated along the lateral road north of the forest to 141 Fd. Amb. at Dahlenburg. The A.D.S. of 164 Fd. Amb. then closed. 53 F.D.S. opened in Bevensen in a school and dealt with the local sick.

Between May 1–3 the division advanced from the Elbe to Lübeck, having been relieved in the sector between Uelzen and the Elbe by U.S. XVIII Airborne Corps. During the night of April 30/May 1, 15th Bde. with a C.C.P. of 158 Fd. Amb. crossed the Elbe at Lauenburg to the centre of the bridgehead established by 15th Division. The brigade advanced from this bridgehead towards Büchen. 158 Fd. Amb. established its C.C.P., reinforced by a light A.D.S., in Basedow. Evacuation was by M.A.C. cars to 34 C.C.S. in Lüneburg *via* Artlenburg. Cases needing urgent surgery were sent to a field ambulance of 15th Division at Lauenburg. On the night of May 1/2, 13th and 17th Bdes. followed. A C.C.P. was with each of the brigades. On the afternoon of May 2, 164 Fd. Amb. opened its A.D.S. in Breitenfelde with 24 F.D.S. (VIII Corps Adv. Surg. Centre) nearby.

On the 3rd, 13th Bde. entered Lübeck where 141 Fd. Amb. opened an A.D.S. in a large school. 158 Fd. Amb. was in Breitenfelde nearby 164 Fd. Amb., but closed. 53 F.D.S. had been left far behind in Bevensen near Uelzen. It was not missed, for casualties were light and the roads good.

6TH AIRBORNE DIVISION

This division, in an infantry rôle, took a prominent part in the advance to the Elbe and beyond. It passed to the south of Osnabrück through Steinhude, north-west of Hanover, where a fierce action was fought, through Uelzen and Lüneburg Heath to Mecklenberg, where the oncoming Russians were met, and then on to Wismar which was reached on May 2. On May 17 the division began to head west once again and concentrated around Lüneburg whence it departed for the United Kingdom to make ready for its further employment in the Far East. Before this could happen, however, Japan capitulated. A brigade

ADVANCE TO AND CROSSING OF THE ELBE

of the division did go to the Far East and actually landed on the Morib beaches on the west coast of Malaya. The rest of the division went to Palestine. The brigade in the Far East became the 5th Independent Brigade and went to Singapore after the Japanese surrender. Late in December 1945 this brigade went to Batavia to reinforce the Indian corps then in Java. Thereafter this brigade rejoined the division in Palestine.

During the advance to the Elbe and beyond the field ambulances were distributed along the divisional axis. Casualties were few in number and only on two occasions was it necessary to nest casualties and to leave a small party with them until evacuation into a F.D.S. or C.C.S. became possible. The uncovering of P.o.W. camps and the waves of German sick and wounded withdrawing from the east as the Russians advanced provided a great deal of work for the divisional medical units.

225 Para. Fd. Amb. was the unit to go with the brigade to the Far East and so added to its most varied experience that of providing a medical service in Semarang, where it took over a Dutch hospital.

15TH DIVISION

Following the crossing of the Rhine and the Ijssel, 11th Armoured, 6th Airborne and 15th Divisions crossed the Dortmund–Ems Canal and the Weser. 15th Division, passing from XII to VIII Corps, moved *via* Lengerich, where 6th Gds. Armd. Bde. came under command on April 4, to the forest of Minden and was north-west of Hanover on April 10. Thence the advance to the Aller was on two axes and a light A.D.S. was established at Neustadt, the main A.D.S. being opened at Mellendorf by 194 Fd. Amb. on April 11. During the evening of this day the leading battalions entered Celle and crossed the Aller.

In Celle there were ten German hospitals with 1,200 of the 2,000 beds occupied and also a temporary concentration camp into which had been crowded the occupants of a train which had been bombed. These starved, neglected and ill-treated creatures were taken into a hospital and the civil population of Celle required to provide the means for their succour.

On April 14 the advance to Uelzen was resumed but progress was slow for the roads were extensively cratered and mined. On the left axis cases were held in Holxen where an abandoned ambulance train was available.

On the 15th Veerssen was captured and, being relieved by 6th Airborne Division, 46th Bde. moved to Holdenstedt. 11th Armoured Division reached Hermannsburg and Bergen on the 16th.

On the 17th, 44th Bde. infiltrated into Uelzen after the town had been heavily bombed from the air, but 46th Bde. was checked and the town did not fall until the evening of the 18th. 153 Fd. Amb. established an A.D.S. in Holdenstedt on the 17th.

490   THE ARMY MEDICAL SERVICES

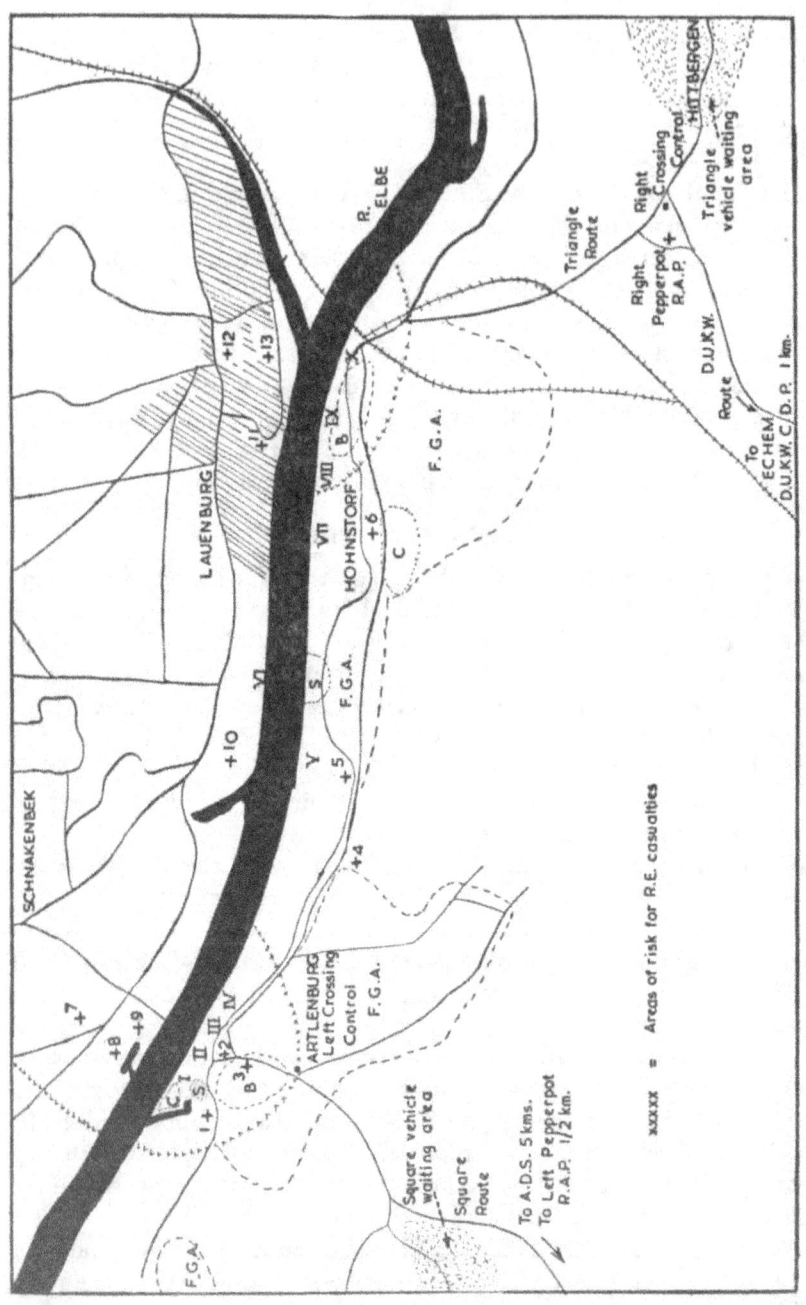

FIG. 91. 15th Division. Operation 'Enterprise'. Medical Cover.
See key on opposite page

ADVANCE TO AND CROSSING OF THE ELBE

In Uelzen there were three main hospitals containing several hundred German military and civilian sick and wounded and some 500 Russian, Polish, French, Belgian, Dutch and Italian P.o.W.

On the 19th the division moved forward of Uelzen to Barum and 194 Fd. Amb. opened a light A.D.S. at Bevensen. Thence the division moved towards the Elbe *via* Lüneburg which had been taken by 11th Armoured Division. On April 21, 227th Bde. cleared Artlenburg and Avendorf and, on the 22nd, the division closed up to the line of the Elbe between Tespe and Bleckede. 1st Cdo. Bde. came under command.

In planning for Operation 'Enterprise'—the crossing of the Elbe—the lessons learnt from the crossing of the Rhine were applied. To insure against a hold-up in evacuation by L.V.T. or by jeep or ambulance car to Lauenburg and thence by D.U.K.W., 194 Fd. Amb. was to send an A.D.S. and an advanced surgical centre consisting of one F.S.U. and one F.T.U., later to be reinforced by a second F.S.U. across the river in the evening of the first day of the battle by raft ferry. Both 193 and 194 Fd. Ambs. were to be ready to hold their cases overnight. Urgent surgical cases were to be sent to 194 Fd. Amb's. A.D.S. at Schnakenbek.

As the planning for this operation proceeded many modifications were made. The main alteration was the abandoning of the intended airdrop in which an airborne M.D.S. was to have been included. Instead 46th Bde. was to make a crossing of the river and was to be followed by 1st Cdo. Bde. The medical detachments with the assaulting battalions were increased by the attachment of eight field ambulance S.Bs. to each battalion and of two sections of a second field ambulance company to each brigade.

Medical provision had to be made for the very large numbers of R.A. and R.E. units on the near bank. Special courses in first aid and stretcher-bearing were arranged for the R.E. units.

Key to Fig. 91.

B = Bridge Maintenance Areas
C = Collecting and Loading Areas
S = Stormboat Areas
F.G.A. = Forward Gun Areas

I.   L.V.T. Ferry. *Iris*
II. Class 40 Raft. *Woodbine*
III. Class 40 Bridge. *Shamrock*
IV. L.V.T. Ferry. *Clover*
V.   L.V.T. Ferry. *Seapink*
VI. Stormboat Ferry
VII. L.V.T. Ferry. *Columbine*
VIII. Class 9 Ferry. *Aster*
IX. Class 9 Bridge. *Primrose*
X.   D.U.K.W. Ferry. *Harebell*

1. C.D.P.
2. C.D.P.
3. L.V.T. R.A.P.
4. C.D.P.
5. C.P.
6. C.D.P.
7. C.E.P. 153 Fd. Amb.
8. C.E.P. 194 Fd. Amb.
9. C.E.P. 194 Fd. Amb.
10. C.E.P. 193 Fd. Amb.
11. C.E.P. 193 Fd. Amb.
12. C.C.P. 1st Cdo. Bde.
13. C.C.P. 193 Fd. Amb.

The casualty disembarkation posts were established before H-hour (0200 hours on April 29). 44th Bde., reinforced by a battalion of 227th Bde., crossed on the left, 1st Cdo. Bde. on the right. Bad weather precluded air support.

On the left 194 Fd. Amb's. C.E.P. parties in the L.V.T. landed on the far shore between 0215 and 0245 hours and quickly established themselves. By 0900 hours the C.E.Ps. had their jeeps and by 1000 hours a C.C.P. of 153 Fd. Amb. with 227th Bde. was evacuating to the right C.E.P. The continuous shelling, mortaring and air attack impeded the establishment of the raft ferries and there was no chance of 194 Fd. Amb. getting across and opening its A.D.S. in Schnakenbek.

On the right two sections of 21 Lt. Fd. Amb. were with 1st Cdo. Bde. and followed the brigade into Lauenburg. 193 Fd. Amb. crossed by D.U.K.W. and opened its A.D.S. in Lauenburg by 1530 hours. This A.D.S. was subjected to much shelling and bombing but its work was not seriously interrupted.

194 Fd. Amb. was then instructed to cross with 44th Bde. and make for Juliusburg. The A.D.S. reached this town at 0400 hours on April 30 and opened on May 1 in Gülzow.

On May 2, 15th Division cleared the Sachsen Wald and established itself on the line Aumühle–Bornsen. The German Chief of Staff, Army

TABLE 49

15th Division. Casualties. April–June 1945

Ratio of Exhaustion Cases to Battle Casualties

Operation	Exhaustion	Wounded	Exhaustion	K.W.M.
'Veritable'	1 :	7	1 :	9·6
'Torchlight'	1 :	19	1 :	24·9
'Advance to the Elbe'	1 :	24	1 :	35
'Enterprise'	1 :	25·3	1 :	32

Admissions. April–June 1945:

	Battle Casualties	Non-Battle Casualties
193 Fd. Amb.	363	307
194 ,, ,,	134	150
153 ,, ,,	443	305
23 F.D.S.	1	141
	941	903

ADVANCE TO AND CROSSING OF THE ELBE

Group North, passed through the line to negotiate the surrender of his formations.

Casualties during Operation 'Enterprise' were comparatively few. Of the 244 divisional casualties 162 were recorded as slight. 165 divisional sick and 650 sick and wounded of other formations passed through the medical units of 15th Division.

43RD DIVISION

For the advance on Bremen the field ambulances were placed under command of the brigades for movement. The break-out from the bridgehead across the Rhine took place on April 1 and on this day Main Divisional H.Q. reached Borculo. 129 Fd. Amb. was with 214th Bde., 168 Lt. Fd. Amb. with 129th Bde. and 130 Fd. Amb. with 130th Bde. 15 F.D.S. moved to Anholt Schloss. On the 2nd, 213 Fd. Amb. reached Borculo and opened for the divisional sick, exhaustion and V.D. cases.

On April 3 Hengelo was captured by 130th Bde. Gp. 15 F.D.S. joined 213 Fd. Amb. in Borculo. On the 4th, 130 Fd. Amb. opened an A.D.S. in Hengelo and was joined there by 168 Lt. Fd. Amb. On the 5th, 129 Fd. Amb. moved on to Nordhorn with 214th Bde. which was relieving 8th Bde. of 3rd Division. 15 F.D.S. moved forward to Hengelo and opened for the divisional sick, exhaustion and V.D. cases. On April 6 the divisional H.Q. moved to Lingen and 213 Fd. Amb. to Hengelo. Casualties were evacuated to 81 B.G.H. in Rheine. On the 8th, 214th Bde. was nearing Haselünne and 129 Fd. Amb. opened its A.D.S. in Lingen. Haselünne was taken on the 10th and 129th Bde. passed through 214th Bde. On April 12, 130th Bde. captured Lastrup and 214th Cloppenburg on the following day. The division was now advancing on two axes, 130th Bde. on the right and 129th Bde. on the left. The divisional H.Q. reached Cloppenburg on the 14th. Here 15 F.D.S. opened for the divisional sick. On the 16th, 35 F.D.S. in Vechta opened to admit P.o.W. casualties. British casualties were evacuated to 24 C.C.S. in Diepholz. On the 18th, Lt. Sec. 15 F.D.S. moved forward to Barnstorf and, on the 20th, 129 Fd. Amb. was required to provide one medical officer and six O.Rs. to take charge of a German T.B. hospital in Wildeshausen with 132 military patients.

On April 21, 213 Fd. Amb. evacuated some 130 German wounded from a German military hospital in Quakenbrück to Vechta and 129 Fd. Amb. moved to Wildeshausen. Evacuation was now to 10 C.C.S. in Bassum.

On the 22nd, 130 Fd. Amb's. A.D.S. opened in Verden and 213 Fd. Amb. was in Schwarme with 214th Bde. but moved to Verden on the following day. On the 24th, 15 F.D.S. also moved to Verden, as did 168 Lt. Fd. Amb. on the following day.

On the 26th Bremen was entered. Three hospitals were overrun. One, at Osterholz, was a large one with 900 beds. 213 Fd. Amb. took it over. The second was a tuberculosis hospital for German marines at Oberneuland and was taken over by 130 Fd. Amb. The third was St. Joseph Stift Hospital (400 beds) and this was also taken over by 130 Fd. Amb.

When the advance north-east of Bremen began on April 27, 130 and 213 Fd. Ambs. joined 129 Fd. Amb. in Osterholz and 168 Lt. Fd. Amb. moved to Achim. On the 28th divisional H.Q. moved to Bassum and 168 Lt. Fd. Amb. was required by D.D.M.S. XXX Corps to proceed to Sandbostel P.o.W. and political prisoners' camp. The capture of Bremen was completed; 52nd Division was placed in charge of the city and 43rd Division handed over the three hospitals mentioned above.

43rd Division then drove towards Bremerhaven. 213 Fd. Amb. moved forward to Quelkhorn, 129 Fd. Amb. to Buchholz and 130 Fd. Amb. to Wilstedt.

On May 2, 129 Fd. Amb. moved on to Tarmstedt and 213 to Westertimke. 130 Fd. Amb. and 38 Fd. Hyg. Sec. sent detachments to a large P.o.W. camp at Westertimke.

On the 3rd, 130 Fd. Amb. and 38 Fd. Hyg. Sec. set up a transit camp in Seedorf for the fit personnel from the Sandbostel P.o.W. camp. These detachments were relieved by XXX Corps units on May 8 and the division moved to the Uelzen–Bevensen–Neetze area.

52ND DIVISION

This division advanced from the Rhine to Bremen on the axis Rheine–Recke–Vilsen–Verden–Hemelingen–Bremen. Resistance was encountered in the areas of Rheine and of Verden. No evacuation problems were encountered during the advance. Field ambulance sections were deployed with the battalions, a field officer from each field ambulance maintaining contact with brigade H.Q.

Successive A.D.Ss. were opened:

April 1– 3	155 Fd. Amb.		Heek
2– 9	156 ,,	,,	Rheine
7–19	155 ,,	,,	Recke
19–23	157 ,,	,,	Verden
May 2–12	156 ,,	,,	Achim

After the cessation of hostilities the division was engaged in static administrative duties until June 11 when it moved to the area of Ghent. 'A' Coy. 155 Fd. Amb. proceeded to Ostend on May 13 for participation in Operation 'Doomsday'—the liberation of Norway—and reached Norway *via* the United Kingdom on May 23, to pass under command A.D.M.S. Allied Liberation Force, Norway.

ADVANCE TO AND CROSSING OF THE ELBE 495

On May 28 the remainder of the unit with 533 and 534 M.D.Us. proceeded to Hamburg *en route* for Norway.

TABLE 50

52nd Division. Admissions to Medical Units. April–June 1945

	B.C.	Sick	Exhaustion	Totals
British and Allied Tps.	897	1,693	77	2,667
P.o.W.	257	32	—	289
Civilians	34	23	—	57
	1,188	1,748	77	3,013

(iii)
Medical Arrangements

VIII CORPS

In Operation 'Plunder', VIII Corps, with 6th Airborne and U.S. 17th Airborne Division under command, was given a limited objective. It was to seal off the area north of the Ruhr and the River Lippe and then remain *in situ* while XII and U.S. XVIII Corps moved forward. But in fact VIII Corps did not become stationary for, having crossed the Rhine, it continued to move forward to the Elbe. The advance was rapid and casualties light. A C.C.S. was opened about 10 km. from the front. This would then recede until it was 40 km. away. A F.D.S. would then open as an advanced surgical centre, taking over from a forward field ambulance. The front would move another 40 km. forward. A second F.D.S. would then open and the first F.D.S. become a staging post and holding unit. The front would move forward another 40 km. A second C.C.S. would then be moved forward (always with difficulty because of lack of transport). In this way surgical facilities were provided at all times.

VIII Corps moved from Issum on March 26 and crossed the Rhine to concentrate north-west of Wesel. 34 C.C.S. took over the Schloss at Gemen. During its stay here 2,988 casualties passed through the C.C.S.

On April 1, 11th Armoured Division, now under command VIII Corps, crossed the Ems at Emsdetten and 6th Airborne Division at Greven where an advanced surgical centre was established by 22 F.D.S.

on April 2. By the 4th the length of the line of evacuation was about a hundred miles from Diepenau to Greven and another forty-six miles to Gemen. 227 M.A.C. was stretched to its utmost.

On the 5th, 6th Airborne crossed the Weser at Petershagen and, on the 6th, 1 F.D.S. opened an advanced surgical centre in Uchte. 24 C.C.S. opened at Bohmte on April 6 to stage casualties on their way to 81 B.G.H. in Rheine. On the 8th, 3 C.C.S. and 11 F.D.S. took over from 1 F.D.S. in Uchte and their transport was sent back to lift 33 C.C.S. in Greven.

15th Division now joined VIII Corps for the crossing of the Elbe and 24 F.D.S. was placed under its command, prepared to open an advanced surgical centre either in Celle or Uelzen. Celle was captured by 15th Division on April 12 and a Polish concentration camp nearby was uncovered. In Celle were several German military hospitals. O.C. 21 Lt. Fd. Amb. was appointed as S.M.O. of these.

On April 12 negotiations concerning Belsen camp opened. On the 15th, 32 C.C.S. arrived in the corps area and came under command. 32 C.C.S., 11 Lt. Fd. Amb. and 76 Fd. Hyg. Sec. were moved into Belsen camp. 86 B.G.H. arrived and opened in Celle. On April 18, 11th Armoured Division took Lüneburg. 33 C.C.S. and 22 F.D.S. moved into this town and 24 F.D.S. to Uelzen. On the 24th, 34 C.C.S. arrived in the corps area from Gemen and opened in Lübeck on May 4.

Operation 'Enterprise', the crossing of the Elbe, began on April 29 and was immediately successful, casualties being extremely slight. They were evacuated across the Elbe by D.U.K.W.

By May 2 it had become apparent that in so far as VIII Corps' front was concerned the war had ended. The roads were thronged with masses of disorganised German troops and transport. The troops had jettisoned their weapons and were moving north, south, east and west. In every town and village large numbers of Germans were found in hospitals and improvised hospitals; some 120,000 altogether in 300 hospitals. Stationary ambulance trains full of wounded were found in many of the stations and on the line. Displaced persons swarmed everywhere.

XII CORPS

On April 1, 7th Armoured, 15th, 52nd and 53rd Divisions and 4th Armd. Bde. were under command XII Corps, which having crossed the Rhine was driving on Bremen. The advance was rapid and the movement of the medical units consequently numerous.

As the advance continued numerous German military hospitals were uncovered. It was decided that the division uncovering such a hospital would administer it until corps could take it over.

When 7th Armoured Division was in the outskirts of Bremen the plan was changed so that XXX Corps took over the direct attack on the city

ADVANCE TO AND CROSSING OF THE ELBE

Date	D.D.M.S.	23 C.C.S.	24 C.C.S.	4 F.D.S.	9 F.D.S.	14 F.D.S.	10 Fd. Hyg. Sec.	Remarks
April 1	Wettringen	Wüllen	Gross Baarlo	Wüllen	Hamminkeln	Gross Baarlo		15 Div. to VIII Corps
2								
3		Ahaus			Rheine			
4				Rheine				3 Div. u/c XII Corps directed on Hamburg
6	Mesum							
7	Westerkappeln							
8			Air cushion, Diepholz	Air cushion, Diepholz	Adv. Surg. Cen. Diepholz	Minor sick, V.D. Ibbenbüren		
10								
13	Gandesbergen				Adv. Surg. Cen. Hoya	Adv. Surg. Cen. Hoya		3 Div. to XXX Corps Gds. Armd. Div. u/c
16								
17	Walsrode			Immobiles, Walsrode	Adv. Surg. Cen. Walsrode			
19								
20		Schneverdingen			Schneverdingen	Schneverdingen		52 Div. to XXX Corps
26		Wintermoor		Wintermoor				
28			Kampen					
30	Lübberstedt							Gds. Armd. Div. to XXX Corps
May 4	Harburg	(closed)		Minor sick, V.D. Tötensen	Hamburg Schloss Breitenburg	Hamburg	Moorege	
7	Hamburg	Wintermoor						

while XII Corps was switched to cross the Weser at Hoya and Verden and then swing north to Hamburg.

The successive moves of the office of the D.D.M.S. and of the corps medical units during this final phase of the campaign were as indicated in the table on p. 497.

XXX CORPS

THE POLITICAL PRISONERS CAMP, SANDBOSTEL

It was known that there was a P.o.W. camp at Sandbostel, but from an escaped P.o.W. who reached the British lines on April 28 it was learnt that in addition to the 15,000 or so P.o.W. in this camp there were, in a separate compound, some 7,000–8,000 political prisoners whose condition, there was every reason to think, was very far from satisfactory. At this time XXX Corps, having captured Bremen, was thrusting northwards to clear and occupy the area between the Weser and the Elbe. Though in no sense was the Sandbostel camp a tactical objective, it was decided, in view of this information, immediately to free its inmates. Application was made to the Germans facing the corps for permission to enter the camp and, this being refused, Guards Armoured Division turned aside to make an assault crossing of the Oste and, on the evening of April 29, overran the camp.

On April 30, senior administrative medical officers of 21 Army Group, Second Army and XXX Corps visited the camp to decide what should and could be done in the matter of providing medical care. It is to be noted that fighting was still proceeding and that action had still to be based upon the assumption that it would continue for an indefinite period of time. It was decided that the medical services of XXX Corps should do everything possible to provide the medical attention that was so very obviously required. It must be remembered, however, that these services belonged to a formation still heavily involved operationally. Accompanying D.D.M.S. XXX Corps on this visit were the officers commanding 168 Lt. Fd. Amb. (8th Armd. Bde.) and 10 C.C.S., the latter having recently returned from a visit to the camp at Belsen.

The P.o.W. portion of the camp was overcrowded but otherwise fairly satisfactory. In its hospital there were 1,840 patients whose condition was likewise fairly satisfactory. But in the compound occupied by the political prisoners the conditions were utterly horrifying. In hutted accommodation, adequate for about 2,000, were between 7,000 and 8,000 emaciated males of fifteen years and upwards. The great majority of them were in a deplorable state of malnutrition. Starved and gravely ill men in filthy rags lay huddled on the bare floor boards. Everywhere the dead and the dying sprawled amid the slime of human excrement. To 168 Lt. Fd. Amb. and 31 Fd. Hyg. Sec. (XXX Corps) was assigned the herculean task of coping with the problems that these conditions

ADVANCE TO AND CROSSING OF THE ELBE

presented. There were no interior sanitary arrangements, and even if there had been, large numbers of the prisoners were far too weak and far too apathetic to have made use of them. Diarrhoea was universal and so everywhere inside and outside the huts was gross pollution. There was no food and apparently no facilities for providing it. It was learnt that periodically a cartload of raw turnips had been thrown into the compound to be seized by such as were still able to compete. For water the prisoners had depended solely upon a large stagnant pool in the compound and this had inevitably become grossly contaminated and evil-smelling.

Full details of the work done by units of the Army Medical Services in the camp at Belsen have been published and it is therefore not intended to re-present them herein. Sandbostel will serve to illustrate the exceptional rôles such medical units were called upon to play during the course of this campaign. In Belsen there were some 40,000 political prisoners, about half of them women and young children, whose deliberate and systematic degradation and dehumanisation added so greatly to the horror of that vast abomination. In Sandbostel there were far fewer and all were males and they had been in this camp only about a month, too short a time to yield the ghastly heaps of piled corpses that so horrified those who uncovered Belsen. But between Belsen and Sandbostel there was no essential difference; the underlying policy of extermination was the same in both places.*

There were medical men among the prisoners and they informed the officer commanding 168 Lt. Fd. Amb. that there were some 1,500 of their fellows who stood in urgent need of hospitalisation, and this figure, which as will be seen was a gross underestimate, formed the basis for immediate action. Huts which stood apart from the camp and which had been occupied by the German staff were selected for conversion into an improvised hospital. They were rapidly cleansed and on May 1 the more seriously ill were moved into them. They were first passed through a 'human laundry' (see Plate XXXI), a large marquee, in the P.o.W. camp close to the political prisoners compound, with twenty tables. The patient from the compound was brought in at the 'dirty' end, his clothing, such as it was, removed and all hair-bearing areas shaved. He was then carried to one of the tables and washed thoroughly with soap and hot water. Then he was dried and dusted with D.D.T., wrapped in a clean blanket, placed on a stretcher and transported to the improvised hospital about half a mile away. From May 1 to May 6, 300 patients each day were thus transferred. The R.A.M.C. officers were reinforced by about half a dozen German civilian doctors,

---

* As photographic records of the conditions in Belsen only are available, a selection of these, which illustrate adequately the appalling conditions prevailing in these camps is included in this chapter (see Plates xxvii to xxxii).

an uncertain number of doctors among the political prisoners, about 50 German nurses, 20 German P.o.W. and a variable number of German female workers, some of these being resident in the camp and some reporting daily, under Military Government arrangements. A corporal and three privates of the A.C.C., and borrowed from 8th Armd. Bde., did all the cooking, aided by some half a dozen French cooks from among the ex-P.o.W.

By May 5 it had become clearly recognised that the task was far beyond the powers of the light field ambulance, and D.D.M.S. XXX Corps moved 10 C.C.S. into the area from Seedorf to take over the improvised hospital, leaving 168 Lt. Fd. Amb. to look after the political prisoners compound and its remaining inmates.

Accommodation. The hospital consisted of:

(a) Six wooden huts each about 40 yards long, with a central corridor and a number of small rooms on either side of this fitted with accommodation for about 200 patients.
(b) Five wooden huts of a different pattern which could accommodate about 600 patients altogether.
(c) One hut, in process of being evacuated by German civilian female workers, which could accommodate about 200 patients.

This gave a total of 2,000 beds. There was no lighting system and the water supply was intermittent and the water unfit for drinking. There were washing and bathing facilities of sorts but the drains were blocked and the floors under water. The area around these huts was cluttered with litter and débris of all kinds and pockmarked with stagnant pools.

In the huts were already over 1,500 patients, living skeletons, naked, suffering from acute and advanced disease as well as from starvation and famine diarrhoea. Typhus was rampant but segregation was impossible. Each patient had a straw palliasse and two, or even three, blankets. Most of them were far too weak to leave their beds and the staff could not possibly answer their insistent demands for water or for bedpans. Everywhere in the huts and outside naked men crouched over some form of receptacle or over no receptacle at all in the stress of acute diarrhoea. But they were apathetic and indifferent to everything save the urgency of hunger and of pain. Liberation meant nothing to them. They displayed no sense of modesty and no emotion save a fretful clamorous impatience to satisfy the pangs of hunger.

10 C.C.S. took over the hospital compound at 1800 hours on May 6, when the number of patients was 1,713 and the number of vacant beds 211. Deaths in the hospital up to this time had numbered 137. The number of those still awaiting transfer to the hospital was thought to be about 200. This estimate proved to be very wide of the mark.

Staff. 10 C.C.S., 14 and 50 F.S.Us. and 24 F.T.U., personnel of 11

ADVANCE TO AND CROSSING OF THE ELBE

F.D.S. and the forward delivery truck of 'Y' Adv. Blood Bank. The officer commanding the C.C.S. appointed the medical specialist of the C.C.S. as medical director and made him responsible for the most advantageous utilisation of the medical staff, which by May 14 had come to consist of:

Officer commanding (O.C. 10 C.C.S.)	1
Administrative staff. B.O.Rs.	6
Chaplains	4
Medical Director	1
Officers R.A.M.C.	13
Officer U.S. A.M.C.	1
Ex-internee doctors	23
German civilian doctors	8

He appointed the senior nursing officer of the C.C.S. director of nursing and made her responsible for the most advantageous employment of the nursing personnel, which by May 14 had come to consist of:

Director of Nursing	1
Q.A.I.M.N.S.	9
Red Cross worker	1
N.Os. R.A.M.C.	70
German nurses	141

He nominated the unit Q.M. director of stores and supplies:

Director of Stores and Supplies	1
B.O.Rs.	25
French ex-P.o.W.	4
German resident kitchen and stores workers	20

The non-medical officer of 10 C.C.S. was appointed director of labour:

Director of Labour	1
B.O.Rs.	135
Ex-internee workers	20
German resident female hospital workers	175
German P.o.W.	55
German daily workers	55

Feeding. The kitchen thus far used by 168 Lt. Fd. Amb. became the hospital kitchen with the C.C.S. sgt. cook in charge. A staff kitchen was established in a garage building and staffed by the A.C.C. cooks to serve the German doctors and nurses and the resident German female workers. A company kitchen was established to serve the personnel of 10 C.C.S., the ex-internee doctors and the German P.o.W.

Ration Scales—Patients:

First stage: Two-hourly feeds of 5 oz., making a total of 60 oz. in twenty-four hours.

Skimmed milk, fresh	2 litres
or	
Dried skimmed milk	4 oz.
Sugar	1 ,,
Salt	4 ,,
Compound vitamin tablets	4 tablets

Second stage:

Skimmed milk, fresh	1½ litres
or	
Dried skimmed milk	3 oz.
Sugar	1 ,,
Bread	5 ,,
Tinned vegetables (peas or beans)	2 ,,
Tinned meat	1 ,,
Potatoes	2 ,,
Margarine or butter	1 ,,
Concentrated soup	½ ,,
Salt	¼ ,,
Compound vitamin tablets	2 tablets

Third stage: The light diet

24 F.T.U. transfused 367 of the patients, those suffering from extreme dehydration, those unable to take fluids by the mouth because of weakness or apathy and typhus cases who were comatose. Plasma and 5 per cent. glucose were given intravenously.

Equipment. The officer commanding 10 C.C.S. himself undertook the gigantic task of obtaining from one source or another:

Pyjamas, shirts and other bedwear	3,000
Pillows	3,000
Pillowcases	6,000
Sheets	3,000
Knives, forks, spoons *each*	3,000
Plates	4,000
Feeding cups	500
Sputum mugs	500
Bowls, washing	200
Air cushions	200
Thermometers	60

plus towels, soap, face cloths, toothbrushes, rubber aprons, nursing overalls, washing tubs, water jugs, primus stoves, slippers, civilian clothes, more blankets, straw, beds, stoves, containers, ladles, baking trays, mincing machines, tin openers and other kitchen equipment.

The Q.M. made contact with the nearest D.I.D. to arrange for the daily supply of milk, eggs and bread. Military Government quickly succeeded in making available everything that was asked for.

At the end of the first day following the take-over, during which 199 more patients were admitted, there was a general feeling of utter despondency; the task seemed quite hopeless. But on the following day D.D.H. XXX Corps brought the good news that 86 B.G.H. was being moved to Rotenburg on May 11 and would be accepting patients from 10 C.C.S. The effect of this was dissipated, however, when it was found that not 200 but about 2,500 more of the political prisoners would need to be taken into the hospital. Typhus was rife among them and those who were ambulant at the time of the uncovering had now collapsed. By May 10 the hospital had 2,277 patients and had to expect an intake of 300 a day during the next week. Deaths were averaging 300 a day. Tentage now filled all available space around the huts. In the hospital area much had been done. The huts were beginning to acquire a neatness. The arrival of pyjamas had an astonishing effect upon the patients, previously seemingly unaffected by the change in their fortune; they began to display an interest in their personal appearance; modesty and dignity began to find expression. The admired attributes of socialised man, compassion, consideration for others, co-operation and the like, disappear when the food intake falls below a certain minimum and stays there and reappear quite quickly as the food intake is increased. With the pyjamas came hope to tinge the atmosphere of the wards and to affect profoundly all who breathed it. Since death was now no longer inevitable the continuance of living became a matter of individual interest and importance. And the weather was fine and warm.

Evacuation. On May 11, evacuation to 86 B.G.H. began, just in time to prevent a crisis. From then to the 15th, 1,529 new patients were admitted to 10 C.C.S's. hospital and 1,382 patients were transferred to 86 B.G.H. or to a convalescent camp that had been established by 3 F.D.S. (XXX Corps) at Seedorf. It was now arranged that 168 Lt. Fd. Amb. in the camp should not send patients to the hospital before 1100 hours daily. This gave time for 111 M.A.C. to get away with its daily load of transfers to hospital in the early morning. The convalescents for 3 F.D.S. were evacuated during the afternoons, when the screening examinations of the patients and of the inmates of the political prisoners camp was conducted.

The number of typhus cases rose to 600 on May 12 and to 760 on May 16. The arrival of 8 Mob. Bact. Lab. on May 15 provided a much needed reinforcement. No case of this disease occurred among the personnel of 10 C.C.S. and its associated units. The patients in the hospital were not permitted to stray beyond the confines of the hospital and visitors were not allowed. Everyone associated with them and all ambulance cars were dusted daily. Separate bathing facilities were provided for the different groups within the hospital population.

On May 17 the last batch of admissions, 92, arrived from the camp and, since 7 Cdn. G.H. at Bassum had begun to accept transfers on the previous day, the bedstate of 10 C.C.S's. hospital began to show a downward trend for the first time since its opening. By May 18 it was down to about 1,835, having been 2,184 on the 12th, but since only non-typhus cases had been sent to the general hospitals the proportion of typhus cases had grown increasingly larger. With the easing of the burden and the passing of the crisis, sickness among the staff began to increase. The commonest ailment was a febrile, non-specific dysentery. This declined when only watercart water was used for drinking and cooking.

Closure. It now became possible to consider the closing down of the hospital. A Military Government hospital at Farge, near Bremen, and 8 B.G.H. at Bassum were now accepting cases from 10 C.C.S. A start was made on May 25 with the burning of the camp. The staff of the hospital was progressively reduced by the departure of 50 F.S.U., the detachment of 11 F.D.S., 14 F.S.U., of the internee doctors and of the German nurses. Surplus equipment was sent to 3 F.D.S. By 1600 hours on June 3 the last 350 patients had been evacuated and the hospital wards were empty and silent. A fence enclosed the cemetery in which a notice commemorating the dead had been erected. Of the rest of those who had passed through this hospital very many were shortly to die, for their health had been far too greatly destroyed.

Records. Under the conditions that obtained sufficient staff and time for the maintenance of accurate records could not be found, but in round numbers the record of this hospital's work was as follows:

Evacuated to D.P. camps direct	2,000
Evacuated to the hospital (791 typhus)	4,102
Died in the camp	1,500
Died in the hospital (102 typhus)	389
Died in other hospitals after transfer	500

Not the least of the causes of the difficulties encountered by the staff was the heterogeneity in respect of nationality of the patients. Of 4,663 examined by the Board of Review there were:

Austrian	4	Estonian	2
Belgian	148	French	757
Canadian	1	German	50
Chinese	1	Greek	94
Czech	93	Hungarian	94
Danish	1	Italian	93
Dutch	243	Latvian	134

ADVANCE TO AND CROSSING OF THE ELBE

Lithuanian	.	.	26	Russian . . .	1,828
Luxembourger	.	.	1	Spanish . . .	20
Polish	.	.	994	Yugoslav . . .	73
Rumanian	.	.	6		

They were equally heterogeneous in respect of social status and of the causes of their being in the camp. They included university lecturers, physicians, architects and habitual criminals. They consisted mainly of such as had been:

(1) taken from home as forced labour and placed immediately into a concentration camp;
(2) taken from home as forced labour and caught after attempting to run away from the place of employment;
(3) P.o.W. taken from P.o.W. camps for labour and thereafter treated as civilians and sent to a concentration camp;
(4) taken from prison during or at the end of their sentences;
(5) arrested because of their political views;
(6) arrested as members of resistance groups;
(7) arrested because they were Jews;
(8) arrested being found in possession of lethal weapons;
(9) arrested after the uprising in Warsaw.

They had been transferred to Sandbostel for extermination. Some 9,000 of them had arrived by rail in open cattle trucks, 100 to a truck, after a journey lasting eight days, during which they were without water and food and were never permitted to leave the trucks. About 2,000 were dead on arrival. Those who could move were made to march the 2 km. to the camp. Those who could not, being either dead or else too weak, were bundled into small sand-carrying tip trucks and taken by rail to the camp where they were tipped in heaps, to lie until their fellows came to fetch them. This was between April 13–18. Between then and May 1 their deliberate elimination proceeded. The seeds of typhus and respiratory tuberculosis were widely sown as malnutrition, gross overcrowding and a complete absence of any measure of environmental sanitation produced their dire effects.

Thus it was that the deep satisfaction that was to be derived from the merciful work that was done by the R.A.M.C., Q.A.I.M.N.S., R.A.S.C., R.A.O.C. and Pioneer Corps personnel and by those associated with them in Sandbostel was greatly diminished by the knowledge that among those they tended with such tender compassion there were very many whose lives could not be saved and whose hurts could not be healed.

SECOND ARMY

The swift advance from the Rhine to the Baltic; the surrender of the German forces, the redeployment of its constituent corps to their respective corps districts and finally the disbandment of H.Q. Second Army provided a multiplicity of problems for the Army Medical Services quite different from those that had been associated with the set-piece battles and far exceeding these in magnitude and complexity.

The evacuation of casualties during the early stages of the advance presented difficulties for the advance was staggered, the left flank being held back while the right moved forward. At one time a distance of over two hundred miles had to be covered by ambulance cars between the forward units and the general hospitals to the west of the Rhine. At this time air evacuation was not feasible but as soon as airfields could be used the problems that stemmed from excessive distance ceased to trouble.

During this advance P.W.X., D.Ps. and innumerable German military hospital populations presented problems of very great magnitude. Supervision and service had to be provided for these commitments. The uncovering of concentration camps such as Belsen and Sandbostel immediately demanded that the Army Medical Services should turn aside from their routine duties and provide for those who had literally been snatched from death the care that they needed. To begin with none but the Army Medical Services could provide this care. To do so laid a very heavy strain upon the medical units and the personnel that were so employed.

The Army Medical Services were obliged to be much involved in the collection and classifying of captured German medical stores and equipment. These were discovered in small dumps widely scattered.

In Schleswig-Holstein there was great congestion caused by the retreat of the German Army from many quarters to this region and by the arrival there of German wounded by land and sea from Denmark and elsewhere. Steps had to be taken to prevent the spread of infection and the outbreak of disease.

It had to be assumed that, although the German forces facing 21 Army Group were disorganised, it was not improbable that resistance stouter than that encountered during the drive through northern France and Belgium would be encountered in places if not everywhere. The medical services therefore had to be prepared to deal with casualties in varying numbers throughout the advance. It was obvious that the main difficulty would be that of evacuating casualties down a rapidly lengthening line. D.Ds.M.S. corps were warned that they must be prepared to hold cases and, if necessary, to increase the holding capacity of the C.C.S.

There were four corps under command Second Army for this advance, VIII, XII, XXX and U.S. XVIII, as well as I Corps District. The advance was to be on four axes, the right well forward and the left held back as a protective flank. This being so it was considered possible to step up corps medical installations *en echelon* to conform and to provide medical services throughout the long L. of C.

[*Imperial War Museum*]

PLATE XXVI. A Half-track Ambulance Car crossing the Dortmund–Ems Canal at a ford made by Bulldozers. April 1945.

Plate XXVII. Belsen Camp, April 1945.

[Imperial War Museum]

PLATE XXVIII. Belsen Camp, April 1945.

[Imperial War Museum

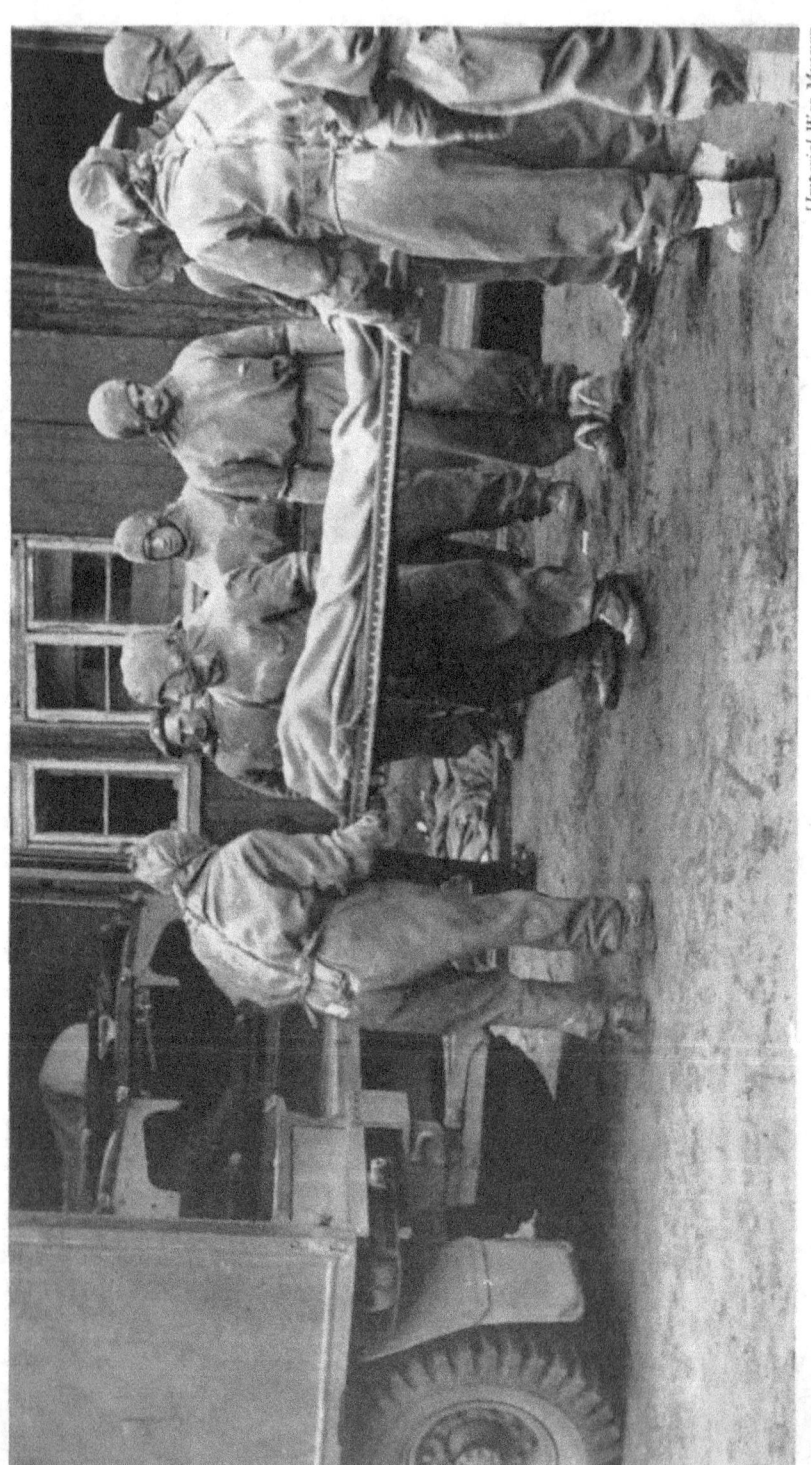

[*Imperial War Museum*

PLATE XXIX. Belsen, April 1945. 11 Light Field Ambulance transferring Typhus cases from the huts to the improvised hospital in the S.S. Barracks.

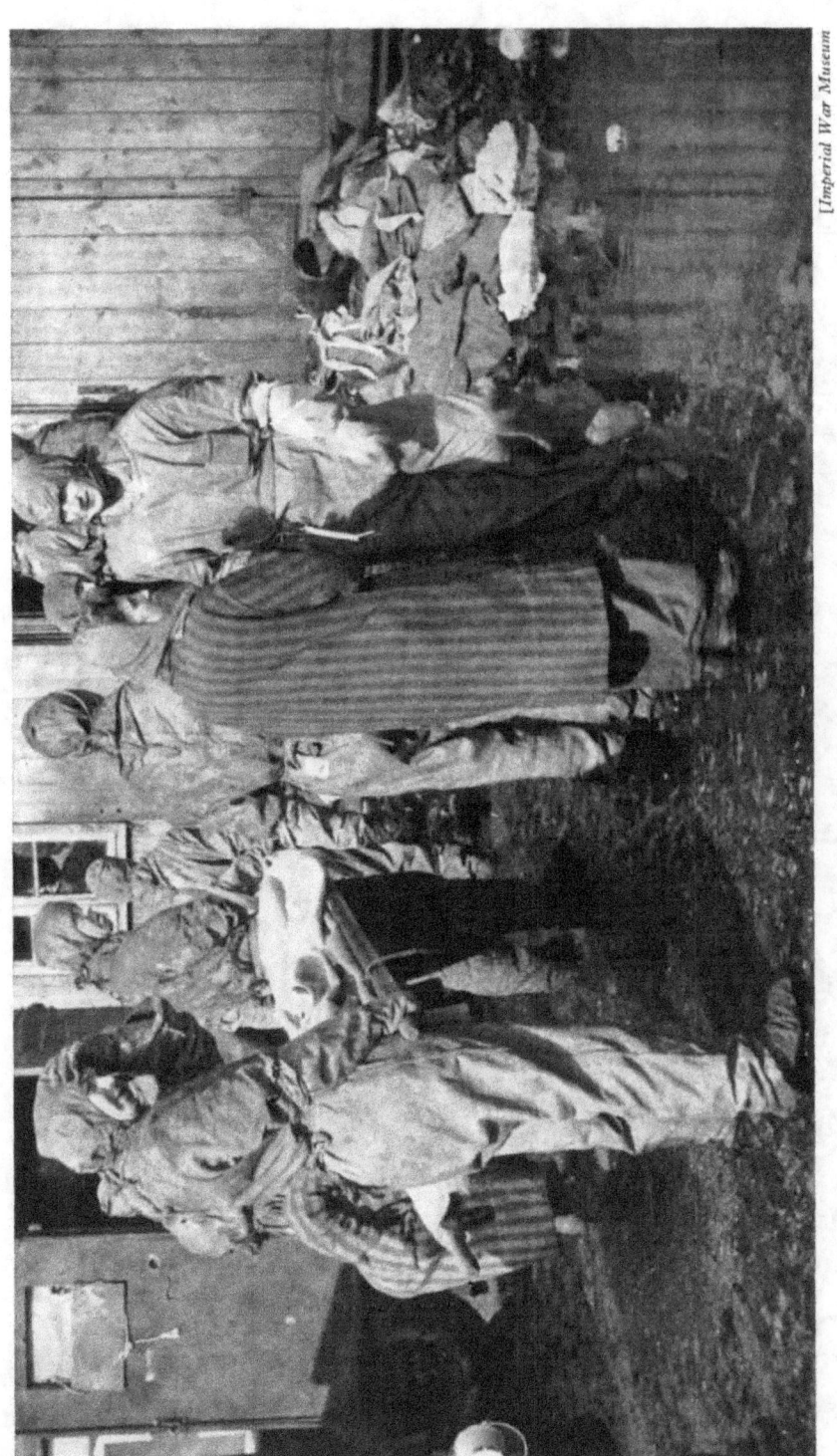

PLATE XXX. Belsen, April 1945. German women transferring the inmates of the huts to Ambulance Cars.

PLATE XXXI. Belsen Camp, April 1945. The Human Laundry.

[*Imperial War Museum*

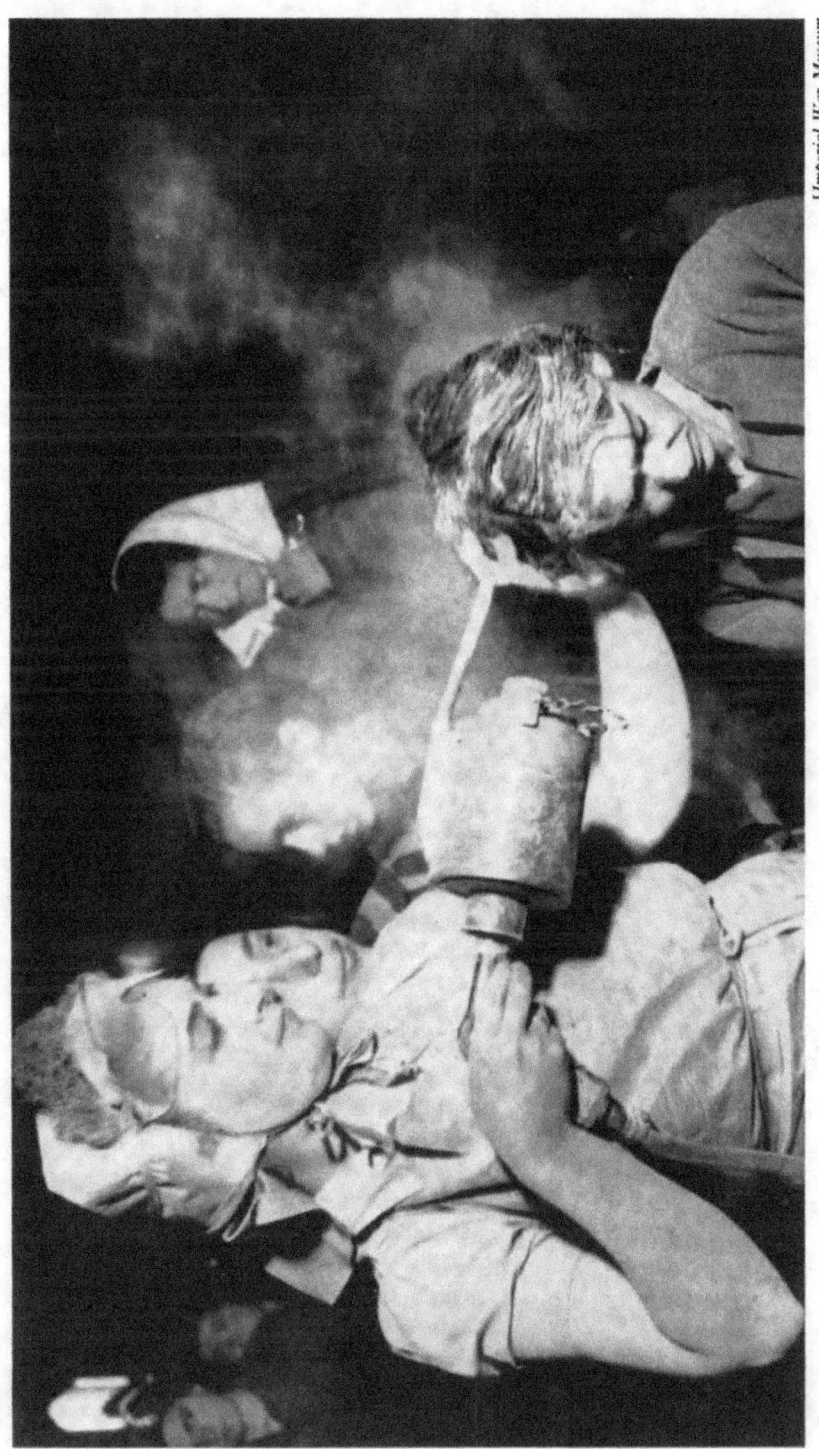

PLATE XXXII. Belsen Camp, April 1945. After having been bathed the inmates are dusted with Anti-louse Powder.

Imperial War Museum

ADVANCE TO AND CROSSING OF THE ELBE

The 200-bed hospitals and the C.C.Ss. were pooled and moved forward by Army according to a co-ordinated plan known to and endorsed by D.Ds.M.S. corps. The following sites were preselected for them:

23 C.C.S.	area of Ahaus
81 B.G.H.	Rheine
3 C.C.S.	Bramsche
24 C.C.S.	Diepholz
33 C.C.S.	Nienburg
84 B.G.H.	Bremen
34 C.C.S.	Soltau
10 C.C.S. and a B.G.H.	Hamburg
35 C.C.S.	to remain, initially, at Airfield B.100

D.Ds.M.S. were asked to ensure that if A.S.Cs. were opened within the corps these would be sited as far as possible in these selected areas and on ground or in buildings suitable for the C.C.S. or hospital that was to come to that area later. Details for the phasing of transport were arranged with S. and T. through Q. and it was hoped that there would always be at least one C.C.S. on wheels or moving forward.

Of the Army hospitals 79 B.G.H. was to revert to command L. of C. with effect from April 1; 9 B.G.H. was to remain in the Venraij area and in the initial stages under command Army but administered by I Corps. 77 B.G.H. was to move to Bedburg on April 1 under command Army but administered by I Corps. 25 B.G.H. was to be available to move to the Rheine area on completion of the move of 77 B.G.H. Other hospitals would be made available by 21 Army Group at a later date for the Bremen and Hamburg areas. 86 B.G.H. (200) was to remain initially at Schloss Wissen near Airfield B.100 and was to continue to admit neuro-surgical and maxillo-facial cases. 35 C.C.S. would move from Airfield B.100 to the area of Rheine when the airfield there was available.

Of the field dressing stations, 2 F.D.S. was to replace 19 and be available for forward movement. 19 F.D.S. was to remain at Bourg-Léopold until the final move to 101 Reinforcement Group. 21 F.D.S. was to remain in the Venraij area; 31, 49 and 50 F.D.Ss. were to close and be available for forward movement and 6 F.D.S. was to open in the Technical College in Helmond for minor sick, exhaustion, infectious and V.D. cases.

Of the advanced depots of medical stores 8 was to remain in Venraij, prepared to move forward, 9 was moved to 86 B.G.H. in Schloss Wissen and 11 was to be prepared to move forward into the Rheine area. If necessary, before 11 was established in Rheine, medical stores would be flown forward from airfield B.100 to Rheine for issue.

'Y' Blood Bank H.Q. at Schloss Wissen was to move forward to Rheine.

257 and 218 A.C.Cs. were to provide ambulance transport, but the latter unit unless otherwise ordered was not to move east of the Rhine.

Evacuation. Amb. R.H. was to remain at Sevenum initially and be moved to Bedburg at a later date. It might be necessary to continue to make use of Sevenum to clear cases from the Venraij area. Airfield B.100 would continue to be used until the Rheine airfield came into use.

It was proposed to establish large reception camps at the Rhine barrier, east of the river, for displaced persons. Forward of this barrier corps were to be responsible for establishing transit camps on their axes at the lateral water obstacles, the Dortmund–Ems Canal, the Weser and the Elbe. It was intended that corps light A.A. regiments should supervise and control these camps. Army was to make available one field hygiene section for the reception camp at the Rhine barrier and another for the supervision of the Dortmund–Ems and Weser laterals and the corps transit camps thereon. Those in P.W.X. camps in the area of Goch who needed hospitalisation were to be evacuated to 77 B.G.H. in Bedburg.

During the advance to the Weser evacuation by road was by 257 A.C.C. from corps C.C.S. to 81 B.G.H. in Wettringen and thence to the hospitals west of the Rhine. The ambulance car resources were stretched to the extreme for the journey from Wettringen to Bedburg and back took twenty-four hours. Ambulance railhead moved forward to Bedburg on April 10. Casualties being evacuated from east of the Rhine were staged at 77 B.G.H. in Bedburg prior to evacuation. Air evacuation became possible when airfield B.108 at Rheine was opened on April 10. The opening of this airfield had been delayed by shell-fire interfering with the construction work. No other suitable airfield could be made available. The C.A.E.U. on this airfield was provided by 83 Group R.A.F.

During the advance to the Elbe evacuation by road continued to be by 257 A.C.C., of which one platoon was allotted to each corps, from corps C.C.S. rearwards. From A.S.Cs. and C.C.Ss. south and west of the Weser, casualties were evacuated first to 84 B.G.H. in Sulingen. Such as were fit for evacuation by air were then transferred to 24 C.C.S. (the air cushion). The rest were conveyed by 257 A.C.C. to 25 B.G.H. in Wettringen. Casualties from 3 C.C.S., or from 10 C.C.S. which opened later east of the river, who had received surgical treatment and were fit for evacuation by air were taken by 257 A.C.C. direct to 24 C.C.S. From A.S.Cs. and C.C.Ss. east of the Weser casualties were evacuated to 86 B.G.H. in Celle. This hospital was kept as clear as possible by air evacuation through 'B' Flight 1 C.A.E.U. on the B.118 airstrip at Celle. 121 B.G.H. opened 300 beds on April 20 and began to receive casualties alternately with 86 B.G.H. and 21 F.D.S. Convales-

ADVANCE TO AND CROSSING OF THE ELBE

cent cases requiring seven to ten days' further treatment on discharge from hospital or Army F.D.S. were evacuated to 13 Con. Depot at Lengerich.

The ambulance railhead remained at Bedburg under control I Corps.

Air evacuation from I Corps area was through 35 C.C.S. at Neuenkirchen (the air cushion) for B.108 airstrip and thence to 25 B.G.H. From Army rear area the air cushion was 24 C.C.S. at Diepholz for B.114 airstrip and thence to 84 B.G.H. From east of the Weser the air cushion was 'B' Flight 1 C.A.E.U. at Celle for B.118 airstrip and thence to 86 and 121 B.G.Hs. From west of the Dortmund–Ems Canal evacuation was under arrangements made by D.D.M.S. I Corps. A platoon of 218 A.C.C. was employed to cover evacuation by road and evacuation to the airfield from the Rheine area. Later a second platoon of 218 A.C.C. was made available to cover road evacuation from Borken to Bedburg.

During the assault crossing of the Elbe evacuation from corps areas was by 257 A.C.C. from corps C.C.Ss. 'B' platoon of 257 A.C.C. in support of XXX Corps evacuated from 23 C.C.S. at Wintermoor to Celle until XII Corps had established itself east of the river when evacuation of XII Corps casualties was switched to 81 B.G.H. in Lüneburg. 'C' platoon of 257 A.C.C. evacuated from 33 C.C.S. and when this unit closed the platoon moved forward to evacuate casualties from 34 C.C.S., east of the Elbe, to Celle. 'D' platoon of 257 A.C.C. less one section evacuated from 3 C.C.S. in Verden to Celle.

Road evacuation within Second Army was undertaken by 257 A.C.C. ('A' platoon and one section of 'D' platoon) between Lüneburg and Celle and from Celle to airstrip B.118. When 'C' platoon moved across the river, 'A' platoon also accepted responsibility for the conveyance of casualties to airstrip B.156. Evacuation from 74 and 81 B.G.Hs. by air was to the air cushion, 35 C.C.S., the overflow going to R.A.F. 52 M.F.H., for airstrip 156 at Lüneburg, while from 84 B.G.H. and 7 Cdn. G.H. evacuation was to the C.A.E.U. at airstrip B.111 at Ahlhorn. From 25 B.G.H. evacuation was as before, to 'A' Flight 1 C.A.E.U. on airstrip B.108 at Rheine.

The moves of the medical units during the advance to the Elbe and beyond illustrate the reactions of the Army Medical Services to the problems set them by the actions of the combatant formations. The location statement as at April 16 and as at May 1 will suffice.

LOCATION STATEMENT. APRIL 16

General hospitals
  West of the Weser
    25 B.G.H. (600) u/c I Corps, open St. Joseph's Lazarett, in Wettringen.
    84 „   (200) open in Sulingen.

East of the Weser
>86 B.G.H. (200) to open April 18, in Celle.
>121 „ (600) to open April 20, in Celle.
>81 „ closed, in Borghorst.

West of the Rhine
>77 B.G.H. u/c I Corps, open in Bedburg.

Convalescent Depot
>13 Con. Depot (forward wing) (500 beds), open in Lengerich.

Light Field Ambulances
>11 Lt. Fd. Amb. for 6th Guards Armoured Brigade . VIII Corps
>   (released for duty in Belsen, April 17)
>21 „ for 1st Commando Brigade . . VIII Corps
>14 „ for 4th Armoured Brigade . . XII Corps
>168 „ for 8th Armoured Brigade . . XXX Corps

Casualty Clearing Stations
>3 C.C.S. open until April 18, in Uchte.
>10 „ u/c XXX Corps.
>23 „ closed in Wüllen. To be moved forward to XII Corps rear area, not before April 19, under Army arrangements.
>24 „ open in Diepholz, acting as temporary air cushion for casualty evacuation.
>32 „ moving to Belsen on April 17.
>33 „ u/c VIII Corps, moving forward to open in area south-west of Uelzen.
>34 „ in Gemen, temporarily u/c I Corps. To be called forward by Second Army if required for operational rôle after April 19.
>35 „ serving as Army air cushion on airstrip B.108, at Rheine.

Field Dressing Stations allotted to Corps
>11, 14 and 22 u/c XXX, XII and VIII Corps respectively to provide additional medical resources to meet commitments to Military Government and to supervise such German military medical installations as are overrun.

>6 F.D.S. in Oldenzaal
>19 „ „ Burgsteinfurt
>26 „ „ Ochtrup

placed u/c I Corps for supervision and control of German military and para-military hospitals and for the organisation of Allied P.W.X. hospital for non-British, U.S. and Dominion P.W.X.

(6 F.D.S. was nominated by D.M.S. 21 Army Group for the Netherlands District and was not to be given commitments outside Holland.)
(26 F.D.S. was to revert to Army on April 23.)

ADVANCE TO AND CROSSING OF THE ELBE

Army Field Dressing Stations

    2 F.D.S. staging at Bohmte. Closed after April 18 in preparation for move forward with 81 B.G.H.
    21 ,, open on April 18, in Celle, acting as a screen for 86 B.G.H.
    31 ,, open in Sulingen, acting as a screen for 84 B.G.H.
    49 ,, moving to area north-east of Osnabrück, under A.D.M.S. Army Troops.
    50 ,, to open on April 17 in Osnabrück under A.D.M.S. Army Troops.

Field Surgical and Transfusion Units

To VIII Corps	33, 48, 52, 53 F.S.Us.; 21 and 22 F.T.Us.
XII Corps	12, 15, 27, 41, 42, 51 and 56 F.S.Us.; 13, 30 and 37 F.T.Us.
XXX Corps	6, 14, 43, 44, 49 and 50 F.S.Us.; 7, 24 and 35 F.T.Us.
I Corps District	13 F.S.U. (with 25 B.G.H.); 14 and 36 F.T.Us.
Second Army	45 F.S.U. (with 84 B.G.H.); 47 and 54 F.S.Us. (with 86 B.G.H.); 6 F.T.U. (84 B.G.H.); 31 F.T.U. (temporarily with 86 B.G.H.)

Special Units

    4 Mob. Bact. Lab. with 84 B.G.H. in Sulingen.
    7 ,, to move on April 17 to Belsen.
    8 ,, with 33 F.D.S. in Wembe u/c I Corps.
    4 Mob. Hyg. Lab. with 84 B.G.H. in Sulingen.
    2 Traumatic Shock Team at 84 B.G.H. To pass u/c XXX Corps on April 21 for attachment to the forward corps C.C.S.

Field Hygiene Sections

    61 Fd. Hyg. Sec. Army Roadhead area. On routine duties and supervising P.W.X. installations and P.o.W. cages in this area.
    75 ,, Army Area. Supervising D.P. camps.
    30 ,, 10 Garrison Area. u/c 10 Garrison. Supervising P.W.X. installations and P.o.W. cages.

Hospitals for Allied P.W.X. exclusive of British and United States

    Gescher, Burgsteinfurt and Nienburg (the last being attached to the P.o.W. camp with effect from April 20).

German Military Hospitals for P.o.W. Sick and Wounded

St. Nicholas Kestricht, Denekamp	Diepholz
Burgsteinfurt	Celle
Gronau	Mettingen
Bentlage	Ibbenbüren
Gr. Burgwedel	Lemforde

Location Statement as at May 1

General Hospitals

West of the Weser

    25 B.G.H. (unchanged) St. Joseph's Lazarett, Wettringen. u/c I Corps.
    7 Cdn. G.H. (600) in civil hospital Bassum, to open May 3.
    84 B.G.H. (unchanged) in Sulingen.

East of the Weser

    81 B.G.H. (200) open in Scharnhorst Barracks, Lüneburg.
    86   „   open in St. Joseph's Lazarett, Celle.
    121   „   open, in school in Celle.
    74   „   (600) moving to Lüneburg to take over from 33 C.C.S.

West of the Rhine

    77 B.G.H. (unchanged) open in Bedburg. u/c I Corps.

Convalescent Depot

    13 Con. Depot forward wing (unchanged), moving forward to Celle.

Light Field Ambulances and Field Ambulances

    11 Lt. Fd. Amb. u/c Second Army for Belsen.
    14   „   u/c VIII Corps for Elbe crossing and thereafter for temporary duty in Neuen Gamme concentration camp.
    21   „   u/c Second Army for P.o.W. and P.W.X. duties. Two sections with 1st Commando Brigade (unchanged).
    168   „   u/c XXX Corps.
    163 Fd. Amb. u/c Second Army as from May 2 for duty in Neuen Gamme concentration camp.

Casualty Clearing Stations

    3 C.C.S. u/c XXX Corps, open in Verden.
    10   „   u/c XXX Corps for duty in P.o.W. camp.
    23   „   u/c XII Corps, open Wintermoor.
    24   „   u/c XII Corps, for duty in Neuen Gamme concentration camp.
    32   „   in Belsen concentration camp.
    33   „   u/c VIII Corps, open in Lüneburg.
    34   „   u/c VIII Corps, closed, moving to the east of the Elbe.
    35   „   u/c Second Army, serving as air cushion at Lüneburg.

Field Dressing Stations allotted to Corps

    11, 14 and 22 F.D.S. (unchanged) with XXX, XII and VIII Corps.
    19 F.D.S. (unchanged) u/c I Corps.

ADVANCE TO AND CROSSING OF THE ELBE

Army Field Dressing Stations

    2 F.D.S. open in Diepholz for local sick and for 'Eclipse' commitments in Army Troops area.

    21 ,, still in Celle, open for minor sick.

    31 ,, open in Scharnhorst Barracks, Lüneburg, a screen for 81 B.G.H.

    49 ,, open in Nienburg for minor sick, acting as V.D.T.C. and supervising P.W.X. hospitals.

    50 ,, (unchanged) open in Osnabrück for local Army troops, V.D.T.C. and minor sick.

Field Surgical and Transfusion Units

With VIII Corps	.	33, 48, 52, 53, 54, and 56 F.S.Us.; 21, 22 and 31 F.T.Us.
	XII Corps	. 12, 15, 27, 41, 42 and 51 F.S.Us.; 13, 30 and 37 F.T.Us.
	XXX Corps	. 6, 14, 43, 44, 49, 50 F.S.Us.; 7, 24 and 35 F.T.Us.
	I Corps District	46 F.S.U. with 25 B.G.H.; 14 F.T.U. with 25 B.G.H.
	Second Army	. 13 and 34 F.S.Us. with 81 B.G.H.; 36 F.T.U. with 81 B.G.H.
		45 and 47 F.S.Us. with 86 B.G.H.; 6 F.T.U. with 86 B.G.H.
		55 F.S.U. with 121 B.G.H.

Special Units

    4 Mob. Bact. Lab. attached to 24 C.C.S. for Neuen Gamme concentration camp.

    7 ,, attached to 32 C.C.S. for Belsen concentration camp.

    8 ,, still with 33 F.D.S.

    4 Mob. Hyg. Lab. attached to 121 B.G.H. in Celle.

    2 Traumatic Shock Team u/c VIII Corps for attachment to forward C.C.S.

    1 Vascular Research Team attached to 81 B.G.H. in Lüneburg.

    M.R.C. Nutritional Team attached to 32 C.C.S. in Belsen concentration camp.

    6 M.N.S.U. attached to 121 B.G.H. in Celle.

    5 M.F.S.U. attached to 121 B.G.H. in Celle.

8 Adv. Depot Med. Stores moved from Venraij to Celle on April 21; 9 Adv. Depot Med. Stores from Venraij to the Schloss Wissen area on April 4 and on to Lüneburg on May 6, and 11 Adv. Depot Med. Stores from Eindhoven to Rheine on April 10 and on to Burgdorf on June 2. 13 Base Depot of Medical Stores opened on April 18 in Neuenkirchen u/c Second Army. The arrival of 1 Captured Enemy Equipment Section

(C.E.E.S.) greatly lightened the tasks of the advanced depots of medical stores. The unit was attached first to 11 Adv. Depot Med. Stores in Rheine and later to 8 Adv. Depot in Celle. During the advance, mobile elements of the advanced depots of medical stores were in constant use and ensured a regular supply of medical equipment to the forward medical units and R.M.Os. These mobile elements could go forward when the advanced depot itself was halted through lack of transport. Two such elements were based on one advanced depot. As the distances from the nearest base depot lengthened, the value of the medical maintenance block became increasingly apparent. A small detachment from an advanced depot with two half-blocks was located at a forward general hospital and this arrangement proved satisfactory in supplying the needs of the general hospitals and of the smaller medical units in the area.

The W.E. transport of advanced depots of medical stores, general hospitals and C.C.Ss. proved to be utterly inadequate. Stores and supplies of all kinds had to be collected over long distances, often necessitating a two-days' journey over damaged and congested roads. It was not uncommon for two corps to obtain all their requirements of medical equipment from one advanced depot. It was necessary therefore for the advanced depots to have available a reserve of essential medical equipment to meet a situation such as this. When such units as V.D.T.Cs. were attached to F.D.Ss. in corps and divisional areas it was necessary for the advanced depots to supply many items not included in the I.1248.

In so far as ordnance stores were concerned, because large numbers of stretchers, blankets, pillows, pyjamas, stomach warmers, etc., were sent out of Army area along with casualties being evacuated by air, it was necessary to maintain very large reserves of these items. These reserves were held at the advanced depots of medical stores with smaller stocks at the air cushions or on airfields. An Army reserve, controlled by D.D.M.S. Second Army, consisted of:

Stretchers . . 9,000	Pyjama suits . . 7,500
Blankets . . . 29,000	Stomach warmers . 437

and a further reserve of 3,500 stretchers, 7,500 blankets and 2,650 pyjama suits was frozen in ordnance stores. In addition the following reserves were held permanently by formations and units over and above the normal G.1098.

	Stretchers	Blankets	Pyjama suits
Corps	1,500	4,500	1,000
Infantry Division .	150	450	—
Armoured Division .	50	150	—
Armoured Brigade .	50	150	—

ADVANCE TO AND CROSSING OF THE ELBE

	Stretchers	Blankets	Pyjama suits
B.G.H. (600 beds)	400	1,200	400
(200)	200	600	100
C.C.S. (Army)	150	450	75
F.D.S. (Army)	100	300	75

The supervision and control of the German military medical services by 21 Army Group added greatly to the tasks that the British and Canadian Army Medical Services were required to undertake. H.Q. Corps District Basic Control Increment included a medical element but the general shortage of medically qualified personnel was such that vacancies could not be filled. The staff increment allotted to Army was authorised with effect from March 8 and the staff of Second Army was completed in the first week of April. Medical stores reconnaissance teams did not become available until June 2.

During the period April 1–June 25, 212 German hospitals and groups of hospitals were uncovered by Second Army in Germany. A group contained anything from 6–10 small institutions. This number does not include the German hospitals subsequently taken over from U.S. Ninth Army. 16 of these hospitals in the Bremen Enclave were handed over to the U.S. 29th Infantry Division as were also a hospital ship and a hospital train. Everywhere in these hospitals there was gross overcrowding and grave deficiencies of expendible medical equipment.

About 60 ambulance trains were uncovered; they consisted of three main types, ambulance trains proper, converted passenger coaches and converted goods wagons. Many of them arrived, ahead of the Russian advance in the east, full of patients; others were found in sidings, having been used as stationary hospitals. Seven of these trains were taken over for conversion into 'leave' trains for British troops.

One hospital ship was uncovered in Bremen and three more in the Neustadt–Flensburg area.

During April the greater part of the job of organising the collection and control of captured medical stores was undertaken by Second Army medical units as the corps units were fully occupied with operational commitments. During May corps units became available for 'Eclipse' undertakings and by the end of the month decentralisation of control of organised dumps to D.Ds.M.S. corps was possible. It was estimated that between five and six thousand tons of German medical equipment were moved by British medical transport, supplemented towards the end of May by a few captured German vehicles.

It was observed that the most notable shortages in this German material were ether and chloroform, the stocks of which seemed to be almost completely exhausted, and the sulphonamides, especially the more recently developed.

CHAPTER 8

THE LIBERATION OF HOLLAND.*
CANADIAN FIRST ARMY

THE objectives of 21 Army Group were to reach the line of the Elbe and to reduce the ports of Bremen and Hamburg. As part of this plan Canadian First Army was to clear north-east Holland and the German coast as far as the mouth of the Weser, using Canadian II Corps, while Canadian I Corps freed western Holland.

Canadian 3rd Division of Canadian II Corps was set the task of clearing the east bank of the River Ijssel which links the Ijsselmeer—the Zuider Zee—and the Rhine near Arnhem. Advancing northward from Emmerich on April 1, leading elements of the division soon crossed into Holland again. The field ambulances moved with their respective brigades. During the evening of April 1, 14 (Cdn.) Fd. Amb. established its A.D.S. in 's Heerenberg, about three miles north of Emmerich and for the first three days of the advance all casualties in the divisional area were cleared from this A.D.S. by M.A.C. to Bedburg, crossing the Rhine first at Rees and later at Emmerich. On April 3, 2 (Cdn.) C.C.S. opened in 's Heerenberg and thereafter casualties were evacuated thereto. The advance was so rapid that the moves of the field ambulances were very frequent and their stay in any one site exceedingly brief. 14 (Cdn.) Fd. Amb., for example, moved eleven times during the month of April. The A.D.Ss. were put in support of the brigades and moved with them, though remaining under command of A.D.M.S. division. In the case of units that were being used to contain pockets of enemy resistance and being left behind by the advancing brigades, the R.A.Ps. usually evacuated casualties to the nearest C.C.P. or A.D.S., even though this was not attached to their own brigade. Similarly the C.C.Ps. of the field ambulances evacuated their casualties into the nearest open A.D.S. no matter whether or not this belonged to the same field ambulance as themselves or to some other.

By April 18 the leading elements of Canadian 3rd Division had reached the coast north of Leeuwarden. Up to the 21st the medical units of this division had evacuated 1,703 casualties, of which only 613 were due to enemy action.

Canadian 2nd Division, on the right of Canadian 3rd Division, had followed an almost parallel course which took it across the Twente

---

* For a fuller account the Canadian Official Medical History should be consulted.

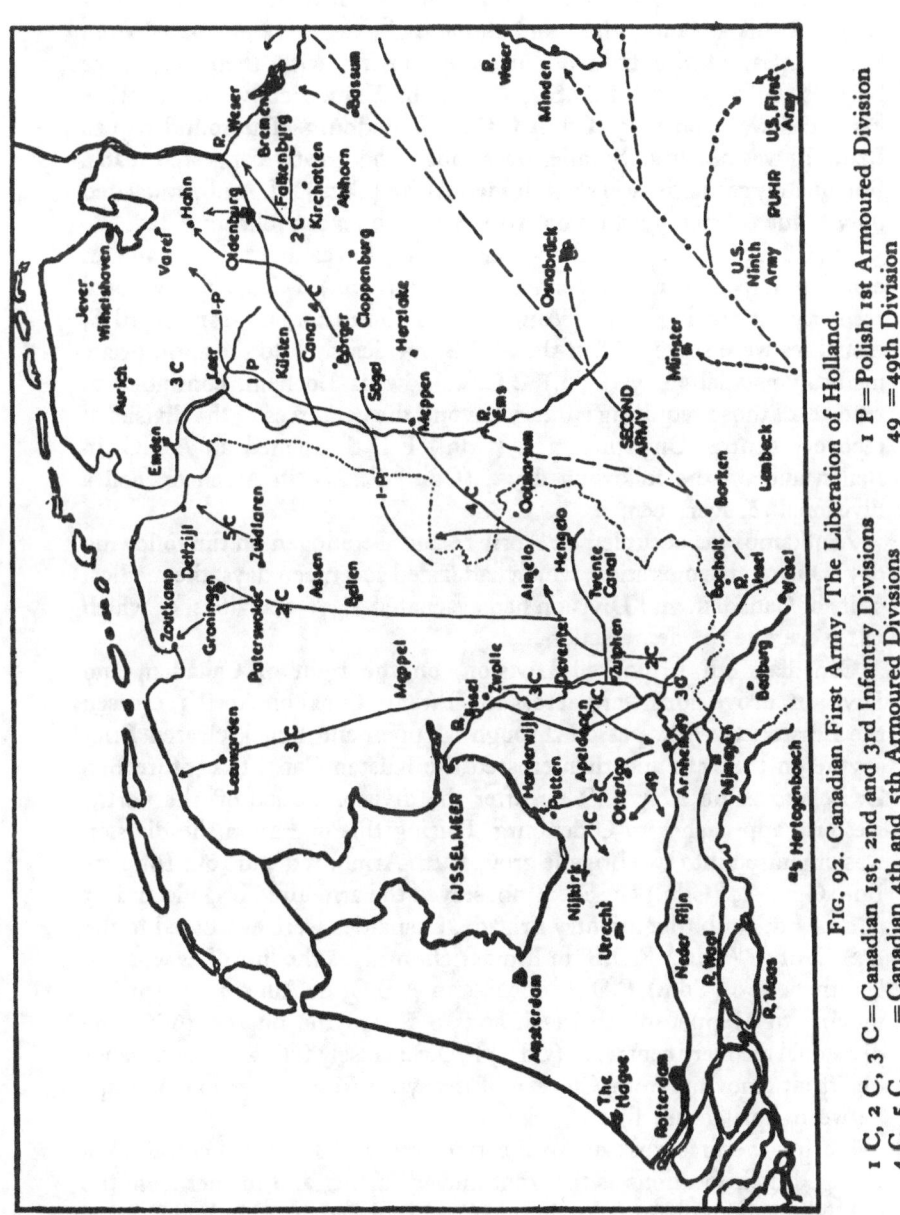

FIG. 92. Canadian First Army. The Liberation of Holland.

1 C, 2 C, 3 C = Canadian 1st, 2nd and 3rd Infantry Divisions
4 C, 5 C = Canadian 4th and 5th Armoured Divisions
1 P = Polish 1st Armoured Division
49 = 49th Division

Canal and on to Groningen and Zoutkamp on the North Sea coast. The pace of the advance was so swift that the medical units had great difficulty in keeping up with the advancing formations. In the early stages of this advance, chest and abdominal cases were evacuated from the A.D.Ss. of the field ambulances moving with their respective brigades to 21 (Cdn.) F.D.S's. A.S.C. in Emmerich while all other casualties went on to 3 (Cdn.) C.C.S. in Bedburg. The round trip to Bedburg was nearly sixty miles over rough and greatly congested roads. Fortunately casualties were not numerous, 18 (Cdn.) Fd. Amb. evacuated only 6 due to enemy action on April 6 and 39 on the following day.

10 (Cdn.) F.D.S. opened a venereal disease treatment centre and an exhaustion centre in Diepenheim and 4 (Cdn.) F.D.S. a divisional recovery centre in Kasteel Ampsen and thereafter, as from April 8, casualties were segregated at the A.D.S. for despatch to the appropriate medical installation. 3 (Cdn.) C.C.S., now at Lochem, continued to receive all those requiring surgery beyond the resources of the divisional recovery centre. On April 13, 5 (Cdn.) F.D.S. opened an A.S.C. in Beilen and on the following day 4 (Cdn.) F.D.S. in Assen opened a divisional recovery centre.

Zoutkamp was occupied on April 15 and Groningen on the following day. During this operation, which had lasted seventeen days, the medical units of Canadian 2nd Division had evacuated 1,376 casualties, of which 581 were due to enemy action.

Canadian 4th Armoured Division, on the right of Canadian 2nd Division, drove northward across the Twente Canal on April 3, crossed the Ems on the 7th, passed through Meppen and Sögel, cleared Friesoythe on the 15th and then crossed the Küsten Canal to capture Bad Zwischenahn on May 1. Thereafter the division sealed off the north-westerly approaches to Oldenburg. During this operation the division was organised into two brigade groups, 4th Armoured and 10th Infantry Bde. Gps. 12 (Cdn.) Lt. Fd. Amb. served the armoured brigade and 15 (Cdn.) Fd. Amb. the infantry brigade. Casualties were evacuated to the A.S.C. of 21 (Cdn.) F.D.S. in Emmerich until, as the line of evacuation lengthened, 6 (Cdn.) F.D.S. opened an A.S.C. in Almelo on April 7, moving to Meppen on the 11th and to Friesoythe on the 16th. The divisional recovery centre, 12 (Cdn.) F.D.S., closely followed the advancing front, moving from Cleve to Friesoythe in a succession of leaps between April 1 and 19.

During the first week of April certain corps and Army medical units changed their locations as the front moved further and further from the old Nijmegen salient. 4 (Cdn.) C.C.S. replaced 2 (Cdn.) C.C.S. in Nijmegen to allow the latter unit to move forward to 's Heerenberg; 3 (Cdn.) C.C.S. moved from Bedburg to Lochem. The specialist units, exhaustion, maxillo-facial, neurosurgical, ophthalmic as well as that which dealt with self-inflicted wounds, were grouped in Nijmegen. All casualties from corps areas were directed to the ambulance control post at Marienboom, just outside Nijmegen. There they were directed to the appropriate medical unit. On April 11, 6 Cdn. G.H. was moved from St. Michielsgestel to Ootmarsum and on the 13th, 2 (Cdn.) C.C.S. moved forward from 's Heerenberg to Meppen.

Canadian I Corps, with 49th Division under command, was occupying, on April 1, positions in the Nijmegen bridgehead south of Arnhem. Its first task was to clear the 'island' between the Neder Rijn and the Waal in 49th Division's sector. This was achieved by 49th Division with Cdn. 11th Inf. Bde. under command, on April 2 and 3. It was thought probable that the Germans might evacuate western Holland but since there was no sign of them doing so and in view of the continued appeals by the Dutch Government on behalf of the Dutch population it was decided, on April 5, to undertake the methodical clearing of western Holland.

On April 14, 49th Division cleared Arnhem and Canadian 1st Division reached the outskirts of Apeldoorn. On the 15th Canadian 5th Armoured Division began a drive from Arnhem to the shore of the Ijsselmeer in an attempt to cut off the German forces around Apeldoorn. The Germans withdrew and the Canadians entered Apeldoorn on the 17th. At Otterloo part of the retreating German force blundered into Canadian 5th Armoured Division's H.Q. to cause the utmost confusion. A violent struggle ensued in which everybody joined. 24 (Cdn.) Fd. Amb. became involved. However, things sorted themselves out ultimately and on the 18th the division completed its drive to the Zuider Zee.

For the initial thrust by 49th Division and Cdn. 11th Inf. Bde. 24 (Cdn.) Fd. Amb. did not open an A.D.S. but evacuated directly to a British field ambulance. On April 4, 4 (Cdn.) C.C.S., with F.S.U. and F.T.U. attached, opened near Nijmegen to receive casualties from Cdn. 11th Inf. Bde. as well as those from 49th Division. Exhaustion and venereal disease cases were sent to 1 Canadian Exhaustion Unit or to 1 Canadian V.D.T.U. which were with 10 (Cdn.) F.D.S. near Nijmegen.

For the drive of Canadian 1st Division towards Apeldoorn each field ambulance formed C.C.Ps. for its brigade while 9 (Cdn.) Fd. Amb. provided a divisional A.D.S. in Gorssel from April 9–17. Priority I and II cases were evacuated to 3 (Cdn.) C.C.S. in Lochem and the rest to 2 (Cdn.) C.C.S. in 's Heerenberg. On April 13, 2 (Cdn.) F.D.S. crossed the Ijssel and on the following day, when F.S.Us. and F.T.U. arrived, established an A.S.C. for Priority I and II cases. The evacuation line was thus shortened from seven to two and a half hours. Priority III cases were now sent to 3 (Cdn.) C.C.S. in Lochem. The advance of the division now became exceedingly rapid. 9 (Cdn.) Fd. Amb. opened an

A.D.S. in Apeldoorn on April 17 and on the following day moved forward to a point north-east of Barneveld. 4 (Cdn.) Fd. Amb. then moved into Apeldoorn to serve as a recovery centre for the minor sick.

To cover Canadian 5th Armoured Division drive from Arnhem to the Zuider Zee, 7 (Cdn.) Lt. Fd. Amb. opened an A.D.S. in Arnhem on April 15. Casualties were evacuated therefrom over the Ijssel by a bridge, over the Neder Rijn by ferry and thence to 4 (Cdn.) C.C.S. in Nijmegen. The journey took two and a half hours by day and three hours by night. The opening of a pontoon bridge at the ferry site shortened the time to one hour. 13 (Cdn.) F.D.S. moved into Arnhem on the 16th and opened an A.S.C. which during the first two days of the operation admitted 65 casualties of which 32 required surgical intervention. Many of these were from the affair at Otterloo where 24 (Cdn.) Fd. Amb. had established an A.D.S. on April 16.

As the division advanced, 7 (Cdn.) Lt. Fd. Amb. opened its A.D.S. in Barneveld on the 18th and a light A.D.S. in Putten, some eight miles further north in the afternoon of the same day. During the rest of the operation Priority I and II cases continued to be evacuated to the A.S.C. in Arnhem and the rest to 3 Cdn. G.H. which had opened in Marienboom, near Nijmegen, on the 7th.

By April 18 Canadian I Corps was in position on an arc running from Harderwijk on the Ijsselmeer, through Barneveld to Renkum on the Neder Rijn. By April 21, 2 (Cdn.) F.D.S. had taken over a German military hospital in Apeldoorn from 5 (Cdn.) Fd. Amb. which then assumed responsibility for holding the minor sick in the area. This arrangement left 4 (Cdn.) Fd. Amb. free for normal operational deployment and so on April 29 this unit moved to Nieuw-Milligen and there opened a M.I. Room and C.C.P. whence casualties were evacuated to the A.D.S. of 9 (Cdn.) Fd. Amb. still located north-east of Barneveld.

On the 28th a truce came into effect on Canadian I Corps' front. Canadian 1st Division was thereafter employed in containing the German formations in western Holland. Canadian 5th Armoured Division then assisted in the clearing of north-east Holland by rounding up the German forces in and around Delfzijl. This task was completed by May 2. The medical units of the division provided cover for this operation by opening respectively at Groningen (7 (Cdn.) Lt. Fd. Amb.) on April 22 and in Ten Boer (24 (Cdn.) Fd. Amb.) on April 26. Evacuation was to 13 (Cdn.) F.D.S. now in Beilen, Priority III cases being sent on from there to 6 Cdn. G.H. in Ootmarsum.

In Canadian I Corps area 5 (Cdn.) C.C.S. opened in Harskamp, three miles north of Otterloo, on April 23. Corps casualties continued to be evacuated through 5 (Cdn.) C.C.S. (corps C.C.S.) to the Nijmegen group of hospitals. In Canadian II Corps area 3 (Cdn.) C.C.S. opened in Borger, near Sögel, on April 23 and 88 B.G.H. had moved to Cloppenburg east of Sögel.

Casualties arriving at the ambulance control post at 3 Cdn. G.H. were directed to the appropriate medical unit. Evacuation rearwards of Nijmegen was the responsibility of A.D.M.S. 4 L. of C. S.A. The appointment of an officer responsible for the arrangements in connexion with evacuation from the Nijmegen hospitals had resulted in better co-ordination of air and rail evacuation and had assisted in keeping the forward medical units cleared of evacuable casualties. The policy of keeping Army C.C.Ss. and hospitals clear of all cases except those unfit to be moved was thus retained. Cases expected to recover within forty-two days were held at the base hospitals in Holland and Belgium.

On April 21 Canadian 2nd and 3rd Divisions, being relieved by Canadian 5th Armoured Division in north-east Holland, moved to positions on the left of the Polish Armoured Division, Canadian 3rd Division taking over from the Poles responsibility for the section of the front west of the River Ems and preparing to cross the river and move on Leer, Aurich and Emden. Canadian 2nd Division prepared to relieve pressure on the flank of Second Army further east. The attack on Leer, begun on April 28, required that there should be an assault crossing of the River Leda. In order that casualties might be evacuated as speedily as possible, 23 (Cdn.) Fd. Amb. opened a C.E.P. and a C.D.P. on either side of the river to evacuate from the C.C.Ps. with the infantry brigades. All casualties were taken from the C.D.P. to the A.D.S. of 22 (Cdn.) Fd. Amb. which sent on the seriously wounded to 2 (Cdn.) C.C.S. in Meppen. Leer was cleared by May 1 when 23 (Cdn.) Fd. Amb. moved in to establish an A.D.S. in a school building. This A.D.S. served the whole division.

On May 3, 22 (Cdn.) Fd. Amb. moved forward to Bagband, ten miles north-east of Leer to provide medical cover for the division in its attack upon Aurich. 14 (Cdn.) Fd. Amb. meanwhile had moved to Leer and 7 (Cdn.) F.D.S. was now in Aschendorf, still serving as a divisional recovery centre.

Canadian 2nd Division's assignment was to relieve the flanking formations of Second Army during the attack on Bremen and to form the northern jaw of a pincer movement aimed at that city. It was also ordered to take the city of Oldenburg. The division began to move on April 18 and casualties *en route* were collected at a light A.D.S. of 18 (Cdn.) Fd. Amb. in Herzlake and evacuated thence to 2 (Cdn.) C.C.S. in Meppen. By the 21st the take-over from the flanking units of Second Army was complete and the necessary medical cover provided. 11 (Cdn.) Fd. Amb. opened an A.D.S. in Cloppenburg on April 19. On the 21st, 4 (Cdn.) F.D.S. established a divisional recovery centre just west of Ahlhorn and 18 (Cdn.) Fd. Amb. opened its A.D.S. just to the north of the same town, whereupon 11 (Cdn.) Fd. Amb. in Cloppenburg closed. Only slight opposition was encountered and the bulk of the wounds that were endured were due to mine or booby-trap.

By the 23rd Kirchatten, on the road south of Oldenburg was in Canadian hands. A.D.Ss. were opened successively as the advance continued, the rear one closing in preparation for a move through those in front of it. When 88 B.G.H. opened in Cloppenburg on April 25 casualty evacuation was greatly eased for the evacuation line was shortened by about thirty miles. It was shortened still further on the following day when 21 (Cdn.) F.D.S. established an A.S.C. near 4 (Cdn.) F.D.S. now in Delmenhorst.

As Canadian 2nd Division drove towards Oldenburg resistance became more severe. 10 (Cdn.) Fd. Amb. opened its A.D.S. in Kirchatten on the 28th and on the 29th 11 and 18 (Cdn.) Fd. Ambs. opened in Falkenburg. On the morning of May 3, 10 (Cdn.) Fd. Amb., which had moved up into the Oldenburg Forest on the 2nd, opened its A.D.S. in the southern part of Oldenburg. The remainder of the city was cleared during the afternoon whereupon this A.D.S. moved into the centre of the city and 11 and 18 (Cdn.) Fd. Ambs. opened north of the city in preparation for the drive to the sea.

During this period, April 21–May 4, the medical units of the division were not hard pressed though the pace of the advance, the ceaseless rain and the lengthening of the evacuation line had made their tasks difficult. The total divisional casualties evacuated between April 21 and May 4 were 925, 235 being due to enemy action. The most difficult day for the medical units was April 26 when, during the thrust towards Oldenburg from Delmenhorst, 127 casualties were evacuated.

Following the capitulation, the Canadian divisions remained where they were at the time of the cessation of hostilities, Canadian 2nd Division around Oldenburg, Canadian 4th Armoured Division around Bad Zwischenahn and Canadian 3rd Division around Aurich. By May 13 Canadian 2nd Division had congregated all German wounded P.o.W. into one hospital in Oldenburg and had begun to take charge of the areas occupied by the other two Canadian divisions and to assume the responsibilities of Canadian II Corps in this corps' area. By May 22 these responsibilities included the supervision of some 9,000 German hospital beds. On the 29th the advance party of the German Twenty-fifth Army arrived from Holland. The Germans were made responsible for the care of their own troops on the line of march from Holland to Germany and for the care of their own sick and wounded being transferred to Germany. Canadian 2nd Division Area received between 5,000 and 10,000 German troops a day plus about 150 sick and wounded. Those likely to recover within a reasonable time were retained on the mainland while hospitals on the Frisian Islands were used for long-term convalescents

THE LIBERATION OF HOLLAND

and amputees. Canadian medical officers stationed at staging points along the various routes taken by these returning Germans directed and co-ordinated the movement of the sick and wounded among them. By the end of June Canadian 2nd Division, now u/c XXX Corps, had supervision of 31 German hospitals plus six trains that were being used as hospitals, a total of 18,000 beds and 13,000 patients.

On July 11, Canadian 2nd Division handed over to Canadian 3rd Division, which, having been reconstructed, had become Canadian Army Occupation Force, and moved into Holland. All the divisional medical units moved to the vicinity of Utrecht. By the end of the month of September Canadian 2nd Division's medical units had either been disbanded or else were in process of returning to Canada.

Canadian 4th Armoured Division in the area of Bad Zwischenahn handed over to Canadian 2nd Division on May 26 and moved back to the vicinity of Almelo in Holland. 12 (Cdn.) Lt. Fd. Amb. supervised a staging camp at Denekamp for wounded Germans being returned to their own country. On June 18, 17 (Cdn.) Lt. Fd. Amb. of Canadian 1st Armoured Brigade joined the division to be disbanded on August 18. The division moved back to Amersfoort in September; its medical personnel with low priorities in respect of the date of their discharge were transferred to Canadian 3rd Division. By the end of the year this division, which had secured a very proud record, had been disbanded.

Canadian 1st Division, when hostilities ceased, was poised for a drive towards Utrecht. After the armistice the division advanced on this axis to ensure that German stragglers were rounded up and congregated into five selected main camp areas. During the move a number of German hospitals and P.o.W. camps were overrun. The German medical staff and patients were concentrated into three of the larger hospitals.

The German troops returning from Holland to Germany were examined by their own medical officers, under Canadian supervision, and all fit to march were started on their way. Staging camps were established and each group of soldiers was accompanied by a German medical officer and ambulances were provided for the evacuatiou of such as broke down on the march. By June 7 all fit German troops had been moved out of Holland and a beginning had been made of the disposal of the inmates of hospitals. On June 26 Canadian 1st Division moved into a concentration area around Utrecht and began its own disbandment. By September 15 the division had ceased to exist.

On May 3 it was decided to spread Canadian 5th Armoured Division throughout the three northern provinces of Holland, Friesland, Groningen and Drenthe, as soon as hostilities ceased. The problems that would face its medical services were the evacuation of Allied personnel from German hospitals in these provinces and the concentration into a certain number of selected hospitals of German sick and wounded. The number of Allied personnel discovered was small and the concentration of German sick and wounded into hospitals in Zuidlaren, Steenwijk and Leeuwarden was straightforward. On May 25 the first convoy carrying German casualties left Zuidlaren for Aurich and by June 15 all except six seriously ill patients, who were transferred to 6 Cdn. G.H. in Zuidlaren, had been moved out. The disbandment of the divisional medical units began on June 30 and soon was complete.

In mid-May, when Canadian 3rd Division moved back into Holland, a new formation known as Canadian 3rd Division, Canadian Army Occupation Force, was created alongside the original 3rd Division. Volunteers, men with low priority scores in respect of the date of their discharge and reinforcements from the United Kingdom who had not seen service on the Continent were used to build up this reconstituted Canadian 3rd Division. For a time there were two A.Ds.M.S. dealing with the medical affairs of the two formations. On July 8 the new Canadian 3rd Division (C.A.O.F.—Canadian Army Occupation Force) moved into Germany and the old Canadian 3rd Division proceeded to disband itself.

By the end of July Canadian First Army became known officially as Canadian Forces in the Netherlands. Among the first of the Army medical units to leave Canadian First Army were 39 and 88 B.G.Hs. with their attached surgical and transfusion units which had been with the Canadians since the days of the Normandy bridgehead. After these had gone, and except for an ambulance car company, only Canadian medical units remained with Canadian First Army. By the end of June seven Canadian F.T.Us., eleven F.S.Us., two exhaustion units and one F.D.S. had been disbanded. On June 25 Canadian II Corps handed over its remaining medical units to Canadian First Army as did Canadian I Corps at the end of the month. It had been decided that all Canadian medical units would be disbanded on the Continent, none returning to Canada intact. By September 7 Canadian Forces in the Netherlands had under command, exclusive of the divisional medical units and those with the Canadian Army Occupation Force, six C.C.Ss. two F.D.Ss., six field hygiene sections, three V.D.T.Us., one advanced depot of medical stores, two mobile bacteriological laboratories, one mobile hygiene laboratory, eight P.A.Cs. and two general hospitals.

Of the general hospitals 2, 10 and 12 Cdn. G.Hs. remained in Ghent, Turnhout and St. André until disbanded, 2 and 10 in September, 12 in November 1945. 20 Cdn. G.H. moved from Antwerp to Turnhout in March and remained there until it was disbanded in September. 21 Cdn. G.H. moved from Mesnières-en-Bray to St. Omer on January 9, 1945, and remained there until proceeding to Turnhout where it was disbanded on September 10. 7 Cdn. G.H. had been moved from Martigny to Turnhout in November and was moved again to Bassum. Because of the persistent rocket attacks on Antwerp 6 and 8 Cdn. G.Hs.

had to be moved in December to St. Michielsgestel. 8 was disbanded in May. 16 Cdn. G.H. moved from Oost Dunkerke to St. Michielsgestel on April 12 and to Sögel on April 25. During March, 1, 3 and 5 Cdn. G.Hs. reached Canadian First Army from Italy. 5 Cdn. G.H. opened in Turnhout on March 25; it was disbanded there on September 12. 1 Cdn. G.H. opened in the Nijmegen hospital area at the end of March. In May it took over the patients of other Canadian hospitals as these were disbanded and by December 1945 it had become the only Canadian general hospital under the command of the Canadian Forces in the Netherlands. It was disbanded on January 18, 1946. 3 Cdn. G.H. relieved 88 B.G.H. in Tilburg on March 15. On April 5 this 200-bed unit moved up to Marienboom, near Nijmegen. On May 9 it moved to Apeldoorn where it remained until July 17 when it was disbanded.

7 and 16 Cdn. G.Hs. were the two hospitals that were included in C.A.O.F. They remained in Europe until 1946. 7 Cdn. G.H. moved from Turnhout to Bassum on May 1 where it admitted 1,236 patients, including 556 civilians released from concentration camps in the area and liberated military personnel from no less than eight European countries. Most of those from the concentration camps were suffering from severe malnutrition and among them were 31 deaths. 35 per cent. of the civilian patients admitted were found to be suffering from respiratory tuberculosis. On May 25, 7 Cdn. G.H. closed, handing its patients over to 8 B.G.H. In June it moved up to Hahn opening there on the 20th. On July 3 it moved again to Sanderbusch where the unit functioned as a garrison hospital. It was closed on May 23, 1946.

16 Cdn. G.H. moved to Sögel in April and admitted civilians and Allied military personnel from concentration and P.o.W. camps. During the month of June it treated some 15,000 released P.o.W. of whom 12,770 were Russians, 1,989 Poles and the remainder representatives of seven other nationalities. This task being finished, the hospital moved to Oldenburg in August where it was reduced to a 200-bed unit and served Canadian 3rd Division (Canadian Army Occupation Force). On March 28, 1946, it left Germany for the United Kingdom where it was disbanded.

Much is to be learnt concerning the differences between the first six months of this campaign, which included the assault landings, the bitter struggle in the bridgehead, the break-out and pursuit and the clearance of the Scheldt and the last five months during which the strength of the German military machine became speedily and progressively diminished, from the differences in the numbers of the killed and wounded Canadians in these two periods.

The figures in Table 51 relate to Canadians and, moreover, to Canadians admitted to hospital. They show that the major Canadian medical installations treated 83,943 Canadian casualties, battle and otherwise. In addition, over 60,000 Allied personnel were treated in Canadian medical units during this campaign, a total of about 150,000.

TABLE 51

Canadian Casualties during the Campaign

June 6–December 31
    Fatalities . . 8,140 including 7,753 killed in action or died of wounds.
    Wounded . . 23,355

January 1–May 31
    Fatalities . . 3,271 including 2,976 killed in action or died of wounds.
    Wounded . . 9,973

Hospital admissions for causes other than enemy action

1944		1945	
June	362	January	5,145
July	1,462	February	5,390
August	3,646	March	5,828
September	2,680	April	6,681
October	4,759	May	6,463
November	3,875		
December	4,160		

The Canadian Government had agreed in December 1944 that Canada should contribute one division, about 25,000 men, to the occupation forces when hostilities ceased. As has been stated the division chosen was a new creation built around Canadian 3rd Division. By July 11, 1945, this new division had assumed its responsibilities. Its medical component consisted of five F.D.Ss., one of them a British unit, one field hygiene section, eighteen R.M.Os., one company of a motor ambulance convoy and two general hospitals. Each R.M.O. established a sick-bay of 10 beds, holding sick and injured expected to recover within forty-eight hours. The F.D.S. had forty beds and could hold its patients up to fourteen days. General hospitals held patients likely to recover within six weeks, discharging their patients to the divisional reception centre or returning them to their units.

During November a new war establishment for the two general hospitals, 7 and 16 Cdn. G.Hs., was approved. 7 became a 600-bed with a 100-bed expansion; 16 a 200-bed.

The G.O.C. division was also Military Governor of the area and so the A.D.M.S. was medical adviser to the military governor as well as to the G.O.C. The divisional medical services were called upon to deal

THE LIBERATION OF HOLLAND

with problems arising from the presence in the area of large numbers of fit Wehrmacht personnel and of large numbers of convalescent German soldiers. Other problems were such as related to the restoration of the civil medical and sanitary services of the area.

In December 1945 the Canadian Government decided that the Canadian troops of the Occupation Force should be withdrawn, beginning in April 1946. When this happened 52nd (Lowland) Division took over from Canadian 3rd Division (C.A.O.F.). On March 20, 1946, the first of the F.D.Ss. moved to a transit camp at Delmenhorst *en route* for the United Kingdom. By May 15 all the Canadian medical units had been closed and were on their way out of the country.

CHAPTER 9

THE OCCUPATION OF GERMANY AND THE END OF THE WAR IN EUROPE

(i)

Operation 'Eclipse' (Second Army)

THIS operation dealt with certain aspects of the advance into Germany and with the occupation of that country following the surrender. It was divided into three phases:

1. The advance into Germany, this proceeding as a purely military operation during which D.Ds.M.S. corps were responsible for all medical matters within their corps boundaries.
2. The period between the completion of this operational advance and the redeployment into National Zones, during which static corps districts were established. Corps H.Qs. were responsible for all dealings with the German Army and civil administration. Medical aspects of the civil administration were dealt with by D.Ds.M.S. corps through the appropriate representative of Military Government. All matters of policy regarding the German Army and civil medical administration were referred to H.Q. (Medical) Second Army so as to ensure uniformity and co-ordination.
3. The period after permanent corps districts had been established. Co-ordination of policy and action now became the responsibility of Zone H.Q.

THE TASKS OF THE ARMY MEDICAL SERVICES

(a) The medical care of the British and Allied troops under 21 Army Group.

In the initial phase of the operation few hospitals other than the 200-bed were in the forward zone. Air evacuation was the rule. Rail evacuation across the Rhine was impracticable. 600-bed hospitals were moved forward as soon as possible.

(b) The medical care of Allied P.o.W. and internees.

An organisation (P.W.X.) to deal with these was established at

S.H.A.E.F. and this had representatives at all levels down to and including corps.

Responsibility for the control, maintenance and evacuation of the P.o.W. and internees, both before and after the signing of the Instrument of Surrender, was that of the commander of the formation in the area in which they were discovered. U.S. and British internees were treated as released P.o.W. P.o.W. who had failed to comply with the 'stay put' order were treated as Displaced Persons until 'I' Branch had passed them as genuine P.o.W.

When a P.o.W. camp or hospital was overrun, D.D.M.S. corps immediately notified H.Q. Second Army, giving details of location, numbers, existing medical arrangements, numbers and types of medical personnel, numbers of sick and wounded and of the arrangements made for their care. Corps were responsible for providing medical personnel and equipment for P.o.W. camps and for the evacuation of the sick and wounded. Medical officers placed in charge of these camps acted as agents of the P.W.X. organisation and dealt with the representatives of this organisation at corps level and also with P.W.X. liaison detachments.

Corps were responsible for the formation of corps collecting centres for the P.o.W. and for the provision of medical staffs for them. An Army transit camp was established, A.D.M.S. Army Tps. being responsible for the provision of medical and hygiene services therein.

Where German medical personnel had remained at duty they were directed to continue their work, save in those cases in which, in the opinion of the D.D.M.S. concerned, such continuance was for any reason undesirable.

U.S. and British sick and wounded P.o.W. were evacuated along the usual medical channels to the United Kingdom. Other Allied P.o.W. were grouped by nationality and evacuated to their own countries whenever arrangements for their reception had been made by the governments concerned.

(c) The supervision and control of the medical administration of the German Army, para-military organisations and other elements of the German armed forces not controlled by the R.N. or R.A.F.

The purpose of this was to ensure the efficient and economical operation of the German Army Medical Services, to control the disposal of medical stores and equipment and to regulate the rate of disbandment or conversion to a civil status so that the medical requirements of the German armed forces were met.

(d) The seizure and control of medical stores, equipment and property, including hospitals of the German military medical services, except those required by, and under the control of, the R.N. and R.A.F.

A zone pool of medical stores visiting teams was formed. Each team consisted of a Q.M., a Q.M.S. interpreter and a driver with a 15 cwt. G.S. truck. Particular attention was given to equipment and drugs of special value in the war against Japan—e.g. anti-malarials, insecticides, disinfectants, sulphaguanidine, X-ray and laboratory equipment.

(e) The maintenance of close liaison with the Public Health section of Military Government, especially in connexion with:

1. The control of infectious and communicable disease.
2. The hospitalisation and medical care of D.Ps. and refugees.
3. The restoration of water and sewage systems.
4. The restoration of an efficient civil medical service.
5. The provision of adequate hospital services.
6. The early restoration of civil laboratory services.

The Military Government Branch was responsible for all civil public health matters.

The ways in which these most onerous tasks were tackled can best be illustrated by reference to the activities of Second Army, I Corps District, VIII Corps and 15th Division.

Second Army. Medical Administrative Plan for the Final Deployment of Formations to their Occupation Areas

The basic allotment of G.H.Q. and Army medical units to each corps district would be:

General hospital (600 or 1,200 beds)	1
,, ,, (600)	1
,, ,, (200)	1
C.C.S.	1
Light field ambulance.	1
F.D.Ss.	2
F.S.Us.	3

(D.Ds.M.S. corps were warned that demands for medical units for the Far East and the withdrawal of personnel for demobilisation would inevitably necessitate some reduction in this allotment at some later date.)

The medical holding policy would be:

General

Field ambulances and F.D.Ss. would hold minor sick and casualties up to ten days.

THE OCCUPATION OF GERMANY

200-bed hospitals and C.C.Ss. would hold cases up to one month's expectancy of hospital treatment. C.C.Ss. would function as station hospitals.

Special Cases

It was the intention that in each corps district there would be one central hospital with facilities for E.N.T., Skin, V.D., psychiatric and possibly orthopaedic cases.

Army Troops V.D.T.C. would remain attached to the hospital in Celle.

ALLOTMENT OF SPECIALISTS

District Hospital	Physician	Surgeon	V.D.	E.N.T.	Ophthalmologist	Neurologist	Dermatologist	Psychiatrist	Anaesthetist	Pathologist	Radiologist	Totals
L. of C.												
*105	—	1	1	—	1	—	—	1	—	—	—	4
*106	—	1	2	1	—	—	—	—	—	—	—	4
*108	—	1 Gyn.	—	1	—	—	1	1	—	—	—	4
*111	—	1	1	—	1	1	—	—	—	—	—	4
XXX Corps (plus corps psychiatrist)												
†8	1	—	1	1	—	—	—	—	—	—	—	3
†74	1	—	1	—	1	—	—	—	—	—	—	3
†121	1	—	—	1	1	—	—	—	—	—	—	3
*29	—	1	1	—	—	—	1	1	—	—	—	4
VIII Corps (plus corps psychiatrist)												
†9 (or 67)	1	—	2	—	1	—	—	—	—	—	—	4
*94	—	1	1	1	1	—	—	—	—	—	—	4
*96	—	1	1	—	—	—	1	1	—	—	—	4
I Corps (plus corps psychiatrist)												
†25	1	—	1	—	1	—	—	1	—	—	—	4
†39	1	—	1	1	1	—	—	—	—	—	—	4
*6	—	1	1	1	—	—	1	—	—	—	—	4
*23 (under 21 A. Gp. control)	—	1	1 Berlin	1	1	—	—	—	—	—	—	4
* 1200-bed hospitals have basically in addition to above	1	1	—	—	—	—	—	—	1	1	1	—
† 600-bed hospitals have basically in addition to above	—	1	—	—	—	—	—	—	1	1	1	—

XII Corps V.D.T.C. would remain attached to 94 B.G.H. in Hamburg.

VIII and XXX Corps would arrange that their corps V.D.T.Cs. were attached to suitable hospitals in the corps areas.

Psychiatric cases. The Army psychiatrist would remain at the hospital in Celle.

XII Corps psychiatrist would remain attached temporarily to 94 B.G.H.

VIII and XXX Corps would arrange for, say, 20–30 hospital beds to be reserved for psychiatric cases under treatment by the corps psychiatrist, who would remain attached to a hospital in the corps district.

General

Before Hamburg became fully established as a medical base, evacuation of cases of from 6 weeks to 3 months expectancy of hospital treatment (and of cases for which special treatment facilities did not exist in Army Area) would continue to be to the L. of C. Evacuation would be by road to the hospitals in Hamburg, Lüneburg, Celle or Bassum. Full use would be made of air evacuation for cases requiring evacuation to the L. of C. Air evacuation would continue to be available from:

B.156 at Lüneburg	83 Gp. R.A.F.
Schleswig or Lübeck	83 Gp. R.A.F.
B.118 at Celle	84 Gp. R.A.F.
B.111 at Ahlhorn	84 Gp. R.A.F.

Ambulance train evacuation would be restricted to cases unsuitable for evacuation by air. Initially the ambulance railhead would be at Lüneburg, with halts at Celle and Hanover. A.D.M.S. 8 Base Sub-area would despatch by ambulance car direct to ambulance R.H. at Lüneburg any cases for rail evacuation. Requests for evacuation by ambulance train would be made to the Medical Branch H.Q. Second Army, where requirements would be co-ordinated before being submitted to Med. Evac. 21 Army Group and Q Mov. (Rail).

After the Hamburg medical base had become fully established it was to be expected that air evacuation would be substantially reduced and that evacuation from Hanover would be by ambulance train, with halts at Celle and Lüneburg, to Hamburg for evacuation to the United Kingdom by hospital ship or carrier.

It was intended that corps districts would be fully responsible for the organisation and control of all ambulance car evacuation within their areas. For this purpose 111 M.A.C. would remain u/c XXX Corps, and 227 M.A.C. u/c VIII Corps. One platoon of 257 A.C.C. would be allotted

THE OCCUPATION OF GERMANY

to 8 Base Sub-area, one platoon to XXX Corps and two platoons would remain in XXX Corps area—Lüneburg–Celle—as Army reserve. 302 M.A.C. might be withdrawn from Army at an early date.

P.o.W. and German Military Medical Installations

German military hospitals and lazarette would continue to be controlled by British medical units. Large numbers of German wounded would still have to be evacuated from Holland, Belgium and Denmark. It would be essential that the British medical units controlling the German military medical installations should ensure the immediate discharge of cases no longer requiring hospital treatment so that the maximum number of hospital beds was available to receive further patients transferred from these countries. The reserve lazarette and civil hospitals with military wings would not be closed without written authority from D.D.M.S. Second Army. Corps districts would be notified weekly, seven days in advance, of the number of German sick and wounded that they would be required to accept in existing German hospitals.

Allied P.W.X. and D.Ps.

The following hospital facilities would be available for ex-P.o.W. and D.Ps.

Osnabrück (Eversheide)	Jugoslavs. 75 beds
Nienburg	Mixed. Medical. 200 beds
Bad Rehburg	Mixed. Tuberculosis and surgical. 150 beds
Fallingbostel	Russian. 2,000 beds
Weisendorf	Italian. 120 beds expanding to 220
Celle	Western European. 250 beds
	Polish. 300 beds
Bomlitz	Western European. 300 beds
Flensburg	Those from Denmark
Husum	For D.Ps.
Schleswig	Eastern European
Lübeck	Eastern European

A hospital transit centre for medical evacuation of west-bound Allied ex-P.o.W. and D.Ps., chronic sick and casualties would be established in Celle by 21 Lt. Fd. Amb. The actual evacuation would be controlled by Medical, Second Army.

French patients would be evacuated by French aircraft from B.118 and B.156 except for those unfit to travel by air. These would be evacuated by rail.

Belgian and Dutch patients would be evacuated by special ambulance trains.

East-bound Allied ex-P.o.W. chronic sick and casualties would be retained in corps districts in existing P.W.X. hospitals until such time as their evacuation could be arranged. There would be no rearward evacuation of the east-bound sick. If additional hospital accommodation became necessary this would have to be organised under corps arrangements.

Belsen Hospital Area

Because of the complex nature of the Army Medical Services' commitments in this area it was recommended that the general supervision of it should remain an Army responsibility and, later, a responsibility of 21 Army Group itself.

13 Convalescent Depot

Except for purposes of local administration this would remain u/c Second Army and later u/c 21 Army Group. It would be located north of Hamburg to serve VIII and XXX Corps and 8 Base Sub-area.

Denmark

The medical administration of Denmark would be under the direct control of A.D.M.S. Denmark, H.Q. 1st Para. Brigade. The following medical units would be under his control.

   32 C.C.S., less light section, at Snoghøj with one section of 257 A.C.C. attached.
   14 F.S.U. and Lt. Sec. 32 C.C.S. at Copenhagen for Zeeland.
   15 F.S.U. and 56 F.S.U. attached 32 C.C.S. for Jutland and Fun.

Arrangements for the evacuation of German sick and convalescents from Denmark would be controlled by Second Army. Corps Districts would be informed by Second Army concerning the reception of cases as and when necessary. Later the control of these evacuation arrangements would be taken over by 21 Army Group.

Blood Supplies

Supplies would be organised by corps districts and D.Ds.M.S. would make the necessary arrangements for corps panels of volunteer donors.

H.Q. 'Y' Blood Bank, together with F.T.Us., would probably be withdrawn under 21 Army Group arrangements in the near future. Until this happened these units would remain where they were.

Field Surgical Units

The following units would remain for the time being u/c Second Army.

   14, 15 and 56 F.S.Us. u/c 1st Para. Bde. for Denmark.
   33 and 54 F.S.Us. u/c VIII Corps.
   45 and 47 F.S.Us. u/c XXX Corps.
   13 and 55 F.S.Us. u/c Second Army (passing u/c XXX Corps later).

It was to be expected that further F.S.Us. would be withdrawn later. A request had been made for one F.S.U. per corps district plus one F.S.U. per 200-bed hospital, this being considered the minimum requirement.

Supply of Medical Equipment

8 Adv. Depot Med. Stores would remain in Celle for the time being but would move later to VIII Corps area, remaining subject to the technical control of Med. Second Army and later to Med. 21 Army Group.

9 Adv. Depot Med. Stores would remain in Lüneburg and shortly pass u/c XXX Corps. It would continue to supply XXX Corps medical units until 12 Base Depot of Medical Stores opened in Hamburg. Thereafter 9 Adv. Depot Med. Stores would become available for withdrawal, medical stores being drawn by general hospitals direct from 12 and 13 Base Depots.

The smaller medical units would continue to draw their supplies from the hospitals.

11 Adv. Depot Med. Stores in Burgdorf would be in charge of the centralisation of Wehrkreis Sanitatspark No. XI and would remain under the technical control of Second Army, later passing to 21 Army Group.

1 C.E.E.S. at Celle would remain the central collecting point for captured equipment from the area west of the Elbe and would continue to receive from outlying captured medical stores under corps control all medical stores required for the war against Japan. Technical control of this unit would remain with Second Army, later passing to 21 Army Group.

The Naval Medical Stores, Schloss Hagen, would be frozen and its contents remain under the control of Second Army as an Army reserve, later as a zone medical store.

Medical stores controlled by corps districts and A.D.M.S. Denmark would be:

VIII Corps	Flensburg, Rendsburg, Lübeck and Neustadt. It might be necessary to form a fifth store in Schleswig-Holstein when the hand-over from XII Corps to VIII Corps is completed.
XXX Corps	Winsen, Vilsen.

A.D.M.S., S.H.A.E.F. Mission Denmark, Randers, Velje and Copenhagen.

H.Q. Second Army, having completed its tasks as an operational formation was disbanded on June 24/25, 1945. H.Q. British Army of the Rhine—the occupation force—was then in process of formation and this was to replace not only H.Q. Second Army but also, on August 24/25, 1945, H.Q. 21 Army Group itself. The Medical Branch H.Q., 21 Army Group then became the medical branch of H.Q., B.A.O.R.

Immediately following the cessation of hostilities the Army Medical Services became much concerned with the supply of medical units and personnel for service in the Far East and with the consequences of the system of demobilisation that had been adopted. As the responsibilities of the medical services were distributed among the corps districts and as the task of providing care for the vast numbers of P.W.X., D.Ps. and German military casualties grew lighter and as the British armed forces on the Continent became smaller, it became possible to disband units as they became surplus to requirements and to distribute their personnel of low priority in respect of demobilisation among other units that were to be retained or to be ear-marked for service in the Far East.

As will have been noted, man-power was saved in the medical field by distributing medical officers on an area as opposed to a unit basis and by posting the advisers at H.Q. 21 Army Group to general hospitals to fill the posts of officers i/c divisions.

I CORPS DISTRICT

On April 3, H.Q. I Corps moved from Tilburg to Walbeck in Germany to take over the local administration from the Maas to the Rhine. Later this area was progressively increased (1) by the inclusion of the Rhine barrier zone from Wesel to Rees and the establishment of large D.P. camps in the areas of Haldern and Hamminkeln; (2) by the extension of the boundary to Borken on April 11; (3) by the handing over of the local administration of the above to 15 L. of C. Sub-area on April 14 and the move of corps H.Q. to Rhede on the 16th; (4) by the extension of the corps boundary to the Dortmund–Ems Canal, excluding Osnabrück and Münster, on the 17th; (5) by the taking over, on the 22nd, of the area comprising the Landkreise of Steinhurt, Ahaus and half of Nordhorn; (6) by the extension of the boundaries so that the corps area ran from the Maas in the west to beyond Minden in the east and south of the fringe of the Ruhr, and (7) the final extension which resulted in the corps district comprising the whole of Westphalia, the North Rhine Province and the Landkreise of Lippe and Schaumburg Lippe.

ORDER OF BATTLE I CORPS DISTRICT AS AT JUNE 30

	Came under command on
15 L. of C. Sub-area	April 7
308th A.A. Bde.	June 7
115th Indep. Inf. Bde.	April 2
19 L. of C. Sub-area	April 22
9th A.G.R.A.	,, 2
76th A.A. Bde.	,, 2
34th Tk. Bde.	,, 2

THE OCCUPATION OF GERMANY

	Came under command on
3rd Division	May 5
Belgian 1st Bde. Gp.	,, 15
49th Division	May 23
103rd A.A. Bde.	
53rd Division	June 4
17th A.G.R.A.	,, 2
Guards Armoured Division	June 15

Medical Units
 6, 9, 25, 77 and 86 B.G.Hs.
 23 C.C.S.
 6, 20, 26, and 33 F.D.Ss.
 13 F.S.U.
 36 F.T.U.
 8 Mob. Bact. Lab.
 6 and 22 Fd. Hyg. Secs.

DISEASES PREVALENT AMONG THE CIVIL POPULATION

The rural population and the inhabitants of the smaller towns were well fed, but in the large towns and cities malnutrition was common. The Public Health Officer of Military Government reported that among them there had been a recent marked increase in the incidence of pellagra and nutritional oedema.

There was a serious outbreak of typhoid in Bochum in June, 406 Germans and 101 Russians being stricken. There were 50 cases notified in Lippstadt and 74 in Ineschedt.

Diphtheria was very prevalent and 30 cases of poliomyelitis were found in Bad Pyrmont, just outside I Corps District.

MEDICAL CONTROL OF DISPLACED PERSONS

The slender resources of Military Government could never have hoped to cope with this problem and the work was, in fact, taken over by I Corps District, the Public Health Officer, Military Government acting as a staff officer (D.Ps.) to D.D.M.S.

There were over 700 D.P. camps with more than 750,000 D.Ps. to be looked after. Hospital accommodation was provided in special D.P. hospitals, in D.P. wings of German civil hospitals or in infectious diseases blocks. Medical officers were obtained from U.N.R.R.A., from among the D.Ps. and from the French and Belgian Army Medical Services. All were under the direct supervision of British S.M.Os. The admission rate for the D.Ps. was around 1 per cent.

Anti-typhus measures were instituted in all parts of the corps district.

Medical supplies were obtained from civil sources or from Military Government stocks.

As I Corps District enlarged, the commitment in respect of P.o.W., D.Ps. and German P.o.W. expanded.

P.W.X./D.P.
　　In camps . . . 750,000
　　In hospitals . . 20,000
P.o.W.
　　In cages . . . 210,000
　　In hospitals . . 40,000

(P.W.X. = Prisoners-of-war other than German)

The sick and wounded P.W.X./D.P. were congregated in German military hospitals (247 in all) and P.W.X./D.P. staffs installed.

The initial evacuation policy for P.W.X./D.P. was:

British/U.S.	Normal British channels.
Westbound	Ambulance trains to France and Belgium. Ambulance cars to Holland.
Russians	The Russians were unable to accept their own nationals.
Eastbound, other than Russian	No arrangements.

The fit among the German sick and wounded in P.o.W. hospitals were sent to the P.o.W. cage, the unfit but movable were transferred to the care of the local burgomaster, who was responsible for making arrangements for their boarding out.

Surplus German medical personnel were demobilised and returned to their home towns under A.A.G. arrangements.

VIII CORPS

After May 2 the medical units were mainly concerned with 'Eclipse' tasks. In every town and village large numbers of German wounded were found in hospitals and improvised hospitals. Many P.o.W. camps were discovered and also many 'Belsens' in miniature. The D.Ps. were quite uncontrollable; they were found on every farm and in every village and town. On the whole they were well fed, but usually lousy. Ambulance trains full of wounded, about 500 in each, were found standing in stations or stranded on the line. It became apparent that Schleswig-Holstein had been one of the main German hospital areas.

A miniature Belsen was uncovered at Neustadt, where 200 D.Ps., women and children, coming ashore in barges from sinking ships had been butchered on May 2. One woman was found still alive among them. 14 Lt. Fd. Amb. was sent to take over this camp, in which typhus was raging.

The first considerable aggregation of German wounded was found in Celle, but this was vastly overtopped by the large numbers in and

THE OCCUPATION OF GERMANY

around Molin and Ratzeburg (15,000), Lübeck (12,000), Neumünster (10,000), Rendsburg (5,000), Flensburg (10,000), and Wismar (20,000). By the end of June the corps had become burdened with about 120,000 German casualties in some 300 hospitals and had to expect that another 30,000 would come into the corps district from Denmark, Holland, Norway and from the east. The D.Ps. were sorted out into national groups. Vast stores of medical equipment were uncovered.

The German Control Section (2 officers and 2 clerks R.A.M.C.) arrived at corps H.Q. to reinforce the medical branch.

The medical stores were collected into three central depots in Flensburg, Rendsburg and Lübeck. A large marine medical depot in Schloss Hagen was 'frozen' by Second Army. All British troops, all P.o.W., all D.Ps. and all German P.o.W. on discharge from the P.o.W. concentration areas were dusted with D.D.T. (5 per cent.). No more than this could be done for the supply to corps was only 1,100 lb. per day. Three tons per day for two to three months were required.

The S.M.Os. appointed to 'Eclipse' tasks were appointed by divisions in divisional areas only and by corps in non-divisional areas.

Liaison with the R.N. and R.A.F. was maintained. It was found that although before the war the hospitals in Schleswig-Holstein had been predominantly naval, now 95 per cent. of the patients in the naval and Luftwaffe hospitals were army. The R.N. handed over these hospitals to the Army. The R.A.F. appeared to have no 'Eclipse' M.Os. so that the R.A.F. control of Luftwaffe hospitals was largely nominal.

In the hospitals the German medical staffs did the bulk of the work and the system of control that had been instituted functioned smoothly. The numbers of sick and wounded Germans coming into the corps district from Denmark and elsewhere were less than had been expected and the D.Ps. were soon reduced to the hard core of immovables, mainly Poles and those from south-east Europe.

Two P.o.W. concentration areas containing some 600,000 and 400,000 German troops respectively, were formed in the corps district. The medical control of their disbandment was provided by the Germans themselves under supervision.

As the corps became gradually converted to its static rôle as a corps district, 9 B.G.H. (600), 94 B.G.H. (1,200) and 81 B.G.H. (200) were placed under command, 81 being replaced in Rendsburg at the end of June by 67 B.G.H. (600).

LOCATIONS OF MEDICAL UNITS AT THE END OF JUNE

Unit	Attached Units	Location
67 B.G.H.	34 F.S.U. and 4 Mob. Bact. Lab.	Rendsburg

Unit	Attached Units	Location
32 C.C.S.	14, 15, 56 F.S.Us., 11 Med. Stores Recce. Team	Snoghøj
33 C.C.S.		Schleswig
34 C.C.S.	54 F.S.U., 31 F.T.U., V.D.T.C., Corps Psychiatrist	Strecknitz
1 F.D.S.	516 M.D.U.	Rendsburg
22 F.D.S.		Bad Segeberg
24 F.D.S.	517 M.D.U.	Kiel
14 Lt. Fd. Amb.		Neustadt
27 Fd. Hyg. Sec.		Lübeck
75 Fd. Hyg. Sec.		Neustadt
13 Con. Depot		Glückstadt
27 and 48 F.S.Us. attached 15th Div. for 'Eclipse' tasks		
13 Med. Stores Recce. Team attached 179 Fd. Amb. (11th Armd. Div.)		Flensburg
15 Med. Stores Recce. Team attached 153 Fd. Amb. (15th Div.)		Lübeck
510 M.D.U.		Kiel
204 F.D.C.		Lübeck
8 Adv. Depot Med. Stores		Celle
65 P.A.C.		Lübeck
227 M.A.C.		Malente
302 M.A.C.		Hamburg

15TH DIVISION

After the cessation of hostilities the divisional medical units visited and took under control members of the German armed forces for discipline, administration, rations and medical supplies and for treatment, guarding and discharge from hospital. P.o.W. cages were supervised and medical arrangements made for columns of P.o.W. passing through the divisional area and for formations coming in to surrender. Allied P.o.W. were cared for and their evacuation assisted, and since Military Government was not provided with suitable medical staff, medical arrangements for refugees and D.Ps. in their camps were made and the wasteful use of stores and petrol for medical purposes prevented. Dumps of medical stores were sought for, examined and guarded. Gradually much of the responsibility for many of these activities was placed upon the German medical services, under British supervision.

The clerical work in connexion with these tasks was literally enormous. A complete summary—*15th Division Medical 'Eclipse' Instructions*—was prepared by D.A.D.M.S. It included, in English and in German, orders for all German military hospitals, giving to each a war establishment of vehicles, and instituted a rationing system for petrol.

A team of British medical officers examined every patient in these

German hospitals and by discharging such as were fit soon reduced the hospital population to a manageable size. Such as were mobile were placed in the care of the local burgomaster for boarding out. The hospital population thereafter varied in size from 30,000 to nearly 50,000. S.S. patients were congregated in certain hospitals under guard. The different nationals were congregated in separate hospitals, as far as possible.

153 Fd. Amb. took over 'Eclipse' commitments in Lübeck, Travemünde and Bad Oldesloe. A C.R.S. was opened in Lübeck. There were some 50,000 D.Ps. in Lübeck and trainloads of German wounded arrived from all directions and without warning.

193 Fd. Amb. went with 46th Bde. to Kiel on May 11. The officer commanding became S.M.O. to the brigade. The unit was fully engaged in organising and supervising the work of the German naval medical services and of the P.o.W. and D.P. camps. 194 Fd. Amb. did similar work in Celle, Uelzen, Rohlsdorf and Schwerin, with companies in Kreise Hagenau and Ludwigslust. This unit discharged 7,278 German patients to the cages and 124 to burgomasters.

23 F.D.S. functioned in Lauenburg, the officer commanding acting as S.M.O. to 15th Divisional R.A. A company of 193 Fd. Amb. was also in this area with 27 F.S.U. and 48 F.S.U. Two C.R.Ss., one in Molin and the other in Geesthacht, with five and, later, three officers of field rank, were established so that this area was well provided for. But there was much to do; large numbers of German sick and wounded were coming into the area by train.

40 Fd. Hyg. Sec. undertook 'Eclipse' tasks in Lahde, Celle, Lüneburg, Geesthacht, Lübeck and Neustadt. 38,240 persons were dusted with A.L.63 up to June 8. Personnel of the unit supervised D.P. camps, repaired and constructed shower baths and generally controlled the sanitation of the area. Eleven O.Rs. R.A. were posted to the unit on June 20 for employment as a spraying team (residual D.D.T.) working under the supervision of a sanitary assistant.

(ii)

The Specialist Services

THE ARMY DENTAL SERVICE (SECOND ARMY)

During the swift advance from the Rhine to the Elbe and beyond it was not possible to do more than deal with the daily (dental) sick. The completion of treatment at a single visit was the aim. This work was magnified for the reason that in corps and army areas the sick parades at C.C.Ss. and general hospitals included large numbers of released P.o.W. from camps that had been overrun. The total sick rate in Second Army rose to 63 per 1,000 (it had been 34 per 1,000 following the break-out from the Normandy bridgehead). The ratio of dental personnel was now approximately 1 dental officer and 1 dental clerk orderly per 3,500 troops and 1 dental mechanic per 5,000.

During the assault crossing of the Rhine the sick rate among rearward units rose. Following the crossing rearward evacuation became difficult and emergency dental treatment had to be provided by the dental officers attached to the A.D.Ss. of the field ambulances on the right bank of the river. During the advance to the Elbe the sick rate fell, to rise again when fighting ceased, sick parades at dental units then averaging 30 patients a day. The sick rate in corps and army areas was at all times higher than that among divisional troops, many attendances being for preventive oral hygiene and the treatment of incipient caries.

The advance was associated with an increase in the demands for denture work of all kinds and with a corresponding rise in the output by the three M.D.Us. attached to each of the divisions.

In mid-April, 58 Fd. Dental Lab. had to be transferred from Second Army to L. of C. for the reason that transport for the unit could not be provided. The unit was in Helmond and its control by H.Q. Second Army had become increasingly difficult as the advance continued.

The incidence of acute ulcerative gingivitis/stomatitis dropped from 2·52/1,000/mensem in March to 1·43 in April, but owing to the rapid movement of formations in some cases the initiation of treatment was delayed and many severe cases had to be evacuated to the C.C.Ss.

5 M.F.S.U., having come u/c Second Army on February 19 to receive casualties from the Reichswald battle, remained with Army until the end. At Eindhoven it was attached to 86 B.G.H., at Wettringen to 25 B.G.H., at Sulingen to 84 B.G.H. and at Celle to 121 B.G.H. During the advance the unit was split into advanced and rear sections, less effective than when combined, in order to shorten the length of the line of evacuation. This division was necessary because the three corps were *en echelon* in a line almost parallel with the main axis of advance and almost a hundred miles in length.

The incidence of maxillo-facial casualties rose during the assault crossings of the Rhine, the Weser and the Aller. A high proportion of the wounds were caused by small-arms missiles, sniper and spandau fire.

Before the advance all dental units were instructed to provide themselves with a month's supply of consumable equipment. As the advance continued much German equipment, expendible and non-expendible, was uncovered and taken into use. Its quality was found to be variable.

The Army Dental Service entered upon this last phase of the campaign with an organisation and equipment that gave to Second Army a dental cover of a quality and comprehensiveness of the highest order. Its contribution to military effectiveness, though it cannot be measured, was surely immense. It was able to provide three M.D.Us. to each division, two to each corps for use with independent brigades and two to Army. The senior dental officer of the trio of M.D.Us. with a division, experienced in the tactical handling of these units, acted as an adviser to the A.D.M.S.

The following principles now governed the use of these M.D.Us.:

(a) During 'quiet' periods they were sited in the vicinity of field ambulance A.D.Ss. and worked in conjunction with the dental officers attached to these medical units.
(b) During battle they moved with the field ambulances and received denture work from the C.C.Ps., at which level the dental officers of the field ambulances were commonly employed.
(c) In the case of the M.D.Us. attached to brigade groups of armoured divisions, the M.D.U. was sited at rear divisional H.Q. It was not feasible to site them further forward because of the high mobility of the brigade groups and the tenuous nature of communications in the areas in which these were operating.

The field dental centres (operational) were distributed to provide 'stops' for the possible rearward drift of dental patients.

147 F.D.C. (Op.) Type B, with one dental mechanic and dental mechanical equipment, was sited at the main east–west bridge over the Maas at Well. 125 F.D.C. (Op.) Type A was sited at the other Maas bridge at Gennep. Denture work was carried out by the dental mechanic

TABLE 52

Army Dental Service. Summary of Work. June 1944–March 1945

	Attendances at Dental Units	New Dentures Supplied	Dentures Repaired
June 1944	6,470	219	377
July	28,016	1,358	1,847
Aug.	41,760	2,040	2,253
Sept.	46,354	2,123	2,293
Oct.	61,626	2,757	3,174
Nov.	63,313	2,862	2,875
Dec.	69,271	3,101	2,875
Jan. 1945	88,450	3,692	3,893
Feb.	80,347	3,375	3,175
Mar.	91,053	3,640	3,592
	576,660	25,167	26,354

with 147 F.D.C. 207 F.D.C. (Op.) Type B remained with 101 Rft. Group at 31 R.H.U. in Diest and Bourg-Léopold.

During the final phase A.D.D.S. was with Main H.Q. Second Army, an arrangement which continued to be most effective.

On June 24/25, D.D.D.S. H.Q. B.A.O.R. took over administrative control of all Second Army dental personnel and units.

THE ARMY TRANSFUSION SERVICE (21 ARMY GROUP)

At the end of March 'Y' Bank crossed the Maas to Weeze and a week later it moved across the Rhine to Rheine, keeping close to the main airstrip and the C.A.E.U. It took with it an extra refrigerator from base and was thus able to maintain three forward sections, each of which, because of the large areas it was likely to cover, was given in addition a small vehicle or M/C. As the Army overran North-west Germany the bank moved forward to Diepholz and then to Celle, its three sections moving ahead with corps as they spread rapidly over the wide areas of liberated territory. Consumption of blood was as high now as at any time since D-day; there was some sharp fighting and, in addition, much transfusion material was used on liberated Allied P.o.W. and a certain amount on the victims of the horror camps at Sandbostel and Belsen.

It was at this point that the great distances between the Bank and the base made it appear that a further movement of at least part of the base would be essential. Fortunately the use of air transport enabled a smooth and efficient supply to be maintained and postponed the need of a move until the sudden ending of hostilities rendered it unnecessary. Meanwhile, 'X' Bank, having moved into Nijmegen, continued to supply Canadian First Army, which had now turned back to the east and north and advanced into northern Holland. Distances here were nothing like as great and only one move by the Bank, from Nijmegen north to Almelo, was necessary to keep pace with the advances. Such then was the final set-out of the transfusion service when the campaign in Northwest Europe ended. Work continued, however, on a diminishing scale for some weeks after the official end of the fighting, mainly occasioned by road mines and booby-trap accidents, sporadic local fights between Allied troops and armed bands of the countless displaced persons of many nationalities and liberated Allied ex-prisoners-of-war, many of whom required a considerable amount of medical treatment before being repatriated.

Prior to being withdrawn from this theatre of war to provide and prepare reinforcements of personnel and equipment for the Far East (very few of which, fortunately, were required), several weeks were spent in making arrangements, similar to those previously made in Normandy, whereby medical units remaining with the occupying army were able to obtain all their transfusion requirements locally and provide their own supplies of whole blood. Transfusion units were withdrawn from the field and gradually disbanded, while 1 B.T.U. returned to the United Kingdom on August 4 and was in its turn also disbanded, having been in existence and on continuous active service from its inception in the Middle East five years previously.

FIELD TRANSFUSION UNITS

It is not possible to follow in detail the movements and dispositions of these units throughout the fighting. Being corps troops they were placed according to the wishes of D.D.M.S. corps and the general policy was to site them at the level of rear corps H.Q. with a C.C.S. Usually corps medical area consisted of two C.C.Ss. with one or more F.S.Us. and a transfusion unit each. These C.C.Ss. worked alternate shifts, either according to time or to numbers of cases admitted. The medical area was completed by a F.D.S. to deal with sick and lightly wounded cases so that the vast majority of admissions to C.C.Ss. were battle casualties requiring surgical treatment.

The C.C.Ss. carried two surgeons of their own and, in addition, had the surgical potential of one or more F.S.Us. added. This meant that surgeons could work a shift system with suitable rest periods, whereas the transfusion officers and orderlies had no such relief, being responsible for the whole of the pre-operative ward and the selection of cases for the ever-open theatre.

The new W.E. of a C.C.S. only allowed two G.D.Os., who were fully occupied in the reception and evacuation departments and the wards and, therefore, were not available to stand in for the transfusion officer. To get over this difficulty the B.T.U. maintained a pool of six officers who were attached to F.T.Us. in the sectors most heavily engaged, while the nursing orderlies of the C.C.S's. pre-operative ward supplied a certain amount of relief to the two orderlies of the F.T.U. This arrangement worked well and was incorporated in amendment No. 2 to the W.E. of a B.T.U., dated September 17, 1943, which allowed transfusion officers on a scale of two per corps for attachment to medical units.

Certain of the F.T.Us. were employed as parts of advanced surgical centres along with two or three F.S.Us. attached to a F.D.S. This scheme was not so successful as the C.C.S., its surgical and holding capacity being considerably less. It was much favoured in the Canadian Army and is of definite value during a phase of rapid advance, where it can be sent forward quickly to deal with urgent cases until first one and then another of the C.C.Ss. can be moved forward to establish a more complete medical centre.

Life in a F.T.U., as with all forward medical units, consisted of periods of intense activity when the pre-operative ward never seemed to be empty in spite of the number of cases sent to the theatre after resuscitation, and periods when the post-operative wards seemed to contain nothing but cases requiring further transfusion or gastric suction with intravenous replacement of fluids. Between these crises there might be a hurried packing and moving to a new site or long tedious intervals when only sporadic casualties or road accidents required attention. It was during such lulls that the B.T.U. tried, as far as possible, to recall units for a short period of rest and refitting at the base.

EXPERIENCES OF BATTLE

The total number of casualties incurred by 21 Army Group, excluding those killed, was 144,649. Of these approximately 12 per cent. were transfused by F.T.Us. using an average of 4·3 pints of intravenous protein fluid to each case, in the ratio of 2·6 of whole blood to 1·7 of plasma, or a proportion of blood to plasma of 1 : 0·6. These figures are derived from daily work sheets of F.T.Us. which were returned to advanced blood banks, which consolidated them and forwarded the results to H.Q. of the B.T.U., which had thus an accurate picture of the

TABLE 53

Casualties Transfused and total fluids used by all units
June 6, 1944–May 10, 1945

	Wounded	Blood	Plasma	Saline	Protein Fluid per 100 Wounded			Saline per 100 Wounded
					Blood	Plasma	Total	
Totals	144,649	60,590	66,781	103,952	42	46	88	72
Daily average	428	179	197	307				

Total of main Intravenous Fluids issued by 1 B.T.U.,
June 6, 1944–May 31, 1945

	Blood	Plasma	Glucose-Saline	Normal Saline	Glucose Solution
Total issues	90,975	88,653	133,857	60,097	19,246
Daily average	253	246	372	167	53

amount of material used and existing stocks in forward areas. The statistics for work done by F.T.Us. can therefore be regarded as accurate.

As regards general hospitals, figures available from monthly returns, which were submitted by the majority, but not all, of the hospitals, show that at least 7·5 per cent. of the total casualties were transfused in general hospitals, using an average of 2·3 pints of protein fluid per case; 1·3 of blood to 1 of plasma: a ratio of 1 : 0·8.

The difference in figures for blood used and blood issued, 30,000 bottles, is accounted for partly by return of over-age blood 18,000 bottles, issues to non-accounting units 1,500, R.A.F. medical units, certain Canadian hospitals and field medical units without transfusion officers.

It is impossible to give accurate figures of the amount of blood given to non-battle casualties, e.g. accidental injuries, P.o.W. and civilians but it was estimated that an over-all figure of 88 pints of protein per 100 battle casualties would include these and be reasonably accurate.

The amount of plasma used by the field ambulances brought the blood-plasma ratio to 1 : 1.

Field Transfusion Units. Of the 18,000-odd cases transfused by these units, the vast majority were done at C.C.S. level. An investigation was carried out with the help of 2nd Echelon to find out the fate of these cases. Available records showed that 75 per cent. of all cases transfused were alive; of the remaining 25 per cent. the large majority died at C.C.S. level.

TRANSFUSION AT DIVISIONAL LEVEL

Statistics are not available of the number of cases transfused by divisional units. These were supplied with dried plasma for the most part, though occasionally very small amounts of blood were available to them.

Travelling transfusions too were used on a considerable scale by these units, but with only a limited degree of success.

On the whole, there was a tendency, due to excessive enthusiasm, to overdo transfusion at very forward levels, sometimes to the detriment of sound first-aid treatment.

On several occasions it was necessary for the B.D.O. to visit field ambulances in certain divisions to point out the fact that resuscitation must not be divorced from surgery, and that to waste time in fully resuscitating a wounded man and then to evacuate him a considerable distance to a surgical centre was not good therapy. Incidentally, intravenous therapy under difficult conditions and by officers whose work did not allow of sufficient practice of transfusion, frequently increased the difficulty of later resuscitation by using up the available superficial veins. This was particularly true of travelling transfusions, a large percentage of which were not running at the end of the journey.

It was necessary finally for D.D.P. 21 Army Group to send out a directive urging field ambulance officers to curb their zeal for transfusion at this level and to concentrate on speedy evacuation.

STATISTICS OF WORK AND MATERIAL PREPARED BY I B.T.U.

Although the most important single activity of the B.T.U. was the receipt and distribution of whole blood, by far the greater part of its work concerned the local production of transfusion material and equipment. When the supply of whole blood is from outside the theatre, a very small part of the unit's man-power is required to deal with it. The incoming blood is received by a refrigerator vehicle with a driver-orderly on the main airfield and transferred to base refrigerators. It is advisable to detail the same orderly-drivers for this duty, as far as possible, as they get to know the organisations of the airfield, especially air freight reception departments, and also to acquire a knowledge of schedules of the different air services; it is most important that these become acquainted personally with their opposite numbers on the airfield staff and aircrews. The same team that receives the blood on the airfield should also be responsible for the despatch of blood to advanced banks when internal air transport is being used and may on occasion fly with the blood to see it arrives safely. In addition they are responsible for the back-loading of empty insulated containers to the United Kingdom, the steady flow of which must be maintained. A similar arrangement is made where blood is being received by sea at a base port.

At the B.T.U. storage and re-issue of the blood does not take up a great deal of time or man-power. It may be said, however, that more supervision is required of blood received from outside than of that taken locally. Owing to the time lag, blood arriving in the theatre is always at least several days old, the average in this campaign being 5–6 days. By the time it leaves the base and is sent to the advanced blood banks, then to forward trucks, it may easily be 10–14 days old before reaching the F.T.Us. and even older by the time it is used on patients. This means that if wastage is to be minimised much turning over and 'juggling' with stocks must be done. Attempts were made by the blood bank officers to exchange blood approaching the age limit (21 days) from units in quiet sectors with units in active sectors who were more likely to use it quickly. This was not a practical solution and finally it was decided to stop issuing blood from base over 10 days old, and from advanced blood banks over 14 days old. This system worked better but entailed a wastage on a moderately large scale, the approximate figure being 18 per cent. These problems do not arise when bleeding is being done locally and can be controlled directly by demands and size and age of stocks.

Local Production. Intravenous Solutions prepared by 1 B.T.U.

	Glucose-Saline	Normal Saline	Glucose Solution	Total 540 c.c. Bottles
540 c.c. Bottles.	65,142	54,201	17,139	136,482

These figures give some idea of the productive capacity of the B.T.U. and if to them is added the amount of other odd solutions required to be produced, it is estimated that the unit must be capable of turning out in the neighbourhood of 750 litres of distilled water a day. Of this a considerable amount must be used for washing out apparatus and preparing distilled water for penicillin in 5 c.c., 10 c.c., 25 c.c., as well as small amounts for the following solutions:

8 per cent.	.	.	Alkali solution
50 ,, ,,	.	.	Glucose solution
30 ,, ,,	.	.	Saline solution
3.8 ,, ,,	.	.	Sodium cit. solution; sodium sulphate isotonic solution
50 ,, ,,	.	.	Sucrose solution

The stills carried by the unit were not capable of producing this amount. The paraffin burning models were abandoned and production maintained with (a) electric stills, local power being used when available and at other times a 22 kw. generator was employed; (b) a large steam still worked by either its own boiler or some existing steam supply such as a large civilian hospital or other institution possesses. The latter proved an excellent method of producing distilled water in large amounts (10 gallons per hour).

The small departments concerned in producing these solutions, filling them into bottles, autoclaving, sealing, checking and packing them, claimed a large proportion of the available personnel of the unit and additional labour, 20 extra O.Rs. R.A.M.C. from R.H.Us. and 50 full-time civilian employees, was found necessary to supplement the W.E.

With regard to the solutions themselves, the method of sealing them was not entirely satisfactory. A screw-cap bottle with aluminium cap and rubber diaphragm screwed down while the bottle was still hot and sealed with a solution of cellulose in acetone cutin which hardened immediately did not prevent loss of vacuum and growth of moulds in a certain number of bottles.

Production of Transfusion-giving Sets. It became apparent early on that the number of giving sets received from the United Kingdom both for blood and saline was insufficient and local production was instituted; in the latter stages nearly all giving sets were prepared by the B.T.U. The used apparatus returned from units was stripped down, cleaned and assembled, new components being supplied from the United Kingdom when necessary. The institution of continuous intramuscular penicillin therapy further increased the need for set production and involved certain difficulties. It was finally decided to use the saline set for this purpose, but pure rubber tubing was used in place of synthetic types which had been found to destroy penicillin.

Actual numbers produced daily varied greatly both according to demand and to the speed with which used sets were returned, which in its turn varied with the activity of the transfusion units. Battle periods meant large consumption of sets, large returns and large numbers remade; quiet periods, the reverse. The average daily figure for all types was 450–500 a day; the greatest number produced was 750 per day.

This department, including stripping, cleaning, rubber washing, needle sharpening and reassembling, accounted for most of the remaining labour available and had, in addition, 12 part-time voluntary women workers of the Belgian Red Cross who wrapped and packed the sets.

LESSONS OF THE CAMPAIGN. TACTICAL AND ADMINISTRATIVE

(a) Base Transfusion Unit.

The war establishment provided for this campaign was certainly an improvement on previous establishments but it was felt that still further additions were necessary for efficient working.

Officers. It was found necessary to maintain a pool of six officers at the B.T.U. One of these was employed on B.T.U. duties in place of the Blood Distribution Officer, the others were allocated to F.T.Us. in busy sectors. Experience showed that there was great need for the appointment of a commissioned quartermaster in view of the large amount of technical stores carried by the unit. These came to exceed in quantity and complexity the stores of other units having commissioned quartermasters, e.g. field ambulances, C.C.Ss. and 200-bed general hospitals.

Other Ranks. Extra labour was always required. The unit had to employ 30 O.Rs. R.A.M.C. on loan from R.H.Us. and 50 full-time civilian employees. In particular these extra workers would be most essential should large-scale local bleeding be necessary.

Transport. The heavy commitments and extensive ramifications of the Transfusion Service threw a great strain on the available transport. The amount provided was barely adequate and an increased allocation seemed fully justified, including at least one large staff car for the long journeys from base to field units undertaken by the C.O. and B.D.O. Refrigerator vehicles were sufficient but there was a shortage of smaller load-carrying vehicles.

Movements. The difficulties encountered in the long move from Normandy to Brussels would seem to indicate that changes of location of a B.T.U. should be as few as possible. It was only with the greatest difficulty that the B.T.U. was able to maintain supplies while attempting to move with its own limited transport. In particular, the production of solutions suffered badly and for some weeks none was produced locally.

Air Transport. Air transport was used on many occasions. For delivery of blood from the United Kingdom it was used almost exclusively and with complete satisfaction, probably because definite arrangements had been made between the service and the air authorities at a high level. Inside the theatre there was no such definite authority to use air transport, and only makeshift arrangements were made between the B.T.U. and local air authorities. The ideal system would allocate at least two aircraft exclusively to the Transfusion Service and these could be used for other medical purposes after fulfilling their transfusion duties. Representatives of the B.T.U. would, of course, travel with the aircraft to ensure safe delivery of stores.

Accommodation. Suitable premises must be allocated to a B.T.U., with due regard to water and electricity supplies, storage space, multiplicity of departments, laboratory facilities, accommodation of F.T.Us. from the field, and garage space. The unit worked, with difficulty, for a short time under canvas, but with buildings for the essential departments.

Training. This is an important duty of the B.T.U. There was a constant demand for replacements of transfusion officers and orderlies in hospitals and C.C.Ss. as well as in F.T.Us., and these could only come from the B.T.U. Training should be practical, as far as possible, and personnel should spend part of their course of instruction attached to a F.T.U. engaged in operations.

(b) *Field Transfusion Units.*

Most F.T.U. officers preferred working with C.C.Ss. rather than with advanced surgical centres with adequate relief provided either by an extra officer from B.T.U. pool or a second F.T.U.; conditions of working were much superior in the former site. The addition of a third orderly to the W.E. would greatly increase the efficiency of this unit. As far as possible units should be kept within the same corps so that they come to feel part of the parent unit and to understand the idiosyncrasies of the surgeons and M.Os.

Equipment. Most F.T.U. officers expressed themselves satisfied with the scale of equipment and transport provided. Frequent, often daily, visits by the advanced banks enabled them to obtain fresh supplies of stores regularly and kept them informed of future developments and problems. The petrol-driven refrigerators used gave complete satisfaction under all conditions.

Personnel. The suggestion is made that a third orderly should be added along with the second officer to increase the efficiency of this unit.

(c) General Hospitals.

These did not present any great administrative problems. Their proximity to the H.Q. or advanced banks and the less urgent nature of their work made it relatively easy to satisfy their needs. Some hospitals did not appoint official transfusion officers with the duty of looking after the storage of blood. In these, and also in some who did have transfusion officers, it was discovered that there was a certain amount of carelessness in this matter and refrigerators were found containing over-age haemolysed, or even grossly contaminated, blood. Indeed one fatality can be directly attributed to such neglect. There was a tendency among hospitals to rely too much on the B.T.U. for supplies, and even when they were in a position to obtain their own whole blood they were most reluctant to do so. This attitude was not shown by hospitals with previous experience in the Middle East which took a pride in maintaining their own blood banks. Some of the difficulty can be attributed to the lack of understanding among the troops generally, due to the fact that such large supplies were available from civilian sources in the United Kingdom and that the troops had not been submitted to such intense propaganda as they had been, and had to be, in the Middle East.

Refrigerators. The refrigerators supplied to general hospitals were of the paraffin-burning type which are difficult to adjust satisfactorily and not easily repaired locally. It would be an advantage to supply an electric or petrol-driven model which can be serviced by B.T.U. technicians.

LESSONS OF THE CAMPAIGN. MEDICAL AND TECHNICAL

Base Transfusion Unit. It was possible for a B.T.U. to supply all the intravenous fluids required by an army group, conditions regarding accommodation, water and power supply being favourable. Main or R.E. sources of water are indispensable and power should be in the form of electric main supply or large generator (22 kw.). Failing this, a reasonable alternative is a large steam still and boiler or steam from a large installation such as exists in a civilian hospital. Sufficient water must be produced for washing apparatus as well as for the solutions themselves. Great care must be taken throughout to minimise the infection of solutions with growths of moulds.

Blood. When supply was maintained by air from the United Kingdom the condition of the blood was, in general, satisfactory. Medical officers complained that frequently the pressure required to force blood through the filter was sufficient to force air back through the non-return air valve. This may have been partly due to defects in the rubber membrane of the valve. This fault occurred sufficiently often to be a source of great annoyance to transfusion officers and a new type of valve might with advantage be designed. Some sort of mechanical device to prevent the occurrence of air embolism when a bottle runs dry should also be incorporated in any new type of apparatus, if only to avoid the reproaches of surgeons in cases of deaths occurring in transfusion patients from conditions not necessarily connected with blood transfusions.

Plasma. It was observed that mild reactions occurred to an appreciable extent in transfusing casualties with plasma, both wet and dry. The exact cause was not discovered but in practice it was found that the majority were of a mild variety and seemed to depend on the speed of administration of the plasma. Most of them stopped when the rate of flow was reduced. A few bottles of the older dried plasma used was found to form a 'gel' on reconstitution, possibly due to excessive moisture in the powder, a further argument for the necessity of improving on the present method of sealing bottles. During the winter on one or two occasions several bottles of wet plasma and saline became frozen and cracked on thawing. It was thought advisable to institute heating in stock rooms during cold weather, especially in view of the size of stocks —up to 25,000 bottles—which had to be maintained as a reserve.

THE ARMY PATHOLOGY SERVICE. SECOND ARMY

In this campaign the organisation for carrying out routine pathologic examination was:

(a) For simple tests each 200-bed hospital and each C.C.S. had a clinical side room in charge of a (corporal) laboratory assistant.
(b) For epidemiological problems in the field two mobile bacteriological laboratories, and later a third, were available.
(c) For clinical pathology the laboratories of the 600 and 1,200-bed hospitals were used.

This organisation was found to be very satisfactory. In the beachhead phase of the campaign the laboratories were usually tented and it was found that the minimal requirements for laboratory accommodation in a general hospital were 'tent hospital expanding' with one section for a 600-bed and two sections for a 1,200-bed hospital plus in each case one 160 lb. tent for sterilising and washing up purposes. Concrete floors were considered essential in a tented laboratory.

With the advance the laboratories were in permanent buildings and the accommodation as a rule very good indeed. The demands of the laboratories were exceedingly heavy.

July–September	25,149 investigations
October–December	48,619 „
January–March	77,746 „
April–June	74,916 „

The war establishment of the pathological laboratories was unsatisfactory for it failed to provide an adequate reserve of trained pathologists and of trained laboratory assistants. The need for experienced biochemists was keenly felt.

The four mobile bacteriological laboratories did most valuable work. Two were reserved for special purposes: (1) control of penicillin therapy and (2) investigation of anaerobic wound infection. The other two were used for general routine work and for carrying out serological and bacteriological tests, mainly for corps units. Since the mobile bacteriological laboratory was commonly attached to a unit under canvas, it had to borrow tentage and this was often difficult. It required tentage of its own (2 × 160 lb. + a No. 10 shelter).

The work undertaken was mainly of an epidemiological nature. During the late summer and autumn dysentery and malaria were common. During the winter diphtheria became a serious problem but it was not considered necessary to immunise the armies, apart from the medical and associated personnel. All suspicious throats were regarded as possibly diphtheritic and so throat swabs provided a very great deal of work for the laboratories. There was but one outbreak of enteric fever and this was confined to one unit. Throughout the campaign the demand for Kahn tests steadily increased. In March 1945, 7,120 such tests were carried out by the British laboratories.

Complete active immunisation against enteric, tetanus, typhus and smallpox was carried out, with excellent results. Tetanus toxoid was used and only two doubtful and mild cases of tetanus occurred among 21 Army Group troops. Cox's vaccine also proved its worth. Considerable numbers of troops came into contact with typhus cases but no fatal case occurred in 21 Army Group.

THE ARMY PSYCHIATRIC SERVICE. SECOND ARMY

During the period January to May 1945, psychiatric battle casualties in Second Army totalled 1,579, the incidence being 8·9 per cent. of surgical battle casualties. Early in February XXX Corps went under command Canadian First Army in preparation for the beginning of the drive into Germany in the Reichswald Forest–Cleve–Goch sector. This offensive—February 8–March 10, 1945—produced 1,170 cases of exhaustion among the British units engaged, the incidence being 14·5 per cent. of surgical battle casualties. XXX Corps' psychiatrist commented in his report on the large percentage of psychiatric casualties among men who had been previously wounded. This group comprised 50 per cent. of the total. A second group was composed of young, immature youths experiencing their first severe action. Many were of poor combatant temperament and often below average intelligence.

The incidence of exhaustion cases and comparison with battle casualties among British divisions engaged in this offensive was:

TABLE 54

XXX Corps. Psychiatric Casualties. February 8–March 10, 1945

	Battle Casualties	Exhaustion Cases	Exhaustion Cases as Percentage of Total Casualties
53rd Inf. Div.	1,695	456	21
51st „ „	1,211	173	12·5
3rd „ „	706	113	13·5
43rd „ „	640	98	13·2
15th „ „	1,084	98	8·3
52nd „ „	376	93	20
Gds. Armd. Div.	449	55	10·9

During the assault crossing of the Rhine morale was high and the percentage of psychiatric casualties low. One infantry battalion in XXX Corps showed a particularly high admission rate to the corps exhaustion centre. The explanation for this was later forthcoming when the commanding officer himself was evacuated with obvious symptoms of a neurotic breakdown.

Thereafter the incidence of exhaustion was as follows:

TABLE 55

XXX Corps. Psychiatric Casualties. April 7–May 5, 1945

Week ending	Total Wounded (a)	Total Exhaustion (b)	$\dfrac{b \times 100}{a+b}$
April 7	2,040	122	7·2
14	2,207	130	6·4
21	2,107	192	8·1
18	1,260	156	9·3
May 5	1,089	208	6·8

Up to 60 per cent. of those who broke down in battle were returned to duty after treatment without evacuation beyond Army level. Of these approximately half returned to full duty, the other half to duty in a lower medical category. The remainder, 40 per cent. were evacuated to 32 B.G.H. at Thildonck.

With the cessation of hostilities came an increase in the number of officers and men breaking down with psychoses. This was particularly noticeable among men of officer status in para-military bodies such as the B.R.C.S. and U.N.R.R.A. While the great majority of those in the Army now wished to leave it, many of those who had gone overseas as members of a para-military organisation, who had left home because they were eager to get away from it, now, with the end of the war, were faced with insecurity. Many of those in Military Government were likewise unstable. Among army personnel there were many of the high age and service groups whose morale was lowered by the prospect of a long and boring occupation and many who had become so accustomed to Army life as to look forward to a resumption of life as a civilian with considerable distaste and anxiety. The non-fraternisation order was another factor which, in certain instances, led to emotional disturbance.

The end of a campaign such as this is a very disturbing event emotionally. The change from life in the Army to life as a civilian calls for considerable adjustment on the part of the individual. In the Army with its hierarchical structure, its groups and sub-groups, its tradition and its rituals, many had encountered comradeship and had been relieved of the necessity of deciding for themselves what to think and what to do, and had found great comfort and security in becoming absorbed into the groups. With peace comes a tomorrow when the individual must make decisions for himself, must assume much personal responsibility. So it is that pessimism and cynicism enlarge and that restlessness, discontent and frustration become expressed. Thus the V.D. rate and the incidence of psychosomatic complaints rise when the guns are silent. Of course there were tens of thousands of men to whom this abrupt change brought benefit, who had done their duty and who now welcomed the bright prospect of a resumption of a peaceful and constructive life.

The number of psychiatric battle casualties during the entire campaign was 13,255.

The obvious inference from these figures is that the treatment of exhaustion constitutes a major activity of the Army Medical Services. Fortunately the psychiatric organisation for Second Army came into existence well in advance of events and so B.L.A. arrived complete with its psychiatric elements. This satisfactory state of affairs had never been achieved in other theatres where psychiatric help was always called for when confusion had already established itself.

The accepted policy of early forward treatment of these casualties, treatment in specialist units and the return of recovered cases to their own units, paid great dividends. The proportion of psychiatric patients

TABLE 56

21 Army Group. Psychiatric Casualties. June 1944–May 1945

	Exhaustion as Percentage of All Casualties	Total No. Exhaustion Cases	No. of Battle Casualties	Exhaustion as Percentage of Battle Casualties
June 6–June 30, 1944	8·6	928	8,818	9·5
July, August and September, 1944	10·3	8,930	35,266	20·2
October, November and December, 1944	4·8	1,736	10,466	14·3
January, February and March, 1945	2·9	980	8,904	9·9
April 1–May 9, 1945	2·6	681	7,929	7·9
Entire Campaign	—	13,255	71,383	15·6

who after treatment returned to full duties necessarily fluctuated according to circumstances. For instance, during the early bridgehead days it was not possible to hold and treat cases for more than a few days, with the result that appreciable numbers were evacuated to the United Kingdom. However, when conditions improved, the policy of evacuation of psychiatric casualties was reversed and emphasis was laid on conservation of man-power by all possible means. Throughout the whole campaign this policy was deliberately directed to the return of too many to duty rather than too few. Relapses were expected and occurred.

TABLE 57

21 Army Group. Percentage of Exhaustion Cases returned to Unit without Evacuation to the L. of C. Feb.–March 1945

Week Ending	British			Canadian		
	Without Change of Category or of Employment	With Change	Totals	Without Change	With Change	Totals
Feb. 3	22	50	72	5	31	36
10	23	30	53	7	14	21
17	16	12	28	11	33	44
24	21	24	45	9	30	39
Mar. 3	20	19	39	8	23	31
10	28	29	57	28	12	40
17	29	45	74	10	37	47
24	12	33	45	3	39	42
31	24	16	40	3	37	40

Table 57 (continued)
British Psychiatric Casualties. February 1945

	Mental Dullness and Deficiency		Psychoneurosis and Psychopathic Personality		Psychosis		Totals	
	Offrs.	O.Rs.	Offrs.	O.Rs.	Offrs.	O.Rs.	Offrs.	O.Rs.
R.T.U.:								
Div. Level	—	—	—	187	—	—	—	187
Army and Corps Level	—	73	12	644	—	—	12	717
L. of C.	—	44	21	614	—	—	21	658
Admitted to Hospital:								
Br. Hosp.	—	35	44	940	5	48	49	1,023
Cdn. Hosp.	—	2	19	321	—	5	19	328
U.S. Hosp.	—	—	—	1	—	—	—	1
Totals	—	154	96	2,707	5	53	101	2,914

During the first month of the campaign the average return to full duties rate was 30–40 per cent. When divisional exhaustion centres were set up in July 1944, medical officers employed therein were extremely enthusiastic and the average return to duty rate was nearer 60 per cent. Thus the corps centres received the poor prognosis type of case and relatively few could be pronounced fit for full duties.

In spite of an appreciable relapse rate it can be stated that over the entire campaign about one-third of exhaustion cases treated eventually remained at full duties. This represents just over 4,400 men saved for further battle at a time when the man-power situation was most critical.

A F.D.S. was used an an army psychiatric centre and served an extremely useful purpose. It was usually situated in the vicinity of R.H.Us. and the convalescent depot and its psychiatrist was always fully occupied. To it was sent the type of patient for whom short-term treatment was sufficient, and on a few occasions it acted as an extremely useful stop-gap, taking overflow cases from a corps centre filled to capacity.

When hostilities ceased it was considered that an Army psychiatric centre could still serve a useful purpose and it was set up as a wing to a general hospital.

To the Army Psychiatric Service nothing gave greater satisfaction than the increasing respect given to psychiatric opinion concerning those imprisoned for desertion or for refusing to obey an order. This aspect of the work is illustrated in Table 58:

TABLE 58

Results of Review of Sentence on 373 men serving various terms of imprisonment for Desertion or Refusing to obey an Order. November 17–December 30, 1944

A. Sentence suspended and returned to full duties in the line . . . 238
  1. Good type of man likely to acquit himself well . 178
  2. Type of man for whom prospect of further good service is only fair . 17
  3. Type of man for whom prospect of further service is doubtful . . 26
  4. Type of man for whom prospect of further service is poor . . 17

C. To remain in prison . 28

B. Referred for Psychiatric opinion . . . 105
  1. Suspend sentence and return to full duties in the line . . . 11
  2. Suspend sentence and regrade to Med. Cat. C and suitable employment . . . 49
  3. Suspend sentence and transfer to Armed Pioneers . . . 30
  4. Suspend sentence and admit to psychiatric hospital for treatment 9
  5. Incorrigible type—to serve further period of sentence . . . 6

D. Conscientious objections. Transferred to R.A.M.C. 2

Total returned to full duties	249	66·7 per cent.
" downgraded in Med. Cat.	49	13·2 "
" transferred to A.M.P.C.	30	8·0 "
" admitted to psychiatric hospital	9	2·4 "
" to remain in prison	34	9·11 "
" transferred to R.A.M.C.	2	0·54 "
	373	

CHAPTER 10
THE HEALTH OF THE TROOPS*

'No account of this campaign would be complete without some mention of the truly remarkable success of the medical organisation. But it must be remembered that there were two factors which contributed greatly to the results achieved; probably no group of doctors has ever worked on better material, and secondly they were caring for the men of a winning army. The men of 21 Army Group were fully immunised and fully trained; their morale was at its highest; they were well-clothed and well-fed; they were fighting in a climate to which the average British soldier is accustomed; hygiene, both personal and unit, was exceptionally good; welfare services were well organised. The exhilarating effect of success also played its part in reducing the rates of sickness.

'Commanders in the field must realise that the medical state of an army is not dependent on the doctors alone. Their efforts are immeasurably facilitated when morale is at its highest, and of all the factors which ensure a high state of morale, there is none more important than success.

'The sickness among troops was almost halved as compared with the last war. It is striking that, as we swept through Germany, liberating prison camps such as Belsen and Sandbostel where thousands of persons were dying of typhus, only twenty-five British troops contracted this disease. None died of it. This was due to preventive inoculations and to the adequate supply and use of a powder called D.D.T.

'Air transport has been of great importance in the evacuation of casualties. By this means over a hundred thousand wounded men were evacuated to base hospitals from front-line units. In the sphere of transfusion, great quantities of blood and blood plasma were used. A co-ordinated service of air transport and refrigerator trucks ensured that fresh blood was always at hand for surgeons working directly behind the lines—even during the rapid advance into Belgium.

'Another interesting fact is that, in the last war, two out of every three men wounded in the belly, died. Field surgical units, operating close behind the lines, greatly reduced this danger. In the Normandy campaign two out of every three wounded in the belly recovered.

'The healing of war wounds has been revolutionised by the use of penicillin. Many men who in the last war would have been permanent invalids, were fit and ready to go back to the line within a month of being wounded.

---

* The volumes on *Surgery* and on *Medicine and Pathology* in this series should be consulted.

THE HEALTH OF THE TROOPS

'*To sum up, the doctors were prepared to lay 15 to 1 that once a man got into their hands, whatever his injury, they would save his life and restore him to health. It is a fine thing that these odds were achieved with a handsome margin*'.

FIELD MARSHAL MONTGOMERY.
Despatch, *The London Gazette*, September 3, 1946.

There is much in this appreciation that invites careful consideration. It will be best to deal first with the comparison of the two wars. The figures given are those which existed and which were available in 1945. It is possible that some of them have since been corrected as additional information was secured.

TABLE 59

A Comparison of the Casualties in This and Other Campaigns

Admissions to Hospital per Week per 1,000 Strength

	1914–18	October–December 1944 (21 Army Group)
Sick and Injuries not due to Enemy Action	12·3	5·5
Injuries due to Enemy Action	7·0	2·4
	19·3	7·9

Mean Monthly Rate per 1,000 Strength

Disease	South African War 1898–1901	First World War 1914–18	Second World War	
			June 1944–March 1945 (incl.)	January 1945–March 1945
Venereal Disease	2·919	2·474	2·116	2·907
Jaundice	0·935	0·082	0·327	0·549
Diphtheria	0·005	0·110	0·235	0·454
Enteric Group	8·704	1·525	0·007	0·003
Dysentery	5·748	0·466	0·355	0·093
Pneumonia	0·383	0·419	0·068	0·100
Mumps	—	0·233	0·030	0·067
Rubella	—	0·190	0·013	0·027
Measles	0·183	0·85	0·012	0·022
Cerebro-spinal Fever	—	0·026	0·007	0·008
Influenza	1·342	0·890 (1914–15)	0·253	0·290
Scabies	—	—	2·633	4·287
Pediculosis	—	—	1·159	1·523
Trench-foot	—	0·503 (1914–15)	—	0·049 (Nov. 5–Mar. 31)

Mean Monthly Rates per 1,000 Strength (excluding Wounded remaining at Duty)

	1914–1918			June 6, 1944–April 13, 1945		
	Offrs.	O.Rs.	Totals	Offrs.	O.Rs.	Totals
Battle Casualties						
Killed	9·5	5·7	5·8	6·1	3·5	3·7
Missing	1·7	2·2	2·2	1·4	0·8	0·9
P.o.W.	2·7	2·7	2·7	1·4	1·6	1·6
Died of Wounds	3·4	2·3	2·3	1·5	1·0	1·0
Wounded, admitted to Medical Units (excl. died of wounds)	30·9	27·9	28·1	18·1	13·8	14·0
Totals	48·2	40·8	41·1	28·5	20·7	21·2
Non-battle Casualties						
Died of Disease	0·5	0·5	0·5	0·1	0·1	0·1
Died of Injuries				0·2	0·2	0·2
Sick or injured, admitted to Medical Units (excl. died)	51·1	53·5	53·4	16·7	23·7	23·3
Totals	51·6	54·0	53·9	17·0	24·0	23·6
Total Casualties	99·8	94·8	95·0	45·5	44·7	44·8
Percentage died of wounds to total wounded admitted to med. units	10·0	7·5	7·6	7·4	6·5	6·6
Percentage died of disease or injury to total sick and injured admitted to medical units	1·0	0·9	0·9	1·5	0·8	0·8
Proportion of battle casualties to non-battle casualties	1:1·1	1:1·3	1:1·3	1:0·6	1:1·2	1:1·1

The casualty rate in 1914–18 (95·0/1,000/month) was more than double that in 1944–45 (44·8/1,000/month). The ratio of battle to non-battle admissions to the medical units was about the same in the two campaigns in North-west Europe, the figures for 1944–45 being battle 167,551, non-battle 206,419. The sickness rate in 1944–45 (23·6/1,000/month) was less than half of the 1914–18 figure (53·9/1,000/month).

Differences in respect of tactics lie at the root of the differences in respect of the battle casualty rate. The difference in respect of the sick rate in the two campaigns was a reflection of the operation of many

THE HEALTH OF THE TROOPS

causes. The 1944–45 campaign in North-west Europe lasted less than a year; the greater part of this time was filled with victory as the armies pressed on towards the final objective. There was no deepening gloom born of disaster, no debilitation and enlarging pessimism that stemmed from long months of static existence in deep trenches amid utter desolation. The troops could be maintained in a high state of physical fitness and they could keep themselves clean. D.D.T. and benzyl benzoate gave control over the louse and the mite. In 1944–45 there was no pandemic of influenza. The venereal disease rate was much the same in both campaigns. The Army Medical Services cannot provide any adequate alternative for that self-care which alone can protect a man from the spirochaete. They were able, however, by means of the sulpha drugs and penicillin to slash the period of military ineffectiveness due to these diseases to a fraction of what it was in 1914–18. The incidence of jaundice in 1944–45 was about four times and that of diphtheria twice that in 1914–18. On the other hand, the incidence of enteric fever was about one-two-hundredth, that of pneumonia one-sixth and that of cerebro-spinal fever one-fourth of the rates in 1914–18.

Undoubtedly the most striking contrast between this and previous campaigns was in respect of the degree of control over the three great hazards to which the wounded man was exposed—haemorrhage, shock and sepsis, the greatest of these being sepsis. D.M.S. 21 Army Group, referring to a report submitted by Consulting Surgeon 21 Army Group, commented that in this campaign thousands of men had received skin closure within 3–5 days of wounding as compared with 10–14 days in previous campaigns and that the results had been between 90 and 95 per cent. successful, this being largely due to the aid afforded by penicillin therapy. This meant that a man with a flesh wound was out of hospital in about a fortnight from the date of wounding and after a week or two at a convalescent depot was ready to return to duty in from a month to six weeks. D.M.S. called attention to the very considerable saving in hospitalisation and in man-power that this meant. He also remarked upon the soldier's reaction to this speed up of cure. Traditionally the soldier regards a wound as a ticket to the United Kingdom. He was not particularly enthusiastic about the shortening of his ineffectiveness. D.M.S. suggested that the introduction of a system of short-term leave would do much to counteract such disappointment.

To some it seemed that possibly this considerable reduction in the period of ineffectiveness following wounding was not without its disadvantages, though these could easily be removed. To speak of a flesh wound is to place oneself in danger of erroneous thinking for it is the total man and not part of him that is wounded. It is but reasonable that a man, wounded but having escaped grievous hurt, should wish strongly to move into a safe place. The strength of his desire wanes with the passing of time, the actual time varying from man to man in different circumstances. Time is required for the wound and also for the total man to heal, less for the wound than for the man in most cases. Thus as surgical methods improve it is possible that their efficacy will be assessed not so much by the shortening of the time interval between wounding and return to the line as by the frequency of early breakdown (exhaustion) on the part of those whose flesh wounds had healed and who had returned to duty before they themselves were hale.

In the following pages a selection of tables which relate to the incidence of disease in Second Army is presented. It is to be understood that the figures given are those which were in existence and which were available to R.M.Os., A.Ds.M.S. and the like at the time when these tables were constructed. Information that was forthcoming later may have led to correction of these figures. But these were the figures that formed the basis of policy and the springboard of action during the actual campaign. It cannot be too strongly emphasised that it is not that which was, but that which was at the time thought to be, that determined policy and action on the part of the medical services.

TABLE 60

I Corps. Casualties. July–September 1944

	July	August	September
Total sick admitted to the Medical Units	2,777	4,093	857
Ratio per 1,000 per annum	392·04	566·0	120·9
Total battle casualties admitted to the Medical Units	3,975	3,339	1,116
Ratio per 1,000 per annum	561·2	459·6	157·5
Total number of Deaths in the Medical Units	72	74	27
Ratio per 1,000 per annum	10·1	10·4	3·7
Total Exhaustion cases admitted to the Medical Units	1,406	591	91
Ratio per 1,000 per annum	198·5	83·4	12·8

Principal Causes of Morbidity

	Actual Admissions	Ratio per 1,000 per annum
Battle Casualties	8,430	1,176
Diseases of the Digestive System	2,102	296·4
Exhaustion	2,088	294
I.A.T.	1,947	274·8
Skin Diseases	1,446	204·12
Malaria	1,056	148·8
P.U.O.	557	78

Diarrhoea and Dysentery

There was a severe outbreak, mainly Flexner, in August while the corps was fighting in the Caen area. It particularly affected the independent brigades and 49th Division.

	Number of Cases		
	July	August	September
6th Airborne Division	73	148	—
3rd Division	182	—	—
Canadian 3rd Division	25	—	—
51st Division	52	101	79
49th Division	27	445	147
Polish Armd. Division	—	—	14
Corps Troops and Independent Brigades	257	468	54

The battlefield was exceedingly filthy, flies abundant and cooks careless. It was difficult to control the breeding of flies during this period of bitter fighting.

Malaria

Malaria was rife in 51st Division which had served in Sicily. At least three of the men who suffered from this disease had never been out of England until they sailed for Normandy. They had been infected (B.T.) in June or July either in the marshalling area in the United Kingdom or else in the valley of the Orne.

	July		August		September	
	Fresh	Relapse	Fresh	Relapse	Fresh	Relapse
6th Airborne Division	1	14	—	—	—	—
3rd Division	—	—	—	—	—	—
Canadian 3rd Division	—	—	—	—	—	—
51st Division	133	340	12	140	17	127
49th Division	—	2	2	6	—	—
Polish Armd. Division	—	—	—	—	—	—
Corps Troops and Independent Brigades	—	104	1	82	—	73
	134	460	15	228	17	200

TABLE 61

I Corps. Casualties. October–December 1944

	October	November	December
Total sick admitted to Medical Units	2,326	2,733	1,873
Ratio per 1,000 per annum	446·6	369·4	438·1
Total battle casualties admitted to the Medical Units	2,232	1,132	96
Ratio per 1,000 per annum	428·4	153·2	22·4
Total Exhaustion cases admitted to the Medical Units	246	96	36
Ratio per 1,000 per annum	47·2	17·1	6·5
Total Deaths in the Medical Units	73	53	4
Ratio per 1,000 per annum	14	12	0·9

Principal Causes of Morbidity

	Total Admissions	Ratio per 1,000 per annum
Battle Casualties	3,469	234·6
Diseases of the Respiratory System	1,243	96·2
Diseases of the Skin	1,092	73·8
Accidental Injuries	986	66·6
Diseases of the Digestive System	752	58·1
I.A.T.	457	30·9
Exhaustion	369	24·8
P.U.O.	114	7·7

TABLE 62

I Corps. Casualties. March–June 1945

Admissions to I Corps Medical Units

	March	April	May	June	Ratio per 1,000 per annum	
					June	January
Total Sick	1,129	437	1,735	4,279	230·88	541·03
Total Battle Casualties	59	12	68	7	—	87·1
Total Injuries	529	159	573	1,098	58·07	52·5
Total Deaths	4	10	39	27	1·11	2·3

The large variation reflects fluctuations in respect of strength.

Admissions to and Discharges from I Corps Medical Units

	April	May	June	Totals
Total admissions	606	2,471	5,384	8,461
Total discharged R.T.U. or R.H.U.	549	1,955	3,157	5,661
Total evacuated from Corps area	459	1,906	1,272	3,637

About 67 per cent. of all admissions were returned to duty.

Principal Causes of Morbidity. April–June 1945

	April	May	June	Total Numbers	Rates per 1,000 per annum for June	Rates per 1,000 per annum Jan.–March
Injuries accidental	144	510	1,022	1,676	58·07	52·5
Diseases of Respiratory System	98	324	806	1,228	44·53	85·1
Diseases of the Skin	60	240	469	769	24·18	55·6
Diseases of the Digestive System	56	218	414	688	23·53	52·9
I.A.T.	89	180	299	568	15·60	12·48

Venereal Diseases

Sources of Infection:

- Germany . . . . 339 cases (non-fraternisation the rule)
- Belgium . . . . 271 (Brussels 206)
- Holland 169
- United Kingdom . . 114 (42 marital)
- France . . . . 47 (Paris 12)

940

A marked increase in incidence occurred after the cessation of the fighting.

Table 63

VIII Corps. Principal Diseases affecting the Troops. July–September 1944

	Cases	
Typhoid Fever	79	Treated in 24 F.D.S., 33 C.C.S., 110 B.G.H., 9 B.G.H.
Diphtheria	2	In hospital
Dysentery, Clinical	3	,,
Erysipelas	1	,,
Infective Jaundice	20	,,
Malaria: Primary	2	,,
Relapse	64	,,
Measles	1	,,
Meningococcal Meningitis	1	,,
Tuberculosis (bone)	1	,,
Scabies	84	In unit lines
Pediculosis corporis	23	,,
P. pubis	36	,,
V.D.: Gonorrhoea	15	Partly in unit lines, partly in field medical units and partly in general hospitals
Syphilis	6	
Other	13	

Only three diseases claimed importance. Save for them the health of the troops was remarkably good.

A generalised and widespread outbreak of gastro-enteritis occurred during July, August and the early part of September and affected all formations and units. For the most part the attacks were mild and lasted for 3–4 days. Not more than five per cent. of the cases required admission to the field medical units. It was decided that the cause was lax cook-house discipline. Flies were very prevalent at this time.

A serious outbreak of typhoid fever occurred in 6th Guards Tank Brigade during late August and September, being confined to Brigade H.Q. No officers were affected. 8 Mob. Bact. Lab. was attached to the brigade but, despite exhaustive tests and the complete control of all the cooks, the cause was not traced to its source. It was most probably an intermittent carrier among the cooks.

There was a sudden outbreak of malaria in 4th Armoured Brigade and especially in 44th R. Tks. This unit, newly from the M.E., was still on atebrin. Wastage through evacuation to the United Kingdom was beginning to be serious when the general hospitals arrived so that these patients could be held there for treatment.

Table 64

XXX Corps. Casualties. January–March 1945

Total Admissions to Medical Units		24,941
(Br. 22,290; Cdn. 811; P.o.W. 1,840)		
Battle Casualties		9,163
(Br. 8,680; Cdn. 483)		
Lower extremity . . .	41 per cent.	
Upper ,, . . .	29 ,, ,,	
Head and Neck . . .	18 ,, ,,	
Chest	7 ,, ,,	
Abdomen and Pelvis . .	5 ,, ,,	
Battle Accidents (including 23 S.I.W.)		1,738
(Br. 1,687; Cdn. 51)		
Sick		12,200
(Br. 11,923; Cdn. 277)		
Respiratory System . .	2,315	19 per cent.
Exhaustion	1,543	13 ,, ,,
Skin	1,504	12 ,, ,,
Digestive System . .	1,359	11 ,, ,,
I.A.T.	1,275	10 ,, ,,
V.D.	626	5 ,, ,,
Trench Foot . . .	45	0.5 ,, ,,
Miscellaneous . . .	3,533	29.5 ,, ,,
British Troops only:		
Total R.T.U.		6,414
Total Died		296
Total Evacuated		15,472
Total lost to Corps		15,768
Average Strength of Corps		108,419
Loss to Corps per 1,000; All Causes . . .		136·80
Average Daily Sick and Accident Admissions per 1,000 .		1·32
Average Daily Sick per 1,000 First Attendances .		5·38
Total Fresh Cases of V.D. per 1,000 (Total cases 626) .		5·70
Total Fresh Cases of Pediculosis		319
Quarterly Incidence of Pediculosis per 1,000 . .		3·07
Total Fresh Cases of Scabies		1,057
Quarterly Incidence of Scabies per 1,000 . .		9·74

TABLE 65

VIII Corps. Casualties. *Other Ranks*. April 1945

Direct Admissions only to Field Medical Units	11 Armd. Div.	15 Div.	5 Div.	6 A.B. Div.	6 Gds. Armd. Bde.	1 Cdo. Bde.	33 Armd. Bde.	8 A.G.R.A.	VIII Corps Tps.	Army Tps.	Other Formations	Cdn.	U.S.	Br. P.o.W.	R.N.	R.A.F.	Dutch	Totals
Battle Casualties	620	469	123	462	44	161	13	22	42	34	29	3	65	—	—	—	—	2,087
Battle Accidents	87	98	28	133	32	13	—	8	45	25	32	3	5	2	—	5	—	516
Accidental Injuries	—	3	—	3	3	—	—	—	—	—	—	—	—	—	—	—	—	6
Burns	19	33	8	13	9	—	—	1	13	8	5	—	—	1	—	1	—	112
Self-Inflicted Wounds	—	—	—	5	—	1	—	—	—	—	1	—	—	—	—	—	—	5
Total Wounded	726	603	159	616	85	175	13	31	100	67	66	6	70	3	—	6	—	2,726
Dysentery	2	1	1	1	1	—	—	—	—	—	—	—	—	—	—	—	—	7
Gastro-enteritis	20	30	10	30	7	1	—	2	5	7	3	—	—	1	—	2	—	124
V.D.: Gonorrhoea	3	5	—	5	2	—	—	—	3	3	—	—	—	7	—	1	—	22
Syphilis	—	—	—	—	—	—	—	—	1	—	—	—	—	—	—	—	—	1
Other	20	47	21	22	7	3	—	15	14	6	7	—	—	—	—	2	—	165
Malaria	—	4	2	—	—	—	—	—	—	1	—	—	—	—	1	—	—	7
Typhus Fever	—	—	—	—	—	—	—	—	—	—	—	—	—	—	—	—	—	—
Enteric Fever	—	—	—	—	—	—	—	—	—	—	—	—	—	—	—	—	—	—
Meningococcal Infection	—	—	—	—	—	—	—	—	—	—	—	—	—	—	—	—	—	—
Infective Hepatitis	10	7	4	4	3	6	—	3	2	2	2	1	2	—	—	—	—	37
Respiratory Diseases	52	52	18	50	13	3	—	7	21	13	3	—	2	—	—	2	—	240
Neurological Diseases	44	37	21	19	3	4	—	—	21	3	6	1	2	1	1	—	—	160
Skin Diseases	32	40	15	21	10	1	—	6	13	8	3	—	—	—	—	—	—	154
Diphtheria	2	—	—	—	—	—	—	—	—	—	—	—	—	1	—	—	1	3
All Other Sick	169	245	155	317	55	34	—	37	106	47	49	2	5	1	—	—	—	1,224
Total Sick	354	468	247	469	101	52	—	70	186	90	73	4	9	10	2	8	1	2,144
Total Wounded and Sick	1,080	1,071	406	1,085	186	227	13	101	286	157	139	10	79	13	2	13	1	4,870
Deaths in Medical Units	45	17	6	25	5	10	—	—	10	2	13	—	5	—	—	—	—	138
R.T.U.	105	210	71	156	37	26	—	26	93	45	51	2	1	—	1	5	—	829
Evacuated from Corps Area	1,017	737	269	1,044	155	219	4	219	241	223	1,424	35	87	25	—	25	4	5,728

TABLE 66

*Second Army. Admissions to Medical Units classified by Cause.
Thirteen Weeks ending September 30, 1944*

	Total No.	Average Rate per 1,000 per week	Rate per 1,000 per year
Injuries, wounds			
Battle Casualties	29,860	7·71	400·92
Accidental	4,929	1·27	66·04
Self-inflicted	179	0·05	2·60
Burns	914	0·23	11·96
Exhaustion	8,005	2·06	107·12
Diseases of Digestive System	4,864	1·25	24·96
Diseases of Respiratory System	1,746	0·48	52·00
Diseases of Skin	2,933	0·76	39·52
Diseases of Neurological System	643	0·17	8·84
P.U.O.	2,172	0·52	29·12
I.A.T.	2,797	0·72	37·44

Numbers returned to units from Corps and Divisional Medical Units.
Total = 12,395

Wounds by Causal Missile

Shell splinter	30 per cent.
Mortar	15 ,,
Unclassified	15 ,,
G.S.W.	30 ,,
Burns / Mines / Aerial Blast	10 ,,

The ratio of the causal agent varied in the different engagements

Wounds by Anatomical Region

Head, Face and Neck	12 per cent.
Shoulders	6 ,,
Arm and Hand	22 ,,
Chest	6 ,,
Buttock	3 ,,
Thigh and Leg	30 ,,
Others multiple	18 ,,

Table 67

Second Army. Infectious Diseases notified during the Thirteen Weeks ending September 30, 1944

Chicken Pox	3
Diphtheria	5
Dysentery	
Protozoal	—
Bacillary	2
Clinical	130
Enteric	
Typhoid / Clinical	82
Enteritis, infective	5,618
Erysipelas	7
Influenza	42
Jaundice	
Catarrhal	67
Other	48
Malaria	
Primary	688
Relapse	1,572
Measles	6
Meningococcal Infection	4
Mumps	2
Pneumonia	
Pneumococcal	8
Other forms	10
Poliomyelitis	—
Rubella	8
Scarlet Fever	3
Tuberculosis	
Pulmonary	6
Others	1
Pyrexia N.Y.D.	77
Diarrhoea	120
Scabies	814
Pediculosis	
corporis	253
capitis	17
pubis	359
V.D.	
Gonorrhoea	69 treated in unit
	103 admitted to medical unit
Syphilis	58
Other forms	159
Total	**10,341**

TABLE 68

Second Army. The Average Weekly Incidence per 1,000 of the Principal Diseases. October 1944–March 1945

	Oct.	Nov.	Dec.	Jan.	Feb.	Mar.
Diseases of the Respiratory System	1·15	1·76	1·4	1·99	1·64	1·30
Diseases of the Digestive System	0·92	1·18	0·83	0·93	0·72	0·67
Diseases of the Skin	0·58	0·87	0·68	0·84	0·97	0·89
I.A.T.	0·85	0·99	0·72	1·04	1·0	0·68
Venereal Diseases, all types	0·30	0·38	0·43	0·41	0·63	0·53
Enteritis	0·60	0·90	1·28	1·53	1·65	1·01
Malaria	0·19	0·06	0·02	0·03	0·01	0·02
Diphtheria	0·03	0·07	0·11	0·11	0·15	0·09
Scabies	0·24	0·36	0·48	0·56	0·82	0·81
Pediculosis	0·12	0·23	0·21	0·22	0·27	0·23
Other Diseases	1·15	1·84	0·68	0·29	0·2	1·05
Injuries						
Battle	4·1	3·88	0·82	2·37	0·42	3·95
Accidental	0·90	1·04	0·79	0·90	0·78	—
Self-inflicted	0·07	0·02	0·01	0·03	0·008	1·25
Burns	0·12	0·16	0·10	0·14	0·11	—
Exhaustion	0·81	0·53	0·14	—	—	—

Diphtheria was the only infectious disease that caused anxiety. Cases occurred sporadically and infection was undoubtedly due to the fact that the troops were living in close contact with the civilian population. Control was difficult therefore. Only the immediate contacts of cases of diphtheria were swabbed and men with the organism in their throats were admitted to hospital and treated as carriers. This course was necessary for the reason that there were no available means of carrying out virulence tests.

In the circumstances that prevailed the incidence of trench-foot was remarkably low. There were no cases in October, 17 in November and 18 in December. The rate per 1,000 per week was 0·08 in January, 0·04 in February and 0·02 in March.

TABLE 69

Second Army Troops. Incidence of Diseases, New Cases, as Percentage of Total New Cases seen by R.M.Os. and in M.I. Rooms.

June 6–30, 1944

Gastro-enteritis	5·4
All other Digestive Diseases	8·24
Diseases of Upper Respiratory Tract	4·6
Scabies	1·48

	June 6–30, 1944
Other Skin Diseases	14·3
Exhaustion	6·68
I.A.T.	5·77
Injuries, accidental	15·09
Injuries, self-inflicted	0·028
Gonorrhoea, fresh	0·23
relapse	0·28
Syphilis	0·34
Pediculosis corporis	0·57
P. pubis	0·82
Malaria	0·71

(1944)	July	August	September
Dysentery	—	0·41	0·35
Gastro-enteritis	6·41	20·6	13·3
Jaundice	0·142	0·024	0·08
All other Digestive Diseases	9·43	9·6	5·03
Diseases of the Upper Respiratory Tract	4·01	3·14	6·44
Other Diseases of Respiratory Tract	1·40	1·0	1·7
Scabies	1·13	0·53	0·72
Other Skin Diseases	14·8	9·97	10·6
Exhaustion	1·6	2·15	1·32
Neurological Diseases	1·04	0·93	0·84
I.A.T.	8·23	6·24	9·7
Pyrexia N.Y.D.	0·334	0·44	0·69
Injuries, battle casualties	1·0	0·36	0·35
accidental	16·1	12·5	12·7
self-inflicted	0·025	—	—
burns	1·43	1·3	1·4
Gonorrhoea, fresh	0·092	0·072	0·87
relapse	0·050	0·064	0·08
Syphilis	0·201	0·032	—
Other V.D.	0·075	0·22	0·38
Pediculosis capitis	0·050	0·008	—
P. corporis	0·786	0·25	0·017
P. pubis	0·660	0·31	0·23
Malaria	0·410	0·55	0·25
Rubella	—	—	—
Measles	0·008	—	—
Gingivitis	0·092	0·056	—
Scarlet Fever	0·008	—	—
Other Diseases	30·5	29·1	32·9

(1944)	October	November	December
Dysentery	0·17	0·027	0·006
Gastro-enteritis	5·99	3·16	3·6
Jaundice	0·046	0·189	0·19

THE HEALTH OF THE TROOPS

(1944)	October	November	December
All other Digestive Diseases	6·25	7·02	7·0
Diseases of Upper Respiratory Tract	12·47	12·6	12·6
Other Diseases of Respiratory Tract	4·0	5·31	5·4
Scabies	0·77	0·67	1·0
Other Skin Diseases	10·26	10·7	10·1
Exhaustion	0·77	0·75	0·77
Neurological Diseases	0·71	0·70	0·53
I.A.T.	9·88	11·2	9·5
Pyrexia N.Y.D.	0·32	0·52	0·29
Injuries, battle casualties	1·02	0·48	0·54
accidental	10·59	11·0	8·6
self-inflicted	0·011	0·009	0·02
burns	1·68	0·70	1·1
Gonorrhoea, fresh	0·99	0·8	0·62
relapse	0·19	0·34	0·16
Syphilis	0·023	0·09	0·064
Other V.D.	0·41	0·21	0·057
Pediculosis capitis	0·011	0·009	—
P. corporis	0·057	0·045	0·057
P. pubis	0·54	0·66	0·71
Malaria	0·23	0·09	0·07
Gingivitis	0·023	0·018	0·004
Diphtheria	0·011	0·13	0·25
Rubella	—	0·009	0·013
Scarlet Fever	—	0·018	—
Chicken Pox	—	0·027	0·020
Tuberculosis, chronic	—	0·009	0·006
Trench foot	—	0·009	—
Erysipelas	—	—	0·013
Pneumonia	—	—	0·006
Scarlet Fever	—	—	0·006
Other Diseases	32·6	32·5	37·0

(1945)	January	February	March
Dysentery	0·016	0·024	0·035
Gastro-enteritis	3·13	3·09	2·37
Jaundice	0·31	0·09	0·1
All other Digestive Diseases	5·40	7·24	6·08
Diseases of Upper Respiratory Tract	16·9	14·27	13·41
Other Diseases of Respiratory Tract	7·26	3·97	3·28
Scabies	1·01	0·89	1·52
Other Skin Diseases	9·11	11·35	12·22
Exhaustion	0·42	0·87	0·83
Neurological Diseases	0·62	0·64	1·04
I.A.T.	10·07	5·59	8·08
Pyrexia N.Y.D.	0·75	0·88	0·67
Injuries, battle casualties	0·74	0·18	0·13

	(1945)	January	February	March
Injuries, accidental	. . . .	8·04	6·68	7·09
self-inflicted	. . . .	—	—	—
burns	. . . .	1·09	1·15	1·07
Gonorrhoea, fresh	. . . .	0·53	0·43	0·36
relapse	. . . .	0·072	0·07	0·035
Syphilis	. . . .	0·08	0·06	0·079
Other V.D.	. . . .	0·136	0·21	0·16
Pediculosis capitis	. . . .	—	0·008	—
P. corporis	. . . .	0·104	0·03	0·021
P. pubis	. . . .	0·50	0·33	0·39
Malaria (R)	. . . .	0·056	0·016	0·042
Gingivitis	. . . .	0·024	0·05	0·084
Diphtheria	. . . .	0·23	0·25	0·17
Chicken Pox	. . . .	0·016	—	—
Parotitis	. . . .	0·008	—	—
Erysipelas	. . . .	0·008	0·008	0·007
Pneumonia	. . . .	0·024	—	0·014
Pulmonary Tuberculosis	. . . .	0·016	0·016	—
Tuberculosis of Spine	. . . .	0·008	—	—
Rubella	. . . .	—	0·024	0·028
Tonsillitis	. . . .	—	0·04	0·063
Cerebro-spinal Fever	. . . .	—	0·008	0·007
Trench Foot	. . . .	—	0·008	0·007
Mumps	. . . .	—	0·008	0·014
Measles	. . . .	—	—	0·035
Scarlet Fever	. . . .	—	0·008	—
Other Diseases	. . . .	33·38	13·15	39·9

TABLE 70

21 Army Group. Analysis of Admissions to British Medical Units. July–December 1944

Analysis of 10,333 Medical Cases admitted to 600- and 1,200-bed Hospitals. July–September 1944

Acute Diarrhoea		3,172	31 per cent.	
Skin Diseases		1,838	18 ,,	
Respiratory Diseases		1,478	14 ,,	(acute 1,148)
Malaria		1,084	11 ,,	(chronic 330)
Psychoneurosis		638	6 ,,	
Infectious Diseases		522	5 ,,	
Diphtheria	42			
Enteric	73			
Weil's	39			
P.U.O.	277			
C.S.M.	5			
Acute Rheumatism	23			

THE HEALTH OF THE TROOPS

Chronic Rheumatism	402	4 per cent.
Dyspepsia and Peptic Ulcer	333	3 ,,
Renal Disease	155	1·5 ,,
Acute Infective Hepatitis	157	1·5 ,,
Sciatica	106	1 ,,
Organic Nervous Disease	109	1 ,,
Cardiovascular Disease	52	0·5 ,,
Sundry	287	2·5 ,,

Routes of Infection:

Bowel . 33 per cent. of medical admissions on account of disease
Droplet 13 ,, ,, ,, ,, ,, ,, ,, ,,
Insect . 13 ,, ,, ,, ,, ,, ,, ,, ,,
  (and thus theoretically preventable)
Typhoid 72 cases in H.Q. 6th Gds. Tk. Bde. (230 men), 6 died. Source not identified.

Analysis of a Series of 4,115 Medical Admissions to seven C.C.Ss. October–December 1944

Exhaustion	1,608	40 per cent.
Diarrhoea	617	15 ,,
Malaria	582	15 ,,
Respiratory Diseases	351	9 ,,
Skin Diseases	324	8 ,,
Short-term Fevers	346	8 ,,
'Rheumatism'	173	4 ,,
Chronic Dyspepsia	66	1·5 ,,
Acute Infective Hepatitis	48	1 ,,

Analysis of a Series of 3,029 Medical Admissions to Four 200-bed Hospitals. October–December 1944

Diarrhoea	929	31 per cent.
Malaria	663	22 ,,
Exhaustion	540	18 ,,
Skin Diseases	301	10 ,,
Respiratory Disease	224	7 ,,
'Rheumatism'	218	7 ,,
Short-term Fevers	104	3 ,,
Chronic Dyspepsia	29	1 ,,
Acute Infective Hepatitis	21	less than 1 per cent.

TABLE 71

21 Army Group. Summary of Surgical Results (Forward Units)

(A) June 1944–February 1945 and (B) March 1945

	A			B		
	Totals	Deaths	Percentage Recovery	Totals	Deaths	Percentage Recovery
Head Penetrating	1,009	97	90·4	59	10	83·1
,, non-Pen.	1,039	30	97·1	46	1	97·8
Max.-Fac.	2,721	44	98·4	139	0	100·0
Chest Pen.	1,782	176	90·1	179	17	90·5
Abdominal Pen.	2,909	893	69·3	216	58	73·1
,, non-Pen.	576	57	90·1	65	6	90·7
Total Abdominal	3,485	950	72·7	281	64	77·2
Acute Abdominal	445	6	98·6	69	0	100·0
Abdomino-Thoracic	600	258	57·0	47	17	63·8
Amputation, above and below elbow	444	14	96·8	25	1	96·0
Amputation, above and below knee	1,582	143	90·9	89	10	88·7
Fractured spine, cord injury	255	46	81·9	60	5	91·6
Fractured spine, without cord injury	99	3	96·9	12	0	100·0
Compound fracture						
Pelvis	242	17	92·9	39	0	100·0
Femur	1,740	97	94·4	236	3	98·7
Tibia-Fibula	2,016	17	99·1	312	1	99·6
Humerus	1,194	11	99·1	205	1	99·5
Radius-Ulna	999	0	100·0	152	0	100·0
Penetrating wounds of Joints						
Shoulder	187	1	99·5	28	0	100·0
Elbow	263	1	99·6	40	0	100·0
Wrist	102	0	100·0	15	0	100·0
Hip	34	0	100·0	4	0	100·0
Knee	1,011	7	99·3	137	0	100·0
Ankle	238	0	100·0	38	0	100·0
Burns						
slight	411	0	100·0	73	0	100·0
severe	316	18	94·3	46	1	97·8
Flesh wounds	7,518	51	99·3	1,416	0	100·0
with main nerve injuries	565	1	99·8	78	0	100·0
with main vessel injuries	807	41	94·9	112	4	96·4
Anaerobic Myositis	256	60	76·6	12	1	91·7
,, Cellulitis	45	6	86·7	8	0	100·0
Miscellaneous	5,515	13	99·7	1,003	3	99·7
Totals	36,920	2,108	94·3	4,960	139	97·2

TABLE 72: 21 Army Group. Analysis of Surgical Results. October–December, 1944

	Direct Admissions		No.	Average per Hospital	Percentage of Admissions
A.	Battle Casualties	..	8,792	517·2	43·4
B.	Non-Battle Casualties	..			
	Traumatic	..	5,341	314·2	26·4
	Non-Traumatic	..	6,124	360·2	30·2
	Totals	..	20,257		100·0

	A. No.	A. Aver. per Hosp.	Percentage of total A.	B. No.	B. Aver. per Hosp.	Percentage of total B.	C. No.	C. Aver. per Hosp.	Percentage of total C.	Total Casualties No.	Aver. per Hosp.	Percentage of Total
Abdomens	151	8·88	1·72	17	1·0	0·32	—	—	—	168	9·88	0·83
Abdomino-Thoracic	31	1·82	0·35	—	—	—	—	—	—	31	1·82	0·15
Amputations	254	14·9	2·89	—	—	—	—	—	—	254	14·9	1·26
Burns	167	9·82	1·90	409	24·1	7·66	—	—	—	576	33·92	2·86
Chests	187	10·7	2·07	27	1·59	0·51	—	—	—	214	12·29	1·03
E.N.T.	—	—	—	—	—	—	648	38·1	10·6	648	38·1	3·20
Eyes	164	9·65	1·87	151	8·88	2·83	443	26·1	7·23	758	44·6	3·76
Femurs	98	5·76	1·11	59	3·47	1·10	—	—	—	157	9·23	0·78
Gas Gangrene	5	0·29	0·06	—	—	—	—	—	—	5	0·29	0·02
Heads	626	36·8	7·12	490	28·8	9·18	—	—	—	1,116	65·6	5·53
Major Joints	271	15·9	3·08	766	45·1	14·3	—	—	—	1,037	61·0	5·15
Max.-Fac.	379	22·3	4·31	235	13·8	4·42	—	—	—	614	36·1	3·03
Spines	61	3·59	0·69	71	4·18	1·33	—	—	—	132	7·77	0·65

Deaths	No.	Average per Hospital	Percentage of Battle Casualty Admissions	Percentage of Deaths
Battle Casualties	151	8·86	1·72	68·6
Non-Battle Casualties				
Traumatic	55	3·22	1·03	25·0
Non-Traumatic	14	0·82	0·23	6·4
Totals	220		1·98	100·0

TABLE 72 (continued)

Deaths in relation to Lesion

	No.	Average per Hospital	Percentage of Total Deaths	Percentage of particular B.C. Lesion
Abdomens	13	0·76	8·61	8·6
Abdomino-Thoracic	5	0·29	3·31	16·1
Amputations	2	0·12	1·33	0·8
Burns	4	0·24	2·65	2·4
Chest	9	0·53	5·96	4·9
E.N.T.	—	—	—	—
Eyes	—	—	—	—
Femurs	4	0·24	2·65	4·1
Gas Gangrene	3	0·18	1·98	60·0
Heads	55	3·24	36·43	8·8
Major Joints	3	0·18	1·98	1·1
Max.-Fac.	5	0·29	3·32	1·1
Spines	7	0·41	4·63	11·5
Others	41	2·41	27·15	0·6

Operations	No.	Average per Hospital	Percentage of Operations	Percentage of Direct Surgical Admissions
Major	5,269	309·9	36·7	26·0
Minor	9,076	533·9	63·3	44·8
Totals	14,345		100·0	70·8

TABLE 73
21 Army Group. Admissions to all British Medical Units

	October 1944 British Offrs.	October 1944 British O.Rs.	October 1944 All Others Offrs.	October 1944 All Others O.Rs.	November 1944 British Offrs.	November 1944 British O.Rs.	November 1944 All Others Offrs.	November 1944 All Others O.Rs.
Beds equipped	1,066	15,014	44	476	1,209	14,600	32	630
Beds occupied:								
Sick	209	5,451	134	1,822	227	5,399	96	2,019
Wounded	96	2,198	95	2,156	86	1,824	32	868
Totals	305	7,649	229	3,978	313	7,223	128	2,887
Infections								
Malaria	5	207	2	41	9	159	4	22
Venereal Disease	8	600	8	474	8	902	23	641
All others	20	254	3	79	23	344	10	280
Infestations								
Scabies	—	28	—	18	—	35	—	26
Others	1	15	—	2	—	2	—	4
Psychiatric Conditions	40	685	11	227	32	863	10	71
Neurological Diseases	10	177	9	32	7	132	5	31
Diseases of the Eye	10	355	1	55	10	259	3	57
" " " Ear	8	335	—	69	7	367	1	94
" " " Nose and Throat	31	368	8	102	36	584	21	231
" " " Respiratory System	50	608	22	174	37	685	8	188
" " " Mouth and Gums	6	64	—	17	9	64	2	25
" " " Digestive System	97	1,531	34	384	106	1,491	31	547
" " " Musculo-skeletal System	37	725	11	146	31	756	13	242
" " " Skin	21	761	6	126	30	842	4	182
" " " Areolar Tissue	20	749	10	114	39	855	13	237
Injuries due to Enemy Action	424	6,886	487	7,550	333	4,056	183	2,998
" " " N.E.A.	131	2,786	105	1,331	113	2,461	70	1,036
Other Causes	141	2,144	162	2,151	108	1,949	129	1,858
Total Admissions	1,060	19,278	879	13,092	938	16,806	530	8,770
Deaths:								
Due to Disease	—	16	—	6	1	13	2	17
" " Injury E.A.	1	74	6	142	6	59	6	87
" " " N.E.A.	1	22	1	1	—	11	1	21
Total Deaths	2	112	7	149	7	83	9	125

TABLE 73 (continued)
21 Army Group. Admissions to all British Medical Units

	December 1944				January 1945			
	British		All Others		British		All Others	
	Offrs.	O.Rs.	Offrs.	O.Rs.	Offrs.	O.Rs.	Offrs.	O.Rs.
Beds equipped . . .	1,325	20,206	11	426	1,259	20,501	61	987
Beds occupied:								
Sick . . .	339	7,171	178	3,741	386	8,726	181	4,417
Wounded . . .	54	1,460	58	642	100	1,692	51	733
Totals . . .	393	8,631	236	4,383	486	10,418	232	5,150
Infections								
Malaria . . .	3	76	2	11	3	79	1	16
Venereal Disease . .	20	1,030	20	782	16	1,407	37	850
All others . . .	53	640	13	224	43	633	14	237
Infestations								
Scabies . . .	1	40	1	18	—	46	1	42
Others . . .	1	22	—	—	—	16	—	—
Psychiatric Conditions .	31	445	5	29	45	579	8	37
Neurological Diseases .	12	134	7	45	12	84	3	15
Diseases of the Eye .	11	311	2	61	8	329	3	66
,, ,, Ear . .	3	249	5	73	13	218	6	32
,, ,, Nose and Throat	40	648	15	232	81	852	31	274
,, ,, Respiratory System	41	643	13	162	54	97	25	227
,, ,, Mouth and Gums	13	49	1	17	12	99	2	27
,, ,, Digestive System	101	1,434	32	510	106	1,432	32	437
,, ,, Musculo-skeletal System	28	671	16	204	45	751	11	149
,, ,, Skin . .	25	849	6	147	34	893	7	120
,, ,, Areolar Tissue .	26	881	26	193	21	940	15	142
Injuries due to Enemy Action .	82	1,524	53	1,066	193	2,536	78	975
Other ,, ,, N.E.A. .	113	2,424	102	1,316	126	2,248	87	1,250
Other Causes . . .	114	2,070	129	2,263	123	2,643	206	3,803
Total Admissions . .	718	14,140	448	7,353	935	15,882	566	8,699
Deaths:								
Due to Disease . .	—	25	—	19	—	11	—	13
,, ,, Injury E.A. .	2	37	5	51	—	19	9	27
,, ,, ,, N.E.A. .	2	13	1	11	1	11	2	7
Total Deaths . .	4	75	6	86	1	41	12	47

TABLE 74

21 Army Group (less Canadian First Army)

Deaths in Medical Units. June 6, 1944–April 13, 1945

	Offrs.	O.Rs.	Totals
Wounded admitted and died of wounds			
British	9,127	121,571	130,698
Allied	351	4,033	4,384
Sick and injured admitted and died			
British	5,423	140,267	145,690
Allied	150	6,655	6,805
Total British	14,550	261,838	276,388
Total Allied	501	10,688	11,189
	15,051	272,526	287,577

The Canadian dead numbered 12,411 of whom 10,729 were killed in action or died of their wounds. (*Official Canadian Medical History, Vol. 1.*)

TABLE 75

21 Army Group. Hospital Bed State (excluding 200-bed hospitals u/c Armies). Dec. 1944–May 1945

Week ending	No. of Beds occupied	No. of Beds vacant	Total number of beds open	W.E. of beds in Theatre
Dec. 2	11,000	9,800	20,800	28,300
9	10,517	11,683	22,200	29,500
16	11,693	13,707	25,400	30,700
23	10,216	14,834	25,050	30,700
30	11,931	15,869	27,800	30,700
Jan. 6	13,458	15,142	28,600	31,900
13	14,190	14,610	28,800	31,900
20	14,733	13,667	28,400	33,100
27	15,839	12,961	28,800	33,100
Feb. 3	16,061	13,138	29,199	33,100
10	14,317	16,551	30,868	33,100
17	15,767	15,120	30,887	33,100
24	16,933	13,862	30,795	33,100
March 3	18,351	13,408	31,759	33,100
10	17,901	14,493	32,394	33,100
17	16,783	15,155	31,938	33,100
24	16,570	15,785	32,355	33,700
30	18,646	14,507	33,153	34,300
April 7	20,176	12,336	32,512	34,900
14	21,230	11,094	32,324	34,900
21	22,111	10,653	32,764	34,900
28	21,737	11,382	33,119	34,900
May 5	21,195	11,762	32,957	34,900
12	20,136	13,924	34,060	36,100
19	21,210	13,806	35,016	36,100
26	14,102	14,863	28,965	35,500

TABLE 76

21 Army Group. Admissions to all Medical Units. Dec. 1944–May 1945

(Rates per 1,000 per week)

Second Army

Week ending	Strength	Injuries E.A.	Injuries N.E.A.	Sick incl. exhaustion			Totals
Dec. 2	314,000	2·08	0·88	4·16	Exh.	0·24	7·12
9	281,000	1·00	1·16	7·37	,,	0·19	9·53
16	301,000	0·30	1·03	6·75	,,	0·07	8·08
23	313,000	0·63	0·92	5·34	,,	0·11	6·89
30	322,000	0·49	1·18	5·39	,,	0·11	7·06
Jan. 6	334,000	1·64	0·99	7·32			9·95
13	320,000	1·82	1·08	8·36			11·26
20	318,000	1·76	1·08	7·41			10·25
27	242,000	3·12	1·06	8·08			12·26
Feb. 3	237,000	0·42	0·86	6·77			8·05
10	215,000	0·28	0·80	6·08			7·16
17	195,000	0·18	0·82	6·68			7·68
24	176,000	0·10	0·81	5·17			6·08
March 3		0·13	0·82	5·87			6·82
10	206,000	3·73	1·44	5·8			10·97
17	340,000	0·36	1·16	6·14			7·66
24	365,000	2·47	1·42	6·67			10·56
31	369,000	12·00	1·44	7·84			21·28
April 7	374,000	5·38	1·30	4·30			10·98
14	399,000	5·18	1·21	4·62			11·01
21	401,000	5·11	1·41	5·87			12·39
28	404,000	3·00	1·55	5·96			10·51
May 5	420,000	2·59	1·57	6·07			10·23
12	417,000	0·11	1·52	5·64			7·27
19	417,000	0·06	1·42	5·94			7·42
26	347,000	0·02	1·00	4·28			5·30

Canadian First Army

Week ending	Strength	Injuries E.A.	Injuries N.E.A.	Sick incl. exhaustion			Totals
Dec. 2	221,000	0·90	1·11	7·44	Exh.	0·15	9·45
9	218,000	0·90	1·26	7·46	,,	0·17	9·62
16	216,000	0·55	1·01	7·80	,,	0·10	9·36
23	201,000	0·88	1·09	5·88	,,	0·13	7·85
30	192,000	0·66	1·94	6·91	,,	0·09	9·51
Jan. 6	191,000	0·92	1·19	7·05			9·16
13	214,000	0·64	1·17	7·07			8·88
20	214,000	1·05	1·06	7·49			9·60
27	288,000	0·98	1·06	7·10			9·14
Feb. 3	294,000	0·56	0·82	8·32			9·70
10	320,000	3·11	1·00	7·67			11·78
17	346,000	6·96	1·13	9·21			17·30
24	374,000	6·29	1·20	9·41			16·90
March 3		9·08	1·17	9·03			19·28
10	290,000	4·34	0·94	6·03			11·31
17	218,000	0·45	0·98	5·84			7·27
24	246,000	0·29	1·11	5·92			7·32
31	269,000	1·41	1·28	6·06			8·75
April 7	245,000	3·43	1·38	5·75			10·56
14	277,000	4·79	1·53	5·40			11·72
21	288,000	3·48	1·45	4·72			9·65
28	266,000	3·82	1·06	5·41			10·29
May 5	266,000	1·78	1·32	5·02			8·12
12	267,000	0·19	1·57	5·07			6·83
19	267,000	0·04	1·28	5·11			6·43
26	249,000	0·02	1·43	6·25			7·70

L. of C.

Week ending	Strength	Injuries E.A.	Injuries N.E.A.	Sick incl. exhaustion	Totals
Dec. 2	280,000	0·41	1·09	6·18	7·68
9	320,000	0·11	1·04	5·45	6·60
16	300,000	0·32	1·10	5·98	7·40
23	303,000	0·55	1·22	6·14	7·91
30	302,000	0·27	1·60	6·23	8·10
Jan. 6	303,000	0·36	1·37	7·56	9·29
13	295,000	0·18	0·89	8·0	9·07
20	301,000	0·21	1·18	8·47	9·86
27	312,000	0·11	1·09	8·00	9·20
Feb. 3	310,000	0·23	1·09	8·65	9·97
10	314,000	0·17	1·23	8·05	9·45
17	315,000	0·16	1·18	8·10	9·44
24	311,000	0·29	1·09	7·96	9·34
March 3		0·13	1·15	7·69	8·97
10	310,000	0·26	1·04	8·03	9·33
17	336,000	0·12	1·32	8·09	9·53
24	328,000	0·13	1·57	8·83	10·53
31	323,000	0·42	1·66	8·29	10·37
April 7	343,000	0·06	1·34	7·70	9·10
14	300,000	0·78	1·52	8·90	11·20
21	288,000	1·36	1·36	8·38	11·10
28	277,000	0·05	1·02	6·90	7·97
May 5	265,000	0·06	0·90	6·66	7·62
12	268,000	0·01	1·26	6·28	7·55
19	268,000	—	0·76	6·53	7·29
26	96,000	0·01	1·44	6·20	7·65

Average Whole Force

Week ending	Injuries E.A.	Injuries N.E.A.	Sick incl. exhaustion	Totals
Nov. 25	1·96	0·99	6·66	9·61
Dec. 2	1·13	1·03	5·92	8·08
9	0·67	1·15	6·76	8·58
16	0·37	1·05	6·74	8·16
23	0·66	1·07	5·72	7·45
30	0·45	1·51	6·05	8·01
Jan. 6	1·00	1·18	7·32	9·50
13	0·93	1·03	7·92	9·88
20	1·01	1·11	7·83	9·95
27	1·28	1·07	7·68	10·03
Feb. 3	0·40	0·93	8·00	9·33
10	1·31	1·03	7·39 Exh. 0·36	9·73
17	2·95	1·08	8·23 ,, 0·89	12·26
24	2·86	1·08	8·03	11·97
March 3	4·32	1·10	8·00	13·42
10	2·61	1·11	7·25	10·97
17	0·29	1·18	6·80	8·27
24	1·08	1·39	7·25	9·72
31	5·13	1·47	7·36	13·96
April 7	2·99	1·33	5·89	10·21
14	3·72	1·39	6·18	11·29
21	3·52	1·41	6·29	11·22
28	2·36	1·26	6·07	9·69
May 5	1·66	1·31	5·94	8·91
12	0·11	1·46	5·66	7·23
19	0·04	1·19	5·87	7·10
26	0·01	1·08	5·32	6·41

TABLE 77

21 Army Group. Direct Admissions to the Medical Divisions of All British Hospitals (excluding 32 B.G.H.) January–March 1945

(The figures in brackets are those for October–December 1944)

Infectious Diseases

Diphtheria		
(faucial)	1,080	(647)
(cutaneous)	9	(8)
Mumps	87	(42)
Typhoid Fever	2	(13)
Paratyphoid A	2	(1)
Measles, all forms	76	(13)
Meningitis		
Meningococcal	23	(11)
Benign lymphatic	4	(4)
Other forms	1	(2)
Poliomyelitis	1	(4)
Encephalitis	–	(1)
Scarlatina	99	(49)
Chicken Pox	32	(35)
Weil's Disease	3	(9)
Influenza	42	(30)
Erysipelas	36	(11)
Glandular Fever	89	(26)
Malaria		
B.T.	3	(8)
B.T. relapse	192	(327)
M.T.	–	(1)
Clinical and other	7	(12)
Short-term Fever N.Y.D.	122	(160)
Long-term Fever N.Y.D.	17	(15)
Acute Rheumatism	172	(93)
	2,099	(1,522)

Rheumatic Disorders

Chronic		
Rheumatoid Arthritis	80	(47)
Osteoarthritis	55	(63)
Spondylitis	14	(13)
Unclassified types	36	(48)
Other types	24	(75)

Fibrositis myalgia neuralgia	95	(769)
Fibrositic pains, functional	50	(37)
	754	(1,052)

Acute Digestive Disorders

Acute Infective Hepatitis	837	(585)
Acute Gastro-enteritis	436	(569)
Acute Diarrhoea	334	(478)
Bacillary Dysentery	134	(260)
Amoebic Dysentery	13	(14)
Other forms	270	(138)
	2,024	(2,044)

Acute Respiratory Diseases

Tonsillitis and Pharyngitis	3,408	(1,857)
Laryngitis and Tracheitis	189	(131)
Bronchitis	738	(778)
Coryza	619	(434)
Vincent's Angina	337	(131)
Pneumonia Prim.	497	(330)
	5,788	(3,661)

Chronic Respiratory Disorders

Pulmonary Tuberculosis	125	(83)
Chronic Bronchitis	469	(404)
Bronchiectasis	16	(27)
Emphysema	20	(27)
Asthma	58	(89)
Neoplasms	2	(15)
Pleurisy, dry	96	(168)
Pleurisy, with effusion	76	(83)
	862	(896)

THE HEALTH OF THE TROOPS

Sciatic Pain

Prolapsed Intra-vertebral disc	87	(54)
Fibrositis type	84	(109)
Functional type	26	(4)
Intermediate type	41	(40)
	238	**(207)**

Dermatological Cases

Scabies	386	(159)
Body louse, infected lesions	6	(3)
Crab louse, infected lesions	4	(2)
Other animal parasites	—	(1)
Impetigo	640	(671)
Ecthyma septic ulceration	62	(62)
Furunculosis	174	(205)
Sycosis	62	(67)
Acne	27	(35)
Dermatitis	1,248	(910)
Psoriasis	79	(69)
Tinea cruris	15	(21)
T. pedis	32	(17)
Warts	55	(53)
Urticaria	64	(54)
Herpes zoster	11	(18)
Other conditions	410	(381)
	3,275	**(2,727)**

Urinary Disorders

Acute Nephritis	45	(63)
Chronic Nephritis	23	(2)
Acute Pyelocystitis	87	(81)
Renal Colic	33	(42)
Stone Oxaluria, etc.	14	(26)
Other Diseases	162	(330)
	364	**(544)**

Circulatory Disorders

Valvular Disease of the Heart	18	(12)
Effort Syndrome	26	(32)
Hyperpiesia	23	(23)
Others	168	(119)
	235	**(186)**

Psychosomatic Disorders

Chronic Dyspepsia	—	(97)
Mucous Colitis	3	(19)
Colon Disorders	10	(12)
Effort Syndrome	26	(23)
Asthma	—	(25)
	39	**(176)**

Psychiatric Conditions

Psychoneurosis	767	(1,813)
Psychosis	21	(51)
	785	**(1,864)**

Organic Nervous Disorders

Epilepsy	68	(67)
Migraine	41	(47)
Other Disorders of the C.N.S.	185	(134)
	294	**(248)**

Miscellaneous Cases, unspecified . . 2,932 (1,627)

Total Admissions . 20,650 (16,754)

Deaths from Disease
British and Canadians
January–March 1945

Acute Infections	
Diphtheria	6
Pneumonias, primary	6
Septicaemia	2
C.S.F.	1
Tuberculosis	2
Infective Hepatitis	3
Poliomyelitis	1
Poisoning	
Strychnine	1
Cardiovascular	
Aortic Incompetence	1
Aortic Aneurysm	1
Rupture, heart valve	1
Rheumatic Carditis	1
Subarachnoid haemorrhage	1
Paroxysmal Tachycardia	1
Coronary Thrombosis	1
Cerebral Haemorrhage	1
Miscellaneous	
Acute Pulmonary Oedema	1
Ruptured Cerebral Abscess	1
N.Y.D. Brain	1

Percentage of Total Admissions

Infectious Diseases	10
Acute Digestive Disorders	10
Chronic ,, ,,	5
Urinary Disorders	1·5
Acute Respiratory Disorders	28
Chronic Respiratory Disorders	4
Sciatic Pain	1
Rheumatic Disorders	3·5
Circulatory Disorders	1
Psychosomatic	–
Dermatological Cases	16
Psychiatric Conditions	–
Organic Nervous Disorders	1·5
Miscellaneous	–

TABLE 78

21 Army Group. Numbers evacuated from the Theatre to the United Kingdom (excluding P.o.W.) Dec. 1944–May 1945

Week ending	1. By air 2. By sea	Injuries E.A.	Injuries N.E.A.	Sick (incl. Exhaustion)	Cumulative Total since D-day	Grand Total
Dec. 2	1.	689	296	560	47,901 }	113,097
	2.	155	139	426	65,196 }	
9	1.	390	215	349	48,885 }	114,320
	2.	63	66	110	65,435 }	
16	1.	184	113	190	49,342 }	115,087
	2.	36	22	252	65,745 }	
23	1.	202	151	278	50,016 }	115,761
	2.	—	—	—	65,745 }	
30	1.	105	151	230	50,502 }	116,537
	2.	43	50	197	66,035 }	
						June 6– Dec. 31 116,760

Week ending	1. By air 2. By sea	Injuries E.A.	Injuries N.E.A.	Sick (incl. Exhaustion)	Cumulative Total since D-day	Grand Total
						From Jan. 1
Jan. 6	1.	342	342	513	974 }	974
	2.	—	—	—	
13	1.	75	84	191	1,324 }	1,580
	2.	30	34	192	256
20	1.	125	120	262	1,831 }	2,695
	2.	161	77	371	865
27	1.	235	77	186	2,329 }	3,542
	2.	50	59	239	1,213
Feb. 3	1.	374	156	420	3,279 }	4,890
	2.	90	66	222	1,591
10	1.	370	330	776	4,755 }	7,395
	2.	153	183	713	2,640
17	1.	417	117	306	5,595 }	8,489
	2.	70	35	149	2,894
24	1.	1,087	174	586	7,442 }	10,569
	2.	83	16	134	3,129
Mar. 3	1.	1,568	159	614	9,783 }	13,034
	2.	11	22	591	3,251
10	1.	1,176	105	371	11,435 }	14,708
	2.	—	11	11	3,273
17	1.	766	130	399	12,730 }	16,205
	2.	48	17	137	3,475
24	1.	411	124	417	13,694 }	17,192
	2.	—	6	17	3,498
31	1.	1,093	164	432	15,383 }	18,991
	2.	11	20	79	3,608
April 7	1.	1,115	168	474	17,140 }	20,811
	2.	7	3	53	3,671
14	1.	1,205	166	348	18,859 }	22,531
	2.	—	1	—	3,672
21	1.	1,438	218	929	21,444 }	25,455
	2.	68	28	243	4,011
28	1.	915	418	966	23,743 }	27,764
	2.	—	3	7	4,021
May 5	1.	553	279	486	25,174 }	29,605
	2.	94	34	282	4,431
12	1.	703	436	694	27,007 }	31,438
	2.	—	—	—	4,431
19	1.	279	341	589	28,216 }	33,071
	2.	133	56	236	4,855
26	1.	176	218	433	29,043 }	34,711
	2.	233	178	402	5,668

Grand Total By Air 79,545
By Sea 71,703

151,248

Note: See R.A.F. Medical Services, Vol. 1, pp. 501–23.

Table 79

Medical Evacuations from North-west Europe to the United Kingdom expressed as Percentage of Admissions to Hospital (British Army only)

	First World War 1914–18		Second World War (Nov. 44–Apr. 45 only)	
	Offrs.	O.Rs.	Offrs.	O.Rs.
Wounded	71	62	47	38
Sick and Injured	40	29	19	13

Table 80

21 Army Group. Summary of Work of Mobile Ophthalmic Units. June 6–September 30, 1944

(a) Total number of cases seen		4,181
(b) Refractions		1,142
Prescriptions following refraction		832
Replacement and repairs by opticians		1,498
(c) Non-refractions		1,550
Sick		550
Casualties		
Non-battle	289	
Battle E.A.	513	
Battle accidental	41	
Total casualties		843
Miscellaneous		700

Summary of Work of Ophthalmic Departments of 600- and 200-bed Hospitals

(a) Total number of cases seen		5,687
(b) Refractions		2,355
Prescriptions following refraction		1,574
(c) Non-refractions		2,350
Sick		1,000
Casualties		
Non-battle	258	
Battle E.A.	927	
Battle accidental	160	
Total casualties		1,345
Unaccounted for		100
R.T.U.		1,000

Common Conditions

Blepharitis	149	10 per cent.
Conjunctivitis	609	43 ,,
Cornea		
Ulcer	241	17 ,,
Superficial keratitis	125	9 ,,
Deep keratitis	22	1·5 ,,
Scleritis	11	0·8 ,,
Iritis and cyclitis	40	3 ,,
Fundus conditions	74	5 ,,
Nervous system	41	3 ,,
Functional	106	7 ,,

(a) Casualties
    Non-battle 547
    Battle E.A. 1,440
    Battle accidental . . . 201
Total casualties 2,188

(b) Casualties

With other wounds	760	40 per cent. of B.Cs.	
Superficial injuries only	768		
Burns	172	10 ,,	,, ,,
Injury to orbital structures	203		
Non-penetrating eye injuries	557		
Penetrating eye injuries	480	30 ,,	,, ,,
Intra-ocular foreign bodies total	157		
,, ,, ,, removed	51	30 ,,	of total
Eye disorganised	244	14 ,,	of B.Cs.
Both eyes injured	198	12 ,,	,, ,,
Patient blinded	38	2 ,,	,, ,,

Causal Agent

Shell	30 per cent.
Bomb, air or mortar	20 ,,
Mine	14 ,,
Bullet	11 ,,
Bomb grenade	6 ,,
Booby traps	2 ,,
Blast, origin unspecified	16 ,,

Operations

Minor	539
Major	517
Plastic to lids, etc.	99
Abscission of uvea	105
Corneal suture	19

Scleral suture	41
Conjunctival flap	146
Cataract extraction or evacuation	5
I.O.F.Bs. magnetic	
Extraction by anterior routes	15
,, ,, posterior ,,	17
Non-magnetic extraction	11
Detachment of retina	1
Enucleation or evisceration	195

Optical Work at Optical Sections of Base Depots of Medical Stores and Mobile Ophthalmic Units

First issue or change of prescription	3,131
Replacement of lens	2,362
Broken lenses	1,464
Broken frames	547

TABLE 81

Incidence of Skin Diseases among Patients admitted to British General Hospitals. July–September 1944

Dermatitis, Eczema, etc.	692	Psoriasis	43
Impetigo	617	Warts	35
Furunculosis	134	T. cruris	30
Scabies	113	Ecthyma	30
Tinea pedis	94	Acne	18
Sycosis	54	Other Conditions	530
Urticaria	47		
			2,437

TABLE 82

21 Army Group. Venereal Diseases. Rates per 1,000 per week Nov. 1944–June 1945

Week ending	Second Army	Canadian First Army	L. of C.
Nov. 4	0·30	1·11	0·58
11	0·29	1·03	0·72
18	0·31	1·37	0·68
25	0·36	1·37	0·64
Dec. 2	0·36	1·23	0·64
9	0·47	1·38	0·64
16	0·32	1·32	0·57
23	0·30	1·26	0·66
30	0·26	1·24	0·58

Week ending	Second Army	Canadian First Army	L. of C.
Jan. 6	0·37	1·44	0·71
13	0·39	1·10	0·66
20	0·34	1·10	0·60
27	0·48	0·82	0·70
Feb. 3	0·31	1·14	0·58
10	0·53	1·00	0·47
17	0·54	0·85	0·71
24	0·37	0·72	0·61
March 3	0·46	0·74	0·71
10	0·51	0·73	0·67
17	0·44	0·92	0·52
24	0·41	1·27	0·64
31	0·49	0·99	0·81
April 7	0·33	0·93	1·10
14	0·25	0·95	0·85
21	0·27	0·65	1·18
28	0·40	0·84	0·86
May 5	0·32	1·16	0·65
12	0·46	1·16	1·19
19	0·43	1·37	1·21
26	0·55	1·73	0·85
June 2	0·51	2·14	0·90

21 Army Group. Venereal Diseases. Rates per 1,000 per week
June–July 1945

Week ending	I Corps District	VIII Corps District	XXX Corps District	Canadian First Army	L. of C.	Overall rate
June 2	0·57	n.a.	n.a.	2·14	0·85	1·04
9	0·86	n.a.	0·57	3·02	0·91	1·29
16	1·03	1·08	1·50	2·47	0·95	1·46
23	1·04	1·40	1·47	2·94	1·08	1·60
30	1·45	1·67	1·24	3·29	0·99	1·67
July 7	1·87	2·44	1·44	2·55	1·30	1·80
14	2·63	1·70	1·68	3·60	1·08	2·07

TABLE 83

13 Convalescent Depot. Summary of First, Second and Third 1,000 Convalescents

	First 1,000	Second 1,000	Third 1,000
Total Surgical	348	309	445
Total Medical	534	588	555
Due to E.A.	118	103	193

	First 1,000	Second 1,000	Third 1,000
Category on Admission: A	937	929	925
B	53	65	64
C	10	5	11
Category on Discharge: A	900	885	868
B	80	102	110
C	20	13	32
Percentage A.1 on discharge	90	88·5	86·8
No. in Infantry	460	418	495
No. in other Arms of Services	540	582	505
No. N.C.Os., sgt. and above	66 (6·6 per cent. of Intake)	55 5·5 per cent.	49 4·9 per cent.
No. requiring special remedial exercises daily	90	200	250
Percentage requiring inoculation	20 per cent.	20 per cent.	33·3 per cent.
Percentage requiring vaccination	30 ,,	25 ,,	20 ,,
Percentage requiring dental treatment	50 ,,	47·7 ,,	40·1 ,,
Percentage requiring:			
Blouses B.D.	25 ,,	25 ,,	10 ,,
Trousers B.D.	25 ,,	35 ,,	15 ,,
Shirts	75 ,,	91 ,,	33 ,,
Socks	80 ,,	97 ,,	100 ,,
Towels	76 ,,	91 ,,	90 ,,
Drawers	76 ,,		
Boots	25 ,,	35 ,,	20 ,,
Greatcoats	12 ,,	20 ,,	7 ,,
Average Length of Stay	14 days	13 days	9 days
Average number reporting sick daily	55	70	65
Average number requiring daily dressings	51	66	94
Average number requiring daily electro-therapy	44	52	50

APPENDIX XI

Surgical Casualties*

§1. *The Assessment of Battle Casualties in the Normandy Campaign. June–July 1944*

This section, in common with those that follow, refers to battle casualties among British troops of 21 Army Group during June and July 1944. It covers the landing on the Normandy beaches and the subsequent close country fighting in the *bocage* country of the bridgehead. It does not cover the mobile war following the final breakout. It was therefore a period of good recovery of wounded and short evacuation through forward medical units. Hospital attention was available in the bridgehead, but owing to the necessity for keeping it so, all casualties requiring hospital accommodation were evacuated as soon as possible to the U.K.

What follows is concerned with estimating the number of troops rendered non-effective during the battle. It is not concerned with those killed outright, but is intended to show the total number that had to be sent back from the battlefield for any medical reason.

The documentary sources were individual case records, respectively compiled at forward medical units (A.F. W.3118) and in hospital (A.F. I.1220). In forward areas, one Field Medical Card (A.F. W.3118) is prepared for each patient, initially by the first medical officer who attends him. It records regimental particulars, diagnosis and notes on clinical progress, and remains with the patient while in a medical unit. On arrival in hospital the patient sees a specialist who confirms the diagnosis. His particulars are entered at this stage on the Hospital Record Card (A.F. I.1220), to which the A.F. W.3118 is attached. Throughout his further progress in hospital and convalescent depot his relevant clinical history is entered on A.F. I.1220. On discharge the patient's documents are sent to the War Office.

It follows that cases not evacuated beyond forward medical units, either because they returned to duty from there or because they died, are recorded only on A.F. W.3118. Since military general hospitals in France during the period under review acted almost exclusively as casualty clearing stations, and were, in fact, keeping their clinical histories on A.Fs. W.3118, cases which received medical attention solely in France were recorded entirely on A.F. W.3118, and those which required hospital treatment were evacuated to the U.K. to be recorded on A.F. I.1220. A.Fs. W.3118 were therefore soon available in the War Office; but it was necessary to wait for a considerable period before complete rendition of A.Fs. I.1220. A.Fs. W.3118 were sampled directly from the sealed bags as received at the War Office. To start with, sampling procedure was truly random, i.e. contents of bags were thoroughly mixed before sorting. Data of this first sort were separately recorded. Since the sample of officers and N.C.Os. obtained therefrom was too small for further break-down, these groups were built up for a second sort by extracting cards referring specifically to these classes. Analysis of a 10 per cent. sample of

---

* From the *Statistical Report on the Health of the Army*. 1943–45. 1948. H.M.S.O.

A.Fs. I.1220 was made by use of the Hollerith machinery, cards used being those on which the Army Number cited ended in the digit 5, and received before February 25, 1945. This was supplemented by direct sorting of cards as they arrived at the War Office until April 9. It is known that this sample is incomplete inasmuch as a small proportion of men wounded during June–July were not then out of hospital, and there is delay between the date of discharge from hospital and arrival of A.F. I.1220 at the War Office.

Figures based on the A.F. I.1220 sample are, therefore, to some extent biased in favour of the exclusion of the longer term cases. The sample includes men wounded over the 8-week period June 6, 1944–July 31, 1944, and would, therefore, include all cases remaining not more than 34 weeks in hospital or convalescent depot, if:

(a) rendition were complete;
(b) individual cards were complete on receipt;
(c) there were no appreciable time lag involved in transmission of the documents to War Office.

A leakage of A.Fs. I.1220 is known to exist from the smaller E.M.S. hospitals and probably involves relatively more short- than long-term cases, since the latter pass through convalescent depots, which check the receipt of documents from the patient's hospital. If we assume that the time lag involved in transmission is rarely greater than 4 weeks, our sample should include nearly all cases whose total stay in medical units did not exceed 7 months.

The following consolidation of Arms of the Service is based roughly upon employment of the various arms involved and their relative position on the battlefield:

1. Armoured Forces
    Household Cavalry; R.A.C.; Recce.
2. Artillery
    Royal Artillery Field; Anti-Tank; Others.
3. Infantry
    All Infantry Regiments; Motor; M.G. and specialised; Guards; Commandos; Army Air Corps, Parachute Regiments, Glider Regiments and S.A.S.
4. Forward Services
    R.E.; R. Signals; R.A.M.C. (and A.D.C.).
5. Others
    R.A.S.C.; R.A.O.C.; R.E.M.E.; Pioneer Corps; Others.

Proportions of wounded treated in the field and evacuated to hospital can be assessed only by reference to sources of information other than A.Fs. W.3118 and I.1220. The responsible Adjutant-General's branch (A.G. (Stats.)) records figures for battle casualties based on regimental reports to 2nd Echelon; and a medical branch (A.M.D. 12), received figures for casualties evacuated to the U.K. Since all hospitalised cases were evacuated to the U.K. during the period under review, the A.M.D. 12 figures subtracted from the total given by A.G. (Stats.) might be assumed to give us the number of

THE HEALTH OF THE TROOPS

cases treated in forward units. This is not wholly true, because of disparity with respect to definition of casualties. The total figure for wounded given by A.G. (Stats.) includes besides personnel wounded by direct enemy action, persons injured by the following:

(i) blast;
(ii) concussion due to blast;
(iii) blast injury;
(iv) accidental injuries sustained in action or in proximity to the enemy; also accidental injuries which are not sustained in action or in proximity to the enemy provided they are caused by fixed apparatus (e.g. land mines) laid as defence against the enemy, as distinct from those employed for training purposes, and provided the personnel injured are on duty and not to blame.

It does not include:

(i) exhaustion, nervous or physical;
(ii) anxiety neurosis;
(iii) hysteria;
(iv) accidental injuries sustained in forward areas but not in action or in proximity to the enemy.

Thus, A.G. (Stats.) definition of wounded is juridical rather than medical, being based on the victim's employment at the time of sustaining injury. In issuing their figures, A.G. (Stats.) do running corrections by transferring from 'Wounded' to 'Killed' individuals notified as 'Died of Wounds' up to the date of issue. Since some individuals die of wounds after admission to medical units, it is necessary therefore to add the corresponding figure to the total wounded in order to get a figure comparable by definition to that derived from medical sources:

	Offrs.	O.Rs.	Totals
'Wounded,' June 6, 44–0600 hours Aug. 1, 44	1,934	29,283	31,217
Died of Wounds, June 6, 44–0600 hours Aug. 1, 44	157	1,623	1,780
	2,091	30,906	32,997

Progress of evacuation to the U.K. as transmitted to A.M.D. 12 was recorded by the medical authorities in charge at the points of disembarkation, a straight count of heads being supported by nominal rolls citing in most cases, a diagnosis. At the start, there was inevitably disparity between the figures, and the June nominal rolls register only 92 per cent. of the numbers counted; but in July 99·3 per cent cases were supported by names. If we weight the June figures derived from nominal rolls with due regard to this leakage we get the following:

Personnel Evacuated from Normandy

	Sick	Wounded	Injured Unspec.	No Diagnosis	Totals
Officers					
June	132	702	140	64	1,038
July	218	730	129	27	1,104
Other Ranks					
June	3,692	9,784	2,171	1,349	16,996
July	6,331	12,182	2,914	1,077	22,504
Totals					
June	3,824	10,486	2,311	1,413	18,034
July	6,549	12,912	3,043	1,104	23,608

For reasons stated Injury Unspecified in the figures cited above does not necessarily mean accidentally injured. It merely records lack of information with respect to the source of the injury. If we assume that the cases for which there is no diagnosis are divided between sick and injured in the same proportions as those for which a diagnosis is cited we get the following budget:

Injured Personnel Evacuated from Normandy

	Officers			Other Ranks		
	Wounds	Unspec.	Total	Wounds	Unspec.	Totals
1. June, Crude Figures	702	140	842	9,784	2,171	11,955
2. No diagnosis cases, divided proportionately	46	9	55	844	187	1,031
3. *Total June*	748	149	897	10,628	2,358	12,986
4. July, Crude Figures	730	129	859	12,182	2,914	15,096
5. No diagnosis cases, divided proportionately	18	3	21	612	146	758
6. *Total July*	748	132	880	12,794	3,060	15,854
7. *Total* 3 and 6	1,496	281	1,777	23,422	5,418	28,840

For two reasons, the above figure (28,840) for total injured O.Rs. evacuated to the U.K. is not exactly comparable with the A.G. (Stats.) figure for wounded, since:

(a) it refers to persons arriving in the U.K. up to the end of July, and therefore excludes those wounded at the end of the month but not as yet evacuated;

THE HEALTH OF THE TROOPS

(b) figures for total injuries derived from medical sources and for wounded from 2nd Echelon each contain an unknown proportion of individuals with unspecified injuries.

Fortunately, combination of the data from both sources on the basis of two extreme assumptions yields figures which do not diverge excessively for our present purpose.

	Percentage Evacuated		
	Offrs.	O.Rs.	Totals
I. If all injuries unspecified were reported as wounded	85·0	93·3	92·8
II. If no injuries unspecified were reported as wounded	71·6	75·8	75·5

Thus we cannot be far out if we assume that the proportions of officers and O.Rs. evacuated are respectively about 80 per cent. and 85 per cent. On this basis we can combine the information supplied by A.Fs. W.3118 and I.1220 without introducing a serious error.

The total figure from the A.M.D. 12 nominal rolls can also be used as a control whereby the completeness of our sample of A.Fs. I.1220 can be checked. We find, in fact:

	Offrs.	O.Rs.	Totals
A.F. I.1220 sample, supposedly 10 per cent.	85	2,034	2,119
A.M.D. 12 Nominal roll of cases evacuated.	1,777	28,840	30,617
Actual percentage of A.M.D. 12 figures represented by A.F. I.1220 sample	4·8	7·1	6·9

It is believed that the deficiency may be due more to incompleteness of rendition of A.Fs. I.1220 than to the known exclusion from our sample of the very long-term cases. Since there is ample evidence that officers do not in fact spend longer in hospital than O.Rs., this supposition is to some extent borne out by greater deficiency among officers.

Relative Importance of Sickness and Battle Injuries

Even in a highly selected army such as that which invaded France in 1944, there is sickness; and the proportion of battle to total casualties differs greatly in different medical units, as disclosed by information derived from A.F. W.3118 and from A.M.D. 12 nominal rolls. The ensuing figures are based on the former.

Cases Dealt with Entirely in forward Medical Units

		Injuries* E.A.	Injuries* N.E.A.	Exhaustion and Psychiatric	Sick
Officers	Percentage of total	40·9	10·4	3·0	45·7
	Standard error	2·07	1·28	0·71	2·10
O.Rs.	Percentage of total	23·8	10·9	17·8	47·5
	Standard error	0·49	0·36	0·44	0·57

* In this table, as elsewhere, E.A.=Enemy Action; N.E.A.=Not Enemy Action.

The next table is based on information supplied by the nominal rolls. No standard errors are given, since the figures are a historical record of a unique event, being complete as such. Thus sampling methods are not applicable, and even if we do elect to regard all battle casualties as a homogeneous universe of which our figures record a sample, it is obviously not random and there is no reason to suppose that samples so defined and so chosen are normally distributed.

Cases Evacuated to Hospital (Percentages)

	Injuries E.A.	Injuries Unspecified	Exhaustion and Psychiatric	Sick
Officers . .	69·2	13·0	2·3	15·6
Other Ranks .	59·5	13·8	8·0	18·8

Comparing the two tables, the character of injury as a relatively more serious contribution to wastage than sickness is clearly seen. To present the differential incidence of the various types of casualties in the two classes of medical units and their respective contributions to the grand total, we have to take into account the limits set by alternative assumptions with respect to allocation of unspecified injuries. The table following gives a representative mid-way figure, subject to a maximum and minimum as indicated by the $\pm$ (or $\mp$) sign. Accordingly, the higher values for those evacuated are always associated with lower values for those treated in forward units. Thus, our estimate of the proportions of different types of casualties admitted to medical units of the same type will lie between closer limits than the ones for persons evacuated or not evacuated. Also, higher values for any category of officers are comparable only with higher values for the similar category of other ranks. This tabulation neglects the sampling error for cases treated in forward units as trivial with respect to our present purpose.

Disposal and Nature of All Cases Admitted to Medical Units

		Injuries E.A.	Injuries N.E.A.	Exhaustion and Psychiatric	Sick	Total
Officers	Treated in Forward units	13·05 ±4·05	3·35 ±1·05	0·95 ±0·35	14·6 ±4·5	31·95 ±9·95
	Evacuated	47·05 ∓6·85	8·85 ∓1·25	1·55 ∓0·25	10·65 ∓1·55	68·1 ∓9·9
	Total	60·1 ∓2·8	12·2 ∓0·2	2·5 ±0·1	25·25 ±2·95	100·0
Other Ranks	Treated in Forward units	7·05 ±3·55	3·2 ±1·6	5·25 ±2·65	14·0 ±7·0	29·5 ±14·8
	Evacuated	41·85 ∓8·85	9·75 ∓2·05	5·6 ∓1·2	13·2 ∓2·8	70·4 ∓14·9
	Total	48·9 ∓5·3	12·95 ∓0·45	10·85 ±1·45	27·2 ±4·2	100·0

Evacuation Policy

One further item of information can be extracted from the nominal rolls of A.M.D.12. As soon as airfields had been captured in Normandy, air evacuation of casualties supplemented evacuation by sea. The nominal rolls show the method employed. Tables 84 and 84a give separate figures from this source with due regard to allocation of 'No Diagnosis' as above.

The table below shows the emergence of a policy with respect to air and sea evacuation. The ratio of the percentage of all wounded evacuated by air to the percentage of air-evacuated sick can be determined separately for Officers and Other Ranks. The June figures show little variation between the four categories, and such as there is follows no clear system. In July, however, the picture is entirely different. The chances of being evacuated by air were about 1·9 times as great for an injured person as for a sick one, and 1·4 times as great for an Officer as for an Other Rank. It would appear that a policy favouring air-evacuation for injury and, to a less extent, for Officers, was being implemented.

The Growth of Evacuation Policy (Percentages evacuated by air)

	June			July		
	(a) Sick	(b) Injured	Ratio (b)÷(a)	(a) Sick	(b) Injured	Ratio (b)÷(a)
A. Other Ranks	18·0	16·4	0·91	14·7	28·1	1·91
B. Officers	19·3	20·8	1·08	20·9	37·8	1·81
C. Ratio B÷A.	1·07	1·27	—	1·42	1·35	—

The Relative Distribution of Injuries E.A. and N.E.A.

As shown above, the demarcation between wounds and accidental injuries is not easy to determine. The criterion employed in sorting A.Fs. W.3118 and I.1220 was whether clinical notes directly recorded information relating injury to employment or an enemy weapon. Thus wounds caused by secondary missiles or burns sustained in a tank set on fire by enemy guns were counted as E.A. So were injuries from land mines or booby traps. Men described as injured by falling debris, in default of evidence associating the casualty with explosion of a shell or bomb, were counted as N.E.A. Self-inflicted wounds were also counted as N.E.A. This is, in fact, a more restricted specification than either:

(a) E.A. cases, the definition of wounded by A.G. (Stats.) on the testimony of the reporting unit, and hence their own interpretation of 'accidental injuries sustained in proximity to the enemy';
(b) N.E.A. cases, the list of injuries unspecified in the nominal roll of A.M.D. 12.

It is, however, the only definition easily applicable to the data of this enquiry; and some divergence between estimates based on such different definitions is regrettably inevitable as the following figures indicate:

	Injuries E.A.		Injuries N.E.A.	
	Crude Figures	Per cent.	Crude Figures	Per cent.
A.F. I.1220 Sample	1,899	89·6	220	10·4
A.M.D. 12 Nominal Rolls	24,918	81·4	5,699	18·6

To some extent conclusions relating to division of casualties as E.A. and N.E.A. are thus limited by the arbitrary definitions necessarily adopted. In so far as they depend on a more precise definition, figures based on A.F. I.1220 give us a clearer picture than those based on nominal rolls of A.M.D. 12, but it must be borne in mind that any subdivision into E.A. and N.E.A. in the analysis which follows has to be interpreted with due regard to the definition of N.E.A. implied. In Tables 85–89 as in other sections, the term N.C.O. has been interpreted to include L/Cpl. and its equivalent.

The salient conclusions that emerge therefrom are:

(a) as one would expect, the ratio between injuries E.A. and N.E.A. varies considerably between ranks and Arms of the Service (Tables 85, 88);
(b) a greater proportion of the injured dealt with in forward areas and not evacuated, in contradistinction to those evacuated, were N.E.A. This preponderance is accounted for almost exclusively by cases returned to duty. Very few of the injured N.E.A. died. (Tables 85, 87);
(c) of cases dealt with in forward areas without being evacuated, about half returned to duty and about half died. About two-thirds are E.A. and one-third N.E.A. (Table 86);
(d) although nearly a third of such injuries are, in fact, Infantrymen (Table 88), injuries N.E.A. are relatively least common among the infantry;
(e) we can, of course, get no fresh estimate of the proportions evacuated and not evacuated from samples of A.Fs. W.3118 and I.1220 selected

TABLE 84

Evacuation from Normandy, June–July 1944

		Officers			O.Rs.		
		Sick	Injured	Total Cases	Sick	Injured	Total Cases
June	Sea	13·71	86·29	100·0	23·24	76·76	100·0
	Air	12·62	87·38	100·0	25·30	74·70	100·0
	Totals	13·49	86·51	100·0	23·58	76·42	100·0
June Totals (cases)	Sea			824			14,146
	Air			214			2,850
	Totals			1,038			16,996
July	Sea	24·55	75·45	100·0	33·42	66·58	100·0
	Air	12·40	87·60	100·0	18·12	81·88	100·0
	Totals	20·38	79·62	100·0	29·73	70·27	100·0
July Totals (cases)	Sea			725			17,080
	Air			379			5,424
	Totals			1,104			22,504
Totals	Sea	18·79	81·21	100·0	28·81	71·20	100·0
	Air	12·48	87·52	100·0	20·59	79·41	100·0
	Totals	17·04	82·96	100·0	27·09	72·91	100·0
Totals (cases)	Sea			1,549			31,226
	Air			593			8,274
	Totals			2,142			39,500

TABLE 84a

		Officers		Other Ranks	
		Sick	Injured	Sick	Injured
June	Sea	80.7	79.2	82.0	83.6
	Air	19.3	20.8	18.0	16.4
	Totals	100.0	100.0	100.0	100.0
July	Sea	79.1	62.2	85.3	71.9
	Air	20.9	37.8	14.7	28.1
	Totals	100.0	100.0	100.0	100.0

TABLE 85

Ratio of Casualties E.A. and N.E.A. by Rank (Numbers in brackets give crude figures in samples)

A. (i) Not Evacuated

	Officers	N.C.O.	Pte.	Total Cases
E.A.	8.6	24.4	67.0	100.0 (1,848)
N.E.A.	5.9	24.1	70.0	100.0 (888)
Totals	7.7	24.3	68.0	100.0 (2,736)

(ii) Evacuated

	Officers	N.C.O.	Pte.	Total Cases
E.A.	4.2	25.0	70.8	100.0 (1,899)
N.E.A.	2.3	22.7	75.0	100.0 (220)
Totals	4.0	24.8	71.2	100.0 (2,119)

B. (i) Not Evacuated

	Officers	N.C.O.	Pte.	Total Cases
E.A.	75.4	67.8	66.6	67.5
N.E.A.	24.6	32.2	33.4	32.5
Totals	100.0 (211)	100.0 (665)	100.0 (1,860)	100.0 (2,736)

(ii) Evacuated

	Officers	N.C.O.	Pte.	Total Cases
E.A.	94.1	90.5	89.1	89.6
N.E.A.	5.9	9.5	10.9	10.4
Totals	100.0 (85)	100.0 (525)	100.0 (1,509)	100.0 (2,119)

TABLE 86
Disposal and Nature of Casualties Not Evacuated Beyond Forward Medical Units

	All Ranks		
	E.A.	N.E.A.	Totals
Returned to duty	27·1	31·2	58·3
Died	40·5	1·3	41·8
Total (2,736)	67·6	32·5	100·0

TABLE 87
Distribution of Casualties Not Evacuated by Rank

A. (i) Returned to Duty

	Officers	N.C.O.	Pte.	Total Cases
E.A.	10·0	25·2	64·8	100·0 (741)
N.E.A.	5·4	24·7	69·9	100·0 (853)
Totals	7·5	25·0	67·5	100·0 (1,594)

(ii) Died

	Officers	N.C.O.	Pte.	Total Cases
E.A.	7·7	23·8	68·5	100·0 (1,107)
N.E.A.	17·1	8·6	74·2	100·0 (35)*
Totals	8·0	23·4	68·7	100·0 (1,142)

B. (i) Returned to Duty

	Officers	N.C.O.	Pte.	Total Cases
E.A.	61·7	47·0	44·6	46·5
N.E.A.	38·3	53·0	55·4	53·5
Totals	100·0 (120)	100·0 (398)	100·0 (1,076)	100·0 (1,594)

(ii) Died

	Officers	N.C.O.	Pte.	Total Cases
E.A.	93·4	98·9	96·7	96·9
N.E.A.	6·6	1·1	3·3	3·1
Totals	100·0 (91)	100·0 (267)	100·0 (784)	100·0 (1,142)

* Based on a small number of cases.

TABLE 88

Distribution of Casualties by Arm of Service

(i) Not Evacuated

	A						B					
	Armd.	Arty.	Inf.	Fwd. Services	Others	Total Cases	Armd.	Arty.	Inf.	Fwd. Services	Others	Total Cases
E.A.	7.8	12.3	67.4	6.8	5.7	100.0 (1,848)	74.6	62.5	81.9	43.6	28.7	67.6
N.E.A.	5.5	15.5	31.1	18.3	29.5	100.0 (888)	25.4	37.5	18.1	56.4	71.3	32.4
Totals	7.1	13.4	55.7	10.5	13.4	100.0 (2,736)	100.0 (193)	100.0 (365)	100.0 (1,521)	100.0 (287)	100.0 (370)	100.0 (2,736)

(ii) Evacuated

	Armd.	Arty.	Inf.	Fwd. Services	Others	Total Cases	Armd.	Arty.	Inf.	Fwd. Services	Others	Total Cases
E.A.	7.3	8.7	72.8	5.9	5.3	100.0 (1,899)	87.4	82.9	94.1	74.2	71.4	89.6
N.E.A.	9.1	15.5	39.5	17.7	18.2	100.0 (220)	12.6	17.1	5.9	25.8	28.6	10.4
Totals	7.5	9.4	69.4	7.1	6.6	100.0 (2,119)	100.0 (159)	100.0 (199)	100.0 (1,470)	100.0 (151)	100.0 (140)	100.0 (2,119)

TABLE 89

Limits of Overall Disposal and Nature of Casualties

	Died	Returned to Duty	Evacuated	Totals
E.A.	7.55 ± 4.63	5.05 ± 3.10	72.90 ∓ 10.25	85.5 ∓ 2.51
N.E.A.	0.24 ± 0.15	5.79 ∓ 3.55	8.47 ∓ 1.18	14.5 ± 2.51
Totals	7.79 ± 4.78	10.84 ± 6.65	81.37 ∓ 11.43	100.0

as these were. Indeed, application of the method discussed on page 599 breaks down in this respect, as a result of the wide margin of error assignable to the ratio of injuries N.E.A. to E.A. among cases treated in forward areas. Such a calculation does, however, give us a better delineation of the overall proportion of injuries that were N.E.A. within the scope of the definition adopted above. This is found to be $14 \cdot 5 \pm 2 \cdot 5$ per cent. (Table 89).

§2. *Injury and Man-power Wastage—Normandy. June–July 1944*

Downgrading as a Measure of Wastage

Two criteria of the gravity of injuries as a source of wastage are available:

(i) resulting number of days off duty;
(ii) physical deterioration as indicated by downgrading or invaliding.

This section is concerned to show how the two are associated. For this purpose 'days off duty' signifies the number of days that elapse between injury and final disposal by discharge from hospital, by death or by appearance before a Medical Board for discharge from the Army (Category E). It therefore covers time spent in all medical units including convalescent depots, but excludes sick leave, out-patient attendance, or stay in hospital after invaliding. Though A.F. I.1220 specifically calls for the patient's medical category on admission and discharge, failure to give such information is unfortunately common. In consequence it is necessary to limit enquiry with reference to downgrading to cases shown as Category C or E on discharge. These are known to have been downgraded, since only men in Categories A and B landed in France during the period covered. Relevant data are incomplete in two ways:

(a) some cards do not state medical category on discharge;
(b) the proportion of our sample in E is far below reasonable expectation in the light of other estimates, and hence suspect.

Almost certainly these two deficiencies are not, as might at first be supposed, mutually explanatory. All cards not citing medical category on discharge were carefully examined; and no case recorded thereon had as yet come before a board at the time when the documents were dispatched. Hence figures here presented have been separately calculated on each of two assumptions with respect to unspecified cases:

Assumption I: No case of category unspecified was in fact downgraded;
Assumption II: We know nothing about them, and should therefore neglect them.

Tables 90 and 91 are designed to show the increasing proportion of patients downgraded among groups spending longer periods away from duty. As for compilation of other tables given below, the basis of sample classification is a decile split with respect to date of discharge from medical units, i.e. division of the whole sample, after arrangement in order of precedence with respect to day of discharge, into groups composed of a number of individuals approximately equivalent to one-tenth of the total. Thus the first decile is composed of 10 per cent. of the sample and is made up of individuals all of whom obtained discharge before any of the residual 90 per cent. The second decile, also composed of 10 per cent. of the sample, is made up of individuals all of whom obtained discharge after those in the first decile and before those in the deciles including the residual 80 per cent.

Table 90 shows separately for E.A. and N.E.A. in accordance with each Assumption I and II above, the proportions downgraded within each tenth of the sample split as above, with the corresponding date of discharge from hospital of the last man in a given sample tenth. The salient feature is a progressive increase of downgradings in successive sample-tenths, i.e. increasing proportion of downgrading associated with longer duration of stay. The N.E.A. sample is too small to justify acceptance at its face value of what appears to be less severe deterioration. Since the sample is defective in respect of some who spent 7–10 months and all who spent a longer time in hospital, the very high downgrading rate in the terminal sample-tenths furnishes an acceptable explanation of the absolute deficiency of E category personnel as mentioned above.

Table 91 shows the proportionate contribution of each sample-tenth to the total downgraded. It is notable that:

(i) over 40 per cent. of E.A. downgradings occurred in the terminal tenth (remaining between 142 and 292 days)
(ii) downgradings in the first 5 tenths (remaining less than 55 days) were trivial.

Table 92 shows separately for E.A. and N.E.A., in accordance with Assumptions I and II above, the proportions downgraded within each Arm of Service group, as delimited in §1. What emerges is that the chances of downgrading, if wounded or injured, do not materially differ with different Arms of Service. Analogous remarks apply *mutatis mutandis* to proportions downgraded in the three categories of rank (Table 93).

Man-Day Wastage

From the standpoint of man-power planning we have at our disposal four criteria of wastage: (*a*) death; (*b*) invaliding; (*c*) downgrading; (*d*) days off duty. Available data concerning (*b*) and (*c*) have been set forth above. What follows refers to (*a*) and (*d*). It will be convenient to consider separately the data respectively derived wholly from A.F. W.3118 (not evacuated to the U.K.) and those taken from A.F. I.1220 (evacuated).

(i) *Deaths and Cases Returned to Unit (R.T.U.) in the theatre.* The A.F. I.1220 sample survey disclosed no case of death in a U.K. hospital. Hence the proportion of such deaths appears to have been negligible from a statistical viewpoint. Table 94 thus shows that:

(*a*) over 50 per cent. of deaths in all medical units occurred on the day of admission;
(*b*) over 80 per cent. of the deaths occurred in the first three days;
(*c*) under 5 per cent. of deaths occurred later than one week after admission.

THE HEALTH OF THE TROOPS

Table 95 refers only to survivors discharged from medical units without evacuation. The figures therefore indicate what the evacuation policy was. The salient conclusions are:

(a) nearly a quarter of such admissions remained only a day for treatment;
(b) over a half remained for a period less than 4 days;
(c) less than one-fifth remained longer than a week.

(ii) *Cases evacuated to the U.K.* Since the tables above exhibit a decile classification with respect to days to disposal, little remains to be said about man-day wastage among evacuated cases. Table 96 exhibits the same data in another way, showing:

(a) over 20 per cent. remained not more than one month;
(b) over 70 per cent. remained not more than three months;
(c) about 15 per cent. still remained at the end of four months.

Accompanying figures illustrate some features not stressed in the text above. Fig. 93 shows the decile classification in respect of days to disposal referred to in the tables accompanying this section. It emphasises the fairly constant proportion of injuries N.E.A. and E.A. in each sample tenth, and also embodies, in the second half of the chart, the data of Table 96. The two histograms on page 611 compare rates of disposal of E.A. and N.E.A. injuries in accordance with our standard conventions, viz.: that part of the histogram which is common to both E.A. and N.E.A. is stippled while excess of E.A. and of N.E.A. is represented by lined and unshaded parts respectively. Fig. 94, which refers to casualties not evacuated to U.K., embodies the data of Tables 94-95, exhibited separately for injuries E.A. and N.E.A.

Time Spent at Different Stages of Evacuation

Time off-duty is amenable to a threefold split:

(a) time to hospital, i.e. the period between injury and arrival at a hospital in the U.K. Since all but a few cases first received medical attention on the day of injury this coincides with time spent in forward units;
(b) time in hospital;
(c) time in convalescent depots.

The last two, (b) and (c), are self-explanatory except in so far as the latter refers solely to military convalescent depots, i.e. B.R.C.S. or Order of St. John auxiliary hospitals and convalescent homes were counted as hospitals.

In assessing relative distribution of time-off-duty between the three stages of treatment, we are concerned solely with man-day wastage. The unit taken is loss to the Army of the services of one man for one day or, what comes to the same thing, the occupation of a bed in a medical unit for one day.* The distribution of man-days off duty as between the three stages of treatment for

---

* Strictly speaking, of course, cases invalided from the Army should not be assessed in this way. For the sake of simplicity, we have to consider them in terms of man-day wastage from injury to medical boarding.

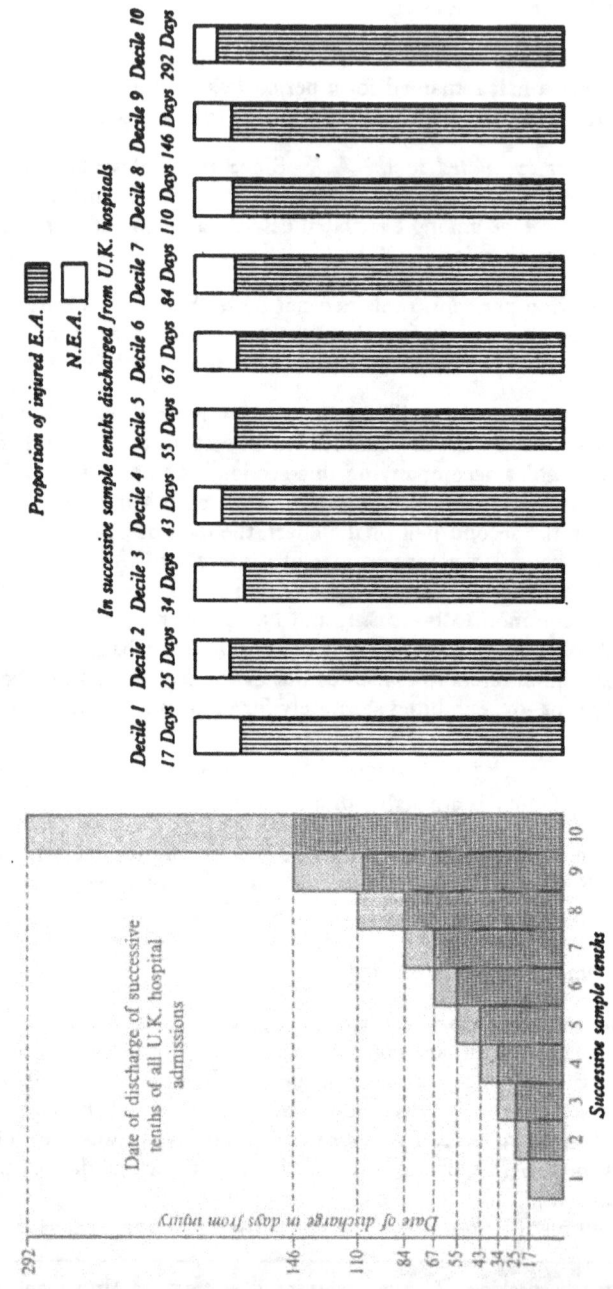

Figure 93
CASUALTIES (INJURED) NORMANDY D-DAY TO END OF JULY 1944

THE HEALTH OF THE TROOPS

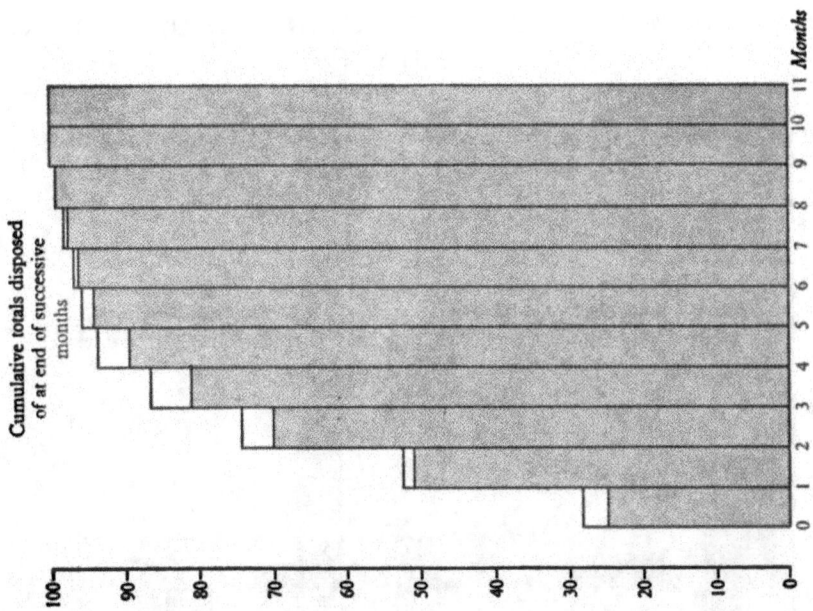

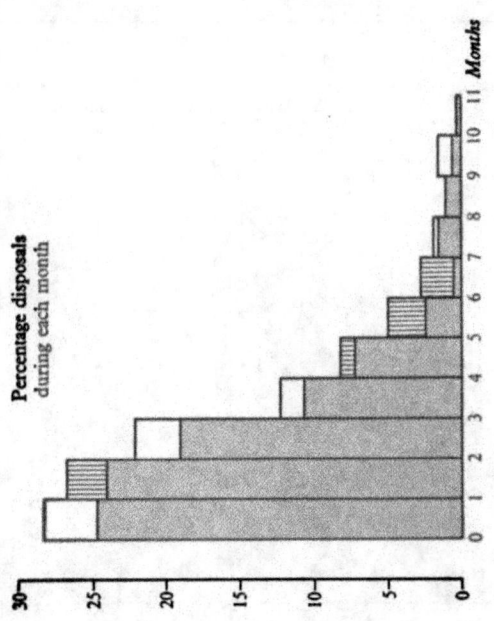

Figure 94
CASUALTIES (INJURED) NORMANDY D-DAY TO END OF JULY 1944

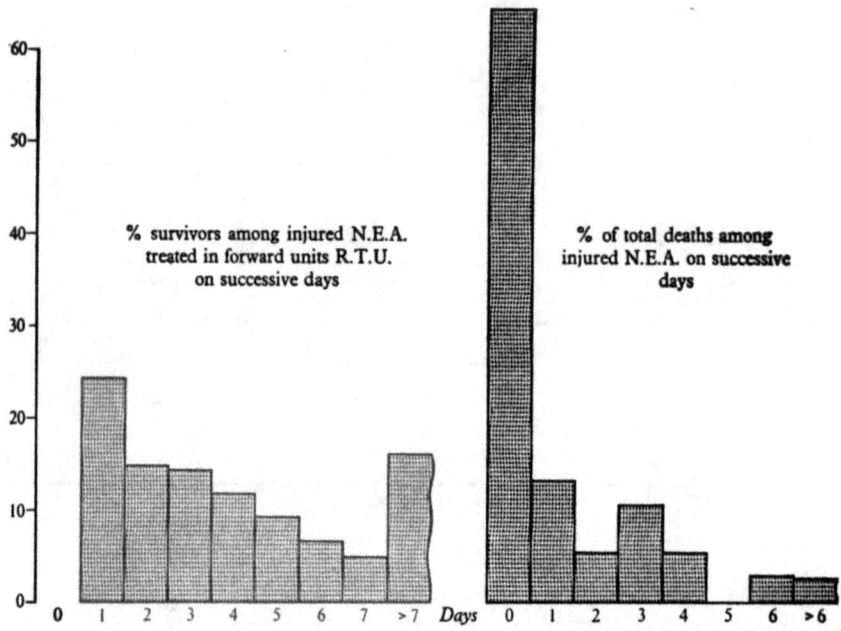

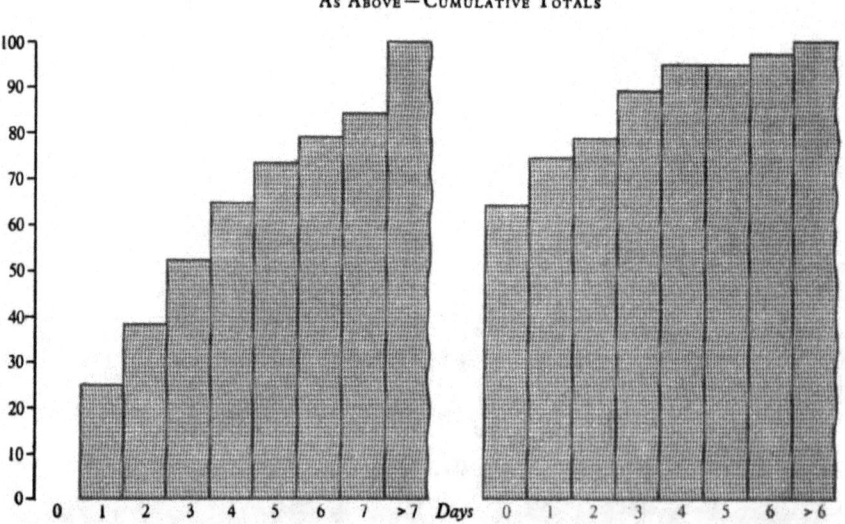

As Above—Cumulative Totals

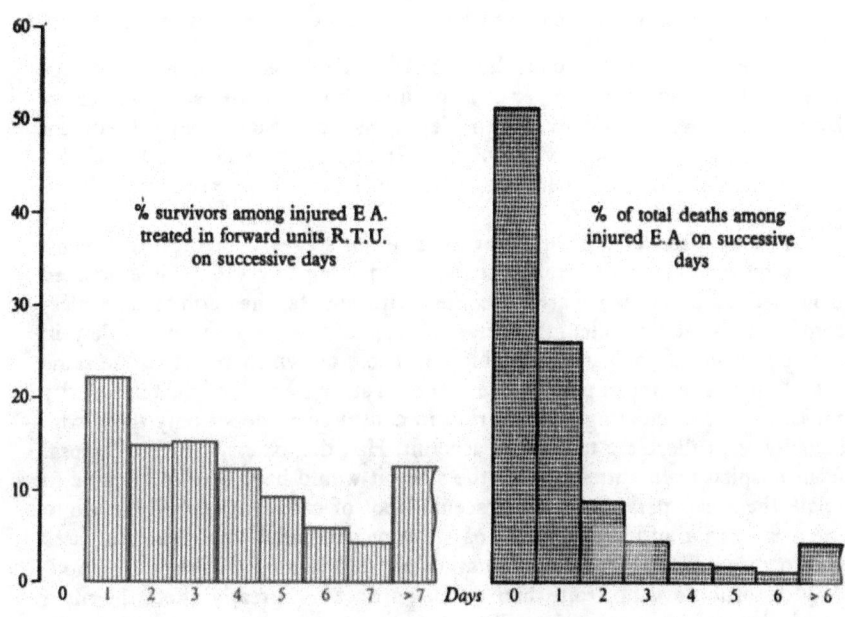
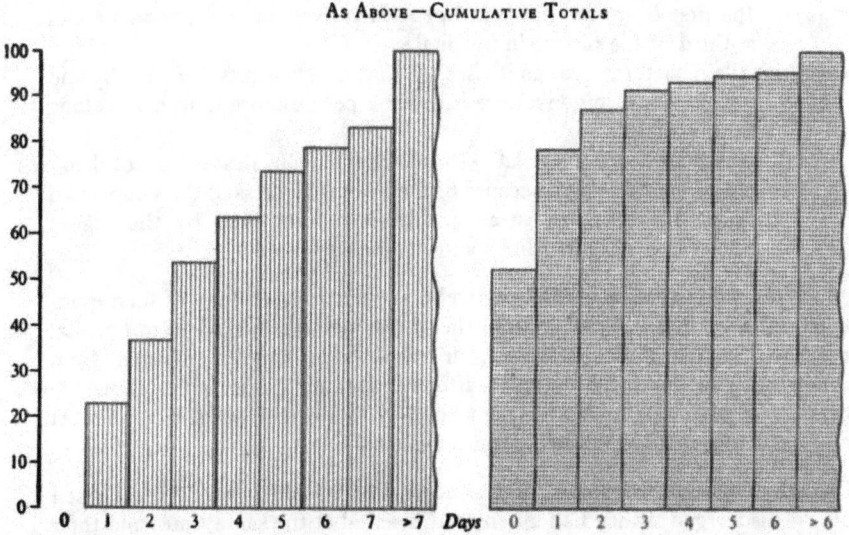

each of the ten severity grades specified by the decile split described above is given in Table 97 and shows:

(a) that 22 per cent. of total time lost to duty by all the men in the sample was spent in convalescent depots;
(b) that the last 10 per cent. of the men to return to duty or to be invalided from the Service accounted for 25 per cent. of the total time lost.

Not every case goes to a convalescent depot. Table 98 shows the percentage of each of the successive 10 per cent. groups who in fact did so. While 50 per cent. of all cases go to convalescent depot, the frequency of such treatment increases with length of stay in hospital. Since officers seldom go to military convalescent depots, the percentages shown in this table are a trifle lower than they should be.

For comparison of time spent at the relevant stages of medical treatment, Table 97 gives us an overall picture, as affecting any group of evacuated wounded. In so far as we are concerned with how far the period in convalescent depot is related to length of stay in hospital, we are interested solely in the sub-group of the cases of Table 98. Table 99 which refers to the same sample shows the mean periods spent at each stage by each of the ten severity ranks, i.e. for calculating mean period in convalescent depot only those who actually went there are taken into account. Had the extent of direct disposal from hospital been anticipated at the start, it would have been preferable to relate the mean period in convalescent depot of cases despatched thereto to the mean period of hospitalisation of the same personnel, i.e. to exclude cases not so disposed of for the computation of the mean hospitalisation period. Any distortion arising from their inclusion does not greatly affect the main conclusions which emerge from Table 99, viz.:

(a) in the first 6 groups the time spent in convalescent depot was about one-third of the period in hospital;
(b) for the next three groups it rises, so that men off duty between 85 and 142 days spent in convalescent depot a period more than half as long as in hospital;
(c) for the final decile the relative time spent in convalescent depot drops again, possibly in part because of the incompleteness of the sample and in part due to administrative procedure prompted by the higher proportion of downgradings and invalidings therein.

Tables 100, 101 and 102, respectively, show the percentage of men evacuated for each day after wounding, the percentage discharged from hospital for each month after admission, and the percentage discharged from convalescent depot for each week after admission. These tables show the bedstate position for a fixed intake at each of the three stages. To interpret them aright two considerations are important:

(i) these figures present the rate at which casualties would have been discharged if they had all entered hospital at the same time; and their use for bedstate planning pre-supposes due regard to the rate of admission;

THE HEALTH OF THE TROOPS

(ii) since there is a high association (*see* Table 99) between time spent at different levels, it is not legitimate to treat the information of Tables 100, 101 and 102 cumulatively. The use of different time units in these tables is intentional with a view to emphasising this.

The main conclusions that emerge from this analysis are:

(i) The first 50 per cent. of wounded to return to duty account for only 22 per cent. of the man-days lost, and the last 10 per cent. account for 25 per cent. Since we have already seen that the final decile includes 60 per cent. of the cases subsequently invalided from the Army, it accounts for a very high concentration of all wastage.

(ii) Of this total man-day wastage 95 per cent. was accommodated in the U.K.—in hospitals 73 per cent. and in military convalescent depots 22 per cent. Roughly speaking, one bed in a convalescent depot was occupied for one day on account of injury for every 3 days a bed was so occupied in hospital. Needless to say, this does not necessarily mean that the hospital population was three times the convalescent depot population of wounded at a given time.

(iii) Almost exactly 50 per cent. of all injured attended a convalescent depot; and the proportion of injured who went to one increased with length of stay in hospital, but not more than 80 per cent. of the highest severity grade go there.

(iv) Time spent in convalescent depot increased with time spent in hospital.

(v) Time from wounding to arrival in hospital was remarkably low, since 90 per cent. were in U.K. hospitals within a week of wounding.

(vi) Of injured, 70 per cent. spent under two months in hospital and 97 per cent. under six months. Of cases going to convalescent depot 50 per cent. spent over one month there.

The data of Tables 97–102 are shown graphically in Figs. 95 and 96.

It is necessary to emphasise that we have to rely on more or less arbitrary, if plausible, assumptions to co-ordinate the data supplied by different documentary sources with a view to an overall estimate of wastage, such as the foregoing survey of the first 8 weeks of the Normandy campaign sets forth. With due regard to the limitations inherent in such assumptions and also to the exclusion of exceptionally long-term cases from the hospital sample on which this analysis relies, the broad general picture which emerges is the following rough and ready balance sheet, in which the most dubious figure refers to invalidings. In view of the known sources of leakage and of the long time lag frequently involved before invaliding, the true rate is almost certainly very much higher than the 5 per cent. cited.

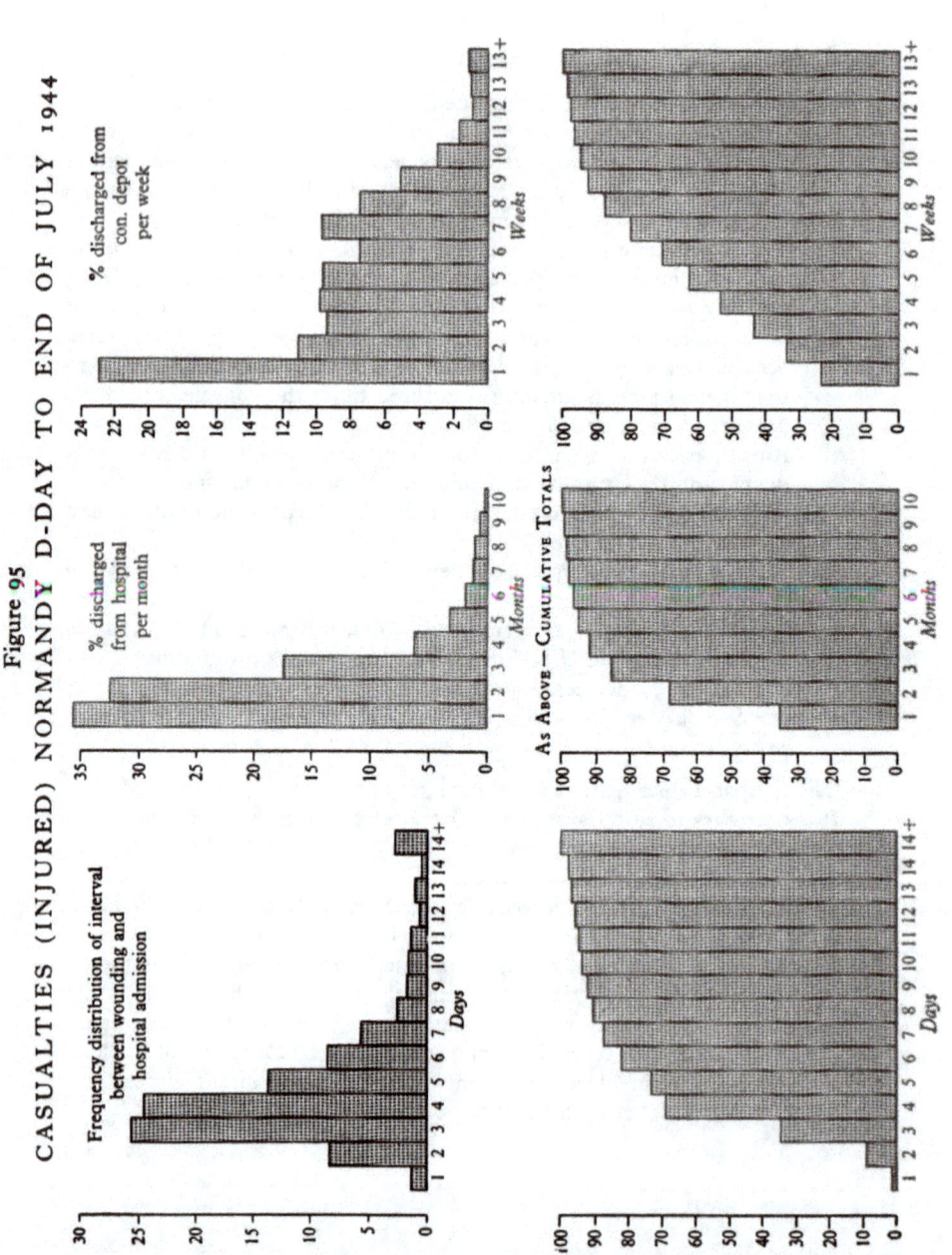

Figure 95

CASUALTIES (INJURED) NORMANDY D-DAY TO END OF JULY 1944

Figure 96
CASUALTIES (INJURED) NORMANDY D-DAY TO END OF JULY 1944

Relation of duration in different types of medical units to decile severity grades

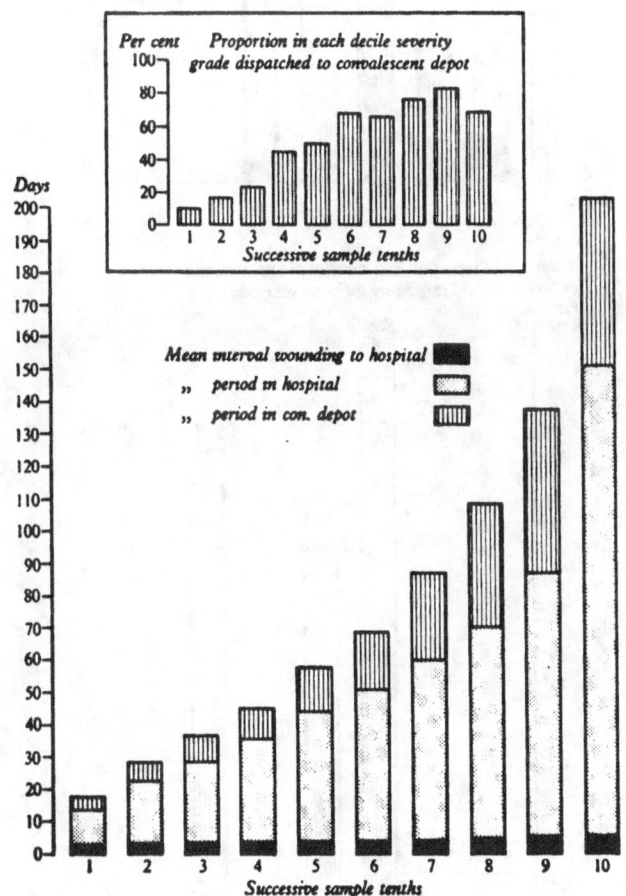

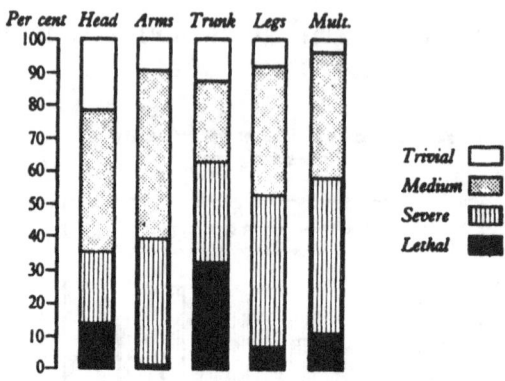

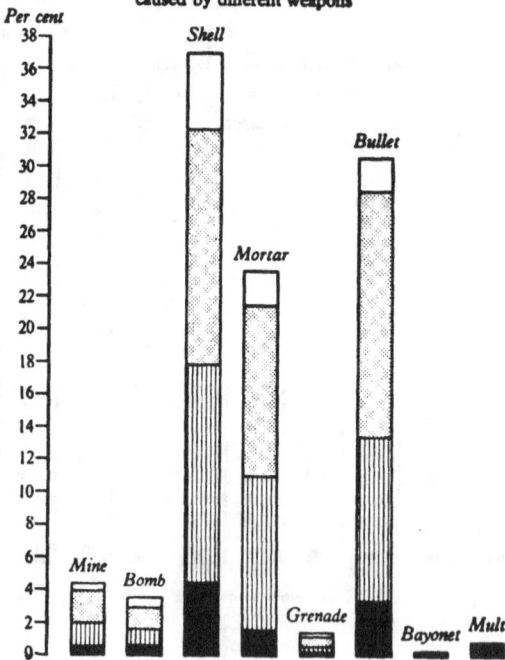

THE HEALTH OF THE TROOPS

Approximate Disposal of 1,000 Cases Admitted to All Medical Units; 21 Army Group; June–July 1944

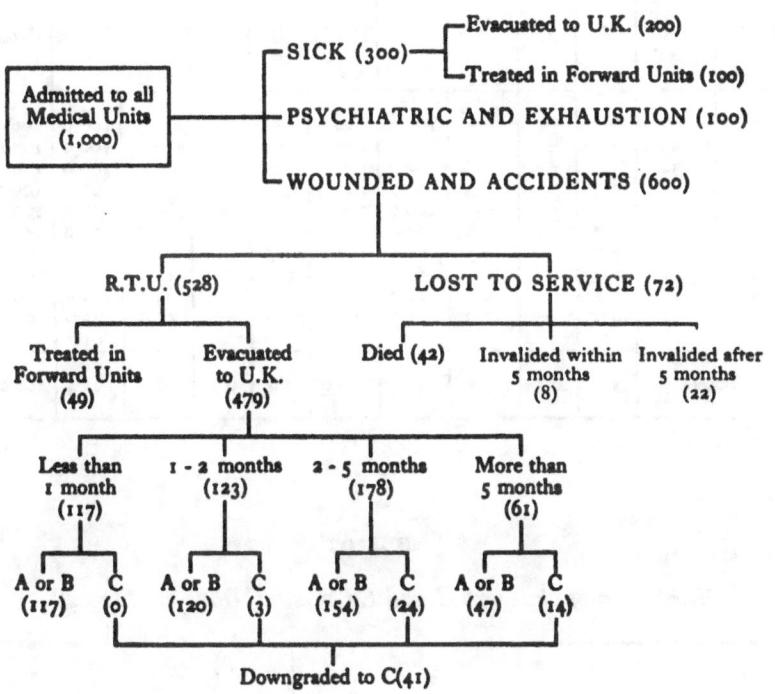

TABLE 90

Relationship Between 'Days to Disposal' and Downgrading

		(a) E.A. (Assumption I)					(b) E.A. (Assumption II)				
Decile	Days to Disposal	C	E	C+E	Others	Totals	C	E	C+E	Others	Totals
1.	17	—	—	—	100·0	100·0	—	—	—	100·0	100·0
2.	25	1·0	—	1·0	99·0	100·0	3·0	—	3·0	97·0	100·0
3.	34	—	—	—	100·0	100·0	—	—	—	100·0	100·0
4.	43	0·5	—	0·5	99·5	100·0	0·9	—	0·9	99·1	100·0
5.	55	3·8	0·5	4·3	95·7	100·0	5·8	0·8	6·6	93·4	100·0
6.	67	1·6	2·2	3·8	96·2	100·0	2·2	2·9	5·1	94·9	100·0
7.	84	7·9	2·1	10·0	90·0	100·0	9·7	2·6	12·3	87·9	100·0
8.	111	9·9	3·1	13·0	87·0	100·0	12·8	4·0	16·8	83·2	100·0
9.	142	19·5	3·2	22·7	77·4	100·0	21·5	3·5	25·0	75·0	100·0
10.	292	25·1	14·8	39·9	60·2	100·0	27·2	16·0	43·1	56·8	100·0
Totals		6·9	2·5	9·4	90·6	100·0	10·8	4·0	14·7	85·3	100·0

(a) N.E.A. (Assumption I)   (b) N.E.A. (Assumption II)

Decile	Days to Disposal	C	E	C+E	Others	Totals	C	E	C+E	Others	Totals
1.	17	—	—	—	100·0	100·0	—	—	—	100·0	100·0
2.	25	—	—	—	100·0	100·0	—	—	—	100·0	100·0
3.	34	—	—	—	100·0	100·0	—	—	—	100·0	100·0
4.	43	6·3	—	6·3	93·7	100·0	7·1	—	7·1	92·9	100·0
5.	55	—	—	—	100·0	100·0	—	—	—	100·0	100·0
6.	67	4·2	—	4·2	95·8	100·0	5·0	—	5·0	95·0	100·0
7.	84	12·5	—	12·5	87·5	100·0	17·7	—	17·7	82·4	100·0
8.	111	8·7	4·4	13·1	87·0	100·0	9·5	4·8	14·3	85·7	100·0
9.	142	9·1	—	9·1	90·9	100·0	9·1	—	9·1	90·9	100·0
10.	292	16·7	—	16·7	83·3	100·0	25·0	—	25·0	75·0	100·0
Totals		5·0	0·5	5·5	94·4	100·0	7·9	0·7	8·6	91·4	100·0

TABLE 91

Distribution of Category C and E Cases by 'Days to Disposal'

		E.A.			N.E.A.		
Decile	Days to Disposal	C	E	C+E	C	E	C+E
1.	17	—	—	—	—	—	—
2.	25	1·5	—	1·1	—	—	—
3.	34	—	—	—	—	—	—
4.	43	0·7	—	0·6	9·1	—	8·3
5.	55	5·4	2·1	4·5	—	—	—
6.	67	2·3	8·3	3·9	9·1	—	8·3
7.	84	11·5	8·3	10·7	27·3	—	25·0
8.	111	14·6	12·5	14·0	18·2	100·0	25·0
9.	142	28·5	12·5	24·2	18·2	—	16·7
10.	292	35·4	56·3	41·0	18·2	—	16·7
Totals .		100·0	100·0	100·0	100·0	100·0	100·0

Table 92

Downgrading by Arm of Service

(a) E.A. (Assumption I)						(b) E.A. (Assumption II)				
	C	E	C+E	Others	Totals	C	E	C+E	Others	Totals
Armoured	7·0	3·5	10·5	89·5	100·0	11·1	5·6	16·7	83·3	100·0
Artillery	8·6	3·1	11·7	88·3	100·0	13·7	5·0	18·7	81·2	100·0
Infantry	6·7	2·3	9·0	91·0	100·0	10·5	3·6	14·1	85·9	100·0
Fwd. Services	7·1	1·8	8·9	91·0	100·0	12·5	3·1	15·6	84·4	100·0
Others	5·0	4·0	9·0	91·0	100·0	7·1	5·7	12·8	87·1	100·0
All Arms	6·9	2·5	9·4	90·6	100·0	10·8	4·0	14·8	85·3	100·0

(a) N.E.A. (Assumption I)						(b) N.E.A. (Assumption II)				
	C	E	C+E	Others	Totals	C	E	C+E	Others	Totals
Armoured	5·0	—	5·0	95·0	100·0	5·3	—	5·3	94·7	100·0
Artillery	—	—	—	100·0	100·0	—	—	—	100·0	100·0
Infantry	4·6	1·2	5·8	94·3	100·0	7·1	1·8	8·9	91·1	100·0
Fwd. Services	7·7	—	7·7	92·3	100·0	15·0	—	15·0	85·0	100·0
Others	7·5	—	7·5	92·5	100·0	12·0	—	12·0	88·0	100·0
All Arms	5·0	0·5	5·5	94·6	100·0	7·9	0·7	8·6	91·4	100·0

Table 93

Downgrading by Rank

(a) E.A. (Assumption I)						(b) E.A. (Assumption II)				
	C	E	C+E	Others	Totals	C	E	C+E	Others	Totals
Officers	5·0	1·3	6·3	93·8	100·0	12·1	3·0	15·2	84·8	100·0
N.C.Os.	8·6	3·4	12·0	88·0	100·0	13·1	5·1	18·2	81·8	100·0
Ptes.	6·3	2·3	8·6	91·4	100·0	9·9	3·6	13·5	86·6	100·0

(a) N.E.A. (Assumption I)						(b) N.E.A. (Assumption II)				
	C	E	C+E	Others	Totals	C	E	C+E	Others	Totals
Officers	—	—	—	100·0	100·0	—	—	—	—	100·0
N.C.Os.	10·0	2·0	12·0	88·0	100·0	14·3	2·9	17·1	82·9	100·0
Ptes.	3·6	—	3·6	96·3	100·0	5·9	—	5·9	94·1	100·0

TABLE 94
Deaths in Forward Medical Units

	(a) E.A.				(b) N.E.A.			
Days to Death	Offrs.	N.C.Os.	Ptes.	Totals	Offrs.	N.C.Os.	Ptes.	Totals
0–1	56·8	56·1	50·5	52·3	42·9	66·7	69·0	64·1
1–2	21·1	25·0	26·6	25·8	14·3	33·3	6·9	10·3
2–3	6·3	8·1	9·4	8·9	—	—	6·9	5·1
3–4	7·4	4·4	4·1	4·4	42·9	—	3·4	10·3
4–5	2·1	2·4	1·4	1·7	—	—	6·9	5·1
5–6	2·1	1·4	1·6	1·6	—	—	—	—
6–7	1·1	0·3	1·5	1·2	—	—	3·4	2·6
7 and over	3·2	2·4	4·9	4·2	—	—	3·4	2·6
Totals	100·0	100·0	100·0	100·0	100·0	100·0	100·0	100·0

TABLE 95
Days off Duty in Forward Medical Units

	(a) E.A.				(b) N.E.A.			
Days off Duty	Offrs.	N.C.Os.	Ptes.	Totals	Offrs.	N.C.Os.	Ptes.	Totals
1.	20·9	26·6	20·6	22·1	21·6	22·1	24·9	24·1
2.	12·2	13·9	15·2	14·6	11·8	17·3	13·8	14·6
3.	13·9	14·3	15·4	15·0	9·8	14·4	14·3	14·1
4.	13·9	9·8	12·7	12·2	17·6	13·7	10·5	11·6
5.	7·8	9·0	9·5	9·2	2·0	10·3	9·0	9·0
6.	2·6	8·6	5·0	5·6	11·8	3·7	6·7	6·2
7.	3·5	5·3	4·1	4·3	5·9	4·1	4·8	4·6
7+	25·2	12·3	17·4	17·1	19·6	14·4	16·0	15·8
Totals	100·0	100·0	100·0	100·0	100·0	100·0	100·0	100·0

TABLE 96

Percentage Disposed per 4-week Month. Cases Evacuated to the U.K.

Month	(a) Month by Month		(b) Cumulative	
	E.A.	N.E.A.	E.A.	N.E.A.
1	24·6	28·2	24·6	28·2
2	26·5	24·1	51·1	52·3
3	19·1	21·8	70·2	74·1
4	10·7	12·3	80·9	86·4
5	8·4	7·3	89·3	93·7
6	4·8	2·3	94·1	96·0
7	2·6	0·5	96·7	96·5
8	1·7	1·4	98·4	97·9
9	0·9	0·9	99·3	98·8
10	0·5	1·4	99·8	100·0
11	0·2	0·0	100·0	100·0
	100·0 (1,899)	100·0 (220)	(1,899)	(220)

TABLE 97

Percentage of Total Man-Day Wastage in Each Decile Group and at Each Stage of Treatment

	Group										Totals
	1	2	3	4	5	6	7	8	9	10	
Man-days to Hospital	0·4	0·5	0·5	0·5	0·5	0·5	0·5	0·6	0·7	0·7	5·3
Man-days in Hospital	1·5	2·8	3·5	4·5	5·6	6·6	8·0	9·5	11·7	19·3	73·1
Man-days in Convalescent Depot	0·04	0·1	0·3	0·5	0·9	1·7	2·5	4·2	5·9	5·3	21·6
Total Man-day Wastage	1·9	3·4	4·3	5·5	7·0	8·8	11·0	14·3	18·3	25·3	100·0 (145,555)
Totals by 1st and 2nd 50 per cent.	22·1					77·7					

Table 98

Percentage of Cases in Each Group (including Officers) who Attended Convalescent Depot

	Group									
	1	2	3	4	5	6	7	8	9	10
Percentage attending Convalescent Depot	8·0	14·4	21·9	42·3	47·8	67·9	64·3	74·9	80·7	76·4

Table 99

Mean Days for Each Group at Different Medical Levels

	Group									
	1	2	3	4	5	6	7	8	9	10
1. Days to Hospital	2·8	3·4	3·6	3·9	3·9	3·9	4·4	4·5	5·7	5·4
2. Days in Hospital	9·8	17·9	24·3	31·6	39·5	46·2	55·0	64·4	80·1	144·3
3. Days in Convalescent Depot	3·7	5·9	8·4	9·0	13·4	17·6	26·2	38·0	50·3	51·9
4. 3 ÷ 2	0·38	0·33	0·35	0·28	0·34	0·38	0·48	0·59	0·63	0·39

Table 100

Percentage Evacuated (a) Per day after wounding; (b) Per day after wounding—Cumulative

	Days														
	1	2	3	4	5	6	7	8	9	10	11	12	13	14	14+
(a) Percentage Transferred to Hospital per day	1·2	8·5	25·6	24·6	13·8	8·6	5·5	2·8	1·6	1·5	1·3	0·7	1·0	0·6	2·7
(b) Percentage Transferred to Hospital per day—Cumulative	1·2	9·7	35·3	59·9	73·7	82·3	87·8	90·6	92·2	93·7	95·0	95·7	96·7	97·3	100·0 (1,889)

Table 101
Percentage Discharged from Hospital (a) Per 4 weeks after admission; (b) Per 4 weeks—Cumulative

	Months									
	1	2	3	4	5	6	7	8	9	10
(a) Percentage Discharged from Hospital per 4 weeks	35·7	32·8	17·2	6·2	3·5	1·8	1·1	1·0	0·5	0·1
(b) Percentage Discharged from Hospital per 4 weeks—Cumulative	35·7	68·5	85·7	91·9	95·4	97·2	98·3	99·3	99·8	99·9 (2,119)

Table 102
Percentage Discharged from Convalescent Depot (a) Per week after admission; (b) Per week—Cumulative

	Weeks													
	1	2	3	4	5	6	7	8	9	10	11	12	13	13+
(a) Percentage Discharged from Conv. Depot per week	22·9	11·1	9·4	9·8	9·6	7·5	9·7	7·5	5·1	2·9	1·6	0·9	0·9	1·1
(b) Percentage Discharged from Conv. Depot per week—Cumulative	22·9	34·0	43·4	53·2	62·8	70·3	80·0	87·5	92·6	95·5	97·1	98·0	98·9	100·0

§3. Sites and Severity of Injuries—Normandy. June–July 1944

In this section there is no separation of injuries N.E.A. from injuries E.A.; and the nature of the data excludes the possibility of any but a gross classification of wounds by anatomical site. Casualties with more than one wound are here defined as *multiple*, without regard to the severity of the several components. The classification into single injuries is fourfold: (a) head and neck, (b) arms, (c) trunk and (d) legs. Arms are delimited to include the shoulder girdle, and legs to include flesh of the buttocks. Any involvement of the pelvic contents is assigned to trunk.

The data of this section refer to 2,293 cases documented exclusively on A.F. W.3118 and 2,111 evacuated to hospital in the U.K. Of the former, 1,042 returned to duty from forward medical units and 1,251 died. Of those evacuated to hospital, and recorded as such on A.Fs. I.1220, none died. Evacuated cases assigned to the 10 severity grades were consolidated in two classes, respectively composed of the first and the last five groups, i.e. one class of the first 50 per cent. to leave hospital and one of the last 50 per cent. The casualties recorded on A.F. W.3118 also give us two broad divisions, trivial and lethal. Altogether, we thus have four grades of severity:

(a) trivial, i.e. treated in, and returned to duty from, forward units;
(b) medium, i.e. evacuated to U.K. hospitals and discharged therefrom among the first 50 per cent.;
(c) severe, i.e. evacuated to U.K. hospitals and discharged among the second 50 per cent.;
(d) lethal, i.e. those who died of wounds after receiving some medical attention.

We have already seen (Section 2) that 50 per cent. of the last named group died on the day they were first admitted to a medical unit. To a large extent, it therefore refers to cases so severely wounded as to be past medical aid though able to survive some hours after injury. Needless to say, our fourfold classification gives no indication of the distribution of all battle casualties, since data concerning instantaneously fatal cases are not here included.

With due regard to the last qualification, Table 103 shows the percentage distribution of injuries at different sites in these four severity grades. To get an overall picture of relative frequency and severity of wounds at individual sites—subject to the same qualification—it is necessary to know the distribution of all injuries between the four severity grades chosen. As shown in a previous instalment of this analysis, it is not possible to give precise figures; but it is clearly of the order: 10 per cent. trivial, 10 per cent. died and 80 per cent. evacuated. Tables 104 and 105 have therefore been prepared on the assumption that the overall distribution is: trivial 10 per cent.; medium and severe 80 per cent.; lethal 10 per cent. *See* also Fig. 96. With respect to hospitalised cases, some additional information is available. For medium and severe groups separately Table 106 therefore shows the distribution of all hospitalised casualties by the number of wounds received.

Table 107 shows distribution of wounds by site separately for each Arm of Service. Tables 108 and 109 show the results of an attempt to classify evacuated injuries by type as well as by site. The original intention to make a more detailed analysis of the data on A.Fs. I.1220 with reference to types of wound failed owing to inadequacy of the clinical notes. However, it has been possible to make a classification based on five broad categories. Of these, (a) concussion and (b) burns are self explanatory. The other three are: (c) superficial, (d) flesh, (e) bone, the last including any involvement of bone whatsoever. Demarcation between superficial and flesh wounds is largely referable to the judgment of the investigators. Unfortunately, it has been possible to classify this information only for single injuries. So the figures are representative only on the assumption that the distribution for multiple wounds is comparable. Table 108 shows the overall distribution of types of wound and Table 109 shows their distribution for each of the four major anatomical sites. The main conclusions that stand out from these tables are:

(i) head and neck wounds are less likely to cause long term hospitalisation although relatively important as a cause of death;

(ii) trunk injuries are about as common as head and neck wounds; but make by far the largest contribution to death from wounds;
(iii) under 1 per cent. of arm wounds prove fatal;
(iv) nearly two thirds of long-term hospital cases are either leg injuries or multiple wounds; but there are relatively more slight leg injuries and more lethal multiple injuries;
(v) nearly 30 per cent. of casualties evacuated as a result of injury are due to multiple wounds, over half of which have only two wounds. About 5 per cent. of all injured receive more than four wounds. Seemingly, multiple injuries spend longer in hospital than single wounds;
(vi) with one notable exception, there is little difference with reference to distribution of wounds by site among the different Arms of the Service. Among troops serving with armour about 40 per cent. of hospitalised wounded as opposed to under 30 per cent. for other Arms have multiple injuries;
(vii) among single wounds about 15 per cent. involve bone injury; and such injury greatly increases liability to long term hospitalisation;
(viii) among single injuries bone injuries of the arm are relatively commoner than of the leg;
(ix) burns, which account for under 3 per cent. of single injuries, are most common on the arm.

TABLE 103

Distribution of Injuries (E.A. and N.E.A.) by Site

	Trivial	Medium	Severe	Lethal
Head and Neck	27·3	12·9	6·6	16·7
Arms	20·4	26·2	19·6	1·9
Trunk	15·8	7·6	9·2	38·5
Legs	26·9	26·9	32·4	14·9
Multiple	9·6	26·4	32·3	27·9
	100 (1,042)	100 (1,074)	100 (1,037)	100 (1,251)

TABLE 104

Relative Severity of Injuries (E.A. and N.E.A.) at Different Sites

	Trivial	Medium	Severe	Lethal	Total
Head and Neck	22·4	42·3	21·6	13·7	100
Arms	9·9	51·0	38·2	0·9	100
Trunk	13·0	25·0	30·3	31·7	100
Legs	9·6	38·6	46·5	5·3	100
Multiple	3·5	38·8	47·4	10·2	100

TABLE 105
Overall Distribution of all Injuries by Site

Head and Neck	12·2
Arms	20·6
Trunk	12·2
Legs	27·9
Multiple	27·2
Total	100

TABLE 106
Distribution of Hospitalised Injuries (E.A. and N.E.A.) by Number of Wounds

Number of Wounds	Medium	Severe	Total
1	73·7	67·9	70·8
2	17·4	18·6	18·0
3	4·1	6·0	5·1
4	0·7	1·7	1·1
over 4	4·1	6·0	5·1
Totals	100	100	100

TABLE 107
Distribution of Hospitalised Injuries by Site and Arm of Service

Site	Armoured	Artillery	Infantry	Forward Services	Others
Head and Neck	6·9	11·2	9·9	12·7	6·3
Arms	19·4	22·3	23·0	22·7	26·4
Trunk	6·9	9·6	8·5	8·7	6·9
Legs	26·3	29·9	30·0	26·0	33·3
Multiple	40·6	26·9	28·6	30·0	27·1
Totals	100 (160)	100 (197)	100 (1,465)	100 (150)	100 (144)

Table 108
Distribution of Injuries by Type and Severity (single injuries only)

	Medium	Severe	All Hospitalised
Superficial	10·1	4·9	7·6
Flesh	79·9	68·4	74·4
Bone	5·4	24·7	14·7
Concussion	0·4	0·6	0·5
Burns	4·1	1·2	2·7
Totals	100 (701)	100 (651)	100 (1,352)

Table 109
Distribution of Hospitalised Single Injuries by Type and Site

	Head and Neck	Arms	Trunk	Legs
Superficial	10·4	7·0	10·7	5·3
Flesh	70·9	68·1	86·7	78·9
Bone	12·6	20·4	2·7	14·5
Concussion	2·7	—	—	—
Burns	3·3	4·5	—	1·3
Totals	100 (182)	100 (445)	100 (150)	100 (545)

§4. *Weapons and Wounds—Normandy. June–July 1944*

Attempts to assess relative efficacy of weapons from clinical records of injuries they cause call for caution. At best, they rest on the soldier's impression of what hit him, sometimes supplemented by a surgeon's estimate of its plausibility checked by the nature of the wound and of any foreign body removed. Often the soldier in modern battle does not know what wounded him, and a civilian surgeon of an E.M.S. hospital is not necessarily an expert on missile identification. Nevertheless, clinical records do attempt to specify the causal weapon in the majority of cases; and since such information is sparse we can at best present a picture of what appear to be the effects of different weapons from such data as are available on the understanding that what follows be accepted with reserve. The main issues involving known bias are:

(a) Gunshot wound (G.S.W.) may be referred indiscriminately to a wound caused by any weapon, a hangover from the practice of 1914–18.

Fortunately, a more specific definition of the weapon is often in the notes. So far as is possible from such indications we here use the term to cover small-arms wounds.

(b) Differential diagnosis of shell and mortar wounds is inevitably crude, since mortar wounds are sometimes described as shell, though the reverse rarely, if ever, happens. So we cannot be certain that mortar or shell here refers to a random sample of wounds so specified.

(c) Statements about enemy weapons are likely to be most reliable if made nearest the place and time of their use. When there were discrepancies between notes made at different stages of treatment, we have therefore relied where possible on information in A.F. W.3118.

(d) As with respect to sites of injury, we have no information regarding what weapons cause instantaneous death.

Ensuing tables conform to patterns discussed earlier. Table 110 and Fig. 96 show distribution of wounds caused by different weapons among four severity grades. For trivial, evacuated and lethal wounds Table 111 shows separately the distribution of wounds caused by the major weapons vis-a-vis anatomical site. Table 112 shows the proportion of men with 1, 2, 3 . . . wounds caused by different weapons. Proportions downgraded after wounding by individual weapons are in Table 113. Distributions of wounds caused by different weapons in the various Arms of the Service and as between officers, N.C.Os., and privates are in Tables 114–117.

The main conclusions which emerge are as follows:

(i) About 90 per cent. of all wounds are due to shells, mortar bombs and gunshot in about equal proportions. There is no dramatic difference with reference to relative severity of wounds caused by different weapons; except in so far as bomb and gunshot wounds tend to produce a higher proportion of fatal injuries.

(ii) With respect to anatomical sites, the main difference between weapons concerns greater or less propensity for inflicting multiple wounds. Gunshot wounds of the head and neck and trunk are relatively rare among evacuated injuries and relatively common among lethal ones, a fact probably referable to greater missile velocity.

(iii) Nearly 80 per cent. of gunshot wounds are single injuries, whereas under 70 per cent. of any other type are such. 'Pepper-pot' injuries are relatively most common from mines and grenades.

(iv) Assessed by downgrading, gunshot wounds appear to cause more permanent damage than other types.

(v) The characteristics of different weapons are clearly reflected in the distribution of wounds by Arm of Service. Similar proportions of shell, mortar and gunshot wounds in the sample as a whole is largely due to the high proportion of infantry among casualties. Among other Arms the proportions are quite different. Whereas about 80 per cent. of all mortar casualties are infantrymen only about 50 per cent. of mine casualties are such, and it is clear that the mine and the bomb are relatively of more effect among supporting troops. Artillery suffer over 50 per cent. of their casualties from shelling. In so far as such differences accord with common sense, they impart confidence in the data.

(vi) Distributions of wounds by weapon are much the same for officers, N.C.Os., and privates.

TABLE 110
Overall Distribution of Wounds by Weapon and Severity Grades

	Trivial	Medium	Severe	Lethal
Mine	3·7	5·0	3·9	2·5
Bomb	6·9	2·6	3·1	3·5
Shell	48·4	35·6	33·7	35·7
Mortar	19·8	26·8	23·8	13·5
Grenade	1·4	1·2	0·9	0·5
Gunshot	19·4	28·0	34·0	43·9
Bayonet	0·3	0·5	0·1	0·4
Multiple	—	0·4	0·6	—
Totals	100 (930)	100 (851)	100 (835)	100 (996)

	Trivial	Medium	Severe	Lethal	Totals
Mine	8·9	47·6	37·4	6·0	100
Bomb	20·7	31·4	37·2	10·6	100
Shell	13·4	39·7	36·9	9·9	100
Mortar	8·3	46·1	40·0	5·7	100
Grenade	13·1	47·9	34·8	4·3	100
Gunshot	6·3	36·3	43·3	14·2	100
Bayonet	—	—	—	—	Negligible
Multiple	—	—	—	—	,,

TABLE 111
Distribution of Wounds by Weapon and Site of Injury

A—Trivial

	Head and Neck	Arms	Trunk	Legs	Multiple	Totals
Mine	34·3	20·0	2·9	25·7	17·1	100 (35)
Bomb	21·9	20·3	12·5	26·6	18·8	100 (64)
Shell	28·9	20·7	16·0	25·6	8·9	100 (450)
Mortar	25·5	20·1	19·6	21·7	13·0	100 (184)
Gunshot	23·8	24·9	16·6	30·9	3·8	100 (181)

B—Evacuated

	Head and Neck	Arms	Trunk	Legs	Multiple	Totals
Mine	14·7	6·7	8·0	14·7	56·0	100 (75)
Bomb	14·6	25·0	10·4	12·5	37·5	100 (48)
Shell	10·1	20·8	9·1	27·6	32·3	100 (582)
Mortar	11·8	21·3	9·5	26·5	31·0	100 (423)
Gunshot	6·9	30·8	8·3	32·9	21·2	100 (520)

C—Lethal

	Head and Neck	Arms	Trunk	Legs	Multiple	Totals
Mine	8·0	—	20·0	20·0	52·0	100 (25)
Bomb	5·7	2·9	60·0	8·6	22·9	100 (35)
Shell	16·2	1·8	35·2	17·6	29·1	100 (437)
Mortar	11·9	3·7	31·3	21·6	31·3	100 (134)
Gunshot	17·1	2·0	50·8	9·3	20·8	100 (356)

Table 112
Number of Wounds Caused by Different Weapons (Evacuated cases only)

	1	2	3	4	5	5+	Total
Mine	43·9	31·9	8·0	1·3	—	14·7	100 (75)
Bomb	62·4	20·8	6·2	2·1	—	8·3	100 (48)
Shell	67·9	20·0	5·5	0·6	0·6	5·2	100 (583)
Mortar	69·3	20·7	5·9	1·9	—	2·4	100 (426)
Grenade	57·9	10·5	15·8	—	—	15·8	100 (19)
Gunshot	78·6	14·7	6·2	0·5	0·1	—	100 (520)
Bayonet	—	—	—	—	—	—	Negligible
Multiple	—	—	—	—	—	—	Negligible

Table 113
Percentage of Personnel Wounded by Individual Weapons Downgraded to Categories C and E

	Assumption I*	Assumption II*
Mine	5·3	10·0
Bomb	6·3	10·7
Shell	8·7	13·7
Mortar	6·8	12·8
Grenade†	—	—
Gunshot	11·5	17·1
Bayonet†	—	—
Multiple†	—	—

* For basis of Assumptions I and II see §2, p. 599.
† Insufficient cases.

TABLE 114

Distribution of Trivial Wounds by Weapon and Arm of Service

	Armoured	Artillery	Infantry	Forward	Others	Totals
Mine	—	4·4	2·2	16·4	8·8	3·9
Bomb	2·3	14·9	5·2	8·2	14·0	7·1
Shell	64·8	51·8	45·4	43·8	52·5	46·9
Mortar	10·2	15·8	23·4	16·4	8·8	20·4
Grenade	3·4	—	1·3	1·4	1·8	1·4
Gunshot	18·2	13·2	22·0	13·7	14·0	20·1
Bayonet	1·1	—	0·3	—	—	0·3
Multiple	—	—	—	—	—	—
Totals	100 (88)	100 (114)	100 (598)	100 (73)	100 (57)	100 (930)
Mine	—	14·3	37·2	34·3	14·3	100 (35)
Bomb	3·1	26·5	48·4	9·4	12·5	100 (64)
Shell	12·7	13·1	60·4	7·1	6·7	100 (450)
Mortar	4·9	9·8	76·0	6·5	2·7	100 (184)
Grenade	—	—	—	—	—	Negligible
Gunshot	8·8	8·3	72·9	5·5	4·4	100 (181)
Bayonet	—	—	—	—	—	Negligible
Multiple	—	—	—	—	—	Negligible

TABLE 115

Distribution of Evacuated Wounds by Weapon and Arm of Service

	Armoured	Artillery	Infantry	Forward	Others	Totals
Mine	9·4	0·7	3·3	11·5	12·8	4·4
Bomb	4·7	5·6	1·7	10·4	4·6	2·8
Shell	47·7	54·5	30·7	29·2	47·6	34·6
Mortar	13·1	15·4	28·8	15·6	15·1	25·3
Grenade	1·9	—	1·0	4·2	—	1·1
Gunshot	21·5	22·4	33·6	29·4	18·6	30·8
Bayonet	—	—	0·5	—	—	0·4
Multiple	1·9	1·4	0·3	—	1·2	0·5
Totals	100 (107)	100 (143)	100 (1,254)	100 (96)	100 (86)	100 (1,686)
Mine	13·3	1·3	55·9	14·6	14·6	100 (75)
Bomb	10·4	16·6	43·7	20·8	8·3	100 (48)
Shell	8·8	13·4	66·2	4·8	7·0	100 (583)
Mortar	3·3	5·2	85·1	3·5	3·1	100 (426)
Grenade	—	—	—	—	—	Negligible
Gunshot	4·4	6·1	80·8	5·4	3·1	100 (520)
Bayonet	—	—	—	—	—	Negligible
Multiple	—	—	—	—	—	Negligible

TABLE 116

Distribution of Lethal Wounds by Weapon and Arm of Service

	Armoured	Artillery	Infantry	Forward	Others	Totals
Mine	1·6	3·1	1·6	7·7	9·3	2·5
Bomb	—	4·7	2·3	9·6	14·8	3·5
Shell	49·9	50·4	42·8	40·3	40·7	43·9
Mortar	6·4	8·7	16·2	9·6	1·9	13·5
Grenade	—	—	0·4	—	3·7	0·5
Gunshot	41·9	33·0	36·5	32·6	29·6	35·7
Bayonet	—	—	—	—	—	—
Multiple	—	—	0·6	—	—	0·4
Totals	100 (62)	100 (127)	100 (701)	100 (52)	100 (54)	100 (996)
Mine	4·0	16·0	44·0	16·0	20·0	100 (25)
Bomb	—	17·2	45·8	14·3	22·9	100 (35)
Shell	7·1	14·7	68·5	4·8	5·0	100 (437)
Mortar	3·0	8·2	84·3	3·7	0·7	100 (134)
Grenade	—	—	—	—	—	Negligible
Gunshot	7·3	11·8	71·7	4·8	4·8	100 (356)
Bayonet	—	—	—	—	—	Negligible
Multiple	—	—	—	—	—	Negligible

TABLE 117

Distribution of Wounds by Weapon and Rank

	Trivial		
	Officers	N.C.Os.	Ptes.
Mine	3·3	5·4	3·3
Bomb	8·5	3·1	7·9
Shell	49·8	50·0	47·8
Mortar	21·3	17·6	20·2
Grenade	—	2·8	1·1
Gunshot	17·0	21·2	19·3
Bayonet	—	—	—
Multiple	—	—	0·4
Totals	100 (101)	100 (216)	100 (613)

Severe

	Officers	N.C.Os.	Ptes.
Mine	2·9	4·1	4·0
Bomb	2·9	3·2	3·2
Shell	31·4	27·8	35·9
Mortar	34·3	24·6	22·7
Grenade	—	2·7	0·3
Gunshot	25·7	37·3	33·0
Bayonet	—	—	0·3
Multiple	2·9	0·4	0·5
Totals	100 (35)	100 (220)	100 (580)

Medium

	Officers	N.C.Os.	Ptes.
Mine	7·5	4·5	4·9
Bomb	—	3·5	2·5
Shell	40·0	38·3	34·3
Mortar	25·0	21·9	28·5
Grenade	2·5	2·0	1·0
Gunshot	22·5	29·9	27·5
Bayonet	—	—	0·8
Multiple	2·5	—	0·5
Totals	100 (40)	100 (201)	100 (610)

Lethal

	Officers	N.C.Os.	Ptes.
Mine	4·2	3·0	2·0
Bomb	5·4	3·8	3·2
Shell	39·3	44·8	43·9
Mortar	11·8	14·1	13·5
Grenade	—	1·1	0·6
Gunshot	39·3	33·3	36·1
Bayonet	—	—	—
Multiple	—	—	0·6
Totals	100 (73)	100 (242)	100 (681)

CHAPTER 11

REFLECTIONS ON THE CAMPAIGN. D.D.M.S. SECOND ARMY

'OVERLORD' was the first campaign in which the medical services were organised on the scale of units and W.Es. recommended by the Hartgill Committee. It was therefore the first full test of the organisation. The broad principles of the organisation stood the test well, but it early became evident that there was somewhat too much weight forward and not quite enough in corps and army areas.

FIELD DRESSING STATIONS

Infantry divisions were allotted two as divisional troops. It was rare that all F.D.Ss. in divisional, corps and army areas were fully employed. In rapid advances many had to be left behind and their transport used to assist the move forward of the heavier units such as C.C.Ss. and general hospitals.

A new scale of

>one per army as army troops;
>two per corps as corps troops;
>one per infantry division as divisional troops;
>one per armoured division as divisional troops;
>one per corps as G.H.Q. troops

was considered adequate and agreed.

The F.D.S. fulfilled many rôles from holding minor sick or exhaustion cases, acting as the nucleus of an advanced surgical centre, P.o.W. hospital or V.D. treatment centre, to forming camp reception stations on the L. of C. In this latter rôle it was definitely wasteful in personnel.

Experience showed that although the advanced surgical centre based on a F.D.S. was definitely not equal to the C.C.S., its value in a rapid advance or in very mobile warfare was considerable.

LIGHT FIELD AMBULANCES

Each armoured brigade that was not an integral part of an armoured division was allotted a light field ambulance. Experience showed that the requirements of the independent armoured brigade operating with a division could be met from divisional resources and its light field ambulance was often redundant. It did, however, require a light field ambulance if operating in an entirely independent rôle. It was agreed that a scale of one light field ambulance to every two armoured brigades not in an armoured division was adequate. These were held as army troops and allotted as required. They also formed a very useful reserve in the hands of D.D.M.S. to meet unexpected situations. This reorganisation was effected early in 1945 and proved successful.

CASUALTY CLEARING STATIONS

From the very beginning of the campaign it was necessary to attach a F.D.S. to a C.C.S. to increase its capacity by filtering off the lightly wounded and sick. An increase in nominal capacity from 50 patients in beds and 70 on stretchers to 100 in beds and 150 on stretchers was recommended. The Standardisation Conference in December 1944, modified the increase to 80 in beds and 120 on stretchers but agreed to an increase of general duty M.Os., to the restoration of nursing officers Q.A.I.M.N.S. on the W.E. and to minor increases in domestic transport. The value of sufficient fully trained nursing sisters in forward units was proved beyond all doubt.

C.C.Ss. were allotted on a scale of two per corps as corps troops and one per army. This rigid arrangement proved wasteful and uneconomic and greater flexibility was achieved by making all C.C.Ss. into army troops and allotting them as required by D.D.M.S. army. This arrangement allowed the weight to be applied where it was most needed without argument from commanders about losing their basic units.

In set battles C.C.Ss. were best used in pairs or more, receiving alternately, with a buffer F.D.S. for light cases and sick in the same area. Forward surgery was best carried out in the C.C.S.

FIELD AND SPECIAL SURGICAL UNITS

The value of small complete mobile surgical units was abundantly demonstrated. It was found that F.S.Us. were best employed at C.C.Ss. but that when occasion demanded they could be attached to a F.D.S. forward in the corps areas to form an advanced surgical centre. A C.C.S. was moved forward to take over as early as possible.

GENERAL HOSPITALS (200 beds)

Throughout the campaign these units were used as C.C.Ss. and their place could well have been taken by C.C.Ss. They require more transport to move and have so low a surgical potential that F.S.Us. always had to be attached. A general hospital of this size would be most usefully employed with a small force or serving a small but distant or isolated garrison. Their mobile ophthalmic sections were of the highest value in saving man-power by issue of spectacles in forward areas, but these could have been attached, and on occasions were, to C.C.Ss. with equal effect.

GENERAL HOSPITALS (600 and 1,200 beds)

The major lessons concerning the use of large general hospitals were:

(i) The 1,200-bed general hospital was too big to be efficient. Adequate accommodation in buildings was difficult to find and control in scattered buildings difficult. The amount of transport required to move the unit always caused difficulties in provision. The largest hospital in the field should not be bigger than 1,000 beds.

(ii) During mobile warfare or in moving a base, hospitals were most easily moved by allotment of at least a G.T. Coy. to Medical. By using the same company in a phased programme vehicles were constantly employed and movement more efficient.

CONVALESCENT DEPOTS

The usefulness of convalescent depots was late in becoming effective in the campaign owing to the inadequacy of their equipment. No provision was made for adequate tentage when buildings were not available. Beds or bunks had to be obtained locally as accommodation stores. Both should be carried by the unit as part of its A.F. G.1098 equipment.

The value, as a means of saving man-power, of small convalescent depots, e.g. for 1,000 men, in Army areas was proved. Attachment of a F.D.S. for minor sick or exhaustion cases really converted these into light casualty treatment and rehabilitation units. A composite unit on the lines of a light casualty hospital would be even more valuable.

A flaw in the organisation of convalescent depots was the absence of wings for officers. It was apparently agreed that officers would be taken care of, during convalescence, either by voluntary organisations such as Red Cross hospitals or by permitting them to go on sick leave. It is obviously wrong that the Army should rely, in part of its personnel recovery system, on outside organisations; it is even more so to consider that sick leave is an adequate substitute for the planned and organised rehabilitation work of a convalescent depot. All convalescent depots should have officer wings.

TRANSFUSION SERVICE

The organisation of the base transfusion unit with its forward sections or blood banks forward with armies was satisfactory, but blood banks required more transport to enable them to maintain constant touch with every corps and to collect blood from forward airfields.

Field transfusion units were best employed at C.C.Ss. but were also attached to F.D.Ss. forming advanced surgical centres.

SPECIALIST SERVICES

There are a certain number of basic specialists on the war establishment of every general hospital, but in addition four per hospital may be selected from any of the following categories: surgeon, physician, orthopaedic surgeon, dermatologist, neurologist, ophthalmologist, oto-rhino-laryngologist, psychiatrist or venereologist. The number of each category present with the force depends on its size and function. These additional specialists were originally posted to a particular general hospital which also carried the necessary specialist equipment. The moves and deployment of the hospitals rarely corresponded with the requirements for moves and deployment of the specialist by areas. Specialists therefore had to be attached to hospitals other than those on whose W.E. they and their equipment were held. This led to considerable administrative confusion as the officers and equipment were often away from the unit to which they were posted for an indefinite period. The original unit still had to account for the personnel and equipment without any control over their moves and attachments.

A central pool of specialists controlled by a small administrative H.Q. would have been an infinitely more satisfactory basis for these specialist services. The specialist could then have been attached to any hospital and would have taken his equipment with him, but the accounting would all have been centralised at pool H.Q. Such a unit would also solve transport problems and might include the advisers in the various specialities. The specialists pool or unit might be extended to include the special surgical teams—e.g. neurosurgical, maxillo-facial, chest surgery—and their equipment.

During the campaign five 100-bed venereal disease expansions to general hospitals were employed from the very beginning as the specialist element of V.D.T.Cs. These centres proved a real necessity but the expansions forming them were accounted for by a multiplicity of general hospitals which never saw the expansions concerned. The special V.D. treatment personnel could also be administered by the specialist pool. In this way only one unit H.Q. would be dealing with attachments and detachments and would relieve every general hospital of much unnecessary administrative work.

MEDICAL ESTABLISHMENTS IN THE L. OF C.

Two field ambulances and a varying number of F.D.Ss. were employed in the L. of C. either for M.I. room or camp reception station work. Useful as these units were, both as a reserve and for providing extra transport, they were uneconomical in medical man-power for the tasks they usually undertook. A definite allotment of camp reception stations for work on the L. of C. in place of the L. of C. field ambulances would be most useful.

MOBILE DENTAL UNITS

The use of mobile dental units enabled practically all kinds of dental work to be done in the forward areas. As a result, it need never have been necessary for men to go more than a few miles from their units to receive dental treatment.

EVACUATION

Ambulance cars were unsatisfactory; they were merely modifications of 1914–18 types.

To allow flexibility M.A.Cs. which were allotted as corps troops were converted to army troops.

Air evacuation proved to be most satisfactory when a definite number of aircraft was allotted for casualty evacuation. The 'Sparrow' flight, which was controlled by the Principal Medical Officer, Second Tactical Air Force, and used for the shuttle back from forward areas so successfully, was always more reliable than the utilisation of Transport Command aircraft which arrived at uncertain times and in varying numbers.

The holding unit for casualties awaiting air evacuation was best formed by an Army unit close to the airfield concerned. It could be provided with surgical and other specialist facilities and could cater for patients held up by delays in evacuation much more easily than could the R.A.F. unit on the airfield. The R.A.F. unit need only be of waiting-room type, holding for an hour or two. There must, of course, be the closest communication between the Army and the R.A.F. unit both by telephone and personal liaison.

During battle, evacuation by all means from Army areas was controlled by a single officer with a small staff. A.D.M.S. Army Troops is a suitable officer for the task but should establish himself in the Army medical area for the period of the battle.

FORWARD SUPPLY OF MEDICAL EQUIPMENT

It was found necessary to form a mobile element of advanced depots medical stores by attaching two 3-ton lorries to each of these units. These lorries carried a store of essential supplies. By this means corps could be supplied during long advances when it would have been impossible to move forward the whole advanced depot in sufficient time.

In Army areas the introduction of detail issue dispensaries attached to a central F.D.S. for R.M.Os. was entirely successful.

FORWARD STOCKS OF STRETCHERS AND BLANKETS

Medical disaster is never surer than when adequate stocks of stretchers and blankets are not maintained well forward. This is an old and tried principle but was proved once again during the campaign when, owing to lack of transport, Second Army was deprived of its reserve during its

REFLECTIONS ON THE CAMPAIGN

advance into Belgium. Only by sacrificing part of an ammunition lift was the balance restored when disaster seemed imminent. Massive air evacuation leads to a constant drain rearwards and replacement has to be by ground transport, unless aircraft are allotted for purely medical use.

PROVISION OF HOSPITAL BEDS FOR THE FORCE

In 'Overlord' beds for only four per cent. of the force were in the theatre and not six per cent. as originally planned. In fact, on the number of casualties handled and with the excellence of evacuation, beds for three per cent. of the force would have been adequate. It must not be forgotten, however, that casualties were relatively light and the sick rate unexpectedly low. Had either gone up to the figure expected before the campaign started, all the available beds would have been required.

STANDARDISED MEDICAL AND SURGICAL TREATMENT

The laying down of standard forms of treatment for common injuries and diseases by clinical memoranda produced by the consultants and advisers gave a continuity of treatment throughout all medical units. Although this tended to be dogmatic it did mean that the sick or wounded man who had to pass through many medical units and the hands of many doctors was able to have a constant form of treatment wherever he went. The success of the system fully justified the means and was one of the major lessons of the campaign.

INTERCOMMUNICATION—MEDICAL SERVICES

The Use of Wireless. During the preliminary period of training in the United Kingdom prior to the invasion of the Continent, it was left to the discretion of D.Ds.M.S. corps as to whether they made use of wireless for intercommunication, although the medical services generally were encouraged to practise wireless procedure. VIII Corps (comprising mainly armoured formations) arranged for its medical units to undergo thorough training in the use of wireless and established corps and divisional medical wireless nets. XXX Corps medical services and Army medical units were also practised in wireless procedure and limited use was made of W.T. and R.T. as a means of intercommunication for corps medical services. On the other hand, XII Corps medical services had decided that there was no need for separate medical wireless nets.

It is interesting to note that as a result of their experience in the Normandy bridgehead fighting the medical services of two of the three divisions originally comprising XII Corps were persuaded that wireless was essential and succeeded in obtaining an allotment of wireless sets for their medical units from the divisional administrative pool of sets. XII Corps medical services later adopted a limited use of wireless.

It was conclusively demonstrated that in mobile warfare the medical services could not keep pace with a rapid advance, whether it be an armoured or an infantry pursuit, unless they had their own wireless net to provide a speedy means of intercommunication. Without a separate medical wireless net orders could not get through to medical units sufficiently quickly for them to keep pace with a rapid advance, and as a result the medical units tended to lag behind the fighting formations. This inevitably resulted in a thinning out of medical resources in the forward areas so that there was a serious risk of initial delay in the evacuation and treatment of casualties incurred during the contact battle as the pursuit closed.

The medical services of an infantry division were normally allotted four wireless sets from the divisional administrative pool of sets. The control set, a 19 set manned by Signals, was located with the A.D.M.S. at Main H.Q. with three out-stations (all 19 or 22 sets) allotted one to each field ambulance and, depending on the local man-power situation, these sets were either manned entirely by Signals operators or jointly manned by one Signals operator assisted by a R.A.M.C. orderly (trained in wireless procedure under formation arrangements).

When field ambulances were placed under command of brigades (for moves, etc.), it was usual for them to be 'netted' to the brigade 'Q' Net only while operating and moving under command of brigade, and during this time contact would be maintained with the A.D.M.S. by 'flicking' at pre-arranged times. For general purposes, however, field ambulance sets were netted to the A.D.M.S. at divisional H.Q. and, if necessary, 'flicked' to the brigade 'Q' net only when required. The A.D.M.S. set usually flicked to the corps medical net at pre-arranged times, for 15-20 minutes every third hour. This flick was doubly useful to divisions in as much as it enabled them to pass messages either through corps or direct to A.Ds.M.S. of flanking divisions also flicking to the corps net.

The medical wireless net for an armoured division normally comprised three sets—control set with the A.D.M.S. at divisional H.Q. and one set each for the field ambulance and light field ambulance. On occasions an additional set was provided for the divisional F.D.S.

Sets were normally netted to the A.D.M.S. set, but during moves or in the advance the field ambulance and light field ambulance sets went on to the brigade and armoured brigade 'Q' nets respectively, maintaining contact with the A.D.M.S. by flicking.

The corps medical wireless net normally comprised three sets, a control set at rear corps H.Q. with two out-stations.

(i) One set with the principal area covering the open C.C.S., one F.D.S. and the M.A.C.
(ii) The second set either with a closed C.C.S. awaiting orders to move forward or with an advanced surgical centre.

REFLECTIONS ON THE CAMPAIGN

Divisions flicked to corps medical net at specified intervals as described above; D.Ds.M.S. corps flicked to the Army medical net twice daily.

The army medical wireless net's control set was located at rear army with one out-station (a 19 set) at ambulance railhead, serving the general hospitals and ambulance car company. On occasions call was made on a second set to cover air evacuation or a subsidiary hospital area at some distance from the principal hospital area. Corps were able to pass messages to Army or to other corps medical branches at their twice daily 'flicks'.

The Slidex Code. The original slidex medical cards issued prior to the invasion were general unsatisfactory, including as they did many phrases which were most unlikely to be used in R.T. and omitting other phrases in frequent use. It is, however, difficult to satisfy in one medical slidex card the demands both of divisional medical units and of corps and Army medical units. Forward units have frequently needed to use 'operational phrases' and to refer to 'A' echelons, centre lines, etc., whereas many phrases like casualty air evacuation, ambulance railhead, are never used by field ambulances, though obviously required for use in R.T. conversation in corps or Army.

ALTERNATIVE MEANS OF INTERCOMMUNICATION

Within divisions the only effective alternative means of intercommunication was by M.C. D.Rs. from field ambulances, augmented by the use of liaison officers. In practice it was a general rule that each field ambulance attached one D.R. for permanent duty at the A.D.M.S's. office and these D.Rs. were utilised to run a medical D.R.L.S. service covering all divisional medical units. Messages sent by this means were delivered reasonably quickly, but the medical D.R.L.S. service was by no means a substitute for wireless communication.

Within corps and Army intercommunication proved a much greater problem. Telephone lines could only be laid to C.C.Ss. or general hospitals if these units were reasonably accessible from existing telephone lines and, moreover, the units themselves were certain to remain *in situ* for at least ten days. During an advance line communication to medical units was obviously impossible and frequently there would be no line communication between rear Army and rear corps for several days in succession. At such times the Army medical wireless net was invaluable. Medical D.R.L.S. services were organised within corps and Army by using two M.C. D.Rs. from the M.A.C. (for corps) or the A.C.C. (for Army). As F.D.Ss. and C.C.Ss. both had only one motor cycle available for D.R. duties, it was clearly impracticable to make general use of these, as they were obviously insufficient to meet the domestic needs of their own units.

Wireless for Special Operational Rôles. On several occasions a 'unit' wireless net was provided for field ambulances or light field ambulances engaged in special rôles, e.g. casualty evacuation from a minefield gapping operation or casualty evacuation from an assault river crossing. For operational rôles of this nature the field ambulance had its own wireless net comprising a 19 set at field ambulance H.Q. with two 22 sets forward with the companies or forward sections. The field ambulance maintained communication to the H.Q. controlling the operation by flicking at specified times. Communication to the A.D.M.S. was usually by D.R. or L.O., as a second flick was not advisable.

CONCLUSIONS

Wireless.

(i) The provision of a medical wireless net at division, corps and Army is essential.
(ii) Division and corps require a definite allocation of wireless sets and the system of 'bidding' to 'Q' for pool sets proved to be both unreliable and unsatisfactory. The absolute minimum scale of sets required is:

Infantry divisional medical services	4 sets
Armoured ,, ,, ,,	3 sets
Corps medical services	3 sets
Army medical services	2 sets (with call on a third when required)

D.Rs. Medical D.R. communications within divisions could easily be organised, using field ambulance D.Rs., and the scale of D.Rs. provided on the W.E. of a field ambulance was adequate to meet this need as well as covering the unit's domestic requirements.

The scale of D.Rs. provided for F.D.Ss., C.C.Ss. and general hospitals proved inadequate. An additional M.C. D.R. for each F.D.S. and also for each 200-bed general hospital would have been exceedingly helpful.

APPENDIX XII

21 ARMY GROUP. LOCATION STATEMENT. GENERAL HOSPITALS. APRIL–MAY 15, 1945

During this period the following moves occurred:

81 B.G.H.	.	St. Paschale, Oostrum–Wettringen–Borghorst–Lüneburg–Kiel.
84 ,,	.	Venraij–Sulingen–Hamburg.
86 ,,	.	Eindhoven–Schloss Wissen–Hoya–Celle–Rotenburg.
88 ,,	.	Nijmegen–Tilburg–Cloppenburg.

REFLECTIONS ON THE CAMPAIGN 645

3 Cdn. G.H.	.	Tilburg–Nijmegen.
6 ,,	.	St. Michielsgestel–Ootmarsum–Bad Zwischenahn.
9 B.G.H.	.	Venraij–Belsen.
25 ,,	.	Amiens–Wettringen.
39 ,,	.	Hasselt–Utrecht.
74 ,,	.	Bruges–Lüneburg.
77 ,,	.	Ghent–Bedburg.
121 ,,	.	Amiens–Hasselt–Celle.
7 Cdn. G.H.	.	St. Michielsgestel–Turnhout–Bassum.
16 ,,	.	Oost Dunkerke–St. Michielsgestel–Sögel.
106 B.G.H.	.	Wavre Notre Dame—Antwerp.
15 Con. Depot	.	Knocke–Hasselt.
13 ,, ,,	.	Sterksel–Lengerich.

So that on May 15 the distribution was as follows:

81 B.G.H.	.	Kiel	Second Army
84 ,,	.	Hamburg	8 B.S.A.
86 ,,	.	Rotenburg	Second Army
88 ,,	.	Cloppenburg	Canadian First Army
3 Cdn. G.H.	.	Nijmegen, Marienboom	,, ,, ,,
6 ,,	.	Bad Zwischenahn	,, ,, ,,
8 B.G.H.	.	Brussels	20 L. of C. S.A.
9 ,,	.	Belsen	Second Army
25 ,,	.	Wettringen	,, ,,
30 ,,	.	Lille (2 × 100)	17 L. of C. S.A.
32 ,,	.	Thildonck	20 ,, ,,
39 ,,	.	moving to Utrecht	Netherlands District
67 ,,	.	Ghent (1 × 100)	16 L. of C. S.A.
74 ,,	.	Lüneburg	Second Army
75 ,,	.	Brussels	20 L. of C. S.A.
77 ,,	.	Bedburg (3 × 100)	Second Army
79 ,,	.	Eindhoven	21 L. of C. S.A.
121 ,,	.	Celle	Second Army
1 Cdn. G.H.	.	Nijmegen, Nebo	L. of C. u/c Cdn. First Army Tps. for local administration
5 ,,	.	Oost Dunkerke	9 L. of C. S.A.
7 ,,	.	Bassum	Second Army
8 ,,	.	St. Michielsgestel	5 L. of C. S.A.
16 ,,	.	Sögel	Canadian First Army
6 B.G.H.	.	Oostakker	16 L. of C. S.A.
23 ,,	.	Lille	17 ,, ,,
29 ,,	.	Eecloo (moving to Belsen)	16 ,, ,,
94 ,,	.	Hamburg (staging)	8 B.S.A.
96 ,,	.	Kain (nr. Tournai)	13 Garrison
101 ,,	.	Heverlee (nr. Louvain) (7 × 100)	20 L. of C. S.A.

646 THE ARMY MEDICAL SERVICES

105 B.G.H.	. .	Ostend (4 × 100)	9 L. of C. S.A.
106 ,,	. .	Antwerp (1 × 100)	7 B.S.A.
108 ,,	. .	Brussels (3 × 100)	20 L. of C. S.A.
109 ,,	. .	Duffel	7 B.S.A.
110 ,,	. .	Bruges (4 × 100)	9 L. of C. S.A.
111 ,,	. .	Brussels	20 ,, ,,
113 ,,	. .	Renaix	13 Garrison
115 ,,	. .	De Haan (6 × 100)	9 L. of C. S.A.
2 Cdn. G.H.	. .	Ghent	16 ,, ,,
10 ,,	. .	Turnhout	7 B.S.A.
12 ,,	. .	Bruges	9 L. of C. S.A.
20 ,,	. .	Turnhout	7 B.S.A.
21 ,,	. .	St. Omer. Detach. 400 beds Hardinghem	17 L. of C. S.A.
5 Con. Depot	.	Knocke	9 ,, ,,
12 ,, ,,	.	De Haan	9 ,, ,,
14 ,, ,,	.	Tournai	13 Garrison
15 ,, ,,	.	Hasselt	9 L. of C. S.A.
2 Cdn. Con. Depot		Knocke	9 L. of C. S.A.
13 Con. Depot	.	Lengerich	Second Army
3 Cdn. Con. Depot		Vught	L. of C.

Hospital Beds in Theatre

Beds occupied	19,910
,, vacant	13,400
,, equipped	33,310
W.E.	36,100

(excluding the 200-bed hospitals u/c armies)

APPENDIX XIII

21 ARMY GROUP. MEDICAL LOCATION STATEMENT AS AT JUNE 25, 1945

General Hospitals

(200 beds)

Unit	Formation	Expansions	Location	Remarks
81 B.G.H.	VIII Corps District		Rendsburg	To Belsen, 28th
84 ,,	XXX ,, ,,		Belsen	Closed for 4 L. of C. (Berlin)
86 ,,	XXX ,, ,,		Rotenburg	Closing, leaving theatre
88 ,,	7 Base S.A.		Duffel	Closing, leaving theatre
3 Cdn. G.H.	Cdn. First Army		Apeldoorn	Closed
6 ,,	,, ,, ,,		Bad Zwischenahn	

REFLECTIONS ON THE CAMPAIGN

(600 beds)

Unit	Formation	Expansions	Location	Remarks
8 B.G.H.	XXX Corps District		Bassum	
9 ,,	VIII ,, ,,		Rissen (nr. Hamburg)	
25 ,,	I ,, ,,		Münster	
32 ,,	20 L. of C. S.A.		Thildonck	
39 ,,	I Corps District		Bensberg	
67 ,,	VIII ,, ,,	1 × 100	Rendsburg	Opening, 200 beds, 28th
74 ,,	XXX ,, ,,		Lüneburg	
77 ,,	I ,, ,,	3 × 100	Bedburg	To leave theatre
121 ,,	XXX ,, ,,		Brunswick	Open 30th
1 Cdn. G.H.	L. of C.		Nijmegen, Nebo	
5 ,,	9 L. of C. S.A.		Oost Dunkerke	Closed
7 ,,	XXX Corps District		Hahn	
8 ,,	5 L. of C. S.A.		St Michielsgestel	
16 ,,	Cnd. First Army		Sögel	For Russian ex P.o.W.

(1,200 beds)

Unit	Formation	Expansions	Location	Remarks
6 B.G.H.	I Corps District		Iserlohn	
23 ,,	17 L. of C. S.A.		Lille (St. André)	Moving to Wittenindsdorf, Bergkirchen
29 ,,	XXX Corps District		Belsen	Moving to Hanover
94 ,,	VIII ,, ,,		Hamburg	
101 ,,	20 L. of C. S.A.	7 × 100	Heverlee (nr. Louvain)	Closed
96 ,,	16 ,, ,,		Kain	Moving to Hamburg
105 ,,	9 ,, ,,	6 × 100	Bruges	
106 ,,	7 B.S.A.	1 × 100	Antwerp	
108 ,,	20 L. of C. S.A.	5 × 100	Brussels	
109 ,,	7 B.S.A.		Duffel	Closed to leave theatre
110 ,,	9 L. of C. S.A.	2 × 100	Bruges	Closed to leave theatre
111 ,,	20 ,, ,,		Brussels	
113 ,,	16 ,, ,,		Renaix	Closed to leave theatre
115 ,,	9 ,, ,,	6 × 100	De Haan	
2 Cdn. G.H.	16 ,, ,,		Ghent	
10 ,,	7 B.S.A.		Turnhout	
12 ,,	9 L. of C. S.A.		Bruges	
20 ,,	9 ,, ,,		Turnhout	Closed
21 ,,	17 ,, ,,		St. Omer detach. 400 beds Hardinghem	

Casualty Clearing Stations

Unit	Formation	Location	Remarks
3 C.C.S.	XXX Corps District	Hanover	
10 ,,	XXX ,, ,,	Gandersheim	
16 ,,	5 L. of C. S.A.	Tilburg	
23 ,,	I Corps District	Salzuflen	
24 ,,	I ,, ,,	Lünen	To leave theatre
32 ,,	VIII ,, ,,	Snoghøj, Denmark	,, ,, ,,

Unit	Formation	Location	Remarks
33 C.C.S.	VIII Corps District	Schleswig	To leave theatre
34 ,,	VIII ,, ,,	Strecknitz	
35 ,,	XXX ,, ,,	Belsen	Closed, for Berlin

Convalescent Depots
(2,000 beds)

5 Con. Depot	9 L. of C. S.A.	Knocke	
9 ,, ,,	21 ,, ,, ,,	Sonnis	Closed. Disbanding
12 ,, ,,	16 ,, ,, ,,	De Haan	Closed. Disbanding
14 ,, ,,	16 ,, ,, ,,	Tournai	Closed, to leave theatre
15 ,, ,,	21 ,, ,, ,,	Hasselt	Closed, to leave theatre
2 Cdn. Con. Depot	9 ,, ,, ,,	Knocke	

(1,000 beds)

13 Con. Depot	VIII Corps District	Glückstadt	
3 Cdn. Con. Depot	L. of C.	Vught	Closed

Field Ambulances

162 Fd.Amb.'A' Coy.	7 B.S.A.	Antwerp	
'B' Coy.	308th Inf. Bde.	Goes	
163 ,, ,,	XXX Corps District	Goslar	
14 Lt. Fd. Amb.	VIII ,, ,,	Neustadt	
16 ,, ,, ,,	79th Armd. Div.	Lorineker	To leave theatre
21 ,, ,, ,,	XXX Corps District	Celle	,, ,, ,,
168 ,, ,, ,,	XXX ,, ,,	Hanover	

Field Dressing Stations

1 F.D.S.	VIII Corps District	Rendsburg	
2 ,,	VIII ,, ,,	Hamburg	
3 ,,	XXX ,, ,,	Göttingen	
4 ,,	VIII ,, ,,	Tötensen	
6 ,,	Netherlands District		
9 ,,	XXX Corps District	Schloss Derneberg	
12 ,,	20 L. of C.	Brussels	
14 ,,	VIII Corps District	Hamburg	
17 ,,	Netherlands District		
20 ,,	I Corps District	Kapellen	
21 ,,	I ,, ,,	Salzuflen	
22 ,,	VIII ,, ,,	Bad Segeberg	
24 ,,	VIII ,, ,,	Nehmten	
25 ,,	36 Beach Brick	Calais	
26 ,,	XXX Corps District	Fallingbostel	
30 ,,	I ,, ,,	München-Gladbach	
31 ,,	XXX ,, ,,	Lüneburg	
32 ,,	9 L. of C. S.A.	Ostend	
33 ,,	I Corps District	Gemen	
34 ,,	25 Garrison	Bayeux	
35 ,,	XXX Corps District	Peine	
49 ,,	XXX ,, ,,	Nienburg	
50 ,,	XXX ,, ,,	Osnabrück	
62 ,,	21 L. of C. S.A.	Eindhoven	

Field Surgical Units

Unit	Formation	Location	Remarks
6 F.S.U.	L. of C.	Knocke	Att. 5 Con. Depot To leave theatre
13 ,,	,,	,,	,,
14 ,,	VIII Corps District	Snoghøj, Denmark	Att. 32 C.C.S.
15 ,,	VIII ,, ,,	,, ,,	,,
27 ,,	VIII ,, ,,	Lauenberg	
33 ,,	L. of C.	Knocke	Att. 5 Con. Depot To leave theatre
34 ,,	VIII Corps District	Rendsburg	Att. 81 B.G.H.
37 ,,	I ,, ,,	Bensberg	,, 39 ,,
38 ,,	21 L. of C. S.A.	Eindhoven	,, 62 F.D.S.
39 ,,	I Corps District	Bensberg	,, 39 B.G.H.
40 ,,	L. of C.	Calais	,, 25 F.D.S.
41 ,,	,,	Knocke	,, 5 Con. Depot To leave theatre
42 ,,	XXX Corps District	Rotenburg	Att. 86 B.G.H.
43 ,,	XXX ,, ,, (5th Div.)	Halberstadt	,, 53 F.D.S.
44 ,,	L. of C.	Knocke	,, 5 Con. Depot To leave theatre
45 ,,	XXX Corps District	Gardelegen	Att. 84 B.G.H.
46 ,,	L. of C.	Knocke	,, 5 Con. Depot To leave theatre
47 ,,	,,	,,	,,
48 ,,	VIII Corps District	Molin	With 15th Div.
49 ,,	XXX ,, ,,	Göttingen	Att. 3 F.D.S.
50 ,,	XXX ,, ,,	Duhnen	,, 175 Fd. Amb. 51st Div.
51 ,,	XXX ,, ,,	Rotenburg	Att. 86 B.G.H.
52 ,,	L. of C.	Knocke	,, 5 Con. Depot To leave theatre
53 ,,	VIII Corps District	Schleswig	Att. 33 C.C.S.
54 ,,	VIII ,, ,,	Strecknitz	,, 34 ,,
55 ,,	XXX ,, ,,	Celle	,, 121 B.G.H.
56 ,,	VIII ,, ,,	Snoghøj	,, 32 C.C.S.
4 M.F.S.U.	20 L. of C. S.A.	Brussels	,, 111 B.G.H.
5 ,,	XXX Corps District	Brunswick	,, 121 ,,
6 ,,	L. of C.	Antwerp	,, 106 ,,
6 M.N.S.U.	,,	Knocke	,, 5 Con. Depot
3 Chest Surgical Team	,,	,,	,, ,,
1 Vascular Injuries Section	XXX Corps District	Belsen	,, 29 B.G.H.

Hospital Beds in Theatre of Operations

Occupied	11,505
Vacant	10,549
Equipped	22,054
W.E.	35,500

APPENDIX XIV

21 ARMY GROUP. MEDICAL LOCATION STATEMENT AS AT AUGUST 13, 1945

General Hospitals

(200 beds)

Unit	Formations	Location	Remarks
81 B.G.H.	XXX Corps District	Hanover	Detach. in Belsen
84 ,,	4 L. of C. S.A.	Kladow Airfield	,, Babelsburg
86 ,,	L. of C.	De Haan, Ostend	Closed To leave theatre
88 ,,	9 L. of C. S.A.	De Haan, Ostend	,, ,, ,,
6 Cdn. G.H.	Canadian Forces, Netherlands	Zuidlaren	

(600 bed)

Unit	Formations	Location	Remarks
8 B.G.H.	XXX Corps District	Bassum	
9 ,,	VIII ,, ,,	Rissen (nr. Hamburg)	
25 ,,	I ,, ,,	Münster	
32 ,,	20 L. of C. S.A.	Thildonck	
39 ,,	I Corps District	Bensberg	
67 ,,	VIII ,, ,,	Rendsburg	
74 ,,	XXX ,, ,,	Lüneburg	
77 ,,	I ,, ,,	Bedburg	To leave theatre
121 ,,	XXX ,, ,,	Brunswick	
1 Cdn. G.H.	L. of C.	Nijmegen, Nebo	
5 ,,	9 L. of C. S.A.	Oost Dunkerke	Closed
7 ,,	XXX Corps District	Sande	
16 ,,	XXX ,, ,,	Sögel	

(1,200 beds)

Unit	Formations	Location	Remarks
6 B.G.H.	I Corps District	Iserlohn	
23 ,,	I ,, ,,	Wittenindsdorf, Bergkirchen	
29 ,,	XXX ,, ,,	Hanover	
94 ,,	VIII ,, ,,	Hamburg	
96 ,,	16 L. of C. S.A.	Kain (nr. Tournai)	To be disbanded
101 ,,	20 ,, ,,	Heverlee (nr. Louvain)	To leave theatre
105 ,,	9 ,, ,,	Bruges	
106 ,,	7 B.S.A.	Antwerp	
108 ,,	20 L. of C. S.A.	Brussels	
109 ,,	7 B.S.A.	Duffel	To leave theatre
110 ,,	9 L. of C. S.A.	Bruges	,, ,, ,,
111 ,,	20 ,, ,,	Brussels	
113 ,,	16 ,, ,,	Renaix	,, ,, ,,
115 ,,	9 ,, ,,	De Haan	
2 Cdn. G.H.	16 ,, ,,	Ghent	
10 ,,	7 B.S.A.	Turnhout	Closed
12 ,,	9 L. of C. S.A.	Bruges	
20 ,,	7 B.S.A.	Turnhout	,,
21 ,,	L. of C.	St. Omer	,,

REFLECTIONS ON THE CAMPAIGN 651

Casualty Clearing Stations

Unit	Formations	Location	Remarks
3 C.C.S.	XXX Corps District	Rotenburg	
10 "	XXX " "	Gandersheim	
16 "	5 L. of C. S.A.	Tilburg	
24 "	I Corps District	Lünen	
32 "	9 L. of C. S.A.	De Haan, Ostend	To leave theatre
33 "	VIII Corps District	Schleswig	" " "
34 "	VIII " "	Strecknitz	
35 "	Berlin Area	Berlin	Closing

Convalescent Depots

(2,000)

5 Con. Depot	9 L. of C. S.A.	Knocke	
14 " "	9 " "	De Haan	To leave theatre
15 " "	21 " "	Sonnis	Closed
2 Cdn. Con. Depot	9 " "	Knocke	"

(1,000)

13 Con. Depot	VIII Corps District	Hamburg	Disbanding
3 Cdn. Con. Depot	L. of C.	Vught	Closed

Field Ambulances

162 Fd. Amb.	5 L. of C. S.A.	Tilburg	
163 " "	XXX Corps District	Hanover	
140 " "	16 L. of C. S.A.	Tournai	
14 Lt. Fd. Amb.	VIII Corps District	Neustadt	
16 " " "	79th Armd. Div.	Lorineker	To leave theatre
21 " " "	XXX Corps District	Celle	" " "
168 " " "	Berlin Area	Berlin	Moving to Peine for disbandment XXX Corps

Field Dressing Stations

1 F.D.S.	VIII Corps District	Rendsburg	
2 "	VIII " "	Hamburg	
3 "	XXX " "	Celle	
4 "	79th Armd. Div.	Tötensen	
6 "	6 L. of C. S.A.	De Haan, Ostend	For conversion
9 "	XXX Corps District	Nordhorn	
12 "	7 B.S.A.	Antwerp	
14 "	VIII Corps District	Hamburg	
17 "	6 L. of C. S.A.	Rotterdam	
20 "	I Corps District	Kapellen	
21 "	I " "	Bad Lippspringe	
22 "	VIII " "	Snoghøj, Denmark	
24 "	VIII " "	Kiel	
25 "	36 Beach Brick	Calais	
26 "	XXX Corps District	Fallingbostel	
30 "	I " "	München-Gladbach	To leave theatre
31 "	XXX " "	Belsen	
32 "	9 L. of C. S.A.	Ostend-Bredene	
33 "	I Corps District	Gemen	

Unit	Formations	Location	Remarks
34 F.D.S.	25 Garrison	Bayeux	
35 ,,	XXX Corps District	Peine	
49 ,,	XXX ,, ,,	Verden	
50 ,,	XXX ,, ,,	Osnabrück	
62 ,,	21 L. of C. S.A.	Eindhoven	

Field Surgical Units

Unit	Formations	Location	Remarks
6 F.S.U.			Attached 5 Con. Depot, to leave theatre
13 ,,			
33 ,,			
41 ,,	L. of C.	Knocke	
44 ,,			
46 ,,			
47 ,,			
14 ,,	I Corps District	Bad Lippspringe	Att. 21 F.D.S.
15 ,,	VIII ,, ,,	Snoghøj	,, 22 ,,
27 ,,	VIII ,, ,,	Hamburg	,, 94 B.G.H.
34 ,,	I ,, ,,	Bergkirchen	,, 23 ,,
37 ,,	6 L. of C. S.A.	Rotterdam	,, 17 F.D.S.
38 ,,	21 ,, ,,	Eindhoven	,, 62 ,,
39 ,,	6 ,, ,,	Amsterdam	,, 6 ,,
40 ,,	L. of C.	Calais	,, 25 ,,
42 ,,	I Corps District	Iserlohn	,, 6 B.G.H.
43 ,,	XXX ,, ,,	Gandersheim	,, 10 C.C.S.
45 ,,	4 L. of C. S.A.	Babelsburg	,, detach. 84 B.G.H.
48 ,,	VIII Corps District	Hamburg	Att. 94 B.G.H.
49 ,,	XXX ,, ,,	Belsen	Moved to Hanover with rear party 81 B.G.H.
50 ,,	XXX ,, ,,	Duhnen	Att. 175 Fd. Amb., 51st Div.
51 ,,	XXX ,, ,,	Rotenburg	Att. 3 C.C.S.
53 ,,	I ,, ,,	München-Gladbach	,, 30 F.D.S.
54 ,,	VIII ,, ,,	Strecknitz	,, 34 C.C.S.
55 ,,	XXX ,, ,,	Brunswick	,, 121 B.G.H., disbanding
56 ,,	VIII ,, ,,	Snoghøj	Att. 22 F.D.S.

Field Hygiene Sections

Unit	Formations	Location
6 Fd. Hyg. Sec.	I Corps District	Iserlohn
22 ,, ,, ,,	19 L. of C. S.A.	Burgsteinfurt
27 ,, ,, ,,	VIII Corps District	Lübeck
30 ,, ,, ,,	4 L. of C. S.A.	Babelsburg
31 ,, ,, ,,	XXX Corps District	Hanover
45 ,, ,, ,,	I ,, ,,	Bad Lippspringe
61 ,, ,, ,,	XXX ,, ,,	Linsburg
68 ,, ,, ,,	16 L. of C. S.A.	Ghent
73 ,, ,, ,,	G.H.Q. Tps.	Salzuflen
80 ,, ,, ,,	20 L. of C. S.A.	Brussels
84 ,, ,, ,,	21 ,, ,,	Helmond
85 ,, ,, ,,	L. of C.	Lambersart

Field Sanitary Sections

Unit	Formations	Location
1	9 L. of C. S.A.	Ostend
2	Berlin Area	Berlin

Unit	Formations	Location	Remarks
3	VIII Corps District	Hamburg	
4	6 L. of C. S.A.	Overschie	
6	VIII Corps District	Molfsee	

Base Depots of Medical Stores

Unit	Formations	Location	Remarks
5	9 L. of C. S.A.	Ostend	
11	20 ,, ,,	Herent (nr. Louvain)	
12	VIII Corps District	Wedel, Hamburg	
13	I ,, ,,	Neuenkirchen	
16	20 L. of C. S.A.	Zaventem	

Advanced Depots of Medical Stores

Unit	Formations	Location	Remarks
8	VIII Corps District	Wedel, Hamburg	
9	XXX ,, ,,	Peine	
11	XXX ,, ,,	Burgdorf	
12	VIII ,, ,,	Schloss Hagen (nr. Kiel)	
14	I ,, ,,	Wuppertal	
15	XXX ,, ,,	Verden	
16	20 L. of C. S.A.	Brussels	
17	20 ,, ,,	Herent (nr. Louvain)	

Mobile Laboratories

Unit	Formations	Location	Remarks
3 Mob. Bact. Lab.	20 L. of C. S.A.	Brussels	
4 ,, ,, ,,	VIII Corps District	Rendsburg	Att. 67 B.G.H.
7 ,, ,, ,,	Berlin Area	Berlin	Att. 35 C.C.S.
8 ,, ,, ,,	XXX Corps District	Rotenburg	,, 3 ,,
4 ,, Hyg. ,,	I ,, ,,	Bad Lippspringe	

Special Teams

Unit	Formations	Location	Remarks
4 M.F.S.U.	20 L. of C. S.A.	Brussels	Att. 111 B.G.H.
6 ,,	L. of C.	Antwerp	,, 106 ,,
6 M.N.S.U.	,,	Knocke	,, 5 Con. Depot

APPENDIX XV

H.Q. SECOND ARMY. SUCCESSIVE LOCATIONS

1944		*Main*	*Rear*
June	11	Creully	Banville
July	6	—	Vaux-sur-Seulles
Aug.	5	Tracy Bocage	—
	23	—	Bazoches-en-Houlme
	27	La Trinité des Laitiers	—
Sept.	2	—	Jouy-sur-Eure (nr. Pacy)
	3	Menantissart (nr. Romescamps)	—
	4	—	Poix (nr. Amiens)
	6	Lombeek Ste. Marie (nr. Brussels)	—
	7	—	Temeeren (nr. Hal)
	14	Holsbeek (nr. Louvain)	—
	21	Lindel	—
	29	—	Holsbeek
	30	Helmond	—
Oct.	7	—	Sonnis
Nov.	7	Neerpelt	—

1945			
March	10	Walbeck	—
	16	—	Horst
April	1	Dingden	—
	5	—	Dingden
	7	Burgsteinfurt	—
	10	—	Borghorst
	11	Ibbenbüren	—
	15	Borstel	—
	17	—	Ohlendorf
	25	Woltem (nr. Soltau)	—
	28	—	Riepe (nr. Soltau)
May	5	Lüneburg	—
	10	—	Rettmer (nr. Lüneburg)
June	14	H.Q. Second Army moved to Bunde near to H.Q. 21 Army Group at Herford and Bad Oeynhausen and handed over its functions to H.Q. B.A.O.R. H.Q. Second Army disbanded on June 24/25, having completed its task as an operational formation.	

APPENDIX XVI

THE L. OF C.

	November	December	January	March	April	May
H.Q. L. of C.	Malines	Roubaix				Roubaix
11 L. of C. Area	Amiens	Malines				Malines
12 L. of C. Area	Cabourg	Amiens				Helmond
4 L. of C. Sub-area	Boitsfort, Brussels (H.Q. L. of C.)			Arras	Eindhoven then Helmond	Canadian First Army
5 L. of C. Sub-area	Bayeux (12 L. of C.A.)				Ginneken H.Q. L. of C. then Breda 12 L. of C.S.A. Tilburg, H.Q. Netherlands District	Breda (12 L. of C.A.)
6 L. of C. Sub-area	St. Vaast, nr. Dieppe (11 L of C.A.)				Ostend (11 L. of C.A.)	Canadian First Army
9 L. of C. Sub-area	Rouen (12 L. of C. C.A.)				(11 L. of C.A.)	Ostend (11 L. of C.A.) I Corps District
15 L. of C. Sub-area	Lille (11 L. of C.A.)				(11 L. of C.A.)	
16 L. of C. Sub-area	Ghent, 7 B.S.A.				Lille (15 L. of C.S.A.) (12 L. of C.A.)	Ghent (11 L. of C.A.) Lille (12 L. of C.A.)
17 L. of C. Sub-area					Renaix (4, L. of C.S.A.) (11 L. of C.A.)	
18 L. of C. Sub-area					Ghent (16 L. of C.S.A.) Boitsfort (11 L. of C.A.)	Netherlands District
19 L. of C. Sub-area				Ypres (12 L. of C.A.)	Eindhoven (12 L. of C.A.)	I Corps District Boitsfort (11 L. of C.A.)
20 L. of C. Sub-area						Eindhoven (12 L. of C.A.)
21 L. of C. Sub-area						Antwerp (11 L. of C.A.)
7 Base Sub-area	Antwerp (H.Q. L. of C.)				(Second Army)	Second Army
8 Base Sub-area	Ostend (H.Q. L. of C.)					
H.Q. 13 Garrison	Renaix (8 B.S.A.)				(16 L. of C.S.A.)	Renaix (16 L. of C.S.A.)
H.Q. Brussels Garrison	Brussels (4 L. of C. S.A.)					Brussels (11 L. of C.A.)
H.Q. 4 Beach Brick	Saleux (6 L. of C.S.A.)	Amiens (6 L. of C.S.A.)	Saleux (6 L. of C.S.A.)		(11 L. of C.A.) Rouen	Rouen (11 L. of C.A.)
H.Q. 25 Garrison	Boulogne (11 L. of C.A.)	Calais (H.Q. L. of C.)			Bayeux (H.Q. L. of C.)	Bayeux (12 L. of C.A.)
H.Q. 36 Beach Brick						Calais
H.Q. 101 Beach Brick	Caen (12 L. of C.A.)					(17 L. of C.S.A.)

APPENDIX XVII

Commando Medical Service

There came to be a shortage of R.A.M.C. personnel in the Commando Group serving with 21 Army Group and an invitation for R.A.M.C. officers and other ranks serving in the theatre was issued. From this the following excerpts have been taken:

1. The Commando Group is an independent volunteer organisation comprising both Army and Royal Marines personnel. There is also a small naval component. The Group consists of a number of commando brigades, each of which includes Army and R.M. commandos.
2. Those who join do so voluntarily and subject to the discretion of the commanding officer may leave whenever they wish to do so. At their commanding officer's discretion too they may at any time be required to leave.
3. A commando unit is analogous to an infantry battalion. It is organised and equipped to carry out raids and assaults requiring highly mobile troops capable of approaching the objective by sea, over coasts and by air. The organisation is designed to allow the easy detachment of parties suitable for a wide variety of independent tasks.
4. When not engaged either in preparing for an operation or in its execution, commando personnel are usually accommodated in civilian billets.
5. Each commando has its own medical section comprising a medical officer, a sergeant, 6 lance corporals and 2 privates.
6. The primary requirement of R.A.M.C. personnel in commandos is medical proficiency. All R.A.M.C. O.Rs. must be N.Os. class III at least.
7. Before posting the R.A.M.C. volunteer undergoes the commando basic training. The successful completion of this entitles him to wear the Green Beret.
8. R.A.M.C. volunteers must be at least eighteen years and five months old and within 21 weeks of completing any period of service for qualifying as a N.O. class III.
9. The volunteer undertakes to serve with the Commando Group for at least six months if required to do so and has to be willing to revert to any rank in which he can be absorbed into the Commando Group W.E.

Medical Standard

S.G. not less than 3 minus.
Can undergo severe strain suitable to a man less than 36 years old.
Height 66 ins.
Weight 120 lb.
Chest girth when fully expanded 34 in.
Range of expansion 2 in.
Unaided vision not less than:
    shooting eye   6/9
    other eye   6/12

Needing no spectacles.
Hearing Standard 1.
Able to march 25 miles.

No significant disabilities or progressive organic disease, and, in particular,

    otorrhoea or otitis
    perforation of drums
    inability to masticate effectively
    chronic dyspepsia
    intractable skin disease
    significant varicose veins
    rupture
    pronounced varicocele
    internal derangement of the knee
    hallux regidus
    disabling flat foot

A deficiency in physique can be compensated for by an over-abundance of spirit. S.G. less than 3 can be compensated for by an unusual excellence in physique.

Tests (in battle order) required at the Commando Basic Training Centre

Agility:
1. Sprint 75 yards and then score 75 per cent. with 5 rounds in 30 seconds (rifle loaded).
2. Vault, with foot assisting, a 4 ft. 6 in. beam or gate.
3. Jump a ditch 8 ft. 6 in. landing on both feet.

Endurance:
4. Two miles cross country in 15 minutes.
5. Forced march of 10 miles in 1 hour 40 minutes and then score 50 per cent. at 30 yards with 5 rounds in 30 seconds.
6. 100 yards crawl consisting of 40 yards hand-and-knee crawl, 10 yards roll and 50 yards leopard crawl, and then score with 2 out of 5 grenades through a window 3 ft. × 5 ft., 10 yards range, to be completed in $3\frac{1}{2}$ minutes.

Strength:
7. Carry a man of equal weight 200 yards on the flat in 1 minute 15 seconds.
8. Scale a 6 ft. wall.
9. Climb a vertical height of 18 ft., traverse a 30 ft. span of horizontal rope and come down with the aid of a rope.

Swimming:
10. Swim 30 yards, respirator not carried. Boots attached to rifle or slung round neck.
11. Swim 100 yards in fresh water or 200 yards in salt water in clothing without boots or equipment, then remain afloat out of depth for 5 minutes.

INDEX

PART I

Aachen, 6, 8, 222, 226, 351, 355 (*Figs. 26, 70, 85*)
Achim, 494 (*Fig. 90*)
Achterbroek (S. of Roosendaal, N. of Brasschaat), 343
Achterste Steeg, 364 (*Fig. 57*)
Administrative Planning Staff, 26, 29, 32, 47, 48, 81
Advance to the Seine, 221 (*Fig. 26*)
    medical cover for 50th Division, *Fig. 29*
Advance to the Somme, medical cover for 50th Division, *Fig. 30*
Aerschot (N.E. of Louvain), 446
Afwaterings Canal, 370 (*Fig. 61*)
Ahaus, 450, 484, 497, 507, 536 (*Fig. 88*)
Ahlhorn, 509, 521, 522, 532 (*Fig. 92*)
Air Evacuation Headquarters, U.K., 69
Airborne Military Hospital, Apeldoorn, 278, 279, 299
Airfield B.100 (Hees), 507, 508
    B.108 (Rheine), 508, 509, 510
    B.111 (Ahlhorn), 509, 532
    B.114 (Diepholz), 509
    B.118 (Celle), 508, 509, 532, 533
    B.156 (Lüneburg), 509, 532, 533
'Alan', Operation, casualties, 382
    medical arrangements, 380–382 (*Figs. 66, 67*)
    medical cover, 379 (*Fig. 65*)
    medical tactical plan, 378
Albert Canal, 6, 222, 224, 232, 233, 236, 243, 247, 250, 251, 252, 294, 330 (*Figs. 31, 49, 53, 70, 71*)
Algemeene Ziekenhuizen, Apeldoorn, 278, 279
Allied Command (Ground Forces), Autumn 1944, 333
Allonville (N.W. of Amiens), 233, 292, 293, 298, 314
Almelo, 518, 523, 544 (*Fig. 92*)
Alost (on the Brussels–Ghent Rd.), 224, 225, 251, 261, 293
Amayé-sur-Orne (S.E. of Evrecy), 239
Amblie, 139 (*Fig. 8*)
Amfreville, 283 (*Fig. 22*)
Amiens, 5, 223, 236, 292, 309, 310, 311, 315, 316, 317, 321, 323, 324, 333, 398, 401, 402, 409, 410, 411, 412, 465, 475, 645, 655 (*Figs. 26, 48*)
Amsterdam, 652 (*Fig. 92*)
Andelst (W. of Valburg), 244
Anholt Schloss, 493
Antwerp, 5, 8, 9, 222, 223, 224, 225, 233, 236, 239, 251, 256, 261, 262, 266, 298, 309, 311, 313, 319, 324, 330, 331, 334, 335, 336, 340, 341, 342, 344, 346, 347, 348, 350, 355, 357, 379, 386, 401, 402, 409, 411, 456, 463, 464, 465, 475, 524, 645, 646, 647, 648, 649, 650, 651, 653, 655 (*Figs. 26, 42, 48, 49, 51, 53, 77*)

Antwerp–Turnhout Canal, 330, 337
'Anvil' ('Dragoon'), Operation, 5, 17, 18, 222
Apeldoorn, 274, 275, 276, 277, 278, 279, 481, 519, 520, 525, 646 (*Figs. 88, 92*)
Appeldorn, 444, 445 (*Fig. 84*)
Ardenne, 141, 314, 329, 332 (*Fig. 8*)
Ardennes, 9, 10, 222, 463, 464, 465 (*Figs. 71, 85*)
    German counter-offensive in the, 351, 353–358, 379, 384, 402, 456, 457
    medical arrangements, 53rd Division, 379
    medical arrangements, XXX Corps, 387–390
Argentan, 4, 219, 220, 236, 242, 292 (*Figs. 24, 25, 29, 46, 47, 52*)
Armentières (N.W. of Lille), 265
Army Dental Service (Second Army), 89, 200, 319, 464, 541
Army Medical Directorate, 24, 28, 34, 35, 36, 38
Army Pathological Service (Second Army), 85, 553
Army Psychiatric Service (Second Army), 206, 324, 403, 554
Army School of Hygiene, 197, 198
Army Transfusion Service (21 Army Group), 87, 203, 320, 465, 544
Arnhem, 5, 6, 7, 8, 226, 227, 228, 229, 230, 231, 232, 244, 268–278, 280, 295, 299, 300, 302, 324, 354, 376, 477, 480, 516, 519, 520 (*Figs. 44, 49, 64, 69, 77, 88, 92*)
Arques-la-Bataille (S.E. of Dieppe), 316, 334, 409, 411
Arras, 223, 232, 292, 655 (*Figs. 48, 51*)
Arromanches, 3, 117, 118, 123, 169, 190, 204, 283, 284, 315, 401 (*Figs. 2, 5, 8, 22, 23, 50*)
Artlenburg, 481, 488, 491 (*Figs. 90, 91*)
Aschendorf, 521
'Ascot', Operation, 373–375 (*Figs. 62, 63*)
Asile Ave Maria, St. Servais (nr. Namur), 458
Asnelles-sur-Mer, 117, 184, 185, 190 (*Figs. 2, 5, 8, 20, 22*)
Assault and lodgement, medical arrangements for 21 Army Group Formations, 174
    medical cover for 21 Army Group Formations, 127
Assche, 293, 298
Assen, 518 (*Fig. 92*)
Asten, 237, 364 (*Figs. 57, 62, 72, 73, 74, 76*)
Aubigny (N. of Falaise on the Caen Rd.), 264, 306, 314
Aunay-sur-Odon, 124, 171, 216, 234, 242, 292, 298, 314 (*Figs. 29, 45*)
Aurich, 521, 522, 524 (*Fig. 92*)
Autryve (on the Escaut, N. of Tournai), 239
'Avalanche', Operation, 16
Avesnes-le-Comte (W. of Arras), 265
'Ayr' Route, 427 (*Fig. 86*)

INDEX

Babelsburg, 650, 652
Bad Lippspringe, 651, 652, 653
Bad Oldesloe, 541
Bad Rehburg, 533
Bad Segeberg, 540, 648
Bad Zwischenahn, 518, 522, 523, 645, 646
Baelen, 262, 266 (*Figs. 73, 74, 75, 76*)
Baexem (on the Roermond–Weert Rd., S. of Heythuijzen), 378, 379
Bailleul, 264
Bagband (N.E. of Leer), 521
Balberger Wald, 416, 417, 470 (*Figs. 78, 79*)
Balleroy, 291, 298 (*Figs. 37, 45*)
Banville, 138, 189, 654 (*Figs. 8, 22*)
Barneveld (E. of Amersfoort, S. of the Amersfoort–Apeldoorn Rd.), 520
Barnstorf, 484, 487, 493 (*Fig. 90*)
Baron, 263 (*Figs. 10, 11, 12*)
Basedow, 488
Basly, 141 (*Fig. 8*)
Basse, 330 (*Fig. 52*)
Bassevelde, 342 (*Fig. 53*)
Bassum, 487, 493, 494, 504, 512, 524, 525, 532, 645, 647, 650 (*Figs. 89, 90, 92*)
Bastogne, 9, 355, 356, 357 (*Figs. 54, 85*)
Bayeux (including Bayeux Medical Area), 3, 18, 19, 23, 116, 117, 118, 121, 122, 143, 154, 169, 176, 177, 179, 182, 183, 189, 190, 191, 193, 194, 198, 200, 205, 209, 237, 298, 307, 309, 310, 313, 314, 315, 317, 321, 323, 324, 325, 326, 329, 330, 332, 333, 334, 347, 348, 399, 401, 405, 409, 410, 411, 412, 475, 476, 648, 651, 655 (*Figs. 1, 2, 3, 4, 5, 6, 8, 15, 19, 20, 21, 22, 23, 24, 45*)
Bazoches-en-Houlme, 320, 654
'Beach Group', 41, 42, 44
Beauregard Château, 143
Beauvais, 250, 292, 293, 323 (*Figs. 30, 47*)
Bedburg, 420, 429, 437, 438, 439, 453, 455, 459, 460, 470, 471, 472, 473, 507, 508, 509, 510, 512, 516, 518, 645, 647, 650 (*Figs. 78, 81, 84, 86, 87, 92*)
Beek (S.E. of Nijmegen on the Kranenburg Rd.), 439, 469 (*Fig. 81*)
Beeringen (N.E. of Diest), 224, 233, 243, 252, 293 (*Figs. 42, 70, 72, 73, 74, 75, 76*)
Beilen, 518, 520 (*Fig. 92*)
Belsen, 486, 496, 498, 499, 506, 510, 511, 512, 513, 534, 538, 544, 560, 645, 646, 647, 648, 649, 650, 651, 652
Bénouville, 142, 151 (*Figs. 2, 8, 9, 14, 18*)
(le) Bény-Bocage, 215, 216, 232 (*Figs. 37, 45*)
Bény-sur-Mer, 119, 138, 141, 170
Bensberg, 641, 649, 650
Bentlage, 511
Berchmanium College, Nijmegen, 306
Berghem, 376 (*Fig. 65*)
Berg-en-Dal, 427, 429, 467 (*Fig. 86*)
Bergen-op-Zoom, 335, 336, 343, 352 (*Figs. 53, 77*)
Bergeyk (S.W. of Valkenswaard on the Lommel Rd.), 266, 378
Bergharen, 367, 376 (*Fig. 64*)
Berlin, 5, 12, 13, 483, 484, 646, 648, 651, 652, 653

Beringen (on the Noorder Vaart), 375 (*Figs. 57, 63*)
Bernières-sur-Mer, 119, 139, 185, 186, 190 (*Figs. 2, 8, 20, 22*)
Best, 242, 362, 369, 370 (*Figs. 56, 59, 60, 72, 73, 75, 76*)
Betekom (W. of Aerschot), 446, 458, 459
Béthune, 261, 265 (*Fig. 48*)
Beveland Canal, 337, 341 (*Fig. 53*)
Beveland Peninsula, 8, 341
Bevensen, 488, 491, 494 (*Fig. 90*)
Bienen, 474 (*Figs. 78, 87*)
Biervliet, 342, 345 (*Fig. 53*)
Bies, 383, 388, 458 (*Fig. 70*)
Biesme, 379, 388 (*Fig. 71*)
Biéville, 119, 151, 152, 255 (*Figs. 2, 9*)
Birten, 430 (*Figs. 79, 80*)
Bislich, 425, 430, 432, 433 (*Figs. 79, 80*)
Bisselt (S. of Nijmegen, nr. Malden), 467
'Blackcock', Operation, 359, 361, 445, 456, 463
    casualties, 437
    medical arrangements, 383–384
    Second Army medical units, 458
    43rd Division, 436, 437
Blakehill Farm Airfield (nr. Swindon), 69
Bleckede, 481, 488, 491 (*Fig. 90*)
Blerick, 352, 364, 365, 366, 367, 430 (*Figs. 55, 58*)
'Blockbuster', Operation, 416, 469, 474
    Canadian II Corps, 470, 471
    casualties, 471
'Bluecoat', Operation, 215, 216
    medical arrangements, 284–292 (*Fig. 37*)
    medical cover, 232, 234, 236, 238, 242, 250
Bocholt (Belgium), 379 (*Figs. 72, 74, 75, 76*)
Boekel (N.E. of Eindhoven), 379 (*Figs. 72, 73, 75*)
Bohmte, 496, 511 (*Fig. 89*)
Bois Halbout, 264
Boitsfort (S.E. of Brussels), 655
'Bolero', Operation, 15
Bomlitz, 533
Bomshof (between Kranenburg and Cleve), 428
Bonneville, 262, 265 (*Fig. 34*)
Boom (N.W. of Malines on the Brussels–Antwerp Rd.), 379
Borculo, 493 (*Fig. 88*)
Börger, 521 (*Fig. 92*)
Borghorst, 510, 644, 654
Borken, 450, 509, 536 (*Figs. 88, 92*)
Borsbeek (S.E. of Antwerp), 266
Borstel, 654
Bosquentin, 265
Botzelaer, 423, 455
Bouchout, 410
Boulogne, 225, 256, 316, 323, 331, 334, 655 (*Fig. 48*)
Bourg-Léopold, 243, 253, 293, 311, 384, 390, 394, 396, 399, 411, 412, 458, 459, 464, 475, 476, 507, 544 (*Figs. 31, 42, 49, 70, 72, 74, 75, 76*)
Bourguébus, 123, 124, 126, 169, 216, 255 (*Figs. 8, 29, 33*)

INDEX

Boxtel, 370, 380, 382, 387, 390, 429, 450 (*Figs. 49, 56, 60, 66, 67*)
Braakman Inlet (between Biervliet and Terneuzen, 342 (*Fig. 53*)
Bradley, General Omar N. (U.S.), 3, 5, 12, 17, 125, 214, 216, 221, 356
Brakkenstein Hospital, Nijmegen, 233, 297, 384, 451, 467 (*Fig. 83*)
Bramsche, 507
Brasschaat (Brasschaet), 341, 343, 347, 349, 380 (*Fig. 53*)
Break-out and advance into Holland, medical cover (21 Army Group Formations), 232
Breda, 352, 380, 466, 654 (*Fig. 77*)
Bree, 360, 361, 378 (*Figs. 70, 72, 73, 74, 75, 76*)
Breitenfelde, 488 (*Fig. 90*)
Bremen, 13, 457, 477, 478, 480, 484, 487, 493, 494, 496, 498, 504, 507, 515, 516, 521 (*Figs. 89, 90, 92*)
Breskens (opposite Flushing across the Scheldt), 335, 337, 340, 345
Breskens Pocket, 8, 336, 337
Breteuil (S.W. of Evreux and W. of Domville), 242 (*Fig. 29*)
Bretteville-l'Orgueilleuse, 121, 141, 156, 162, 170, 193, 220 (*Figs. 2, 8, 10, 11, 13, 15, 17, 33*)
Brieux, 262, 263, 264, 266
Brionne (on the Risle, on the Bernay–Bourgtheroulde Rd.), 329, 330, 332
British Red Cross Society, 68, 69, 135, 281, 282, 556, 609
Broadwell Airfield (nr. Swindon), 69
Brouay, 170 (*Fig. 15*)
Bruges, 223, 331, 348, 350, 401, 409, 410, 411, 412, 465, 475, 476, 645, 646, 647, 650 (*Figs. 51, 77*)
Bruges–Ghent Canal, 225
Brunnsum (S.E. of Sittard and S.W. of Geilenkirchen), 436
Brunswick, 13, 647, 649, 650, 652
Brussels, 5, 23, 222, 223, 224, 233, 239, 240, 243, 250, 251, 278, 293, 306, 309, 310, 311, 314, 316, 317, 319, 321, 322, 323, 324, 355, 356, 357, 379, 387, 388, 390, 398, 399, 401, 409, 410, 411, 412, 456, 461, 462, 465, 466, 475, 476, 551, 645, 646, 647, 648, 649, 650, 651, 653, 655 (*Figs. 26, 48, 49, 51, 71, 77, 85*)
Buchten (N. of Sittard), 421
Buchholz, 494
Budel, 366, 379, 382, 383 (*Figs. 62, 68*)
Bully Grenay, 265
Buron, 141, 142 (*Figs. 2, 8*)
Burgdorf, 513, 535, 653
Burgsteinfurt, 510, 511, 652, 654

Cabourg, 655 (*Figs. 1, 8, 22*)
Caen, 1, 2, 3, 16, 18, 19, 116, 118, 119, 121, 122, 123, 124, 125, 126, 127, 141, 142, 143, 151, 152, 172, 176, 183, 189, 198, 200, 203, 205, 219, 222, 234, 244, 250, 256, 322, 326, 329, 565, 655 (*Figs. 1, 2, 3, 4, 8, 9, 13, 15, 16, 18, 22, 23, 25, 29, 33, 45*)

Caen Canal, 130, 151, 179 (*Figs. 16, 18, 22*)
Cahaignes (on the Vernon–Gisors Rd.), 293
Caillouet, 292, 298, 306, 309, 314 (*Fig. 48*)
Cairon, 137, 141, 142 (*Fig. 8*)
Calais, 23, 225, 323, 331, 648, 649, 651, 652, 655 (*Fig. 48*)
Calcar, 416, 426, 439, 444, 452, 470 (*Figs. 78, 79, 81, 86*)
Cambes, 256 (*Fig. 16*)
Capellen (Kapellen), 343 (*Figs. 53, 77*)
Carentan, 3, 16, 115, 121, 125 (*Figs. 1, 3, 4, 24*)
Carentan Canal, 19, 115
Carpiquet, 125, 141, 179 (*Figs. 2, 13, 15*)
Carpiquet Airfield, 118, 124, 125, 141, 401 (*Figs. 8, 17*)
Casualties, battle, assessment of, in Normandy Campaign, June–July 1944, 595–635
  evacuation of, 45–61
  Operation 'Alan', 382
    'Blackcock', 437
    'Blockbuster', 471
    'Clipper', 386
    'Enterprise', 492, 493
    'Epsom', 159
    'Goodwood Meeting', 127, 153
    'Mallard', 383
    'Neptune', 184
    'Plunder', 423, 425, 443, 445, 450, 456, 473, 495
    'Torchlight', 433, 492
    'Totalize', 327, 328, 330
    'Varsity', 425
    'Veritable', 420, 422, 429, 434, 435, 439, 443, 453, 470, 471, 492, 554, 555
  psychiatric, 207, 554–559
  R.A.M.C., assault and lodgement, 130
  reception and distribution in U.K., 61–75
  21 Army Group, 212, 546, 557, 576–635
    Canadian First Army, 186, 213, 330, 349, 350, 470, 471, 525, 526, 569, 570, 583, 592, 593
    Second Army, 184, 191, 195, 307, 461, 571–577
      I Corps, 127, 176, 564–567
      VIII Corps, 127, 286, 570
      XII Corps, 382, 383, 450
      XXX Corps, 182, 453, 456, 555, 569
      Guards Armd. Division, 127, 153, 234, 420
      3rd Division, 153, 238, 422, 423, 487, 565
      5th Division, 570
      6th Airborne Division, 130, 131, 425, 565
      7th Armd. Division, 127, 235, 421, 485
      11th Armd. Division, 127, 237, 486, 570
      15th Division, 159, 161, 240, 241, 429, 433–436, 492, 570
      43rd Division, 437, 439

INDEX

Casualties—*cont.*
  21 Army Group—*cont.*
    Second Army—*cont.*
      49th Division, 164, 166, 247–249, 367, 368, 565
      50th Division, 137
      51st Division, 260, 376, 443, 445, 565
      52nd Division, 346, 495
      53rd Division, 171, 261, 267
Casualty Clearing Stations, reflections on, 637
Caumont, 2, 3, 19, 121, 122, 215, 232, 234, 236, 238, 242 (*Figs. 1, 3, 4, 24, 37*)
Caucourt, 262, 265 (*Fig. 19*)
Cazelle, 142, 151, 176, 234, 244, 256, 327, 328, 329 (*Figs. 8, 9, 16*)
Celle, 477, 489, 496, 508, 509, 510, 511, 512, 513, 514, 531, 532, 533, 535, 538, 540, 541, 542, 544, 644, 645, 648, 649, 651 (*Figs. 89, 90*)
Celles (nr. Dinant), 357, 358, 361, 379
Chambord, 265
Charleroi, 388 (*Figs. 54, 71, 85*)
Château de Mouen, 162, 170, 263
Château Liblion, 379
Château Mesnières (nr. Dieppe), 412
Cherbourg, 1, 2, 3, 14, 17, 19, 23, 81, 115, 123, 124, 125, 334, 401 (*Figs. 1, 2, 3, 4, 24*)
Cheux (W. of Caen), 155, 156, 157, 158, 162, 169, 170, 263 (*Figs. 8, 10, 11, 12, 13, 15, 17*)
Children's Hospital, Nijmegen, 244
Churchill, Rt. Hon. Winston S. (Sir Winston), 14, 15, 16, 21
Ciney, 388, 440, 458, 459 (*Figs. 54, 71, 85*)
Cintheaux, 220, 327, 330 (*Fig. 52*)
Civil Affairs, 83, 101, 147, 205
Civil population (I Corps District), diseases prevalent among, 537
Cleve, 10, 414, 415, 416, 419, 422, 426, 428, 429, 437, 438, 439, 450, 451, 467, 469, 470, 471, 473, 474, 518, 554 (*Figs. 78, 81, 83, 84, 86, 87, 88*)
Cloppenburg, 493, 521, 522, 644, 645 (*Figs. 88, 89, 92*)
'Clipper', Operation, 386–387
  casualties, 386
  medical arrangements, *Fig. 70*
'Cobra', Operation, 126, 214, 215
'Colin', Operation, 370–372
  medical cover, *Figs. 60, 61*
Colleville-sur-Orne, 124, 157, 169, 170 (*Figs. 10, 11, 12, 14, 15*)
Cologne, 10, 11, 12, 353, 413, 417 (*Fig. 26*)
Colombelles, 126, 154, 169 (*Figs. 2, 8, 9*)
Colombiers-sur-Seulles, 141, 176 (*Figs. 8, 16*)
Combined Commanders, 14, 16
Combined Chiefs of Staff, 14, 15, 16, 17, 18
Combined Operations Command, 14, 21
Commander, Allied Naval Expeditionary Force, 18, 48, 51, 52, 57, 91
Commando Medical Service, 655
Communicable diseases, precautions against, 80
Condé-sur-Noireau, 232, 236, 250 (*Figs. 1, 6, 29, 45*)

Convalescent Depots, 21 Army Group, 409, 474
  reflections on, 637
Copenhagen, 534, 535
Corbie, 317
Cormelles, 256 (*Figs. 8, 33*)
Cormeilles (on the Lisieux–Pont Audemer Rd.), 245, 284
Corps Medical Area, layout, *Fig. 40*
C.O.S.S.A.C., 16, 18, 21, 31, 50, 51, 52
Cotentin Peninsula, 1, 2, 3, 18, 19, 124
Coudewater (N.E. of s'Hertogenbosch on the Heesch Rd.), 378
Coulombs, 170 (*Fig. 15*)
Courseulles-sur-Mer, 187 (*Figs. 2, 8, 20, 22, 23, 50*)
Coutances, 3, 123, 214 (*Figs. 1, 3, 4, 24*)
Cuverville, 153, 154 (*Figs. 9, 18*)
Couvre Chef, 142 (*Fig. 8*)
Cristot, 164, 264 (*Fig. 13*)
Croisilles, 292
Cruelly, 171, 189, 654 (*Figs. 2, 5, 8, 15, 22*)

Dahlenburg, 488 (*Fig. 90*)
Deelen Airfield, Arnhem, 306
De Heibloem, 367
Delmenhorst (S.W. of Bremen), 487, 522, 527
Denekamp (S.W. of Nordhorn and N. of Enschede on the Nordhorn–Hengelo Rd.), 511, 523
De Haan, 401, 410, 411, 412, 476, 646, 647, 648, 650, 651
Denmark, 534, 535
Depot de Mendicité, 366
Deurne, 363 (*Figs. 43, 57, 72, 73, 75*)
Diarrhoea and dysentery, I Corps, July–September 1944, 565
Diepenheim (W. of Enschede on the Hengelo–Lochem–Zutphen Rd.), 518
Dieppe (including Dieppe Medical Area), 16, 223, 225, 247, 309, 313, 314, 315, 316, 317, 330, 332, 334, 399, 401, 409, 410, 412, 465, 475 (*Figs. 24, 48, 51*)
Diepholz, 484, 487, 493, 497, 507, 509, 510, 511, 513, 544 (*Figs. 88, 89, 90*)
Diest, 252, 253, 293, 298, 306, 309, 311, 314, 323, 360, 386, 390, 446, 458, 464, 544 (*Figs. 31, 42, 49, 51, 71, 72, 73, 74, 75, 76, 85*)
Dieteren (N. of Susteren), 361, 421
Dinant, 355, 356, 357, 358, 388 (*Figs. 54, 71, 85*)
Dingden, 654
Director General, Army Medical Services, 26, 29, 32, 48, 50, 52, 53, 54, 55
Displaced Persons, 506, 511, 529, 533, 536, 537, 538, 539, 541
Dixmude, 331, 332 (*Fig. 52*)
Doenitz, Grand Admiral Karl, 484
Domart, 265
Domberg (in N.W. corner of Walcheren), 344
Donsbruggen, 428 (*Fig. 86*)

INDEX

'Doomsday', Operation, 494
Dortmund–Ems Canal, 477, 478, 486, 489, 508, 509, 536 (*Fig. 88*)
Douvres, 143, 179, 180 (*Figs. 2, 8, 9, 15, 16, 18, 20, 22, 23*)
Down Ampney Airfield (nr. Swindon), 69
Dover, 21, 61, 62
Dozulé (E. of Troarn on the Pont l'Eveque Rd.), 283, 284
'Dragoon', see 'Anvil'
Driel, 230, 231, 244, 277, 278, 297, 298, 306 (*Figs. 43, 44*)
Ducy Ste. Marguerite, 164 (*Fig. 13*)
Duffel (on the Malines–Lierre Rd.), 402, 409, 410, 412, 476, 646, 647, 650
Duhnen, 649, 652
Dunkirk, 225, 256, 323, 330, 348, 369 (*Fig. 48*)
Düsseldorf, 5, 8, 10, 11, 413, 417
Dutch Resistance Movement, 275, 280

'Eclipse', Operation, 460, 486, 513, 515, 528–541
Ecarde, 131, 176, 283 (*Fig. 16*)
Ecouis, 265
Ecouché, 236, 242 (*Figs. 25, 46*)
Eecloo, 331, 342, 347, 412, 474, 475, 645 (*Fig. 53*)
Eersel, 262, 266 (*Figs. 73, 74*)
Eindhoven, 6, 7, 12, 13, 226, 228, 233, 242, 244, 253, 277, 293, 295, 297, 300, 309, 311, 314, 324, 369, 370, 373, 378, 379, 380, 382, 390, 395, 398, 399, 403, 410, 411, 412, 437, 451, 458, 459, 460, 461, 462, 464, 466, 475, 513, 542, 644, 645, 648, 649, 652, 655 (*Figs. 32, 43, 49, 51, 56, 59, 60, 65, 66, 67, 68, 72, 74*)
Eisenhower, General Dwight D. (U.S.), 1, 4, 5, 9, 10, 12, 13, 15, 16, 17, 18, 20, 22, 23, 222, 223, 335, 356, 413, 484
Elbe, advance to and crossing of the, 477–484 (*Figs. 88–90*)
    medical arrangements, 495–515
    medical cover, 484–495 (*Fig. 91*)
'Elephant', Operation, 349
Emergency Medical Services of the Ministry of Health and the Department of Health for Scotland, 27, 36, 37, 43, 64, 65, 66, 67, 69, 70, 71, 72, 73, 74, 75, 89, 103, 405
Emmerich, 10, 413, 418, 445, 472, 473, 480, 516, 518 (*Figs. 78, 81, 84, 87, 88*)
Engter, 487 (*Fig. 88*)
'Enterprise', Operation, 477, 481, 482 (*Fig. 90*)
    casualties, 492, 493
    evacuation, 509
    medical arrangements, 495, 496
    medical cover, 485, 486, 487–493 (*Fig. 91*)
Epecamps, 265
'Epsom', Operation, 124, 125
    casualties, 159
    medical arrangements, 176–180 (*Fig. 17*)
    medical cover, 154–159, 162 (*Figs. 10, 11*)
Erichshof, 487
Erpen, 437

Erps–Querbs, 379
Escaut Canal, 6, 7, 222, 233, 237, 262, 295 (*Figs. 42, 43*)
Escoville, 152 (*Fig. 9*)
Estrues, 314
Evacuation of casualties, 45
Evacuation, reflections on, 640
Evacuation system, September 1944, *Fig. 51*
Evere Airfield, Brussels, 293, 311, 323
Everlo, 367
Evrecy, 3, 116, 121, 161, 179, 216, 238, 263 (*Figs. 8, 12*)
Evreux, 292, 307, 309 (*Figs. 29, 47*)
Exmes, 242
Eysden, 360, 383, 386, 388, 458, 466 (*Figs. 70, 72, 73, 74, 75, 76*)
Exercise 'Fabius', 24
Expeditionary Force, assembly and dispatch, 91

Falaise, 4, 5, 122, 124, 125, 142, 143, 219, 220, 221, 236, 250, 262, 264, 267, 284, 306, 309, 318, 319, 322, 326, 327, 328, 329 (*Figs. 1, 3, 4, 24, 25, 29, 46, 47, 52*)
Fallingbostel, 533, 648, 651
Falkenburg, 522 (*Fig. 92*)
Farge (nr. Bremen), 504
Field and Special Surgical Units, reflections on, 637
Field Dressing Stations, reflections on, 636
Flensburg, 484, 515, 533, 535, 539, 540
Fleurbaix, 262, 265
Fleury-sur-Orne, 143, 326 (*Figs. 8, 52*)
Flushing, 8, 335, 339, 340, 345, 347 (*Figs. 53, 77*)
Fontaine, 162, 265
Fontaine-Henri, 139 (*Fig. 8*)
Fontenay (W. of Caen), 164 (*Fig. 13*)
Forêt de la Londe, 317 (*Fig. 34*)
Forêt Grimbosq (N. of Thury Harcourt), 264
'Fortitude', Operation, 21
Frankfurt, 5, 12, 335, 419, 482
Frasselt, 427, 428, 430, 451 (*Figs. 86, 87*)
French Resistance Movement (Les Forces Françaises de l'Intérieur), 2, 20, 129, 216, 221, 222, 223, 245
Fresnay, 264
Fresney-le-Vieux, 239, 263
Fresnoy (on the Arras–Lens Rd.), 233, 251, 293, 298
Friesland Province, 523
Friesoythe (W. of Falkenburg, S. of Küsten Canal), 518
Frisian Islands, 484, 522
Freudenburg, 438 (*Fig. 81*)
Fun (Denmark), 534

Gacé, 242, 292, 298 (*Figs. 29, 46*)
Gandersheim, 647, 651, 652
Gandesbergen, 497
Gangelt, 420, 436, 437 (*Fig. 70*)
Gardelegen, 649
Gaumesnil, 327 (*Fig. 52*)

INDEX

Geertruidenberg (on the Maas, N. of Breda), 352, 360, 370
Geesthacht, 481, 541 (*Fig. 90*)
Geilenkirchen, 9, 352, 354, 360, 386, 436 (*Figs. 55, 74, 75, 76*)
Geldern, 11, 413, 416, 417, 420, 440, 459, 460 (*Figs. 78, 79*)
Geldrop, 254, 373, 382, 390, 459 (*Figs. 68, 72, 73, 74, 75, 76*)
Geleen (S.W. of Sittard on the Maestricht Rd.), 361, 421
Gemen (N.E. of Borken), 460, 495, 496, 510, 648, 651
Gemonde (S. of s'Hertogenbosch, S.E. of Vught), 450
Gendringen, 474 (*Fig. 87*)
Gennep, 416, 420, 428, 437, 441, 451, 543 (*Figs. 72, 78, 83, 86*)
German counter-attack at Mortain (U.S. 12 Army Group), 216 (*Fig. 24*)
Germany, occupation of, 528
Gerpinnes, 388 (*Fig. 71*)
Gescher, 511
Gheel, 224, 225, 239, 251, 293 (*Figs. 31, 42, 75, 76*)
Gheluvelt (on the Ypres–Menin Rd.), 262, 265
Ghent, 224, 225, 235, 261, 337, 342, 347, 348, 401, 410, 412, 465, 472, 475, 476, 487, 494, 524, 645, 646, 647, 650, 652, 655 (*Figs. 48, 77*)
Ginneken, 655
Giverny (on the Seine, S.E. of Vernon), 243
Glisy, 317 (*Fig. 48*)
Glos-la-Ferrière, 265
Glückstadt, 540, 648
Goch, 414, 416, 419, 420, 422, 426, 429, 438, 439, 441, 446, 450, 452, 470, 508, 554 (*Figs. 78, 79, 81, 83, 84, 86, 88*)
Goderville, 260 (*Fig. 35*)
Goes, 342, 346, 648 (*Fig. 53*)
Goirle, 380 (*Fig. 65*)
'Gold' Beach, 18, 114, 117, 118 (*Figs. 1, 2*)
Gonneville-la-Mallet, 260 (*Fig. 35*)
'Goodwood Meeting', Operation, 125–127, 172, 214
   casualties, 127, 153
   medical arrangements, 178–180 (*Fig. 18*)
   medical cover:
      Canadian, 142, 143
      British, 153–155
Gorssel (S.E. of Deventer on the Zutphen Rd.), 519
Goslar, 648
Gosport, 52, 61, 62
Gossoncourt (S. of Tirlemont on the Huy Rd.), 360
Göttingen, 648, 649
Gournay, 263, 265
Grainville-sur-Odon, 156, 183, 184, 263 (*Figs. 10, 11, 12*)
Grand Val, 264
Grave, 6, 226, 228, 231, 244, 277, 295, 297, 300, 336, 350, 351, 378, 380, 386, 403, 450 (*Figs. 32, 43, 44, 49, 64, 67, 69, 72, 73*)
Grave-sur-Mer, 139, 185, 186, 190, 194, 200 (*Figs. 2, 8, 20*)

'Greenline', Operation, 160, 161
   medical cover, *Fig. 12*
'Grenade', Operation, 416
Greven, 457, 495, 496 (*Fig. 83*)
Grenay, 262, 265
Grimbosq (N. of Thury Harcourt), 264
Groede (S.W. of Breskens), 342
Groesbeek, 415, 427, 441 (*Figs. 44, 69, 78, 82, 86*)
Groin (N.W. of Rees), 423
Groningen, 480, 518, 520 (*Fig. 92*)
Gross Baarlo, 497
Gross Burgwedel, 511
Gronau, 511
'Grouse', Operation, 284
Gruitrode (S. of Bree), 378
Gülzow, 492
'Guy Fawkes', Operation, 370

Haecht, 446
Haffen, 430, 432 (*Figs. 79, 80*)
Hahn, 525, 647 (*Fig. 92*)
Halberstadt, 649
Haldern, 430, 444, 453, 536 (*Fig. 80*)
Halle-Boyenhoven, 360
Halsche Water (nr. Tilburg), 370
Hamb, 431 (*Fig. 79*)
Hamburg, 13, 422, 477, 478, 481, 484, 485, 495, 497, 498, 507, 516, 532, 535, 540, 644, 645, 647, 648, 650, 651, 652, 653 (*Fig. 90*)
Hamminkeln, 424, 430, 450, 497, 536 (*Figs. 78, 79, 80, 88*)
Hamont, 366, 375, 379, 382 (*Figs. 62, 68, 72, 73, 74, 75, 76*)
Hanover, 485, 488, 489, 532, 647, 648, 650, 651, 652
Hapert, 378 (*Fig. 65*)
Harburg, 478, 484, 497 (*Fig. 90*)
Hardinghem, 331, 332, 475, 476, 646, 647
Hartgill Committee, 28, 32, 41, 286, 636
Hartenstein, *see* Hotel Hartenstein
Harskamp (N.W. of Arnhem and S.W. of Apeldoorn), 520
'Hat' Route, 160, 161 (*Fig. 12*)
Hasselt, 224, 360, 387, 388, 393, 394, 399, 400, 410, 411, 458, 459, 460, 462, 475, 645, 646, 648 (*Figs. 42, 70, 72, 73, 74, 75, 76, 85*)
Hautmesnil, 329 (*Fig. 52*)
'Hawick' Route, 156 (*Figs. 10, 11*)
Health of the troops, 560
Hechtel, 233, 244, 252, 294, 295, 386 (*Figs. 42, 70, 72, 73, 74, 75, 76*)
Heek (on the Stadtlohn–Ochtrup Rd., N.E. of Ahaus), 494
s'Heerenberg (N. of Emmerich), 516, 518, 519
Heerle, 343
Hees, 295, 296, 297, 384, 451, 460, 461, 467 (*Fig. 78*)
Heesch, 378 (*Fig. 65*)
Heeze, 361, 410 (*Figs. 62, 72, 74, 75, 76*)
Hekkens, 440, 441 (*Fig. 83*)
Helden, 375, 379 (*Fig. 63*)
Helenaveen, 364 (*Fig. 57*)

INDEX

Helmond, 237, 352, 361, 363, 364, 388, 458, 459, 461, 507, 542, 652, 654, 655 (*Figs. 32, 43, 57, 72, 75, 76*)
Helvoirt, 370 (*Fig. 61*)
Hengelo, 493 (*Figs. 88, 92*)
Herent (N.W. of Louvain), 653
Hermanville, 119, 151, 169, 185, 186, 190, 193 (*Figs. 2, 8, 20, 22*)
Hermeville, 245, 247 (*Fig. 28*)
Herpen, 378 (*Fig. 65*)
s'Hertogenbosch, 336, 352, 360, 370, 376, 378, 380, 419, 467 (*Figs. 32, 49, 60, 61, 65, 67, 77, 92*)
Hervieux, 238
Herzlake, 521 (*Fig. 92*)
Het Loo, 278, 280
Heubécourt (N.E. of Vernon), 243
Heusden (S.E. of Beeringen), 233
Heveadorp Ferry, 7, 230, 231 (*Fig. 64*)
Heverlee (S. of Louvain), 360, 379, 412, 476, 645, 647, 650
Heythuyzen (Heythuijzen), 375, 378 (*Figs. 62, 63, 72, 76*)
'Hill 309', 215
'Hill 361', 215, 216
Hilvarenbeek, 362 (*Figs. 56, 75, 76*)
Hochwald, 416, 417, 452, 470, 471 (*Figs. 78, 79*)
Hochwald Xanten, 431 (*Figs. 79, 80*)
Hoensbroek (E. of Nuth and S.E. of Sittard), 436
Hof, 266
Holland, advance into, medical arrangements, 284
    medical cover, 232
Holland, liberation of, Canadian First Army, 516 (*Fig. 92*)
Holsbeek (nr. Louvain), 654
Holxen, 489
Home Forces, reorganisation 1944, 97
Hoogboom, 347 (*Fig. 53*)
Hoogstraten (S. of Breda and W. of Turnhout), 379
Hôpital Brugmann, Brussels, 309
Hôpital St. Gilles, Brussels, 309
Hôpital St. Pierre, Brussels, 233, 293, 309
Hornoy, 262, 265
Horst, 364, 441, 461, 654 (*Fig. 57*)
Hospital accommodation in U.K., 70
Hospital beds, provision of for 'Overlord', 641
Hospital for Incurables, Lille, 317
Hospitals (General), location of (21 Army Group), 333, 409, 474, 644
Hospitals (General—200 beds), reflection on, 637
    (General—600 and 1,200 beds), reflection on, 638
Hotel Hartenstein, Oosterbeek, 230, 231, 269, 270, 271
Hotel Schoonoord, Oosterbeek, 269, 270, 272, 273, 274, 277
Hotel Tafelberg, Oosterbeek, 269, 271, 272, 273, 274
Hoya (on the Weser), 478, 497, 498, 644
'Howe' Beach, 185 (*Fig. 20*)

Huijbergen (S.E. of Bergen-op-Zoom and E. of Woensdrecht), 343
Huis Oosterhout, 378
'Humid', Operation, 366
Hunsel (S.E. of Weert), 378
'Husky', Operation, 16
Husum, 533

Ibbenbüren, 477, 478, 484, 497, 511, 654 (*Fig. 88*)
Ifs, 143, 326 (*Figs. 8, 52*)
Ijsselmeer (Zuider Zee), 516, 519, 520 (*Fig. 92*)
Ijzendijke, 342 (*Fig. 53*)
'Infatuate I', Operation, 339, 340
    medical arrangements, 347 (*Fig. 53*)
    medical cover, 345
'Infatuate II', Operation, 339, 340
    medical arrangements, 347 (*Fig. 53*)
    medical cover, 343–346
Ingonville, 256
Intercommunication—medical services, reflections on, 640
Iserlohn, 647, 650, 651
'Item' Beach, 117, 186 (*Fig. 20*)

Jerusalem, 136, 182, 183, 184, 298 (*Figs. 6, 22*)
'Jig' Beach, 117, 186, 187 (*Fig. 20*)
Juaye-Mondaye, 136, 202 (*Figs. 6, 7*)
Jonker Bosch Hospital, Nijmegen, 233, 295, 296, 297, 306, 384, 385, 451, 467 (*Fig. 44*)
Jouy-sur-Eure (N.W. of Pacy), 654
Julich, 10, 353, 413 (*Fig. 55*)
Juliusburg, 492
'Juno' Beach, 18, 114, 118, 119, 162, 170 (*Figs. 1, 2*)
'Jupiter', Operation, 124, 125
    medical arrangements, 176, 177, 179 (*Fig. 17*)
    medical cover, 162
Jutland, 534

Kain (N. of Tournai), 474, 476, 645, 647, 650
Kampen, 497
Kapellen (N.E. of Geldern), 420, 422, 452, 459, 460, 648, 651 (*Fig. 79*)
Kapellen (Capellen) (N. of Antwerp), 343 (*Figs. 53, 77*)
Kaserne Willem III, Apeldoorn, 278
Kasteel Ampsen, 518
Katholijke Ziekenhuizen, Apeldoorn, 278, 279
Kattenbosch, 266
Kaulille (N.W. of Bree), 382
Keent, 378
Kerkhoven, 266
Kervenheim, 422 (*Fig. 79*)
Kessel (S.W. of Baarlo), 379 (*Fig. 63*)
Kevelaer, 420, 449, 450 (*Fig. 79*)
Kiel, 540, 541, 644, 645, 651
'King' Beach, 117, 186 (*Fig. 20*)

666 INDEX

Kinroy (Kinroij), 360, 378 (*Figs. 72, 75, 76*)
Kirchatten, 522 (*Fig. 92*)
Kladow Airfield, 650
Kleine Brogel (Petit Broghel) (N.E. of Hechtel and N. of Peer), 237
Knocke-sur-Mer, 337, 411, 412, 476, 645, 646, 648, 649, 651, 652, 653 (*Fig. 53*)
Krabbendijke (S. of Kruiningen on the S. Beveland Isthmus), 342
Kranenburg, 414, 426, 427, 428, 429, 437, 441, 450, 451, 469, 471 (*Figs. 78, 81, 86, 87*)
Kreis Hagenau, 541
Kruiningen, 342 (*Fig. 52*)
Küsten Canal, 480, 518 (*Fig. 92*)

Laak (N. of Hasselt), 293 (*Fig. 42*)
La Blanchère, 292, 298
La Corderie (nr. Bayeux), 23
La Chapelle-du-Bois, 262, 265
La Délivrande, 141, 142, 143, 155, 169, 176, 179, 180, 190, 191, 193, 194, 196, 283 (*Figs. 8, 14, 16, 22*)
La Haye-St. Sylvestre (E. of Vimoutiers and S. of Broglie), 262, 265
La Hulpe (S.E. of Brussels and S. of Waterloo), 379
La Lazarette, Bayeux, 193, 194
La Londe (W. of Aunay-sur-Orne), 242
La Prevotière, 163
La Rivière, 117, 118 (*Fig. 2*)
La Trinité des Laitiers, 320, 654
La Villeneuve, 142 (*Fig. 8*)
Lahde, 541
Lambersart, 652
Lanklaar, 360, 361 (*Figs. 72, 74, 75, 76*)
Lauenburg, 488, 491, 492, 541, 649 (*Figs. 90, 91*)
Lazarett, Stalag XIB, 280–283
Le Bocq, 232
Leende, *Figs. 62, 72, 73, 75, 76*
Le Hamel (N. of Orbec and S.E. of Lisieux), 329
Le Haut d'Audrieu, 164 (*Fig. 13*)
Le Havre, 23, 223, 225, 245, 247, 256, 283, 284, 323, 334, 356 (*Figs. 1, 3, 4, 24, 28, 35*)
Le Mariquet (S. of Ranville), 130, 283
Le Mesnil (nr. the coast W. of Arromanches), 130 (*Fig. 5*)
Le Mesnil (E. of Aunay-sur-Orne), 263
Le Mesnil-Patry, 158, 170 (*Figs. 8, 10, 11, 15*)
Le Mont, 263, 264
Le Plein (nr. Amfreville in the Orne Estuary), 283
Le Plessis (on the Seine, S.E. of Caudebec), 245
Le Sevich, 265
Le Thuit, 262, 265
Le Tilleul (S. of Etretat on the Le Havre Rd.), 260
Le Tourneur (N. of Bény-Bocage), 232
Le Translay, 332
Leer, 521 (*Fig. 92*)
Leeuwarden, 516, 524 (*Fig. 92*)
Leffard, 264

Lemforde, 484, 487 (*Fig. 89*)
Lengerich, 489, 509, 510, 645, 646 (*Fig. 88*)
Lens, 239, 292
Léopold Canal, 331, 335, 336, 337, 342, 347 (*Fig. 53*)
Leveroij (E. of Weert, between Weert and Heythuyzen), 375 (*Fig. 63*)
Les Andelys (between Pont de l'Arche and Vernon on the Seine), 237, 262
Les Authieux, 332
Les Bottereaux, 265
Les Buissons, 141
Les Faux, 265
Les Moulins (S.E. of Thury Harcourt), 264
Les Moutiers-en-Cinglais (W. of Bretteville-sur-Laize on the Thury Harcourt–Caen Rd.), 263, 264
Les Planches, 265
Les Saullets, 162 (*Figs. 10, 11*)
Liége, 5, 9, 355, 356, 357, 369, 384, 440 (*Figs. 26, 85*)
Lierre, 247, 266, 284, 324, 380, 437 (*Fig. 49*)
Liesel, 363, 364 (*Fig. 57*)
Light Field Ambulances, reflections on, 636
Lille, 223, 224, 239, 251, 261, 316, 317, 398, 401, 410, 411, 475, 524, 645, 655 (*Figs. 26, 48, 51*)
Lillebonne, 245, 260, 284 (*Fig. 35*)
Lille St. Hubert, 237, 366 (*Figs. 75, 76*)
Lindel, 654
Lingen, 477, 478, 486, 493 (*Fig. 88*)
Linsburg, 652
Lippstadt, 12, 419, 483, 537
Lisieux, 234, 255, 284, 329, 332 (*Figs. 1, 3, 4, 24, 29, 33*)
Livarot (on the Lisieux–Alençon Rd.), 330
Location of General Hospitals, 21 Army Group, 333
Location of medical units, 53rd Division, August and September 1944, 263–266
Lochem (E. of Zutphen on the Hengelo Rd.), 518, 519
Lokeren (on the Antwerp–Ghent Rd.), 331, 332, 347
Lombeek Ste. Marie (nr. Brussels), 654
Longueval, 154 (*Figs. 9, 14*)
Loon-op-Zand, 349, 360, 370 (*Fig. 77*)
Lorineker, 648, 651
Loucelles, 162 (*Fig. 13*)
Louvain, 244, 277, 357, 360, 379, 388, 390, 393, 398, 410, 412, 422, 462, 465, 476, 645, 647, 650, 653, 654 (*Figs. 42, 49, 71, 72, 85*)
'Love' Beach, 118, 185 (*Fig. 20*)
Lübberstedt, 497
Lübeck, 13, 481, 486, 488, 496, 532, 533, 535, 539, 540, 541, 652
Ludendorf Bridge, Remagen, 417
Ludwigslust (nr. Hamburg), 481, 541
Luijksgestel (Luyksgestel), 266
Lüneburg, 13, 477, 486, 488, 491, 496, 509, 512, 513, 532, 533, 535, 541, 644, 645, 647, 648, 650, 654 (*Figs. 89, 90*)
Lüneburg Heath, 484, 488
Lünen, 647, 651

INDEX 667

Maas, advance to, medical arrangements, 380
　medical cover, 360
Maasbree, 364, 366, 367 (*Figs. 57, 58*)
Maas–Waal Canal, 6, 226, 228, 360 (*Figs. 32, 43, 64, 69*)
Maestricht, 355, 387, 440, 466 (*Figs. 55, 70, 72, 74, 75, 76, 85*)
Maeseyck, 384, 386, 420, 456 (*Figs. 55, 70, 72, 73, 74, 75, 76*)
Maillen, 388
Malaria, I Corps, July–September 1944, 565
Maldegem (between Aadenburg and Eecloo), 342, 349
Malden, 233, 467 (*Figs. 44, 73, 82*)
Malente, 540
Malines (Mechlin, Mechelen), 224, 401, 403, 655 (*Fig. 42*)
'Mallard', Operation:
　casualties, 383
　medical arrangements, 382, 383 (*Fig. 68*)
　medical cover, 379
Mantes-Gassicourt, 4, 221 (*Fig. 47*)
Marcelet, 170, 263 (*Fig. 15*)
Marche, 355, 356, 388, 440, 456 (*Figs. 71, 85*)
Mardilly (E. of Vimoutiers on the Alençon Rd.), 265
Marienbaum, 444, 445, 471 (*Figs. 78, 79*)
Marienboom, Nijmegen, 427, 525, 530, 645
Marienbosch (Pensionaat), Nijmegen, 295, 296, 297, 384, 386, 450, 453, 467
'Market Garden', Operation, 6, 8, 226–232, 335, 345, 360
　medical arrangements:
　　XXX Corps, 293–299 (*Fig. 43*)
　　H.Q. Airborne Troops, 299–306 (*Fig. 44*)
　　Second Army, 309, 317, 320
　medical cover:
　　Guards Armd. Division, 233, 234
　　1st Airborne Division, 267–283 (*Fig. 36*)
　　43rd Division, 243, 244
　　50th Division, 253
Marnefer (S. of La Haye-St. Sylvestre), 265
Martigny, 316, 332, 347, 350, 409, 524
Materborn, 428, 437, 438, 439, 450 (*Figs. 81, 86, 87*)
Mechelen, 383, 386 (*Fig. 70*)
Medical Arrangements, advance into Holland, 284
　advance to and crossing of the Rhine, 445
　opening of Estuary of the Scheldt, 347 (*Fig. 53*)
　the attack on Caen, *Fig. 16*
　'Bluecoat', Operation, *Fig. 37*
　'Clipper', Operation, *Fig. 70*
　'Epsom' and 'Jupiter', Operations, *Fig. 17*
　'Goodwood Meeting', Operation, *Fig. 18*
　'Market Garden', Operation, *Fig. 43*
　'Plunder', Operation, 453 (*Fig. 84*)
　21 Army Group formations, 174
　　Canadian First Army, 347, 466 (*Fig. 53*)

Canadian II Corps, 347
Second Army, 184, 390, 456, 505 (*Fig. 85*)
　I Corps, 380
　VIII Corps, 495
　XII Corps, 180, 380, 445, 496 (*Figs. 66, 67*)
　XXX Corps, 181, 379, 384, 450, 498 (*Figs. 42, 69, 70, 71*)
　L. of C., 400
　11 L. of C. Area, 463
Medical Branch, H.Q. 21 Army Group, 23, 24
Medical Cover:
　advance to and crossing of, the Rhine, 419
　assault and lodgement of 21 Army Group Formations, 127
　break out and advance into Holland (21 Army Group Formations), 232
　opening of Estuary of the Scheldt, 341
　Canadian First Army, *Fig. 86*
　　Canadian 2nd Division, 341
　　Canadian 3rd Division, 138, 342
　　Canadian 4th Armd. Division, 343
　Guards Armd. Division, 360, 419
　3rd Division, 422, 486
　4th Special Service Brigade, 343
　5th Division, 487
　6th Airborne Division, 127, 361, 423, 488
　7th Armd. Division, 360, 420, 484
　11th Armd. Division, 485
　15th Division, 361, 426, 489 (*Figs. 10, 11, 12, 56, 57, 58, 80, 91*)
　43rd Division, 436, 493 (*Fig. 81*)
　49th Division, 246 (*Fig. 28*)
　50th Division, 132, 136 (*Figs. 29, 30, 31, 32*)
　51st Division, 369, 371 (*Figs. 14, 33, 34, 35, 61, 62, 63, 64, 82, 83*)
　52nd (Lowland) Division, 345, 445, 494
　53rd Division, *Fig. 65*
Medical equipment, forward supply of, 640
Medical establishments (L. of C.), reflections on, 639
Medical Order of Battle, Second Army, 407
Medical Planning:
　Canadian First Army, 101
　Operation 'Overlord', 23
　Second Army, 25
　3rd Division, 144
Medical Planning Committee, 33, 45, 83
Medical Planning Section (of the Administrative Planning Staff), 29, 30, 31, 32, 45, 47, 48
Medical Research Council, 80
Medical Services—intercommunication reflections on, 641
Medical Situation, Second Army (*Figs. 72, 73, 74, 75, 76*)
Medical supplies, 75
Medical supplies by air, 1st Airborne Division, 302
Medical Tactical Plan, 101
　Airborne Division (Operation 'Market Garden'), 268

INDEX

Medical Units: distribution of,
   in 11 L. of C. Area, *Fig. 50*
   21 Army Group locations, 539, 646, 650
Meerveldhoven (S. of Zeelst, S.W. of Eindhoven), 242, 262, 390
Mehr, 430 (*Figs. 79, 80, 86*)
Meijel, 364, 375 (*Fig. 57*)
Mellendorf, 489
Menantissart (nr. Romescamps), 654
Menin, 265
Menzelen (on the Rhine opposite Rees), 448
Meppen, 480, 518, 519, 521 (*Figs. 88, 92*)
Méricourt-en-Vimeux, 265
Meslay, 264
Mesnil-Lieubray, 265
Mesnil-Verclives, 262, 265
Mesnières-en-Bray (nr. Dieppe), 347, 348, 524
Mesum, 497 (*Fig. 88*)
Mettingen, 511
Meuse–Escaut Canal, 222, 224, 225, 226, 237, 252, 293, 297, 319 (*Figs. 31, 42*)
Mézidon, 245, 317, 332 (*Fig. 25*)
'Mike' Beach, 118, 131, 186, 187 (*Fig. 20*)
Military Government, 429, 500, 503, 504, 510, 528, 530, 537, 540, 556
Military Hospital, Avenue de la Couronne, Brussels, 293
Mill, 419, 440 (*Fig. 82*)
Mingoval, 265
Ministry of Health, 26, 62, 64, 65, 67, 71, 72, 73
Mirbord, 162 (*Fig. 12*)
Mobile Dental Units, reflections on, 639
Moergestel (E. of Tilburg), 362 (*Fig. 56*)
Molenhoek (S.E. of Eecloo), 345
Molfsee, 653
Molin, 529, 541, 649
Moll, 393, 395, 400, 458 (*Figs. 74, 75, 76*)
Mondrainville, 155, 169, 263 (*Figs. 10, 11, 12, 13, 15*)
Montgaroult, 292, 298, 314
Montgomery, Field Marshal, Sir Bernard (Viscount), 2, 3, 4, 5, 6, 9, 10, 12, 17, 18, 19, 21, 24, 122, 123, 124, 125, 126, 215, 216, 220, 222, 223, 226, 335, 351, 356, 357, 418, 484, 560, 561
Mont Pinçon, 171, 215, 216, 242, 250, 292 (*Fig. 24*)
Montroty, 265
Montivilliers, 245, 247 (*Figs. 28, 35*)
Mook, 349, 416, 419, 420, 441, 452 (*Figs. 44, 77, 78, 81, 82, 83, 86*)
Moorege, 497
Mortain, 3, 4, 5, 214, 216, 217, 219 (*Fig. 24*)
Mörs (W. of Duisburg and E. of Venlo), 413
Mouen, 162, 263 (*Figs. 10, 11, 12, 13, 15*)
Moulineaux, 141 (*Fig. 8*)
'Mulberries', 3, 17, 21, 123, 125, 189, 190, 204
München-Gladbach, 10, 648, 651, 652 (*Fig. 55*)
Municipal Hospital, Arnhem, 268, 269
Münster, 536, 647, 650 (*Fig. 92*)

Namur, 355, 356, 358, 383, 384, 388, 390, 440 (*Figs. 26, 53, 85*)

'Nan' Beach, 118, 186 (*Fig. 20*)
Nebo, Nijmegen, 427, 475, 645, 647, 650 (*Fig. 86*)
Nécy (S.E. of Falaise), 264
Nederasselt, 306 (*Fig. 44*)
Nederweert, 366, 373 (*Figs. 62, 63, 73*)
Neerloon, 306 (*Fig. 44*)
Neeroeteren (on the Lanklaar–Bree Rd. at the level of Bourg Leopold), 378
Neerpelt, 225, 306, 654 (*Figs. 49, 73, 75, 76*)
Nehmten, 494, 648
'Neptune' Operation, 18, 19, 104, 114–124 (*Figs. 1, 2*)
   casualties, 184
   medical arrangements, 174
   medical cover, 127
Netherlands District, 510
Neu Darchau (on the Elbe), 479, 488
Neuen Gamme, 512, 513
Neuenkirchen, 509, 513, 653
Neuf Mer, 138, 141 (*Fig. 8*)
Neumünster, 539
Neustadt, 489, 515, 535, 538, 540, 541, 648, 651 (*Fig. 89*)
Neuve Eglise, 265
Nienburg, 477, 507, 511, 513, 533, 648 (*Figs. 89, 90*)
Nieuw-Millingen (W. of Apeldoorn on the Amersfoort Rd.), 520
Nijmegen 'Island', 376, 378, 385, 386, 519
Nijmegen, 6, 7, 8, 10, 226, 227, 228, 229, 230, 231, 233, 237, 244, 253, 277, 294, 295, 297, 298, 300, 306, 311, 324, 336, 340, 349, 350, 352, 354, 360, 366, 367, 369, 375, 376, 380, 384, 385, 390, 399, 403, 413, 415, 419, 420, 427, 428, 437, 438, 439, 441, 450, 451, 456, 466, 467, 470, 471, 472, 475, 480, 518, 519, 520, 521, 525, 544, 644, 645 (*Figs. 32, 42, 44, 49, 59, 64, 69, 72, 73, 77, 78, 82, 86, 92*)
Nijmegen Bridgehead, medical cover of 50th Division (*Fig. 32*)
Noeux-les-Mines, 265, 266
Nonant, 184, 291, 292, 298 (*Figs. 6, 29*)
Nordhorn, 486, 493, 536, 650 (*Fig. 88*)
Noorder Canal, 373, 378 (*Figs. 62, 63*)
Noron l'Abbaye, 264
Nuland, 378 (*Fig. 68*)
Nune, 265
Nuth, 360, 383, 386, 388, 436 (*Fig. 70*)
Nütterden, 426, 428, 429, 437, 438 (*Figs. 81, 86, 87*)

'Oban' Route, 156, 157 (*Figs. 10, 11*)
'Oboe' Beach, 118, 185 (*Fig. 20*)
Oberneuland, 494
Ochtrup (nr. the German frontier at the level of Enschede), 510
Occupation areas, deployment of medical formations to, 530
   VIII Corps, 538
   15th Division, 540
Occupation of Germany, 528
Oerle (S.W. of Eindhoven), 266, 378
Ohlendorf, 654

INDEX

Oirschot, 362, 363 (*Fig. 56*)
Oldenburg, 480, 518, 521, 522, 525 (*Figs. 89, 90*)
Oldenzaal, 486, 510
Oler, 379
'Omaha' Beach, 18, 114, 115, 118, 119, 121 (*Fig. 1*)
Oostakker (N. of Ghent), 410, 412, 475, 645
Oost Dunkerke (on the coast N.E. of Dunkirk), 350, 412, 474, 475, 525, 645, 647, 650
Oostmalle (on the Antwerp–Turnhout Rd.), 247
Oosterbeek, 7, 228, 229, 230, 269, 270, 271, 272, 273, 274, 275, 276, 277 (*Figs. 36, 44*)
Oosterhout (N.W. of Nijmegen, beyond the Waal), 231, 352, 367
Oostrum, 459, 475, 644
Ootmarsum, 519, 520, 645 (*Fig. 92*)
Operation 'Alan', 377, 378, 380, 382
    'Anvil' ('Dragoon'), 5, 17, 18, 222
    'Ascot', 373, 374
    'Avalanche', 16
    'Blackcock', 359, 383, 384, 436, 437, 445, 456, 458, 463
    'Blockbuster', 416, 469, 470, 471, 474
    'Bluecoat', 215, 216, 236, 238, 284, 285, 291
    'Bolero', 15
    'Clipper', 386, 387
    'Cobra', 126, 214, 215
    'Colin', 370, 371, 372
    'Doomsday', 494
    'Dragoon' (*see* 'Anvil')
    'Eclipse', 460, 486, 513, 515, 528, 538, 539, 540, 541
    'Elephant', 349
    'Enterprise', 477, 481, 482, 490, 491, 492, 493, 496
    'Epsom', 124, 176, 177
    'Fortitude', 21
    'Goodwood Meeting', 125, 126, 127, 142, 153, 155, 172, 176, 177, 178, 179, 214
    'Greenline', 160
    'Grenade', 416
    'Grouse', 284
    'Guy Fawkes', 370
    'Humid', 366
    'Husky', 16
    'Infatuate I', 339
    'Infatuate II', 340, 343, 347
    'Jupiter', 124, 162, 176, 177, 179
    'Mallard', 379, 382, 383
    'Market Garden', 6, 8, 226, 233, 243, 253, 267, 293, 295, 296, 299, 303, 309, 317, 320, 335, 345, 360
    'Neptune', 18, 114
    'Overlord', 2, 14, 16, 17, 18, 24, 31, 101, 103, 104, 128, 133, 222, 312, 636, 641
    'Plunder', 418, 422, 439, 444, 446, 450, 453, 454, 455, 456, 459, 461, 462, 463, 472, 473, 495
    'Rebound', 366
    'Round-Up', 15
    'Shears', 383
    'Sledgehammer', 15
    'Spring', 143
    'Suitcase', 343
    'Switchback', 337, 342, 347
    'Torch', 15, 16, 31, 77
    'Torchlight', 430, 431, 433, 436, 492
    'Totalize', 218, 219, 255, 256, 257, 326
    'Varsity', 418, 456
    'Veritable', 349, 360, 366, 387, 390, 416, 419, 420, 422, 426, 429, 430, 437, 438, 439, 440, 441, 442, 443, 445, 450, 453, 456, 458, 461, 463, 466, 467, 471, 492
    'Vitality I', 337, 341, 342, 347
    'Vitality II', 337
Order of Battle, Second Army, 104, 406
    I Corps District, 536
Orville, 262, 264
Osnabrück, 477, 486, 487, 488, 511, 513, 533, 536, 648, 652 (*Figs. 88, 89, 92*)
Oss, 352, 370, 378 (*Fig. 65*)
Ostend, 225, 316, 317, 323, 344, 347, 348, 361, 398, 401, 410, 411, 412, 465, 476, 494, 646, 648, 650, 651, 652, 653, 655 (*Fig. 51*)
Ostend-Bredene, 651
Osterholz (nr. Bremen), 494
Otterloo, 299, 519, 520 (*Fig. 92*)
Ottersum, 419, 441 (*Fig. 83*)
Ouistreham, 118, 119, 151, 179, 189 (*Figs. 2, 8, 9, 16, 22*)
Ouilly-le-Vicomte (N. of Lisieux), 245
'Overlord', Civil Affairs, 101
'Overlord', Operation, 2, 128, 133, 222, 312
    genesis and development of, 14–23
    medical planning, 24–104
        Second Army, 25–101
        Canadian First Army, 101–104
    Second Army, Order of Battle, 104–106
    21 Army Group Medical Services, 106–113
    raising of the medical component, 32
    reflections on the campaign, 636–644
Overpelt, 398 (*Figs. 51, 72, 75, 76*)
Overschie, 653
Overyssche (S.E. of Brussels on the Wavre Rd.), 379
Oxelear (nr. Diest), 266

Paris, 4, 20, 221, 222, 318 (*Figs. 47, 48*)
Pas-de-Calais, 2, 21, 221, 222, 323, 335
'Pearl Black' Route, 427 (*Fig. 86*)
'Pearl Red' Route, 427
Pédouzes, 256 (*Fig. 33*)
Peer, 236, 237 (*Figs. 72, 73, 75*)
Peine, 648, 651, 652, 653
Pensionaat Marienbosch, Nijmegen (*see* Marienbosch)
Périers (N.E. of Caen), 125, 152 (*Fig. 9*)
Perigny, 232, 314 (*Fig. 37*)
Pernes, 265
Petegem, 471
'Peter' Beach, 118, 186 (*Fig. 20*)
Petersberg, Oosterbeek, 274, 275 (*Fig. 36*)
Petit Broghel (Kleine Broghel) (S. of Neerpelt and N. of Peer), 237

INDEX

Pierrepont, 138, 141, 142 (*Fig. 8*)
'Plunder' Operation, 418 (*Fig. 78*)
    casualties, 423, 425, 433, 445, 450, 456, 473, 495
    medical arrangements:
        VIII Corps, 495
        XII Corps, 446–450
        XXX Corps, 453–456 (*Fig. 84*)
        Canadian First Army, 472–474 (*Fig. 87*)
        Second Army, 456, 459–463, 466
    medical cover, 422, 423–426 ('Varsity'), 430–436 ('Torchlight'), 439, 444, 445
Point 112, 179 (*Figs. 12, 17*)
Poix (nr. Amiens), 654
Political Prisoners Camp, Sandbostel, 498
Pt. Sains, 265
Pont Audemer, 245, 284 (*Fig. 34*)
Poppel, 352, 366, 380 (*Fig. 65*)
Port-en-Bessin, 116, 118, 121, 189 (*Figs. 2, 22*)
Portsmouth, 14, 22, 24, 61, 62, 103, 204
Postel (S.E. of Turnhout, N.E. of the frontier), 266, 377
Praest, 444, 473, 474 (*Figs. 78, 87*)
Pulle (E. of Antwerp and N. of the Antwerp–Herenthals Rd.), 379
Pursuit to Albert and Meuse–Escaut Canals, 222
Putten, 520 (*Fig. 92*)
Putte (N. of Antwerp), 341 (*Fig. 53*)
Pûtot-en-Bessin, 121, 156, 162 (*Figs. 2, 8, 10, 11, 13, 15*)
P.W.X., 506, 508, 510, 511, 512, 513, 528, 533, 534, 536, 538

Quakenbrück, 493 (*Figs. 88, 89*)
Qualburg, 453, 455 (*Figs. 84, 86, 87*)
'Queen' Beach, 118, 186 (*Fig. 20*)
Quelkhorn, 494
Quesnay, 220 (*Figs. 7, 25*)

Ranchy, 194
Randers, Denmark, 535
Ranville, 117, 119, 129, 130, 131, 152, 153, 168, 169, 244 (*Figs. 14, 16, 18, 22*)
Ranst (nr. Antwerp), 266
Rations, 78
Ratzeburg, 539
Rauray, 124, 164, 179 (*Figs. 13, 17*)
'Rebound', Operation, 366
Recke (between Rheine and Vilsen), 494
Reckheim, 386 (*Fig. 70*)
Rees, 11, 416, 423, 430, 444, 445, 453, 455, 460, 472, 475, 516, 536 (*Figs. 78, 84, 88*)
Reflections on the campaign (D.D.M.S., Second Army), 636
Rehden, 487 (*Fig. 90*)
Reichswald, 10, 230, 335, 353, 356, 359, 384, 386, 542 (*Figs. 43, 69*)
    Attack on the, (Operation 'Veritable'), 413–417 (*Figs. 77, 78, 81*)
        medical arrangements, 450–453, 458–459

    medical cover, 419–445 (*Figs. 82, 83*)
    medical cover Canadian First Army, 466–472 (*Fig. 86*)
    psychiatric battle casualties, 554, 555
Remagen, 11, 12, 417, 418, 482
Renaix (on the Audenarde–Leuze Rd.), 236, 251, 293, 398, 411, 412, 476, 646, 647, 650, 655
Rendsburg, 535, 539, 540, 646, 647, 648, 649, 650, 651, 653
Retersbeek, 437
Rettmer (nr. Lüneburg), 654
Reusel, 265, 378 (*Fig. 65*)
Reviers, 139, 176, 189, 190, 191, 193, 194, 195, 196, 314, 315, 334, 409, 410 (*Figs. 8, 16, 20, 22, 23, 50*)
Rhede, 536
Rheims, 13, 354, 355, 356, 484
Rheine, 457, 477, 478, 480, 484, 486, 493, 494, 496, 497, 507, 508, 509, 510, 513, 514, 544 (*Fig. 88*)
Rhine, advance to and crossing of, 413–419, (*Figs. 77, 78*)
    medical arrangements, 445–466 (*Figs. 84, 85*)
    medical cover, 419–445 (*Figs. 79–83*)
    medical cover Canadian First Army, 466–474 (*Figs. 86, 87*)
    psychiatric battle casualties, 554–557
Riepe (nr. Soltau), 654
Riethoven (S. of Eindhoven, W. of Valkenswaard), 262, 266
Ripdorf, 488
Rissen, 647, 650
River
    Aller, 477, 478, 484, 486, 489, 542 (*Fig. 90*)
    Dives, 116, 220, 245, 283 (*Figs. 1, 8, 16, 25, 33*)
    Dommel, 370
    Elbe, 12, 13, 418, 419, 477, 478, 479, 481, 483, 484, 486, 487, 488, 491, 495, 496, 498, 508, 509, 512, 516, 535, 541, 542 (*Figs. 90, 91*)
    Ems, 457, 477, 480, 485, 486, 495, 518, 521 (*Fig. 92*)
    Ijssel, 227, 480, 489, 516, 519, 520 (in Germany the Issel; in Holland the Ijssel) (*Fig. 92*)
    Issel, 432, 445 (*Figs. 78, 80, 92*)
    Leda, 521
    Lézarde, 248 (*Figs. 28, 35*)
    Maas, 6, 8, 9, 224, 226, 228, 230, 231, 236, 254, 295, 324, 335, 336, 340, 349, 351, 352, 355, 359, 360, 361, 364, 365, 366, 367, 370, 375, 378, 379, 380, 382, 386, 399, 420, 422, 440, 441, 442, 444, 456, 458, 472, 480, 481, 536, 544 (*Figs. 32, 43, 44, 55, 64, 66, 67, 68, 69, 70, 77, 78, 81, 82, 86, 92*)
    Meuse, 9, 10, 20, 355, 356, 358, 361, 369, 384, 386, 387, 388 (in Belgium the Meuse; in Holland the Maas)(*Figs. 26, 54, 85*)

INDEX

Moselle, 9, 10, 11, 353, 355, 413, 417, 418
Neder Rijn, 6, 8, 10, 226, 229, 230, 231, 244, 274, 276, 278, 297, 299, 376, 384, 386, 480, 519, 520 (*Figs. 36, 44, 49, 64, 69, 77, 92*)
Niers, 416, 428, 429, 437, 441 (*Figs. 81, 83, 86*)
Odon, 122, 124, 125, 126, 155, 156, 162, 163, 171, 176 (*Figs. 3, 4, 8, 12, 17, 22*)
Orne, 1, 3, 18, 116, 117, 119, 122, 124, 125, 126, 130, 141, 142, 151, 152, 153, 155, 168, 169, 176, 179, 215, 219, 236, 244, 245, 261, 267, 283, 326, 565 (*Figs. 1, 2, 3, 4, 8, 14, 18, 22, 24, 25*)
Rhine, 4, 5, 8, 10, 11, 12, 222, 223, 224, 226, 351, 353, 413, 414, 416, 417, 418, 419, 422, 423, 424, 430, 432, 433, 439, 440, 444, 445, 449, 450, 453, 455, 456, 457, 460, 463, 465, 466, 472, 473, 474, 477, 480, 482, 483, 484, 485, 489, 491, 493, 495, 496, 505, 506, 516, 536, 541, 542, 544 (*Figs. 78, 79 80, 81, 84, 86*)
Roer, 9, 10, 351, 359, 361, 379, 416, 420, 452 (*Figs. 55, 70*)
Saar, 10, 11, 223, 413, 417
Scheldt, 5, 8, 225, 335, 336, 337, 340, 345, 349, 351 (*Figs. 49, 77*)
Seine, 1, 2, 3, 4, 5, 20, 23, 221, 222, 223, 225, 232, 234, 236, 237, 239, 242, 243, 244, 245, 250, 255, 261, 262, 283, 284, 292, 306, 307, 309, 311, 312, 313, 315, 316, 317, 322, 323, 329, 330, 331, 332, 348, 401, 409 (*Figs. 3, 4, 26, 28, 30, 34, 35, 47, 48*)
Seulles, 119, 141 (*Figs. 2, 8, 19, 22, 37*)
Somme, 223, 224, 232, 250, 262, 286, 316
Vire, 3, 18, 19, 125, 214, 215
Waal, 6, 226, 228, 230, 244, 253, 352, 360, 366, 376, 380, 386, 415, 467, 519 (*Figs. 43, 44, 49, 64, 69, 77, 78, 82, 83, 92*)
Würm, 352, 359, 361, 421 (*Fig. 55*)
Weser, 13, 477, 478, 479, 480, 483, 486, 487, 489, 496, 498, 508, 509, 512, 516, 542 (*Figs. 90, 92*)
Rocquancourt, 327 (*Figs. 25, 52*)
Roer, advance to, 353, 355, 356, 413
  medical arrangements, 380
  medical cover, 360
Roer Triangle, clearing of, 359 (*Fig. 55*)
  medical arrangements, 380
  medical cover, 360
Roermond, 352, 359, 361, 379, 382, 421 (*Figs. 35, 68, 70, 72, 73, 74, 75, 76*)
'Roger' Beach, 118, 186 (*Fig. 20*)
Roggel, 375 (*Figs., 62, 63*)
Rohlsdorf, 541
Rolleville, 245, 246 (*Fig. 28*)
Roosendaal, 336, 343, 352, 366, 380 (*Fig. 53*)
Roosevelt, President Franklin, D., 14, 15
Rotenburg, 503, 644, 645, 646, 649, 651, 652, 653
Rotterdam, 313, 651, 652 (*Fig. 92*)
Rots, 141 (*Fig. 8*)
Roubaix (N.E. of Lille), 239, 655
Rouen, 221, 245, 310, 315, 316, 317, 333, 334, 401, 409, 410, 465, 655 (*Figs. 3, 4, 47, 48, 51*)
'Round-up', Operation, 15
R.A.F. Medical Services, 85
R.N. Medical Services, 30, 56, 85
Rucqueville, 170 (*Fig. 15*)
Rugles (W. of Breteuil), 306, 309, 314
Ruhr, 4, 5, 10, 11, 12, 222, 223, 227, 232, 335, 351, 418, 419, 482, 483, 495, 536 (*Fig. 26*)
Ryckevorsel (on the Oostemalle–Hoogstraten–Breda Rd., E. of St. Léonard), 366
Ryes, 182, 190, 191, 194, 196, 314 (*Figs. 5, 19, 22, 23*)

Saar, 9, 10, 11, 223, 335, 353, 354, 356 (*Fig. 26*)
Sacquenville, 265
Saeffeler Beck (nr. the Sittard–Heinsberg Rd., S. of Echterbosch), 359
St. Amands, 412
St. André, Bruges, 342, 347, 348, 350 (*Fig. 53*)
St. André, Lille, 410, 412, 475, 524, 647
St. André d'Herbetot (on the Pont l'Eveque–Beuzeville Rd.), 284
St. André-sur-Cailly (N.E. of Rouen), 332
St. Aubin-sur-Mer, 118 (*Figs. 2, 8, 22, 50*)
St. Aubin d'Arquenay, 153, 168, 169 (*Fig. 14*)
St. Aubin-sur-Algot, 284
St. Augustine's College, Eindhoven, 390
St. Canisius' Hospital, Nijmegen, 467
St. Clair, 264
St. Elizabeth Hospital, Arnhem, 229, 268, 269, 270, 272, 273, 274, 275, 276
St. Gabriel, 155
St. Gatien-des-Bois (on the Pont l'Evêque–Honfleur Rd.), 283
St. Germain la Blanche Herbe, 143, 256, 284, 326, 327, 329, 330 (*Figs. 8, 16, 52*)
St. Germain-Langot, 264
St. Hubert, 136, 388 (*Figs. 54, 72, 82, 85*)
St. Hugh's College, Oxford, 69
St. Hymer, 330, 332
St. Jean-des-Essartiers, 232 (*Fig. 37*)
St. Joseph's Hospital, Bourg-Léopold, 295
St. Joseph's Kriegs Lazarett, Celle, 512
St. Joseph's Kriegs Lazarett, Apeldoorn, 278
St. Joseph's Hospital, Eindhoven, 253
St. Joseph's Lazarett, Wettringen, 509, 512
St. Joseph Stift Hospital, Bremen, 494
St. Laurent-de-Condel, 263, 264
St. Léger, 117, 163, 164, 170, 181, 314 (*Figs. 2, 13, 15*)
St. Lô, 2, 3, 19, 123, 125, 127, 214, 215 (*Figs. 1, 3, 4, 24*)
St. Louis Pensionaat, Weert, 382
St. Maartin's Orthopaedic Klinik, Nijmegen, 384
St. Mauvieu, 141, 156, 170, 174, 263 (*Figs. 10, 11, 13, 15*)
Ste. Mariaburg, 341 (*Fig. 53*)
St. Martin-des-Besaces, 215, 232 (*Fig. 37*)

St. Martin de Mieux, 264
St. Michel (nr. Bruges), 344
St. Michielsgestel, 350, 370, 380, 410, 411, 412, 451, 467, 472, 475, 519, 525, 645, 647 (*Fig. 61*)
St. Nicholas Kestricht in Denekamp, 511
St. Oedenrode, 244, 253, 256, 266, 294, 295, 297, 352, 362, 369, 370, 378 (*Figs. 32, 43, 59, 61, 72*)
St. Omer, 323, 324, 332, 334, 347, 348, 350, 401, 409, 412, 474, 475, 476, 524, 646, 647, 650 (*Fig. 51*)
St. Paschale, Oostrum, 475, 644
St. Pierre (E. of Tilly-sur-Seulles), 163, 164
St. Pierre-sur-Dives, 255, 329, 330 (*Figs. 25, 52*)
St. Pierre-du-Fresne (S. of Caumont and N. of Jurques), 242
St. Pol (W. of Arras), 223, 239, 261, 401, 411, 412, 476
St. Romain, 245 (*Fig. 35*)
St. Richier (on the Troarn–Dozulé Rd.), 283
St. Samson (E. of Troarn on the Dozulé Rd.), 283
St. Servais (nr. Namur), 388, 458
St. Vaast (nr. Dieppe), 655
St. Valéry-en-Caux (on the coast W. of Dieppe), 225, 255, 256
St. Vigor-le-Grand, 183, 190, 291 (*Fig. 5*)
Saleux (nr. Amiens), 316, 655
Sallen (N.W. of Caumont), 232
Salzuflen, 647, 648, 652
Samer (S.E. of Boulogne), 316
Sandbostel, 494, 498, 505, 506, 544, 560
Sanderbusch (S.W. of Wilhelmshaven), 525
Sande, 650
Saussay-la-Campagne, 265
Schaijk, 378 (*Fig. 65*)
Schaffen (N.W. of Diest), 233
Scheldt Estuary, opening of the, 335–350
  casualties, 349
  medical arrangements, 347–350 (*Fig. 53*)
  medical cover, 341–346
  operations, 335–340
Schleswig, 532, 533, 540, 648, 649, 651
Schleswig-Holstein, 13, 484, 485, 486, 506, 535, 538, 539
Schloss Breitenburg, 497
Schloss Calbeck (between Goch and Üdem), 429
Schloss Derneberg, 648
Schloss Hagen (nr. Kiel), 535, 539, 653
Schloss Wissen, 450, 452, 459, 460, 507, 508, 513, 644 (*Fig. 84*)
Schmidt Dams (*see* Roer Dams)
Schnakenbek, 491, 492 (*Fig. 91*)
Schneverdingen, 497
Schwarme, 493
Schwerin, 541
Sea-sickness, 95
Second Army
  Army Dental Service, 89, 200, 319
  Army Pathological Service, 85
  Army Psychiatric Service, 324
  casualties, 184, 191, 195, 307, 461, 571–576

  distribution of medical units, 192
  medical arrangements, 184
  medical planning, 25
  medical situation, *Figs. 45, 46, 47, 48, 49*
  order of battle, 104
Secqueville-en-Bessin, 139, 141, 142, 170, 193 (*Figs. 8, 15, 17, 22*)
Seedorf, 494, 500, 503
Selincourt, 265
Sept Vents (S.W. of Caumont), 232
Sevenum, 364, 366, 367, 383, 461, 508 (*Figs. 57, 68*)
'Shears', Operation, 383
'Ship' Route, 160, 161 (*Fig. 12*)
Siegfried Line, 6, 9, 226, 358, 359, 366, 414, 416, 417, 426, 451, 452, 466 (*Figs. 26, 55*)
Sittard, 360, 361, 387, 421, 456, 458 (*Figs. 55, 70, 73, 74, 75, 76*)
'Sledge Hammer', Operation, 15
Slidex Code, 330, 643
Slijk Ewijk, 467 (*Figs. 44, 64*)
Slooe Channel, Walcheren, 339, 340 (*Fig. 53*)
Snoghøj (Denmark), 534, 540, 647, 649, 651, 652
Soex, 331
Sögel, 518, 521, 525, 645, 647, 650 (*Fig. 92*)
Soltau, 478, 484, 507, 654 (*Figs. 89, 90*)
Someren, 363 (*Figs. 57, 62*)
Son, 6, 7, 226, 228, 230, 295, 297, 384 (*Figs. 43, 59*)
Sonnis, 465, 648, 651, 654 (*Fig. 70*)
South Beveland, 8, 337, 339, 341, 345, 346
South Beveland Isthmus, 335, 336, 337, 352
Southampton, 23, 52, 61, 62, 66
Specialist Services, reflections on, 639
Spiekelspode, 233
Spoy Canal (N. of the Wyler–Cleve Rd., S.E. of Nijmegen), 426, 428
'Spring', Operation, 143
Staatsforst Cleve, 429
Stalag XIB Lazarett, 280
Stamproy, 378 (*Figs. 73, 75, 76*)
Stratton St. Margaret (nr. Swindon), 69, 75
Steensel (on the Eindhoven–Eersel Rd.), 378, 379
Steenvorde (on the Poperinghe–Cassel Rd., N. of Hazebrouck), 331, 332
Steenwijk (N. of Zwolle on the Leeuwarden Rd.), 524
Stein (S.W. of Sittard and near the frontier), 383
Sterksel, 390, 393, 410, 411, 458, 459, 475, 476, 645
Stoppel Burg (S.E. of Nijmegen on the edge of the Reichswald), 426, 450
Strecknitz, 540, 647, 648, 650, 651
Stretchers and blankets, forward stocks, 640
Subles, 170 (*Fig. 21*)
Sudweyhe, 487
'Suitcase', Operation, 343
  medical arrangements, *Fig. 53*
  medical cover, 343
Sulingen, 508, 509, 511, 512, 542, 644

INDEX

Supreme Headquarters, Allied Expeditionary Force (S.H.A.E.F.), 17, 18, 20, 24, 52, 101, 104, 213, 333, 335, 355, 529
'Switchback', Operation, 337
    medical arrangements, 347 (*Fig. 53*)
    medical cover, 342
'Sword' Beach, 18, 114, 116, 118, 119 (*Figs. 1, 2*)

Tarmstedt (nr. Bremen), 494
Temeeren (nr. Hal), 654
Ten Boer (N.E. of Groningen on the Delfzijl Rd.), 520
Terneuzen, 337, 342, 345 (*Fig. 55*)
Tentage lay-out, 33 C.C.S., *Fig. 38*
    34 C.C.S., *Fig. 39*
    Advanced Surgical Centre, *Fig. 41*
Tessenderloo, 233 (*Fig. 74*)
Thaon, 141, 142, 143 (*Fig. 8*)
Thildonck, 475, 556, 645, 647, 650
Tilburg, 324, 349, 352, 360, 361, 362, 363, 370, 378, 380, 410, 411, 419, 427, 429, 466, 474, 475, 525, 536, 644, 645, 647, 651, 655 (*Figs. 49, 56, 61, 65, 66, 67, 77*)
Tilbury, 52, 61, 62, 74, 361
Tilly (N.E. of Vernon on the Vernon–Gisors Rd.), 243
Tilly-la-Campagne, 255, 326 (*Fig. 33*)
Tilly-sur-Seulles, 121, 122, 137, 183, 250 (*Figs. 6, 15, 19, 45*)
Tirlemont, 360, 388 (*Figs. 71, 76*)
'Torch', Operation, 15, 16, 31, 77
'Torchlight', Operation, *Fig. 79*
    casualties, 433, 492
    medical cover, 430–436 (*Fig. 80*)
'Totalize' Operation, Canadian First Army, 218–221 (*Fig. 25*)
    casualties, 327, 328, 330
    medical arrangements, 326–329
        51st Division, 255
            medical cover, 256 (*Fig. 33*)
Tötensen, 497, 647, 650
Touffreville, 126, 264 (*Fig. 22*)
Tournai (E. of Lille), 251, 293, 401, 411, 412, 474, 476, 644, 645, 647, 649, 650
Tourville, 262 (*Figs. 10, 11*)
Tracy-Bocage, 654
Transfusion Service, reflections on, 637
Travemünde, 541
Treebeek (S. of Sittard, nr. Nuth), 436
Tremeloo, 458, 459
'Triangle' Route, 160, 161, 163 (*Fig. 12*)
Troarn, 117, 126, 151, 152, 169, 283 (*Figs. 2, 8, 9, 16, 22, 25, 33*)
Trouville, 17, 284
Trungy, 291, 292, 298 (*Fig. 7*)
Turnhout, 348, 350, 366, 380, 410, 412, 429, 437, 439, 440, 451, 467, 472, 475, 476, 524, 525, 644, 645, 646, 649 (*Figs. 31, 49, 65, 77*)
Turnhout Canal, 249, 267, 366
Twente Canal, 516, 518 (*Fig. 92*)

Uchte, 486, 496, 510 (*Fig. 89*)
Udem, 416, 422, 426, 438, 444, 452, 470, 471 (*Figs. 78, 79, 81, 84, 86*)

Uden, 6, 231, 244, 360, 376, 380, 386, 390 (*Fig. 43*)
Udenhout, 360, 370 (*Fig. 61*)
Uelzen, 477, 487, 488, 489, 491, 494, 496, 510 (*Fig. 89*)
Uitwaterings Canal, 375 (*Fig. 63*)
Urquhart, Major General R. E., 227
'Utah' Beach, 18, 114, 115, 119, 121, 124 (*Fig. 1*)
Utrecht, 355, 523, 645 (*Fig. 92*)

Vacognes (on the Aunay–Evrecy Rd.), 263, 264
Valburg, 244, 277, 295, 297 (*Figs. 43, 44, 64*)
Valkenswaard, 7, 228, 277, 295, 390, 398, 399, 458, 460, 462 (*Figs. 31, 43, 72, 73, 74, 75, 76*)
'Varsity', Operation, 418
    casualties, 425
    medical arrangements, 447, 456
    medical cover, 423–426
Vaux, 187, 189, 194, 654 (*Figs. 8, 22, 23, 50*)
Vechta, 493 (*Figs. 88, 89, 90*)
Veerle, 262, 266
Veghel, 6, 226, 227, 228, 231, 233, 253, 295, 352, 360 (*Figs. 32, 43, 61, 72*)
Velje (Denmark), 535
Venlo, 10, 336, 352, 361, 366, 369, 382, 383 (*Figs. 55, 58, 68, 73, 76*)
Venraij, 336, 352, 449, 459, 461, 462, 466, 475, 507, 508, 513, 644, 645 (*Figs. 72, 75*)
Verden, 493, 494, 498, 509, 512, 652, 653 (*Fig. 90*)
'Veritable', Operation, 349, 360, 366, 387, 390, 413–417, 463 (*Figs. 77, 78*)
    casualties, 420, 422, 429, 434, 435, 439, 443, 453, 470, 471, 492
        psychiatric, 554, 555
    medical arrangements
        XXX Corps, 450–453
        Canadian First Army, 466–471 (*Fig. 86*)
        Second Army, 456, 458, 459, 461, 466
    medical cover, 419, 420, 422, 426–430, 437–439, 440–444 (*Figs. 81, 82, 83*)
Vernon, 221, 232, 236, 243, 250, 292, 293 (*Fig. 30*)
Ver-sur-Mer, 185, 186, 190 (*Figs. 5, 20, 50*)
Vignats, 264
Villers-Bocage, 2, 3, 19, 116, 121, 124, 171, 216, 234, 250, 292 (*Figs. 1, 8, 15, 45*)
Villers Canivet, 264
Villers-sur-Mer (S.W. of Deauville), 283
Vilsen, 494, 535, 541
Vimont, 126, 245 (*Figs. 8, 25, 33*)
Vire, 4, 215, 216, 232, 237 (*Figs. 1, 24, 45*)
Vissel, 432 (*Fig. 70*)
'Vitality I', Operation, 337
    medical arrangements, 347 (*Fig. 53*)
    medical cover, 341, 342
'Vitality II', Operation, 337
    medical arrangements, 347 (*Fig. 53*)
    medical cover, 345
Vlasmer, 233

INDEX

Voorheide (S.W. of Reusel on the Turnhout Rd.), 378
Vught, 370, 476, 645, 648, 651 (*Fig. 61*)

Wageningen, 269
Wailly-Beauchamp (S. of Montreuil and Etaples), 331, 332
Walbeck, 465, 536, 654
Walcheren, 8, 324, 335, 336, 339, 341, 342, 343, 344, 346, 350 (*Fig. 53*)
Walsrode, 484, 497 (*Fig. 90*)
War Wounds Committee, 87
Watchfield Airfield (nr. Swindon), 69
Water, 80
Wavre Notre Dame (N.E. of Malines), 325, 398, 403, 410, 411, 463, 475, 476, 645
Wedel, Hamburg, 653
Weert, 361, 367, 369, 373, 378, 379, 382, 421, 444, 458, 459 (*Figs. 62, 63, 72, 73*)
Weeze, 420, 421, 422, 429, 453, 544 (*Figs. 78, 79, 84*)
Weisendorf, 533
Well (on the Maas, E. of Venraij and W. of Geldern), 439, 543
Wembe, 511
Wervicq, 265
Wessem Canal, 373, 378, 379 (*Figs. 62, 63*)
Wesel, 11, 12, 413, 416, 417, 418, 420, 422, 430, 445, 453, 456, 495, 536 (*Figs. 78, 79, 80, 84, 88, 92*)
Westkapelle, 340, 344, 347 (*Fig. 53*)
Westmalle (on the Antwerp–Turnhout Rd.), 366
Westertimke, 494
Wetten, 420, 431 (*Fig. 79*)
Wettringen, 484, 486, 497, 508, 509, 512, 542, 644, 645 (*Fig. 88*)
Wezel (S.W. of Lommel), 266
Wietmarschen, 487
Wilhelmina Canal, 6, 228, 242, 262, 362 (*Fig. 56*)

Wijchen, 360, 472 (*Figs. 44, 64*)
Wijchmaal (Wychmaal), 388, 390 (*Fig. 68*)
Wildeshausen, 493
Willebroeck (W. of Malines on the Brussels–Antwerp Rd.), 293
Wilstedt, 494
Winnekendonk, 420, 422 (*Fig. 79*)
Winsen, 535
Wintermoor, 497, 509, 512
Wireless, reflections on use of, 641
Wismar, 481, 482, 488, 539
Wissman (S. of Hamminkeln), 430
Wittenindsdorf Bergkirchen, 647, 650
Wolfheze, 269, 270, 277, 299, 302 (*Fig. 44*)
Woltem (N.E. Soltau), 654
Wommerson (just N. of the Tirlemont–St. Trond Rd.), 360
Wüllen, 497, 510
Wuppertal, 653
Wychmaal (*see* Wijchmaal)
Wyler, 414, 426, 427, 451, 469 (*Figs. 78, 86*)

Xanten, 413, 416, 417, 420, 422, 439, 446, 460, 470 (*Figs. 78, 79, 80, 84, 88*)

Ypres (on the Poperinghe–Menin Rd.), 357, 471, 472, 655
Yvetot, 260, 284 (*Fig. 35*)

Zammel, 266
Zaventem, 653
Zeeland, 380, 450, 534 (*Fig. 82*)
Zeelst, 242, 380, 382, 390 (*Figs. 59, 60, 66, 67*)
Zoutelande (on the W. coast of Walcheren), 344
Zuider Zee (*see also* Ijsselmeer), 6, 20, 227, 480, 481, 519, 520
Zuidlaren, 524, 650 (*Fig. 92*)
Zuid Willems Vaart, 254 (*Figs. 57, 62, 63*)

PART II

British and Allied Formations and Medical Units

Allied Formation and Units

Allied First Airborne Army, 1, 11, 226, 333
Airborne Troops, 106, 130, 295, 299–306
I Airborne Corps, 226, 233, 277, 297, 298, 299, 300
1st Airborne Division, 6, 8, 77, 107, 108, 128, 226, 227, 229, 230, 231, 244, 267–283, 297, 298, 299, 300, 301, 302, 304, 305, 311, 324, 386
1st Airlanding Brigade, 228, 268, 269, 300
1st Parachute Brigade, 228, 229, 268, 272, 300, 534
4th Parachute Brigade, 229, 269, 270, 272, 276, 300

Sea-borne Echelon, 1st A.B. Division, 277, 278, 297
6th Airborne Division, 11, 18, 19, 105, 107, 108, 114, 116, 117, 119, 120, 127–133, 146, 151, 168, 169, 174, 200, 206, 207, 219, 283, 284, 358, 361, 379, 388, 406, 418, 423–426, 430, 432, 433, 446, 447, 456, 457, 477, 481, 482, 486, 488, 489, 495, 496, 565, 570
6th Airlanding Brigade, 119, 120, 131, 425, 426
3rd Parachute Brigade, 116, 117, 120, 131, 284, 425, 426
5th Parachute Brigade, 105, 116, 120, 131, 284, 425, 426

INDEX

Land Element, 6th A.B. Division, 424, 447
Glider Pilot Regiment, 231, 273
1st Parachute Battalion, 228, 229
2nd Parachute Battalion, 228, 272
3rd Parachute Battalion, 228, 229
7th Parachute Battalion, 130
8th Parachute Battalion, 130
9th Parachute Battalion, 117, 130
21st Independent Parachute Company (Pathfinders), 273
Airborne Forward Delivery Airfield Group, 301, 305, 306

Belgian Formation

1st Belgian Brigade Group, 224, 283, 378, 390, 406, 407, 537

British Formations and Units

Army at Home, 35, 97
Home Forces, 15, 32, 36
21 Army Group, 1, 2, 4, 5, 8, 10, 11, 12, 13, 17, 24, 35, 36, 37, 38, 39, 44, 81, 82, 83, 84, 85, 86, 91, 101, 106, 114, 149, 173, 180, 199, 206, 207, 212, 213, 216, 223, 225, 231, 283, 286, 307, 311, 313, 314, 315, 322, 333, 335, 336, 353, 400, 404, 405, 409, 413, 416, 418, 465, 472, 481, 484, 498, 506, 507, 510, 515, 516, 528, 534, 535, 536, 546, 554, 557, 560, 576–593, 619
Second Army, 1, 4, 6, 8, 11, 12, 13, 17, 18, 24, 25, 44, 89, 90, 91, 96, 101, 104, 106, 108, 109, 110, 111, 112, 113, 114, 116, 121, 122, 125, 151, 161, 182, 184–200, 205, 208, 215, 216, 217, 219, 221, 222, 223, 224, 226, 227, 236, 238, 242, 279, 299, 300, 301, 306–314, 315, 316, 317, 321, 323, 324, 325, 333, 336, 351, 352, 359, 366, 383, 386, 390–400, 401, 402, 406, 409, 411, 412, 418, 423, 424, 432, 445, 453, 456–463, 464, 465, 466, 475, 476, 477, 479, 480, 483, 484, 498, 505–515, 521, 528, 530, 536, 539, 542, 564, 571–576, 644, 645, 646, 654, 655
British Army of the Rhine, 535, 544, 654

Corps

I Corps, 1, 2, 18, 19, 102, 105, 106, 109, 110, 113, 114, 118, 120, 124, 125, 126, 127, 130, 145, 149, 152, 153, 163, 172, 174–176, 179, 181, 182, 189, 190, 193, 204, 211, 219, 221, 225, 234, 237, 244, 255, 256, 284, 314, 323, 326, 328, 329, 337, 343, 351, 352, 366, 380, 472, 480, 507, 509, 510, 511, 512, 531, 536, 564, 566
I Corps District, 506, 511, 513, 530, 534, 536–538, 593, 647, 648, 649, 650, 651, 652, 653, 655
VIII Corps, 7, 8, 85, 104, 105, 106, 109, 110, 113, 122, 123, 124, 125, 126, 127, 152, 162, 170, 171, 176, 177, 178, 179, 180, 182, 193, 215, 216, 223, 226, 227, 231, 232, 234, 236, 237, 238, 253, 284–291, 311, 336, 352, 365, 373, 378, 382, 388, 390, 406, 407, 450, 453, 456, 457, 458, 459, 460, 462, 477, 478, 479, 481, 482, 484, 487, 488, 489, 495, 496, 497, 506, 510, 511, 512, 513, 530, 531, 532, 534, 535, 538–540, 568, 641
VIII Corps District, 534, 539, 593, 646, 647, 648, 649, 650, 651, 653
XII Corps, 7, 105, 106, 108, 109, 110, 113, 180, 181, 193, 211, 221, 223, 224, 225, 226, 227, 231, 239, 261, 262, 311, 346, 351, 352, 359, 360, 361, 366, 367, 369, 373, 375, 377, 380–384, 386, 388, 390, 393, 394, 403, 406, 407, 418, 430, 432, 436, 445–450, 453, 456, 457, 458, 459, 460, 462, 477, 478, 479, 481, 484, 485, 487, 489, 495, 496, 497, 498, 506, 509, 510, 511, 512, 513, 532, 535, 641
XXX Corps, 1, 2, 6, 7, 8, 18, 19, 105, 106, 108, 109, 110, 113, 114, 116, 117, 119, 120, 121, 122, 124, 134, 161, 163, 171, 179, 180, 181–184, 188, 189, 190, 193, 204, 208, 211, 215, 216, 219, 221, 223, 224, 225, 226, 227, 228, 231, 234, 236, 238, 243, 244, 250, 253, 261, 262, 276, 286, 291–299, 301, 302, 306, 311, 324, 353, 356, 357, 358, 360, 365, 373, 378, 379, 382, 383, 384–390, 393, 403, 406, 407, 413, 416, 417, 418, 419, 420, 422, 428, 429, 430, 439, 440, 444, 445, 446, 450–456, 457, 458, 459, 460, 462, 465, 471, 477, 478, 479, 480, 487, 494, 496, 497, 498, 500, 503, 506, 509, 510, 511, 512, 513, 523, 531, 532, 533, 534, 535, 554, 569, 641, 651
XXX Corps District, 593, 646, 647, 648, 649, 650, 651, 652, 653

Divisions

Guards Armoured Division, 7, 104, 106, 107, 108, 109, 126, 127, 143, 153, 155, 215, 216, 223, 226, 227, 230, 232–234, 243, 250, 252, 286, 291, 293, 319, 353, 357, 360, 383, 386, 387, 388, 406, 415, 417, 419, 423, 426, 441, 445, 450, 451, 452, 453, 455, 456, 477, 478, 479, 486, 497, 498, 537, 554
3rd Infantry Division, 18, 19, 105, 107, 108, 109, 114, 118, 119, 125, 126, 129, 130, 144–153, 169, 172, 174, 175, 201, 226, 232, 236, 237, 336, 406, 415, 422, 429, 444, 445, 452, 453, 456, 460, 477, 478, 479, 486, 487, 493, 497, 537, 554, 565
5th Infantry Division, 481, 487, 570, 649
7th Armoured Division, 18, 105, 106, 107, 109, 114, 121, 122, 126, 127, 143, 154, 155, 172, 181, 183, 215, 216, 219, 221, 223, 224, 226, 234, 239, 261, 291, 319, 336, 352, 359, 360, 361, 370, 373, 378, 380, 382, 383, 406, 420–422, 446, 477, 478, 479, 481, 484, 485, 486, 496
9th Armoured Division, 100
11th Armoured Division, 104, 106, 107, 108, 109, 122, 124, 126, 127, 154, 155,

2 Z

Divisions—cont.

11th Armoured Division—cont.
156, 215, 216, 219, 223, 224, 226, 232, 236–237, 243, 250, 286, 292, 293, 319, 335, 390, 406, 415, 416, 452, 456, 457, 477, 478, 479, 481, 485, 486, 489, 491, 495, 496, 540, 570

15th (Scottish) Infantry Division, 104, 106, 107, 108, 109, 122, 124, 155–161, 163, 171, 180, 215, 221, 223, 225, 226, 232, 238–242, 252, 261, 262, 291, 336, 352, 353, 361–366, 367, 369, 370, 373, 380, 382, 383, 406, 414, 415, 416, 418, 419, 420, 422, 424, 426–436, 437, 438, 439, 446, 447, 450, 451, 452, 456, 457, 460, 469, 477, 479, 481, 488, 489–493, 496, 497, 530, 540, 541, 554, 570, 649

38th Infantry Division, 100

43rd (Wessex) Infantry Division, 106, 107, 108, 109, 122, 124, 155, 156, 158, 160, 161, 162, 171, 180, 208, 215, 216, 221, 226, 230, 231, 232, 233, 238, 242–244, 250, 292, 295, 297, 302, 353, 357, 359, 360, 383, 384, 386, 387, 388, 394, 406, 415, 416, 417, 419, 422, 426, 428, 429, 436–440, 445, 450, 451, 452, 453, 455, 460, 469, 470, 477, 479, 493, 494, 554

45th Infantry Division, 100

47th Infantry Division, 100

48th Reserve Infantry Division, 100

49th (West Riding) Infantry Division, 18, 104, 106, 107, 108, 109, 114, 124, 163–168, 181, 182, 183, 201, 219, 221, 225, 232, 244–250, 255, 256, 336, 352, 364, 366–368, 375, 376, 382, 383, 406, 472, 480, 517, 519, 537, 565

50th (Northumbrian) Infantry Division, 18, 19, 105, 106, 107, 108, 109, 114, 117, 118, 121, 122, 132–138, 170, 181, 183, 201, 202, 215, 216, 219, 223, 224, 226, 228, 233, 239, 243, 250–255, 291, 293, 294, 319, 367, 376, 378, 380, 384, 386, 394, 406

51st (Highland) Infantry Division, 18, 105, 107, 108, 109, 114, 122, 168, 174, 206, 207, 219, 221, 225, 244, 245, 255–261, 336, 352, 357, 362, 367, 369–377, 378, 380, 382, 383, 387, 388, 406, 414, 415, 416, 418, 419, 422, 426, 428, 429, 430, 437, 440–445, 450, 451, 452, 453, 454, 455, 456, 460, 469, 472, 473, 477, 479, 554, 565, 649

52nd (Lowland) Infantry Division, 8, 226, 300, 301, 303, 305, 306, 336, 337, 339, 340, 341, 342, 345, 346, 347, 359, 383, 406, 407, 415, 416, 417, 421, 422, 429, 430, 433, 436, 437, 441, 445, 446, 452, 456, 460, 469, 477, 478, 494, 495, 496, 497, 527, 554

53rd (Welsh) Infantry Division, 104, 106, 107, 108, 109, 161, 169, 171, 180, 219, 223, 224, 226, 238, 261–267, 336, 352, 353, 357, 369, 370, 377–379, 380, 382, 387, 388, 406, 407, 414, 415, 416, 420, 426, 428, 429, 433, 438, 440, 441, 446, 450, 451, 452, 456, 460, 469, 477, 478, 479, 496, 537, 554

55th Infantry Division, 100

59th (Staffordshire) Infantry Division, 104, 106, 107, 108, 109, 125, 151, 171, 172, 219, 261, 267

61st Infantry Division, 100

76th Reserve Infantry Division, 100

77th Holding Division, 100

79th Armoured Division, 18, 21, 106, 121, 172–174, 352, 359, 414, 416, 430, 450, 648, 651

80th Reserve Infantry Division, 100

Brigades

1st Special Service Brigade, 18, 105, 114, 116, 118, 130, 146, 151

1st Commando Brigade, 415, 418, 421, 430, 446, 448, 460, 477, 481, 486, 491, 492, 510, 512, 570

3rd Armoured Brigade, 243

4th Armoured Brigade, 18, 105, 107, 226, 367, 378, 380, 406, 407, 432, 464, 496, 510, 568

4th Special Service Brigade, 18, 114, 118, 256, 340, 343, 344, 347

5th Guards Armoured Brigade (Gds. Armd. Div.), 153, 180, 233, 234, 360, 419, 420

5th Independent Brigade (5 Div.), 489

6th Guards Tank (Armd.) Brigade, 215, 238, 383, 406, 407, 436, 477, 489, 510, 568, 570

8th Armoured Brigade, 18, 107, 114, 117, 163, 167, 183, 215, 226, 359, 383, 384, 385, 406, 407, 421, 438, 498, 500, 510

8th Infantry Brigade (3 Div.), 118, 119, 120, 150, 151, 487, 493

9th Infantry Brigade (3 Div.), 118, 120, 150, 151, 237, 423, 487

13th Infantry Brigade (5 Div.), 487, 488

15th Infantry Brigade (5 Div.), 487, 488

17th Infantry Brigade (5 Div.), 487, 488

19th Infantry Brigade (59 Div.), 172

22nd Armoured Brigade (7 Armd. Div.), 121, 154, 235

27th Armoured Brigade, 18, 105, 107, 114, 118, 145, 149, 150

29th Armoured Brigade (11 Armd. Div.), 154, 357, 361, 379, 387, 388, 390, 406, 407, 456, 485

30th Armoured Brigade, 105, 107, 380

31st Armoured Brigade, 107, 124, 446

32nd Guards Brigade (Gds. Armd. Div.), 153, 162, 179, 231, 233, 234, 360, 415, 419, 420

33rd Armoured Brigade, 107, 184, 219, 255, 256, 370, 379, 387, 406, 407, 570

34th Tank Brigade, 106, 107, 161, 170, 180, 245, 387, 406, 407, 536

44th (Lowland) Infantry Brigade (15 Div.), 155, 156, 157, 160, 241, 362, 364, 427, 428, 429, 430, 432, 436, 437, 489, 492

46th (Highland) Infantry Brigade (15

INDEX

Div.), 155, 156, 160, 266, 428, 430, 432, 489, 491
56th Infantry Brigade (Independent), 108, 117, 118, 120, 135, 138, 154, 184, 245, 366, 367
69th Infantry Brigade (50 Div.), 117, 118, 120, 133, 251, 253
70th Infantry Brigade (49 Div.), 163, 166
71st Infantry Brigade (53 Div.), 169, 261, 262, 378, 379
115th Independent Infantry Brigade, 536
129th Infantry Brigade (43 Div.), 162, 216, 437, 438, 439, 493
130th Infantry Brigade (43 Div.), 162, 243, 244, 298, 437, 438, 439, 493
131st Infantry Brigade (7 Armd. Div.), 154, 235
146th Infantry Brigade (49 Div.), 163, 166, 247, 367
147th Infantry Brigade (49 Div.), 163, 166, 245, 247, 367
151st Infantry Brigade (50 Div.), 117, 118, 120, 133, 135, 251, 253
152nd Infantry Brigade (51 Div.), 168, 169, 255, 370, 373, 375, 376, 440, 441, 444
153rd Infantry Brigade (51 Div.), 168, 169, 370, 373, 375, 376, 440, 444
154th Infantry Brigade (51 Div.), 168, 219, 255, 256, 369, 370, 373, 375, 376, 440, 441, 444, 445
155th Infantry Brigade (52 Div.), 345
156th Infantry Brigade (52 Div.), 345, 346
157th Infantry Brigade (52 Div.), 306, 345, 346, 421, 432
158th Infantry Brigade (53 Div.), 169, 261, 262, 263, 266, 369, 370, 377, 378, 379
159th Infantry Brigade (11 Armd. Div.), 154, 486
160th Infantry Brigade (53 Div.), 169, 261, 262, 378, 379
176th Infantry Brigade (59 Div.), 172
177th Infantry Brigade (59 Div.), 172
185th Infantry Brigade (3 Div.), 118, 119, 120, 150, 151, 237, 487
214th Infantry Brigade (43 Div.), 162, 244, 437, 439, 493
227th Infantry Brigade (15 Div.), 155, 156, 362, 364, 428, 429, 430, 432, 491, 492
231st Infantry Brigade (50 Div.), 117, 120, 133, 233, 250
308th Infantry Brigade, 648

Regiments and Battalions

4th/7th Royal Dragoon Guards, 231
1st Royal Dragoons, 454
11th Hussars (Prince Albert's Own), 484
13th/18th Royal Hussars (Queen Mary's Own), 119, 216
23rd Hussars, 358
3rd Royal Tank Regiment, 357, 358
44th Royal Tank Regiment, 568
107th Royal Tank Regiment, 443
Derbyshire Yeomanry (T.A.), 370
Grenadier Guards, 230
Irish Guards, 228, 230
2nd Scots Guards, 419, 420
1st Welsh Guards, 230, 420
2nd Argyll & Sutherland Highlanders (Princess Louise's), 481
1st Border Regt., 269, 271, 272, 274
6th Cameronians (Scottish Rifles), 339, 359
1st Dorset Regt., 117
4th Dorset Regt., 231, 299
5th Duke of Cornwall's Light Infantry, 231
6th Duke of Wellington's Regt. (West Riding), 163, 164
7th Duke of Wellington's Regt. (West Riding), 164, 247
10th Durham Light Infantry, 163, 164, 166
2nd East Yorkshire Regt. (Duke of York's Own), 118
5th East Yorkshire Regt. (Duke of York's Own), 117
Glasgow Highlanders (T.A.), 339
1st Gordon Highlanders, 441
6th Green Howards (Alexandra, Princess of Wales's Own) (Yorkshire Regt.), 117, 118
7th Green Howards (Alexandra, Princess of Wales's Own) (Yorkshire Regt.), 118
Hallamshire Battalion, York & Lancaster Regt. (T.A.), 166
1st Hampshire Regt., 117
7th Hampshire Regt., 243
5th Highland Light Infantry (City of Glasgow Regt.), 340
6th Highland Light Infantry (City of Glasgow Regt.), 340
2nd Kensington Regt. (T.A.), 165
4th King's Own Scottish Borderers, 340, 359
7th King's Own Scottish Borderers, 271, 272
1st/4th King's Own Yorkshire Light Infantry, 164, 166
2nd King's Own Shropshire Light Infantry, 119
1st Leicestershire Regt., 247
4th Lincolnshire Regt., 166
5th Royal Berkshire Regt. (Princess Charlotte of Wales's), 315
7th/9th Royal Scots (The Royal Regiment), 340, 359
4th/5th Royal Scots Fusiliers, 359
11th Royal Scots Fusiliers, 166, 247
7th Seaforth Highlanders (Ross-shire Buffs, The Duke of Albany's), 428
4th Somerset Light Infantry (Prince Albert's), 216
1st South Lancashire Regt. (The Prince of Wales's Volunteers), 118
2nd South Staffordshire Regt., 272
1st Tyneside Scottish (T.A.), 166
5th Wiltshire Regt. (Duke of Edinburgh's), 216

INDEX

Units

3rd Commando, 105
4th Commando, 118, 119, 340
6th Commando, 105
10th Inter-Allied, 340
41st Commando, 105, 118, 340, 344
45th Royal Marine, 105
46th Commando, 106
47th Royal Marine, 105, 117, 118, 120, 340
48th Royal Marine, 105, 118, 340, 344
5th Beach Group, 108, 144, 145, 150, 151, 174, 185, 186, 201
6th Beach Group, 108, 144, 145, 150, 151, 174, 185, 186
7th Beach Group, 108, 174, 185, 186, 201
8th Beach Group, 109, 174, 185, 186, 201
9th Beach Group, 109, 181, 185, 186, 201
10th Beach Group, 109, 181, 185, 186, 201
4th Beach Brick, 655
36th Beach Brick, 648, 651, 655
101st Beach Brick, 655
Brussels Garrison, 655
10 Garrison, 106, 189, 211, 408, 511
13 Garrison, 411, 412, 474, 476, 645, 646, 655
25 Garrison, 648, 652
10 Holding and Selection Unit, 405
31 Holding and Selection Unit, 544
32 (later 33) Holding and Selection Unit, 465
34 Holding and Selection Unit, 202, 464
37 Holding and Selection Unit, 405
101 Reinforcement Group, 464, 507, 544
113 Transit Camp, 464
1 Army Roadhead, 211
2 Army Roadhead, 189, 211
10 Army Roadhead, 480
12 Army Roadhead, 480

Lines of Communication Units

L. of C., 108, 109, 111, 112, 113, 180, 209, 223, 294, 311, 316, 325, 378, 390, 395, 400, 402, 405, 459, 475, 506, 507, 532, 542, 592, 645, 647, 648, 649, 650, 651, 652, 655
11 L. of C. Area, 106, 107, 109, 176, 185, 188, 189, 190, 193, 194, 197, 211, 315, 316, 317, 318, 401, 402, 409, 410, 463, 655
12 L. of C. Area, 107, 315, 316, 402, 409, 475, 655
4 L. of C. Sub-Area, 106, 107, 211, 311, 315, 316, 402, 409, 410, 411, 412, 475, 476, 521, 646, 650, 652, 655
5 L. of C. Sub-Area, 105, 107, 189, 211, 315, 409, 411, 412, 645, 647, 651, 655
6 L. of C. Sub-Area, 315, 316, 409, 411, 412, 652, 655
9 L. of C. Sub-Area, 645, 646, 647, 648, 650, 651, 652, 655
15 L. of C. Sub-Area, 316, 409, 410, 411, 412, 475, 476, 536, 655
16 L. of C. Sub-Area, 316, 410, 411, 412, 474, 475, 476, 645, 646, 647, 648, 650, 651, 655
17 L. of C. Sub-Area, 645, 646, 647, 655
18 L. of C. Sub-Area, 655
19 L. of C. Sub-Area, 536, 652, 655
20 L. of C. Sub-Area, 645, 646, 647, 648, 649, 650, 652, 655
21 L. of C. Sub-Area, 645, 648, 649, 651, 652, 655
7 Base Sub-Area, 107, 189, 262, 402, 409, 410, 411, 412, 475, 476, 646, 647, 648, 650, 651, 655
8 Base Sub-Area, 107, 316, 409, 410, 411, 412, 474, 475, 476, 532, 533, 534, 645, 655
101 Beach Sub-Area, 106, 107, 149, 150, 174, 186, 189, 211
102 Beach Sub-Area, 106, 107, 139, 174, 189, 211, 315
104 Beach Sub-Area, 106, 107, 133, 181, 189, 211, 315
Berlin Area, 651, 652
Netherlands District, 645, 648, 655

Canadian Formations and Units

Canadian First Army, 1, 4, 8, 10, 11, 12, 13, 17, 21, 24, 101, 102, 114, 176, 189, 194, 205, 211, 217, 219, 222, 223, 225, 314, 316, 317, 321, 323, 324, 326–332, 333, 336, 340, 347–350, 351, 353, 357, 359, 360, 366, 379, 383, 386, 410, 411, 412, 413, 415, 418, 450, 456, 466–474, 475, 476, 477, 480, 481, 516–527, 544, 545, 554, 592, 645, 646, 647, 655
Canadian Forces in the Netherlands, 524, 525, 650
Canadian I Corps, 471, 472, 480, 481, 516, 519, 520, 524
Canadian II Corps, 101, 102, 126, 142–144, 154, 180, 219, 220, 221, 225, 231, 255, 284, 314, 323, 326, 328, 329, 331, 347, 352, 366, 367, 376, 384, 386, 416, 428, 439, 450, 453, 469, 470, 471, 472, 473, 474, 480, 516, 520, 522, 524
Canadian 1st Infantry Division, 471, 472, 480, 481, 517, 519, 520, 523
Canadian 2nd Infantry Division, 102, 142, 143, 219, 220, 225, 326, 327, 329, 330, 337, 339, 340, 341, 342, 347, 349, 414, 415, 416, 426, 440, 450, 467, 469, 470, 471, 473, 474, 480, 516, 517, 518, 521, 522, 523
Canadian 3rd Infantry Division, 1, 3, 18, 19, 101, 102, 105, 114, 118, 119, 121, 125, 126, 138–142, 143, 151, 172, 174, 179, 201, 219, 220, 221, 225, 327, 329, 331, 337, 340, 342, 347, 349, 414, 415, 416, 426, 428, 439, 444, 445, 450, 453, 467, 469, 470, 471, 473, 474, 480, 516, 517
Canadian 3rd Division (Canadian Army Occupation Force), 523, 524, 525, 526, 527
Canadian 4th Armoured Division, 219, 220, 221, 225, 326, 327, 328, 329, 331, 336, 337, 340, 342, 343, 344, 349, 352, 380, 415, 416, 417, 452, 470, 471, 474, 480, 517, 518, 522, 523

INDEX

Canadian 5th Armoured Division, 471, 472, 480, 517, 519, 520, 521, 523
Canadian 1st Armoured Brigade, 480, 523
Canadian 2nd Armoured Brigade, 18, 101, 105, 114, 118, 141, 142, 219, 220, 326, 350, 366, 474
Canadian 4th Armoured Brigade (Cdn. 4 Armd. Div.), 219, 327, 343, 518
Canadian 4th Infantry Brigade (Cdn. 2 Div.), 142, 219, 467, 469, 470
Canadian 5th Infantry Brigade (Cdn. 2 Div.), 142, 326, 467, 470
Canadian 6th Infantry Brigade (Cdn. 2 Div.), 142, 326, 467, 474
Canadian 7th Infantry Brigade (Cdn. 3 Div.), 118, 119, 120, 138, 141, 142, 342, 349, 428, 467, 469, 470, 473
Canadian 8th Infantry Brigade (Cdn. 3 Div.), 118, 119, 120, 138, 141, 142, 342, 439, 467, 469, 473
Canadian 9th Infantry Brigade (Cdn. 3 Div.), 120, 138, 141, 142, 342, 444, 472, 473, 474
Canadian 10th Infantry Brigade (Cdn. 4 Armd. Div.), 343, 518
Canadian 11th Infantry Brigade (Cdn. 5 Armd. Div.), 519
Canadian 1st Parachute Battalion, 130, 482
Canadian 1st Rocket Unit, 359
Calgary Highlanders, 339
Canadian Black Watch (The Black Watch (Royal Regiment of Canada)), 339
North Shore (New Brunswick) Regt., 118
Queen's Own Rifles of Canada, 118
Régiment de Maisonneuve, 329
Regina Rifle Regt., 118
Royal Regt. of Canada, 339
Royal Winnepeg Rifles, 118
1st Canadian Scottish Regt., 121

Czechoslovak Formation

1st Czechoslovak Independent Armoured Brigade, 225, 256

Dutch Formation

Royal Netherlands Infantry Brigade (Princess Irene's), 226, 243, 283, 303, 306, 406, 407

French Formations

French First Army, 1, 8, 9, 13, 222, 333, 353, 417, 482, 483
French 2nd Armoured Division, 219, 220, 222
French 2nd Infantry Division, 222

German Formations

German Army Group North, 492
German Fifth Panzer Army, 9, 355
German Sixth S.S. Panzer Army, 9, 355
German Seventh Army, 9, 355
German Fifteenth Army, 355
German Twenty-fifth Army, 522
German 2nd Panzer Division, 355
German Panzer Lehr Division, 355
German 116th Panzer Division, 355

Polish Formations

Polish 1st Armoured Division, 4, 219, 220, 225, 328, 336, 352, 366, 380, 480, 517, 521, 565
Polish 1st Independent Parachute Brigade, 226, 227, 229, 230, 231, 277, 300, 301, 303, 304, 305, 306

Russian Unit

Russian Guards Division, 483

United States of America: Formations and Units

U.S. 6 Army Group, 1, 9, 11, 13, 222, 223, 333, 353, 482
U.S. 12 Army Group, 1, 3, 5, 9, 10, 12, 13, 216, 333, 356, 413
U.S. First Army, 1, 2, 3, 4, 5, 8, 9, 10, 11, 12, 13, 18, 19, 24, 114, 116, 122, 124, 125, 126, 214, 216, 222, 333, 335, 351, 353, 354, 356, 357, 358, 359, 387, 413, 416, 417, 419, 482, 483
U.S. Third Army, 1, 3, 4, 5, 8, 9, 10, 11, 12, 13, 21, 216, 219, 221, 222, 333, 353, 356, 357, 358, 413, 417, 418, 419, 482, 483
U.S. Fifth Army, 483
U.S. Seventh Army, 1, 2, 5, 8, 9, 10, 222, 333, 353, 357, 413, 417, 418, 482, 483, 484
U.S. Ninth Army, 1, 9, 10, 11, 12, 13, 333, 353, 355, 359, 361, 403, 413, 416, 417, 418, 419, 421, 483, 515
U.S. V Corps, 2, 18, 19, 114, 115, 116, 119, 121, 215, 220, 222, 353, 355, 482, 483
U.S. VII Corps, 2, 4, 11, 12, 18, 19, 114, 115, 121, 123, 125, 214, 216, 223, 357, 358, 384, 388, 390, 419
U.S. VIII Corps, 3, 123, 125, 214, 215, 216, 354, 355, 357, 358, 384, 388, 390
U.S. XII Corps, 221
U.S. XV Corps, 217, 219, 220, 221, 483
U.S. Airborne XVIII Corps, 303, 354, 358, 418, 456, 460, 481, 488, 495, 506
U.S. XIX Corps, 125, 221, 223
U.S. XX Corps, 221
U.S. 1st Infantry Division, 114, 121, 122, 214, 355
U.S. 2nd Armoured Division, 114, 214, 217, 221, 358, 483
U.S. 2nd Infantry Division, 355
U.S. 3rd Armoured Division, 214, 217
U.S. 4th Armoured Division, 215
U.S. 4th Infantry Division, 114, 121, 123, 124, 214, 222, 354
U.S. 5th Infantry Division, 238
U.S. 6th Armoured Division, 3
U.S. 7th Armoured Division, 221, 237, 355, 357, 363, 407, 481

INDEX

United States of America: Formations and Units—*cont.*

U.S. 8th Infantry Division, 481
U.S. 9th Armoured Division, 11, 354, 417
U.S. 9th Infantry Division, 114, 123, 214
U.S. 10th Armoured Division, 356, 357
U.S. 17th Airborne Division, 11, 418, 430, 432, 447, 495
U.S. 28th Infantry Division, 354, 355
U.S. 29th Infantry Division, 114, 121, 515
U.S. 30th Infantry Division, 214, 217, 355, 418
U.S. 35th Infantry Division, 417
U.S. 69th Infantry Division, 483
U.S. 79th Infantry Division, 123, 221, 418
U.S. 82nd Airborne Division, 6, 7, 18, 19, 114, 115, 119, 121, 226, 227, 228, 229, 230, 294, 295, 300, 301, 305, 306, 354, 357, 360, 384, 390, 407, 481
U.S. 83rd Infantry Division, 483
U.S. 84th Infantry Division, 353, 379, 386
U.S. 88th Infantry Division, 483
U.S. 90th Infantry Division, 114, 220
U.S. 99th Infantry Division, 355
U.S. 101st Airborne Division, 6, 7, 9, 18, 19, 114, 115, 121, 226, 227, 228, 233, 295, 299, 300, 301, 305, 354, 356, 376, 380, 384, 386, 390, 407
U.S. 104th Infantry Division, 336, 352
U.S. 106th Infantry Division, 354
U.S. 504th Parachute Regt., 7, 230
U.S. 359th Regimental Combat Team of U.S. 90th Division, 114
U.S. 8th Airforce, 219

British Medical Units

Advanced Blood Banks
'X' Advanced Blood Bank, 203, 321, 322, 323, 324, 451, 466, 544
'Y' Advanced Blood Bank, 147, 203, 321, 322, 323, 324, 385, 390, 394, 408, 448, 451, 465, 466, 501, 508, 534, 544

Ambulance Trains
Nos. 40, 41, 42, 43, 44, 45, 46, 47, 48, 49, 50, 51, 52, 53, 112

Army Blood Supply Depot, Bristol, 85, 87, 204

Army Medical Store, Ludgershall, 75, 77, 78

Base Transfusion Units
1 B.T.U., 86, 111, 203, 320, 321, 322, 323, 324, 465, 466, 545, 546, 548–550
6 B.T.U., 111

1 Casualty Air Evacuation Unit (R.A.F.), 461, 508, 509, 544

Casualty Clearing Stations
3 C.C.S., 110, 133, 135, 136, 137, 177, 179, 181, 184, 190, 193, 233, 250, 278, 292, 293, 294, 295, 296, 297, 298, 303, 306, 307, 308, 310, 312, 339, 360, 383, 384, 385, 386, 387, 388, 389, 391, 392, 393, 395, 438, 442, 443, 450, 451, 452, 453, 454, 455, 457, 458, 459, 460, 467, 469, 496, 507, 508, 509, 510, 512, 647, 651, 652, 653
10 C.C.S., 110, 133, 135, 181, 182, 183, 190, 193, 201, 233, 250, 251, 252, 291, 292, 293, 294, 295, 296, 297, 298, 303, 307, 308, 310, 312, 360, 383, 384, 385, 386, 387, 388, 391, 392, 393, 395, 396, 420, 423, 442, 450, 451, 452, 454, 455, 458, 459, 460, 487, 493, 498, 500, 501, 502, 503, 504, 507, 508, 510, 512, 647, 651, 652
16 C.C.S., 110, 144, 145, 147, 149, 151, 168, 174, 175, 176, 190, 193, 256, 257, 258, 284, 380, 647, 651
23 C.C.S., 110, 180, 307, 308, 310, 312, 369, 371, 379, 380, 381, 382, 384, 391, 392, 393, 395, 410, 443, 446, 448, 449, 450, 452, 453, 458, 459, 460, 497, 507, 509, 510, 512, 537, 647
24 C.C.S., 110, 180, 181, 307, 308, 312, 373, 379, 380, 381, 382, 383, 385, 386, 388, 392, 395, 396, 446, 448, 449, 450, 457, 458, 459, 460, 493, 496, 497, 507, 508, 509, 510, 512, 513, 647, 651
32 C.C.S., 110, 174, 175, 176, 177, 179, 190, 191, 193, 257, 259, 260, 283, 284, 380, 496, 510, 512, 513, 539, 540, 647, 648, 651
33 C.C.S., 110, 141, 179, 180, 193, 287, 307, 312, 328, 373, 388, 389, 391, 392, 393, 395, 396, 450, 457, 458, 459, 460, 488, 496, 507, 509, 510, 512, 513, 540, 568, 648, 649, 651
34 C.C.S., 110, 179, 180, 193, 254, 287, 307, 312, 388, 391, 392, 393, 395, 396, 450, 458, 459, 460, 488, 495, 496, 507, 509, 510, 512, 540, 648, 649, 652
35 C.C.S., 110, 190, 191, 193, 253, 297, 307, 308, 309, 312, 390, 391, 392, 393, 394, 395, 396, 398, 407, 458, 459, 460, 461, 507, 509, 510, 512, 648, 651, 653

Casualty Embarkation Points
1 C.E.P., 144, 146, 149, 150, 174, 186
2 C.E.P., 174, 186, 187, 193, 194
3 C.E.P., 186, 187

Convalescent Depots
5 Con. Depot, 111, 411, 412, 476, 646, 648, 649, 651, 652, 653
9 Con. Depot, 648
12 Con. Depot, 111, 315, 411, 412, 476, 646, 648
13 Con. Depot, 112, 206, 209, 311, 324, 393, 394, 395, 396, 397, 398, 407, 411, 412, 458, 459, 464, 475, 476, 509, 510, 534, 540, 593, 645, 646, 648, 651

INDEX

14 Con. Depot, 112, 403, 411, 412, 476, 512, 646, 648, 651
15 Con. Depot, 112, 191, 411, 412, 476, 645, 646, 648, 651
16 Con. Depot, 112, 191

Depots of Medical Stores
5 Base Depot, 112, 191, 196, 409, 653
11 Base Depot, 112, 409, 464, 653
12 Base Depot, 112, 191, 196, 409, 535, 653
13 Base Depot, 112, 191, 316, 409, 513, 535, 653
16 Base Depot, 653
6 Advanced Depot, 112, 195, 196, 314
8 Advanced Depot, 112, 195, 196, 293, 314, 385, 387, 394, 399, 408, 457, 462, 465, 507, 513, 514, 535, 540, 653
9 Advanced Depot, 112, 195, 196, 312, 314, 394, 399, 408, 448, 450, 462, 465, 507, 513, 535, 653
11 Advanced Depot, 112, 195, 196, 312, 314, 390, 394, 399, 408, 451, 462, 465, 507, 513, 514, 535, 653
12 Advanced Depot, 653
14 Advanced Depot, 653
15 Advanced Depot, 653
16 Advanced Depot, 653
17 Advanced Depot, 653

Medical Stores Reconnaissance Teams
Nos. 11, 13 and 15, 540

1 Captured Enemy Equipment Section (Medical), 400, 513, 535

Field Ambulances
2 Lt. Fd. Amb., 107, 154, 181, 183, 234, 235, 319, 360, 361, 484
7 Fd. Amb., 100
8 Fd. Amb., 107, 129, 146, 148, 149, 150, 152, 422, 423, 455, 473, 486, 487
9 Fd. Amb., 107, 145, 148, 149, 150, 152, 237, 422, 423, 486, 487
11 Lt. Fd. Amb., 107, 145, 149, 150, 238, 428, 430, 432, 433, 436, 446, 447, 450, 457, 460, 496, 510, 512
14 Lt. Fd. Amb., 107, 163, 367, 374, 378, 444, 454, 455, 460, 510, 512, 538, 540, 648, 651
16 Lt. Fd. Amb., 107, 173, 648, 651
16 Para. Fd. Amb., 108, 127, 268, 269, 270, 272, 275, 276, 300, 302, 486
18 Lt. Fd. Amb., 104, 154, 155, 232, 379, 388, 389, 390
19 Lt. Fd. Amb., 107, 153, 154, 232, 233, 360, 419, 420
21 Lt. Fd. Amb., 107, 160, 173, 446, 448, 486, 492, 496, 510, 512, 533, 648, 651
22 Lt. Fd. Amb., 107, 256, 260, 371, 379, 380, 383
23 Lt. Fd. Amb., 107, 160, 161, 170, 180, 245, 246, 247, 262

128 Fd. Amb., 107, 153, 154, 162, 232, 233, 234, 360, 419, 420
129 Fd. Amb., 107, 162, 163, 242, 243, 244, 292, 436, 437, 438, 439, 440, 493, 494
130 Fd. Amb., 107, 160, 162, 163, 242, 243, 244, 297, 302, 436, 437, 438, 439, 440, 493, 494
131 Fd. Amb., 107, 154, 181, 183, 234, 235, 319, 360, 361, 378, 383, 421, 484
133 Para. Fd. Amb., 108, 268, 269, 270, 276, 278, 280, 299, 300, 302
140 Fd. Amb., 651
141 Fd. Amb., 487, 488
146 Fd. Amb., 107, 163, 164, 166, 183, 244, 245, 246, 247, 366, 367
147 Fd. Amb., 107, 169, 170, 171, 261, 263, 264, 265, 266, 378, 379
149 Fd. Amb., 107, 133, 135, 137, 170, 183, 250, 251, 252, 253, 254
153 Fd. Amb., 108, 155, 157, 159, 160, 161, 238, 240, 242, 362, 363, 364, 373, 428, 429, 433, 435, 469, 489, 491, 492, 540, 541
155 Fd. Amb., 300, 345, 445, 494
156 Fd. Amb., 300, 345, 346, 445, 494
157 Fd. Amb., 300, 303, 306, 345, 433, 445, 494
158 Fd. Amb., 487, 488
160 Fd. Amb., 108, 163, 164, 183, 244, 245, 246, 247, 366, 367
162 Fd. Amb., 108, 648, 651
163 Fd. Amb., 108, 137, 244, 276, 277, 278, 291, 292, 293, 294, 295, 296, 297, 298, 299, 302, 384, 385, 386, 463, 512, 648, 651
164 Fd. Amb., 487, 488
168 Lt. Fd. Amb., 107, 133, 137, 163, 183, 243, 438, 493, 494, 498, 499, 500, 501, 503, 510, 512, 648, 651
171 Fd. Amb., 100
172 Fd. Amb., 100
174 Fd. Amb., 108, 168, 169, 257, 258, 259, 260, 369, 371, 372, 373, 374, 375, 376, 442, 443, 444, 445
175 Fd. Amb., 108, 168, 169, 257, 259, 260, 369, 371, 372, 373, 374, 375, 376, 442, 443, 444, 649, 652
176 Fd. Amb., 108, 168, 169, 257, 258, 259, 260, 369, 371, 372, 373, 374, 375, 419, 442, 443, 444, 445
177 Fd. Amb., 100
178 Fd. Amb., 100
179 Fd. Amb., 108, 154, 155, 486, 540
180 Fd. Amb., 100
181 A/L Fd. Amb., 108, 267, 268, 269, 270, 271, 272, 274, 275, 276, 277, 278, 299, 300, 302
186 Fd. Amb., 108, 135, 137, 183, 250, 251, 252, 254, 297
187 Fd. Amb., 108, 163, 164, 183, 244, 245, 246, 247, 366, 367, 383
190 Fd. Amb., 100
191 Fd. Amb., 100
193 Fd. Amb., 108, 155, 156, 157, 158,

British Medical Units—*cont.*

Field Ambulances—*cont.*
193 Fd. Amb.—*cont.*
    159, 160, 161, 238, 239, 240, 266, 362, 363, 364, 427, 428, 429, 432, 433, 435, 438, 469, 491, 492, 541
194 Fd. Amb., 108, 155, 156, 157, 158, 159, 160, 161, 162, 238, 239, 240, 242, 362, 363, 364, 365, 427, 428, 429, 432, 433, 435, 436, 469, 489, 491, 492, 541
195 A/L Fd. Amb., 108, 130, 131, 283, 424, 425, 426, 433
199 Fd. Amb., 100
200 Fd. Amb., 108, 133, 135, 137, 183, 233, 250, 251, 252, 253, 254
201 Lt. Fd. Amb., 100
202 Fd. Amb., 108, 169, 170, 261, 263, 264, 265, 266, 369, 377, 378, 379, 428
203 Fd. Amb., 108, 133, 135, 137, 172, 183
207 Fd. Amb., 100
209 Fd. Amb., 100
210 Fd. Amb., 108, 172
211 Fd. Amb., 108, 172
212 Fd. Amb., 108, 169, 170, 171, 261, 262, 263, 264, 265, 266, 378, 379, 380, 420
213 Fd. Amb., 108, 162, 163, 242, 243, 244, 436, 437, 438, 439, 493, 494
223 Fd. Amb., 108, 148, 149, 150, 152, 237, 422, 423, 455, 473, 486, 487
224 Para. Fd. Amb., 108, 127, 130, 131, 283, 284, 425, 432, 433
225 Para. Fd. Amb., 108, 127, 129, 130, 131, 133, 168, 283, 425, 433, 489

Field Dental Centres
125 F.D.C., 464, 543
147 F.D.C., 464, 543, 544
204 F.D.C., 540
207 F.D.C., 464, 544

58 Field Dental Laboratory, 542

Field Dressing Stations
1 F.D.S., 108, 174, 185, 190, 193, 201, 395, 396, 407, 486, 496, 540, 648, 651
2 F.D.S., 108, 174, 185, 187, 190, 193, 201, 311, 312, 390, 391, 392, 393, 395, 396, 407, 458, 459, 507, 511, 513, 648, 651
3 F.D.S., 108, 181, 182, 183, 184, 291, 292, 293, 294, 295, 296, 297, 302, 360, 383, 384, 385, 386, 387, 388, 389, 393, 395, 396, 422, 450, 452, 454, 455, 457, 487, 503, 504, 648, 649, 651
4 F.D.S., 108, 180, 181, 373, 379, 380, 381, 382, 383, 394, 395, 396, 407, 446, 449, 450, 458, 497, 648, 651
5 F.D.S., 108, 168, 169, 258, 259, 260, 369, 371, 372, 374, 442
6 F.D.S., 108, 168, 257, 258, 259, 260, 369, 371, 372, 373, 442, 460, 507, 510, 537, 648, 651, 652
7 F.D.S., 108, 154
8 F.D.S., 108, 153, 232, 233, 234, 360, 419, 420
9 F.D.S., 108, 150, 174, 181, 184, 185, 190, 379, 380, 381, 382, 383, 393, 395, 396, 407, 432, 446, 448, 450, 497, 648, 651
10 F.D.S., 108, 149, 150
11 F.D.S., 108, 149, 150, 237, 422, 460, 496, 500, 504, 510, 512
12 F.D.S., 108, 150, 174, 185, 190, 193, 315, 317, 648, 651
13 F.D.S., 108, 169, 170, 171, 263, 264, 265, 266, 378, 379, 388, 389
14 F.D.S., 108, 162, 163, 242, 243, 253, 293, 311, 312, 383, 390, 391, 393, 394, 395, 399, 407, 436, 439, 460, 497, 510, 512, 648, 651
15 F.D.S., 108, 162, 163, 242, 243, 244, 436, 439, 493
16 F.D.S., 108, 163, 164, 181, 182, 183, 201, 244, 293, 366, 367
17 F.D.S., 108, 163, 201, 244, 245, 246, 366, 367, 648, 651, 652
18 F.D.S., 300, 345, 346, 445
19 F.D.S., 300, 345, 460, 507, 510, 512
20 F.D.S., 108, 148, 150, 174, 185, 190, 193, 201, 259, 260, 283, 284, 380, 537, 648, 651
21 F.D.S., 108, 148, 150, 174, 185, 190, 193, 201, 292, 316, 394, 395, 396, 403, 458, 459, 460, 507, 508, 511, 513, 648, 651, 652
22 F.D.S., 109, 155, 156, 157, 158, 159, 160, 161, 238, 239, 242, 361, 362, 363, 364, 427, 435, 460, 486, 495, 496, 510, 512, 540, 648, 651, 652
23 F.D.S., 109, 155, 161, 238, 239, 242, 362, 363, 364, 427, 431, 433, 435, 436, 492, 541
24 F.D.S., 109, 193, 395, 396, 488, 496, 540, 568, 648, 651
25 F.D.S., 109, 181, 185, 190, 193, 648, 649, 651, 652
26 F.D.S., 108, 169, 170, 262, 263, 264, 265, 266, 378, 379, 460, 510, 537, 648, 651
27 F.D.S., 109, 172
28 F.D.S., 109, 172
29 F.D.S., 109, 154, 183, 234, 235, 361, 484
30 F.D.S., 109, 175, 176, 258, 284, 343, 380, 648, 651, 652
31 F.D.S., 109, 181, 185, 190, 193, 201, 293, 309, 311, 312, 316, 390, 391, 392, 393, 394, 395, 396, 400, 407, 457, 458, 459, 507, 511, 513, 648, 651
32 F.D.S., 109, 181, 185, 190, 317, 648, 651
33 F.D.S., 109, 174, 175, 176, 185, 190, 193, 201, 284, 511, 537, 648, 651
34 F.D.S., 109, 174, 185, 187, 190, 201, 315, 317, 648, 652
35 F.D.S., 109, 181, 182, 183, 184, 185, 190, 201, 233, 291, 292, 293, 294,

INDEX

295, 296, 297, 383, 384, 385, 386, 387, 388, 389, 396, 407, 442, 450, 451, 453, 454, 455, 457, 493, 648, 652
47 F.D.S., 109, 133, 137, 250, 251, 252, 293, 312, 390, 391, 392, 393, 394, 407
48 F.D.S., 109, 133, 135, 137, 183, 250, 251, 252, 253, 254, 293, 295, 296
49 F.D.S., 109, 185, 190, 193, 292, 306, 311, 312, 390, 391, 392, 393, 394, 395, 396, 407, 458, 459, 507, 511, 513, 648, 652
50 F.D.S., 109, 193, 194, 390, 391, 392, 393, 394, 395, 396, 400, 407, 458, 459, 507, 511, 513, 648, 652
53 F.D.S., 487, 488, 649
62 F.D.S., 648, 649, 652
190 F.D.S., 100
191 F.D.S., 100
199 F.D.S., 100
207 F.D.S., 100

Field Hygiene Sections
6 Fd. Hyg. Sec., 109, 174, 175, 176, 284, 537, 652
7 Fd. Hyg. Sec., 100
10 Fd. Hyg. Sec., 109, 180, 380, 383, 449, 497
17 Fd. Hyg. Sec., 100
22 Fd. Hyg. Sec., 109, 133, 537, 652
24 Fd. Hyg. Sec., 487
26 Fd. Hyg. Sec., 109, 149, 150, 487
27 Fd. Hyg. Sec., 109, 540, 652
28 Fd. Hyg. Sec., 100
29 Fd. Hyg. Sec., 109, 168, 441
30 Fd. Hyg. Sec., 109, 172, 408, 511, 652
31 Fd. Hyg. Sec., 109, 183, 291, 293, 384, 386, 387, 388, 498, 652
32 Fd. Hyg. Sec., 300, 345, 445
35 Fd. Hyg. Sec., 109, 163
38 Fd. Hyg. Sec., 109, 162, 242, 439, 494
40 Fd. Hyg. Sec., 109, 155, 429, 541
45 Fd. Hyg. Sec., 44, 109, 652
53 Fd. Hyg. Sec., 109, 169, 170, 263, 264, 265, 266, 379
55 Fd. Hyg. Sec., 100
60 Fd. Hyg. Sec., 109, 153, 232, 233, 234, 360
61 Fd. Hyg. Sec., 109, 195, 511, 652
68 Fd. Hyg. Sec., 100, 652
70 Fd. Hyg. Sec., 109, 154, 181
72 Fd. Hyg. Sec., 100
73 Fd. Hyg. Sec., 100, 652
74 Fd. Hyg. Sec., 185
75 Fd. Hyg. Sec., 109, 315, 511, 540
76 Fd. Hyg. Sec., 109, 154, 496
79 Fd. Hyg. Sec., 100
80 Fd. Hyg. Sec., 100, 652
81 Fd. Hyg. Sec., 100
84 Fd. Hyg. Sec., 652
85 Fd. Hyg. Sec., 652

Field Sanitary Sections
1 Fd. San. Sec., 109, 150, 174, 652
2 Fd. San. Sec., 109, 150, 174, 652
3 Fd. San. Sec., 109, 174, 315, 653
4 Fd. San. Sec., 109, 174, 315, 653
6 Fd. San. Sec., 653

Field Surgical Units
6 F.S.U., 109, 181, 292, 388, 407, 450, 511, 513, 649, 652
12 F.S.U., 109, 181, 380, 383, 407, 448, 511, 513
13 F.S.U., 109, 181, 380, 407, 511, 513, 534, 537, 649, 652
14 F.S.U., 109, 383, 407, 450, 500, 504, 511, 513, 534, 540, 649, 652
15 F.S.U., 110, 181, 380, 383, 407, 448, 511, 513, 534, 540, 649, 652
27 F.S.U., 110, 181, 380, 407, 448, 511, 513, 540, 541, 649, 652
30 F.S.U., 181
32 F.S.U., 181
33 F.S.U., 110, 174, 185, 287, 408, 511, 513, 534, 649, 652
34 F.S.U., 110, 174, 185, 513, 539, 649, 652
37 F.S.U., 110, 150, 174, 185, 649, 652
38 F.S.U., 110, 150, 174, 185, 287, 288, 408, 448, 450, 649, 652
39 F.S.U., 110, 150, 174, 185, 649, 652
40 F.S.U., 110, 150, 174, 185, 292, 408, 649, 652
41 F.S.U., 110, 181, 185, 383, 408, 448, 450, 511, 513, 649, 652
42 F.S.U., 110, 181, 185, 380, 408, 446, 448, 511, 513, 649, 652
43 F.S.U., 110, 183, 293, 383, 386, 388, 408, 450, 452, 453, 455, 511, 513, 649, 652
44 F.S.U., 110, 292, 388, 408, 450, 510, 513, 649, 652
45 F.S.U., 110, 174, 185, 187, 315, 408, 511, 513, 534, 649, 652
46 F.S.U., 110, 174, 185, 187, 408, 513, 649, 652
47 F.S.U., 110, 181, 183, 185, 408, 511, 513, 534, 649, 652
48 F.S.U., 110, 181, 185, 283, 511, 513, 540, 541, 649, 652
49 F.S.U., 110, 243, 292, 295, 296, 383, 386, 388, 408, 450, 452, 453, 455, 511, 513, 649, 652
50 F.S.U., 110, 293, 383, 408, 450, 500, 504, 511, 513, 649, 652
51 F.S.U., 110, 408, 511, 513, 649, 652
52 F.S.U., 110, 408, 511, 513, 649
53 F.S.U., 110, 408, 511, 513, 649, 652
54 F.S.U., 110, 185, 288, 408, 511, 513, 534, 649, 652
55 F.S.U., 110, 145, 149, 174, 513, 534, 649, 652
56 F.S.U., 110, 174, 408, 446, 511, 513, 534, 540, 649, 652

Field Transfusion Units
6 F.T.U., 110, 181, 408, 511, 513
7 F.T.U., 110, 181, 183, 292, 295, 296, 383, 386, 388, 408, 455, 511, 513

British Medical Units—*cont.*

Field Transfusion Units—*cont.*
13 F.T.U., 110, 174, 185, 187, 203, 380, 383, 408, 448, 511, 513
14 F.T.U., 110, 174, 185, 203, 511, 513
21 F.T.U., 110, 150, 174, 185, 203, 408, 448, 511, 513
22 F.T.U., 110, 150, 162, 174, 185, 203, 408, 511, 513
24 F.T.U., 110, 181, 185, 203, 383, 408, 450, 500, 502, 511, 513
29 F.T.U., 110, 145, 147, 149, 174
30 F.T.U., 110, 181, 185, 203, 380, 383, 408, 448, 450, 511, 513
31 F.T.U., 110, 156, 157, 158, 408, 511, 513, 540
35 F.T.U., 110, 292, 388, 408, 450, 511, 513
36 F.T.U., 110, 174, 511, 513, 537
37 F.T.U., 110, 380, 408, 448, 450, 511, 513

General Hospitals
6 B.G.H., 111, 191, 317, 333, 334, 409, 410, 412, 475, 531, 537, 645, 647, 650, 652
8 B.G.H., 111, 309, 333, 388, 389, 398, 407, 411, 457, 475, 504, 525, 531, 645, 647, 650
9 B.G.H., 111, 191, 309, 310, 316, 317, 333, 347, 402, 409, 411, 459, 463, 475, 507, 531, 537, 539, 568, 645, 647, 650
20 B.G.H., 111, 191, 193, 194, 333, 409, 410
23 B.G.H., 111, 191, 333, 334, 409, 410, 412, 475, 531, 645, 647, 650, 652
24 B.G.H., 111, 333, 334, 409, 410
25 B.G.H., 111, 191, 309, 316, 317, 333, 409, 411, 475, 507, 508, 509, 511, 513, 531, 537, 542, 645, 647, 650
29 B.G.H., 111, 191, 333, 334, 409, 410, 412, 474, 475, 531, 645, 647, 649, 650
30 B.G.H., 111, 191, 193, 333, 347, 409, 410, 411, 475, 645
32 B.G.H., 111, 191, 193, 206, 209, 324, 325, 333, 398, 403, 404, 409, 410, 411, 412, 475, 556, 586, 645, 647, 650
39 B.G.H., 111, 309, 333, 360, 387, 388, 393, 394, 395, 396, 407, 409, 410, 411, 457, 458, 459, 475, 524, 531, 645, 647, 649, 650
67 B.G.H., 531, 539, 645, 647, 650, 653
73 B.G.H., 111, 191, 333, 334, 409, 410
74 B.G.H., 111, 191, 333, 409, 410, 411, 475, 509, 512, 531, 645, 647, 650
75 B.G.H., 111, 190, 193, 333, 409, 410, 412, 475, 645
77 B.G.H., 111, 190, 193, 194, 195, 315, 333, 334, 409, 410, 412, 475, 507, 508, 510, 512, 537, 645, 647, 650
79 B.G.H., 111, 177, 179, 183, 185, 190, 191, 193, 333, 334, 369, 371, 379, 390, 391, 392, 393, 394, 395, 396, 403, 407, 409, 410, 412, 458, 459, 475, 507, 645

81 B.G.H., 111, 182, 183, 190, 191, 193, 194, 306, 307, 308, 309, 310, 312, 316, 333, 360, 386, 387, 388, 390, 391, 392, 393, 394, 395, 396, 403, 407, 409, 410, 411, 457, 458, 459, 475, 486, 493, 496, 507, 508, 509, 510, 511, 512, 513, 539, 644, 645, 646, 649, 650, 652
84 B.G.H., 111, 190, 191, 193, 194, 306, 307, 308, 309, 310, 312, 333, 379, 390, 391, 392, 393, 394, 395, 396, 407, 409, 410, 411, 458, 459, 475, 507, 508, 509, 511, 512, 542, 644, 645, 646, 649, 650, 652
86 B.G.H., 111, 168, 176, 191, 193, 194, 233, 251, 252, 293, 306, 307, 308, 309, 310, 312, 333, 390, 391, 392, 393, 394, 395, 396, 407, 409, 410, 411, 458, 459, 460, 464, 475, 496, 503, 507, 508, 509, 510, 511, 512, 513, 537, 542, 644, 645, 646, 649, 650
88 B.G.H., 111, 168, 191, 193, 194, 329, 330, 332, 333, 409, 410, 411, 475, 522, 524, 525, 644, 645, 646, 650
94 B.G.H., 531, 532, 539, 645, 647, 650, 652
96 B.G.H., 412, 474, 476, 531, 645, 647, 650
101 B.G.H., 111, 191, 333, 334, 360, 388, 389, 409, 410, 412, 457, 476, 645, 647, 650
102 B.G.H., 111, 191, 333, 334, 409, 410
105 B.G.H., 111, 191, 333, 334, 409, 410, 412, 476, 531, 646, 647, 650
106 B.G.H., 111, 191, 333, 334, 409, 412, 463, 475, 476, 531, 645, 646, 647, 649, 650, 653
107 B.G.H., 111, 191, 333, 334, 409, 410
108 B.G.H., 111, 191, 333, 334, 409, 410, 412, 457, 476, 531, 646, 647, 650
109 B.G.H., 111, 333, 334, 402, 410, 412, 476, 646, 647, 650
110 B.G.H., 111, 191, 333, 334, 409, 410, 412, 476, 568, 646, 647, 650
111 B.G.H., 111, 333, 334, 410, 412, 476, 531, 646, 647, 649, 650, 653
112 B.G.H., 111, 333, 334
113 B.G.H., 111, 333, 334, 409, 411, 412, 476, 646, 647, 650
114 B.G.H., 111, 333, 334
115 B.G.H., 111, 333, 334, 410, 412, 476, 646, 647, 650
121 B.G.H., 111, 191, 316, 317, 333, 334, 409, 410, 412, 475, 508, 509, 510, 513, 531, 542, 645, 647, 649, 650, 652

British Military Hospital (163 Field Ambulance), Antwerp, 463

Maxillo-Facial Surgical Units
4 M.F.S.U., 649, 653
5 M.F.S.U., 111, 203, 408, 458, 459, 464, 513, 542, 649
6 M.F.S.U., 111, 203, 472, 649, 653

303 Medical Pioneer Company, 144, 145, 148, 150, 152

INDEX 685

Medical Research Council's Nutritional Research Team, 513

Mobile Bacteriological Laboratories
3 Mob. Bact. Lab., 86, 112, 322, 653
4 Mob. Bact. Lab., 112, 408, 511, 513, 539, 653
7 Mob. Bact. Lab., 112, 322, 511, 513, 653
8 Mob. Bact. Lab., 112, 503, 511, 513, 537, 568, 658

Mobile Dental Units
27 M.D.U., 169
31 M.D.U., 169
134 M.D.U., 133, 154, 319
204 M.D.U., 113, 202, 319
205 M.D.U., 113, 163
206 M.D.U., 113
207 M.D.U., 113, 202, 319
208 M.D.U., 113, 202
209 M.D.U., 113, 319
210 M.D.U., 113, 319
211 M.D.U., 113, 181
212 M.D.U., 113, 319
214 M.D.U., 113, 319
215 M.D.U., 133, 181
501 M.D.U., 345, 445
510 M.D.U., 540
514 M.D.U., 465
516 M.D.U., 540
517 M.D.U., 464, 540
533 M.D.U., 345, 445, 495
534 M.D.U., 345, 445, 495

52 Mobile Field Hospital (R.A.F.), 509

4 Mobile Hygiene Laboratory, 112, 408, 513, 653

Mobile Neuro-Surgical Unit, 111, 408, 459, 513, 649, 653

Naval Medical Stores, Schloss Hagen, 535

Port Detachments
20 Port Detachment, 112, 144, 149, 150, 174
21 Port Detachment, 112, 174
22 Port Detachment, 112, 181
23 Port Detachment, 112, 181
24 Port Detachment, 112
25 Port Detachment, 112, 408
26 Port Detachment, 112
27 Port Detachment, 112
28 Port Detachment, 112, 408
29 Port Detachment, 112
30 Port Detachment, 112

Prophylactic Ablution Centres
60 P.A.C., 113
61 P.A.C., 113
62 P.A.C., 113, 408
63 P.A.C., 113
64 P.A.C., 113, 408
65 P.A.C., 113, 408, 540
66 P.A.C., 113, 408
67 P.A.C., 113
68 P.A.C., 113, 181, 408
69–79 (inclusive) P.A.C., 113

Rest Centre (Second Army), 206, 209

Surgical Teams
3 Chest Surgery Surgical Team, 111, 649
23 Surg. Team, 174
24 Surg. Team, 174
29 Surg. Team, 174
73 Surg. Team, 174
109 Surg. Team, 150, 174
112 Surg. Team, 174, 185

2 Traumatic Shock Research Team, 511, 513

1 Vascular Injuries Research Team, 513, 649

Motor Ambulance Convoys and Ambulance Car Companies (R.A.S.C.)
111 M.A.C., 183, 291, 293, 294, 295, 296, 297, 384, 385, 386, 388, 450, 451, 503, 532
132 M.A.C., 175, 176, 256
227 M.A.C., 309, 496, 532, 540
302 M.A.C., 169, 170, 180, 263, 264, 265, 266, 378, 432, 446, 450, 451, 453, 533, 540
218 A.C.C., 193, 311, 462, 508, 509
257 A.C.C., 191, 193, 293, 294, 295, 296, 309, 311, 385, 390, 394, 398, 408, 449, 461, 462, 508, 509, 532, 534
403 M.A.C., 311
753 M.A.C., 311, 316, 317

Canadian Medical Units

Casualty Clearing Stations
2 Cdn. C.C.S., 142, 327, 328, 329, 330, 332, 342, 347, 349, 516, 518, 519, 521
3 Cdn. C.C.S., 142, 327, 328, 330, 331, 332, 375, 376, 423, 443, 451, 452, 467, 470, 472, 473, 518, 519, 520
4 Cdn. C.C.S., 471, 518, 519, 520
5 Cdn. C.C.S., 520
6 Cdn. C.C.S., 142, 327, 328, 329, 339, 341, 343, 347, 442, 451, 452, 467, 470

Convalescent Depots
2 Cdn. Con. Depot, 191, 330, 411, 412, 476, 646, 648, 651
3 Cdn. Con. Depot, 411, 412, 476, 646, 648, 651
4 Cdn. Con. Depot, 103

Cdn. Convalescent Hospital, 103

Depots of Medical Stores
2 Cdn. Base Depot, 191, 409
2 Cdn. Advanced Depot, 196, 314

1 Cdn. Exhaustion Unit, 142, 143, 518, 519

Canadian Medical Units—*cont.*

Field Ambulances
  4 Cdn. Fd. Amb., 520
  5 Cdn. Fd. Amb., 520
  7 Cdn. Lt. Fd. Amb., 520
  8 Cdn. Lt. Fd. Amb., 472
  9 Cdn. Fd. Amb., 142, 519, 520
  10 Cdn. Fd. Amb., 142, 143, 326, 327, 341, 342, 467, 470, 471, 474, 522
  11 Cdn. Fd. Amb., 142, 143, 326, 327, 341, 342, 467, 469, 470, 474, 521, 522
  12 Cdn. Lt. Fd. Amb., 327, 331, 342, 343, 471, 474, 518, 523
  14 Cdn. Fd. Amb., 102, 138, 141, 142, 143, 327, 331, 342, 349, 469, 471, 516, 521
  15 Cdn. Fd. Amb., 326, 327, 329, 343, 349, 471, 474, 518
  17 Cdn. Lt. Fd. Amb., 141, 331, 343, 344, 350, 474, 523
  18 Cdn. Fd. Amb., 142, 143, 326, 327, 341, 467, 470, 471, 474, 518, 521, 522
  22 Cdn. Fd. Amb., 102, 138, 141, 142, 143, 327, 331, 342, 349, 467, 469, 471, 521
  23 Cdn. Fd. Amb., 102, 138, 139, 141, 142, 143, 327, 329, 331, 342, 349, 469, 471, 473, 521
  24 Cdn. Fd. Amb. (Lt)., 472, 519, 520

Field Dressing Stations
  2 Cdn. F.D.S., 519, 520
  4 Cdn. F.D.S., 142, 326, 329, 339, 341, 349, 474, 518, 521, 522
  5 Cdn. F.D.S., 142, 143, 329, 331, 332, 339, 342, 347, 349, 451, 467, 470, 518
  6 Cdn. F.D.S., 142, 194, 329, 330, 332, 339, 344, 346, 347, 518
  7 Cdn. F.D.S., 142, 143, 326, 327, 331, 339, 342, 349, 470, 473, 521
  8 Cdn. F.D.S., 472
  9 Cdn. F.D.S., 328, 331, 332, 339, 341, 347
  10 Cdn. F.D.S., 142, 328, 329, 344, 518, 519
  11 Cdn. F.D.S., 329, 332
  12 Cdn. F.D.S., 331, 339, 343, 349, 470, 471, 518
  13 Cdn. F.D.S., 472, 520
  21 Cdn. F.D.S., 142, 143, 326, 339, 341, 342, 349, 518, 522

Field Hygiene Sections
  7 Cdn. Fd. Hyg. Sec., 142
  11 Cdn. Fd. Hyg. Sec., 472
  13 Cdn. Fd. Hyg. Sec., 142

Field Surgical Units
  6 Cdn. F.S.U., 349
  8 Cdn. F.S.U., 344, 347
  9 Cdn. F.S.U., 329, 344, 347
  10 Cdn. F.S.U., 329, 347
  11 Cdn. F.S.U., 347

Field Transfusion Units
  4 Cdn. F.T.U., 347
  5 Cdn. F.T.U., 344, 347
  7 Cdn. F.T.U., 329

General Hospitals
  1 Cdn. G.H., 103, 472, 475, 525, 645, 647, 650
  2 Cdn. G.H., 103, 143, 330, 333, 334, 347, 348, 409, 410, 412, 472, 524, 646, 647, 650
  3 Cdn. G.H., 103, 475, 520, 521, 525, 645, 646
  4 Cdn. G.H., 103, 143
  5 Cdn. G.H., 525, 645, 647, 650
  6 Cdn. G.H., 143, 194, 330, 331, 332, 333, 339, 341, 347, 348, 350, 409, 410, 411, 451, 467, 475, 519, 520, 524, 645, 646, 650
  7 Cdn. G.H., 103, 143, 191, 316, 317, 332, 333, 334, 347, 348, 350, 409, 410, 412, 451, 475, 504, 509, 512, 524, 525, 526, 645, 647, 650
  8 Cdn. G.H., 103, 143, 191, 316, 317, 332, 333, 334, 339, 347, 348, 350, 409, 410, 412, 451, 467, 472, 475, 524, 525, 645, 647
  9 Cdn. G.H., 103, 143
  10 Cdn. G.H., 103, 143, 191, 333, 334, 347, 348, 409, 410, 412, 451, 467, 472, 476, 524, 646, 647, 650
  11 Cdn. G.H., 103
  12 Cdn. G.H., 103, 143, 330, 333, 334, 339, 342, 347, 348, 350, 409, 412, 476, 524, 646, 647, 650
  13 Cdn. G.H., 103, 143
  16 Cdn. G.H., 103, 143, 332, 333, 334, 347, 348, 350, 409, 412, 474, 475, 525, 526, 645, 647, 650
  17 Cdn. G.H., 103, 143, 144
  18 Cdn. G.H., 103
  19 Cdn. G.H., 103
  20 Cdn. G.H., 103, 143, 333, 334, 402, 411, 412, 463, 475, 476, 524, 646, 647, 650
  21 Cdn. G.H., 143, 333, 334, 347, 348, 409, 412, 475, 476, 524, 646, 647, 650
  22 Cdn. G.H., 143

1 Cdn. Mobile Neuro-Surgical Unit, 472, 518

Motor Ambulance Convoys
  1 Cdn. M.A.C., 471
  2 Cdn. M.A.C., 143, 256, 326, 329, 341, 342, 467

1 Cdn. Venereal Diseases Treatment Unit, 142, 519

German Medical Unit
Wehrkreis Sanitatspark XI, 535

Polish Medical Unit
1 Polish Para. Fd. Amb., 300, 302, 303, 306

INDEX

United States Medical Units
- 24 Evacuation Hospital, 294, 295, 312, 386, 390, 391, 392
- 82 Evacuation Hospital, 233
- 50 Field Hospital, 302
- 183 Medical Battalion, 430
- 307 Airborne Medical Company, 295, 296, 297, 300, 384, 385, 386
- 326 Airborne Medical Company, 295, 296, 300, 384, 385, 386
- 384 Ambulance Company, 294, 295

www.ingramcontent.com/pod-product-compliance
Lightning Source LLC
Chambersburg PA
CBHW050522300426
44113CB00012B/1919